International ~~Financial Reporting~~ rting S...

as issued at 1 January 2012

This edition published in two parts

PART A

International Financial Reporting Standards®

as issued at 1 January 2012

This edition published in two parts

PART A

The Conceptual Framework for Financial Reporting,
the Preface to International Financial Reporting Standards (IFRSs®) and
the consolidated text of IFRSs
including International Accounting Standards (IASs®) and Interpretations,
as issued at 1 January 2012

(Glossary of Terms and index included)

For the accompanying documents published with IFRSs,
and other relevant material, see Part B of this edition

International Accounting Standards Board®
30 Cannon Street
London EC4M 6XH
United Kingdom

Telephone: +44 (0)20 7246 6410
Fax: +44 (0)20 7246 6411
Email: iasb@ifrs.org

Publications Telephone: +44 (0)20 7332 2730
Publications Fax: +44 (0)20 7332 2749
Publications Email: publications@ifrs.org
Web: www.ifrs.org

International Financial Reporting Standards (IFRSs) together with their accompanying documents are issued by the International Accounting Standards Board (IASB),
30 Cannon Street, London EC4M 6XH, United Kingdom.
Tel: +44 (0)20 7246 6410 Fax: +44 (0)20 7246 6411
Email: iasb@ifrs.org Web: www.ifrs.org

ISBN for this part: 978-1-907877-46-9
ISBN for complete publication (two parts): 978-1-907877-45-2

⊛IFRS

Contents

Interpretations

© IFRS Foundation

* * * * *

Changes in this edition

This section is a brief guide to the changes to International Financial Reporting Standards (IFRSs) since the publication of the 2011 edition of the Bound Volume of International Financial Reporting Standards (the 'Red Book').

Introduction

This volume includes the latest consolidated versions of all IFRSs, including IASs and Interpretations.

This volume includes amendments to IFRSs that have an effective date after 1 January 2012. Readers seeking the consolidated text of IFRSs that are effective on 1 January 2012 should refer to the single-part edition of the Bound Volume (the 'Blue Book').

New requirements introduced in 2011

The following changes were made during 2011:

- four new standards—IFRSs 10, 11, 12 and 13
- one new Interpretation—IFRIC 20
- seven revised standards—IFRSs 7 and 9 and IASs 1, 12, 19, 27 and 28
- amendments to IFRSs that were issued as separate documents
- amendments to other IFRSs resulting from those amended standards.

New pronouncements

Details of the new, revised and amended standards, new Interpretation and amendments to IFRSs included in this edition are as follows.

IFRS 10, IFRS 11, IFRS 12, IAS 27 and IAS 28

In May 2011 the IASB issued IFRS 10 *Consolidated Financial Statements*, IFRS 11 *Joint Arrangements* and IFRS 12 *Disclosure of Interests in Other Entities* and two revised standards, IAS 27 *Separate Financial Statements* and IAS 28 *Investments in Associates and Joint Ventures*. All of the new standards are effective for annual periods beginning on or after 1 January 2013, and earlier application is permitted.

IFRS 10 supersedes IAS 27 *Consolidated and Separate Financial Statements* and SIC-12 *Consolidated—Special Purpose Entities*, IFRS 11 supersedes IAS 31 *Interests in Joint Ventures* and SIC-13 *Jointly Controlled Entities—Non-monetary Contributions by Venturers* and IFRS 12 applies to entities that have an interest in a subsidiary, a joint arrangement, an associate or an unconsolidated structured entity.

IAS 27, together with IFRS 10 and IFRS 12, supersedes IAS 27 *Consolidated and Separate Financial Statements* (as amended in 2008). IAS 28 prescribes the accounting for investments in associates and sets out the requirements for the application of the equity method when accounting for investments in associates and joint ventures.

IFRS 13

IFRS 13 *Fair Value Measurement* was issued in May 2011. It defines fair value, sets out a framework for measuring fair value and requires disclosures about fair value measurement. It is effective for annual periods beginning on or after 1 January 2013. Earlier application is permitted.

IFRIC 20

IFRIC 20 *Stripping Costs in the Production Phase of a Surface Mine* was issued in October 2011. It clarifies how an entity allocates the stripping costs it incurs during the production phase of a surface mine between inventory and other assets, as well as the period over which it should amortise any capitalised stripping costs. It is effective for annual periods beginning on or after 1 January 2013. Earlier application is permitted.

Amendments to IFRSs issued as separate documents

Amendments to IFRS 7

Disclosures—Offsetting Financial Assets and Financial Liabilities (Amendments to IFRS 7) was issued in December 2011. These amendments require entities to disclose information so that users of its financial statements are able to evaluate the effect or potential effect of netting arrangements and similar agreements on the entity's financial position. It is required to be applied for annual periods beginning on or before 1 January 2013. Earlier application is permitted.

Amendments to IFRS 9

Mandatory Effective Date and Transition Disclosures (Amendments to IFRS 9 and IFRS 7) was issued in December 2011. The amendments require IFRS 9 to be applied for annual periods beginning on or after 1 January 2015, and must be applied when IFRS 9 is first applied. Earlier application of IFRS 9 is permitted. These amendments to IFRS 9 modify the relief from restating prior periods, and also added transition disclosures to IFRS 7 that are required to be applied when IFRS 9 is first applied.

Amendments to IAS 1

Presentation of Items of Other Comprehensive Income (Amendments to IAS 1) was issued in June 2011. The amendment is required to be applied for annual periods beginning on or after 1 July 2012. Earlier application is permitted.

Amendments to IAS 19

IAS 19 *Employee Benefits* was issued in June 2011. It prescribes the accounting and disclosure by employers for employee benefits and is effective for annual periods beginning on or after 1 January 2013. Earlier application is permitted.

Amendments to IAS 32

Offsetting Financial Assets and Financial Liabilities (Amendments to IAS 32) was issued in December 2011. The amendments clarify (a) the meaning of 'currently has a legally enforceable right of set-off'; and (b) that some gross settlement systems would be considered equivalent to net settlement if they eliminate or result in insignificant credit and liquidity risk and process receivables and payables in a single settlement process or cycle. The amendment is required to be applied for annual periods beginning on or before 1 January 2014. Earlier application is permitted.

Other material that has changed

The Glossary of Terms has been revised.

Minor editorial corrections to IFRSs (including necessary updating) have been made; a list of these is available on the website.

We have included a reference table ('Table of IFRSs') at the back of the Red Bound Volume. This lists all IFRSs that have been published before 1 January 2012.

Introduction to this edition

Overview

The International Accounting Standards Board (IASB), based in London, began operations in 2001. The IASB is committed to developing, in the public interest, a single set of high quality, global accounting standards that require transparent and comparable information in general purpose financial statements. In pursuit of this objective, the IASB co-operates with national accounting standard-setters to achieve convergence in accounting standards around the world. The IASB members have a broad range of professional backgrounds and have liaison responsibilities throughout the world. The IASB is selected, overseen and funded by the IFRS Foundation (formerly called the International Accounting Standards Committee (IASC) Foundation). The IFRS Foundation is financed through a number of national financing regimes, which include levies and payments from regulatory and standard-setting bodies, international organisations and other accounting bodies.

Trustees

The Trustees provide oversight of the operations of the IFRS Foundation and the IASB. The responsibilities of the Trustees include the appointment of members of the IASB, the IFRS Advisory Council and the IFRS Interpretations Committee; overseeing and monitoring the IASB's effectiveness and adherence to its due process and consultation procedures; establishing and maintaining appropriate financing arrangements; approval of the budget for the IFRS Foundation; and responsibility for constitutional changes. The Trustees have established a public accountability link to a Monitoring Board comprising public capital market authorities.

The Trustees comprise individuals that as a group provide an appropriate balance of professional backgrounds, including auditors, preparers, users, academics, and other officials serving the public interest. Under the Constitution of the IFRS Foundation as revised in 2010 (see below), the Trustees are appointed so that there are six from the Asia/Oceania region, six from Europe, six from North America, one from Africa and one from South America, and two others from any area, as long as geographical balance is maintained.

IFRS Foundation's Constitution

The IFRS Foundation's Constitution requires the Trustees to review the constitutional arrangements every five years. The Trustees completed a full review and revision of the Constitution in June 2005, and a revised Constitution came into effect on 1 July 2005. In 2008 the Trustees began the next review, with the first part focusing on the creation of a formal link to public authorities to enhance public accountability and considering the size and composition of the IASB. The Trustees concluded the first part of the review in January 2009 and issued a revised Constitution for effect from 1 February 2009. The changes included the expansion of the IASB from fourteen to sixteen members, selected by geographical origins, by 1 July 2012, with an option to include up to three part-time members. The revised Constitution established the link to the new Monitoring Board to ensure public accountability. The remaining part of the review was concluded in January 2010, when the Constitution was further revised with effect from 1 March 2010.

Among the changes introduced were the renaming of the IASC Foundation as the IFRS Foundation, the International Financial Reporting Interpretations Committee (IFRIC) as the IFRS Interpretations Committee, and the Standards Advisory Council (SAC) as the IFRS Advisory Council. Other changes included revised objectives for the organisation, and specific provision for Trustees to be appointed from Africa and South America.

IASB

The IASB consists of fifteen members (all full-time), which will increase to sixteen in July 2012. The IASB has full discretion in developing and pursuing the technical agenda for setting accounting standards, subject to consultation with the Trustees and a public consultation every three years, the first of which began in 2011. The main qualifications for membership of the IASB are professional competence and practical experience. The Trustees are required to select members so that the IASB, as a group, will comprise the best available combination of technical expertise and international business and market experience. The IASB is also expected to provide an appropriate mix of recent practical experience among auditors, preparers, users and academics. The IASB, in consultation with the Trustees, is expected to establish and maintain liaison with national standard-setters and other official bodies concerned with standard-setting in order to promote the convergence of national standards and the IASB's standards (IFRSs). The publication of a standard, exposure draft, or Interpretation requires approval by nine of the IASB's fifteen members. At 1 January 2012 the IASB members were:

Hans Hoogervorst, *Chairman*	Wei-Guo Zhang
Ian Mackintosh, *Vice-Chairman*	Stephen Cooper
Philippe Danjou	Jan Engström
Patrick Finnegan	Amaro Luiz de Oliveira Gomes
Prabhakar Kalavacherla	Takatsugu Ochi
Patricia McConnell	Darrel Scott
Paul Pacter	
John T Smith	

The IASB issues a summary of its decisions after each Board meeting. This *IASB Update* is published in electronic format on the website www.iasb.org.

IFRS Advisory Council

The IFRS Advisory Council provides a forum for participation by organisations and individuals with an interest in international financial reporting, and diverse geographical and functional backgrounds. The objective of the Advisory Council is to give the IASB advice on agenda decisions and priorities in its work, inform the IASB of the views of Advisory Council members on major standard-setting projects, and give other advice to the IASB or the Trustees.

The Advisory Council comprises about fifty members, representing stakeholder organisations internationally. The Advisory Council normally meets at least three times a year. Its meetings are open to the public. The chair of the Advisory Council is appointed by the Trustees, and cannot be a member of the IASB or its staff. The chair of the Advisory Council is invited to attend and participate in the Trustees' meetings.

Details of the members of the Advisory Council are available on the website www.ifrs.org.

IFRS Interpretations Committee

The IFRS Interpretations Committee is appointed by the Trustees to assist the IASB in establishing and improving standards of financial accounting and reporting for the benefit of users, preparers and auditors of financial statements. The Trustees established the Interpretations Committee (then called the International Financial Reporting Interpretations Committee (IFRIC)) in March 2002, when it replaced the previous interpretations committee, the Standing Interpretations Committee (SIC). The role of the Interpretations Committee is to provide timely guidance on newly identified financial reporting issues not specifically addressed in IFRSs or issues where unsatisfactory or conflicting interpretations have developed, or seem likely to develop. It thus promotes the rigorous and uniform application of IFRSs.

The Interpretations Committee assists the IASB in achieving international convergence of accounting standards by working with similar groups sponsored by national standard-setters to reach similar conclusions on issues where underlying standards are substantially similar.

The Interpretations Committee has fourteen voting members in addition to a non-voting chair, currently Wayne Upton. The chair has the right to speak about the technical issues being considered but not to vote. The Trustees, as they deem necessary, may appoint as non-voting observers regulatory organisations, whose representatives have the right to attend and speak at meetings. Currently, the International Organization of Securities Commissions (IOSCO) and the European Commission are non-voting observers.

The Interpretations Committee publishes a summary of its decisions promptly after each meeting. This *IFRIC Update* is published in electronic format on the website www.ifrs.org.

Details of the members of the Interpretations Committee are available on the website www.ifrs.org.

IASB technical staff

A staff based in London, headed by the Chairman of the IASB, supports the IASB. At 1 January 2012 the technical staff included people from Australia, Argentina, Belgium, Bosnia-Herzegovina, Brazil, Canada, China, France, Germany, Iceland, India, Ireland, Italy, Japan, Republic of Korea, Malaysia, Mexico, The Netherlands, New Zealand, Poland, Russia, South Africa, Spain, Sweden, the UK and the US.

Due process

IASB due process

IFRSs are developed through a formal system of due process and broad international consultation.

The IASB has complete responsibility for all IASB technical matters including the preparation and issuing of IFRSs and exposure drafts, and final approval of Interpretations developed by the IFRS Interpretations Committee. The IASB has full discretion in developing and pursuing its technical agenda, subject to the consultations described above. Formal due process for projects normally, but not necessarily, involves the following steps (the steps that are required under the terms of the IFRS Foundation's Constitution are indicated by an asterisk*):

(a) The IASB staff are asked to identify, review and raise issues that might warrant the Board's attention. The IASB's discussion of potential projects and its decisions to adopt new projects take place in public Board meetings. Before reaching such decisions the IASB consults the IFRS Advisory Council on proposed agenda items and setting priorities.*

(b) When adding an item to its active agenda, the IASB decides whether to conduct the project alone or jointly with another standard-setter.

(c) After considering the nature of the issues and the level of interest among constituents, the IASB may establish a working group.

(d) Although a discussion paper is not a mandatory step in its due process, the IASB normally publishes a discussion paper as its first publication on any major new topic. Typically, a discussion paper includes a comprehensive overview of the issue, possible approaches in addressing the issue, the preliminary views of its authors or the IASB, and an invitation to comment. If the IASB decides to omit this step, it will state its reasons.

(e) Publication of an exposure draft is a mandatory step in the due process.* The development of an exposure draft is carried out during IASB meetings, conducted in public. It involves the IASB considering and reaching decisions on issues on the basis of staff research and recommendations, as well as comments from any discussion paper, suggestions made by the Advisory Council, working groups and national standard-setters and arising from public education sessions conducted for the IASB. An exposure draft must be approved by at least nine members of the IASB.* An exposure draft will be accompanied by a basis for conclusions and include any alternative views held by dissenting IASB members.

(f) The IASB reviews the comment letters received* and the results of other consultations. As a means of exploring the issues further, and soliciting further comments and suggestions, the IASB may conduct field visits, or arrange public hearings and round-table meetings.

(g) The development of an IFRS is carried out during IASB meetings, conducted in public. After resolving issues arising from the exposure draft, the IASB considers whether it should expose any revised proposals for public comment. When the IASB is satisfied that it has reached a conclusion on the issues arising from the exposure draft, it instructs the staff to draft the IFRS. An IFRS must be approved by at least nine members of the IASB.* An IFRS will be accompanied by a basis for conclusions and include any dissenting opinions held by IASB members voting against the IFRS.

Adopting the 'comply or explain' approach that is used by various regulatory bodies, the IASB explains its reasons if it decides to omit any non-mandatory step of its consultative process.

The publication of an exposure draft, a standard or a final Interpretation requires approval by nine of the fifteen members of the IASB (or ten when there are sixteen members). Other decisions of the IASB, including the publication of a discussion paper, require a simple majority of the members of the IASB present at a meeting that is attended by at least 60 per cent of the members of the IASB, in person or by telecommunications.

The IASB has documented and described its consultative procedures in the *Due Process Handbook for the IASB*, which has been approved by the Trustees.

IFRS Interpretations Committee due process

Interpretations of IFRSs are developed through a formal system of due process and broad international consultation. The Interpretations Committee discusses technical matters in meetings that are open to public observation. The due process for each issue normally, but not necessarily, involves the following steps (the steps that are required under the terms of the IFRS Foundation's Constitution are indicated by an asterisk*):

(a) The Interpretations Committee assesses issues suggested by constituents for addition to its agenda. Where the Interpretations Committee decides not to deal with an issue, it publishes the reason for this decision. The tentative agenda decision with reasons is published in draft immediately following the Interpretations Committee's meeting at which it is presented. This allows time for public comment before the recommendation not to deal with an issue is considered at the Interpretations Committee's following meeting.

(b) For those issues added to the agenda, the IASB staff prepare an issues summary. This describes the issue and provides the information necessary for Interpretations Committee members to gain an understanding of the issue and make decisions about it. Preparation of an issues summary involves a review of the authoritative accounting literature including the IASB's *Conceptual Framework*, consideration of alternatives, and consultation with national standard-setters, including national committees that have responsibility for interpretations of national standards.

(c) A consensus on a draft Interpretation is reached if no more than four Interpretations Committee members have voted against the proposal.* The draft Interpretation is released for public comment unless five or more IASB members object to its release within a week of being informed of its completion.*

(d) Comments received during the comment period are considered by the Interpretations Committee before an Interpretation is finalised.*

(e) A consensus on an Interpretation is reached if no more than four Interpretations Committee members have voted against the proposal.* The Interpretation is put to the IASB for approval. Approval by the IASB requires at least nine IASB members to be in favour.* Approved Interpretations are issued by the IASB.

Each voting member of the Interpretations Committee has one vote. Ten voting members constitute a quorum. Members vote in accordance with their own independent views, not as representatives voting according to the views of any firm, organisation or constituency with which they may be associated. Approval of draft or final Interpretations requires that not more than four voting members vote against the draft or final Interpretation.

The Interpretations Committee has documented and described its consultative procedures in the *Due Process Handbook for the IFRS Interpretations Committee*, which has been approved by the Trustees.

Openness of meetings

Meetings of the Trustees, the IASB, the Advisory Council and the Interpretations Committee are all open to public observation. However, some discussions (normally about selection, appointment and other personnel issues) are held in private.

The IASB continues to explore how technology can be used to overcome geographical barriers and other logistical problems and thus facilitate public observation of open meetings. Examples of innovations for that purpose include the introduction of audio and video and webcasting on the website www.ifrs.org.

The agenda for each meeting of the Trustees, the IASB, the Advisory Council and the Interpretations Committee is published in advance on the website, together with Observer Notes, which contain the papers tabled for the meeting. The IASB also publishes promptly a summary of the technical decisions made at meetings of the IASB and the Interpretations Committee and, where appropriate, decisions of the Trustees.

Comment periods

The IASB publishes, for public comment, discussion papers and an exposure draft of each standard, with a normal comment period of 120 days. In some circumstances, the IASB may expose proposals for a longer or shorter period. Draft Interpretations are normally exposed for a 60–day comment period, although a shorter period of not less than 30 days may be used in some circumstances.

Co-ordination with national due process

The IASB meets regularly with national standard-setters and other official bodies concerned with accounting standard-setting. In addition, staff members of the IASB and accounting standard-setters co-operate on a daily basis on projects, sharing resources whenever necessary and appropriate. Close co-ordination with those bodies is important to the success of the IASB.

Opportunities for input

The development of an International Financial Reporting Standard (IFRS) involves an open, public process of debating technical issues and evaluating input sought through several mechanisms. Opportunities for interested parties to participate in the development of IFRSs include, depending on the nature of the project:

- participation in the development of views as a member of the Advisory Council;

- participation in working groups;

© IFRS Foundation

- submission of an issue to the Interpretations Committee (see the website for details);
- submission of a comment letter in response to a discussion paper;
- submission of a comment letter in response to an exposure draft;
- submission of a comment letter in response to a draft Interpretation;
- participation in public hearings and round-table discussions; and
- participation in field visits.

The IASB publishes an annual report on its activities during the past year and priorities for the next year. The report provides a basis and opportunity for comment by interested parties.

Preface to International Financial Reporting Standards

The *Preface to International Financial Reporting Standards* sets out the objectives and due process of the IASB and explains the scope, authority and timing of application of IFRSs (including Interpretations).

IASB Conceptual Framework

The IASB is developing a *Conceptual Framework for Financial Reporting*. The first edition of the *Conceptual Framework* was issued in September 2010, replacing the *Framework for the Preparation and Presentation of Financial Statements* developed by the IASB's predecessor body. The *Conceptual Framework* assists the IASB:

(a) in the development of future IFRSs and in its review of existing IFRSs; and

(b) in promoting the harmonisation of regulations, accounting standards and procedures relating to the presentation of financial statements by providing a basis for reducing the number of alternative accounting treatments permitted by IFRSs.

In addition, the *Conceptual Framework* may assist:

- preparers of financial statements in applying IFRSs and in dealing with topics that have yet to form the subject of a standard or an Interpretation;
- auditors in forming an opinion on whether financial statements comply with IFRSs;
- users of financial statements in interpreting the information contained in financial statements prepared in conformity with IFRSs; and
- those who are interested in the work of the IASB, providing them with information about its approach to the formulation of accounting standards.

The *Conceptual Framework* is not an IFRS. However, when developing an accounting policy in the absence of a standard or an Interpretation that specifically applies to an item, an entity's management is required to refer to, and consider the applicability of, the concepts in the *Conceptual Framework* (see IAS 8 *Accounting Policies, Changes in Accounting Estimates and Errors*).

In a limited number of cases there may be a conflict between the *Conceptual Framework* and a requirement within a standard or an Interpretation. In those cases where there is a conflict, the requirements of the standard or Interpretation prevail over those of the *Conceptual Framework*.

Accounting standards

The IASB publishes its standards in a series of pronouncements called International Financial Reporting Standards (IFRSs). Upon its inception the IASB adopted the body of International Accounting Standards (IASs) issued by its predecessor, the Board of the International Accounting Standards Committee. The term 'International Financial Reporting Standards' includes IFRSs, IASs and Interpretations developed by the Interpretations Committee or the former Standing Interpretations Committee (SIC).

Staff advice

The IASB's operating procedures do not generally allow IASB staff to give advice on the meaning of IFRSs.

Current technical activities

Details of the current technical activities of the IASB and the Interpretations Committee, including the progress of their deliberations, are available on the website. As projects are completed, the IASB expects to add new projects. The Interpretations Committee adds topics to its agenda on the basis of an assessment of issues submitted to it by constituents.

The IASB reports on its technical projects on the website www.ifrs.org. The IASB publishes a report on its decisions promptly after each Board meeting in *IASB Update*. The Interpretations Committee publishes a report on its decisions promptly after each meeting in *IFRIC Update*.

IASB/IFRS Foundation publications and translations

The IFRS Foundation holds the copyright of International Financial Reporting Standards, International Accounting Standards, Interpretations, exposure drafts, and other IASB publications in all countries, except where the Foundation has expressly waived copyright on portions of that material. For more information regarding the Foundation's copyright, please refer to the copyright notice with this edition or the website (www.ifrs.org).

Translations of International Financial Reporting Standards have been created in over 40 languages. The IFRS Foundation considers additional translations as needs arise. For more information, contact the Foundation's Director—IFRS Content Services.

Although the IFRS Foundation makes every reasonable effort to translate IFRSs into other languages on a timely basis, a rigorous process must be followed to ensure that the translations are as accurate as possible. For that reason, there may well be a lag between when a standard or an Interpretation is issued by the IASB (in English) and when it is issued in other languages. Further details are available on the website (www.ifrs.org) and from the IFRS Foundation's Publications department.

More information

The website, www.ifrs.org, provides news, updates and other resources related to the IASB and the IFRS Foundation. The latest publications and subscription services can also be ordered from the Foundation's Shop at www.ifrs.org.

For more information about the IASB, or to obtain copies of its publications and details of the IFRS Foundation's subscription services, visit www.ifrs.org, or write to:

IFRS Foundation Publications Department
30 Cannon Street,
London EC4M 6XH
United Kingdom

Telephone: +44 (0)20 7332 2730
Fax: +44 (0)20 7332 2749
Email: publications@ifrs.org
Web: www.ifrs.org

Preface to International Financial Reporting Standards[1]

This *Preface* is issued to set out the objectives and due process of the International Accounting Standards Board and to explain the scope, authority and timing of application of International Financial Reporting Standards. The *Preface* was approved by the IASB in April 2002 and superseded the *Preface* published in January 1975 (amended November 1982). In 2007 the *Preface* was amended in January and October to reflect changes in the IASC Foundation's[2] Constitution and in September as a consequence of the changes made by IAS 1 *Presentation of Financial Statements* (as revised in 2007). In January 2008 paragraph 9 was amended to update the reference to the body now known as the IPSASB. In 2010 the *Preface* was amended to reflect the Constitution as revised in January 2009 and January 2010 and the publication of the *Conceptual Framework* in September 2010.

1   The International Accounting Standards Board (IASB) was established in 2001 as part of the International Accounting Standards Committee (IASC) Foundation. In 2010 the IASC Foundation was renamed the IFRS Foundation. The governance of the IFRS Foundation rests with twenty-two Trustees. The Trustees' responsibilities include appointing the members of the IASB and associated councils and committees, as well as securing financing for the organisation. The IASB comprises fifteen full-time members (the IFRS Foundation's Constitution provides for membership to rise to sixteen by 1 July 2012). Approval of International Financial Reporting Standards (IFRSs) and related documents, such as the *Conceptual Framework for Financial Reporting*, exposure drafts, and other discussion documents, is the responsibility of the IASB.

2   The IFRS Interpretations Committee[3] comprises fourteen voting members and a non-voting Chairman, all appointed by the Trustees. The role of the Committee is to prepare interpretations of IFRSs for approval by the IASB and, in the context of the *Conceptual Framework*, to provide timely guidance on financial reporting issues. The Committee (then called the International Financial Reporting Interpretations Committee) replaced the former Standing Interpretations Committee (SIC) in 2002.

3   The IFRS Advisory Council[4] is appointed by the Trustees. It provides a formal vehicle for participation by organisations and individuals with an interest in international financial reporting. The participants have diverse geographical and functional backgrounds. The Council's objective is to give advice to the IASB on priorities, agenda decisions and on major standard-setting projects.

4   The IASB was preceded by the Board of IASC, which came into existence on 29 June 1973 as a result of an agreement by professional accountancy bodies in Australia, Canada, France, Germany, Japan, Mexico, the Netherlands, the United Kingdom and Ireland, and the United States of America. A revised Agreement and Constitution were signed in November 1982. The Constitution was further revised in October 1992 and May 2000 by the IASC Board. Under the May 2000

---

1   including IFRIC and SIC Interpretations

2   In July 2010 the IASC Foundation was renamed the IFRS Foundation.

3   Before March 2010 the Interpretations Committee was called the International Financial Reporting Interpretations Committee (IFRIC).

4   Before March 2010 the IFRS Advisory Council was called the Standards Advisory Council (SAC).

Constitution, the professional accountancy bodies adopted a mechanism enabling the appointed Trustees to put the May 2000 Constitution into force. The Trustees activated the new Constitution in January 2001, and revised it in March 2002.[5]

5   At its meeting on 20 April 2001 the IASB passed the following resolution:

> All Standards and Interpretations issued under previous Constitutions continue to be applicable unless and until they are amended or withdrawn. The International Accounting Standards Board may amend or withdraw International Accounting Standards and SIC Interpretations issued under previous Constitutions of IASC as well as issue new Standards and Interpretations.

When the term IFRSs is used in this *Preface*, it includes standards and Interpretations approved by the IASB, and International Accounting Standards (IASs) and SIC Interpretations issued under previous Constitutions.

Objectives of the IASB

6   The objectives of the IASB are:

(a)   to develop, in the public interest, a single set of high quality, understandable, enforceable and globally accepted financial reporting standards based on clearly articulated principles. These standards should require high quality, transparent and comparable information in financial statements and other financial reporting to help investors, other participants in the various capital markets of the world and other users of financial information make economic decisions;

(b)   to promote the use and rigorous application of those standards;

(c)   in fulfilling the objectives associated with (a) and (b), to take account of, as appropriate, the needs of a range of sizes and types of entities in diverse economic settings;

(d)   to promote and facilitate the adoption of IFRSs, being the standards and interpretations issued by the IASB, through the convergence of national accounting standards and IFRSs.

Scope and authority of International Financial Reporting Standards

7   The IASB achieves its objectives primarily by developing and publishing IFRSs and promoting the use of those standards in general purpose financial statements and other financial reporting. Other financial reporting comprises information provided outside financial statements that assists in the interpretation of a complete set of financial statements or improves users' ability to make efficient economic decisions. In developing IFRSs, the IASB works with national standard-setters to promote and facilitate adoption of IFRSs through convergence of national accounting standards and IFRSs.

---

5   The Constitution was further revised in July 2002, June 2005, October 2007, January 2009 and January 2010.

8 IFRSs set out recognition, measurement, presentation and disclosure requirements dealing with transactions and events that are important in general purpose financial statements. They may also set out such requirements for transactions and events that arise mainly in specific industries. IFRSs are based on the *Conceptual Framework*, which addresses the concepts underlying the information presented in general purpose financial statements. Although the *Conceptual Framework* was not issued until September 2010, it was developed from the previous *Framework for the Preparation and Presentation of Financial Statements*, which the IASB adopted in 2001. The objective of the *Conceptual Framework* is to facilitate the consistent and logical formulation of IFRSs. The *Conceptual Framework* also provides a basis for the use of judgement in resolving accounting issues.

9 IFRSs are designed to apply to the general purpose financial statements and other financial reporting of profit-oriented entities. Profit-oriented entities include those engaged in commercial, industrial, financial and similar activities, whether organised in corporate or in other forms. They include organisations such as mutual insurance companies and other mutual co-operative entities that provide dividends or other economic benefits directly and proportionately to their owners, members or participants. Although IFRSs are not designed to apply to not-for-profit activities in the private sector, public sector or government, entities with such activities may find them appropriate. The International Public Sector Accounting Standards Board (IPSASB) prepares accounting standards for governments and other public sector entities, other than government business entities, based on IFRSs.

10 IFRSs apply to all general purpose financial statements. Such financial statements are directed towards the common information needs of a wide range of users, for example, shareholders, creditors, employees and the public at large. The objective of financial statements is to provide information about the financial position, performance and cash flows of an entity that is useful to those users in making economic decisions.

11 A complete set of financial statements includes a statement of financial position, a statement of comprehensive income, a statement of changes in equity, a statement of cash flows, and accounting policies and explanatory notes. When a separate income statement is presented in accordance with IAS 1 *Presentation of Financial Statements* (as revised in 2007), it is part of that complete set. In the interest of timeliness and cost considerations and to avoid repeating information previously reported, an entity may provide less information in its interim financial statements than in its annual financial statements. IAS 34 *Interim Financial Reporting* prescribes the minimum content of complete or condensed financial statements for an interim period. The term 'financial statements' includes a complete set of financial statements prepared for an interim or annual period, and condensed financial statements for an interim period.

12 Some IFRSs permit different treatments for given transactions and events. The IASB's objective is to require like transactions and events to be accounted for and reported in a like way and unlike transactions and events to be accounted for and reported differently, both within an entity over time and

among entities. Consequently, the IASB intends not to permit choices in accounting treatment. Also, the IASB has reconsidered, and will continue to reconsider, those transactions and events for which IFRSs permit a choice of accounting treatment, with the objective of reducing the number of those choices.

13　Standards approved by the IASB include paragraphs in bold type and plain type, which have equal authority. Paragraphs in bold type indicate the main principles. An individual standard should be read in the context of the objective stated in that standard and this *Preface*.

14　Interpretations of IFRSs are prepared by the Interpretations Committee to give authoritative guidance on issues that are likely to receive divergent or unacceptable treatment, in the absence of such guidance.

15　IAS 1 (as revised in 2007) includes the following requirement:

> An entity whose financial statements comply with IFRSs shall make an explicit and unreserved statement of such compliance in the notes. An entity shall not describe financial statements as complying with IFRSs unless they comply with all the requirements of IFRSs.

16　Any limitation of the scope of an IFRS is made clear in the standard.

Due process

17　IFRSs are developed through an international due process that involves accountants, financial analysts and other users of financial statements, the business community, stock exchanges, regulatory and legal authorities, academics and other interested individuals and organisations from around the world. The IASB consults, in public meetings, the Advisory Council on major projects, agenda decisions and work priorities, and discusses technical matters in meetings that are open to public observation. Due process for projects normally, but not necessarily, involves the following steps (the steps that are required under the terms of the IFRS Foundation's Constitution are indicated by an asterisk[*]):

(a)　the staff are asked to identify and review all the issues associated with the topic and to consider the application of the *Conceptual Framework* to the issues;

(b)　study of national accounting requirements and practice and an exchange of views about the issues with national standard-setters;

(c)　consulting the Trustees and the Advisory Council about the advisability of adding the topic to the IASB's agenda;[*][6]

(d)　formation of an advisory group to give advice to the IASB on the project;

(e)　publishing for public comment a discussion document;

(f)　publishing for public comment an exposure draft (including any dissenting opinions held by IASB members) approved by at least nine votes of the IASB if there are fewer than sixteen members, or by ten of its members if there are sixteen members;[*]

6　Beginning no later than 30 June 2011 the IASB is required to carry out a public consultation on its agenda every three years.

(g) normally publishing with an exposure draft a basis for conclusions and the alternative views of any IASB member who opposes publication;*

(h) consideration of all comments received within the comment period on discussion documents and exposure drafts;*

(i) consideration of the desirability of holding a public hearing and of the desirability of conducting field tests and, if considered desirable, holding such hearings and conducting such tests;

(j) approval of a standard by at least nine votes of the IASB if there are fewer than sixteen members, or by ten of its members if there are sixteen members;* and

(k) publishing with a standard (i) a basis for conclusions, explaining, among other things, the steps in the IASB's due process and how the IASB dealt with public comments on the exposure draft, and (ii) the dissenting opinion of any IASB member.*

18   Interpretations of IFRSs are developed through an international due process that involves accountants, financial analysts and other users of financial statements, the business community, stock exchanges, regulatory and legal authorities, academics and other interested individuals and organisations from around the world. The Interpretations Committee discusses technical matters in meetings that are open to public observation. The due process for each project normally, but not necessarily, involves the following steps (the steps that are required under the terms of the IFRS Foundation's Constitution are indicated by an asterisk*):

(a) the staff are asked to identify and review all the issues associated with the topic and to consider the application of the *Conceptual Framework* to the issues;

(b) consideration of the implications for the issues of the hierarchy of IAS 8 *Accounting Policies, Changes in Accounting Estimates and Errors*;

(c) publication of a draft Interpretation for public comment if no more than four Committee members have voted against the proposal;*

(d) consideration of all comments received within the comment period on a draft Interpretation;*

(e) approval by the Interpretations Committee of an Interpretation if no more than four Committee members have voted against the Interpretation after considering public comments on the draft Interpretation;* and

(f) approval of the Interpretation by at least nine votes of the IASB if there are fewer than sixteen members, or by ten of its members if there are sixteen members.*

Timing of application of International Financial Reporting Standards

19   IFRSs apply from a date specified in the document. New or revised IFRSs set out transitional provisions to be applied on their initial application.

20   The IASB has no general policy of exempting transactions occurring before a specific date from the requirements of new IFRSs. When financial statements are used to monitor compliance with contracts and agreements, a new IFRS may have consequences that were not foreseen when the contract or agreement was finalised. For example, covenants contained in banking and loan agreements may impose limits on measures shown in a borrower's financial statements. The IASB believes the fact that financial reporting requirements evolve and change over time is well understood and would be known to the parties when they entered into the agreement. It is up to the parties to determine whether the agreement should be insulated from the effects of a future IFRS, or, if not, the manner in which it might be renegotiated to reflect changes in reporting rather than changes in the underlying financial condition.

21   Exposure drafts are issued for comment and their proposals are subject to revision. Until the effective date of an IFRS, the requirements of any IFRS that would be affected by proposals in an exposure draft remain in force.

Language

22   The approved text of any discussion document, exposure draft or IFRS is that approved by the IASB in the English language. The IASB may approve translations in other languages, provided that the translation is prepared in accordance with a process that provides assurance of the quality of the translation, and the IASB may license other translations.

The *Conceptual Framework for Financial Reporting*

The Conceptual Framework *was issued by the IASB in September 2010. It superseded the* Framework for the Preparation and Presentation of Financial Statements.

CONTENTS

Foreword

The International Accounting Standards Board is currently in the process of updating its conceptual framework. This conceptual framework project is conducted in phases.

As a chapter is finalised, the relevant paragraphs in the *Framework for the Preparation and Presentation of Financial Statements* that was published in 1989 will be replaced. When the conceptual framework project is completed, the Board will have a complete, comprehensive and single document called the *Conceptual Framework for Financial Reporting*.

This version of the *Conceptual Framework* includes the first two chapters the Board published as a result of its first phase of the conceptual framework project—Chapter 1 *The objective of general purpose financial reporting* and Chapter 3 *Qualitative characteristics of useful financial information*. Chapter 2 will deal with the reporting entity concept. The Board published an exposure draft on this topic in March 2010 with a comment period that ended on 16 July 2010. Chapter 4 contains the remaining text of the *Framework* (1989). The table of concordance, at the end of this publication, shows how the contents of the *Framework* (1989) and the *Conceptual Framework* (2010) correspond.

> The Introduction has been carried forward from the *Framework* (1989). This will be updated when the IASB considers the purpose of the *Conceptual Framework*. Until then, the purpose and the status of the *Conceptual Framework* are the same as before.

Introduction

Financial statements are prepared and presented for external users by many entities around the world. Although such financial statements may appear similar from country to country, there are differences which have probably been caused by a variety of social, economic and legal circumstances and by different countries having in mind the needs of different users of financial statements when setting national requirements.

These different circumstances have led to the use of a variety of definitions of the elements of financial statements: for example, assets, liabilities, equity, income and expenses. They have also resulted in the use of different criteria for the recognition of items in the financial statements and in a preference for different bases of measurement. The scope of the financial statements and the disclosures made in them have also been affected.

The International Accounting Standards Board is committed to narrowing these differences by seeking to harmonise regulations, accounting standards and procedures relating to the preparation and presentation of financial statements. It believes that further harmonisation can best be pursued by focusing on financial statements that are prepared for the purpose of providing information that is useful in making economic decisions.

The Board believes that financial statements prepared for this purpose meet the common needs of most users. This is because nearly all users are making economic decisions, for example:

(a)   to decide when to buy, hold or sell an equity investment.

(b)   to assess the stewardship or accountability of management.

(c)   to assess the ability of the entity to pay and provide other benefits to its employees.

(d)   to assess the security for amounts lent to the entity.

(e)   to determine taxation policies.

(f)   to determine distributable profits and dividends.

(g)   to prepare and use national income statistics.

(h)   to regulate the activities of entities.

The Board recognises, however, that governments, in particular, may specify different or additional requirements for their own purposes. These requirements should not, however, affect financial statements published for the benefit of other users unless they also meet the needs of those other users.

Financial statements are most commonly prepared in accordance with an accounting model based on recoverable historical cost and the nominal financial capital maintenance concept. Other models and concepts may be more appropriate in order to meet the objective of providing information that is useful for making economic decisions although there is at present no consensus for change. This *Conceptual Framework* has been developed so that it is applicable to a range of accounting models and concepts of capital and capital maintenance.

Purpose and status

This *Conceptual Framework* sets out the concepts that underlie the preparation and presentation of financial statements for external users. The purpose of the *Conceptual Framework* is:

(a) to assist the Board in the development of future IFRSs and in its review of existing IFRSs;

(b) to assist the Board in promoting harmonisation of regulations, accounting standards and procedures relating to the presentation of financial statements by providing a basis for reducing the number of alternative accounting treatments permitted by IFRSs;

(c) to assist national standard-setting bodies in developing national standards;

(d) to assist preparers of financial statements in applying IFRSs and in dealing with topics that have yet to form the subject of an IFRS;

(e) to assist auditors in forming an opinion on whether financial statements comply with IFRSs;

(f) to assist users of financial statements in interpreting the information contained in financial statements prepared in compliance with IFRSs; and

(g) to provide those who are interested in the work of the IASB with information about its approach to the formulation of IFRSs.

This *Conceptual Framework* is not an IFRS and hence does not define standards for any particular measurement or disclosure issue. Nothing in this *Conceptual Framework* overrides any specific IFRS.

The Board recognises that in a limited number of cases there may be a conflict between the *Conceptual Framework* and an IFRS. In those cases where there is a conflict, the requirements of the IFRS prevail over those of the *Conceptual Framework*. As, however, the Board will be guided by the *Conceptual Framework* in the development of future IFRSs and in its review of existing IFRSs, the number of cases of conflict between the *Conceptual Framework* and IFRSs will diminish through time.

The *Conceptual Framework* will be revised from time to time on the basis of the Board's experience of working with it.

Scope

The *Conceptual Framework* deals with:

(a) the objective of financial reporting;

(b) the qualitative characteristics of useful financial information;

(c) the definition, recognition and measurement of the elements from which financial statements are constructed; and

(d) concepts of capital and capital maintenance.

CHAPTER 1: *THE OBJECTIVE OF GENERAL PURPOSE FINANCIAL REPORTING*

Chapter 1: *The objective of general purpose financial reporting*

Introduction

OB1   The objective of general purpose financial reporting forms the foundation of the *Conceptual Framework*. Other aspects of the *Conceptual Framework*—a reporting entity concept, the qualitative characteristics of, and the constraint on, useful financial information, elements of financial statements, recognition, measurement, presentation and disclosure—flow logically from the objective.

Objective, usefulness and limitations of general purpose financial reporting

OB2   The objective of general purpose financial reporting[1] is to provide financial information about the reporting entity that is useful to existing and potential investors, lenders and other creditors in making decisions about providing resources to the entity. Those decisions involve buying, selling or holding equity and debt instruments, and providing or settling loans and other forms of credit.

OB3   Decisions by existing and potential investors about buying, selling or holding equity and debt instruments depend on the returns that they expect from an investment in those instruments, for example dividends, principal and interest payments or market price increases. Similarly, decisions by existing and potential lenders and other creditors about providing or settling loans and other forms of credit depend on the principal and interest payments or other returns that they expect. Investors', lenders' and other creditors' expectations about returns depend on their assessment of the amount, timing and uncertainty of (the prospects for) future net cash inflows to the entity. Consequently, existing and potential investors, lenders and other creditors need information to help them assess the prospects for future net cash inflows to an entity.

OB4   To assess an entity's prospects for future net cash inflows, existing and potential investors, lenders and other creditors need information about the resources of the entity, claims against the entity, and how efficiently and effectively the entity's management and governing board[2] have discharged their responsibilities to use the entity's resources. Examples of such responsibilities include protecting the entity's resources from unfavourable effects of economic factors such as price and technological changes and ensuring that the entity complies with applicable laws, regulations and contractual provisions. Information about management's discharge of its responsibilities is also useful for decisions by existing investors, lenders and other creditors who have the right to vote on or otherwise influence management's actions.

---

1   Throughout this *Conceptual Framework*, the terms *financial reports* and *financial reporting* refer to *general purpose financial reports* and *general purpose financial reporting* unless specifically indicated otherwise.

2   Throughout this *Conceptual Framework*, the term *management* refers to *management and the governing board of an entity* unless specifically indicated otherwise.

OB5   Many existing and potential investors, lenders and other creditors cannot require reporting entities to provide information directly to them and must rely on general purpose financial reports for much of the financial information they need. Consequently, they are the primary users to whom general purpose financial reports are directed.

OB6   However, general purpose financial reports do not and cannot provide all of the information that existing and potential investors, lenders and other creditors need. Those users need to consider pertinent information from other sources, for example, general economic conditions and expectations, political events and political climate, and industry and company outlooks.

OB7   General purpose financial reports are not designed to show the value of a reporting entity; but they provide information to help existing and potential investors, lenders and other creditors to estimate the value of the reporting entity.

OB8   Individual primary users have different, and possibly conflicting, information needs and desires. The Board, in developing financial reporting standards, will seek to provide the information set that will meet the needs of the maximum number of primary users. However, focusing on common information needs does not prevent the reporting entity from including additional information that is most useful to a particular subset of primary users.

OB9   The management of a reporting entity is also interested in financial information about the entity. However, management need not rely on general purpose financial reports because it is able to obtain the financial information it needs internally.

OB10   Other parties, such as regulators and members of the public other than investors, lenders and other creditors, may also find general purpose financial reports useful. However, those reports are not primarily directed to these other groups.

OB11   To a large extent, financial reports are based on estimates, judgements and models rather than exact depictions. The *Conceptual Framework* establishes the concepts that underlie those estimates, judgements and models. The concepts are the goal towards which the Board and preparers of financial reports strive. As with most goals, the *Conceptual Framework*'s vision of ideal financial reporting is unlikely to be achieved in full, at least not in the short term, because it takes time to understand, accept and implement new ways of analysing transactions and other events. Nevertheless, establishing a goal towards which to strive is essential if financial reporting is to evolve so as to improve its usefulness.

Information about a reporting entity's economic resources, claims against the entity and changes in resources and claims

OB12   General purpose financial reports provide information about the financial position of a reporting entity, which is information about the entity's economic resources and the claims against the reporting entity. Financial reports also provide information about the effects of transactions and other events that change a reporting entity's economic resources and claims. Both types of information provide useful input for decisions about providing resources to an entity.

Economic resources and claims

OB13   Information about the nature and amounts of a reporting entity's economic resources and claims can help users to identify the reporting entity's financial strengths and weaknesses. That information can help users to assess the reporting entity's liquidity and solvency, its needs for additional financing and how successful it is likely to be in obtaining that financing. Information about priorities and payment requirements of existing claims helps users to predict how future cash flows will be distributed among those with a claim against the reporting entity.

OB14   Different types of economic resources affect a user's assessment of the reporting entity's prospects for future cash flows differently. Some future cash flows result directly from existing economic resources, such as accounts receivable. Other cash flows result from using several resources in combination to produce and market goods or services to customers. Although those cash flows cannot be identified with individual economic resources (or claims), users of financial reports need to know the nature and amount of the resources available for use in a reporting entity's operations.

Changes in economic resources and claims

OB15   Changes in a reporting entity's economic resources and claims result from that entity's financial performance (see paragraphs OB17–OB20) and from other events or transactions such as issuing debt or equity instruments (see paragraph OB21). To properly assess the prospects for future cash flows from the reporting entity, users need to be able to distinguish between both of these changes.

OB16   Information about a reporting entity's financial performance helps users to understand the return that the entity has produced on its economic resources. Information about the return the entity has produced provides an indication of how well management has discharged its responsibilities to make efficient and effective use of the reporting entity's resources. Information about the variability and components of that return is also important, especially in assessing the uncertainty of future cash flows. Information about a reporting entity's past financial performance and how its management discharged its responsibilities is usually helpful in predicting the entity's future returns on its economic resources.

Financial performance reflected by accrual accounting

OB17 Accrual accounting depicts the effects of transactions and other events and circumstances on a reporting entity's economic resources and claims in the periods in which those effects occur, even if the resulting cash receipts and payments occur in a different period. This is important because information about a reporting entity's economic resources and claims and changes in its economic resources and claims during a period provides a better basis for assessing the entity's past and future performance than information solely about cash receipts and payments during that period.

OB18 Information about a reporting entity's financial performance during a period, reflected by changes in its economic resources and claims other than by obtaining additional resources directly from investors and creditors (see paragraph OB21), is useful in assessing the entity's past and future ability to generate net cash inflows. That information indicates the extent to which the reporting entity has increased its available economic resources, and thus its capacity for generating net cash inflows through its operations rather than by obtaining additional resources directly from investors and creditors.

OB19 Information about a reporting entity's financial performance during a period may also indicate the extent to which events such as changes in market prices or interest rates have increased or decreased the entity's economic resources and claims, thereby affecting the entity's ability to generate net cash inflows.

Financial performance reflected by past cash flows

OB20 Information about a reporting entity's cash flows during a period also helps users to assess the entity's ability to generate future net cash inflows. It indicates how the reporting entity obtains and spends cash, including information about its borrowing and repayment of debt, cash dividends or other cash distributions to investors, and other factors that may affect the entity's liquidity or solvency. Information about cash flows helps users understand a reporting entity's operations, evaluate its financing and investing activities, assess its liquidity or solvency and interpret other information about financial performance.

Changes in economic resources and claims not resulting from financial performance

OB21 A reporting entity's economic resources and claims may also change for reasons other than financial performance, such as issuing additional ownership shares. Information about this type of change is necessary to give users a complete understanding of why the reporting entity's economic resources and claims changed and the implications of those changes for its future financial performance.

CHAPTER 2: *THE REPORTING ENTITY*

[to be added]

CHAPTER 3: *QUALITATIVE CHARACTERISTICS OF USEFUL FINANCIAL INFORMATION*

Chapter 3: *Qualitative characteristics of useful financial information*

Introduction

QC1   The qualitative characteristics of useful financial information discussed in this chapter identify the types of information that are likely to be most useful to the existing and potential investors, lenders and other creditors for making decisions about the reporting entity on the basis of information in its financial report (financial information).

QC2   Financial reports provide information about the reporting entity's economic resources, claims against the reporting entity and the effects of transactions and other events and conditions that change those resources and claims. (This information is referred to in the *Conceptual Framework* as information about the economic phenomena.) Some financial reports also include explanatory material about management's expectations and strategies for the reporting entity, and other types of forward-looking information.

QC3   The qualitative characteristics of useful financial information[3] apply to financial information provided in financial statements, as well as to financial information provided in other ways. Cost, which is a pervasive constraint on the reporting entity's ability to provide useful financial information, applies similarly. However, the considerations in applying the qualitative characteristics and the cost constraint may be different for different types of information. For example, applying them to forward-looking information may be different from applying them to information about existing economic resources and claims and to changes in those resources and claims.

Qualitative characteristics of useful financial information

QC4   If financial information is to be useful, it must be relevant and faithfully represent what it purports to represent. The usefulness of financial information is enhanced if it is comparable, verifiable, timely and understandable.

Fundamental qualitative characteristics

QC5   The fundamental qualitative characteristics are *relevance* and *faithful representation*.

Relevance

QC6   Relevant financial information is capable of making a difference in the decisions made by users. Information may be capable of making a difference in a decision even if some users choose not to take advantage of it or are already aware of it from other sources.

QC7   Financial information is capable of making a difference in decisions if it has predictive value, confirmatory value or both.

---

3   Throughout this *Conceptual Framework*, the terms *qualitative characteristics* and *constraint* refer to the qualitative characteristics of, and the constraint on, useful financial information.

QC8   Financial information has predictive value if it can be used as an input to processes employed by users to predict future outcomes. Financial information need not be a prediction or forecast to have predictive value. Financial information with predictive value is employed by users in making their own predictions.

QC9   Financial information has confirmatory value if it provides feedback about (confirms or changes) previous evaluations.

QC10   The predictive value and confirmatory value of financial information are interrelated. Information that has predictive value often also has confirmatory value. For example, revenue information for the current year, which can be used as the basis for predicting revenues in future years, can also be compared with revenue predictions for the current year that were made in past years. The results of those comparisons can help a user to correct and improve the processes that were used to make those previous predictions.

Materiality

QC11   Information is material if omitting it or misstating it could influence decisions that users make on the basis of financial information about a specific reporting entity. In other words, materiality is an entity-specific aspect of relevance based on the nature or magnitude, or both, of the items to which the information relates in the context of an individual entity's financial report. Consequently, the Board cannot specify a uniform quantitative threshold for materiality or predetermine what could be material in a particular situation.

Faithful representation

QC12   Financial reports represent economic phenomena in words and numbers. To be useful, financial information must not only represent relevant phenomena, but it must also faithfully represent the phenomena that it purports to represent. To be a perfectly faithful representation, a depiction would have three characteristics. It would be *complete*, *neutral* and *free from error*. Of course, perfection is seldom, if ever, achievable. The Board's objective is to maximise those qualities to the extent possible.

QC13   A complete depiction includes all information necessary for a user to understand the phenomenon being depicted, including all necessary descriptions and explanations. For example, a complete depiction of a group of assets would include, at a minimum, a description of the nature of the assets in the group, a numerical depiction of all of the assets in the group, and a description of what the numerical depiction represents (for example, original cost, adjusted cost or fair value). For some items, a complete depiction may also entail explanations of significant facts about the quality and nature of the items, factors and circumstances that might affect their quality and nature, and the process used to determine the numerical depiction.

QC14   A neutral depiction is without bias in the selection or presentation of financial information. A neutral depiction is not slanted, weighted, emphasised, de-emphasised or otherwise manipulated to increase the probability that financial information will be received favourably or unfavourably by users. Neutral information does not mean information with no purpose or no influence on behaviour. On the contrary, relevant financial information is, by definition, capable of making a difference in users' decisions.

QC15   Faithful representation does not mean accurate in all respects. Free from error means there are no errors or omissions in the description of the phenomenon, and the process used to produce the reported information has been selected and applied with no errors in the process. In this context, free from error does not mean perfectly accurate in all respects. For example, an estimate of an unobservable price or value cannot be determined to be accurate or inaccurate. However, a representation of that estimate can be faithful if the amount is described clearly and accurately as being an estimate, the nature and limitations of the estimating process are explained, and no errors have been made in selecting and applying an appropriate process for developing the estimate.

QC16   A faithful representation, by itself, does not necessarily result in useful information. For example, a reporting entity may receive property, plant and equipment through a government grant. Obviously, reporting that an entity acquired an asset at no cost would faithfully represent its cost, but that information would probably not be very useful. A slightly more subtle example is an estimate of the amount by which an asset's carrying amount should be adjusted to reflect an impairment in the asset's value. That estimate can be a faithful representation if the reporting entity has properly applied an appropriate process, properly described the estimate and explained any uncertainties that significantly affect the estimate. However, if the level of uncertainty in such an estimate is sufficiently large, that estimate will not be particularly useful. In other words, the relevance of the asset being faithfully represented is questionable. If there is no alternative representation that is more faithful, that estimate may provide the best available information.

Applying the fundamental qualitative characteristics

QC17   Information must be both relevant and faithfully represented if it is to be useful. Neither a faithful representation of an irrelevant phenomenon nor an unfaithful representation of a relevant phenomenon helps users make good decisions.

QC18   The most efficient and effective process for applying the fundamental qualitative characteristics would usually be as follows (subject to the effects of enhancing characteristics and the cost constraint, which are not considered in this example). First, identify an economic phenomenon that has the potential to be useful to users of the reporting entity's financial information. Second, identify the type of information about that phenomenon that would be most relevant if it is available and can be faithfully represented. Third, determine whether that information is available and can be faithfully represented. If so, the process of satisfying the fundamental qualitative characteristics ends at that point. If not, the process is repeated with the next most relevant type of information.

Enhancing qualitative characteristics

QC19   *Comparability, verifiability, timeliness* and *understandability* are qualitative characteristics that enhance the usefulness of information that is relevant and faithfully represented. The enhancing qualitative characteristics may also help determine which of two ways should be used to depict a phenomenon if both are considered equally relevant and faithfully represented.

Comparability

QC20   Users' decisions involve choosing between alternatives, for example, selling or holding an investment, or investing in one reporting entity or another. Consequently, information about a reporting entity is more useful if it can be compared with similar information about other entities and with similar information about the same entity for another period or another date.

QC21   Comparability is the qualitative characteristic that enables users to identify and understand similarities in, and differences among, items. Unlike the other qualitative characteristics, comparability does not relate to a single item. A comparison requires at least two items.

QC22   Consistency, although related to comparability, is not the same. Consistency refers to the use of the same methods for the same items, either from period to period within a reporting entity or in a single period across entities. Comparability is the goal; consistency helps to achieve that goal.

QC23   Comparability is not uniformity. For information to be comparable, like things must look alike and different things must look different. Comparability of financial information is not enhanced by making unlike things look alike any more than it is enhanced by making like things look different.

QC24   Some degree of comparability is likely to be attained by satisfying the fundamental qualitative characteristics. A faithful representation of a relevant economic phenomenon should naturally possess some degree of comparability with a faithful representation of a similar relevant economic phenomenon by another reporting entity.

QC25   Although a single economic phenomenon can be faithfully represented in multiple ways, permitting alternative accounting methods for the same economic phenomenon diminishes comparability.

Verifiability

QC26   Verifiability helps assure users that information faithfully represents the economic phenomena it purports to represent. Verifiability means that different knowledgeable and independent observers could reach consensus, although not necessarily complete agreement, that a particular depiction is a faithful representation. Quantified information need not be a single point estimate to be verifiable. A range of possible amounts and the related probabilities can also be verified.

QC27   Verification can be direct or indirect. Direct verification means verifying an amount or other representation through direct observation, for example, by counting cash. Indirect verification means checking the inputs to a model, formula or other technique and recalculating the outputs using the same methodology. An example is verifying the carrying amount of inventory by checking the inputs (quantities and costs) and recalculating the ending inventory using the same cost flow assumption (for example, using the first-in, first-out method).

QC28   It may not be possible to verify some explanations and forward-looking financial information until a future period, if at all. To help users decide whether they want to use that information, it would normally be necessary to disclose the underlying assumptions, the methods of compiling the information and other factors and circumstances that support the information.

Timeliness

QC29   Timeliness means having information available to decision-makers in time to be capable of influencing their decisions. Generally, the older the information is the less useful it is. However, some information may continue to be timely long after the end of a reporting period because, for example, some users may need to identify and assess trends.

Understandability

QC30   Classifying, characterising and presenting information clearly and concisely makes it *understandable*.

QC31   Some phenomena are inherently complex and cannot be made easy to understand. Excluding information about those phenomena from financial reports might make the information in those financial reports easier to understand. However, those reports would be incomplete and therefore potentially misleading.

QC32   Financial reports are prepared for users who have a reasonable knowledge of business and economic activities and who review and analyse the information diligently. At times, even well-informed and diligent users may need to seek the aid of an adviser to understand information about complex economic phenomena.

Applying the enhancing qualitative characteristics

QC33   Enhancing qualitative characteristics should be maximised to the extent possible. However, the enhancing qualitative characteristics, either individually or as a group, cannot make information useful if that information is irrelevant or not faithfully represented.

QC34 Applying the enhancing qualitative characteristics is an iterative process that does not follow a prescribed order. Sometimes, one enhancing qualitative characteristic may have to be diminished to maximise another qualitative characteristic. For example, a temporary reduction in comparability as a result of prospectively applying a new financial reporting standard may be worthwhile to improve relevance or faithful representation in the longer term. Appropriate disclosures may partially compensate for non-comparability.

The cost constraint on useful financial reporting

QC35 Cost is a pervasive constraint on the information that can be provided by financial reporting. Reporting financial information imposes costs, and it is important that those costs are justified by the benefits of reporting that information. There are several types of costs and benefits to consider.

QC36 Providers of financial information expend most of the effort involved in collecting, processing, verifying and disseminating financial information, but users ultimately bear those costs in the form of reduced returns. Users of financial information also incur costs of analysing and interpreting the information provided. If needed information is not provided, users incur additional costs to obtain that information elsewhere or to estimate it.

QC37 Reporting financial information that is relevant and faithfully represents what it purports to represent helps users to make decisions with more confidence. This results in more efficient functioning of capital markets and a lower cost of capital for the economy as a whole. An individual investor, lender or other creditor also receives benefits by making more informed decisions. However, it is not possible for general purpose financial reports to provide all the information that every user finds relevant.

QC38 In applying the cost constraint, the Board assesses whether the benefits of reporting particular information are likely to justify the costs incurred to provide and use that information. When applying the cost constraint in developing a proposed financial reporting standard, the Board seeks information from providers of financial information, users, auditors, academics and others about the expected nature and quantity of the benefits and costs of that standard. In most situations, assessments are based on a combination of quantitative and qualitative information.

QC39 Because of the inherent subjectivity, different individuals' assessments of the costs and benefits of reporting particular items of financial information will vary. Therefore, the Board seeks to consider costs and benefits in relation to financial reporting generally, and not just in relation to individual reporting entities. That does not mean that assessments of costs and benefits always justify the same reporting requirements for all entities. Differences may be appropriate because of different sizes of entities, different ways of raising capital (publicly or privately), different users' needs or other factors.

CHAPTER 4: *THE 1989 FRAMEWORK: THE REMAINING TEXT*

Chapter 4: *The* Framework *(1989): the remaining text*

> *The remaining text of the* Framework for the Preparation and Presentation of Financial Statements *(1989) has not been amended to reflect changes made by IAS 1* Presentation of Financial Statements *(as revised in 2007).*
>
> *The remaining text will also be updated when the Board has considered the elements of financial statements and their measurement bases.*

Underlying assumption

Going concern

4.1 The financial statements are normally prepared on the assumption that an entity is a going concern and will continue in operation for the foreseeable future. Hence, it is assumed that the entity has neither the intention nor the need to liquidate or curtail materially the scale of its operations; if such an intention or need exists, the financial statements may have to be prepared on a different basis and, if so, the basis used is disclosed.

The elements of financial statements

4.2 Financial statements portray the financial effects of transactions and other events by grouping them into broad classes according to their economic characteristics. These broad classes are termed the elements of financial statements. The elements directly related to the measurement of financial position in the balance sheet are assets, liabilities and equity. The elements directly related to the measurement of performance in the income statement are income and expenses. The statement of changes in financial position usually reflects income statement elements and changes in balance sheet elements; accordingly, this *Conceptual Framework* identifies no elements that are unique to this statement.

4.3 The presentation of these elements in the balance sheet and the income statement involves a process of sub-classification. For example, assets and liabilities may be classified by their nature or function in the business of the entity in order to display information in the manner most useful to users for purposes of making economic decisions.

Financial position

4.4 The elements directly related to the measurement of financial position are assets, liabilities and equity. These are defined as follows:

(a) An asset is a resource controlled by the entity as a result of past events and from which future economic benefits are expected to flow to the entity.

(b) A liability is a present obligation of the entity arising from past events, the settlement of which is expected to result in an outflow from the entity of resources embodying economic benefits.

(c) Equity is the residual interest in the assets of the entity after deducting all its liabilities.

4.5   The definitions of an asset and a liability identify their essential features but do not attempt to specify the criteria that need to be met before they are recognised in the balance sheet. Thus, the definitions embrace items that are not recognised as assets or liabilities in the balance sheet because they do not satisfy the criteria for recognition discussed in paragraphs 4.37–4.53. In particular, the expectation that future economic benefits will flow to or from an entity must be sufficiently certain to meet the probability criterion in paragraph 4.38 before an asset or liability is recognised.

4.6   In assessing whether an item meets the definition of an asset, liability or equity, attention needs to be given to its underlying substance and economic reality and not merely its legal form. Thus, for example, in the case of finance leases, the substance and economic reality are that the lessee acquires the economic benefits of the use of the leased asset for the major part of its useful life in return for entering into an obligation to pay for that right an amount approximating to the fair value of the asset and the related finance charge. Hence, the finance lease gives rise to items that satisfy the definition of an asset and a liability and are recognised as such in the lessee's balance sheet.

4.7   Balance sheets drawn up in accordance with current IFRSs may include items that do not satisfy the definitions of an asset or liability and are not shown as part of equity. The definitions set out in paragraph 4.4 will, however, underlie future reviews of existing IFRSs and the formulation of further IFRSs.

Assets

4.8   The future economic benefit embodied in an asset is the potential to contribute, directly or indirectly, to the flow of cash and cash equivalents to the entity. The potential may be a productive one that is part of the operating activities of the entity. It may also take the form of convertibility into cash or cash equivalents or a capability to reduce cash outflows, such as when an alternative manufacturing process lowers the costs of production.

4.9   An entity usually employs its assets to produce goods or services capable of satisfying the wants or needs of customers; because these goods or services can satisfy these wants or needs, customers are prepared to pay for them and hence contribute to the cash flow of the entity. Cash itself renders a service to the entity because of its command over other resources.

4.10   The future economic benefits embodied in an asset may flow to the entity in a number of ways. For example, an asset may be:

(a)   used singly or in combination with other assets in the production of goods or services to be sold by the entity;

(b)   exchanged for other assets;

(c)   used to settle a liability; or

(d)   distributed to the owners of the entity.

4.11   Many assets, for example, property, plant and equipment, have a physical form. However, physical form is not essential to the existence of an asset; hence patents and copyrights, for example, are assets if future economic benefits are expected to flow from them to the entity and if they are controlled by the entity.

4.12 Many assets, for example, receivables and property, are associated with legal rights, including the right of ownership. In determining the existence of an asset, the right of ownership is not essential; thus, for example, property held on a lease is an asset if the entity controls the benefits which are expected to flow from the property. Although the capacity of an entity to control benefits is usually the result of legal rights, an item may nonetheless satisfy the definition of an asset even when there is no legal control. For example, know-how obtained from a development activity may meet the definition of an asset when, by keeping that know-how secret, an entity controls the benefits that are expected to flow from it.

4.13 The assets of an entity result from past transactions or other past events. Entities normally obtain assets by purchasing or producing them, but other transactions or events may generate assets; examples include property received by an entity from government as part of a programme to encourage economic growth in an area and the discovery of mineral deposits. Transactions or events expected to occur in the future do not in themselves give rise to assets; hence, for example, an intention to purchase inventory does not, of itself, meet the definition of an asset.

4.14 There is a close association between incurring expenditure and generating assets but the two do not necessarily coincide. Hence, when an entity incurs expenditure, this may provide evidence that future economic benefits were sought but is not conclusive proof that an item satisfying the definition of an asset has been obtained. Similarly the absence of a related expenditure does not preclude an item from satisfying the definition of an asset and thus becoming a candidate for recognition in the balance sheet; for example, items that have been donated to the entity may satisfy the definition of an asset.

Liabilities

4.15 An essential characteristic of a liability is that the entity has a present obligation. An obligation is a duty or responsibility to act or perform in a certain way. Obligations may be legally enforceable as a consequence of a binding contract or statutory requirement. This is normally the case, for example, with amounts payable for goods and services received. Obligations also arise, however, from normal business practice, custom and a desire to maintain good business relations or act in an equitable manner. If, for example, an entity decides as a matter of policy to rectify faults in its products even when these become apparent after the warranty period has expired, the amounts that are expected to be expended in respect of goods already sold are liabilities.

4.16 A distinction needs to be drawn between a present obligation and a future commitment. A decision by the management of an entity to acquire assets in the future does not, of itself, give rise to a present obligation. An obligation normally arises only when the asset is delivered or the entity enters into an irrevocable agreement to acquire the asset. In the latter case, the irrevocable nature of the agreement means that the economic consequences of failing to honour the obligation, for example, because of the existence of a substantial penalty, leave the entity with little, if any, discretion to avoid the outflow of resources to another party.

4.17   The settlement of a present obligation usually involves the entity giving up resources embodying economic benefits in order to satisfy the claim of the other party. Settlement of a present obligation may occur in a number of ways, for example, by:

(a)   payment of cash;

(b)   transfer of other assets;

(c)   provision of services;

(d)   replacement of that obligation with another obligation; or

(e)   conversion of the obligation to equity.

An obligation may also be extinguished by other means, such as a creditor waiving or forfeiting its rights.

4.18   Liabilities result from past transactions or other past events. Thus, for example, the acquisition of goods and the use of services give rise to trade payables (unless paid for in advance or on delivery) and the receipt of a bank loan results in an obligation to repay the loan. An entity may also recognise future rebates based on annual purchases by customers as liabilities; in this case, the sale of the goods in the past is the transaction that gives rise to the liability.

4.19   Some liabilities can be measured only by using a substantial degree of estimation. Some entities describe these liabilities as provisions. In some countries, such provisions are not regarded as liabilities because the concept of a liability is defined narrowly so as to include only amounts that can be established without the need to make estimates. The definition of a liability in paragraph 4.4 follows a broader approach. Thus, when a provision involves a present obligation and satisfies the rest of the definition, it is a liability even if the amount has to be estimated. Examples include provisions for payments to be made under existing warranties and provisions to cover pension obligations.

Equity

4.20   Although equity is defined in paragraph 4.4 as a residual, it may be sub-classified in the balance sheet. For example, in a corporate entity, funds contributed by shareholders, retained earnings, reserves representing appropriations of retained earnings and reserves representing capital maintenance adjustments may be shown separately. Such classifications can be relevant to the decision-making needs of the users of financial statements when they indicate legal or other restrictions on the ability of the entity to distribute or otherwise apply its equity. They may also reflect the fact that parties with ownership interests in an entity have differing rights in relation to the receipt of dividends or the repayment of contributed equity.

4.21   The creation of reserves is sometimes required by statute or other law in order to give the entity and its creditors an added measure of protection from the effects of losses. Other reserves may be established if national tax law grants exemptions from, or reductions in, taxation liabilities when transfers to such reserves are made. The existence and size of these legal, statutory and tax reserves is information that can be relevant to the decision-making needs of users. Transfers to such reserves are appropriations of retained earnings rather than expenses.

4.22   The amount at which equity is shown in the balance sheet is dependent on the measurement of assets and liabilities. Normally, the aggregate amount of equity only by coincidence corresponds with the aggregate market value of the shares of the entity or the sum that could be raised by disposing of either the net assets on a piecemeal basis or the entity as a whole on a going concern basis.

4.23   Commercial, industrial and business activities are often undertaken by means of entities such as sole proprietorships, partnerships and trusts and various types of government business undertakings. The legal and regulatory framework for such entities is often different from that applying to corporate entities. For example, there may be few, if any, restrictions on the distribution to owners or other beneficiaries of amounts included in equity. Nevertheless, the definition of equity and the other aspects of this *Conceptual Framework* that deal with equity are appropriate for such entities.

Performance

4.24   Profit is frequently used as a measure of performance or as the basis for other measures, such as return on investment or earnings per share. The elements directly related to the measurement of profit are income and expenses. The recognition and measurement of income and expenses, and hence profit, depends in part on the concepts of capital and capital maintenance used by the entity in preparing its financial statements. These concepts are discussed in paragraphs 4.57–4.65.

4.25   The elements of income and expenses are defined as follows:

(a)   Income is increases in economic benefits during the accounting period in the form of inflows or enhancements of assets or decreases of liabilities that result in increases in equity, other than those relating to contributions from equity participants.

(b)   Expenses are decreases in economic benefits during the accounting period in the form of outflows or depletions of assets or incurrences of liabilities that result in decreases in equity, other than those relating to distributions to equity participants.

4.26   The definitions of income and expenses identify their essential features but do not attempt to specify the criteria that would need to be met before they are recognised in the income statement. Criteria for the recognition of income and expenses are discussed in paragraphs 4.37–4.53.

4.27   Income and expenses may be presented in the income statement in different ways so as to provide information that is relevant for economic decision-making. For example, it is common practice to distinguish between those items of income and expenses that arise in the course of the ordinary activities of the entity and those that do not. This distinction is made on the basis that the source of an item is relevant in evaluating the ability of the entity to generate cash and cash equivalents in the future; for example, incidental activities such as the disposal of a long-term investment are unlikely to recur on a regular basis. When distinguishing between items in this way consideration needs to be given to the nature of the entity and its operations. Items that arise from the ordinary activities of one entity may be unusual in respect of another.

4.28   Distinguishing between items of income and expense and combining them in different ways also permits several measures of entity performance to be displayed. These have differing degrees of inclusiveness. For example, the income statement could display gross margin, profit or loss from ordinary activities before taxation, profit or loss from ordinary activities after taxation, and profit or loss.

Income

4.29   The definition of income encompasses both revenue and gains. Revenue arises in the course of the ordinary activities of an entity and is referred to by a variety of different names including sales, fees, interest, dividends, royalties and rent.

4.30   Gains represent other items that meet the definition of income and may, or may not, arise in the course of the ordinary activities of an entity. Gains represent increases in economic benefits and as such are no different in nature from revenue. Hence, they are not regarded as constituting a separate element in this *Conceptual Framework*.

4.31   Gains include, for example, those arising on the disposal of non-current assets. The definition of income also includes unrealised gains; for example, those arising on the revaluation of marketable securities and those resulting from increases in the carrying amount of long-term assets. When gains are recognised in the income statement, they are usually displayed separately because knowledge of them is useful for the purpose of making economic decisions. Gains are often reported net of related expenses.

4.32   Various kinds of assets may be received or enhanced by income; examples include cash, receivables and goods and services received in exchange for goods and services supplied. Income may also result from the settlement of liabilities. For example, an entity may provide goods and services to a lender in settlement of an obligation to repay an outstanding loan.

Expenses

4.33   The definition of expenses encompasses losses as well as those expenses that arise in the course of the ordinary activities of the entity. Expenses that arise in the course of the ordinary activities of the entity include, for example, cost of sales, wages and depreciation. They usually take the form of an outflow or depletion of assets such as cash and cash equivalents, inventory, property, plant and equipment.

4.34   Losses represent other items that meet the definition of expenses and may, or may not, arise in the course of the ordinary activities of the entity. Losses represent decreases in economic benefits and as such they are no different in nature from other expenses. Hence, they are not regarded as a separate element in this *Conceptual Framework*.

4.35   Losses include, for example, those resulting from disasters such as fire and flood, as well as those arising on the disposal of non-current assets. The definition of expenses also includes unrealised losses, for example, those arising from the effects of increases in the rate of exchange for a foreign currency in respect of the borrowings of an entity in that currency. When losses are recognised in the income statement, they are usually displayed separately because knowledge of them is useful for the purpose of making economic decisions. Losses are often reported net of related income.

Capital maintenance adjustments

4.36   The revaluation or restatement of assets and liabilities gives rise to increases or decreases in equity. While these increases or decreases meet the definition of income and expenses, they are not included in the income statement under certain concepts of capital maintenance. Instead these items are included in equity as capital maintenance adjustments or revaluation reserves. These concepts of capital maintenance are discussed in paragraphs 4.57–4.65 of this *Conceptual Framework*.

Recognition of the elements of financial statements

4.37   Recognition is the process of incorporating in the balance sheet or income statement an item that meets the definition of an element and satisfies the criteria for recognition set out in paragraph 4.38. It involves the depiction of the item in words and by a monetary amount and the inclusion of that amount in the balance sheet or income statement totals. Items that satisfy the recognition criteria should be recognised in the balance sheet or income statement. The failure to recognise such items is not rectified by disclosure of the accounting policies used nor by notes or explanatory material.

4.38   An item that meets the definition of an element should be recognised if:

(a)   it is probable that any future economic benefit associated with the item will flow to or from the entity; and

(b)   the item has a cost or value that can be measured with reliability.[4]

4.39   In assessing whether an item meets these criteria and therefore qualifies for recognition in the financial statements, regard needs to be given to the materiality considerations discussed in Chapter 3 *Qualitative characteristics of useful financial information*. The interrelationship between the elements means that an item that meets the definition and recognition criteria for a particular element, for example, an asset, automatically requires the recognition of another element, for example, income or a liability.

The probability of future economic benefit

4.40   The concept of probability is used in the recognition criteria to refer to the degree of uncertainty that the future economic benefits associated with the item will flow to or from the entity. The concept is in keeping with the uncertainty that characterises the environment in which an entity operates. Assessments of the degree of uncertainty attaching to the flow of future economic benefits are made on the basis of the evidence available when the financial statements are prepared. For example, when it is probable that a receivable owed to an entity will be paid,

---

4   Information is reliable when it is complete, neutral and free from error.

it is then justifiable, in the absence of any evidence to the contrary, to recognise the receivable as an asset. For a large population of receivables, however, some degree of non-payment is normally considered probable; hence an expense representing the expected reduction in economic benefits is recognised.

Reliability of measurement

4.41   The second criterion for the recognition of an item is that it possesses a cost or value that can be measured with reliability. In many cases, cost or value must be estimated; the use of reasonable estimates is an essential part of the preparation of financial statements and does not undermine their reliability. When, however, a reasonable estimate cannot be made the item is not recognised in the balance sheet or income statement. For example, the expected proceeds from a lawsuit may meet the definitions of both an asset and income as well as the probability criterion for recognition; however, if it is not possible for the claim to be measured reliably, it should not be recognised as an asset or as income; the existence of the claim, however, would be disclosed in the notes, explanatory material or supplementary schedules.

4.42   An item that, at a particular point in time, fails to meet the recognition criteria in paragraph 4.38 may qualify for recognition at a later date as a result of subsequent circumstances or events.

4.43   An item that possesses the essential characteristics of an element but fails to meet the criteria for recognition may nonetheless warrant disclosure in the notes, explanatory material or in supplementary schedules. This is appropriate when knowledge of the item is considered to be relevant to the evaluation of the financial position, performance and changes in financial position of an entity by the users of financial statements.

Recognition of assets

4.44   An asset is recognised in the balance sheet when it is probable that the future economic benefits will flow to the entity and the asset has a cost or value that can be measured reliably.

4.45   An asset is not recognised in the balance sheet when expenditure has been incurred for which it is considered improbable that economic benefits will flow to the entity beyond the current accounting period. Instead such a transaction results in the recognition of an expense in the income statement. This treatment does not imply either that the intention of management in incurring expenditure was other than to generate future economic benefits for the entity or that management was misguided. The only implication is that the degree of certainty that economic benefits will flow to the entity beyond the current accounting period is insufficient to warrant the recognition of an asset.

Recognition of liabilities

4.46   A liability is recognised in the balance sheet when it is probable that an outflow of resources embodying economic benefits will result from the settlement of a present obligation and the amount at which the settlement will take place can be measured reliably. In practice, obligations under contracts that are equally proportionately unperformed (for example, liabilities for inventory ordered but not yet received) are generally not recognised as liabilities in the financial statements. However, such obligations may meet the definition of liabilities and, provided the recognition criteria are met in the particular circumstances, may qualify for recognition. In such circumstances, recognition of liabilities entails recognition of related assets or expenses.

Recognition of income

4.47   Income is recognised in the income statement when an increase in future economic benefits related to an increase in an asset or a decrease of a liability has arisen that can be measured reliably. This means, in effect, that recognition of income occurs simultaneously with the recognition of increases in assets or decreases in liabilities (for example, the net increase in assets arising on a sale of goods or services or the decrease in liabilities arising from the waiver of a debt payable).

4.48   The procedures normally adopted in practice for recognising income, for example, the requirement that revenue should be earned, are applications of the recognition criteria in this *Conceptual Framework*. Such procedures are generally directed at restricting the recognition as income to those items that can be measured reliably and have a sufficient degree of certainty.

Recognition of expenses

4.49   Expenses are recognised in the income statement when a decrease in future economic benefits related to a decrease in an asset or an increase of a liability has arisen that can be measured reliably. This means, in effect, that recognition of expenses occurs simultaneously with the recognition of an increase in liabilities or a decrease in assets (for example, the accrual of employee entitlements or the depreciation of equipment).

4.50   Expenses are recognised in the income statement on the basis of a direct association between the costs incurred and the earning of specific items of income. This process, commonly referred to as the matching of costs with revenues, involves the simultaneous or combined recognition of revenues and expenses that result directly and jointly from the same transactions or other events; for example, the various components of expense making up the cost of goods sold are recognised at the same time as the income derived from the sale of the goods. However, the application of the matching concept under this *Conceptual Framework* does not allow the recognition of items in the balance sheet which do not meet the definition of assets or liabilities.

4.51   When economic benefits are expected to arise over several accounting periods and the association with income can only be broadly or indirectly determined, expenses are recognised in the income statement on the basis of systematic and rational allocation procedures. This is often necessary in recognising the expenses associated with the using up of assets such as property, plant, equipment, goodwill, patents and trademarks; in such cases the expense is referred to as depreciation or amortisation. These allocation procedures are intended to recognise expenses in the accounting periods in which the economic benefits associated with these items are consumed or expire.

4.52   An expense is recognised immediately in the income statement when an expenditure produces no future economic benefits or when, and to the extent that, future economic benefits do not qualify, or cease to qualify, for recognition in the balance sheet as an asset.

4.53   An expense is also recognised in the income statement in those cases when a liability is incurred without the recognition of an asset, as when a liability under a product warranty arises.

Measurement of the elements of financial statements

4.54   Measurement is the process of determining the monetary amounts at which the elements of the financial statements are to be recognised and carried in the balance sheet and income statement. This involves the selection of the particular basis of measurement.

4.55   A number of different measurement bases are employed to different degrees and in varying combinations in financial statements. They include the following:

(a)   *Historical cost.* Assets are recorded at the amount of cash or cash equivalents paid or the fair value of the consideration given to acquire them at the time of their acquisition. Liabilities are recorded at the amount of proceeds received in exchange for the obligation, or in some circumstances (for example, income taxes), at the amounts of cash or cash equivalents expected to be paid to satisfy the liability in the normal course of business.

(b)   *Current cost.* Assets are carried at the amount of cash or cash equivalents that would have to be paid if the same or an equivalent asset was acquired currently. Liabilities are carried at the undiscounted amount of cash or cash equivalents that would be required to settle the obligation currently.

(c)   *Realisable (settlement) value.* Assets are carried at the amount of cash or cash equivalents that could currently be obtained by selling the asset in an orderly disposal. Liabilities are carried at their settlement values; that is, the undiscounted amounts of cash or cash equivalents expected to be paid to satisfy the liabilities in the normal course of business.

(d)   *Present value.* Assets are carried at the present discounted value of the future net cash inflows that the item is expected to generate in the normal course of business. Liabilities are carried at the present discounted value of the future net cash outflows that are expected to be required to settle the liabilities in the normal course of business.

4.56   The measurement basis most commonly adopted by entities in preparing their financial statements is historical cost. This is usually combined with other measurement bases. For example, inventories are usually carried at the lower of cost and net realisable value, marketable securities may be carried at market value and pension liabilities are carried at their present value. Furthermore, some entities use the current cost basis as a response to the inability of the historical cost accounting model to deal with the effects of changing prices of non-monetary assets.

Concepts of capital and capital maintenance

Concepts of capital

4.57   A financial concept of capital is adopted by most entities in preparing their financial statements. Under a financial concept of capital, such as invested money or invested purchasing power, capital is synonymous with the net assets or equity of the entity. Under a physical concept of capital, such as operating capability, capital is regarded as the productive capacity of the entity based on, for example, units of output per day.

4.58   The selection of the appropriate concept of capital by an entity should be based on the needs of the users of its financial statements. Thus, a financial concept of capital should be adopted if the users of financial statements are primarily concerned with the maintenance of nominal invested capital or the purchasing power of invested capital. If, however, the main concern of users is with the operating capability of the entity, a physical concept of capital should be used. The concept chosen indicates the goal to be attained in determining profit, even though there may be some measurement difficulties in making the concept operational.

Concepts of capital maintenance and the determination of profit

4.59   The concepts of capital in paragraph 4.57 give rise to the following concepts of capital maintenance:

   (a)   *Financial capital maintenance.* Under this concept a profit is earned only if the financial (or money) amount of the net assets at the end of the period exceeds the financial (or money) amount of net assets at the beginning of the period, after excluding any distributions to, and contributions from, owners during the period. Financial capital maintenance can be measured in either nominal monetary units or units of constant purchasing power.

   (b)   *Physical capital maintenance.* Under this concept a profit is earned only if the physical productive capacity (or operating capability) of the entity (or the resources or funds needed to achieve that capacity) at the end of the period exceeds the physical productive capacity at the beginning of the period, after excluding any distributions to, and contributions from, owners during the period.

4.60   The concept of capital maintenance is concerned with how an entity defines the capital that it seeks to maintain. It provides the linkage between the concepts of capital and the concepts of profit because it provides the point of reference by which profit is measured; it is a prerequisite for distinguishing between an entity's return on capital and its return of capital; only inflows of assets in excess of amounts needed to maintain capital may be regarded as profit and therefore as a return on capital. Hence, profit is the residual amount that remains after expenses (including capital maintenance adjustments, where appropriate) have been deducted from income. If expenses exceed income the residual amount is a loss.

4.61   The physical capital maintenance concept requires the adoption of the current cost basis of measurement. The financial capital maintenance concept, however, does not require the use of a particular basis of measurement. Selection of the basis under this concept is dependent on the type of financial capital that the entity is seeking to maintain.

4.62   The principal difference between the two concepts of capital maintenance is the treatment of the effects of changes in the prices of assets and liabilities of the entity. In general terms, an entity has maintained its capital if it has as much capital at the end of the period as it had at the beginning of the period. Any amount over and above that required to maintain the capital at the beginning of the period is profit.

4.63   Under the concept of financial capital maintenance where capital is defined in terms of nominal monetary units, profit represents the increase in nominal money capital over the period. Thus, increases in the prices of assets held over the period, conventionally referred to as holding gains, are, conceptually, profits. They may not be recognised as such, however, until the assets are disposed of in an exchange transaction. When the concept of financial capital maintenance is defined in terms of constant purchasing power units, profit represents the increase in invested purchasing power over the period. Thus, only that part of the increase in the prices of assets that exceeds the increase in the general level of prices is regarded as profit. The rest of the increase is treated as a capital maintenance adjustment and, hence, as part of equity.

4.64   Under the concept of physical capital maintenance when capital is defined in terms of the physical productive capacity, profit represents the increase in that capital over the period. All price changes affecting the assets and liabilities of the entity are viewed as changes in the measurement of the physical productive capacity of the entity; hence, they are treated as capital maintenance adjustments that are part of equity and not as profit.

4.65   The selection of the measurement bases and concept of capital maintenance will determine the accounting model used in the preparation of the financial statements. Different accounting models exhibit different degrees of relevance and reliability and, as in other areas, management must seek a balance between relevance and reliability. This Conceptual Framework is applicable to a range of accounting models and provides guidance on preparing and presenting the financial statements constructed under the chosen model. At the present time, it is not the intention of the Board to prescribe a particular model other than in exceptional circumstances, such as for those entities reporting in the currency of a hyperinflationary economy. This intention will, however, be reviewed in the light of world developments.

International Financial Reporting Standard 1

First-time Adoption of International Financial Reporting Standards

In April 2001 the International Accounting Standards Board (IASB) adopted SIC-8 *First-time Application of IASs as the Primary Basis of Accounting*, which had been issued by the Standing Interpretations Committee of the International Accounting Standards Committee in July 1998.

In June 2003 the IASB issued IFRS 1 *First-time Adoption of International Financial Reporting Standards* to replace SIC-8. IAS 1 *Presentation of Financial Statements* (as revised in 2007) amended the terminology used throughout IFRSs, including IFRS 1.

The IASB restructured IFRS 1 in November 2008. In December 2010 the IASB amended IFRS 1 to reflect that a first-time adopter would restate past transactions from the date of transition to IFRSs instead of at 1 January 2004.

Since it was issued in 2003, IFRS 1 was amended to accommodate first-time adoption requirements resulting from new or amended IFRSs.

Contents

FOR THE ACCOMPANYING DOCUMENTS LISTED BELOW, SEE PART B OF THIS EDITION

APPROVAL BY THE BOARD OF IFRS 1 ISSUED IN NOVEMBER 2008

APPROVAL BY THE BOARD OF AMENDMENTS TO IFRS 1:

Additional Exemptions For First-time Adopters issued in July 2009

Limited Exemption from Comparative IFRS 7 Disclosures for First-time Adopters issued in January 2010

Severe Hyperinflation and Removal of Fixed Dates for First-time Adopters issued in December 2010

BASIS FOR CONCLUSIONS

APPENDIX
Amendments to Basis for Conclusions on other IFRSs

IMPLEMENTATION GUIDANCE

TABLE OF CONCORDANCE

International Financial Reporting Standard 1 *First-time Adoption of International Financial Reporting Standards* (IFRS 1) is set out in paragraphs 1–40 and Appendices A–E. All the paragraphs have equal authority. Paragraphs in **bold type** state the main principles. Terms defined in Appendix A are in *italics* the first time they appear in the IFRS. Definitions of other terms are given in the Glossary for International Financial Reporting Standards. IFRS 1 should be read in the context of its objective and the Basis for Conclusions, the *Preface to International Financial Reporting Standards* and the *Conceptual Framework for Financial Reporting*. IAS 8 *Accounting Policies, Changes in Accounting Estimates and Errors* provides a basis for selecting and applying accounting policies in the absence of explicit guidance

Introduction

Reasons for issuing the IFRS

IN1 The International Accounting Standards Board issued IFRS 1 in June 2003. IFRS 1 replaced SIC-8 *First-time Application of IASs as the Primary Basis of Accounting*. The Board developed the IFRS to address concerns about the full retrospective application of IFRSs required by SIC-8.

IN2 Subsequently, IFRS 1 was amended many times to accommodate first-time adoption requirements resulting from new or amended IFRSs. As a result, the IFRS became more complex and less clear. In 2007, therefore, the Board proposed, as part of its annual improvements project, to change IFRS 1 to make it easier for the reader to understand and to design it to better accommodate future changes. The version of IFRS 1 issued in 2008 retains the substance of the previous version, but within a changed structure. It replaces the previous version and is effective for entities applying IFRSs for the first time for annual periods beginning on or after 1 July 2009. Earlier application is permitted.

Main features of the IFRS

IN3 The IFRS applies when an entity adopts IFRSs for the first time by an explicit and unreserved statement of compliance with IFRSs.

IN4 In general, the IFRS requires an entity to comply with each IFRS effective at the end of its first IFRS reporting period. In particular, the IFRS requires an entity to do the following in the opening IFRS statement of financial position that it prepares as a starting point for its accounting under IFRSs:

(a) recognise all assets and liabilities whose recognition is required by IFRSs;

(b) not recognise items as assets or liabilities if IFRSs do not permit such recognition;

(c) reclassify items that it recognised under previous GAAP as one type of asset, liability or component of equity, but are a different type of asset, liability or component of equity under IFRSs; and

(d) apply IFRSs in measuring all recognised assets and liabilities.

IN5 The IFRS grants limited exemptions from these requirements in specified areas where the cost of complying with them would be likely to exceed the benefits to users of financial statements. The IFRS also prohibits retrospective application of IFRSs in some areas, particularly where retrospective application would require judgements by management about past conditions after the outcome of a particular transaction is already known.

IN6 The IFRS requires disclosures that explain how the transition from previous GAAP to IFRSs affected the entity's reported financial position, financial performance and cash flows.

IN7 An entity is required to apply the IFRS if its first IFRS financial statements are for a period beginning on or after 1 July 2009. Earlier application is encouraged.

International Financial Reporting Standard 1
First-time Adoption of International Financial Reporting Standards

Objective

1   The objective of this IFRS is to ensure that an entity's *first IFRS financial statements*, and its interim financial reports for part of the period covered by those financial statements, contain high quality information that:

(a)   is transparent for users and comparable over all periods presented;

(b)   provides a suitable starting point for accounting in accordance with *International Financial Reporting Standards (IFRSs)*; and

(c)   can be generated at a cost that does not exceed the benefits.

Scope

2   An entity shall apply this IFRS in:

(a)   its first IFRS financial statements; and

(b)   each interim financial report, if any, that it presents in accordance with IAS 34 *Interim Financial Reporting* for part of the period covered by its first IFRS financial statements.

3   An entity's first IFRS financial statements are the first annual financial statements in which the entity adopts IFRSs, by an explicit and unreserved statement in those financial statements of compliance with IFRSs. Financial statements in accordance with IFRSs are an entity's first IFRS financial statements if, for example, the entity:

(a)   presented its most recent previous financial statements:

(i)   in accordance with national requirements that are not consistent with IFRSs in all respects;

(ii)   in conformity with IFRSs in all respects, except that the financial statements did not contain an explicit and unreserved statement that they complied with IFRSs;

(iii) containing an explicit statement of compliance with some, but not all, IFRSs;

(iv)   in accordance with national requirements inconsistent with IFRSs, using some individual IFRSs to account for items for which national requirements did not exist; or

(v)   in accordance with national requirements, with a reconciliation of some amounts to the amounts determined in accordance with IFRSs;

(b)   prepared financial statements in accordance with IFRSs for internal use only, without making them available to the entity's owners or any other external users;

(c)   prepared a reporting package in accordance with IFRSs for consolidation purposes without preparing a complete set of financial statements as defined in IAS 1 *Presentation of Financial Statements* (as revised in 2007); or

(d)   did not present financial statements for previous periods.

4   This IFRS applies when an entity first adopts IFRSs. It does not apply when, for example, an entity:

(a)   stops presenting financial statements in accordance with national requirements, having previously presented them as well as another set of financial statements that contained an explicit and unreserved statement of compliance with IFRSs;

(b)   presented financial statements in the previous year in accordance with national requirements and those financial statements contained an explicit and unreserved statement of compliance with IFRSs; or

(c)   presented financial statements in the previous year that contained an explicit and unreserved statement of compliance with IFRSs, even if the auditors qualified their audit report on those financial statements.

5   This IFRS does not apply to changes in accounting policies made by an entity that already applies IFRSs. Such changes are the subject of:

(a)   requirements on changes in accounting policies in IAS 8 *Accounting Policies, Changes in Accounting Estimates and Errors*; and

(b)   specific transitional requirements in other IFRSs.

Recognition and measurement

Opening IFRS statement of financial position

6   An entity shall prepare and present an *opening IFRS statement of financial position* at the *date of transition to IFRSs*. This is the starting point for its accounting in accordance with IFRSs.

Accounting policies

7   **An entity shall use the same accounting policies in its opening IFRS statement of financial position and throughout all periods presented in its first IFRS financial statements. Those accounting policies shall comply with each IFRS effective at the end of its first IFRS reporting period, except as specified in paragraphs 13–19 and Appendices B–E.**

8   An entity shall not apply different versions of IFRSs that were effective at earlier dates. An entity may apply a new IFRS that is not yet mandatory if that IFRS permits early application.

Example: Consistent application of latest version of IFRSs

Background

The end of entity A's first IFRS reporting period is 31 December 20X5. Entity A decides to present comparative information in those financial statements for one year only (see paragraph 21). Therefore, its date of transition to IFRSs is the beginning of business on 1 January 20X4 (or, equivalently, close of business on 31 December 20X3). Entity A presented financial statements in accordance with its *previous GAAP* annually to 31 December each year up to, and including, 31 December 20X4.

Application of requirements

Entity A is required to apply the IFRSs effective for periods ending on 31 December 20X5 in:

(a)   preparing and presenting its opening IFRS statement of financial position at 1 January 20X4; and

(b)   preparing and presenting its statement of financial position for 31 December 20X5 (including comparative amounts for 20X4), statement of comprehensive income, statement of changes in equity and statement of cash flows for the year to 31 December 20X5 (including comparative amounts for 20X4) and disclosures (including comparative information for 20X4).

If a new IFRS is not yet mandatory but permits early application, entity A is permitted, but not required, to apply that IFRS in its first IFRS financial statements.

---

9   The transitional provisions in other IFRSs apply to changes in accounting policies made by an entity that already uses IFRSs; they do not apply to a *first-time adopter*'s transition to IFRSs, except as specified in Appendices B–E.

10   Except as described in paragraphs 13–19 and Appendices B–E, an entity shall, in its opening IFRS statement of financial position:

(a)   recognise all assets and liabilities whose recognition is required by IFRSs;

(b)   not recognise items as assets or liabilities if IFRSs do not permit such recognition;

(c)   reclassify items that it recognised in accordance with previous GAAP as one type of asset, liability or component of equity, but are a different type of asset, liability or component of equity in accordance with IFRSs; and

(d)   apply IFRSs in measuring all recognised assets and liabilities.

11   The accounting policies that an entity uses in its opening IFRS statement of financial position may differ from those that it used for the same date using its previous GAAP. The resulting adjustments arise from events and transactions before the date of transition to IFRSs. Therefore, an entity shall recognise those adjustments directly in retained earnings (or, if appropriate, another category of equity) at the date of transition to IFRSs.

12   This IFRS establishes two categories of exceptions to the principle that an entity's opening IFRS statement of financial position shall comply with each IFRS:

(a)   paragraphs 14–17 and Appendix B prohibit retrospective application of some aspects of other IFRSs.

(b)   Appendices C–E grant exemptions from some requirements of other IFRSs.

Exceptions to the retrospective application of other IFRSs

13   This IFRS prohibits retrospective application of some aspects of other IFRSs. These exceptions are set out in paragraphs 14–17 and Appendix B.

Estimates

14   **An entity's estimates in accordance with IFRSs at the date of transition to IFRSs shall be consistent with estimates made for the same date in accordance with previous GAAP (after adjustments to reflect any difference in accounting policies), unless there is objective evidence that those estimates were in error.**

15   An entity may receive information after the date of transition to IFRSs about estimates that it had made under previous GAAP. In accordance with paragraph 14, an entity shall treat the receipt of that information in the same way as non-adjusting events after the reporting period in accordance with IAS 10 *Events after the Reporting Period*. For example, assume that an entity's date of transition to IFRSs is 1 January 20X4 and new information on 15 July 20X4 requires the revision of an estimate made in accordance with previous GAAP at 31 December 20X3. The entity shall not reflect that new information in its opening IFRS statement of financial position (unless the estimates need adjustment for any differences in accounting policies or there is objective evidence that the estimates were in error). Instead, the entity shall reflect that new information in profit or loss (or, if appropriate, other comprehensive income) for the year ended 31 December 20X4.

16   An entity may need to make estimates in accordance with IFRSs at the date of transition to IFRSs that were not required at that date under previous GAAP. To achieve consistency with IAS 10, those estimates in accordance with IFRSs shall reflect conditions that existed at the date of transition to IFRSs. In particular, estimates at the date of transition to IFRSs of market prices, interest rates or foreign exchange rates shall reflect market conditions at that date.

17   Paragraphs 14–16 apply to the opening IFRS statement of financial position. They also apply to a comparative period presented in an entity's first IFRS financial statements, in which case the references to the date of transition to IFRSs are replaced by references to the end of that comparative period.

Exemptions from other IFRSs

18 An entity may elect to use one or more of the exemptions contained in Appendices C–E. An entity shall not apply these exemptions by analogy to other items.

19 [Deleted]

Presentation and disclosure

20 This IFRS does not provide exemptions from the presentation and disclosure requirements in other IFRSs.

Comparative information

21 To comply with IAS 1, an entity's first IFRS financial statements shall include at least three statements of financial position, two statements of profit or loss and other comprehensive income, two separate statements of profit or loss (if presented), two statements of cash flows and two statements of changes in equity and related notes, including comparative information.

Non-IFRS comparative information and historical summaries

22 Some entities present historical summaries of selected data for periods before the first period for which they present full comparative information in accordance with IFRSs. This IFRS does not require such summaries to comply with the recognition and measurement requirements of IFRSs. Furthermore, some entities present comparative information in accordance with previous GAAP as well as the comparative information required by IAS 1. In any financial statements containing historical summaries or comparative information in accordance with previous GAAP, an entity shall:

   (a) label the previous GAAP information prominently as not being prepared in accordance with IFRSs; and

   (b) disclose the nature of the main adjustments that would make it comply with IFRSs. An entity need not quantify those adjustments.

Explanation of transition to IFRSs

23 An entity shall explain how the transition from previous GAAP to IFRSs affected its reported financial position, financial performance and cash flows.

Reconciliations

24 To comply with paragraph 23, an entity's first IFRS financial statements shall include:

   (a) reconciliations of its equity reported in accordance with previous GAAP to its equity in accordance with IFRSs for both of the following dates:

      (i) the date of transition to IFRSs; and

> > (ii) the end of the latest period presented in the entity's most recent annual financial statements in accordance with previous GAAP.
>
> (b) a reconciliation to its total comprehensive income in accordance with IFRSs for the latest period in the entity's most recent annual financial statements. The starting point for that reconciliation shall be total comprehensive income in accordance with previous GAAP for the same period or, if an entity did not report such a total, profit or loss under previous GAAP.
>
> (c) if the entity recognised or reversed any impairment losses for the first time in preparing its opening IFRS statement of financial position, the disclosures that IAS 36 *Impairment of Assets* would have required if the entity had recognised those impairment losses or reversals in the period beginning with the date of transition to IFRSs.

25   The reconciliations required by paragraph 24(a) and (b) shall give sufficient detail to enable users to understand the material adjustments to the statement of financial position and statement of comprehensive income. If an entity presented a statement of cash flows under its previous GAAP, it shall also explain the material adjustments to the statement of cash flows.

26   If an entity becomes aware of errors made under previous GAAP, the reconciliations required by paragraph 24(a) and (b) shall distinguish the correction of those errors from changes in accounting policies.

27   IAS 8 does not apply to the changes in accounting policies an entity makes when it adopts IFRSs or to changes in those policies until after it presents its first IFRS financial statements. Therefore, IAS 8's requirements about changes in accounting policies do not apply in an entity's first IFRS financial statements.

27A   If during the period covered by its first IFRS financial statements an entity changes its accounting policies or its use of the exemptions contained in this IFRS, it shall explain the changes between its first IFRS interim financial report and its first IFRS financial statements, in accordance with paragraph 23, and it shall update the reconciliations required by paragraph 24(a) and (b).

28   If an entity did not present financial statements for previous periods, its first IFRS financial statements shall disclose that fact.

Designation of financial assets or financial liabilities

29   An entity is permitted to designate a previously recognised financial asset as a financial asset measured at fair value through profit or loss in accordance with paragraph D19A. The entity shall disclose the fair value of financial assets so designated at the date of designation and their classification and carrying amount in the previous financial statements.

29A   An entity is permitted to designate a previously recognised financial liability as a financial liability at fair value through profit or loss in accordance with paragraph D19. The entity shall disclose the fair value of financial liabilities so designated at the date of designation and their classification and carrying amount in the previous financial statements.

Use of fair value as deemed cost

30   If an entity uses fair value in its opening IFRS statement of financial position as *deemed cost* for an item of property, plant and equipment, an investment property or an intangible asset (see paragraphs D5 and D7), the entity's first IFRS financial statements shall disclose, for each line item in the opening IFRS statement of financial position:

(a)   the aggregate of those fair values; and

(b)   the aggregate adjustment to the carrying amounts reported under previous GAAP.

Use of deemed cost for investments in subsidiaries, joint ventures and associates

31   Similarly, if an entity uses a deemed cost in its opening IFRS statement of financial position for an investment in a subsidiary, joint venture or associate in its separate financial statements (see paragraph D15), the entity's first IFRS separate financial statements shall disclose:

(a)   the aggregate deemed cost of those investments for which deemed cost is their previous GAAP carrying amount;

(b)   the aggregate deemed cost of those investments for which deemed cost is fair value; and

(c)   the aggregate adjustment to the carrying amounts reported under previous GAAP.

Use of deemed cost for oil and gas assets

31A   If an entity uses the exemption in paragraph D8A(b) for oil and gas assets, it shall disclose that fact and the basis on which carrying amounts determined under previous GAAP were allocated.

Use of deemed cost for operations subject to rate regulation

31B   If an entity uses the exemption in paragraph D8B for operations subject to rate regulation, it shall disclose that fact and the basis on which carrying amounts were determined under previous GAAP.

Use of deemed cost after severe hyperinflation

31C   If an entity elects to measure assets and liabilities at fair value and to use that fair value as the deemed cost in its opening IFRS statement of financial position because of severe hyperinflation (see paragraphs D26–D30), the entity's first IFRS financial statements shall disclose an explanation of how, and why, the entity had, and then ceased to have, a functional currency that has both of the following characteristics:

(a)   a reliable general price index is not available to all entities with transactions and balances in the currency.

(b)   exchangeability between the currency and a relatively stable foreign currency does not exist.

Interim financial reports

32 To comply with paragraph 23, if an entity presents an interim financial report in accordance with IAS 34 for part of the period covered by its first IFRS financial statements, the entity shall satisfy the following requirements in addition to the requirements of IAS 34:

(a) Each such interim financial report shall, if the entity presented an interim financial report for the comparable interim period of the immediately preceding financial year, include:

(i) a reconciliation of its equity in accordance with previous GAAP at the end of that comparable interim period to its equity under IFRSs at that date; and

(ii) a reconciliation to its total comprehensive income in accordance with IFRSs for that comparable interim period (current and year to date). The starting point for that reconciliation shall be total comprehensive income in accordance with previous GAAP for that period or, if an entity did not report such a total, profit or loss in accordance with previous GAAP.

(b) In addition to the reconciliations required by (a), an entity's first interim financial report in accordance with IAS 34 for part of the period covered by its first IFRS financial statements shall include the reconciliations described in paragraph 24(a) and (b) (supplemented by the details required by paragraphs 25 and 26) or a cross-reference to another published document that includes these reconciliations.

(c) If an entity changes its accounting policies or its use of the exemptions contained in this IFRS, it shall explain the changes in each such interim financial report in accordance with paragraph 23 and update the reconciliations required by (a) and (b).

33 IAS 34 requires minimum disclosures, which are based on the assumption that users of the interim financial report also have access to the most recent annual financial statements. However, IAS 34 also requires an entity to disclose 'any events or transactions that are material to an understanding of the current interim period'. Therefore, if a first-time adopter did not, in its most recent annual financial statements in accordance with previous GAAP, disclose information material to an understanding of the current interim period, its interim financial report shall disclose that information or include a cross-reference to another published document that includes it.

Effective date

34 An entity shall apply this IFRS if its first IFRS financial statements are for a period beginning on or after 1 July 2009. Earlier application is permitted.

35 An entity shall apply the amendments in paragraphs D1(n) and D23 for annual periods beginning on or after 1 July 2009. If an entity applies IAS 23 *Borrowing Costs* (as revised in 2007) for an earlier period, those amendments shall be applied for that earlier period.

36   IFRS 3 *Business Combinations* (as revised in 2008) amended paragraphs 19, C1 and C4(f) and (g). If an entity applies IFRS 3 (revised 2008) for an earlier period, the amendments shall also be applied for that earlier period.

37   IAS 27 *Consolidated and Separate Financial Statements* (as amended in 2008) amended paragraphs B1 and B7. If an entity applies IAS 27 (amended 2008) for an earlier period, the amendments shall be applied for that earlier period.

38   *Cost of an Investment in a Subsidiary, Jointly Controlled Entity or Associate* (Amendments to IFRS 1 and IAS 27), issued in May 2008, added paragraphs 31, D1(g), D14 and D15. An entity shall apply those paragraphs for annual periods beginning on or after 1 July 2009. Earlier application is permitted. If an entity applies the paragraphs for an earlier period, it shall disclose that fact.

39   Paragraph B7 was amended by *Improvements to IFRSs* issued in May 2008. An entity shall apply those amendments for annual periods beginning on or after 1 July 2009. If an entity applies IAS 27 (amended 2008) for an earlier period, the amendments shall be applied for that earlier period.

39A   *Additional Exemptions for First-time Adopters* (Amendments to IFRS 1), issued in July 2009, added paragraphs 31A, D8A, D9A and D21A and amended paragraph D1(c), (d) and (l). An entity shall apply those amendments for annual periods beginning on or after 1 January 2010. Earlier application is permitted. If an entity applies the amendments for an earlier period it shall disclose that fact.

39B   [Deleted]

39C   IFRIC 19 *Extinguishing Financial Liabilities with Equity Instruments* added paragraph D25. An entity shall apply that amendment when it applies IFRIC 19.

39D   *Limited Exemption from Comparative IFRS 7 Disclosures for First-time Adopters* (Amendment to IFRS 1), issued in January 2010, added paragraph E3. An entity shall apply that amendment for annual periods beginning on or after 1 July 2010. Earlier application is permitted. If an entity applies the amendment for an earlier period, it shall disclose that fact.

39E   *Improvements to IFRSs* issued in May 2010 added paragraphs 27A, 31B and D8B and amended paragraphs 27, 32, D1(c) and D8. An entity shall apply those amendments for annual periods beginning on or after 1 January 2011. Earlier application is permitted. If an entity applies the amendments for an earlier period it shall disclose that fact. Entities that adopted IFRSs in periods before the effective date of IFRS 1 or applied IFRS 1 in a previous period are permitted to apply the amendment to paragraph D8 retrospectively in the first annual period after the amendment is effective. An entity applying paragraph D8 retrospectively shall disclose that fact.

39F   *Disclosures—Transfers of Financial Assets* (Amendments to IFRS 7), issued in October 2010, added paragraph E4. An entity shall apply that amendment for annual periods beginning on or after 1 July 2011. Earlier application is permitted. If an entity applies the amendment for an earlier period, it shall disclose that fact.

39G   IFRS 9 *Financial Instruments*, issued in October 2010, amended paragraphs 29, B1–B5, D1(j), D14, D15, D19 and D20, added paragraphs 29A, B8, B9, D19A–D19D, E1 and E2 and deleted paragraph 39B. An entity shall apply those amendments when it applies IFRS 9 as issued in October 2010.

39H   *Severe Hyperinflation and Removal of Fixed Dates for First-time Adopters* (Amendments to IFRS 1), issued in December 2010, amended paragraphs B2, D1 and D20 and added paragraphs 31C and D26–D30. An entity shall apply those amendments for annual periods beginning on or after 1 July 2011. Earlier application is permitted.

39I   IFRS 10 *Consolidated Financial Statements* and IFRS 11 *Joint Arrangements*, issued in May 2011, amended paragraphs 31, B7, C1, D1, D14 and D15 and added paragraph D31. An entity shall apply those amendments when it applies IFRS 10 and IFRS 11.

39J   IFRS 13 *Fair Value Measurement*, issued in May 2011, deleted paragraph 19, amended the definition of fair value in Appendix A and amended paragraphs D15 and D20. An entity shall apply those amendments when it applies IFRS 13.

39K   *Presentation of Items of Other Comprehensive Income* (Amendments to IAS 1), issued in June 2011, amended paragraph 21. An entity shall apply that amendment when it applies IAS 1 as amended in June 2011.

39L   IAS 19 *Employee Benefits* (as amended in June 2011) amended paragraph D1, deleted paragraphs D10 and D11 and added paragraph E5. An entity shall apply those amendments when it applies IAS 19 (as amended in June 2011).

39M   IFRIC 20 *Stripping Costs in the Production Phase of a Surface Mine* added paragraph D32 and amended paragraph D1. An entity shall apply that amendment when it applies IFRIC 20.

Withdrawal of IFRS 1 (issued 2003)

40   This IFRS supersedes IFRS 1 (issued in 2003 and amended at May 2008).

Appendix A
Defined terms

This appendix is an integral part of the IFRS.

date of transition to IFRSs	The beginning of the earliest period for which an entity presents full comparative information under IFRSs in its **first IFRS financial statements**.
deemed cost	An amount used as a surrogate for cost or depreciated cost at a given date. Subsequent depreciation or amortisation assumes that the entity had initially recognised the asset or liability at the given date and that its cost was equal to the deemed cost.
fair value	*Fair value* is the price that would be received to sell an asset or paid to transfer a liability in an orderly transaction between market participants at the measurement date. (See IFRS 13.)
first IFRS financial statements	The first annual financial statements in which an entity adopts **International Financial Reporting Standards (IFRSs)**, by an explicit and unreserved statement of compliance with IFRSs.
first IFRS reporting period	The latest reporting period covered by an entity's **first IFRS financial statements**.
first-time adopter	An entity that presents its **first IFRS financial statements**.
International Financial Reporting Standards (IFRSs)	Standards and Interpretations issued by the International Accounting Standards Board (IASB). They comprise:
	(a) International Financial Reporting Standards;
	(b) International Accounting Standards;
	(c) IFRIC Interpretations; and
	(d) SIC Interpretations.[a]
opening IFRS statement of financial position	An entity's statement of financial position at the **date of transition to IFRSs**.
previous GAAP	The basis of accounting that a **first-time adopter** used immediately before adopting IFRSs.

[a] Definition of IFRSs amended after the name changes introduced by the revised Constitution of the IFRS Foundation in 2010.

Appendix B
Exceptions to the retrospective application of other IFRSs

This appendix is an integral part of the IFRS.

B1 An entity shall apply the following exceptions:

(a) derecognition of financial assets and financial liabilities (paragraphs B2 and B3);

(b) hedge accounting (paragraphs B4–B6);

(c) non-controlling interests (paragraph B7);

(d) classification and measurement of financial assets (paragraph B8); and

(e) embedded derivatives (paragraph B9).

Derecognition of financial assets and financial liabilities

B2 Except as permitted by paragraph B3, a first-time adopter shall apply the derecognition requirements in IFRS 9 prospectively for transactions occurring on or after the date of transition to IFRSs. For example, if a first-time adopter derecognised non-derivative financial assets or non-derivative financial liabilities in accordance with its previous GAAP as a result of a transaction that occurred before the date of transition to IFRSs, it shall not recognise those assets and liabilities in accordance with IFRSs (unless they qualify for recognition as a result of a later transaction or event).

B3 Despite paragraph B2, an entity may apply the derecognition requirements in IFRS 9 retrospectively from a date of the entity's choosing, provided that the information needed to apply IFRS 9 to financial assets and financial liabilities derecognised as a result of past transactions was obtained at the time of initially accounting for those transactions.

Hedge accounting

B4 As required by IFRS 9, at the date of transition to IFRSs an entity shall:

(a) measure all derivatives at fair value; and

(b) eliminate all deferred losses and gains arising on derivatives that were reported in accordance with previous GAAP as if they were assets or liabilities.

B5 An entity shall not reflect in its opening IFRS statement of financial position a hedging relationship of a type that does not qualify for hedge accounting in accordance with IAS 39 (for example, many hedging relationships where the hedging instrument is a cash instrument or written option; or where the hedged item is a net position). However, if an entity designated a net position as a hedged item in accordance with previous GAAP, it may designate an individual item within that net position as a hedged item in accordance with IFRSs, provided that it does so no later than the date of transition to IFRSs.

B6   If, before the date of transition to IFRSs, an entity had designated a transaction as a hedge but the hedge does not meet the conditions for hedge accounting in IAS 39, the entity shall apply paragraphs 91 and 101 of IAS 39 to discontinue hedge accounting. Transactions entered into before the date of transition to IFRSs shall not be retrospectively designated as hedges.

Non-controlling interests

B7   A first-time adopter shall apply the following requirements of IFRS 10 prospectively from the date of transition to IFRSs:

(a)   the requirement in paragraph B94 that total comprehensive income is attributed to the owners of the parent and to the non-controlling interests even if this results in the non-controlling interests having a deficit balance;

(b)   the requirements in paragraphs 23 and B93 for accounting for changes in the parent's ownership interest in a subsidiary that do not result in a loss of control; and

(c)   the requirements in paragraphs B97–B99 for accounting for a loss of control over a subsidiary, and the related requirements of paragraph 8A of IFRS 5 *Non-current Assets Held for Sale and Discontinued Operations*.

However, if a first-time adopter elects to apply IFRS 3 retrospectively to past business combinations, it shall also apply IFRS 10 in accordance with paragraph C1 of this IFRS.

Classification and measurement of financial assets

B8   An entity shall assess whether a financial asset meets the conditions in paragraph 4.1.2 of IFRS 9 on the basis of the facts and circumstances that exist at the date of transition to IFRSs.

Embedded derivatives

B9   A first-time adopter shall assess whether an embedded derivative is required to be separated from the host contract and accounted for as a derivative on the basis of the conditions that existed at the later of the date it first became a party to the contract and the date a reassessment is required by paragraph B4.3.11 of IFRS 9.

Appendix C
Exemptions for business combinations

This appendix is an integral part of the IFRS. An entity shall apply the following requirements to business combinations that the entity recognised before the date of transition to IFRSs.

C1 A first-time adopter may elect not to apply IFRS 3 retrospectively to past business combinations (business combinations that occurred before the date of transition to IFRSs). However, if a first-time adopter restates any business combination to comply with IFRS 3, it shall restate all later business combinations and shall also apply IFRS 10 from that same date. For example, if a first-time adopter elects to restate a business combination that occurred on 30 June 20X6, it shall restate all business combinations that occurred between 30 June 20X6 and the date of transition to IFRSs, and it shall also apply IFRS 10 from 30 June 20X6.

C2 An entity need not apply IAS 21 *The Effects of Changes in Foreign Exchange Rates* retrospectively to fair value adjustments and goodwill arising in business combinations that occurred before the date of transition to IFRSs. If the entity does not apply IAS 21 retrospectively to those fair value adjustments and goodwill, it shall treat them as assets and liabilities of the entity rather than as assets and liabilities of the acquiree. Therefore, those goodwill and fair value adjustments either are already expressed in the entity's functional currency or are non-monetary foreign currency items, which are reported using the exchange rate applied in accordance with previous GAAP.

C3 An entity may apply IAS 21 retrospectively to fair value adjustments and goodwill arising in either:

(a) all business combinations that occurred before the date of transition to IFRSs; or

(b) all business combinations that the entity elects to restate to comply with IFRS 3, as permitted by paragraph C1 above.

C4 If a first-time adopter does not apply IFRS 3 retrospectively to a past business combination, this has the following consequences for that business combination:

(a) The first-time adopter shall keep the same classification (as an acquisition by the legal acquirer, a reverse acquisition by the legal acquiree, or a uniting of interests) as in its previous GAAP financial statements.

(b) The first-time adopter shall recognise all its assets and liabilities at the date of transition to IFRSs that were acquired or assumed in a past business combination, other than:

(i) some financial assets and financial liabilities derecognised in accordance with previous GAAP (see paragraph B2); and

(ii) assets, including goodwill, and liabilities that were not recognised in the acquirer's consolidated statement of financial position in accordance with previous GAAP and also would not qualify for recognition in accordance with IFRSs in the separate statement of financial position of the acquiree (see (f)–(i) below).

The first-time adopter shall recognise any resulting change by adjusting retained earnings (or, if appropriate, another category of equity), unless the change results from the recognition of an intangible asset that was previously subsumed within goodwill (see (g)(i) below).

(c)   The first-time adopter shall exclude from its opening IFRS statement of financial position any item recognised in accordance with previous GAAP that does not qualify for recognition as an asset or liability under IFRSs. The first-time adopter shall account for the resulting change as follows:

    (i)   the first-time adopter may have classified a past business combination as an acquisition and recognised as an intangible asset an item that does not qualify for recognition as an asset in accordance with IAS 38 *Intangible Assets*. It shall reclassify that item (and, if any, the related deferred tax and non-controlling interests) as part of goodwill (unless it deducted goodwill directly from equity in accordance with previous GAAP, see (g)(i) and (i) below).

    (ii)   the first-time adopter shall recognise all other resulting changes in retained earnings.[1]

(d)   IFRSs require subsequent measurement of some assets and liabilities on a basis that is not based on original cost, such as fair value. The first-time adopter shall measure these assets and liabilities on that basis in its opening IFRS statement of financial position, even if they were acquired or assumed in a past business combination. It shall recognise any resulting change in the carrying amount by adjusting retained earnings (or, if appropriate, another category of equity), rather than goodwill.

(e)   Immediately after the business combination, the carrying amount in accordance with previous GAAP of assets acquired and liabilities assumed in that business combination shall be their deemed cost in accordance with IFRSs at that date. If IFRSs require a cost-based measurement of those assets and liabilities at a later date, that deemed cost shall be the basis for cost-based depreciation or amortisation from the date of the business combination.

(f)   If an asset acquired, or liability assumed, in a past business combination was not recognised in accordance with previous GAAP, it does not have a deemed cost of zero in the opening IFRS statement of financial position. Instead, the acquirer shall recognise and measure it in its consolidated statement of financial position on the basis that IFRSs would require in the statement of financial position of the acquiree. To illustrate: if the acquirer had not, in accordance with its previous GAAP, capitalised finance leases acquired in a past business combination, it shall capitalise those leases in its consolidated financial statements, as IAS 17 *Leases* would require the acquiree to do in its IFRS statement of financial position. Similarly, if the acquirer had not, in accordance with its previous GAAP, recognised a contingent liability that still exists at the date of transition to

---

1   Such changes include reclassifications from or to intangible assets if goodwill was not recognised in accordance with previous GAAP as an asset. This arises if, in accordance with previous GAAP, the entity (a) deducted goodwill directly from equity or (b) did not treat the business combination as an acquisition.

IFRSs, the acquirer shall recognise that contingent liability at that date unless IAS 37 *Provisions, Contingent Liabilities and Contingent Assets* would prohibit its recognition in the financial statements of the acquiree. Conversely, if an asset or liability was subsumed in goodwill in accordance with previous GAAP but would have been recognised separately under IFRS 3, that asset or liability remains in goodwill unless IFRSs would require its recognition in the financial statements of the acquiree.

(g) The carrying amount of goodwill in the opening IFRS statement of financial position shall be its carrying amount in accordance with previous GAAP at the date of transition to IFRSs, after the following two adjustments:

    (i) If required by (c)(i) above, the first-time adopter shall increase the carrying amount of goodwill when it reclassifies an item that it recognised as an intangible asset in accordance with previous GAAP. Similarly, if (f) above requires the first-time adopter to recognise an intangible asset that was subsumed in recognised goodwill in accordance with previous GAAP, the first-time adopter shall decrease the carrying amount of goodwill accordingly (and, if applicable, adjust deferred tax and non-controlling interests).

    (ii) Regardless of whether there is any indication that the goodwill may be impaired, the first-time adopter shall apply IAS 36 in testing the goodwill for impairment at the date of transition to IFRSs and in recognising any resulting impairment loss in retained earnings (or, if so required by IAS 36, in revaluation surplus). The impairment test shall be based on conditions at the date of transition to IFRSs.

(h) No other adjustments shall be made to the carrying amount of goodwill at the date of transition to IFRSs. For example, the first-time adopter shall not restate the carrying amount of goodwill:

    (i) to exclude in-process research and development acquired in that business combination (unless the related intangible asset would qualify for recognition in accordance with IAS 38 in the statement of financial position of the acquiree);

    (ii) to adjust previous amortisation of goodwill;

    (iii) to reverse adjustments to goodwill that IFRS 3 would not permit, but were made in accordance with previous GAAP because of adjustments to assets and liabilities between the date of the business combination and the date of transition to IFRSs.

(i) If the first-time adopter recognised goodwill in accordance with previous GAAP as a deduction from equity:

    (i) it shall not recognise that goodwill in its opening IFRS statement of financial position. Furthermore, it shall not reclassify that goodwill to profit or loss if it disposes of the subsidiary or if the investment in the subsidiary becomes impaired.

(ii) adjustments resulting from the subsequent resolution of a contingency affecting the purchase consideration shall be recognised in retained earnings.

(j) In accordance with its previous GAAP, the first-time adopter may not have consolidated a subsidiary acquired in a past business combination (for example, because the parent did not regard it as a subsidiary in accordance with previous GAAP or did not prepare consolidated financial statements). The first-time adopter shall adjust the carrying amounts of the subsidiary's assets and liabilities to the amounts that IFRSs would require in the subsidiary's statement of financial position. The deemed cost of goodwill equals the difference at the date of transition to IFRSs between:

(i) the parent's interest in those adjusted carrying amounts; and

(ii) the cost in the parent's separate financial statements of its investment in the subsidiary.

(k) The measurement of non-controlling interests and deferred tax follows from the measurement of other assets and liabilities. Therefore, the above adjustments to recognised assets and liabilities affect non-controlling interests and deferred tax.

C5 The exemption for past business combinations also applies to past acquisitions of investments in associates and of interests in joint ventures. Furthermore, the date selected for paragraph C1 applies equally for all such acquisitions.

Appendix D
Exemptions from other IFRSs

This appendix is an integral part of the IFRS.

D1　An entity may elect to use one or more of the following exemptions:

(a)　share-based payment transactions (paragraphs D2 and D3);

(b)　insurance contracts (paragraph D4);

(c)　deemed cost (paragraphs D5–D8B);

(d)　leases (paragraphs D9 and D9A);

(e)　[deleted]

(f)　cumulative translation differences (paragraphs D12 and D13);

(g)　investments in subsidiaries, joint ventures and associates (paragraphs D14 and D15);

(h)　assets and liabilities of subsidiaries, associates and joint ventures (paragraphs D16 and D17);

(i)　compound financial instruments (paragraph D18);

(j)　designation of previously recognised financial instruments (paragraphs D19–D19D);

(k)　fair value measurement of financial assets or financial liabilities at initial recognition (paragraph D20);

(l)　decommissioning liabilities included in the cost of property, plant and equipment (paragraphs D21 and D21A);

(m)　financial assets or intangible assets accounted for in accordance with IFRIC 12 *Service Concession Arrangements* (paragraph D22);

(n)　borrowing costs (paragraph D23);

(o)　transfers of assets from customers (paragraph D24);

(p)　extinguishing financial liabilities with equity instruments (paragraph D25);

(q)　severe hyperinflation (paragraphs D26–D30);

(r)　joint arrangements (paragraph D31); and

(s)　stripping costs in the production phase of a surface mine (paragraph D32).

An entity shall not apply these exemptions by analogy to other items.

Share-based payment transactions

D2   A first-time adopter is encouraged, but not required, to apply IFRS 2 *Share-based Payment* to equity instruments that were granted on or before 7 November 2002. A first-time adopter is also encouraged, but not required, to apply IFRS 2 to equity instruments that were granted after 7 November 2002 and vested before the later of (a) the date of transition to IFRSs and (b) 1 January 2005. However, if a first-time adopter elects to apply IFRS 2 to such equity instruments, it may do so only if the entity has disclosed publicly the fair value of those equity instruments, determined at the measurement date, as defined in IFRS 2. For all grants of equity instruments to which IFRS 2 has not been applied (eg equity instruments granted on or before 7 November 2002), a first-time adopter shall nevertheless disclose the information required by paragraphs 44 and 45 of IFRS 2. If a first-time adopter modifies the terms or conditions of a grant of equity instruments to which IFRS 2 has not been applied, the entity is not required to apply paragraphs 26–29 of IFRS 2 if the modification occurred before the date of transition to IFRSs.

D3   A first-time adopter is encouraged, but not required, to apply IFRS 2 to liabilities arising from share-based payment transactions that were settled before the date of transition to IFRSs. A first-time adopter is also encouraged, but not required, to apply IFRS 2 to liabilities that were settled before 1 January 2005. For liabilities to which IFRS 2 is applied, a first-time adopter is not required to restate comparative information to the extent that the information relates to a period or date that is earlier than 7 November 2002.

Insurance contracts

D4   A first-time adopter may apply the transitional provisions in IFRS 4 *Insurance Contracts*. IFRS 4 restricts changes in accounting policies for insurance contracts, including changes made by a first-time adopter.

Deemed cost

D5   An entity may elect to measure an item of property, plant and equipment at the date of transition to IFRSs at its fair value and use that fair value as its deemed cost at that date.

D6   A first-time adopter may elect to use a previous GAAP revaluation of an item of property, plant and equipment at, or before, the date of transition to IFRSs as deemed cost at the date of the revaluation, if the revaluation was, at the date of the revaluation, broadly comparable to:

(a)   fair value; or

(b)   cost or depreciated cost in accordance with IFRSs, adjusted to reflect, for example, changes in a general or specific price index.

D7   The elections in paragraphs D5 and D6 are also available for:

(a)   investment property, if an entity elects to use the cost model in IAS 40 *Investment Property*; and

(b)   intangible assets that meet:

    (i)   the recognition criteria in IAS 38 (including reliable measurement of original cost); and

    (ii)   the criteria in IAS 38 for revaluation (including the existence of an active market).

An entity shall not use these elections for other assets or for liabilities.

D8   A first-time adopter may have established a deemed cost in accordance with previous GAAP for some or all of its assets and liabilities by measuring them at their fair value at one particular date because of an event such as a privatisation or initial public offering.

    (a)   If the measurement date is *at or before* the date of transition to IFRSs, the entity may use such event-driven fair value measurements as deemed cost for IFRSs at the date of that measurement.

    (b)   If the measurement date is *after* the date of transition to IFRSs, but during the period covered by the first IFRS financial statements, the event-driven fair value measurements may be used as deemed cost when the event occurs. An entity shall recognise the resulting adjustments directly in retained earnings (or if appropriate, another category of equity) at the measurement date. At the date of transition to IFRSs, the entity shall either establish the deemed cost by applying the criteria in paragraphs D5–D7 or measure assets and liabilities in accordance with the other requirements in this IFRS.

D8A   Under some national accounting requirements exploration and development costs for oil and gas properties in the development or production phases are accounted for in cost centres that include all properties in a large geographical area. A first-time adopter using such accounting under previous GAAP may elect to measure oil and gas assets at the date of transition to IFRSs on the following basis:

    (a)   exploration and evaluation assets at the amount determined under the entity's previous GAAP; and

    (b)   assets in the development or production phases at the amount determined for the cost centre under the entity's previous GAAP. The entity shall allocate this amount to the cost centre's underlying assets pro rata using reserve volumes or reserve values as of that date.

The entity shall test exploration and evaluation assets and assets in the development and production phases for impairment at the date of transition to IFRSs in accordance with IFRS 6 *Exploration for and Evaluation of Mineral Resources* or IAS 36 respectively and, if necessary, reduce the amount determined in accordance with (a) or (b) above. For the purposes of this paragraph, oil and gas assets comprise only those assets used in the exploration, evaluation, development or production of oil and gas.

D8B   Some entities hold items of property, plant and equipment or intangible assets that are used, or were previously used, in operations subject to rate regulation. The carrying amount of such items might include amounts that were determined under previous GAAP but do not qualify for capitalisation in accordance with IFRSs. If this is the case, a first-time adopter may elect to use the previous GAAP carrying amount of such an item at the date of transition to IFRSs as deemed cost. If an entity applies this exemption to an item, it need not apply it to all items. At the date of transition to IFRSs, an entity shall test for impairment in accordance with IAS 36 each item for which this exemption is used. For the purposes of this paragraph, operations are subject to rate regulation if they provide goods or services to customers at prices (ie rates) established by an authorised body empowered to establish rates that bind the customers and that are designed to recover the specific costs the entity incurs in providing the regulated goods or services and to earn a specified return. The specified return could be a minimum or range and need not be a fixed or guaranteed return.

Leases

D9   A first-time adopter may apply the transitional provisions in IFRIC 4 *Determining whether an Arrangement contains a Lease*. Therefore, a first-time adopter may determine whether an arrangement existing at the date of transition to IFRSs contains a lease on the basis of facts and circumstances existing at that date.

D9A   If a first-time adopter made the same determination of whether an arrangement contained a lease in accordance with previous GAAP as that required by IFRIC 4 but at a date other than that required by IFRIC 4, the first-time adopter need not reassess that determination when it adopts IFRSs. For an entity to have made the same determination of whether the arrangement contained a lease in accordance with previous GAAP, that determination would have to have given the same outcome as that resulting from applying IAS 17 *Leases* and IFRIC 4.

D10-D11 [Deleted]

Cumulative translation differences

D12   IAS 21 requires an entity:

(a)   to recognise some translation differences in other comprehensive income and accumulate these in a separate component of equity; and

(b)   on disposal of a foreign operation, to reclassify the cumulative translation difference for that foreign operation (including, if applicable, gains and losses on related hedges) from equity to profit or loss as part of the gain or loss on disposal.

D13   However, a first-time adopter need not comply with these requirements for cumulative translation differences that existed at the date of transition to IFRSs. If a first-time adopter uses this exemption:

(a)   the cumulative translation differences for all foreign operations are deemed to be zero at the date of transition to IFRSs; and

(b)   the gain or loss on a subsequent disposal of any foreign operation shall exclude translation differences that arose before the date of transition to IFRSs and shall include later translation differences.

Investments in subsidiaries, joint ventures and associates

D14   When an entity prepares separate financial statements, IAS 27 requires it to account for its investments in subsidiaries, joint ventures and associates either:

(a)   at cost; or

(b)   in accordance with IFRS 9.

D15   If a first-time adopter measures such an investment at cost in accordance with IAS 27, it shall measure that investment at one of the following amounts in its separate opening IFRS statement of financial position:

(a)   cost determined in accordance with IAS 27; or

(b)   deemed cost. The deemed cost of such an investment shall be its:

(i)   fair value at the entity's date of transition to IFRSs in its separate financial statements; or

(ii)   previous GAAP carrying amount at that date.

A first-time adopter may choose either (i) or (ii) above to measure its investment in each subsidiary, joint venture or associate that it elects to measure using a deemed cost.

Assets and liabilities of subsidiaries, associates and joint ventures

D16   If a subsidiary becomes a first-time adopter later than its parent, the subsidiary shall, in its financial statements, measure its assets and liabilities at either:

(a)   the carrying amounts that would be included in the parent's consolidated financial statements, based on the parent's date of transition to IFRSs, if no adjustments were made for consolidation procedures and for the effects of the business combination in which the parent acquired the subsidiary; or

(b)   the carrying amounts required by the rest of this IFRS, based on the subsidiary's date of transition to IFRSs. These carrying amounts could differ from those described in (a):

(i)   when the exemptions in this IFRS result in measurements that depend on the date of transition to IFRSs.

(ii)   when the accounting policies used in the subsidiary's financial statements differ from those in the consolidated financial statements. For example, the subsidiary may use as its accounting policy the cost model in IAS 16 *Property, Plant and Equipment*, whereas the group may use the revaluation model.

A similar election is available to an associate or joint venture that becomes a first-time adopter later than an entity that has significant influence or joint control over it.

D17   However, if an entity becomes a first-time adopter later than its subsidiary (or associate or joint venture) the entity shall, in its consolidated financial statements, measure the assets and liabilities of the subsidiary (or associate or joint venture) at the same carrying amounts as in the financial statements of the subsidiary (or associate or joint venture), after adjusting for consolidation and equity accounting adjustments and for the effects of the business combination in which the entity acquired the subsidiary. Similarly, if a parent becomes a first-time adopter for its separate financial statements earlier or later than for its consolidated financial statements, it shall measure its assets and liabilities at the same amounts in both financial statements, except for consolidation adjustments.

Compound financial instruments

D18   IAS 32 *Financial Instruments: Presentation* requires an entity to split a compound financial instrument at inception into separate liability and equity components. If the liability component is no longer outstanding, retrospective application of IAS 32 involves separating two portions of equity. The first portion is in retained earnings and represents the cumulative interest accreted on the liability component. The other portion represents the original equity component. However, in accordance with this IFRS, a first-time adopter need not separate these two portions if the liability component is no longer outstanding at the date of transition to IFRSs.

Designation of previously recognised financial instruments

D19   IFRS 9 permits a financial liability (provided it meets certain criteria) to be designated as a financial liability at fair value through profit or loss. Despite this requirement an entity is permitted to designate, at the date of transition to IFRSs, any financial liability as at fair value through profit or loss provided the liability meets the criteria in paragraph 4.2.2 of IFRS 9 at that date.

D19A   An entity may designate a financial asset as measured at fair value through profit or loss in accordance with paragraph 4.1.5 of IFRS 9 on the basis of the facts and circumstances that exist at the date of transition to IFRSs.

D19B   An entity may designate an investment in an equity instrument as at fair value through other comprehensive income in accordance with paragraph 5.7.5 of IFRS 9 on the basis of the facts and circumstances that exist at the date of transition to IFRSs.

D19C   If it is impracticable (as defined in IAS 8) for an entity to apply retrospectively the effective interest method or the impairment requirements in paragraphs 58–65 and AG84–AG93 of IAS 39, the fair value of the financial asset at the date of transition to IFRSs shall be the new amortised cost of that financial asset at the date of transition to IFRSs.

D19D   An entity shall determine whether the treatment in paragraph 5.7.7 of IFRS 9 would create an accounting mismatch in profit or loss on the basis of the facts and circumstances that exist at the date of transition to IFRSs.

Fair value measurement of financial assets or financial liabilities at initial recognition

D20 Despite the requirements of paragraphs 7 and 9, an entity may apply the requirements in the last sentence of paragraph B5.4.8 and in paragraph B5.4.9 of IFRS 9 prospectively to transactions entered into on or after the date of transition to IFRSs.

Decommissioning liabilities included in the cost of property, plant and equipment

D21 IFRIC 1 *Changes in Existing Decommissioning, Restoration and Similar Liabilities* requires specified changes in a decommissioning, restoration or similar liability to be added to or deducted from the cost of the asset to which it relates; the adjusted depreciable amount of the asset is then depreciated prospectively over its remaining useful life. A first-time adopter need not comply with these requirements for changes in such liabilities that occurred before the date of transition to IFRSs. If a first-time adopter uses this exemption, it shall:

(a) measure the liability as at the date of transition to IFRSs in accordance with IAS 37;

(b) to the extent that the liability is within the scope of IFRIC 1, estimate the amount that would have been included in the cost of the related asset when the liability first arose, by discounting the liability to that date using its best estimate of the historical risk-adjusted discount rate(s) that would have applied for that liability over the intervening period; and

(c) calculate the accumulated depreciation on that amount, as at the date of transition to IFRSs, on the basis of the current estimate of the useful life of the asset, using the depreciation policy adopted by the entity in accordance with IFRSs.

D21A An entity that uses the exemption in paragraph D8A(b) (for oil and gas assets in the development or production phases accounted for in cost centres that include all properties in a large geographical area under previous GAAP) shall, instead of applying paragraph D21 or IFRIC 1:

(a) measure decommissioning, restoration and similar liabilities as at the date of transition to IFRSs in accordance with IAS 37; and

(b) recognise directly in retained earnings any difference between that amount and the carrying amount of those liabilities at the date of transition to IFRSs determined under the entity's previous GAAP.

Financial assets or intangible assets accounted for in accordance with IFRIC 12

D22 A first-time adopter may apply the transitional provisions in IFRIC 12.

Borrowing costs

D23   A first-time adopter may apply the transitional provisions set out in paragraphs 27 and 28 of IAS 23, as revised in 2007. In those paragraphs references to the effective date shall be interpreted as 1 January 2009 or the date of transition to IFRSs, whichever is later.

Transfers of assets from customers

D24   A first-time adopter may apply the transitional provisions set out in paragraph 22 of IFRIC 18 *Transfers of Assets from Customers*. In that paragraph, reference to the effective date shall be interpreted as 1 July 2009 or the date of transition to IFRSs, whichever is later. In addition, a first-time adopter may designate any date before the date of transition to IFRSs and apply IFRIC 18 to all transfers of assets from customers received on or after that date.

Extinguishing financial liabilities with equity instruments

D25   A first-time adopter may apply the transitional provisions in IFRIC 19 *Extinguishing Financial Liabilities with Equity Instruments*.

Severe hyperinflation

D26   If an entity has a functional currency that was, or is, the currency of a hyperinflationary economy, it shall determine whether it was subject to severe hyperinflation before the date of transition to IFRSs. This applies to entities that are adopting IFRSs for the first time, as well as entities that have previously applied IFRSs.

D27   The currency of a hyperinflationary economy is subject to severe hyperinflation if it has both of the following characteristics:

(a)   a reliable general price index is not available to all entities with transactions and balances in the currency.

(b)   exchangeability between the currency and a relatively stable foreign currency does not exist.

D28   The functional currency of an entity ceases to be subject to severe hyperinflation on the functional currency normalisation date. That is the date when the functional currency no longer has either, or both, of the characteristics in paragraph D27, or when there is a change in the entity's functional currency to a currency that is not subject to severe hyperinflation.

D29   When an entity's date of transition to IFRSs is on, or after, the functional currency normalisation date, the entity may elect to measure all assets and liabilities held before the functional currency normalisation date at fair value on the date of transition to IFRSs. The entity may use that fair value as the deemed cost of those assets and liabilities in the opening IFRS statement of financial position.

D30   When the functional currency normalisation date falls within a 12-month comparative period, the comparative period may be less than 12 months, provided that a complete set of financial statements (as required by paragraph 10 of IAS 1) is provided for that shorter period.

Joint arrangements

D31   A first-time adopter may apply the transition provisions in IFRS 11 with the following exception. When changing from proportionate consolidation to the equity method, a first-time adopter shall test for impairment the investment in accordance with IAS 36 as at the beginning of the earliest period presented, regardless of whether there is any indication that the investment may be impaired. Any resulting impairment shall be recognised as an adjustment to retained earnings at the beginning of the earliest period presented.

Stripping costs in the production phase of a surface mine

D32   A first-time adopter may apply the transitional provisions set out in paragraphs A1 to A4 of IFRIC 20 *Stripping Costs in the Production Phase of a Surface Mine*. In that paragraph, reference to the effective date shall be interpreted as 1 January 2013 or the beginning of the first IFRS reporting period, whichever is later.

Appendix E
Short-term exemptions from IFRSs

This appendix is an integral part of the IFRS.

Exemption from the requirement to restate comparative information for IFRS 9

E1   In its first IFRS financial statements, an entity that (a) adopts IFRSs for annual periods beginning before 1 January 2012 and (b) applies IFRS 9 shall present at least one year of comparative information. However, this comparative information need not comply with IFRS 7 *Financial Instruments: Disclosures* or IFRS 9, to the extent that the disclosures required by IFRS 7 relate to items within the scope of IFRS 9. For such entities, references to the 'date of transition to IFRSs' shall mean, in the case of IFRS 7 and IFRS 9 only, the beginning of the first IFRS reporting period.

E2   An entity that chooses to present comparative information that does not comply with IFRS 7 and IFRS 9 in its first year of transition shall:

(a)   apply the recognition and measurement requirements of its previous GAAP in place of the requirements of IFRS 9 to comparative information about items within the scope of IFRS 9.

(b)   disclose this fact together with the basis used to prepare this information.

(c)   treat any adjustment between the statement of financial position at the comparative period's reporting date (ie the statement of financial position that includes comparative information under previous GAAP) and the statement of financial position at the start of the *first IFRS reporting period* (ie the first period that includes information that complies with IFRS 7 and IFRS 9) as arising from a change in accounting policy and give the disclosures required by paragraph 28(a)–(e) and (f)(i) of IAS 8. Paragraph 28(f)(i) applies only to amounts presented in the statement of financial position at the comparative period's reporting date.

(d)   apply paragraph 17(c) of IAS 1 to provide additional disclosures when compliance with the specific requirements in IFRSs is insufficient to enable users to understand the impact of particular transactions, other events and conditions on the entity's financial position and financial performance.

Disclosures about financial instruments

E3   A first-time adopter may apply the transition provisions in paragraph 44G of IFRS 7.[2]

E4   A first-time adopter may apply the transition provisions in paragraph 44M of IFRS 7.[3]

Employee benefits

E5   A first-time adopter may apply the transition provisions in paragraph 173(b) of IAS 19.

---

2   Paragraph E3 was added as a consequence of *Limited Exemption from Comparative IFRS 7 Disclosures for First-time Adopters* (Amendment to IFRS 1) issued in January 2010. To avoid the potential use of hindsight and to ensure that first-time adopters are not disadvantaged as compared with current IFRS preparers, the Board decided that first-time adopters should be permitted to use the same transition provisions permitted for existing preparers of financial statements prepared in accordance with IFRSs that are included in *Improving Disclosures about Financial Instruments* (Amendments to IFRS 7).

3   Paragraph E4 was added as a consequence of *Disclosures—Transfers of Financial Assets* (Amendments to IFRS 7) issued in October 2010. To avoid the potential use of hindsight and to ensure that first-time adopters are not disadvantaged as compared with current IFRS preparers, the Board decided that first-time adopters should be permitted to use the same transition provisions permitted for existing preparers of financial statements prepared in accordance with IFRSs that are included in *Disclosures—Transfers of Financial Assets* (Amendments to IFRS 7).

International Financial Reporting Standard 2

Share-based Payment

In February 2004 the International Accounting Standards Board (IASB) issued IFRS 2 *Share-based Payment*. The IASB amended IFRS 2 to clarify its scope in January 2008 and to incorporate the guidance contained in two related Interpretations (IFRIC 8 *Scope of IFRS 2* and IFRIC 11 *IFRS 2—Group and Treasury Share Transactions*) in June 2009.

Other IFRSs have made minor consequential amendments to IFRS 2. They include IFRS 3 *Business Combinations* (as revised in January 2008), *Improvements to IFRSs* (issued April 2009) and IFRS 9 *Financial Instruments* (issued November 2009 and October 2010) .

CONTENTS

FOR THE ACCOMPANYING DOCUMENTS LISTED BELOW, SEE PART B OF THIS EDITION

APPROVAL BY THE BOARD OF IFRS 2 ISSUED IN FEBRUARY 2004

APPROVAL BY THE BOARD OF AMENDMENTS TO IFRS 2:

Vesting Conditions and Cancellations issued in January 2008

Group Cash-settled Share-based Payment Transactions issued in June 2009

BASIS FOR CONCLUSIONS

IMPLEMENTATION GUIDANCE

TABLE OF CONCORDANCE

International Financial Reporting Standard 2 *Share-based Payment* (IFRS 2) is set out in paragraphs 1–64 and Appendices A–C. All the paragraphs have equal authority. Paragraphs in **bold type** state the main principles. Terms defined in Appendix A are in *italics* the first time they appear in the Standard. Definitions of other terms are given in the Glossary for International Financial Reporting Standards. IFRS 2 should be read in the context of its objective and the Basis for Conclusions, the *Preface to International Financial Reporting Standards* and the *Conceptual Framework for Financial Reporting*. IAS 8 *Accounting Policies, Changes in Accounting Estimates and Errors* provides a basis for selecting and applying accounting policies in the absence of explicit guidance.

Introduction

Reasons for issuing the IFRS

IN1   Entities often grant shares or share options to employees or other parties. Share plans and share option plans are a common feature of employee remuneration, for directors, senior executives and many other employees. Some entities issue shares or share options to pay suppliers, such as suppliers of professional services.

IN2   Until this IFRS was issued, there was no IFRS covering the recognition and measurement of these transactions. Concerns were raised about this gap in IFRSs, given the increasing prevalence of share-based payment transactions in many countries.

Reasons for amending IFRS 2 in June 2009

IN2A   In June 2009 the International Accounting Standards Board amended IFRS 2 to clarify its scope and the accounting for group cash-settled share-based payment transactions in the separate or individual financial statements of the entity receiving the goods or services when that entity has no obligation to settle the share-based payment transaction. The amendments also incorporate the guidance contained in the following Interpretations:

- IFRIC 8 *Scope of IFRS 2*

- IFRIC 11 *IFRS 2—Group and Treasury Share Transactions*.

As a result, the Board withdrew IFRIC 8 and IFRIC 11.

Main features of the IFRS

IN3   The IFRS requires an entity to recognise share-based payment transactions in its financial statements, including transactions with employees or other parties to be settled in cash, other assets, or equity instruments of the entity. There are no exceptions to the IFRS, other than for transactions to which other Standards apply.

IN4   The IFRS sets out measurement principles and specific requirements for three types of share-based payment transactions:

(a)   equity-settled share-based payment transactions, in which the entity receives goods or services as consideration for equity instruments of the entity (including shares or share options);

(b)   cash-settled share-based payment transactions, in which the entity acquires goods or services by incurring liabilities to the supplier of those goods or services for amounts that are based on the price (or value) of the entity's shares or other equity instruments of the entity;and

(c)   transactions in which the entity receives or acquires goods or services and the terms of the arrangement provide either the entity or the supplier of those goods or services with a choice of whether the entity settles the transaction in cash or by issuing equity instruments.

IN5   For equity-settled share-based payment transactions, the IFRS requires an entity to measure the goods or services received, and the corresponding increase in equity, directly, at the fair value of the goods or services received, unless that fair value cannot be estimated reliably. If the entity cannot estimate reliably the fair value of the goods or services received, the entity is required to measure their value, and the corresponding increase in equity, indirectly, by reference to the fair value of the equity instruments granted. Furthermore:

(a)   for transactions with employees and others providing similar services, the entity is required to measure the fair value of the equity instruments granted, because it is typically not possible to estimate reliably the fair value of employee services received. The fair value of the equity instruments granted is measured at grant date.

(b)   for transactions with parties other than employees (and those providing similar services), there is a rebuttable presumption that the fair value of the goods or services received can be estimated reliably. That fair value is measured at the date the entity obtains the goods or the counterparty renders service. In rare cases, if the presumption is rebutted, the transaction is measured by reference to the fair value of the equity instruments granted, measured at the date the entity obtains the goods or the counterparty renders service.

(c)   for goods or services measured by reference to the fair value of the equity instruments granted, the IFRS specifies that all non-vesting conditions are taken into account in the estimate of the fair value of the equity instruments. However, vesting conditions that are not market conditions are not taken into account when estimating the fair value of the shares or options at the relevant measurement date (as specified above). Instead, vesting conditions are taken into account by adjusting the number of equity instruments included in the measurement of the transaction amount so that, ultimately, the amount recognised for goods or services received as consideration for the equity instruments granted is based on the number of equity instruments that eventually vest. Hence, on a cumulative basis, no amount is recognised for goods or services received if the equity instruments granted do not vest because of failure to satisfy a vesting condition (other than a market condition).

(d)   the IFRS requires the fair value of equity instruments granted to be based on market prices, if available, and to take into account the terms and conditions upon which those equity instruments were granted. In the absence of market prices, fair value is estimated, using a valuation technique to estimate what the price of those equity instruments would have been on the measurement date in an arm's length transaction between knowledgeable, willing parties.

(e)   the IFRS also sets out requirements if the terms and conditions of an option or share grant are modified (eg an option is repriced) or if a grant is cancelled, repurchased or replaced with another grant of equity instruments. For example, irrespective of any modification, cancellation or settlement of a grant of equity instruments to employees, the IFRS generally requires the entity to recognise, as a minimum, the services received measured at the grant date fair value of the equity instruments granted.

IN6   For cash-settled share-based payment transactions, the IFRS requires an entity to measure the goods or services acquired and the liability incurred at the fair value of the liability. Until the liability is settled, the entity is required to remeasure the fair value of the liability at the end of each reporting period and at the date of settlement, with any changes in value recognised in profit or loss for the period.

IN7   For share-based payment transactions in which the terms of the arrangement provide either the entity or the supplier of goods or services with a choice of whether the entity settles the transaction in cash or by issuing equity instruments, the entity is required to account for that transaction, or the components of that transaction, as a cash-settled share-based payment transaction if, and to the extent that, the entity has incurred a liability to settle in cash (or other assets), or as an equity-settled share-based payment transaction if, and to the extent that, no such liability has been incurred.

IN8   The IFRS prescribes various disclosure requirements to enable users of financial statements to understand:

(a)   the nature and extent of share-based payment arrangements that existed during the period;

(b)   how the fair value of the goods or services received, or the fair value of the equity instruments granted, during the period was determined; and

(c)   the effect of share-based payment transactions on the entity's profit or loss for the period and on its financial position.

International Financial Reporting Standard 2
Share-based Payment

Objective

1   The objective of this IFRS is to specify the financial reporting by an entity when it undertakes a *share-based payment transaction*. In particular, it requires an entity to reflect in its profit or loss and financial position the effects of share-based payment transactions, including expenses associated with transactions in which *share options* are granted to employees.

Scope

2   An entity shall apply this IFRS in accounting for all share-based payment transactions, whether or not the entity can identify specifically some or all of the goods or services received, including:

    (a)   *equity-settled share-based payment transactions*,

    (b)   *cash-settled share-based payment transactions*, and

    (c)   transactions in which the entity receives or acquires goods or services and the terms of the arrangement provide either the entity or the supplier of those goods or services with a choice of whether the entity settles the transaction in cash (or other assets) or by issuing equity instruments,

      except as noted in paragraphs 3A–6. In the absence of specifically identifiable goods or services, other circumstances may indicate that goods or services have been (or will be) received, in which case this IFRS applies.

3   [Deleted]

3A   A share-based payment transaction may be settled by another group entity (or a shareholder of any group entity) on behalf of the entity receiving or acquiring the goods or services. Paragraph 2 also applies to an entity that

    (a)   receives goods or services when another entity in the same group (or a shareholder of any group entity) has the obligation to settle the share-based payment transaction, or

    (b)   has an obligation to settle a share-based payment transaction when another entity in the same group receives the goods or services

      unless the transaction is clearly for a purpose other than payment for goods or services supplied to the entity receiving them.

4   For the purposes of this IFRS, a transaction with an employee (or other party) in his/her capacity as a holder of equity instruments of the entity is not a share-based payment transaction. For example, if an entity grants all holders of a particular class of its equity instruments the right to acquire additional equity instruments of the entity at a price that is less than the fair value of those equity instruments, and an employee receives such a right because he/she is a holder of equity instruments of that particular class, the granting or exercise of that right is not subject to the requirements of this IFRS.

5   As noted in paragraph 2, this IFRS applies to share-based payment transactions in which an entity acquires or receives goods or services. Goods include inventories, consumables, property, plant and equipment, intangible assets and other non-financial assets. However, an entity shall not apply this IFRS to transactions in which the entity acquires goods as part of the net assets acquired in a business combination as defined by IFRS 3 *Business Combinations* (as revised in 2008), in a combination of entities or businesses under common control as described in paragraphs B1–B4 of IFRS 3, or the contribution of a business on the formation of a joint venture as defined by IFRS 11 *Joint Arrangements*. Hence, equity instruments issued in a business combination in exchange for control of the acquiree are not within the scope of this IFRS. However, equity instruments granted to employees of the acquiree in their capacity as employees (eg in return for continued service) are within the scope of this IFRS. Similarly, the cancellation, replacement or other modification of *share-based payment arrangements* because of a business combination or other equity restructuring shall be accounted for in accordance with this IFRS. IFRS 3 provides guidance on determining whether equity instruments issued in a business combination are part of the consideration transferred in exchange for control of the acquiree (and therefore within the scope of IFRS 3) or are in return for continued service to be recognised in the post-combination period (and therefore within the scope of this IFRS).

6   This IFRS does not apply to share-based payment transactions in which the entity receives or acquires goods or services under a contract within the scope of paragraphs 8–10 of IAS 32 *Financial Instruments: Presentation* (as revised in 2003)[1] or paragraphs 5–7 of IAS 39 *Financial Instruments: Recognition and Measurement* (as revised in 2003).

6A   This IFRS uses the term 'fair value' in a way that differs in some respects from the definition of fair value in IFRS 13 *Fair Value Measurement*. Therefore, when applying IFRS 2 an entity measures fair value in accordance with this IFRS, not IFRS 13.

Recognition

7   **An entity shall recognise the goods or services received or acquired in a share-based payment transaction when it obtains the goods or as the services are received. The entity shall recognise a corresponding increase in equity if the goods or services were received in an equity-settled share-based payment transaction, or a liability if the goods or services were acquired in a cash-settled share-based payment transaction.**

8   **When the goods or services received or acquired in a share-based payment transaction do not qualify for recognition as assets, they shall be recognised as expenses.**

9   Typically, an expense arises from the consumption of goods or services. For example, services are typically consumed immediately, in which case an expense is recognised as the counterparty renders service. Goods might be consumed over a period of time or, in the case of inventories, sold at a later date, in which case an expense is recognised when the goods are consumed or sold. However, sometimes it is necessary to recognise an expense before the goods or

1   The title of IAS 32 was amended in 2005.

services are consumed or sold, because they do not qualify for recognition as assets. For example, an entity might acquire goods as part of the research phase of a project to develop a new product. Although those goods have not been consumed, they might not qualify for recognition as assets under the applicable IFRS.

Equity-settled share-based payment transactions

Overview

10   **For equity-settled share-based payment transactions, the entity shall measure the goods or services received, and the corresponding increase in equity, directly, at the fair value of the goods or services received, unless that fair value cannot be estimated reliably. If the entity cannot estimate reliably the fair value of the goods or services received, the entity shall measure their value, and the corresponding increase in equity, indirectly, by reference to[2] the fair value of the equity instruments granted.**

11   To apply the requirements of paragraph 10 to transactions with *employees and others providing similar services*,[3] the entity shall measure the fair value of the services received by reference to the fair value of the equity instruments granted, because typically it is not possible to estimate reliably the fair value of the services received, as explained in paragraph 12. The fair value of those equity instruments shall be measured at *grant date*.

12   Typically, shares, share options or other equity instruments are granted to employees as part of their remuneration package, in addition to a cash salary and other employment benefits. Usually, it is not possible to measure directly the services received for particular components of the employee's remuneration package. It might also not be possible to measure the fair value of the total remuneration package independently, without measuring directly the fair value of the equity instruments granted. Furthermore, shares or share options are sometimes granted as part of a bonus arrangement, rather than as a part of basic remuneration, eg as an incentive to the employees to remain in the entity's employ or to reward them for their efforts in improving the entity's performance. By granting shares or share options, in addition to other remuneration, the entity is paying additional remuneration to obtain additional benefits. Estimating the fair value of those additional benefits is likely to be difficult. Because of the difficulty of measuring directly the fair value of the services received, the entity shall measure the fair value of the employee services received by reference to the fair value of the equity instruments granted.

---

2   This IFRS uses the phrase 'by reference to' rather than 'at', because the transaction is ultimately measured by multiplying the fair value of the equity instruments granted, measured at the date specified in paragraph 11 or 13 (whichever is applicable), by the number of equity instruments that vest, as explained in paragraph 19.

3   In the remainder of this IFRS, all references to employees also include others providing similar services.

13   To apply the requirements of paragraph 10 to transactions with parties other than employees, there shall be a rebuttable presumption that the fair value of the goods or services received can be estimated reliably. That fair value shall be measured at the date the entity obtains the goods or the counterparty renders service. In rare cases, if the entity rebuts this presumption because it cannot estimate reliably the fair value of the goods or services received, the entity shall measure the goods or services received, and the corresponding increase in equity, indirectly, by reference to the fair value of the equity instruments granted, measured at the date the entity obtains the goods or the counterparty renders service.

13A   In particular, if the identifiable consideration received (if any) by the entity appears to be less than the fair value of the equity instruments granted or liability incurred, typically this situation indicates that other consideration (ie unidentifiable goods or services) has been (or will be) received by the entity. The entity shall measure the identifiable goods or services received in accordance with this IFRS. The entity shall measure the unidentifiable goods or services received (or to be received) as the difference between the fair value of the share-based payment and the fair value of any identifiable goods or services received (or to be received). The entity shall measure the unidentifiable goods or services received at the grant date. However, for cash-settled transactions, the liability shall be remeasured at the end of each reporting period until it is settled in accordance with paragraphs 30–33.

Transactions in which services are received

14   If the equity instruments granted *vest* immediately, the counterparty is not required to complete a specified period of service before becoming unconditionally entitled to those equity instruments. In the absence of evidence to the contrary, the entity shall presume that services rendered by the counterparty as consideration for the equity instruments have been received. In this case, on grant date the entity shall recognise the services received in full, with a corresponding increase in equity.

15   If the equity instruments granted do not vest until the counterparty completes a specified period of service, the entity shall presume that the services to be rendered by the counterparty as consideration for those equity instruments will be received in the future, during the *vesting period*. The entity shall account for those services as they are rendered by the counterparty during the vesting period, with a corresponding increase in equity. For example:

(a)   if an employee is granted share options conditional upon completing three years' service, then the entity shall presume that the services to be rendered by the employee as consideration for the share options will be received in the future, over that three-year vesting period.

(b)   if an employee is granted share options conditional upon the achievement of a performance condition and remaining in the entity's employ until that performance condition is satisfied, and the length of the vesting period varies depending on when that performance condition is satisfied, the entity shall presume that the services to be rendered by the employee as consideration for the share options will be received in the future, over the expected vesting period. The entity shall estimate the length of the expected vesting period at grant date, based on the most likely outcome of the performance condition. If the performance condition is a *market condition*, the estimate of the length of the expected vesting period shall be consistent with the assumptions used in estimating the fair value of the options granted, and shall not be subsequently revised. If the performance condition is not a market condition, the entity shall revise its estimate of the length of the vesting period, if necessary, if subsequent information indicates that the length of the vesting period differs from previous estimates.

Transactions measured by reference to the fair value of the equity instruments granted

Determining the fair value of equity instruments granted

16   For transactions measured by reference to the fair value of the equity instruments granted, an entity shall measure the fair value of equity instruments granted at the *measurement date*, based on market prices if available, taking into account the terms and conditions upon which those equity instruments were granted (subject to the requirements of paragraphs 19–22).

17   If market prices are not available, the entity shall estimate the fair value of the equity instruments granted using a valuation technique to estimate what the price of those equity instruments would have been on the measurement date in an arm's length transaction between knowledgeable, willing parties. The valuation technique shall be consistent with generally accepted valuation methodologies for pricing financial instruments, and shall incorporate all factors and assumptions that knowledgeable, willing market participants would consider in setting the price (subject to the requirements of paragraphs 19–22).

18   Appendix B contains further guidance on the measurement of the fair value of shares and share options, focusing on the specific terms and conditions that are common features of a grant of shares or share options to employees.

Treatment of vesting conditions

19   A grant of equity instruments might be conditional upon satisfying specified *vesting conditions*. For example, a grant of shares or share options to an employee is typically conditional on the employee remaining in the entity's employ for a specified period of time. There might be performance conditions that must be satisfied, such as the entity achieving a specified growth in profit or a specified increase in the entity's share price. Vesting conditions, other than market conditions, shall not be taken into account when estimating the fair value of the shares or share options at the measurement date. Instead, vesting conditions shall be taken into account by adjusting the number of equity instruments included in the measurement of the transaction amount so that, ultimately, the amount recognised for goods or services received as consideration for the equity instruments granted shall be based on the number of equity instruments that eventually vest. Hence, on a cumulative basis, no amount is recognised for goods

or services received if the equity instruments granted do not vest because of failure to satisfy a vesting condition, eg the counterparty fails to complete a specified service period, or a performance condition is not satisfied, subject to the requirements of paragraph 21.

20   To apply the requirements of paragraph 19, the entity shall recognise an amount for the goods or services received during the vesting period based on the best available estimate of the number of equity instruments expected to vest and shall revise that estimate, if necessary, if subsequent information indicates that the number of equity instruments expected to vest differs from previous estimates. On vesting date, the entity shall revise the estimate to equal the number of equity instruments that ultimately vested, subject to the requirements of paragraph 21.

21   Market conditions, such as a target share price upon which vesting (or exercisability) is conditioned, shall be taken into account when estimating the fair value of the equity instruments granted. Therefore, for grants of equity instruments with market conditions, the entity shall recognise the goods or services received from a counterparty who satisfies all other vesting conditions (eg services received from an employee who remains in service for the specified period of service), irrespective of whether that market condition is satisfied.

Treatment of non-vesting conditions

21A   Similarly, an entity shall take into account all non-vesting conditions when estimating the fair value of the equity instruments granted. Therefore, for grants of equity instruments with non-vesting conditions, the entity shall recognise the goods or services received from a counterparty that satisfies all vesting conditions that are not market conditions (eg services received from an employee who remains in service for the specified period of service), irrespective of whether those non-vesting conditions are satisfied.

Treatment of a reload feature

22   For options with a *reload feature*, the reload feature shall not be taken into account when estimating the fair value of options granted at the measurement date. Instead, a *reload option* shall be accounted for as a new option grant, if and when a reload option is subsequently granted.

After vesting date

23   Having recognised the goods or services received in accordance with paragraphs 10–22, and a corresponding increase in equity, the entity shall make no subsequent adjustment to total equity after vesting date. For example, the entity shall not subsequently reverse the amount recognised for services received from an employee if the vested equity instruments are later forfeited or, in the case of share options, the options are not exercised. However, this requirement does not preclude the entity from recognising a transfer within equity, ie a transfer from one component of equity to another.

If the fair value of the equity instruments cannot be estimated reliably

24 The requirements in paragraphs 16–23 apply when the entity is required to measure a share-based payment transaction by reference to the fair value of the equity instruments granted. In rare cases, the entity may be unable to estimate reliably the fair value of the equity instruments granted at the measurement date, in accordance with the requirements in paragraphs 16–22. In these rare cases only, the entity shall instead:

(a) measure the equity instruments at their *intrinsic value*, initially at the date the entity obtains the goods or the counterparty renders service and subsequently at the end of each reporting period and at the date of final settlement, with any change in intrinsic value recognised in profit or loss. For a grant of share options, the share-based payment arrangement is finally settled when the options are exercised, are forfeited (eg upon cessation of employment) or lapse (eg at the end of the option's life).

(b) recognise the goods or services received based on the number of equity instruments that ultimately vest or (where applicable) are ultimately exercised. To apply this requirement to share options, for example, the entity shall recognise the goods or services received during the vesting period, if any, in accordance with paragraphs 14 and 15, except that the requirements in paragraph 15(b) concerning a market condition do not apply. The amount recognised for goods or services received during the vesting period shall be based on the number of share options expected to vest. The entity shall revise that estimate, if necessary, if subsequent information indicates that the number of share options expected to vest differs from previous estimates. On vesting date, the entity shall revise the estimate to equal the number of equity instruments that ultimately vested. After vesting date, the entity shall reverse the amount recognised for goods or services received if the share options are later forfeited, or lapse at the end of the share option's life.

25 If an entity applies paragraph 24, it is not necessary to apply paragraphs 26–29, because any modifications to the terms and conditions on which the equity instruments were granted will be taken into account when applying the intrinsic value method set out in paragraph 24. However, if an entity settles a grant of equity instruments to which paragraph 24 has been applied:

(a) if the settlement occurs during the vesting period, the entity shall account for the settlement as an acceleration of vesting, and shall therefore recognise immediately the amount that would otherwise have been recognised for services received over the remainder of the vesting period.

(b) any payment made on settlement shall be accounted for as the repurchase of equity instruments, ie as a deduction from equity, except to the extent that the payment exceeds the intrinsic value of the equity instruments, measured at the repurchase date. Any such excess shall be recognised as an expense.

Modifications to the terms and conditions on which equity instruments were granted, including cancellations and settlements

26 An entity might modify the terms and conditions on which the equity instruments were granted. For example, it might reduce the exercise price of options granted to employees (ie reprice the options), which increases the fair value of those options. The requirements in paragraphs 27–29 to account for the effects of modifications are expressed in the context of share-based payment transactions with employees. However, the requirements shall also be applied to share-based payment transactions with parties other than employees that are measured by reference to the fair value of the equity instruments granted. In the latter case, any references in paragraphs 27–29 to grant date shall instead refer to the date the entity obtains the goods or the counterparty renders service.

27 The entity shall recognise, as a minimum, the services received measured at the grant date fair value of the equity instruments granted, unless those equity instruments do not vest because of failure to satisfy a vesting condition (other than a market condition) that was specified at grant date. This applies irrespective of any modifications to the terms and conditions on which the equity instruments were granted, or a cancellation or settlement of that grant of equity instruments. In addition, the entity shall recognise the effects of modifications that increase the total fair value of the share-based payment arrangement or are otherwise beneficial to the employee. Guidance on applying this requirement is given in Appendix B.

28 If a grant of equity instruments is cancelled or settled during the vesting period (other than a grant cancelled by forfeiture when the vesting conditions are not satisfied):

(a) the entity shall account for the cancellation or settlement as an acceleration of vesting, and shall therefore recognise immediately the amount that otherwise would have been recognised for services received over the remainder of the vesting period.

(b) any payment made to the employee on the cancellation or settlement of the grant shall be accounted for as the repurchase of an equity interest, ie as a deduction from equity, except to the extent that the payment exceeds the fair value of the equity instruments granted, measured at the repurchase date. Any such excess shall be recognised as an expense. However, if the share-based payment arrangement included liability components, the entity shall remeasure the fair value of the liability at the date of cancellation or settlement. Any payment made to settle the liability component shall be accounted for as an extinguishment of the liability.

(c) if new equity instruments are granted to the employee and, on the date when those new equity instruments are granted, the entity identifies the new equity instruments granted as replacement equity instruments for the cancelled equity instruments, the entity shall account for the granting of replacement equity instruments in the same way as a modification of the original grant of equity instruments, in accordance with paragraph 27 and the guidance in Appendix B.. The incremental fair value granted is the difference between the fair value of the replacement equity instruments and the net fair value of the cancelled equity instruments, at the date the replacement equity instruments are granted. The net fair value of the cancelled equity instruments is their fair value, immediately before the cancellation, less the amount of any payment made to the employee on cancellation of the equity instruments that is accounted for as a deduction from equity in accordance with (b) above. If the entity does not identify new equity instruments granted as replacement equity instruments for the cancelled equity instruments, the entity shall account for those new equity instruments as a new grant of equity instruments.

28A   If an entity or counterparty can choose whether to meet a non-vesting condition, the entity shall treat the entity's or counterparty's failure to meet that non-vesting condition during the vesting period as a cancellation.

29   If an entity repurchases vested equity instruments, the payment made to the employee shall be accounted for as a deduction from equity, except to the extent that the payment exceeds the fair value of the equity instruments repurchased, measured at the repurchase date. Any such excess shall be recognised as an expense.

Cash-settled share-based payment transactions

30   **For cash-settled share-based payment transactions, the entity shall measure the goods or services acquired and the liability incurred at the fair value of the liability. Until the liability is settled, the entity shall remeasure the fair value of the liability at the end of each reporting period and at the date of settlement, with any changes in fair value recognised in profit or loss for the period.**

31   For example, an entity might grant share appreciation rights to employees as part of their remuneration package, whereby the employees will become entitled to a future cash payment (rather than an equity instrument), based on the increase in the entity's share price from a specified level over a specified period of time. Or an entity might grant to its employees a right to receive a future cash payment by granting to them a right to shares (including shares to be issued upon the exercise of share options) that are redeemable, either mandatorily (eg upon cessation of employment) or at the employee's option.

32   The entity shall recognise the services received, and a liability to pay for those services, as the employees render service. For example, some share appreciation rights vest immediately, and the employees are therefore not required to complete a specified period of service to become entitled to the cash payment. In the absence of evidence to the contrary, the entity shall presume that the services rendered by the employees in exchange for the share appreciation rights have been received. Thus, the entity shall recognise immediately the services received and a liability to pay for them. If the share appreciation rights do not vest until the employees have completed a specified period of service, the entity shall recognise the services received, and a liability to pay for them, as the employees render service during that period.

33   The liability shall be measured, initially and at the end of each reporting period until settled, at the fair value of the share appreciation rights, by applying an option pricing model, taking into account the terms and conditions on which the share appreciation rights were granted, and the extent to which the employees have rendered service to date.

Share-based payment transactions with cash alternatives

34   **For share-based payment transactions in which the terms of the arrangement provide either the entity or the counterparty with the choice of whether the entity settles the transaction in cash (or other assets) or by issuing equity instruments, the entity shall account for that transaction, or the components of that transaction, as a cash-settled share-based payment transaction if, and to the extent that, the entity has incurred a liability to settle in cash or other assets, or as an equity-settled share-based payment transaction if, and to the extent that, no such liability has been incurred.**

Share-based payment transactions in which the terms of the arrangement provide the counterparty with a choice of settlement

35   If an entity has granted the counterparty the right to choose whether a share-based payment transaction is settled in cash[4] or by issuing equity instruments, the entity has granted a compound financial instrument, which includes a debt component (ie the counterparty's right to demand payment in cash) and an equity component (ie the counterparty's right to demand settlement in equity instruments rather than in cash). For transactions with parties other than employees, in which the fair value of the goods or services received is measured directly, the entity shall measure the equity component of the compound financial instrument as the difference between the fair value of the goods or services received and the fair value of the debt component, at the date when the goods or services are received.

36   For other transactions, including transactions with employees, the entity shall measure the fair value of the compound financial instrument at the measurement date, taking into account the terms and conditions on which the rights to cash or equity instruments were granted.

37   To apply paragraph 36, the entity shall first measure the fair value of the debt component, and then measure the fair value of the equity component—taking into account that the counterparty must forfeit the right to receive cash in order to receive the equity instrument. The fair value of the compound financial instrument is the sum of the fair values of the two components. However, share-based payment transactions in which the counterparty has the choice of settlement are often structured so that the fair value of one settlement alternative is the same as the other. For example, the counterparty might have the choice of receiving share options or cash-settled share appreciation rights. In such cases, the fair value of the equity component is zero, and hence the fair

---

4   In paragraphs 35–43, all references to cash also include other assets of the entity.

value of the compound financial instrument is the same as the fair value of the debt component. Conversely, if the fair values of the settlement alternatives differ, the fair value of the equity component usually will be greater than zero, in which case the fair value of the compound financial instrument will be greater than the fair value of the debt component.

38   The entity shall account separately for the goods or services received or acquired in respect of each component of the compound financial instrument. For the debt component, the entity shall recognise the goods or services acquired, and a liability to pay for those goods or services, as the counterparty supplies goods or renders service, in accordance with the requirements applying to cash-settled share-based payment transactions (paragraphs 30–33). For the equity component (if any), the entity shall recognise the goods or services received, and an increase in equity, as the counterparty supplies goods or renders service, in accordance with the requirements applying to equity-settled share-based payment transactions (paragraphs 10–29).

39   At the date of settlement, the entity shall remeasure the liability to its fair value. If the entity issues equity instruments on settlement rather than paying cash, the liability shall be transferred direct to equity, as the consideration for the equity instruments issued.

40   If the entity pays in cash on settlement rather than issuing equity instruments, that payment shall be applied to settle the liability in full. Any equity component previously recognised shall remain within equity. By electing to receive cash on settlement, the counterparty forfeited the right to receive equity instruments. However, this requirement does not preclude the entity from recognising a transfer within equity, ie a transfer from one component of equity to another.

Share-based payment transactions in which the terms of the arrangement provide the entity with a choice of settlement

41   For a share-based payment transaction in which the terms of the arrangement provide an entity with the choice of whether to settle in cash or by issuing equity instruments, the entity shall determine whether it has a present obligation to settle in cash and account for the share-based payment transaction accordingly. The entity has a present obligation to settle in cash if the choice of settlement in equity instruments has no commercial substance (eg because the entity is legally prohibited from issuing shares), or the entity has a past practice or a stated policy of settling in cash, or generally settles in cash whenever the counterparty asks for cash settlement.

42   If the entity has a present obligation to settle in cash, it shall account for the transaction in accordance with the requirements applying to cash-settled share-based payment transactions, in paragraphs 30–33.

43   If no such obligation exists, the entity shall account for the transaction in accordance with the requirements applying to equity-settled share-based payment transactions, in paragraphs 10–29. Upon settlement:

(a)   if the entity elects to settle in cash, the cash payment shall be accounted for as the repurchase of an equity interest, ie as a deduction from equity, except as noted in (c) below.

(b) if the entity elects to settle by issuing equity instruments, no further accounting is required (other than a transfer from one component of equity to another, if necessary), except as noted in (c) below.

(c) if the entity elects the settlement alternative with the higher fair value, as at the date of settlement, the entity shall recognise an additional expense for the excess value given, ie the difference between the cash paid and the fair value of the equity instruments that would otherwise have been issued, or the difference between the fair value of the equity instruments issued and the amount of cash that would otherwise have been paid, whichever is applicable.

Share-based payment transactions among group entities (2009 amendments)

43A For share-based payment transactions among group entities, in its separate or individual financial statements, the entity receiving the goods or services shall measure the goods or services received as either an equity-settled or a cash-settled share-based payment transaction by assessing:

(a) the nature of the awards granted, and

(b) its own rights and obligations.

The amount recognised by the entity receiving the goods or services may differ from the amount recognised by the consolidated group or by another group entity settling the share-based payment transaction.

43B The entity receiving the goods or services shall measure the goods or services received as an equity-settled share-based payment transaction when:

(a) the awards granted are its own equity instruments, or

(b) the entity has no obligation to settle the share-based payment transaction.

The entity shall subsequently remeasure such an equity-settled share-based payment transaction only for changes in non-market vesting conditions in accordance with paragraphs 19–21. In all other circumstances, the entity receiving the goods or services shall measure the goods or services received as a cash-settled share-based payment transaction.

43C The entity settling a share-based payment transaction when another entity in the group receives the goods or services shall recognise the transaction as an equity-settled share-based payment transaction only if it is settled in the entity's own equity instruments. Otherwise, the transaction shall be recognised as a cash-settled share-based payment transaction.

43D Some group transactions involve repayment arrangements that require one group entity to pay another group entity for the provision of the share-based payments to the suppliers of goods or services. In such cases, the entity that receives the goods or services shall account for the share-based payment transaction in accordance with paragraph 43B regardless of intragroup repayment arrangements.

Disclosures

44   **An entity shall disclose information that enables users of the financial statements to understand the nature and extent of share-based payment arrangements that existed during the period.**

45   To give effect to the principle in paragraph 44, the entity shall disclose at least the following:

(a)   a description of each type of share-based payment arrangement that existed at any time during the period, including the general terms and conditions of each arrangement, such as vesting requirements, the maximum term of options granted, and the method of settlement (eg whether in cash or equity). An entity with substantially similar types of share-based payment arrangements may aggregate this information, unless separate disclosure of each arrangement is necessary to satisfy the principle in paragraph 44.

(b)   the number and weighted average exercise prices of share options for each of the following groups of options:

(i)   outstanding at the beginning of the period;

(ii)   granted during the period;

(iii)   forfeited during the period;

(iv)   exercised during the period;

(v)   expired during the period;

(vi)   outstanding at the end of the period; and

(vii)   exercisable at the end of the period.

(c)   for share options exercised during the period, the weighted average share price at the date of exercise. If options were exercised on a regular basis throughout the period, the entity may instead disclose the weighted average share price during the period.

(d)   for share options outstanding at the end of the period, the range of exercise prices and weighted average remaining contractual life. If the range of exercise prices is wide, the outstanding options shall be divided into ranges that are meaningful for assessing the number and timing of additional shares that may be issued and the cash that may be received upon exercise of those options.

46   **An entity shall disclose information that enables users of the financial statements to understand how the fair value of the goods or services received, or the fair value of the equity instruments granted, during the period was determined.**

47   If the entity has measured the fair value of goods or services received as consideration for equity instruments of the entity indirectly, by reference to the fair value of the equity instruments granted, to give effect to the principle in paragraph 46, the entity shall disclose at least the following:

(a) for share options granted during the period, the weighted average fair value of those options at the measurement date and information on how that fair value was measured, including:

    (i) the option pricing model used and the inputs to that model, including the weighted average share price, exercise price, expected volatility, option life, expected dividends, the risk-free interest rate and any other inputs to the model, including the method used and the assumptions made to incorporate the effects of expected early exercise;

    (ii) how expected volatility was determined, including an explanation of the extent to which expected volatility was based on historical volatility; and

    (iii) whether and how any other features of the option grant were incorporated into the measurement of fair value, such as a market condition.

(b) for other equity instruments granted during the period (ie other than share options), the number and weighted average fair value of those equity instruments at the measurement date, and information on how that fair value was measured, including:

    (i) if fair value was not measured on the basis of an observable market price, how it was determined;

    (ii) whether and how expected dividends were incorporated into the measurement of fair value; and

    (iii) whether and how any other features of the equity instruments granted were incorporated into the measurement of fair value.

(c) for share-based payment arrangements that were modified during the period:

    (i) an explanation of those modifications;

    (ii) the incremental fair value granted (as a result of those modifications); and

    (iii) information on how the incremental fair value granted was measured, consistently with the requirements set out in (a) and (b) above, where applicable.

48   If the entity has measured directly the fair value of goods or services received during the period, the entity shall disclose how that fair value was determined, eg whether fair value was measured at a market price for those goods or services.

49   If the entity has rebutted the presumption in paragraph 13, it shall disclose that fact, and give an explanation of why the presumption was rebutted.

50   **An entity shall disclose information that enables users of the financial statements to understand the effect of share-based payment transactions on the entity's profit or loss for the period and on its financial position.**

51 To give effect to the principle in paragraph 50, the entity shall disclose at least the following:

(a) the total expense recognised for the period arising from share-based payment transactions in which the goods or services received did not qualify for recognition as assets and hence were recognised immediately as an expense, including separate disclosure of that portion of the total expense that arises from transactions accounted for as equity-settled share-based payment transactions;

(b) for liabilities arising from share-based payment transactions:

(i) the total carrying amount at the end of the period; and

(ii) the total intrinsic value at the end of the period of liabilities for which the counterparty's right to cash or other assets had vested by the end of the period (eg vested share appreciation rights).

52 If the information required to be disclosed by this IFRS does not satisfy the principles in paragraphs 44, 46 and 50, the entity shall disclose such additional information as is necessary to satisfy them.

Transitional provisions

53 For equity-settled share-based payment transactions, the entity shall apply this IFRS to grants of shares, share options or other equity instruments that were granted after 7 November 2002 and had not yet vested at the effective date of this IFRS.

54 The entity is encouraged, but not required, to apply this IFRS to other grants of equity instruments if the entity has disclosed publicly the fair value of those equity instruments, determined at the measurement date.

55 For all grants of equity instruments to which this IFRS is applied, the entity shall restate comparative information and, where applicable, adjust the opening balance of retained earnings for the earliest period presented.

56 For all grants of equity instruments to which this IFRS has not been applied (eg equity instruments granted on or before 7 November 2002), the entity shall nevertheless disclose the information required by paragraphs 44 and 45.

57 If, after the IFRS becomes effective, an entity modifies the terms or conditions of a grant of equity instruments to which this IFRS has not been applied, the entity shall nevertheless apply paragraphs 26–29 to account for any such modifications.

58 For liabilities arising from share-based payment transactions existing at the effective date of this IFRS, the entity shall apply the IFRS retrospectively. For these liabilities, the entity shall restate comparative information, including adjusting the opening balance of retained earnings in the earliest period presented for which comparative information has been restated, except that the entity is not required to restate comparative information to the extent that the information relates to a period or date that is earlier than 7 November 2002.

59   The entity is encouraged, but not required, to apply retrospectively the IFRS to other liabilities arising from share-based payment transactions, for example, to liabilities that were settled during a period for which comparative information is presented.

Effective date

60   An entity shall apply this IFRS for annual periods beginning on or after 1 January 2005. Earlier application is encouraged. If an entity applies the IFRS for a period beginning before 1 January 2005, it shall disclose that fact.

61   IFRS 3 (as revised in 2008) and *Improvements to IFRSs* issued in April 2009 amended paragraph 5. An entity shall apply those amendments for annual periods beginning on or after 1 July 2009. Earlier application is permitted. If an entity applies IFRS 3 (revised 2008) for an earlier period, the amendments shall also be applied for that earlier period.

62   An entity shall apply the following amendments retrospectively in annual periods beginning on or after 1 January 2009:

    (a)   the requirements in paragraph 21A in respect of the treatment of non-vesting conditions;

    (b)   the revised definitions of 'vest' and 'vesting conditions' in Appendix A;

    (c)   the amendments in paragraphs 28 and 28A in respect of cancellations.

Earlier application is permitted. If an entity applies these amendments for a period beginning before 1 January 2009, it shall disclose that fact.

63   An entity shall apply the following amendments made by *Group Cash-settled Share-based Payment Transactions* issued in June 2009 retrospectively, subject to the transitional provisions in paragraphs 53–59, in accordance with IAS 8 *Accounting Policies, Changes in Accounting Estimates and Errors* for annual periods beginning on or after 1 January 2010:

    (a)   the amendment of paragraph 2, the deletion of paragraph 3 and the addition of paragraphs 3A and 43A–43D and of paragraphs B45, B47, B50, B54, B56–B58 and B60 in Appendix B in respect of the accounting for transactions among group entities.

    (b)   the revised definitions in Appendix A of the following terms:

        •   cash-settled share-based payment transaction,

        •   equity-settled share-based payment transaction,

        •   share-based payment arrangement, and

        •   share-based payment transaction.

If the information necessary for retrospective application is not available, an entity shall reflect in its separate or individual financial statements the amounts previously recognised in the group's consolidated financial statements. Earlier application is permitted. If an entity applies the amendments for a period beginning before 1 January 2010, it shall disclose that fact.

63A   IFRS 10 *Consolidated Financial Statements* and IFRS 11, issued in May 2011, amended paragraph 5 and Appendix A. An entity shall apply those amendments when it applies IFRS 10 and IFRS 11.

Withdrawal of Interpretations

64   *Group Cash-settled Share-based Payment Transactions* issued in June 2009 supersedes IFRIC 8 *Scope of IFRS 2* and IFRIC 11 *IFRS 2—Group and Treasury Share Transactions*. The amendments made by that document incorporated the previous requirements set out in IFRIC 8 and IFRIC 11 as follows:

(a)   amended paragraph 2 and added paragraph 13A in respect of the accounting for transactions in which the entity cannot identify specifically some or all of the goods or services received. Those requirements were effective for annual periods beginning on or after 1 May 2006.

(b)   added paragraphs B46, B48, B49, B51–B53, B55, B59 and B61 in Appendix B in respect of the accounting for transactions among group entities. Those requirements were effective for annual periods beginning on or after 1 March 2007.

Those requirements were applied retrospectively in accordance with the requirements of IAS 8, subject to the transitional provisions of IFRS 2.

Appendix A
Defined terms

This appendix is an integral part of the IFRS.

cash-settled share-based payment transaction	A **share-based payment transaction** in which the entity acquires goods or services by incurring a liability to transfer cash or other assets to the supplier of those goods or services for amounts that are based on the price (or value) of **equity instruments** (including shares or **share options**) of the entity or another group entity.
employees and others providing similar services	Individuals who render personal services to the entity and either (a) the individuals are regarded as employees for legal or tax purposes, (b) the individuals work for the entity under its direction in the same way as individuals who are regarded as employees for legal or tax purposes, or (c) the services rendered are similar to those rendered by employees. For example, the term encompasses all management personnel, ie those persons having authority and responsibility for planning, directing and controlling the activities of the entity, including non-executive directors.
equity instrument	A contract that evidences a residual interest in the assets of an entity after deducting all of its liabilities.[a]
equity instrument granted	The right (conditional or unconditional) to an **equity instrument** of the entity conferred by the entity on another party, under a **share-based payment arrangement**.
equity-settled share-based payment transaction	A **share-based payment transaction** in which the entity (a) receives goods or services as consideration for its own **equity instruments** (including shares or **share options**), or (b) receives goods or services but has no obligation to settle the transaction with the supplier.
fair value	The amount for which an asset could be exchanged, a liability settled, or an **equity instrument granted** could be exchanged, between knowledgeable, willing parties in an arm's length transaction.
grant date	The date at which the entity and another party (including an employee) agree to a **share-based payment arrangement**, being when the entity and the counterparty have a shared understanding of the terms and conditions of the arrangement. At grant date the entity confers on the counterparty the right to cash, other assets, or **equity instruments** of the entity, provided the specified **vesting conditions**, if any, are met. If that agreement is subject to an approval process (for example, by shareholders), grant date is the date when that approval is obtained.

intrinsic value	The difference between the **fair value** of the shares to which the counterparty has the (conditional or unconditional) right to subscribe or which it has the right to receive, and the price (if any) the counterparty is (or will be) required to pay for those shares. For example, a **share option** with an exercise price of CU15,[b] on a share with a **fair value** of CU20, has an intrinsic value of CU5.
market condition	A condition upon which the exercise price, vesting or exercisability of an **equity instrument** depends that is related to the market price of the entity's **equity instruments**, such as attaining a specified share price or a specified amount of **intrinsic value** of a **share option**, or achieving a specified target that is based on the market price of the entity's **equity instruments** relative to an index of market prices of **equity instruments** of other entities.
measurement date	The date at which the **fair value** of the **equity instruments granted** is measured for the purposes of this IFRS. For transactions with **employees and others providing similar services**, the measurement date is **grant date**. For transactions with parties other than employees (and those providing similar services), the measurement date is the date the entity obtains the goods or the counterparty renders service.
reload feature	A feature that provides for an automatic grant of additional **share options** whenever the option holder exercises previously granted options using the entity's shares, rather than cash, to satisfy the exercise price.
reload option	A new **share option** granted when a share is used to satisfy the exercise price of a previous **share option**.
share-based payment arrangement	An agreement between the entity (or another group[c] entity or any shareholder of any group entity) and another party (including an employee) that entitles the other party to receive

       (a)   cash or other assets of the entity for amounts that are based on the price (or value) of **equity instruments** (including shares or **share options**) of the entity or another group entity, or

       (b)   **equity instruments** (including shares or **share options**) of the entity or another group entity,

provided the specified **vesting conditions**, if any, are met.

share-based payment transaction	A transaction in which the entity

       (a)   receives goods or services from the supplier of those goods or services (including an employee) in a **share-based payment arrangement**, or

       (b)   incurs an obligation to settle the transaction with the supplier in a **share-based payment arrangement** when another group entity receives those goods or services.

share option	A contract that gives the holder the right, but not the obligation, to subscribe to the entity's shares at a fixed or determinable price for a specified period of time.
vest	To become an entitlement. Under a **share-based payment arrangement**, a counterparty's right to receive cash, other assets or **equity instruments** of the entity vests when the counterparty's entitlement is no longer conditional on the satisfaction of any **vesting conditions**.
vesting conditions	The conditions that determine whether the entity receives the services that entitle the counterparty to receive cash, other assets or **equity instruments** of the entity, under a **share-based payment arrangement**. Vesting conditions are either service conditions or performance conditions. Service conditions require the counterparty to complete a specified period of service. Performance conditions require the counterparty to complete a specified period of service and specified performance targets to be met (such as a specified increase in the entity's profit over a specified period of time). A performance condition might include a **market condition**.
vesting period	The period during which all the specified **vesting conditions** of a **share-based payment arrangement** are to be satisfied.

[a] The *Conceptual Framework for Financial Reporting* defines a liability as a present obligation of the entity arising from past events, the settlement of which is expected to result in an outflow from the entity of resources embodying economic benefits (ie an outflow of cash or other assets of the entity).

[b] In this appendix, monetary amounts are denominated in 'currency units (CU)'.

[c] A 'group' is defined in Appendix A of IFRS 10 *Consolidated Financial Statements* as 'a parent and its subsidiaries' from the perspective of the reporting entity's ultimate parent.

Appendix B
Application guidance

This appendix is an integral part of the IFRS.

Estimating the fair value of equity instruments granted

B1 Paragraphs B2–B41 of this appendix discuss measurement of the fair value of shares and share options granted, focusing on the specific terms and conditions that are common features of a grant of shares or share options to employees. Therefore, it is not exhaustive. Furthermore, because the valuation issues discussed below focus on shares and share options granted to employees, it is assumed that the fair value of the shares or share options is measured at grant date. However, many of the valuation issues discussed below (eg determining expected volatility) also apply in the context of estimating the fair value of shares or share options granted to parties other than employees at the date the entity obtains the goods or the counterparty renders service.

Shares

B2 For shares granted to employees, the fair value of the shares shall be measured at the market price of the entity's shares (or an estimated market price, if the entity's shares are not publicly traded), adjusted to take into account the terms and conditions upon which the shares were granted (except for vesting conditions that are excluded from the measurement of fair value in accordance with paragraphs 19–21).

B3 For example, if the employee is not entitled to receive dividends during the vesting period, this factor shall be taken into account when estimating the fair value of the shares granted. Similarly, if the shares are subject to restrictions on transfer after vesting date, that factor shall be taken into account, but only to the extent that the post-vesting restrictions affect the price that a knowledgeable, willing market participant would pay for that share. For example, if the shares are actively traded in a deep and liquid market, post-vesting transfer restrictions may have little, if any, effect on the price that a knowledgeable, willing market participant would pay for those shares. Restrictions on transfer or other restrictions that exist during the vesting period shall not be taken into account when estimating the grant date fair value of the shares granted, because those restrictions stem from the existence of vesting conditions, which are accounted for in accordance with paragraphs 19–21.

Share options

B4 For share options granted to employees, in many cases market prices are not available, because the options granted are subject to terms and conditions that do not apply to traded options. If traded options with similar terms and conditions do not exist, the fair value of the options granted shall be estimated by applying an option pricing model.

B5 The entity shall consider factors that knowledgeable, willing market participants would consider in selecting the option pricing model to apply. For example, many employee options have long lives, are usually exercisable during the period between vesting date and the end of the options' life, and are often exercised early. These factors should be considered when estimating the grant date fair value of the options. For many entities, this might preclude the use of the Black-Scholes-Merton formula, which does not allow for the possibility of exercise before the end of the option's life and may not adequately reflect the effects of expected early exercise. It also does not allow for the possibility that expected volatility and other model inputs might vary over the option's life. However, for share options with relatively short contractual lives, or that must be exercised within a short period of time after vesting date, the factors identified above may not apply. In these instances, the Black-Scholes-Merton formula may produce a value that is substantially the same as a more flexible option pricing model.

B6 All option pricing models take into account, as a minimum, the following factors:

(a) the exercise price of the option;

(b) the life of the option;

(c) the current price of the underlying shares;

(d) the expected volatility of the share price;

(e) the dividends expected on the shares (if appropriate); and

(f) the risk-free interest rate for the life of the option.

B7 Other factors that knowledgeable, willing market participants would consider in setting the price shall also be taken into account (except for vesting conditions and reload features that are excluded from the measurement of fair value in accordance with paragraphs 19–22).

B8 For example, a share option granted to an employee typically cannot be exercised during specified periods (eg during the vesting period or during periods specified by securities regulators). This factor shall be taken into account if the option pricing model applied would otherwise assume that the option could be exercised at any time during its life. However, if an entity uses an option pricing model that values options that can be exercised only at the end of the options' life, no adjustment is required for the inability to exercise them during the vesting period (or other periods during the options' life), because the model assumes that the options cannot be exercised during those periods.

B9 Similarly, another factor common to employee share options is the possibility of early exercise of the option, for example, because the option is not freely transferable, or because the employee must exercise all vested options upon cessation of employment. The effects of expected early exercise shall be taken into account, as discussed in paragraphs B16–B21.

B10   Factors that a knowledgeable, willing market participant would not consider in setting the price of a share option (or other equity instrument) shall not be taken into account when estimating the fair value of share options (or other equity instruments) granted. For example, for share options granted to employees, factors that affect the value of the option from the individual employee's perspective only are not relevant to estimating the price that would be set by a knowledgeable, willing market participant.

Inputs to option pricing models

B11   In estimating the expected volatility of and dividends on the underlying shares, the objective is to approximate the expectations that would be reflected in a current market or negotiated exchange price for the option. Similarly, when estimating the effects of early exercise of employee share options, the objective is to approximate the expectations that an outside party with access to detailed information about employees' exercise behaviour would develop based on information available at the grant date.

B12   Often, there is likely to be a range of reasonable expectations about future volatility, dividends and exercise behaviour. If so, an expected value should be calculated, by weighting each amount within the range by its associated probability of occurrence.

B13   Expectations about the future are generally based on experience, modified if the future is reasonably expected to differ from the past. In some circumstances, identifiable factors may indicate that unadjusted historical experience is a relatively poor predictor of future experience. For example, if an entity with two distinctly different lines of business disposes of the one that was significantly less risky than the other, historical volatility may not be the best information on which to base reasonable expectations for the future.

B14   In other circumstances, historical information may not be available. For example, a newly listed entity will have little, if any, historical data on the volatility of its share price. Unlisted and newly listed entities are discussed further below.

B15   In summary, an entity should not simply base estimates of volatility, exercise behaviour and dividends on historical information without considering the extent to which the past experience is expected to be reasonably predictive of future experience.

Expected early exercise

B16   Employees often exercise share options early, for a variety of reasons. For example, employee share options are typically non-transferable. This often causes employees to exercise their share options early, because that is the only way for the employees to liquidate their position. Also, employees who cease employment are usually required to exercise any vested options within a short period of time, otherwise the share options are forfeited. This factor also causes the early exercise of employee share options. Other factors causing early exercise are risk aversion and lack of wealth diversification.

B17   The means by which the effects of expected early exercise are taken into account depends upon the type of option pricing model applied. For example, expected early exercise could be taken into account by using an estimate of the option's expected life (which, for an employee share option, is the period of time from grant date to the date on which the option is expected to be exercised) as an input into an option pricing model (eg the Black-Scholes-Merton formula). Alternatively, expected early exercise could be modelled in a binomial or similar option pricing model that uses contractual life as an input.

B18   Factors to consider in estimating early exercise include:

(a)   the length of the vesting period, because the share option typically cannot be exercised until the end of the vesting period. Hence, determining the valuation implications of expected early exercise is based on the assumption that the options will vest. The implications of vesting conditions are discussed in paragraphs 19–21.

(b)   the average length of time similar options have remained outstanding in the past.

(c)   the price of the underlying shares. Experience may indicate that the employees tend to exercise options when the share price reaches a specified level above the exercise price.

(d)   the employee's level within the organisation. For example, experience might indicate that higher-level employees tend to exercise options later than lower-level employees (discussed further in paragraph B21).

(e)   expected volatility of the underlying shares. On average, employees might tend to exercise options on highly volatile shares earlier than on shares with low volatility.

B19   As noted in paragraph B17, the effects of early exercise could be taken into account by using an estimate of the option's expected life as an input into an option pricing model. When estimating the expected life of share options granted to a group of employees, the entity could base that estimate on an appropriately weighted average expected life for the entire employee group or on appropriately weighted average lives for subgroups of employees within the group, based on more detailed data about employees' exercise behaviour (discussed further below).

B20   Separating an option grant into groups for employees with relatively homogeneous exercise behaviour is likely to be important. Option value is not a linear function of option term; value increases at a decreasing rate as the term lengthens. For example, if all other assumptions are equal, although a two-year option is worth more than a one-year option, it is not worth twice as much. That means that calculating estimated option value on the basis of a single weighted average life that includes widely differing individual lives would overstate the total fair value of the share options granted. Separating options granted into several groups, each of which has a relatively narrow range of lives included in its weighted average life, reduces that overstatement.

B21 Similar considerations apply when using a binomial or similar model. For example, the experience of an entity that grants options broadly to all levels of employees might indicate that top-level executives tend to hold their options longer than middle-management employees hold theirs and that lower-level employees tend to exercise their options earlier than any other group. In addition, employees who are encouraged or required to hold a minimum amount of their employer's equity instruments, including options, might on average exercise options later than employees not subject to that provision. In those situations, separating options by groups of recipients with relatively homogeneous exercise behaviour will result in a more accurate estimate of the total fair value of the share options granted.

Expected volatility

B22 Expected volatility is a measure of the amount by which a price is expected to fluctuate during a period. The measure of volatility used in option pricing models is the annualised standard deviation of the continuously compounded rates of return on the share over a period of time. Volatility is typically expressed in annualised terms that are comparable regardless of the time period used in the calculation, for example, daily, weekly or monthly price observations.

B23 The rate of return (which may be positive or negative) on a share for a period measures how much a shareholder has benefited from dividends and appreciation (or depreciation) of the share price.

B24 The expected annualised volatility of a share is the range within which the continuously compounded annual rate of return is expected to fall approximately two-thirds of the time. For example, to say that a share with an expected continuously compounded rate of return of 12 per cent has a volatility of 30 per cent means that the probability that the rate of return on the share for one year will be between −18 per cent (12% − 30%) and 42 per cent (12% + 30%) is approximately two-thirds. If the share price is CU100 at the beginning of the year and no dividends are paid, the year-end share price would be expected to be between CU83.53 (CU100 × $e^{-0.18}$) and CU152.20 (CU100 × $e^{0.42}$) approximately two-thirds of the time.

B25 Factors to consider in estimating expected volatility include:

(a) implied volatility from traded share options on the entity's shares, or other traded instruments of the entity that include option features (such as convertible debt), if any.

(b) the historical volatility of the share price over the most recent period that is generally commensurate with the expected term of the option (taking into account the remaining contractual life of the option and the effects of expected early exercise).

(c) the length of time an entity's shares have been publicly traded. A newly listed entity might have a high historical volatility, compared with similar entities that have been listed longer. Further guidance for newly listed entities is given below.

(d)   the tendency of volatility to revert to its mean, ie its long-term average level, and other factors indicating that expected future volatility might differ from past volatility. For example, if an entity's share price was extraordinarily volatile for some identifiable period of time because of a failed takeover bid or a major restructuring, that period could be disregarded in computing historical average annual volatility.

(e)   appropriate and regular intervals for price observations. The price observations should be consistent from period to period. For example, an entity might use the closing price for each week or the highest price for the week, but it should not use the closing price for some weeks and the highest price for other weeks. Also, the price observations should be expressed in the same currency as the exercise price.

Newly listed entities

B26   As noted in paragraph B25, an entity should consider historical volatility of the share price over the most recent period that is generally commensurate with the expected option term. If a newly listed entity does not have sufficient information on historical volatility, it should nevertheless compute historical volatility for the longest period for which trading activity is available. It could also consider the historical volatility of similar entities following a comparable period in their lives. For example, an entity that has been listed for only one year and grants options with an average expected life of five years might consider the pattern and level of historical volatility of entities in the same industry for the first six years in which the shares of those entities were publicly traded.

Unlisted entities

B27   An unlisted entity will not have historical information to consider when estimating expected volatility. Some factors to consider instead are set out below.

B28   In some cases, an unlisted entity that regularly issues options or shares to employees (or other parties) might have set up an internal market for its shares. The volatility of those share prices could be considered when estimating expected volatility.

B29   Alternatively, the entity could consider the historical or implied volatility of similar listed entities, for which share price or option price information is available, to use when estimating expected volatility. This would be appropriate if the entity has based the value of its shares on the share prices of similar listed entities.

B30   If the entity has not based its estimate of the value of its shares on the share prices of similar listed entities, and has instead used another valuation methodology to value its shares, the entity could derive an estimate of expected volatility consistent with that valuation methodology. For example, the entity might value its shares on a net asset or earnings basis. It could consider the expected volatility of those net asset values or earnings.

Expected dividends

B31   Whether expected dividends should be taken into account when measuring the fair value of shares or options granted depends on whether the counterparty is entitled to dividends or dividend equivalents.

B32   For example, if employees were granted options and are entitled to dividends on the underlying shares or dividend equivalents (which might be paid in cash or applied to reduce the exercise price) between grant date and exercise date, the options granted should be valued as if no dividends will be paid on the underlying shares, ie the input for expected dividends should be zero.

B33   Similarly, when the grant date fair value of shares granted to employees is estimated, no adjustment is required for expected dividends if the employee is entitled to receive dividends paid during the vesting period.

B34   Conversely, if the employees are not entitled to dividends or dividend equivalents during the vesting period (or before exercise, in the case of an option), the grant date valuation of the rights to shares or options should take expected dividends into account. That is to say, when the fair value of an option grant is estimated, expected dividends should be included in the application of an option pricing model. When the fair value of a share grant is estimated, that valuation should be reduced by the present value of dividends expected to be paid during the vesting period.

B35   Option pricing models generally call for expected dividend yield. However, the models may be modified to use an expected dividend amount rather than a yield. An entity may use either its expected yield or its expected payments. If the entity uses the latter, it should consider its historical pattern of increases in dividends. For example, if an entity's policy has generally been to increase dividends by approximately 3 per cent per year, its estimated option value should not assume a fixed dividend amount throughout the option's life unless there is evidence that supports that assumption.

B36   Generally, the assumption about expected dividends should be based on publicly available information. An entity that does not pay dividends and has no plans to do so should assume an expected dividend yield of zero. However, an emerging entity with no history of paying dividends might expect to begin paying dividends during the expected lives of its employee share options. Those entities could use an average of their past dividend yield (zero) and the mean dividend yield of an appropriately comparable peer group.

Risk-free interest rate

B37   Typically, the risk-free interest rate is the implied yield currently available on zero-coupon government issues of the country in whose currency the exercise price is expressed, with a remaining term equal to the expected term of the option being valued (based on the option's remaining contractual life and taking into account the effects of expected early exercise). It may be necessary to use an appropriate substitute, if no such government issues exist or circumstances indicate that the implied yield on zero-coupon government issues is not representative of the risk-free interest rate (for example, in high inflation economies). Also, an appropriate substitute should be used if market participants would typically determine the risk-free interest rate by using that substitute, rather than the implied yield of zero-coupon government issues, when estimating the fair value of an option with a life equal to the expected term of the option being valued.

Capital structure effects

B38 Typically, third parties, not the entity, write traded share options. When these share options are exercised, the writer delivers shares to the option holder. Those shares are acquired from existing shareholders. Hence the exercise of traded share options has no dilutive effect.

B39 In contrast, if share options are written by the entity, new shares are issued when those share options are exercised (either actually issued or issued in substance, if shares previously repurchased and held in treasury are used). Given that the shares will be issued at the exercise price rather than the current market price at the date of exercise, this actual or potential dilution might reduce the share price, so that the option holder does not make as large a gain on exercise as on exercising an otherwise similar traded option that does not dilute the share price.

B40 Whether this has a significant effect on the value of the share options granted depends on various factors, such as the number of new shares that will be issued on exercise of the options compared with the number of shares already issued. Also, if the market already expects that the option grant will take place, the market may have already factored the potential dilution into the share price at the date of grant.

B41 However, the entity should consider whether the possible dilutive effect of the future exercise of the share options granted might have an impact on their estimated fair value at grant date. Option pricing models can be adapted to take into account this potential dilutive effect.

Modifications to equity-settled share-based payment arrangements

B42 Paragraph 27 requires that, irrespective of any modifications to the terms and conditions on which the equity instruments were granted, or a cancellation or settlement of that grant of equity instruments, the entity should recognise, as a minimum, the services received measured at the grant date fair value of the equity instruments granted, unless those equity instruments do not vest because of failure to satisfy a vesting condition (other than a market condition) that was specified at grant date. In addition, the entity should recognise the effects of modifications that increase the total fair value of the share-based payment arrangement or are otherwise beneficial to the employee.

B43 To apply the requirements of paragraph 27:

(a) if the modification increases the fair value of the equity instruments granted (eg by reducing the exercise price), measured immediately before and after the modification, the entity shall include the incremental fair value granted in the measurement of the amount recognised for services received as consideration for the equity instruments granted. The incremental fair value granted is the difference between the fair value of the modified equity instrument and that of the original equity instrument, both estimated as at the date of the modification. If the modification occurs during the vesting period, the incremental fair value granted is included in the measurement of the amount recognised for services received over the period from the modification date until the date when the modified equity instruments vest, in addition to the amount based on the grant date fair value of the original equity instruments, which is recognised over the remainder of the original vesting period. If the modification occurs after vesting date, the incremental fair value granted is recognised immediately, or over the vesting period if the employee is required to complete an additional period of service before becoming unconditionally entitled to those modified equity instruments.

(b)   similarly, if the modification increases the number of equity instruments granted, the entity shall include the fair value of the additional equity instruments granted, measured at the date of the modification, in the measurement of the amount recognised for services received as consideration for the equity instruments granted, consistently with the requirements in (a) above. For example, if the modification occurs during the vesting period, the fair value of the additional equity instruments granted is included in the measurement of the amount recognised for services received over the period from the modification date until the date when the additional equity instruments vest, in addition to the amount based on the grant date fair value of the equity instruments originally granted, which is recognised over the remainder of the original vesting period.

(c)   if the entity modifies the vesting conditions in a manner that is beneficial to the employee, for example, by reducing the vesting period or by modifying or eliminating a performance condition (other than a market condition, changes to which are accounted for in accordance with (a) above), the entity shall take the modified vesting conditions into account when applying the requirements of paragraphs 19–21.

B44   Furthermore, if the entity modifies the terms or conditions of the equity instruments granted in a manner that reduces the total fair value of the share-based payment arrangement, or is not otherwise beneficial to the employee, the entity shall nevertheless continue to account for the services received as consideration for the equity instruments granted as if that modification had not occurred (other than a cancellation of some or all the equity instruments granted, which shall be accounted for in accordance with paragraph 28). For example:

(a)   if the modification reduces the fair value of the equity instruments granted, measured immediately before and after the modification, the entity shall not take into account that decrease in fair value and shall continue to measure the amount recognised for services received as consideration for the equity instruments based on the grant date fair value of the equity instruments granted.

(b)   if the modification reduces the number of equity instruments granted to an employee, that reduction shall be accounted for as a cancellation of that portion of the grant, in accordance with the requirements of paragraph 28.

(c) if the entity modifies the vesting conditions in a manner that is not beneficial to the employee, for example, by increasing the vesting period or by modifying or adding a performance condition (other than a market condition, changes to which are accounted for in accordance with (a) above), the entity shall not take the modified vesting conditions into account when applying the requirements of paragraphs 19–21.

Share-based payment transactions among group entities (2009 amendments)

B45 Paragraphs 43A–43C address the accounting for share-based payment transactions among group entities in each entity's separate or individual financial statements. Paragraphs B46–B61 discuss how to apply the requirements in paragraphs 43A–43C. As noted in paragraph 43D, share-based payment transactions among group entities may take place for a variety of reasons depending on facts and circumstances. Therefore, this discussion is not exhaustive and assumes that when the entity receiving the goods or services has no obligation to settle the transaction, the transaction is a parent's equity contribution to the subsidiary, regardless of any intragroup repayment arrangements.

B46 Although the discussion below focuses on transactions with employees, it also applies to similar share-based payment transactions with suppliers of goods or services other than employees. An arrangement between a parent and its subsidiary may require the subsidiary to pay the parent for the provision of the equity instruments to the employees. The discussion below does not address how to account for such an intragroup payment arrangement.

B47 Four issues are commonly encountered in share-based payment transactions among group entities. For convenience, the examples below discuss the issues in terms of a parent and its subsidiary.

Share-based payment arrangements involving an entity's own equity instruments

B48 The first issue is whether the following transactions involving an entity's own equity instruments should be accounted for as equity-settled or as cash-settled in accordance with the requirements of this IFRS:

(a) an entity grants to its employees rights to equity instruments of the entity (eg share options), and either chooses or is required to buy equity instruments (ie treasury shares) from another party, to satisfy its obligations to its employees; and

(b) an entity's employees are granted rights to equity instruments of the entity (eg share options), either by the entity itself or by its shareholders, and the shareholders of the entity provide the equity instruments needed.

B49 The entity shall account for share-based payment transactions in which it receives services as consideration for its own equity instruments as equity-settled. This applies regardless of whether the entity chooses or is required to buy those equity instruments from another party to satisfy its obligations to its employees under the share-based payment arrangement. It also applies regardless of whether:

(a)   the employee's rights to the entity's equity instruments were granted by the entity itself or by its shareholder(s); or

(b)   the share-based payment arrangement was settled by the entity itself or by its shareholder(s).

B50   If the shareholder has an obligation to settle the transaction with its investee's employees, it provides equity instruments of its investee rather than its own. Therefore, if its investee is in the same group as the shareholder, in accordance with paragraph 43C, the shareholder shall measure its obligation in accordance with the requirements applicable to cash-settled share-based payment transactions in the shareholder's separate financial statements and those applicable to equity-settled share-based payment transactions in the shareholder's consolidated financial statements.

Share-based payment arrangements involving equity instruments of the parent

B51   The second issue concerns share-based payment transactions between two or more entities within the same group involving an equity instrument of another group entity. For example, employees of a subsidiary are granted rights to equity instruments of its parent as consideration for the services provided to the subsidiary.

B52   Therefore, the second issue concerns the following share-based payment arrangements:

(a)   a parent grants rights to its equity instruments directly to the employees of its subsidiary: the parent (not the subsidiary) has the obligation to provide the employees of the subsidiary with the equity instruments; and

(b)   a subsidiary grants rights to equity instruments of its parent to its employees: the subsidiary has the obligation to provide its employees with the equity instruments.

A parent grants rights to its equity instruments to the employees of its subsidiary (paragraph B52(a))

B53   The subsidiary does not have an obligation to provide its parent's equity instruments to the subsidiary's employees. Therefore, in accordance with paragraph 43B, the subsidiary shall measure the services received from its employees in accordance with the requirements applicable to equity-settled share-based payment transactions, and recognise a corresponding increase in equity as a contribution from the parent.

B54   The parent has an obligation to settle the transaction with the subsidiary's employees by providing the parent's own equity instruments. Therefore, in accordance with paragraph 43C, the parent shall measure its obligation in accordance with the requirements applicable to equity-settled share-based payment transactions.

A subsidiary grants rights to equity instruments of its parent to its employees (paragraph B52(b))

B55   Because the subsidiary does not meet either of the conditions in paragraph 43B, it shall account for the transaction with its employees as cash-settled. This requirement applies irrespective of how the subsidiary obtains the equity instruments to satisfy its obligations to its employees.

Share-based payment arrangements involving cash-settled payments to employees

B56   The third issue is how an entity that receives goods or services from its suppliers (including employees) should account for share-based arrangements that are cash-settled when the entity itself does not have any obligation to make the required payments to its suppliers. For example, consider the following arrangements in which the parent (not the entity itself) has an obligation to make the required cash payments to the employees of the entity:

(a)   the employees of the entity will receive cash payments that are linked to the price of its equity instruments.

(b)   the employees of the entity will receive cash payments that are linked to the price of its parent's equity instruments.

B57   The subsidiary does not have an obligation to settle the transaction with its employees. Therefore, the subsidiary shall account for the transaction with its employees as equity-settled, and recognise a corresponding increase in equity as a contribution from its parent. The subsidiary shall remeasure the cost of the transaction subsequently for any changes resulting from non-market vesting conditions not being met in accordance with paragraphs 19–21. This differs from the measurement of the transaction as cash-settled in the consolidated financial statements of the group.

B58   Because the parent has an obligation to settle the transaction with the employees, and the consideration is cash, the parent (and the consolidated group) shall measure its obligation in accordance with the requirements applicable to cash-settled share-based payment transactions in paragraph 43C.

Transfer of employees between group entities

B59   The fourth issue relates to group share-based payment arrangements that involve employees of more than one group entity. For example, a parent might grant rights to its equity instruments to the employees of its subsidiaries, conditional upon the completion of continuing service with the group for a specified period. An employee of one subsidiary might transfer employment to another subsidiary during the specified vesting period without the employee's rights to equity instruments of the parent under the original share-based payment arrangement being affected. If the subsidiaries have no obligation to settle the share-based payment transaction with their employees, they account for it as an equity-settled transaction. Each subsidiary shall measure the services received from the employee by reference to the fair value of the equity instruments at the date the rights to those equity instruments were originally granted by the parent as defined in Appendix A, and the proportion of the vesting period the employee served with each subsidiary.

B60 If the subsidiary has an obligation to settle the transaction with its employees in its parent's equity instruments, it accounts for the transaction as cash-settled. Each subsidiary shall measure the services received on the basis of grant date fair value of the equity instruments for the proportion of the vesting period the employee served with each subsidiary. In addition, each subsidiary shall recognise any change in the fair value of the equity instruments during the employee's service period with each subsidiary.

B61 Such an employee, after transferring between group entities, may fail to satisfy a vesting condition other than a market condition as defined in Appendix A, eg the employee leaves the group before completing the service period. In this case, because the vesting condition is service to the group, each subsidiary shall adjust the amount previously recognised in respect of the services received from the employee in accordance with the principles in paragraph 19. Hence, if the rights to the equity instruments granted by the parent do not vest because of an employee's failure to meet a vesting condition other than a market condition, no amount is recognised on a cumulative basis for the services received from that employee in the financial statements of any group entity.

Appendix C
Amendments to other IFRSs

The amendments in this appendix become effective for annual financial statements covering periods beginning on or after 1 January 2005. If an entity applies this IFRS for an earlier period, these amendments become effective for that earlier period.

* * * * *

The amendments contained in this appendix when this Standard was issued in 2004 have been incorporated into the relevant IFRSs published in this volume.

International Financial Reporting Standard 3

Business Combinations

In April 2001 the International Accounting Standards Board (IASB) adopted IAS 22 *Business Combinations*, which had originally been issued by the International Accounting Standards Committee in October 1998. IAS 22 was itself a revised version of IAS 22 *Business Combinations* that was issued in November 1983.

In March 2004 the IASB replaced IAS 22 and three related Interpretations (SIC-9 *Business Combinations—Classification either as Acquisitions or Unitings of Interests*, SIC-22 *Business Combinations—Subsequent Adjustment of Fair Values and Goodwill Initially Reported* and SIC-28 *Business Combinations—'Date of Exchange' and Fair Value of Equity Instruments*) when it issued IFRS 3 *Business Combinations*.

Minor amendments were made to IFRS 3 in March 2004 by IFRS 5 *Non-current Assets Held for Sale and Discontinued Operations* and IAS 1 *Presentation of Financial Statements* (as revised in September 2007), which amended the terminology used throughout IFRSs, including IFRS 3.

In January 2008 the IASB issued a revised IFRS 3. IFRS 3 was amended in May 2010 by *Improvements to IFRSs*.

Other IFRSs have made minor consequential amendments to IFRS 3. They include IFRS 9 *Financial Instruments* (issued November 2009 and October 2010), IFRS 10 *Consolidated Financial Statements* (issued May 2011), IFRS 11 *Joint Arrangements* (issued May 2011) and IFRS 13 *Fair Value Measurement* (issued May 2011).

Contents

FOR THE ACCOMPANYING DOCUMENTS LISTED BELOW, SEE PART B OF THIS EDITION

APPROVAL BY THE BOARD OF IFRS 3 ISSUED IN JANUARY 2008

BASIS FOR CONCLUSIONS

APPENDIX
Amendments to the Basis for Conclusions on other IFRSs

DISSENTING OPINIONS

ILLUSTRATIVE EXAMPLES

APPENDIX
Amendments to guidance on other IFRSs

COMPARISON OF IFRS 3 (AS REVISED IN 2008) AND SFAS 141(R)

TABLE OF CONCORDANCE

International Financial Reporting Standard 3 *Business Combinations* (IFRS 3) is set out in paragraphs 1–68 and Appendices A–C. All the paragraphs have equal authority. Paragraphs in **bold type** state the main principles. Terms defined in Appendix A are in *italics* the first time they appear in the IFRS. Definitions of other terms are given in the Glossary for International Financial Reporting Standards. IFRS 3 should be read in the context of its objective and the Basis for Conclusions, the *Preface to International Financial Reporting Standards* and the *Conceptual Framework for Financial Reporting*. IAS 8 *Accounting Policies, Changes in Accounting Estimates and Errors* provides a basis for selecting and applying accounting policies in the absence of explicit guidance.

Introduction

Reasons for issuing the IFRS

IN1   The revised International Financial Reporting Standard 3 *Business Combinations* (IFRS 3) is part of a joint effort by the International Accounting Standards Board (IASB) and the US Financial Accounting Standards Board (FASB) to improve financial reporting while promoting the international convergence of accounting standards.   Each board decided to address the accounting for business combinations in two phases. The IASB and the FASB deliberated the first phase separately. The FASB concluded its first phase in June 2001 by issuing FASB Statement No. 141 *Business Combinations*. The IASB concluded its first phase in March 2004 by issuing the previous version of IFRS 3 *Business Combinations*. The boards' primary conclusion in the first phase was that virtually all business combinations are acquisitions. Accordingly, the boards decided to require the use of one method of accounting for business combinations—the acquisition method.

IN2   The second phase of the project addressed the guidance for applying the acquisition method. The boards decided that a significant improvement could be made to financial reporting if they had similar standards for accounting for business combinations. Thus, they decided to conduct the second phase of the project as a joint effort with the objective of reaching the same conclusions. The boards concluded the second phase of the project by issuing this IFRS and FASB Statement No. 141 (revised 2007) *Business Combinations* and the related amendments to IAS 27 *Consolidated and Separate Financial Statements* and FASB Statement No. 160 *Noncontrolling Interests in Consolidated Financial Statements*.[1]

IN3   The IFRS replaces IFRS 3 (as issued in 2004) and comes into effect for business combinations for which the acquisition date is on or after the beginning of the first annual reporting period beginning on or after 1 July 2009.   Earlier application is permitted, provided that IAS 27 (as amended in 2008) is applied at the same time.

Main features of the IFRS

IN4   The objective of the IFRS is to enhance the relevance, reliability and comparability of the information that an entity provides in its financial statements about a business combination and its effects. It does that by establishing principles and requirements for how an acquirer:

(a)   recognises and measures in its financial statements the identifiable assets acquired, the liabilities assumed and any non-controlling interest in the acquiree;

(b)   recognises and measures the goodwill acquired in the business combination or a gain from a bargain purchase; and

---

1   The requirements for consolidated financial statements in IAS 27 were superseded by IFRS 10 *Consolidated Financial Statements*, issued in May 2011. Topic 810 *Consolidation* in the *FASB Accounting Standards Codification*® codified the guidance in SFAS 160.

(c)   determines what information to disclose to enable users of the financial statements to evaluate the nature and financial effects of the business combination.

Core principle

IN5   An acquirer of a business recognises the assets acquired and liabilities assumed at their acquisition-date fair values and discloses information that enables users to evaluate the nature and financial effects of the acquisition.

Applying the acquisition method

IN6   A business combination must be accounted for by applying the acquisition method, unless it is a combination involving entities or businesses under common control.One of the parties to a business combination can always be identified as the acquirer, being the entity that obtains control of the other business (the acquiree).Formations of a joint venture or the acquisition of an asset or a group of assets that does not constitute a business are not business combinations.

IN7   The IFRS establishes principles for recognising and measuring the identifiable assets acquired, the liabilities assumed and any non-controlling interest in the acquiree. Any classifications or designations made in recognising these items must be made in accordance with the contractual terms, economic conditions, acquirer's operating or accounting policies and other factors that exist at the acquisition date.

IN8   Each identifiable asset and liability is measured at its acquisition-date fair value. Non-controlling interests in an acquiree that are present ownership interests and entitle their holders to a proportionate share of the entity's net assets in the event of liquidation are measured at either fair value or the present ownership instruments' proportionate share in the recognised amounts of the acquiree's net identifiable assets. All other components of non-controlling interests shall be measured at their acquisition-date fair values, unless another measurement basis is required by IFRSs.

IN9   The IFRS provides limited exceptions to these recognition and measurement principles:

(a)   Leases and insurance contracts are required to be classified on the basis of the contractual terms and other factors at the inception of the contract (or when the terms have changed) rather than on the basis of the factors that exist at the acquisition date.

(b)   Only those contingent liabilities assumed in a business combination that are a present obligation and can be measured reliably are recognised.

(c)   Some assets and liabilities are required to be recognised or measured in accordance with other IFRSs, rather than at fair value. The assets and liabilities affected are those falling within the scope of IAS 12 *Income Taxes*, IAS 19 *Employee Benefits*, IFRS 2 *Share-based Payment* and IFRS 5 *Non-current Assets Held for Sale and Discontinued Operations*.

(d)   There are special requirements for measuring a reacquired right.

(e)   Indemnification assets are recognised and measured on a basis that is consistent with the item that is subject to the indemnification, even if that measure is not fair value.

IN10   The IFRS requires the acquirer, having recognised the identifiable assets, the liabilities and any non-controlling interests, to identify any difference between:

(a)   the aggregate of the consideration transferred, any non-controlling interest in the acquiree and, in a business combination achieved in stages, the acquisition-date fair value of the acquirer's previously held equity interest in the acquiree; and

(b)   the net identifiable assets acquired.

The difference will, generally, be recognised as goodwill. If the acquirer has made a gain from a bargain purchase that gain is recognised in profit or loss.

IN11   The consideration transferred in a business combination (including any contingent consideration) is measured at fair value.

IN12   In general, an acquirer measures and accounts for assets acquired and liabilities assumed or incurred in a business combination after the business combination has been completed in accordance with other applicable IFRSs. However, the IFRS provides accounting requirements for reacquired rights, contingent liabilities, contingent consideration and indemnification assets.

Disclosure

IN13   The IFRS requires the acquirer to disclose information that enables users of its financial statements to evaluate the nature and financial effect of business combinations that occurred during the current reporting period or after the reporting date but before the financial statements are authorised for issue. After a business combination, the acquirer must disclose any adjustments recognised in the current reporting period that relate to business combinations that occurred in the current or previous reporting periods.

International Financial Reporting Standard 3
Business Combinations

Objective

1   The objective of this IFRS is to improve the relevance, reliability and comparability of the information that a reporting entity provides in its financial statements about a *business combination* and its effects. To accomplish that, this IFRS establishes principles and requirements for how the *acquirer*:

(a)   recognises and measures in its financial statements the *identifiable* assets acquired, the liabilities assumed and any *non-controlling interest* in the *acquiree*;

(b)   recognises and measures the *goodwill* acquired in the business combination or a gain from a bargain purchase; and

(c)   determines what information to disclose to enable users of the financial statements to evaluate the nature and financial effects of the business combination.

Scope

2   This IFRS applies to a transaction or other event that meets the definition of a business combination. This IFRS does not apply to:

(a)   the formation of a joint venture.

(b)   the acquisition of an asset or a group of assets that does not constitute a *business*. In such cases the acquirer shall identify and recognise the individual identifiable assets acquired (including those assets that meet the definition of, and recognition criteria for, *intangible assets* in IAS 38 *Intangible Assets*) and liabilities assumed. The cost of the group shall be allocated to the individual identifiable assets and liabilities on the basis of their relative *fair values* at the date of purchase. Such a transaction or event does not give rise to goodwill.

(c)   a combination of entities or businesses under common control (paragraphs B1–B4 provide related application guidance).

Identifying a business combination

3   An entity shall determine whether a transaction or other event is a business combination by applying the definition in this IFRS, which requires that the assets acquired and liabilities assumed constitute a business. If the assets acquired are not a business, the reporting entity shall account for the transaction or other event as an asset acquisition. Paragraphs B5–B12 provide guidance on identifying a business combination and the definition of a business.

The acquisition method

4   **An entity shall account for each business combination by applying the acquisition method.**

5   Applying the acquisition method requires:

   (a)   identifying the acquirer;

   (b)   determining the *acquisition date*;

   (c)   recognising and measuring the identifiable assets acquired, the liabilities assumed and any non-controlling interest in the acquiree; and

   (d)   recognising and measuring goodwill or a gain from a bargain purchase.

Identifying the acquirer

6   **For each business combination, one of the combining entities shall be identified as the acquirer.**

7   The guidance in IFRS 10 *Consolidated Financial Statements* shall be used to identify the acquirer—the entity that obtains *control* of another entity, ie the acquiree. If a business combination has occurred but applying the guidance in IFRS 10 does not clearly indicate which of the combining entities is the acquirer, the factors in paragraphs B14–B18 shall be considered in making that determination.

Determining the acquisition date

8   **The acquirer shall identify the acquisition date, which is the date on which it obtains control of the acquiree.**

9   The date on which the acquirer obtains control of the acquiree is generally the date on which the acquirer legally transfers the consideration, acquires the assets and assumes the liabilities of the acquiree—the closing date. However, the acquirer might obtain control on a date that is either earlier or later than the closing date. For example, the acquisition date precedes the closing date if a written agreement provides that the acquirer obtains control of the acquiree on a date before the closing date. An acquirer shall consider all pertinent facts and circumstances in identifying the acquisition date.

Recognising and measuring the identifiable assets acquired, the liabilities assumed and any non-controlling interest in the acquiree

Recognition principle

10   **As of the acquisition date, the acquirer shall recognise, separately from goodwill, the identifiable assets acquired, the liabilities assumed and any non-controlling interest in the acquiree. Recognition of identifiable assets acquired and liabilities assumed is subject to the conditions specified in paragraphs 11 and 12.**

Recognition conditions

11   To qualify for recognition as part of applying the acquisition method, the identifiable assets acquired and liabilities assumed must meet the definitions of assets and liabilities in the *Framework*[2] *for the Preparation and Presentation of Financial Statements* at the acquisition date. For example, costs the acquirer expects but is not obliged to incur in the future to effect its plan to exit an activity of an acquiree or to terminate the employment of or relocate an acquiree's employees are not liabilities at the acquisition date. Therefore, the acquirer does not recognise those costs as part of applying the acquisition method. Instead, the acquirer recognises those costs in its post-combination financial statements in accordance with other IFRSs.

12   In addition, to qualify for recognition as part of applying the acquisition method, the identifiable assets acquired and liabilities assumed must be part of what the acquirer and the acquiree (or its former *owners*) exchanged in the business combination transaction rather than the result of separate transactions. The acquirer shall apply the guidance in paragraphs 51–53 to determine which assets acquired or liabilities assumed are part of the exchange for the acquiree and which, if any, are the result of separate transactions to be accounted for in accordance with their nature and the applicable IFRSs.

13   The acquirer's application of the recognition principle and conditions may result in recognising some assets and liabilities that the acquiree had not previously recognised as assets and liabilities in its financial statements. For example, the acquirer recognises the acquired identifiable intangible assets, such as a brand name, a patent or a customer relationship, that the acquiree did not recognise as assets in its financial statements because it developed them internally and charged the related costs to expense.

14   Paragraphs B28–B40 provide guidance on recognising operating leases and intangible assets. Paragraphs 22–28 specify the types of identifiable assets and liabilities that include items for which this IFRS provides limited exceptions to the recognition principle and conditions.

Classifying or designating identifiable assets acquired and liabilities assumed in a business combination

15   At the acquisition date, the acquirer shall classify or designate the identifiable assets acquired and liabilities assumed as necessary to apply other IFRSs subsequently. The acquirer shall make those classifications or designations on the basis of the contractual terms, economic conditions, its operating or accounting policies and other pertinent conditions as they exist at the acquisition date.

16   In some situations, IFRSs provide for different accounting depending on how an entity classifies or designates a particular asset or liability. Examples of classifications or designations that the acquirer shall make on the basis of the pertinent conditions as they exist at the acquisition date include but are not limited to:

---

2   IASC's *Framework for the Preparation and Presentation of Financial Statements* was adopted by the IASB in 2001. In September 2010 the IASB replaced the *Framework* with the *Conceptual Framework for Financial Reporting*.

(a)   classification of particular financial assets and liabilities as measured at fair value or at amortised cost, in accordance with IFRS 9 *Financial Instruments*;

(b)   designation of a derivative instrument as a hedging instrument in accordance with IAS 39; and

(c)   assessment of whether an embedded derivative should be separated from a host contract in accordance with IFRS 9 (which is a matter of 'classification' as this IFRS uses that term).

17   This IFRS provides two exceptions to the principle in paragraph 15:

(a)   classification of a lease contract as either an operating lease or a finance lease in accordance with IAS 17 *Leases*; and

(b)   classification of a contract as an insurance contract in accordance with IFRS 4 *Insurance Contracts*.

The acquirer shall classify those contracts on the basis of the contractual terms and other factors at the inception of the contract (or, if the terms of the contract have been modified in a manner that would change its classification, at the date of that modification, which might be the acquisition date).

Measurement principle

18   The acquirer shall measure the identifiable assets acquired and the liabilities assumed at their acquisition-date fair values.

19   For each business combination, the acquirer shall measure at the acquisition date components of non-controlling interests in the acquiree that are present ownership interests and entitle their holders to a proportionate share of the entity's net assets in the event of liquidation at either:

(a)   fair value; or

(b)   the present ownership instruments' proportionate share in the recognised amounts of the acquiree's identifiable net assets.

All other components of non-controlling interests shall be measured at their acquisition-date fair values, unless another measurement basis is required by IFRSs.

20   Paragraphs 24–31 specify the types of identifiable assets and liabilities that include items for which this IFRS provides limited exceptions to the measurement principle.

Exceptions to the recognition or measurement principles

21   This IFRS provides limited exceptions to its recognition and measurement principles. Paragraphs 22–31 specify both the particular items for which exceptions are provided and the nature of those exceptions. The acquirer shall account for those items by applying the requirements in paragraphs 22–31, which will result in some items being:

(a) recognised either by applying recognition conditions in addition to those in paragraphs 11 and 12 or by applying the requirements of other IFRSs, with results that differ from applying the recognition principle and conditions.

(b) measured at an amount other than their acquisition-date fair values.

Exception to the recognition principle

Contingent liabilities

22   IAS 37 *Provisions, Contingent Liabilities and Contingent Assets* defines a contingent liability as:

(a) a possible obligation that arises from past events and whose existence will be confirmed only by the occurrence or non-occurrence of one or more uncertain future events not wholly within the control of the entity; or

(b) a present obligation that arises from past events but is not recognised because:

(i) it is not probable that an outflow of resources embodying economic benefits will be required to settle the obligation; or

(ii) the amount of the obligation cannot be measured with sufficient reliability.

23   The requirements in IAS 37 do not apply in determining which contingent liabilities to recognise as of the acquisition date. Instead, the acquirer shall recognise as of the acquisition date a contingent liability assumed in a business combination if it is a present obligation that arises from past events and its fair value can be measured reliably. Therefore, contrary to IAS 37, the acquirer recognises a contingent liability assumed in a business combination at the acquisition date even if it is not probable that an outflow of resources embodying economic benefits will be required to settle the obligation. Paragraph 56 provides guidance on the subsequent accounting for contingent liabilities.

Exceptions to both the recognition and measurement principles

Income taxes

24   The acquirer shall recognise and measure a deferred tax asset or liability arising from the assets acquired and liabilities assumed in a business combination in accordance with IAS 12 *Income Taxes*.

25   The acquirer shall account for the potential tax effects of temporary differences and carryforwards of an acquiree that exist at the acquisition date or arise as a result of the acquisition in accordance with IAS 12.

Employee benefits

26   The acquirer shall recognise and measure a liability (or asset, if any) related to the acquiree's employee benefit arrangements in accordance with IAS 19 *Employee Benefits*.

Indemnification assets

27   The seller in a business combination may contractually indemnify the acquirer for the outcome of a contingency or uncertainty related to all or part of a specific asset or liability. For example, the seller may indemnify the acquirer against losses above a specified amount on a liability arising from a particular contingency; in other words, the seller will guarantee that the acquirer's liability will not exceed a specified amount. As a result, the acquirer obtains an indemnification asset. The acquirer shall recognise an indemnification asset at the same time that it recognises the indemnified item measured on the same basis as the indemnified item, subject to the need for a valuation allowance for uncollectible amounts. Therefore, if the indemnification relates to an asset or a liability that is recognised at the acquisition date and measured at its acquisition-date fair value, the acquirer shall recognise the indemnification asset at the acquisition date measured at its acquisition-date fair value. For an indemnification asset measured at fair value, the effects of uncertainty about future cash flows because of collectibility considerations are included in the fair value measure and a separate valuation allowance is not necessary (paragraph B41 provides related application guidance).

28   In some circumstances, the indemnification may relate to an asset or a liability that is an exception to the recognition or measurement principles. For example, an indemnification may relate to a contingent liability that is not recognised at the acquisition date because its fair value is not reliably measurable at that date. Alternatively, an indemnification may relate to an asset or a liability, for example, one that results from an employee benefit, that is measured on a basis other than acquisition-date fair value. In those circumstances, the indemnification asset shall be recognised and measured using assumptions consistent with those used to measure the indemnified item, subject to management's assessment of the collectibility of the indemnification asset and any contractual limitations on the indemnified amount. Paragraph 57 provides guidance on the subsequent accounting for an indemnification asset.

Exceptions to the measurement principle

Reacquired rights

29   The acquirer shall measure the value of a reacquired right recognised as an intangible asset on the basis of the remaining contractual term of the related contract regardless of whether market participants would consider potential contractual renewals when measuring its fair value. Paragraphs B35 and B36 provide related application guidance.

Share-based payment transactions

30   The acquirer shall measure a liability or an equity instrument related to share-based payment transactions of the acquiree or the replacement of an acquiree's share-based payment transactions with share-based payment transactions of the acquirer in accordance with the method in IFRS 2 *Share-based Payment* at the acquisition date. (This IFRS refers to the result of that method as the 'market-based measure' of the share-based payment transaction.)

Assets held for sale

31   The acquirer shall measure an acquired non-current asset (or disposal group) that is classified as held for sale at the acquisition date in accordance with IFRS 5 *Non-current Assets Held for Sale and Discontinued Operations* at fair value less costs to sell in accordance with paragraphs 15–18 of that IFRS.

Recognising and measuring goodwill or a gain from a bargain purchase

32   The acquirer shall recognise goodwill as of the acquisition date measured as the excess of (a) over (b) below:

    (a)   the aggregate of:

        (i)   the consideration transferred measured in accordance with this IFRS, which generally requires acquisition-date fair value (see paragraph 37);

        (ii)   the amount of any non-controlling interest in the acquiree measured in accordance with this IFRS; and

        (iii)   in a business combination achieved in stages (see paragraphs 41 and 42), the acquisition-date fair value of the acquirer's previously held equity interest in the acquiree.

    (b)   the net of the acquisition-date amounts of the identifiable assets acquired and the liabilities assumed measured in accordance with this IFRS.

33   In a business combination in which the acquirer and the acquiree (or its former owners) exchange only equity interests, the acquisition-date fair value of the acquiree's equity interests may be more reliably measurable than the acquisition-date fair value of the acquirer's equity interests. If so, the acquirer shall determine the amount of goodwill by using the acquisition-date fair value of the acquiree's equity interests instead of the acquisition-date fair value of the equity interests transferred. To determine the amount of goodwill in a business combination in which no consideration is transferred, the acquirer shall use the acquisition-date fair value of the acquirer's interest in the acquiree in place of the acquisition-date fair value of the consideration transferred (paragraph 32(a)(i)). Paragraphs B46–B49 provide related application guidance.

Bargain purchases

34   Occasionally, an acquirer will make a bargain purchase, which is a business combination in which the amount in paragraph 32(b) exceeds the aggregate of the amounts specified in paragraph 32(a). If that excess remains after applying the requirements in paragraph 36, the acquirer shall recognise the resulting gain in profit or loss on the acquisition date. The gain shall be attributed to the acquirer.

35   A bargain purchase might happen, for example, in a business combination that is a forced sale in which the seller is acting under compulsion. However, the recognition or measurement exceptions for particular items discussed in paragraphs 22–31 may also result in recognising a gain (or change the amount of a recognised gain) on a bargain purchase.

36   Before recognising a gain on a bargain purchase, the acquirer shall reassess whether it has correctly identified all of the assets acquired and all of the liabilities assumed and shall recognise any additional assets or liabilities that are identified in that review. The acquirer shall then review the procedures used to measure the amounts this IFRS requires to be recognised at the acquisition date for all of the following:

(a)   the identifiable assets acquired and liabilities assumed;

(b)   the non-controlling interest in the acquiree, if any;

(c)   for a business combination achieved in stages, the acquirer's previously held equity interest in the acquiree; and

(d)   the consideration transferred.

The objective of the review is to ensure that the measurements appropriately reflect consideration of all available information as of the acquisition date.

Consideration transferred

37   The consideration transferred in a business combination shall be measured at fair value, which shall be calculated as the sum of the acquisition-date fair values of the assets transferred by the acquirer, the liabilities incurred by the acquirer to former owners of the acquiree and the equity interests issued by the acquirer. (However, any portion of the acquirer's share-based payment awards exchanged for awards held by the acquiree's employees that is included in consideration transferred in the business combination shall be measured in accordance with paragraph 30 rather than at fair value.) Examples of potential forms of consideration include cash, other assets, a business or a subsidiary of the acquirer, *contingent consideration*, ordinary or preference equity instruments, options, warrants and member interests of *mutual entities*.

38   The consideration transferred may include assets or liabilities of the acquirer that have carrying amounts that differ from their fair values at the acquisition date (for example, non-monetary assets or a business of the acquirer). If so, the acquirer shall remeasure the transferred assets or liabilities to their fair values as of the acquisition date and recognise the resulting gains or losses, if any, in profit or loss. However, sometimes the transferred assets or liabilities remain within the combined entity after the business combination (for example, because the assets or liabilities were transferred to the acquiree rather than to its former owners), and the acquirer therefore retains control of them. In that situation, the acquirer shall measure those assets and liabilities at their carrying amounts immediately before the acquisition date and shall not recognise a gain or loss in profit or loss on assets or liabilities it controls both before and after the business combination.

Contingent consideration

39   The consideration the acquirer transfers in exchange for the acquiree includes any asset or liability resulting from a contingent consideration arrangement (see paragraph 37). The acquirer shall recognise the acquisition-date fair value of contingent consideration as part of the consideration transferred in exchange for the acquiree.

40   The acquirer shall classify an obligation to pay contingent consideration as a liability or as equity on the basis of the definitions of an equity instrument and a financial liability in paragraph 11 of IAS 32 *Financial Instruments: Presentation*, or other applicable IFRSs. The acquirer shall classify as an asset a right to the return of previously transferred consideration if specified conditions are met. Paragraph 58 provides guidance on the subsequent accounting for contingent consideration.

Additional guidance for applying the acquisition method to particular types of business combinations

A business combination achieved in stages

41   An acquirer sometimes obtains control of an acquiree in which it held an equity interest immediately before the acquisition date. For example, on 31 December 20X1, Entity A holds a 35 per cent non-controlling equity interest in Entity B. On that date, Entity A purchases an additional 40 per cent interest in Entity B, which gives it control of Entity B. This IFRS refers to such a transaction as a business combination achieved in stages, sometimes also referred to as a step acquisition.

42   In a business combination achieved in stages, the acquirer shall remeasure its previously held equity interest in the acquiree at its acquisition-date fair value and recognise the resulting gain or loss, if any, in profit or loss or other comprehensive income, as appropriate. In prior reporting periods, the acquirer may have recognised changes in the value of its equity interest in the acquiree in other comprehensive income. If so, the amount that was recognised in other comprehensive income shall be recognised on the same basis as would be required if the acquirer had disposed directly of the previously held equity interest.

A business combination achieved without the transfer of consideration

43   An acquirer sometimes obtains control of an acquiree without transferring consideration. The acquisition method of accounting for a business combination applies to those combinations. Such circumstances include:

(a)   The acquiree repurchases a sufficient number of its own shares for an existing investor (the acquirer) to obtain control.

(b)   Minority veto rights lapse that previously kept the acquirer from controlling an acquiree in which the acquirer held the majority voting rights.

(c)   The acquirer and acquiree agree to combine their businesses by contract alone. The acquirer transfers no consideration in exchange for control of an acquiree and holds no equity interests in the acquiree, either on the acquisition date or previously. Examples of business combinations achieved by contract alone include bringing two businesses together in a stapling arrangement or forming a dual listed corporation.

44   In a business combination achieved by contract alone, the acquirer shall attribute to the owners of the acquiree the amount of the acquiree's net assets recognised in accordance with this IFRS. In other words, the equity interests in the acquiree held by parties other than the acquirer are a non-controlling interest in the acquirer's post-combination financial statements even if the result is that all of the equity interests in the acquiree are attributed to the non-controlling interest.

Measurement period

45   **If the initial accounting for a business combination is incomplete by the end of the reporting period in which the combination occurs, the acquirer shall report in its financial statements provisional amounts for the items for which the accounting is incomplete. During the measurement period, the acquirer shall retrospectively adjust the provisional amounts recognised at the acquisition date to reflect new information obtained about facts and circumstances that existed as of the acquisition date and, if known, would have affected the measurement of the amounts recognised as of that date. During the measurement period, the acquirer shall also recognise additional assets or liabilities if new information is obtained about facts and circumstances that existed as of the acquisition date and, if known, would have resulted in the recognition of those assets and liabilities as of that date. The measurement period ends as soon as the acquirer receives the information it was seeking about facts and circumstances that existed as of the acquisition date or learns that more information is not obtainable. However, the measurement period shall not exceed one year from the acquisition date.**

46   The measurement period is the period after the acquisition date during which the acquirer may adjust the provisional amounts recognised for a business combination. The measurement period provides the acquirer with a reasonable time to obtain the information necessary to identify and measure the following as of the acquisition date in accordance with the requirements of this IFRS:

(a)   the identifiable assets acquired, liabilities assumed and any non-controlling interest in the acquiree;

(b)   the consideration transferred for the acquiree (or the other amount used in measuring goodwill);

(c)   in a business combination achieved in stages, the equity interest in the acquiree previously held by the acquirer; and

(d)   the resulting goodwill or gain on a bargain purchase.

47   The acquirer shall consider all pertinent factors in determining whether information obtained after the acquisition date should result in an adjustment to the provisional amounts recognised or whether that information results from events that occurred after the acquisition date. Pertinent factors include the date when additional information is obtained and whether the acquirer can identify a reason for a change to provisional amounts. Information that is obtained shortly after the acquisition date is more likely to reflect circumstances that existed at the acquisition date than is information obtained several months later.

For example, unless an intervening event that changed its fair value can be identified, the sale of an asset to a third party shortly after the acquisition date for an amount that differs significantly from its provisional fair value measured at that date is likely to indicate an error in the provisional amount.

48　　The acquirer recognises an increase (decrease) in the provisional amount recognised for an identifiable asset (liability) by means of a decrease (increase) in goodwill. However, new information obtained during the measurement period may sometimes result in an adjustment to the provisional amount of more than one asset or liability. For example, the acquirer might have assumed a liability to pay damages related to an accident in one of the acquiree's facilities, part or all of which are covered by the acquiree's liability insurance policy. If the acquirer obtains new information during the measurement period about the acquisition-date fair value of that liability, the adjustment to goodwill resulting from a change to the provisional amount recognised for the liability would be offset (in whole or in part) by a corresponding adjustment to goodwill resulting from a change to the provisional amount recognised for the claim receivable from the insurer.

49　　During the measurement period, the acquirer shall recognise adjustments to the provisional amounts as if the accounting for the business combination had been completed at the acquisition date. Thus, the acquirer shall revise comparative information for prior periods presented in financial statements as needed, including making any change in depreciation, amortisation or other income effects recognised in completing the initial accounting.

50　　After the measurement period ends, the acquirer shall revise the accounting for a business combination only to correct an error in accordance with IAS 8 *Accounting Policies, Changes in Accounting Estimates and Errors*.

Determining what is part of the business combination transaction

51　　The acquirer and the acquiree may have a pre-existing relationship or other arrangement before negotiations for the business combination began, or they may enter into an arrangement during the negotiations that is separate from the business combination. In either situation, the acquirer shall identify any amounts that are not part of what the acquirer and the acquiree (or its former owners) exchanged in the business combination, ie amounts that are not part of the exchange for the acquiree. The acquirer shall recognise as part of applying the acquisition method only the consideration transferred for the acquiree and the assets acquired and liabilities assumed in the exchange for the acquiree. Separate transactions shall be accounted for in accordance with the relevant IFRSs.

52　　A transaction entered into by or on behalf of the acquirer or primarily for the benefit of the acquirer or the combined entity, rather than primarily for the benefit of the acquiree (or its former owners) before the combination, is likely to be a separate transaction. The following are examples of separate transactions that are not to be included in applying the acquisition method:

(a)　　a transaction that in effect settles pre-existing relationships between the acquirer and acquiree;

(b)   a transaction that remunerates employees or former owners of the acquiree for future services; and

(c)   a transaction that reimburses the acquiree or its former owners for paying the acquirer's acquisition-related costs.

Paragraphs B50–B62 provide related application guidance.

Acquisition-related costs

53   Acquisition-related costs are costs the acquirer incurs to effect a business combination. Those costs include finder's fees; advisory, legal, accounting, valuation and other professional or consulting fees; general administrative costs, including the costs of maintaining an internal acquisitions department; and costs of registering and issuing debt and equity securities. The acquirer shall account for acquisition-related costs as expenses in the periods in which the costs are incurred and the services are received, with one exception. The costs to issue debt or equity securities shall be recognised in accordance with IAS 32 and IFRS 9.

Subsequent measurement and accounting

54   **In general, an acquirer shall subsequently measure and account for assets acquired, liabilities assumed or incurred and equity instruments issued in a business combination in accordance with other applicable IFRSs for those items, depending on their nature. However, this IFRS provides guidance on subsequently measuring and accounting for the following assets acquired, liabilities assumed or incurred and equity instruments issued in a business combination:**

(a)   **reacquired rights;**

(b)   **contingent liabilities recognised as of the acquisition date;**

(c)   **indemnification assets; and**

(d)   **contingent consideration.**

Paragraph B63 provides related application guidance.

Reacquired rights

55   A reacquired right recognised as an intangible asset shall be amortised over the remaining contractual period of the contract in which the right was granted. An acquirer that subsequently sells a reacquired right to a third party shall include the carrying amount of the intangible asset in determining the gain or loss on the sale.

Contingent liabilities

56   After initial recognition and until the liability is settled, cancelled or expires, the acquirer shall measure a contingent liability recognised in a business combination at the higher of:

(a)   the amount that would be recognised in accordance with IAS 37; and

(b) the amount initially recognised less, if appropriate, cumulative amortisation recognised in accordance with IAS 18 *Revenue*.

This requirement does not apply to contracts accounted for in accordance with IFRS 9.

Indemnification assets

57 At the end of each subsequent reporting period, the acquirer shall measure an indemnification asset that was recognised at the acquisition date on the same basis as the indemnified liability or asset, subject to any contractual limitations on its amount and, for an indemnification asset that is not subsequently measured at its fair value, management's assessment of the collectibility of the indemnification asset. The acquirer shall derecognise the indemnification asset only when it collects the asset, sells it or otherwise loses the right to it.

Contingent consideration

58 Some changes in the fair value of contingent consideration that the acquirer recognises after the acquisition date may be the result of additional information that the acquirer obtained after that date about facts and circumstances that existed at the acquisition date. Such changes are measurement period adjustments in accordance with paragraphs 45–49. However, changes resulting from events after the acquisition date, such as meeting an earnings target, reaching a specified share price or reaching a milestone on a research and development project, are not measurement period adjustments. The acquirer shall account for changes in the fair value of contingent consideration that are not measurement period adjustments as follows:

(a) Contingent consideration classified as equity shall not be remeasured and its subsequent settlement shall be accounted for within equity.

(b) Contingent consideration classified as an asset or a liability that:

(i) is a financial instrument and is within the scope of IFRS 9 or IAS 39 shall be measured at fair value, with any resulting gain or loss recognised either in profit or loss or in other comprehensive income in accordance with IFRS 9.

(ii) is not within the scope of IFRS 9 shall be accounted for in accordance with IAS 37 or other IFRSs as appropriate.

Disclosures

59 The acquirer shall disclose information that enables users of its financial statements to evaluate the nature and financial effect of a business combination that occurs either:

(a) during the current reporting period; or

(b) after the end of the reporting period but before the financial statements are authorised for issue.

60   To meet the objective in paragraph 59, the acquirer shall disclose the information specified in paragraphs B64—B66.

61   **The acquirer shall disclose information that enables users of its financial statements to evaluate the financial effects of adjustments recognised in the current reporting period that relate to business combinations that occurred in the period or previous reporting periods.**

62   To meet the objective in paragraph 61, the acquirer shall disclose the information specified in paragraph B67.

63   If the specific disclosures required by this and other IFRSs do not meet the objectives set out in paragraphs 59 and 61, the acquirer shall disclose whatever additional information is necessary to meet those objectives.

Effective date and transition

Effective date

64   This IFRS shall be applied prospectively to business combinations for which the acquisition date is on or after the beginning of the first annual reporting period beginning on or after 1 July 2009. Earlier application is permitted. However, this IFRS shall be applied only at the beginning of an annual reporting period that begins on or after 30 June 2007. If an entity applies this IFRS before 1 July 2009, it shall disclose that fact and apply IAS 27 (as amended in 2008) at the same time.

64A   [Deleted]

64B   *Improvements to IFRSs* issued in May 2010 amended paragraphs 19, 30 and B56 and added paragraphs B62A and B62B. An entity shall apply those amendments for annual periods beginning on or after 1 July 2010. Earlier application is permitted. If an entity applies the amendments for an earlier period it shall disclose that fact. Application should be prospective from the date when the entity first applied this IFRS.

64C   Paragraphs 65A–65E were added by *Improvements to IFRSs* issued in May 2010. An entity shall apply those amendments for annual periods beginning on or after 1 July 2010. Earlier application is permitted. If an entity applies the amendments for an earlier period it shall disclose that fact. The amendments shall be applied to contingent consideration balances arising from business combinations with an acquisition date prior to the application of this IFRS, as issued in 2008.

64D   IFRS 9, issued in October 2010, amended paragraphs 16, 42, 53, 56 and 58(b) and deleted paragraph 64A. An entity shall apply those amendments when it applies IFRS 9 as issued in October 2010.

64E   IFRS 10, issued in May 2011, amended paragraphs 7, B13, B63(e) and Appendix A. An entity shall apply those amendments when it applies IFRS 10.

64F   IFRS 13 *Fair Value Measurement*, issued in May 2011, amended paragraphs 20, 29, 33, 47, amended the definition of fair value in Appendix A and amended paragraphs B22, B40, B43–B46, B49 and B64. An entity shall apply those amendments when it applies IFRS 13.

Transition

65 Assets and liabilities that arose from business combinations whose acquisition dates preceded the application of this IFRS shall not be adjusted upon application of this IFRS.

65A Contingent consideration balances arising from business combinations whose acquisition dates preceded the date when an entity first applied this IFRS as issued in 2008 shall not be adjusted upon first application of this IFRS. Paragraphs 65B–65E shall be applied in the subsequent accounting for those balances. Paragraphs 65B–65E shall not apply to the accounting for contingent consideration balances arising from business combinations with acquisition dates on or after the date when the entity first applied this IFRS as issued in 2008. In paragraphs 65B–65E business combination refers exclusively to business combinations whose acquisition date preceded the application of this IFRS as issued in 2008.

65B If a business combination agreement provides for an adjustment to the cost of the combination contingent on future events, the acquirer shall include the amount of that adjustment in the cost of the combination at the acquisition date if the adjustment is probable and can be measured reliably.

65C A business combination agreement may allow for adjustments to the cost of the combination that are contingent on one or more future events. The adjustment might, for example, be contingent on a specified level of profit being maintained or achieved in future periods, or on the market price of the instruments issued being maintained. It is usually possible to estimate the amount of any such adjustment at the time of initially accounting for the combination without impairing the reliability of the information, even though some uncertainty exists. If the future events do not occur or the estimate needs to be revised, the cost of the business combination shall be adjusted accordingly.

65D However, when a business combination agreement provides for such an adjustment, that adjustment is not included in the cost of the combination at the time of initially accounting for the combination if it either is not probable or cannot be measured reliably. If that adjustment subsequently becomes probable and can be measured reliably, the additional consideration shall be treated as an adjustment to the cost of the combination.

65E In some circumstances, the acquirer may be required to make a subsequent payment to the seller as compensation for a reduction in the value of the assets given, equity instruments issued or liabilities incurred or assumed by the acquirer in exchange for control of the acquiree. This is the case, for example, when the acquirer guarantees the market price of equity or debt instruments issued as part of the cost of the business combination and is required to issue additional equity or debt instruments to restore the originally determined cost. In such cases, no increase in the cost of the business combination is recognised. In the case of equity instruments, the fair value of the additional payment is offset by an equal reduction in the value attributed to the instruments initially issued. In the case of debt instruments, the additional payment is regarded as a reduction in the premium or an increase in the discount on the initial issue.

66 An entity, such as a mutual entity, that has not yet applied IFRS 3 and had one or more business combinations that were accounted for using the purchase method shall apply the transition provisions in paragraphs B68 and B69.

Income taxes

67 For business combinations in which the acquisition date was before this IFRS is applied, the acquirer shall apply the requirements of paragraph 68 of IAS 12, as amended by this IFRS, prospectively. That is to say, the acquirer shall not adjust the accounting for prior business combinations for previously recognised changes in recognised deferred tax assets. However, from the date when this IFRS is applied, the acquirer shall recognise, as an adjustment to profit or loss (or, if IAS 12 requires, outside profit or loss), changes in recognised deferred tax assets.

Withdrawal of IFRS 3 (2004)

68 This IFRS supersedes IFRS 3 *Business Combinations* (as issued in 2004).

Appendix A
Defined terms

This appendix is an integral part of the IFRS.

acquiree	The business or businesses that the **acquirer** obtains control of in a **business combination**.
acquirer	The entity that obtains control of the **acquiree**.
acquisition date	The date on which the **acquirer** obtains control of the **acquiree**.
business	An integrated set of activities and assets that is capable of being conducted and managed for the purpose of providing a return in the form of dividends, lower costs or other economic benefits directly to investors or other owners, members or participants.
business combination	A transaction or other event in which an **acquirer** obtains control of one or more **businesses**. Transactions sometimes referred to as 'true mergers' or 'mergers of equals' are also **business combinations** as that term is used in this IFRS.
contingent consideration	Usually, an obligation of the **acquirer** to transfer additional assets or **equity interests** to the former owners of an **acquiree** as part of the exchange for **control** of the **acquiree** if specified future events occur or conditions are met. However, contingent consideration also may give the **acquirer** the right to the return of previously transferred consideration if specified conditions are met.
equity interests	For the purposes of this IFRS, *equity interests* is used broadly to mean ownership interests of investor-owned entities and owner, member or participant interests of **mutual entities**.
fair value	*Fair value* is the price that would be received to sell an asset or paid to transfer a liability in an orderly transaction between market participants at the measurement date. (See IFRS 13.)
goodwill	An asset representing the future economic benefits arising from other assets acquired in a **business combination** that are not individually identified and separately recognised.
identifiable	An asset is *identifiable* if it either:

    (a) is separable, ie capable of being separated or divided from the entity and sold, transferred, licensed, rented or exchanged, either individually or together with a related contract, identifiable asset or liability, regardless of whether the entity intends to do so; or

    (b) arises from contractual or other legal rights, regardless of whether those rights are transferable or separable from the entity or from other rights and obligations.

intangible asset	An **identifiable** non-monetary asset without physical substance.
mutual entity	An entity, other than an investor-owned entity, that provides dividends, lower costs or other economic benefits directly to its **owners**, members or participants. For example, a mutual insurance company, a credit union and a co-operative entity are all mutual entities.
non-controlling interest	The equity in a subsidiary not attributable, directly or indirectly, to a parent.
owners	For the purposes of this IFRS, *owners* is used broadly to include holders of **equity interests** of investor-owned entities and owners or members of, or participants in, **mutual entities**.

Appendix B
Application guidance

This appendix is an integral part of the IFRS.

Business combinations of entities under common control (application of paragraph 2(c))

B1 This IFRS does not apply to a business combination of entities or businesses under common control. A business combination involving entities or businesses under common control is a business combination in which all of the combining entities or businesses are ultimately controlled by the same party or parties both before and after the business combination, and that control is not transitory.

B2 A group of individuals shall be regarded as controlling an entity when, as a result of contractual arrangements, they collectively have the power to govern its financial and operating policies so as to obtain benefits from its activities. Therefore, a business combination is outside the scope of this IFRS when the same group of individuals has, as a result of contractual arrangements, ultimate collective power to govern the financial and operating policies of each of the combining entities so as to obtain benefits from their activities, and that ultimate collective power is not transitory.

B3 An entity may be controlled by an individual or by a group of individuals acting together under a contractual arrangement, and that individual or group of individuals may not be subject to the financial reporting requirements of IFRSs. Therefore, it is not necessary for combining entities to be included as part of the same consolidated financial statements for a business combination to be regarded as one involving entities under common control.

B4 The extent of non-controlling interests in each of the combining entities before and after the business combination is not relevant to determining whether the combination involves entities under common control. Similarly, the fact that one of the combining entities is a subsidiary that has been excluded from the consolidated financial statements is not relevant to determining whether a combination involves entities under common control.

Identifying a business combination (application of paragraph 3)

B5 This IFRS defines a business combination as a transaction or other event in which an acquirer obtains control of one or more businesses. An acquirer might obtain control of an acquiree in a variety of ways, for example:

(a) by transferring cash, cash equivalents or other assets (including net assets that constitute a business);

(b) by incurring liabilities;

(c) by issuing equity interests;

(d) by providing more than one type of consideration; or

(e) without transferring consideration, including by contract alone (see paragraph 43).

B6   A business combination may be structured in a variety of ways for legal, taxation or other reasons, which include but are not limited to:

(a)   one or more businesses become subsidiaries of an acquirer or the net assets of one or more businesses are legally merged into the acquirer;

(b)   one combining entity transfers its net assets, or its owners transfer their equity interests, to another combining entity or its owners;

(c)   all of the combining entities transfer their net assets, or the owners of those entities transfer their equity interests, to a newly formed entity (sometimes referred to as a roll-up or put-together transaction); or

(d)   a group of former owners of one of the combining entities obtains control of the combined entity.

Definition of a business (application of paragraph 3)

B7   A business consists of inputs and processes applied to those inputs that have the ability to create outputs. Although businesses usually have outputs, outputs are not required for an integrated set to qualify as a business. The three elements of a business are defined as follows:

(a)   **Input:** Any economic resource that creates, or has the ability to create, outputs when one or more processes are applied to it. Examples include non-current assets (including intangible assets or rights to use non-current assets), intellectual property, the ability to obtain access to necessary materials or rights and employees.

(b)   **Process:** Any system, standard, protocol, convention or rule that when applied to an input or inputs, creates or has the ability to create outputs. Examples include strategic management processes, operational processes and resource management processes. These processes typically are documented, but an organised workforce having the necessary skills and experience following rules and conventions may provide the necessary processes that are capable of being applied to inputs to create outputs. (Accounting, billing, payroll and other administrative systems typically are not processes used to create outputs.)

(c)   **Output:** The result of inputs and processes applied to those inputs that provide or have the ability to provide a return in the form of dividends, lower costs or other economic benefits directly to investors or other owners, members or participants.

B8   To be capable of being conducted and managed for the purposes defined, an integrated set of activities and assets requires two essential elements—inputs and processes applied to those inputs, which together are or will be used to create outputs. However, a business need not include all of the inputs or processes that the seller used in operating that business if market participants are capable of acquiring the business and continuing to produce outputs, for example, by integrating the business with their own inputs and processes.

B9   The nature of the elements of a business varies by industry and by the structure of an entity's operations (activities), including the entity's stage of development. Established businesses often have many different types of inputs, processes and outputs, whereas new businesses often have few inputs and processes and sometimes only a single output (product). Nearly all businesses also have liabilities, but a business need not have liabilities.

B10   An integrated set of activities and assets in the development stage might not have outputs. If not, the acquirer should consider other factors to determine whether the set is a business. Those factors include, but are not limited to, whether the set:

(a)   has begun planned principal activities;

(b)   has employees, intellectual property and other inputs and processes that could be applied to those inputs;

(c)   is pursuing a plan to produce outputs; and

(d)   will be able to obtain access to customers that will purchase the outputs.

Not all of those factors need to be present for a particular integrated set of activities and assets in the development stage to qualify as a business.

B11   Determining whether a particular set of assets and activities is a business should be based on whether the integrated set is capable of being conducted and managed as a business by a market participant. Thus, in evaluating whether a particular set is a business, it is not relevant whether a seller operated the set as a business or whether the acquirer intends to operate the set as a business.

B12   In the absence of evidence to the contrary, a particular set of assets and activities in which goodwill is present shall be presumed to be a business. However, a business need not have goodwill.

Identifying the acquirer (application of paragraphs 6 and 7)

B13   The guidance in IFRS 10 *Consolidated Financial Statements* shall be used to identify the acquirer—the entity that obtains control of the acquiree. If a business combination has occurred but applying the guidance in IFRS 10 does not clearly indicate which of the combining entities is the acquirer, the factors in paragraphs B14–B18 shall be considered in making that determination.

B14   In a business combination effected primarily by transferring cash or other assets or by incurring liabilities, the acquirer is usually the entity that transfers the cash or other assets or incurs the liabilities.

B15   In a business combination effected primarily by exchanging equity interests, the acquirer is usually the entity that issues its equity interests. However, in some business combinations, commonly called 'reverse acquisitions', the issuing entity is the acquiree. Paragraphs B19–B27 provide guidance on accounting for reverse acquisitions. Other pertinent facts and circumstances shall also be considered in identifying the acquirer in a business combination effected by exchanging equity interests, including:

(a)   *the relative voting rights in the combined entity after the business combination*—The acquirer is usually the combining entity whose owners as a group retain or receive the largest portion of the voting rights in the combined entity.

In determining which group of owners retains or receives the largest portion of the voting rights, an entity shall consider the existence of any unusual or special voting arrangements and options, warrants or convertible securities.

(b) *the existence of a large minority voting interest in the combined entity if no other owner or organised group of owners has a significant voting interest*—The acquirer is usually the combining entity whose single owner or organised group of owners holds the largest minority voting interest in the combined entity.

(c) *the composition of the governing body of the combined entity*—The acquirer is usually the combining entity whose owners have the ability to elect or appoint or to remove a majority of the members of the governing body of the combined entity.

(d) *the composition of the senior management of the combined entity*—The acquirer is usually the combining entity whose (former) management dominates the management of the combined entity.

(e) *the terms of the exchange of equity interests*—The acquirer is usually the combining entity that pays a premium over the pre-combination fair value of the equity interests of the other combining entity or entities.

B16 The acquirer is usually the combining entity whose relative size (measured in, for example, assets, revenues or profit) is significantly greater than that of the other combining entity or entities.

B17 In a business combination involving more than two entities, determining the acquirer shall include a consideration of, among other things, which of the combining entities initiated the combination, as well as the relative size of the combining entities.

B18 A new entity formed to effect a business combination is not necessarily the acquirer. If a new entity is formed to issue equity interests to effect a business combination, one of the combining entities that existed before the business combination shall be identified as the acquirer by applying the guidance in paragraphs B13–B17. In contrast, a new entity that transfers cash or other assets or incurs liabilities as consideration may be the acquirer.

Reverse acquisitions

B19 A reverse acquisition occurs when the entity that issues securities (the legal acquirer) is identified as the acquiree for accounting purposes on the basis of the guidance in paragraphs B13–B18. The entity whose equity interests are acquired (the legal acquiree) must be the acquirer for accounting purposes for the transaction to be considered a reverse acquisition. For example, reverse acquisitions sometimes occur when a private operating entity wants to become a public entity but does not want to register its equity shares. To accomplish that, the private entity will arrange for a public entity to acquire its equity interests in exchange for the equity interests of the public entity. In this example, the public entity is the **legal acquirer** because it issued its equity interests, and the private entity is the **legal acquiree** because its equity interests were acquired. However, application of the guidance in paragraphs B13–B18 results in identifying:

(a)   the public entity as the **acquiree** for accounting purposes (the accounting acquiree); and

(b)   the private entity as the **acquirer** for accounting purposes (the accounting acquirer).

The accounting acquiree must meet the definition of a business for the transaction to be accounted for as a reverse acquisition, and all of the recognition and measurement principles in this IFRS, including the requirement to recognise goodwill, apply.

Measuring the consideration transferred

B20   In a reverse acquisition, the accounting acquirer usually issues no consideration for the acquiree. Instead, the accounting acquiree usually issues its equity shares to the owners of the accounting acquirer. Accordingly, the acquisition-date fair value of the consideration transferred by the accounting acquirer for its interest in the accounting acquiree is based on the number of equity interests the legal subsidiary would have had to issue to give the owners of the legal parent the same percentage equity interest in the combined entity that results from the reverse acquisition. The fair value of the number of equity interests calculated in that way can be used as the fair value of consideration transferred in exchange for the acquiree.

Preparation and presentation of consolidated financial statements

B21   Consolidated financial statements prepared following a reverse acquisition are issued under the name of the legal parent (accounting acquiree) but described in the notes as a continuation of the financial statements of the legal subsidiary (accounting acquirer), with one adjustment, which is to adjust retroactively the accounting acquirer's legal capital to reflect the legal capital of the accounting acquiree. That adjustment is required to reflect the capital of the legal parent (the accounting acquiree). Comparative information presented in those consolidated financial statements also is retroactively adjusted to reflect the legal capital of the legal parent (accounting acquiree).

B22   Because the consolidated financial statements represent the continuation of the financial statements of the legal subsidiary except for its capital structure, the consolidated financial statements reflect:

(a)   the assets and liabilities of the legal subsidiary (the accounting acquirer) recognised and measured at their pre-combination carrying amounts.

(b)   the assets and liabilities of the legal parent (the accounting acquiree) recognised and measured in accordance with this IFRS.

(c)   the retained earnings and other equity balances of the legal subsidiary (accounting acquirer) **before** the business combination.

(d)   the amount recognised as issued equity interests in the consolidated financial statements determined by adding the issued equity interest of the legal subsidiary (the accounting acquirer) outstanding immediately before the business combination to the fair value of the legal parent (accounting acquiree). However, the equity structure (ie the number and type of equity interests issued) reflects the equity structure of the legal parent (the accounting acquiree), including the equity interests the legal parent issued to effect the combination. Accordingly, the equity structure of the legal subsidiary (the accounting acquirer) is restated using the exchange ratio established in the acquisition agreement to reflect the number of shares of the legal parent (the accounting acquiree) issued in the reverse acquisition.

(e) the non-controlling interest's proportionate share of the legal subsidiary's (accounting acquirer's) pre-combination carrying amounts of retained earnings and other equity interests as discussed in paragraphs B23 and B24.

Non-controlling interest

B23 In a reverse acquisition, some of the owners of the legal acquiree (the accounting acquirer) might not exchange their equity interests for equity interests of the legal parent (the accounting acquiree). Those owners are treated as a non-controlling interest in the consolidated financial statements after the reverse acquisition. That is because the owners of the legal acquiree that do not exchange their equity interests for equity interests of the legal acquirer have an interest in only the results and net assets of the legal acquiree—not in the results and net assets of the combined entity. Conversely, even though the legal acquirer is the acquiree for accounting purposes, the owners of the legal acquirer have an interest in the results and net assets of the combined entity.

B24 The assets and liabilities of the legal acquiree are measured and recognised in the consolidated financial statements at their pre-combination carrying amounts (see paragraph B22(a)). Therefore, in a reverse acquisition the non-controlling interest reflects the non-controlling shareholders' proportionate interest in the pre-combination carrying amounts of the legal acquiree's net assets even if the non-controlling interests in other acquisitions are measured at their fair value at the acquisition date.

Earnings per share

B25 As noted in paragraph B22(d), the equity structure in the consolidated financial statements following a reverse acquisition reflects the equity structure of the legal acquirer (the accounting acquiree), including the equity interests issued by the legal acquirer to effect the business combination.

B26 In calculating the weighted average number of ordinary shares outstanding (the denominator of the earnings per share calculation) during the period in which the reverse acquisition occurs:

(a) the number of ordinary shares outstanding from the beginning of that period to the acquisition date shall be computed on the basis of the weighted average number of ordinary shares of the legal acquiree (accounting acquirer) outstanding during the period multiplied by the exchange ratio established in the merger agreement; and

(b) the number of ordinary shares outstanding from the acquisition date to the end of that period shall be the actual number of ordinary shares of the legal acquirer (the accounting acquiree) outstanding during that period.

B27 The basic earnings per share for each comparative period before the acquisition date presented in the consolidated financial statements following a reverse acquisition shall be calculated by dividing:

(a) the profit or loss of the legal acquiree attributable to ordinary shareholders in each of those periods by

(b) the legal acquiree's historical weighted average number of ordinary shares outstanding multiplied by the exchange ratio established in the acquisition agreement.

Recognising particular assets acquired and liabilities assumed (application of paragraphs 10–13)

Operating leases

B28 The acquirer shall recognise no assets or liabilities related to an operating lease in which the acquiree is the lessee except as required by paragraphs B29 and B30.

B29 The acquirer shall determine whether the terms of each operating lease in which the acquiree is the lessee are favourable or unfavourable. The acquirer shall recognise an intangible asset if the terms of an operating lease are favourable relative to market terms and a liability if the terms are unfavourable relative to market terms. Paragraph B42 provides guidance on measuring the acquisition-date fair value of assets subject to operating leases in which the acquiree is the lessor.

B30 An identifiable intangible asset may be associated with an operating lease, which may be evidenced by market participants' willingness to pay a price for the lease even if it is at market terms. For example, a lease of gates at an airport or of retail space in a prime shopping area might provide entry into a market or other future economic benefits that qualify as identifiable intangible assets, for example, as a customer relationship. In that situation, the acquirer shall recognise the associated identifiable intangible asset(s) in accordance with paragraph B31.

Intangible assets

B31 The acquirer shall recognise, separately from goodwill, the identifiable intangible assets acquired in a business combination. An intangible asset is identifiable if it meets either the separability criterion or the contractual-legal criterion.

B32 An intangible asset that meets the contractual-legal criterion is identifiable even if the asset is not transferable or separable from the acquiree or from other rights and obligations. For example:

(a) an acquiree leases a manufacturing facility under an operating lease that has terms that are favourable relative to market terms. The lease terms explicitly prohibit transfer of the lease (through either sale or sublease). The amount by which the lease terms are favourable compared with the terms of current market transactions for the same or similar items is an intangible asset that meets the contractual-legal criterion for recognition separately from goodwill, even though the acquirer cannot sell or otherwise transfer the lease contract.

(b)   an acquiree owns and operates a nuclear power plant. The licence to operate that power plant is an intangible asset that meets the contractual-legal criterion for recognition separately from goodwill, even if the acquirer cannot sell or transfer it separately from the acquired power plant. An acquirer may recognise the fair value of the operating licence and the fair value of the power plant as a single asset for financial reporting purposes if the useful lives of those assets are similar.

(c)   an acquiree owns a technology patent. It has licensed that patent to others for their exclusive use outside the domestic market, receiving a specified percentage of future foreign revenue in exchange. Both the technology patent and the related licence agreement meet the contractual-legal criterion for recognition separately from goodwill even if selling or exchanging the patent and the related licence agreement separately from one another would not be practical.

B33   The separability criterion means that an acquired intangible asset is capable of being separated or divided from the acquiree and sold, transferred, licensed, rented or exchanged, either individually or together with a related contract, identifiable asset or liability. An intangible asset that the acquirer would be able to sell, license or otherwise exchange for something else of value meets the separability criterion even if the acquirer does not intend to sell, license or otherwise exchange it. An acquired intangible asset meets the separability criterion if there is evidence of exchange transactions for that type of asset or an asset of a similar type, even if those transactions are infrequent and regardless of whether the acquirer is involved in them. For example, customer and subscriber lists are frequently licensed and thus meet the separability criterion. Even if an acquiree believes its customer lists have characteristics different from other customer lists, the fact that customer lists are frequently licensed generally means that the acquired customer list meets the separability criterion. However, a customer list acquired in a business combination would not meet the separability criterion if the terms of confidentiality or other agreements prohibit an entity from selling, leasing or otherwise exchanging information about its customers.

B34   An intangible asset that is not individually separable from the acquiree or combined entity meets the separability criterion if it is separable in combination with a related contract, identifiable asset or liability. For example:

(a)   market participants exchange deposit liabilities and related depositor relationship intangible assets in observable exchange transactions. Therefore, the acquirer should recognise the depositor relationship intangible asset separately from goodwill.

(b)   an acquiree owns a registered trademark and documented but unpatented technical expertise used to manufacture the trademarked product. To transfer ownership of a trademark, the owner is also required to transfer everything else necessary for the new owner to produce a product or service indistinguishable from that produced by the former owner. Because the unpatented technical expertise must be separated from the acquiree or combined entity and sold if the related trademark is sold, it meets the separability criterion.

Reacquired rights

B35   As part of a business combination, an acquirer may reacquire a right that it had previously granted to the acquiree to use one or more of the acquirer's recognised or unrecognised assets. Examples of such rights include a right to use the acquirer's trade name under a franchise agreement or a right to use the acquirer's technology under a technology licensing agreement. A reacquired right is an identifiable intangible asset that the acquirer recognises separately from goodwill. Paragraph 29 provides guidance on measuring a reacquired right and paragraph 55 provides guidance on the subsequent accounting for a reacquired right.

B36   If the terms of the contract giving rise to a reacquired right are favourable or unfavourable relative to the terms of current market transactions for the same or similar items, the acquirer shall recognise a settlement gain or loss. Paragraph B52 provides guidance for measuring that settlement gain or loss.

Assembled workforce and other items that are not identifiable

B37   The acquirer subsumes into goodwill the value of an acquired intangible asset that is not identifiable as of the acquisition date. For example, an acquirer may attribute value to the existence of an assembled workforce, which is an existing collection of employees that permits the acquirer to continue to operate an acquired business from the acquisition date. An assembled workforce does not represent the intellectual capital of the skilled workforce—the (often specialised) knowledge and experience that employees of an acquiree bring to their jobs. Because the assembled workforce is not an identifiable asset to be recognised separately from goodwill, any value attributed to it is subsumed into goodwill.

B38   The acquirer also subsumes into goodwill any value attributed to items that do not qualify as assets at the acquisition date. For example, the acquirer might attribute value to potential contracts the acquiree is negotiating with prospective new customers at the acquisition date. Because those potential contracts are not themselves assets at the acquisition date, the acquirer does not recognise them separately from goodwill. The acquirer should not subsequently reclassify the value of those contracts from goodwill for events that occur after the acquisition date. However, the acquirer should assess the facts and circumstances surrounding events occurring shortly after the acquisition to determine whether a separately recognisable intangible asset existed at the acquisition date.

B39   After initial recognition, an acquirer accounts for intangible assets acquired in a business combination in accordance with the provisions of IAS 38 *Intangible Assets*. However, as described in paragraph 3 of IAS 38, the accounting for some acquired intangible assets after initial recognition is prescribed by other IFRSs.

B40   The identifiability criteria determine whether an intangible asset is recognised separately from goodwill. However, the criteria neither provide guidance for measuring the fair value of an intangible asset nor restrict the assumptions used in measuring the fair value of an intangible asset. For example, the acquirer would take into account the assumptions that market participants would use when pricing the intangible asset, such as expectations of future contract renewals, in measuring fair value. It is not necessary for the renewals themselves to meet the identifiability criteria. (However, see paragraph 29, which establishes an exception to the fair value measurement principle for reacquired rights recognised in a business combination.) Paragraphs 36 and 37 of IAS 38 provide guidance for determining whether intangible assets should be combined into a single unit of account with other intangible or tangible assets.

Measuring the fair value of particular identifiable assets and a non-controlling interest in an acquiree (application of paragraphs 18 and 19)

Assets with uncertain cash flows (valuation allowances)

B41 The acquirer shall not recognise a separate valuation allowance as of the acquisition date for assets acquired in a business combination that are measured at their acquisition-date fair values because the effects of uncertainty about future cash flows are included in the fair value measure. For example, because this IFRS requires the acquirer to measure acquired receivables, including loans, at their acquisition-date fair values, the acquirer does not recognise a separate valuation allowance for the contractual cash flows that are deemed to be uncollectible at that date.

Assets subject to operating leases in which the acquiree is the lessor

B42 In measuring the acquisition-date fair value of an asset such as a building or a patent that is subject to an operating lease in which the acquiree is the lessor, the acquirer shall take into account the terms of the lease. In other words, the acquirer does not recognise a separate asset or liability if the terms of an operating lease are either favourable or unfavourable when compared with market terms as paragraph B29 requires for leases in which the acquiree is the lessee.

Assets that the acquirer intends not to use or to use in a way that is different from the way other market participants would use them

B43 To protect its competitive position, or for other reasons, the acquirer may intend not to use an acquired non-financial asset actively, or it may not intend to use the asset according to its highest and best use. For example, that might be the case for an acquired research and development intangible asset that the acquirer plans to use defensively by preventing others from using it. Nevertheless, the acquirer shall measure the fair value of the non-financial asset assuming its highest and best use by market participants in accordance with the appropriate valuation premise, both initially and when measuring fair value less costs of disposal for subsequent impairment testing.

Non-controlling interest in an acquiree

B44 This IFRS allows the acquirer to measure a non-controlling interest in the acquiree at its fair value at the acquisition date. Sometimes an acquirer will be able to measure the acquisition-date fair value of a non-controlling interest on the basis of a quoted price in an active market for the equity shares (ie those not held by the acquirer). In other situations, however, a quoted price in an active market for the equity shares will not be available. In those situations, the acquirer would measure the fair value of the non-controlling interest using other valuation techniques.

B45 The fair values of the acquirer's interest in the acquiree and the non-controlling interest on a per-share basis might differ. The main difference is likely to be the inclusion of a control premium in the per-share fair value of the acquirer's interest in the acquiree or, conversely, the inclusion of a discount for lack of control (also referred to as a non-controlling interest discount) in the per-share fair value of the non-controlling interest if market participants would take into account such a premium or discount when pricing the non-controlling interest.

Measuring goodwill or a gain from a bargain purchase

Measuring the acquisition-date fair value of the acquirer's interest in the acquiree using valuation techniques (application of paragraph 33)

B46 In a business combination achieved without the transfer of consideration, the acquirer must substitute the acquisition-date fair value of its interest in the acquiree for the acquisition-date fair value of the consideration transferred to measure goodwill or a gain on a bargain purchase (see paragraphs 32–34).

Special considerations in applying the acquisition method to combinations of mutual entities (application of paragraph 33)

B47 When two mutual entities combine, the fair value of the equity or member interests in the acquiree (or the fair value of the acquiree) may be more reliably measurable than the fair value of the member interests transferred by the acquirer. In that situation, paragraph 33 requires the acquirer to determine the amount of goodwill by using the acquisition-date fair value of the acquiree's equity interests instead of the acquisition-date fair value of the acquirer's equity interests transferred as consideration. In addition, the acquirer in a combination of mutual entities shall recognise the acquiree's net assets as a direct addition to capital or equity in its statement of financial position, not as an addition to retained earnings, which is consistent with the way in which other types of entities apply the acquisition method.

B48 Although they are similar in many ways to other businesses, mutual entities have distinct characteristics that arise primarily because their members are both customers and owners. Members of mutual entities generally expect to receive benefits for their membership, often in the form of reduced fees charged for goods and services or patronage dividends. The portion of patronage dividends allocated to each member is often based on the amount of business the member did with the mutual entity during the year.

B49 A fair value measurement of a mutual entity should include the assumptions that market participants would make about future member benefits as well as any other relevant assumptions market participants would make about the mutual entity. For example, a present value technique may be used to measure the fair value of a mutual entity. The cash flows used as inputs to the model should be based on the expected cash flows of the mutual entity, which are likely to reflect reductions for member benefits, such as reduced fees charged for goods and services.

Determining what is part of the business combination transaction (application of paragraphs 51 and 52)

B50 The acquirer should consider the following factors, which are neither mutually exclusive nor individually conclusive, to determine whether a transaction is part of the exchange for the acquiree or whether the transaction is separate from the business combination:

(a) **the reasons for the transaction**—Understanding the reasons why the parties to the combination (the acquirer and the acquiree and their owners, directors and managers—and their agents) entered into a particular transaction or arrangement may provide insight into whether it is part of the consideration transferred and the assets acquired or liabilities assumed. For example, if a transaction is arranged primarily for the benefit of the acquirer or the combined entity rather than primarily for the benefit of the acquiree or its former owners before the combination, that portion of the transaction price paid (and any related assets or liabilities) is less likely to be part of the exchange for the acquiree. Accordingly, the acquirer would account for that portion separately from the business combination.

(b) **who initiated the transaction**—Understanding who initiated the transaction may also provide insight into whether it is part of the exchange for the acquiree. For example, a transaction or other event that is initiated by the acquirer may be entered into for the purpose of providing future economic benefits to the acquirer or combined entity with little or no benefit received by the acquiree or its former owners before the combination. On the other hand, a transaction or arrangement initiated by the acquiree or its former owners is less likely to be for the benefit of the acquirer or the combined entity and more likely to be part of the business combination transaction.

(c) **the timing of the transaction**—The timing of the transaction may also provide insight into whether it is part of the exchange for the acquiree. For example, a transaction between the acquirer and the acquiree that takes place during the negotiations of the terms of a business combination may have been entered into in contemplation of the business combination to provide future economic benefits to the acquirer or the combined entity. If so, the acquiree or its former owners before the business combination are likely to receive little or no benefit from the transaction except for benefits they receive as part of the combined entity.

Effective settlement of a pre-existing relationship between the acquirer and acquiree in a business combination (application of paragraph 52(a))

B51　The acquirer and acquiree may have a relationship that existed before they contemplated the business combination, referred to here as a 'pre-existing relationship'. A pre-existing relationship between the acquirer and acquiree may be contractual (for example, vendor and customer or licensor and licensee) or non-contractual (for example, plaintiff and defendant).

B52　If the business combination in effect settles a pre-existing relationship, the acquirer recognises a gain or loss, measured as follows:

(a)　for a pre-existing non-contractual relationship (such as a lawsuit), fair value.

(b)　for a pre-existing contractual relationship, the lesser of (i) and (ii):

(i)　the amount by which the contract is favourable or unfavourable from the perspective of the acquirer when compared with terms for current market transactions for the same or similar items. (An unfavourable contract is a contract that is unfavourable in terms of current market terms. It is not necessarily an onerous contract in which the unavoidable costs of meeting the obligations under the contract exceed the economic benefits expected to be received under it.)

(ii)　the amount of any stated settlement provisions in the contract available to the counterparty to whom the contract is unfavourable.

If (ii) is less than (i), the difference is included as part of the business combination accounting.

The amount of gain or loss recognised may depend in part on whether the acquirer had previously recognised a related asset or liability, and the reported gain or loss therefore may differ from the amount calculated by applying the above requirements.

B53　A pre-existing relationship may be a contract that the acquirer recognises as a reacquired right. If the contract includes terms that are favourable or unfavourable when compared with pricing for current market transactions for the same or similar items, the acquirer recognises, separately from the business combination, a gain or loss for the effective settlement of the contract, measured in accordance with paragraph B52.

Arrangements for contingent payments to employees or selling shareholders (application of paragraph 52(b))

B54 Whether arrangements for contingent payments to employees or selling shareholders are contingent consideration in the business combination or are separate transactions depends on the nature of the arrangements. Understanding the reasons why the acquisition agreement includes a provision for contingent payments, who initiated the arrangement and when the parties entered into the arrangement may be helpful in assessing the nature of the arrangement.

B55 If it is not clear whether an arrangement for payments to employees or selling shareholders is part of the exchange for the acquiree or is a transaction separate from the business combination, the acquirer should consider the following indicators:

(a) *Continuing employment*—The terms of continuing employment by the selling shareholders who become key employees may be an indicator of the substance of a contingent consideration arrangement. The relevant terms of continuing employment may be included in an employment agreement, acquisition agreement or some other document. A contingent consideration arrangement in which the payments are automatically forfeited if employment terminates is remuneration for post-combination services. Arrangements in which the contingent payments are not affected by employment termination may indicate that the contingent payments are additional consideration rather than remuneration.

(b) *Duration of continuing employment*—If the period of required employment coincides with or is longer than the contingent payment period, that fact may indicate that the contingent payments are, in substance, remuneration.

(c) *Level of remuneration*—Situations in which employee remuneration other than the contingent payments is at a reasonable level in comparison with that of other key employees in the combined entity may indicate that the contingent payments are additional consideration rather than remuneration.

(d) *Incremental payments to employees*—If selling shareholders who do not become employees receive lower contingent payments on a per-share basis than the selling shareholders who become employees of the combined entity, that fact may indicate that the incremental amount of contingent payments to the selling shareholders who become employees is remuneration.

(e) *Number of shares owned*—The relative number of shares owned by the selling shareholders who remain as key employees may be an indicator of the substance of the contingent consideration arrangement. For example, if the selling shareholders who owned substantially all of the shares in the acquiree continue as key employees, that fact may indicate that the arrangement is, in substance, a profit-sharing arrangement intended to provide remuneration for post-combination services. Alternatively, if selling shareholders who continue as key employees owned only a small number of shares of the acquiree and all selling shareholders receive the same amount of contingent consideration on a per-share basis, that fact may indicate that the contingent payments are additional consideration.

The pre-acquisition ownership interests held by parties related to selling shareholders who continue as key employees, such as family members, should also be considered.

(f) *Linkage to the valuation*—If the initial consideration transferred at the acquisition date is based on the low end of a range established in the valuation of the acquiree and the contingent formula relates to that valuation approach, that fact may suggest that the contingent payments are additional consideration. Alternatively, if the contingent payment formula is consistent with prior profit-sharing arrangements, that fact may suggest that the substance of the arrangement is to provide remuneration.

(g) *Formula for determining consideration*—The formula used to determine the contingent payment may be helpful in assessing the substance of the arrangement. For example, if a contingent payment is determined on the basis of a multiple of earnings, that might suggest that the obligation is contingent consideration in the business combination and that the formula is intended to establish or verify the fair value of the acquiree. In contrast, a contingent payment that is a specified percentage of earnings might suggest that the obligation to employees is a profit-sharing arrangement to remunerate employees for services rendered.

(h) *Other agreements and issues*—The terms of other arrangements with selling shareholders (such as agreements not to compete, executory contracts, consulting contracts and property lease agreements) and the income tax treatment of contingent payments may indicate that contingent payments are attributable to something other than consideration for the acquiree. For example, in connection with the acquisition, the acquirer might enter into a property lease arrangement with a significant selling shareholder. If the lease payments specified in the lease contract are significantly below market, some or all of the contingent payments to the lessor (the selling shareholder) required by a separate arrangement for contingent payments might be, in substance, payments for the use of the leased property that the acquirer should recognise separately in its post-combination financial statements. In contrast, if the lease contract specifies lease payments that are consistent with market terms for the leased property, the arrangement for contingent payments to the selling shareholder may be contingent consideration in the business combination.

Acquirer share-based payment awards exchanged for awards held by the acquiree's employees (application of paragraph 52(b))

B56 An acquirer may exchange its share-based payment awards[3] (replacement awards) for awards held by employees of the acquiree. Exchanges of share options or other share-based payment awards in conjunction with a business combination are accounted for as modifications of share-based payment awards in accordance with IFRS 2 *Share-based Payment*. If the acquirer replaces the acquiree awards, either all or a portion of the market-based measure of the acquirer's replacement

---

3 In paragraphs B56–B62 the term 'share-based payment awards' refers to vested or unvested share-based payment transactions.

awards shall be included in measuring the consideration transferred in the business combination. Paragraphs B57–B62 provide guidance on how to allocate the market-based measure. However, in situations in which acquiree awards would expire as a consequence of a business combination and if the acquirer replaces those awards when it is not obliged to do so, all of the market-based measure of the replacement awards shall be recognised as remuneration cost in the post-combination financial statements in accordance with IFRS 2. That is to say, none of the market-based measure of those awards shall be included in measuring the consideration transferred in the business combination. The acquirer is obliged to replace the acquiree awards if the acquiree or its employees have the ability to enforce replacement. For example, for the purposes of applying this guidance, the acquirer is obliged to replace the acquiree's awards if replacement is required by:

(a)   the terms of the acquisition agreement;

(b)   the terms of the acquiree's awards; or

(c)   applicable laws or regulations.

B57   To determine the portion of a replacement award that is part of the consideration transferred for the acquiree and the portion that is remuneration for post-combination service, the acquirer shall measure both the replacement awards granted by the acquirer and the acquiree awards as of the acquisition date in accordance with IFRS 2. The portion of the market-based measure of the replacement award that is part of the consideration transferred in exchange for the acquiree equals the portion of the acquiree award that is attributable to pre-combination service.

B58   The portion of the replacement award attributable to pre-combination service is the market-based measure of the acquiree award multiplied by the ratio of the portion of the vesting period completed to the greater of the total vesting period or the original vesting period of the acquiree award. The vesting period is the period during which all the specified vesting conditions are to be satisfied. Vesting conditions are defined in IFRS 2.

B59   The portion of a non-vested replacement award attributable to post-combination service, and therefore recognised as remuneration cost in the post-combination financial statements, equals the total market-based measure of the replacement award less the amount attributed to pre-combination service. Therefore, the acquirer attributes any excess of the market-based measure of the replacement award over the market-based measure of the acquiree award to post-combination service and recognises that excess as remuneration cost in the post-combination financial statements. The acquirer shall attribute a portion of a replacement award to post-combination service if it requires post-combination service, regardless of whether employees had rendered all of the service required for their acquiree awards to vest before the acquisition date.

B60   The portion of a non-vested replacement award attributable to pre-combination service, as well as the portion attributable to post-combination service, shall reflect the best available estimate of the number of replacement awards expected to vest. For example, if the market-based measure of the portion of a replacement award attributed to pre-combination service is CU100 and the acquirer expects that only 95 per cent of the award will vest, the amount included in consideration transferred in the business combination is CU95. Changes in the estimated number of replacement awards expected to vest are reflected in remuneration cost for the periods in which the changes or forfeitures occur not as adjustments to the consideration transferred in the business combination. Similarly, the effects of other events, such as modifications or the ultimate outcome of awards with performance conditions, that occur after the acquisition date are accounted for in accordance with IFRS 2 in determining remuneration cost for the period in which an event occurs.

B61   The same requirements for determining the portions of a replacement award attributable to pre-combination and post-combination service apply regardless of whether a replacement award is classified as a liability or as an equity instrument in accordance with the provisions of IFRS 2. All changes in the market-based measure of awards classified as liabilities after the acquisition date and the related income tax effects are recognised in the acquirer's post-combination financial statements in the period(s) in which the changes occur.

B62   The income tax effects of replacement awards of share-based payments shall be recognised in accordance with the provisions of IAS 12 *Income Taxes*.

Equity-settled share-based payment transactions of the acquiree

B62A   The acquiree may have outstanding share-based payment transactions that the acquirer does not exchange for its share-based payment transactions. If vested, those acquiree share-based payment transactions are part of the non-controlling interest in the acquiree and are measured at their market-based measure. If unvested, they are measured at their market-based measure as if the acquisition date were the grant date in accordance with paragraphs 19 and 30.

B62B   The market-based measure of unvested share-based payment transactions is allocated to the non-controlling interest on the basis of the ratio of the portion of the vesting period completed to the greater of the total vesting period and the original vesting period of the share-based payment transaction. The balance is allocated to post-combination service.

Other IFRSs that provide guidance on subsequent measurement and accounting (application of paragraph 54)

B63   Examples of other IFRSs that provide guidance on subsequently measuring and accounting for assets acquired and liabilities assumed or incurred in a business combination include:

(a)   IAS 38 prescribes the accounting for identifiable intangible assets acquired in a business combination. The acquirer measures goodwill at the amount recognised at the acquisition date less any accumulated impairment losses. IAS 36 *Impairment of Assets* prescribes the accounting for impairment losses.

(b)   IFRS 4 *Insurance Contracts* provides guidance on the subsequent accounting for an insurance contract acquired in a business combination.

(c) IAS 12 prescribes the subsequent accounting for deferred tax assets (including unrecognised deferred tax assets) and liabilities acquired in a business combination.

(d) IFRS 2 provides guidance on subsequent measurement and accounting for the portion of replacement share-based payment awards issued by an acquirer that is attributable to employees' future services.

(e) IFRS 10 provides guidance on accounting for changes in a parent's ownership interest in a subsidiary after control is obtained.

Disclosures (application of paragraphs 59 and 61)

B64 To meet the objective in paragraph 59, the acquirer shall disclose the following information for each business combination that occurs during the reporting period:

(a) the name and a description of the acquiree.

(b) the acquisition date.

(c) the percentage of voting equity interests acquired.

(d) the primary reasons for the business combination and a description of how the acquirer obtained control of the acquiree.

(e) a qualitative description of the factors that make up the goodwill recognised, such as expected synergies from combining operations of the acquiree and the acquirer, intangible assets that do not qualify for separate recognition or other factors.

(f) the acquisition-date fair value of the total consideration transferred and the acquisition-date fair value of each major class of consideration, such as:

(i) cash;

(ii) other tangible or intangible assets, including a business or subsidiary of the acquirer;

(iii) liabilities incurred, for example, a liability for contingent consideration; and

(iv) equity interests of the acquirer, including the number of instruments or interests issued or issuable and the method of measuring the fair value of those instruments or interests.

(g) for contingent consideration arrangements and indemnification assets:

(i) the amount recognised as of the acquisition date;

(ii) a description of the arrangement and the basis for determining the amount of the payment; and

(iii) an estimate of the range of outcomes (undiscounted) or, if a range cannot be estimated, that fact and the reasons why a range cannot be estimated. If the maximum amount of the payment is unlimited, the acquirer shall disclose that fact.

(h) for acquired receivables:

    (i) the fair value of the receivables;

    (ii) the gross contractual amounts receivable; and

    (iii) the best estimate at the acquisition date of the contractual cash flows not expected to be collected.

The disclosures shall be provided by major class of receivable, such as loans, direct finance leases and any other class of receivables.

(i) the amounts recognised as of the acquisition date for each major class of assets acquired and liabilities assumed.

(j) for each contingent liability recognised in accordance with paragraph 23, the information required in paragraph 85 of IAS 37 *Provisions, Contingent Liabilities and Contingent Assets*. If a contingent liability is not recognised because its fair value cannot be measured reliably, the acquirer shall disclose:

    (i) the information required by paragraph 86 of IAS 37; and

    (ii) the reasons why the liability cannot be measured reliably.

(k) the total amount of goodwill that is expected to be deductible for tax purposes.

(l) for transactions that are recognised separately from the acquisition of assets and assumption of liabilities in the business combination in accordance with paragraph 51:

    (i) a description of each transaction;

    (ii) how the acquirer accounted for each transaction;

    (iii) the amounts recognised for each transaction and the line item in the financial statements in which each amount is recognised; and

    (iv) if the transaction is the effective settlement of a pre-existing relationship, the method used to determine the settlement amount.

(m) the disclosure of separately recognised transactions required by (l) shall include the amount of acquisition-related costs and, separately, the amount of those costs recognised as an expense and the line item or items in the statement of comprehensive income in which those expenses are recognised. The amount of any issue costs not recognised as an expense and how they were recognised shall also be disclosed.

(n) in a bargain purchase (see paragraphs 34–36):

    (i) the amount of any gain recognised in accordance with paragraph 34 and the line item in the statement of comprehensive income in which the gain is recognised; and

    (ii) a description of the reasons why the transaction resulted in a gain.

(o) for each business combination in which the acquirer holds less than 100 per cent of the equity interests in the acquiree at the acquisition date:

    (i) the amount of the non-controlling interest in the acquiree recognised at the acquisition date and the measurement basis for that amount; and

    (ii) for each non-controlling interest in an acquiree measured at fair value, the valuation technique(s) and significant inputs used to measure that value.

(p) in a business combination achieved in stages:

    (i) the acquisition-date fair value of the equity interest in the acquiree held by the acquirer immediately before the acquisition date; and

    (ii) the amount of any gain or loss recognised as a result of remeasuring to fair value the equity interest in the acquiree held by the acquirer before the business combination (see paragraph 42) and the line item in the statement of comprehensive income in which that gain or loss is recognised.

(q) the following information:

    (i) the amounts of revenue and profit or loss of the acquiree since the acquisition date included in the consolidated statement of comprehensive income for the reporting period; and

    (ii) the revenue and profit or loss of the combined entity for the current reporting period as though the acquisition date for all business combinations that occurred during the year had been as of the beginning of the annual reporting period.

If disclosure of any of the information required by this subparagraph is impracticable, the acquirer shall disclose that fact and explain why the disclosure is impracticable. This IFRS uses the term 'impracticable' with the same meaning as in IAS 8 *Accounting Policies, Changes in Accounting Estimates and Errors*.

B65 For individually immaterial business combinations occurring during the reporting period that are material collectively, the acquirer shall disclose in aggregate the information required by paragraph B64(e)–(q).

B66 If the acquisition date of a business combination is after the end of the reporting period but before the financial statements are authorised for issue, the acquirer shall disclose the information required by paragraph B64 unless the initial accounting for the business combination is incomplete at the time the financial statements are authorised for issue. In that situation, the acquirer shall describe which disclosures could not be made and the reasons why they cannot be made.

B67 To meet the objective in paragraph 61, the acquirer shall disclose the following information for each material business combination or in the aggregate for individually immaterial business combinations that are material collectively:

(a) if the initial accounting for a business combination is incomplete (see paragraph 45) for particular assets, liabilities, non-controlling interests or items of consideration and the amounts recognised in the financial statements for the business combination thus have been determined only provisionally:

    (i)   the reasons why the initial accounting for the business combination is incomplete;

    (ii)   the assets, liabilities, equity interests or items of consideration for which the initial accounting is incomplete; and

    (iii) the nature and amount of any measurement period adjustments recognised during the reporting period in accordance with paragraph 49.

(b)   for each reporting period after the acquisition date until the entity collects, sells or otherwise loses the right to a contingent consideration asset, or until the entity settles a contingent consideration liability or the liability is cancelled or expires:

    (i)   any changes in the recognised amounts, including any differences arising upon settlement;

    (ii)   any changes in the range of outcomes (undiscounted) and the reasons for those changes; and

    (iii) the valuation techniques and key model inputs used to measure contingent consideration.

(c)   for contingent liabilities recognised in a business combination, the acquirer shall disclose the information required by paragraphs 84 and 85 of IAS 37 for each class of provision.

(d)   a reconciliation of the carrying amount of goodwill at the beginning and end of the reporting period showing separately:

    (i)   the gross amount and accumulated impairment losses at the beginning of the reporting period.

    (ii)   additional goodwill recognised during the reporting period, except goodwill included in a disposal group that, on acquisition, meets the criteria to be classified as held for sale in accordance with IFRS 5 *Non-current Assets Held for Sale and Discontinued Operations*.

    (iii) adjustments resulting from the subsequent recognition of deferred tax assets during the reporting period in accordance with paragraph 67.

    (iv) goodwill included in a disposal group classified as held for sale in accordance with IFRS 5 and goodwill derecognised during the reporting period without having previously been included in a disposal group classified as held for sale.

    (v)   impairment losses recognised during the reporting period in accordance with IAS 36. (IAS 36 requires disclosure of information about the recoverable amount and impairment of goodwill in addition to this requirement.)

(vi) net exchange rate differences arising during the reporting period in accordance with IAS 21 *The Effects of Changes in Foreign Exchange Rates*.

(vii) any other changes in the carrying amount during the reporting period.

(viii) the gross amount and accumulated impairment losses at the end of the reporting period.

(e) the amount and an explanation of any gain or loss recognised in the current reporting period that both:

(i) relates to the identifiable assets acquired or liabilities assumed in a business combination that was effected in the current or previous reporting period; and

(ii) is of such a size, nature or incidence that disclosure is relevant to understanding the combined entity's financial statements.

Transitional provisions for business combinations involving only mutual entities or by contract alone (application of paragraph 66)

B68 Paragraph 64 provides that this IFRS applies prospectively to business combinations for which the acquisition date is on or after the beginning of the first annual reporting period beginning on or after 1 July 2009. Earlier application is permitted. However, an entity shall apply this IFRS only at the beginning of an annual reporting period that begins on or after 30 June 2007. If an entity applies this IFRS before its effective date, the entity shall disclose that fact and shall apply IAS 27 (as amended in 2008) at the same time.

B69 The requirement to apply this IFRS prospectively has the following effect for a business combination involving only mutual entities or by contract alone if the acquisition date for that business combination is before the application of this IFRS:

(a) *Classification*—An entity shall continue to classify the prior business combination in accordance with the entity's previous accounting policies for such combinations.

(b) *Previously recognised goodwill*—At the beginning of the first annual period in which this IFRS is applied, the carrying amount of goodwill arising from the prior business combination shall be its carrying amount at that date in accordance with the entity's previous accounting policies. In determining that amount, the entity shall eliminate the carrying amount of any accumulated amortisation of that goodwill and the corresponding decrease in goodwill. No other adjustments shall be made to the carrying amount of goodwill.

(c) *Goodwill previously recognised as a deduction from equity*—The entity's previous accounting policies may have resulted in goodwill arising from the prior business combination being recognised as a deduction from equity. In that situation the entity shall not recognise that goodwill as an asset at the beginning of the first annual period in which this IFRS is applied. Furthermore, the entity shall not recognise in profit or loss any part of that goodwill when it disposes of all or part of the business to which that goodwill relates or when a cash-generating unit to which the goodwill relates becomes impaired.

(d) *Subsequent accounting for goodwill*—From the beginning of the first annual period in which this IFRS is applied, an entity shall discontinue amortising goodwill arising from the prior business combination and shall test goodwill for impairment in accordance with IAS 36.

(e) *Previously recognised negative goodwill*—An entity that accounted for the prior business combination by applying the purchase method may have recognised a deferred credit for an excess of its interest in the net fair value of the acquiree's identifiable assets and liabilities over the cost of that interest (sometimes called negative goodwill). If so, the entity shall derecognise the carrying amount of that deferred credit at the beginning of the first annual period in which this IFRS is applied with a corresponding adjustment to the opening balance of retained earnings at that date.

Appendix C
Amendments to other IFRSs

The amendments in this appendix shall be applied for annual reporting periods beginning on or after 1 July 2009. If an entity applies this IFRS for an earlier period, these amendments shall be applied for that earlier period. Amended paragraphs are shown with new text underlined and deleted text struck through.

* * * * *

The amendments contained in this appendix when this revised IFRS was issued in 2008 have been incorporated into the relevant IFRSs published in this volume.

International Financial Reporting Standard 4

Insurance Contracts

In March 2004 the International Accounting Standards Board (IASB) issued IFRS 4 *Insurance Contracts*. In August 2005 the IASB amended the scope of IFRS 4 to clarify that most financial guarantee contracts would apply the financial instruments requirements. In December 2005 the IASB published revised guidance on implementing IFRS 4.

Other IFRSs have made minor consequential amendments to IFRS 4. They include IFRS 7 *Financial Instruments: Disclosures* (amendments in March 2009) and IFRS 9 *Financial Instruments* (issued November 2009 and October 2010).

CONTENTS

INTERNATIONAL FINANCIAL REPORTING STANDARD 4
INSURANCE CONTRACTS

FOR THE ACCOMPANYING DOCUMENTS LISTED BELOW, SEE PART B OF THIS EDITION

© IFRS Foundation

International Financial Reporting Standard 4 *Insurance Contracts* (IFRS 4) is set out in paragraphs 1–45 and Appendices A–C. All the paragraphs have equal authority. Paragraphs in **bold type** state the main principles. Terms defined in Appendix A are in *italics* the first time they appear in the Standard. Definitions of other terms are given in the Glossary for International Financial Reporting Standards. IFRS 4 should be read in the context of its objective and the Basis for Conclusions, the *Preface to International Financial Reporting Standards* and the *Conceptual Framework for Financial Reporting*. IAS 8 *Accounting Policies, Changes in Accounting Estimates and Errors* provides a basis for selecting and applying accounting policies in the absence of explicit guidance.

Introduction

Reasons for issuing the IFRS

IN1   This is the first IFRS to deal with insurance contracts. Accounting practices for insurance contracts have been diverse, and have often differed from practices in other sectors. Because many entities will adopt IFRSs in 2005, the International Accounting Standards Board has issued this IFRS:

(a)   to make limited improvements to accounting for insurance contracts until the Board completes the second phase of its project on insurance contracts.

(b)   to require any entity issuing insurance contracts (an insurer) to disclose information about those contracts.

IN2   This IFRS is a stepping stone to phase II of this project. The Board is committed to completing phase II without delay once it has investigated all relevant conceptual and practical questions and completed its full due process.

Main features of the IFRS

IN3   The IFRS applies to all insurance contracts (including reinsurance contracts) that an entity issues and to reinsurance contracts that it holds, except for specified contracts covered by other IFRSs. It does not apply to other assets and liabilities of an insurer, such as financial assets and financial liabilities within the scope of IFRS 9 *Financial Instruments*. Furthermore, it does not address accounting by policyholders.

IN4   The IFRS exempts an insurer temporarily (ie during phase I of this project) from some requirements of other IFRSs, including the requirement to consider the *Framework*[1] in selecting accounting policies for insurance contracts. However, the IFRS:

(a)   prohibits provisions for possible claims under contracts that are not in existence at the end of the reporting period (such as catastrophe and equalisation provisions).

(b)   requires a test for the adequacy of recognised insurance liabilities and an impairment test for reinsurance assets.

(c)   requires an insurer to keep insurance liabilities in its statement of financial position until they are discharged or cancelled, or expire, and to present insurance liabilities without offsetting them against related reinsurance assets.

IN5   The IFRS permits an insurer to change its accounting policies for insurance contracts only if, as a result, its financial statements present information that is more relevant and no less reliable, or more reliable and no less relevant. In particular, an insurer cannot introduce any of the following practices, although it may continue using accounting policies that involve them:

---

1   The reference to the *Framework* is to IASC's *Framework for the Preparation and Presentation of Financial Statements*, adopted by the IASB in 2001. In September 2010 the IASB replaced the *Framework* with the *Conceptual Framework for Financial Reporting*.

(a) measuring insurance liabilities on an undiscounted basis.

(b) measuring contractual rights to future investment management fees at an amount that exceeds their fair value as implied by a comparison with current fees charged by other market participants for similar services.

(c) using non-uniform accounting policies for the insurance liabilities of subsidiaries.

IN6 The IFRS permits the introduction of an accounting policy that involves remeasuring designated insurance liabilities consistently in each period to reflect current market interest rates (and, if the insurer so elects, other current estimates and assumptions). Without this permission, an insurer would have been required to apply the change in accounting policies consistently to all similar liabilities.

IN7 An insurer need not change its accounting policies for insurance contracts to eliminate excessive prudence. However, if an insurer already measures its insurance contracts with sufficient prudence, it should not introduce additional prudence.

IN8 There is a rebuttable presumption that an insurer's financial statements will become less relevant and reliable if it introduces an accounting policy that reflects future investment margins in the measurement of insurance contracts.

IN9 When an insurer changes its accounting policies for insurance liabilities, it may reclassify some or all financial assets as 'at fair value through profit or loss'.

IN10 The IFRS:

(a) clarifies that an insurer need not account for an embedded derivative separately at fair value if the embedded derivative meets the definition of an insurance contract.

(b) requires an insurer to unbundle (ie account separately for) deposit components of some insurance contracts, to avoid the omission of assets and liabilities from its statement of financial position.

(c) clarifies the applicability of the practice sometimes known as 'shadow accounting'.

(d) permits an expanded presentation for insurance contracts acquired in a business combination or portfolio transfer.

(e) addresses limited aspects of discretionary participation features contained in insurance contracts or financial instruments.

IN11 The IFRS requires disclosure to help users understand:

(a) the amounts in the insurer's financial statements that arise from insurance contracts.

(b) the nature and extent of risks arising from insurance contracts.

IN12 [Deleted]

Potential impact of future proposals

IN13 [Deleted]

International Financial Reporting Standard 4
Insurance Contracts

Objective

1   The objective of this IFRS is to specify the financial reporting for *insurance contracts* by any entity that issues such contracts (described in this IFRS as an *insurer*) until the Board completes the second phase of its project on insurance contracts. In particular, this IFRS requires:

(a)   limited improvements to accounting by insurers for insurance contracts.

(b)   disclosure that identifies and explains the amounts in an insurer's financial statements arising from insurance contracts and helps users of those financial statements understand the amount, timing and uncertainty of future cash flows from insurance contracts.

Scope

2   An entity shall apply this IFRS to:

(a)   insurance contracts (including *reinsurance contracts*) that it issues and reinsurance contracts that it holds.

(b)   financial instruments that it issues with a *discretionary participation feature* (see paragraph 35). IFRS 7 *Financial Instruments: Disclosures* requires disclosure about financial instruments, including financial instruments that contain such features.

3   This IFRS does not address other aspects of accounting by insurers, such as accounting for financial assets held by insurers and financial liabilities issued by insurers (see IAS 32 *Financial Instruments: Presentation*, IAS 39 *Financial Instruments: Recognition and Measurement*, IFRS 7 and IFRS 9 *Financial Instruments*), except in the transitional provisions in paragraph 45.

4   An entity shall not apply this IFRS to:

(a)   product warranties issued directly by a manufacturer, dealer or retailer (see IAS 18 *Revenue* and IAS 37 *Provisions, Contingent Liabilities and Contingent Assets*).

(b)   employers' assets and liabilities under employee benefit plans (see IAS 19 *Employee Benefits* and IFRS 2 *Share-based Payment*) and retirement benefit obligations reported by defined benefit retirement plans (see IAS 26 *Accounting and Reporting by Retirement Benefit Plans*).

(c)   contractual rights or contractual obligations that are contingent on the future use of, or right to use, a non-financial item (for example, some licence fees, royalties, contingent lease payments and similar items), as well as a lessee's residual value guarantee embedded in a finance lease (see IAS 17 *Leases*, IAS 18 *Revenue* and IAS 38 *Intangible Assets*).

(d)   financial guarantee contracts unless the issuer has previously asserted explicitly that it regards such contracts as insurance contracts and has used accounting applicable to insurance contracts, in which case the issuer may elect to apply either IAS 32, IFRS 7 and IFRS 9 or this IFRS to such financial guarantee contracts. The issuer may make that election contract by contract, but the election for each contract is irrevocable.

(e) contingent consideration payable or receivable in a business combination (see IFRS 3 *Business Combinations*).

(f) *direct insurance contracts* that the entity holds (ie direct insurance contracts in which the entity is the *policyholder*). However, a *cedant* shall apply this IFRS to reinsurance contracts that it holds.

5   For ease of reference, this IFRS describes any entity that issues an insurance contract as an insurer, whether or not the issuer is regarded as an insurer for legal or supervisory purposes.

6   A reinsurance contract is a type of insurance contract. Accordingly, all references in this IFRS to insurance contracts also apply to reinsurance contracts.

Embedded derivatives

7   IFRS 9 requires an entity to separate some embedded derivatives from their host contract, measure them at *fair value* and include changes in their fair value in profit or loss. IFRS 9 applies to derivatives embedded in an insurance contract unless the embedded derivative is itself an insurance contract.

8   As an exception to the requirements in IFRS 9, an insurer need not separate, and measure at fair value, a policyholder's option to surrender an insurance contract for a fixed amount (or for an amount based on a fixed amount and an interest rate), even if the exercise price differs from the carrying amount of the host *insurance liability*. However, the requirements in IFRS 9 do apply to a put option or cash surrender option embedded in an insurance contract if the surrender value varies in response to the change in a financial variable (such as an equity or commodity price or index), or a non-financial variable that is not specific to a party to the contract. Furthermore, those requirements also apply if the holder's ability to exercise a put option or cash surrender option is triggered by a change in such a variable (for example, a put option that can be exercised if a stock market index reaches a specified level).

9   Paragraph 8 applies equally to options to surrender a financial instrument containing a discretionary participation feature.

Unbundling of deposit components

10   Some insurance contracts contain both an insurance component and a *deposit component*. In some cases, an insurer is required or permitted to *unbundle* those components:

(a) unbundling is required if both the following conditions are met:

(i) the insurer can measure the deposit component (including any embedded surrender options) separately (ie without considering the insurance component).

(ii) the insurer's accounting policies do not otherwise require it to recognise all obligations and rights arising from the deposit component.

(b) unbundling is permitted, but not required, if the insurer can measure the deposit component separately as in (a)(i) but its accounting policies require it to recognise all obligations and rights arising from the deposit component, regardless of the basis used to measure those rights and obligations.

(c) unbundling is prohibited if an insurer cannot measure the deposit component separately as in (a)(i).

11 The following is an example of a case when an insurer's accounting policies do not require it recognise all obligations arising from a deposit component. A cedant receives compensation for losses from a *reinsurer*, but the contract obliges the cedant to repay the compensation in future years. That obligation arises from a deposit component. If the cedant's accounting policies would otherwise permit it to recognise the compensation as income without recognising the resulting obligation, unbundling is required.

12 To unbundle a contract, an insurer shall:

(a) apply this IFRS to the insurance component.

(b) apply IFRS 9 to the deposit component.

Recognition and measurement

Temporary exemption from some other IFRSs

13 Paragraphs 10–12 of IAS 8 *Accounting Policies, Changes in Accounting Estimates and Errors* specify criteria for an entity to use in developing an accounting policy if no IFRS applies specifically to an item. However, this IFRS exempts an insurer from applying those criteria to its accounting policies for:

(a) insurance contracts that it issues (including related acquisition costs and related intangible assets, such as those described in paragraphs 31 and 32); and

(b) reinsurance contracts that it holds.

14 Nevertheless, this IFRS does not exempt an insurer from some implications of the criteria in paragraphs 10–12 of IAS 8. Specifically, an insurer:

(a) shall not recognise as a liability any provisions for possible future claims, if those claims arise under insurance contracts that are not in existence at the end of the reporting period (such as catastrophe provisions and equalisation provisions).

(b) shall carry out the *liability adequacy test* described in paragraphs 15–19.

(c) shall remove an insurance liability (or a part of an insurance liability) from its statement of financial position when, and only when, it is extinguished—ie when the obligation specified in the contract is discharged or cancelled or expires.

(d)   shall not offset:

(i)   *reinsurance assets* against the related insurance liabilities; or

(ii)   income or expense from reinsurance contracts against the expense or income from the related insurance contracts.

(e)   shall consider whether its reinsurance assets are impaired (see paragraph 20).

Liability adequacy test

15   **An insurer shall assess at the end of each reporting period whether its recognised insurance liabilities are adequate, using current estimates of future cash flows under its insurance contracts. If that assessment shows that the carrying amount of its insurance liabilities (less related deferred acquisition costs and related intangible assets, such as those discussed in paragraphs 31 and 32) is inadequate in the light of the estimated future cash flows, the entire deficiency shall be recognised in profit or loss.**

16   If an insurer applies a liability adequacy test that meets specified minimum requirements, this IFRS imposes no further requirements. The minimum requirements are the following:

(a)   The test considers current estimates of all contractual cash flows, and of related cash flows such as claims handling costs, as well as cash flows resulting from embedded options and guarantees.

(b)   If the test shows that the liability is inadequate, the entire deficiency is recognised in profit or loss.

17   If an insurer's accounting policies do not require a liability adequacy test that meets the minimum requirements of paragraph 16, the insurer shall:

(a)   determine the carrying amount of the relevant insurance liabilities[2] less the carrying amount of:

(i)   any related deferred acquisition costs; and

(ii)   any related intangible assets, such as those acquired in a business combination or portfolio transfer (see paragraphs 31 and 32). However, related reinsurance assets are not considered because an insurer accounts for them separately (see paragraph 20).

(b)   determine whether the amount described in (a) is less than the carrying amount that would be required if the relevant insurance liabilities were within the scope of IAS 37. If it is less, the insurer shall recognise the entire difference in profit or loss and decrease the carrying amount of the related deferred acquisition costs or related intangible assets or increase the carrying amount of the relevant insurance liabilities.

---

2   The relevant insurance liabilities are those insurance liabilities (and related deferred acquisition costs and related intangible assets) for which the insurer's accounting policies do not require a liability adequacy test that meets the minimum requirements of paragraph 16.

18   If an insurer's liability adequacy test meets the minimum requirements of paragraph 16, the test is applied at the level of aggregation specified in that test. If its liability adequacy test does not meet those minimum requirements, the comparison described in paragraph 17 shall be made at the level of a portfolio of contracts that are subject to broadly similar risks and managed together as a single portfolio.

19   The amount described in paragraph 17(b) (ie the result of applying IAS 37) shall reflect future investment margins (see paragraphs 27–29) if, and only if, the amount described in paragraph 17(a) also reflects those margins.

Impairment of reinsurance assets

20   If a cedant's reinsurance asset is impaired, the cedant shall reduce its carrying amount accordingly and recognise that impairment loss in profit or loss. A reinsurance asset is impaired if, and only if:

(a)   there is objective evidence, as a result of an event that occurred after initial recognition of the reinsurance asset, that the cedant may not receive all amounts due to it under the terms of the contract; and

(b)   that event has a reliably measurable impact on the amounts that the cedant will receive from the reinsurer.

Changes in accounting policies

21   Paragraphs 22–30 apply both to changes made by an insurer that already applies IFRSs and to changes made by an insurer adopting IFRSs for the first time.

22   **An insurer may change its accounting policies for insurance contracts if, and only if, the change makes the financial statements more relevant to the economic decision-making needs of users and no less reliable, or more reliable and no less relevant to those needs. An insurer shall judge relevance and reliability by the criteria in IAS 8.**

23   To justify changing its accounting policies for insurance contracts, an insurer shall show that the change brings its financial statements closer to meeting the criteria in IAS 8, but the change need not achieve full compliance with those criteria. The following specific issues are discussed below:

(a)   current interest rates (paragraph 24);

(b)   continuation of existing practices (paragraph 25);

(c)   prudence (paragraph 26);

(d)   future investment margins (paragraphs 27–29); and

(e)   shadow accounting (paragraph 30).

Current market interest rates

24   An insurer is permitted, but not required, to change its accounting policies so that it remeasures designated insurance liabilities[3] to reflect current market interest rates and recognises changes in those liabilities in profit or loss. At that time, it may also introduce accounting policies that require other current estimates and assumptions for the designated liabilities. The election in this paragraph permits an insurer to change its accounting policies for designated liabilities, without applying those policies consistently to all similar liabilities as IAS 8 would otherwise require. If an insurer designates liabilities for this election, it shall continue to apply current market interest rates (and, if applicable, the other current estimates and assumptions) consistently in all periods to all these liabilities until they are extinguished.

Continuation of existing practices

25   An insurer may continue the following practices, but the introduction of any of them does not satisfy paragraph 22:

    (a)   measuring insurance liabilities on an undiscounted basis.

    (b)   measuring contractual rights to future investment management fees at an amount that exceeds their fair value as implied by a comparison with current fees charged by other market participants for similar services. It is likely that the fair value at inception of those contractual rights equals the origination costs paid, unless future investment management fees and related costs are out of line with market comparables.

    (c)   using non-uniform accounting policies for the insurance contracts (and related deferred acquisition costs and related intangible assets, if any) of subsidiaries, except as permitted by paragraph 24. If those accounting policies are not uniform, an insurer may change them if the change does not make the accounting policies more diverse and also satisfies the other requirements in this IFRS.

Prudence

26   An insurer need not change its accounting policies for insurance contracts to eliminate excessive prudence. However, if an insurer already measures its insurance contracts with sufficient prudence, it shall not introduce additional prudence.

Future investment margins

27   An insurer need not change its accounting policies for insurance contracts to eliminate future investment margins. However, there is a rebuttable presumption that an insurer's financial statements will become less relevant and reliable if it introduces an accounting policy that reflects future investment

---

3   In this paragraph, insurance liabilities include related deferred acquisition costs and related intangible assets, such as those discussed in paragraphs 31 and 32.

margins in the measurement of insurance contracts, unless those margins affect the contractual payments. Two examples of accounting policies that reflect those margins are:

(a)   using a discount rate that reflects the estimated return on the insurer's assets; or

(b)   projecting the returns on those assets at an estimated rate of return, discounting those projected returns at a different rate and including the result in the measurement of the liability.

28   An insurer may overcome the rebuttable presumption described in paragraph 27 if, and only if, the other components of a change in accounting policies increase the relevance and reliability of its financial statements sufficiently to outweigh the decrease in relevance and reliability caused by the inclusion of future investment margins. For example, suppose that an insurer's existing accounting policies for insurance contracts involve excessively prudent assumptions set at inception and a discount rate prescribed by a regulator without direct reference to market conditions, and ignore some embedded options and guarantees. The insurer might make its financial statements more relevant and no less reliable by switching to a comprehensive investor-oriented basis of accounting that is widely used and involves:

(a)   current estimates and assumptions;

(b)   a reasonable (but not excessively prudent) adjustment to reflect risk and uncertainty;

(c)   measurements that reflect both the intrinsic value and time value of embedded options and guarantees; and

(d)   a current market discount rate, even if that discount rate reflects the estimated return on the insurer's assets.

29   In some measurement approaches, the discount rate is used to determine the present value of a future profit margin. That profit margin is then attributed to different periods using a formula. In those approaches, the discount rate affects the measurement of the liability only indirectly. In particular, the use of a less appropriate discount rate has a limited or no effect on the measurement of the liability at inception. However, in other approaches, the discount rate determines the measurement of the liability directly. In the latter case, because the introduction of an asset-based discount rate has a more significant effect, it is highly unlikely that an insurer could overcome the rebuttable presumption described in paragraph 27.

Shadow accounting

30   In some accounting models, realised gains or losses on an insurer's assets have a direct effect on the measurement of some or all of (a) its insurance liabilities, (b) related deferred acquisition costs and (c) related intangible assets, such as those described in paragraphs 31 and 32. An insurer is permitted, but not required, to change its accounting policies so that a recognised but unrealised gain or loss on an asset affects those measurements in the same way that a realised gain or loss

does. The related adjustment to the insurance liability (or deferred acquisition costs or intangible assets) shall be recognised in other comprehensive income if, and only if, the unrealised gains or losses are recognised in other comprehensive income. This practice is sometimes described as 'shadow accounting'.

Insurance contracts acquired in a business combination or portfolio transfer

31 To comply with IFRS 3, an insurer shall, at the acquisition date, measure at fair value the insurance liabilities assumed and *insurance assets* acquired in a business combination. However, an insurer is permitted, but not required, to use an expanded presentation that splits the fair value of acquired insurance contracts into two components:

(a) a liability measured in accordance with the insurer's accounting policies for insurance contracts that it issues; and

(b) an intangible asset, representing the difference between (i) the fair value of the contractual insurance rights acquired and insurance obligations assumed and (ii) the amount described in (a). The subsequent measurement of this asset shall be consistent with the measurement of the related insurance liability.

32 An insurer acquiring a portfolio of insurance contracts may use the expanded presentation described in paragraph 31.

33 The intangible assets described in paragraphs 31 and 32 are excluded from the scope of IAS 36 *Impairment of Assets* and IAS 38. However, IAS 36 and IAS 38 apply to customer lists and customer relationships reflecting the expectation of future contracts that are not part of the contractual insurance rights and contractual insurance obligations that existed at the date of a business combination or portfolio transfer.

Discretionary participation features

Discretionary participation features in insurance contracts

34 Some insurance contracts contain a discretionary participation feature as well as a *guaranteed element*. The issuer of such a contract:

(a) may, but need not, recognise the guaranteed element separately from the discretionary participation feature. If the issuer does not recognise them separately, it shall classify the whole contract as a liability. If the issuer classifies them separately, it shall classify the guaranteed element as a liability.

(b) shall, if it recognises the discretionary participation feature separately from the guaranteed element, classify that feature as either a liability or a separate component of equity. This IFRS does not specify how the issuer determines whether that feature is a liability or equity. The issuer may split that feature into liability and equity components and shall use a consistent accounting policy for that split. The issuer shall not classify that feature as an intermediate category that is neither liability nor equity.

(c)   may recognise all premiums received as revenue without separating any portion that relates to the equity component. The resulting changes in the guaranteed element and in the portion of the discretionary participation feature classified as a liability shall be recognised in profit or loss. If part or all of the discretionary participation feature is classified in equity, a portion of profit or loss may be attributable to that feature (in the same way that a portion may be attributable to non-controlling interests). The issuer shall recognise the portion of profit or loss attributable to any equity component of a discretionary participation feature as an allocation of profit or loss, not as expense or income (see IAS 1 *Presentation of Financial Statements*).

(d)   shall, if the contract contains an embedded derivative within the scope of IFRS 9, apply IFRS 9 to that embedded derivative.

(e)   shall, in all respects not described in paragraphs 14–20 and 34(a)–(d), continue its existing accounting policies for such contracts, unless it changes those accounting policies in a way that complies with paragraphs 21–30.

Discretionary participation features in financial instruments

35   The requirements in paragraph 34 also apply to a financial instrument that contains a discretionary participation feature. In addition:

(a)   if the issuer classifies the entire discretionary participation feature as a liability, it shall apply the liability adequacy test in paragraphs 15–19 to the whole contract (ie both the guaranteed element and the discretionary participation feature). The issuer need not determine the amount that would result from applying IFRS 9 to the guaranteed element.

(b)   if the issuer classifies part or all of that feature as a separate component of equity, the liability recognised for the whole contract shall not be less than the amount that would result from applying IFRS 9 to the guaranteed element. That amount shall include the intrinsic value of an option to surrender the contract, but need not include its time value if paragraph 9 exempts that option from measurement at fair value. The issuer need not disclose the amount that would result from applying IFRS 9 to the guaranteed element, nor need it present that amount separately. Furthermore, the issuer need not determine that amount if the total liability recognised is clearly higher.

(c)   although these contracts are financial instruments, the issuer may continue to recognise the premiums for those contracts as revenue and recognise as an expense the resulting increase in the carrying amount of the liability.

(d)   although these contracts are financial instruments, an issuer applying paragraph 20(b) of IFRS 7 to contracts with a discretionary participation feature shall disclose the total interest expense recognised in profit or loss, but need not calculate such interest expense using the effective interest method.

Disclosure

Explanation of recognised amounts

36   **An insurer shall disclose information that identifies and explains the amounts in its financial statements arising from insurance contracts.**

37   To comply with paragraph 36, an insurer shall disclose:

(a)   its accounting policies for insurance contracts and related assets, liabilities, income and expense.

(b)   the recognised assets, liabilities, income and expense (and, if it presents its statement of cash flows using the direct method, cash flows) arising from insurance contracts.   Furthermore, if the insurer is a cedant, it shall disclose:

(i)   gains and losses recognised in profit or loss on buying reinsurance; and

(ii)   if the cedant defers and amortises gains and losses arising on buying reinsurance, the amortisation for the period and the amounts remaining unamortised at the beginning and end of the period.

(c)   the process used to determine the assumptions that have the greatest effect on the measurement of the recognised amounts described in (b). When practicable, an insurer shall also give quantified disclosure of those assumptions.

(d)   the effect of changes in assumptions used to measure insurance assets and insurance liabilities, showing separately the effect of each change that has a material effect on the financial statements.

(e)   reconciliations of changes in insurance liabilities, reinsurance assets and, if any, related deferred acquisition costs.

Nature and extent of risks arising from insurance contracts

38   **An insurer shall disclose information that enables users of its financial statements to evaluate the nature and extent of risks arising from insurance contracts.**

39   To comply with paragraph 38, an insurer shall disclose:

(a)   its objectives, policies and processes for managing risks arising from insurance contracts and the methods used to manage those risks.

(b)   [deleted]

(c)   information about *insurance risk* (both before and after risk mitigation by reinsurance), including information about:

(i)   sensitivity to insurance risk (see paragraph 39A).

(ii)   concentrations of insurance risk, including a description of how management determines concentrations and a description of the shared characteristic that identifies each concentration (eg type of insured event, geographical area, or currency).

      (iii)   actual claims compared with previous estimates (ie claims development). The disclosure about claims development shall go back to the period when the earliest material claim arose for which there is still uncertainty about the amount and timing of the claims payments, but need not go back more than ten years. An insurer need not disclose this information for claims for which uncertainty about the amount and timing of claims payments is typically resolved within one year.

(d)   information about credit risk, liquidity risk and market risk that paragraphs 31–42 of IFRS 7 would require if the insurance contracts were within the scope of IFRS 7. However:

      (i)   an insurer need not provide the maturity analyses required by paragraph 39(a) and (b) of IFRS 7 if it discloses information about the estimated timing of the net cash outflows resulting from recognised insurance liabilities instead. This may take the form of an analysis, by estimated timing, of the amounts recognised in the statement of financial position.

      (ii)   if an insurer uses an alternative method to manage sensitivity to market conditions, such as an embedded value analysis, it may use that sensitivity analysis to meet the requirement in paragraph 40(a) of IFRS 7. Such an insurer shall also provide the disclosures required by paragraph 41 of IFRS 7.

(e)   information about exposures to market risk arising from embedded derivatives contained in a host insurance contract if the insurer is not required to, and does not, measure the embedded derivatives at fair value.

39A   To comply with paragraph 39(c)(i), an insurer shall disclose either (a) or (b) as follows:

(a)   a sensitivity analysis that shows how profit or loss and equity would have been affected if changes in the relevant risk variable that were reasonably possible at the end of the reporting period had occurred; the methods and assumptions used in preparing the sensitivity analysis; and any changes from the previous period in the methods and assumptions used. However, if an insurer uses an alternative method to manage sensitivity to market conditions, such as an embedded value analysis, it may meet this requirement by disclosing that alternative sensitivity analysis and the disclosures required by paragraph 41 of IFRS 7.

(b)   qualitative information about sensitivity, and information about those terms and conditions of insurance contracts that have a material effect on the amount, timing and uncertainty of the insurer's future cash flows.

Effective date and transition

40   The transitional provisions in paragraphs 41–45 apply both to an entity that is already applying IFRSs when it first applies this IFRS and to an entity that applies IFRSs for the first time (a first-time adopter).

41　An entity shall apply this IFRS for annual periods beginning on or after 1 January 2005. Earlier application is encouraged. If an entity applies this IFRS for an earlier period, it shall disclose that fact.

41A　*Financial Guarantee Contracts* (Amendments to IAS 39 and IFRS 4), issued in August 2005, amended paragraphs 4(d), B18(g) and B19(f). An entity shall apply those amendments for annual periods beginning on or after 1 January 2006. Earlier application is encouraged. If an entity applies those amendments for an earlier period, it shall disclose that fact and apply the related amendments to IAS 39 and IAS 32[4] at the same time.

41B　IAS 1 (as revised in 2007) amended the terminology used throughout IFRSs. In addition it amended paragraph 30. An entity shall apply those amendments for annual periods beginning on or after 1 January 2009. If an entity applies IAS 1 (revised 2007) for an earlier period, the amendments shall be applied for that earlier period.

41C　[Deleted]

41D　IFRS 9, issued in October 2010, amended paragraphs 3, 4(d), 7, 8, 12, 34(d), 35, 45 and B18–B20 and Appendix A and deleted paragraph 41C. An entity shall apply those amendments when it applies IFRS 9 as issued in October 2010.

41E　IFRS 13 *Fair Value Measurement*, issued in May 2011, amended the definition of fair value in Appendix A. An entity shall apply that amendment when it applies IFRS 13.

Disclosure

42　An entity need not apply the disclosure requirements in this IFRS to comparative information that relates to annual periods beginning before 1 January 2005, except for the disclosures required by paragraph 37(a) and (b) about accounting policies, and recognised assets, liabilities, income and expense (and cash flows if the direct method is used).

43　If it is impracticable to apply a particular requirement of paragraphs 10–35 to comparative information that relates to annual periods beginning before 1 January 2005, an entity shall disclose that fact. Applying the liability adequacy test (paragraphs 15–19) to such comparative information might sometimes be impracticable, but it is highly unlikely to be impracticable to apply other requirements of paragraphs 10–35 to such comparative information. IAS 8 explains the term 'impracticable'.

44　In applying paragraph 39(c)(iii), an entity need not disclose information about claims development that occurred earlier than five years before the end of the first financial year in which it applies this IFRS. Furthermore, if it is impracticable, when an entity first applies this IFRS, to prepare information about claims development that occurred before the beginning of the earliest period for which an entity presents full comparative information that complies with this IFRS, the entity shall disclose that fact.

4　When an entity applies IFRS 7, the reference to IAS 32 is replaced by a reference to IFRS 7.

Redesignation of financial assets

45 Notwithstanding paragraph 4.4.1 of IFRS 9, when an insurer changes its accounting policies for insurance liabilities, it is permitted, but not required, to reclassify some or all of its financial assets so that they are measured at fair value. This reclassification is permitted if an insurer changes accounting policies when it first applies this IFRS and if it makes a subsequent policy change permitted by paragraph 22. The reclassification is a change in accounting policy and IAS 8 applies.

Appendix A
Defined terms

This appendix is an integral part of the IFRS.

cedant	The **policyholder** under a **reinsurance contract**.
deposit component	A contractual component that is not accounted for as a derivative under IFRS 9 and would be within the scope of IFRS 9 if it were a separate instrument.
direct insurance contract	An **insurance contract** that is not a **reinsurance contract**.

discretionary participation feature

A contractual right to receive, as a supplement to **guaranteed benefits**, additional benefits:

(a) that are likely to be a significant portion of the total contractual benefits;

(b) whose amount or timing is contractually at the discretion of the issuer; and

(c) that are contractually based on:

    (i) the performance of a specified pool of contracts or a specified type of contract;

    (ii) realised and/or unrealised investment returns on a specified pool of assets held by the issuer; or

    (iii) the profit or loss of the company, fund or other entity that issues the contract.

fair value	*Fair value* is the price that would be received to sell an asset or paid to transfer a liability in an orderly transaction between market participants at the measurement date. (See IFRS 13.)
financial guarantee contract	A contract that requires the issuer to make specified payments to reimburse the holder for a loss it incurs because a specified debtor fails to make payment when due in accordance with the original or modified terms of a debt instrument.
financial risk	The risk of a possible future change in one or more of a specified interest rate, financial instrument price, commodity price, foreign exchange rate, index of prices or rates, credit rating or credit index or other variable, provided in the case of a non-financial variable that the variable is not specific to a party to the contract.
guaranteed benefits	Payments or other benefits to which a particular **policyholder** or investor has an unconditional right that is not subject to the contractual discretion of the issuer.

guaranteed element	An obligation to pay **guaranteed benefits**, included in a contract that contains a **discretionary participation feature**.
insurance asset	An **insurer's** net contractual rights under an **insurance contract**.
insurance contract	A contract under which one party (the **insurer**) accepts significant **insurance risk** from another party (the **policyholder**) by agreeing to compensate the policyholder if a specified uncertain future event (the **insured event**) adversely affects the policyholder. (See Appendix B for guidance on this definition.)
insurance liability	An **insurer's** net contractual obligations under an **insurance contract**.
insurance risk	Risk, other than **financial risk**, transferred from the holder of a contract to the issuer.
insured event	An uncertain future event that is covered by an **insurance contract** and creates **insurance risk**.
insurer	The party that has an obligation under an **insurance contract** to compensate a **policyholder** if an **insured event** occurs.
liability adequacy test	An assessment of whether the carrying amount of an **insurance liability** needs to be increased (or the carrying amount of related deferred acquisition costs or related intangible assets decreased), based on a review of future cash flows.
policyholder	A party that has a right to compensation under an **insurance contract** if an **insured event** occurs.
reinsurance assets	A **cedant's** net contractual rights under a **reinsurance contract**.
reinsurance contract	An **insurance contract** issued by one insurer (the **reinsurer**) to compensate another insurer (the **cedant**) for losses on one or more contracts issued by the cedant.
reinsurer	The party that has an obligation under a **reinsurance contract** to compensate a **cedant** if an **insured event** occurs.
unbundle	Account for the components of a contract as if they were separate contracts.

Appendix B
Definition of an insurance contract

This appendix is an integral part of the IFRS.

B1   This appendix gives guidance on the definition of an insurance contract in Appendix A. It addresses the following issues:

   (a)   the term 'uncertain future event' (paragraphs B2–B4);

   (b)   payments in kind (paragraphs B5–B7);

   (c)   insurance risk and other risks (paragraphs B8–B17);

   (d)   examples of insurance contracts (paragraphs B18–B21);

   (e)   significant insurance risk (paragraphs B22–B28); and

   (f)   changes in the level of insurance risk (paragraphs B29 and B30).

Uncertain future event

B2   Uncertainty (or risk) is the essence of an insurance contract. Accordingly, at least one of the following is uncertain at the inception of an insurance contract:

   (a)   whether an *insured event* will occur;

   (b)   when it will occur; or

   (c)   how much the insurer will need to pay if it occurs.

B3   In some insurance contracts, the insured event is the discovery of a loss during the term of the contract, even if the loss arises from an event that occurred before the inception of the contract. In other insurance contracts, the insured event is an event that occurs during the term of the contract, even if the resulting loss is discovered after the end of the contract term.

B4   Some insurance contracts cover events that have already occurred, but whose financial effect is still uncertain. An example is a reinsurance contract that covers the direct insurer against adverse development of claims already reported by policyholders. In such contracts, the insured event is the discovery of the ultimate cost of those claims.

Payments in kind

B5   Some insurance contracts require or permit payments to be made in kind. An example is when the insurer replaces a stolen article directly, instead of reimbursing the policyholder. Another example is when an insurer uses its own hospitals and medical staff to provide medical services covered by the contracts.

B6   Some fixed-fee service contracts in which the level of service depends on an uncertain event meet the definition of an insurance contract in this IFRS but are not regulated as insurance contracts in some countries. One example is a maintenance contract in which the service provider agrees to repair specified equipment after a malfunction. The fixed service fee is based on the expected number of malfunctions, but it is uncertain whether a particular machine will break down. The malfunction of the equipment adversely affects its owner and the contract compensates the owner (in kind, rather than cash). Another example is a contract for car breakdown services in which the provider agrees, for a fixed annual fee, to provide roadside assistance or tow the car to a nearby garage. The latter contract could meet the definition of an insurance contract even if the provider does not agree to carry out repairs or replace parts.

B7 Applying the IFRS to the contracts described in paragraph B6 is likely to be no more burdensome than applying the IFRSs that would be applicable if such contracts were outside the scope of this IFRS:

(a) There are unlikely to be material liabilities for malfunctions and breakdowns that have already occurred.

(b) If IAS 18 *Revenue* applied, the service provider would recognise revenue by reference to the stage of completion (and subject to other specified criteria). That approach is also acceptable under this IFRS, which permits the service provider (i) to continue its existing accounting policies for these contracts unless they involve practices prohibited by paragraph 14 and (ii) to improve its accounting policies if so permitted by paragraphs 22–30.

(c) The service provider considers whether the cost of meeting its contractual obligation to provide services exceeds the revenue received in advance. To do this, it applies the liability adequacy test described in paragraphs 15–19 of this IFRS. If this IFRS did not apply to these contracts, the service provider would apply IAS 37 to determine whether the contracts are onerous.

(d) For these contracts, the disclosure requirements in this IFRS are unlikely to add significantly to disclosures required by other IFRSs.

Distinction between insurance risk and other risks

B8 The definition of an insurance contract refers to insurance risk, which this IFRS defines as risk, other than *financial risk*, transferred from the holder of a contract to the issuer. A contract that exposes the issuer to financial risk without significant insurance risk is not an insurance contract.

B9 The definition of financial risk in Appendix A includes a list of financial and non-financial variables. That list includes non-financial variables that are not specific to a party to the contract, such as an index of earthquake losses in a particular region or an index of temperatures in a particular city. It excludes non-financial variables that are specific to a party to the contract, such as the occurrence or non-occurrence of a fire that damages or destroys an asset of that party. Furthermore, the risk of changes in the fair value of a non-financial asset is not a financial risk if the fair value reflects not only changes in market prices for such assets (a financial variable) but also the condition of a specific non-financial asset held by a party to a contract (a non-financial variable). For example, if a guarantee of the residual value of a specific car exposes the guarantor to the risk of changes in the car's physical condition, that risk is insurance risk, not financial risk.

B10   Some contracts expose the issuer to financial risk, in addition to significant insurance risk. For example, many life insurance contracts both guarantee a minimum rate of return to policyholders (creating financial risk) and promise death benefits that at some times significantly exceed the policyholder's account balance (creating insurance risk in the form of mortality risk). Such contracts are insurance contracts.

B11   Under some contracts, an insured event triggers the payment of an amount linked to a price index. Such contracts are insurance contracts, provided the payment that is contingent on the insured event can be significant. For example, a life-contingent annuity linked to a cost-of-living index transfers insurance risk because payment is triggered by an uncertain event—the survival of the annuitant. The link to the price index is an embedded derivative, but it also transfers insurance risk. If the resulting transfer of insurance risk is significant, the embedded derivative meets the definition of an insurance contract, in which case it need not be separated and measured at fair value (see paragraph 7 of this IFRS).

B12   The definition of insurance risk refers to risk that the insurer accepts from the policyholder. In other words, insurance risk is a pre-existing risk transferred from the policyholder to the insurer. Thus, a new risk created by the contract is not insurance risk.

B13   The definition of an insurance contract refers to an adverse effect on the policyholder. The definition does not limit the payment by the insurer to an amount equal to the financial impact of the adverse event. For example, the definition does not exclude 'new-for-old' coverage that pays the policyholder sufficient to permit replacement of a damaged old asset by a new asset. Similarly, the definition does not limit payment under a term life insurance contract to the financial loss suffered by the deceased's dependants, nor does it preclude the payment of predetermined amounts to quantify the loss caused by death or an accident.

B14   Some contracts require a payment if a specified uncertain event occurs, but do not require an adverse effect on the policyholder as a precondition for payment. Such a contract is not an insurance contract even if the holder uses the contract to mitigate an underlying risk exposure. For example, if the holder uses a derivative to hedge an underlying non-financial variable that is correlated with cash flows from an asset of the entity, the derivative is not an insurance contract because payment is not conditional on whether the holder is adversely affected by a reduction in the cash flows from the asset. Conversely, the definition of an insurance contract refers to an uncertain event for which an adverse effect on the policyholder is a contractual precondition for payment. This contractual precondition does not require the insurer to investigate whether the event actually caused an adverse effect, but permits the insurer to deny payment if it is not satisfied that the event caused an adverse effect.

B15   Lapse or persistency risk (ie the risk that the counterparty will cancel the contract earlier or later than the issuer had expected in pricing the contract) is not insurance risk because the payment to the counterparty is not contingent on an uncertain future event that adversely affects the counterparty. Similarly, expense risk (ie the risk of unexpected increases in the administrative costs associated with the servicing of a contract, rather than in costs associated with insured events) is not insurance risk because an unexpected increase in expenses does not adversely affect the counterparty.

B16　Therefore, a contract that exposes the issuer to lapse risk, persistency risk or expense risk is not an insurance contract unless it also exposes the issuer to insurance risk. However, if the issuer of that contract mitigates that risk by using a second contract to transfer part of that risk to another party, the second contract exposes that other party to insurance risk.

B17　An insurer can accept significant insurance risk from the policyholder only if the insurer is an entity separate from the policyholder. In the case of a mutual insurer, the mutual accepts risk from each policyholder and pools that risk. Although policyholders bear that pooled risk collectively in their capacity as owners, the mutual has still accepted the risk that is the essence of an insurance contract.

Examples of insurance contracts

B18　The following are examples of contracts that are insurance contracts, if the transfer of insurance risk is significant:

(a)　insurance against theft or damage to property.

(b)　insurance against product liability, professional liability, civil liability or legal expenses.

(c)　life insurance and prepaid funeral plans (although death is certain, it is uncertain when death will occur or, for some types of life insurance, whether death will occur within the period covered by the insurance).

(d)　life-contingent annuities and pensions (ie contracts that provide compensation for the uncertain future event—the survival of the annuitant or pensioner—to assist the annuitant or pensioner in maintaining a given standard of living, which would otherwise be adversely affected by his or her survival).

(e)　disability and medical cover.

(f)　surety bonds, fidelity bonds, performance bonds and bid bonds (ie contracts that provide compensation if another party fails to perform a contractual obligation, for example an obligation to construct a building).

(g)　credit insurance that provides for specified payments to be made to reimburse the holder for a loss it incurs because a specified debtor fails to make payment when due under the original or modified terms of a debt instrument. These contracts could have various legal forms, such as that of a guarantee, some types of letter of credit, a credit derivative default contract or an insurance contract. However, although these contracts meet the definition of an insurance contract, they also meet the definition of a financial guarantee contract in IFRS 9 and are within the scope of IAS 32[5] and IFRS 9, not this IFRS (see paragraph 4(d)).

5　When an entity applies IFRS 7, the reference to IAS 32 is replaced by a reference to IFRS 7.

Nevertheless, if an issuer of financial guarantee contracts has previously asserted explicitly that it regards such contracts as insurance contracts and has used accounting applicable to insurance contracts, the issuer may elect to apply either IAS 32[6] and IFRS 9 or this IFRS to such financial guarantee contracts.

(h) product warranties. Product warranties issued by another party for goods sold by a manufacturer, dealer or retailer are within the scope of this IFRS. However, product warranties issued directly by a manufacturer, dealer or retailer are outside its scope, because they are within the scope of IAS 18 and IAS 37.

(i) title insurance (ie insurance against the discovery of defects in title to land that were not apparent when the insurance contract was written). In this case, the insured event is the discovery of a defect in the title, not the defect itself.

(j) travel assistance (ie compensation in cash or in kind to policyholders for losses suffered while they are travelling). Paragraphs B6 and B7 discuss some contracts of this kind.

(k) catastrophe bonds that provide for reduced payments of principal, interest or both if a specified event adversely affects the issuer of the bond (unless the specified event does not create significant insurance risk, for example if the event is a change in an interest rate or foreign exchange rate).

(l) insurance swaps and other contracts that require a payment based on changes in climatic, geological or other physical variables that are specific to a party to the contract.

(m) reinsurance contracts.

B19 The following are examples of items that are not insurance contracts:

(a) investment contracts that have the legal form of an insurance contract but do not expose the insurer to significant insurance risk, for example life insurance contracts in which the insurer bears no significant mortality risk (such contracts are non-insurance financial instruments or service contracts, see paragraphs B20 and B21).

(b) contracts that have the legal form of insurance, but pass all significant insurance risk back to the policyholder through non-cancellable and enforceable mechanisms that adjust future payments by the policyholder as a direct result of insured losses, for example some financial reinsurance contracts or some group contracts (such contracts are normally non-insurance financial instruments or service contracts, see paragraphs B20 and B21).

(c) self-insurance, in other words retaining a risk that could have been covered by insurance (there is no insurance contract because there is no agreement with another party).

---

6   When an entity applies IFRS 7, the reference to IAS 32 is replaced by a reference to IFRS 7.

(d) contracts (such as gambling contracts) that require a payment if a specified uncertain future event occurs, but do not require, as a contractual precondition for payment, that the event adversely affects the policyholder. However, this does not preclude the specification of a predetermined payout to quantify the loss caused by a specified event such as death or an accident (see also paragraph B13).

(e) derivatives that expose one party to financial risk but not insurance risk, because they require that party to make payment based solely on changes in one or more of a specified interest rate, financial instrument price, commodity price, foreign exchange rate, index of prices or rates, credit rating or credit index or other variable, provided in the case of a non-financial variable that the variable is not specific to a party to the contract (see IFRS 9).

(f) a credit-related guarantee (or letter of credit, credit derivative default contract or credit insurance contract) that requires payments even if the holder has not incurred a loss on the failure of the debtor to make payments when due (see IFRS 9).

(g) contracts that require a payment based on a climatic, geological or other physical variable that is not specific to a party to the contract (commonly described as weather derivatives).

(h) catastrophe bonds that provide for reduced payments of principal, interest or both, based on a climatic, geological or other physical variable that is not specific to a party to the contract.

B20 If the contracts described in paragraph B19 create financial assets or financial liabilities, they are within the scope of IFRS 9. Among other things, this means that the parties to the contract use what is sometimes called deposit accounting, which involves the following:

(a) one party recognises the consideration received as a financial liability, rather than as revenue.

(b) the other party recognises the consideration paid as a financial asset, rather than as an expense.

B21 If the contracts described in paragraph B19 do not create financial assets or financial liabilities, IAS 18 applies. Under IAS 18, revenue associated with a transaction involving the rendering of services is recognised by reference to the stage of completion of the transaction if the outcome of the transaction can be estimated reliably.

Significant insurance risk

B22 A contract is an insurance contract only if it transfers significant insurance risk. Paragraphs B8–B21 discuss insurance risk. The following paragraphs discuss the assessment of whether insurance risk is significant.

B23 Insurance risk is significant if, and only if, an insured event could cause an insurer to pay significant additional benefits in any scenario, excluding scenarios that lack commercial substance (ie have no discernible effect on the economics of the transaction). If significant additional benefits would be payable in scenarios that have commercial substance, the condition in the previous sentence may be met even if the insured event is extremely unlikely or even if the expected (ie probability-weighted) present value of contingent cash flows is a small proportion of the expected present value of all the remaining contractual cash flows.

B24 The additional benefits described in paragraph B23 refer to amounts that exceed those that would be payable if no insured event occurred (excluding scenarios that lack commercial substance). Those additional amounts include claims handling and claims assessment costs, but exclude:

(a) the loss of the ability to charge the policyholder for future services. For example, in an investment-linked life insurance contract, the death of the policyholder means that the insurer can no longer perform investment management services and collect a fee for doing so. However, this economic loss for the insurer does not reflect insurance risk, just as a mutual fund manager does not take on insurance risk in relation to the possible death of the client. Therefore, the potential loss of future investment management fees is not relevant in assessing how much insurance risk is transferred by a contract.

(b) waiver on death of charges that would be made on cancellation or surrender. Because the contract brought those charges into existence, the waiver of these charges does not compensate the policyholder for a pre-existing risk. Hence, they are not relevant in assessing how much insurance risk is transferred by a contract.

(c) a payment conditional on an event that does not cause a significant loss to the holder of the contract. For example, consider a contract that requires the issuer to pay one million currency units if an asset suffers physical damage causing an insignificant economic loss of one currency unit to the holder. In this contract, the holder transfers to the insurer the insignificant risk of losing one currency unit. At the same time, the contract creates non-insurance risk that the issuer will need to pay 999,999 currency units if the specified event occurs. Because the issuer does not accept significant insurance risk from the holder, this contract is not an insurance contract.

(d) possible reinsurance recoveries. The insurer accounts for these separately.

B25 An insurer shall assess the significance of insurance risk contract by contract, rather than by reference to materiality to the financial statements.[7] Thus, insurance risk may be significant even if there is a minimal probability of material losses for a whole book of contracts. This contract-by-contract assessment makes it easier to classify a contract as an insurance contract. However, if a relatively homogeneous book of small contracts is known to consist of contracts that all transfer insurance risk, an insurer need not examine each contract within that book to identify a few non-derivative contracts that transfer insignificant insurance risk.

---

[7] For this purpose, contracts entered into simultaneously with a single counterparty (or contracts that are otherwise interdependent) form a single contract.

B26 It follows from paragraphs B23–B25 that if a contract pays a death benefit exceeding the amount payable on survival, the contract is an insurance contract unless the additional death benefit is insignificant (judged by reference to the contract rather than to an entire book of contracts). As noted in paragraph B24(b), the waiver on death of cancellation or surrender charges is not included in this assessment if this waiver does not compensate the policyholder for a pre-existing risk. Similarly, an annuity contract that pays out regular sums for the rest of a policyholder's life is an insurance contract, unless the aggregate life-contingent payments are insignificant.

B27 Paragraph B23 refers to additional benefits. These additional benefits could include a requirement to pay benefits earlier if the insured event occurs earlier and the payment is not adjusted for the time value of money. An example is whole life insurance for a fixed amount (in other words, insurance that provides a fixed death benefit whenever the policyholder dies, with no expiry date for the cover). It is certain that the policyholder will die, but the date of death is uncertain. The insurer will suffer a loss on those individual contracts for which policyholders die early, even if there is no overall loss on the whole book of contracts.

B28 If an insurance contract is unbundled into a deposit component and an insurance component, the significance of insurance risk transfer is assessed by reference to the insurance component. The significance of insurance risk transferred by an embedded derivative is assessed by reference to the embedded derivative.

Changes in the level of insurance risk

B29 Some contracts do not transfer any insurance risk to the issuer at inception, although they do transfer insurance risk at a later time. For example, consider a contract that provides a specified investment return and includes an option for the policyholder to use the proceeds of the investment on maturity to buy a life-contingent annuity at the current annuity rates charged by the insurer to other new annuitants when the policyholder exercises the option. The contract transfers no insurance risk to the issuer until the option is exercised, because the insurer remains free to price the annuity on a basis that reflects the insurance risk transferred to the insurer at that time. However, if the contract specifies the annuity rates (or a basis for setting the annuity rates), the contract transfers insurance risk to the issuer at inception.

B30 A contract that qualifies as an insurance contract remains an insurance contract until all rights and obligations are extinguished or expire.

Appendix C
Amendments to other IFRSs

The amendments in this appendix shall be applied for annual periods beginning on or after 1 January 2005. If an entity adopts this IFRS for an earlier period, these amendments shall be applied for that earlier period.

* * * * *

The amendments contained in this appendix when this IFRS was issued in 2004 have been incorporated into the relevant IFRSs published in this volume.

International Financial Reporting Standard 5

Non-current Assets Held for Sale and Discontinued Operations

In April 2001 the International Accounting Standards Board (IASB) adopted IAS 35 *Discontinuing Operations*, which had originally been issued by the International Accounting Standards Committee in June 1998.

In March 2004 the IASB issued IFRS 5 *Non-current Assets Held for Sale and Discontinued Operations* to replace IAS 35.

Other IFRSs have made minor consequential amendments to IFRS 5. They include IFRS 3 *Business Combinations* (as revised in January 2008), *Improvements to IFRSs* (issued May 2008 and April 2009), IFRIC 17 *Distributions of Non-cash Assets to Owners* (issued November 2008) and IFRS 9 *Financial Instruments* (issued November 2009 and October 2010).

CONTENTS

FOR THE ACCOMPANYING DOCUMENTS LISTED BELOW, SEE PART B OF THIS EDITION

APPROVAL BY THE BOARD OF IFRS 5 ISSUED IN MARCH 2004

BASIS FOR CONCLUSIONS

DISSENTING OPINIONS

IMPLEMENTATION GUIDANCE

International Financial Reporting Standard 5 *Non-current Assets Held for Sale and Discontinued Operations* (IFRS 5) is set out in paragraphs 1–45 and Appendices A–C. All the paragraphs have equal authority. Paragraphs in **bold type** state the main principles. Terms defined in Appendix A are in *italics* the first time they appear in the Standard. Definitions of other terms are given in the Glossary for International Financial Reporting Standards. IFRS 5 should be read in the context of its objective and the Basis for Conclusions, the *Preface to International Financial Reporting Standards* and the *Conceptual Framework for Financial Reporting*. IAS 8 *Accounting Policies, Changes in Accounting Estimates and Errors* provides a basis for selecting and applying accounting policies in the absence of explicit guidance.

Introduction

Reasons for issuing the IFRS

IN1   International Financial Reporting Standard 5 *Non-current Assets Held for Sale and Discontinued Operations* (IFRS 5) sets out requirements for the classification, measurement and presentation of non-current assets held for sale and replaces IAS 35 *Discontinuing Operations*.

IN2   Achieving convergence of accounting standards around the world is one of the prime objectives of the International Accounting Standards Board. In pursuit of that objective, one of the strategies adopted by the Board has been to enter into a memorandum of understanding with the Financial Accounting Standards Board (FASB) in the United States that sets out the two boards' commitment to convergence. As a result of that understanding the boards have undertaken a joint short-term project with the objective of reducing differences between IFRSs and US GAAP that are capable of resolution in a relatively short time and can be addressed outside major projects.

IN3   One aspect of that project involves the two boards considering each other's recent standards with a view to adopting high quality accounting solutions. The IFRS arises from the IASB's consideration of FASB Statement No. 144 *Accounting for the Impairment or Disposal of Long-Lived Assets* (SFAS 144), issued in 2001.

IN4   SFAS 144 addresses three areas: (i) the impairment of long-lived assets to be held and used, (ii) the classification, measurement and presentation of assets held for sale and (iii) the classification and presentation of discontinued operations. The impairment of long-lived assets to be held and used is an area in which there are extensive differences between IFRSs and US GAAP. However, those differences were not thought to be capable of resolution in a relatively short time. Convergence on the other two areas was thought to be worth pursuing within the context of the short-term project.

IN5   The IFRS achieves substantial convergence with the requirements of SFAS 144 relating to assets held for sale, the timing of the classification of operations as discontinued and the presentation of such operations.

Main features of the IFRS

IN6   The IFRS:

(a)   adopts the classification 'held for sale'.

(b)   introduces the concept of a disposal group, being a group of assets to be disposed of, by sale or otherwise, together as a group in a single transaction, and liabilities directly associated with those assets that will be transferred in the transaction.

(c)   specifies that assets or disposal groups that are classified as held for sale are carried at the lower of carrying amount and fair value less costs to sell.

(d) specifies that an asset classified as held for sale, or included within a disposal group that is classified as held for sale, is not depreciated.

(e) specifies that an asset classified as held for sale, and the assets and liabilities included within a disposal group classified as held for sale, are presented separately in the statement of financial position.

(f) withdraws IAS 35 *Discontinuing Operations* and replaces it with requirements that:

(i) change the timing of the classification of an operation as discontinued. IAS 35 classified an operation as discontinuing at the earlier of (a) the entity entering into a binding sale agreement and (b) the board of directors approving and announcing a formal disposal plan. The IFRS classifies an operation as discontinued at the date the operation meets the criteria to be classified as held for sale or when the entity has disposed of the operation.

(ii) specify that the results of discontinued operations are to be shown separately in the statement of comprehensive income.

(iii) prohibit retroactive classification of an operation as discontinued, when the criteria for that classification are not met until after the reporting period.

International Financial Reporting Standard 5
Non-current Assets Held for Sale and Discontinued Operations

Objective

1   The objective of this IFRS is to specify the accounting for assets held for sale, and the presentation and disclosure of *discontinued operations*. In particular, the IFRS requires:

(a)   assets that meet the criteria to be classified as held for sale to be measured at the lower of carrying amount and *fair value* less *costs to sell*, and depreciation on such assets to cease; and

(b)   assets that meet the criteria to be classified as held for sale to be presented separately in the statement of financial position and the results of discontinued operations to be presented separately in the statement of comprehensive income.

Scope

2   The classification and presentation requirements of this IFRS apply to all recognised *non-current assets*[1] and to all *disposal groups* of an entity. The measurement requirements of this IFRS apply to all recognised non-current assets and disposal groups (as set out in paragraph 4), except for those assets listed in paragraph 5 which shall continue to be measured in accordance with the Standard noted.

3   Assets classified as non-current in accordance with IAS 1 *Presentation of Financial Statements* shall not be reclassified as *current assets* until they meet the criteria to be classified as held for sale in accordance with this IFRS. Assets of a class that an entity would normally regard as non-current that are acquired exclusively with a view to resale shall not be classified as current unless they meet the criteria to be classified as held for sale in accordance with this IFRS.

4   Sometimes an entity disposes of a group of assets, possibly with some directly associated liabilities, together in a single transaction. Such a disposal group may be a group of *cash-generating units*, a single cash-generating unit, or part of a cash-generating unit.[2] The group may include any assets and any liabilities of the entity, including current assets, current liabilities and assets excluded by paragraph 5 from the measurement requirements of this IFRS. If a non-current asset within the scope of the measurement requirements of this IFRS is part of a disposal group, the measurement requirements of this IFRS apply to the group as

---

1   For assets classified according to a liquidity presentation, non-current assets are assets that include amounts expected to be recovered more than twelve months after the reporting period. Paragraph 3 applies to the classification of such assets.

2   However, once the cash flows from an asset or group of assets are expected to arise principally from sale rather than continuing use, they become less dependent on cash flows arising from other assets, and a disposal group that was part of a cash-generating unit becomes a separate cash-generating unit.

a whole, so that the group is measured at the lower of its carrying amount and fair value less costs to sell. The requirements for measuring the individual assets and liabilities within the disposal group are set out in paragraphs 18, 19 and 23.

5   The measurement provisions of this IFRS[3] do not apply to the following assets, which are covered by the IFRSs listed, either as individual assets or as part of a disposal group:

(a)   deferred tax assets (IAS 12 *Income Taxes*).

(b)   assets arising from employee benefits (IAS 19 *Employee Benefits*).

(c)   financial assets within the scope of IFRS 9 *Financial Instruments*.

(d)   non-current assets that are accounted for in accordance with the fair value model in IAS 40 *Investment Property*.

(e)   non-current assets that are measured at fair value less costs to sell in accordance with IAS 41 *Agriculture*.

(f)   contractual rights under insurance contracts as defined in IFRS 4 *Insurance Contracts*.

5A   The classification, presentation and measurement requirements in this IFRS applicable to a non-current asset (or disposal group) that is classified as held for sale apply also to a non-current asset (or disposal group) that is classified as held for distribution to owners acting in their capacity as owners (held for distribution to owners).

5B   This IFRS specifies the disclosures required in respect of non-current assets (or disposal groups) classified as held for sale or discontinued operations. Disclosures in other IFRSs do not apply to such assets (or disposal groups) unless those IFRSs require:

(a)   specific disclosures in respect of non-current assets (or disposal groups) classified as held for sale or discontinued operations; or

(b)   disclosures about measurement of assets and liabilities within a disposal group that are not within the scope of the measurement requirement of IFRS 5 and such disclosures are not already provided in the other notes to the financial statements.

Additional disclosures about non-current assets (or disposal groups) classified as held for sale or discontinued operations may be necessary to comply with the general requirements of IAS 1, in particular paragraphs 15 and 125 of that Standard.

---

3   Other than paragraphs 18 and 19, which require the assets in question to be measured in accordance with other applicable IFRSs.

Classification of non-current assets (or disposal groups) as held for sale or as held for distribution to owners

6   **An entity shall classify a non-current asset (or disposal group) as held for sale if its carrying amount will be recovered principally through a sale transaction rather than through continuing use.**

7   For this to be the case, the asset (or disposal group) must be available for immediate sale in its present condition subject only to terms that are usual and customary for sales of such assets (or disposal groups) and its sale must be *highly probable*.

8   For the sale to be highly probable, the appropriate level of management must be committed to a plan to sell the asset (or disposal group), and an active programme to locate a buyer and complete the plan must have been initiated. Further, the asset (or disposal group) must be actively marketed for sale at a price that is reasonable in relation to its current fair value. In addition, the sale should be expected to qualify for recognition as a completed sale within one year from the date of classification, except as permitted by paragraph 9, and actions required to complete the plan should indicate that it is unlikely that significant changes to the plan will be made or that the plan will be withdrawn. The probability of shareholders' approval (if required in the jurisdiction) should be considered as part of the assessment of whether the sale is highly probable.

8A   An entity that is committed to a sale plan involving loss of control of a subsidiary shall classify all the assets and liabilities of that subsidiary as held for sale when the criteria set out in paragraphs 6–8 are met, regardless of whether the entity will retain a non-controlling interest in its former subsidiary after the sale.

9   Events or circumstances may extend the period to complete the sale beyond one year. An extension of the period required to complete a sale does not preclude an asset (or disposal group) from being classified as held for sale if the delay is caused by events or circumstances beyond the entity's control and there is sufficient evidence that the entity remains committed to its plan to sell the asset (or disposal group). This will be the case when the criteria in Appendix B are met.

10   Sale transactions include exchanges of non-current assets for other non-current assets when the exchange has commercial substance in accordance with IAS 16 *Property, Plant and Equipment*.

11   When an entity acquires a non-current asset (or disposal group) exclusively with a view to its subsequent disposal, it shall classify the non-current asset (or disposal group) as held for sale at the acquisition date only if the one-year requirement in paragraph 8 is met (except as permitted by paragraph 9) and it is highly probable that any other criteria in paragraphs 7 and 8 that are not met at that date will be met within a short period following the acquisition (usually within three months).

12   If the criteria in paragraphs 7 and 8 are met after the reporting period, an entity shall not classify a non-current asset (or disposal group) as held for sale in those financial statements when issued. However, when those criteria are met after the reporting period but before the authorisation of the financial statements for issue, the entity shall disclose the information specified in paragraph 41(a), (b) and (d) in the notes.

12A   A non-current asset (or disposal group) is classified as held for distribution to owners when the entity is committed to distribute the asset (or disposal group) to the owners. For this to be the case, the assets must be available for immediate distribution in their present condition and the distribution must be highly probable. For the distribution to be highly probable, actions to complete the distribution must have been initiated and should be expected to be completed within one year from the date of classification. Actions required to complete the distribution should indicate that it is unlikely that significant changes to the distribution will be made or that the distribution will be withdrawn. The probability of shareholders' approval (if required in the jurisdiction) should be considered as part of the assessment of whether the distribution is highly probable.

Non-current assets that are to be abandoned

13   An entity shall not classify as held for sale a non-current asset (or disposal group) that is to be abandoned. This is because its carrying amount will be recovered principally through continuing use. However, if the disposal group to be abandoned meets the criteria in paragraph 32(a)–(c), the entity shall present the results and cash flows of the disposal group as discontinued operations in accordance with paragraphs 33 and 34 at the date on which it ceases to be used. Non-current assets (or disposal groups) to be abandoned include non-current assets (or disposal groups) that are to be used to the end of their economic life and non-current assets (or disposal groups) that are to be closed rather than sold.

14   An entity shall not account for a non-current asset that has been temporarily taken out of use as if it had been abandoned.

Measurement of non-current assets (or disposal groups) classified as held for sale

Measurement of a non-current asset (or disposal group)

15   **An entity shall measure a non-current asset (or disposal group) classified as held for sale at the lower of its carrying amount and fair value less costs to sell.**

15A   **An entity shall measure a non-current asset (or disposal group) classified as held for distribution to owners at the lower of its carrying amount and fair value less costs to distribute.[4]**

16   If a newly acquired asset (or disposal group) meets the criteria to be classified as held for sale (see paragraph 11), applying paragraph 15 will result in the asset (or disposal group) being measured on initial recognition at the lower of its carrying amount had it not been so classified (for example, cost) and fair value less costs to sell. Hence, if the asset (or disposal group) is acquired as part of a business combination, it shall be measured at fair value less costs to sell.

---

4   Costs to distribute are the incremental costs directly attributable to the distribution, excluding finance costs and income tax expense.

17   When the sale is expected to occur beyond one year, the entity shall measure the costs to sell at their present value. Any increase in the present value of the costs to sell that arises from the passage of time shall be presented in profit or loss as a financing cost.

18   Immediately before the initial classification of the asset (or disposal group) as held for sale, the carrying amounts of the asset (or all the assets and liabilities in the group) shall be measured in accordance with applicable IFRSs.

19   On subsequent remeasurement of a disposal group, the carrying amounts of any assets and liabilities that are not within the scope of the measurement requirements of this IFRS, but are included in a disposal group classified as held for sale, shall be remeasured in accordance with applicable IFRSs before the fair value less costs to sell of the disposal group is remeasured.

Recognition of impairment losses and reversals

20   An entity shall recognise an impairment loss for any initial or subsequent write-down of the asset (or disposal group) to fair value less costs to sell, to the extent that it has not been recognised in accordance with paragraph 19.

21   An entity shall recognise a gain for any subsequent increase in fair value less costs to sell of an asset, but not in excess of the cumulative impairment loss that has been recognised either in accordance with this IFRS or previously in accordance with IAS 36 *Impairment of Assets*.

22   An entity shall recognise a gain for any subsequent increase in fair value less costs to sell of a disposal group:

(a)   to the extent that it has not been recognised in accordance with paragraph 19; but

(b)   not in excess of the cumulative impairment loss that has been recognised, either in accordance with this IFRS or previously in accordance with IAS 36, on the non-current assets that are within the scope of the measurement requirements of this IFRS.

23   The impairment loss (or any subsequent gain) recognised for a disposal group shall reduce (or increase) the carrying amount of the non-current assets in the group that are within the scope of the measurement requirements of this IFRS, in the order of allocation set out in paragraphs 104(a) and (b) and 122 of IAS 36 (as revised in 2004).

24   A gain or loss not previously recognised by the date of the sale of a non-current asset (or disposal group) shall be recognised at the date of derecognition. Requirements relating to derecognition are set out in:

(a)   paragraphs 67–72 of IAS 16 (as revised in 2003) for property, plant and equipment, and

(b)   paragraphs 112–117 of IAS 38 *Intangible Assets* (as revised in 2004) for intangible assets.

25   An entity shall not depreciate (or amortise) a non-current asset while it is classified as held for sale or while it is part of a disposal group classified as held for sale. Interest and other expenses attributable to the liabilities of a disposal group classified as held for sale shall continue to be recognised.

Changes to a plan of sale

26   If an entity has classified an asset (or disposal group) as held for sale, but the criteria in paragraphs 7–9 are no longer met, the entity shall cease to classify the asset (or disposal group) as held for sale.

27   The entity shall measure a non-current asset that ceases to be classified as held for sale (or ceases to be included in a disposal group classified as held for sale) at the lower of:

(a)   its carrying amount before the asset (or disposal group) was classified as held for sale, adjusted for any depreciation, amortisation or revaluations that would have been recognised had the asset (or disposal group) not been classified as held for sale, and

(b)   its *recoverable amount* at the date of the subsequent decision not to sell.[5]

28   The entity shall include any required adjustment to the carrying amount of a non-current asset that ceases to be classified as held for sale in profit or loss[6] from continuing operations in the period in which the criteria in paragraphs 7–9 are no longer met. Financial statements for the periods since classification as held for sale shall be amended accordingly if the disposal group or non-current asset that ceases to be classified as held for sale is a subsidiary, joint operation, joint venture, associate, or a portion of an interest in a joint venture or an associate. The entity shall present that adjustment in the same caption in the statement of comprehensive income used to present a gain or loss, if any, recognised in accordance with paragraph 37.

29   If an entity removes an individual asset or liability from a disposal group classified as held for sale, the remaining assets and liabilities of the disposal group to be sold shall continue to be measured as a group only if the group meets the criteria in paragraphs 7–9. Otherwise, the remaining non-current assets of the group that individually meet the criteria to be classified as held for sale shall be measured individually at the lower of their carrying amounts and fair values less costs to sell at that date. Any non-current assets that do not meet the criteria shall cease to be classified as held for sale in accordance with paragraph 26.

---

5   If the non-current asset is part of a cash-generating unit, its recoverable amount is the carrying amount that would have been recognised after the allocation of any impairment loss arising on that cash-generating unit in accordance with IAS 36.

6   Unless the asset is property, plant and equipment or an intangible asset that had been revalued in accordance with IAS 16 or IAS 38 before classification as held for sale, in which case the adjustment shall be treated as a revaluation increase or decrease.

Presentation and disclosure

30 An entity shall present and disclose information that enables users of the financial statements to evaluate the financial effects of discontinued operations and disposals of non-current assets (or disposal groups).

Presenting discontinued operations

31 A *component of an entity* comprises operations and cash flows that can be clearly distinguished, operationally and for financial reporting purposes, from the rest of the entity. In other words, a component of an entity will have been a cash-generating unit or a group of cash-generating units while being held for use.

32 A discontinued operation is a component of an entity that either has been disposed of, or is classified as held for sale, and

 (a) represents a separate major line of business or geographical area of operations,

 (b) is part of a single co-ordinated plan to dispose of a separate major line of business or geographical area of operations or

 (c) is a subsidiary acquired exclusively with a view to resale.

33 An entity shall disclose:

 (a) a single amount in the statement of comprehensive income comprising the total of:

  (i) the post-tax profit or loss of discontinued operations and

  (ii) the post-tax gain or loss recognised on the measurement to fair value less costs to sell or on the disposal of the assets or disposal group(s) constituting the discontinued operation.

 (b) an analysis of the single amount in (a) into:

  (i) the revenue, expenses and pre-tax profit or loss of discontinued operations;

  (ii) the related income tax expense as required by paragraph 81(h) of IAS 12;

  (iii) the gain or loss recognised on the measurement to fair value less costs to sell or on the disposal of the assets or disposal group(s) constituting the discontinued operation; and

  (iv) the related income tax expense as required by paragraph 81(h) of IAS 12.

 The analysis may be presented in the notes or in the statement of comprehensive income. If it is presented in the statement of comprehensive income it shall be presented in a section identified as relating to discontinued operations, ie separately from continuing operations. The analysis is not required for disposal groups that are newly acquired subsidiaries that meet the criteria to be classified as held for sale on acquisition (see paragraph 11).

(c)   the net cash flows attributable to the operating, investing and financing activities of discontinued operations. These disclosures may be presented either in the notes or in the financial statements. These disclosures are not required for disposal groups that are newly acquired subsidiaries that meet the criteria to be classified as held for sale on acquisition (see paragraph 11).

(d)   the amount of income from continuing operations and from discontinued operations attributable to owners of the parent. These disclosures may be presented either in the notes or in the statement of comprehensive income.

33A   If an entity presents the items of profit or loss in a separate statement as described in paragraph 10A of IAS 1 (as amended in 2011), a section identified as relating to discontinued operations is presented in that statement.

34   An entity shall re-present the disclosures in paragraph 33 for prior periods presented in the financial statements so that the disclosures relate to all operations that have been discontinued by the end of the reporting period for the latest period presented.

35   Adjustments in the current period to amounts previously presented in discontinued operations that are directly related to the disposal of a discontinued operation in a prior period shall be classified separately in discontinued operations. The nature and amount of such adjustments shall be disclosed. Examples of circumstances in which these adjustments may arise include the following:

(a)   the resolution of uncertainties that arise from the terms of the disposal transaction, such as the resolution of purchase price adjustments and indemnification issues with the purchaser.

(b)   the resolution of uncertainties that arise from and are directly related to the operations of the component before its disposal, such as environmental and product warranty obligations retained by the seller.

(c)   the settlement of employee benefit plan obligations, provided that the settlement is directly related to the disposal transaction.

36   If an entity ceases to classify a component of an entity as held for sale, the results of operations of the component previously presented in discontinued operations in accordance with paragraphs 33–35 shall be reclassified and included in income from continuing operations for all periods presented. The amounts for prior periods shall be described as having been re-presented.

36A   An entity that is committed to a sale plan involving loss of control of a subsidiary shall disclose the information required in paragraphs 33–36 when the subsidiary is a disposal group that meets the definition of a discontinued operation in accordance with paragraph 32.

Gains or losses relating to continuing operations

37   Any gain or loss on the remeasurement of a non-current asset (or disposal group) classified as held for sale that does not meet the definition of a discontinued operation shall be included in profit or loss from continuing operations.

Presentation of a non-current asset or disposal group classified as held for sale

38   An entity shall present a non-current asset classified as held for sale and the assets of a disposal group classified as held for sale separately from other assets in the statement of financial position. The liabilities of a disposal group classified as held for sale shall be presented separately from other liabilities in the statement of financial position. Those assets and liabilities shall not be offset and presented as a single amount. The major classes of assets and liabilities classified as held for sale shall be separately disclosed either in the statement of financial position or in the notes, except as permitted by paragraph 39. An entity shall present separately any cumulative income or expense recognised in other comprehensive income relating to a non-current asset (or disposal group) classified as held for sale.

39   If the disposal group is a newly acquired subsidiary that meets the criteria to be classified as held for sale on acquisition (see paragraph 11), disclosure of the major classes of assets and liabilities is not required.

40   An entity shall not reclassify or re-present amounts presented for non-current assets or for the assets and liabilities of disposal groups classified as held for sale in the statements of financial position for prior periods to reflect the classification in the statement of financial position for the latest period presented.

Additional disclosures

41   An entity shall disclose the following information in the notes in the period in which a non-current asset (or disposal group) has been either classified as held for sale or sold:

(a)   a description of the non-current asset (or disposal group);

(b)   a description of the facts and circumstances of the sale, or leading to the expected disposal, and the expected manner and timing of that disposal;

(c)   the gain or loss recognised in accordance with paragraphs 20–22 and, if not separately presented in the statement of comprehensive income, the caption in the statement of comprehensive income that includes that gain or loss;

(d)   if applicable, the reportable segment in which the non-current asset (or disposal group) is presented in accordance with IFRS 8 *Operating Segments*.

42   If either paragraph 26 or paragraph 29 applies, an entity shall disclose, in the period of the decision to change the plan to sell the non-current asset (or disposal group), a description of the facts and circumstances leading to the decision and the effect of the decision on the results of operations for the period and any prior periods presented.

Transitional provisions

43 The IFRS shall be applied prospectively to non-current assets (or disposal groups) that meet the criteria to be classified as held for sale and operations that meet the criteria to be classified as discontinued after the effective date of the IFRS. An entity may apply the requirements of the IFRS to all non-current assets (or disposal groups) that meet the criteria to be classified as held for sale and operations that meet the criteria to be classified as discontinued after any date before the effective date of the IFRS, provided the valuations and other information needed to apply the IFRS were obtained at the time those criteria were originally met.

Effective date

44 An entity shall apply this IFRS for annual periods beginning on or after 1 January 2005. Earlier application is encouraged. If an entity applies the IFRS for a period beginning before 1 January 2005, it shall disclose that fact.

44A IAS 1 (as revised in 2007) amended the terminology used throughout IFRSs. In addition it amended paragraphs 3 and 38, and added paragraph 33A. An entity shall apply those amendments for annual periods beginning on or after 1 January 2009. If an entity applies IAS 1 (revised 2007) for an earlier period, the amendments shall be applied for that earlier period.

44B IAS 27 *Consolidated and Separate Financial Statements* (as amended in 2008) added paragraph 33(d). An entity shall apply that amendment for annual periods beginning on or after 1 July 2009. If an entity applies IAS 27 (amended 2008) for an earlier period, the amendment shall be applied for that earlier period. The amendment shall be applied retrospectively.

44C Paragraphs 8A and 36A were added by *Improvements to IFRSs* issued in May 2008. An entity shall apply those amendments for annual periods beginning on or after 1 July 2009. Earlier application is permitted. However, an entity shall not apply the amendments for annual periods beginning before 1 July 2009 unless it also applies IAS 27 (as amended in January 2008). If an entity applies the amendments before 1 July 2009 it shall disclose that fact. An entity shall apply the amendments prospectively from the date at which it first applied IFRS 5, subject to the transitional provisions in paragraph 45 of IAS 27 (amended January 2008).

44D Paragraphs 5A, 12A and 15A were added and paragraph 8 was amended by IFRIC 17 *Distributions of Non-cash Assets to Owners* in November 2008. Those amendments shall be applied prospectively to non-current assets (or disposal groups) that are classified as held for distribution to owners in annual periods beginning on or after 1 July 2009. Retrospective application is not permitted. Earlier application is permitted. If an entity applies the amendments for a period beginning before 1 July 2009 it shall disclose that fact and also apply IFRS 3 *Business Combinations* (as revised in 2008), IAS 27 (as amended in January 2008) and IFRIC 17.

44E   Paragraph 5B was added by *Improvements to IFRSs* issued in April 2009. An entity shall apply that amendment prospectively for annual periods beginning on or after 1 January 2010. Earlier application is permitted. If an entity applies the amendment for an earlier period it shall disclose that fact.

44F   IFRS 9, issued in October 2010, amended paragraph 5. An entity shall apply that amendment when it applies IFRS 9 as issued in October 2010.

44G   IFRS 11 *Joint Arrangements*, issued in May 2011, amended paragraph 28. An entity shall apply that amendment when it applies IFRS 11.

44H   IFRS 13 *Fair Value Measurement*, issued in May 2011, amended the definition of fair value in Appendix A. An entity shall apply that amendment when it applies IFRS 13.

44I   *Presentation of Items of Other Comprehensive Income* (Amendments to IAS 1), issued in June 2011, amended paragraph 33A. An entity shall apply that amendment when it applies IAS 1 as amended in June 2011.

Withdrawal of IAS 35

45   This IFRS supersedes IAS 35 *Discontinuing Operations*.

Appendix A
Defined terms

This appendix is an integral part of the IFRS.

cash-generating unit	The smallest identifiable group of assets that generates cash inflows that are largely independent of the cash inflows from other assets or groups of assets.
component of an entity	Operations and cash flows that can be clearly distinguished, operationally and for financial reporting purposes, from the rest of the entity.
costs to sell	The incremental costs directly attributable to the disposal of an asset (or **disposal group**), excluding finance costs and income tax expense.
current asset	An entity shall classify an asset as current when:

    (a)   it expects to realise the asset, or intends to sell or consume it, in its normal operating cycle;

    (b)   it holds the asset primarily for the purpose of trading;

    (c)   it expects to realise the asset within twelve months after the reporting period; or

    (d)   the asset is cash or a cash equivalent (as defined in IAS 7) unless the asset is restricted from being exchanged or used to settle a liability for at least twelve months after the reporting period.

discontinued operation	A **component of an entity** that either has been disposed of or is classified as held for sale and:

    (a)   represents a separate major line of business or geographical area of operations,

    (b)   is part of a single co-ordinated plan to dispose of a separate major line of business or geographical area of operations or

    (c)   is a subsidiary acquired exclusively with a view to resale.

disposal group	A group of assets to be disposed of, by sale or otherwise, together as a group in a single transaction, and liabilities directly associated with those assets that will be transferred in the transaction. The group includes goodwill acquired in a business combination if the group is a **cash-generating unit** to which goodwill has been allocated in accordance with the requirements of paragraphs 80–87 of IAS 36 *Impairment of Assets* (as revised in 2004) or if it is an operation within such a cash-generating unit.
fair value	*Fair value* is the price that would be received to sell an asset or paid to transfer a liability in an orderly transaction between market participants at the measurement date. (See IFRS 13.)

firm purchase commitment	An agreement with an unrelated party, binding on both parties and usually legally enforceable, that (a) specifies all significant terms, including the price and timing of the transactions, and (b) includes a disincentive for non-performance that is sufficiently large to make performance **highly probable.**
highly probable	Significantly more likely than **probable**.
non-current asset	An asset that does not meet the definition of a **current asset**.
probable	More likely than not.
recoverable amount	The higher of an asset's **fair value** less **costs to sell** and its **value in use**.
value in use	The present value of estimated future cash flows expected to arise from the continuing use of an asset and from its disposal at the end of its useful life.

Appendix B
Application supplement

This appendix is an integral part of the IFRS.

Extension of the period required to complete a sale

B1   As noted in paragraph 9, an extension of the period required to complete a sale does not preclude an asset (or disposal group) from being classified as held for sale if the delay is caused by events or circumstances beyond the entity's control and there is sufficient evidence that the entity remains committed to its plan to sell the asset (or disposal group). An exception to the one-year requirement in paragraph 8 shall therefore apply in the following situations in which such events or circumstances arise:

   (a)   at the date an entity commits itself to a plan to sell a non-current asset (or disposal group) it reasonably expects that others (not a buyer) will impose conditions on the transfer of the asset (or disposal group) that will extend the period required to complete the sale, and:

      (i)   actions necessary to respond to those conditions cannot be initiated until after a *firm purchase commitment* is obtained, and

      (ii)   a firm purchase commitment is highly probable within one year.

   (b)   an entity obtains a firm purchase commitment and, as a result, a buyer or others unexpectedly impose conditions on the transfer of a non-current asset (or disposal group) previously classified as held for sale that will extend the period required to complete the sale, and:

      (i)   timely actions necessary to respond to the conditions have been taken, and

      (ii)   a favourable resolution of the delaying factors is expected.

   (c)   during the initial one-year period, circumstances arise that were previously considered unlikely and, as a result, a non-current asset (or disposal group) previously classified as held for sale is not sold by the end of that period, and:

      (i)   during the initial one-year period the entity took action necessary to respond to the change in circumstances,

      (ii)   the non-current asset (or disposal group) is being actively marketed at a price that is reasonable, given the change in circumstances, and

      (iii) the criteria in paragraphs 7 and 8 are met.

Appendix C
Amendments to other IFRSs

The amendments in this appendix shall be applied for annual periods beginning on or after 1 January 2005. If an entity adopts this IFRS for an earlier period, these amendments shall be applied for that earlier period.

* * * * *

The amendments contained in this appendix when this IFRS was issued in 2004 have been incorporated into the relevant IFRSs published in this volume.

International Financial Reporting Standard 6

Exploration for and Evaluation of Mineral Resources

In December 2004 the International Accounting Standards Board (IASB) issued IFRS 6 *Exploration for and Evaluation of Mineral Resources*.

Other IFRSs have made minor consequential amendments to IFRS 6. They include IFRS 8 *Operating Segments* (issued November 2006), IFRS 1 *First-time Adoption of International Financial Reporting Standards* (as revised in November 2008) and *Improvements to IFRSs* (issued April 2009).

CONTENTS

from paragraph

FOR THE ACCOMPANYING DOCUMENTS LISTED BELOW, SEE PART B OF THIS EDITION

APPROVAL BY THE BOARD OF IFRS 6 ISSUED IN DECEMBER 2004

APPROVAL BY THE BOARD OF AMENDMENTS TO IFRS 1 AND IFRS 6 ISSUED IN JUNE 2005

BASIS FOR CONCLUSIONS

DISSENTING OPINIONS

International Financial Reporting Standard 6 *Exploration for and Evaluation of Mineral Resources* (IFRS 6) is set out in paragraphs 1–27 and Appendices A and B. All the paragraphs have equal authority. Paragraphs in **bold type** state the main principles. Terms defined in Appendix A are in *italics* the first time they appear in the Standard. Definitions of other terms are given in the Glossary for International Financial Reporting Standards. IFRS 6 should be read in the context of its objective and the Basis for Conclusions, the *Preface to International Financial Reporting Standards* and the *Conceptual Framework for Financial Reporting*. IAS 8 *Accounting Policies, Changes in Accounting Estimates and Errors* provides a basis for selecting and applying accounting policies in the absence of explicit guidance.

Introduction

Reasons for issuing the IFRS

IN1 The International Accounting Standards Board decided to develop an International Financial Reporting Standard (IFRS) on exploration for and evaluation of mineral resources because:

(a) until now there has been no IFRS that specifically addresses the accounting for those activities and they are excluded from the scope of IAS 38 *Intangible Assets*. In addition, 'mineral rights and mineral resources such as oil, natural gas and similar non-regenerative resources' are excluded from the scope of IAS 16 *Property, Plant and Equipment*. Consequently, an entity was required to determine its accounting policy for the exploration for and evaluation of mineral resources in accordance with paragraphs 10–12 of IAS 8 *Accounting Policies, Changes in Accounting Estimates and Errors*.

(b) there are different views on how exploration and evaluation expenditures should be accounted for in accordance with IFRSs.

(c) accounting practices for exploration and evaluation assets under the requirements of other standard-setting bodies are diverse and often differ from practices in other sectors for expenditures that may be considered analogous (eg accounting practices for research and development costs in accordance with IAS 38).

(d) exploration and evaluation expenditures are significant to entities engaged in extractive activities.

(e) an increasing number of entities incurring exploration and evaluation expenditures present their financial statements in accordance with IFRSs, and many more are expected to do so from 2005.

IN2 The Board's predecessor organisation, the International Accounting Standards Committee, established a Steering Committee in 1998 to carry out initial work on accounting and financial reporting by entities engaged in extractive activities. In November 2000 the Steering Committee published an Issues Paper *Extractive Industries*.

IN3 In July 2001 the Board announced that it would restart the project only when agenda time permitted. Although the Board recognised the importance of accounting for extractive activities generally, it decided in September 2002 that it was not feasible to complete the detailed analysis required for this project, obtain appropriate input from constituents and undertake the Board's normal due process in time to implement changes before many entities adopted IFRSs in 2005.

IN4 The Board's objectives for this phase of its extractive activities project are:

(a) to make limited improvements to accounting practices for exploration and evaluation expenditures, without requiring major changes that might be reversed when the Board undertakes a comprehensive review of accounting practices used by entities engaged in the exploration for and evaluation of mineral resources.

(b) to specify the circumstances in which entities that recognise exploration and evaluation assets should test such assets for impairment in accordance with IAS 36 *Impairment of Assets*.

(c) to require entities engaged in the exploration for and evaluation of mineral resources to disclose information about exploration and evaluation assets, the level at which such assets are assessed for impairment and any impairment losses recognised.

Main features of the IFRS

IN5 The IFRS:

(a) permits an entity to develop an accounting policy for exploration and evaluation assets without specifically considering the requirements of paragraphs 11 and 12 of IAS 8. Thus, an entity adopting IFRS 6 may continue to use the accounting policies applied immediately before adopting the IFRS. This includes continuing to use recognition and measurement practices that are part of those accounting policies.

(b) requires entities recognising exploration and evaluation assets to perform an impairment test on those assets when facts and circumstances suggest that the carrying amount of the assets may exceed their recoverable amount.

(c) varies the recognition of impairment from that in IAS 36 but measures the impairment in accordance with that Standard once the impairment is identified.

International Financial Reporting Standard 6
Exploration for and Evaluation of Mineral Resources

Objective

1   The objective of this IFRS is to specify the financial reporting for the *exploration for and evaluation of mineral resources.*

2   In particular, the IFRS requires:

(a)   limited improvements to existing accounting practices for *exploration and evaluation expenditures.*

(b)   entities that recognise *exploration and evaluation assets* to assess such assets for impairment in accordance with this IFRS and measure any impairment in accordance with IAS 36 *Impairment of Assets.*

(c)   disclosures that identify and explain the amounts in the entity's financial statements arising from the exploration for and evaluation of mineral resources and help users of those financial statements understand the amount, timing and certainty of future cash flows from any exploration and evaluation assets recognised.

Scope

3   An entity shall apply the IFRS to exploration and evaluation expenditures that it incurs.

4   The IFRS does not address other aspects of accounting by entities engaged in the exploration for and evaluation of mineral resources.

5   An entity shall not apply the IFRS to expenditures incurred:

(a)   before the exploration for and evaluation of mineral resources, such as expenditures incurred before the entity has obtained the legal rights to explore a specific area.

(b)   after the technical feasibility and commercial viability of extracting a mineral resource are demonstrable.

Recognition of exploration and evaluation assets

Temporary exemption from IAS 8 paragraphs 11 and 12

6   When developing its accounting policies, an entity recognising exploration and evaluation assets shall apply paragraph 10 of IAS 8 *Accounting Policies, Changes in Accounting Estimates and Errors.*

7   Paragraphs 11 and 12 of IAS 8 specify sources of authoritative requirements and guidance that management is required to consider in developing an accounting policy for an item if no IFRS applies specifically to that item. Subject to paragraphs 9 and 10 below, this IFRS exempts an entity from applying those paragraphs to its accounting policies for the recognition and measurement of exploration and evaluation assets.

Measurement of exploration and evaluation assets

Measurement at recognition

8   **Exploration and evaluation assets shall be measured at cost.**

Elements of cost of exploration and evaluation assets

9   An entity shall determine an accounting policy specifying which expenditures are recognised as exploration and evaluation assets and apply the policy consistently. In making this determination, an entity considers the degree to which the expenditure can be associated with finding specific mineral resources. The following are examples of expenditures that might be included in the initial measurement of exploration and evaluation assets (the list is not exhaustive):

(a)   acquisition of rights to explore;

(b)   topographical, geological, geochemical and geophysical studies;

(c)   exploratory drilling;

(d)   trenching;

(e)   sampling; and

(f)   activities in relation to evaluating the technical feasibility and commercial viability of extracting a mineral resource.

10   Expenditures related to the development of mineral resources shall not be recognised as exploration and evaluation assets. The *Framework*[1] and IAS 38 *Intangible Assets* provide guidance on the recognition of assets arising from development.

11   In accordance with IAS 37 *Provisions, Contingent Liabilities and Contingent Assets* an entity recognises any obligations for removal and restoration that are incurred during a particular period as a consequence of having undertaken the exploration for and evaluation of mineral resources.

---

1   The reference to the *Framework* is to IASC's *Framework for the Preparation and Presentation of Financial Statements*, adopted by the IASB in 2001. In September 2010 the IASB replaced the *Framework* with the *Conceptual Framework for Financial Reporting*.

Measurement after recognition

12   After recognition, an entity shall apply either the cost model or the revaluation model to the exploration and evaluation assets. If the revaluation model is applied (either the model in IAS 16 *Property, Plant and Equipment* or the model in IAS 38) it shall be consistent with the classification of the assets (see paragraph 15).

Changes in accounting policies

13   **An entity may change its accounting policies for exploration and evaluation expenditures if the change makes the financial statements more relevant to the economic decision-making needs of users and no less reliable, or more reliable and no less relevant to those needs. An entity shall judge relevance and reliability using the criteria in IAS 8.**

14   To justify changing its accounting policies for exploration and evaluation expenditures, an entity shall demonstrate that the change brings its financial statements closer to meeting the criteria in IAS 8, but the change need not achieve full compliance with those criteria.

Presentation

Classification of exploration and evaluation assets

15   An entity shall classify exploration and evaluation assets as tangible or intangible according to the nature of the assets acquired and apply the classification consistently.

16   Some exploration and evaluation assets are treated as intangible (eg drilling rights), whereas others are tangible (eg vehicles and drilling rigs). To the extent that a tangible asset is consumed in developing an intangible asset, the amount reflecting that consumption is part of the cost of the intangible asset. However, using a tangible asset to develop an intangible asset does not change a tangible asset into an intangible asset.

Reclassification of exploration and evaluation assets

17   An exploration and evaluation asset shall no longer be classified as such when the technical feasibility and commercial viability of extracting a mineral resource are demonstrable. Exploration and evaluation assets shall be assessed for impairment, and any impairment loss recognised, before reclassification.

Impairment

Recognition and measurement

18   Exploration and evaluation assets shall be assessed for impairment when facts and circumstances suggest that the carrying amount of an exploration and evaluation asset may exceed its recoverable amount. When facts and circumstances suggest that the carrying amount exceeds the recoverable amount, an entity shall measure, present and disclose any resulting impairment loss in accordance with IAS 36, except as provided by paragraph 21 below.

19   For the purposes of exploration and evaluation assets only, paragraph 20 of this IFRS shall be applied rather than paragraphs 8–17 of IAS 36 when identifying an exploration and evaluation asset that may be impaired. Paragraph 20 uses the term 'assets' but applies equally to separate exploration and evaluation assets or a cash-generating unit.

20   One or more of the following facts and circumstances indicate that an entity should test exploration and evaluation assets for impairment (the list is not exhaustive):

   (a)   the period for which the entity has the right to explore in the specific area has expired during the period or will expire in the near future, and is not expected to be renewed.

   (b)   substantive expenditure on further exploration for and evaluation of mineral resources in the specific area is neither budgeted nor planned.

   (c)   exploration for and evaluation of mineral resources in the specific area have not led to the discovery of commercially viable quantities of mineral resources and the entity has decided to discontinue such activities in the specific area.

   (d)   sufficient data exist to indicate that, although a development in the specific area is likely to proceed, the carrying amount of the exploration and evaluation asset is unlikely to be recovered in full from successful development or by sale.

In any such case, or similar cases, the entity shall perform an impairment test in accordance with IAS 36. Any impairment loss is recognised as an expense in accordance with IAS 36.

Specifying the level at which exploration and evaluation assets are assessed for impairment

21   An entity shall determine an accounting policy for allocating exploration and evaluation assets to cash-generating units or groups of cash-generating units for the purpose of assessing such assets for impairment. Each cash-generating unit or group of units to which an exploration and evaluation asset is allocated shall not be larger than an operating segment determined in accordance with IFRS 8 *Operating Segments*.

22   The level identified by the entity for the purposes of testing exploration and evaluation assets for impairment may comprise one or more cash-generating units.

Disclosure

23   An entity shall disclose information that identifies and explains the amounts recognised in its financial statements arising from the exploration for and evaluation of mineral resources.

24   To comply with paragraph 23, an entity shall disclose:

(a)   its accounting policies for exploration and evaluation expenditures including the recognition of exploration and evaluation assets.

(b)   the amounts of assets, liabilities, income and expense and operating and investing cash flows arising from the exploration for and evaluation of mineral resources.

25   An entity shall treat exploration and evaluation assets as a separate class of assets and make the disclosures required by either IAS 16 or IAS 38 consistent with how the assets are classified.

Effective date

26   An entity shall apply this IFRS for annual periods beginning on or after 1 January 2006. Earlier application is encouraged. If an entity applies the IFRS for a period beginning before 1 January 2006, it shall disclose that fact.

Transitional provisions

27   If it is impracticable to apply a particular requirement of paragraph 18 to comparative information that relates to annual periods beginning before 1 January 2006, an entity shall disclose that fact. IAS 8 explains the term 'impracticable'.

Appendix A
Defined terms

This appendix is an integral part of the IFRS.

exploration and evaluation assets	**Exploration and evaluation expenditures** recognised as assets in accordance with the entity's accounting policy.
exploration and evaluation expenditures	Expenditures incurred by an entity in connection with the **exploration for and evaluation of mineral resources** before the technical feasibility and commercial viability of extracting a mineral resource are demonstrable.
exploration for and evaluation of mineral resources	The search for mineral resources, including minerals, oil, natural gas and similar non-regenerative resources after the entity has obtained legal rights to explore in a specific area, as well as the determination of the technical feasibility and commercial viability of extracting the mineral resource.

Appendix B
Amendments to other IFRSs

The amendments in this appendix shall be applied for annual periods beginning on or after 1 January 2006. If an entity applies this IFRS for an earlier period, these amendments shall be applied for that earlier period.

* * * * *

The amendments contained in this appendix when this IFRS was issued in 2004 have been incorporated into the relevant IFRSs published in this volume.

International Financial Reporting Standard 7

Financial Instruments: Disclosures

In April 2001 the International Accounting Standards Board (IASB) adopted IAS 30 *Disclosures in the Financial Statements of Banks and Similar Financial Institutions*, which had originally been issued by the International Accounting Standards Committee in August 1990.

In August 2005 the IASB issued IFRS 7 *Financial Instruments*, which replaced IAS 30 and carried forward the disclosure requirements in IAS 32 *Financial Instruments: Disclosure and Presentation*. IAS 32 was subsequently renamed as IAS 32 *Financial Instruments: Presentation*. IAS 1 *Presentation of Financial Statements* (as revised in 2007) amended the terminology used throughout IFRSs, including IFRS 7. In March 2009 the IASB enhanced the disclosures about fair value and liquidity risks in IFRS 7.

The IASB also amended IFRS 7 to reflect that a new financial instruments standard was issued—IFRS 9 *Financial Instruments*, issued in November 2009, related to the classification of financial assets and the updated IFRS 9 *Financial Instruments*, issued in October 2010, related to the classification of financial liabilities.

IFRS 7 was also amended in October 2010 to require entities to supplement disclosures for all transferred financial assets that are not derecognised where there has been some continuing involvement in a transferred asset. The IASB amended IFRS 7 in December 2011 to improve disclosures in netting arrangements associated with financial assets and financial liabilities.

Other IFRSs have made minor consequential amendments to IFRS 7. They include IFRS 3 *Business Combinations* (as revised in January 2008), *Puttable Financial Instruments and Obligations arising on Liquidation* (Amendments to IAS 32 and IAS 1) (issued February 2008), *Improvements to IFRSs* (issued May 2008 and May 2010) and IFRS 1 *First-time Adoption of IFRSs* (as revised in January 2010).

Contents

FOR THE ACCOMPANYING DOCUMENTS LISTED BELOW, SEE PART B OF THIS EDITION

APPROVAL BY THE BOARD OF IFRS 7 ISSUED IN AUGUST 2005

APPROVAL BY THE BOARD OF AMENDMENTS TO IFRS 7:

Reclassification of Financial Assets (Amendments to IAS 39 and IFRS 7)
issued in October 2008

Reclassification of Financial Assets—Effective Date and Transition
(Amendments to IAS 39 and IFRS 7) issued in October 2008

Improving Disclosures about Financial Instruments issued in March 2009

Disclosures—Transfers of Financial Assets issued in October 2010

Mandatory Effective Date of IFRS 9 and Transition Disclosures
(Amendments to IFRS 9 (2009), IFRS 9 (2010) and IFRS 7) issued in December 2011

Disclosures—Offsetting Financial Assets and Financial Liabilities
(Amendments to IFRS 7) issued in December 2011

BASIS FOR CONCLUSIONS

APPENDIX
Amendments to Basis for Conclusions on other IFRSs

IMPLEMENTATION GUIDANCE

APPENDIX
Amendments to guidance on other IFRSs

International Financial Reporting Standard 7 *Financial Instruments: Disclosures* (IFRS 7) is set out in paragraphs 1–45 and Appendices A–C. All the paragraphs have equal authority. Paragraphs in **bold type** state the main principles. Terms defined in Appendix A are in *italics* the first time they appear in the Standard. Definitions of other terms are given in the Glossary for International Financial Reporting Standards. IFRS 7 should be read in the context of its objective and the Basis for Conclusions, the *Preface to International Financial Reporting Standards* and the *Conceptual Framework for Financial Reporting*. IAS 8 *Accounting Policies, Changes in Accounting Estimates and Errors* provides a basis for selecting and applying accounting policies in the absence of explicit guidance.

Introduction

Reasons for issuing the IFRS

IN1 In recent years, the techniques used by entities for measuring and managing exposure to risks arising from financial instruments have evolved and new risk management concepts and approaches have gained acceptance. In addition, many public and private sector initiatives have proposed improvements to the disclosure framework for risks arising from financial instruments.

IN2 The International Accounting Standards Board believes that users of financial statements need information about an entity's exposure to risks and how those risks are managed. Such information can influence a user's assessment of the financial position and financial performance of an entity or of the amount, timing and uncertainty of its future cash flows. Greater transparency regarding those risks allows users to make more informed judgements about risk and return.

IN3 Consequently, the Board concluded that there was a need to revise and enhance the disclosures in IAS 30 *Disclosures in the Financial Statements of Banks and Similar Financial Institutions* and IAS 32 *Financial Instruments: Disclosure and Presentation*. As part of this revision, the Board removed duplicative disclosures and simplified the disclosures about concentrations of risk, credit risk, liquidity risk and market risk in IAS 32.

Main features of the IFRS

IN4 IFRS 7 applies to all risks arising from all financial instruments, except those instruments listed in paragraph 3. The IFRS applies to all entities, including entities that have few financial instruments (eg a manufacturer whose only financial instruments are accounts receivable and accounts payable) and those that have many financial instruments (eg a financial institution most of whose assets and liabilities are financial instruments). However, the extent of disclosure required depends on the extent of the entity's use of financial instruments and of its exposure to risk.

IN5 The IFRS requires disclosure of:

(a) the significance of financial instruments for an entity's financial position and performance. These disclosures incorporate many of the requirements previously in IAS 32.

(b) qualitative and quantitative information about exposure to risks arising from financial instruments, including specified minimum disclosures about credit risk, liquidity risk and market risk. The qualitative disclosures describe management's objectives, policies and processes for managing those risks. The quantitative disclosures provide information about the extent to which the entity is exposed to risk, based on information provided internally to the entity's key management personnel. Together, these disclosures provide an overview of the entity's use of financial instruments and the exposures to risks they create.

IN5A   Amendments to the IFRS, issued in March 2009, require enhanced disclosures about fair value measurements and liquidity risk. These have been made to address application issues and provide useful information to users.

IN5B   *Disclosures—Transfers of Financial Assets* (Amendments to IFRS 7), issued in October 2010, amended the required disclosures to help users of financial statements evaluate the risk exposures relating to transfers of financial assets and the effect of those risks on an entity's financial position.

IN5C   In May 2011 the Board relocated the disclosures about fair value measurements to IFRS 13 *Fair Value Measurement*.

IN6   The IFRS includes in Appendix B mandatory application guidance that explains how to apply the requirements in the IFRS. The IFRS is accompanied by non-mandatory Implementation Guidance that describes how an entity might provide the disclosures required by the IFRS.

IN7   The IFRS supersedes IAS 30 and the disclosure requirements of IAS 32. The presentation requirements of IAS 32 remain unchanged.

IN8   The IFRS is effective for annual periods beginning on or after 1 January 2007. Earlier application is encouraged.

IN9   *Disclosures—Offsetting Financial Assets and Financial Liabilities* (Amendments to IFRS 7), issued in December 2011, amended the required disclosures to include information that will enable users of an entity's financial statements to evaluate the effect or potential effect of netting arrangements, including rights of set-off associated with the entity's recognised financial assets and recognised financial liabilities, on the entity's financial position.

International Financial Reporting Standard 7
Financial Instruments: Disclosures

Objective

1   The objective of this IFRS is to require entities to provide disclosures in their financial statements that enable users to evaluate:

   (a)   the significance of financial instruments for the entity's financial position and performance; and

   (b)   the nature and extent of risks arising from financial instruments to which the entity is exposed during the period and at the end of the reporting period, and how the entity manages those risks.

2   The principles in this IFRS complement the principles for recognising, measuring and presenting financial assets and financial liabilities in IAS 32 *Financial Instruments: Presentation* and IFRS 9 *Financial Instruments*.

Scope

3   This IFRS shall be applied by all entities to all types of financial instruments, except:

   (a)   those interests in subsidiaries, associates or joint ventures that are accounted for in accordance with IFRS 10 *Consolidated Financial Statements*, IAS 27 *Separate Financial Statements* or IAS 28 *Investments in Associates and Joint Ventures*. However, in some cases, IAS 27 or IAS 28 permits an entity to account for an interest in a subsidiary, associate or joint venture using IAS 39; in those cases, entities shall apply the requirements of this IFRS and, for those measured at fair value, the requirements of IFRS 13 *Fair Value Measurement*. Entities shall also apply this IFRS to all derivatives linked to interests in subsidiaries, associates or joint ventures unless the derivative meets the definition of an equity instrument in IAS 32.

   (b)   employers' rights and obligations arising from employee benefit plans, to which IAS 19 *Employee Benefits* applies.

   (c)   [deleted]

   (d)   insurance contracts as defined in IFRS 4 *Insurance Contracts*. However, this IFRS applies to derivatives that are embedded in insurance contracts if IFRS 9 requires the entity to account for them separately. Moreover, an issuer shall apply this IFRS to *financial guarantee contracts* if the issuer applies IFRS 9 in recognising and measuring the contracts, but shall apply IFRS 4 if the issuer elects, in accordance with paragraph 4(d) of IFRS 4, to apply IFRS 4 in recognising and measuring them.

   (e)   financial instruments, contracts and obligations under share-based payment transactions to which IFRS 2 *Share-based Payment* applies, except that this IFRS applies to contracts within the scope of IFRS 9.

   (f)   instruments that are required to be classified as equity instruments in accordance with paragraphs 16A and 16B or paragraphs 16C and 16D of IAS 32.

4   This IFRS applies to recognised and unrecognised financial instruments. Recognised financial instruments include financial assets and financial liabilities that are within the scope of IFRS 9. Unrecognised financial instruments include some financial instruments that, although outside the scope of IFRS 9, are within the scope of this IFRS (such as some loan commitments).

5   This IFRS applies to contracts to buy or sell a non-financial item that are within the scope of IFRS 9.

Classes of financial instruments and level of disclosure

6   When this IFRS requires disclosures by class of financial instrument, an entity shall group financial instruments into classes that are appropriate to the nature of the information disclosed and that take into account the characteristics of those financial instruments. An entity shall provide sufficient information to permit reconciliation to the line items presented in the statement of financial position.

Significance of financial instruments for financial position and performance

7   **An entity shall disclose information that enables users of its financial statements to evaluate the significance of financial instruments for its financial position and performance.**

Statement of financial position

Categories of financial assets and financial liabilities

8   The carrying amounts of each of the following categories, as specified in IFRS 9, shall be disclosed either in the statement of financial position or in the notes:

(a)   financial assets measured at fair value through profit or loss, showing separately (i) those designated as such upon initial recognition and (ii) those mandatorily measured at fair value in accordance with IFRS 9.

(b)   [deleted]

(c)   [deleted]

(d)   [deleted]

(e)   financial liabilities at fair value through profit or loss, showing separately (i) those designated as such upon initial recognition and (ii) those that meet the definition of held for trading in IFRS 9.

(f)   financial assets measured at amortised cost.

(g)   financial liabilities measured at amortised cost.

(h)   financial assets measured at fair value through other comprehensive income.

Financial assets or financial liabilities at fair value through profit or loss

9   If the entity has designated as measured at fair value a financial asset (or group of financial assets) that would otherwise be measured at amortised cost, it shall disclose:

    (a)   the maximum exposure to *credit risk* (see paragraph 36(a)) of the financial asset (or group of financial assets) at the end of the reporting period.

    (b)   the amount by which any related credit derivatives or similar instruments mitigate that maximum exposure to credit risk.

    (c)   the amount of change, during the period and cumulatively, in the fair value of the financial asset (or group of financial assets) that is attributable to changes in the credit risk of the financial asset determined either:

        (i)   as the amount of change in its fair value that is not attributable to changes in market conditions that give rise to *market risk* ; or

        (ii)   using an alternative method the entity believes more faithfully represents the amount of change in its fair value that is attributable to changes in the credit risk of the asset.

    Changes in market conditions that give rise to market risk include changes in an observed (benchmark) interest rate, commodity price, foreign exchange rate or index of prices or rates.

    (d)   the amount of the change in the fair value of any related credit derivatives or similar instruments that has occurred during the period and cumulatively since the financial asset was designated.

10   If the entity has designated a financial liability as at fair value through profit or loss in accordance with paragraph 4.2.2 of IFRS 9 and is required to present the effects of changes in that liability's credit risk in other comprehensive income (see paragraph 5.7.7 of IFRS 9), it shall disclose:

    (a)   the amount of change, cumulatively, in the fair value of the financial liability that is attributable to changes in the credit risk of that liability (see paragraphs B5.7.13–B5.7.20 of IFRS 9 for guidance on determining the effects of changes in a liability's credit risk).

    (b)   the difference between the financial liability's carrying amount and the amount the entity would be contractually required to pay at maturity to the holder of the obligation.

    (c)   any transfers of the cumulative gain or loss within equity during the period including the reason for such transfers.

    (d)   if a liability is derecognised during the period, the amount (if any) presented in other comprehensive income that was realised at derecognition.

10A   If an entity has designated a financial liability as at fair value through profit or loss in accordance with paragraph 4.2.2 of IFRS 9 and is required to present all changes in the fair value of that liability (including the effects of changes in the credit risk of the liability) in profit or loss (see paragraphs 5.7.7 and 5.7.8 of IFRS 9), it shall disclose:

(a)   the amount of change, during the period and cumulatively, in the fair value of the financial liability that is attributable to changes in the credit risk of that liability (see paragraphs B5.7.13–B5.7.20 of IFRS 9 for guidance on determining the effects of changes in a liability's credit risk); and

(b)   the difference between the financial liability's carrying amount and the amount the entity would be contractually required to pay at maturity to the holder of the obligation.

11   The entity shall also disclose:

(a)   a detailed description of the methods used to comply with the requirements in paragraphs 9(c), 10(a) and 10A(a) and paragraph 5.7.7(a) of IFRS 9, including an explanation of why the method is appropriate.

(b)   if the entity believes that the disclosure it has given, either in the statement of financial position or in the notes, to comply with the requirements in paragraph 9(c), 10(a) or 10A(a) or paragraph 5.7.7(a) of IFRS 9 does not faithfully represent the change in the fair value of the financial asset or financial liability attributable to changes in its credit risk, the reasons for reaching this conclusion and the factors it believes are relevant.

(c)   a detailed description of the methodology or methodologies used to determine whether presenting the effects of changes in a liability's credit risk in other comprehensive income would create or enlarge an accounting mismatch in profit or loss (see paragraphs 5.7.7 and 5.7.8 of IFRS 9). If an entity is required to present the effects of changes in a liability's credit risk in profit or loss (see paragraph 5.7.8 of IFRS 9), the disclosure must include a detailed description of the economic relationship described in paragraph B5.7.6 of IFRS 9.

Financial assets measured at fair value through other comprehensive income

11A   If an entity has designated investments in equity instruments to be measured at fair value through other comprehensive income, as permitted by paragraph 5.7.5 of IFRS 9, it shall disclose:

(a)   which investments in equity instruments have been designated to be measured at fair value through other comprehensive income.

(b)   the reasons for using this presentation alternative.

(c)   the fair value of each such investment at the end of the reporting period.

(d)   dividends recognised during the period, showing separately those related to investments derecognised during the reporting period and those related to investments held at the end of the reporting period.

(e)   any transfers of the cumulative gain or loss within equity during the period including the reason for such transfers.

11B   If an entity derecognised investments in equity instruments measured at fair value through other comprehensive income during the reporting period, it shall disclose:

(a)   the reasons for disposing of the investments.

(b)   the fair value of the investments at the date of derecognition.

(c)   the cumulative gain or loss on disposal.

Reclassification

12–12A   [Deleted]

12B   An entity shall disclose if, in the current or previous reporting periods, it has reclassified any financial assets in accordance with paragraph 4.4.1 of IFRS 9. For each such event, an entity shall disclose:

(a)   the date of reclassification.

(b)   a detailed explanation of the change in business model and a qualitative description of its effect on the entity's financial statements.

(c)   the amount reclassified into and out of each category.

12C   For each reporting period following reclassification until derecognition, an entity shall disclose for assets reclassified so that they are measured at amortised cost in accordance with paragraph 4.4.1 of IFRS 9:

(a)   the effective interest rate determined on the date of reclassification; and

(b)   the interest income or expense recognised.

12D   If an entity has reclassified financial assets so that they are measured at amortised cost since its last annual reporting date, it shall disclose:

(a)   the fair value of the financial assets at the end of the reporting period; and

(b)   the fair value gain or loss that would have been recognised in profit or loss during the reporting period if the financial assets had not been reclassified.

13   [Deleted]

Offsetting financial assets and financial liabilities

13A   The disclosures in paragraphs 13B–13E supplement the other disclosure requirements of this IFRS and are required for all recognised financial instruments that are set off in accordance with paragraph 42 of IAS 32. These disclosures also apply to recognised financial instruments that are subject to an enforceable master netting arrangement or similar agreement, irrespective of whether they are set off in accordance with paragraph 42 of IAS 32.

13B   An entity shall disclose information to enable users of its financial statements to evaluate the effect or potential effect of netting arrangements on the entity's financial position. This includes the effect or potential effect of rights of set-off associated with the entity's recognised financial assets and recognised financial liabilities that are within the scope of paragraph 13A.

13C   To meet the objective in paragraph 13B, an entity shall disclose, at the end of the reporting period, the following quantitative information separately for recognised financial assets and recognised financial liabilities that are within the scope of paragraph 13A:

(a)   the gross amounts of those recognised financial assets and recognised financial liabilities;

(b)   the amounts that are set off in accordance with the criteria in paragraph 42 of IAS 32 when determining the net amounts presented in the statement of financial position;

(c)   the net amounts presented in the statement of financial position;

(d)   the amounts subject to an enforceable master netting arrangement or similar agreement that are not otherwise included in paragraph 13C(b), including:

(i)   amounts related to recognised financial instruments that do not meet some or all of the offsetting criteria in paragraph 42 of IAS 32; and

(ii)   amounts related to financial collateral (including cash collateral); and

(e)   the net amount after deducting the amounts in (d) from the amounts in (c) above.

The information required by this paragraph shall be presented in a tabular format, separately for financial assets and financial liabilities, unless another format is more appropriate.

13D   The total amount disclosed in accordance with paragraph 13C(d) for an instrument shall be limited to the amount in paragraph 13C(c) for that instrument.

13E   An entity shall include a description in the disclosures of the rights of set-off associated with the entity's recognised financial assets and recognised financial liabilities subject to enforceable master netting arrangements and similar agreements that are disclosed in accordance with paragraph 13C(d), including the nature of those rights.

13F   If the information required by paragraphs 13B–13E is disclosed in more than one note to the financial statements, an entity shall cross-refer between those notes.

Collateral

14   An entity shall disclose:

(a)   the carrying amount of financial assets it has pledged as collateral for liabilities or contingent liabilities, including amounts that have been reclassified in accordance with paragraph 3.2.23(a) of IFRS 9; and

(b)   the terms and conditions relating to its pledge.

15   When an entity holds collateral (of financial or non-financial assets) and is permitted to sell or repledge the collateral in the absence of default by the owner of the collateral, it shall disclose:

    (a)   the fair value of the collateral held;

    (b)   the fair value of any such collateral sold or repledged, and whether the entity has an obligation to return it; and

    (c)   the terms and conditions associated with its use of the collateral.

Allowance account for credit losses

16   When financial assets are impaired by credit losses and the entity records the impairment in a separate account (eg an allowance account used to record individual impairments or a similar account used to record a collective impairment of assets) rather than directly reducing the carrying amount of the asset, it shall disclose a reconciliation of changes in that account during the period for each class of financial assets.

Compound financial instruments with multiple embedded derivatives

17   If an entity has issued an instrument that contains both a liability and an equity component (see paragraph 28 of IAS 32) and the instrument has multiple embedded derivatives whose values are interdependent (such as a callable convertible debt instrument), it shall disclose the existence of those features.

Defaults and breaches

18   For *loans payable* recognised at the end of the reporting period, an entity shall disclose:

    (a)   details of any defaults during the period of principal, interest, sinking fund, or redemption terms of those loans payable;

    (b)   the carrying amount of the loans payable in default at the end of the reporting period; and

    (c)   whether the default was remedied, or the terms of the loans payable were renegotiated, before the financial statements were authorised for issue.

19   If, during the period, there were breaches of loan agreement terms other than those described in paragraph 18, an entity shall disclose the same information as required by paragraph 18 if those breaches permitted the lender to demand accelerated repayment (unless the breaches were remedied, or the terms of the loan were renegotiated, on or before the end of the reporting period).

Statement of comprehensive income

Items of income, expense, gains or losses

20   An entity shall disclose the following items of income, expense, gains or losses either in the statement of comprehensive income or in the notes:

    (a)   net gains or net losses on:

(i) financial assets or financial liabilities measured at fair value through profit or loss, showing separately those on financial assets or financial liabilities designated as such upon initial recognition, and those on financial assets or financial liabilities that are mandatorily measured at fair value in accordance with IFRS 9 (eg financial liabilities that meet the definition of held for trading in IFRS 9). For financial liabilities designated as at fair value through profit or loss, an entity shall show separately the amount of gain or loss recognised in other comprehensive income and the amount recognised in profit or loss.

(ii) [deleted]

(iii) [deleted]

(iv) [deleted]

(v) financial liabilities measured at amortised cost.

(vi) financial assets measured at amortised cost.

(vii) financial assets measured at fair value through other comprehensive income.

(b) total interest income and total interest expense (calculated using the effective interest method) for financial assets that are measured at amortised cost or financial liabilities not at fair value through profit or loss.

(c) fee income and expense (other than amounts included in determining the effective interest rate) arising from:

(i) financial assets measured at amortised cost or financial liabilities that are not at fair value through profit or loss; and

(ii) trust and other fiduciary activities that result in the holding or investing of assets on behalf of individuals, trusts, retirement benefit plans, and other institutions.

(d) interest income on impaired financial assets accrued in accordance with paragraph AG93 of IAS 39 *Financial Instruments: Recognition and Measurement*

(e) the amount of any impairment loss for each class of financial asset.

20A An entity shall disclose an analysis of the gain or loss recognised in the statement of comprehensive income arising from the derecognition of financial assets measured at amortised cost, showing separately gains and losses arising from derecognition of those financial assets. This disclosure shall include the reasons for derecognising those financial assets.

Other disclosures

Accounting policies

21 In accordance with paragraph 117 of IAS 1 *Presentation of Financial Statements* (as revised in 2007), an entity discloses, in the summary of significant accounting policies, the measurement basis (or bases) used in preparing the financial statements and the other accounting policies used that are relevant to an understanding of the financial statements.

Hedge accounting

22   An entity shall disclose the following separately for each type of hedge described in IAS 39 (ie fair value hedges, cash flow hedges, and hedges of net investments in foreign operations):

(a)   a description of each type of hedge;

(b)   a description of the financial instruments designated as hedging instruments and their fair values at the end of the reporting period; and

(c)   the nature of the risks being hedged.

23   For cash flow hedges, an entity shall disclose:

(a)   the periods when the cash flows are expected to occur and when they are expected to affect profit or loss;

(b)   a description of any forecast transaction for which hedge accounting had previously been used, but which is no longer expected to occur;

(c)   the amount that was recognised in other comprehensive income during the period;

(d)   the amount that was reclassified from equity to profit or loss for the period, showing the amount included in each line item in the statement of comprehensive income; and

(e)   the amount that was removed from equity during the period and included in the initial cost or other carrying amount of a non-financial asset or non-financial liability whose acquisition or incurrence was a hedged highly probable forecast transaction.

24   An entity shall disclose separately:

(a)   in fair value hedges, gains or losses:

(i)   on the hedging instrument; and

(ii)   on the hedged item attributable to the hedged risk.

(b)   the ineffectiveness recognised in profit or loss that arises from cash flow hedges.

(c)   the ineffectiveness recognised in profit or loss that arises from hedges of net investments in foreign operations.

Fair value

25   Except as set out in paragraph 29, for each class of financial assets and financial liabilities (see paragraph 6), an entity shall disclose the fair value of that class of assets and liabilities in a way that permits it to be compared with its carrying amount.

26   In disclosing fair values, an entity shall group financial assets and financial liabilities into classes, but shall offset them only to the extent that their carrying amounts are offset in the statement of financial position.

27–27B   [Deleted]

28   In some cases, an entity does not recognise a gain or loss on initial recognition of a financial asset or financial liability because the fair value is neither evidenced by a quoted price in an active market for an identical asset or liability (ie a Level 1 input) nor based on a valuation technique that uses only data from observable markets (see paragraph AG76 of IAS 39). In such cases, the entity shall disclose by class of financial asset or financial liability:

(a)   its accounting policy for recognising in profit or loss the difference between the fair value at initial recognition and the transaction price to reflect a change in factors (including time) that market participants would take into account when pricing the asset or liability (see paragraph B5.4.9 of IFRS 9).

(b)   the aggregate difference yet to be recognised in profit or loss at the beginning and end of the period and a reconciliation of changes in the balance of this difference.

(c)   why the entity concluded that the transaction price was not the best evidence of fair value, including a description of the evidence that supports the fair value.

29   Disclosures of fair value are not required:

(a)   when the carrying amount is a reasonable approximation of fair value, for example, for financial instruments such as short-term trade receivables and payables;

(b)   [deleted]

(c)   for a contract containing a discretionary participation feature (as described in IFRS 4) if the fair value of that feature cannot be measured reliably.

30   In the cases described in paragraph 29(c), an entity shall disclose information to help users of the financial statements make their own judgements about the extent of possible differences between the carrying amount of those contracts and their fair value, including:

(a)   the fact that fair value information has not been disclosed for these instruments because their fair value cannot be measured reliably;

(b)   a description of the financial instruments, their carrying amount, and an explanation of why fair value cannot be measured reliably;

(c)   information about the market for the instruments;

(d)   information about whether and how the entity intends to dispose of the financial instruments; and

(e)   if financial instruments whose fair value previously could not be reliably measured are derecognised, that fact, their carrying amount at the time of derecognition, and the amount of gain or loss recognised.

Nature and extent of risks arising from financial instruments

31 **An entity shall disclose information that enables users of its financial statements to evaluate the nature and extent of risks arising from financial instruments to which the entity is exposed at the end of the reporting period.**

32 The disclosures required by paragraphs 33–42 focus on the risks that arise from financial instruments and how they have been managed. These risks typically include, but are not limited to, credit risk, *liquidity risk* and market risk.

32A Providing qualitative disclosures in the context of quantitative disclosures enables users to link related disclosures and hence form an overall picture of the nature and extent of risks arising from financial instruments. The interaction between qualitative and quantitative disclosures contributes to disclosure of information in a way that better enables users to evaluate an entity's exposure to risks.

Qualitative disclosures

33 For each type of risk arising from financial instruments, an entity shall disclose:

(a) the exposures to risk and how they arise;

(b) its objectives, policies and processes for managing the risk and the methods used to measure the risk; and

(c) any changes in (a) or (b) from the previous period.

Quantitative disclosures

34 For each type of risk arising from financial instruments, an entity shall disclose:

(a) summary quantitative data about its exposure to that risk at the end of the reporting period. This disclosure shall be based on the information provided internally to key management personnel of the entity (as defined in IAS 24 *Related Party Disclosures*), for example the entity's board of directors or chief executive officer.

(b) the disclosures required by paragraphs 36–42, to the extent not provided in accordance with (a)

(c) concentrations of risk if not apparent from the disclosures made in accordance with (a) and (b).

35 If the quantitative data disclosed as at the end of the reporting period are unrepresentative of an entity's exposure to risk during the period, an entity shall provide further information that is representative.

Credit risk

36 An entity shall disclose by class of financial instrument:

(a) the amount that best represents its maximum exposure to credit risk at the end of the reporting period without taking account of any collateral held or other credit enhancements (eg netting agreements that do not qualify for offset in accordance with IAS 32); this disclosure is not required for financial instruments whose carrying amount best represents the maximum exposure to credit risk.

(b) a description of collateral held as security and other credit enhancements, and their financial effect (eg a quantification of the extent to which collateral and other credit enhancements mitigate credit risk) in respect of the amount that best represents the maximum exposure to credit risk (whether disclosed in accordance with (a) or represented by the carrying amount of a financial instrument).

(c) information about the credit quality of financial assets that are neither *past due* nor impaired.

(d) [deleted]

Financial assets that are either past due or impaired

37 An entity shall disclose by class of financial asset:

(a) an analysis of the age of financial assets that are past due as at the end of the reporting period but not impaired; and

(b) an analysis of financial assets that are individually determined to be impaired as at the end of the reporting period, including the factors the entity considered in determining that they are impaired.

(c) [deleted]

Collateral and other credit enhancements obtained

38 When an entity obtains financial or non-financial assets during the period by taking possession of collateral it holds as security or calling on other credit enhancements (eg guarantees), and such assets meet the recognition criteria in other IFRSs, an entity shall disclose for such assets held at the reporting date:

(a) the nature and carrying amount of the assets; and

(b) when the assets are not readily convertible into cash, its policies for disposing of such assets or for using them in its operations.

Liquidity risk

39 An entity shall disclose:

(a) a maturity analysis for non-derivative financial liabilities (including issued financial guarantee contracts) that shows the remaining contractual maturities.

(b) a maturity analysis for derivative financial liabilities. The maturity analysis shall include the remaining contractual maturities for those derivative financial liabilities for which contractual maturities are essential for an understanding of the timing of the cash flows (see paragraph B11B).

(c) a description of how it manages the liquidity risk inherent in (a) and (b).

Market risk

Sensitivity analysis

40   Unless an entity complies with paragraph 41, it shall disclose:

(a)   a sensitivity analysis for each type of market risk to which the entity is exposed at the end of the reporting period, showing how profit or loss and equity would have been affected by changes in the relevant risk variable that were reasonably possible at that date;

(b)   the methods and assumptions used in preparing the sensitivity analysis; and

(c)   changes from the previous period in the methods and assumptions used, and the reasons for such changes.

41   If an entity prepares a sensitivity analysis, such as value-at-risk, that reflects interdependencies between risk variables (eg interest rates and exchange rates) and uses it to manage financial risks, it may use that sensitivity analysis in place of the analysis specified in paragraph 40. The entity shall also disclose:

(a)   an explanation of the method used in preparing such a sensitivity analysis, and of the main parameters and assumptions underlying the data provided; and

(b)   an explanation of the objective of the method used and of limitations that may result in the information not fully reflecting the fair value of the assets and liabilities involved.

Other market risk disclosures

42   When the sensitivity analyses disclosed in accordance with paragraph 40 or 41 are unrepresentative of a risk inherent in a financial instrument (for example because the year-end exposure does not reflect the exposure during the year), the entity shall disclose that fact and the reason it believes the sensitivity analyses are unrepresentative.

Transfers of financial assets

42A   The disclosure requirements in paragraphs 42B–42H relating to transfers of financial assets supplement the other disclosure requirements of this IFRS. An entity shall present the disclosures required by paragraphs 42B–42H in a single note in its financial statements. An entity shall provide the required disclosures for all transferred financial assets that are not derecognised and for any continuing involvement in a transferred asset, existing at the reporting date, irrespective of when the related transfer transaction occurred. For the purposes of applying the disclosure requirements in those paragraphs, an entity transfers all or a part of a financial asset (the transferred financial asset) if, and only if, it either:

(a)   transfers the contractual rights to receive the cash flows of that financial asset; or

(b)   retains the contractual rights to receive the cash flows of that financial asset, but assumes a contractual obligation to pay the cash flows to one or more recipients in an arrangement.

42B   An entity shall disclose information that enables users of its financial statements:

(a)   to understand the relationship between transferred financial assets that are not derecognised in their entirety and the associated liabilities; and

(b)   to evaluate the nature of, and risks associated with, the entity's continuing involvement in derecognised financial assets.

42C   For the purposes of applying the disclosure requirements in paragraphs 42E–42H, an entity has continuing involvement in a transferred financial asset if, as part of the transfer, the entity retains any of the contractual rights or obligations inherent in the transferred financial asset or obtains any new contractual rights or obligations relating to the transferred financial asset. For the purposes of applying the disclosure requirements in paragraphs 42E–42H, the following do not constitute continuing involvement:

(a)   normal representations and warranties relating to fraudulent transfer and concepts of reasonableness, good faith and fair dealings that could invalidate a transfer as a result of legal action;

(b)   forward, option and other contracts to reacquire the transferred financial asset for which the contract price (or exercise price) is the fair value of the transferred financial asset; or

(c)   an arrangement whereby an entity retains the contractual rights to receive the cash flows of a financial asset but assumes a contractual obligation to pay the cash flows to one or more entities and the conditions in paragraph 3.2.5(a)–(c) of IFRS 9 are met.

Transferred financial assets that are not derecognised in their entirety

42D   An entity may have transferred financial assets in such a way that part or all of the transferred financial assets do not qualify for derecognition. To meet the objectives set out in paragraph 42B(a), the entity shall disclose at each reporting date for each class of transferred financial assets that are not derecognised in their entirety:

(a)   the nature of the transferred assets.

(b)   the nature of the risks and rewards of ownership to which the entity is exposed.

(c)   a description of the nature of the relationship between the transferred assets and the associated liabilities, including restrictions arising from the transfer on the reporting entity's use of the transferred assets.

(d)   when the counterparty (counterparties) to the associated liabilities has (have) recourse only to the transferred assets, a schedule that sets out the fair value of the transferred assets, the fair value of the associated liabilities and the net position (the difference between the fair value of the transferred assets and the associated liabilities).

(e) when the entity continues to recognise all of the transferred assets, the carrying amounts of the transferred assets and the associated liabilities.

(f) when the entity continues to recognise the assets to the extent of its continuing involvement (see paragraphs 3.2.6(c)(ii) and 3.2.16 of IFRS 9), the total carrying amount of the original assets before the transfer, the carrying amount of the assets that the entity continues to recognise, and the carrying amount of the associated liabilities.

Transferred financial assets that are derecognised in their entirety

42E To meet the objectives set out in paragraph 42B(b), when an entity derecognises transferred financial assets in their entirety (see paragraph 3.2.6(a) and (c)(i) of IFRS 9) but has continuing involvement in them, the entity shall disclose, as a minimum, for each type of continuing involvement at each reporting date:

(a) the carrying amount of the assets and liabilities that are recognised in the entity's statement of financial position and represent the entity's continuing involvement in the derecognised financial assets, and the line items in which the carrying amount of those assets and liabilities are recognised.

(b) the fair value of the assets and liabilities that represent the entity's continuing involvement in the derecognised financial assets.

(c) the amount that best represents the entity's maximum exposure to loss from its continuing involvement in the derecognised financial assets, and information showing how the maximum exposure to loss is determined.

(d) the undiscounted cash outflows that would or may be required to repurchase derecognised financial assets (eg the strike price in an option agreement) or other amounts payable to the transferee in respect of the transferred assets. If the cash outflow is variable then the amount disclosed should be based on the conditions that exist at each reporting date.

(e) a maturity analysis of the undiscounted cash outflows that would or may be required to repurchase the derecognised financial assets or other amounts payable to the transferee in respect of the transferred assets, showing the remaining contractual maturities of the entity's continuing involvement.

(f) qualitative information that explains and supports the quantitative disclosures required in (a)–(e).

42F An entity may aggregate the information required by paragraph 42E in respect of a particular asset if the entity has more than one type of continuing involvement in that derecognised financial asset, and report it under one type of continuing involvement.

42G   In addition, an entity shall disclose for each type of continuing involvement:

(a)   the gain or loss recognised at the date of transfer of the assets.

(b)   income and expenses recognised, both in the reporting period and cumulatively, from the entity's continuing involvement in the derecognised financial assets (eg fair value changes in derivative instruments).

(c)   if the total amount of proceeds from transfer activity (that qualifies for derecognition) in a reporting period is not evenly distributed throughout the reporting period (eg if a substantial proportion of the total amount of transfer activity takes place in the closing days of a reporting period):

(i)   when the greatest transfer activity took place within that reporting period (eg the last five days before the end of the reporting period),

(ii)   the amount (eg related gains or losses) recognised from transfer activity in that part of the reporting period, and

(iii) the total amount of proceeds from transfer activity in that part of the reporting period.

An entity shall provide this information for each period for which a statement of comprehensive income is presented.

Supplementary information

42H   An entity shall disclose any additional information that it considers necessary to meet the disclosure objectives in paragraph 42B.

Effective date and transition

43   An entity shall apply this IFRS for annual periods beginning on or after 1 January 2007. Earlier application is encouraged. If an entity applies this IFRS for an earlier period, it shall disclose that fact.

44   If an entity applies this IFRS for annual periods beginning before 1 January 2006, it need not present comparative information for the disclosures required by paragraphs 31–42 about the nature and extent of risks arising from financial instruments.

44A   IAS 1 (as revised in 2007) amended the terminology used throughout IFRSs. In addition it amended paragraphs 20, 21, 23(c) and (d), 27(c) and B5 of Appendix B. An entity shall apply those amendments for annual periods beginning on or after 1 January 2009. If an entity applies IAS 1 (revised 2007) for an earlier period, the amendments shall be applied for that earlier period.

44B   IFRS 3 (as revised in 2008) deleted paragraph 3(c). An entity shall apply that amendment for annual periods beginning on or after 1 July 2009. If an entity applies IFRS 3 (revised 2008) for an earlier period, the amendment shall also be applied for that earlier period. However, the amendment does not apply to contingent consideration that arose from a business combination for which the acquisition date preceded the application of IFRS 3 (revised 2008). Instead, an entity shall account for such consideration in accordance with paragraphs 65A–65E of IFRS 3 (as amended in 2010).

44C   An entity shall apply the amendment in paragraph 3 for annual periods beginning on or after 1 January 2009. If an entity applies *Puttable Financial Instruments and Obligations Arising on Liquidation* (Amendments to IAS 32 and IAS 1), issued in February 2008, for an earlier period, the amendment in paragraph 3 shall be applied for that earlier period.

44D   Paragraph 3(a) was amended by *Improvements to IFRSs* issued in May 2008. An entity shall apply that amendment for annual periods beginning on or after 1 January 2009. Earlier application is permitted. If an entity applies the amendment for an earlier period it shall disclose that fact and apply for that earlier period the amendments to paragraph 1 of IAS 28, paragraph 1 of IAS 31 and paragraph 4 of IAS 32 issued in May 2008. An entity is permitted to apply the amendment prospectively.

44E–44F   [Deleted]

44G   *Improving Disclosures about Financial Instruments* (Amendments to IFRS 7), issued in March 2009, amended paragraphs 27, 39 and B11 and added paragraphs 27A, 27B, B10A and B11A–B11F. An entity shall apply those amendments for annual periods beginning on or after 1 January 2009. An entity need not provide the disclosures required by the amendments for:

(a)   any annual or interim period, including any statement of financial position, presented within an annual comparative period ending before 31 December 2009, or

(b)   any statement of financial position as at the beginning of the earliest comparative period as at a date before 31 December 2009.

Earlier application is permitted. If an entity applies the amendments for an earlier period, it shall disclose that fact.[1]

44H   [Deleted]

44I   When an entity first applies IFRS 9, it shall disclose for each class of financial assets and financial liabilities at the date of initial application:

(a)   the original measurement category and carrying amount determined in accordance with IAS 39;

(b)   the new measurement category and carrying amount determined in accordance with IFRS 9;

(c)   the amount of any financial assets and financial liabilities in the statement of financial position that were previously designated as measured at fair value through profit or loss but are no longer so designated, distinguishing between those that IFRS 9 requires an entity to reclassify and those that an entity elects to reclassify.

An entity shall present these quantitative disclosures in tabular format unless another format is more appropriate.

---

1   Paragraph 44G was amended as a consequence of *Limited Exemption from Comparative IFRS 7 Disclosures for First-time Adopters* (Amendment to IFRS 1) issued in January 2010. The Board amended paragraph 44G to clarify its conclusions and intended transition for *Improving Disclosures about Financial Instruments* (Amendments to IFRS 7).

44J   When an entity first applies IFRS 9, it shall disclose qualitative information to enable users to understand:

(a)   how it applied the classification requirements in IFRS 9 to those financial assets whose classification has changed as a result of applying IFRS 9.

(b)   the reasons for any designation or de-designation of financial assets or financial liabilities as measured at fair value through profit or loss.

44K   Paragraph 44B was amended by *Improvements to IFRSs* issued in May 2010. An entity shall apply that amendment for annual periods beginning on or after 1 July 2010. Earlier application is permitted.

44L   *Improvements to IFRSs* issued in May 2010 added paragraph 32A and amended paragraphs 34 and 36–38. An entity shall apply those amendments for annual periods beginning on or after 1 January 2011. Earlier application is permitted. If an entity applies the amendments for an earlier period it shall disclose that fact.

44M   *Disclosures—Transfers of Financial Assets* (Amendments to IFRS 7), issued in October 2010, deleted paragraph 13 and added paragraphs 42A–42H and B29–B39. An entity shall apply those amendments for annual periods beginning on or after 1 July 2011. Earlier application is permitted. If an entity applies the amendments from an earlier date, it shall disclose that fact. An entity need not provide the disclosures required by those amendments for any period presented that begins before the date of initial application of the amendments.

44N   IFRS 9, issued in October 2010, amended paragraphs 2–5, 8–10, 11, 14, 20, 28, 30 and 42C–42E, Appendix A, and paragraphs B1, B5, B10(a), B22 and B27, added paragraphs 10A, 11A, 11B, 12B–12D, 20A, 44I and 44J, and deleted paragraphs 12, 12A, 29(b), 44E, 44F, 44H and B4 and Appendix D. An entity shall apply those amendments when it applies IFRS 9 as issued in October 2010.

44O   IFRS 10 and IFRS 11 *Joint Arrangements*, issued in May 2011, amended paragraph 3. An entity shall apply that amendment when it applies IFRS 10 and IFRS 11.

44P   IFRS 13, issued in May 2011, amended paragraphs 3, 28 and 29 and Appendix A and deleted paragraphs 27–27B. An entity shall apply those amendments when it applies IFRS 13.

44Q   *Presentation of Items of Other Comprehensive Income* (Amendments to IAS 1), issued in June 2011, amended paragraph 27B. An entity shall apply that amendment when it applies IAS 1 as amended in June 2011.

44R   *Disclosures—Offsetting Financial Assets and Financial Liabilities* (Amendments to IFRS 7), issued in December 2011, added paragraphs IN9, 13A–13F and B40–B53. An entity shall apply those amendments for annual periods beginning on or after 1 January 2013 and interim periods within those annual periods. An entity shall provide the disclosures required by those amendments retrospectively.

44S   When an entity first applies the classification and measurement requirements of IFRS 9, it shall present the disclosures set out in paragraphs 44T–44W of this IFRS if it elects to, or is required to, provide these disclosures in accordance with IFRS 9 (see paragraph 8.2.12 of IFRS 9 (2009) and paragraph 7.2.14 of IFRS 9 (2010)).

44T   If required by paragraph 44S, at the date of initial application of IFRS 9 an entity shall disclose the changes in the classifications of financial assets and financial liabilities, showing separately:

(a)   the changes in the carrying amounts on the basis of their measurement categories in accordance with IAS 39 (ie not resulting from a change in measurement attribute on transition to IFRS 9); and

(b)   the changes in the carrying amounts arising from a change in measurement attribute on transition to IFRS 9.

The disclosures in this paragraph need not be made after the annual period in which IFRS 9 is initially applied.

44U   In the reporting period in which IFRS 9 is initially applied, an entity shall disclose the following for financial assets and financial liabilities that have been reclassified so that they are measured at amortised cost as a result of the transition to IFRS 9:

(a)   the fair value of the financial assets or financial liabilities at the end of the reporting period;

(b)   the fair value gain or loss that would have been recognised in profit or loss or other comprehensive income during the reporting period if the financial assets or financial liabilities had not been reclassified;

(c)   the effective interest rate determined on the date of reclassification; and

(d)   the interest income or expense recognised.

If an entity treats the fair value of a financial asset or a financial liability as its amortised cost at the date of initial application (see paragraph 8.2.10 of IFRS 9 (2009) and paragraph 7.2.10 of IFRS 9 (2010)), the disclosures in (c) and (d) of this paragraph shall be made for each reporting period following reclassification until derecognition. Otherwise, the disclosures in this paragraph need not be made after the reporting period containing the date of initial application.

44V   If an entity presents the disclosures set out in paragraphs 44S–44U at the date of initial application of IFRS 9, those disclosures, and the disclosures in paragraph 28 of IAS 8 during the reporting period containing the date of initial application, must permit reconciliation between:

(a)   the measurement categories in accordance with IAS 39 and IFRS 9; and

(b)   the line items presented in the statements of financial position.

44W   If an entity presents the disclosures set out in paragraphs 44S–44U at the date of initial application of IFRS 9, those disclosures, and the disclosures in paragraph 25 of this IFRS at the date of initial application, must permit reconciliation between:

(a)   of the measurement categories presented in accordance with IAS 39 and IFRS 9; and

(b)   the class of financial instrument at the date of initial application.

Withdrawal of IAS 30

45   This IFRS supersedes IAS 30 *Disclosures in the Financial Statements of Banks and Similar Financial Institutions*.

Appendix A
Defined terms

This appendix is an integral part of the IFRS.

credit risk	The risk that one party to a financial instrument will cause a financial loss for the other party by failing to discharge an obligation.
currency risk	The risk that the fair value or future cash flows of a financial instrument will fluctuate because of changes in foreign exchange rates.
interest rate risk	The risk that the fair value or future cash flows of a financial instrument will fluctuate because of changes in market interest rates.
liquidity risk	The risk that an entity will encounter difficulty in meeting obligations associated with that are settled by delivering or another.
loans payable	Loans payable are financial liabilities, other than short-term trade payables on normal credit terms.
market risk	The risk that the fair value or future cash flows of a financial instrument will fluctuate because of changes in market prices. Market risk comprises three types of risk: **currency risk**, **interest rate risk** and **other price risk**.
other price risk	The risk that the fair value or future cash flows of a financial instrument will fluctuate because of changes in market prices (other than those arising from **interest rate risk** or **currency risk**), whether those changes are caused by factors specific to the individual financial instrument or its issuer or by factors affecting all similar financial instruments traded in the market.
past due	A financial asset is past due when a counterparty has failed to make a payment when contractually due.

The following terms are defined in paragraph 11 of IAS 32, paragraph 9 of IAS 39 or Appendix A of IFRS 9 and are used in the IFRS with the meaning specified in IAS 32, IAS 39 and IFRS 9.

- amortised cost of a financial asset or financial liability
- derecognition
- derivative
- effective interest method
- equity instrument
- fair value
- financial asset
- financial guarantee contract
- financial instrument
- financial liability
- financial liability at fair value through profit or loss
- forecast transaction
- hedging instrument
- held for trading
- reclassification date
- regular way purchase or sale.

Appendix B
Application guidance

This appendix is an integral part of the IFRS.

Classes of financial instruments and level of disclosure (paragraph 6)

B1   Paragraph 6 requires an entity to group financial instruments into classes that are appropriate to the nature of the information disclosed and that take into account the characteristics of those financial instruments. The classes described in paragraph 6 are determined by the entity and are, thus, distinct from the categories of financial instruments specified in IFRS 9 (which determine how financial instruments are measured and where changes in fair value are recognised).

B2   In determining classes of financial instrument, an entity shall, at a minimum:

   (a)   distinguish instruments measured at amortised cost from those measured at fair value.

   (b)   treat as a separate class or classes those financial instruments outside the scope of this IFRS.

B3   An entity decides, in the light of its circumstances, how much detail it provides to satisfy the requirements of this IFRS, how much emphasis it places on different aspects of the requirements and how it aggregates information to display the overall picture without combining information with different characteristics. It is necessary to strike a balance between overburdening financial statements with excessive detail that may not assist users of financial statements and obscuring important information as a result of too much aggregation. For example, an entity shall not obscure important information by including it among a large amount of insignificant detail. Similarly, an entity shall not disclose information that is so aggregated that it obscures important differences between individual transactions or associated risks.

Significance of financial instruments for financial position and performance

B4   [Deleted]

Other disclosure – accounting policies (paragraph 21)

B5   Paragraph 21 requires disclosure of the measurement basis (or bases) used in preparing the financial statements and the other accounting policies used that are relevant to an understanding of the financial statements. For financial instruments, such disclosure may include:

   (a)   for financial liabilities designated as at fair value through profit or loss:

      (i)   the nature of the financial liabilities the entity has designated as at fair value through profit or loss;

© IFRS Foundation

(ii)   the criteria for so designating such financial liabilities on initial recognition; and

(iii) how the entity has satisfied the conditions in paragraph 4.2.2 of IFRS 9 for such designation.

(aa) for financial assets designated as measured at fair value through profit or loss:

    (i)   the nature of the financial assets the entity has designated as measured at fair value through profit or loss; and

    (ii)   how the entity has satisfied the criteria in paragraph 4.1.5 of IFRS 9 for such designation.

(b)   [deleted]

(c)   whether regular way purchases and sales of financial assets are accounted for at trade date or at settlement date (see paragraph 3.1.2 of IFRS 9).

(d)   when an allowance account is used to reduce the carrying amount of financial assets impaired by credit losses:

    (i)   the criteria for determining when the carrying amount of impaired financial assets is reduced directly (or, in the case of a reversal of a write-down, increased directly) and when the allowance account is used; and

    (ii)   the criteria for writing off amounts charged to the allowance account against the carrying amount of impaired financial assets (see paragraph 16).

(e)   how net gains or net losses on each category of financial instrument are determined (see paragraph 20(a)), for example, whether the net gains or net losses on items at fair value through profit or loss include interest or dividend income.

(f)   the criteria the entity uses to determine that there is objective evidence that an impairment loss has occurred (see paragraph 20(e)).

(g)   when the terms of financial assets that would otherwise be past due or impaired have been renegotiated, the accounting policy for financial assets that are the subject of renegotiated terms (see paragraph 36(d)).

Paragraph 122 of IAS 1 (as revised in 2007) also requires entities to disclose, in the summary of significant accounting policies or other notes, the judgements, apart from those involving estimations, that management has made in the process of applying the entity's accounting policies and that have the most significant effect on the amounts recognised in the financial statements.

Nature and extent of risks arising from financial instruments (paragraphs 31–42)

B6 The disclosures required by paragraphs 31–42 shall be either given in the financial statements or incorporated by cross-reference from the financial statements to some other statement, such as a management commentary or risk report, that is available to users of the financial statements on the same terms as the financial statements and at the same time. Without the information incorporated by cross-reference, the financial statements are incomplete.

Quantitative disclosures (paragraph 34)

B7 Paragraph 34(a) requires disclosures of summary quantitative data about an entity's exposure to risks based on the information provided internally to key management personnel of the entity. When an entity uses several methods to manage a risk exposure, the entity shall disclose information using the method or methods that provide the most relevant and reliable information. IAS 8 *Accounting Policies, Changes in Accounting Estimates and Errors* discusses relevance and reliability.

B8 Paragraph 34(c) requires disclosures about concentrations of risk. Concentrations of risk arise from financial instruments that have similar characteristics and are affected similarly by changes in economic or other conditions. The identification of concentrations of risk requires judgement taking into account the circumstances of the entity. Disclosure of concentrations of risk shall include:

(a) a description of how management determines concentrations;

(b) a description of the shared characteristic that identifies each concentration (eg counterparty, geographical area, currency or market); and

(c) the amount of the risk exposure associated with all financial instruments sharing that characteristic.

Maximum credit risk exposure (paragraph 36(a))

B9 Paragraph 36(a) requires disclosure of the amount that best represents the entity's maximum exposure to credit risk. For a financial asset, this is typically the gross carrying amount, net of:

(a) any amounts offset in accordance with IAS 32; and

(b) any impairment losses recognised in accordance with IAS 39.

B10 Activities that give rise to credit risk and the associated maximum exposure to credit risk include, but are not limited to:

(a) granting loans to customers and placing deposits with other entities. In these cases, the maximum exposure to credit risk is the carrying amount of the related financial assets.

(b) entering into derivative contracts, eg foreign exchange contracts, interest rate swaps and credit derivatives. When the resulting asset is measured at fair value, the maximum exposure to credit risk at the end of the reporting period will equal the carrying amount.

(c)   granting financial guarantees. In this case, the maximum exposure to credit risk is the maximum amount the entity could have to pay if the guarantee is called on, which may be significantly greater than the amount recognised as a liability.

(d)   making a loan commitment that is irrevocable over the life of the facility or is revocable only in response to a material adverse change. If the issuer cannot settle the loan commitment net in cash or another financial instrument, the maximum credit exposure is the full amount of the commitment. This is because it is uncertain whether the amount of any undrawn portion may be drawn upon in the future. This may be significantly greater than the amount recognised as a liability.

Quantitative liquidity risk disclosures (paragraphs 34(a) and 39(a) and (b))

B10A   In accordance with paragraph 34(a) an entity discloses summary quantitative data about its exposure to liquidity risk on the basis of the information provided internally to key management personnel. An entity shall explain how those data are determined. If the outflows of cash (or another financial asset) included in those data could either:

(a)   occur significantly earlier than indicated in the data, or

(b)   be for significantly different amounts from those indicated in the data (eg for a derivative that is included in the data on a net settlement basis but for which the counterparty has the option to require gross settlement),

the entity shall state that fact and provide quantitative information that enables users of its financial statements to evaluate the extent of this risk unless that information is included in the contractual maturity analyses required by paragraph 39(a) or (b).

B11   In preparing the maturity analyses required by paragraph 39(a) and (b), an entity uses its judgement to determine an appropriate number of time bands. For example, an entity might determine that the following time bands are appropriate:

(a)   not later than one month;

(b)   later than one month and not later than three months;

(c)   later than three months and not later than one year; and

(d)   later than one year and not later than five years.

B11A   In complying with paragraph 39(a) and (b), an entity shall not separate an embedded derivative from a hybrid (combined) financial instrument. For such an instrument, an entity shall apply paragraph 39(a).

B11B   Paragraph 39(b) requires an entity to disclose a quantitative maturity analysis for derivative financial liabilities that shows remaining contractual maturities if the contractual maturities are essential for an understanding of the timing of the cash flows. For example, this would be the case for:

    (a)   an interest rate swap with a remaining maturity of five years in a cash flow hedge of a variable rate financial asset or liability.

    (b)   all loan commitments.

B11C   Paragraph 39(a) and (b) requires an entity to disclose maturity analyses for financial liabilities that show the remaining contractual maturities for some financial liabilities. In this disclosure:

    (a)   when a counterparty has a choice of when an amount is paid, the liability is allocated to the earliest period in which the entity can be required to pay. For example, financial liabilities that an entity can be required to repay on demand (eg demand deposits) are included in the earliest time band.

    (b)   when an entity is committed to make amounts available in instalments, each instalment is allocated to the earliest period in which the entity can be required to pay. For example, an undrawn loan commitment is included in the time band containing the earliest date it can be drawn down.

    (c)   for issued financial guarantee contracts the maximum amount of the guarantee is allocated to the earliest period in which the guarantee could be called.

B11D   The contractual amounts disclosed in the maturity analyses as required by paragraph 39(a) and (b) are the contractual undiscounted cash flows, for example:

    (a)   gross finance lease obligations (before deducting finance charges);

    (b)   prices specified in forward agreements to purchase financial assets for cash;

    (c)   net amounts for pay-floating/receive-fixed interest rate swaps for which net cash flows are exchanged;

    (d)   contractual amounts to be exchanged in a derivative financial instrument (eg a currency swap) for which gross cash flows are exchanged; and

    (e)   gross loan commitments.

Such undiscounted cash flows differ from the amount included in the statement of financial position because the amount in that statement is based on discounted cash flows. When the amount payable is not fixed, the amount disclosed is determined by reference to the conditions existing at the end of the reporting period. For example, when the amount payable varies with changes in an index, the amount disclosed may be based on the level of the index at the end of the period.

B11E   Paragraph 39(c) requires an entity to describe how it manages the liquidity risk inherent in the items disclosed in the quantitative disclosures required in paragraph 39(a) and (b). An entity shall disclose a maturity analysis of financial assets it holds for managing liquidity risk (eg financial assets that are readily saleable or expected to generate cash inflows to meet cash outflows on financial liabilities), if that information is necessary to enable users of its financial statements to evaluate the nature and extent of liquidity risk.

B11F   Other factors that an entity might consider in providing the disclosure required in paragraph 39(c) include, but are not limited to, whether the entity:

(a)   has committed borrowing facilities (eg commercial paper facilities) or other lines of credit (eg stand-by credit facilities) that it can access to meet liquidity needs;

(b)   holds deposits at central banks to meet liquidity needs;

(c)   has very diverse funding sources;

(d)   has significant concentrations of liquidity risk in either its assets or its funding sources;

(e)   has internal control processes and contingency plans for managing liquidity risk;

(f)   has instruments that include accelerated repayment terms (eg on the downgrade of the entity's credit rating);

(g)   has instruments that could require the posting of collateral (eg margin calls for derivatives);

(h)   has instruments that allow the entity to choose whether it settles its financial liabilities by delivering cash (or another financial asset) or by delivering its own shares; or

(i)   has instruments that are subject to master netting agreements.

B12–B16 [Deleted]

Market risk – sensitivity analysis (paragraphs 40 and 41)

B17   Paragraph 40(a) requires a sensitivity analysis for each type of market risk to which the entity is exposed. In accordance with paragraph B3, an entity decides how it aggregates information to display the overall picture without combining information with different characteristics about exposures to risks from significantly different economic environments. For example:

(a)   an entity that trades financial instruments might disclose this information separately for financial instruments held for trading and those not held for trading.

(b)   an entity would not aggregate its exposure to market risks from areas of hyperinflation with its exposure to the same market risks from areas of very low inflation.

If an entity has exposure to only one type of market risk in only one economic environment, it would not show disaggregated information.

B18   Paragraph 40(a) requires the sensitivity analysis to show the effect on profit or loss and equity of reasonably possible changes in the relevant risk variable (eg prevailing market interest rates, currency rates, equity prices or commodity prices). For this purpose:

(a)   entities are not required to determine what the profit or loss for the period would have been if relevant risk variables had been different. Instead, entities disclose the effect on profit or loss and equity at the end of the reporting period assuming that a reasonably possible change in the relevant risk variable had occurred at the end of the reporting period and had been applied to the risk exposures in existence at that date. For example, if an entity has a floating rate liability at the end of the year, the entity would disclose the effect on profit or loss (ie interest expense) for the current year if interest rates had varied by reasonably possible amounts.

(b) entities are not required to disclose the effect on profit or loss and equity for each change within a range of reasonably possible changes of the relevant risk variable. Disclosure of the effects of the changes at the limits of the reasonably possible range would be sufficient.

B19 In determining what a reasonably possible change in the relevant risk variable is, an entity should consider:

(a) the economic environments in which it operates. A reasonably possible change should not include remote or 'worst case' scenarios or 'stress tests'. Moreover, if the rate of change in the underlying risk variable is stable, the entity need not alter the chosen reasonably possible change in the risk variable. For example, assume that interest rates are 5 per cent and an entity determines that a fluctuation in interest rates of ±50 basis points is reasonably possible. It would disclose the effect on profit or loss and equity if interest rates were to change to 4.5 per cent or 5.5 per cent. In the next period, interest rates have increased to 5.5 per cent. The entity continues to believe that interest rates may fluctuate by ±50 basis points (ie that the rate of change in interest rates is stable). The entity would disclose the effect on profit or loss and equity if interest rates were to change to 5 per cent or 6 per cent. The entity would not be required to revise its assessment that interest rates might reasonably fluctuate by ±50 basis points, unless there is evidence that interest rates have become significantly more volatile.

(b) the time frame over which it is making the assessment. The sensitivity analysis shall show the effects of changes that are considered to be reasonably possible over the period until the entity will next present these disclosures, which is usually its next annual reporting period.

B20 Paragraph 41 permits an entity to use a sensitivity analysis that reflects interdependencies between risk variables, such as a value-at-risk methodology, if it uses this analysis to manage its exposure to financial risks. This applies even if such a methodology measures only the potential for loss and does not measure the potential for gain. Such an entity might comply with paragraph 41(a) by disclosing the type of value-at-risk model used (eg whether the model relies on Monte Carlo simulations), an explanation about how the model works and the main assumptions (eg the holding period and confidence level). Entities might also disclose the historical observation period and weightings applied to observations within that period, an explanation of how options are dealt with in the calculations, and which volatilities and correlations (or, alternatively, Monte Carlo probability distribution simulations) are used.

B21 An entity shall provide sensitivity analyses for the whole of its business, but may provide different types of sensitivity analysis for different classes of financial instruments.

Interest rate risk

B22   *Interest rate risk* arises on interest-bearing financial instruments recognised in the statement of financial position (eg debt instruments acquired or issued) and on some financial instruments not recognised in the statement of financial position (eg some loan commitments).

Currency risk

B23   *Currency risk* (or foreign exchange risk) arises on financial instruments that are denominated in a foreign currency, ie in a currency other than the functional currency in which they are measured. For the purpose of this IFRS, currency risk does not arise from financial instruments that are non-monetary items or from financial instruments denominated in the functional currency.

B24   A sensitivity analysis is disclosed for each currency to which an entity has significant exposure.

Other price risk

B25   *Other price risk* arises on financial instruments because of changes in, for example, commodity prices or equity prices. To comply with paragraph 40, an entity might disclose the effect of a decrease in a specified stock market index, commodity price, or other risk variable. For example, if an entity gives residual value guarantees that are financial instruments, the entity discloses an increase or decrease in the value of the assets to which the guarantee applies.

B26   Two examples of financial instruments that give rise to equity price risk are (a) a holding of equities in another entity and (b) an investment in a trust that in turn holds investments in equity instruments. Other examples include forward contracts and options to buy or sell specified quantities of an equity instrument and swaps that are indexed to equity prices. The fair values of such financial instruments are affected by changes in the market price of the underlying equity instruments.

B27   In accordance with paragraph 40(a), the sensitivity of profit or loss (that arises, for example, from instruments measured at fair value through profit or loss) is disclosed separately from the sensitivity of other comprehensive income (that arises, for example, from investments in equity instruments whose changes in fair value are presented in other comprehensive income).

B28   Financial instruments that an entity classifies as equity instruments are not remeasured. Neither profit or loss nor equity will be affected by the equity price risk of those instruments. Accordingly, no sensitivity analysis is required.

Derecognition (paragraphs 42C–42H)

Continuing involvement (paragraph 42C)

B29   The assessment of continuing involvement in a transferred financial asset for the purposes of the disclosure requirements in paragraphs 42E–42H is made at the level of the reporting entity. For example, if a subsidiary transfers to an unrelated third party a financial asset in which the parent of the subsidiary has continuing involvement, the subsidiary does not include the parent's involvement in the assessment of whether it has continuing involvement in the transferred asset in its separate or individual financial statements (ie when the subsidiary is the reporting entity). However, a parent would include its continuing involvement (or that of another member of the group) in a financial asset transferred by its subsidiary in determining whether it has continuing involvement in the transferred asset in its consolidated financial statements (ie when the reporting entity is the group).

B30 An entity does not have a continuing involvement in a transferred financial asset if, as part of the transfer, it neither retains any of the contractual rights or obligations inherent in the transferred financial asset nor acquires any new contractual rights or obligations relating to the transferred financial asset. An entity does not have continuing involvement in a transferred financial asset if it has neither an interest in the future performance of the transferred financial asset nor a responsibility under any circumstances to make payments in respect of the transferred financial asset in the future.

B31 Continuing involvement in a transferred financial asset may result from contractual provisions in the transfer agreement or in a separate agreement with the transferee or a third party entered into in connection with the transfer.

Transferred financial assets that are not derecognised in their entirety (paragraph 42D)

B32 Paragraph 42D requires disclosures when part or all of the transferred financial assets do not qualify for derecognition. Those disclosures are required at each reporting date at which the entity continues to recognise the transferred financial assets, regardless of when the transfers occurred.

Types of continuing involvement (paragraphs 42E–42H)

B33 Paragraphs 42E–42H require qualitative and quantitative disclosures for each type of continuing involvement in derecognised financial assets. An entity shall aggregate its continuing involvement into types that are representative of the entity's exposure to risks. For example, an entity may aggregate its continuing involvement by type of financial instrument (eg guarantees or call options) or by type of transfer (eg factoring of receivables, securitisations and securities lending).

Maturity analysis for undiscounted cash outflows to repurchase transferred assets (paragraph 42E(e))

B34 Paragraph 42E(e) requires an entity to disclose a maturity analysis of the undiscounted cash outflows to repurchase derecognised financial assets or other amounts payable to the transferee in respect of the derecognised financial assets, showing the remaining contractual maturities of the entity's continuing involvement. This analysis distinguishes cash flows that are required to be paid (eg forward contracts), cash flows that the entity may be required to pay (eg written put options) and cash flows that the entity might choose to pay (eg purchased call options).

B35 An entity shall use its judgement to determine an appropriate number of time bands in preparing the maturity analysis required by paragraph 42E(e). For example, an entity might determine that the following maturity time bands are appropriate:

(a) not later than one month;

(b) later than one month and not later than three months;

(c) later than three months and not later than six months;

(d) later than six months and not later than one year;

(e) later than one year and not later than three years;

(f) later than three years and not later than five years; and

(g) more than five years.

B36 If there is a range of possible maturities, the cash flows are included on the basis of the earliest date on which the entity can be required or is permitted to pay.

Qualitative information (paragraph 42E(f))

B37 The qualitative information required by paragraph 42E(f) includes a description of the derecognised financial assets and the nature and purpose of the continuing involvement retained after transferring those assets. It also includes a description of the risks to which an entity is exposed, including:

(a) a description of how the entity manages the risk inherent in its continuing involvement in the derecognised financial assets.

(b) whether the entity is required to bear losses before other parties, and the ranking and amounts of losses borne by parties whose interests rank lower than the entity's interest in the asset (ie its continuing involvement in the asset).

(c) a description of any triggers associated with obligations to provide financial support or to repurchase a transferred financial asset.

Gain or loss on derecognition (paragraph 42G(a))

B38 Paragraph 42G(a) requires an entity to disclose the gain or loss on derecognition relating to financial assets in which the entity has continuing involvement. The entity shall disclose if a gain or loss on derecognition arose because the fair values of the components of the previously recognised asset (ie the interest in the asset derecognised and the interest retained by the entity) were different from the fair value of the previously recognised asset as a whole. In that situation, the entity shall also disclose whether the fair value measurements included significant inputs that were not based on observable market data, as described in paragraph 27A.

Supplementary information (paragraph 42H)

B39 The disclosures required in paragraphs 42D–42G may not be sufficient to meet the disclosure objectives in paragraph 42B. If this is the case, the entity shall disclose whatever additional information is necessary to meet the disclosure objectives. The entity shall decide, in the light of its circumstances, how much additional information it needs to provide to satisfy the information needs of users and how much emphasis it places on different aspects of the additional information. It is necessary to strike a balance between burdening financial statements with excessive detail that may not assist users of financial statements and obscuring information as a result of too much aggregation.

Offsetting financial assets and financial liabilities (paragraphs 13A–13F)

Scope (paragraph 13A)

B40 The disclosures in paragraphs 13B–13E are required for all recognised financial instruments that are set off in accordance with paragraph 42 of IAS 32. In addition, financial instruments are within the scope of the disclosure requirements in paragraphs 13B–13E if they are subject to an enforceable master netting arrangement or similar agreement that covers similar financial instruments and transactions, irrespective of whether the financial instruments are set off in accordance with paragraph 42 of IAS 32.

B41 The similar agreements referred to in paragraphs 13A and B40 include derivative clearing agreements, global master repurchase agreements, global master securities lending agreements, and any related rights to financial collateral. The similar financial instruments and transactions referred to in paragraph B40 include derivatives, sale and repurchase agreements, reverse sale and repurchase agreements, securities borrowing, and securities lending agreements. Examples of financial instruments that are not within the scope of paragraph 13A are loans and customer deposits at the same institution (unless they are set off in the statement of financial position), and financial instruments that are subject only to a collateral agreement.

Disclosure of quantitative information for recognised financial assets and recognised financial liabilities within the scope of paragraph 13A (paragraph 13C)

B42 Financial instruments disclosed in accordance with paragraph 13C may be subject to different measurement requirements (for example, a payable related to a repurchase agreement may be measured at amortised cost, while a derivative will be measured at fair value). An entity shall include instruments at their recognised amounts and describe any resulting measurement differences in the related disclosures.

Disclosure of the gross amounts of recognised financial assets and recognised financial liabilities within the scope of paragraph 13A (paragraph 13C(a))

B43   The amounts required by paragraph 13C(a) relate to recognised financial instruments that are set off in accordance with paragraph 42 of IAS 32. The amounts required by paragraph 13C(a) also relate to recognised financial instruments that are subject to an enforceable master netting arrangement or similar agreement irrespective of whether they meet the offsetting criteria. However, the disclosures required by paragraph 13C(a) do not relate to any amounts recognised as a result of collateral agreements that do not meet the offsetting criteria in paragraph 42 of IAS 32. Instead, such amounts are required to be disclosed in accordance with paragraph 13C(d).

Disclosure of the amounts that are set off in accordance with the criteria in paragraph 42 of IAS 32 (paragraph 13C(b))

B44   Paragraph 13C(b) requires that entities disclose the amounts set off in accordance with paragraph 42 of IAS 32 when determining the net amounts presented in the statement of financial position. The amounts of both the recognised financial assets and the recognised financial liabilities that are subject to set-off under the same arrangement will be disclosed in both the financial asset and financial liability disclosures. However, the amounts disclosed (in, for example, a table) are limited to the amounts that are subject to set-off. For example, an entity may have a recognised derivative asset and a recognised derivative liability that meet the offsetting criteria in paragraph 42 of IAS 32. If the gross amount of the derivative asset is larger than the gross amount of the derivative liability, the financial asset disclosure table will include the entire amount of the derivative asset (in accordance with paragraph 13C(a)) and the entire amount of the derivative liability (in accordance with paragraph 13C(b)). However, while the financial liability disclosure table will include the entire amount of the derivative liability (in accordance with paragraph 13C(a)), it will only include the amount of the derivative asset (in accordance with paragraph 13C(b)) that is equal to the amount of the derivative liability.

Disclosure of the net amounts presented in the statement of financial position (paragraph 13C(c))

B45   If an entity has instruments that meet the scope of these disclosures (as specified in paragraph 13A), but that do not meet the offsetting criteria in paragraph 42 of IAS 32, the amounts required to be disclosed by paragraph 13C(c) would equal the amounts required to be disclosed by paragraph 13C(a).

B46   The amounts required to be disclosed by paragraph 13C(c) must be reconciled to the individual line item amounts presented in the statement of financial position. For example, if an entity determines that the aggregation or disaggregation of individual financial statement line item amounts provides more relevant information, it must reconcile the aggregated or disaggregated amounts disclosed in paragraph 13C(c) back to the individual line item amounts presented in the statement of financial position.

Disclosure of the amounts subject to an enforceable master netting arrangement or similar agreement that are not otherwise included in paragraph 13C(b) (paragraph 13C(d))

B47 Paragraph 13C(d) requires that entities disclose amounts that are subject to an enforceable master netting arrangement or similar agreement that are not otherwise included in paragraph 13C(b). Paragraph 13C(d)(i) refers to amounts related to recognised financial instruments that do not meet some or all of the offsetting criteria in paragraph 42 of IAS 32 (for example, current rights of set-off that do not meet the criterion in paragraph 42(b) of IAS 32, or conditional rights of set-off that are enforceable and exercisable only in the event of default, or only in the event of insolvency or bankruptcy of any of the counterparties).

B48 Paragraph 13C(d)(ii) refers to amounts related to financial collateral, including cash collateral, both received and pledged. An entity shall disclose the fair value of those financial instruments that have been pledged or received as collateral. The amounts disclosed in accordance with paragraph 13C(d)(ii) should relate to the actual collateral received or pledged and not to any resulting payables or receivables recognised to return or receive back such collateral.

Limits on the amounts disclosed in paragraph 13C(d) (paragraph 13D)

B49 When disclosing amounts in accordance with paragraph 13C(d), an entity must take into account the effects of over-collateralisation by financial instrument. To do so, the entity must first deduct the amounts disclosed in accordance with paragraph 13C(d)(i) from the amount disclosed in accordance with paragraph 13C(c). The entity shall then limit the amounts disclosed in accordance with paragraph 13C(d)(ii) to the remaining amount in paragraph 13C(c) for the related financial instrument. However, if rights to collateral can be enforced across financial instruments, such rights can be included in the disclosure provided in accordance with paragraph 13D.

Description of the rights of set-off subject to enforceable master netting arrangements and similar agreements (paragraph 13E)

B50 An entity shall describe the types of rights of set-off and similar arrangements disclosed in accordance with paragraph 13C(d), including the nature of those rights. For example, an entity shall describe its conditional rights. For instruments subject to rights of set-off that are not contingent on a future event but that do not meet the remaining criteria in paragraph 42 of IAS 32, the entity shall describe the reason(s) why the criteria are not met. For any financial collateral received or pledged, the entity shall describe the terms of the collateral agreement (for example, when the collateral is restricted).

Disclosure by type of financial instrument or by counterparty

B51 The quantitative disclosures required by paragraph 13C(a)–(e) may be grouped by type of financial instrument or transaction (for example, derivatives, repurchase and reverse repurchase agreements or securities borrowing and securities lending agreements).

B52 Alternatively, an entity may group the quantitative disclosures required by paragraph 13C(a)–(c) by type of financial instrument, and the quantitative disclosures required by paragraph 13C(c)–(e) by counterparty. If an entity provides the required information by counterparty, the entity is not required to identify the counterparties by name. However, designation of counterparties (Counterparty A, Counterparty B, Counterparty C, etc) shall remain consistent from year to year for the years presented to maintain comparability. Qualitative disclosures shall be considered so that further information can be given about the types of counterparties. When disclosure of the amounts in paragraph 13C(c)–(e) is provided by counterparty, amounts that are individually significant in terms of total counterparty amounts shall be separately disclosed and the remaining individually insignificant counterparty amounts shall be aggregated into one line item.

Other

B53 The specific disclosures required by paragraphs 13C–13E are minimum requirements. To meet the objective in paragraph 13B an entity may need to supplement them with additional (qualitative) disclosures, depending on the terms of the enforceable master netting arrangements and related agreements, including the nature of the rights of set-off, and their effect or potential effect on the entity's financial position.

Appendix C
Amendments to other IFRSs

The amendments in this appendix shall be applied for annual periods beginning on or after 1 January 2007. If an entity applies this IFRS for an earlier period, these amendments shall be applied for that earlier period.

* * * * *

The amendments contained in this appendix when this IFRS was issued in 2005 have been incorporated into the text of the relevant IFRSs included in this volume.

International Financial Reporting Standard 8

Operating Segments

In April 2001 the International Accounting Standards Board (IASB) adopted IAS 14 *Segment Reporting*, which had originally been issued by the International Accounting Standards Committee in August 1997. IAS 14 *Segment Reporting* replaced IAS 14 *Reporting Financial Information by Segment*, issued in August 1981.

In November 2006 the IASB issued IFRS 8 *Operating Segments* to replace IAS 14. IAS 1 *Presentation of Financial Statements* (as revised in 2007) amended the terminology used throughout IFRSs, including IFRS 8.

Other IFRSs have made minor consequential amendments to IAS 14 and IFRS 8. They include IAS 1 *Presentation of Financial Statements* (as revised in September 2007), *Improvements to IFRSs* (issued April 2009) and IAS 24 *Related Party Disclosures* (issued November 2009).

CONTENTS

FOR THE ACCOMPANYING DOCUMENTS LISTED BELOW, SEE PART B OF THIS EDITION

International Financial Reporting Standard 8 *Operating Segments* (IFRS 8) is set out in paragraphs 1–37 and Appendices A and B. All the paragraphs have equal authority. Paragraphs in **bold type** state the main principles. Definitions of terms are given in the Glossary for International Financial Reporting Standards. IFRS 8 should be read in the context of its core principle and the Basis for Conclusions, the *Preface to International Financial Reporting Standards* and the *Conceptual Framework for Financial Reporting*. IAS 8 *Accounting Policies, Changes in Accounting Estimates and Errors* provides a basis for selecting and applying accounting policies in the absence of explicit guidance.

Introduction

Reasons for issuing the IFRS

IN1   International Financial Reporting Standard 8 *Operating Segments* sets out requirements for disclosure of information about an entity's operating segments and also about the entity's products and services, the geographical areas in which it operates, and its major customers.

IN2   Achieving convergence of accounting standards around the world is one of the prime objectives of the International Accounting Standards Board. In pursuit of that objective, the Board and the Financial Accounting Standards Board (FASB) in the United States have undertaken a joint short-term project with the objective of reducing differences between International Financial Reporting Standards (IFRSs) and US generally accepted accounting principles (US GAAP) that are capable of resolution in a relatively short time and can be addressed outside major projects. One aspect of that project involves the two boards considering each other's recent standards with a view to adopting high quality financial reporting solutions. The IFRS arises from the IASB's consideration of FASB Statement No.131 *Disclosures about Segments of an Enterprise and Related Information* (SFAS 131) issued in 1997, compared with IAS 14 *Segment Reporting*, which was issued in substantially its present form by the IASB's predecessor body, the International Accounting Standards Committee, in 1997.

IN3   The IFRS achieves convergence with the requirements of SFAS 131, except for minor differences listed in paragraph BC60 of the Basis for Conclusions. The wording of the IFRS is the same as that of SFAS 131 except for changes necessary to make the terminology consistent with that in other IFRSs.

Main features of the IFRS

IN4   The IFRS specifies how an entity should report information about its operating segments in annual financial statements and, as a consequential amendment to IAS 34 *Interim Financial Reporting*, requires an entity to report selected information about its operating segments in interim financial reports. It also sets out requirements for related disclosures about products and services, geographical areas and major customers.

IN5   The IFRS requires an entity to report financial and descriptive information about its reportable segments. Reportable segments are operating segments or aggregations of operating segments that meet specified criteria. Operating segments are components of an entity about which separate financial information is available that is evaluated regularly by the chief operating decision maker in deciding how to allocate resources and in assessing performance. Generally, financial information is required to be reported on the same basis as is used internally for evaluating operating segment performance and deciding how to allocate resources to operating segments.

IN6   The IFRS requires an entity to report a measure of operating segment profit or loss and of segment assets. It also requires an entity to report a measure of segment liabilities and particular income and expense items if such measures are regularly provided to the chief operating decision maker. It requires reconciliations of total reportable segment revenues, total profit or loss, total assets, liabilities and other amounts disclosed for reportable segments to corresponding amounts in the entity's financial statements.

IN7   The IFRS requires an entity to report information about the revenues derived from its products or services (or groups of similar products and services), about the countries in which it earns revenues and holds assets, and about major customers, regardless of whether that information is used by management in making operating decisions. However, the IFRS does not require an entity to report information that is not prepared for internal use if the necessary information is not available and the cost to develop it would be excessive.

IN8   The IFRS also requires an entity to give descriptive information about the way the operating segments were determined, the products and services provided by the segments, differences between the measurements used in reporting segment information and those used in the entity's financial statements, and changes in the measurement of segment amounts from period to period.

IN9   An entity shall apply this IFRS for annual periods beginning on or after 1 January 2009. Earlier application is permitted. If an entity applies this IFRS for an earlier period, it shall disclose that fact.

Changes from previous requirements

IN10   The IFRS replaces IAS 14 *Segment Reporting*. The main changes from IAS 14 are described below.

Identification of segments

IN11   The requirements of the IFRS are based on the information about the components of the entity that management uses to make decisions about operating matters. The IFRS requires identification of operating segments on the basis of internal reports that are regularly reviewed by the entity's chief operating decision maker in order to allocate resources to the segment and assess its performance. IAS 14 required identification of two sets of segments—one based on related products and services, and the other on geographical areas. IAS 14 regarded one set as primary segments and the other as secondary segments.

IN12   A component of an entity that sells primarily or exclusively to other operating segments of the entity is included in the IFRS's definition of an operating segment if the entity is managed that way. IAS 14 limited reportable segments to those that earn a majority of their revenue from sales to external customers and therefore did not require the different stages of vertically integrated operations to be identified as separate segments.

Measurement of segment information

IN13   The IFRS requires the amount reported for each operating segment item to be the measure reported to the chief operating decision maker for the purposes of allocating resources to the segment and assessing its performance. IAS 14 required segment information to be prepared in conformity with the accounting policies adopted for preparing and presenting the financial statements of the consolidated group or entity.

IN14   IAS 14 defined segment revenue, segment expense, segment result, segment assets and segment liabilities. The IFRS does not define these terms, but requires an explanation of how segment profit or loss, segment assets and segment liabilities are measured for each reportable segment.

Disclosure

IN15   The IFRS requires an entity to disclose the following information:

(a)   factors used to identify the entity's operating segments, including the basis of organisation (for example, whether management organises the entity around differences in products and services, geographical areas, regulatory environments, or a combination of factors and whether segments have been aggregated), and

(b)   types of products and services from which each reportable segment derives its revenues.

IN16   IAS 14 required the entity to disclose specified items of information about its primary segments. The IFRS requires an entity to disclose specified amounts about each reportable segment, if the specified amounts are included in the measure of segment profit or loss and are reviewed by or otherwise regularly provided to the chief operating decision maker.

IN17   The IFRS requires an entity to report interest revenue separately from interest expense for each reportable segment unless a majority of the segment's revenues are from interest and the chief operating decision maker relies primarily on net interest revenue to assess the performance of the segment and to make decisions about resources to be allocated to the segment. IAS 14 did not require disclosure of interest income and expense.

IN18   The IFRS requires an entity, including an entity with a single reportable segment, to disclose information for the entity as a whole about its products and services, geographical areas, and major customers. This requirement applies, regardless of the entity's organisation, if the information is not included as part of the disclosures about segments. IAS 14 required the disclosure of secondary segment information for either industry or geographical segments, to supplement the information given for the primary segments.

International Financial Reporting Standard 8
Operating Segments

Core principle

1   An entity shall disclose information to enable users of its financial statements to evaluate the nature and financial effects of the business activities in which it engages and the economic environments in which it operates.

Scope

2   This IFRS shall apply to:

    (a)   the separate or individual financial statements of an entity:

        (i)   whose debt or equity instruments are traded in a public market (a domestic or foreign stock exchange or an over-the-counter market, including local and regional markets), or

        (ii)   that files, or is in the process of filing, its financial statements with a securities commission or other regulatory organisation for the purpose of issuing any class of instruments in a public market; and

    (b)   the consolidated financial statements of a group with a parent:

        (i)   whose debt or equity instruments are traded in a public market (a domestic or foreign stock exchange or an over-the-counter market, including local and regional markets), or

        (ii)   that files, or is in the process of filing, the consolidated financial statements with a securities commission or other regulatory organisation for the purpose of issuing any class of instruments in a public market.

3   If an entity that is not required to apply this IFRS chooses to disclose information about segments that does not comply with this IFRS, it shall not describe the information as segment information.

4   If a financial report contains both the consolidated financial statements of a parent that is within the scope of this IFRS as well as the parent's separate financial statements, segment information is required only in the consolidated financial statements.

Operating segments

5   An operating segment is a component of an entity:

    (a)   that engages in business activities from which it may earn revenues and incur expenses (including revenues and expenses relating to transactions with other components of the same entity),

(b)   whose operating results are regularly reviewed by the entity's chief operating decision maker to make decisions about resources to be allocated to the segment and assess its performance, and

(c)   for which discrete financial information is available.

An operating segment may engage in business activities for which it has yet to earn revenues, for example, start-up operations may be operating segments before earning revenues.

6   Not every part of an entity is necessarily an operating segment or part of an operating segment. For example, a corporate headquarters or some functional departments may not earn revenues or may earn revenues that are only incidental to the activities of the entity and would not be operating segments. For the purposes of this IFRS, an entity's post-employment benefit plans are not operating segments.

7   The term 'chief operating decision maker' identifies a function, not necessarily a manager with a specific title. That function is to allocate resources to and assess the performance of the operating segments of an entity. Often the chief operating decision maker of an entity is its chief executive officer or chief operating officer but, for example, it may be a group of executive directors or others.

8   For many entities, the three characteristics of operating segments described in paragraph 5 clearly identify its operating segments. However, an entity may produce reports in which its business activities are presented in a variety of ways. If the chief operating decision maker uses more than one set of segment information, other factors may identify a single set of components as constituting an entity's operating segments, including the nature of the business activities of each component, the existence of managers responsible for them, and information presented to the board of directors.

9   Generally, an operating segment has a segment manager who is directly accountable to and maintains regular contact with the chief operating decision maker to discuss operating activities, financial results, forecasts, or plans for the segment. The term 'segment manager' identifies a function, not necessarily a manager with a specific title. The chief operating decision maker also may be the segment manager for some operating segments. A single manager may be the segment manager for more than one operating segment. If the characteristics in paragraph 5 apply to more than one set of components of an organisation but there is only one set for which segment managers are held responsible, that set of components constitutes the operating segments.

10   The characteristics in paragraph 5 may apply to two or more overlapping sets of components for which managers are held responsible. That structure is sometimes referred to as a matrix form of organisation. For example, in some entities, some managers are responsible for different product and service lines worldwide, whereas other managers are responsible for specific geographical areas. The chief operating decision maker regularly reviews the operating results of both sets of components, and financial information is available for both. In that situation, the entity shall determine which set of components constitutes the operating segments by reference to the core principle.

Reportable segments

11   An entity shall report separately information about each operating segment that:

(a)   has been identified in accordance with paragraphs 5–10 or results from aggregating two or more of those segments in accordance with paragraph 12, and

(b)   exceeds the quantitative thresholds in paragraph 13.

Paragraphs 14–19 specify other situations in which separate information about an operating segment shall be reported.

Aggregation criteria

12   Operating segments often exhibit similar long-term financial performance if they have similar economic characteristics. For example, similar long-term average gross margins for two operating segments would be expected if their economic characteristics were similar. Two or more operating segments may be aggregated into a single operating segment if aggregation is consistent with the core principle of this IFRS, the segments have similar economic characteristics, and the segments are similar in each of the following respects:

(a)   the nature of the products and services;

(b)   the nature of the production processes;

(c)   the type or class of customer for their products and services;

(d)   the methods used to distribute their products or provide their services; and

(e)   if applicable, the nature of the regulatory environment, for example, banking, insurance or public utilities.

Quantitative thresholds

13   An entity shall report separately information about an operating segment that meets any of the following quantitative thresholds:

(a)   Its reported revenue, including both sales to external customers and intersegment sales or transfers, is 10 per cent or more of the combined revenue, internal and external, of all operating segments.

(b)   The absolute amount of its reported profit or loss is 10 per cent or more of the greater, in absolute amount, of (i) the combined reported profit of all operating segments that did not report a loss and (ii) the combined reported loss of all operating segments that reported a loss.

(c)   Its assets are 10 per cent or more of the combined assets of all operating segments.

Operating segments that do not meet any of the quantitative thresholds may be considered reportable, and separately disclosed, if management believes that information about the segment would be useful to users of the financial statements.

14 An entity may combine information about operating segments that do not meet the quantitative thresholds with information about other operating segments that do not meet the quantitative thresholds to produce a reportable segment only if the operating segments have similar economic characteristics and share a majority of the aggregation criteria listed in paragraph 12.

15 If the total external revenue reported by operating segments constitutes less than 75 per cent of the entity's revenue, additional operating segments shall be identified as reportable segments (even if they do not meet the criteria in paragraph 13) until at least 75 per cent of the entity's revenue is included in reportable segments.

16 Information about other business activities and operating segments that are not reportable shall be combined and disclosed in an 'all other segments' category separately from other reconciling items in the reconciliations required by paragraph 28. The sources of the revenue included in the 'all other segments' category shall be described.

17 If management judges that an operating segment identified as a reportable segment in the immediately preceding period is of continuing significance, information about that segment shall continue to be reported separately in the current period even if it no longer meets the criteria for reportability in paragraph 13.

18 If an operating segment is identified as a reportable segment in the current period in accordance with the quantitative thresholds, segment data for a prior period presented for comparative purposes shall be restated to reflect the newly reportable segment as a separate segment, even if that segment did not satisfy the criteria for reportability in paragraph 13 in the prior period, unless the necessary information is not available and the cost to develop it would be excessive.

19 There may be a practical limit to the number of reportable segments that an entity separately discloses beyond which segment information may become too detailed. Although no precise limit has been determined, as the number of segments that are reportable in accordance with paragraphs 13–18 increases above ten, the entity should consider whether a practical limit has been reached.

Disclosure

20 **An entity shall disclose information to enable users of its financial statements to evaluate the nature and financial effects of the business activities in which it engages and the economic environments in which it operates.**

21 To give effect to the principle in paragraph 20, an entity shall disclose the following for each period for which a statement of comprehensive income is presented:

(a) general information as described in paragraph 22;

(b) information about reported segment profit or loss, including specified revenues and expenses included in reported segment profit or loss, segment assets, segment liabilities and the basis of measurement, as described in paragraphs 23–27; and

(c)   reconciliations of the totals of segment revenues, reported segment profit or loss, segment assets, segment liabilities and other material segment items to corresponding entity amounts as described in paragraph 28.

Reconciliations of the amounts in the statement of financial position for reportable segments to the amounts in the entity's statement of financial position are required for each date at which a statement of financial position is presented. Information for prior periods shall be restated as described in paragraphs 29 and 30.

General information

22   An entity shall disclose the following general information:

(a)   factors used to identify the entity's reportable segments, including the basis of organisation (for example, whether management has chosen to organise the entity around differences in products and services, geographical areas, regulatory environments, or a combination of factors and whether operating segments have been aggregated), and

(b)   types of products and services from which each reportable segment derives its revenues.

Information about profit or loss, assets and liabilities

23   An entity shall report a measure of profit or loss for each reportable segment. An entity shall report a measure of total assets and liabilities for each reportable segment if such amounts are regularly provided to the chief operating decision maker. An entity shall also disclose the following about each reportable segment if the specified amounts are included in the measure of segment profit or loss reviewed by the chief operating decision maker, or are otherwise regularly provided to the chief operating decision maker, even if not included in that measure of segment profit or loss:

(a)   revenues from external customers;

(b)   revenues from transactions with other operating segments of the same entity;

(c)   interest revenue;

(d)   interest expense;

(e)   depreciation and amortisation;

(f)   material items of income and expense disclosed in accordance with paragraph 97 of IAS 1 *Presentation of Financial Statements* (as revised in 2007);

(g)   the entity's interest in the profit or loss of associates and joint ventures accounted for by the equity method;

(h)   income tax expense or income; and

(i)   material non-cash items other than depreciation and amortisation.

An entity shall report interest revenue separately from interest expense for each reportable segment unless a majority of the segment's revenues are from interest and the chief operating decision maker relies primarily on net interest revenue to assess the performance of the segment and make decisions about resources to be allocated to the segment. In that situation, an entity may report that segment's interest revenue net of its interest expense and disclose that it has done so.

24 An entity shall disclose the following about each reportable segment if the specified amounts are included in the measure of segment assets reviewed by the chief operating decision maker or are otherwise regularly provided to the chief operating decision maker, even if not included in the measure of segment assets:

(a) the amount of investment in associates and joint ventures accounted for by the equity method, and

(b) the amounts of additions to non-current assets[1] other than financial instruments, deferred tax assets, net defined benefit assets (see IAS 19 *Employee Benefits*) and rights arising under insurance contracts.

Measurement

25 The amount of each segment item reported shall be the measure reported to the chief operating decision maker for the purposes of making decisions about allocating resources to the segment and assessing its performance. Adjustments and eliminations made in preparing an entity's financial statements and allocations of revenues, expenses, and gains or losses shall be included in determining reported segment profit or loss only if they are included in the measure of the segment's profit or loss that is used by the chief operating decision maker. Similarly, only those assets and liabilities that are included in the measures of the segment's assets and segment's liabilities that are used by the chief operating decision maker shall be reported for that segment. If amounts are allocated to reported segment profit or loss, assets or liabilities, those amounts shall be allocated on a reasonable basis.

26 If the chief operating decision maker uses only one measure of an operating segment's profit or loss, the segment's assets or the segment's liabilities in assessing segment performance and deciding how to allocate resources, segment profit or loss, assets and liabilities shall be reported at those measures. If the chief operating decision maker uses more than one measure of an operating segment's profit or loss, the segment's assets or the segment's liabilities, the reported measures shall be those that management believes are determined in accordance with the measurement principles most consistent with those used in measuring the corresponding amounts in the entity's financial statements.

27 An entity shall provide an explanation of the measurements of segment profit or loss, segment assets and segment liabilities for each reportable segment. At a minimum, an entity shall disclose the following:

(a) the basis of accounting for any transactions between reportable segments.

---

1 For assets classified according to a liquidity presentation, non-current assets are assets that include amounts expected to be recovered more than twelve months after the reporting period.

(b)   the nature of any differences between the measurements of the reportable segments' profits or losses and the entity's profit or loss before income tax expense or income and discontinued operations (if not apparent from the reconciliations described in paragraph 28).   Those differences could include accounting policies and policies for allocation of centrally incurred costs that are necessary for an understanding of the reported segment information.

(c)   the nature of any differences between the measurements of the reportable segments' assets and the entity's assets (if not apparent from the reconciliations described in paragraph 28). Those differences could include accounting policies and policies for allocation of jointly used assets that are necessary for an understanding of the reported segment information.

(d)   the nature of any differences between the measurements of the reportable segments' liabilities and the entity's liabilities (if not apparent from the reconciliations described in paragraph 28).   Those differences could include accounting policies and policies for allocation of jointly utilised liabilities that are necessary for an understanding of the reported segment information.

(e)   the nature of any changes from prior periods in the measurement methods used to determine reported segment profit or loss and the effect, if any, of those changes on the measure of segment profit or loss.

(f)   the nature and effect of any asymmetrical allocations to reportable segments. For example, an entity might allocate depreciation expense to a segment without allocating the related depreciable assets to that segment.

Reconciliations

28   An entity shall provide reconciliations of all of the following:

(a)   the total of the reportable segments' revenues to the entity's revenue.

(b)   the total of the reportable segments' measures of profit or loss to the entity's profit or loss before tax expense (tax income) and discontinued operations. However, if an entity allocates to reportable segments items such as tax expense (tax income), the entity may reconcile the total of the segments' measures of profit or loss to the entity's profit or loss after those items.

(c)   the total of the reportable segments' assets to the entity's assets.

(d)   the total of the reportable segments' liabilities to the entity's liabilities if segment liabilities are reported in accordance with paragraph 23.

(e)   the total of the reportable segments' amounts for every other material item of information disclosed to the corresponding amount for the entity.

All material reconciling items shall be separately identified and described. For example, the amount of each material adjustment needed to reconcile reportable segment profit or loss to the entity's profit or loss arising from different accounting policies shall be separately identified and described.

Restatement of previously reported information

29   If an entity changes the structure of its internal organisation in a manner that causes the composition of its reportable segments to change, the corresponding information for earlier periods, including interim periods, shall be restated unless the information is not available and the cost to develop it would be excessive. The determination of whether the information is not available and the cost to develop it would be excessive shall be made for each individual item of disclosure. Following a change in the composition of its reportable segments, an entity shall disclose whether it has restated the corresponding items of segment information for earlier periods.

30   If an entity has changed the structure of its internal organisation in a manner that causes the composition of its reportable segments to change and if segment information for earlier periods, including interim periods, is not restated to reflect the change, the entity shall disclose in the year in which the change occurs segment information for the current period on both the old basis and the new basis of segmentation, unless the necessary information is not available and the cost to develop it would be excessive.

Entity-wide disclosures

31   Paragraphs 32–34 apply to all entities subject to this IFRS including those entities that have a single reportable segment. Some entities' business activities are not organised on the basis of differences in related products and services or differences in geographical areas of operations. Such an entity's reportable segments may report revenues from a broad range of essentially different products and services, or more than one of its reportable segments may provide essentially the same products and services. Similarly, an entity's reportable segments may hold assets in different geographical areas and report revenues from customers in different geographical areas, or more than one of its reportable segments may operate in the same geographical area. Information required by paragraphs 32–34 shall be provided only if it is not provided as part of the reportable segment information required by this IFRS.

Information about products and services

32   An entity shall report the revenues from external customers for each product and service, or each group of similar products and services, unless the necessary information is not available and the cost to develop it would be excessive, in which case that fact shall be disclosed. The amounts of revenues reported shall be based on the financial information used to produce the entity's financial statements.

Information about geographical areas

33   An entity shall report the following geographical information, unless the necessary information is not available and the cost to develop it would be excessive:

(a)   revenues from external customers (i) attributed to the entity's country of domicile and (ii) attributed to all foreign countries in total from which the entity derives revenues. If revenues from external customers attributed to an individual foreign country are material, those revenues shall be disclosed separately. An entity shall disclose the basis for attributing revenues from external customers to individual countries.

(b)   non-current assets[2] other than financial instruments, deferred tax assets, post-employment benefit assets, and rights arising under insurance contracts (i) located in the entity's country of domicile and (ii) located in all foreign countries in total in which the entity holds assets. If assets in an individual foreign country are material, those assets shall be disclosed separately.

The amounts reported shall be based on the financial information that is used to produce the entity's financial statements. If the necessary information is not available and the cost to develop it would be excessive, that fact shall be disclosed. An entity may provide, in addition to the information required by this paragraph, subtotals of geographical information about groups of countries.

Information about major customers

34   An entity shall provide information about the extent of its reliance on its major customers. If revenues from transactions with a single external customer amount to 10 per cent or more of an entity's revenues, the entity shall disclose that fact, the total amount of revenues from each such customer, and the identity of the segment or segments reporting the revenues. The entity need not disclose the identity of a major customer or the amount of revenues that each segment reports from that customer. For the purposes of this IFRS, a group of entities known to a reporting entity to be under common control shall be considered a single customer. However, judgement is required to assess whether a government (including government agencies and similar bodies whether local, national or international) and entities known to the reporting entity to be under the control of that government are considered a single customer. In assessing this, the reporting entity shall consider the extent of economic integration between those entities.

Transition and effective date

35   An entity shall apply this IFRS in its annual financial statements for periods beginning on or after 1 January 2009. Earlier application is permitted. If an entity applies this IFRS in its financial statements for a period before 1 January 2009, it shall disclose that fact.

35A   Paragraph 23 was amended by *Improvements to IFRSs* issued in April 2009. An entity shall apply that amendment for annual periods beginning on or after 1 January 2010. Earlier application is permitted. If an entity applies the amendment for an earlier period it shall disclose that fact.

---

2   For assets classified according to a liquidity presentation, non-current assets are assets that include amounts expected to be recovered more than twelve months after the reporting period.

36 Segment information for prior years that is reported as comparative information for the initial year of application (including application of the amendment to paragraph 23 made in April 2009) shall be restated to conform to the requirements of this IFRS, unless the necessary information is not available and the cost to develop it would be excessive.

36A IAS 1 (as revised in 2007) amended the terminology used throughout IFRSs. In addition it amended paragraph 23(f). An entity shall apply those amendments for annual periods beginning on or after 1 January 2009. If an entity applies IAS 1 (revised 2007) for an earlier period, the amendments shall be applied for that earlier period.

36B IAS 24 *Related Party Disclosures* (as revised in 2009) amended paragraph 34 for annual periods beginning on or after 1 January 2011. If an entity applies IAS 24 (revised 2009) for an earlier period, it shall apply the amendment to paragraph 34 for that earlier period.

Withdrawal of IAS 14

37 This IFRS supersedes IAS 14 *Segment Reporting*.

Appendix A
Defined term

This appendix is an integral part of the IFRS.

operating segment An operating segment is a component of an entity:

> (a) that engages in business activities from which it may earn revenues and incur expenses (including revenues and expenses relating to transactions with other components of the same entity),
>
> (b) whose operating results are regularly reviewed by the entity's chief operating decision maker to make decisions about resources to be allocated to the segment and assess its performance, and
>
> (c) for which discrete financial information is available.

Appendix B
Amendments to other IFRSs

The amendments in this appendix shall be applied for annual periods beginning on or after 1 January 2009. If an entity applies this IFRS for an earlier period, these amendments shall be applied for that earlier period. In the amended paragraphs, new text is underlined and deleted text is struck through.

* * * * *

The amendments contained in this appendix when this IFRS was issued in 2006 have been incorporated into the text of the relevant IFRSs in this volume.

International Financial Reporting Standard 9

Financial Instruments

In April 2001 the International Accounting Standards Board (IASB) adopted IAS 39 *Financial Instruments: Recognition and Measurement*, which had originally been issued by the International Accounting Standards Committee in March 1999.

The IASB intends to ultimately replace IAS 39 in its entirety. However, in response to requests from interested parties that the accounting for financial instruments should be improved quickly, the IASB divided its project to replace IAS 39 into phases. As the IASB completes each phase, it will replace portions of IAS 39 with chapters in IFRS 9.

In November 2009, the IASB issued the chapters of IFRS 9 *Financial Instruments* relating to the classification and measurement of financial assets. In October 2010 the IASB added the requirements related to the classification and measurement of financial liabilities to IFRS 9. This includes requirements on embedded derivatives and how to account for own credit risks for financial liabilities that are measured at fair value.

In October 2010 the IASB also decided to carry forward unchanged from IAS 39 the requirements related to the derecognition of financial assets and financial liabilities. Because of these changes, in October 2010 the IASB restructured IFRS 9 and its Basis for Conclusions. In December 2011 the IASB deferred the effective date to January 2015.

CONTENTS

from paragraph

FOR THE ACCOMPANYING DOCUMENTS LISTED BELOW, SEE PART B OF THIS EDITION

APPROVAL BY THE BOARD OF IFRS 9 ISSUED IN NOVEMBER 2009

APPROVAL BY THE BOARD OF THE REQUIREMENTS ADDED TO IFRS 9 IN OCTOBER 2010

APPROVAL BY THE BOARD OF *MANDATORY EFFECTIVE DATE OF IFRS 9 AND TRANSITION DISCLOSURES* (AMENDMENTS TO IFRS 9 (2009), IFRS 9 (2010) AND IFRS 7) ISSUED IN DECEMBER 2011

BASIS FOR CONCLUSIONS

APPENDIX
Amendments to the Basis for Conclusions on other IFRSs

DISSENTING OPINIONS

ILLUSTRATIVE EXAMPLES

QUESTIONS AND ANSWERS ON IMPLEMENTING IFRS 9

APPENDIX
Amendments to the guidance on other IFRSs

TABLES OF CONCORDANCE

International Financial Reporting Standard 9 *Financial Instruments* (IFRS 9) is set out in paragraphs 1.1–7.3.2 and Appendices A–C. All the paragraphs have equal authority. Paragraphs in **bold type** state the main principles. Terms defined in Appendix A are in *italics* the first time they appear in the IFRS. Definitions of other terms are given in the Glossary for International Financial Reporting Standards. IFRS 9 should be read in the context of its objective and the Basis for Conclusions, the *Preface to International Financial Reporting Standards* and the *Conceptual Framework for Financial Reporting*. IAS 8 *Accounting Policies, Changes in Accounting Estimates and Errors* provides a basis for selecting and applying accounting policies in the absence of explicit guidance .

Introduction

Reasons for issuing the IFRS

IN1   IAS 39 *Financial Instruments: Recognition and Measurement* sets out the requirements for recognising and measuring financial assets, financial liabilities and some contracts to buy or sell non-financial items. The International Accounting Standards Board inherited IAS 39 from its predecessor body, the International Accounting Standards Committee.

IN2   Many users of financial statements and other interested parties told the Board that the requirements in IAS 39 were difficult to understand, apply and interpret. They urged the Board to develop a new standard for the financial reporting of financial instruments that was principle-based and less complex. Although the Board amended IAS 39 several times to clarify requirements, add guidance and eliminate internal inconsistencies, it had not previously undertaken a fundamental reconsideration of reporting for financial instruments.

IN3   In 2005 the Board and the US Financial Accounting Standards Board (FASB) began working towards a long-term objective to improve and simplify the reporting for financial instruments. This work resulted in the publication of a discussion paper, *Reducing Complexity in Reporting Financial Instruments*, in March 2008. Focusing on the measurement of financial instruments and hedge accounting, the paper identified several possible approaches for improving and simplifying the accounting for financial instruments. The responses to the paper indicated support for a significant change in the requirements for reporting financial instruments. In November 2008 the Board added this project to its active agenda, and in December 2008 the FASB also added the project to its agenda.

IN4   In April 2009, in response to the input received on its work responding to the financial crisis, and following the conclusions of the G20 leaders and the recommendations of international bodies such as the Financial Stability Board, the Board announced an accelerated timetable for replacing IAS 39. As a result, in July 2009 the Board published an exposure draft *Financial Instruments: Classification and Measurement*, followed by the first chapters of IFRS 9 *Financial Instruments* in November 2009.

The Board's approach to replacing IAS 39

IN5   The Board intends that IFRS 9 will ultimately replace IAS 39 in its entirety. However, in response to requests from interested parties that the accounting for financial instruments should be improved quickly, the Board divided its project to replace IAS 39 into three main phases. As the Board completes each phase, it will delete the relevant portions of IAS 39 and create chapters in IFRS 9 that replace the requirements in IAS 39.

IN6　The three main phases of the Board's project to replace IAS 39 are:

(a)　**Phase 1: Classification and measurement of financial assets and financial liabilities.** In November 2009 the Board issued the chapters of IFRS 9 relating to the classification and measurement of financial assets. Those chapters require all financial assets to be classified on the basis of the entity's business model for managing the financial assets and the contractual cash flow characteristics of the financial asset. Assets are initially measured at fair value plus, in the case of a financial asset not at fair value through profit or loss, particular transaction costs. Assets are subsequently measured at amortised cost or fair value. In October 2010 the Board added to IFRS 9 the requirements related to the classification and measurement of financial liabilities. Those additional requirements are described further in paragraph IN7.

(b)　**Phase 2: Impairment methodology.** In June 2009 the Board published a Request for Information on the feasibility of an expected loss model for the impairment of financial assets. This formed the basis of an exposure draft, *Financial Instruments: Amortised Cost and Impairment*, published in November 2009. The Board also set up a panel of credit and risk experts to consider and advise on the operational issues arising from an expected cash flow approach. The Board is redeliberating the proposals in the exposure draft to address the comments received from respondents, and suggestions from the expert advisory panel and other outreach activities.

(c)　**Phase 3: Hedge accounting.** The Board is considering how to improve and simplify the hedge accounting requirements of IAS 39. It expects to publish proposals for a comprehensive new approach before the end of 2010.

IN7　In October 2010 the Board added to IFRS 9 the requirements for classification and measurement of financial liabilities:

(a)　Most of the requirements in IAS 39 for classification and measurement of financial liabilities were carried forward unchanged to IFRS 9. Under IAS 39 most liabilities were subsequently measured at amortised cost or bifurcated into a host, which is measured at amortised cost, and an embedded derivative, which is measured at fair value. Liabilities that are held for trading (including all derivative liabilities) were measured at fair value. Although the Board had originally proposed a symmetrical approach for financial assets and financial liabilities in the exposure draft published in 2009, the Board decided to retain most of the requirements in IAS 39 for classifying and measuring financial liabilities because constituents told the Board that those requirements were working well in practice. Consistently with its objective to replace IAS 39 in its entirety, the Board relocated those requirements from IAS 39 to IFRS 9.

(b)　Consistently with the requirements in IFRS 9 for investments in equity instruments that do not have a quoted price in an active market for an identical instrument (ie a Level 1 input) (and derivative assets linked to those investments), the exception from fair value measurement was eliminated for derivative liabilities that are linked to and must be settled by delivery of such an equity instrument. Under IAS 39, if those derivatives were not reliably measurable, they were required to be measured at cost. IFRS 9 requires them to be measured at fair value.

(c) The requirements related to the fair value option for financial liabilities were changed to address own credit risk. Those improvements respond to consistent feedback from users of financial statements and others that the effects of changes in a liability's credit risk ought not to affect profit or loss unless the liability is held for trading. The improvements followed from the proposals published in May 2010 in the exposure draft *Fair Value Option for Financial Liabilities*.

IN8 In addition to the three phases described above, the Board published in March 2009 an exposure draft *Derecognition* (proposed amendments to IAS 39 and IFRS 7 *Financial Instruments: Disclosures*). However, in June 2010 the Board revised its strategy and work plan and decided to retain the existing requirements in IAS 39 for the derecognition of financial assets and financial liabilities but to finalise improved disclosure requirements. The new requirements were issued in October 2010 as an amendment to IFRS 7 and have an effective date of 1 July 2011. Later in October 2010 the requirements in IAS 39 related to the derecognition of financial assets and financial liabilities were carried forward unchanged to IFRS 9.

IN9 As a result of the added requirements described in paragraphs IN7 and IN8, IFRS 9 and its Basis for Conclusions were restructured. Many paragraphs were renumbered and some were re-sequenced. New paragraphs were added to accommodate the guidance that was carried forward unchanged from IAS 39. Also, new sections were added to IFRS 9 as placeholders for the guidance that will result from subsequent phases of this project. Otherwise, the restructuring did not change the requirements in IFRS 9 issued in 2009. The Basis for Conclusions on IFRS 9 has been expanded to include material from the Basis for Conclusions on IAS 39 that discusses guidance that was carried forward without being reconsidered. Minor necessary edits have been made to that material.

IN10 The Board and the FASB are committed to achieving increased comparability internationally in the accounting for financial instruments. However, those efforts have been complicated by the differing project timetables established to respond to the respective stakeholder groups. In May 2010 the FASB published a proposed Accounting Standards Update (ASU) on accounting for financial instruments that contained proposals for a new comprehensive standard on financial instruments, including proposals on the classification and measurement of financial assets and financial liabilities, impairment methodology and hedge accounting. The proposed ASU had a comment deadline of 30 September 2010 and the FASB has begun to redeliberate its proposals. The Board asked its constituents to provide feedback to the FASB on the proposals in the FASB's exposure draft because this is a joint project with an objective of increasing international comparability. Feedback from IFRS constituents will be helpful to the FASB as it redeliberates its proposals. Moreover, after the FASB redeliberates its proposals, the Board will use that feedback to consider what steps (if any) should be taken to reconcile any remaining differences between IFRSs and US GAAP. Any possible changes as a result of that comparison will be subject to the Board's normal due process.

IN11   *Mandatory Effective Date of IFRS 9 and Transition Disclosures* (Amendments to IFRS 9 (2009), IFRS 9 (2010) and IFRS 7), issued in December 2011, amended the effective date of IFRS 9 (2009) and IFRS 9 (2010) so that IFRS 9 is required to be applied for annual periods beginning on or after 1 January 2015. Early application is permitted. The amendments also modified the relief from restating prior periods. The Board has published amendments to IFRS 7 to require additional disclosures on transition from IAS 39 to IFRS 9. Entities that initially apply IFRS 9 in periods:

(a)   beginning before 1 January 2012 need not restate prior periods and are not required to provide the disclosures set out in paragraphs 44S–44W of IFRS 7;

(b)   beginning on or after 1 January 2012 and before 1 January 2013 must elect either to provide the disclosures set out in paragraphs 44S–44W of IFRS 7 or to restate prior periods; and

(c)   beginning on or after 1 January 2013 shall provide the disclosures set out in paragraphs 44S–44W of IFRS 7. The entity need not restate prior periods.

International Financial Reporting Standard 9
Financial Instruments

Chapter 1 Objective

1.1 The objective of this IFRS is to establish principles for the financial reporting of *financial assets* and *financial liabilities* that will present relevant and useful information to users of financial statements for their assessment of the amounts, timing and uncertainty of an entity's future cash flows.

Chapter 2 Scope

2.1 An entity shall apply this IFRS to all items within the scope of IAS 39 *Financial Instruments: Recognition and Measurement*.

Chapter 3 Recognition and derecognition

3.1 Initial recognition

3.1.1 **An entity shall recognise a financial asset or a financial liability in its statement of financial position when, and only when, the entity becomes party to the contractual provisions of the instrument (see paragraphs B3.1.1 and B3.1.2). When an entity first recognises a financial asset, it shall classify it in accordance with paragraphs 4.1.1–4.1.5 and measure it in accordance with paragraphs 5.1.1 and 5.1.2. When an entity first recognises a financial liability, it shall classify it in accordance with paragraphs 4.2.1 and 4.2.2 and measure it in accordance with paragraph 5.1.1.**

Regular way purchase or sale of financial assets

3.1.2 A *regular way purchase or sale* of financial assets shall be recognised and derecognised, as applicable, using trade date accounting or settlement date accounting (see paragraphs B3.1.3–B3.1.6).

3.2 Derecognition of financial assets

3.2.1 In consolidated financial statements, paragraphs 3.2.2–3.2.9, B3.1.1, B3.1.2 and B3.2.1–B3.2.17 are applied at a consolidated level. Hence, an entity first consolidates all subsidiaries in accordance with IFRS 10 *Consolidated Financial Statements* and then applies those paragraphs to the resulting group.

3.2.2 **Before evaluating whether, and to what extent, *derecognition* is appropriate under paragraphs 3.2.3–3.2.9, an entity determines whether those paragraphs should be applied to a part of a financial asset (or a part of a group of similar financial assets) or a financial asset (or a group of similar financial assets) in its entirety, as follows.**

(a) Paragraphs 3.2.3–3.2.9 are applied to a part of a financial asset (or a part of a group of similar financial assets) if, and only if, the part being considered for derecognition meets one of the following three conditions.

    (i) The part comprises only specifically identified cash flows from a financial asset (or a group of similar financial assets). For example, when an entity enters into an interest rate strip whereby the counterparty obtains the right to the interest cash flows, but not the principal cash flows from a debt instrument, paragraphs 3.2.3–3.2.9 are applied to the interest cash flows.

    (ii) The part comprises only a fully proportionate (pro rata) share of the cash flows from a financial asset (or a group of similar financial assets). For example, when an entity enters into an arrangement whereby the counterparty obtains the rights to a 90 per cent share of all cash flows of a debt instrument, paragraphs 3.2.3–3.2.9 are applied to 90 per cent of those cash flows. If there is more than one counterparty, each counterparty is not required to have a proportionate share of the cash flows provided that the transferring entity has a fully proportionate share.

    (iii) The part comprises only a fully proportionate (pro rata) share of specifically identified cash flows from a financial asset (or a group of similar financial assets). For example, when an entity enters into an arrangement whereby the counterparty obtains the rights to a 90 per cent share of interest cash flows from a financial asset, paragraphs 3.2.3–3.2.9 are applied to 90 per cent of those interest cash flows. If there is more than one counterparty, each counterparty is not required to have a proportionate share of the specifically identified cash flows provided that the transferring entity has a fully proportionate share.

(b) In all other cases, paragraphs 3.2.3–3.2.9 are applied to the financial asset in its entirety (or to the group of similar financial assets in their entirety). For example, when an entity transfers (i) the rights to the first or the last 90 per cent of cash collections from a financial asset (or a group of financial assets), or (ii) the rights to 90 per cent of the cash flows from a group of receivables, but provides a guarantee to compensate the buyer for any credit losses up to 8 per cent of the principal amount of the receivables, paragraphs 3.2.3–3.2.9 are applied to the financial asset (or a group of similar financial assets) in its entirety.

In paragraphs 3.2.3–3.2.12, the term 'financial asset' refers to either a part of a financial asset (or a part of a group of similar financial assets) as identified in (a) above or, otherwise, a financial asset (or a group of similar financial assets) in its entirety.

3.2.3 An entity shall derecognise a financial asset when, and only when:

(a) the contractual rights to the cash flows from the financial asset expire, or

(b) it transfers the financial asset as set out in paragraphs 3.2.4 and 3.2.5 and the transfer qualifies for derecognition in accordance with paragraph 3.2.6.

(See paragraph 3.1.2 for regular way sales of financial assets.)

3.2.4   An entity transfers a financial asset if, and only if, it either:

(a)   transfers the contractual rights to receive the cash flows of the financial asset, or

(b)   retains the contractual rights to receive the cash flows of the financial asset, but assumes a contractual obligation to pay the cash flows to one or more recipients in an arrangement that meets the conditions in paragraph 3.2.5.

3.2.5   When an entity retains the contractual rights to receive the cash flows of a financial asset (the 'original asset'), but assumes a contractual obligation to pay those cash flows to one or more entities (the 'eventual recipients'), the entity treats the transaction as a transfer of a financial asset if, and only if, all of the following three conditions are met.

(a)   The entity has no obligation to pay amounts to the eventual recipients unless it collects equivalent amounts from the original asset. Short-term advances by the entity with the right of full recovery of the amount lent plus accrued interest at market rates do not violate this condition.

(b)   The entity is prohibited by the terms of the transfer contract from selling or pledging the original asset other than as security to the eventual recipients for the obligation to pay them cash flows.

(c)   The entity has an obligation to remit any cash flows it collects on behalf of the eventual recipients without material delay. In addition, the entity is not entitled to reinvest such cash flows, except for investments in cash or cash equivalents (as defined in IAS 7 *Statement of Cash Flows*) during the short settlement period from the collection date to the date of required remittance to the eventual recipients, and interest earned on such investments is passed to the eventual recipients.

3.2.6   When an entity transfers a financial asset (see paragraph 3.2.4), it shall evaluate the extent to which it retains the risks and rewards of ownership of the financial asset. In this case:

(a)   if the entity transfers substantially all the risks and rewards of ownership of the financial asset, the entity shall derecognise the financial asset and recognise separately as assets or liabilities any rights and obligations created or retained in the transfer.

(b)   if the entity retains substantially all the risks and rewards of ownership of the financial asset, the entity shall continue to recognise the financial asset.

(c)   if the entity neither transfers nor retains substantially all the risks and rewards of ownership of the financial asset, the entity shall determine whether it has retained control of the financial asset. In this case:

(i)   if the entity has not retained control, it shall derecognise the financial asset and recognise separately as assets or liabilities any rights and obligations created or retained in the transfer.

(ii)   if the entity has retained control, it shall continue to recognise the financial asset to the extent of its continuing involvement in the financial asset (see paragraph 3.2.16).

3.2.7 The transfer of risks and rewards (see paragraph 3.2.6) is evaluated by comparing the entity's exposure, before and after the transfer, with the variability in the amounts and timing of the net cash flows of the transferred asset. An entity has retained substantially all the risks and rewards of ownership of a financial asset if its exposure to the variability in the present value of the future net cash flows from the financial asset does not change significantly as a result of the transfer (eg because the entity has sold a financial asset subject to an agreement to buy it back at a fixed price or the sale price plus a lender's return). An entity has transferred substantially all the risks and rewards of ownership of a financial asset if its exposure to such variability is no longer significant in relation to the total variability in the present value of the future net cash flows associated with the financial asset (eg because the entity has sold a financial asset subject only to an option to buy it back at its *fair value* at the time of repurchase or has transferred a fully proportionate share of the cash flows from a larger financial asset in an arrangement, such as a loan sub-participation, that meets the conditions in paragraph 3.2.5).

3.2.8 Often it will be obvious whether the entity has transferred or retained substantially all risks and rewards of ownership and there will be no need to perform any computations. In other cases, it will be necessary to compute and compare the entity's exposure to the variability in the present value of the future net cash flows before and after the transfer. The computation and comparison are made using as the discount rate an appropriate current market interest rate. All reasonably possible variability in net cash flows is considered, with greater weight being given to those outcomes that are more likely to occur.

3.2.9 Whether the entity has retained control (see paragraph 3.2.6(c)) of the transferred asset depends on the transferee's ability to sell the asset. If the transferee has the practical ability to sell the asset in its entirety to an unrelated third party and is able to exercise that ability unilaterally and without needing to impose additional restrictions on the transfer, the entity has not retained control. In all other cases, the entity has retained control.

Transfers that qualify for derecognition

3.2.10 If an entity transfers a financial asset in a transfer that qualifies for derecognition in its entirety and retains the right to service the financial asset for a fee, it shall recognise either a servicing asset or a servicing liability for that servicing contract. If the fee to be received is not expected to compensate the entity adequately for performing the servicing, a servicing liability for the servicing obligation shall be recognised at its fair value. If the fee to be received is expected to be more than adequate compensation for the servicing, a servicing asset shall be recognised for the servicing right at an amount determined on the basis of an allocation of the carrying amount of the larger financial asset in accordance with paragraph 3.2.13.

3.2.11 If, as a result of a transfer, a financial asset is derecognised in its entirety but the transfer results in the entity obtaining a new financial asset or assuming a new financial liability, or a servicing liability, the entity shall recognise the new financial asset, financial liability or servicing liability at fair value.

3.2.12 On derecognition of a financial asset in its entirety, the difference between:

(a) the carrying amount (measured at the date of derecognition) and

(b) the consideration received (including any new asset obtained less any new liability assumed)

shall be recognised in profit or loss.

3.2.13 If the transferred asset is part of a larger financial asset (eg when an entity transfers interest cash flows that are part of a debt instrument, see paragraph 3.2.2(a)) and the part transferred qualifies for derecognition in its entirety, the previous carrying amount of the larger financial asset shall be allocated between the part that continues to be recognised and the part that is derecognised, on the basis of the relative fair values of those parts on the date of the transfer. For this purpose, a retained servicing asset shall be treated as a part that continues to be recognised. The difference between:

(a) the carrying amount (measured at the date of derecognition) allocated to the part derecognised and

(b) the consideration received for the part derecognised (including any new asset obtained less any new liability assumed)

shall be recognised in profit or loss.

3.2.14 When an entity allocates the previous carrying amount of a larger financial asset between the part that continues to be recognised and the part that is derecognised, the fair value of the part that continues to be recognised needs to be measured. When the entity has a history of selling parts similar to the part that continues to be recognised or other market transactions exist for such parts, recent prices of actual transactions provide the best estimate of its fair value. When there are no price quotes or recent market transactions to support the fair value of the part that continues to be recognised, the best estimate of the fair value is the difference between the fair value of the larger financial asset as a whole and the consideration received from the transferee for the part that is derecognised.

Transfers that do not qualify for derecognition

3.2.15 If a transfer does not result in derecognition because the entity has retained substantially all the risks and rewards of ownership of the transferred asset, the entity shall continue to recognise the transferred asset in its entirety and shall recognise a financial liability for the consideration received. In subsequent periods, the entity shall recognise any income on the transferred asset and any expense incurred on the financial liability.

Continuing involvement in transferred assets

3.2.16 If an entity neither transfers nor retains substantially all the risks and rewards of ownership of a transferred asset, and retains control of the transferred asset, the entity continues to recognise the transferred asset to the extent of its continuing involvement. The extent of the entity's continuing involvement in the transferred asset is the extent to which it is exposed to changes in the value of the transferred asset. For example:

(a) When the entity's continuing involvement takes the form of guaranteeing the transferred asset, the extent of the entity's continuing involvement is the lower of (i) the amount of the asset and (ii) the maximum amount of the consideration received that the entity could be required to repay ('the guarantee amount').

(b) When the entity's continuing involvement takes the form of a written or purchased option (or both) on the transferred asset, the extent of the entity's continuing involvement is the amount of the transferred asset that the entity may repurchase. However, in the case of a written put option on an asset that is measured at fair value, the extent of the entity's continuing involvement is limited to the lower of the fair value of the transferred asset and the option exercise price (see paragraph B3.2.13).

(c) When the entity's continuing involvement takes the form of a cash-settled option or similar provision on the transferred asset, the extent of the entity's continuing involvement is measured in the same way as that which results from non-cash settled options as set out in (b) above.

3.2.17 When an entity continues to recognise an asset to the extent of its continuing involvement, the entity also recognises an associated liability. Despite the other measurement requirements in this IFRS, the transferred asset and the associated liability are measured on a basis that reflects the rights and obligations that the entity has retained. The associated liability is measured in such a way that the net carrying amount of the transferred asset and the associated liability is:

(a) the *amortised cost* of the rights and obligations retained by the entity, if the transferred asset is measured at amortised cost, or

(b) equal to the fair value of the rights and obligations retained by the entity when measured on a stand-alone basis, if the transferred asset is measured at fair value.

3.2.18 The entity shall continue to recognise any income arising on the transferred asset to the extent of its continuing involvement and shall recognise any expense incurred on the associated liability.

3.2.19 For the purpose of subsequent measurement, recognised changes in the fair value of the transferred asset and the associated liability are accounted for consistently with each other in accordance with paragraph 5.7.1, and shall not be offset.

3.2.20 If an entity's continuing involvement is in only a part of a financial asset (eg when an entity retains an option to repurchase part of a transferred asset, or retains a residual interest that does not result in the retention of substantially all the risks and rewards of ownership and the entity retains control), the entity allocates the previous carrying amount of the financial asset between the part it continues to recognise under continuing involvement, and the part it no longer recognises on the basis of the relative fair values of those parts on the date of the transfer. For this purpose, the requirements of paragraph 3.2.14 apply. The difference between:

(a) the carrying amount (measured at the date of derecognition) allocated to the part that is no longer recognised and

(b) the consideration received for the part no longer recognised

shall be recognised in profit or loss.

3.2.21   If the transferred asset is measured at amortised cost, the option in this IFRS to designate a financial liability as at fair value through profit or loss is not applicable to the associated liability.

All transfers

3.2.22   If a transferred asset continues to be recognised, the asset and the associated liability shall not be offset. Similarly, the entity shall not offset any income arising from the transferred asset with any expense incurred on the associated liability (see IAS 32 *Financial Instruments: Presentation* paragraph 42).

3.2.23   If a transferor provides non-cash collateral (such as debt or equity instruments) to the transferee, the accounting for the collateral by the transferor and the transferee depends on whether the transferee has the right to sell or repledge the collateral and on whether the transferor has defaulted. The transferor and transferee shall account for the collateral as follows:

(a)   If the transferee has the right by contract or custom to sell or repledge the collateral, then the transferor shall reclassify that asset in its statement of financial position (eg as a loaned asset, pledged equity instruments or repurchase receivable) separately from other assets.

(b)   If the transferee sells collateral pledged to it, it shall recognise the proceeds from the sale and a liability measured at fair value for its obligation to return the collateral.

(c)   If the transferor defaults under the terms of the contract and is no longer entitled to redeem the collateral, it shall derecognise the collateral, and the transferee shall recognise the collateral as its asset initially measured at fair value or, if it has already sold the collateral, derecognise its obligation to return the collateral.

(d)   Except as provided in (c), the transferor shall continue to carry the collateral as its asset, and the transferee shall not recognise the collateral as an asset.

3.3 Derecognition of financial liabilities

3.3.1   An entity shall remove a financial liability (or a part of a financial liability) from its statement of financial position when, and only when, it is extinguished—ie when the obligation specified in the contract is discharged or cancelled or expires.

3.3.2   An exchange between an existing borrower and lender of debt instruments with substantially different terms shall be accounted for as an extinguishment of the original financial liability and the recognition of a new financial liability. Similarly, a substantial modification of the terms of an existing financial liability or a part of it (whether or not attributable to the financial difficulty of the debtor) shall be accounted for as an extinguishment of the original financial liability and the recognition of a new financial liability.

3.3.3 **The difference between the carrying amount of a financial liability (or part of a financial liability) extinguished or transferred to another party and the consideration paid, including any non-cash assets transferred or liabilities assumed, shall be recognised in profit or loss.**

3.3.4 If an entity repurchases a part of a financial liability, the entity shall allocate the previous carrying amount of the financial liability between the part that continues to be recognised and the part that is derecognised based on the relative fair values of those parts on the date of the repurchase. The difference between (a) the carrying amount allocated to the part derecognised and (b) the consideration paid, including any non-cash assets transferred or liabilities assumed, for the part derecognised shall be recognised in profit or loss.

Chapter 4 Classification

4.1 Classification of financial assets

4.1.1 **Unless paragraph 4.1.5 applies, an entity shall classify financial assets as subsequently measured at either amortised cost or fair value on the basis of both:**

(a) **the entity's business model for managing the financial assets and**

(b) **the contractual cash flow characteristics of the financial asset.**

4.1.2 **A financial asset shall be measured at amortised cost if both of the following conditions are met:**

(a) **The asset is held within a business model whose objective is to hold assets in order to collect contractual cash flows.**

(b) **The contractual terms of the financial asset give rise on specified dates to cash flows that are solely payments of principal and interest on the principal amount outstanding.**

Paragraphs B4.1.1–B4.1.26 provide guidance on how to apply these conditions.

4.1.3 **For the purpose of applying paragraph 4.1.2(b), interest is consideration for the time value of money and for the credit risk associated with the principal amount outstanding during a particular period of time.**

4.1.4 **A financial asset shall be measured at fair value unless it is measured at amortised cost in accordance with paragraph 4.1.2.**

Option to designate a financial asset at fair value through profit or loss

4.1.5 **Despite paragraphs 4.1.1–4.1.4, an entity may, at initial recognition, irrevocably designate a financial asset as measured at fair value through profit or loss if doing so eliminates or significantly reduces a measurement or recognition inconsistency (sometimes referred to as an 'accounting mismatch') that would otherwise arise from measuring assets or liabilities or recognising the gains and losses on them on different bases (see paragraphs B4.1.29–B4.1.32).**

4.1.6 IFRS 7 *Financial Instruments: Disclosures* requires the entity to provide disclosures about financial assets it has designated as at fair value through profit or loss.

4.2 Classification of financial liabilities

4.2.1   An entity shall classify all financial liabilities as subsequently measured at amortised cost using the *effective interest method*, except for:

(a)   *financial liabilities at fair value through profit or loss*. Such liabilities, including *derivatives* that are liabilities, shall be subsequently measured at fair value.

(b)   financial liabilities that arise when a transfer of a financial asset does not qualify for derecognition or when the continuing involvement approach applies. Paragraphs 3.2.15 and 3.2.17 apply to the measurement of such financial liabilities.

(c)   *financial guarantee contracts* as defined in Appendix A. After initial recognition, an issuer of such a contract shall (unless paragraph 4.2.1(a) or (b) applies) subsequently measure it at the higher of:

(i)   the amount determined in accordance with IAS 37 *Provisions, Contingent Liabilities and Contingent Assets* and

(ii)   the amount initially recognised (see paragraph 5.1.1) less, when appropriate, cumulative amortisation recognised in accordance with IAS 18 *Revenue*.

(d)   commitments to provide a loan at a below-market interest rate. After initial recognition, an issuer of such a commitment shall (unless paragraph 4.2.1(a) applies) subsequently measure it at the higher of:

(i)   the amount determined in accordance with IAS 37 and

(ii)   the amount initially recognised (see paragraph 5.1.1) less, when appropriate, cumulative amortisation recognised in accordance with IAS 18.

Option to designate a financial liability at fair value through profit or loss

4.2.2   An entity may, at initial recognition, irrevocably designate a financial liability as measured at fair value through profit or loss when permitted by paragraph 4.3.5, or when doing so results in more relevant information, because either:

(a)   it eliminates or significantly reduces a measurement or recognition inconsistency (sometimes referred to as 'an accounting mismatch') that would otherwise arise from measuring assets or liabilities or recognising the gains and losses on them on different bases; or

(b)   a group of financial liabilities or financial assets and financial liabilities is managed and its performance is evaluated on a fair value basis, in accordance with a documented risk management or investment strategy, and information about the group is provided internally on that basis to the entity's key management personnel (as defined in IAS 24 *Related Party Disclosures*), for example the entity's board of directors and chief executive officer.

4.2.3   IFRS 7 requires the entity to provide disclosures about financial liabilities it has designated as at fair value through profit or loss.

4.3 Embedded derivatives

4.3.1   An embedded derivative is a component of a hybrid contract that also includes a non-derivative host—with the effect that some of the cash flows of the combined instrument vary in a way similar to a stand-alone derivative. An embedded derivative causes some or all of the cash flows that otherwise would be required by the contract to be modified according to a specified interest rate, financial instrument price, commodity price, foreign exchange rate, index of prices or rates, credit rating or credit index, or other variable, provided in the case of a non-financial variable that the variable is not specific to a party to the contract. A derivative that is attached to a *financial instrument* but is contractually transferable independently of that instrument, or has a different counterparty, is not an embedded derivative, but a separate financial instrument.

Hybrid contracts with financial asset hosts

4.3.2   If a hybrid contract contains a host that is an asset within the scope of this IFRS, an entity shall apply the requirements in paragraphs 4.1.1–4.1.5 to the entire hybrid contract.

Other hybrid contracts

4.3.3   If a hybrid contract contains a host that is not an asset within the scope of this IFRS, an embedded derivative shall be separated from the host and accounted for as a derivative under this IFRS if, and only if:

(a)   the economic characteristics and risks of the embedded derivative are not closely related to the economic characteristics and risks of the host (see paragraphs B4.3.5 and B4.3.8);

(b)   a separate instrument with the same terms as the embedded derivative would meet the definition of a derivative; and

(c)   the hybrid contract is not measured at fair value with changes in fair value recognised in profit or loss (ie a derivative that is embedded in a financial liability at fair value through profit or loss is not separated).

4.3.4   If an embedded derivative is separated, the host contract shall be accounted for in accordance with the appropriate IFRSs. This IFRS does not address whether an embedded derivative shall be presented separately in the statement of financial position.

4.3.5   Despite paragraphs 4.3.3 and 4.3.4, if a contract contains one or more embedded derivatives and the host is not an asset within the scope of this IFRS, an entity may designate the entire hybrid contract as at fair value through profit or loss unless:

(a)   the embedded derivative(s) do(es) not significantly modify the cash flows that otherwise would be required by the contract; or

(b)   it is clear with little or no analysis when a similar hybrid instrument is first considered that separation of the embedded derivative(s) is prohibited, such as a prepayment option embedded in a loan that permits the holder to prepay the loan for approximately its amortised cost.

4.3.6   **If an entity is required by this IFRS to separate an embedded derivative from its host, but is unable to measure the embedded derivative separately either at acquisition or at the end of a subsequent financial reporting period, it shall designate the entire hybrid contract as at fair value through profit or loss.**

4.3.7   If an entity is unable to measure reliably the fair value of an embedded derivative on the basis of its terms and conditions, the fair value of the embedded derivative is the difference between the fair value of the hybrid contract and the fair value of the host. If the entity is unable to measure the fair value of the embedded derivative using this method, paragraph 4.3.6 applies and the hybrid contract is designated as at fair value through profit or loss.

4.4 Reclassification

4.4.1   **When, and only when, an entity changes its business model for managing financial assets it shall reclassify all affected financial assets in accordance with paragraphs 4.1.1–4.1.4.**

4.4.2   **An entity shall not reclassify any financial liability.**

4.4.3   The following changes in circumstances are not reclassifications for the purposes of paragraphs 4.4.1 and 4.4.2:

(a)   A derivative that was previously a designated and effective hedging instrument in a cash flow hedge or net investment hedge no longer qualifies as such.

(b)   A derivative becomes a designated and effective hedging instrument in a cash flow hedge or net investment hedge.

Chapter 5 Measurement

5.1 Initial measurement

5.1.1   **At initial recognition, an entity shall measure a financial asset or financial liability at its fair value plus or minus, in the case of a financial asset or financial liability not at fair value through profit or loss, transaction costs that are directly attributable to the acquisition or issue of the financial asset or financial liability.**

5.1.1A   **However, if the fair value of the financial asset or financial liability at initial recognition differs from the transaction price, an entity shall apply paragraph B5.1.2A.**

5.1.2   When an entity uses settlement date accounting for an asset that is subsequently measured at amortised cost, the asset is recognised initially at its fair value on the trade date (see paragraphs B3.1.3–B3.1.6).

5.2 Subsequent measurement of financial assets

5.2.1 After initial recognition, an entity shall measure a financial asset in accordance with paragraphs 4.1.1–4.1.5 at fair value or amortised cost (see paragraphs 9 and AG5–AG8 of IAS 39).

5.2.2 An entity shall apply the impairment requirements in paragraphs 58–65 and AG84–AG93 of IAS 39 to financial assets measured at amortised cost.

5.2.3 An entity shall apply the hedge accounting requirements in paragraphs 89–102 of IAS 39 to a financial asset that is designated as a hedged item (see paragraphs 78–84 and AG98–AG101 of IAS 39).

5.3 Subsequent measurement of financial liabilities

5.3.1 After initial recognition, an entity shall measure a financial liability in accordance with paragraphs 4.2.1–4.2.2 (see paragraphs 5.4.1–5.4.3 and B5.4.1–B5.4.17 and paragraphs 9 and AG5–AG8 of IAS 39).

5.3.2 An entity shall apply the hedge accounting requirements in paragraphs 89–102 of IAS 39 to a financial liability that is designated as a hedged item (see paragraphs 78–84 and AG98–AG101 of IAS 39).

5.4.1– [Deleted]
5.4.3

5.5 Amortised cost measurement – *not used*

5.6 Reclassification of financial assets

5.6.1 If an entity reclassifies financial assets in accordance with paragraph 4.4.1, it shall apply the reclassification prospectively from the *reclassification date*. The entity shall not restate any previously recognised gains, losses or interest.

5.6.2 If, in accordance with paragraph 4.4.1, an entity reclassifies a financial asset so that it is measured at fair value, its fair value is measured at the reclassification date. Any gain or loss arising from a difference between the previous carrying amount and fair value is recognised in profit or loss.

5.6.3 If, in accordance with paragraph 4.4.1, an entity reclassifies a financial asset so that it is measured at amortised cost, its fair value at the reclassification date becomes its new carrying amount.

5.7 Gains and losses

5.7.1 A gain or loss on a financial asset or financial liability that is measured at fair value shall be recognised in profit or loss unless:

(a) it is part of a hedging relationship (see paragraphs 89-102 of IAS 39);

(b)   it is an investment in an *equity instrument* and the entity has elected to present gains and losses on that investment in other comprehensive income in accordance with paragraph 5.7.5; or

(c)   it is a financial liability designated as at fair value through profit or loss and the entity is required to present the effects of changes in the liability's *credit risk* in other comprehensive income in accordance with paragraph 5.7.7.

5.7.2   A gain or loss on a financial asset that is measured at amortised cost and is not part of a hedging relationship (see paragraphs 89–102 of IAS 39) shall be recognised in profit or loss when the financial asset is derecognised, impaired or reclassified in accordance with paragraph 5.6.2, and through the amortisation process. A gain or loss on a financial liability that is measured at amortised cost and is not part of a hedging relationship (see paragraphs 89–102 of IAS 39) shall be recognised in profit or loss when the financial liability is derecognised and through the amortisation process.

5.7.3   A gain or loss on financial assets or financial liabilities that are hedged items (see paragraphs 78–84 and AG98–AG101 of IAS 39) shall be recognised in accordance with paragraphs 89–102 of IAS 39.

5.7.4   If an entity recognises financial assets using settlement date accounting (see paragraph 3.1.2 and paragraphs B3.1.3 and B3.1.6), any change in the fair value of the asset to be received during the period between the trade date and the settlement date is not recognised for assets measured at amortised cost (other than impairment losses). For assets measured at fair value, however, the change in fair value shall be recognised in profit or loss or in other comprehensive income, as appropriate under paragraph 5.7.1.

Investments in equity instruments

5.7.5   At initial recognition, an entity may make an irrevocable election to present in other comprehensive income subsequent changes in the fair value of an investment in an equity instrument within the scope of this IFRS that is not *held for trading*.

5.7.6   If an entity makes the election in paragraph 5.7.5, it shall recognise in profit or loss dividends from that investment when the entity's right to receive payment of the dividend is established in accordance with IAS 18.

Liabilities designated as at fair value through profit or loss

5.7.7   An entity shall present a gain or loss on a financial liability designated as at fair value through profit or loss as follows:

(a)   The amount of change in the fair value of the financial liability that is attributable to changes in the credit risk of that liability shall be presented in other comprehensive income (see paragraphs B5.7.13–B5.7.20), and

(b)   the remaining amount of change in the fair value of the liability shall be presented in profit or loss unless the treatment of the effects of changes in the liability's credit risk described in (a) would create or enlarge an accounting mismatch in profit or loss (in which case paragraph 5.7.8 applies). Paragraphs B5.7.5–B5.7.7 and B5.7.10–B5.7.12 provide guidance on determining whether an accounting mismatch would be created or enlarged.

5.7.8 If the requirements in paragraph 5.7.7 would create or enlarge an accounting mismatch in profit or loss, an entity shall present all gains or losses on that liability (including the effects of changes in the credit risk of that liability) in profit or loss.

5.7.9 Despite the requirements in paragraphs 5.7.7 and 5.7.8, an entity shall present in profit or loss all gains and losses on loan commitments and financial guarantee contracts that are designated as at fair value through profit or loss.

Chapter 6 Hedge accounting – *not used*

Chapter 7 Effective date and transition

7.1 Effective date

7.1.1 An entity shall apply this IFRS for annual periods beginning on or after 1 January 2015. Earlier application is permitted. However, if an entity elects to apply this IFRS early and has not already applied IFRS 9 issued in 2009, it must apply all of the requirements in this IFRS at the same time (but see also paragraph 7.3.2). If an entity applies this IFRS in its financial statements for a period beginning before 1 January 2015, it shall disclose that fact and at the same time apply the amendments in Appendix C.

7.1.2 IFRS 10 and IFRS 11 *Joint Arrangements*, issued in May 2011, amended paragraphs 3.2.1, B3.2.1–B3.2.3, B4.3.12(c), B5.7.15, C11 and C30 and deleted paragraphs C23–C28 and the related headings. An entity shall apply those amendments when it applies IFRS 10 and IFRS 11.

7.1.3 IFRS 13 *Fair Value Measurement*, issued in May 2011, amended paragraphs 3.2.14, 4.3.7, 5.1.1, 5.2.1, 5.4.1, 5.6.2, 7.2.5, 7.2.11, 7.2.12, amended the definition of fair value in Appendix A, amended paragraphs B3.2.11, B3.2.17, B5.1.1, B5.2.2, B5.4.8, B5.4.14, B5.4.16, B5.7.20, C3, C11, C26, C28, C30, C49 and C53, deleted paragraphs 5.4.2, B5.4.1–B5.4.13 and added paragraphs 5.1.1A, B5.1.2A and B5.2.2A. An entity shall apply those amendments when it applies IFRS 13.

7.2 Transition

7.2.1 An entity shall apply this IFRS retrospectively, in accordance with IAS 8 *Accounting Policies, Changes in Accounting Estimates and Errors*, except as specified in paragraphs 7.2.4–7.2.15. This IFRS shall not be applied to items that have already been derecognised at the date of initial application.

7.2.2　For the purposes of the transition provisions in paragraphs 7.2.1 and 7.2.3–7.2.16, the date of initial application is the date when an entity first applies the requirements of this IFRS. The date of initial application may be:

(a)　any date between the issue of this IFRS and 31 December 2010, for entities initially applying this IFRS before 1 January 2011; or

(b)　the beginning of the first reporting period in which the entity adopts this IFRS, for entities initially applying this IFRS on or after 1 January 2011.

7.2.3　If the date of initial application is not at the beginning of a reporting period, the entity shall disclose that fact and the reasons for using that date of initial application.

7.2.4　At the date of initial application, an entity shall assess whether a financial asset meets the condition in paragraph 4.1.2(a) on the basis of the facts and circumstances that exist at the date of initial application. The resulting classification shall be applied retrospectively irrespective of the entity's business model in prior reporting periods.

7.2.5　If an entity measures a hybrid contract at fair value in accordance with paragraph 4.1.4 or paragraph 4.1.5 but the fair value of the hybrid contract had not been measured in comparative reporting periods, the fair value of the hybrid contract in the comparative reporting periods shall be the sum of the fair values of the components (ie the non-derivative host and the embedded derivative) at the end of each comparative reporting period.

7.2.6　At the date of initial application, an entity shall recognise any difference between the fair value of the entire hybrid contract at the date of initial application and the sum of the fair values of the components of the hybrid contract at the date of initial application:

(a)　in the opening retained earnings of the reporting period of initial application if the entity initially applies this IFRS at the beginning of a reporting period, or

(b)　in profit or loss if the entity initially applies this IFRS during a reporting period.

7.2.7　At the date of initial application, an entity may designate:

(a)　a financial asset as measured at fair value through profit or loss in accordance with paragraph 4.1.5, or

(b)　an investment in an equity instrument as at fair value through other comprehensive income in accordance with paragraph 5.7.5.

Such designation shall be made on the basis of the facts and circumstances that exist at the date of initial application. That classification shall be applied retrospectively.

7.2.8　At the date of initial application, an entity:

(a)　shall revoke its previous designation of a financial asset as measured at fair value through profit or loss if that financial asset does not meet the condition in paragraph 4.1.5.

(b) may revoke its previous designation of a financial asset as measured at fair value through profit or loss if that financial asset meets the condition in paragraph 4.1.5.

Such revocation shall be made on the basis of the facts and circumstances that exist at the date of initial application. That classification shall be applied retrospectively.

7.2.9 At the date of initial application, an entity:

(a) may designate a financial liability as measured at fair value through profit or loss in accordance with paragraph 4.2.2(a).

(b) shall revoke its previous designation of a financial liability as measured at fair value through profit or loss if such designation was made at initial recognition in accordance with the condition now in paragraph 4.2.2(a) and such designation does not satisfy that condition at the date of initial application.

(c) may revoke its previous designation of a financial liability as measured at fair value through profit or loss if such designation was made at initial recognition in accordance with the condition now in paragraph 4.2.2(a) and such designation satisfies that condition at the date of initial application.

Such designation and revocation shall be made on the basis of the facts and circumstances that exist at the date of initial application. That classification shall be applied retrospectively.

7.2.10 If it is impracticable (as defined in IAS 8) for an entity to apply retrospectively the effective interest method or the impairment requirements in paragraphs 58–65 and AG84–AG93 of IAS 39, the entity shall treat the fair value of the financial asset or financial liability at the end of each comparative period as its amortised cost if the entity restates prior periods. If it is impracticable (as defined in IAS 8) for an entity to apply retrospectively the effective interest method or the impairment requirements in paragraphs 58–65 and AG84–AG93 of IAS 39, the fair value of the financial asset or financial liability at the date of initial application shall be treated as the new amortised cost of that financial asset or financial liability at the date of initial application of this IFRS.

7.2.11 If an entity previously accounted for an investment in an equity instrument that does not have a quoted price in an active market for an identical instrument (ie a Level 1 input) (or a derivative asset that is linked to and must be settled by delivery of such an equity instrument) at cost in accordance with IAS 39, it shall measure that instrument at fair value at the date of initial application. Any difference between the previous carrying amount and fair value shall be recognised in the opening retained earnings of the reporting period that includes the date of initial application.

7.2.12   If an entity previously accounted for a derivative liability that is linked to and must be settled by delivery of an equity instrument that does not have a quoted price in an active market for an identical instrument (ie a Level 1 input) at cost in accordance with IAS 39, it shall measure that derivative liability at fair value at the date of initial application. Any difference between the previous carrying amount and fair value shall be recognised in the opening retained earnings of the reporting period that includes the date of initial application.

7.2.13   At the date of initial application, an entity shall determine whether the treatment in paragraph 5.7.7 would create or enlarge an accounting mismatch in profit or loss on the basis of the facts and circumstances that exist at the date of initial application. This IFRS shall be applied retrospectively on the basis of that determination.

7.2.14   Despite the requirement in paragraph 7.2.1, an entity that adopts the classification and measurement requirements of this IFRS for reporting periods:

(a)   beginning before 1 January 2012 need not restate prior periods and is not required to provide the disclosures set out in paragraphs 44S–44W of IFRS 7;

(b)   beginning on or after 1 January 2012 and before 1 January 2013 shall elect either to provide the disclosures set out in paragraphs 44S–44W of IFRS 7 or to restate prior periods; and

(c)   beginning on or after 1 January 2013 shall provide the disclosures set out in paragraphs 44S–44W of IFRS 7. The entity need not restate prior periods.

If an entity does not restate prior periods, the entity shall recognise any difference between the previous carrying amount and the carrying amount at the beginning of the annual reporting period that includes the date of initial application in the opening retained earnings (or other component of equity, as appropriate) of the annual reporting period that includes the date of initial application. However, if an entity restates prior periods, the restated financial statements must reflect all of the requirements in this IFRS.

7.2.15   If an entity prepares interim financial reports in accordance with IAS 34 *Interim Financial Reporting* the entity need not apply the requirements in this IFRS to interim periods prior to the date of initial application if it is impracticable (as defined in IAS 8).

Entities that have applied early IFRS 9 issued in 2009

7.2.16   An entity shall apply the transition requirements in paragraphs 7.2.1–7.2.15 at the relevant date of initial application. In other words, an entity shall apply paragraphs 7.2.4–7.2.11 if it applies IFRS 9 (issued in 2009) or, not having done so, when it applies IFRS 9 (issued in 2010) in its entirety. An entity is not permitted to apply those paragraphs more than once.

7.3 Withdrawal of IFRIC 9 and IFRS 9 (2009)

7.3.1   This IFRS supersedes IFRIC 9 *Reassessment of Embedded Derivatives*. The requirements added to IFRS 9 in October 2010 incorporated the requirements previously set out in paragraphs 5 and 7 of IFRIC 9. As a consequential amendment, IFRS 1 *First-time Adoption of International Financial Reporting Standards* incorporated the requirements previously set out in paragraph 8 of IFRIC 9.

7.3.2   This IFRS supersedes IFRS 9 issued in 2009. However, for annual periods beginning before 1 January 2015, an entity may elect to apply IFRS 9 issued in 2009 instead of applying this IFRS.

Appendix A
Defined terms

This appendix is an integral part of the IFRS.

derecognition	The removal of a previously recognised financial asset or financial liability from an entity's statement of financial position.
derivative	A financial instrument or other contract within the scope of this IFRS (see paragraph 2.1) with all three of the following characteristics.

(a)   Its value changes in response to the change in a specified interest rate, financial instrument price, commodity price, foreign exchange rate, index of prices or rates, credit rating or credit index, or other variable, provided in the case of a non-financial variable that the variable is not specific to a party to the contract (sometimes called the 'underlying').

(b)   It requires no initial net investment or an initial net investment that is smaller than would be required for other types of contracts that would be expected to have a similar response to changes in market factors.

(c)   It is settled at a future date.

fair value	*Fair value* is the price that would be received to sell an asset or paid to transfer a liability in an orderly transaction between market participants at the measurement date. (See IFRS 13.)
financial guarantee contract	A contract that requires the issuer to make specified payments to reimburse the holder for a loss it incurs because a specified debtor fails to make payment when due in accordance with the original or modified terms of a debt instrument.
financial liability at fair value through profit or loss	A financial liability that meets either of the following conditions.

(a)   It meets the definition of **held for trading**.

(b)   Upon initial recognition it is designated by the entity as at fair value through profit or loss in accordance with paragraph 4.2.2 or 4.3.5.

held for trading	A financial asset or financial liability that:

    (a)   is acquired or incurred principally for the purpose of selling or repurchasing it in the near term;

    (b)   on initial recognition is part of a portfolio of identified financial instruments that are managed together and for which there is evidence of a recent actual pattern of short-term profit-taking; or

    (c)   is a derivative (except for a derivative that is a financial guarantee contract or a designated and effective hedging instrument).

reclassification date	The first day of the first reporting period following the change in business model that results in an entity reclassifying financial assets.
regular way purchase or sale	A purchase or sale of a financial asset under a contract whose terms require delivery of the asset within the time frame established generally by regulation or convention in the marketplace concerned.

The following terms are defined in paragraph 11 of IAS 32, paragraph 9 of IAS 39 or Appendix A of IFRS 7 and are used in this IFRS with the meanings specified in IAS 32, IAS 39 or IFRS 7:

(a)   amortised cost of a financial asset or financial liability

(b)   credit risk

(c)   effective interest method

(d)   equity instrument

(e)   financial asset

(f)   financial instrument

(g)   financial liability

(h)   hedged item

(i)   hedging instrument

(j)   transaction costs.

Appendix B
Application guidance

This appendix is an integral part of the IFRS.

Recognition and derecognition (chapter 3)

Initial recognition (section 3.1)

B3.1.1   As a consequence of the principle in paragraph 3.1.1, an entity recognises all of its contractual rights and obligations under derivatives in its statement of financial position as assets and liabilities, respectively, except for derivatives that prevent a transfer of financial assets from being accounted for as a sale (see paragraph B3.2.14). If a transfer of a financial asset does not qualify for derecognition, the transferee does not recognise the transferred asset as its asset (see paragraph B3.2.15).

B3.1.2   The following are examples of applying the principle in paragraph 3.1.1:

    (a)   Unconditional receivables and payables are recognised as assets or liabilities when the entity becomes a party to the contract and, as a consequence, has a legal right to receive or a legal obligation to pay cash.

    (b)   Assets to be acquired and liabilities to be incurred as a result of a firm commitment to purchase or sell goods or services are generally not recognised until at least one of the parties has performed under the agreement. For example, an entity that receives a firm order does not generally recognise an asset (and the entity that places the order does not recognise a liability) at the time of the commitment but, rather, delays recognition until the ordered goods or services have been shipped, delivered or rendered. If a firm commitment to buy or sell non-financial items is within the scope of this IFRS in accordance with paragraphs 5–7 of IAS 39, its net fair value is recognised as an asset or liability on the commitment date (see (c) below). In addition, if a previously unrecognised firm commitment is designated as a hedged item in a fair value hedge, any change in the net fair value attributable to the hedged risk is recognised as an asset or liability after the inception of the hedge (see paragraphs 93 and 94 of IAS 39).

    (c)   A forward contract that is within the scope of this IFRS (see paragraph 2.1) is recognised as an asset or a liability on the commitment date, rather than on the date on which settlement takes place. When an entity becomes a party to a forward contract, the fair values of the right and obligation are often equal, so that the net fair value of the forward is zero. If the net fair value of the right and obligation is not zero, the contract is recognised as an asset or liability.

    (d)   Option contracts that are within the scope of this IFRS (see paragraph 2.1) are recognised as assets or liabilities when the holder or writer becomes a party to the contract.

    (e)   Planned future transactions, no matter how likely, are not assets and liabilities because the entity has not become a party to a contract.

Regular way purchase or sale of financial assets

B3.1.3   A regular way purchase or sale of financial assets is recognised using either trade date accounting or settlement date accounting as described in paragraphs B3.1.5 and B3.1.6. An entity shall apply the same method consistently for all purchases and sales of financial assets that are classified in the same way in accordance with this IFRS. For this purpose assets that are mandatorily measured at fair value through profit or loss form a separate classification from assets designated as measured at fair value through profit or loss. In addition, investments in equity instruments accounted for using the option provided in paragraph 5.7.5 form a separate classification.

B3.1.4   A contract that requires or permits net settlement of the change in the value of the contract is not a regular way contract. Instead, such a contract is accounted for as a derivative in the period between the trade date and the settlement date.

B3.1.5   The trade date is the date that an entity commits itself to purchase or sell an asset. Trade date accounting refers to (a) the recognition of an asset to be received and the liability to pay for it on the trade date, and (b) derecognition of an asset that is sold, recognition of any gain or loss on disposal and the recognition of a receivable from the buyer for payment on the trade date. Generally, interest does not start to accrue on the asset and corresponding liability until the settlement date when title passes.

B3.1.6   The settlement date is the date that an asset is delivered to or by an entity. Settlement date accounting refers to (a) the recognition of an asset on the day it is received by the entity, and (b) the derecognition of an asset and recognition of any gain or loss on disposal on the day that it is delivered by the entity. When settlement date accounting is applied an entity accounts for any change in the fair value of the asset to be received during the period between the trade date and the settlement date in the same way as it accounts for the acquired asset. In other words, the change in value is not recognised for assets measured at amortised cost; it is recognised in profit or loss for assets classified as financial assets measured at fair value through profit or loss; and it is recognised in other comprehensive income for investments in equity instruments accounted for in accordance with paragraph 5.7.5.

Derecognition of financial assets (section 3.2)

B3.2.1 The following flow chart illustrates the evaluation of whether and to what extent a financial asset is derecognised.

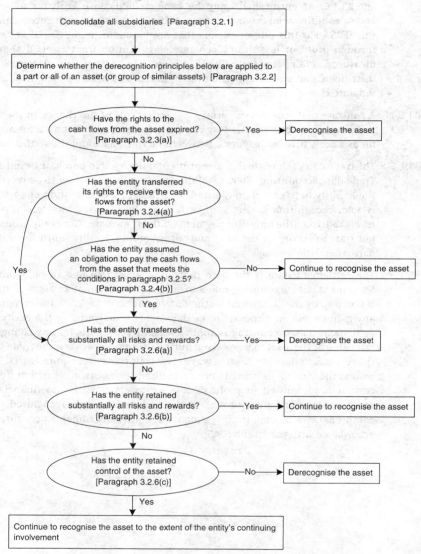

Arrangements under which an entity retains the contractual rights to receive the cash flows of a financial asset, but assumes a contractual obligation to pay the cash flows to one or more recipients (paragraph 3.2.4(b))

B3.2.2   The situation described in paragraph 3.2.4(b) (when an entity retains the contractual rights to receive the cash flows of the financial asset, but assumes a contractual obligation to pay the cash flows to one or more recipients) occurs, for example, if the entity is a trust, and issues to investors beneficial interests in the underlying financial assets that it owns and provides servicing of those financial assets. In that case, the financial assets qualify for derecognition if the conditions in paragraphs 3.2.5 and 3.2.6 are met.

B3.2.3   In applying paragraph 3.2.5, the entity could be, for example, the originator of the financial asset, or it could be a group that includes a subsidiary that has acquired the financial asset and passes on cash flows to unrelated third party investors.

Evaluation of the transfer of risks and rewards of ownership (paragraph 3.2.6)

B3.2.4   Examples of when an entity has transferred substantially all the risks and rewards of ownership are:

(a)   an unconditional sale of a financial asset;

(b)   a sale of a financial asset together with an option to repurchase the financial asset at its fair value at the time of repurchase; and

(c)   a sale of a financial asset together with a put or call option that is deeply out of the money (ie an option that is so far out of the money it is highly unlikely to go into the money before expiry).

B3.2.5   Examples of when an entity has retained substantially all the risks and rewards of ownership are:

(a)   a sale and repurchase transaction where the repurchase price is a fixed price or the sale price plus a lender's return;

(b)   a securities lending agreement;

(c)   a sale of a financial asset together with a total return swap that transfers the market risk exposure back to the entity;

(d)   a sale of a financial asset together with a deep in-the-money put or call option (ie an option that is so far in the money that it is highly unlikely to go out of the money before expiry); and

(e)   a sale of short-term receivables in which the entity guarantees to compensate the transferee for credit losses that are likely to occur.

B3.2.6   If an entity determines that as a result of the transfer, it has transferred substantially all the risks and rewards of ownership of the transferred asset, it does not recognise the transferred asset again in a future period, unless it reacquires the transferred asset in a new transaction.

Evaluation of the transfer of control

B3.2.7 An entity has not retained control of a transferred asset if the transferee has the practical ability to sell the transferred asset. An entity has retained control of a transferred asset if the transferee does not have the practical ability to sell the transferred asset. A transferee has the practical ability to sell the transferred asset if it is traded in an active market because the transferee could repurchase the transferred asset in the market if it needs to return the asset to the entity. For example, a transferee may have the practical ability to sell a transferred asset if the transferred asset is subject to an option that allows the entity to repurchase it, but the transferee can readily obtain the transferred asset in the market if the option is exercised. A transferee does not have the practical ability to sell the transferred asset if the entity retains such an option and the transferee cannot readily obtain the transferred asset in the market if the entity exercises its option.

B3.2.8 The transferee has the practical ability to sell the transferred asset only if the transferee can sell the transferred asset in its entirety to an unrelated third party and is able to exercise that ability unilaterally and without imposing additional restrictions on the transfer. The critical question is what the transferee is able to do in practice, not what contractual rights the transferee has concerning what it can do with the transferred asset or what contractual prohibitions exist. In particular:

(a) a contractual right to dispose of the transferred asset has little practical effect if there is no market for the transferred asset, and

(b) an ability to dispose of the transferred asset has little practical effect if it cannot be exercised freely. For that reason:

(i) the transferee's ability to dispose of the transferred asset must be independent of the actions of others (ie it must be a unilateral ability), and

(ii) the transferee must be able to dispose of the transferred asset without needing to attach restrictive conditions or 'strings' to the transfer (eg conditions about how a loan asset is serviced or an option giving the transferee the right to repurchase the asset).

B3.2.9 That the transferee is unlikely to sell the transferred asset does not, of itself, mean that the transferor has retained control of the transferred asset. However, if a put option or guarantee constrains the transferee from selling the transferred asset, then the transferor has retained control of the transferred asset. For example, if a put option or guarantee is sufficiently valuable it constrains the transferee from selling the transferred asset because the transferee would, in practice, not sell the transferred asset to a third party without attaching a similar option or other restrictive conditions. Instead, the transferee would hold the transferred asset so as to obtain payments under the guarantee or put option. Under these circumstances the transferor has retained control of the transferred asset.

Transfers that qualify for derecognition

B3.2.10 An entity may retain the right to a part of the interest payments on transferred assets as compensation for servicing those assets. The part of the interest payments that the entity would give up upon termination or transfer of the servicing contract is allocated to the servicing asset or servicing liability. The part of the interest payments that the entity would not give up is an interest-only strip receivable. For example, if the entity would not give up any interest upon termination or transfer of the servicing contract, the entire interest spread is an interest-only strip receivable. For the purposes of applying paragraph 3.2.13, the fair values of the servicing asset and interest-only strip receivable are used to allocate the carrying amount of the receivable between the part of the asset that is derecognised and the part that continues to be recognised. If there is no servicing fee specified or the fee to be received is not expected to compensate the entity adequately for performing the servicing, a liability for the servicing obligation is recognised at fair value.

B3.2.11 When measuring the fair values of the part that continues to be recognised and the part that is derecognised for the purposes of applying paragraph 3.2.13, an entity applies the fair value measurement requirements in IFRS 13 in addition to paragraph 3.2.14.

Transfers that do not qualify for derecognition

B3.2.12 The following is an application of the principle outlined in paragraph 3.2.15. If a guarantee provided by the entity for default losses on the transferred asset prevents a transferred asset from being derecognised because the entity has retained substantially all the risks and rewards of ownership of the transferred asset, the transferred asset continues to be recognised in its entirety and the consideration received is recognised as a liability.

Continuing involvement in transferred assets

B3.2.13 The following are examples of how an entity measures a transferred asset and the associated liability under paragraph 3.2.16.

All assets

(a) If a guarantee provided by an entity to pay for default losses on a transferred asset prevents the transferred asset from being derecognised to the extent of the continuing involvement, the transferred asset at the date of the transfer is measured at the lower of (i) the carrying amount of the asset and (ii) the maximum amount of the consideration received in the transfer that the entity could be required to repay ('the guarantee amount'). The associated liability is initially measured at the guarantee amount plus the fair value of the guarantee (which is normally the consideration received for the guarantee). Subsequently, the initial fair value of the guarantee is recognised in profit or loss on a time proportion basis (see IAS 18) and the carrying value of the asset is reduced by any impairment losses.

Assets measured at amortised cost

(b)　If a put option obligation written by an entity or call option right held by an entity prevents a transferred asset from being derecognised and the entity measures the transferred asset at amortised cost, the associated liability is measured at its cost (ie the consideration received) adjusted for the amortisation of any difference between that cost and the amortised cost of the transferred asset at the expiration date of the option. For example, assume that the amortised cost and carrying amount of the asset on the date of the transfer is CU98 and that the consideration received is CU95. The amortised cost of the asset on the option exercise date will be CU100. The initial carrying amount of the associated liability is CU95 and the difference between CU95 and CU100 is recognised in profit or loss using the effective interest method. If the option is exercised, any difference between the carrying amount of the associated liability and the exercise price is recognised in profit or loss.

Assets measured at fair value

(c)　If a call option right retained by an entity prevents a transferred asset from being derecognised and the entity measures the transferred asset at fair value, the asset continues to be measured at its fair value. The associated liability is measured at (i) the option exercise price less the time value of the option if the option is in or at the money, or (ii) the fair value of the transferred asset less the time value of the option if the option is out of the money. The adjustment to the measurement of the associated liability ensures that the net carrying amount of the asset and the associated liability is the fair value of the call option right. For example, if the fair value of the underlying asset is CU80, the option exercise price is CU95 and the time value of the option is CU5, the carrying amount of the associated liability is CU75 (CU80 – CU5) and the carrying amount of the transferred asset is CU80 (ie its fair value).

(d)　If a put option written by an entity prevents a transferred asset from being derecognised and the entity measures the transferred asset at fair value, the associated liability is measured at the option exercise price plus the time value of the option. The measurement of the asset at fair value is limited to the lower of the fair value and the option exercise price because the entity has no right to increases in the fair value of the transferred asset above the exercise price of the option. This ensures that the net carrying amount of the asset and the associated liability is the fair value of the put option obligation. For example, if the fair value of the underlying asset is CU120, the option exercise price is CU100 and the time value of the option is CU5, the carrying amount of the associated liability is CU105 (CU100 + CU5) and the carrying amount of the asset is CU100 (in this case the option exercise price).

(e)　If a collar, in the form of a purchased call and written put, prevents a transferred asset from being derecognised and the entity measures the asset at fair value, it continues to measure the asset at fair value. The associated liability is measured at (i) the sum of the call exercise price and fair value of the put option less the time value of the call option, if the call option is in or at the money, or (ii) the sum of the fair value of the asset and the fair value of the put option less the time value of the call option if the call option is out of the money. The adjustment to the associated liability ensures that the net carrying amount of the asset and the associated liability is the fair value of the options held and written by the entity. For example, assume an entity transfers a financial asset that is measured at fair value while simultaneously purchasing a call with an exercise price of CU120 and writing a put with an exercise price of CU80. Assume also that the fair value of the asset is CU100 at the date of the transfer. The time value of the put and call are CU1 and CU5 respectively. In this case, the entity recognises an asset of CU100 (the fair value of the asset) and a liability of CU96 [(CU100 + CU1) – CU5]. This gives a net asset value of CU4, which is the fair value of the options held and written by the entity.

All transfers

B3.2.14 To the extent that a transfer of a financial asset does not qualify for derecognition, the transferor's contractual rights or obligations related to the transfer are not accounted for separately as derivatives if recognising both the derivative and either the transferred asset or the liability arising from the transfer would result in recognising the same rights or obligations twice. For example, a call option retained by the transferor may prevent a transfer of financial assets from being accounted for as a sale. In that case, the call option is not separately recognised as a derivative asset.

B3.2.15 To the extent that a transfer of a financial asset does not qualify for derecognition, the transferee does not recognise the transferred asset as its asset. The transferee derecognises the cash or other consideration paid and recognises a receivable from the transferor. If the transferor has both a right and an obligation to reacquire control of the entire transferred asset for a fixed amount (such as under a repurchase agreement), the transferee may measure its receivable at amortised cost if it meets the criteria in paragraph 4.1.2.

Examples

B3.2.16 The following examples illustrate the application of the derecognition principles of this IFRS.

   (a) *Repurchase agreements and securities lending.* If a financial asset is sold under an agreement to repurchase it at a fixed price or at the sale price plus a lender's return or if it is loaned under an agreement to return it to the transferor, it is not derecognised because the transferor retains substantially all the risks and rewards of ownership. If the transferee obtains the right to sell or pledge the asset, the transferor reclassifies the asset in its statement of financial position, for example, as a loaned asset or repurchase receivable.

   (b) *Repurchase agreements and securities lending—assets that are substantially the same.* If a financial asset is sold under an agreement to repurchase the same or substantially the same asset at a fixed price or at the sale price plus a lender's return or if a financial asset is borrowed or loaned under an agreement to return the same or substantially the same asset to the transferor, it is not derecognised because the transferor retains substantially all the risks and rewards of ownership.

(c) *Repurchase agreements and securities lending—right of substitution.* If a repurchase agreement at a fixed repurchase price or a price equal to the sale price plus a lender's return, or a similar securities lending transaction, provides the transferee with a right to substitute assets that are similar and of equal fair value to the transferred asset at the repurchase date, the asset sold or lent under a repurchase or securities lending transaction is not derecognised because the transferor retains substantially all the risks and rewards of ownership.

(d) *Repurchase right of first refusal at fair value.* If an entity sells a financial asset and retains only a right of first refusal to repurchase the transferred asset at fair value if the transferee subsequently sells it, the entity derecognises the asset because it has transferred substantially all the risks and rewards of ownership.

(e) *Wash sale transaction.* The repurchase of a financial asset shortly after it has been sold is sometimes referred to as a wash sale. Such a repurchase does not preclude derecognition provided that the original transaction met the derecognition requirements. However, if an agreement to sell a financial asset is entered into concurrently with an agreement to repurchase the same asset at a fixed price or the sale price plus a lender's return, then the asset is not derecognised.

(f) *Put options and call options that are deeply in the money.* If a transferred financial asset can be called back by the transferor and the call option is deeply in the money, the transfer does not qualify for derecognition because the transferor has retained substantially all the risks and rewards of ownership. Similarly, if the financial asset can be put back by the transferee and the put option is deeply in the money, the transfer does not qualify for derecognition because the transferor has retained substantially all the risks and rewards of ownership.

(g) *Put options and call options that are deeply out of the money.* A financial asset that is transferred subject only to a deep out-of-the-money put option held by the transferee or a deep out-of-the-money call option held by the transferor is derecognised. This is because the transferor has transferred substantially all the risks and rewards of ownership.

(h) *Readily obtainable assets subject to a call option that is neither deeply in the money nor deeply out of the money.* If an entity holds a call option on an asset that is readily obtainable in the market and the option is neither deeply in the money nor deeply out of the money, the asset is derecognised. This is because the entity (i) has neither retained nor transferred substantially all the risks and rewards of ownership, and (ii) has not retained control. However, if the asset is not readily obtainable in the market, derecognition is precluded to the extent of the amount of the asset that is subject to the call option because the entity has retained control of the asset.

(i)   *A not readily obtainable asset subject to a put option written by an entity that is neither deeply in the money nor deeply out of the money.* If an entity transfers a financial asset that is not readily obtainable in the market, and writes a put option that is not deeply out of the money, the entity neither retains nor transfers substantially all the risks and rewards of ownership because of the written put option. The entity retains control of the asset if the put option is sufficiently valuable to prevent the transferee from selling the asset, in which case the asset continues to be recognised to the extent of the transferor's continuing involvement (see paragraph B3.2.9). The entity transfers control of the asset if the put option is not sufficiently valuable to prevent the transferee from selling the asset, in which case the asset is derecognised.

(j)   *Assets subject to a fair value put or call option or a forward repurchase agreement.* A transfer of a financial asset that is subject only to a put or call option or a forward repurchase agreement that has an exercise or repurchase price equal to the fair value of the financial asset at the time of repurchase results in derecognition because of the transfer of substantially all the risks and rewards of ownership.

(k)   *Cash-settled call or put options.* An entity evaluates the transfer of a financial asset that is subject to a put or call option or a forward repurchase agreement that will be settled net in cash to determine whether it has retained or transferred substantially all the risks and rewards of ownership. If the entity has not retained substantially all the risks and rewards of ownership of the transferred asset, it determines whether it has retained control of the transferred asset. That the put or the call or the forward repurchase agreement is settled net in cash does not automatically mean that the entity has transferred control (see paragraphs B3.2.9 and (g), (h) and (i) above).

(l)   *Removal of accounts provision.* A removal of accounts provision is an unconditional repurchase (call) option that gives an entity the right to reclaim assets transferred subject to some restrictions. Provided that such an option results in the entity neither retaining nor transferring substantially all the risks and rewards of ownership, it precludes derecognition only to the extent of the amount subject to repurchase (assuming that the transferee cannot sell the assets). For example, if the carrying amount and proceeds from the transfer of loan assets are CU100,000 and any individual loan could be called back but the aggregate amount of loans that could be repurchased could not exceed CU10,000, CU90,000 of the loans would qualify for derecognition.

(m)   *Clean-up calls.* An entity, which may be a transferor, that services transferred assets may hold a clean-up call to purchase remaining transferred assets when the amount of outstanding assets falls to a specified level at which the cost of servicing those assets becomes burdensome in relation to the benefits of servicing. Provided that such a clean-up call results in the entity neither retaining nor transferring substantially all the risks and rewards of ownership and the transferee cannot sell the assets, it precludes derecognition only to the extent of the amount of the assets that is subject to the call option.

(n)   *Subordinated retained interests and credit guarantees.* An entity may provide the transferee with credit enhancement by subordinating some or all of its interest retained in the transferred asset. Alternatively, an entity may provide the transferee with credit enhancement in the form of a credit guarantee that could be unlimited or limited to a specified amount. If the entity retains substantially all the risks and rewards of ownership of the transferred asset, the asset continues to be recognised in its entirety. If the entity retains some, but not substantially all, of the risks and rewards of ownership and has retained control, derecognition is precluded to the extent of the amount of cash or other assets that the entity could be required to pay.

(o)   *Total return swaps.* An entity may sell a financial asset to a transferee and enter into a total return swap with the transferee, whereby all of the interest payment cash flows from the underlying asset are remitted to the entity in exchange for a fixed payment or variable rate payment and any increases or declines in the fair value of the underlying asset are absorbed by the entity. In such a case, derecognition of all of the asset is prohibited.

(p)   *Interest rate swaps.* An entity may transfer to a transferee a fixed rate financial asset and enter into an interest rate swap with the transferee to receive a fixed interest rate and pay a variable interest rate based on a notional amount that is equal to the principal amount of the transferred financial asset. The interest rate swap does not preclude derecognition of the transferred asset provided the payments on the swap are not conditional on payments being made on the transferred asset.

(q)   *Amortising interest rate swaps.* An entity may transfer to a transferee a fixed rate financial asset that is paid off over time, and enter into an amortising interest rate swap with the transferee to receive a fixed interest rate and pay a variable interest rate based on a notional amount. If the notional amount of the swap amortises so that it equals the principal amount of the transferred financial asset outstanding at any point in time, the swap would generally result in the entity retaining substantial prepayment risk, in which case the entity either continues to recognise all of the transferred asset or continues to recognise the transferred asset to the extent of its continuing involvement. Conversely, if the amortisation of the notional amount of the swap is not linked to the principal amount outstanding of the transferred asset, such a swap would not result in the entity retaining prepayment risk on the asset. Hence, it would not preclude derecognition of the transferred asset provided the payments on the swap are not conditional on interest payments being made on the transferred asset and the swap does not result in the entity retaining any other significant risks and rewards of ownership on the transferred asset.

B3.2.17 This paragraph illustrates the application of the continuing involvement approach when the entity's continuing involvement is in a part of a financial asset.

Assume an entity has a portfolio of prepayable loans whose coupon and effective interest rate is 10 per cent and whose principal amount and amortised cost is CU10,000. It enters into a transaction in which, in return for a payment of CU9,115, the transferee obtains the right to CU9,000 of any collections of principal plus interest thereon at 9.5 per cent. The entity retains rights to CU1,000 of any collections of principal plus interest thereon at 10 per cent, plus the excess spread of 0.5 per cent on the remaining CU9,000 of principal. Collections from prepayments are allocated between the entity and the transferee proportionately in the ratio of 1:9, but any defaults are deducted from the entity's interest of CU1,000 until that interest is exhausted. The fair value of the loans at the date of the transaction is CU10,100 and the fair value of the excess spread of 0.5 per cent is CU40.

The entity determines that it has transferred some significant risks and rewards of ownership (for example, significant prepayment risk) but has also retained some significant risks and rewards of ownership (because of its subordinated retained interest) and has retained control. It therefore applies the continuing involvement approach.

To apply this IFRS, the entity analyses the transaction as (a) a retention of a fully proportionate retained interest of CU1,000, plus (b) the subordination of that retained interest to provide credit enhancement to the transferee for credit losses.

The entity calculates that CU9,090 (90 per cent × CU10,100) of the consideration received of CU9,115 represents the consideration for a fully proportionate 90 per cent share. The remainder of the consideration received (CU25) represents consideration received for subordinating its retained interest to provide credit enhancement to the transferee for credit losses. In addition, the excess spread of 0.5 per cent represents consideration received for the credit enhancement. Accordingly, the total consideration received for the credit enhancement is CU65 (CU25 + CU40).

The entity calculates the gain or loss on the sale of the 90 per cent share of cash flows. Assuming that separate fair values of the 90 per cent part transferred and the 10 per cent part retained are not available at the date of the transfer, the entity allocates the carrying amount of the asset in accordance with paragraph 3.2.14 as follows:

	Fair value	Percentage	Allocated carrying amount
Portion transferred	9,090	90%	9,000
Portion retained	1,010	10%	1,000
Total	**10,100**		**10,000**

continued...

...continued

The entity computes its gain or loss on the sale of the 90 per cent share of the cash flows by deducting the allocated carrying amount of the portion transferred from the consideration received, ie CU90 (CU9,090 – CU9,000). The carrying amount of the portion retained by the entity is CU1,000.

In addition, the entity recognises the continuing involvement that results from the subordination of its retained interest for credit losses. Accordingly, it recognises an asset of CU1,000 (the maximum amount of the cash flows it would not receive under the subordination), and an associated liability of CU1,065 (which is the maximum amount of the cash flows it would not receive under the subordination, ie CU1,000 plus the fair value of the subordination of CU65).

The entity uses all of the above information to account for the transaction as follows:

	Debit	Credit
Original asset	—	9,000
Asset recognised for subordination or the residual interest	1,000	—
Asset for the consideration received in the form of excess spread	40	—
Profit or loss (gain on transfer)	—	90
Liability	—	1,065
Cash received	9,115	—
Total	**10,155**	**10,155**

Immediately following the transaction, the carrying amount of the asset is CU2,040 comprising CU1,000, representing the allocated cost of the portion retained, and CU1,040, representing the entity's additional continuing involvement from the subordination of its retained interest for credit losses (which includes the excess spread of CU40).

In subsequent periods, the entity recognises the consideration received for the credit enhancement (CU65) on a time proportion basis, accrues interest on the recognised asset using the effective interest method and recognises any credit impairment on the recognised assets. As an example of the latter, assume that in the following year there is a credit impairment loss on the underlying loans of CU300. The entity reduces its recognised asset by CU600 (CU300 relating to its retained interest and CU300 relating to the additional continuing involvement that arises from the subordination of its retained interest for credit losses), and reduces its recognised liability by CU300. The net result is a charge to profit or loss for credit impairment of CU300.

Derecognition of financial liabilities (section 3.3)

B3.3.1 A financial liability (or part of it) is extinguished when the debtor either:

(a) discharges the liability (or part of it) by paying the creditor, normally with cash, other financial assets, goods or services; or

(b) is legally released from primary responsibility for the liability (or part of it) either by process of law or by the creditor. (If the debtor has given a guarantee this condition may still be met.)

B3.3.2 If an issuer of a debt instrument repurchases that instrument, the debt is extinguished even if the issuer is a market maker in that instrument or intends to resell it in the near term.

B3.3.3 Payment to a third party, including a trust (sometimes called 'in-substance defeasance'), does not, by itself, relieve the debtor of its primary obligation to the creditor, in the absence of legal release.

B3.3.4 If a debtor pays a third party to assume an obligation and notifies its creditor that the third party has assumed its debt obligation, the debtor does not derecognise the debt obligation unless the condition in paragraph B3.3.1(b) is met. If the debtor pays a third party to assume an obligation and obtains a legal release from its creditor, the debtor has extinguished the debt. However, if the debtor agrees to make payments on the debt to the third party or direct to its original creditor, the debtor recognises a new debt obligation to the third party.

B3.3.5 Although legal release, whether judicially or by the creditor, results in derecognition of a liability, the entity may recognise a new liability if the derecognition criteria in paragraphs 3.2.1–3.2.23 are not met for the financial assets transferred. If those criteria are not met, the transferred assets are not derecognised, and the entity recognises a new liability relating to the transferred assets.

B3.3.6 For the purpose of paragraph 3.3.2, the terms are substantially different if the discounted present value of the cash flows under the new terms, including any fees paid net of any fees received and discounted using the original effective interest rate, is at least 10 per cent different from the discounted present value of the remaining cash flows of the original financial liability. If an exchange of debt instruments or modification of terms is accounted for as an extinguishment, any costs or fees incurred are recognised as part of the gain or loss on the extinguishment. If the exchange or modification is not accounted for as an extinguishment, any costs or fees incurred adjust the carrying amount of the liability and are amortised over the remaining term of the modified liability.

B3.3.7 In some cases, a creditor releases a debtor from its present obligation to make payments, but the debtor assumes a guarantee obligation to pay if the party assuming primary responsibility defaults. In these circumstances the debtor:

(a) recognises a new financial liability based on the fair value of its obligation for the guarantee, and

(b) recognises a gain or loss based on the difference between (i) any proceeds paid and (ii) the carrying amount of the original financial liability less the fair value of the new financial liability.

Classification (chapter 4)

Classification of financial assets (section 4.1)

The entity's business model for managing financial assets

B4.1.1   Paragraph 4.1.1(a) requires an entity to classify financial assets as subsequently measured at amortised cost or fair value on the basis of the entity's business model for managing the financial assets. An entity assesses whether its financial assets meet this condition on the basis of the objective of the business model as determined by the entity's key management personnel (as defined in IAS 24).

B4.1.2   The entity's business model does not depend on management's intentions for an individual instrument. Accordingly, this condition is not an instrument-by-instrument approach to classification and should be determined on a higher level of aggregation. However, a single entity may have more than one business model for managing its financial instruments. Therefore, classification need not be determined at the reporting entity level. For example, an entity may hold a portfolio of investments that it manages in order to collect contractual cash flows and another portfolio of investments that it manages in order to trade to realise fair value changes.

B4.1.3   Although the objective of an entity's business model may be to hold financial assets in order to collect contractual cash flows, the entity need not hold all of those instruments until maturity. Thus an entity's business model can be to hold financial assets to collect contractual cash flows even when sales of financial assets occur. For example, the entity may sell a financial asset if:

   (a)   the financial asset no longer meets the entity's investment policy (eg the credit rating of the asset declines below that required by the entity's investment policy);

   (b)   an insurer adjusts its investment portfolio to reflect a change in expected duration (ie the expected timing of payouts); or

   (c)   an entity needs to fund capital expenditures.

   However, if more than an infrequent number of sales are made out of a portfolio, the entity needs to assess whether and how such sales are consistent with an objective of collecting contractual cash flows.

B4.1.4   The following are examples of when the objective of an entity's business model may be to hold financial assets to collect the contractual cash flows. This list of examples is not exhaustive.

Example	Analysis
Example 1 An entity holds investments to collect their contractual cash flows but would sell an investment in particular circumstances.	Although an entity may consider, among other information, the financial assets' fair values from a liquidity perspective (ie the cash amount that would be realised if the entity needs to sell assets), the entity's objective is to hold the financial assets and collect the contractual cash flows. Some sales would not contradict that objective.
Example 2 An entity's business model is to purchase portfolios of financial assets, such as loans. Those portfolios may or may not include financial assets with incurred credit losses. If payment on the loans is not made on a timely basis, the entity attempts to extract the contractual cash flows through various means—for example, by making contact with the debtor by mail, telephone or other methods. In some cases, the entity enters into interest rate swaps to change the interest rate on particular financial assets in a portfolio from a floating interest rate to a fixed interest rate.	The objective of the entity's business model is to hold the financial assets and collect the contractual cash flows. The entity does not purchase the portfolio to make a profit by selling them. The same analysis would apply even if the entity does not expect to receive all of the contractual cash flows (eg some of the financial assets have incurred credit losses). Moreover, the fact that the entity has entered into derivatives to modify the cash flows of the portfolio does not in itself change the entity's business model. If the portfolio is not managed on a fair value basis, the objective of the business model could be to hold the assets to collect the contractual cash flows.
Example 3 An entity has a business model with the objective of originating loans to customers and subsequently to sell those loans to a securitisation vehicle. The securitisation vehicle issues instruments to investors. The originating entity controls the securitisation vehicle and thus consolidates it. The securitisation vehicle collects the contractual cash flows from the loans and passes them on to its investors. It is assumed for the purposes of this example that the loans continue to be recognised in the consolidated statement of financial position because they are not derecognised by the securitisation vehicle.	The consolidated group originated the loans with the objective of holding them to collect the contractual cash flows. However, the originating entity has an objective of realising cash flows on the loan portfolio by selling the loans to the securitisation vehicle, so for the purposes of its separate financial statements it would not be considered to be managing this portfolio in order to collect the contractual cash flows.

B4.1.5 One business model in which the objective is not to hold instruments to collect the contractual cash flows is if an entity manages the performance of a portfolio of financial assets with the objective of realising cash flows through the sale of the assets. For example, if an entity actively manages a portfolio of assets in order to realise fair value changes arising from changes in credit spreads and yield curves, its business model is not to hold those assets to collect the contractual cash flows. The entity's objective results in active buying and selling and the entity is managing the instruments to realise fair value gains rather than to collect the contractual cash flows.

B4.1.6 A portfolio of financial assets that is managed and whose performance is evaluated on a fair value basis (as described in paragraph 4.2.2(b)) is not held to collect contractual cash flows. Also, a portfolio of financial assets that meets the definition of held for trading is not held to collect contractual cash flows. Such portfolios of instruments must be measured at fair value through profit or loss.

Contractual cash flows that are solely payments of principal and interest on the principal amount outstanding

B4.1.7 Paragraph 4.1.1 requires an entity (unless paragraph 4.1.5 applies) to classify a financial asset as subsequently measured at amortised cost or fair value on the basis of the contractual cash flow characteristics of the financial asset that is in a group of financial assets managed for the collection of the contractual cash flows.

B4.1.8 An entity shall assess whether contractual cash flows are solely payments of principal and interest on the principal amount outstanding for the currency in which the financial asset is denominated (see also paragraph B5.7.2).

B4.1.9 Leverage is a contractual cash flow characteristic of some financial assets. Leverage increases the variability of the contractual cash flows with the result that they do not have the economic characteristics of interest. Stand-alone option, forward and swap contracts are examples of financial assets that include leverage. Thus such contracts do not meet the condition in paragraph 4.1.2(b) and cannot be subsequently measured at amortised cost.

B4.1.10 Contractual provisions that permit the issuer (ie the debtor) to prepay a debt instrument (eg a loan or a bond) or permit the holder (ie the creditor) to put a debt instrument back to the issuer before maturity result in contractual cash flows that are solely payments of principal and interest on the principal amount outstanding only if:

(a) the provision is not contingent on future events, other than to protect:

(i) the holder against the credit deterioration of the issuer (eg defaults, credit downgrades or loan covenant violations), or a change in control of the issuer; or

(ii) the holder or issuer against changes in relevant taxation or law; and

(b) the prepayment amount substantially represents unpaid amounts of principal and interest on the principal amount outstanding, which may include reasonable additional compensation for the early termination of the contract.

B4.1.11 Contractual provisions that permit the issuer or holder to extend the contractual term of a debt instrument (ie an extension option) result in contractual cash flows that are solely payments of principal and interest on the principal amount outstanding only if:

(a) the provision is not contingent on future events, other than to protect:

(i) the holder against the credit deterioration of the issuer (eg defaults, credit downgrades or loan covenant violations) or a change in control of the issuer; or

(ii) the holder or issuer against changes in relevant taxation or law; and

(b) the terms of the extension option result in contractual cash flows during the extension period that are solely payments of principal and interest on the principal amount outstanding.

B4.1.12 A contractual term that changes the timing or amount of payments of principal or interest does not result in contractual cash flows that are solely principal and interest on the principal amount outstanding unless it:

(a) is a variable interest rate that is consideration for the time value of money and the credit risk (which may be determined at initial recognition only, and so may be fixed) associated with the principal amount outstanding; and

(b) if the contractual term is a prepayment option, meets the conditions in paragraph B4.1.10; or

(c) if the contractual term is an extension option, meets the conditions in paragraph B4.1.11.

B4.1.13 The following examples illustrate contractual cash flows that are solely payments of principal and interest on the principal amount outstanding. This list of examples is not exhaustive.

Instrument	Analysis
Instrument A Instrument A is a bond with a stated maturity date. Payments of principal and interest on the principal amount outstanding are linked to an inflation index of the currency in which the instrument is issued. The inflation link is not leveraged and the principal is protected.	The contractual cash flows are solely payments of principal and interest on the principal amount outstanding. Linking payments of principal and interest on the principal amount outstanding to an unleveraged inflation index resets the time value of money to a current level. In other words, the interest rate on the instrument reflects 'real' interest. Thus, the interest amounts are consideration for the time value of money on the principal amount outstanding. However, if the interest payments were indexed to another variable such as the debtor's performance (eg the debtor's net income) or an equity index, the contractual cash flows are not payments of principal and interest on the principal amount outstanding. That is because the interest payments are not consideration for the time value of money and for credit risk associated with the principal amount outstanding. There is variability in the contractual interest payments that is inconsistent with market interest rates.

continued...

...continued **Instrument**	**Analysis**
Instrument B Instrument B is a variable interest rate instrument with a stated maturity date that permits the borrower to choose the market interest rate on an ongoing basis. For example, at each interest rate reset date, the borrower can choose to pay three-month LIBOR for a three-month term or one-month LIBOR for a one-month term.	The contractual cash flows are solely payments of principal and interest on the principal amount outstanding as long as the interest paid over the life of the instrument reflects consideration for the time value of money and for the credit risk associated with the instrument. The fact that the LIBOR interest rate is reset during the life of the instrument does not in itself disqualify the instrument. However, if the borrower is able to choose to pay one-month LIBOR for three months and that one-month LIBOR is not reset each month, the contractual cash flows are not payments of principal and interest. The same analysis would apply if the borrower is able to choose between the lender's published one-month variable interest rate and the lender's published three-month variable interest rate. However, if the instrument has a contractual interest rate that is based on a term that exceeds the instrument's remaining life, its contractual cash flows are not payments of principal and interest on the principal amount outstanding. For example, a constant maturity bond with a five-year term that pays a variable rate that is reset periodically but always reflects a five-year maturity does not result in contractual cash flows that are payments of principal and interest on the principal amount outstanding. That is because the interest payable in each period is disconnected from the term of the instrument (except at origination).

continued...

...continued **Instrument**	**Analysis**
Instrument C Instrument C is a bond with a stated maturity date and pays a variable market interest rate. That variable interest rate is capped.	The contractual cash flows of both: (a) an instrument that has a fixed interest rate and (b) an instrument that has a variable interest rate are payments of principal and interest on the principal amount outstanding as long as the interest reflects consideration for the time value of money and for the credit risk associated with the instrument during the term of the instrument. Therefore, an instrument that is a combination of (a) and (b) (eg a bond with an interest rate cap) can have cash flows that are solely payments of principal and interest on the principal amount outstanding. Such a feature may reduce cash flow variability by setting a limit on a variable interest rate (eg an interest rate cap or floor) or increase the cash flow variability because a fixed rate becomes variable.
Instrument D Instrument D is a full recourse loan and is secured by collateral.	The fact that a full recourse loan is collateralised does not in itself affect the analysis of whether the contractual cash flows are solely payments of principal and interest on the principal amount outstanding.

B4.1.14   The following examples illustrate contractual cash flows that are not payments of principal and interest on the principal amount outstanding. This list of examples is not exhaustive.

Instrument	**Analysis**
Instrument E Instrument E is a bond that is convertible into equity instruments of the issuer.	The holder would analyse the convertible bond in its entirety. The contractual cash flows are not payments of principal and interest on the principal amount outstanding because the interest rate does not reflect only consideration for the time value of money and the credit risk. The return is also linked to the value of the equity of the issuer.
	continued...

...continued **Instrument**	**Analysis**
Instrument F Instrument F is a loan that pays an inverse floating interest rate (ie the interest rate has an inverse relationship to market interest rates).	The contractual cash flows are not solely payments of principal and interest on the principal amount outstanding. The interest amounts are not consideration for the time value of money on the principal amount outstanding.
Instrument G Instrument G is a perpetual instrument but the issuer may call the instrument at any point and pay the holder the par amount plus accrued interest due. Instrument G pays a market interest rate but payment of interest cannot be made unless the issuer is able to remain solvent immediately afterwards. Deferred interest does not accrue additional interest.	The contractual cash flows are not payments of principal and interest on the principal amount outstanding. That is because the issuer may be required to defer interest payments and additional interest does not accrue on those deferred interest amounts. As a result, interest amounts are not consideration for the time value of money on the principal amount outstanding. If interest accrued on the deferred amounts, the contractual cash flows could be payments of principal and interest on the principal amount outstanding.
	The fact that Instrument G is perpetual does not in itself mean that the contractual cash flows are not payments of principal and interest on the principal amount outstanding. In effect, a perpetual instrument has continuous (multiple) extension options. Such options may result in contractual cash flows that are payments of principal and interest on the principal amount outstanding if interest payments are mandatory and must be paid in perpetuity. Also, the fact that Instrument G is callable does not mean that the contractual cash flows are not payments of principal and interest on the principal amount outstanding unless it is callable at an amount that does not substantially reflect payment of outstanding principal and interest on that principal. Even if the callable amount includes an amount that compensates the holder for the early termination of the instrument, the contractual cash flows could be payments of principal and interest on the principal amount outstanding.

B4.1.15　In some cases a financial asset may have contractual cash flows that are described as principal and interest but those cash flows do not represent the payment of principal and interest on the principal amount outstanding as described in paragraphs 4.1.2(b) and 4.1.3 of this IFRS.

B4.1.16　This may be the case if the financial asset represents an investment in particular assets or cash flows and hence the contractual cash flows are not solely payments of principal and interest on the principal amount outstanding. For example, the contractual cash flows may include payment for factors other than consideration for the time value of money and for the credit risk associated with the principal amount outstanding during a particular period of time. As a result, the instrument would not satisfy the condition in paragraph 4.1.2(b). This could be the case when a creditor's claim is limited to specified assets of the debtor or the cash flows from specified assets (for example, a 'non-recourse' financial asset).

B4.1.17　However, the fact that a financial asset is non-recourse does not in itself necessarily preclude the financial asset from meeting the condition in paragraph 4.1.2(b). In such situations, the creditor is required to assess ('look through to') the particular underlying assets or cash flows to determine whether the contractual cash flows of the financial asset being classified are payments of principal and interest on the principal amount outstanding. If the terms of the financial asset give rise to any other cash flows or limit the cash flows in a manner inconsistent with payments representing principal and interest, the financial asset does not meet the condition in paragraph 4.1.2(b). Whether the underlying assets are financial assets or non-financial assets does not in itself affect this assessment.

B4.1.18　If a contractual cash flow characteristic is not genuine, it does not affect the classification of a financial asset. A cash flow characteristic is not genuine if it affects the instrument's contractual cash flows only on the occurrence of an event that is extremely rare, highly abnormal and very unlikely to occur.

B4.1.19　In almost every lending transaction the creditor's instrument is ranked relative to the instruments of the debtor's other creditors. An instrument that is subordinated to other instruments may have contractual cash flows that are payments of principal and interest on the principal amount outstanding if the debtor's non-payment is a breach of contract and the holder has a contractual right to unpaid amounts of principal and interest on the principal amount outstanding even in the event of the debtor's bankruptcy. For example, a trade receivable that ranks its creditor as a general creditor would qualify as having payments of principal and interest on the principal amount outstanding. This is the case even if the debtor issued loans that are collateralised, which in the event of bankruptcy would give that loan holder priority over the claims of the general creditor in respect of the collateral but does not affect the contractual right of the general creditor to unpaid principal and other amounts due.

Contractually linked instruments

B4.1.20　In some types of transactions, an entity may prioritise payments to the holders of financial assets using multiple contractually linked instruments that create concentrations of credit risk (tranches). Each tranche has a subordination ranking that specifies the order in which any cash flows generated by the issuer are allocated to the tranche. In such situations, the holders of a tranche have the right to payments of principal and interest on the principal amount outstanding only if the issuer generates sufficient cash flows to satisfy higher-ranking tranches.

B4.1.21 In such transactions, a tranche has cash flow characteristics that are payments of principal and interest on the principal amount outstanding only if:

(a) the contractual terms of the tranche being assessed for classification (without looking through to the underlying pool of financial instruments) give rise to cash flows that are solely payments of principal and interest on the principal amount outstanding (eg the interest rate on the tranche is not linked to a commodity index);

(b) the underlying pool of financial instruments has the cash flow characteristics set out in paragraphs B4.1.23 and B4.1.24; and

(c) the exposure to credit risk in the underlying pool of financial instruments inherent in the tranche is equal to or lower than the exposure to credit risk of the underlying pool of financial instruments (for example, this condition would be met if the underlying pool of instruments were to lose 50 per cent as a result of credit losses and under all circumstances the tranche would lose 50 per cent or less).

B4.1.22 An entity must look through until it can identify the underlying pool of instruments that are creating (rather than passing through) the cash flows. This is the underlying pool of financial instruments.

B4.1.23 The underlying pool must contain one or more instruments that have contractual cash flows that are solely payments of principal and interest on the principal amount outstanding.

B4.1.24 The underlying pool of instruments may also include instruments that:

(a) reduce the cash flow variability of the instruments in paragraph B4.1.23 and, when combined with the instruments in paragraph B4.1.23, result in cash flows that are solely payments of principal and interest on the principal amount outstanding (eg an interest rate cap or floor or a contract that reduces the credit risk on some or all of the instruments in paragraph B4.1.23); or

(b) align the cash flows of the tranches with the cash flows of the pool of underlying instruments in paragraph B4.1.23 to address differences in and only in:

(i) whether the interest rate is fixed or floating;

(ii) the currency in which the cash flows are denominated, including inflation in that currency; or

(iii) the timing of the cash flows.

B4.1.25 If any instrument in the pool does not meet the conditions in either paragraph B4.1.23 or paragraph B4.1.24, the condition in paragraph B4.1.21(b) is not met.

B4.1.26 If the holder cannot assess the conditions in paragraph B4.1.21 at initial recognition, the tranche must be measured at fair value. If the underlying pool of instruments can change after initial recognition in such a way that the pool may not meet the conditions in paragraphs B4.1.23 and B4.1.24, the tranche does not meet the conditions in paragraph B4.1.21 and must be measured at fair value.

Option to designate a financial asset or financial liability as at fair value through profit or loss (sections 4.1 and 4.2)

B4.1.27 Subject to the conditions in paragraphs 4.1.5 and 4.2.2, this IFRS allows an entity to designate a financial asset, a financial liability, or a group of financial instruments (financial assets, financial liabilities or both) as at fair value through profit or loss provided that doing so results in more relevant information.

B4.1.28 The decision of an entity to designate a financial asset or financial liability as at fair value through profit or loss is similar to an accounting policy choice (although, unlike an accounting policy choice, it is not required to be applied consistently to all similar transactions). When an entity has such a choice, paragraph 14(b) of IAS 8 requires the chosen policy to result in the financial statements providing reliable and more relevant information about the effects of transactions, other events and conditions on the entity's financial position, financial performance or cash flows. For example, in the case of designation of a financial liability as at fair value through profit or loss, paragraph 4.2.2 sets out the two circumstances when the requirement for more relevant information will be met. Accordingly, to choose such designation in accordance with paragraph 4.2.2, the entity needs to demonstrate that it falls within one (or both) of these two circumstances.

Designation eliminates or significantly reduces an accounting mismatch

B4.1.29 Measurement of a financial asset or financial liability and classification of recognised changes in its value are determined by the item's classification and whether the item is part of a designated hedging relationship. Those requirements can create a measurement or recognition inconsistency (sometimes referred to as an 'accounting mismatch') when, for example, in the absence of designation as at fair value through profit or loss, a financial asset would be classified as subsequently measured at fair value and a liability the entity considers related would be subsequently measured at amortised cost (with changes in fair value not recognised). In such circumstances, an entity may conclude that its financial statements would provide more relevant information if both the asset and the liability were measured as at fair value through profit or loss.

B4.1.30 The following examples show when this condition could be met. In all cases, an entity may use this condition to designate financial assets or financial liabilities as at fair value through profit or loss only if it meets the principle in paragraph 4.1.5 or 4.2.2(a).

(a) An entity has liabilities under insurance contracts whose measurement incorporates current information (as permitted by IFRS 4, paragraph 24), and financial assets it considers related that would otherwise be measured at amortised cost.

(b) An entity has financial assets, financial liabilities or both that share a risk, such as interest rate risk, that gives rise to opposite changes in fair value that tend to offset each other. However, only some of the instruments would be measured at fair value through profit or loss (ie are derivatives, or are classified as held for trading). It may also be the case that the requirements for hedge accounting are not met, for example because the requirements for effectiveness in paragraph 88 of IAS 39 are not met.

(c)   An entity has financial assets, financial liabilities or both that share a risk, such as interest rate risk, that gives rise to opposite changes in fair value that tend to offset each other and the entity does not qualify for hedge accounting because none of the instruments is a derivative. Furthermore, in the absence of hedge accounting there is a significant inconsistency in the recognition of gains and losses. For example, the entity has financed a specified group of loans by issuing traded bonds whose changes in fair value tend to offset each other. If, in addition, the entity regularly buys and sells the bonds but rarely, if ever, buys and sells the loans, reporting both the loans and the bonds at fair value through profit or loss eliminates the inconsistency in the timing of recognition of gains and losses that would otherwise result from measuring them both at amortised cost and recognising a gain or loss each time a bond is repurchased.

B4.1.31   In cases such as those described in the preceding paragraph, to designate, at initial recognition, the financial assets and financial liabilities not otherwise so measured as at fair value through profit or loss may eliminate or significantly reduce the measurement or recognition inconsistency and produce more relevant information. For practical purposes, the entity need not enter into all of the assets and liabilities giving rise to the measurement or recognition inconsistency at exactly the same time. A reasonable delay is permitted provided that each transaction is designated as at fair value through profit or loss at its initial recognition and, at that time, any remaining transactions are expected to occur.

B4.1.32   It would not be acceptable to designate only some of the financial assets and financial liabilities giving rise to the inconsistency as at fair value through profit or loss if to do so would not eliminate or significantly reduce the inconsistency and would therefore not result in more relevant information. However, it would be acceptable to designate only some of a number of similar financial assets or similar financial liabilities if doing so achieves a significant reduction (and possibly a greater reduction than other allowable designations) in the inconsistency. For example, assume an entity has a number of similar financial liabilities that sum to CU100 and a number of similar financial assets that sum to CU50 but are measured on a different basis. The entity may significantly reduce the measurement inconsistency by designating at initial recognition all of the assets but only some of the liabilities (for example, individual liabilities with a combined total of CU45) as at fair value through profit or loss. However, because designation as at fair value through profit or loss can be applied only to the whole of a financial instrument, the entity in this example must designate one or more liabilities in their entirety. It could not designate either a component of a liability (eg changes in value attributable to only one risk, such as changes in a benchmark interest rate) or a proportion (ie percentage) of a liability.

A group of financial liabilities or financial assets and financial liabilities is managed and its performance is evaluated on a fair value basis

B4.1.33 An entity may manage and evaluate the performance of a group of financial liabilities or financial assets and financial liabilities in such a way that measuring that group at fair value through profit or loss results in more relevant information. The focus in this instance is on the way the entity manages and evaluates performance, rather than on the nature of its financial instruments.

B4.1.34 For example, an entity may use this condition to designate financial liabilities as at fair value through profit or loss if it meets the principle in paragraph 4.2.2(b) and the entity has financial assets and financial liabilities that share one or more risks and those risks are managed and evaluated on a fair value basis in accordance with a documented policy of asset and liability management. An example could be an entity that has issued 'structured products' containing multiple embedded derivatives and manages the resulting risks on a fair value basis using a mix of derivative and non-derivative financial instruments.

B4.1.35 As noted above, this condition relies on the way the entity manages and evaluates performance of the group of financial instruments under consideration. Accordingly, (subject to the requirement of designation at initial recognition) an entity that designates financial liabilities as at fair value through profit or loss on the basis of this condition shall so designate all eligible financial liabilities that are managed and evaluated together.

B4.1.36 Documentation of the entity's strategy need not be extensive but should be sufficient to demonstrate compliance with paragraph 4.2.2(b). Such documentation is not required for each individual item, but may be on a portfolio basis. For example, if the performance management system for a department—as approved by the entity's key management personnel—clearly demonstrates that its performance is evaluated on a total return basis, no further documentation is required to demonstrate compliance with paragraph 4.2.2(b).

Embedded derivatives (section 4.3)

B4.3.1 When an entity becomes a party to a hybrid contract with a host that is not an asset within the scope of this IFRS, paragraph 4.3.3 requires the entity to identify any embedded derivative, assess whether it is required to be separated from the host contract and, for those that are required to be separated, measure the derivatives at fair value at initial recognition and subsequently.

B4.3.2 If a host contract has no stated or predetermined maturity and represents a residual interest in the net assets of an entity, then its economic characteristics and risks are those of an equity instrument, and an embedded derivative would need to possess equity characteristics related to the same entity to be regarded as closely related. If the host contract is not an equity instrument and meets the definition of a financial instrument, then its economic characteristics and risks are those of a debt instrument.

B4.3.3 An embedded non-option derivative (such as an embedded forward or swap) is separated from its host contract on the basis of its stated or implied substantive terms, so as to result in it having a fair value of zero at initial recognition. An embedded option-based derivative (such as an embedded put, call, cap, floor or swaption) is separated from its host contract on the basis of the stated terms of the option feature. The initial carrying amount of the host instrument is the residual amount after separating the embedded derivative.

B4.3.4 Generally, multiple embedded derivatives in a single hybrid contract are treated as a single compound embedded derivative. However, embedded derivatives that are classified as equity (see IAS 32) are accounted for separately from those classified as assets or liabilities. In addition, if a hybrid contract has more than one embedded derivative and those derivatives relate to different risk exposures and are readily separable and independent of each other, they are accounted for separately from each other.

B4.3.5 The economic characteristics and risks of an embedded derivative are not closely related to the host contract (paragraph 4.3.3(a)) in the following examples. In these examples, assuming the conditions in paragraph 4.3.3(b) and (c) are met, an entity accounts for the embedded derivative separately from the host contract.

(a) A put option embedded in an instrument that enables the holder to require the issuer to reacquire the instrument for an amount of cash or other assets that varies on the basis of the change in an equity or commodity price or index is not closely related to a host debt instrument.

(b) An option or automatic provision to extend the remaining term to maturity of a debt instrument is not closely related to the host debt instrument unless there is a concurrent adjustment to the approximate current market rate of interest at the time of the extension. If an entity issues a debt instrument and the holder of that debt instrument writes a call option on the debt instrument to a third party, the issuer regards the call option as extending the term to maturity of the debt instrument provided the issuer can be required to participate in or facilitate the remarketing of the debt instrument as a result of the call option being exercised.

(c) Equity-indexed interest or principal payments embedded in a host debt instrument or insurance contract—by which the amount of interest or principal is indexed to the value of equity instruments—are not closely related to the host instrument because the risks inherent in the host and the embedded derivative are dissimilar.

(d) Commodity-indexed interest or principal payments embedded in a host debt instrument or insurance contract—by which the amount of interest or principal is indexed to the price of a commodity (such as gold)—are not closely related to the host instrument because the risks inherent in the host and the embedded derivative are dissimilar.

(e) A call, put, or prepayment option embedded in a host debt contract or host insurance contract is not closely related to the host contract unless:

(i) the option's exercise price is approximately equal on each exercise date to the amortised cost of the host debt instrument or the carrying amount of the host insurance contract; or

      (ii)   the exercise price of a prepayment option reimburses the lender for an amount up to the approximate present value of lost interest for the remaining term of the host contract. Lost interest is the product of the principal amount prepaid multiplied by the interest rate differential. The interest rate differential is the excess of the effective interest rate of the host contract over the effective interest rate the entity would receive at the prepayment date if it reinvested the principal amount prepaid in a similar contract for the remaining term of the host contract.

The assessment of whether the call or put option is closely related to the host debt contract is made before separating the equity element of a convertible debt instrument in accordance with IAS 32.

(f)   Credit derivatives that are embedded in a host debt instrument and allow one party (the 'beneficiary') to transfer the credit risk of a particular reference asset, which it may not own, to another party (the 'guarantor') are not closely related to the host debt instrument. Such credit derivatives allow the guarantor to assume the credit risk associated with the reference asset without directly owning it.

B4.3.6   An example of a hybrid contract is a financial instrument that gives the holder a right to put the financial instrument back to the issuer in exchange for an amount of cash or other financial assets that varies on the basis of the change in an equity or commodity index that may increase or decrease (a 'puttable instrument'). Unless the issuer on initial recognition designates the puttable instrument as a financial liability at fair value through profit or loss, it is required to separate an embedded derivative (ie the indexed principal payment) under paragraph 4.3.3 because the host contract is a debt instrument under paragraph B4.3.2 and the indexed principal payment is not closely related to a host debt instrument under paragraph B4.3.5(a). Because the principal payment can increase and decrease, the embedded derivative is a non-option derivative whose value is indexed to the underlying variable.

B4.3.7   In the case of a puttable instrument that can be put back at any time for cash equal to a proportionate share of the net asset value of an entity (such as units of an open-ended mutual fund or some unit-linked investment products), the effect of separating an embedded derivative and accounting for each component is to measure the hybrid contract at the redemption amount that is payable at the end of the reporting period if the holder exercised its right to put the instrument back to the issuer.

B4.3.8   The economic characteristics and risks of an embedded derivative are closely related to the economic characteristics and risks of the host contract in the following examples. In these examples, an entity does not account for the embedded derivative separately from the host contract.

(a)   An embedded derivative in which the underlying is an interest rate or interest rate index that can change the amount of interest that would otherwise be paid or received on an interest-bearing host debt contract or insurance contract is closely related to the host contract unless the hybrid contract can be settled in such a way that the holder would not recover substantially all of its recognised investment or the embedded derivative could at least double the holder's initial rate of return on the host contract and could result in a rate of return that is at least twice what the market return would be for a contract with the same terms as the host contract.

(b) An embedded floor or cap on the interest rate on a debt contract or insurance contract is closely related to the host contract, provided the cap is at or above the market rate of interest and the floor is at or below the market rate of interest when the contract is issued, and the cap or floor is not leveraged in relation to the host contract. Similarly, provisions included in a contract to purchase or sell an asset (eg a commodity) that establish a cap and a floor on the price to be paid or received for the asset are closely related to the host contract if both the cap and floor were out of the money at inception and are not leveraged.

(c) An embedded foreign currency derivative that provides a stream of principal or interest payments that are denominated in a foreign currency and is embedded in a host debt instrument (eg a dual currency bond) is closely related to the host debt instrument. Such a derivative is not separated from the host instrument because IAS 21 requires foreign currency gains and losses on monetary items to be recognised in profit or loss.

(d) An embedded foreign currency derivative in a host contract that is an insurance contract or not a financial instrument (such as a contract for the purchase or sale of a non-financial item where the price is denominated in a foreign currency) is closely related to the host contract provided it is not leveraged, does not contain an option feature, and requires payments denominated in one of the following currencies:

    (i) the functional currency of any substantial party to that contract;

    (ii) the currency in which the price of the related good or service that is acquired or delivered is routinely denominated in commercial transactions around the world (such as the US dollar for crude oil transactions); or

    (iii) a currency that is commonly used in contracts to purchase or sell non-financial items in the economic environment in which the transaction takes place (eg a relatively stable and liquid currency that is commonly used in local business transactions or external trade).

(e) An embedded prepayment option in an interest-only or principal-only strip is closely related to the host contract provided the host contract (i) initially resulted from separating the right to receive contractual cash flows of a financial instrument that, in and of itself, did not contain an embedded derivative, and (ii) does not contain any terms not present in the original host debt contract.

(f) An embedded derivative in a host lease contract is closely related to the host contract if the embedded derivative is (i) an inflation-related index such as an index of lease payments to a consumer price index (provided that the lease is not leveraged and the index relates to inflation in the entity's own economic environment), (ii) contingent rentals based on related sales or (iii) contingent rentals based on variable interest rates.

(g)   A unit-linking feature embedded in a host financial instrument or host insurance contract is closely related to the host instrument or host contract if the unit-denominated payments are measured at current unit values that reflect the fair values of the assets of the fund. A unit-linking feature is a contractual term that requires payments denominated in units of an internal or external investment fund.

(h)   A derivative embedded in an insurance contract is closely related to the host insurance contract if the embedded derivative and host insurance contract are so interdependent that an entity cannot measure the embedded derivative separately (ie without considering the host contract).

Instruments containing embedded derivatives

B4.3.9   As noted in paragraph B4.3.1, when an entity becomes a party to a hybrid contract with a host that is not an asset within the scope of this IFRS and with one or more embedded derivatives, paragraph 4.3.3 requires the entity to identify any such embedded derivative, assess whether it is required to be separated from the host contract and, for those that are required to be separated, measure the derivatives at fair value at initial recognition and subsequently. These requirements can be more complex, or result in less reliable measures, than measuring the entire instrument at fair value through profit or loss. For that reason this IFRS permits the entire hybrid contract to be designated as at fair value through profit or loss.

B4.3.10   Such designation may be used whether paragraph 4.3.3 requires the embedded derivatives to be separated from the host contract or prohibits such separation. However, paragraph 4.3.5 would not justify designating the hybrid contract as at fair value through profit or loss in the cases set out in paragraph 4.3.5(a) and (b) because doing so would not reduce complexity or increase reliability.

Reassessment of embedded derivatives

B4.3.11   In accordance with paragraph 4.3.3, an entity shall assess whether an embedded derivative is required to be separated from the host contract and accounted for as a derivative when the entity first becomes a party to the contract. Subsequent reassessment is prohibited unless there is a change in the terms of the contract that significantly modifies the cash flows that otherwise would be required under the contract, in which case reassessment is required. An entity determines whether a modification to cash flows is significant by considering the extent to which the expected future cash flows associated with the embedded derivative, the host contract or both have changed and whether the change is significant relative to the previously expected cash flows on the contract.

B4.3.12   Paragraph B4.3.11 does not apply to embedded derivatives in contracts acquired in:

(a)   a business combination (as defined in IFRS 3 *Business Combinations*);

(b)   a combination of entities or businesses under common control as described in paragraphs B1–B4 of IFRS 3; or

(c)   the formation of a joint venture as defined in IFRS 11 *Joint Arrangements*

or their possible reassessment at the date of acquisition.[1]

---

1   IFRS 3 addresses the acquisition of contracts with embedded derivatives in a business combination.

Reclassification of financial assets (section 4.4)

B4.4.1 Paragraph 4.4.1 requires an entity to reclassify financial assets if the objective of the entity's business model for managing those financial assets changes. Such changes are expected to be very infrequent. Such changes must be determined by the entity's senior management as a result of external or internal changes and must be significant to the entity's operations and demonstrable to external parties. Examples of a change in business model include the following:

(a) An entity has a portfolio of commercial loans that it holds to sell in the short term. The entity acquires a company that manages commercial loans and has a business model that holds the loans in order to collect the contractual cash flows. The portfolio of commercial loans is no longer for sale, and the portfolio is now managed together with the acquired commercial loans and all are held to collect the contractual cash flows.

(b) A financial services firm decides to shut down its retail mortgage business. That business no longer accepts new business and the financial services firm is actively marketing its mortgage loan portfolio for sale.

B4.4.2 A change in the objective of the entity's business model must be effected before the reclassification date. For example, if a financial services firm decides on 15 February to shut down its retail mortgage business and hence must reclassify all affected financial assets on 1 April (ie the first day of the entity's next reporting period), the entity must not accept new retail mortgage business or otherwise engage in activities consistent with its former business model after 15 February.

B4.4.3 The following are not changes in business model:

(a) a change in intention related to particular financial assets (even in circumstances of significant changes in market conditions).

(b) the temporary disappearance of a particular market for financial assets.

(c) a transfer of financial assets between parts of the entity with different business models.

Measurement (chapter 5)

Initial measurement (section 5.1)

B5.1.1 The fair value of a financial instrument at initial recognition is normally the transaction price (ie the fair value of the consideration given or received, see also paragraph B5.1.2A and IFRS 13). However, if part of the consideration given or received is for something other than the financial instrument, an entity shall measure the fair value of the financial instrument. For example, the fair value of a long-term loan or receivable that carries no interest can be measured as the present value of all future cash receipts discounted using the prevailing market rate(s) of interest for a similar instrument (similar as to currency, term, type of interest rate and other factors) with a similar credit rating. Any additional amount lent is an expense or a reduction of income unless it qualifies for recognition as some other type of asset.

B5.1.2   If an entity originates a loan that bears an off-market interest rate (eg 5 per cent when the market rate for similar loans is 8 per cent), and receives an upfront fee as compensation, the entity recognises the loan at its fair value, ie net of the fee it receives.

B5.1.2A   The best evidence of the fair value of a financial instrument at initial recognition is normally the transaction price (ie the fair value of the consideration given or received, see also IFRS 13). If an entity determines that the fair value at initial recognition differs from the transaction price as mentioned in paragraph 5.1.1A, the entity shall account for that instrument at that date as follows:

(a)   at the measurement required by paragraph 5.1.1 if that fair value is evidenced by a quoted price in an active market for an identical asset or liability (ie a Level 1 input) or based on a valuation technique that uses only data from observable markets. An entity shall recognise the difference between the fair value at initial recognition and the transaction price as a gain or loss.

(b)   in all other cases, at the measurement required by paragraph 5.1.1, adjusted to defer the difference between the fair value at initial recognition and the transaction price. After initial recognition, the entity shall recognise that deferred difference as a gain or loss only to the extent that it arises from a change in a factor (including time) that market participants would take into account when pricing the asset or liability.

Subsequent measurement of financial assets (section 5.2)

B5.2.1   If a financial instrument that was previously recognised as a financial asset is measured at fair value and its fair value decreases below zero, it is a financial liability measured in accordance with paragraph 4.2.1. However, hybrid contracts with hosts that are assets within the scope of this IFRS are always measured in accordance with paragraph 4.3.2.

B5.2.2   The following example illustrates the accounting for transaction costs on the initial and subsequent measurement of a financial asset measured at fair value with changes through other comprehensive income in accordance with paragraph 5.7.5. An entity acquires an asset for CU100 plus a purchase commission of CU2. Initially, the entity recognises the asset at CU102. The reporting period ends one day later, when the quoted market price of the asset is CU100. If the asset were sold, a commission of CU3 would be paid. On that date, the entity measures the asset at CU100 (without regard to the possible commission on sale) and recognises a loss of CU2 in other comprehensive income.

B5.2.2A   The subsequent measurement of a financial asset or financial liability and the subsequent recognition of gains and losses described in paragraph B5.1.2A shall be consistent with the requirements of this IFRS.

B5.4.1–   [Deleted]
B5.4.13

Investments in equity instruments and contracts on those investments

B5.4.14 All investments in equity instruments and contracts on those instruments must be measured at fair value. However, in limited circumstances, cost may be an appropriate estimate of fair value. That may be the case if insufficient more recent information is available to measure fair value, or if there is a wide range of possible fair value measurements and cost represents the best estimate of fair value within that range.

B5.4.15 Indicators that cost might not be representative of fair value include:

(a) a significant change in the performance of the investee compared with budgets, plans or milestones.

(b) changes in expectation that the investee's technical product milestones will be achieved.

(c) a significant change in the market for the investee's equity or its products or potential products.

(d) a significant change in the global economy or the economic environment in which the investee operates.

(e) a significant change in the performance of comparable entities, or in the valuations implied by the overall market.

(f) internal matters of the investee such as fraud, commercial disputes, litigation, changes in management or strategy.

(g) evidence from external transactions in the investee's equity, either by the investee (such as a fresh issue of equity), or by transfers of equity instruments between third parties.

B5.4.16 The list in paragraph B5.4.15 is not exhaustive. An entity shall use all information about the performance and operations of the investee that becomes available after the date of initial recognition. To the extent that any such relevant factors exist, they may indicate that cost might not be representative of fair value. In such cases, the entity must measure fair value.

B5.4.17 Cost is never the best estimate of fair value for investments in quoted equity instruments (or contracts on quoted equity instruments).

Gains and losses (section 5.7)

B5.7.1 Paragraph 5.7.5 permits an entity to make an irrevocable election to present in other comprehensive income changes in the fair value of an investment in an equity instrument that is not held for trading. This election is made on an instrument-by-instrument (ie share-by-share) basis. Amounts presented in other comprehensive income shall not be subsequently transferred to profit or loss. However, the entity may transfer the cumulative gain or loss within equity. Dividends on such investments are recognised in profit or loss in accordance with IAS 18 unless the dividend clearly represents a recovery of part of the cost of the investment.

B5.7.2   An entity applies IAS 21 *The Effects of Changes in Foreign Exchange Rates* to financial assets and financial liabilities that are monetary items in accordance with IAS 21 and denominated in a foreign currency. IAS 21 requires any foreign exchange gains and losses on monetary assets and monetary liabilities to be recognised in profit or loss. An exception is a monetary item that is designated as a hedging instrument in either a cash flow hedge (see paragraphs 95–101 of IAS 39) or a hedge of a net investment (see paragraph 102 of IAS 39).

B5.7.3   Paragraph 5.7.5 permits an entity to make an irrevocable election to present in other comprehensive income changes in the fair value of an investment in an equity instrument that is not held for trading. Such an investment is not a monetary item. Accordingly, the gain or loss that is presented in other comprehensive income in accordance with paragraph 5.7.5 includes any related foreign exchange component.

B5.7.4   If there is a hedging relationship between a non-derivative monetary asset and a non-derivative monetary liability, changes in the foreign currency component of those financial instruments are presented in profit or loss.

Liabilities designated as at fair value through profit or loss

B5.7.5   When an entity designates a financial liability as at fair value through profit or loss, it must determine whether presenting in other comprehensive income the effects of changes in the liability's credit risk would create or enlarge an accounting mismatch in profit or loss. An accounting mismatch would be created or enlarged if presenting the effects of changes in the liability's credit risk in other comprehensive income would result in a greater mismatch in profit or loss than if those amounts were presented in profit or loss.

B5.7.6   To make that determination, an entity must assess whether it expects that the effects of changes in the liability's credit risk will be offset in profit or loss by a change in the fair value of another financial instrument measured at fair value through profit or loss. Such an expectation must be based on an economic relationship between the characteristics of the liability and the characteristics of the other financial instrument.

B5.7.7   That determination is made at initial recognition and is not reassessed. For practical purposes the entity need not enter into all of the assets and liabilities giving rise to an accounting mismatch at exactly the same time. A reasonable delay is permitted provided that any remaining transactions are expected to occur. An entity must apply consistently its methodology for determining whether presenting in other comprehensive income the effects of changes in the liability's credit risk would create or enlarge an accounting mismatch in profit or loss. However, an entity may use different methodologies when there are different economic relationships between the characteristics of the liabilities designated as at fair value through profit or loss and the characteristics of the other financial instruments. IFRS 7 requires an entity to provide qualitative disclosures in the notes to the financial statements about its methodology for making that determination.

B5.7.8   If such a mismatch would be created or enlarged, the entity is required to present all changes in fair value (including the effects of changes in the credit risk of the liability) in profit or loss. If such a mismatch would not be created or enlarged, the entity is required to present the effects of changes in the liability's credit risk in other comprehensive income.

B5.7.9   Amounts presented in other comprehensive income shall not be subsequently transferred to profit or loss. However, the entity may transfer the cumulative gain or loss within equity.

B5.7.10   The following example describes a situation in which an accounting mismatch would be created in profit or loss if the effects of changes in the credit risk of the liability were presented in other comprehensive income. A mortgage bank provides loans to customers and funds those loans by selling bonds with matching characteristics (eg amount outstanding, repayment profile, term and currency) in the market. The contractual terms of the loan permit the mortgage customer to prepay its loan (ie satisfy its obligation to the bank) by buying the corresponding bond at fair value in the market and delivering that bond to the mortgage bank. As a result of that contractual prepayment right, if the credit quality of the bond worsens (and, thus, the fair value of the mortgage bank's liability decreases), the fair value of the mortgage bank's loan asset also decreases. The change in the fair value of the asset reflects the mortgage customer's contractual right to prepay the mortgage loan by buying the underlying bond at fair value (which, in this example, has decreased) and delivering the bond to the mortgage bank. Therefore, the effects of changes in the credit risk of the liability (the bond) will be offset in profit or loss by a corresponding change in the fair value of a financial asset (the loan). If the effects of changes in the liability's credit risk were presented in other comprehensive income there would be an accounting mismatch in profit or loss. Therefore, the mortgage bank is required to present all changes in fair value of the liability (including the effects of changes in the liability's credit risk) in profit or loss.

B5.7.11   In the example in paragraph B5.7.10, there is a contractual linkage between the effects of changes in the credit risk of the liability and changes in the fair value of the financial asset (ie as a result of the mortgage customer's contractual right to prepay the loan by buying the bond at fair value and delivering the bond to the mortgage bank). However, an accounting mismatch may also occur in the absence of a contractual linkage.

B5.7.12   For the purposes of applying the requirements in paragraphs 5.7.7 and 5.7.8, an accounting mismatch is not caused solely by the measurement method that an entity uses to determine the effects of changes in a liability's credit risk. An accounting mismatch in profit or loss would arise only when the effects of changes in the liability's credit risk (as defined in IFRS 7) are expected to be offset by changes in the fair value of another financial instrument. A mismatch that arises solely as a result of the measurement method (ie because an entity does not isolate changes in a liability's credit risk from some other changes in its fair value) does not affect the determination required by paragraphs 5.7.7 and 5.7.8. For example, an entity may not isolate changes in a liability's credit risk from changes in liquidity risk. If the entity presents the combined effect of both factors in other comprehensive income, a mismatch may occur because changes in liquidity risk may be included in the fair value measurement of the entity's financial assets and the entire fair value change of those assets is presented in profit or loss. However, such a mismatch is caused by measurement imprecision, not the offsetting relationship described in paragraph B5.7.6 and, therefore, does not affect the determination required by paragraphs 5.7.7 and 5.7.8.

The meaning of 'credit risk'

B5.7.13 IFRS 7 defines credit risk as 'the risk that one party to a financial instrument will cause a financial loss for the other party by failing to discharge an obligation'. The requirement in paragraph 5.7.7(a) relates to the risk that the issuer will fail to perform on that particular liability. It does not necessarily relate to the creditworthiness of the issuer. For example, if an entity issues a collateralised liability and a non-collateralised liability that are otherwise identical, the credit risk of those two liabilities will be different, even though they are issued by the same entity. The credit risk on the collateralised liability will be less than the credit risk of the non-collateralised liability. The credit risk for a collateralised liability may be close to zero.

B5.7.14 For the purposes of applying the requirement in paragraph 5.7.7(a), credit risk is different from asset-specific performance risk. Asset-specific performance risk is not related to the risk that an entity will fail to discharge a particular obligation but rather it is related to the risk that a single asset or a group of assets will perform poorly (or not at all).

B5.7.15 The following are examples of asset-specific performance risk:

(a) a liability with a unit-linking feature whereby the amount due to investors is contractually determined on the basis of the performance of specified assets. The effect of that unit-linking feature on the fair value of the liability is asset-specific performance risk, not credit risk.

(b) a liability issued by a structured entity with the following characteristics. The entity is legally isolated so the assets in the entity are ring-fenced solely for the benefit of its investors, even in the event of bankruptcy. The entity enters into no other transactions and the assets in the entity cannot be hypothecated. Amounts are due to the entity's investors only if the ring-fenced assets generate cash flows. Thus, changes in the fair value of the liability primarily reflect changes in the fair value of the assets. The effect of the performance of the assets on the fair value of the liability is asset-specific performance risk, not credit risk.

Determining the effects of changes in credit risk

B5.7.16 For the purposes of applying the requirement in paragraph 5.7.7(a), an entity shall determine the amount of change in the fair value of the financial liability that is attributable to changes in the credit risk of that liability either:

(a) as the amount of change in its fair value that is not attributable to changes in market conditions that give rise to market risk (see paragraphs B5.7.17 and B5.7.18); or

(b) using an alternative method the entity believes more faithfully represents the amount of change in the liability's fair value that is attributable to changes in its credit risk.

B5.7.17 Changes in market conditions that give rise to market risk include changes in a benchmark interest rate, the price of another entity's financial instrument, a commodity price, a foreign exchange rate or an index of prices or rates.

B5.7.18 If the only significant relevant changes in market conditions for a liability are changes in an observed (benchmark) interest rate, the amount in paragraph B5.7.16(a) can be estimated as follows:

(a) First, the entity computes the liability's internal rate of return at the start of the period using the fair value of the liability and the liability's contractual cash flows at the start of the period. It deducts from this rate of return the observed (benchmark) interest rate at the start of the period, to arrive at an instrument-specific component of the internal rate of return.

(b) Next, the entity calculates the present value of the cash flows associated with the liability using the liability's contractual cash flows at the end of the period and a discount rate equal to the sum of (i) the observed (benchmark) interest rate at the end of the period and (ii) the instrument-specific component of the internal rate of return as determined in (a).

(c) The difference between the fair value of the liability at the end of the period and the amount determined in (b) is the change in fair value that is not attributable to changes in the observed (benchmark) interest rate. This is the amount to be presented in other comprehensive income in accordance with paragraph 5.7.7(a).

B5.7.19 The example in paragraph B5.7.18 assumes that changes in fair value arising from factors other than changes in the instrument's credit risk or changes in observed (benchmark) interest rates are not significant. This method would not be appropriate if changes in fair value arising from other factors are significant. In those cases, an entity is required to use an alternative method that more faithfully measures the effects of changes in the liability's credit risk (see paragraph B5.7.16(b)). For example, if the instrument in the example contains an embedded derivative, the change in fair value of the embedded derivative is excluded in determining the amount to be presented in other comprehensive income in accordance with paragraph 5.7.7(a).

B5.7.20 As with all fair value measurements, an entity's measurement method for determining the portion of the change in the liability's fair value that is attributable to changes in its credit risk must make maximum use of relevant observable inputs and minimum use of unobservable inputs.

Effective date and transition (chapter 7)

Transition (section 7.2)

Financial assets held for trading

B7.2.1   At the date of initial application of this IFRS, an entity must determine whether the objective of the entity's business model for managing any of its financial assets meets the condition in paragraph 4.1.2(a) or if a financial asset is eligible for the election in paragraph 5.7.5. For that purpose, an entity shall determine whether financial assets meet the definition of held for trading as if the entity had acquired the assets at the date of initial application.

Definitions (Appendix A)

Derivatives

BA.1   Typical examples of derivatives are futures and forward, swap and option contracts. A derivative usually has a notional amount, which is an amount of currency, a number of shares, a number of units of weight or volume or other units specified in the contract. However, a derivative instrument does not require the holder or writer to invest or receive the notional amount at the inception of the contract. Alternatively, a derivative could require a fixed payment or payment of an amount that can change (but not proportionally with a change in the underlying) as a result of some future event that is unrelated to a notional amount. For example, a contract may require a fixed payment of CU1,000 if six-month LIBOR increases by 100 basis points. Such a contract is a derivative even though a notional amount is not specified.

BA.2   The definition of a derivative in this IFRS includes contracts that are settled gross by delivery of the underlying item (eg a forward contract to purchase a fixed rate debt instrument). An entity may have a contract to buy or sell a non-financial item that can be settled net in cash or another financial instrument or by exchanging financial instruments (eg a contract to buy or sell a commodity at a fixed price at a future date). Such a contract is within the scope of this IFRS unless it was entered into and continues to be held for the purpose of delivery of a non-financial item in accordance with the entity's expected purchase, sale or usage requirements (see paragraphs 5–7 of IAS 39).

BA.3   One of the defining characteristics of a derivative is that it has an initial net investment that is smaller than would be required for other types of contracts that would be expected to have a similar response to changes in market factors. An option contract meets that definition because the premium is less than the investment that would be required to obtain the underlying financial instrument to which the option is linked. A currency swap that requires an initial exchange of different currencies of equal fair values meets the definition because it has a zero initial net investment.

BA.4   A regular way purchase or sale gives rise to a fixed price commitment between trade date and settlement date that meets the definition of a derivative. However, because of the short duration of the commitment it is not recognised as a derivative financial instrument. Rather, this IFRS provides for special accounting for such regular way contracts (see paragraphs 3.1.2 and B3.1.3–B3.1.6).

BA.5   The definition of a derivative refers to non-financial variables that are not specific to a party to the contract. These include an index of earthquake losses in a particular region and an index of temperatures in a particular city. Non-financial variables specific to a party to the contract include the occurrence or non-occurrence of a fire that damages or destroys an asset of a party to the contract. A change in the fair value of a non-financial asset is specific to the owner if the fair value reflects not only changes in market prices for such assets (a financial variable) but also the condition of the specific non-financial asset held (a non-financial variable). For example, if a guarantee of the residual value of a specific car exposes the guarantor to the risk of changes in the car's physical condition, the change in that residual value is specific to the owner of the car.

Financial assets and liabilities held for trading

BA.6   Trading generally reflects active and frequent buying and selling, and financial instruments held for trading generally are used with the objective of generating a profit from short-term fluctuations in price or dealer's margin.

BA.7   Financial liabilities held for trading include:

     (a)   derivative liabilities that are not accounted for as hedging instruments;

     (b)   obligations to deliver financial assets borrowed by a short seller (ie an entity that sells financial assets it has borrowed and does not yet own);

     (c)   financial liabilities that are incurred with an intention to repurchase them in the near term (eg a quoted debt instrument that the issuer may buy back in the near term depending on changes in its fair value); and

     (d)   financial liabilities that are part of a portfolio of identified financial instruments that are managed together and for which there is evidence of a recent pattern of short-term profit-taking.

BA.8   The fact that a liability is used to fund trading activities does not in itself make that liability one that is held for trading.

Appendix C
Amendments to other IFRSs

Except where otherwise stated, an entity shall apply the amendments in this appendix when it applies IFRS 9 issued in October 2010. These amendments incorporate with additions the amendments issued in Appendix C of IFRS 9 in 2009.

* * * * *

The amendments contained in this appendix when this IFRS was issued in 2010 have been incorporated into the relevant IFRSs published in this volume.

International Financial Reporting Standard 10

Consolidated Financial Statements

In April 2001 the International Accounting Standards Board (IASB) adopted IAS 27 *Consolidated Financial Statements and Accounting for Investments in Subsidiaries*, which had originally been issued by the International Accounting Standards Committee in April 1989. IAS 27 replaced most of IAS 3 *Consolidated Financial Statements* (issued in June 1976).

In December 2003, the IASB amended and renamed IAS 27 with a new title—*Consolidated and Separate Financial Statements*. The amended IAS 27 also incorporated the guidance contained in two related Interpretations (SIC-12 *Consolidation-Special Purpose Entities* and SIC-33 *Consolidation and Equity Method—Potential Voting Rights and Allocation of Ownership Interests*).

In June 2008, the IASB amended IAS 27. This amendment, which related to accounting for non-controlling interests and the loss of control of subsidiaries, was done in conjunction with amendments to IFRS 3 *Business Combinations*.

In May 2011 the IASB issued IFRS 10 *Consolidated Financial Statements* to replace IAS 27. IFRS 12 *Disclosure of Interests in Other Entities*, also issued in May 2011, replaced the disclosure requirements in IAS 27. IFRS 10 incorporates the guidance contained in two related Interpretations (SIC-12 *Consolidation-Special Purpose Entities* and SIC-33 *Consolidation*).

CONTENTS

FOR THE ACCOMPANYING DOCUMENTS LISTED BELOW, SEE PART B OF THIS EDITION

APPROVAL BY THE BOARD OF IFRS 10 ISSUED IN MAY 2011

BASIS FOR CONCLUSIONS

APPENDIX
Previous Board approvals and dissenting opinions

APPENDIX
Amendments to the Basis for Conclusions on other IFRSs

AMENDMENTS TO THE GUIDANCE ON OTHER IFRSs

International Financial Reporting Standard 10 *Consolidated Financial Statements* (IFRS 10) is set out in paragraphs 1–26 and Appendices A–D. All the paragraphs have equal authority. Paragraphs in **bold type** state the main principles. Terms defined in Appendix A are in *italics* the first time they appear in the Standard. Definitions of other terms are given in the Glossary for International Financial Reporting Standards. IFRS 10 should be read in the context of its objective and the Basis for Conclusions, the *Preface to International Financial Reporting Standards* and the *Conceptual Framework for Financial Reporting*. IAS 8 *Accounting Policies, Changes in Accounting Estimates and Errors* provides a basis for selecting and applying accounting policies in the absence of explicit guidance.

Introduction

IN1   IFRS 10 *Consolidated Financial Statements* establishes principles for the presentation and preparation of consolidated financial statements when an entity controls one or more other entities.

IN2   The IFRS supersedes IAS 27 *Consolidated and Separate Financial Statements* and SIC-12 *Consolidation—Special Purpose Entities* and is effective for annual periods beginning on or after 1 January 2013. Earlier application is permitted.

Reasons for issuing the IFRS

IN3   The Board added a project on consolidation to its agenda to deal with divergence in practice in applying IAS 27 and SIC-12. For example, entities varied in their application of the control concept in circumstances in which a reporting entity controls another entity but holds less than a majority of the voting rights of the entity, and in circumstances involving agency relationships.

IN4   In addition, a perceived conflict of emphasis between IAS 27 and SIC-12 had led to inconsistent application of the concept of control. IAS 27 required the consolidation of entities that are controlled by a reporting entity, and it defined control as the power to govern the financial and operating policies of an entity so as to obtain benefits from its activities. SIC-12, which interpreted the requirements of IAS 27 in the context of special purpose entities, placed greater emphasis on risks and rewards.

IN5   The global financial crisis that started in 2007 highlighted the lack of transparency about the risks to which investors were exposed from their involvement with 'off balance sheet vehicles' (such as securitisation vehicles), including those that they had set up or sponsored. As a result, the G20 leaders, the Financial Stability Board and others asked the Board to review the accounting and disclosure requirements for such 'off balance sheet vehicles'.

Main features of the IFRS

IN6   The IFRS requires an entity that is a parent to present consolidated financial statements. A limited exemption is available to some entities.

General requirements

IN7   The IFRS defines the principle of control and establishes control as the basis for determining which entities are consolidated in the consolidated financial statements. The IFRS also sets out the accounting requirements for the preparation of consolidated financial statements.

IN8   An investor controls an investee when it is exposed, or has rights, to variable returns from its involvement with the investee and has the ability to affect those returns through its power over the investee; Thus, the principle of control sets out the following three elements of control:

(a) power over the investee;

(b) exposure, or rights, to variable returns from involvement with the investee; and

(c) the ability to use power over the investee to affect the amount of the investor's returns.

IN9 The IFRS sets out requirements on how to apply the control principle:

(a) in circumstances when voting rights or similar rights give an investor power, including situations where the investor holds less than a majority of voting rights and in circumstances involving potential voting rights.

(b) in circumstances when an investee is designed so that voting rights are not the dominant factor in deciding who controls the investee, such as when any voting rights relate to administrative tasks only and the relevant activities are directed by means of contractual arrangements.

(c) in circumstances involving agency relationships.

(d) in circumstances when the investor has control over specified assets of an investee.

IN10 The IFRS requires an investor to reassess whether it controls an investee if facts and circumstances indicate that there are changes to one or more of the three elements of control.

IN11 When preparing consolidated financial statements, an entity must use uniform accounting policies for reporting like transactions and other events in similar circumstances. Intragroup balances and transactions must be eliminated. Non-controlling interests in subsidiaries must be presented in the consolidated statement of financial position within equity, separately from the equity of the owners of the parent.

IN12 The disclosure requirements for interests in subsidiaries are specified in IFRS 12 *Disclosure of Interests in Other Entities*.

International Financial Reporting Standard 10
Consolidated Financial Statements

Objective

1   The objective of this IFRS is to establish principles for the presentation and preparation of consolidated financial statements when an entity controls one or more other entities.

Meeting the objective

2   To meet the objective in paragraph 1, this IFRS:

(a)   requires an entity (the *parent*) that controls one or more other entities (*subsidiaries*) to present consolidated financial statements;

(b)   defines the principle of *control*, and establishes control as the basis for consolidation;

(c)   sets out how to apply the principle of control to identify whether an investor controls an investee and therefore must consolidate the investee; and

(d)   sets out the accounting requirements for the preparation of consolidated financial statements.

3   This IFRS does not deal with the accounting requirements for business combinations and their effect on consolidation, including goodwill arising on a business combination (see IFRS 3 *Business Combinations*).

Scope

4   An entity that is a parent shall present consolidated financial statements. This IFRS applies to all entities, except as follows:

(a)   a parent need not present consolidated financial statements if it meets all the following conditions:

(i)   it is a wholly-owned subsidiary or is a partially-owned subsidiary of another entity and all its other owners, including those not otherwise entitled to vote, have been informed about, and do not object to, the parent not presenting consolidated financial statements;

(ii)   its debt or equity instruments are not traded in a public market (a domestic or foreign stock exchange or an over-the-counter market, including local and regional markets);

(iii)   it did not file, nor is it in the process of filing, its financial statements with a securities commission or other regulatory organisation for the purpose of issuing any class of instruments in a public market; and

      (iv)   its ultimate or any intermediate parent produces consolidated financial statements that are available for public use and comply with IFRSs.

    (b)   post-employment benefit plans or other long-term employee benefit plans to which IAS 19 *Employee Benefits* applies.

Control

5   **An investor, regardless of the nature of its involvement with an entity (the investee), shall determine whether it is a parent by assessing whether it controls the investee.**

6   **An investor controls an investee when it is exposed, or has rights, to variable returns from its involvement with the investee and has the ability to affect those returns through its power over the investee.**

7   **Thus, an investor controls an investee if and only if the investor has all the following:**

    (a)   **power over the investee (see paragraphs 10–14);**

    (b)   **exposure, or rights, to variable returns from its involvement with the investee (see paragraphs 15 and 16); and**

    (c)   **the ability to use its power over the investee to affect the amount of the investor's returns (see paragraphs 17 and 18).**

8   An investor shall consider all facts and circumstances when assessing whether it controls an investee. The investor shall reassess whether it controls an investee if facts and circumstances indicate that there are changes to one or more of the three elements of control listed in paragraph 7 (see paragraphs B80–B85).

9   Two or more investors collectively control an investee when they must act together to direct the relevant activities. In such cases, because no investor can direct the activities without the co-operation of the others, no investor individually controls the investee. Each investor would account for its interest in the investee in accordance with the relevant IFRSs, such as IFRS 11 *Joint Arrangements*, IAS 28 *Investments in Associates and Joint Ventures* or IFRS 9 *Financial Instruments*.

Power

10   An investor has power over an investee when the investor has existing rights that give it the current ability to direct the *relevant activities*, ie the activities that significantly affect the investee's returns.

11   Power arises from rights. Sometimes assessing power is straightforward, such as when power over an investee is obtained directly and solely from the voting rights granted by equity instruments such as shares, and can be assessed by considering the voting rights from those shareholdings. In other cases, the assessment will be more complex and require more than one factor to be considered, for example when power results from one or more contractual arrangements.

12   An investor with the current ability to direct the relevant activities has power even if its rights to direct have yet to be exercised. Evidence that the investor has been directing relevant activities can help determine whether the investor has power, but such evidence is not, in itself, conclusive in determining whether the investor has power over an investee.

13   If two or more investors each have existing rights that give them the unilateral ability to direct different relevant activities, the investor that has the current ability to direct the activities that most significantly affect the returns of the investee has power over the investee.

14   An investor can have power over an investee even if other entities have existing rights that give them the current ability to participate in the direction of the relevant activities, for example when another entity has *significant influence*. However, an investor that holds only protective rights does not have power over an investee (see paragraphs B26–B28), and consequently does not control the investee.

Returns

15   An investor is exposed, or has rights, to variable returns from its involvement with the investee when the investor's returns from its involvement have the potential to vary as a result of the investee's performance. The investor's returns can be only positive, only negative or both positive and negative.

16   Although only one investor can control an investee, more than one party can share in the returns of an investee. For example, holders of non-controlling interests can share in the profits or distributions of an investee.

Link between power and returns

17   An investor controls an investee if the investor not only has power over the investee and exposure or rights to variable returns from its involvement with the investee, but also has the ability to use its power to affect the investor's returns from its involvement with the investee.

18   Thus, an investor with decision-making rights shall determine whether it is a principal or an agent. An investor that is an agent in accordance with paragraphs B58–B72 does not control an investee when it exercises decision-making rights delegated to it.

Accounting requirements

19   **A parent shall prepare consolidated financial statements using uniform accounting policies for like transactions and other events in similar circumstances.**

20   Consolidation of an investee shall begin from the date the investor obtains control of the investee and cease when the investor loses control of the investee.

21   Paragraphs B86–B93 set out guidance for the preparation of consolidated financial statements.

Non-controlling interests

22   A parent shall present non-controlling interests in the consolidated statement of financial position within equity, separately from the equity of the owners of the parent.

23   Changes in a parent's ownership interest in a subsidiary that do not result in the parent losing control of the subsidiary are equity transactions (ie transactions with owners in their capacity as owners).

24   Paragraphs B94–B96 set out guidance for the accounting for non-controlling interests in consolidated financial statements.

Loss of control

25   If a parent loses control of a subsidiary, the parent:

(a)   derecognises the assets and liabilities of the former subsidiary from the consolidated statement of financial position.

(b)   recognises any investment retained in the former subsidiary at its fair value when control is lost and subsequently accounts for it and for any amounts owed by or to the former subsidiary in accordance with relevant IFRSs. That fair value shall be regarded as the fair value on initial recognition of a financial asset in accordance with IFRS 9 or, when appropriate, the cost on initial recognition of an investment in an associate or joint venture.

(c)   recognises the gain or loss associated with the loss of control attributable to the former controlling interest.

26   Paragraphs B97–B99 set out guidance for the accounting for the loss of control.

Appendix A
Defined terms

This appendix is an integral part of the IFRS.

consolidated financial statements	The financial statements of a **group** in which the assets, liabilities, equity, income, expenses and cash flows of the **parent** and its **subsidiaries** are presented as those of a single economic entity.
control of an investee	An investor controls an investee when the investor is exposed, or has rights, to variable returns from its involvement with the investee and has the ability to affect those returns through its power over the investee.
decision maker	An entity with decision-making rights that is either a principal or an agent for other parties.
group	A **parent** and its **subsidiaries**.
non-controlling interest	Equity in a **subsidiary** not attributable, directly or indirectly, to a **parent**.
parent	An entity that **controls** one or more entities.
power	Existing rights that give the current ability to direct the **relevant activities**.
protective rights	Rights designed to protect the interest of the party holding those rights without giving that party power over the entity to which those rights relate.
relevant activities	For the purpose of this IFRS, relevant activities are activities of the investee that significantly affect the investee's returns.
removal rights	Rights to deprive the decision maker of its decision-making authority.
subsidiary	An entity that is controlled by another entity.

The following terms are defined in IFRS 11, IFRS 12 *Disclosure of Interests in Other Entities*, IAS 28 (as amended in 2011) or IAS 24 *Related Party Disclosures* and are used in this IFRS with the meanings specified in those IFRSs:

- associate
- interest in another entity
- joint venture
- key management personnel
- related party
- significant influence.

Appendix B
Application guidance

This appendix is an integral part of the IFRS. It describes the application of paragraphs 1–26 and has the same authority as the other parts of the IFRS.

B1   The examples in this appendix portray hypothetical situations. Although some aspects of the examples may be present in actual fact patterns, all facts and circumstances of a particular fact pattern would need to be evaluated when applying IFRS 10.

Assessing control

B2   To determine whether it controls an investee an investor shall assess whether it has all the following:

(a)   power over the investee;

(b)   exposure, or rights, to variable returns from its involvement with the investee; and

(c)   the ability to use its power over the investee to affect the amount of the investor's returns.

B3   Consideration of the following factors may assist in making that determination:

(a)   the purpose and design of the investee (see paragraphs B5–B8);

(b)   what the relevant activities are and how decisions about those activities are made (see paragraphs B11–B13);

(c)   whether the rights of the investor give it the current ability to direct the relevant activities (see paragraphs B14–B54);

(d)   whether the investor is exposed, or has rights, to variable returns from its involvement with the investee (see paragraphs B55–B57); and

(e)   whether the investor has the ability to use its power over the investee to affect the amount of the investor's returns (see paragraphs B58–B72).

B4   When assessing control of an investee, an investor shall consider the nature of its relationship with other parties (see paragraphs B73–B75).

Purpose and design of an investee

B5   When assessing control of an investee, an investor shall consider the purpose and design of the investee in order to identify the relevant activities, how decisions about the relevant activities are made, who has the current ability to direct those activities and who receives returns from those activities.

B6   When an investee's purpose and design are considered, it may be clear that an investee is controlled by means of equity instruments that give the holder proportionate voting rights, such as ordinary shares in the investee. In this case, in the absence of any additional arrangements that alter decision-making, the assessment of control focuses on which party, if any, is able to exercise voting rights sufficient to determine the investee's operating and financing policies (see paragraphs B34–B50). In the most straightforward case, the investor that holds a majority of those voting rights, in the absence of any other factors, controls the investee.

B7 To determine whether an investor controls an investee in more complex cases, it may be necessary to consider some or all of the other factors in paragraph B3.

B8 An investee may be designed so that voting rights are not the dominant factor in deciding who controls the investee, such as when any voting rights relate to administrative tasks only and the relevant activities are directed by means of contractual arrangements. In such cases, an investor's consideration of the purpose and design of the investee shall also include consideration of the risks to which the investee was designed to be exposed, the risks it was designed to pass on to the parties involved with the investee and whether the investor is exposed to some or all of those risks. Consideration of the risks includes not only the downside risk, but also the potential for upside.

Power

B9 To have power over an investee, an investor must have existing rights that give it the current ability to direct the relevant activities. For the purpose of assessing power, only substantive rights and rights that are not protective shall be considered (see paragraphs B22–B28).

B10 The determination about whether an investor has power depends on the relevant activities, the way decisions about the relevant activities are made and the rights the investor and other parties have in relation to the investee.

Relevant activities and direction of relevant activities

B11 For many investees, a range of operating and financing activities significantly affect their returns. Examples of activities that, depending on the circumstances, can be relevant activities include, but are not limited to:

(a)   selling and purchasing of goods or services;

(b)   managing financial assets during their life (including upon default);

(c)   selecting, acquiring or disposing of assets;

(d)   researching and developing new products or processes; and

(e)   determining a funding structure or obtaining funding.

B12 Examples of decisions about relevant activities include but are not limited to:

(a)   establishing operating and capital decisions of the investee, including budgets; and

(b)   appointing and remunerating an investee's key management personnel or service providers and terminating their services or employment.

B13   In some situations, activities both before and after a particular set of circumstances arises or event occurs may be relevant activities. When two or more investors have the current ability to direct relevant activities and those activities occur at different times, the investors shall determine which investor is able to direct the activities that most significantly affect those returns consistently with the treatment of concurrent decision-making rights (see paragraph 13). The investors shall reconsider this assessment over time if relevant facts or circumstances change.

Application examples

Example 1

Two investors form an investee to develop and market a medical product. One investor is responsible for developing and obtaining regulatory approval of the medical product—that responsibility includes having the unilateral ability to make all decisions relating to the development of the product and to obtaining regulatory approval. Once the regulator has approved the product, the other investor will manufacture and market it—this investor has the unilateral ability to make all decisions about the manufacture and marketing of the project. If all the activities—developing and obtaining regulatory approval as well as manufacturing and marketing of the medical product—are relevant activities, each investor needs to determine whether it is able to direct the activities that *most* significantly affect the investee's returns. Accordingly, each investor needs to consider whether developing and obtaining regulatory approval or the manufacturing and marketing of the medical product is the activity that most significantly affects the investee's returns and whether it is able to direct that activity. In determining which investor has power, the investors would consider:

(a)   the purpose and design of the investee;

(b)   the factors that determine the profit margin, revenue and value of the investee as well as the value of the medical product;

(c)   the effect on the investee's returns resulting from each investor's decision-making authority with respect to the factors in (b); and

(d)   the investors' exposure to variability of returns.

In this particular example, the investors would also consider:

(e)   the uncertainty of, and effort required in, obtaining regulatory approval (considering the investor's record of successfully developing and obtaining regulatory approval of medical products); and

(f)   which investor controls the medical product once the development phase is successful.

continued...

...continued

Application examples

Example 2

An investment vehicle (the investee) is created and financed with a debt instrument held by an investor (the debt investor) and equity instruments held by a number of other investors. The equity tranche is designed to absorb the first losses and to receive any residual return from the investee. One of the equity investors who holds 30 per cent of the equity is also the asset manager. The investee uses its proceeds to purchase a portfolio of financial assets, exposing the investee to the credit risk associated with the possible default of principal and interest payments of the assets. The transaction is marketed to the debt investor as an investment with minimal exposure to the credit risk associated with the possible default of the assets in the portfolio because of the nature of these assets and because the equity tranche is designed to absorb the first losses of the investee. The returns of the investee are significantly affected by the management of the investee's asset portfolio, which includes decisions about the selection, acquisition and disposal of the assets within portfolio guidelines and the management upon default of any portfolio assets. All those activities are managed by the asset manager until defaults reach a specified proportion of the portfolio value (ie when the value of the portfolio is such that the equity tranche of the investee has been consumed). From that time, a third-party trustee manages the assets according to the instructions of the debt investor. Managing the investee's asset portfolio is the relevant activity of the investee. The asset manager has the ability to direct the relevant activities until defaulted assets reach the specified proportion of the portfolio value; the debt investor has the ability to direct the relevant activities when the value of defaulted assets surpasses that specified proportion of the portfolio value. The asset manager and the debt investor each need to determine whether they are able to direct the activities that *most* significantly affect the investee's returns, including considering the purpose and design of the investee as well as each party's exposure to variability of returns.

Rights that give an investor power over an investee

B14   Power arises from rights. To have power over an investee, an investor must have existing rights that give the investor the current ability to direct the relevant activities. The rights that may give an investor power can differ between investees.

B15   Examples of rights that, either individually or in combination, can give an investor power include but are not limited to:

     (a)   rights in the form of voting rights (or potential voting rights) of an investee (see paragraphs B34–B50);

     (b)   rights to appoint, reassign or remove members of an investee's key management personnel who have the ability to direct the relevant activities;

     (c)   rights to appoint or remove another entity that directs the relevant activities;

    (d)   rights to direct the investee to enter into, or veto any changes to, transactions for the benefit of the investor; and

    (e)   other rights (such as decision-making rights specified in a management contract) that give the holder the ability to direct the relevant activities.

B16   Generally, when an investee has a range of operating and financing activities that significantly affect the investee's returns and when substantive decision-making with respect to these activities is required continuously, it will be voting or similar rights that give an investor power, either individually or in combination with other arrangements.

B17   When voting rights cannot have a significant effect on an investee's returns, such as when voting rights relate to administrative tasks only and contractual arrangements determine the direction of the relevant activities, the investor needs to assess those contractual arrangements in order to determine whether it has rights sufficient to give it power over the investee. To determine whether an investor has rights sufficient to give it power, the investor shall consider the purpose and design of the investee (see paragraphs B5–B8) and the requirements in paragraphs B51–B54 together with paragraphs B18–B20.

B18   In some circumstances it may be difficult to determine whether an investor's rights are sufficient to give it power over an investee. In such cases, to enable the assessment of power to be made, the investor shall consider evidence of whether it has the practical ability to direct the relevant activities unilaterally. Consideration is given, but is not limited, to the following, which, when considered together with its rights and the indicators in paragraphs B19 and B20, may provide evidence that the investor's rights are sufficient to give it power over the investee:

    (a)   The investor can, without having the contractual right to do so, appoint or approve the investee's key management personnel who have the ability to direct the relevant activities.

    (b)   The investor can, without having the contractual right to do so, direct the investee to enter into, or can veto any changes to, significant transactions for the benefit of the investor.

    (c)   The investor can dominate either the nominations process for electing members of the investee's governing body or the obtaining of proxies from other holders of voting rights.

    (d)   The investee's key management personnel are related parties of the investor (for example, the chief executive officer of the investee and the chief executive officer of the investor are the same person).

    (e)   The majority of the members of the investee's governing body are related parties of the investor.

B19   Sometimes there will be indications that the investor has a special relationship with the investee, which suggests that the investor has more than a passive interest in the investee. The existence of any individual indicator, or a particular combination of indicators, does not necessarily mean that the power criterion is met. However, having more than a passive interest in the investee may indicate that the investor has other related rights sufficient to give it power or provide evidence of existing power over an investee. For example, the following suggests that the investor has more than a passive interest in the investee and, in combination with other rights, may indicate power:

(a)   The investee's key management personnel who have the ability to direct the relevant activities are current or previous employees of the investor.

(b)   The investee's operations are dependent on the investor, such as in the following situations:

    (i)   The investee depends on the investor to fund a significant portion of its operations.

    (ii)   The investor guarantees a significant portion of the investee's obligations.

    (iii)   The investee depends on the investor for critical services, technology, supplies or raw materials.

    (iv)   The investor controls assets such as licences or trademarks that are critical to the investee's operations.

    (v)   The investee depends on the investor for key management personnel, such as when the investor's personnel have specialised knowledge of the investee's operations.

(c)   A significant portion of the investee's activities either involve or are conducted on behalf of the investor.

(d)   The investor's exposure, or rights, to returns from its involvement with the investee is disproportionately greater than its voting or other similar rights. For example, there may be a situation in which an investor is entitled, or exposed, to more than half of the returns of the investee but holds less than half of the voting rights of the investee.

B20   The greater an investor's exposure, or rights, to variability of returns from its involvement with an investee, the greater is the incentive for the investor to obtain rights sufficient to give it power. Therefore, having a large exposure to variability of returns is an indicator that the investor may have power. However, the extent of the investor's exposure does not, in itself, determine whether an investor has power over the investee.

B21   When the factors set out in paragraph B18 and the indicators set out in paragraphs B19 and B20 are considered together with an investor's rights, greater weight shall be given to the evidence of power described in paragraph B18.

Substantive rights

B22   An investor, in assessing whether it has power, considers only substantive rights relating to an investee (held by the investor and others). For a right to be substantive, the holder must have the practical ability to exercise that right.

B23   Determining whether rights are substantive requires judgement, taking into account all facts and circumstances. Factors to consider in making that determination include but are not limited to:

    (a)   Whether there are any barriers (economic or otherwise) that prevent the holder (or holders) from exercising the rights. Examples of such barriers include but are not limited to:

        (i)   financial penalties and incentives that would prevent (or deter) the holder from exercising its rights.

        (ii)   an exercise or conversion price that creates a financial barrier that would prevent (or deter) the holder from exercising its rights.

        (iii)   terms and conditions that make it unlikely that the rights would be exercised, for example, conditions that narrowly limit the timing of their exercise.

        (iv)   the absence of an explicit, reasonable mechanism in the founding documents of an investee or in applicable laws or regulations that would allow the holder to exercise its rights.

        (v)   the inability of the holder of the rights to obtain the information necessary to exercise its rights.

        (vi)   operational barriers or incentives that would prevent (or deter) the holder from exercising its rights (eg the absence of other managers willing or able to provide specialised services or provide the services and take on other interests held by the incumbent manager).

        (vii)   legal or regulatory requirements that prevent the holder from exercising its rights (eg where a foreign investor is prohibited from exercising its rights).

    (b)   When the exercise of rights requires the agreement of more than one party, or when the rights are held by more than one party, whether a mechanism is in place that provides those parties with the practical ability to exercise their rights collectively if they choose to do so. The lack of such a mechanism is an indicator that the rights may not be substantive. The more parties that are required to agree to exercise the rights, the less likely it is that those rights are substantive. However, a board of directors whose members are independent of the decision maker may serve as a mechanism for numerous investors to act collectively in exercising their rights. Therefore, removal rights exercisable by an independent board of directors are more likely to be substantive than if the same rights were exercisable individually by a large number of investors.

    (c)   Whether the party or parties that hold the rights would benefit from the exercise of those rights. For example, the holder of potential voting rights in an investee (see paragraphs B47–B50) shall consider the exercise or conversion price of the instrument. The terms and conditions of potential voting rights are more likely to be substantive when the instrument is in the money or the investor would benefit for other reasons (eg by realising synergies between the investor and the investee) from the exercise or conversion of the instrument.

B24   To be substantive, rights also need to be exercisable when decisions about the direction of the relevant activities need to be made. Usually, to be substantive, the rights need to be currently exercisable. However, sometimes rights can be substantive, even though the rights are not currently exercisable.

Application examples

Example 3

The investee has annual shareholder meetings at which decisions to direct the relevant activities are made. The next scheduled shareholders' meeting is in eight months. However, shareholders that individually or collectively hold at least 5 per cent of the voting rights can call a special meeting to change the existing policies over the relevant activities, but a requirement to give notice to the other shareholders means that such a meeting cannot be held for at least 30 days. Policies over the relevant activities can be changed only at special or scheduled shareholders' meetings. This includes the approval of material sales of assets as well as the making or disposing of significant investments.

The above fact pattern applies to examples 3A–3D described below. Each example is considered in isolation.

Example 3A

An investor holds a majority of the voting rights in the investee. The investor's voting rights are substantive because the investor is able to make decisions about the direction of the relevant activities when they need to be made. The fact that it takes 30 days before the investor can exercise its voting rights does not stop the investor from having the current ability to direct the relevant activities from the moment the investor acquires the shareholding.

Example 3B

An investor is party to a forward contract to acquire the majority of shares in the investee. The forward contract's settlement date is in 25 days. The existing shareholders are unable to change the existing policies over the relevant activities because a special meeting cannot be held for at least 30 days, at which point the forward contract will have been settled. Thus, the investor has rights that are essentially equivalent to the majority shareholder in example 3A above (ie the investor holding the forward contract can make decisions about the direction of the relevant activities when they need to be made). The investor's forward contract is a substantive right that gives the investor the current ability to direct the relevant activities even before the forward contract is settled.

Example 3C

An investor holds a substantive option to acquire the majority of shares in the investee that is exercisable in 25 days and is deeply in the money. The same conclusion would be reached as in example 3B.

continued...

> ...*continued*
> **Application examples**
>
> **Example 3D**
>
> An investor is party to a forward contract to acquire the majority of shares in the investee, with no other related rights over the investee. The forward contract's settlement date is in six months. In contrast to the examples above, the investor does not have the current ability to direct the relevant activities. The existing shareholders have the current ability to direct the relevant activities because they can change the existing policies over the relevant activities before the forward contract is settled.

B25   Substantive rights exercisable by other parties can prevent an investor from controlling the investee to which those rights relate. Such substantive rights do not require the holders to have the ability to initiate decisions. As long as the rights are not merely protective (see paragraphs B26–B28), substantive rights held by other parties may prevent the investor from controlling the investee even if the rights give the holders only the current ability to approve or block decisions that relate to the relevant activities.

Protective rights

B26   In evaluating whether rights give an investor power over an investee, the investor shall assess whether its rights, and rights held by others, are protective rights. Protective rights relate to fundamental changes to the activities of an investee or apply in exceptional circumstances. However, not all rights that apply in exceptional circumstances or are contingent on events are protective (see paragraphs B13 and B53).

B27   Because protective rights are designed to protect the interests of their holder without giving that party power over the investee to which those rights relate, an investor that holds only protective rights cannot have power or prevent another party from having power over an investee (see paragraph 14).

B28   Examples of protective rights include but are not limited to:

(a)   a lender's right to restrict a borrower from undertaking activities that could significantly change the credit risk of the borrower to the detriment of the lender.

(b)   the right of a party holding a non-controlling interest in an investee to approve capital expenditure greater than that required in the ordinary course of business, or to approve the issue of equity or debt instruments.

(c)   the right of a lender to seize the assets of a borrower if the borrower fails to meet specified loan repayment conditions.

Franchises

B29   A franchise agreement for which the investee is the franchisee often gives the franchisor rights that are designed to protect the franchise brand. Franchise agreements typically give franchisors some decision-making rights with respect to the operations of the franchisee.

B30 Generally, franchisors' rights do not restrict the ability of parties other than the franchisor to make decisions that have a significant effect on the franchisee's returns. Nor do the rights of the franchisor in franchise agreements necessarily give the franchisor the current ability to direct the activities that significantly affect the franchisee's returns.

B31 It is necessary to distinguish between having the current ability to make decisions that significantly affect the franchisee's returns and having the ability to make decisions that protect the franchise brand. The franchisor does not have power over the franchisee if other parties have existing rights that give them the current ability to direct the relevant activities of the franchisee.

B32 By entering into the franchise agreement the franchisee has made a unilateral decision to operate its business in accordance with the terms of the franchise agreement, but for its own account.

B33 Control over such fundamental decisions as the legal form of the franchisee and its funding structure may be determined by parties other than the franchisor and may significantly affect the returns of the franchisee. The lower the level of financial support provided by the franchisor and the lower the franchisor's exposure to variability of returns from the franchisee the more likely it is that the franchisor has only protective rights.

Voting rights

B34 Often an investor has the current ability, through voting or similar rights, to direct the relevant activities. An investor considers the requirements in this section (paragraphs B35–B50) if the relevant activities of an investee are directed through voting rights.

Power with a majority of the voting rights

B35 An investor that holds more than half of the voting rights of an investee has power in the following situations, unless paragraph B36 or paragraph B37 applies:

(a) the relevant activities are directed by a vote of the holder of the majority of the voting rights, or

(b) a majority of the members of the governing body that directs the relevant activities are appointed by a vote of the holder of the majority of the voting rights.

Majority of the voting rights but no power

B36 For an investor that holds more than half of the voting rights of an investee, to have power over an investee, the investor's voting rights must be substantive, in accordance with paragraphs B22–B25, and must provide the investor with the current ability to direct the relevant activities, which often will be through determining operating and financing policies. If another entity has existing rights that provide that entity with the right to direct the relevant activities and that entity is not an agent of the investor, the investor does not have power over the investee.

B37   An investor does not have power over an investee, even though the investor holds the majority of the voting rights in the investee, when those voting rights are not substantive. For example, an investor that has more than half of the voting rights in an investee cannot have power if the relevant activities are subject to direction by a government, court, administrator, receiver, liquidator or regulator.

Power without a majority of the voting rights

B38   An investor can have power even if it holds less than a majority of the voting rights of an investee. An investor can have power with less than a majority of the voting rights of an investee, for example, through:

(a)   a contractual arrangement between the investor and other vote holders (see paragraph B39);

(b)   rights arising from other contractual arrangements (see paragraph B40);

(c)   the investor's voting rights (see paragraphs B41–B45);

(d)   potential voting rights (see paragraphs B47–B50); or

(e)   a combination of (a)–(d).

Contractual arrangement with other vote holders

B39   A contractual arrangement between an investor and other vote holders can give the investor the right to exercise voting rights sufficient to give the investor power, even if the investor does not have voting rights sufficient to give it power without the contractual arrangement. However, a contractual arrangement might ensure that the investor can direct enough other vote holders on how to vote to enable the investor to make decisions about the relevant activities.

Rights from other contractual arrangements

B40   Other decision-making rights, in combination with voting rights, can give an investor the current ability to direct the relevant activities. For example, the rights specified in a contractual arrangement in combination with voting rights may be sufficient to give an investor the current ability to direct the manufacturing processes of an investee or to direct other operating or financing activities of an investee that significantly affect the investee's returns. However, in the absence of any other rights, economic dependence of an investee on the investor (such as relations of a supplier with its main customer) does not lead to the investor having power over the investee.

The investor's voting rights

B41   An investor with less than a majority of the voting rights has rights that are sufficient to give it power when the investor has the practical ability to direct the relevant activities unilaterally.

B42   When assessing whether an investor's voting rights are sufficient to give it power, an investor considers all facts and circumstances, including:

(a)   the size of the investor's holding of voting rights relative to the size and dispersion of holdings of the other vote holders, noting that:

      (i)   the more voting rights an investor holds, the more likely the investor is to have existing rights that give it the current ability to direct the relevant activities;

      (ii)   the more voting rights an investor holds relative to other vote holders, the more likely the investor is to have existing rights that give it the current ability to direct the relevant activities;

      (iii)   the more parties that would need to act together to outvote the investor, the more likely the investor is to have existing rights that give it the current ability to direct the relevant activities;

(b)   potential voting rights held by the investor, other vote holders or other parties (see paragraphs B47–B50);

(c)   rights arising from other contractual arrangements (see paragraph B40); and

(d)   any additional facts and circumstances that indicate the investor has, or does not have, the current ability to direct the relevant activities at the time that decisions need to be made, including voting patterns at previous shareholders' meetings.

B43   When the direction of relevant activities is determined by majority vote and an investor holds significantly more voting rights than any other vote holder or organised group of vote holders, and the other shareholdings are widely dispersed, it may be clear, after considering the factors listed in paragraph 42(a)–(c) alone, that the investor has power over the investee.

Application examples

Example 4

An investor acquires 48 per cent of the voting rights of an investee. The remaining voting rights are held by thousands of shareholders, none individually holding more than 1 per cent of the voting rights. None of the shareholders has any arrangements to consult any of the others or make collective decisions. When assessing the proportion of voting rights to acquire, on the basis of the relative size of the other shareholdings, the investor determined that a 48 per cent interest would be sufficient to give it control. In this case, on the basis of the absolute size of its holding and the relative size of the other shareholdings, the investor concludes that it has a sufficiently dominant voting interest to meet the power criterion without the need to consider any other evidence of power.

continued...

...*continued* **Application examples**
Example 5
Investor A holds 40 per cent of the voting rights of an investee and twelve other investors each hold 5 per cent of the voting rights of the investee. A shareholder agreement grants investor A the right to appoint, remove and set the remuneration of management responsible for directing the relevant activities. To change the agreement, a two-thirds majority vote of the shareholders is required. In this case, investor A concludes that the absolute size of the investor's holding and the relative size of the other shareholdings alone are not conclusive in determining whether the investor has rights sufficient to give it power. However, investor A determines that its contractual right to appoint, remove and set the remuneration of management is sufficient to conclude that it has power over the investee. The fact that investor A might not have exercised this right or the likelihood of investor A exercising its right to select, appoint or remove management shall not be considered when assessing whether investor A has power.

B44   In other situations, it may be clear after considering the factors listed in paragraph B42(a)–(c) alone that an investor does not have power.

Application example
Example 6
Investor A holds 45 per cent of the voting rights of an investee. Two other investors each hold 26 per cent of the voting rights of the investee. The remaining voting rights are held by three other shareholders, each holding 1 per cent. There are no other arrangements that affect decision-making. In this case, the size of investor A's voting interest and its size relative to the other shareholdings are sufficient to conclude that investor A does not have power. Only two other investors would need to co-operate to be able to prevent investor A from directing the relevant activities of the investee.

B45   However, the factors listed in paragraph B42(a)–(c) alone may not be conclusive. If an investor, having considered those factors, is unclear whether it has power, it shall consider additional facts and circumstances, such as whether other shareholders are passive in nature as demonstrated by voting patterns at previous shareholders' meetings. This includes the assessment of the factors set out in paragraph B18 and the indicators in paragraphs B19 and B20. The fewer voting rights the investor holds, and the fewer parties that would need to act together to outvote the investor, the more reliance would be placed on the additional facts and circumstances to assess whether the investor's rights are sufficient to give it power. When the facts and circumstances in paragraphs B18–B20 are considered together with the investor's rights, greater weight shall be given to the evidence of power in paragraph B18 than to the indicators of power in paragraphs B19 and B20.

Application examples

Example 7

An investor holds 45 per cent of the voting rights of an investee. Eleven other shareholders each hold 5 per cent of the voting rights of the investee. None of the shareholders has contractual arrangements to consult any of the others or make collective decisions. In this case, the absolute size of the investor's holding and the relative size of the other shareholdings alone are not conclusive in determining whether the investor has rights sufficient to give it power over the investee. Additional facts and circumstances that may provide evidence that the investor has, or does not have, power shall be considered.

Example 8

An investor holds 35 per cent of the voting rights of an investee. Three other shareholders each hold 5 per cent of the voting rights of the investee. The remaining voting rights are held by numerous other shareholders, none individually holding more than 1 per cent of the voting rights. None of the shareholders has arrangements to consult any of the others or make collective decisions. Decisions about the relevant activities of the investee require the approval of a majority of votes cast at relevant shareholders' meetings—75 per cent of the voting rights of the investee have been cast at recent relevant shareholders' meetings. In this case, the active participation of the other shareholders at recent shareholders' meetings indicates that the investor would not have the practical ability to direct the relevant activities unilaterally, regardless of whether the investor has directed the relevant activities because a sufficient number of other shareholders voted in the same way as the investor.

B46 If it is not clear, having considered the factors listed in paragraph B42(a)–(d), that the investor has power, the investor does not control the investee.

Potential voting rights

B47 When assessing control, an investor considers its potential voting rights as well as potential voting rights held by other parties, to determine whether it has power. Potential voting rights are rights to obtain voting rights of an investee, such as those arising from convertible instruments or options, including forward contracts. Those potential voting rights are considered only if the rights are substantive (see paragraphs B22–B25).

B48 When considering potential voting rights, an investor shall consider the purpose and design of the instrument, as well as the purpose and design of any other involvement the investor has with the investee. This includes an assessment of the various terms and conditions of the instrument as well as the investor's apparent expectations, motives and reasons for agreeing to those terms and conditions.

B49 If the investor also has voting or other decision-making rights relating to the investee's activities, the investor assesses whether those rights, in combination with potential voting rights, give the investor power.

B50   Substantive potential voting rights alone, or in combination with other rights, can give an investor the current ability to direct the relevant activities. For example, this is likely to be the case when an investor holds 40 per cent of the voting rights of an investee and, in accordance with paragraph B23, holds substantive rights arising from options to acquire a further 20 per cent of the voting rights.

Application examples

Example 9

Investor A holds 70 per cent of the voting rights of an investee. Investor B has 30 per cent of the voting rights of the investee as well as an option to acquire half of investor A's voting rights. The option is exercisable for the next two years at a fixed price that is deeply out of the money (and is expected to remain so for that two-year period). Investor A has been exercising its votes and is actively directing the relevant activities of the investee. In such a case, investor A is likely to meet the power criterion because it appears to have the current ability to direct the relevant activities. Although investor B has currently exercisable options to purchase additional voting rights (that, if exercised, would give it a majority of the voting rights in the investee), the terms and conditions associated with those options are such that the options are not considered substantive.

Example 10

Investor A and two other investors each hold a third of the voting rights of an investee. The investee's business activity is closely related to investor A. In addition to its equity instruments, investor A also holds debt instruments that are convertible into ordinary shares of the investee at any time for a fixed price that is out of the money (but not deeply out of the money). If the debt were converted, investor A would hold 60 per cent of the voting rights of the investee. Investor A would benefit from realising synergies if the debt instruments were converted into ordinary shares. Investor A has power over the investee because it holds voting rights of the investee together with substantive potential voting rights that give it the current ability to direct the relevant activities.

Power when voting or similar rights do not have a significant effect on the investee's returns

B51   In assessing the purpose and design of an investee (see paragraphs B5–B8), an investor shall consider the involvement and decisions made at the investee's inception as part of its design and evaluate whether the transaction terms and features of the involvement provide the investor with rights that are sufficient to give it power. Being involved in the design of an investee alone is not sufficient to give an investor control. However, involvement in the design may indicate that the investor had the opportunity to obtain rights that are sufficient to give it power over the investee.

B52   In addition, an investor shall consider contractual arrangements such as call rights, put rights and liquidation rights established at the investee's inception. When these contractual arrangements involve activities that are closely related to the investee, then these activities are, in substance, an integral part of the investee's overall activities, even though they may occur outside the legal boundaries of the investee. Therefore, explicit or implicit decision-making rights embedded in contractual arrangements that are closely related to the investee need to be considered as relevant activities when determining power over the investee.

B53 For some investees, relevant activities occur only when particular circumstances arise or events occur. The investee may be designed so that the direction of its activities and its returns are predetermined unless and until those particular circumstances arise or events occur. In this case, only the decisions about the investee's activities when those circumstances or events occur can significantly affect its returns and thus be relevant activities. The circumstances or events need not have occurred for an investor with the ability to make those decisions to have power. The fact that the right to make decisions is contingent on circumstances arising or an event occurring does not, in itself, make those rights protective.

Application examples

Example 11

An investee's only business activity, as specified in its founding documents, is to purchase receivables and service them on a day-to-day basis for its investors. The servicing on a day-to-day basis includes the collection and passing on of principal and interest payments as they fall due. Upon default of a receivable the investee automatically puts the receivable to an investor as agreed separately in a put agreement between the investor and the investee. The only relevant activity is managing the receivables upon default because it is the only activity that can significantly affect the investee's returns. Managing the receivables before default is not a relevant activity because it does not require substantive decisions to be made that could significantly affect the investee's returns—the activities before default are predetermined and amount only to collecting cash flows as they fall due and passing them on to investors. Therefore, only the investor's right to manage the assets upon default should be considered when assessing the overall activities of the investee that significantly affect the investee's returns. In this example, the design of the investee ensures that the investor has decision-making authority over the activities that significantly affect the returns at the only time that such decision-making authority is required. The terms of the put agreement are integral to the overall transaction and the establishment of the investee. Therefore, the terms of the put agreement together with the founding documents of the investee lead to the conclusion that the investor has power over the investee even though the investor takes ownership of the receivables only upon default and manages the defaulted receivables outside the legal boundaries of the investee.

continued...

...continued
Application examples
Example 12
The only assets of an investee are receivables. When the purpose and design of the investee are considered, it is determined that the only relevant activity is managing the receivables upon default. The party that has the ability to manage the defaulting receivables has power over the investee, irrespective of whether any of the borrowers have defaulted.

B54   An investor may have an explicit or implicit commitment to ensure that an investee continues to operate as designed. Such a commitment may increase the investor's exposure to variability of returns and thus increase the incentive for the investor to obtain rights sufficient to give it power. Therefore a commitment to ensure that an investee operates as designed may be an indicator that the investor has power, but does not, by itself, give an investor power, nor does it prevent another party from having power.

Exposure, or rights, to variable returns from an investee

B55   When assessing whether an investor has control of an investee, the investor determines whether it is exposed, or has rights, to variable returns from its involvement with the investee.

B56   Variable returns are returns that are not fixed and have the potential to vary as a result of the performance of an investee. Variable returns can be only positive, only negative or both positive and negative (see paragraph 15). An investor assesses whether returns from an investee are variable and how variable those returns are on the basis of the substance of the arrangement and regardless of the legal form of the returns. For example, an investor can hold a bond with fixed interest payments. The fixed interest payments are variable returns for the purpose of this IFRS because they are subject to default risk and they expose the investor to the credit risk of the issuer of the bond. The amount of variability (ie how variable those returns are) depends on the credit risk of the bond. Similarly, fixed performance fees for managing an investee's assets are variable returns because they expose the investor to the performance risk of the investee. The amount of variability depends on the investee's ability to generate sufficient income to pay the fee.

B57   Examples of returns include:

(a)   dividends, other distributions of economic benefits from an investee (eg interest from debt securities issued by the investee) and changes in the value of the investor's investment in that investee.

(b)   remuneration for servicing an investee's assets or liabilities, fees and exposure to loss from providing credit or liquidity support, residual interests in the investee's assets and liabilities on liquidation of that investee, tax benefits, and access to future liquidity that an investor has from its involvement with an investee.

(c)   returns that are not available to other interest holders. For example, an investor might use its assets in combination with the assets of the investee, such as combining operating functions to achieve economies of scale, cost savings, sourcing scarce products, gaining access to proprietary knowledge or limiting some operations or assets, to enhance the value of the investor's other assets.

Link between power and returns

Delegated power

B58 When an investor with decision-making rights (a decision maker) assesses whether it controls an investee, it shall determine whether it is a principal or an agent. An investor shall also determine whether another entity with decision-making rights is acting as an agent for the investor. An agent is a party primarily engaged to act on behalf and for the benefit of another party or parties (the principal(s)) and therefore does not control the investee when it exercises its decision-making authority (see paragraphs 17 and 18). Thus, sometimes a principal's power may be held and exercisable by an agent, but on behalf of the principal. A decision maker is not an agent simply because other parties can benefit from the decisions that it makes.

B59 An investor may delegate its decision-making authority to an agent on some specific issues or on all relevant activities. When assessing whether it controls an investee, the investor shall treat the decision-making rights delegated to its agent as held by the investor directly. In situations where there is more than one principal, each of the principals shall assess whether it has power over the investee by considering the requirements in paragraphs B5–B54. Paragraphs B60–B72 provide guidance on determining whether a decision maker is an agent or a principal.

B60 A decision maker shall consider the overall relationship between itself, the investee being managed and other parties involved with the investee, in particular all the factors below, in determining whether it is an agent:

(a) the scope of its decision-making authority over the investee (paragraphs B62 and B63).

(b) the rights held by other parties (paragraphs B64–B67).

(c) the remuneration to which it is entitled in accordance with the remuneration agreement(s) (paragraphs B68–B70).

(d) the decision maker's exposure to variability of returns from other interests that it holds in the investee (paragraphs B71 and B72).

Different weightings shall be applied to each of the factors on the basis of particular facts and circumstances.

B61 Determining whether a decision maker is an agent requires an evaluation of all the factors listed in paragraph B60 unless a single party holds substantive rights to remove the decision maker (removal rights) and can remove the decision maker without cause (see paragraph B65).

The scope of the decision-making authority

B62   The scope of a decision maker's decision-making authority is evaluated by considering:

     (a)   the activities that are permitted according to the decision-making agreement(s) and specified by law, and

     (b)   the discretion that the decision maker has when making decisions about those activities.

B63   A decision maker shall consider the purpose and design of the investee, the risks to which the investee was designed to be exposed, the risks it was designed to pass on to the parties involved and the level of involvement the decision maker had in the design of an investee. For example, if a decision maker is significantly involved in the design of the investee (including in determining the scope of decision-making authority), that involvement may indicate that the decision maker had the opportunity and incentive to obtain rights that result in the decision maker having the ability to direct the relevant activities.

Rights held by other parties

B64   Substantive rights held by other parties may affect the decision maker's ability to direct the relevant activities of an investee. Substantive removal or other rights may indicate that the decision maker is an agent.

B65   When a single party holds substantive removal rights and can remove the decision maker without cause, this, in isolation, is sufficient to conclude that the decision maker is an agent. If more than one party holds such rights (and no individual party can remove the decision maker without the agreement of other parties) those rights are not, in isolation, conclusive in determining that a decision maker acts primarily on behalf and for the benefit of others. In addition, the greater the number of parties required to act together to exercise rights to remove a decision maker and the greater the magnitude of, and variability associated with, the decision maker's other economic interests (ie remuneration and other interests), the less the weighting that shall be placed on this factor.

B66   Substantive rights held by other parties that restrict a decision maker's discretion shall be considered in a similar manner to removal rights when evaluating whether the decision maker is an agent. For example, a decision maker that is required to obtain approval from a small number of other parties for its actions is generally an agent. (See paragraphs B22–B25 for additional guidance on rights and whether they are substantive.)

B67   Consideration of the rights held by other parties shall include an assessment of any rights exercisable by an investee's board of directors (or other governing body) and their effect on the decision-making authority (see paragraph B23(b)).

Remuneration

B68   The greater the magnitude of, and variability associated with, the decision maker's remuneration relative to the returns expected from the activities of the investee, the more likely the decision maker is a principal.

B69   In determining whether it is a principal or an agent the decision maker shall also consider whether the following conditions exist:

(a)   The remuneration of the decision maker is commensurate with the services provided.

(b)   The remuneration agreement includes only terms, conditions or amounts that are customarily present in arrangements for similar services and level of skills negotiated on an arm's length basis.

B70   A decision maker cannot be an agent unless the conditions set out in paragraph B69(a) and (b) are present. However, meeting those conditions in isolation is not sufficient to conclude that a decision maker is an agent.

Exposure to variability of returns from other interests

B71   A decision maker that holds other interests in an investee (eg investments in the investee or provides guarantees with respect to the performance of the investee), shall consider its exposure to variability of returns from those interests in assessing whether it is an agent. Holding other interests in an investee indicates that the decision maker may be a principal.

B72   In evaluating its exposure to variability of returns from other interests in the investee a decision maker shall consider the following:

(a)   the greater the magnitude of, and variability associated with, its economic interests, considering its remuneration and other interests in aggregate, the more likely the decision maker is a principal.

(b)   whether its exposure to variability of returns is different from that of the other investors and, if so, whether this might influence its actions. For example, this might be the case when a decision maker holds subordinated interests in, or provides other forms of credit enhancement to, an investee.

The decision maker shall evaluate its exposure relative to the total variability of returns of the investee. This evaluation is made primarily on the basis of returns expected from the activities of the investee but shall not ignore the decision maker's maximum exposure to variability of returns of the investee through other interests that the decision maker holds.

Application examples

Example 13

A decision maker (fund manager) establishes, markets and manages a publicly traded, regulated fund according to narrowly defined parameters set out in the investment mandate as required by its local laws and regulations. The fund was marketed to investors as an investment in a diversified portfolio of equity securities of publicly traded entities. Within the defined parameters, the fund manager has discretion about the assets in which to invest. The fund manager has made a 10 per cent pro rata investment in the fund and receives a market-based fee for its services equal to 1 per cent of the net asset value of the fund. The fees are commensurate with the services provided. The fund manager does not have any obligation to fund losses beyond its 10 per cent investment. The fund is not required to establish, and has not established, an independent board of directors. The investors do not hold any substantive rights that would affect the decision-making authority of the fund manager, but can redeem their interests within particular limits set by the fund.

Although operating within the parameters set out in the investment mandate and in accordance with the regulatory requirements, the fund manager has decision-making rights that give it the current ability to direct the relevant activities of the fund—the investors do not hold substantive rights that could affect the fund manager's decision-making authority. The fund manager receives a market-based fee for its services that is commensurate with the services provided and has also made a pro rata investment in the fund. The remuneration and its investment expose the fund manager to variability of returns from the activities of the fund without creating exposure that is of such significance that it indicates that the fund manager is a principal.

In this example, consideration of the fund manager's exposure to variability of returns from the fund together with its decision-making authority within restricted parameters indicates that the fund manager is an agent. Thus, the fund manager concludes that it does not control the fund.

Example 14

A decision maker establishes, markets and manages a fund that provides investment opportunities to a number of investors. The decision maker (fund manager) must make decisions in the best interests of all investors and in accordance with the fund's governing agreements. Nonetheless, the fund manager has wide decision-making discretion. The fund manager receives a market-based fee for its services equal to 1 per cent of assets under management and 20 per cent of all the fund's profits if a specified profit level is achieved. The fees are commensurate with the services provided.

continued...

...continued
Application examples

Although it must make decisions in the best interests of all investors, the fund manager has extensive decision-making authority to direct the relevant activities of the fund. The fund manager is paid fixed and performance-related fees that are commensurate with the services provided. In addition, the remuneration aligns the interests of the fund manager with those of the other investors to increase the value of the fund, without creating exposure to variability of returns from the activities of the fund that is of such significance that the remuneration, when considered in isolation, indicates that the fund manager is a principal.

The above fact pattern and analysis applies to examples 14A–14C described below. Each example is considered in isolation.

Example 14A

The fund manager also has a 2 per cent investment in the fund that aligns its interests with those of the other investors. The fund manager does not have any obligation to fund losses beyond its 2 per cent investment. The investors can remove the fund manager by a simple majority vote, but only for breach of contract.

The fund manager's 2 per cent investment increases its exposure to variability of returns from the activities of the fund without creating exposure that is of such significance that it indicates that the fund manager is a principal. The other investors' rights to remove the fund manager are considered to be protective rights because they are exercisable only for breach of contract. In this example, although the fund manager has extensive decision-making authority and is exposed to variability of returns from its interest and remuneration, the fund manager's exposure indicates that the fund manager is an agent. Thus, the fund manager concludes that it does not control the fund.

Example 14B

The fund manager has a more substantial pro rata investment in the fund, but does not have any obligation to fund losses beyond that investment. The investors can remove the fund manager by a simple majority vote, but only for breach of contract.

In this example, the other investors' rights to remove the fund manager are considered to be protective rights because they are exercisable only for breach of contract. Although the fund manager is paid fixed and performance-related fees that are commensurate with the services provided, the combination of the fund manager's investment together with its remuneration could create exposure to variability of returns from the activities of the fund that is of such significance that it indicates that the fund manager is a principal. The greater the magnitude of, and variability associated with, the fund manager's economic interests (considering its remuneration and other interests in aggregate), the more emphasis the fund manager would place on those economic interests in the analysis, and the more likely the fund manager is a principal.

continued...

...continued

Application examples

For example, having considered its remuneration and the other factors, the fund manager might consider a 20 per cent investment to be sufficient to conclude that it controls the fund. However, in different circumstances (ie if the remuneration or other factors are different), control may arise when the level of investment is different.

Example 14C

The fund manager has a 20 per cent pro rata investment in the fund, but does not have any obligation to fund losses beyond its 20 per cent investment. The fund has a board of directors, all of whose members are independent of the fund manager and are appointed by the other investors. The board appoints the fund manager annually. If the board decided not to renew the fund manager's contract, the services performed by the fund manager could be performed by other managers in the industry.

Although the fund manager is paid fixed and performance-related fees that are commensurate with the services provided, the combination of the fund manager's 20 per cent investment together with its remuneration creates exposure to variability of returns from the activities of the fund that is of such significance that it indicates that the fund manager is a principal. However, the investors have substantive rights to remove the fund manager—the board of directors provides a mechanism to ensure that the investors can remove the fund manager if they decide to do so.

In this example, the fund manager places greater emphasis on the substantive removal rights in the analysis. Thus, although the fund manager has extensive decision-making authority and is exposed to variability of returns of the fund from its remuneration and investment, the substantive rights held by the other investors indicate that the fund manager is an agent. Thus, the fund manager concludes that it does not control the fund.

continued...

...*continued*

Application examples

Example 15

An investee is created to purchase a portfolio of fixed rate asset-backed securities, funded by fixed rate debt instruments and equity instruments. The equity instruments are designed to provide first loss protection to the debt investors and receive any residual returns of the investee. The transaction was marketed to potential debt investors as an investment in a portfolio of asset-backed securities with exposure to the credit risk associated with the possible default of the issuers of the asset-backed securities in the portfolio and to the interest rate risk associated with the management of the portfolio. On formation, the equity instruments represent 10 per cent of the value of the assets purchased. A decision maker (the asset manager) manages the active asset portfolio by making investment decisions within the parameters set out in the investee's prospectus. For those services, the asset manager receives a market-based fixed fee (ie 1 per cent of assets under management) and performance-related fees (ie 10 per cent of profits) if the investee's profits exceed a specified level. The fees are commensurate with the services provided. The asset manager holds 35 per cent of the equity in the investee. The remaining 65 per cent of the equity, and all the debt instruments, are held by a large number of widely dispersed unrelated third party investors. The asset manager can be removed, without cause, by a simple majority decision of the other investors.

The asset manager is paid fixed and performance-related fees that are commensurate with the services provided. The remuneration aligns the interests of the fund manager with those of the other investors to increase the value of the fund. The asset manager has exposure to variability of returns from the activities of the fund because it holds 35 per cent of the equity and from its remuneration.

Although operating within the parameters set out in the investee's prospectus, the asset manager has the current ability to make investment decisions that significantly affect the investee's returns—the removal rights held by the other investors receive little weighting in the analysis because those rights are held by a large number of widely dispersed investors. In this example, the asset manager places greater emphasis on its exposure to variability of returns of the fund from its equity interest, which is subordinate to the debt instruments. Holding 35 per cent of the equity creates subordinated exposure to losses and rights to returns of the investee, which are of such significance that it indicates that the asset manager is a principal. Thus, the asset manager concludes that it controls the investee.

continued...

...continued

Application examples

Example 16

A decision maker (the sponsor) sponsors a multi-seller conduit, which issues short-term debt instruments to unrelated third party investors. The transaction was marketed to potential investors as an investment in a portfolio of highly rated medium-term assets with minimal exposure to the credit risk associated with the possible default by the issuers of the assets in the portfolio. Various transferors sell high quality medium-term asset portfolios to the conduit. Each transferor services the portfolio of assets that it sells to the conduit and manages receivables on default for a market-based servicing fee. Each transferor also provides first loss protection against credit losses from its asset portfolio through over-collateralisation of the assets transferred to the conduit. The sponsor establishes the terms of the conduit and manages the operations of the conduit for a market-based fee. The fee is commensurate with the services provided. The sponsor approves the sellers permitted to sell to the conduit, approves the assets to be purchased by the conduit and makes decisions about the funding of the conduit. The sponsor must act in the best interests of all investors.

The sponsor is entitled to any residual return of the conduit and also provides credit enhancement and liquidity facilities to the conduit. The credit enhancement provided by the sponsor absorbs losses of up to 5 per cent of all of the conduit's assets, after losses are absorbed by the transferors. The liquidity facilities are not advanced against defaulted assets. The investors do not hold substantive rights that could affect the decision-making authority of the sponsor.

Even though the sponsor is paid a market-based fee for its services that is commensurate with the services provided, the sponsor has exposure to variability of returns from the activities of the conduit because of its rights to any residual returns of the conduit and the provision of credit enhancement and liquidity facilities (ie the conduit is exposed to liquidity risk by using short-term debt instruments to fund medium-term assets). Even though each of the transferors has decision-making rights that affect the value of the assets of the conduit, the sponsor has extensive decision-making authority that gives it the current ability to direct the activities that most significantly affect the conduit's returns (ie the sponsor established the terms of the conduit, has the right to make decisions about the assets (approving the assets purchased and the transferors of those assets) and the funding of the conduit (for which new investment must be found on a regular basis)). The right to residual returns of the conduit and the provision of credit enhancement and liquidity facilities expose the sponsor to variability of returns from the activities of the conduit that is different from that of the other investors. Accordingly, that exposure indicates that the sponsor is a principal and thus the sponsor concludes that it controls the conduit. The sponsor's obligation to act in the best interest of all investors does not prevent the sponsor from being a principal.

Relationship with other parties

B73 When assessing control, an investor shall consider the nature of its relationship with other parties and whether those other parties are acting on the investor's behalf (ie they are 'de facto agents'). The determination of whether other parties are acting as de facto agents requires judgement, considering not only the nature of the relationship but also how those parties interact with each other and the investor.

B74 Such a relationship need not involve a contractual arrangement. A party is a de facto agent when the investor has, or those that direct the activities of the investor have, the ability to direct that party to act on the investor's behalf. In these circumstances, the investor shall consider its de facto agent's decision-making rights and its indirect exposure, or rights, to variable returns through the de facto agent together with its own when assessing control of an investee.

B75 The following are examples of such other parties that, by the nature of their relationship, might act as de facto agents for the investor:

(a) the investor's related parties.

(b) a party that received its interest in the investee as a contribution or loan from the investor.

(c) a party that has agreed not to sell, transfer or encumber its interests in the investee without the investor's prior approval (except for situations in which the investor and the other party have the right of prior approval and the rights are based on mutually agreed terms by willing independent parties).

(d) a party that cannot finance its operations without subordinated financial support from the investor.

(e) an investee for which the majority of the members of its governing body or for which its key management personnel are the same as those of the investor.

(f) a party that has a close business relationship with the investor, such as the relationship between a professional service provider and one of its significant clients.

Control of specified assets

B76 An investor shall consider whether it treats a portion of an investee as a deemed separate entity and, if so, whether it controls the deemed separate entity.

B77 An investor shall treat a portion of an investee as a deemed separate entity if and only if the following condition is satisfied:

Specified assets of the investee (and related credit enhancements, if any) are the only source of payment for specified liabilities of, or specified other interests in, the investee. Parties other than those with the specified liability do not have rights or obligations related to the specified assets or to residual cash flows from those assets. In substance, none of the returns from the specified assets can be used by the remaining investee and none of the liabilities of the deemed separate entity are payable from the assets of the remaining investee. Thus, in substance, all the assets, liabilities and equity of that deemed separate entity are ring-fenced from the overall investee. Such a deemed separate entity is often called a 'silo'.

B78 When the condition in paragraph B77 is satisfied, an investor shall identify the activities that significantly affect the returns of the deemed separate entity and how those activities are directed in order to assess whether it has power over that portion of the investee. When assessing control of the deemed separate entity, the investor shall also consider whether it has exposure or rights to variable returns from its involvement with that deemed separate entity and the ability to use its power over that portion of the investee to affect the amount of the investor's returns.

B79 If the investor controls the deemed separate entity, the investor shall consolidate that portion of the investee. In that case, other parties exclude that portion of the investee when assessing control of, and in consolidating, the investee.

Continuous assessment

B80 An investor shall reassess whether it controls an investee if facts and circumstances indicate that there are changes to one or more of the three elements of control listed in paragraph 7.

B81 If there is a change in how power over an investee can be exercised, that change must be reflected in how an investor assesses its power over an investee. For example, changes to decision-making rights can mean that the relevant activities are no longer directed through voting rights, but instead other agreements, such as contracts, give another party or parties the current ability to direct the relevant activities.

B82 An event can cause an investor to gain or lose power over an investee without the investor being involved in that event. For example, an investor can gain power over an investee because decision-making rights held by another party or parties that previously prevented the investor from controlling an investee have elapsed.

B83 An investor also considers changes affecting its exposure, or rights, to variable returns from its involvement with an investee. For example, an investor that has power over an investee can lose control of an investee if the investor ceases to be entitled to receive returns or to be exposed to obligations, because the investor would fail to satisfy paragraph 7(b) (eg if a contract to receive performance-related fees is terminated).

B84 An investor shall consider whether its assessment that it acts as an agent or a principal has changed. Changes in the overall relationship between the investor and other parties can mean that an investor no longer acts as an agent, even though it has previously acted as an agent, and vice versa. For example, if changes to the rights of the investor, or of other parties, occur, the investor shall reconsider its status as a principal or an agent.

B85 An investor's initial assessment of control or its status as a principal or an agent would not change simply because of a change in market conditions (eg a change in the investee's returns driven by market conditions), unless the change in market conditions changes one or more of the three elements of control listed in paragraph 7 or changes the overall relationship between a principal and an agent.

Accounting requirements

Consolidation procedures

B86 Consolidated financial statements:

(a) combine like items of assets, liabilities, equity, income, expenses and cash flows of the parent with those of its subsidiaries.

(b) offset (eliminate) the carrying amount of the parent's investment in each subsidiary and the parent's portion of equity of each subsidiary (IFRS 3 explains how to account for any related goodwill).

(c) eliminate in full intragroup assets and liabilities, equity, income, expenses and cash flows relating to transactions between entities of the group (profits or losses resulting from intragroup transactions that are recognised in assets, such as inventory and fixed assets, are eliminated in full). Intragroup losses may indicate an impairment that requires recognition in the consolidated financial statements. IAS 12 *Income Taxes* applies to temporary differences that arise from the elimination of profits and losses resulting from intragroup transactions.

Uniform accounting policies

B87 If a member of the group uses accounting policies other than those adopted in the consolidated financial statements for like transactions and events in similar circumstances, appropriate adjustments are made to that group member's financial statements in preparing the consolidated financial statements to ensure conformity with the group's accounting policies.

Measurement

B88 An entity includes the income and expenses of a subsidiary in the consolidated financial statements from the date it gains control until the date when the entity ceases to control the subsidiary. Income and expenses of the subsidiary are based on the amounts of the assets and liabilities recognised in the consolidated financial statements at the acquisition date. For example, depreciation expense recognised in the consolidated statement of comprehensive income after the acquisition date is based on the fair values of the related depreciable assets recognised in the consolidated financial statements at the acquisition date.

Potential voting rights

B89 When potential voting rights, or other derivatives containing potential voting rights, exist, the proportion of profit or loss and changes in equity allocated to the parent and non-controlling interests in preparing consolidated financial statements is determined solely on the basis of existing ownership interests and does not reflect the possible exercise or conversion of potential voting rights and other derivatives, unless paragraph B90 applies.

B90 In some circumstances an entity has, in substance, an existing ownership interest as a result of a transaction that currently gives the entity access to the returns associated with an ownership interest. In such circumstances, the proportion allocated to the parent and non-controlling interests in preparing consolidated financial statements is determined by taking into account the eventual exercise of those potential voting rights and other derivatives that currently give the entity access to the returns.

B91 IFRS 9 does not apply to interests in subsidiaries that are consolidated. When instruments containing potential voting rights in substance currently give access to the returns associated with an ownership interest in a subsidiary, the instruments are not subject to the requirements of IFRS 9. In all other cases, instruments containing potential voting rights in a subsidiary are accounted for in accordance with IFRS 9.

Reporting date

B92 The financial statements of the parent and its subsidiaries used in the preparation of the consolidated financial statements shall have the same reporting date. When the end of the reporting period of the parent is different from that of a subsidiary, the subsidiary prepares, for consolidation purposes, additional financial information as of the same date as the financial statements of the parent to enable the parent to consolidate the financial information of the subsidiary, unless it is impracticable to do so.

B93 If it is impracticable to do so, the parent shall consolidate the financial information of the subsidiary using the most recent financial statements of the subsidiary adjusted for the effects of significant transactions or events that occur between the date of those financial statements and the date of the consolidated financial statements. In any case, the difference between the date of the subsidiary's financial statements and that of the consolidated financial statements shall be no more than three months, and the length of the reporting periods and any difference between the dates of the financial statements shall be the same from period to period.

Non-controlling interests

B94 An entity shall attribute the profit or loss and each component of other comprehensive income to the owners of the parent and to the non-controlling interests. The entity shall also attribute total comprehensive income to the owners of the parent and to the non-controlling interests even if this results in the non-controlling interests having a deficit balance.

B95　If a subsidiary has outstanding cumulative preference shares that are classified as equity and are held by non-controlling interests, the entity shall compute its share of profit or loss after adjusting for the dividends on such shares, whether or not such dividends have been declared.

Changes in the proportion held by non-controlling interests

B96　When the proportion of the equity held by non-controlling interests changes, an entity shall adjust the carrying amounts of the controlling and non-controlling interests to reflect the changes in their relative interests in the subsidiary. The entity shall recognise directly in equity any difference between the amount by which the non-controlling interests are adjusted and the fair value of the consideration paid or received, and attribute it to the owners of the parent.

Loss of control

B97　A parent might lose control of a subsidiary in two or more arrangements (transactions). However, sometimes circumstances indicate that the multiple arrangements should be accounted for as a single transaction. In determining whether to account for the arrangements as a single transaction, a parent shall consider all the terms and conditions of the arrangements and their economic effects. One or more of the following indicate that the parent should account for the multiple arrangements as a single transaction:

(a)　They are entered into at the same time or in contemplation of each other.

(b)　They form a single transaction designed to achieve an overall commercial effect.

(c)　The occurrence of one arrangement is dependent on the occurrence of at least one other arrangement.

(d)　One arrangement considered on its own is not economically justified, but it is economically justified when considered together with other arrangements. An example is when a disposal of shares is priced below market and is compensated for by a subsequent disposal priced above market.

B98　If a parent loses control of a subsidiary, it shall:

(a)　derecognise:

(i)　the assets (including any goodwill) and liabilities of the subsidiary at their carrying amounts at the date when control is lost; and

(ii)　the carrying amount of any non-controlling interests in the former subsidiary at the date when control is lost (including any components of other comprehensive income attributable to them).

(b)　recognise:

(i)　the fair value of the consideration received, if any, from the transaction, event or circumstances that resulted in the loss of control;

      (ii)   if the transaction, event or circumstances that resulted in the loss of control involves a distribution of shares of the subsidiary to owners in their capacity as owners, that distribution; and

      (iii)   any investment retained in the former subsidiary at its fair value at the date when control is lost.

  (c)   reclassify to profit or loss, or transfer directly to retained earnings if required by other IFRSs, the amounts recognised in other comprehensive income in relation to the subsidiary on the basis described in paragraph B99.

  (d)   recognise any resulting difference as a gain or loss in profit or loss attributable to the parent.

B99   If a parent loses control of a subsidiary, the parent shall account for all amounts previously recognised in other comprehensive income in relation to that subsidiary on the same basis as would be required if the parent had directly disposed of the related assets or liabilities. Therefore, if a gain or loss previously recognised in other comprehensive income would be reclassified to profit or loss on the disposal of the related assets or liabilities, the parent shall reclassify the gain or loss from equity to profit or loss (as a reclassification adjustment) when it loses control of the subsidiary. If a revaluation surplus previously recognised in other comprehensive income would be transferred directly to retained earnings on the disposal of the asset, the parent shall transfer the revaluation surplus directly to retained earnings when it loses control of the subsidiary.

Appendix C
Effective date and transition

This appendix is an integral part of the IFRS and has the same authority as the other parts of the IFRS.

Effective date

C1 An entity shall apply this IFRS for annual periods beginning on or after 1 January 2013. Earlier application is permitted. If an entity applies this IFRS earlier, it shall disclose that fact and apply IFRS 11, IFRS 12, IAS 27 *Separate Financial Statements* and IAS 28 (as amended in 2011) at the same time.

Transition

C2 An entity shall apply this IFRS retrospectively, in accordance with IAS 8 *Accounting Policies, Changes in Accounting Estimates and Errors*, except as specified in paragraphs C3–C6.

C3 When applying this IFRS for the first time, an entity is not required to make adjustments to the accounting for its involvement with either:

    (a) entities that were previously consolidated in accordance with IAS 27 *Consolidated and Separate Financial Statements* and SIC-12 *Consolidation—Special Purpose Entities* and, in accordance with this IFRS, continue to be consolidated; or

    (b) entities that were previously unconsolidated in accordance with IAS 27 and SIC-12 and, in accordance with this IFRS, continue not to be consolidated.

C4 When application of this IFRS for the first time results in an investor consolidating an investee that was not consolidated in accordance with IAS 27 and SIC-12 the investor shall:

    (a) if the investee is a business (as defined in IFRS 3), measure the assets, liabilities and non-controlling interests in that previously unconsolidated investee on the date of initial application as if that investee had been consolidated (and thus applied acquisition accounting in accordance with IFRS 3) from the date when the investor obtained control of that investee on the basis of the requirements of this IFRS.

    (b) if the investee is not a business (as defined in IFRS 3), measure the assets, liabilities and non-controlling interests in that previously unconsolidated investee on the date of initial application as if that investee had been consolidated (applying the acquisition method as described in IFRS 3 without recognising any goodwill for the investee) from the date when the investor obtained control of that investee on the basis of the requirements of this IFRS. Any difference between the amount of assets, liabilities and non-controlling interests recognised and the previous carrying amount of the investor's involvement with the investee shall be recognised as a corresponding adjustment to the opening balance of equity.

(c)   if measuring an investee's assets, liabilities and non-controlling interest in accordance with (a) or (b) is impracticable (as defined in IAS 8), the investor shall:

    (i)   if the investee is a business, apply the requirements of IFRS 3. The deemed acquisition date shall be the beginning of the earliest period for which application of IFRS 3 is practicable, which may be the current period.

    (ii)   if the investee is not a business, apply the acquisition method as described in IFRS 3 without recognising any goodwill for the investee as of the deemed acquisition date. The deemed acquisition date shall be the beginning of the earliest period for which the application of this paragraph is practicable, which may be the current period.

The investor shall recognise any difference between the amount of assets, liabilities and non-controlling interests recognised at the deemed acquisition date and any previously recognised amounts from its involvement as an adjustment to equity for that period. In addition, the investor shall provide comparative information and disclosures in accordance with IAS 8.

C5   When application of this IFRS for the first time results in an investor no longer consolidating an investee that was consolidated in accordance with IAS 27 (as amended in 2008) and SIC-12, the investor shall measure its retained interest in the investee on the date of initial application at the amount at which it would have been measured if the requirements of this IFRS had been effective when the investor became involved with, or lost control of, the investee. If measurement of the retained interest is impracticable (as defined in IAS 8), the investor shall apply the requirements of this IFRS for accounting for a loss of control at the beginning of the earliest period for which application of this IFRS is practicable, which may be the current period. The investor shall recognise any difference between the previously recognised amount of the assets, liabilities and non-controlling interest and the carrying amount of the investor's involvement with the investee as an adjustment to equity for that period. In addition, the investor shall provide comparative information and disclosures in accordance with IAS 8.

C6   Paragraphs 23, 25, B94 and B96–B99 were amendments to IAS 27 made in 2008 that were carried forward into IFRS 10. Except when an entity applies paragraph C3, the entity shall apply the requirements in those paragraphs as follows:

(a)   An entity shall not restate any profit or loss attribution for reporting periods before it applied the amendment in paragraph B94 for the first time.

(b)   The requirements in paragraphs 23 and B96 for accounting for changes in ownership interests in a subsidiary after control is obtained do not apply to changes that occurred before an entity applied these amendments for the first time.

(c)   An entity shall not restate the carrying amount of an investment in a former subsidiary if control was lost before it applied the amendments in paragraphs 25 and B97–B99 for the first time. In addition, an entity shall not recalculate any gain or loss on the loss of control of a subsidiary that occurred before the amendments in paragraphs 25 and B97–B99 were applied for the first time.

References to IFRS 9

C7   If an entity applies this IFRS but does not yet apply IFRS 9, any reference in this IFRS to IFRS 9 shall be read as a reference to IAS 39 *Financial Instruments: Recognition and Measurement*.

Withdrawal of other IFRSs

C8   This IFRS supersedes the requirements relating to consolidated financial statements in IAS 27 (as amended in 2008).

C9   This IFRS also supersedes SIC-12 *Consolidation—Special Purpose Entities*.

Appendix D
Amendments to other IFRSs

This appendix sets out the amendments to other IFRSs that are a consequence of the Board issuing this IFRS. An entity shall apply the amendments for annual periods beginning on or after 1 January 2013. If an entity applies this IFRS for an earlier period, it shall apply these amendments for that earlier period. Amended paragraphs are shown with new text underlined and deleted text struck through.

* * * * *

The amendments contained in this appendix when this IFRS was issued in 2011 have been incorporated into the relevant IFRSs published in this volume.

International Financial Reporting Standard 11

Joint Arrangements

In April 2001 the International Accounting Standards Board (IASB) adopted IAS 31 *Financial Reporting of Interests in Joint Ventures*, which had originally been issued by the International Accounting Standards Committee in December 1990.

In December 2003 the IASB amended and renamed IAS 31 with a new title—*Interests in Joint Ventures*. This amendment was done in conjunction with amendments to IAS 27 *Consolidated Financial Statements and Accounting for Investments in Subsidiaries* and IAS 28 *Accounting for Investments in Associates*.

In May 2011 the IASB issued IFRS 11 *Joint Arrangements* to replace IAS 31. IFRS 12 *Disclosure of Interests in Other Entities*, also issued in May 2011, replaced the disclosure requirements in IAS 31. IFRS 10 incorporated the guidance contained in a related Interpretation (SIC-13 *Jointly Controlled Entities-Non-Monetary Contributions by Venturers*).

CONTENTS

FOR THE ACCOMPANYING DOCUMENTS LISTED BELOW, SEE PART B OF THIS EDITION

APPROVAL BY THE BOARD OF IFRS 11 ISSUED IN MAY 2011

BASIS FOR CONCLUSION

APPENDIX
Amendments to the Basis for Conclusions on other IFRSs

ILLUSTRATIVE EXAMPLES

International Financial Reporting Standard 11 *Joint Arrangements* (IFRS 11) is set out in paragraphs 1–27 and Appendices A–D. All the paragraphs have equal authority. Paragraphs in **bold type** state the main principles. Terms defined in Appendix A are in italics the first time they appear in the Standard. Definitions of other terms are given in the Glossary for International Financial Reporting Standards. IFRS 11 should be read in the context of its objective and the Basis for Conclusions, the *Preface to International Financial Reporting Standards* and the *Conceptual Framework for Financial Reporting*. IAS 8 *Accounting Policies, Changes in Accounting Estimates and Errors* provides a basis for selecting and applying accounting policies in the absence of explicit guidance.

Introduction

Overview

IN1 International Financial Reporting Standard 11 *Joint Arrangements* establishes principles for financial reporting by parties to a joint arrangement.

IN2 The IFRS supersedes IAS 31 *Interests in Joint Ventures* and SIC-13 *Jointly Controlled Entities—Non-Monetary Contributions by Venturers* and is effective for annual periods beginning on or after 1 January 2013. Earlier application is permitted.

Reasons for issuing the IFRS

IN3 The IFRS is concerned principally with addressing two aspects of IAS 31: first, that the structure of the arrangement was the only determinant of the accounting and, second, that an entity had a choice of accounting treatment for interests in jointly controlled entities.

IN4 IFRS 11 improves on IAS 31 by establishing principles that are applicable to the accounting for all joint arrangements.

Main features of the IFRS

IN5 The IFRS requires a party to a joint arrangement to determine the type of joint arrangement in which it is involved by assessing its rights and obligations arising from the arrangement.

General requirements

IN6 The IFRS is to be applied by all entities that are a party to a joint arrangement. A joint arrangement is an arrangement of which two or more parties have joint control. The IFRS defines joint control as the contractually agreed sharing of control of an arrangement, which exists only when decisions about the relevant activities (ie activities that significantly affect the returns of the arrangement) require the unanimous consent of the parties sharing control.

IN7 The IFRS classifies joint arrangements into two types—joint operations and joint ventures. A joint operation is a joint arrangement whereby the parties that have joint control of the arrangement (ie joint operators) have rights to the assets, and obligations for the liabilities, relating to the arrangement. A joint venture is a joint arrangement whereby the parties that have joint control of the arrangement (ie joint venturers) have rights to the net assets of the arrangement.

IN8 An entity determines the type of joint arrangement in which it is involved by considering its rights and obligations. An entity assesses its rights and obligations by considering the structure and legal form of the arrangement, the contractual terms agreed to by the parties to the arrangement and, when relevant, other facts and circumstances.

IN9 The IFRS requires a joint operator to recognise and measure the assets and liabilities (and recognise the related revenues and expenses) in relation to its interest in the arrangement in accordance with relevant IFRSs applicable to the particular assets, liabilities, revenues and expenses.

IN10 The IFRS requires a joint venturer to recognise an investment and to account for that investment using the equity method in accordance with IAS 28 *Investments in Associates and Joint Ventures*, unless the entity is exempted from applying the equity method as specified in that standard.

IN11 The disclosure requirements for parties with joint control of a joint arrangement are specified in IFRS 12 *Disclosure of Interests in Other Entities*.

International Financial Reporting Standard 11
Joint Arrangements

Objective

1   The objective of this IFRS is to establish principles for financial reporting by entities that have an interest in arrangements that are controlled jointly (ie *joint arrangements*).

Meeting the objective

2   To meet the objective in paragraph 1, this IFRS defines *joint control* and requires an entity that is a *party to a joint arrangement* to determine the type of joint arrangement in which it is involved by assessing its rights and obligations and to account for those rights and obligations in accordance with that type of joint arrangement.

Scope

3   This IFRS shall be applied by all entities that are a party to a joint arrangement.

Joint arrangements

4   A joint arrangement is an arrangement of which two or more parties have joint control.

5   A joint arrangement has the following characteristics:

(a)   The parties are bound by a contractual arrangement (see paragraphs B2–B4).

(b)   The contractual arrangement gives two or more of those parties joint control of the arrangement (see paragraphs 7–13).

6   A joint arrangement is either a *joint operation* or a *joint venture*.

Joint control

7   Joint control is the contractually agreed sharing of control of an arrangement, which exists only when decisions about the relevant activities require the unanimous consent of the parties sharing control.

8   An entity that is a party to an arrangement shall assess whether the contractual arrangement gives all the parties, or a group of the parties, control of the arrangement collectively. All the parties, or a group of the parties, control the arrangement collectively when they must act together to direct the activities that significantly affect the returns of the arrangement (ie the relevant activities).

9   Once it has been determined that all the parties, or a group of the parties, control the arrangement collectively, joint control exists only when decisions about the relevant activities require the unanimous consent of the parties that control the arrangement collectively.

10   In a joint arrangement, no single party controls the arrangement on its own. A party with joint control of an arrangement can prevent any of the other parties, or a group of the parties, from controlling the arrangement.

11   An arrangement can be a joint arrangement even though not all of its parties have joint control of the arrangement. This IFRS distinguishes between parties that have joint control of a joint arrangement (*joint operators* or *joint venturers*) and parties that participate in, but do not have joint control of, a joint arrangement.

12   An entity will need to apply judgement when assessing whether all the parties, or a group of the parties, have joint control of an arrangement. An entity shall make this assessment by considering all facts and circumstances (see paragraphs B5–B11).

13   If facts and circumstances change, an entity shall reassess whether it still has joint control of the arrangement.

Types of joint arrangement

14   **An entity shall determine the type of joint arrangement in which it is involved. The classification of a joint arrangement as a joint operation or a joint venture depends upon the rights and obligations of the parties to the arrangement.**

15   **A joint operation is a joint arrangement whereby the parties that have joint control of the arrangement have rights to the assets, and obligations for the liabilities, relating to the arrangement. Those parties are called joint operators.**

16   **A joint venture is a joint arrangement whereby the parties that have joint control of the arrangement have rights to the net assets of the arrangement. Those parties are called joint venturers.**

17   An entity applies judgement when assessing whether a joint arrangement is a joint operation or a joint venture. An entity shall determine the type of joint arrangement in which it is involved by considering its rights and obligations arising from the arrangement. An entity assesses its rights and obligations by considering the structure and legal form of the arrangement, the terms agreed by the parties in the contractual arrangement and, when relevant, other facts and circumstances (see paragraphs B12–B33).

18   Sometimes the parties are bound by a framework agreement that sets up the general contractual terms for undertaking one or more activities. The framework agreement might set out that the parties establish different joint arrangements to deal with specific activities that form part of the agreement. Even though those joint arrangements are related to the same framework agreement, their type might be different if the parties' rights and obligations differ when undertaking the different activities dealt with in the framework agreement. Consequently, joint operations and joint ventures can coexist when the parties undertake different activities that form part of the same framework agreement.

19   If facts and circumstances change, an entity shall reassess whether the type of joint arrangement in which it is involved has changed.

Financial statements of parties to a joint arrangement

Joint operations

20　A joint operator shall recognise in relation to its interest in a joint operation:

    (a)　its assets, including its share of any assets held jointly;

    (b)　its liabilities, including its share of any liabilities incurred jointly;

    (c)　its revenue from the sale of its share of the output arising from the joint operation;

    (d)　its share of the revenue from the sale of the output by the joint operation; and

    (e)　its expenses, including its share of any expenses incurred jointly.

21　A joint operator shall account for the assets, liabilities, revenues and expenses relating to its interest in a joint operation in accordance with the IFRSs applicable to the particular assets, liabilities, revenues and expenses.

22　The accounting for transactions such as the sale, contribution or purchase of assets between an entity and a joint operation in which it is a joint operator is specified in paragraphs B34–B37.

23　A party that participates in, but does not have joint control of, a joint operation shall also account for its interest in the arrangement in accordance with paragraphs 20–22 if that party has rights to the assets, and obligations for the liabilities, relating to the joint operation. If a party that participates in, but does not have joint control of, a joint operation does not have rights to the assets, and obligations for the liabilities, relating to that joint operation, it shall account for its interest in the joint operation in accordance with the IFRSs applicable to that interest.

Joint ventures

24　**A joint venturer shall recognise its interest in a joint venture as an investment and shall account for that investment using the equity method in accordance with IAS 28** *Investments in Associates and Joint Ventures* **unless the entity is exempted from applying the equity method as specified in that standard.**

25　A party that participates in, but does not have joint control of, a joint venture shall account for its interest in the arrangement in accordance with IFRS 9 *Financial Instruments*, unless it has significant influence over the joint venture, in which case it shall account for it in accordance with IAS 28 (as amended in 2011).

Separate financial statements

26 In its separate financial statements, a joint operator or joint venturer shall account for its interest in:

 (a) a joint operation in accordance with paragraphs 20–22;

 (b) a joint venture in accordance with paragraph 10 of IAS 27 *Separate Financial Statements*.

27 In its separate financial statements, a party that participates in, but does not have joint control of, a joint arrangement shall account for its interest in:

 (a) a joint operation in accordance with paragraph 23;

 (b) a joint venture in accordance with IFRS 9, unless the entity has significant influence over the joint venture, in which case it shall apply paragraph 10 of IAS 27 (as amended in 2011).

Appendix A
Defined terms

This appendix is an integral part of the IFRS.

joint arrangement	An arrangement of which two or more parties have **joint control**.
joint control	The contractually agreed sharing of control of an arrangement, which exists only when decisions about the relevant activities require the unanimous consent of the parties sharing control.
joint operation	A **joint arrangement** whereby the parties that have **joint control** of the arrangement have rights to the assets, and obligations for the liabilities, relating to the arrangement.
joint operator	A party to a **joint operation** that has **joint control** of that joint operation.
joint venture	A **joint arrangement** whereby the parties that have **joint control** of the arrangement have rights to the net assets of the arrangement.
joint venturer	A party to a **joint venture** that has **joint control** of that joint venture.
party to a joint arrangement	An entity that participates in a **joint arrangement**, regardless of whether that entity has **joint control** of the arrangement.
separate vehicle	A separately identifiable financial structure, including separate legal entities or entities recognised by statute, regardless of whether those entities have a legal personality.

The following terms are defined in IAS 27 (as amended in 2011), IAS 28 (as amended in 2011) or IFRS 10 *Consolidated Financial Statements* and are used in this IFRS with the meanings specified in those IFRSs:

- control of an investee

- equity method

- power

- protective rights

- relevant activities

- separate financial statements

- significant influence.

Appendix B
Application guidance

This appendix is an integral part of the IFRS. It describes the application of paragraphs 1–27 and has the same authority as the other parts of the IFRS.

B1   The examples in this appendix portray hypothetical situations. Although some aspects of the examples may be present in actual fact patterns, all relevant facts and circumstances of a particular fact pattern would need to be evaluated when applying IFRS 11.

Joint arrangements

Contractual arrangement (paragraph 5)

B2   Contractual arrangements can be evidenced in several ways. An enforceable contractual arrangement is often, but not always, in writing, usually in the form of a contract or documented discussions between the parties. Statutory mechanisms can also create enforceable arrangements, either on their own or in conjunction with contracts between the parties.

B3   When joint arrangements are structured through a *separate vehicle* (see paragraphs B19–B33), the contractual arrangement, or some aspects of the contractual arrangement, will in some cases be incorporated in the articles, charter or by-laws of the separate vehicle.

B4   The contractual arrangement sets out the terms upon which the parties participate in the activity that is the subject of the arrangement. The contractual arrangement generally deals with such matters as:

(a)   the purpose, activity and duration of the joint arrangement.

(b)   how the members of the board of directors, or equivalent governing body, of the joint arrangement, are appointed.

(c)   the decision-making process: the matters requiring decisions from the parties, the voting rights of the parties and the required level of support for those matters. The decision-making process reflected in the contractual arrangement establishes joint control of the arrangement (see paragraphs B5–B11).

(d)   the capital or other contributions required of the parties.

(e)   how the parties share assets, liabilities, revenues, expenses or profit or loss relating to the joint arrangement.

Joint control (paragraphs 7–13)

B5   In assessing whether an entity has joint control of an arrangement, an entity shall assess first whether all the parties, or a group of the parties, control the arrangement. IFRS 10 defines control and shall be used to determine whether all the parties, or a group of the parties, are exposed, or have rights, to variable returns from their involvement with the arrangement and have the ability to affect those returns through their power over the arrangement. When all the parties, or a group of the parties, considered collectively, are able to direct the activities that significantly affect the returns of the arrangement (ie the relevant activities), the parties control the arrangement collectively.

B6 After concluding that all the parties, or a group of the parties, control the arrangement collectively, an entity shall assess whether it has joint control of the arrangement. Joint control exists only when decisions about the relevant activities require the unanimous consent of the parties that collectively control the arrangement. Assessing whether the arrangement is jointly controlled by all of its parties or by a group of the parties, or controlled by one of its parties alone, can require judgement.

B7 Sometimes the decision-making process that is agreed upon by the parties in their contractual arrangement implicitly leads to joint control. For example, assume two parties establish an arrangement in which each has 50 per cent of the voting rights and the contractual arrangement between them specifies that at least 51 per cent of the voting rights are required to make decisions about the relevant activities. In this case, the parties have implicitly agreed that they have joint control of the arrangement because decisions about the relevant activities cannot be made without both parties agreeing.

B8 In other circumstances, the contractual arrangement requires a minimum proportion of the voting rights to make decisions about the relevant activities. When that minimum required proportion of the voting rights can be achieved by more than one combination of the parties agreeing together, that arrangement is not a joint arrangement unless the contractual arrangement specifies which parties (or combination of parties) are required to agree unanimously to decisions about the relevant activities of the arrangement.

Application examples

Example 1

Assume that three parties establish an arrangement: A has 50 per cent of the voting rights in the arrangement, B has 30 per cent and C has 20 per cent. The contractual arrangement between A, B and C specifies that at least 75 per cent of the voting rights are required to make decisions about the relevant activities of the arrangement. Even though A can block any decision, it does not control the arrangement because it needs the agreement of B. The terms of their contractual arrangement requiring at least 75 per cent of the voting rights to make decisions about the relevant activities imply that A and B have joint control of the arrangement because decisions about the relevant activities of the arrangement cannot be made without both A and B agreeing.

continued...

...continued
Application examples

Example 2

Assume an arrangement has three parties: A has 50 per cent of the voting rights in the arrangement and B and C each have 25 per cent. The contractual arrangement between A, B and C specifies that at least 75 per cent of the voting rights are required to make decisions about the relevant activities of the arrangement. Even though A can block any decision, it does not control the arrangement because it needs the agreement of either B or C. In this example, A, B and C collectively control the arrangement. However, there is more than one combination of parties that can agree to reach 75 per cent of the voting rights (ie either A and B or A and C). In such a situation, to be a joint arrangement the contractual arrangement between the parties would need to specify which combination of the parties is required to agree unanimously to decisions about the relevant activities of the arrangement.

Example 3

Assume an arrangement in which A and B each have 35 per cent of the voting rights in the arrangement with the remaining 30 per cent being widely dispersed. Decisions about the relevant activities require approval by a majority of the voting rights. A and B have joint control of the arrangement only if the contractual arrangement specifies that decisions about the relevant activities of the arrangement require both A and B agreeing.

B9   The requirement for unanimous consent means that any party with joint control of the arrangement can prevent any of the other parties, or a group of the parties, from making unilateral decisions (about the relevant activities) without its consent. If the requirement for unanimous consent relates only to decisions that give a party protective rights and not to decisions about the relevant activities of an arrangement, that party is not a party with joint control of the arrangement.

B10　A contractual arrangement might include clauses on the resolution of disputes, such as arbitration. These provisions may allow for decisions to be made in the absence of unanimous consent among the parties that have joint control. The existence of such provisions does not prevent the arrangement from being jointly controlled and, consequently, from being a joint arrangement.

Assessing joint control

Does the contractual arrangement give all the parties, or a group of the parties, control of the arrangement collectively? —No→ Outside the scope of IFRS 11

Yes

Do decisions about the relevant activities require the unanimous consent of all the parties, or of a group of the parties, that collectively control the arrangement? —No→ Outside the scope of IFRS 11

Yes

The arrangement is jointly controlled: the arrangement is a joint arrangement.

B11　When an arrangement is outside the scope of IFRS 11, an entity accounts for its interest in the arrangement in accordance with relevant IFRSs, such as IFRS 10, IAS 28 (as amended in 2011) or IFRS 9.

Types of joint arrangement (paragraphs 14–19)

B12　Joint arrangements are established for a variety of purposes (eg as a way for parties to share costs and risks, or as a way to provide the parties with access to new technology or new markets), and can be established using different structures and legal forms.

B13　Some arrangements do not require the activity that is the subject of the arrangement to be undertaken in a separate vehicle. However, other arrangements involve the establishment of a separate vehicle.

B14　The classification of joint arrangements required by this IFRS depends upon the parties' rights and obligations arising from the arrangement in the normal course of business. This IFRS classifies joint arrangements as either joint operations or joint ventures. When an entity has rights to the assets, and obligations for the liabilities, relating to the arrangement, the arrangement is a joint operation. When an entity has rights to the net assets of the arrangement, the arrangement is a joint venture. Paragraphs B16–B33 set out the assessment an entity carries out to determine whether it has an interest in a joint operation or an interest in a joint venture.

Classification of a joint arrangement

B15   As stated in paragraph B14, the classification of joint arrangements requires the parties to assess their rights and obligations arising from the arrangement. When making that assessment, an entity shall consider the following:

     (a)   the structure of the joint arrangement (see paragraphs B16–B21).

     (b)   when the joint arrangement is structured through a separate vehicle:

         (i)   the legal form of the separate vehicle (see paragraphs B22–B24);

         (ii)   the terms of the contractual arrangement (see paragraphs B25–B28); and

         (iii)   when relevant, other facts and circumstances (see paragraphs B29–B33).

Structure of the joint arrangement

Joint arrangements not structured through a separate vehicle

B16   A joint arrangement that is not structured through a separate vehicle is a joint operation. In such cases, the contractual arrangement establishes the parties' rights to the assets, and obligations for the liabilities, relating to the arrangement, and the parties' rights to the corresponding revenues and obligations for the corresponding expenses.

B17   The contractual arrangement often describes the nature of the activities that are the subject of the arrangement and how the parties intend to undertake those activities together. For example, the parties to a joint arrangement could agree to manufacture a product together, with each party being responsible for a specific task and each using its own assets and incurring its own liabilities. The contractual arrangement could also specify how the revenues and expenses that are common to the parties are to be shared among them. In such a case, each joint operator recognises in its financial statements the assets and liabilities used for the specific task, and recognises its share of the revenues and expenses in accordance with the contractual arrangement.

B18   In other cases, the parties to a joint arrangement might agree, for example, to share and operate an asset together. In such a case, the contractual arrangement establishes the parties' rights to the asset that is operated jointly, and how output or revenue from the asset and operating costs are shared among the parties. Each joint operator accounts for its share of the joint asset and its agreed share of any liabilities, and recognises its share of the output, revenues and expenses in accordance with the contractual arrangement.

Joint arrangements structured through a separate vehicle

B19   A joint arrangement in which the assets and liabilities relating to the arrangement are held in a separate vehicle can be either a joint venture or a joint operation.

B20   Whether a party is a joint operator or a joint venturer depends on the party's rights to the assets, and obligations for the liabilities, relating to the arrangement that are held in the separate vehicle.

B21   As stated in paragraph B15, when the parties have structured a joint arrangement in a separate vehicle, the parties need to assess whether the legal form of the separate vehicle, the terms of the contractual arrangement and, when relevant, any other facts and circumstances give them:

(a)   rights to the assets, and obligations for the liabilities, relating to the arrangement (ie the arrangement is a joint operation); or

(b)   rights to the net assets of the arrangement (ie the arrangement is a joint venture).

Classification of a joint arrangement: assessment of the parties' rights and obligations arising from the arrangement

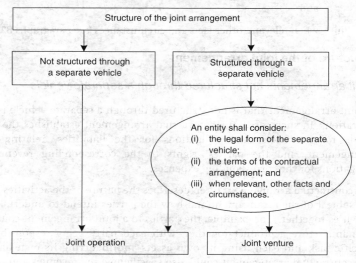

The legal form of the separate vehicle

B22   The legal form of the separate vehicle is relevant when assessing the type of joint arrangement. The legal form assists in the initial assessment of the parties' rights to the assets and obligations for the liabilities held in the separate vehicle, such as whether the parties have interests in the assets held in the separate vehicle and whether they are liable for the liabilities held in the separate vehicle.

B23   For example, the parties might conduct the joint arrangement through a separate vehicle, whose legal form causes the separate vehicle to be considered in its own right (ie the assets and liabilities held in the separate vehicle are the assets and liabilities of the separate vehicle and not the assets and liabilities of the parties). In such a case, the assessment of the rights and obligations conferred upon the parties by the legal form of the separate vehicle indicates that the arrangement is a joint venture. However, the terms agreed by the parties in their contractual arrangement (see paragraphs B25–B28) and, when relevant, other facts and circumstances (see paragraphs B29–B33) can override the assessment of the rights and obligations conferred upon the parties by the legal form of the separate vehicle.

B24   The assessment of the rights and obligations conferred upon the parties by the legal form of the separate vehicle is sufficient to conclude that the arrangement is a joint operation only if the parties conduct the joint arrangement in a separate vehicle whose legal form does not confer separation between the parties and the separate vehicle (ie the assets and liabilities held in the separate vehicle are the parties' assets and liabilities).

Assessing the terms of the contractual arrangement

B25 In many cases, the rights and obligations agreed to by the parties in their contractual arrangements are consistent, or do not conflict, with the rights and obligations conferred on the parties by the legal form of the separate vehicle in which the arrangement has been structured.

B26 In other cases, the parties use the contractual arrangement to reverse or modify the rights and obligations conferred by the legal form of the separate vehicle in which the arrangement has been structured.

Application example

Example 4

Assume that two parties structure a joint arrangement in an incorporated entity. Each party has a 50 per cent ownership interest in the incorporated entity. The incorporation enables the separation of the entity from its owners and as a consequence the assets and liabilities held in the entity are the assets and liabilities of the incorporated entity. In such a case, the assessment of the rights and obligations conferred upon the parties by the legal form of the separate vehicle indicates that the parties have rights to the net assets of the arrangement.

However, the parties modify the features of the corporation through their contractual arrangement so that each has an interest in the assets of the incorporated entity and each is liable for the liabilities of the incorporated entity in a specified proportion. Such contractual modifications to the features of a corporation can cause an arrangement to be a joint operation.

B27 The following table compares common terms in contractual arrangements of parties to a joint operation and common terms in contractual arrangements of parties to a joint venture. The examples of the contractual terms provided in the following table are not exhaustive.

Assessing the terms of the contractual arrangement		
	Joint operation	**Joint venture**
The terms of the contractual arrangement	The contractual arrangement provides the parties to the joint arrangement with rights to the assets, and obligations for the liabilities, relating to the arrangement.	The contractual arrangement provides the parties to the joint arrangement with rights to the net assets of the arrangement (ie it is the separate vehicle, not the parties, that has rights to the assets, and obligations for the liabilities, relating to the arrangement).
		continued...

...continued		
Assessing the terms of the contractual arrangement		
	Joint operation	**Joint venture**
Rights to assets	The contractual arrangement establishes that the parties to the joint arrangement share all interests (eg rights, title or ownership) in the assets relating to the arrangement in a specified proportion (eg in proportion to the parties' ownership interest in the arrangement or in proportion to the activity carried out through the arrangement that is directly attributed to them).	The contractual arrangement establishes that the assets brought into the arrangement or subsequently acquired by the joint arrangement are the arrangement's assets. The parties have no interests (ie no rights, title or ownership) in the assets of the arrangement.
Obligations for liabilities	The contractual arrangement establishes that the parties to the joint arrangement share all liabilities, obligations, costs and expenses in a specified proportion (eg in proportion to the parties' ownership interest in the arrangement or in proportion to the activity carried out through the arrangement that is directly attributed to them).	The contractual arrangement establishes that the joint arrangement is liable for the debts and obligations of the arrangement.
		The contractual arrangement establishes that the parties to the joint arrangement are liable to the arrangement only to the extent of their respective investments in the arrangement or to their respective obligations to contribute any unpaid or additional capital to the arrangement, or both.
	The contractual arrangement establishes that the parties to the joint arrangement are liable for claims raised by third parties.	The contractual arrangement states that creditors of the joint arrangement do not have rights of recourse against any party with respect to debts or obligations of the arrangement.
		continued...

...continued		
Assessing the terms of the contractual arrangement		
	Joint operation	**Joint venture**
Revenues, expenses, profit or loss	The contractual arrangement establishes the allocation of revenues and expenses on the basis of the relative performance of each party to the joint arrangement. For example, the contractual arrangement might establish that revenues and expenses are allocated on the basis of the capacity that each party uses in a plant operated jointly, which could differ from their ownership interest in the joint arrangement. In other instances, the parties might have agreed to share the profit or loss relating to the arrangement on the basis of a specified proportion such as the parties' ownership interest in the arrangement. This would not prevent the arrangement from being a joint operation if the parties have rights to the assets, and obligations for the liabilities, relating to the arrangement.	The contractual arrangement establishes each party's share in the profit or loss relating to the activities of the arrangement.
Guarantees	The parties to joint arrangements are often required to provide guarantees to third parties that, for example, receive a service from, or provide financing to, the joint arrangement. The provision of such guarantees, or the commitment by the parties to provide them, does not, by itself, determine that the joint arrangement is a joint operation. The feature that determines whether the joint arrangement is a joint operation or a joint venture is whether the parties have obligations for the liabilities relating to the arrangement (for some of which the parties might or might not have provided a guarantee).	

B28   When the contractual arrangement specifies that the parties have rights to the assets, and obligations for the liabilities, relating to the arrangement, they are parties to a joint operation and do not need to consider other facts and circumstances (paragraphs B29–B33) for the purposes of classifying the joint arrangement.

Assessing other facts and circumstances

B29   When the terms of the contractual arrangement do not specify that the parties have rights to the assets, and obligations for the liabilities, relating to the arrangement, the parties shall consider other facts and circumstances to assess whether the arrangement is a joint operation or a joint venture.

B30   A joint arrangement might be structured in a separate vehicle whose legal form confers separation between the parties and the separate vehicle. The contractual terms agreed among the parties might not specify the parties' rights to the assets and obligations for the liabilities, yet consideration of other facts and circumstances can lead to such an arrangement being classified as a joint operation. This will be the case when other facts and circumstances give the parties rights to the assets, and obligations for the liabilities, relating to the arrangement.

B31   When the activities of an arrangement are primarily designed for the provision of output to the parties, this indicates that the parties have rights to substantially all the economic benefits of the assets of the arrangement. The parties to such arrangements often ensure their access to the outputs provided by the arrangement by preventing the arrangement from selling output to third parties.

B32   The effect of an arrangement with such a design and purpose is that the liabilities incurred by the arrangement are, in substance, satisfied by the cash flows received from the parties through their purchases of the output. When the parties are substantially the only source of cash flows contributing to the continuity of the operations of the arrangement, this indicates that the parties have an obligation for the liabilities relating to the arrangement.

Application example

Example 5

Assume that two parties structure a joint arrangement in an incorporated entity (entity C) in which each party has a 50 per cent ownership interest. The purpose of the arrangement is to manufacture materials required by the parties for their own, individual manufacturing processes. The arrangement ensures that the parties operate the facility that produces the materials to the quantity and quality specifications of the parties.

The legal form of entity C (an incorporated entity) through which the activities are conducted initially indicates that the assets and liabilities held in entity C are the assets and liabilities of entity C. The contractual arrangement between the parties does not specify that the parties have rights to the assets or obligations for the liabilities of entity C. Accordingly, the legal form of entity C and the terms of the contractual arrangement indicate that the arrangement is a joint venture.

However, the parties also consider the following aspects of the arrangement:

- The parties agreed to purchase all the output produced by entity C in a ratio of 50:50. Entity C cannot sell any of the output to third parties, unless this is approved by the two parties to the arrangement. Because the purpose of the arrangement is to provide the parties with output they require, such sales to third parties are expected to be uncommon and not material.

- The price of the output sold to the parties is set by both parties at a level that is designed to cover the costs of production and administrative expenses incurred by entity C. On the basis of this operating model, the arrangement is intended to operate at a break-even level.

From the fact pattern above, the following facts and circumstances are relevant:

- The obligation of the parties to purchase all the output produced by entity C reflects the exclusive dependence of entity C upon the parties for the generation of cash flows and, thus, the parties have an obligation to fund the settlement of the liabilities of entity C.

- The fact that the parties have rights to all the output produced by entity C means that the parties are consuming, and therefore have rights to, all the economic benefits of the assets of entity C.

These facts and circumstances indicate that the arrangement is a joint operation. The conclusion about the classification of the joint arrangement in these circumstances would not change if, instead of the parties using their share of the output themselves in a subsequent manufacturing process, the parties sold their share of the output to third parties.

If the parties changed the terms of the contractual arrangement so that the arrangement was able to sell output to third parties, this would result in entity C assuming demand, inventory and credit risks. In that scenario, such a change in the facts and circumstances would require reassessment of the classification of the joint arrangement. Such facts and circumstances would indicate that the arrangement is a joint venture.

B33 The following flow chart reflects the assessment an entity follows to classify an arrangement when the joint arrangement is structured through a separate vehicle:

Classification of a joint arrangement structured through a separate vehicle

Legal form of the separate vehicle	Does the legal form of the separate vehicle give the parties rights to the assets, and obligations for the liabilities, relating to the arrangement?	Yes →
	↓ No	
Terms of the contractual arrangement	Do the terms of the contractual arrangement specify that the parties have rights to the assets, and obligations for the liabilities, relating to the arrangement?	Yes → Joint operation
	↓ No	
Other facts and circumstances	Have the parties designed the arrangement so that (a) its activities primarily aim to provide the parties with an output (ie the parties have rights to substantially all of the economic benefits of the assets held in the separate vehicle) and (b) it depends on the parties on a continuous basis for settling the liabilities relating to the activity conducted through the arrangement?	Yes →
	↓ No	
	Joint venture	

Financial statements of parties to a joint arrangement (paragraph 22)

Accounting for sales or contributions of assets to a joint operation

B34 When an entity enters into a transaction with a joint operation in which it is a joint operator, such as a sale or contribution of assets, it is conducting the transaction with the other parties to the joint operation and, as such, the joint operator shall recognise gains and losses resulting from such a transaction only to the extent of the other parties' interests in the joint operation.

B35 When such transactions provide evidence of a reduction in the net realisable value of the assets to be sold or contributed to the joint operation, or of an impairment loss of those assets, those losses shall be recognised fully by the joint operator.

Accounting for purchases of assets from a joint operation

B36   When an entity enters into a transaction with a joint operation in which it is a joint operator, such as a purchase of assets, it shall not recognise its share of the gains and losses until it resells those assets to a third party.

B37   When such transactions provide evidence of a reduction in the net realisable value of the assets to be purchased or of an impairment loss of those assets, a joint operator shall recognise its share of those losses.

Appendix C
Effective date, transition and withdrawal of other IFRSs

This appendix is an integral part of the IFRS and has the same authority as the other parts of the IFRS.

Effective date

C1   An entity shall apply this IFRS for annual periods beginning on or after 1 January 2013. Earlier application is permitted. If an entity applies this IFRS earlier, it shall disclose that fact and apply IFRS 10, IFRS 12 *Disclosure of Interests in Other Entities*, IAS 27 (as amended in 2011) and IAS 28 (as amended in 2011) at the same time.

Transition

Joint ventures—transition from proportionate consolidation to the equity method

C2   When changing from proportionate consolidation to the equity method, an entity shall recognise its investment in the joint venture as at the beginning of the earliest period presented. That initial investment shall be measured as the aggregate of the carrying amounts of the assets and liabilities that the entity had previously proportionately consolidated, including any goodwill arising from acquisition. If the goodwill previously belonged to a larger cash-generating unit, or to a group of cash-generating units, the entity shall allocate goodwill to the joint venture on the basis of the relative carrying amounts of the joint venture and the cash-generating unit or group of cash-generating units to which it belonged.

C3   The opening balance of the investment determined in accordance with paragraph C2 is regarded as the deemed cost of the investment at initial recognition. An entity shall apply paragraphs 40–43 of IAS 28 (as amended in 2011) to the opening balance of the investment to assess whether the investment is impaired and shall recognise any impairment loss as an adjustment to retained earnings at the beginning of the earliest period presented. The initial recognition exception in paragraphs 15 and 24 of IAS 12 *Income Taxes* does not apply when the entity recognises an investment in a joint venture resulting from applying the transition requirements for joint ventures that had previously been proportionately consolidated.

C4   If aggregating all previously proportionately consolidated assets and liabilities results in negative net assets, an entity shall assess whether it has legal or constructive obligations in relation to the negative net assets and, if so, the entity shall recognise the corresponding liability. If the entity concludes that it does not have legal or constructive obligations in relation to the negative net assets, it shall not recognise the corresponding liability but it shall adjust retained earnings at the beginning of the earliest period presented. The entity shall disclose this fact, along with its cumulative unrecognised share of losses of its joint ventures as at the beginning of the earliest period presented and at the date at which this IFRS is first applied.

C5   An entity shall disclose a breakdown of the assets and liabilities that have been aggregated into the single line investment balance as at the beginning of the earliest period presented. That disclosure shall be prepared in an aggregated manner for all joint ventures for which an entity applies the transition requirements referred to in paragraphs C2–C6.

C6   After initial recognition, an entity shall account for its investment in the joint venture using the equity method in accordance with IAS 28 (as amended in 2011).

Joint operations—transition from the equity method to accounting for assets and liabilities

C7   When changing from the equity method to accounting for assets and liabilities in respect of its interest in a joint operation, an entity shall, at the beginning of the earliest period presented, derecognise the investment that was previously accounted for using the equity method and any other items that formed part of the entity's net investment in the arrangement in accordance with paragraph 38 of IAS 28 (as amended in 2011) and recognise its share of each of the assets and the liabilities in respect of its interest in the joint operation, including any goodwill that might have formed part of the carrying amount of the investment.

C8   An entity shall determine its interest in the assets and liabilities relating to the joint operation on the basis of its rights and obligations in a specified proportion in accordance with the contractual arrangement. An entity measures the initial carrying amounts of the assets and liabilities by disaggregating them from the carrying amount of the investment at the beginning of the earliest period presented on the basis of the information used by the entity in applying the equity method.

C9   Any difference arising from the investment previously accounted for using the equity method together with any other items that formed part of the entity's net investment in the arrangement in accordance with paragraph 38 of IAS 28 (as amended in 2011), and the net amount of the assets and liabilities, including any goodwill, recognised shall be:

(a)   offset against any goodwill relating to the investment with any remaining difference adjusted against retained earnings at the beginning of the earliest period presented, if the net amount of the assets and liabilities, including any goodwill, recognised is higher than the investment (and any other items that formed part of the entity's net investment) derecognised.

(b)   adjusted against retained earnings at the beginning of the earliest period presented, if the net amount of the assets and liabilities, including any goodwill, recognised is lower than the investment (and any other items that formed part of the entity's net investment) derecognised.

C10   An entity changing from the equity method to accounting for assets and liabilities shall provide a reconciliation between the investment derecognised, and the assets and liabilities recognised, together with any remaining difference adjusted against retained earnings, at the beginning of the earliest period presented.

C11   The initial recognition exception in paragraphs 15 and 24 of IAS 12 does not apply when the entity recognises assets and liabilities relating to its interest in a joint operation.

Transition provisions in an entity's separate financial statements

C12   An entity that, in accordance with paragraph 10 of IAS 27, was previously accounting in its separate financial statements for its interest in a joint operation as an investment at cost or in accordance with IFRS 9 shall:

(a)   derecognise the investment and recognise the assets and the liabilities in respect of its interest in the joint operation at the amounts determined in accordance with paragraphs C7–C9.

(b)   provide a reconciliation between the investment derecognised, and the assets and liabilities recognised, together with any remaining difference adjusted in retained earnings, at the beginning of the earliest period presented.

C13   The initial recognition exception in paragraphs 15 and 24 of IAS 12 does not apply when the entity recognises assets and liabilities relating to its interest in a joint operation in its separate financial statements resulting from applying the transition requirements for joint operations referred to in paragraph C12.

References to IFRS 9

C14   If an entity applies this IFRS but does not yet apply IFRS 9, any reference to IFRS 9 shall be read as a reference to IAS 39 *Financial Instruments: Recognition and Measurement*.

Withdrawal of other IFRSs

C15   This IFRS supersedes the following IFRSs:

(a)   IAS 31 *Interests in Joint Ventures*; and

(b)   SIC-13 *Jointly Controlled Entities—Non-Monetary Contributions by Venturers*.

Appendix D
Amendments to other IFRSs

This appendix sets out amendments to other IFRSs that are a consequence of the Board issuing IFRS 11. An entity shall apply the amendments for annual periods beginning on or after 1 January 2013. If an entity applies IFRS 11 for an earlier period, it shall apply the amendments for that earlier period. Amended paragraphs are shown with new text underlined and deleted text struck through.

* * * * *

The amendments contained in this appendix when this IFRS was issued in 2011 have been incorporated into the relevant IFRSs published in this volume.

International Financial Reporting Standard 12

Disclosure of Interests in Other Entities

In May 2011 the International Accounting Standards Board (IASB) issued IFRS 12 *Disclosure of Interests in Other Entities*. IFRS 12 replaced the disclosure requirements in IAS 27 *Consolidated and Separate Financial Statements*, IAS 28 *Investments in Associates* and IAS 31 *Interests in Joint Ventures*.

CONTENTS

FOR THE ACCOMPANYING DOCUMENTS LISTED BELOW, SEE PART B OF THIS EDITION

APPROVAL BY THE BOARD OF IFRS 12 ISSUED IN MAY 2011

BASIS FOR CONCLUSIONS ON IFRS 12

International Financial Reporting Standard 12 *Disclosure of Interests in Other Entities* (IFRS 12) is set out in paragraphs 1–31 and Appendices A–D. All the paragraphs have equal authority. Paragraphs in **bold type** state the main principles. Terms defined in Appendix A are in italics the first time they appear in the IFRS. Definitions of other terms are given in the Glossary for International Financial Reporting Standards. IFRS 12 should be read in the context of its objective and the Basis for Conclusions, the *Preface to International Financial Reporting Standards* and the *Conceptual Framework for Financial Reporting*. IAS 8 *Accounting Policies, Changes in Accounting Estimates and Errors* provides a basis for selecting and applying accounting policies in the absence of explicit guidance.

Introduction

IN1　IFRS 12 *Disclosure of Interests in Other Entities* applies to entities that have an interest in a subsidiary, a joint arrangement, an associate or an unconsolidated structured entity.

IN2　The IFRS is effective for annual periods beginning on or after 1 January 2013. Earlier application is permitted.

Reasons for issuing the IFRS

IN3　Users of financial statements have consistently requested improvements to the disclosure of a reporting entity's interests in other entities to help identify the profit or loss and cash flows available to the reporting entity and determine the value of a current or future investment in the reporting entity.

IN4　They highlighted the need for better information about the subsidiaries that are consolidated, as well as an entity's interests in joint arrangements and associates that are not consolidated but with which the entity has a special relationship.

IN5　The global financial crisis that started in 2007 also highlighted a lack of transparency about the risks to which a reporting entity was exposed from its involvement with structured entities, including those that it had sponsored.

IN6　In response to input received from users and others, including the G20 leaders and the Financial Stability Board, the Board decided to address in IFRS 12 the need for improved disclosure of a reporting entity's interests in other entities when the reporting entity has a special relationship with those other entities.

IN7　The Board identified an opportunity to integrate and make consistent the disclosure requirements for subsidiaries, joint arrangements, associates and unconsolidated structured entities and present those requirements in a single IFRS. The Board observed that the disclosure requirements of IAS 27 *Consolidated and Separate Financial Statements*, IAS 28 *Investments in Associates* and IAS 31 *Interests in Joint Ventures* overlapped in many areas. In addition, many commented that the disclosure requirements for interests in unconsolidated structured entities should not be located in a consolidation standard. Therefore, the Board concluded that a combined disclosure standard for interests in other entities would make it easier to understand and apply the disclosure requirements for subsidiaries, joint ventures, associates and unconsolidated structured entities.

Main features of the IFRS

IN8　The IFRS requires an entity to disclose information that enables users of financial statements to evaluate:

(a)　the nature of, and risks associated with, its interests in other entities; and

(b)　the effects of those interests on its financial position, financial performance and cash flows.

General requirements

IN9   The IFRS establishes disclosure objectives according to which an entity discloses information that enables users of its financial statements

(a)   to understand:

    (i)   the significant judgements and assumptions (and changes to those judgements and assumptions) made in determining the nature of its interest in another entity or arrangement (ie control, joint control or significant influence), and in determining the type of joint arrangement in which it has an interest; and

    (ii)   the interest that non-controlling interests have in the group's activities and cash flows; and

(b)   to evaluate:

    (i)   the nature and extent of significant restrictions on its ability to access or use assets, and settle liabilities, of the group;

    (ii)   the nature of, and changes in, the risks associated with its interests in consolidated structured entities;

    (iii)   the nature and extent of its interests in unconsolidated structured entities, and the nature of, and changes in, the risks associated with those interests;

    (iv)   the nature, extent and financial effects of its interests in joint arrangements and associates, and the nature of the risks associated with those interests;

    (v)   the consequences of changes in a parent's ownership interest in a subsidiary that do not result in a loss of control; and

    (vi)   the consequences of losing control of a subsidiary during the reporting period.

IN10   The IFRS specifies minimum disclosures that an entity must provide. If the minimum disclosures required by the IFRS are not sufficient to meet the disclosure objective, an entity discloses whatever additional information is necessary to meet that objective.

IN11   The IFRS requires an entity to consider the level of detail necessary to satisfy the disclosure objective and how much emphasis to place on each of the requirements in the IFRS. An entity shall aggregate or disaggregate disclosures so that useful information is not obscured by either the inclusion of a large amount of insignificant detail or the aggregation of items that have different characteristics.

International Financial Reporting Standard 12
Disclosure of Interests in Other Entities

Objective

1   The objective of this IFRS is to require an entity to disclose information that enables users of its financial statements to evaluate:

   (a)   the nature of, and risks associated with, *its interests in other entities*; and

   (b)   the effects of those interests on its financial position, financial performance and cash flows.

Meeting the objective

2   To meet the objective in paragraph 1, an entity shall disclose:

   (a)   the significant judgements and assumptions it has made in determining the nature of its interest in another entity or arrangement, and in determining the type of joint arrangement in which it has an interest (paragraphs 7–9); and

   (b)   information about its interests in:

      (i)   subsidiaries (paragraphs 10–19);

      (ii)   joint arrangements and associates (paragraphs 20–23); and

      (iii)   *structured entities* that are not controlled by the entity (unconsolidated structured entities) (paragraphs 24–31).

3   If the disclosures required by this IFRS, together with disclosures required by other IFRSs, do not meet the objective in paragraph 1, an entity shall disclose whatever additional information is necessary to meet that objective.

4   An entity shall consider the level of detail necessary to satisfy the disclosure objective and how much emphasis to place on each of the requirements in this IFRS. It shall aggregate or disaggregate disclosures so that useful information is not obscured by either the inclusion of a large amount of insignificant detail or the aggregation of items that have different characteristics (see paragraphs B2–B6).

Scope

5   This IFRS shall be applied by an entity that has an interest in any of the following:

   (a)   subsidiaries

   (b)   joint arrangements (ie joint operations or joint ventures)

   (c)   associates

   (d)   unconsolidated structured entities.

6   This IFRS does not apply to:

(a)   post-employment benefit plans or other long-term employee benefit plans to which IAS 19 *Employee Benefits* applies.

(b)   an entity's separate financial statements to which IAS 27 *Separate Financial Statements* applies. However, if an entity has interests in unconsolidated structured entities and prepares separate financial statements as its only financial statements, it shall apply the requirements in paragraphs 24–31 when preparing those separate financial statements.

(c)   an interest held by an entity that participates in, but does not have joint control of, a joint arrangement unless that interest results in significant influence over the arrangement or is an interest in a structured entity.

(d)   an interest in another entity that is accounted for in accordance with IFRS 9 *Financial Instruments*. However, an entity shall apply this IFRS:

(i)   when that interest is an interest in an associate or a joint venture that, in accordance with IAS 28 *Investments in Associates and Joint Ventures*, is measured at fair value through profit or loss; or

(ii)   when that interest is an interest in an unconsolidated structured entity.

Significant judgements and assumptions

7   **An entity shall disclose information about significant judgements and assumptions it has made (and changes to those judgements and assumptions) in determining:**

(a)   **that it has control of another entity, ie an investee as described in paragraphs 5 and 6 of IFRS 10 *Consolidated Financial Statements*;**

(b)   **that it has joint control of an arrangement or significant influence over another entity; and**

(c)   **the type of joint arrangement (ie joint operation or joint venture) when the arrangement has been structured through a separate vehicle.**

8   The significant judgements and assumptions disclosed in accordance with paragraph 7 include those made by the entity when changes in facts and circumstances are such that the conclusion about whether it has control, joint control or significant influence changes during the reporting period.

9   To comply with paragraph 7, an entity shall disclose, for example, significant judgements and assumptions made in determining that:

(a)   it does not control another entity even though it holds more than half of the voting rights of the other entity.

(b)   it controls another entity even though it holds less than half of the voting rights of the other entity.

(c)   it is an agent or a principal (see paragraphs B58–B72 of IFRS 10).

(d)   it does not have significant influence even though it holds 20 per cent or more of the voting rights of another entity.

(e)   it has significant influence even though it holds less than 20 per cent of the voting rights of another entity.

Interests in subsidiaries

10   An entity shall disclose information that enables users of its consolidated financial statements

(a)   to understand:

(i)   the composition of the group; and

(ii)   the interest that non-controlling interests have in the group's activities and cash flows (paragraph 12); and

(b)   to evaluate:

(i)   the nature and extent of significant restrictions on its ability to access or use assets, and settle liabilities, of the group (paragraph 13);

(ii)   the nature of, and changes in, the risks associated with its interests in consolidated structured entities (paragraphs 14–17);

(iii) the consequences of changes in its ownership interest in a subsidiary that do not result in a loss of control (paragraph 18); and

(iv)   the consequences of losing control of a subsidiary during the reporting period (paragraph 19).

11   When the financial statements of a subsidiary used in the preparation of consolidated financial statements are as of a date or for a period that is different from that of the consolidated financial statements (see paragraphs B92 and B93 of IFRS 10), an entity shall disclose:

(a)   the date of the end of the reporting period of the financial statements of that subsidiary; and

(b)   the reason for using a different date or period.

The interest that non-controlling interests have in the group's activities and cash flows

12   An entity shall disclose for each of its subsidiaries that have non-controlling interests that are material to the reporting entity:

(a)   the name of the subsidiary.

(b)   the principal place of business (and country of incorporation if different from the principal place of business) of the subsidiary.

(c)   the proportion of ownership interests held by non-controlling interests.

(d)   the proportion of voting rights held by non-controlling interests, if different from the proportion of ownership interests held.

(e) the profit or loss allocated to non-controlling interests of the subsidiary during the reporting period.

(f) accumulated non-controlling interests of the subsidiary at the end of the reporting period.

(g) summarised financial information about the subsidiary (see paragraph B10).

The nature and extent of significant restrictions

13 An entity shall disclose:

(a) significant restrictions (eg statutory, contractual and regulatory restrictions) on its ability to access or use the assets and settle the liabilities of the group, such as:

    (i) those that restrict the ability of a parent or its subsidiaries to transfer cash or other assets to (or from) other entities within the group.

    (ii) guarantees or other requirements that may restrict dividends and other capital distributions being paid, or loans and advances being made or repaid, to (or from) other entities within the group.

(b) the nature and extent to which protective rights of non-controlling interests can significantly restrict the entity's ability to access or use the assets and settle the liabilities of the group (such as when a parent is obliged to settle liabilities of a subsidiary before settling its own liabilities, or approval of non-controlling interests is required either to access the assets or to settle the liabilities of a subsidiary).

(c) the carrying amounts in the consolidated financial statements of the assets and liabilities to which those restrictions apply.

Nature of the risks associated with an entity's interests in consolidated structured entities

14 An entity shall disclose the terms of any contractual arrangements that could require the parent or its subsidiaries to provide financial support to a consolidated structured entity, including events or circumstances that could expose the reporting entity to a loss (eg liquidity arrangements or credit rating triggers associated with obligations to purchase assets of the structured entity or provide financial support).

15 If during the reporting period a parent or any of its subsidiaries has, without having a contractual obligation to do so, provided financial or other support to a consolidated structured entity (eg purchasing assets of or instruments issued by the structured entity), the entity shall disclose:

(a) the type and amount of support provided, including situations in which the parent or its subsidiaries assisted the structured entity in obtaining financial support; and

(b) the reasons for providing the support.

16   If during the reporting period a parent or any of its subsidiaries has, without having a contractual obligation to do so, provided financial or other support to a previously unconsolidated structured entity and that provision of support resulted in the entity controlling the structured entity, the entity shall disclose an explanation of the relevant factors in reaching that decision.

17   An entity shall disclose any current intentions to provide financial or other support to a consolidated structured entity, including intentions to assist the structured entity in obtaining financial support.

Consequences of changes in a parent's ownership interest in a subsidiary that do not result in a loss of control

18   An entity shall present a schedule that shows the effects on the equity attributable to owners of the parent of any changes in its ownership interest in a subsidiary that do not result in a loss of control.

Consequences of losing control of a subsidiary during the reporting period

19   An entity shall disclose the gain or loss, if any, calculated in accordance with paragraph 25 of IFRS 10, and:

(a)   the portion of that gain or loss attributable to measuring any investment retained in the former subsidiary at its fair value at the date when control is lost; and

(b)   the line item(s) in profit or loss in which the gain or loss is recognised (if not presented separately).

Interests in joint arrangements and associates

20   An entity shall disclose information that enables users of its financial statements to evaluate:

(a)   the nature, extent and financial effects of its interests in joint arrangements and associates, including the nature and effects of its contractual relationship with the other investors with joint control of, or significant influence over, joint arrangements and associates (paragraphs 21 and 22); and

(b)   the nature of, and changes in, the risks associated with its interests in joint ventures and associates (paragraph 23).

Nature, extent and financial effects of an entity's interests in joint arrangements and associates

21   An entity shall disclose:

(a)   for each joint arrangement and associate that is material to the reporting entity:

(i)   the name of the joint arrangement or associate.

    (ii)   the nature of the entity's relationship with the joint arrangement or associate (by, for example, describing the nature of the activities of the joint arrangement or associate and whether they are strategic to the entity's activities).

    (iii)   the principal place of business (and country of incorporation, if applicable and different from the principal place of business) of the joint arrangement or associate.

    (iv)   the proportion of ownership interest or participating share held by the entity and, if different, the proportion of voting rights held (if applicable).

(b)   for each joint venture and associate that is material to the reporting entity:

    (i)   whether the investment in the joint venture or associate is measured using the equity method or at fair value.

    (ii)   summarised financial information about the joint venture or associate as specified in paragraphs B12 and B13.

    (iii)   if the joint venture or associate is accounted for using the equity method, the fair value of its investment in the joint venture or associate, if there is a quoted market price for the investment.

(c)   financial information as specified in paragraph B16 about the entity's investments in joint ventures and associates that are not individually material:

    (i)   in aggregate for all individually immaterial joint ventures and, separately,

    (ii)   in aggregate for all individually immaterial associates.

22   An entity shall also disclose:

(a)   the nature and extent of any significant restrictions (eg resulting from borrowing arrangements, regulatory requirements or contractual arrangements between investors with joint control of or significant influence over a joint venture or an associate) on the ability of joint ventures or associates to transfer funds to the entity in the form of cash dividends, or to repay loans or advances made by the entity.

(b)   when the financial statements of a joint venture or associate used in applying the equity method are as of a date or for a period that is different from that of the entity:

    (i)   the date of the end of the reporting period of the financial statements of that joint venture or associate; and

    (ii)   the reason for using a different date or period.

(c)   the unrecognised share of losses of a joint venture or associate, both for the reporting period and cumulatively, if the entity has stopped recognising its share of losses of the joint venture or associate when applying the equity method.

Risks associated with an entity's interests in joint ventures and associates

23   An entity shall disclose:

(a)   commitments that it has relating to its joint ventures separately from the amount of other commitments as specified in paragraphs B18–B20.

(b)   in accordance with IAS 37 *Provisions, Contingent Liabilities and Contingent Assets*, unless the probability of loss is remote, contingent liabilities incurred relating to its interests in joint ventures or associates (including its share of contingent liabilities incurred jointly with other investors with joint control of, or significant influence over, the joint ventures or associates), separately from the amount of other contingent liabilities.

Interests in unconsolidated structured entities

24   **An entity shall disclose information that enables users of its financial statements:**

(a)   **to understand the nature and extent of its interests in unconsolidated structured entities (paragraphs 26–28); and**

(b)   **to evaluate the nature of, and changes in, the risks associated with its interests in unconsolidated structured entities (paragraphs 29–31).**

25   The information required by paragraph 24(b) includes information about an entity's exposure to risk from involvement that it had with unconsolidated structured entities in previous periods (eg sponsoring the structured entity), even if the entity no longer has any contractual involvement with the structured entity at the reporting date.

Nature of interests

26   An entity shall disclose qualitative and quantitative information about its interests in unconsolidated structured entities, including, but not limited to, the nature, purpose, size and activities of the structured entity and how the structured entity is financed.

27   If an entity has sponsored an unconsolidated structured entity for which it does not provide information required by paragraph 29 (eg because it does not have an interest in the entity at the reporting date), the entity shall disclose:

(a)   how it has determined which structured entities it has sponsored;

(b)   *income from those structured entities* during the reporting period, including a description of the types of income presented; and

(c)   the carrying amount (at the time of transfer) of all assets transferred to those structured entities during the reporting period.

28   An entity shall present the information in paragraph 27(b) and (c) in tabular format, unless another format is more appropriate, and classify its sponsoring activities into relevant categories (see paragraphs B2–B6).

Nature of risks

29 An entity shall disclose in tabular format, unless another format is more appropriate, a summary of:

(a) the carrying amounts of the assets and liabilities recognised in its financial statements relating to its interests in unconsolidated structured entities.

the line items in the statement of financial position in which those assets and liabilities are recognised.

(b) the amount that best represents the entity's maximum exposure to loss from its interests in unconsolidated structured entities, including how the maximum exposure to loss is determined. If an entity cannot quantify its maximum exposure to loss from its interests in unconsolidated structured entities it shall disclose that fact and the reasons.

(c) a comparison of the carrying amounts of the assets and liabilities of the entity that relate to its interests in unconsolidated structured entities and the entity's maximum exposure to loss from those entities.

30 If during the reporting period an entity has, without having a contractual obligation to do so, provided financial or other support to an unconsolidated structured entity in which it previously had or currently has an interest (for example, purchasing assets of or instruments issued by the structured entity), the entity shall disclose:

(a) the type and amount of support provided, including situations in which the entity assisted the structured entity in obtaining financial support; and

(b) the reasons for providing the support.

31 An entity shall disclose any current intentions to provide financial or other support to an unconsolidated structured entity, including intentions to assist the structured entity in obtaining financial support.

Appendix A
Defined terms

This appendix is an integral part of the IFRS.

income from a structured entity	For the purpose of this IFRS, income from a **structured entity** includes, but is not limited to, recurring and non-recurring fees, interest, dividends, gains or losses on the remeasurement or derecognition of interests in structured entities and gains or losses from the transfer of assets and liabilities to the structured entity.
interest in another entity	For the purpose of this IFRS, an interest in another entity refers to contractual and non-contractual involvement that exposes an entity to variability of returns from the performance of the other entity. An interest in another entity can be evidenced by, but is not limited to, the holding of equity or debt instruments as well as other forms of involvement such as the provision of funding, liquidity support, credit enhancement and guarantees. It includes the means by which an entity has control or joint control of, or significant influence over, another entity. An entity does not necessarily have an interest in another entity solely because of a typical customer supplier relationship.
	Paragraphs B7–B9 provide further information about interests in other entities.
	Paragraphs B55–B57 of IFRS 10 explain variability of returns.
structured entity	An entity that has been designed so that voting or similar rights are not the dominant factor in deciding who controls the entity, such as when any voting rights relate to administrative tasks only and the relevant activities are directed by means of contractual arrangements.
	Paragraphs B22–B24 provide further information about structured entities.

The following terms are defined in IAS 27 (as amended in 2011), IAS 28 (as amended in 2011), IFRS 10 and IFRS 11 *Joint Arrangements* and are used in this IFRS with the meanings specified in those IFRSs:

- associate
- consolidated financial statements
- control of an entity
- equity method
- group
- joint arrangement
- joint control
- joint operation
- joint venture
- non-controlling interest
- parent
- protective rights
- relevant activities
- separate financial statements
- separate vehicle
- significant influence
- subsidiary.

Appendix B
Application guidance

This appendix is an integral part of the IFRS. It describes the application of paragraphs 1–31 and has the same authority as the other parts of the IFRS.

B1 The examples in this appendix portray hypothetical situations. Although some aspects of the examples may be present in actual fact patterns, all relevant facts and circumstances of a particular fact pattern would need to be evaluated when applying IFRS 12.

Aggregation (paragraph 4)

B2 An entity shall decide, in the light of its circumstances, how much detail it provides to satisfy the information needs of users, how much emphasis it places on different aspects of the requirements and how it aggregates the information. It is necessary to strike a balance between burdening financial statements with excessive detail that may not assist users of financial statements and obscuring information as a result of too much aggregation.

B3 An entity may aggregate the disclosures required by this IFRS for interests in similar entities if aggregation is consistent with the disclosure objective and the requirement in paragraph B4, and does not obscure the information provided. An entity shall disclose how it has aggregated its interests in similar entities.

B4 An entity shall present information separately for interests in:

    (a)   subsidiaries;

    (b)   joint ventures;

    (c)   joint operations;

    (d)   associates; and

    (e)   unconsolidated structured entities.

B5 In determining whether to aggregate information, an entity shall consider quantitative and qualitative information about the different risk and return characteristics of each entity it is considering for aggregation and the significance of each such entity to the reporting entity. The entity shall present the disclosures in a manner that clearly explains to users of financial statements the nature and extent of its interests in those other entities.

B6 Examples of aggregation levels within the classes of entities set out in paragraph B4 that might be appropriate are:

    (a)   nature of activities (eg a research and development entity, a revolving credit card securitisation entity).

    (b)   industry classification.

    (c)   geography (eg country or region).

Interests in other entities

B7 An interest in another entity refers to contractual and non-contractual involvement that exposes the reporting entity to variability of returns from the performance of the other entity. Consideration of the purpose and design of the other entity may help the reporting entity when assessing whether it has an interest in that entity and, therefore, whether it is required to provide the disclosures in this IFRS. That assessment shall include consideration of the risks that the other entity was designed to create and the risks the other entity was designed to pass on to the reporting entity and other parties.

B8 A reporting entity is typically exposed to variability of returns from the performance of another entity by holding instruments (such as equity or debt instruments issued by the other entity) or having another involvement that absorbs variability. For example, assume a structured entity holds a loan portfolio. The structured entity obtains a credit default swap from another entity (the reporting entity) to protect itself from the default of interest and principal payments on the loans. The reporting entity has involvement that exposes it to variability of returns from the performance of the structured entity because the credit default swap absorbs variability of returns of the structured entity.

B9 Some instruments are designed to transfer risk from a reporting entity to another entity. Such instruments create variability of returns for the other entity but do not typically expose the reporting entity to variability of returns from the performance of the other entity. For example, assume a structured entity is established to provide investment opportunities for investors who wish to have exposure to entity Z's credit risk (entity Z is unrelated to any party involved in the arrangement). The structured entity obtains funding by issuing to those investors notes that are linked to entity Z's credit risk (credit-linked notes) and uses the proceeds to invest in a portfolio of risk-free financial assets. The structured entity obtains exposure to entity Z's credit risk by entering into a credit default swap (CDS) with a swap counterparty. The CDS passes entity Z's credit risk to the structured entity in return for a fee paid by the swap counterparty. The investors in the structured entity receive a higher return that reflects both the structured entity's return from its asset portfolio and the CDS fee. The swap counterparty does not have involvement with the structured entity that exposes it to variability of returns from the performance of the structured entity because the CDS transfers variability to the structured entity, rather than absorbing variability of returns of the structured entity.

Summarised financial information for subsidiaries, joint ventures and associates (paragraphs 12 and 21)

B10 For each subsidiary that has non-controlling interests that are material to the reporting entity, an entity shall disclose:

(a) dividends paid to non-controlling interests.

(b) summarised financial information about the assets, liabilities, profit or loss and cash flows of the subsidiary that enables users to understand the interest that non-controlling interests have in the group's activities and cash flows. That information might include but is not limited to, for example, current assets, non-current assets, current liabilities non-current liabilities, revenue, profit or loss and total comprehensive income.

B11 The summarised financial information required by paragraph B10(b) shall be the amounts before inter-company eliminations.

B12 For each joint venture and associate that is material to the reporting entity, an entity shall disclose:

(a) dividends received from the joint venture or associate.

(b) summarised financial information for the joint venture or associate (see paragraphs B14 and B15) including, but not necessarily limited to:

(i) current assets.

(ii) non-current assets.

(iii) current liabilities.

(iv) non-current liabilities.

(v) revenue.

(vi) profit or loss from continuing operations.

(vii) post-tax profit or loss from discontinued operations.

(viii) other comprehensive income.

(ix) total comprehensive income.

B13 In addition to the summarised financial information required by paragraph B12, an entity shall disclose for each joint venture that is material to the reporting entity the amount of:

(a) cash and cash equivalents included in paragraph B12(b)(i).

(b) current financial liabilities (excluding trade and other payables and provisions) included in paragraph B12(b)(iii).

(c) non-current financial liabilities (excluding trade and other payables and provisions) included in paragraph B12(b)(iv).

(d) depreciation and amortisation.

(e) interest income.

(f) interest expense.

(g) income tax expense or income.

B14 The summarised financial information presented in accordance with paragraphs B12 and B13 shall be the amounts included in the IFRS financial statements of the joint venture or associate (and not the entity's share of those amounts). If the entity accounts for its interest in the joint venture or associate using the equity method:

(a) the amounts included in the IFRS financial statements of the joint venture or associate shall be adjusted to reflect adjustments made by the entity when using the equity method, such as fair value adjustments made at the time of acquisition and adjustments for differences in accounting policies.

    (b)   the entity shall provide a reconciliation of the summarised financial information presented to the carrying amount of its interest in the joint venture or associate.

B15   An entity may present the summarised financial information required by paragraphs B12 and B13 on the basis of the joint venture's or associate's financial statements if:

    (a)   the entity measures its interest in the joint venture or associate at fair value in accordance with IAS 28 (as amended in 2011); and

    (b)   the joint venture or associate does not prepare IFRS financial statements and preparation on that basis would be impracticable or cause undue cost.

In that case, the entity shall disclose the basis on which the summarised financial information has been prepared.

B16   An entity shall disclose, in aggregate, the carrying amount of its interests in all individually immaterial joint ventures or associates that are accounted for using the equity method. An entity shall also disclose separately the aggregate amount of its share of those joint ventures' or associates':

    (a)   profit or loss from continuing operations.

    (b)   post-tax profit or loss from discontinued operations.

    (c)   other comprehensive income.

    (d)   total comprehensive income.

An entity provides the disclosures separately for joint ventures and associates.

B17   When an entity's interest in a subsidiary, a joint venture or an associate (or a portion of its interest in a joint venture or an associate) is classified as held for sale in accordance with IFRS 5 *Non-current Assets Held for Sale and Discontinued Operations*, the entity is not required to disclose summarised financial information for that subsidiary, joint venture or associate in accordance with paragraphs B10–B16.

Commitments for joint ventures (paragraph 23(a))

B18   An entity shall disclose total commitments it has made but not recognised at the reporting date (including its share of commitments made jointly with other investors with joint control of a joint venture) relating to its interests in joint ventures. Commitments are those that may give rise to a future outflow of cash or other resources.

B19   Unrecognised commitments that may give rise to a future outflow of cash or other resources include:

    (a)   unrecognised commitments to contribute funding or resources as a result of, for example:

        (i)   the constitution or acquisition agreements of a joint venture (that, for example, require an entity to contribute funds over a specific period).

          (ii)   capital-intensive projects undertaken by a joint venture.

          (iii)   unconditional purchase obligations, comprising procurement of equipment, inventory or services that an entity is committed to purchasing from, or on behalf of, a joint venture.

          (iv)   unrecognised commitments to provide loans or other financial support to a joint venture.

          (v)   unrecognised commitments to contribute resources to a joint venture, such as assets or services.

          (vi)   other non-cancellable unrecognised commitments relating to a joint venture.

    (b)   unrecognised commitments to acquire another party's ownership interest (or a portion of that ownership interest) in a joint venture if a particular event occurs or does not occur in the future.

B20   The requirements and examples in paragraphs B18 and B19 illustrate some of the types of disclosure required by paragraph 18 of IAS 24 *Related Party Disclosures*.

Interests in unconsolidated structured entities (paragraphs 24–31)

Structured entities

B21   A structured entity is an entity that has been designed so that voting or similar rights are not the dominant factor in deciding who controls the entity, such as when any voting rights relate to administrative tasks only and the relevant activities are directed by means of contractual arrangements.

B22   A structured entity often has some or all of the following features or attributes:

    (a)   restricted activities.

    (b)   a narrow and well-defined objective, such as to effect a tax-efficient lease, carry out research and development activities, provide a source of capital or funding to an entity or provide investment opportunities for investors by passing on risks and rewards associated with the assets of the structured entity to investors.

    (c)   insufficient equity to permit the structured entity to finance its activities without subordinated financial support.

    (d)   financing in the form of multiple contractually linked instruments to investors that create concentrations of credit or other risks (tranches).

B23   Examples of entities that are regarded as structured entities include, but are not limited to:

    (a)   securitisation vehicles.

    (b)   asset-backed financings.

    (c)   some investment funds.

B24   An entity that is controlled by voting rights is not a structured entity simply because, for example, it receives funding from third parties following a restructuring.

Nature of risks from interests in unconsolidated structured entities (paragraphs 29–31)

B25   In addition to the information required by paragraphs 29–31, an entity shall disclose additional information that is necessary to meet the disclosure objective in paragraph 24(b).

B26   Examples of additional information that, depending on the circumstances, might be relevant to an assessment of the risks to which an entity is exposed when it has an interest in an unconsolidated structured entity are:

(a)   the terms of an arrangement that could require the entity to provide financial support to an unconsolidated structured entity (eg liquidity arrangements or credit rating triggers associated with obligations to purchase assets of the structured entity or provide financial support), including:

(i)   a description of events or circumstances that could expose the reporting entity to a loss.

(ii)   whether there are any terms that would limit the obligation.

(iii)   whether there are any other parties that provide financial support and, if so, how the reporting entity's obligation ranks with those of other parties.

(b)   losses incurred by the entity during the reporting period relating to its interests in unconsolidated structured entities.

(c)   the types of income the entity received during the reporting period from its interests in unconsolidated structured entities.

(d)   whether the entity is required to absorb losses of an unconsolidated structured entity before other parties, the maximum limit of such losses for the entity, and (if relevant) the ranking and amounts of potential losses borne by parties whose interests rank lower than the entity's interest in the unconsolidated structured entity.

(e)   information about any liquidity arrangements, guarantees or other commitments with third parties that may affect the fair value or risk of the entity's interests in unconsolidated structured entities.

(f)   any difficulties an unconsolidated structured entity has experienced in financing its activities during the reporting period.

(g)   in relation to the funding of an unconsolidated structured entity, the forms of funding (eg commercial paper or medium-term notes) and their weighted-average life. That information might include maturity analyses of the assets and funding of an unconsolidated structured entity if the structured entity has longer-term assets funded by shorter-term funding.

Appendix C
Effective date and transition

This appendix is an integral part of the IFRS and has the same authority as the other parts of the IFRS.

Effective date and transition

C1 An entity shall apply this IFRS for annual periods beginning on or after 1 January 2013. Earlier application is permitted.

C2 An entity is encouraged to provide information required by this IFRS earlier than annual periods beginning on or after 1 January 2013. Providing some of the disclosures required by this IFRS does not compel the entity to comply with all the requirements of this IFRS or to apply IFRS 10, IFRS 11, IAS 27 (as amended in 2011) and IAS 28 (as amended in 2011) early.

References to IFRS 9

C3 If an entity applies this IFRS but does not yet apply IFRS 9, any reference to IFRS 9 shall be read as a reference to IAS 39 *Financial Instruments: Recognition and Measurement.*

Appendix D
Amendments to other IFRSs

This appendix sets out amendments to other IFRSs that are a consequence of the Board issuing IFRS 12. An entity shall apply the amendments for annual periods beginning on or after 1 January 2013. If an entity applies IFRS 12 for an earlier period, it shall apply the amendments for that earlier period. Amended paragraphs are shown with new text underlined and deleted text struck through.

* * * * *

The amendments contained in this appendix when this IFRS was issued in 2011 have been incorporated into the relevant IFRSs published in this volume.

International Financial Reporting Standard 13

Fair Value Measurement

In May 2011 the International Accounting Standards Board issued IFRS 13 *Fair Value Measurement*. IFRS 13 defines fair value and replaces the requirement contained in individual standards.

CONTENTS

FOR THE ACCOMPANYING DOCUMENTS LISTED BELOW, SEE PART B OF THIS EDITION

APPROVAL BY THE BOARD OF IFRS 13 ISSUED IN MAY 2011

BASIS FOR CONCLUSIONS

APPENDIX
Amendments to the Basis for Conclusions on other IFRSs

ILLUSTRATIVE EXAMPLES

APPENDIX
Amendments to the guidance on other IFRSs

International Financial Reporting Standard 13 *Fair Value Measurement* (IFRS 13) is set out in paragraphs 1–99 and Appendices A–D. All the paragraphs have equal authority. Paragraphs in **bold type** state the main principles. Terms defined in Appendix A are in *italics* the first time they appear in the IFRS. Definitions of other terms are given in the Glossary for International Financial Reporting Standards. IFRS 13 should be read in the context of its objective and the Basis for Conclusions, the *Preface to International Financial Reporting Standards* and the *Conceptual Framework for Financial Reporting*. IAS 8 *Accounting Policies, Changes in Accounting Estimates and Errors* provides a basis for selecting and applying accounting policies in the absence of explicit guidance.

Introduction

Overview

IN1　International Financial Reporting Standard 13 *Fair Value Measurement* (IFRS 13):

　　(a)　defines fair value;

　　(b)　sets out in a single IFRS a framework for measuring fair value; and

　　(c)　requires disclosures about fair value measurements.

IN2　The IFRS applies to IFRSs that require or permit fair value measurements or disclosures about fair value measurements (and measurements, such as fair value less costs to sell, based on fair value or disclosures about those measurements), except in specified circumstances.

IN3　The IFRS is to be applied for annual periods beginning on or after 1 January 2013. Earlier application is permitted.

IN4　The IFRS explains how to measure fair value for financial reporting. It does not require fair value measurements in addition to those already required or permitted by other IFRSs and is not intended to establish valuation standards or affect valuation practices outside financial reporting.

Reasons for issuing the IFRS

IN5　Some IFRSs require or permit entities to measure or disclose the fair value of assets, liabilities or their own equity instruments. Because those IFRSs were developed over many years, the requirements for measuring fair value and for disclosing information about fair value measurements were dispersed and in many cases did not articulate a clear measurement or disclosure objective.

IN6　As a result, some of those IFRSs contained limited guidance about how to measure fair value, whereas others contained extensive guidance and that guidance was not always consistent across those IFRSs that refer to fair value. Inconsistencies in the requirements for measuring fair value and for disclosing information about fair value measurements have contributed to diversity in practice and have reduced the comparability of information reported in financial statements. IFRS 13 remedies that situation.

IN7　Furthermore, in 2006 the International Accounting Standards Board (IASB) and the US national standard-setter, the Financial Accounting Standards Board (FASB), published a Memorandum of Understanding, which has served as the foundation of the boards' efforts to create a common set of high quality global accounting standards. Consistent with the Memorandum of Understanding and the boards' commitment to achieving that goal, IFRS 13 is the result of the work by the IASB and the FASB to develop common requirements for measuring fair value and for disclosing information about fair value measurements in accordance with IFRSs and US generally accepted accounting principles (GAAP).

Main features

IN8   IFRS 13 defines fair value as the price that would be received to sell an asset or paid to transfer a liability in an orderly transaction between market participants at the measurement date (ie an exit price).

IN9   That definition of fair value emphasises that fair value is a market-based measurement, not an entity-specific measurement. When measuring fair value, an entity uses the assumptions that market participants would use when pricing the asset or liability under current market conditions, including assumptions about risk. As a result, an entity's intention to hold an asset or to settle or otherwise fulfil a liability is not relevant when measuring fair value.

IN10   The IFRS explains that a fair value measurement requires an entity to determine the following:

(a)   the particular asset or liability being measured;

(b)   for a non-financial asset, the highest and best use of the asset and whether the asset is used in combination with other assets or on a stand-alone basis;

(c)   the market in which an orderly transaction would take place for the asset or liability; and

(d)   the appropriate valuation technique(s) to use when measuring fair value. The valuation technique(s) used should maximise the use of relevant observable inputs and minimise unobservable inputs. Those inputs should be consistent with the inputs a market participant would use when pricing the asset or liability.

International Financial Reporting Standard 13
Fair Value Measurement

Objective

1   This IFRS:

(a)   defines *fair value*;

(b)   sets out in a single IFRS a framework for measuring fair value; and

(c)   requires disclosures about fair value measurements.

2   Fair value is a market-based measurement, not an entity-specific measurement. For some assets and liabilities, observable market transactions or market information might be available. For other assets and liabilities, observable market transactions and market information might not be available. However, the objective of a fair value measurement in both cases is the same—to estimate the price at which an *orderly transaction* to sell the asset or to transfer the liability would take place between *market participants* at the measurement date under current market conditions (ie an *exit price* at the measurement date from the perspective of a market participant that holds the asset or owes the liability).

3   When a price for an identical asset or liability is not observable, an entity measures fair value using another valuation technique that maximises the use of relevant *observable inputs* and minimises the use of *unobservable inputs*. Because fair value is a market-based measurement, it is measured using the assumptions that market participants would use when pricing the asset or liability, including assumptions about risk. As a result, an entity's intention to hold an asset or to settle or otherwise fulfil a liability is not relevant when measuring fair value.

4   The definition of fair value focuses on assets and liabilities because they are a primary subject of accounting measurement. In addition, this IFRS shall be applied to an entity's own equity instruments measured at fair value.

Scope

5   This IFRS applies when another IFRS requires or permits fair value measurements or disclosures about fair value measurements (and measurements, such as fair value less costs to sell, based on fair value or disclosures about those measurements), except as specified in paragraphs 6 and 7.

6   The measurement and disclosure requirements of this IFRS do not apply to the following:

(a)   share-based payment transactions within the scope of IFRS 2 *Share-based Payment*;

(b)   leasing transactions within the scope of IAS 17 *Leases*; and

(c)   measurements that have some similarities to fair value but are not fair value, such as net realisable value in IAS 2 *Inventories* or value in use in IAS 36 *Impairment of Assets*.

7 The disclosures required by this IFRS are not required for the following:

 (a) plan assets measured at fair value in accordance with IAS 19 *Employee Benefits*;

 (b) retirement benefit plan investments measured at fair value in accordance with IAS 26 *Accounting and Reporting by Retirement Benefit Plans*; and

 (c) assets for which recoverable amount is fair value less costs of disposal in accordance with IAS 36.

8 The fair value measurement framework described in this IFRS applies to both initial and subsequent measurement if fair value is required or permitted by other IFRSs.

Measurement

Definition of fair value

9 **This IFRS defines fair value as the price that would be received to sell an asset or paid to transfer a liability in an orderly transaction between market participants at the measurement date.**

10 Paragraph B2 describes the overall fair value measurement approach.

The asset or liability

11 **A fair value measurement is for a particular asset or liability. Therefore, when measuring fair value an entity shall take into account the characteristics of the asset or liability if market participants would take those characteristics into account when pricing the asset or liability at the measurement date. Such characteristics include, for example, the following:**

 (a) **the condition and location of the asset; and**

 (b) **restrictions, if any, on the sale or use of the asset.**

12 The effect on the measurement arising from a particular characteristic will differ depending on how that characteristic would be taken into account by market participants.

13 The asset or liability measured at fair value might be either of the following:

 (a) a stand-alone asset or liability (eg a financial instrument or a non-financial asset); or

 (b) a group of assets, a group of liabilities or a group of assets and liabilities (eg a cash-generating unit or a business).

14 Whether the asset or liability is a stand-alone asset or liability, a group of assets, a group of liabilities or a group of assets and liabilities for recognition or disclosure purposes depends on its unit of account. The unit of account for the asset or liability shall be determined in accordance with the IFRS that requires or permits the fair value measurement, except as provided in this IFRS.

The transaction

15 A fair value measurement assumes that the asset or liability is exchanged in an orderly transaction between market participants to sell the asset or transfer the liability at the measurement date under current market conditions.

16 A fair value measurement assumes that the transaction to sell the asset or transfer the liability takes place either:

(a) in the *principal market* for the asset or liability; or

(b) in the absence of a principal market, in the *most advantageous market* for the asset or liability.

17 An entity need not undertake an exhaustive search of all possible markets to identify the principal market or, in the absence of a principal market, the most advantageous market, but it shall take into account all information that is reasonably available. In the absence of evidence to the contrary, the market in which the entity would normally enter into a transaction to sell the asset or to transfer the liability is presumed to be the principal market or, in the absence of a principal market, the most advantageous market.

18 If there is a principal market for the asset or liability, the fair value measurement shall represent the price in that market (whether that price is directly observable or estimated using another valuation technique), even if the price in a different market is potentially more advantageous at the measurement date.

19 The entity must have access to the principal (or most advantageous) market at the measurement date. Because different entities (and businesses within those entities) with different activities may have access to different markets, the principal (or most advantageous) market for the same asset or liability might be different for different entities (and businesses within those entities). Therefore, the principal (or most advantageous) market (and thus, market participants) shall be considered from the perspective of the entity, thereby allowing for differences between and among entities with different activities.

20 Although an entity must be able to access the market, the entity does not need to be able to sell the particular asset or transfer the particular liability on the measurement date to be able to measure fair value on the basis of the price in that market.

21 Even when there is no observable market to provide pricing information about the sale of an asset or the transfer of a liability at the measurement date, a fair value measurement shall assume that a transaction takes place at that date, considered from the perspective of a market participant that holds the asset or owes the liability. That assumed transaction establishes a basis for estimating the price to sell the asset or to transfer the liability.

Market participants

22 An entity shall measure the fair value of an asset or a liability using the assumptions that market participants would use when pricing the asset or liability, assuming that market participants act in their economic best interest.

23   In developing those assumptions, an entity need not identify specific market participants. Rather, the entity shall identify characteristics that distinguish market participants generally, considering factors specific to all the following:

(a)   the asset or liability;

(b)   the principal (or most advantageous) market for the asset or liability; and

(c)   market participants with whom the entity would enter into a transaction in that market.

The price

24   **Fair value is the price that would be received to sell an asset or paid to transfer a liability in an orderly transaction in the principal (or most advantageous) market at the measurement date under current market conditions (ie an exit price) regardless of whether that price is directly observable or estimated using another valuation technique.**

25   The price in the principal (or most advantageous) market used to measure the fair value of the asset or liability shall not be adjusted for *transaction costs*. Transaction costs shall be accounted for in accordance with other IFRSs. Transaction costs are not a characteristic of an asset or a liability; rather, they are specific to a transaction and will differ depending on how an entity enters into a transaction for the asset or liability.

26   Transaction costs do not include *transport costs*. If location is a characteristic of the asset (as might be the case, for example, for a commodity), the price in the principal (or most advantageous) market shall be adjusted for the costs, if any, that would be incurred to transport the asset from its current location to that market.

Application to non-financial assets

Highest and best use for non-financial assets

27   **A fair value measurement of a non-financial asset takes into account a market participant's ability to generate economic benefits by using the asset in its *highest and best* use or by selling it to another market participant that would use the asset in its highest and best use.**

28   The highest and best use of a non-financial asset takes into account the use of the asset that is physically possible, legally permissible and financially feasible, as follows:

(a)   A use that is physically possible takes into account the physical characteristics of the asset that market participants would take into account when pricing the asset (eg the location or size of a property).

(b)   A use that is legally permissible takes into account any legal restrictions on the use of the asset that market participants would take into account when pricing the asset (eg the zoning regulations applicable to a property).

(c) A use that is financially feasible takes into account whether a use of the asset that is physically possible and legally permissible generates adequate income or cash flows (taking into account the costs of converting the asset to that use) to produce an investment return that market participants would require from an investment in that asset put to that use.

29 Highest and best use is determined from the perspective of market participants, even if the entity intends a different use. However, an entity's current use of a non-financial asset is presumed to be its highest and best use unless market or other factors suggest that a different use by market participants would maximise the value of the asset.

30 To protect its competitive position, or for other reasons, an entity may intend not to use an acquired non-financial asset actively or it may intend not to use the asset according to its highest and best use. For example, that might be the case for an acquired intangible asset that the entity plans to use defensively by preventing others from using it. Nevertheless, the entity shall measure the fair value of a non-financial asset assuming its highest and best use by market participants.

Valuation premise for non-financial assets

31 The highest and best use of a non-financial asset establishes the valuation premise used to measure the fair value of the asset, as follows:

(a) The highest and best use of a non-financial asset might provide maximum value to market participants through its use in combination with other assets as a group (as installed or otherwise configured for use) or in combination with other assets and liabilities (eg a business).

(i) If the highest and best use of the asset is to use the asset in combination with other assets or with other assets and liabilities, the fair value of the asset is the price that would be received in a current transaction to sell the asset assuming that the asset would be used with other assets or with other assets and liabilities and that those assets and liabilities (ie its complementary assets and the associated liabilities) would be available to market participants.

(ii) Liabilities associated with the asset and with the complementary assets include liabilities that fund working capital, but do not include liabilities used to fund assets other than those within the group of assets.

(iii) Assumptions about the highest and best use of a non-financial asset shall be consistent for all the assets (for which highest and best use is relevant) of the group of assets or the group of assets and liabilities within which the asset would be used.

(b) The highest and best use of a non-financial asset might provide maximum value to market participants on a stand-alone basis. If the highest and best use of the asset is to use it on a stand-alone basis, the fair value of the asset is the price that would be received in a current transaction to sell the asset to market participants that would use the asset on a stand-alone basis.

32   The fair value measurement of a non-financial asset assumes that the asset is sold consistently with the unit of account specified in other IFRSs (which may be an individual asset). That is the case even when that fair value measurement assumes that the highest and best use of the asset is to use it in combination with other assets or with other assets and liabilities because a fair value measurement assumes that the market participant already holds the complementary assets and the associated liabilities.

33   Paragraph B3 describes the application of the valuation premise concept for non-financial assets.

Application to liabilities and an entity's own equity instruments

General principles

34   **A fair value measurement assumes that a financial or non-financial liability or an entity's own equity instrument (eg equity interests issued as consideration in a business combination) is transferred to a market participant at the measurement date. The transfer of a liability or an entity's own equity instrument assumes the following:**

      (a)   A liability would remain outstanding and the market participant transferee would be required to fulfil the obligation. The liability would not be settled with the counterparty or otherwise extinguished on the measurement date.

      (b)   An entity's own equity instrument would remain outstanding and the market participant transferee would take on the rights and responsibilities associated with the instrument. The instrument would not be cancelled or otherwise extinguished on the measurement date.

35   Even when there is no observable market to provide pricing information about the transfer of a liability or an entity's own equity instrument (eg because contractual or other legal restrictions prevent the transfer of such items), there might be an observable market for such items if they are held by other parties as assets (eg a corporate bond or a call option on an entity's shares).

36   In all cases, an entity shall maximise the use of relevant observable inputs and minimise the use of unobservable inputs to meet the objective of a fair value measurement, which is to estimate the price at which an orderly transaction to transfer the liability or equity instrument would take place between market participants at the measurement date under current market conditions.

Liabilities and equity instruments held by other parties as assets

37   **When a quoted price for the transfer of an identical or a similar liability or entity's own equity instrument is not available and the identical item is held by another party as an asset, an entity shall measure the fair value of the liability or equity instrument from the perspective of a market participant that holds the identical item as an asset at the measurement date.**

38   In such cases, an entity shall measure the fair value of the liability or equity instrument as follows:

(a)   using the quoted price in an *active market* for the identical item held by another party as an asset, if that price is available.

(b)   if that price is not available, using other observable inputs, such as the quoted price in a market that is not active for the identical item held by another party as an asset.

(c)   if the observable prices in (a) and (b) are not available, using another valuation technique, such as:

(i)   an *income approach* (eg a present value technique that takes into account the future cash flows that a market participant would expect to receive from holding the liability or equity instrument as an asset; see paragraphs B10 and B11).

(ii)   a *market approach* (eg using quoted prices for similar liabilities or equity instruments held by other parties as assets; see paragraphs B5–B7).

39   An entity shall adjust the quoted price of a liability or an entity's own equity instrument held by another party as an asset only if there are factors specific to the asset that are not applicable to the fair value measurement of the liability or equity instrument. An entity shall ensure that the price of the asset does not reflect the effect of a restriction preventing the sale of that asset. Some factors that may indicate that the quoted price of the asset should be adjusted include the following:

(a)   The quoted price for the asset relates to a similar (but not identical) liability or equity instrument held by another party as an asset. For example, the liability or equity instrument may have a particular characteristic (eg the credit quality of the issuer) that is different from that reflected in the fair value of the similar liability or equity instrument held as an asset.

(b)   The unit of account for the asset is not the same as for the liability or equity instrument. For example, for liabilities, in some cases the price for an asset reflects a combined price for a package comprising both the amounts due from the issuer and a third-party credit enhancement. If the unit of account for the liability is not for the combined package, the objective is to measure the fair value of the issuer's liability, not the fair value of the combined package. Thus, in such cases, the entity would adjust the observed price for the asset to exclude the effect of the third-party credit enhancement.

Liabilities and equity instruments not held by other parties as assets

40   **When a quoted price for the transfer of an identical or a similar liability or entity's own equity instrument is not available and the identical item is not held by another party as an asset, an entity shall measure the fair value of the liability or equity instrument using a valuation technique from the perspective of a market participant that owes the liability or has issued the claim on equity.**

41 For example, when applying a present value technique an entity might take into account either of the following:

(a) the future cash outflows that a market participant would expect to incur in fulfilling the obligation, including the compensation that a market participant would require for taking on the obligation (see paragraphs B31–B33).

(b) the amount that a market participant would receive to enter into or issue an identical liability or equity instrument, using the assumptions that market participants would use when pricing the identical item (eg having the same credit characteristics) in the principal (or most advantageous) market for issuing a liability or an equity instrument with the same contractual terms.

Non-performance risk

42 **The fair value of a liability reflects the effect of *non-performance risk*. Non-performance risk includes, but may not be limited to, an entity's own credit risk (as defined in IFRS 7 *Financial Instruments: Disclosures*). Non-performance risk is assumed to be the same before and after the transfer of the liability.**

43 When measuring the fair value of a liability, an entity shall take into account the effect of its credit risk (credit standing) and any other factors that might influence the likelihood that the obligation will or will not be fulfilled. That effect may differ depending on the liability, for example:

(a) whether the liability is an obligation to deliver cash (a financial liability) or an obligation to deliver goods or services (a non-financial liability).

(b) the terms of credit enhancements related to the liability, if any.

44 The fair value of a liability reflects the effect of non-performance risk on the basis of its unit of account. The issuer of a liability issued with an inseparable third-party credit enhancement that is accounted for separately from the liability shall not include the effect of the credit enhancement (eg a third-party guarantee of debt) in the fair value measurement of the liability. If the credit enhancement is accounted for separately from the liability, the issuer would take into account its own credit standing and not that of the third party guarantor when measuring the fair value of the liability.

Restriction preventing the transfer of a liability or an entity's own equity instrument

45 When measuring the fair value of a liability or an entity's own equity instrument, an entity shall not include a separate input or an adjustment to other *inputs* relating to the existence of a restriction that prevents the transfer of the item. The effect of a restriction that prevents the transfer of a liability or an entity's own equity instrument is either implicitly or explicitly included in the other inputs to the fair value measurement.

46　For example, at the transaction date, both the creditor and the obligor accepted the transaction price for the liability with full knowledge that the obligation includes a restriction that prevents its transfer. As a result of the restriction being included in the transaction price, a separate input or an adjustment to an existing input is not required at the transaction date to reflect the effect of the restriction on transfer. Similarly, a separate input or an adjustment to an existing input is not required at subsequent measurement dates to reflect the effect of the restriction on transfer.

Financial liability with a demand feature

47　The fair value of a financial liability with a demand feature (eg a demand deposit) is not less than the amount payable on demand, discounted from the first date that the amount could be required to be paid.

Application to financial assets and financial liabilities with offsetting positions in market risks or counterparty credit risk

48　An entity that holds a group of financial assets and financial liabilities is exposed to market risks (as defined in IFRS 7) and to the credit risk (as defined in IFRS 7) of each of the counterparties. If the entity manages that group of financial assets and financial liabilities on the basis of its net exposure to either market risks or credit risk, the entity is permitted to apply an exception to this IFRS for measuring fair value. That exception permits an entity to measure the fair value of a group of financial assets and financial liabilities on the basis of the price that would be received to sell a net long position (ie an asset) for a particular risk exposure or paid to transfer a net short position (ie a liability) for a particular risk exposure in an orderly transaction between market participants at the measurement date under current market conditions. Accordingly, an entity shall measure the fair value of the group of financial assets and financial liabilities consistently with how market participants would price the net risk exposure at the measurement date.

49　An entity is permitted to use the exception in paragraph 48 only if the entity does all the following:

(a)　manages the group of financial assets and financial liabilities on the basis of the entity's net exposure to a particular market risk (or risks) or to the credit risk of a particular counterparty in accordance with the entity's documented risk management or investment strategy;

(b)　provides information on that basis about the group of financial assets and financial liabilities to the entity's key management personnel, as defined in IAS 24 *Related Party Disclosures*; and

(c)　is required or has elected to measure those financial assets and financial liabilities at fair value in the statement of financial position at the end of each reporting period.

50   The exception in paragraph 48 does not pertain to financial statement presentation. In some cases the basis for the presentation of financial instruments in the statement of financial position differs from the basis for the measurement of financial instruments, for example, if an IFRS does not require or permit financial instruments to be presented on a net basis. In such cases an entity may need to allocate the portfolio-level adjustments (see paragraphs 53–56) to the individual assets or liabilities that make up the group of financial assets and financial liabilities managed on the basis of the entity's net risk exposure. An entity shall perform such allocations on a reasonable and consistent basis using a methodology appropriate in the circumstances.

51   An entity shall make an accounting policy decision in accordance with IAS 8 *Accounting Policies, Changes in Accounting Estimates and Errors* to use the exception in paragraph 48. An entity that uses the exception shall apply that accounting policy, including its policy for allocating bid-ask adjustments (see paragraphs 53–55) and credit adjustments (see paragraph 56), if applicable, consistently from period to period for a particular portfolio.

52   The exception in paragraph 48 applies only to financial assets and financial liabilities within the scope of IAS 39 *Financial Instruments: Recognition and Measurement* or IFRS 9 *Financial Instruments*.

Exposure to market risks

53   When using the exception in paragraph 48 to measure the fair value of a group of financial assets and financial liabilities managed on the basis of the entity's net exposure to a particular market risk (or risks), the entity shall apply the price within the bid-ask spread that is most representative of fair value in the circumstances to the entity's net exposure to those market risks (see paragraphs 70 and 71).

54   When using the exception in paragraph 48, an entity shall ensure that the market risk (or risks) to which the entity is exposed within that group of financial assets and financial liabilities is substantially the same. For example, an entity would not combine the interest rate risk associated with a financial asset with the commodity price risk associated with a financial liability because doing so would not mitigate the entity's exposure to interest rate risk or commodity price risk. When using the exception in paragraph 48, any basis risk resulting from the market risk parameters not being identical shall be taken into account in the fair value measurement of the financial assets and financial liabilities within the group.

55   Similarly, the duration of the entity's exposure to a particular market risk (or risks) arising from the financial assets and financial liabilities shall be substantially the same. For example, an entity that uses a 12-month futures contract against the cash flows associated with 12 months' worth of interest rate risk exposure on a five-year financial instrument within a group made up of only those financial assets and financial liabilities measures the fair value of the exposure to 12-month interest rate risk on a net basis and the remaining interest rate risk exposure (ie years 2–5) on a gross basis.

Exposure to the credit risk of a particular counterparty

56　When using the exception in paragraph 48 to measure the fair value of a group of financial assets and financial liabilities entered into with a particular counterparty, the entity shall include the effect of the entity's net exposure to the credit risk of that counterparty or the counterparty's net exposure to the credit risk of the entity in the fair value measurement when market participants would take into account any existing arrangements that mitigate credit risk exposure in the event of default (eg a master netting agreement with the counterparty or an agreement that requires the exchange of collateral on the basis of each party's net exposure to the credit risk of the other party). The fair value measurement shall reflect market participants' expectations about the likelihood that such an arrangement would be legally enforceable in the event of default.

Fair value at initial recognition

57　When an asset is acquired or a liability is assumed in an exchange transaction for that asset or liability, the transaction price is the price paid to acquire the asset or received to assume the liability (an *entry price*). In contrast, the fair value of the asset or liability is the price that would be received to sell the asset or paid to transfer the liability (an exit price). Entities do not necessarily sell assets at the prices paid to acquire them. Similarly, entities do not necessarily transfer liabilities at the prices received to assume them.

58　In many cases the transaction price will equal the fair value (eg that might be the case when on the transaction date the transaction to buy an asset takes place in the market in which the asset would be sold).

59　When determining whether fair value at initial recognition equals the transaction price, an entity shall take into account factors specific to the transaction and to the asset or liability. Paragraph B4 describes situations in which the transaction price might not represent the fair value of an asset or a liability at initial recognition.

60　If another IFRS requires or permits an entity to measure an asset or a liability initially at fair value and the transaction price differs from fair value, the entity shall recognise the resulting gain or loss in profit or loss unless that IFRS specifies otherwise.

Valuation techniques

61　**An entity shall use valuation techniques that are appropriate in the circumstances and for which sufficient data are available to measure fair value, maximising the use of relevant observable inputs and minimising the use of unobservable inputs.**

62　The objective of using a valuation technique is to estimate the price at which an orderly transaction to sell the asset or to transfer the liability would take place between market participants at the measurement date under current market conditions. Three widely used valuation techniques are the market approach, the *cost approach* and the income approach. The main aspects of those approaches are summarised in paragraphs B5–B11. An entity shall use valuation techniques consistent with one or more of those approaches to measure fair value.

63   In some cases a single valuation technique will be appropriate (eg when valuing an asset or a liability using quoted prices in an active market for identical assets or liabilities). In other cases, multiple valuation techniques will be appropriate (eg that might be the case when valuing a cash-generating unit). If multiple valuation techniques are used to measure fair value, the results (ie respective indications of fair value) shall be evaluated considering the reasonableness of the range of values indicated by those results. A fair value measurement is the point within that range that is most representative of fair value in the circumstances.

64   If the transaction price is fair value at initial recognition and a valuation technique that uses unobservable inputs will be used to measure fair value in subsequent periods, the valuation technique shall be calibrated so that at initial recognition the result of the valuation technique equals the transaction price. Calibration ensures that the valuation technique reflects current market conditions, and it helps an entity to determine whether an adjustment to the valuation technique is necessary (eg there might be a characteristic of the asset or liability that is not captured by the valuation technique). After initial recognition, when measuring fair value using a valuation technique or techniques that use unobservable inputs, an entity shall ensure that those valuation techniques reflect observable market data (eg the price for a similar asset or liability) at the measurement date.

65   Valuation techniques used to measure fair value shall be applied consistently. However, a change in a valuation technique or its application (eg a change in its weighting when multiple valuation techniques are used or a change in an adjustment applied to a valuation technique) is appropriate if the change results in a measurement that is equally or more representative of fair value in the circumstances. That might be the case if, for example, any of the following events take place:

(a)   new markets develop;

(b)   new information becomes available;

(c)   information previously used is no longer available;

(d)   valuation techniques improve; or

(e)   market conditions change.

66   Revisions resulting from a change in the valuation technique or its application shall be accounted for as a change in accounting estimate in accordance with IAS 8. However, the disclosures in IAS 8 for a change in accounting estimate are not required for revisions resulting from a change in a valuation technique or its application.

Inputs to valuation techniques

General principles

67   **Valuation techniques used to measure fair value shall maximise the use of relevant observable inputs and minimise the use of unobservable inputs.**

68   Examples of markets in which inputs might be observable for some assets and liabilities (eg financial instruments) include exchange markets, dealer markets, brokered markets and principal-to-principal markets (see paragraph B34).

69   An entity shall select inputs that are consistent with the characteristics of the asset or liability that market participants would take into account in a transaction for the asset or liability (see paragraphs 11 and 12). In some cases those characteristics result in the application of an adjustment, such as a premium or discount (eg a control premium or non-controlling interest discount). However, a fair value measurement shall not incorporate a premium or discount that is inconsistent with the unit of account in the IFRS that requires or permits the fair value measurement (see paragraphs 13 and 14). Premiums or discounts that reflect size as a characteristic of the entity's holding (specifically, a blockage factor that adjusts the quoted price of an asset or a liability because the market's normal daily trading volume is not sufficient to absorb the quantity held by the entity, as described in paragraph 80) rather than as a characteristic of the asset or liability (eg a control premium when measuring the fair value of a controlling interest) are not permitted in a fair value measurement. In all cases, if there is a quoted price in an active market (ie a *Level 1 input*) for an asset or a liability, an entity shall use that price without adjustment when measuring fair value, except as specified in paragraph 79.

Inputs based on bid and ask prices

70   If an asset or a liability measured at fair value has a bid price and an ask price (eg an input from a dealer market), the price within the bid-ask spread that is most representative of fair value in the circumstances shall be used to measure fair value regardless of where the input is categorised within the fair value hierarchy (ie Level 1, 2 or 3; see paragraphs 72–90). The use of bid prices for asset positions and ask prices for liability positions is permitted, but is not required.

71   This IFRS does not preclude the use of mid-market pricing or other pricing conventions that are used by market participants as a practical expedient for fair value measurements within a bid-ask spread.

Fair value hierarchy

72   To increase consistency and comparability in fair value measurements and related disclosures, this IFRS establishes a fair value hierarchy that categorises into three levels (see paragraphs 76–90) the inputs to valuation techniques used to measure fair value. The fair value hierarchy gives the highest priority to quoted prices (unadjusted) in active markets for identical assets or liabilities (Level 1 inputs) and the lowest priority to unobservable inputs (*Level 3 inputs*).

73   In some cases, the inputs used to measure the fair value of an asset or a liability might be categorised within different levels of the fair value hierarchy. In those cases, the fair value measurement is categorised in its entirety in the same level of the fair value hierarchy as the lowest level input that is significant to the entire measurement. Assessing the significance of a particular input to the entire measurement requires judgement, taking into account factors specific to the asset or liability. Adjustments to arrive at measurements based on fair value, such as costs to sell when measuring fair value less costs to sell, shall not be taken into account when determining the level of the fair value hierarchy within which a fair value measurement is categorised.

74   The availability of relevant inputs and their relative subjectivity might affect the selection of appropriate valuation techniques (see paragraph 61). However, the fair value hierarchy prioritises the inputs to valuation techniques, not the valuation techniques used to measure fair value. For example, a fair value measurement developed using a present value technique might be categorised within Level 2 or Level 3, depending on the inputs that are significant to the entire measurement and the level of the fair value hierarchy within which those inputs are categorised.

75   If an observable input requires an adjustment using an unobservable input and that adjustment results in a significantly higher or lower fair value measurement, the resulting measurement would be categorised within Level 3 of the fair value hierarchy. For example, if a market participant would take into account the effect of a restriction on the sale of an asset when estimating the price for the asset, an entity would adjust the quoted price to reflect the effect of that restriction. If that quoted price is a *Level 2 input* and the adjustment is an unobservable input that is significant to the entire measurement, the measurement would be categorised within Level 3 of the fair value hierarchy.

Level 1 inputs

76   Level 1 inputs are quoted prices (unadjusted) in active markets for identical assets or liabilities that the entity can access at the measurement date.

77   A quoted price in an active market provides the most reliable evidence of fair value and shall be used without adjustment to measure fair value whenever available, except as specified in paragraph 79.

78   A Level 1 input will be available for many financial assets and financial liabilities, some of which might be exchanged in multiple active markets (eg on different exchanges). Therefore, the emphasis within Level 1 is on determining both of the following:

   (a)   the principal market for the asset or liability or, in the absence of a principal market, the most advantageous market for the asset or liability; and

   (b)   whether the entity can enter into a transaction for the asset or liability at the price in that market at the measurement date.

79   An entity shall not make an adjustment to a Level 1 input except in the following circumstances:

   (a)   when an entity holds a large number of similar (but not identical) assets or liabilities (eg debt securities) that are measured at fair value and a quoted price in an active market is available but not readily accessible for each of those assets or liabilities individually (ie given the large number of similar assets or liabilities held by the entity, it would be difficult to obtain pricing information for each individual asset or liability at the measurement date). In that case, as a practical expedient, an entity may measure fair value using an alternative pricing method that does not rely exclusively on quoted prices (eg matrix pricing). However, the use of an alternative pricing method results in a fair value measurement categorised within a lower level of the fair value hierarchy.

(b)   when a quoted price in an active market does not represent fair value at the measurement date. That might be the case if, for example, significant events (such as transactions in a principal-to-principal market, trades in a brokered market or announcements) take place after the close of a market but before the measurement date. An entity shall establish and consistently apply a policy for identifying those events that might affect fair value measurements. However, if the quoted price is adjusted for new information, the adjustment results in a fair value measurement categorised within a lower level of the fair value hierarchy.

(c)   when measuring the fair value of a liability or an entity's own equity instrument using the quoted price for the identical item traded as an asset in an active market and that price needs to be adjusted for factors specific to the item or the asset (see paragraph 39). If no adjustment to the quoted price of the asset is required, the result is a fair value measurement categorised within Level 1 of the fair value hierarchy. However, any adjustment to the quoted price of the asset results in a fair value measurement categorised within a lower level of the fair value hierarchy.

80   If an entity holds a position in a single asset or liability (including a position comprising a large number of identical assets or liabilities, such as a holding of financial instruments) and the asset or liability is traded in an active market, the fair value of the asset or liability shall be measured within Level 1 as the product of the quoted price for the individual asset or liability and the quantity held by the entity. That is the case even if a market's normal daily trading volume is not sufficient to absorb the quantity held and placing orders to sell the position in a single transaction might affect the quoted price.

Level 2 inputs

81   Level 2 inputs are inputs other than quoted prices included within Level 1 that are observable for the asset or liability, either directly or indirectly.

82   If the asset or liability has a specified (contractual) term, a Level 2 input must be observable for substantially the full term of the asset or liability. Level 2 inputs include the following:

(a)   quoted prices for similar assets or liabilities in active markets.

(b)   quoted prices for identical or similar assets or liabilities in markets that are not active.

(c)   inputs other than quoted prices that are observable for the asset or liability, for example:

(i)   interest rates and yield curves observable at commonly quoted intervals;

(ii)   implied volatilities; and

(iii) credit spreads.

(d)   *market-corroborated inputs.*

83   Adjustments to Level 2 inputs will vary depending on factors specific to the asset
       or liability. Those factors include the following:

       (a)   the condition or location of the asset;

       (b)   the extent to which inputs relate to items that are comparable to the asset
             or liability (including those factors described in paragraph 39); and

       (c)   the volume or level of activity in the markets within which the inputs
             are observed.

84   An adjustment to a Level 2 input that is significant to the entire measurement
       might result in a fair value measurement categorised within Level 3 of the fair
       value hierarchy if the adjustment uses significant unobservable inputs.

85   Paragraph B35 describes the use of Level 2 inputs for particular assets and
       liabilities.

Level 3 inputs

86   Level 3 inputs are unobservable inputs for the asset or liability.

87   Unobservable inputs shall be used to measure fair value to the extent that
       relevant observable inputs are not available, thereby allowing for situations in
       which there is little, if any, market activity for the asset or liability at the
       measurement date. However, the fair value measurement objective remains
       the same, ie an exit price at the measurement date from the perspective of a
       market participant that holds the asset or owes the liability. Therefore,
       unobservable inputs shall reflect the assumptions that market participants would
       use when pricing the asset or liability, including assumptions about risk.

88   Assumptions about risk include the risk inherent in a particular valuation
       technique used to measure fair value (such as a pricing model) and the risk
       inherent in the inputs to the valuation technique. A measurement that does not
       include an adjustment for risk would not represent a fair value measurement if
       market participants would include one when pricing the asset or liability.
       For example, it might be necessary to include a risk adjustment when there is
       significant measurement uncertainty (eg when there has been a significant
       decrease in the volume or level of activity when compared with normal market
       activity for the asset or liability, or similar assets or liabilities, and the entity has
       determined that the transaction price or quoted price does not represent fair
       value, as described in paragraphs B37–B47).

89   An entity shall develop unobservable inputs using the best information available
       in the circumstances, which might include the entity's own data. In developing
       unobservable inputs, an entity may begin with its own data, but it shall adjust
       those data if reasonably available information indicates that other market
       participants would use different data or there is something particular to the
       entity that is not available to other market participants (eg an entity-specific
       synergy). An entity need not undertake exhaustive efforts to obtain information
       about market participant assumptions. However, an entity shall take into

account all information about market participant assumptions that is reasonably available. Unobservable inputs developed in the manner described above are considered market participant assumptions and meet the objective of a fair value measurement.

90   Paragraph B36 describes the use of Level 3 inputs for particular assets and liabilities.

Disclosure

91   **An entity shall disclose information that helps users of its financial statements assess both of the following:**

(a)   **for assets and liabilities that are measured at fair value on a recurring or non-recurring basis in the statement of financial position after initial recognition, the valuation techniques and inputs used to develop those measurements.**

(b)   **for recurring fair value measurements using significant unobservable inputs (Level 3), the effect of the measurements on profit or loss or other comprehensive income for the period.**

92   To meet the objectives in paragraph 91, an entity shall consider all the following:

(a)   the level of detail necessary to satisfy the disclosure requirements;

(b)   how much emphasis to place on each of the various requirements;

(c)   how much aggregation or disaggregation to undertake; and

(d)   whether users of financial statements need additional information to evaluate the quantitative information disclosed.

If the disclosures provided in accordance with this IFRS and other IFRSs are insufficient to meet the objectives in paragraph 91, an entity shall disclose additional information necessary to meet those objectives.

93   To meet the objectives in paragraph 91, an entity shall disclose, at a minimum, the following information for each class of assets and liabilities (see paragraph 94 for information on determining appropriate classes of assets and liabilities) measured at fair value (including measurements based on fair value within the scope of this IFRS) in the statement of financial position after initial recognition:

(a)   for recurring and non-recurring fair value measurements, the fair value measurement at the end of the reporting period, and for non-recurring fair value measurements, the reasons for the measurement. Recurring fair value measurements of assets or liabilities are those that other IFRSs require or permit in the statement of financial position at the end of each reporting period. Non-recurring fair value measurements of assets or liabilities are those that other IFRSs require or permit in the statement of financial position in particular circumstances (eg when an entity measures an asset held for sale at fair value less costs to sell in accordance with IFRS 5 *Non-current Assets Held for Sale and Discontinued Operations* because the asset's fair value less costs to sell is lower than its carrying amount).

(b) for recurring and non-recurring fair value measurements, the level of the fair value hierarchy within which the fair value measurements are categorised in their entirety (Level 1, 2 or 3).

(c) for assets and liabilities held at the end of the reporting period that are measured at fair value on a recurring basis, the amounts of any transfers between Level 1 and Level 2 of the fair value hierarchy, the reasons for those transfers and the entity's policy for determining when transfers between levels are deemed to have occurred (see paragraph 95). Transfers into each level shall be disclosed and discussed separately from transfers out of each level.

(d) for recurring and non-recurring fair value measurements categorised within Level 2 and Level 3 of the fair value hierarchy, a description of the valuation technique(s) and the inputs used in the fair value measurement. If there has been a change in valuation technique (eg changing from a market approach to an income approach or the use of an additional valuation technique), the entity shall disclose that change and the reason(s) for making it. For fair value measurements categorised within Level 3 of the fair value hierarchy, an entity shall provide quantitative information about the significant unobservable inputs used in the fair value measurement. An entity is not required to create quantitative information to comply with this disclosure requirement if quantitative unobservable inputs are not developed by the entity when measuring fair value (eg when an entity uses prices from prior transactions or third-party pricing information without adjustment). However, when providing this disclosure an entity cannot ignore quantitative unobservable inputs that are significant to the fair value measurement and are reasonably available to the entity.

(e) for recurring fair value measurements categorised within Level 3 of the fair value hierarchy, a reconciliation from the opening balances to the closing balances, disclosing separately changes during the period attributable to the following:

(i) total gains or losses for the period recognised in profit or loss, and the line item(s) in profit or loss in which those gains or losses are recognised.

(ii) total gains or losses for the period recognised in other comprehensive income, and the line item(s) in other comprehensive income in which those gains or losses are recognised.

(iii) purchases, sales, issues and settlements (each of those types of changes disclosed separately).

(iv) the amounts of any transfers into or out of Level 3 of the fair value hierarchy, the reasons for those transfers and the entity's policy for determining when transfers between levels are deemed to have occurred (see paragraph 95). Transfers into Level 3 shall be disclosed and discussed separately from transfers out of Level 3.

(f) for recurring fair value measurements categorised within Level 3 of the fair value hierarchy, the amount of the total gains or losses for the period in (e)(i) included in profit or loss that is attributable to the change in unrealised gains or losses relating to those assets and liabilities held at the end of the reporting period, and the line item(s) in profit or loss in which those unrealised gains or losses are recognised.

(g) for recurring and non-recurring fair value measurements categorised within Level 3 of the fair value hierarchy, a description of the valuation processes used by the entity (including, for example, how an entity decides its valuation policies and procedures and analyses changes in fair value measurements from period to period).

(h) for recurring fair value measurements categorised within Level 3 of the fair value hierarchy:

    (i) for all such measurements, a narrative description of the sensitivity of the fair value measurement to changes in unobservable inputs if a change in those inputs to a different amount might result in a significantly higher or lower fair value measurement. If there are interrelationships between those inputs and other unobservable inputs used in the fair value measurement, an entity shall also provide a description of those interrelationships and of how they might magnify or mitigate the effect of changes in the unobservable inputs on the fair value measurement. To comply with that disclosure requirement, the narrative description of the sensitivity to changes in unobservable inputs shall include, at a minimum, the unobservable inputs disclosed when complying with (d).

    (ii) for financial assets and financial liabilities, if changing one or more of the unobservable inputs to reflect reasonably possible alternative assumptions would change fair value significantly, an entity shall state that fact and disclose the effect of those changes. The entity shall disclose how the effect of a change to reflect a reasonably possible alternative assumption was calculated. For that purpose, significance shall be judged with respect to profit or loss, and total assets or total liabilities, or, when changes in fair value are recognised in other comprehensive income, total equity.

(i) for recurring and non-recurring fair value measurements, if the highest and best use of a non-financial asset differs from its current use, an entity shall disclose that fact and why the non-financial asset is being used in a manner that differs from its highest and best use.

94 An entity shall determine appropriate classes of assets and liabilities on the basis of the following:

(a) the nature, characteristics and risks of the asset or liability; and

(b) the level of the fair value hierarchy within which the fair value measurement is categorised.

The number of classes may need to be greater for fair value measurements categorised within Level 3 of the fair value hierarchy because those measurements have a greater degree of uncertainty and subjectivity. Determining appropriate classes of assets and liabilities for which disclosures about fair value measurements should be provided requires judgement. A class of assets and liabilities will often require greater disaggregation than the line items presented in the statement of financial position. However, an entity shall provide information sufficient to permit reconciliation to the line items presented in the statement of financial position. If another IFRS specifies the class for an asset or a liability, an entity may use that class in providing the disclosures required in this IFRS if that class meets the requirements in this paragraph.

95   An entity shall disclose and consistently follow its policy for determining when transfers between levels of the fair value hierarchy are deemed to have occurred in accordance with paragraph 93(c) and (e)(iv). The policy about the timing of recognising transfers shall be the same for transfers into the levels as for transfers out of the levels. Examples of policies for determining the timing of transfers include the following:

(a)   the date of the event or change in circumstances that caused the transfer.

(b)   the beginning of the reporting period.

(c)   the end of the reporting period.

96   If an entity makes an accounting policy decision to use the exception in paragraph 48, it shall disclose that fact.

97   For each class of assets and liabilities not measured at fair value in the statement of financial position but for which the fair value is disclosed, an entity shall disclose the information required by paragraph 93(b), (d) and (i). However, an entity is not required to provide the quantitative disclosures about significant unobservable inputs used in fair value measurements categorised within Level 3 of the fair value hierarchy required by paragraph 93(d). For such assets and liabilities, an entity does not need to provide the other disclosures required by this IFRS.

98   For a liability measured at fair value and issued with an inseparable third-party credit enhancement, an issuer shall disclose the existence of that credit enhancement and whether it is reflected in the fair value measurement of the liability.

99   An entity shall present the quantitative disclosures required by this IFRS in a tabular format unless another format is more appropriate.

Appendix A
Defined terms

This appendix is an integral part of the IFRS.

active market	A market in which transactions for the asset or liability take place with sufficient frequency and volume to provide pricing information on an ongoing basis.
cost approach	A valuation technique that reflects the amount that would be required currently to replace the service capacity of an asset (often referred to as current replacement cost).
entry price	The price paid to acquire an asset or received to assume a liability in an exchange transaction.
exit price	The price that would be received to sell an asset or paid to transfer a liability.
expected cash flow	The probability-weighted average (ie mean of the distribution) of possible future cash flows.
fair value	The price that would be received to sell an asset or paid to transfer a liability in an orderly transaction between market participants at the measurement date.
highest and best use	The use of a non-financial asset by market participants that would maximise the value of the asset or the group of assets and liabilities (eg a business) within which the asset would be used.
income approach	Valuation techniques that convert future amounts (eg cash flows or income and expenses) to a single current (ie discounted) amount. The fair value measurement is determined on the basis of the value indicated by current market expectations about those future amounts.
inputs	The assumptions that market participants would use when pricing the asset or liability, including assumptions about risk, such as the following:
	(a) the risk inherent in a particular valuation technique used to measure fair value (such as a pricing model); and
	(b) the risk inherent in the inputs to the valuation technique.
	Inputs may be observable or unobservable.
Level 1 inputs	Quoted prices (unadjusted) in active markets for identical assets or liabilities that the entity can access at the measurement date.
Level 2 inputs	Inputs other than quoted prices included within Level 1 that are observable for the asset or liability, either directly or indirectly.
Level 3 inputs	Unobservable inputs for the asset or liability.

market approach	A valuation technique that uses prices and other relevant information generated by market transactions involving identical or comparable (ie similar) assets, liabilities or a group of assets and liabilities, such as a business.
market-corroborated inputs	Inputs that are derived principally from or corroborated by observable market data by correlation or other means.
market participants	Buyers and sellers in the principal (or most advantageous) market for the asset or liability that have all of the following characteristics:

(a)   They are independent of each other, ie they are not related parties as defined in IAS 24, although the price in a related party transaction may be used as an input to a fair value measurement if the entity has evidence that the transaction was entered into at market terms.

(b)   They are knowledgeable, having a reasonable understanding about the asset or liability and the transaction using all available information, including information that might be obtained through due diligence efforts that are usual and customary.

(c)   They are able to enter into a transaction for the asset or liability.

(d)   They are willing to enter into a transaction for the asset or liability, ie they are motivated but not forced or otherwise compelled to do so.

most advantageous market	The market that maximises the amount that would be received to sell the asset or minimises the amount that would be paid to transfer the liability, after taking into account transaction costs and transport costs.
non-performance risk	The risk that an entity will not fulfil an obligation. Non-performance risk includes, but may not be limited to, the entity's own credit risk.
observable inputs	Inputs that are developed using market data, such as publicly available information about actual events or transactions, and that reflect the assumptions that market participants would use when pricing the asset or liability.
orderly transaction	A transaction that assumes exposure to the market for a period before the measurement date to allow for marketing activities that are usual and customary for transactions involving such assets or liabilities; it is not a forced transaction (eg a forced liquidation or distress sale).
principal market	The market with the greatest volume and level of activity for the asset or liability.

risk premium	Compensation sought by risk-averse market participants for bearing the uncertainty inherent in the cash flows of an asset or a liability. Also referred to as a 'risk adjustment'.
transaction costs	The costs to sell an asset or transfer a liability in the principal (or most advantageous) market for the asset or liability that are directly attributable to the disposal of the asset or the transfer of the liability and meet both of the following criteria:

    (a)   They result directly from and are essential to that transaction.

    (b)   They would not have been incurred by the entity had the decision to sell the asset or transfer the liability not been made (similar to costs to sell, as defined in IFRS 5).

transport costs	The costs that would be incurred to transport an asset from its current location to its principal (or most advantageous) market.
unit of account	The level at which an asset or a liability is aggregated or disaggregated in an IFRS for recognition purposes.
unobservable inputs	Inputs for which market data are not available and that are developed using the best information available about the assumptions that market participants would use when pricing the asset or liability.

Appendix B
Application guidance

This appendix is an integral part of the IFRS. It describes the application of paragraphs 1–99 and has the same authority as the other parts of the IFRS.

B1 The judgements applied in different valuation situations may be different. This appendix describes the judgements that might apply when an entity measures fair value in different valuation situations.

The fair value measurement approach

B2 The objective of a fair value measurement is to estimate the price at which an orderly transaction to sell the asset or to transfer the liability would take place between market participants at the measurement date under current market conditions. A fair value measurement requires an entity to determine all the following:

(a) the particular asset or liability that is the subject of the measurement (consistently with its unit of account).

(b) for a non-financial asset, the valuation premise that is appropriate for the measurement (consistently with its highest and best use).

(c) the principal (or most advantageous) market for the asset or liability.

(d) the valuation technique(s) appropriate for the measurement, considering the availability of data with which to develop inputs that represent the assumptions that market participants would use when pricing the asset or liability and the level of the fair value hierarchy within which the inputs are categorised.

Valuation premise for non-financial assets (paragraphs 31–33)

B3 When measuring the fair value of a non-financial asset used in combination with other assets as a group (as installed or otherwise configured for use) or in combination with other assets and liabilities (eg a business), the effect of the valuation premise depends on the circumstances. For example:

(a) the fair value of the asset might be the same whether the asset is used on a stand-alone basis or in combination with other assets or with other assets and liabilities. That might be the case if the asset is a business that market participants would continue to operate. In that case, the transaction would involve valuing the business in its entirety. The use of the assets as a group in an ongoing business would generate synergies that would be available to market participants (ie market participant synergies that, therefore, should affect the fair value of the asset on either a stand-alone basis or in combination with other assets or with other assets and liabilities).

(b) an asset's use in combination with other assets or with other assets and liabilities might be incorporated into the fair value measurement through adjustments to the value of the asset used on a stand-alone basis. That might be the case if the asset is a machine and the fair value measurement is determined using an observed price for a similar machine (not installed or otherwise configured for use), adjusted for transport and installation costs so that the fair value measurement reflects the current condition and location of the machine (installed and configured for use).

(c) an asset's use in combination with other assets or with other assets and liabilities might be incorporated into the fair value measurement through the market participant assumptions used to measure the fair value of the asset. For example, if the asset is work in progress inventory that is unique and market participants would convert the inventory into finished goods, the fair value of the inventory would assume that market participants have acquired or would acquire any specialised machinery necessary to convert the inventory into finished goods.

(d) an asset's use in combination with other assets or with other assets and liabilities might be incorporated into the valuation technique used to measure the fair value of the asset. That might be the case when using the multi-period excess earnings method to measure the fair value of an intangible asset because that valuation technique specifically takes into account the contribution of any complementary assets and the associated liabilities in the group in which such an intangible asset would be used.

(e) in more limited situations, when an entity uses an asset within a group of assets, the entity might measure the asset at an amount that approximates its fair value when allocating the fair value of the asset group to the individual assets of the group. That might be the case if the valuation involves real property and the fair value of improved property (ie an asset group) is allocated to its component assets (such as land and improvements).

Fair value at initial recognition (paragraphs 57–60)

B4 When determining whether fair value at initial recognition equals the transaction price, an entity shall take into account factors specific to the transaction and to the asset or liability. For example, the transaction price might not represent the fair value of an asset or a liability at initial recognition if any of the following conditions exist:

(a) The transaction is between related parties, although the price in a related party transaction may be used as an input into a fair value measurement if the entity has evidence that the transaction was entered into at market terms.

(b) The transaction takes place under duress or the seller is forced to accept the price in the transaction. For example, that might be the case if the seller is experiencing financial difficulty.

(c)   The unit of account represented by the transaction price is different from the unit of account for the asset or liability measured at fair value. For example, that might be the case if the asset or liability measured at fair value is only one of the elements in the transaction (eg in a business combination), the transaction includes unstated rights and privileges that are measured separately in accordance with another IFRS, or the transaction price includes transaction costs.

(d)   The market in which the transaction takes place is different from the principal market (or most advantageous market). For example, those markets might be different if the entity is a dealer that enters into transactions with customers in the retail market, but the principal (or most advantageous) market for the exit transaction is with other dealers in the dealer market.

Valuation techniques (paragraphs 61–66)

Market approach

B5   The market approach uses prices and other relevant information generated by market transactions involving identical or comparable (ie similar) assets, liabilities or a group of assets and liabilities, such as a business.

B6   For example, valuation techniques consistent with the market approach often use market multiples derived from a set of comparables. Multiples might be in ranges with a different multiple for each comparable. The selection of the appropriate multiple within the range requires judgement, considering qualitative and quantitative factors specific to the measurement.

B7   Valuation techniques consistent with the market approach include matrix pricing. Matrix pricing is a mathematical technique used principally to value some types of financial instruments, such as debt securities, without relying exclusively on quoted prices for the specific securities, but rather relying on the securities' relationship to other benchmark quoted securities.

Cost approach

B8   The cost approach reflects the amount that would be required currently to replace the service capacity of an asset (often referred to as current replacement cost).

B9   From the perspective of a market participant seller, the price that would be received for the asset is based on the cost to a market participant buyer to acquire or construct a substitute asset of comparable utility, adjusted for obsolescence. That is because a market participant buyer would not pay more for an asset than the amount for which it could replace the service capacity of that asset. Obsolescence encompasses physical deterioration, functional (technological) obsolescence and economic (external) obsolescence and is broader than depreciation for financial reporting purposes (an allocation of historical cost) or tax purposes (using specified service lives). In many cases the current replacement cost method is used to measure the fair value of tangible assets that are used in combination with other assets or with other assets and liabilities.

Income approach

B10 The income approach converts future amounts (eg cash flows or income and expenses) to a single current (ie discounted) amount. When the income approach is used, the fair value measurement reflects current market expectations about those future amounts.

B11 Those valuation techniques include, for example, the following:

(a) present value techniques (see paragraphs B12–B30);

(b) option pricing models, such as the Black-Scholes-Merton formula or a binomial model (ie a lattice model), that incorporate present value techniques and reflect both the time value and the intrinsic value of an option; and

(c) the multi-period excess earnings method, which is used to measure the fair value of some intangible assets.

Present value techniques

B12 Paragraphs B13–B30 describe the use of present value techniques to measure fair value. Those paragraphs focus on a discount rate adjustment technique and an *expected cash flow* (expected present value) technique. Those paragraphs neither prescribe the use of a single specific present value technique nor limit the use of present value techniques to measure fair value to the techniques discussed. The present value technique used to measure fair value will depend on facts and circumstances specific to the asset or liability being measured (eg whether prices for comparable assets or liabilities can be observed in the market) and the availability of sufficient data.

The components of a present value measurement

B13 Present value (ie an application of the income approach) is a tool used to link future amounts (eg cash flows or values) to a present amount using a discount rate. A fair value measurement of an asset or a liability using a present value technique captures all the following elements from the perspective of market participants at the measurement date:

(a) an estimate of future cash flows for the asset or liability being measured.

(b) expectations about possible variations in the amount and timing of the cash flows representing the uncertainty inherent in the cash flows.

(c) the time value of money, represented by the rate on risk-free monetary assets that have maturity dates or durations that coincide with the period covered by the cash flows and pose neither uncertainty in timing nor risk of default to the holder (ie a risk-free interest rate).

(d) the price for bearing the uncertainty inherent in the cash flows (ie a risk premium).

(e) other factors that market participants would take into account in the circumstances.

(f) for a liability, the non-performance risk relating to that liability, including the entity's (ie the obligor's) own credit risk.

General principles

B14 Present value techniques differ in how they capture the elements in paragraph B13. However, all the following general principles govern the application of any present value technique used to measure fair value:

(a) Cash flows and discount rates should reflect assumptions that market participants would use when pricing the asset or liability.

(b) Cash flows and discount rates should take into account only the factors attributable to the asset or liability being measured.

(c) To avoid double-counting or omitting the effects of risk factors, discount rates should reflect assumptions that are consistent with those inherent in the cash flows. For example, a discount rate that reflects the uncertainty in expectations about future defaults is appropriate if using contractual cash flows of a loan (ie a discount rate adjustment technique). That same rate should not be used if using expected (ie probability-weighted) cash flows (ie an expected present value technique) because the expected cash flows already reflect assumptions about the uncertainty in future defaults; instead, a discount rate that is commensurate with the risk inherent in the expected cash flows should be used.

(d) Assumptions about cash flows and discount rates should be internally consistent. For example, nominal cash flows, which include the effect of inflation, should be discounted at a rate that includes the effect of inflation. The nominal risk-free interest rate includes the effect of inflation. Real cash flows, which exclude the effect of inflation, should be discounted at a rate that excludes the effect of inflation. Similarly, after-tax cash flows should be discounted using an after-tax discount rate. Pre-tax cash flows should be discounted at a rate consistent with those cash flows.

(e) Discount rates should be consistent with the underlying economic factors of the currency in which the cash flows are denominated.

Risk and uncertainty

B15 A fair value measurement using present value techniques is made under conditions of uncertainty because the cash flows used are estimates rather than known amounts. In many cases both the amount and timing of the cash flows are uncertain. Even contractually fixed amounts, such as the payments on a loan, are uncertain if there is risk of default.

B16 Market participants generally seek compensation (ie a risk premium) for bearing the uncertainty inherent in the cash flows of an asset or a liability. A fair value measurement should include a risk premium reflecting the amount that market participants would demand as compensation for the uncertainty inherent in the cash flows. Otherwise, the measurement would not faithfully represent fair value. In some cases determining the appropriate risk premium might be difficult. However, the degree of difficulty alone is not a sufficient reason to exclude a risk premium.

B17 Present value techniques differ in how they adjust for risk and in the type of cash flows they use. For example:

(a) The discount rate adjustment technique (see paragraphs B18–B22) uses a risk-adjusted discount rate and contractual, promised or most likely cash flows.

(b) Method 1 of the expected present value technique (see paragraph B25) uses risk-adjusted expected cash flows and a risk-free rate.

(c) Method 2 of the expected present value technique (see paragraph B26) uses expected cash flows that are not risk-adjusted and a discount rate adjusted to include the risk premium that market participants require. That rate is different from the rate used in the discount rate adjustment technique.

Discount rate adjustment technique

B18 The discount rate adjustment technique uses a single set of cash flows from the range of possible estimated amounts, whether contractual or promised (as is the case for a bond) or most likely cash flows. In all cases, those cash flows are conditional upon the occurrence of specified events (eg contractual or promised cash flows for a bond are conditional on the event of no default by the debtor). The discount rate used in the discount rate adjustment technique is derived from observed rates of return for comparable assets or liabilities that are traded in the market. Accordingly, the contractual, promised or most likely cash flows are discounted at an observed or estimated market rate for such conditional cash flows (ie a market rate of return).

B19 The discount rate adjustment technique requires an analysis of market data for comparable assets or liabilities. Comparability is established by considering the nature of the cash flows (eg whether the cash flows are contractual or non-contractual and are likely to respond similarly to changes in economic conditions), as well as other factors (eg credit standing, collateral, duration, restrictive covenants and liquidity). Alternatively, if a single comparable asset or liability does not fairly reflect the risk inherent in the cash flows of the asset or liability being measured, it may be possible to derive a discount rate using data for several comparable assets or liabilities in conjunction with the risk-free yield curve (ie using a 'build-up' approach).

B20 To illustrate a build-up approach, assume that Asset A is a contractual right to receive CU800[1] in one year (ie there is no timing uncertainty). There is an established market for comparable assets, and information about those assets, including price information, is available. Of those comparable assets:

(a) Asset B is a contractual right to receive CU1,200 in one year and has a market price of CU1,083. Thus, the implied annual rate of return (ie a one-year market rate of return) is 10.8 per cent [(CU1,200/CU1,083) – 1].

(b) Asset C is a contractual right to receive CU700 in two years and has a market price of CU566. Thus, the implied annual rate of return (ie a two-year market rate of return) is 11.2 per cent [(CU700/CU566)^0.5 – 1].

(c) All three assets are comparable with respect to risk (ie dispersion of possible pay-offs and credit).

---

1 In this IFRS monetary amounts are denominated in 'currency units (CU)'.

B21   On the basis of the timing of the contractual payments to be received for Asset A relative to the timing for Asset B and Asset C (ie one year for Asset B versus two years for Asset C), Asset B is deemed more comparable to Asset A. Using the contractual payment to be received for Asset A (CU800) and the one-year market rate derived from Asset B (10.8 per cent), the fair value of Asset A is CU722 (CU800/1.108). Alternatively, in the absence of available market information for Asset B, the one-year market rate could be derived from Asset C using the build-up approach. In that case the two-year market rate indicated by Asset C (11.2 per cent) would be adjusted to a one-year market rate using the term structure of the risk-free yield curve. Additional information and analysis might be required to determine whether the risk premiums for one-year and two-year assets are the same. If it is determined that the risk premiums for one-year and two-year assets are not the same, the two-year market rate of return would be further adjusted for that effect.

B22   When the discount rate adjustment technique is applied to fixed receipts or payments, the adjustment for risk inherent in the cash flows of the asset or liability being measured is included in the discount rate. In some applications of the discount rate adjustment technique to cash flows that are not fixed receipts or payments, an adjustment to the cash flows may be necessary to achieve comparability with the observed asset or liability from which the discount rate is derived.

Expected present value technique

B23   The expected present value technique uses as a starting point a set of cash flows that represents the probability-weighted average of all possible future cash flows (ie the expected cash flows). The resulting estimate is identical to expected value, which, in statistical terms, is the weighted average of a discrete random variable's possible values with the respective probabilities as the weights. Because all possible cash flows are probability-weighted, the resulting expected cash flow is not conditional upon the occurrence of any specified event (unlike the cash flows used in the discount rate adjustment technique).

B24   In making an investment decision, risk-averse market participants would take into account the risk that the actual cash flows may differ from the expected cash flows. Portfolio theory distinguishes between two types of risk:

(a)   unsystematic (diversifiable) risk, which is the risk specific to a particular asset or liability.

(b)   systematic (non-diversifiable) risk, which is the common risk shared by an asset or a liability with the other items in a diversified portfolio.

Portfolio theory holds that in a market in equilibrium, market participants will be compensated only for bearing the systematic risk inherent in the cash flows. (In markets that are inefficient or out of equilibrium, other forms of return or compensation might be available.)

B25   Method 1 of the expected present value technique adjusts the expected cash flows of an asset for systematic (ie market) risk by subtracting a cash risk premium (ie risk-adjusted expected cash flows). Those risk-adjusted expected cash flows represent a certainty-equivalent cash flow, which is discounted at a risk-free interest rate. A certainty-equivalent cash flow refers to an expected cash flow (as defined), adjusted for risk so that a market participant is indifferent to trading a certain cash flow for an expected cash flow. For example, if a market participant was willing to trade an expected cash flow of CU1,200 for a certain cash flow of CU1,000, the CU1,000 is the certainty equivalent of the CU1,200 (ie the CU200 would represent the cash risk premium). In that case the market participant would be indifferent as to the asset held.

B26 In contrast, Method 2 of the expected present value technique adjusts for systematic (ie market) risk by applying a risk premium to the risk-free interest rate. Accordingly, the expected cash flows are discounted at a rate that corresponds to an expected rate associated with probability-weighted cash flows (ie an expected rate of return). Models used for pricing risky assets, such as the capital asset pricing model, can be used to estimate the expected rate of return. Because the discount rate used in the discount rate adjustment technique is a rate of return relating to conditional cash flows, it is likely to be higher than the discount rate used in Method 2 of the expected present value technique, which is an expected rate of return relating to expected or probability-weighted cash flows.

B27 To illustrate Methods 1 and 2, assume that an asset has expected cash flows of CU780 in one year determined on the basis of the possible cash flows and probabilities shown below. The applicable risk-free interest rate for cash flows with a one-year horizon is 5 per cent, and the systematic risk premium for an asset with the same risk profile is 3 per cent.

Possible cash flows	Probability	Probability-weighted cash flows
CU500	15%	CU75
CU800	60%	CU480
CU900	25%	CU225
Expected cash flows		CU780

B28 In this simple illustration, the expected cash flows (CU780) represent the probability-weighted average of the three possible outcomes. In more realistic situations, there could be many possible outcomes. However, to apply the expected present value technique, it is not always necessary to take into account distributions of all possible cash flows using complex models and techniques. Rather, it might be possible to develop a limited number of discrete scenarios and probabilities that capture the array of possible cash flows. For example, an entity might use realised cash flows for some relevant past period, adjusted for changes in circumstances occurring subsequently (eg changes in external factors, including economic or market conditions, industry trends and competition as well as changes in internal factors affecting the entity more specifically), taking into account the assumptions of market participants.

B29 In theory, the present value (ie the fair value) of the asset's cash flows is the same whether determined using Method 1 or Method 2, as follows:

(a) Using Method 1, the expected cash flows are adjusted for systematic (ie market) risk. In the absence of market data directly indicating the amount of the risk adjustment, such adjustment could be derived from an asset pricing model using the concept of certainty equivalents. For example, the risk adjustment (ie the cash risk premium of CU22) could be determined using the systematic risk premium of 3 per cent (CU780 − [CU780 × (1.05/1.08)]), which results in risk-adjusted expected cash flows of CU758 (CU780 − CU22). The CU758 is the certainty equivalent of CU780 and is discounted at the risk-free interest rate (5 per cent). The present value (ie the fair value) of the asset is CU722 (CU758/1.05).

(b) Using Method 2, the expected cash flows are not adjusted for systematic (ie market) risk. Rather, the adjustment for that risk is included in the discount rate. Thus, the expected cash flows are discounted at an expected rate of return of 8 per cent (ie the 5 per cent risk-free interest rate plus the 3 per cent systematic risk premium). The present value (ie the fair value) of the asset is CU722 (CU780/1.08).

B30 When using an expected present value technique to measure fair value, either Method 1 or Method 2 could be used. The selection of Method 1 or Method 2 will depend on facts and circumstances specific to the asset or liability being measured, the extent to which sufficient data are available and the judgements applied.

Applying present value techniques to liabilities and an entity's own equity instruments not held by other parties as assets (paragraphs 40 and 41)

B31 When using a present value technique to measure the fair value of a liability that is not held by another party as an asset (eg a decommissioning liability), an entity shall, among other things, estimate the future cash outflows that market participants would expect to incur in fulfilling the obligation. Those future cash outflows shall include market participants' expectations about the costs of fulfilling the obligation and the compensation that a market participant would require for taking on the obligation. Such compensation includes the return that a market participant would require for the following:

(a) undertaking the activity (ie the value of fulfilling the obligation; eg by using resources that could be used for other activities); and

(b) assuming the risk associated with the obligation (ie a *risk premium* that reflects the risk that the actual cash outflows might differ from the expected cash outflows; see paragraph B33).

B32 For example, a non-financial liability does not contain a contractual rate of return and there is no observable market yield for that liability. In some cases the components of the return that market participants would require will be indistinguishable from one another (eg when using the price a third party contractor would charge on a fixed fee basis). In other cases an entity needs to estimate those components separately (eg when using the price a third party contractor would charge on a cost plus basis because the contractor in that case would not bear the risk of future changes in costs).

B33   An entity can include a risk premium in the fair value measurement of a liability or an entity's own equity instrument that is not held by another party as an asset in one of the following ways:

     (a)   by adjusting the cash flows (ie as an increase in the amount of cash outflows); or

     (b)   by adjusting the rate used to discount the future cash flows to their present values (ie as a reduction in the discount rate).

    An entity shall ensure that it does not double-count or omit adjustments for risk. For example, if the estimated cash flows are increased to take into account the compensation for assuming the risk associated with the obligation, the discount rate should not be adjusted to reflect that risk.

Inputs to valuation techniques (paragraphs 67–71)

B34   Examples of markets in which inputs might be observable for some assets and liabilities (eg financial instruments) include the following:

     (a)   *Exchange markets.* In an exchange market, closing prices are both readily available and generally representative of fair value. An example of such a market is the London Stock Exchange.

     (b)   *Dealer markets.* In a dealer market, dealers stand ready to trade (either buy or sell for their own account), thereby providing liquidity by using their capital to hold an inventory of the items for which they make a market. Typically bid and ask prices (representing the price at which the dealer is willing to buy and the price at which the dealer is willing to sell, respectively) are more readily available than closing prices. Over-the-counter markets (for which prices are publicly reported) are dealer markets. Dealer markets also exist for some other assets and liabilities, including some financial instruments, commodities and physical assets (eg used equipment).

     (c)   *Brokered markets.* In a brokered market, brokers attempt to match buyers with sellers but do not stand ready to trade for their own account. In other words, brokers do not use their own capital to hold an inventory of the items for which they make a market. The broker knows the prices bid and asked by the respective parties, but each party is typically unaware of another party's price requirements. Prices of completed transactions are sometimes available. Brokered markets include electronic communication networks, in which buy and sell orders are matched, and commercial and residential real estate markets.

     (d)   *Principal-to-principal markets.* In a principal-to-principal market, transactions, both originations and resales, are negotiated independently with no intermediary. Little information about those transactions may be made available publicly.

Fair value hierarchy (paragraphs 72–90)

Level 2 inputs (paragraphs 81–85)

B35 Examples of Level 2 inputs for particular assets and liabilities include the following:

(a) *Receive-fixed, pay-variable interest rate swap based on the London Interbank Offered Rate (LIBOR) swap rate.* A Level 2 input would be the LIBOR swap rate if that rate is observable at commonly quoted intervals for substantially the full term of the swap.

(b) *Receive-fixed, pay-variable interest rate swap based on a yield curve denominated in a foreign currency.* A Level 2 input would be the swap rate based on a yield curve denominated in a foreign currency that is observable at commonly quoted intervals for substantially the full term of the swap. That would be the case if the term of the swap is 10 years and that rate is observable at commonly quoted intervals for 9 years, provided that any reasonable extrapolation of the yield curve for year 10 would not be significant to the fair value measurement of the swap in its entirety.

(c) *Receive-fixed, pay-variable interest rate swap based on a specific bank's prime rate.* A Level 2 input would be the bank's prime rate derived through extrapolation if the extrapolated values are corroborated by observable market data, for example, by correlation with an interest rate that is observable over substantially the full term of the swap.

(d) *Three-year option on exchange-traded shares.* A Level 2 input would be the implied volatility for the shares derived through extrapolation to year 3 if both of the following conditions exist:

   (i) Prices for one-year and two-year options on the shares are observable.

   (ii) The extrapolated implied volatility of a three-year option is corroborated by observable market data for substantially the full term of the option.

   In that case the implied volatility could be derived by extrapolating from the implied volatility of the one-year and two-year options on the shares and corroborated by the implied volatility for three-year options on comparable entities' shares, provided that correlation with the one-year and two-year implied volatilities is established.

(e) *Licensing arrangement.* For a licensing arrangement that is acquired in a business combination and was recently negotiated with an unrelated party by the acquired entity (the party to the licensing arrangement), a Level 2 input would be the royalty rate in the contract with the unrelated party at inception of the arrangement.

(f) *Finished goods inventory at a retail outlet.* For finished goods inventory that is acquired in a business combination, a Level 2 input would be either a price to customers in a retail market or a price to retailers in a wholesale market, adjusted for differences between the condition and location of the inventory item and the comparable (ie similar) inventory items so that the fair value measurement reflects the price that would be received in a transaction to sell the inventory to another retailer that would complete the requisite selling efforts. Conceptually, the fair value measurement will be the same, whether adjustments are made to a retail price (downward) or to a wholesale price (upward). Generally, the price that requires the least amount of subjective adjustments should be used for the fair value measurement.

(g) *Building held and used.* A Level 2 input would be the price per square metre for the building (a valuation multiple) derived from observable market data, eg multiples derived from prices in observed transactions involving comparable (ie similar) buildings in similar locations.

(h) *Cash-generating unit.* A Level 2 input would be a valuation multiple (eg a multiple of earnings or revenue or a similar performance measure) derived from observable market data, eg multiples derived from prices in observed transactions involving comparable (ie similar) businesses, taking into account operational, market, financial and non-financial factors.

Level 3 inputs (paragraphs 86–90)

B36 Examples of Level 3 inputs for particular assets and liabilities include the following:

(a) *Long-dated currency swap.* A Level 3 input would be an interest rate in a specified currency that is not observable and cannot be corroborated by observable market data at commonly quoted intervals or otherwise for substantially the full term of the currency swap. The interest rates in a currency swap are the swap rates calculated from the respective countries' yield curves.

(b) *Three-year option on exchange-traded shares.* A Level 3 input would be historical volatility, ie the volatility for the shares derived from the shares' historical prices. Historical volatility typically does not represent current market participants' expectations about future volatility, even if it is the only information available to price an option.

(c) *Interest rate swap.* A Level 3 input would be an adjustment to a mid-market consensus (non-binding) price for the swap developed using data that are not directly observable and cannot otherwise be corroborated by observable market data.

(d) *Decommissioning liability assumed in a business combination.* A Level 3 input would be a current estimate using the entity's own data about the future cash outflows to be paid to fulfil the obligation (including market participants' expectations about the costs of fulfilling the obligation and the compensation that a market participant would require for taking on the obligation to dismantle the asset) if there is no reasonably available information that indicates that market participants would use different assumptions. That Level 3 input would be used in a present value technique together with other inputs, eg a current risk-free interest rate or a credit-adjusted risk-free rate if the effect of the entity's credit standing on the fair value of the liability is reflected in the discount rate rather than in the estimate of future cash outflows.

(e) *Cash-generating unit.* A Level 3 input would be a financial forecast (eg of cash flows or profit or loss) developed using the entity's own data if there is no reasonably available information that indicates that market participants would use different assumptions.

Measuring fair value when the volume or level of activity for an asset or a liability has significantly decreased

B37   The fair value of an asset or a liability might be affected when there has been a significant decrease in the volume or level of activity for that asset or liability in relation to normal market activity for the asset or liability (or similar assets or liabilities). To determine whether, on the basis of the evidence available, there has been a significant decrease in the volume or level of activity for the asset or liability, an entity shall evaluate the significance and relevance of factors such as the following:

(a)   There are few recent transactions.

(b)   Price quotations are not developed using current information.

(c)   Price quotations vary substantially either over time or among market-makers (eg some brokered markets).

(d)   Indices that previously were highly correlated with the fair values of the asset or liability are demonstrably uncorrelated with recent indications of fair value for that asset or liability.

(e)   There is a significant increase in implied liquidity risk premiums, yields or performance indicators (such as delinquency rates or loss severities) for observed transactions or quoted prices when compared with the entity's estimate of expected cash flows, taking into account all available market data about credit and other non-performance risk for the asset or liability.

(f)   There is a wide bid-ask spread or significant increase in the bid-ask spread.

(g)   There is a significant decline in the activity of, or there is an absence of, a market for new issues (ie a primary market) for the asset or liability or similar assets or liabilities.

(h)   Little information is publicly available (eg for transactions that take place in a principal-to-principal market).

B38   If an entity concludes that there has been a significant decrease in the volume or level of activity for the asset or liability in relation to normal market activity for the asset or liability (or similar assets or liabilities), further analysis of the transactions or quoted prices is needed. A decrease in the volume or level of activity on its own may not indicate that a transaction price or quoted price does not represent fair value or that a transaction in that market is not orderly. However, if an entity determines that a transaction or quoted price does not represent fair value (eg there may be transactions that are not orderly), an adjustment to the transactions or quoted prices will be necessary if the entity uses those prices as a basis for measuring fair value and that adjustment may be significant to the fair value measurement in its entirety. Adjustments also may be necessary in other circumstances (eg when a price for a similar asset requires significant adjustment to make it comparable to the asset being measured or when the price is stale).

B39   This IFRS does not prescribe a methodology for making significant adjustments to transactions or quoted prices. See paragraphs 61–66 and B5–B11 for a discussion of the use of valuation techniques when measuring fair value. Regardless of the valuation technique used, an entity shall include appropriate risk adjustments, including a risk premium reflecting the amount that market participants would demand as compensation for the uncertainty inherent in the cash flows of an asset or a liability (see paragraph B17). Otherwise, the measurement does not faithfully represent fair value. In some cases determining the appropriate risk adjustment might be difficult. However, the degree of difficulty alone is not a sufficient basis on which to exclude a risk adjustment. The risk adjustment shall be reflective of an orderly transaction between market participants at the measurement date under current market conditions.

B40   If there has been a significant decrease in the volume or level of activity for the asset or liability, a change in valuation technique or the use of multiple valuation techniques may be appropriate (eg the use of a market approach and a present value technique). When weighting indications of fair value resulting from the use of multiple valuation techniques, an entity shall consider the reasonableness of the range of fair value measurements. The objective is to determine the point within the range that is most representative of fair value under current market conditions. A wide range of fair value measurements may be an indication that further analysis is needed.

B41   Even when there has been a significant decrease in the volume or level of activity for the asset or liability, the objective of a fair value measurement remains the same. Fair value is the price that would be received to sell an asset or paid to transfer a liability in an orderly transaction (ie not a forced liquidation or distress sale) between market participants at the measurement date under current market conditions.

B42   Estimating the price at which market participants would be willing to enter into a transaction at the measurement date under current market conditions if there has been a significant decrease in the volume or level of activity for the asset or liability depends on the facts and circumstances at the measurement date and requires judgement. An entity's intention to hold the asset or to settle or otherwise fulfil the liability is not relevant when measuring fair value because fair value is a market-based measurement, not an entity-specific measurement.

Identifying transactions that are not orderly

B43   The determination of whether a transaction is orderly (or is not orderly) is more difficult if there has been a significant decrease in the volume or level of activity for the asset or liability in relation to normal market activity for the asset or liability (or similar assets or liabilities). In such circumstances it is not appropriate to conclude that all transactions in that market are not orderly (ie forced liquidations or distress sales). Circumstances that may indicate that a transaction is not orderly include the following:

(a) There was not adequate exposure to the market for a period before the measurement date to allow for marketing activities that are usual and customary for transactions involving such assets or liabilities under current market conditions.

(b) There was a usual and customary marketing period, but the seller marketed the asset or liability to a single market participant.

(c) The seller is in or near bankruptcy or receivership (ie the seller is distressed).

(d) The seller was required to sell to meet regulatory or legal requirements (ie the seller was forced).

(e) The transaction price is an outlier when compared with other recent transactions for the same or a similar asset or liability.

An entity shall evaluate the circumstances to determine whether, on the weight of the evidence available, the transaction is orderly.

B44 An entity shall consider all the following when measuring fair value or estimating market risk premiums:

(a) If the evidence indicates that a transaction is not orderly, an entity shall place little, if any, weight (compared with other indications of fair value) on that transaction price.

(b) If the evidence indicates that a transaction is orderly, an entity shall take into account that transaction price. The amount of weight placed on that transaction price when compared with other indications of fair value will depend on the facts and circumstances, such as the following:

(i) the volume of the transaction.

(ii) the comparability of the transaction to the asset or liability being measured.

(iii) the proximity of the transaction to the measurement date.

(c) If an entity does not have sufficient information to conclude whether a transaction is orderly, it shall take into account the transaction price. However, that transaction price may not represent fair value (ie the transaction price is not necessarily the sole or primary basis for measuring fair value or estimating market risk premiums). When an entity does not have sufficient information to conclude whether particular transactions are orderly, the entity shall place less weight on those transactions when compared with other transactions that are known to be orderly.

An entity need not undertake exhaustive efforts to determine whether a transaction is orderly, but it shall not ignore information that is reasonably available. When an entity is a party to a transaction, it is presumed to have sufficient information to conclude whether the transaction is orderly.

Using quoted prices provided by third parties

B45   This IFRS does not preclude the use of quoted prices provided by third parties, such as pricing services or brokers, if an entity has determined that the quoted prices provided by those parties are developed in accordance with this IFRS.

B46   If there has been a significant decrease in the volume or level of activity for the asset or liability, an entity shall evaluate whether the quoted prices provided by third parties are developed using current information that reflects orderly transactions or a valuation technique that reflects market participant assumptions (including assumptions about risk). In weighting a quoted price as an input to a fair value measurement, an entity places less weight (when compared with other indications of fair value that reflect the results of transactions) on quotes that do not reflect the result of transactions.

B47   Furthermore, the nature of a quote (eg whether the quote is an indicative price or a binding offer) shall be taken into account when weighting the available evidence, with more weight given to quotes provided by third parties that represent binding offers.

Appendix C
Effective date and transition

This appendix is an integral part of the IFRS and has the same authority as the other parts of the IFRS.

C1   An entity shall apply this IFRS for annual periods beginning on or after 1 January 2013. Earlier application is permitted. If an entity applies this IFRS for an earlier period, it shall disclose that fact.

C2   This IFRS shall be applied prospectively as of the beginning of the annual period in which it is initially applied.

C3   The disclosure requirements of this IFRS need not be applied in comparative information provided for periods before initial application of this IFRS.

Appendix D
Amendments to other IFRSs

This appendix sets out amendments to other IFRSs that are a consequence of the Board issuing IFRS 13. An entity shall apply the amendments for annual periods beginning on or after 1 January 2013. If an entity applies IFRS 13 for an earlier period, it shall apply the amendments for that earlier period. Amended paragraphs are shown with new text underlined and deleted text struck through.

* * * * *

The amendments contained in this appendix when this IFRS was issued in 2011 have been incorporated into the relevant IFRSs published in this volume.

International Accounting Standard 1

Presentation of Financial Statements

In April 2001 the International Accounting Standards Board (IASB) adopted IAS 1 *Presentation of Financial Statements*, which had originally been issued by the International Accounting Standards Committee in September 1997. IAS 1 *Presentation of Financial Statements* replaced IAS 1 *Disclosure of Accounting Policies* (issued in 1975), IAS 5 *Information to be Disclosed in Financial Statements* (originally approved in 1977) and IAS 13 *Presentation of Current Assets and Current Liabilities* (approved in 1979).

In December 2003 the IASB issued a revised IAS 1 as part of its initial agenda of technical projects. The IASB issued an amended IAS 1 in September 2007, which included an amendment to the presentation of owner changes in equity and comprehensive income and a change in terminology in the titles of financial statements. In June 2011 the IASB amended IAS 1 to improve how items of other income comprehensive income (OCI) should be presented.

Other IFRSs have made minor consequential amendments to IAS 1. They include IFRS 5 *Non-current Assets Held for Sale and Discontinued Operations* (issued March 2004), IFRS 7 *Financial Instruments: Disclosures* (issued August 2005), *Improvements to IFRSs* (issued May 2008, April 2009 and May 2010) and IFRS 9 *Financial Instruments* (issued November 2009 and October 2010).

CONTENTS

APPENDIX
Amendments to other pronouncements

FOR THE ACCOMPANYING DOCUMENTS LISTED BELOW, SEE PART B OF THIS EDITION

APPROVAL BY THE BOARD OF IAS 1 ISSUED IN SEPTEMBER 2007

APPROVAL BY THE BOARD OF *PUTTABLE FINANCIAL INSTRUMENTS AND OBLIGATIONS ARISING ON LIQUIDATION* (AMENDMENTS TO IAS 32 AND IAS 1) ISSUED IN FEBRUARY 2008

BASIS FOR CONCLUSIONS

APPENDIX
Amendments to the Basis for Conclusions on other IFRSs

DISSENTING OPINIONS

IMPLEMENTATION GUIDANCE

APPENDIX
Amendments to guidance on other IFRSs

TABLE OF CONCORDANCE

International Accounting Standard 1 *Presentation of Financial Statements* (IAS 1) is set out in paragraphs 1–140 and the Appendix. All the paragraphs have equal authority. IAS 1 should be read in the context of its objective and the Basis for Conclusions, the *Preface to International Financial Reporting Standards* and the *Conceptual Framework for Financial Reporting*. IAS 8 *Accounting Policies, Changes in Accounting Estimates and Errors* provides a basis for selecting and applying accounting policies in the absence of explicit guidance.

Introduction

IN1   International Accounting Standard 1 *Presentation of Financial Statements* (IAS 1) replaces IAS 1 *Presentation of Financial Statements* (revised in 2003) as amended in 2005. IAS 1 sets overall requirements for the presentation of financial statements, guidelines for their structure and minimum requirements for their content.

Reasons for revising IAS 1

IN2   The main objective of the International Accounting Standards Board in revising IAS 1 was to aggregate information in the financial statements on the basis of shared characteristics. With this in mind, the Board considered it useful to separate changes in equity (net assets) of an entity during a period arising from transactions with owners in their capacity as owners from other changes in equity. Consequently, the Board decided that all owner changes in equity should be presented in the statement of changes in equity, separately from non-owner changes in equity.

IN3   In its review, the Board also considered FASB Statement No. 130 *Reporting Comprehensive Income* (SFAS 130) issued in 1997. The requirements in IAS 1 regarding the presentation of the statement of comprehensive income are similar to those in SFAS 130; however, some differences remain and those are identified in paragraph BC106 of the Basis for Conclusions.

IN4   In addition, the Board's intention in revising IAS 1 was to improve and reorder sections of IAS 1 to make it easier to read. The Board's objective was not to reconsider all the requirements of IAS 1.

Main features of IAS 1

IN5   IAS 1 affects the presentation of owner changes in equity and of comprehensive income. It does not change the recognition, measurement or disclosure of specific transactions and other events required by other IFRSs.

IN6   IAS 1 requires an entity to present, in a statement of changes in equity, all owner changes in equity. All non-owner changes in equity (ie comprehensive income) are required to be presented in one statement of comprehensive income or in two statements (a separate income statement and a statement of comprehensive income). Components of comprehensive income are not permitted to be presented in the statement of changes in equity.

IN7   IAS 1 requires an entity to present a statement of financial position as at the beginning of the earliest comparative period in a complete set of financial statements when the entity applies an accounting policy retrospectively or makes a retrospective restatement, as defined in IAS 8 *Accounting Policies, Changes in Accounting Estimates and Errors*, or when the entity reclassifies items in the financial statements.

IN8   IAS 1 requires an entity to disclose reclassification adjustments and income tax relating to each component of other comprehensive income. Reclassification adjustments are the amounts reclassified to profit or loss in the current period that were previously recognised in other comprehensive income.

IN9   IAS 1 requires the presentation of dividends recognised as distributions to owners and related amounts per share in the statement of changes in equity or in the notes. Dividends are distributions to owners in their capacity as owners and the statement of changes in equity presents all owner changes in equity.

Changes from previous requirements

IN10   The main changes from the previous version of IAS 1 are described below.

A complete set of financial statements

IN11   The previous version of IAS 1 used the titles 'balance sheet' and 'cash flow statement' to describe two of the statements within a complete set of financial statements. IAS 1 uses 'statement of financial position' and 'statement of cash flows' for those statements. The new titles reflect more closely the function of those statements, as described in the *Framework*[1] (see paragraphs BC14–BC21 of the Basis for Conclusions).

IN12   IAS 1 requires an entity to disclose comparative information in respect of the previous period, ie to disclose as a minimum two of each of the statements and related notes. It introduces a requirement to include in a complete set of financial statements a statement of financial position as at the beginning of the earliest comparative period whenever the entity retrospectively applies an accounting policy or makes a retrospective restatement of items in its financial statements, or when it reclassifies items in its financial statements. The purpose is to provide information that is useful in analysing an entity's financial statements (see paragraphs BC31 and BC32 of the Basis for Conclusions).

Reporting owner changes in equity and comprehensive income

IN13   The previous version of IAS 1 required the presentation of an income statement that included items of income and expense recognised in profit or loss. It required items of income and expense not recognised in profit or loss to be presented in the statement of changes in equity, together with owner changes in equity. It also labelled the statement of changes in equity comprising profit or loss, other items of income and expense and the effects of changes in accounting policies and correction of errors as 'statement of recognised income and expense'. IAS 1 now requires:

       (a)   all changes in equity arising from transactions with owners in their capacity as owners (ie owner changes in equity) to be presented separately from non-owner changes in equity. An entity is not permitted to present

---

1   The reference to the *Framework* is to IASC's *Framework for the Preparation and Presentation of Financial Statements*, adopted by the IASB in 2001. In September 2010 the IASB replaced the *Framework* with the *Conceptual Framework for Financial Reporting*.

components of comprehensive income (ie non-owner changes in equity) in the statement of changes in equity. The purpose is to provide better information by aggregating items with shared characteristics and separating items with different characteristics (see paragraphs BC37 and BC38 of the Basis for Conclusions).

(b) income and expenses to be presented in one statement (a statement of comprehensive income) or in two statements (a separate income statement and a statement of comprehensive income), separately from owner changes in equity (see paragraphs BC49–BC54 of the Basis for Conclusions).

(c) components of other comprehensive income to be displayed in the statement of comprehensive income.

(d) total comprehensive income to be presented in the financial statements.

Other comprehensive income—reclassification adjustments and related tax effects

IN14   IAS 1 requires an entity to disclose income tax relating to each component of other comprehensive income. The previous version of IAS 1 did not include such a requirement. The purpose is to provide users with tax information relating to these components because the components often have tax rates different from those applied to profit or loss (see paragraphs BC65–BC68 of the Basis for Conclusions).

IN15   IAS 1 also requires an entity to disclose reclassification adjustments relating to components of other comprehensive income. Reclassification adjustments are amounts reclassified to profit or loss in the current period that were recognised in other comprehensive income in previous periods. The purpose is to provide users with information to assess the effect of such reclassifications on profit or loss (see paragraphs BC69–BC73 of the Basis for Conclusions).

Presentation of dividends

IN16   The previous version of IAS 1 permitted disclosure of the amount of dividends recognised as distributions to equity holders (now referred to as 'owners') and the related amount per share in the income statement, in the statement of changes in equity or in the notes. IAS 1 requires dividends recognised as distributions to owners and related amounts per share to be presented in the statement of changes in equity or in the notes. The presentation of such disclosures in the statement of comprehensive income is not permitted (see paragraph BC75 of the Basis for Conclusions). The purpose is to ensure that owner changes in equity (in this case, distributions to owners in the form of dividends) are presented separately from non-owner changes in equity (presented in the statement of comprehensive income).

Presentation of items of other comprehensive income

IN17　In June 2011 the Board issued *Presentation of Items of Other Comprehensive Income* (Amendments to IAS 1). The amendments improved the consistency and clarity of the presentation of items of other comprehensive income (OCI). The amendments also highlighted the importance that the Board places on presenting profit or loss and OCI together and with equal prominence. As explained in paragraph IN13, in 2007 IAS 1 was amended to require profit or loss and OCI to be presented together. The amendments issued in June 2011 retained that requirement, but focused on improving how items of OCI are presented.

IN18　The main change resulting from the amendments was a requirement for entities to group items presented in OCI on the basis of whether they are potentially reclassifiable to profit or loss subsequently (reclassification adjustments). The amendments did not address which items are presented in OCI.

IN19　The amendments did not change the option to present items of OCI either before tax or net of tax. However, if the items are presented before tax then the tax related to each of the two groups of OCI items (those that might be reclassified and those that will not be reclassified) must be shown separately.

International Accounting Standard 1
Presentation of Financial Statements

Objective

1   This Standard prescribes the basis for presentation of general purpose financial statements to ensure comparability both with the entity's financial statements of previous periods and with the financial statements of other entities. It sets out overall requirements for the presentation of financial statements, guidelines for their structure and minimum requirements for their content.

Scope

2   **An entity shall apply this Standard in preparing and presenting general purpose financial statements in accordance with International Financial Reporting Standards (IFRSs).**

3   Other IFRSs set out the recognition, measurement and disclosure requirements for specific transactions and other events.

4   This Standard does not apply to the structure and content of condensed interim financial statements prepared in accordance with IAS 34 *Interim Financial Reporting*. However, paragraphs 15–35 apply to such financial statements. This Standard applies equally to all entities, including those that present consolidated financial statements in accordance with IFRS 10 *Consolidated Financial Statements* and those that present separate financial statements in accordance with IAS 27 *Separate Financial Statements*.

5   This Standard uses terminology that is suitable for profit-oriented entities, including public sector business entities. If entities with not-for-profit activities in the private sector or the public sector apply this Standard, they may need to amend the descriptions used for particular line items in the financial statements and for the financial statements themselves.

6   Similarly, entities that do not have equity as defined in IAS 32 *Financial Instruments: Presentation* (eg some mutual funds) and entities whose share capital is not equity (eg some co-operative entities) may need to adapt the financial statement presentation of members' or unitholders' interests.

Definitions

7   **The following terms are used in this Standard with the meanings specified:**

General purpose financial statements **(referred to as 'financial statements') are those intended to meet the needs of users who are not in a position to require an entity to prepare reports tailored to their particular information needs.**

Impracticable **Applying a requirement is impracticable when the entity cannot apply it after making every reasonable effort to do so.**

International Financial Reporting Standards (IFRSs) **are Standards and Interpretations issued by the International Accounting Standards Board (IASB). They comprise:**

(a)   **International Financial Reporting Standards;**

(b)   **International Accounting Standards;**

(c)   **IFRIC Interpretations; and**

(d)   **SIC Interpretations.**[2]

Material **Omissions or misstatements of items are material if they could, individually or collectively, influence the economic decisions that users make on the basis of the financial statements. Materiality depends on the size and nature of the omission or misstatement judged in the surrounding circumstances. The size or nature of the item, or a combination of both, could be the determining factor.**

Assessing whether an omission or misstatement could influence economic decisions of users, and so be material, requires consideration of the characteristics of those users. The *Framework for the Preparation and Presentation of Financial Statements* states in paragraph 25[3] that 'users are assumed to have a reasonable knowledge of business and economic activities and accounting and a willingness to study the information with reasonable diligence.' Therefore, the assessment needs to take into account how users with such attributes could reasonably be expected to be influenced in making economic decisions.

Notes **contain information in addition to that presented in the statement of financial position, statement(s) of profit or loss and other comprehensive income, separate income statement (if presented), statement of changes in equity and statement of cash flows. Notes provide narrative descriptions or disaggregations of items presented in those statements and information about items that do not qualify for recognition in those statements.**

Other comprehensive income **comprises items of income and expense (including reclassification adjustments) that are not recognised in profit or loss as required or permitted by other IFRSs.**

The components of other comprehensive income include:

(a)   changes in revaluation surplus (see IAS 16 *Property, Plant and Equipment* and IAS 38 *Intangible Assets*);

(b)   remeasurements of defined benefit plans (see IAS 19 *Employee Benefits*);

(c)   gains and losses arising from translating the financial statements of a foreign operation (see IAS 21 *The Effects of Changes in Foreign Exchange Rates*);

(d)   gains and losses from investments in equity instruments measured at fair value through other comprehensive income in accordance with paragraph 5.7.5 of IFRS 9 *Financial Instruments*;

---

2   Definition of IFRSs amended after the name changes introduced by the revised Constitution of the IFRS Foundation in 2010.

3   In September 2010 the IASB replaced the *Framework* with the *Conceptual Framework for Financial Reporting.* Paragraph 25 was superseded by Chapter 3 of the *Conceptual Framework.*

(e) the effective portion of gains and losses on hedging instruments in a cash flow hedge (see IAS 39 *Financial Instruments: Recognition and Measurement*);

(f) for particular liabilities designated as at fair value through profit or loss, the amount of the change in fair value that is attributable to changes in the liability's credit risk (see paragraph 5.7.7 of IFRS 9).

Owners **are holders of instruments classified as equity.**

Profit or loss **is the total of income less expenses, excluding the components of other comprehensive income.**

Reclassification adjustments **are amounts reclassified to profit or loss in the current period that were recognised in other comprehensive income in the current or previous periods.**

Total comprehensive income **is the change in equity during a period resulting from transactions and other events, other than those changes resulting from transactions with owners in their capacity as owners.**

Total comprehensive income comprises all components of 'profit or loss' and of 'other comprehensive income'.

8   Although this Standard uses the terms 'other comprehensive income', 'profit or loss' and 'total comprehensive income', an entity may use other terms to describe the totals as long as the meaning is clear. For example, an entity may use the term 'net income' to describe profit or loss.

8A   The following terms are described in IAS 32 *Financial Instruments: Presentation* and are used in this Standard with the meaning specified in IAS 32:

(a) puttable financial instrument classified as an equity instrument (described in paragraphs 16A and 16B of IAS 32)

(b) an instrument that imposes on the entity an obligation to deliver to another party a pro rata share of the net assets of the entity only on liquidation and is classified as an equity instrument (described in paragraphs 16C and 16D of IAS 32).

Financial statements

Purpose of financial statements

9   Financial statements are a structured representation of the financial position and financial performance of an entity. The objective of financial statements is to provide information about the financial position, financial performance and cash flows of an entity that is useful to a wide range of users in making economic decisions. Financial statements also show the results of the management's stewardship of the resources entrusted to it. To meet this objective, financial statements provide information about an entity's:

(a) assets;

(b) liabilities;

(c) equity;

(d) income and expenses, including gains and losses;

(e) contributions by and distributions to owners in their capacity as owners; and

(f) cash flows.

This information, along with other information in the notes, assists users of financial statements in predicting the entity's future cash flows and, in particular, their timing and certainty.

Complete set of financial statements

10 A complete set of financial statements comprises:

(a) a statement of financial position as at the end of the period;

(b) a statement of profit or loss and other comprehensive income for the period;

(c) a statement of changes in equity for the period;

(d) a statement of cash flows for the period;

(e) notes, comprising a summary of significant accounting policies and other explanatory information; and

(f) a statement of financial position as at the beginning of the earliest comparative period when an entity applies an accounting policy retrospectively or makes a retrospective restatement of items in its financial statements, or when it reclassifies items in its financial statements.

An entity may use titles for the statements other than those used in this Standard. For example, an entity may use the title 'statement of comprehensive income' instead of 'statement of profit or loss and other comprehensive income'.

10A An entity may present a single statement of profit or loss and other comprehensive income, with profit or loss and other comprehensive income presented in two sections. The sections shall be presented together, with the section presented first followed directly by the other comprehensive income section. An entity may present the profit or loss section in a separate statement of profit or loss. If so, the separate statement of profit or loss shall immediately precede the statement presenting comprehensive income, which shall begin with profit or loss.

11 An entity shall present with equal prominence all of the financial statements in a complete set of financial statements.

12 [Deleted]

13 Many entities present, outside the financial statements, a financial review by management that describes and explains the main features of the entity's financial performance and financial position, and the principal uncertainties it faces. Such a report may include a review of:

(a) the main factors and influences determining financial performance, including changes in the environment in which the entity operates, the entity's response to those changes and their effect, and the entity's policy for investment to maintain and enhance financial performance, including its dividend policy;

(b) the entity's sources of funding and its targeted ratio of liabilities to equity; and

(c) the entity's resources not recognised in the statement of financial position in accordance with IFRSs.

14 Many entities also present, outside the financial statements, reports and statements such as environmental reports and value added statements, particularly in industries in which environmental factors are significant and when employees are regarded as an important user group. Reports and statements presented outside financial statements are outside the scope of IFRSs.

General features

Fair presentation and compliance with IFRSs

15 **Financial statements shall present fairly the financial position, financial performance and cash flows of an entity. Fair presentation requires the faithful representation of the effects of transactions, other events and conditions in accordance with the definitions and recognition criteria for assets, liabilities, income and expenses set out in the *Framework*.[4] The application of IFRSs, with additional disclosure when necessary, is presumed to result in financial statements that achieve a fair presentation.**

16 **An entity whose financial statements comply with IFRSs shall make an explicit and unreserved statement of such compliance in the notes. An entity shall not describe financial statements as complying with IFRSs unless they comply with all the requirements of IFRSs.**

17 In virtually all circumstances, an entity achieves a fair presentation by compliance with applicable IFRSs. A fair presentation also requires an entity:

(a) to select and apply accounting policies in accordance with IAS 8 *Accounting Policies, Changes in Accounting Estimates and Errors*. IAS 8 sets out a hierarchy of authoritative guidance that management considers in the absence of an IFRS that specifically applies to an item.

(b) to present information, including accounting policies, in a manner that provides relevant, reliable, comparable and understandable information.

(c) to provide additional disclosures when compliance with the specific requirements in IFRSs is insufficient to enable users to understand the impact of particular transactions, other events and conditions on the entity's financial position and financial performance.

---

4 Paragraphs 15–24 contain references to the objective of financial statements set out in the *Framework* [*for the Preparation and Presentation of Financial Statements*]. In September 2010 the IASB replaced the *Framework* with the *Conceptual Framework for Financial Reporting*, which replaced the objective of financial statements with the objective of general purpose financial reporting: see Chapter 1 of the *Conceptual Framework*.

18   An entity cannot rectify inappropriate accounting policies either by disclosure of the accounting policies used or by notes or explanatory material.

19   In the extremely rare circumstances in which management concludes that compliance with a requirement in an IFRS would be so misleading that it would conflict with the objective of financial statements set out in the *Framework*, the entity shall depart from that requirement in the manner set out in paragraph 20 if the relevant regulatory framework requires, or otherwise does not prohibit, such a departure.

20   When an entity departs from a requirement of an IFRS in accordance with paragraph 19, it shall disclose:

(a)   that management has concluded that the financial statements present fairly the entity's financial position, financial performance and cash flows;

(b)   that it has complied with applicable IFRSs, except that it has departed from a particular requirement to achieve a fair presentation;

(c)   the title of the IFRS from which the entity has departed, the nature of the departure, including the treatment that the IFRS would require, the reason why that treatment would be so misleading in the circumstances that it would conflict with the objective of financial statements set out in the *Framework*, and the treatment adopted; and

(d)   for each period presented, the financial effect of the departure on each item in the financial statements that would have been reported in complying with the requirement.

21   When an entity has departed from a requirement of an IFRS in a prior period, and that departure affects the amounts recognised in the financial statements for the current period, it shall make the disclosures set out in paragraph 20(c) and (d).

22   Paragraph 21 applies, for example, when an entity departed in a prior period from a requirement in an IFRS for the measurement of assets or liabilities and that departure affects the measurement of changes in assets and liabilities recognised in the current period's financial statements.

23   In the extremely rare circumstances in which management concludes that compliance with a requirement in an IFRS would be so misleading that it would conflict with the objective of financial statements set out in the *Framework*, but the relevant regulatory framework prohibits departure from the requirement, the entity shall, to the maximum extent possible, reduce the perceived misleading aspects of compliance by disclosing:

(a)   the title of the IFRS in question, the nature of the requirement, and the reason why management has concluded that complying with that requirement is so misleading in the circumstances that it conflicts with the objective of financial statements set out in the *Framework*; and

(b)   for each period presented, the adjustments to each item in the financial statements that management has concluded would be necessary to achieve a fair presentation.

24   For the purpose of paragraphs 19–23, an item of information would conflict with
       the objective of financial statements when it does not represent faithfully the
       transactions, other events and conditions that it either purports to represent or
       could reasonably be expected to represent and, consequently, it would be likely to
       influence economic decisions made by users of financial statements. When
       assessing whether complying with a specific requirement in an IFRS would be so
       misleading that it would conflict with the objective of financial statements set
       out in the *Framework*, management considers:

       (a)   why the objective of financial statements is not achieved in the particular
              circumstances; and

       (b)   how the entity's circumstances differ from those of other entities that comply
              with the requirement. If other entities in similar circumstances comply with
              the requirement, there is a rebuttable presumption that the entity's
              compliance with the requirement would not be so misleading that it would
              conflict with the objective of financial statements set out in the *Framework*.

Going concern

25   **When preparing financial statements, management shall make an assessment of
       an entity's ability to continue as a going concern. An entity shall prepare financial
       statements on a going concern basis unless management either intends to
       liquidate the entity or to cease trading, or has no realistic alternative but to do so.
       When management is aware, in making its assessment, of material uncertainties
       related to events or conditions that may cast significant doubt upon the entity's
       ability to continue as a going concern, the entity shall disclose those uncertainties.
       When an entity does not prepare financial statements on a going concern basis, it
       shall disclose that fact, together with the basis on which it prepared the financial
       statements and the reason why the entity is not regarded as a going concern.**

26   In assessing whether the going concern assumption is appropriate, management
       takes into account all available information about the future, which is at least,
       but is not limited to, twelve months from the end of the reporting period.
       The degree of consideration depends on the facts in each case. When an entity has
       a history of profitable operations and ready access to financial resources, the
       entity may reach a conclusion that the going concern basis of accounting is
       appropriate without detailed analysis. In other cases, management may need to
       consider a wide range of factors relating to current and expected profitability,
       debt repayment schedules and potential sources of replacement financing before
       it can satisfy itself that the going concern basis is appropriate.

Accrual basis of accounting

27   **An entity shall prepare its financial statements, except for cash flow information,
       using the accrual basis of accounting.**

28   When the accrual basis of accounting is used, an entity recognises items as assets,
       liabilities, equity, income and expenses (the elements of financial statements)
       when they satisfy the definitions and recognition criteria for those elements in
       the *Framework*.[5]

---

5   replaced by the *Conceptual Framework* in September 2010

Materiality and aggregation

29   **An entity shall present separately each material class of similar items. An entity shall present separately items of a dissimilar nature or function unless they are immaterial.**

30   Financial statements result from processing large numbers of transactions or other events that are aggregated into classes according to their nature or function. The final stage in the process of aggregation and classification is the presentation of condensed and classified data, which form line items in the financial statements. If a line item is not individually material, it is aggregated with other items either in those statements or in the notes. An item that is not sufficiently material to warrant separate presentation in those statements may warrant separate presentation in the notes.

31   An entity need not provide a specific disclosure required by an IFRS if the information is not material.

Offsetting

32   **An entity shall not offset assets and liabilities or income and expenses, unless required or permitted by an IFRS.**

33   An entity reports separately both assets and liabilities, and income and expenses. Offsetting in the statements of comprehensive income or financial position or in the separate income statement (if presented), except when offsetting reflects the substance of the transaction or other event, detracts from the ability of users both to understand the transactions, other events and conditions that have occurred and to assess the entity's future cash flows. Measuring assets net of valuation allowances—for example, obsolescence allowances on inventories and doubtful debts allowances on receivables—is not offsetting.

34   IAS 18 *Revenue* defines revenue and requires an entity to measure it at the fair value of the consideration received or receivable, taking into account the amount of any trade discounts and volume rebates the entity allows. An entity undertakes, in the course of its ordinary activities, other transactions that do not generate revenue but are incidental to the main revenue-generating activities. An entity presents the results of such transactions, when this presentation reflects the substance of the transaction or other event, by netting any income with related expenses arising on the same transaction. For example:

(a)   an entity presents gains and losses on the disposal of non-current assets, including investments and operating assets, by deducting from the proceeds on disposal the carrying amount of the asset and related selling expenses; and

(b)   an entity may net expenditure related to a provision that is recognised in accordance with IAS 37 *Provisions, Contingent Liabilities and Contingent Assets* and reimbursed under a contractual arrangement with a third party (for example, a supplier's warranty agreement) against the related reimbursement.

35   In addition, an entity presents on a net basis gains and losses arising from a group of similar transactions, for example, foreign exchange gains and losses or gains and losses arising on financial instruments held for trading. However, an entity presents such gains and losses separately if they are material.

Frequency of reporting

36   **An entity shall present a complete set of financial statements (including comparative information) at least annually. When an entity changes the end of its reporting period and presents financial statements for a period longer or shorter than one year, an entity shall disclose, in addition to the period covered by the financial statements:**

       (a)   the reason for using a longer or shorter period, and

       (b)   the fact that amounts presented in the financial statements are not entirely comparable.

37   Normally, an entity consistently prepares financial statements for a one-year period. However, for practical reasons, some entities prefer to report, for example, for a 52-week period. This Standard does not preclude this practice.

Comparative information

38   **Except when IFRSs permit or require otherwise, an entity shall disclose comparative information in respect of the previous period for all amounts reported in the current period's financial statements. An entity shall include comparative information for narrative and descriptive information when it is relevant to an understanding of the current period's financial statements.**

39   An entity disclosing comparative information shall present, as a minimum, two statements of financial position, two of each of the other statements, and related notes. When an entity applies an accounting policy retrospectively or makes a retrospective restatement of items in its financial statements or when it reclassifies items in its financial statements, it shall present, as a minimum, three statements of financial position, two of each of the other statements, and related notes. An entity presents statements of financial position as at:

       (a)   the end of the current period,

       (b)   the end of the previous period (which is the same as the beginning of the current period), and

       (c)   the beginning of the earliest comparative period.

40   In some cases, narrative information provided in the financial statements for the previous period(s) continues to be relevant in the current period. For example, an entity discloses in the current period details of a legal dispute whose outcome was uncertain at the end of the immediately preceding reporting period and that is yet to be resolved. Users benefit from information that the uncertainty existed at the end of the immediately preceding reporting period, and about the steps that have been taken during the period to resolve the uncertainty.

41   When the entity changes the presentation or classification of items in its financial statements, the entity shall reclassify comparative amounts unless reclassification is impracticable. When the entity reclassifies comparative amounts, the entity shall disclose:

(a)   the nature of the reclassification;

(b)   the amount of each item or class of items that is reclassified; and

(c)   the reason for the reclassification.

42   When it is impracticable to reclassify comparative amounts, an entity shall disclose:

(a)   the reason for not reclassifying the amounts, and

(b)   the nature of the adjustments that would have been made if the amounts had been reclassified.

43   Enhancing the inter-period comparability of information assists users in making economic decisions, especially by allowing the assessment of trends in financial information for predictive purposes. In some circumstances, it is impracticable to reclassify comparative information for a particular prior period to achieve comparability with the current period. For example, an entity may not have collected data in the prior period(s) in a way that allows reclassification, and it may be impracticable to recreate the information.

44   IAS 8 sets out the adjustments to comparative information required when an entity changes an accounting policy or corrects an error.

Consistency of presentation

45   An entity shall retain the presentation and classification of items in the financial statements from one period to the next unless:

(a)   it is apparent, following a significant change in the nature of the entity's operations or a review of its financial statements, that another presentation or classification would be more appropriate having regard to the criteria for the selection and application of accounting policies in IAS 8; or

(b)   an IFRS requires a change in presentation.

46   For example, a significant acquisition or disposal, or a review of the presentation of the financial statements, might suggest that the financial statements need to be presented differently. An entity changes the presentation of its financial statements only if the changed presentation provides information that is reliable and more relevant to users of the financial statements and the revised structure is likely to continue, so that comparability is not impaired. When making such changes in presentation, an entity reclassifies its comparative information in accordance with paragraphs 41 and 42.

Structure and content

Introduction

47   This Standard requires particular disclosures in the statement of financial position or of comprehensive income, in the separate income statement (if presented), or in the statement of changes in equity and requires disclosure of other line items either in those statements or in the notes. IAS 7 *Statement of Cash Flows* sets out requirements for the presentation of cash flow information.

48   This Standard sometimes uses the term 'disclosure' in a broad sense, encompassing items presented in the financial statements. Disclosures are also required by other IFRSs. Unless specified to the contrary elsewhere in this Standard or in another IFRS, such disclosures may be made in the financial statements.

Identification of the financial statements

49   **An entity shall clearly identify the financial statements and distinguish them from other information in the same published document.**

50   IFRSs apply only to financial statements, and not necessarily to other information presented in an annual report, a regulatory filing, or another document. Therefore, it is important that users can distinguish information that is prepared using IFRSs from other information that may be useful to users but is not the subject of those requirements.

51   **An entity shall clearly identify each financial statement and the notes. In addition, an entity shall display the following information prominently, and repeat it when necessary for the information presented to be understandable:**

    (a)   **the name of the reporting entity or other means of identification, and any change in that information from the end of the preceding reporting period;**

    (b)   **whether the financial statements are of an individual entity or a group of entities;**

    (c)   **the date of the end of the reporting period or the period covered by the set of financial statements or notes;**

    (d)   **the presentation currency, as defined in IAS 21; and**

    (e)   **the level of rounding used in presenting amounts in the financial statements.**

52   An entity meets the requirements in paragraph 51 by presenting appropriate headings for pages, statements, notes, columns and the like. Judgement is required in determining the best way of presenting such information. For example, when an entity presents the financial statements electronically, separate pages are not always used; an entity then presents the above items to ensure that the information included in the financial statements can be understood.

53   An entity often makes financial statements more understandable by presenting information in thousands or millions of units of the presentation currency. This is acceptable as long as the entity discloses the level of rounding and does not omit material information.

Statement of financial position

Information to be presented in the statement of financial position

54 As a minimum, the statement of financial position shall include line items that present the following amounts:

(a) property, plant and equipment;

(b) investment property;

(c) intangible assets;

(d) financial assets (excluding amounts shown under (e), (h) and (i));

(e) investments accounted for using the equity method;

(f) biological assets;

(g) inventories;

(h) trade and other receivables;

(i) cash and cash equivalents;

(j) the total of assets classified as held for sale and assets included in disposal groups classified as held for sale in accordance with IFRS 5 *Non-current Assets Held for Sale and Discontinued Operations*;

(k) trade and other payables;

(l) provisions;

(m) financial liabilities (excluding amounts shown under (k) and (l));

(n) liabilities and assets for current tax, as defined in IAS 12 *Income Taxes*;

(o) deferred tax liabilities and deferred tax assets, as defined in IAS 12;

(p) liabilities included in disposal groups classified as held for sale in accordance with IFRS 5;

(q) non-controlling interests, presented within equity; and

(r) issued capital and reserves attributable to owners of the parent.

55 An entity shall present additional line items, headings and subtotals in the statement of financial position when such presentation is relevant to an understanding of the entity's financial position.

56 When an entity presents current and non-current assets, and current and non-current liabilities, as separate classifications in its statement of financial position, it shall not classify deferred tax assets (liabilities) as current assets (liabilities).

57 This Standard does not prescribe the order or format in which an entity presents items. Paragraph 54 simply lists items that are sufficiently different in nature or function to warrant separate presentation in the statement of financial position. In addition:

(a)   line items are included when the size, nature or function of an item or aggregation of similar items is such that separate presentation is relevant to an understanding of the entity's financial position; and

(b)   the descriptions used and the ordering of items or aggregation of similar items may be amended according to the nature of the entity and its transactions, to provide information that is relevant to an understanding of the entity's financial position. For example, a financial institution may amend the above descriptions to provide information that is relevant to the operations of a financial institution.

58   An entity makes the judgement about whether to present additional items separately on the basis of an assessment of:

(a)   the nature and liquidity of assets;

(b)   the function of assets within the entity; and

(c)   the amounts, nature and timing of liabilities.

59   The use of different measurement bases for different classes of assets suggests that their nature or function differs and, therefore, that an entity presents them as separate line items. For example, different classes of property, plant and equipment can be carried at cost or at revalued amounts in accordance with IAS 16.

Current/non-current distinction

60   **An entity shall present current and non-current assets, and current and non-current liabilities, as separate classifications in its statement of financial position in accordance with paragraphs 66–76 except when a presentation based on liquidity provides information that is reliable and more relevant. When that exception applies, an entity shall present all assets and liabilities in order of liquidity.**

61   **Whichever method of presentation is adopted, an entity shall disclose the amount expected to be recovered or settled after more than twelve months for each asset and liability line item that combines amounts expected to be recovered or settled:**

(a)   **no more than twelve months after the reporting period, and**

(b)   **more than twelve months after the reporting period.**

62   When an entity supplies goods or services within a clearly identifiable operating cycle, separate classification of current and non-current assets and liabilities in the statement of financial position provides useful information by distinguishing the net assets that are continuously circulating as working capital from those used in the entity's long-term operations. It also highlights assets that are expected to be realised within the current operating cycle, and liabilities that are due for settlement within the same period.

63   For some entities, such as financial institutions, a presentation of assets and liabilities in increasing or decreasing order of liquidity provides information that is reliable and more relevant than a current/non-current presentation because the entity does not supply goods or services within a clearly identifiable operating cycle.

64   In applying paragraph 60, an entity is permitted to present some of its assets and liabilities using a current/non-current classification and others in order of liquidity when this provides information that is reliable and more relevant. The need for a mixed basis of presentation might arise when an entity has diverse operations.

65   Information about expected dates of realisation of assets and liabilities is useful in assessing the liquidity and solvency of an entity. IFRS 7 *Financial Instruments: Disclosures* requires disclosure of the maturity dates of financial assets and financial liabilities. Financial assets include trade and other receivables, and financial liabilities include trade and other payables. Information on the expected date of recovery of non-monetary assets such as inventories and expected date of settlement for liabilities such as provisions is also useful, whether assets and liabilities are classified as current or as non-current. For example, an entity discloses the amount of inventories that are expected to be recovered more than twelve months after the reporting period.

Current assets

66   **An entity shall classify an asset as current when:**

      (a)   **it expects to realise the asset, or intends to sell or consume it, in its normal operating cycle;**

      (b)   **it holds the asset primarily for the purpose of trading;**

      (c)   **it expects to realise the asset within twelve months after the reporting period; or**

      (d)   **the asset is cash or a cash equivalent (as defined in IAS 7) unless the asset is restricted from being exchanged or used to settle a liability for at least twelve months after the reporting period.**

      An entity shall classify all other assets as non-current.

67   This Standard uses the term 'non-current' to include tangible, intangible and financial assets of a long-term nature. It does not prohibit the use of alternative descriptions as long as the meaning is clear.

68   The operating cycle of an entity is the time between the acquisition of assets for processing and their realisation in cash or cash equivalents. When the entity's normal operating cycle is not clearly identifiable, it is assumed to be twelve months. Current assets include assets (such as inventories and trade receivables) that are sold, consumed or realised as part of the normal operating cycle even when they are not expected to be realised within twelve months after the reporting period. Current assets also include assets held primarily for the purpose of trading (examples include some financial assets that meet the definition of held for trading in IFRS 9) and the current portion of non-current financial assets.

Current liabilities

69   **An entity shall classify a liability as current when:**

      (a)   **it expects to settle the liability in its normal operating cycle;**

(b)   it holds the liability primarily for the purpose of trading;

(c)   the liability is due to be settled within twelve months after the reporting period; or

(d)   it does not have an unconditional right to defer settlement of the liability for at least twelve months after the reporting period (see paragraph 73). Terms of a liability that could, at the option of the counterparty, result in its settlement by the issue of equity instruments do not affect its classification.

An entity shall classify all other liabilities as non-current.

70   Some current liabilities, such as trade payables and some accruals for employee and other operating costs, are part of the working capital used in the entity's normal operating cycle. An entity classifies such operating items as current liabilities even if they are due to be settled more than twelve months after the reporting period. The same normal operating cycle applies to the classification of an entity's assets and liabilities. When the entity's normal operating cycle is not clearly identifiable, it is assumed to be twelve months.

71   Other current liabilities are not settled as part of the normal operating cycle, but are due for settlement within twelve months after the reporting period or held primarily for the purpose of trading. Examples are some financial liabilities that meet the definition of held for trading in IFRS 9, bank overdrafts, and the current portion of non-current financial liabilities, dividends payable, income taxes and other non-trade payables. Financial liabilities that provide financing on a long-term basis (ie are not part of the working capital used in the entity's normal operating cycle) and are not due for settlement within twelve months after the reporting period are non-current liabilities, subject to paragraphs 74 and 75.

72   An entity classifies its financial liabilities as current when they are due to be settled within twelve months after the reporting period, even if:

(a)   the original term was for a period longer than twelve months, and

(b)   an agreement to refinance, or to reschedule payments, on a long-term basis is completed after the reporting period and before the financial statements are authorised for issue.

73   If an entity expects, and has the discretion, to refinance or roll over an obligation for at least twelve months after the reporting period under an existing loan facility, it classifies the obligation as non-current, even if it would otherwise be due within a shorter period. However, when refinancing or rolling over the obligation is not at the discretion of the entity (for example, there is no arrangement for refinancing), the entity does not consider the potential to refinance the obligation and classifies the obligation as current.

74   When an entity breaches a provision of a long-term loan arrangement on or before the end of the reporting period with the effect that the liability becomes payable on demand, it classifies the liability as current, even if the lender agreed, after the reporting period and before the authorisation of the financial statements for issue, not to demand payment as a consequence of the breach. An entity classifies the liability as current because, at the end of the reporting period, it does not have an unconditional right to defer its settlement for at least twelve months after that date.

75   However, an entity classifies the liability as non-current if the lender agreed by the end of the reporting period to provide a period of grace ending at least twelve months after the reporting period, within which the entity can rectify the breach and during which the lender cannot demand immediate repayment.

76   In respect of loans classified as current liabilities, if the following events occur between the end of the reporting period and the date the financial statements are authorised for issue, those events are disclosed as non-adjusting events in accordance with IAS 10 *Events after the Reporting Period*:

(a)   refinancing on a long-term basis;

(b)   rectification of a breach of a long-term loan arrangement; and

(c)   the granting by the lender of a period of grace to rectify a breach of a long-term loan arrangement ending at least twelve months after the reporting period.

Information to be presented either in the statement of financial position or in the notes

77   **An entity shall disclose, either in the statement of financial position or in the notes, further subclassifications of the line items presented, classified in a manner appropriate to the entity's operations.**

78   The detail provided in subclassifications depends on the requirements of IFRSs and on the size, nature and function of the amounts involved. An entity also uses the factors set out in paragraph 58 to decide the basis of subclassification. The disclosures vary for each item, for example:

(a)   items of property, plant and equipment are disaggregated into classes in accordance with IAS 16;

(b)   receivables are disaggregated into amounts receivable from trade customers, receivables from related parties, prepayments and other amounts;

(c)   inventories are disaggregated, in accordance with IAS 2 *Inventories*, into classifications such as merchandise, production supplies, materials, work in progress and finished goods;

(d)   provisions are disaggregated into provisions for employee benefits and other items; and

(e)   equity capital and reserves are disaggregated into various classes, such as paid-in capital, share premium and reserves.

79   **An entity shall disclose the following, either in the statement of financial position or the statement of changes in equity, or in the notes:**

(a)   **for each class of share capital:**

(i)   **the number of shares authorised;**

(ii)   **the number of shares issued and fully paid, and issued but not fully paid;**

(iii)   **par value per share, or that the shares have no par value;**

   (iv) a reconciliation of the number of shares outstanding at the beginning and at the end of the period;

   (v) the rights, preferences and restrictions attaching to that class including restrictions on the distribution of dividends and the repayment of capital;

   (vi) shares in the entity held by the entity or by its subsidiaries or associates; and

   (vii) shares reserved for issue under options and contracts for the sale of shares, including terms and amounts; and

  (b) a description of the nature and purpose of each reserve within equity.

80 An entity without share capital, such as a partnership or trust, shall disclose information equivalent to that required by paragraph 79(a), showing changes during the period in each category of equity interest, and the rights, preferences and restrictions attaching to each category of equity interest.

80A If an entity has reclassified

  (a) a puttable financial instrument classified as an equity instrument, or

  (b) an instrument that imposes on the entity an obligation to deliver to another party a pro rata share of the net assets of the entity only on liquidation and is classified as an equity instrument

between financial liabilities and equity, it shall disclose the amount reclassified into and out of each category (financial liabilities or equity), and the timing and reason for that reclassification.

Statement of profit or loss and other comprehensive income

81 [Deleted]

81A The statement of profit or loss and other comprehensive income (statement of comprehensive income) shall present, in addition to the profit or loss and other comprehensive income sections:

  (a) profit or loss;

  (b) total other comprehensive income;

  (c) comprehensive income for the period, being the total of profit or loss and other comprehensive income.

If an entity presents a separate statement of profit or loss it does not present the profit or loss section in the statement presenting comprehensive income.

81B An entity shall present the following items, in addition to the profit or loss and other comprehensive income sections, as allocation of profit or loss and other comprehensive income for the period:

  (a) profit or loss for the period attributable to:

   (i) non-controlling interests, and

   (ii) owners of the parent.

(b)   comprehensive income for the period attributable to:

    (i)   non-controlling interests, and

    (ii)   owners of the parent.

If an entity presents profit or loss in a separate statement it shall present (a) in that statement.

Information to be presented in the profit or loss section or the statement of profit or loss

82   In addition to items required by other IFRSs, the profit or loss section or the statement of profit or loss shall include line items that present the following amounts for the period:

(a)   revenue;

(aa)   gains and losses arising from the derecognition of financial assets measured at amortised cost;

(b)   finance costs;

(c)   share of the profit or loss of associates and joint ventures accounted for using the equity method;

(ca)   if a financial asset is reclassified so that it is measured at fair value, any gain or loss arising from a difference between the previous carrying amount and its fair value at the reclassification date (as defined in IFRS 9);

(d)   tax expense;

(e)   [deleted]

(ea)   a single amount for the total of discontinued operations (see IFRS 5).

(f–i)   [deleted]

Information to be presented in the other comprehensive income section

82A   The other comprehensive income section shall present line items for amounts of other comprehensive income in the period, classified by nature (including share of the other comprehensive income of associates and joint ventures accounted for using the equity method) and grouped into those that, in accordance with other IFRSs:

(a)   will not be reclassified subsequently to profit or loss; and

(b)   will be reclassified subsequently to profit or loss when specific conditions are met.

83–84   [Deleted]

85   An entity shall present additional line items, headings and subtotals in the statement(s) presenting profit or loss and other comprehensive income when such presentation is relevant to an understanding of the entity's financial performance.

86　　Because the effects of an entity's various activities, transactions and other events differ in frequency, potential for gain or loss and predictability, disclosing the components of financial performance assists users in understanding the financial performance achieved and in making projections of future financial performance. An entity includes additional line items in the statement(s) presenting profit or loss and other comprehensive income and it amends the descriptions used and the ordering of items when this is necessary to explain the elements of financial performance. An entity considers factors including materiality and the nature and function of the items of income and expense. For example, a financial institution may amend the descriptions to provide information that is relevant to the operations of a financial institution. An entity does not offset income and expense items unless the criteria in paragraph 32 are met.

87　　**An entity shall not present any items of income or expense as extraordinary items, in the statement(s) presenting profit or loss and other comprehensive income or in the notes.**

Profit or loss for the period

88　　**An entity shall recognise all items of income and expense in a period in profit or loss unless an IFRS requires or permits otherwise.**

89　　Some IFRSs specify circumstances when an entity recognises particular items outside profit or loss in the current period. IAS 8 specifies two such circumstances: the correction of errors and the effect of changes in accounting policies. Other IFRSs require or permit components of other comprehensive income that meet the *Framework*'s[6] definition of income or expense to be excluded from profit or loss (see paragraph 7).

Other comprehensive income for the period

90　　**An entity shall disclose the amount of income tax relating to each item other comprehensive income, including reclassification adjustments, either in the statement of profit or loss and other comprehensive income or in the notes.**

91　　An entity may present items of other comprehensive income either:

(a)　　net of related tax effects, or

(b)　　before related tax effects with one amount shown for the aggregate amount of income tax relating to those items.

If an entity elects alternative (b), it shall allocate the tax between the items that might be reclassified subsequently to the profit or loss section and those that will not be reclassified subsequently to the profit or loss section.

92　　**An entity shall disclose reclassification adjustments relating to components of other comprehensive income.**

6　In September 2010 the IASB replaced the *Framework* with the *Conceptual Framework for Financial Reporting*.

93   Other IFRSs specify whether and when amounts previously recognised in other comprehensive income are reclassified to profit or loss. Such reclassifications are referred to in this Standard as reclassification adjustments. A reclassification adjustment is included with the related component of other comprehensive income in the period that the adjustment is reclassified to profit or loss. These amounts may have been recognised in other comprehensive income as unrealised gains in the current or previous periods. Those unrealised gains must be deducted from other comprehensive income in the period in which the realised gains are reclassified to profit or loss to avoid including them in total comprehensive income twice.

94   An entity may present reclassification adjustments in the statement(s) of profit or loss and other comprehensive income or in the notes. An entity presenting reclassification adjustments in the notes presents the items of other comprehensive income after any related reclassification adjustments.

95   Reclassification adjustments arise, for example, on disposal of a foreign operation (see IAS 21) and when a hedged forecast cash flow affects profit or loss (see paragraph 100 of IAS 39).

96   Reclassification adjustments do not arise on changes in revaluation surplus recognised in accordance with IAS 16 or IAS 38 or on remeasurements of defined benefit plans recognised in accordance with IAS 19. These components are recognised in other comprehensive income and are not reclassified to profit or loss in subsequent periods. Changes in revaluation surplus may be transferred to retained earnings in subsequent periods as the asset is used or when it is derecognised (see IAS 16 and IAS 38).

Information to be presented in the statement(s) of profit or loss and other comprehensive income or in the notes

97   **When items of income or expense are material, an entity shall disclose their nature and amount separately.**

98   Circumstances that would give rise to the separate disclosure of items of income and expense include:

(a)   write-downs of inventories to net realisable value or of property, plant and equipment to recoverable amount, as well as reversals of such write-downs;

(b)   restructurings of the activities of an entity and reversals of any provisions for the costs of restructuring;

(c)   disposals of items of property, plant and equipment;

(d)   disposals of investments;

(e)   discontinued operations;

(f)   litigation settlements; and

(g)   other reversals of provisions.

99   **An entity shall present an analysis of expenses recognised in profit or loss using a classification based on either their nature or their function within the entity, whichever provides information that is reliable and more relevant.**

100   Entities are encouraged to present the analysis in paragraph 99 in the statement(s) presenting profit or loss and other comprehensive income.

101   Expenses are subclassified to highlight components of financial performance that may differ in terms of frequency, potential for gain or loss and predictability. This analysis is provided in one of two forms.

102   The first form of analysis is the 'nature of expense' method. An entity aggregates expenses within profit or loss according to their nature (for example, depreciation, purchases of materials, transport costs, employee benefits and advertising costs), and does not reallocate them among functions within the entity. This method may be simple to apply because no allocations of expenses to functional classifications are necessary. An example of a classification using the nature of expense method is as follows:

Revenue	X
Other income	X
Changes in inventories of finished goods and work in progress	X
Raw materials and consumables used	X
Employee benefits expense	X
Depreciation and amortisation expense	X
Other expenses	X
Total expenses	(X)
Profit before tax	X

103   The second form of analysis is the 'function of expense' or 'cost of sales' method and classifies expenses according to their function as part of cost of sales or, for example, the costs of distribution or administrative activities. At a minimum, an entity discloses its cost of sales under this method separately from other expenses. This method can provide more relevant information to users than the classification of expenses by nature, but allocating costs to functions may require arbitrary allocations and involve considerable judgement. An example of a classification using the function of expense method is as follows:

Revenue	X
Cost of sales	(X)
Gross profit	X
Other income	X
Distribution costs	(X)
Administrative expenses	(X)
Other expenses	(X)
Profit before tax	X

104   **An entity classifying expenses by function shall disclose additional information on the nature of expenses, including depreciation and amortisation expense and employee benefits expense.**

105   The choice between the function of expense method and the nature of expense method depends on historical and industry factors and the nature of the entity. Both methods provide an indication of those costs that might vary, directly or indirectly, with the level of sales or production of the entity. Because each method of presentation has merit for different types of entities, this Standard requires management to select the presentation that is reliable and more relevant. However, because information on the nature of expenses is useful in predicting future cash flows, additional disclosure is required when the function of expense classification is used. In paragraph 104, 'employee benefits' has the same meaning as in IAS 19.

Statement of changes in equity

Information to be presented in the statement of changes in equity

106   **An entity shall present a statement of changes in equity as required by paragraph 10. The statement of changes in equity includes the following information:**

(a)   **total comprehensive income for the period, showing separately the total amounts attributable to owners of the parent and to non-controlling interests;**

(b)   **for each component of equity, the effects of retrospective application or retrospective restatement recognised in accordance with IAS 8; and**

(c)   [deleted]

(d)   **for each component of equity, a reconciliation between the carrying amount at the beginning and the end of the period, separately disclosing changes resulting from:**

(i)   **profit or loss;**

(ii)   **other comprehensive income; and**

(iii) **transactions with owners in their capacity as owners, showing separately contributions by and distributions to owners and changes in ownership interests in subsidiaries that do not result in a loss of control.**

Information to be presented in the statement of changes in equity or in the notes

106A   For each component of equity an entity shall present, either in the statement of changes in equity or in the notes, an analysis of other comprehensive income by item (see paragraph 106(d)(ii)).

107   An entity shall present, either in the statement of changes in equity or in the notes, the amount of dividends recognised as distributions to owners during the period, and the related amount of dividends per share.

108   In paragraph 106, the components of equity include, for example, each class of contributed equity, the accumulated balance of each class of other comprehensive income and retained earnings.

109 Changes in an entity's equity between the beginning and the end of the reporting period reflect the increase or decrease in its net assets during the period. Except for changes resulting from transactions with owners in their capacity as owners (such as equity contributions, reacquisitions of the entity's own equity instruments and dividends) and transaction costs directly related to such transactions, the overall change in equity during a period represents the total amount of income and expense, including gains and losses, generated by the entity's activities during that period.

110 IAS 8 requires retrospective adjustments to effect changes in accounting policies, to the extent practicable, except when the transition provisions in another IFRS require otherwise. IAS 8 also requires restatements to correct errors to be made retrospectively, to the extent practicable. Retrospective adjustments and retrospective restatements are not changes in equity but they are adjustments to the opening balance of retained earnings, except when an IFRS requires retrospective adjustment of another component of equity. Paragraph 106(b) requires disclosure in the statement of changes in equity of the total adjustment to each component of equity resulting from changes in accounting policies and, separately, from corrections of errors. These adjustments are disclosed for each prior period and the beginning of the period.

Statement of cash flows

111 Cash flow information provides users of financial statements with a basis to assess the ability of the entity to generate cash and cash equivalents and the needs of the entity to utilise those cash flows. IAS 7 sets out requirements for the presentation and disclosure of cash flow information.

Notes

Structure

112 The notes shall:

   (a) present information about the basis of preparation of the financial statements and the specific accounting policies used in accordance with paragraphs 117–124;

   (b) disclose the information required by IFRSs that is not presented elsewhere in the financial statements; and

   (c) provide information that is not presented elsewhere in the financial statements, but is relevant to an understanding of any of them.

113 An entity shall, as far as practicable, present notes in a systematic manner. An entity shall cross-reference each item in the statements of financial position and of comprehensive income, in the separate income statement (if presented), and in the statements of changes in equity and of cash flows to any related information in the notes.

114 An entity normally presents notes in the following order, to assist users to understand the financial statements and to compare them with financial statements of other entities:

(a)   statement of compliance with IFRSs (see paragraph 16);

(b)   summary of significant accounting policies applied (see paragraph 117);

(c)   supporting information for items presented in the statements of financial position and of comprehensive income, in the separate income statement (if presented), and in the statements of changes in equity and of cash flows, in the order in which each statement and each line item is presented; and

(d)   other disclosures, including:

   (i)   contingent liabilities (see IAS 37) and unrecognised contractual commitments, and

   (ii)   non-financial disclosures, eg the entity's financial risk management objectives and policies (see IFRS 7).

115   In some circumstances, it may be necessary or desirable to vary the order of specific items within the notes. For example, an entity may combine information on changes in fair value recognised in profit or loss with information on maturities of financial instruments, although the former disclosures relate to the statement(s) presenting profit or loss and other comprehensive income and the latter relate to the statement of financial position. Nevertheless, an entity retains a systematic structure for the notes as far as practicable.

116   An entity may present notes providing information about the basis of preparation of the financial statements and specific accounting policies as a separate section of the financial statements.

Disclosure of accounting policies

117   An entity shall disclose in the summary of significant accounting policies:

(a)   the measurement basis (or bases) used in preparing the financial statements, and

(b)   the other accounting policies used that are relevant to an understanding of the financial statements.

118   It is important for an entity to inform users of the measurement basis or bases used in the financial statements (for example, historical cost, current cost, net realisable value, fair value or recoverable amount) because the basis on which an entity prepares the financial statements significantly affects users' analysis. When an entity uses more than one measurement basis in the financial statements, for example when particular classes of assets are revalued, it is sufficient to provide an indication of the categories of assets and liabilities to which each measurement basis is applied.

119   In deciding whether a particular accounting policy should be disclosed, management considers whether disclosure would assist users in understanding how transactions, other events and conditions are reflected in reported financial performance and financial position. Disclosure of particular accounting policies is especially useful to users when those policies are selected from alternatives allowed in IFRSs. An example is disclosure of whether an entity applies the fair value or cost model to its investment property (see IAS 40 *Investment Property*).

Some IFRSs specifically require disclosure of particular accounting policies, including choices made by management between different policies they allow. For example, IAS 16 requires disclosure of the measurement bases used for classes of property, plant and equipment.

120   Each entity considers the nature of its operations and the policies that the users of its financial statements would expect to be disclosed for that type of entity. For example, users would expect an entity subject to income taxes to disclose its accounting policies for income taxes, including those applicable to deferred tax liabilities and assets. When an entity has significant foreign operations or transactions in foreign currencies, users would expect disclosure of accounting policies for the recognition of foreign exchange gains and losses.

121   An accounting policy may be significant because of the nature of the entity's operations even if amounts for current and prior periods are not material. It is also appropriate to disclose each significant accounting policy that is not specifically required by IFRSs but the entity selects and applies in accordance with IAS 8.

122   **An entity shall disclose, in the summary of significant accounting policies or other notes, the judgements, apart from those involving estimations (see paragraph 125), that management has made in the process of applying the entity's accounting policies and that have the most significant effect on the amounts recognised in the financial statements.**

123   In the process of applying the entity's accounting policies, management makes various judgements, apart from those involving estimations, that can significantly affect the amounts it recognises in the financial statements. For example, management makes judgements in determining:

    (a)   [deleted]

    (b)   when substantially all the significant risks and rewards of ownership of financial assets and lease assets are transferred to other entities; and

    (c)   whether, in substance, particular sales of goods are financing arrangements and therefore do not give rise to revenue.

124   Some of the disclosures made in accordance with paragraph 122 are required by other IFRSs. For example, IFRS 12 *Disclosure of Interests in Other Entities* requires an entity to disclose the judgements it has made in determining whether it controls another entity. IAS 40 *Investment Property* requires disclosure of the criteria developed by the entity to distinguish investment property from owner-occupied property and from property held for sale in the ordinary course of business, when classification of the property is difficult.

Sources of estimation uncertainty

125   **An entity shall disclose information about the assumptions it makes about the future, and other major sources of estimation uncertainty at the end of the reporting period, that have a significant risk of resulting in a material adjustment to the carrying amounts of assets and liabilities within the next financial year. In respect of those assets and liabilities, the notes shall include details of:**

    (a)   their nature, and

    (b)   their carrying amount as at the end of the reporting period.

126   Determining the carrying amounts of some assets and liabilities requires estimation of the effects of uncertain future events on those assets and liabilities at the end of the reporting period. For example, in the absence of recently observed market prices, future-oriented estimates are necessary to measure the recoverable amount of classes of property, plant and equipment, the effect of technological obsolescence on inventories, provisions subject to the future outcome of litigation in progress, and long-term employee benefit liabilities such as pension obligations. These estimates involve assumptions about such items as the risk adjustment to cash flows or discount rates, future changes in salaries and future changes in prices affecting other costs.

127   The assumptions and other sources of estimation uncertainty disclosed in accordance with paragraph 125 relate to the estimates that require management's most difficult, subjective or complex judgements. As the number of variables and assumptions affecting the possible future resolution of the uncertainties increases, those judgements become more subjective and complex, and the potential for a consequential material adjustment to the carrying amounts of assets and liabilities normally increases accordingly.

128   The disclosures in paragraph 125 are not required for assets and liabilities with a significant risk that their carrying amounts might change materially within the next financial year if, at the end of the reporting period, they are measured at fair value based on a quoted price in an active market for an identical asset or liability. Such fair values might change materially within the next financial year but these changes would not arise from assumptions or other sources of estimation uncertainty at the end of the reporting period.

129   An entity presents the disclosures in paragraph 125 in a manner that helps users of financial statements to understand the judgements that management makes about the future and about other sources of estimation uncertainty. The nature and extent of the information provided vary according to the nature of the assumption and other circumstances. Examples of the types of disclosures an entity makes are:

(a)   the nature of the assumption or other estimation uncertainty;

(b)   the sensitivity of carrying amounts to the methods, assumptions and estimates underlying their calculation, including the reasons for the sensitivity;

(c)   the expected resolution of an uncertainty and the range of reasonably possible outcomes within the next financial year in respect of the carrying amounts of the assets and liabilities affected; and

(d)   an explanation of changes made to past assumptions concerning those assets and liabilities, if the uncertainty remains unresolved.

130   This Standard does not require an entity to disclose budget information or forecasts in making the disclosures in paragraph 125.

131   Sometimes it is impracticable to disclose the extent of the possible effects of an assumption or another source of estimation uncertainty at the end of the reporting period. In such cases, the entity discloses that it is reasonably possible, on the basis of existing knowledge, that outcomes within the next financial year

that are different from the assumption could require a material adjustment to the carrying amount of the asset or liability affected. In all cases, the entity discloses the nature and carrying amount of the specific asset or liability (or class of assets or liabilities) affected by the assumption.

132 The disclosures in paragraph 122 of particular judgements that management made in the process of applying the entity's accounting policies do not relate to the disclosures of sources of estimation uncertainty in paragraph 125.

133 Other IFRSs require the disclosure of some of the assumptions that would otherwise be required in accordance with paragraph 125. For example, IAS 37 requires disclosure, in specified circumstances, of major assumptions concerning future events affecting classes of provisions. IFRS 13 *Fair Value Measurement* requires disclosure of significant assumptions (including the valuation technique(s) and inputs) the entity uses when measuring the fair values of assets and liabilities that are carried at fair value.

Capital

134 An entity shall disclose information that enables users of its financial statements to evaluate the entity's objectives, policies and processes for managing capital.

135 To comply with paragraph 134, the entity discloses the following:

(a) qualitative information about its objectives, policies and processes for managing capital, including:

(i) a description of what it manages as capital;

(ii) when an entity is subject to externally imposed capital requirements, the nature of those requirements and how those requirements are incorporated into the management of capital; and

(iii) how it is meeting its objectives for managing capital.

(b) summary quantitative data about what it manages as capital. Some entities regard some financial liabilities (eg some forms of subordinated debt) as part of capital. Other entities regard capital as excluding some components of equity (eg components arising from cash flow hedges).

(c) any changes in (a) and (b) from the previous period.

(d) whether during the period it complied with any externally imposed capital requirements to which it is subject.

(e) when the entity has not complied with such externally imposed capital requirements, the consequences of such non-compliance.

The entity bases these disclosures on the information provided internally to key management personnel.

136 An entity may manage capital in a number of ways and be subject to a number of different capital requirements. For example, a conglomerate may include entities that undertake insurance activities and banking activities and those entities may operate in several jurisdictions. When an aggregate disclosure of

capital requirements and how capital is managed would not provide useful information or distorts a financial statement user' understanding of an entity's capital resources, the entity shall disclose separate information for each capital requirement to which the entity is subject.

Puttable financial instruments classified as equity

136A   For puttable financial instruments classified as equity instruments, an entity shall disclose (to the extent not disclosed elsewhere):

(a)   summary quantitative data about the amount classified as equity;

(b)   its objectives, policies and processes for managing its obligation to repurchase or redeem the instruments when required to do so by the instrument holders, including any changes from the previous period;

(c)   the expected cash outflow on redemption or repurchase of that class of financial instruments; and

(d)   information about how the expected cash outflow on redemption or repurchase was determined.

Other disclosures

137   An entity shall disclose in the notes:

(a)   the amount of dividends proposed or declared before the financial statements were authorised for issue but not recognised as a distribution to owners during the period, and the related amount per share; and

(b)   the amount of any cumulative preference dividends not recognised.

138   An entity shall disclose the following, if not disclosed elsewhere in information published with the financial statements:

(a)   the domicile and legal form of the entity, its country of incorporation and the address of its registered office (or principal place of business, if different from the registered office);

(b)   a description of the nature of the entity's operations and its principal activities;

(c)   the name of the parent and the ultimate parent of the group; and

(d)   if it is a limited life entity, information regarding the length of its life.

Transition and effective date

139   An entity shall apply this Standard for annual periods beginning on or after 1 January 2009. Earlier application is permitted. If an entity adopts this Standard for an earlier period, it shall disclose that fact.

139A   IAS 27 (as amended in 2008) amended paragraph 106. An entity shall apply that amendment for annual periods beginning on or after 1 July 2009. If an entity applies IAS 27 (amended 2008) for an earlier period, the amendment shall be applied for that earlier period. The amendment shall be applied retrospectively.

139B   *Puttable Financial Instruments and Obligations Arising on Liquidation* (Amendments to IAS 32 and IAS 1), issued in February 2008, amended paragraph 138 and inserted paragraphs 8A, 80A and 136A. An entity shall apply those amendments for annual periods beginning on or after 1 January 2009. Earlier application is permitted. If an entity applies the amendments for an earlier period, it shall disclose that fact and apply the related amendments to IAS 32, IAS 39, IFRS 7 and IFRIC 2 *Members' Shares in Co-operative Entities and Similar Instruments* at the same time.

139C   Paragraphs 68 and 71 were amended by *Improvements to IFRSs* issued in May 2008. An entity shall apply those amendments for annual periods beginning on or after 1 January 2009. Earlier application is permitted. If an entity applies the amendments for an earlier period it shall disclose that fact.

139D   Paragraph 69 was amended by *Improvements to IFRSs* issued in April 2009. An entity shall apply that amendment for annual periods beginning on or after 1 January 2010. Earlier application is permitted. If an entity applies the amendment for an earlier period it shall disclose that fact.

139E   [Deleted]

139F   Paragraphs 106 and 107 were amended and paragraph 106A was added by *Improvements to IFRSs* issued in May 2010. An entity shall apply those amendments for annual periods beginning on or after 1 January 2011. Earlier application is permitted.

139G   IFRS 9, issued in October 2010, amended paragraphs 7, 68, 71, 82, 93, 95 and 123 and deleted paragraph 139E. An entity shall apply those amendments when it applies IFRS 9 as issued in October 2010.

139H   IFRS 10 and IFRS 12, issued in May 2011, amended paragraphs 4, 119, 123 and 124. An entity shall apply those amendments when it applies IFRS 10 and IFRS 12.

139I   IFRS 13, issued in May 2011, amended paragraphs 128 and 133. An entity shall apply those amendments when it applies IFRS 13.

139J   *Presentation of Items of Other Comprehensive Income* (Amendments to IAS 1), issued in June 2011, amended paragraphs 7, 10, 82, 85–87, 90, 91, 94, 100 and 115, added paragraphs 10A, 81A, 81B and 82A, and deleted paragraphs 12, 81, 83 and 84. An entity shall apply those amendments for annual periods beginning on or after 1 July 2012. Earlier application is permitted. If an entity applies the amendments for an earlier period it shall disclose that fact.

139K   IAS 19 *Employee Benefits* (as amended in June 2011) amended the definition of 'other comprehensive income' in paragraph 7 and paragraph 96. An entity shall apply those amendments when it applies IAS 19 (as amended in June 2011).

Withdrawal of IAS 1 (revised 2003)

140   This Standard supersedes IAS 1 *Presentation of Financial Statements* revised in 2003, as amended in 2005.

Appendix
Amendments to other pronouncements

The amendments in this appendix shall be applied for annual periods beginning on or after 1 January 2009. If an entity applies this Standard for an earlier period, these amendments shall be applied for that earlier period. In the amended paragraphs, new text is underlined and deleted text is struck through.

* * * * *

The amendments contained in this appendix when this Standard was revised in 2007 have been incorporated into the relevant pronouncements published in this volume.

International Accounting Standard 2

Inventories

In April 2001 the International Accounting Standards Board (IASB) adopted IAS 2 *Inventories*, which had originally been issued by the International Accounting Standards Committee in December 2003. IAS 2 *Inventories* replaced IAS 2 *Valuation and Presentation of Inventories in the Context of the Historical Cost System* (issued in October 1975).

In December 2003 the IASB issued a revised IAS 2 as part of its initial agenda of technical projects. The revised IAS 2 also incorporated the guidance contained in a related Interpretation (SIC-1 *Consistency—Different Cost Formulas for Inventories*).

Other IFRSs have made minor consequential amendments to IAS 2. They include *Improvements to IFRSs* (issued May 2008) and IFRS 9 *Financial Instruments* (issued November 2009 and October 2010).

CONTENTS

FOR THE ACCOMPANYING DOCUMENTS LISTED BELOW, SEE PART B OF THIS EDITION

APPROVAL BY THE BOARD OF IAS 2 ISSUED IN DECEMBER 2003

BASIS FOR CONCLUSIONS

International Accounting Standard 2 *Inventories* (IAS 2) is set out in paragraphs 1–42 and the Appendix. All the paragraphs have equal authority but retain the IASC format of the Standard when it was adopted by the IASB. IAS 2 should be read in the context of its objective and the Basis for Conclusions, the *Preface to International Financial Reporting Standards* and the *Conceptual Framework for Financial Reporting*. IAS 8 *Accounting Policies, Changes in Accounting Estimates and Errors* provides a basis for selecting and applying accounting policies in the absence of explicit guidance.

Introduction

IN1   International Accounting Standard 2 *Inventories* (IAS 2) replaces IAS 2 *Inventories* (revised in 1993) and should be applied for annual periods beginning on or after 1 January 2005. Earlier application is encouraged. The Standard also supersedes SIC-1 *Consistency—Different Cost Formulas for Inventories*.

Reasons for revising IAS 2

IN2   The International Accounting Standards Board developed this revised IAS 2 as part of its project on Improvements to International Accounting Standards. The project was undertaken in the light of queries and criticisms raised in relation to the Standards by securities regulators, professional accountants and other interested parties. The objectives of the project were to reduce or eliminate alternatives, redundancies and conflicts within the Standards, to deal with some convergence issues and to make other improvements.

IN3   For IAS 2 the Board's main objective was a limited revision to reduce alternatives for the measurement of inventories. The Board did not reconsider the fundamental approach to accounting for inventories contained in IAS 2.

The main changes

IN4   The main changes from the previous version of IAS 2 are described below.

Objective and scope

IN5   The objective and scope paragraphs of IAS 2 were amended by removing the words 'held under the historical cost system', to clarify that the Standard applies to all inventories that are not specifically excluded from its scope.

Scope clarification

IN6   The Standard clarifies that some types of inventories are outside its scope while certain other types of inventories are exempted only from the measurement requirements in the Standard.

IN7   Paragraph 3 establishes a clear distinction between those inventories that are entirely outside the scope of the Standard (described in paragraph 2) and those inventories that are outside the scope of the measurement requirements but within the scope of the other requirements in the Standard.

Scope exemptions

Producers of agricultural and forest products, agricultural produce after harvest and minerals and mineral products

IN8   The Standard does not apply to the measurement of inventories of producers of agricultural and forest products, agricultural produce after harvest, and minerals and mineral products, to the extent that they are measured at net realisable value in accordance with well-established industry practices. The previous version of IAS 2 was amended to replace the words 'mineral ores' with 'minerals and mineral products' to clarify that the scope exemption is not limited to the early stage of extraction of mineral ores.

Inventories of commodity broker-traders

IN9   The Standard does not apply to the measurement of inventories of commodity broker-traders to the extent that they are measured at fair value less costs to sell.

Cost of inventories

Costs of purchase

IN10   IAS 2 does not permit exchange differences arising directly on the recent acquisition of inventories invoiced in a foreign currency to be included in the costs of purchase of inventories. This change from the previous version of IAS 2 resulted from the elimination of the allowed alternative treatment of capitalising certain exchange differences in IAS 21 *The Effects of Changes in Foreign Exchange Rates*. That alternative had already been largely restricted in its application by SIC-11 *Foreign Exchange—Capitalisation of Losses from Severe Currency Devaluations*. SIC-11 has been superseded as a result of the revision of IAS 21 in 2003.

Other costs

IN11   Paragraph 18 was inserted to clarify that when inventories are purchased with deferred settlement terms, the difference between the purchase price for normal credit terms and the amount paid is recognised as interest expense over the period of financing.

Cost formulas

Consistency

IN12   The Standard incorporates the requirements of SIC-1 *Consistency—Different Cost Formulas for Inventories* that an entity use the same cost formula for all inventories having a similar nature and use to the entity. SIC-1 is superseded.

Prohibition of LIFO as a cost formula

IN13   The Standard does not permit the use of the last-in, first-out (LIFO) formula to measure the cost of inventories.

Recognition as an expense

IN14   The Standard eliminates the reference to the matching principle.

IN15   The Standard describes the circumstances that would trigger a reversal of a write-down of inventories recognised in a prior period.

Disclosure

Inventories carried at fair value less costs to sell

IN16 The Standard requires disclosure of the carrying amount of inventories carried at fair value less costs to sell.

Write-down of inventories

IN17 The Standard requires disclosure of the amount of any write-down of inventories recognised as an expense in the period and eliminates the requirement to disclose the amount of inventories carried at net realisable value.

International Accounting Standard 2
Inventories

Objective

1   The objective of this Standard is to prescribe the accounting treatment for inventories. A primary issue in accounting for inventories is the amount of cost to be recognised as an asset and carried forward until the related revenues are recognised. This Standard provides guidance on the determination of cost and its subsequent recognition as an expense, including any write-down to net realisable value. It also provides guidance on the cost formulas that are used to assign costs to inventories.

Scope

2   This Standard applies to all inventories, except:

(a)   work in progress arising under construction contracts, including directly related service contracts (see IAS 11 *Construction Contracts*);

(b)   financial instruments (see IAS 32 *Financial Instruments: Presentation* and IFRS 9 *Financial Instruments*); and

(c)   biological assets related to agricultural activity and agricultural produce at the point of harvest (see IAS 41 *Agriculture*).

3   This Standard does not apply to the measurement of inventories held by:

(a)   producers of agricultural and forest products, agricultural produce after harvest, and minerals and mineral products, to the extent that they are measured at net realisable value in accordance with well-established practices in those industries. When such inventories are measured at net realisable value, changes in that value are recognised in profit or loss in the period of the change.

(b)   commodity broker-traders who measure their inventories at fair value less costs to sell. When such inventories are measured at fair value less costs to sell, changes in fair value less costs to sell are recognised in profit or loss in the period of the change.

4   The inventories referred to in paragraph 3(a) are measured at net realisable value at certain stages of production. This occurs, for example, when agricultural crops have been harvested or minerals have been extracted and sale is assured under a forward contract or a government guarantee, or when an active market exists and there is a negligible risk of failure to sell. These inventories are excluded from only the measurement requirements of this Standard.

5   Broker-traders are those who buy or sell commodities for others or on their own account. The inventories referred to in paragraph 3(b) are principally acquired with the purpose of selling in the near future and generating a profit from fluctuations in price or broker-traders' margin. When these inventories are measured at fair value less costs to sell, they are excluded from only the measurement requirements of this Standard.

Definitions

6   The following terms are used in this Standard with the meanings specified:

Inventories are assets:

(a)   held for sale in the ordinary course of business;

(b)   in the process of production for such sale; or

(c)   in the form of materials or supplies to be consumed in the production process or in the rendering of services.

Net realisable value is the estimated selling price in the ordinary course of business less the estimated costs of completion and the estimated costs necessary to make the sale.

Fair value is the price that would be received to sell an asset or paid to transfer a liability in an orderly transaction between market participants at the measurement date. (See IFRS 13 *Fair Value Measurement*.)

7   Net realisable value refers to the net amount that an entity expects to realise from the sale of inventory in the ordinary course of business. Fair value reflects the price at which an orderly transaction to sell the same inventory in the principal (or most advantageous) market for that inventory would take place between market participants at the measurement date. The former is an entity-specific value; the latter is not. Net realisable value for inventories may not equal fair value less costs to sell.

8   Inventories encompass goods purchased and held for resale including, for example, merchandise purchased by a retailer and held for resale, or land and other property held for resale. Inventories also encompass finished goods produced, or work in progress being produced, by the entity and include materials and supplies awaiting use in the production process. In the case of a service provider, inventories include the costs of the service, as described in paragraph 19, for which the entity has not yet recognised the related revenue (see IAS 18 *Revenue*).

Measurement of inventories

9   Inventories shall be measured at the lower of cost and net realisable value.

Cost of inventories

10   The cost of inventories shall comprise all costs of purchase, costs of conversion and other costs incurred in bringing the inventories to their present location and condition.

Costs of purchase

11   The costs of purchase of inventories comprise the purchase price, import duties and other taxes (other than those subsequently recoverable by the entity from the taxing authorities), and transport, handling and other costs directly attributable

to the acquisition of finished goods, materials and services. Trade discounts, rebates and other similar items are deducted in determining the costs of purchase.

Costs of conversion

12   The costs of conversion of inventories include costs directly related to the units of production, such as direct labour. They also include a systematic allocation of fixed and variable production overheads that are incurred in converting materials into finished goods. Fixed production overheads are those indirect costs of production that remain relatively constant regardless of the volume of production, such as depreciation and maintenance of factory buildings and equipment, and the cost of factory management and administration. Variable production overheads are those indirect costs of production that vary directly, or nearly directly, with the volume of production, such as indirect materials and indirect labour.

13   The allocation of fixed production overheads to the costs of conversion is based on the normal capacity of the production facilities. Normal capacity is the production expected to be achieved on average over a number of periods or seasons under normal circumstances, taking into account the loss of capacity resulting from planned maintenance. The actual level of production may be used if it approximates normal capacity. The amount of fixed overhead allocated to each unit of production is not increased as a consequence of low production or idle plant. Unallocated overheads are recognised as an expense in the period in which they are incurred. In periods of abnormally high production, the amount of fixed overhead allocated to each unit of production is decreased so that inventories are not measured above cost. Variable production overheads are allocated to each unit of production on the basis of the actual use of the production facilities.

14   A production process may result in more than one product being produced simultaneously. This is the case, for example, when joint products are produced or when there is a main product and a by-product. When the costs of conversion of each product are not separately identifiable, they are allocated between the products on a rational and consistent basis. The allocation may be based, for example, on the relative sales value of each product either at the stage in the production process when the products become separately identifiable, or at the completion of production. Most by-products, by their nature, are immaterial. When this is the case, they are often measured at net realisable value and this value is deducted from the cost of the main product. As a result, the carrying amount of the main product is not materially different from its cost.

Other costs

15   Other costs are included in the cost of inventories only to the extent that they are incurred in bringing the inventories to their present location and condition. For example, it may be appropriate to include non-production overheads or the costs of designing products for specific customers in the cost of inventories.

16   Examples of costs excluded from the cost of inventories and recognised as expenses in the period in which they are incurred are:

(a) abnormal amounts of wasted materials, labour or other production costs;

(b) storage costs, unless those costs are necessary in the production process before a further production stage;

(c) administrative overheads that do not contribute to bringing inventories to their present location and condition; and

(d) selling costs.

17 IAS 23 *Borrowing Costs* identifies limited circumstances where borrowing costs are included in the cost of inventories.

18 An entity may purchase inventories on deferred settlement terms. When the arrangement effectively contains a financing element, that element, for example a difference between the purchase price for normal credit terms and the amount paid, is recognised as interest expense over the period of the financing.

Cost of inventories of a service provider

19 To the extent that service providers have inventories, they measure them at the costs of their production. These costs consist primarily of the labour and other costs of personnel directly engaged in providing the service, including supervisory personnel, and attributable overheads. Labour and other costs relating to sales and general administrative personnel are not included but are recognised as expenses in the period in which they are incurred. The cost of inventories of a service provider does not include profit margins or non-attributable overheads that are often factored into prices charged by service providers.

Cost of agricultural produce harvested from biological assets

20 In accordance with IAS 41 *Agriculture* inventories comprising agricultural produce that an entity has harvested from its biological assets are measured on initial recognition at their fair value less costs to sell at the point of harvest. This is the cost of the inventories at that date for application of this Standard.

Techniques for the measurement of cost

21 Techniques for the measurement of the cost of inventories, such as the standard cost method or the retail method, may be used for convenience if the results approximate cost. Standard costs take into account normal levels of materials and supplies, labour, efficiency and capacity utilisation. They are regularly reviewed and, if necessary, revised in the light of current conditions.

22 The retail method is often used in the retail industry for measuring inventories of large numbers of rapidly changing items with similar margins for which it is impracticable to use other costing methods. The cost of the inventory is determined by reducing the sales value of the inventory by the appropriate percentage gross margin. The percentage used takes into consideration inventory that has been marked down to below its original selling price. An average percentage for each retail department is often used.

Cost formulas

23   **The cost of inventories of items that are not ordinarily interchangeable and goods or services produced and segregated for specific projects shall be assigned by using specific identification of their individual costs.**

24   Specific identification of cost means that specific costs are attributed to identified items of inventory. This is the appropriate treatment for items that are segregated for a specific project, regardless of whether they have been bought or produced. However, specific identification of costs is inappropriate when there are large numbers of items of inventory that are ordinarily interchangeable. In such circumstances, the method of selecting those items that remain in inventories could be used to obtain predetermined effects on profit or loss.

25   **The cost of inventories, other than those dealt with in paragraph 23, shall be assigned by using the first-in, first-out (FIFO) or weighted average cost formula. An entity shall use the same cost formula for all inventories having a similar nature and use to the entity. For inventories with a different nature or use, different cost formulas may be justified.**

26   For example, inventories used in one operating segment may have a use to the entity different from the same type of inventories used in another operating segment. However, a difference in geographical location of inventories (or in the respective tax rules), by itself, is not sufficient to justify the use of different cost formulas.

27   The FIFO formula assumes that the items of inventory that were purchased or produced first are sold first, and consequently the items remaining in inventory at the end of the period are those most recently purchased or produced. Under the weighted average cost formula, the cost of each item is determined from the weighted average of the cost of similar items at the beginning of a period and the cost of similar items purchased or produced during the period. The average may be calculated on a periodic basis, or as each additional shipment is received, depending upon the circumstances of the entity.

Net realisable value

28   The cost of inventories may not be recoverable if those inventories are damaged, if they have become wholly or partially obsolete, or if their selling prices have declined. The cost of inventories may also not be recoverable if the estimated costs of completion or the estimated costs to be incurred to make the sale have increased. The practice of writing inventories down below cost to net realisable value is consistent with the view that assets should not be carried in excess of amounts expected to be realised from their sale or use.

29   Inventories are usually written down to net realisable value item by item. In some circumstances, however, it may be appropriate to group similar or related items. This may be the case with items of inventory relating to the same product line that have similar purposes or end uses, are produced and marketed in the same geographical area, and cannot be practicably evaluated separately from other items in that product line. It is not appropriate to write inventories down on the

basis of a classification of inventory, for example, finished goods, or all the inventories in a particular operating segment. Service providers generally accumulate costs in respect of each service for which a separate selling price is charged. Therefore, each such service is treated as a separate item.

30   Estimates of net realisable value are based on the most reliable evidence available at the time the estimates are made, of the amount the inventories are expected to realise. These estimates take into consideration fluctuations of price or cost directly relating to events occurring after the end of the period to the extent that such events confirm conditions existing at the end of the period.

31   Estimates of net realisable value also take into consideration the purpose for which the inventory is held. For example, the net realisable value of the quantity of inventory held to satisfy firm sales or service contracts is based on the contract price. If the sales contracts are for less than the inventory quantities held, the net realisable value of the excess is based on general selling prices. Provisions may arise from firm sales contracts in excess of inventory quantities held or from firm purchase contracts. Such provisions are dealt with under IAS 37 *Provisions, Contingent Liabilities and Contingent Assets*.

32   Materials and other supplies held for use in the production of inventories are not written down below cost if the finished products in which they will be incorporated are expected to be sold at or above cost. However, when a decline in the price of materials indicates that the cost of the finished products exceeds net realisable value, the materials are written down to net realisable value. In such circumstances, the replacement cost of the materials may be the best available measure of their net realisable value.

33   A new assessment is made of net realisable value in each subsequent period. When the circumstances that previously caused inventories to be written down below cost no longer exist or when there is clear evidence of an increase in net realisable value because of changed economic circumstances, the amount of the write-down is reversed (ie the reversal is limited to the amount of the original write-down) so that the new carrying amount is the lower of the cost and the revised net realisable value. This occurs, for example, when an item of inventory that is carried at net realisable value, because its selling price has declined, is still on hand in a subsequent period and its selling price has increased.

Recognition as an expense

34   **When inventories are sold, the carrying amount of those inventories shall be recognised as an expense in the period in which the related revenue is recognised. The amount of any write-down of inventories to net realisable value and all losses of inventories shall be recognised as an expense in the period the write-down or loss occurs. The amount of any reversal of any write-down of inventories, arising from an increase in net realisable value, shall be recognised as a reduction in the amount of inventories recognised as an expense in the period in which the reversal occurs.**

35 Some inventories may be allocated to other asset accounts, for example, inventory used as a component of self-constructed property, plant or equipment. Inventories allocated to another asset in this way are recognised as an expense during the useful life of that asset.

Disclosure

36 The financial statements shall disclose:

(a) the accounting policies adopted in measuring inventories, including the cost formula used;

(b) the total carrying amount of inventories and the carrying amount in classifications appropriate to the entity;

(c) the carrying amount of inventories carried at fair value less costs to sell;

(d) the amount of inventories recognised as an expense during the period;

(e) the amount of any write-down of inventories recognised as an expense in the period in accordance with paragraph 34;

(f) the amount of any reversal of any write-down that is recognised as a reduction in the amount of inventories recognised as expense in the period in accordance with paragraph 34;

(g) the circumstances or events that led to the reversal of a write-down of inventories in accordance with paragraph 34; and

(h) the carrying amount of inventories pledged as security for liabilities.

37 Information about the carrying amounts held in different classifications of inventories and the extent of the changes in these assets is useful to financial statement users. Common classifications of inventories are merchandise, production supplies, materials, work in progress and finished goods. The inventories of a service provider may be described as work in progress.

38 The amount of inventories recognised as an expense during the period, which is often referred to as cost of sales, consists of those costs previously included in the measurement of inventory that has now been sold and unallocated production overheads and abnormal amounts of production costs of inventories. The circumstances of the entity may also warrant the inclusion of other amounts, such as distribution costs.

39 Some entities adopt a format for profit or loss that results in amounts being disclosed other than the cost of inventories recognised as an expense during the period. Under this format, an entity presents an analysis of expenses using a classification based on the nature of expenses. In this case, the entity discloses the costs recognised as an expense for raw materials and consumables, labour costs and other costs together with the amount of the net change in inventories for the period.

Effective date

40   An entity shall apply this Standard for annual periods beginning on or after 1 January 2005. Earlier application is encouraged. If an entity applies this Standard for a period beginning before 1 January 2005, it shall disclose that fact.

40A   [Deleted]

40B   IFRS 9 issued in October 2010, amended paragraph 2(b) and deleted paragraph 40A. An entity shall apply those amendments when it applies IFRS 9 as issued in October 2010.

40C   IFRS 13, issued in May 2011, amended the definition of fair value in paragraph 6 and amended paragraph 7. An entity shall apply those amendments when it applies IFRS 13.

Withdrawal of other pronouncements

41   This Standard supersedes IAS 2 *Inventories* (revised in 1993).

42   This Standard supersedes SIC-1 *Consistency—Different Cost Formulas for Inventories*.

Appendix
Amendments to other pronouncements

The amendments in this appendix shall be applied for annual periods beginning on or after 1 January 2005. If an entity applies this Standard for an earlier period, these amendments shall be applied for that earlier period.

* * * * *

The amendments contained in this appendix when this Standard was revised in 2003 have been incorporated into the relevant pronouncements published in this volume.

International Accounting Standard 7

Statement of Cash Flows

In April 2001 the International Accounting Standards Board (IASB) adopted IAS 7 *Cash Flow Statements*, which had originally been issued by the International Accounting Standards Committee in December 1992. IAS 7 *Cash Flow Statements* replaced IAS 7 *Statement of Changes in Financial Position* (issued in October 1977).

As a result of the changes in terminology used throughout IFRSs arising from requirements in IAS 1 *Presentation of Financial Statements* (issued in 2007), the title of IAS 7 was changed to *Statement of Changes of Cash Flows*.

Other IFRSs have made minor consequential amendments to IAS 7. They include IAS 8 *Accounting Policies, Changes in Accounting Estimates and Errors* (issued December 2003), IFRS 8 *Operating Segments* (issued November 2006) and *Improvements to IFRSs* (issued May 2008 and April 2009).

CONTENTS

FOR THE ACCOMPANYING DOCUMENTS LISTED BELOW, SEE PART B OF THIS EDITION

International Accounting Standard 7 *Statement of Cash Flows* (IAS 7) is set out in paragraphs 1–57. All the paragraphs have equal authority but retain the IASC format of the Standard when it was adopted by the IASB. IAS 7 should be read in the context of its objective and the Basis for Conclusions, the *Preface to International Financial Reporting Standards* and the *Conceptual Framework for Financial Reporting*. IAS 8 *Accounting Policies, Changes in Accounting Estimates and Errors* provides a basis for selecting and applying accounting policies in the absence of explicit guidance.

International Accounting Standard 7
Statement of Cash Flows[1]

Objective

Information about the cash flows of an entity is useful in providing users of financial statements with a basis to assess the ability of the entity to generate cash and cash equivalents and the needs of the entity to utilise those cash flows. The economic decisions that are taken by users require an evaluation of the ability of an entity to generate cash and cash equivalents and the timing and certainty of their generation.

The objective of this Standard is to require the provision of information about the historical changes in cash and cash equivalents of an entity by means of a statement of cash flows which classifies cash flows during the period from operating, investing and financing activities.

Scope

1   **An entity shall prepare a statement of cash flows in accordance with the requirements of this Standard and shall present it as an integral part of its financial statements for each period for which financial statements are presented.**

2   This Standard supersedes IAS 7 *Statement of Changes in Financial Position*, approved in July 1977.

3   Users of an entity's financial statements are interested in how the entity generates and uses cash and cash equivalents. This is the case regardless of the nature of the entity's activities and irrespective of whether cash can be viewed as the product of the entity, as may be the case with a financial institution. Entities need cash for essentially the same reasons however different their principal revenue-producing activities might be. They need cash to conduct their operations, to pay their obligations, and to provide returns to their investors. Accordingly, this Standard requires all entities to present a statement of cash flows.

Benefits of cash flow information

4   A statement of cash flows, when used in conjunction with the rest of the financial statements, provides information that enables users to evaluate the changes in net assets of an entity, its financial structure (including its liquidity and solvency) and its ability to affect the amounts and timing of cash flows in order to adapt to changing circumstances and opportunities. Cash flow information is useful in assessing the ability of the entity to generate cash and cash equivalents and enables users to develop models to assess and compare the present value of the

---

1   In September 2007 the IASB amended the title of IAS 7 from *Cash Flow Statements* to *Statement of Cash Flows* as a consequence of the revision of IAS 1 *Presentation of Financial Statements* in 2007.

future cash flows of different entities. It also enhances the comparability of the reporting of operating performance by different entities because it eliminates the effects of using different accounting treatments for the same transactions and events.

5   Historical cash flow information is often used as an indicator of the amount, timing and certainty of future cash flows. It is also useful in checking the accuracy of past assessments of future cash flows and in examining the relationship between profitability and net cash flow and the impact of changing prices.

Definitions

6   The following terms are used in this Standard with the meanings specified:

Cash comprises cash on hand and demand deposits.

Cash equivalents are short-term, highly liquid investments that are readily convertible to known amounts of cash and which are subject to an insignificant risk of changes in value.

Cash flows are inflows and outflows of cash and cash equivalents.

Operating activities are the principal revenue-producing activities of the entity and other activities that are not investing or financing activities.

Investing activities are the acquisition and disposal of long-term assets and other investments not included in cash equivalents.

Financing activities are activities that result in changes in the size and composition of the contributed equity and borrowings of the entity.

Cash and cash equivalents

7   Cash equivalents are held for the purpose of meeting short-term cash commitments rather than for investment or other purposes. For an investment to qualify as a cash equivalent it must be readily convertible to a known amount of cash and be subject to an insignificant risk of changes in value. Therefore, an investment normally qualifies as a cash equivalent only when it has a short maturity of, say, three months or less from the date of acquisition. Equity investments are excluded from cash equivalents unless they are, in substance, cash equivalents, for example in the case of preferred shares acquired within a short period of their maturity and with a specified redemption date.

8   Bank borrowings are generally considered to be financing activities. However, in some countries, bank overdrafts which are repayable on demand form an integral part of an entity's cash management. In these circumstances, bank overdrafts are included as a component of cash and cash equivalents. A characteristic of such banking arrangements is that the bank balance often fluctuates from being positive to overdrawn.

9   Cash flows exclude movements between items that constitute cash or cash equivalents because these components are part of the cash management of an entity rather than part of its operating, investing and financing activities. Cash management includes the investment of excess cash in cash equivalents.

Presentation of a statement of cash flows

10 **The statement of cash flows shall report cash flows during the period classified by operating, investing and financing activities.**

11 An entity presents its cash flows from operating, investing and financing activities in a manner which is most appropriate to its business. Classification by activity provides information that allows users to assess the impact of those activities on the financial position of the entity and the amount of its cash and cash equivalents. This information may also be used to evaluate the relationships among those activities.

12 A single transaction may include cash flows that are classified differently. For example, when the cash repayment of a loan includes both interest and capital, the interest element may be classified as an operating activity and the capital element is classified as a financing activity.

Operating activities

13 The amount of cash flows arising from operating activities is a key indicator of the extent to which the operations of the entity have generated sufficient cash flows to repay loans, maintain the operating capability of the entity, pay dividends and make new investments without recourse to external sources of financing. Information about the specific components of historical operating cash flows is useful, in conjunction with other information, in forecasting future operating cash flows.

14 Cash flows from operating activities are primarily derived from the principal revenue-producing activities of the entity. Therefore, they generally result from the transactions and other events that enter into the determination of profit or loss. Examples of cash flows from operating activities are:

(a) cash receipts from the sale of goods and the rendering of services;

(b) cash receipts from royalties, fees, commissions and other revenue;

(c) cash payments to suppliers for goods and services;

(d) cash payments to and on behalf of employees;

(e) cash receipts and cash payments of an insurance entity for premiums and claims, annuities and other policy benefits;

(f) cash payments or refunds of income taxes unless they can be specifically identified with financing and investing activities; and

(g) cash receipts and payments from contracts held for dealing or trading purposes.

Some transactions, such as the sale of an item of plant, may give rise to a gain or loss that is included in recognised profit or loss. The cash flows relating to such transactions are cash flows from investing activities. However, cash payments to manufacture or acquire assets held for rental to others and subsequently held for sale as described in paragraph 68A of IAS 16 *Property, Plant and Equipment* are cash flows from operating activities. The cash receipts from rents and subsequent sales of such assets are also cash flows from operating activities.

15   An entity may hold securities and loans for dealing or trading purposes, in which case they are similar to inventory acquired specifically for resale. Therefore, cash flows arising from the purchase and sale of dealing or trading securities are classified as operating activities. Similarly, cash advances and loans made by financial institutions are usually classified as operating activities since they relate to the main revenue-producing activity of that entity.

Investing activities

16   The separate disclosure of cash flows arising from investing activities is important because the cash flows represent the extent to which expenditures have been made for resources intended to generate future income and cash flows. Only expenditures that result in a recognised asset in the statement of financial position are eligible for classification as investing activities. Examples of cash flows arising from investing activities are:

(a)   cash payments to acquire property, plant and equipment, intangibles and other long-term assets. These payments include those relating to capitalised development costs and self-constructed property, plant and equipment;

(b)   cash receipts from sales of property, plant and equipment, intangibles and other long-term assets;

(c)   cash payments to acquire equity or debt instruments of other entities and interests in joint ventures (other than payments for those instruments considered to be cash equivalents or those held for dealing or trading purposes);

(d)   cash receipts from sales of equity or debt instruments of other entities and interests in joint ventures (other than receipts for those instruments considered to be cash equivalents and those held for dealing or trading purposes);

(e)   cash advances and loans made to other parties (other than advances and loans made by a financial institution);

(f)   cash receipts from the repayment of advances and loans made to other parties (other than advances and loans of a financial institution);

(g)   cash payments for futures contracts, forward contracts, option contracts and swap contracts except when the contracts are held for dealing or trading purposes, or the payments are classified as financing activities; and

(h)   cash receipts from futures contracts, forward contracts, option contracts and swap contracts except when the contracts are held for dealing or trading purposes, or the receipts are classified as financing activities.

When a contract is accounted for as a hedge of an identifiable position the cash flows of the contract are classified in the same manner as the cash flows of the position being hedged.

Financing activities

17   The separate disclosure of cash flows arising from financing activities is important because it is useful in predicting claims on future cash flows by providers of capital to the entity. Examples of cash flows arising from financing activities are:

(a)   cash proceeds from issuing shares or other equity instruments;

(b)   cash payments to owners to acquire or redeem the entity's shares;

(c)   cash proceeds from issuing debentures, loans, notes, bonds, mortgages and other short-term or long-term borrowings;

(d)   cash repayments of amounts borrowed; and

(e)   cash payments by a lessee for the reduction of the outstanding liability relating to a finance lease.

Reporting cash flows from operating activities

18   **An entity shall report cash flows from operating activities using either:**

(a)   **the direct method, whereby major classes of gross cash receipts and gross cash payments are disclosed; or**

(b)   **the indirect method, whereby profit or loss is adjusted for the effects of transactions of a non-cash nature, any deferrals or accruals of past or future operating cash receipts or payments, and items of income or expense associated with investing or financing cash flows.**

19   Entities are encouraged to report cash flows from operating activities using the direct method. The direct method provides information which may be useful in estimating future cash flows and which is not available under the indirect method. Under the direct method, information about major classes of gross cash receipts and gross cash payments may be obtained either:

(a)   from the accounting records of the entity; or

(b)   by adjusting sales, cost of sales (interest and similar income and interest expense and similar charges for a financial institution) and other items in the statement of comprehensive income for:

(i)   changes during the period in inventories and operating receivables and payables;

(ii)   other non-cash items; and

(iii)   other items for which the cash effects are investing or financing cash flows.

20   Under the indirect method, the net cash flow from operating activities is determined by adjusting profit or loss for the effects of:

(a)   changes during the period in inventories and operating receivables and payables;

(b)   non-cash items such as depreciation, provisions, deferred taxes, unrealised foreign currency gains and losses, and undistributed profits of associates; and

(c)   all other items for which the cash effects are investing or financing cash flows.

Alternatively, the net cash flow from operating activities may be presented under the indirect method by showing the revenues and expenses disclosed in the statement of comprehensive income and the changes during the period in inventories and operating receivables and payables.

Reporting cash flows from investing and financing activities

21   **An entity shall report separately major classes of gross cash receipts and gross cash payments arising from investing and financing activities, except to the extent that cash flows described in paragraphs 22 and 24 are reported on a net basis.**

Reporting cash flows on a net basis

22   **Cash flows arising from the following operating, investing or financing activities may be reported on a net basis:**

  (a)   **cash receipts and payments on behalf of customers when the cash flows reflect the activities of the customer rather than those of the entity; and**

  (b)   **cash receipts and payments for items in which the turnover is quick, the amounts are large, and the maturities are short.**

23   Examples of cash receipts and payments referred to in paragraph 22(a) are:

  (a)   the acceptance and repayment of demand deposits of a bank;

  (b)   funds held for customers by an investment entity; and

  (c)   rents collected on behalf of, and paid over to, the owners of properties.

23A   Examples of cash receipts and payments referred to in paragraph 22(b) are advances made for, and the repayment of:

  (a)   principal amounts relating to credit card customers;

  (b)   the purchase and sale of investments; and

  (c)   other short-term borrowings, for example, those which have a maturity period of three months or less.

24   **Cash flows arising from each of the following activities of a financial institution may be reported on a net basis:**

  (a)   **cash receipts and payments for the acceptance and repayment of deposits with a fixed maturity date;**

  (b)   **the placement of deposits with and withdrawal of deposits from other financial institutions; and**

(c)   cash advances and loans made to customers and the repayment of those advances and loans.

Foreign currency cash flows

25   Cash flows arising from transactions in a foreign currency shall be recorded in an entity's functional currency by applying to the foreign currency amount the exchange rate between the functional currency and the foreign currency at the date of the cash flow.

26   The cash flows of a foreign subsidiary shall be translated at the exchange rates between the functional currency and the foreign currency at the dates of the cash flows.

27   Cash flows denominated in a foreign currency are reported in a manner consistent with IAS 21 *The Effects of Changes in Foreign Exchange Rates*. This permits the use of an exchange rate that approximates the actual rate. For example, a weighted average exchange rate for a period may be used for recording foreign currency transactions or the translation of the cash flows of a foreign subsidiary. However, IAS 21 does not permit use of the exchange rate at the end of the reporting period when translating the cash flows of a foreign subsidiary.

28   Unrealised gains and losses arising from changes in foreign currency exchange rates are not cash flows. However, the effect of exchange rate changes on cash and cash equivalents held or due in a foreign currency is reported in the statement of cash flows in order to reconcile cash and cash equivalents at the beginning and the end of the period. This amount is presented separately from cash flows from operating, investing and financing activities and includes the differences, if any, had those cash flows been reported at end of period exchange rates.

29   [Deleted]

30   [Deleted]

Interest and dividends

31   Cash flows from interest and dividends received and paid shall each be disclosed separately. Each shall be classified in a consistent manner from period to period as either operating, investing or financing activities.

32   The total amount of interest paid during a period is disclosed in the statement of cash flows whether it has been recognised as an expense in profit or loss or capitalised in accordance with IAS 23 *Borrowing Costs*.

33   Interest paid and interest and dividends received are usually classified as operating cash flows for a financial institution. However, there is no consensus on the classification of these cash flows for other entities. Interest paid and interest and dividends received may be classified as operating cash flows because they enter into the determination of profit or loss. Alternatively, interest paid and interest and dividends received may be classified as financing cash flows and investing cash flows respectively, because they are costs of obtaining financial resources or returns on investments.

34   Dividends paid may be classified as a financing cash flow because they are a cost of obtaining financial resources. Alternatively, dividends paid may be classified as a component of cash flows from operating activities in order to assist users to determine the ability of an entity to pay dividends out of operating cash flows.

Taxes on income

35   **Cash flows arising from taxes on income shall be separately disclosed and shall be classified as cash flows from operating activities unless they can be specifically identified with financing and investing activities.**

36   Taxes on income arise on transactions that give rise to cash flows that are classified as operating, investing or financing activities in a statement of cash flows. While tax expense may be readily identifiable with investing or financing activities, the related tax cash flows are often impracticable to identify and may arise in a different period from the cash flows of the underlying transaction. Therefore, taxes paid are usually classified as cash flows from operating activities. However, when it is practicable to identify the tax cash flow with an individual transaction that gives rise to cash flows that are classified as investing or financing activities the tax cash flow is classified as an investing or financing activity as appropriate. When tax cash flows are allocated over more than one class of activity, the total amount of taxes paid is disclosed.

Investments in subsidiaries, associates and joint ventures

37   When accounting for an investment in an associate, a joint venture or a subsidiary accounted for by use of the equity or cost method, an investor restricts its reporting in the statement of cash flows to the cash flows between itself and the investee, for example, to dividends and advances.

38   An entity that reports its interest in an associate or a joint venture using the equity method includes in its statement of cash flows the cash flows in respect of its investments in the associate or joint venture, and distributions and other payments or receipts between it and the associate or joint venture.

Changes in ownership interests in subsidiaries and other businesses

39   **The aggregate cash flows arising from obtaining or losing control of subsidiaries or other businesses shall be presented separately and classified as investing activities.**

40   **An entity shall disclose, in aggregate, in respect of both obtaining and losing control of subsidiaries or other businesses during the period each of the following:**

      (a)   the total consideration paid or received;

      (b)   the portion of the consideration consisting of cash and cash equivalents;

(c)   the amount of cash and cash equivalents in the subsidiaries or other businesses over which control is obtained or lost; and

(d)   the amount of the assets and liabilities other than cash or cash equivalents in the subsidiaries or other businesses over which control is obtained or lost, summarised by each major category.

41   The separate presentation of the cash flow effects of obtaining or losing control of subsidiaries or other businesses as single line items, together with the separate disclosure of the amounts of assets and liabilities acquired or disposed of, helps to distinguish those cash flows from the cash flows arising from the other operating, investing and financing activities. The cash flow effects of losing control are not deducted from those of obtaining control.

42   The aggregate amount of the cash paid or received as consideration for obtaining or losing control of subsidiaries or other businesses is reported in the statement of cash flows net of cash and cash equivalents acquired or disposed of as part of such transactions, events or changes in circumstances.

42A   Cash flows arising from changes in ownership interests in a subsidiary that do not result in a loss of control shall be classified as cash flows from financing activities.

42B   Changes in ownership interests in a subsidiary that do not result in a loss of control, such as the subsequent purchase or sale by a parent of a subsidiary's equity instruments, are accounted for as equity transactions (see IFRS 10 *Consolidated Financial Statements*). Accordingly, the resulting cash flows are classified in the same way as other transactions with owners described in paragraph 17.

Non-cash transactions

43   **Investing and financing transactions that do not require the use of cash or cash equivalents shall be excluded from a statement of cash flows. Such transactions shall be disclosed elsewhere in the financial statements in a way that provides all the relevant information about these investing and financing activities.**

44   Many investing and financing activities do not have a direct impact on current cash flows although they do affect the capital and asset structure of an entity. The exclusion of non-cash transactions from the statement of cash flows is consistent with the objective of a statement of cash flows as these items do not involve cash flows in the current period. Examples of non-cash transactions are:

(a)   the acquisition of assets either by assuming directly related liabilities or by means of a finance lease;

(b)   the acquisition of an entity by means of an equity issue; and

(c)   the conversion of debt to equity.

Components of cash and cash equivalents

45 **An entity shall disclose the components of cash and cash equivalents and shall present a reconciliation of the amounts in its statement of cash flows with the equivalent items reported in the statement of financial position.**

46 In view of the variety of cash management practices and banking arrangements around the world and in order to comply with IAS 1 *Presentation of Financial Statements*, an entity discloses the policy which it adopts in determining the composition of cash and cash equivalents.

47 The effect of any change in the policy for determining components of cash and cash equivalents, for example, a change in the classification of financial instruments previously considered to be part of an entity's investment portfolio, is reported in accordance with IAS 8 *Accounting Policies, Changes in Accounting Estimates and Errors*.

Other disclosures

48 **An entity shall disclose, together with a commentary by management, the amount of significant cash and cash equivalent balances held by the entity that are not available for use by the group.**

49 There are various circumstances in which cash and cash equivalent balances held by an entity are not available for use by the group. Examples include cash and cash equivalent balances held by a subsidiary that operates in a country where exchange controls or other legal restrictions apply when the balances are not available for general use by the parent or other subsidiaries.

50 Additional information may be relevant to users in understanding the financial position and liquidity of an entity. Disclosure of this information, together with a commentary by management, is encouraged and may include:

(a) the amount of undrawn borrowing facilities that may be available for future operating activities and to settle capital commitments, indicating any restrictions on the use of these facilities;

(b) [deleted]

(c) the aggregate amount of cash flows that represent increases in operating capacity separately from those cash flows that are required to maintain operating capacity; and

(d) the amount of the cash flows arising from the operating, investing and financing activities of each reportable segment (see IFRS 8 *Operating Segments*).

51 The separate disclosure of cash flows that represent increases in operating capacity and cash flows that are required to maintain operating capacity is useful in enabling the user to determine whether the entity is investing adequately in the maintenance of its operating capacity. An entity that does not invest adequately in the maintenance of its operating capacity may be prejudicing future profitability for the sake of current liquidity and distributions to owners.

52   The disclosure of segmental cash flows enables users to obtain a better understanding of the relationship between the cash flows of the business as a whole and those of its component parts and the availability and variability of segmental cash flows.

Effective date

53   This Standard becomes operative for financial statements covering periods beginning on or after 1 January 1994.

54   IAS 27 (as amended in 2008) amended paragraphs 39–42 and added paragraphs 42A and 42B. An entity shall apply those amendments for annual periods beginning on or after 1 July 2009. If an entity applies IAS 27 (amended 2008) for an earlier period, the amendments shall be applied for that earlier period. The amendments shall be applied retrospectively.

55   Paragraph 14 was amended by *Improvements to IFRSs* issued in May 2008. An entity shall apply that amendment for annual periods beginning on or after 1 January 2009. Earlier application is permitted. If an entity applies the amendment for an earlier period it shall disclose that fact and apply paragraph 68A of IAS 16.

56   Paragraph 16 was amended by *Improvements to IFRSs* issued in April 2009. An entity shall apply that amendment for annual periods beginning on or after 1 January 2010. Earlier application is permitted. If an entity applies the amendment for an earlier period it shall disclose that fact.

57   IFRS 10 and IFRS 11 *Joint Arrangements*, issued in May 2011, amended paragraphs 37, 38 and 42B and deleted paragraph 50(b). An entity shall apply those amendments when it applies IFRS 10 and IFRS 11.

International Accounting Standard 8

Accounting Policies, Changes in Accounting Estimates and Errors

In April 2001 the International Accounting Standards Board (IASB) adopted IAS 8 *Net Profit or Loss for the Period, Fundamental Errors and Changes in Accounting Policies*, which had originally been issued by the International Accounting Standards Committee in December 1993. IAS 8 *Net Profit or Loss for the Period, Fundamental Errors and Changes in Accounting Policies* replaced IAS 8 *Unusual and Prior Period Items and Changes in Accounting Policies* (issued in February 1978).

In December 2003, the IASB issued a revised IAS 8 with a new title—*Accounting Policies, Changes in Accounting Estimates and Errors*. This revised IAS 8 was part of the IASB's initial agenda of technical projects. The revised IAS 8 also incorporated the guidance contained in two related Interpretations (SIC-2 *Consistency—Capitalisation of Borrowing Costs* and SIC-18 *Consistency—Alternative Methods*).

Other IFRSs have made minor consequential amendments to IAS 8. They include IAS 1 *Presentation of Financial Statements* (as revised in December 2003), *Improvements to IFRSs* (issued May 2008) and IFRS 9 *Financial Instruments* (issued November 2009 and October 2010).

CONTENTS

FOR THE ACCOMPANYING DOCUMENTS LISTED BELOW, SEE PART B OF THIS EDITION

APPROVAL BY THE BOARD OF IAS 8 ISSUED IN DECEMBER 2003

BASIS FOR CONCLUSIONS

IMPLEMENTATION GUIDANCE

International Accounting Standard 8 *Accounting Policies, Changes in Accounting Estimates and Errors* (IAS 8) is set out in paragraphs 1–56 and the Appendix. All the paragraphs have equal authority but retain the IASC format of the Standard when it was adopted by the IASB. IAS 8 should be read in the context of its objective and the Basis for Conclusions, the *Preface to International Financial Reporting Standards* and the *Conceptual Framework for Financial Reporting*.

Introduction

IN1 International Accounting Standard 8 *Accounting Policies, Changes in Accounting Estimates and Errors* (IAS 8) replaces IAS 8 *Net Profit or Loss for the Period, Fundamental Errors and Changes in Accounting Policies* (revised in 1993) and should be applied for annual periods beginning on or after 1 January 2005. Earlier application is encouraged. The Standard also replaces the following Interpretations:

- SIC-2 *Consistency—Capitalisation of Borrowing Costs*
- SIC-18 *Consistency—Alternative Methods.*

Reasons for revising IAS 8

IN2 The International Accounting Standards Board developed this revised IAS 8 as part of its project on Improvements to International Accounting Standards. The project was undertaken in the light of queries and criticisms raised in relation to the Standards by securities regulators, professional accountants and other interested parties. The objectives of the project were to reduce or eliminate alternatives, redundancies and conflicts within the Standards, to deal with some convergence issues and to make other improvements.

IN3 For IAS 8, the Board's main objectives were:

(a) to remove the allowed alternative to retrospective application of voluntary changes in accounting policies and retrospective restatement to correct prior period errors;

(b) to eliminate the concept of a fundamental error;

(c) to articulate the hierarchy of guidance to which management refers, whose applicability it considers when selecting accounting policies in the absence of Standards and Interpretations that specifically apply;

(d) to define material omissions or misstatements, and describe how to apply the concept of materiality when applying accounting policies and correcting errors; and

(e) to incorporate the consensus in SIC-2 and in SIC-18.

IN4 The Board did not reconsider the other requirements of IAS 8.

Changes from previous requirements

IN5 The main changes from the previous version of IAS 8 are described below.

Selection of accounting policies

IN6 The requirements for the selection and application of accounting policies in IAS 1 *Presentation of Financial Statements* (as issued in 1997) have been transferred to the Standard. The Standard updates the previous hierarchy of guidance to which management refers and whose applicability it considers when selecting accounting policies in the absence of International Financial Reporting Standards (IFRSs) that specifically apply.

Materiality

IN7 The Standard defines material omissions or misstatements. It stipulates that:

(a) the accounting policies in IFRSs need not be applied when the effect of applying them is immaterial. This complements the statement in IAS 1 that disclosures required by IFRSs need not be made if the information is immaterial.

(b) financial statements do not comply with IFRSs if they contain material errors.

(c) material prior period errors are to be corrected retrospectively in the first set of financial statements authorised for issue after their discovery.

Voluntary changes in accounting policies and corrections of prior period errors

IN8 The Standard requires retrospective application of voluntary changes in accounting policies and retrospective restatement to correct prior period errors. It removes the allowed alternative in the previous version of IAS 8:

(a) to include in profit or loss for the current period the adjustment resulting from changing an accounting policy or the amount of a correction of a prior period error; and

(b) to present unchanged comparative information from financial statements of prior periods.

IN9 As a result of the removal of the allowed alternative, comparative information for prior periods is presented as if new accounting policies had always been applied and prior period errors had never occurred.

Impracticability

IN10 The Standard retains the 'impracticability' criterion for exemption from changing comparative information when changes in accounting policies are applied retrospectively and prior period errors are corrected. The Standard now includes a definition of 'impracticable' and guidance on its interpretation.

IN11 The Standard also states that when it is impracticable to determine the cumulative effect, at the beginning of the current period, of:

(a) applying a new accounting policy to all prior periods, or

(b) an error on all prior periods,

the entity changes the comparative information as if the new accounting policy had been applied, or the error had been corrected, prospectively from the earliest date practicable.

Fundamental errors

IN12 The Standard eliminates the concept of a fundamental error and thus the distinction between fundamental errors and other material errors. The Standard defines prior period errors.

Disclosures

IN13   The Standard now requires, rather than encourages, disclosure of an impending change in accounting policy when an entity has yet to implement a new IFRS that has been issued but not yet come into effect. In addition, it requires disclosure of known or reasonably estimable information relevant to assessing the possible impact that application of the new IFRS will have on the entity's financial statements in the period of initial application.

IN14   The Standard requires more detailed disclosure of the amounts of adjustments resulting from changing accounting policies or correcting prior period errors. It requires those disclosures to be made for each financial statement line item affected and, if IAS 33 *Earnings per Share* applies to the entity, for basic and diluted earnings per share.

Other changes

IN15   The presentation requirements for profit or loss for the period have been transferred to IAS 1.

IN16   The Standard incorporates the consensus in SIC-18, namely that:

(a)   an entity selects and applies its accounting policies consistently for similar transactions, other events and conditions, unless an IFRS specifically requires or permits categorisation of items for which different policies may be appropriate; and

(b)   if an IFRS requires or permits such categorisation, an appropriate accounting policy is selected and applied consistently to each category.

The consensus in SIC-18 incorporated the consensus in SIC-2, and requires that when an entity has chosen a policy of capitalising borrowing costs, it should apply this policy to all qualifying assets.

IN17   The Standard includes a definition of a change in accounting estimate.

IN18   The Standard includes exceptions from including the effects of changes in accounting estimates prospectively in profit or loss. It states that to the extent that a change in an accounting estimate gives rise to changes in assets or liabilities, or relates to an item of equity, it is recognised by adjusting the carrying amount of the related asset, liability or equity item in the period of the change.

International Accounting Standard 8
Accounting Policies, Changes in Accounting Estimates and Errors

Objective

1   The objective of this Standard is to prescribe the criteria for selecting and changing accounting policies, together with the accounting treatment and disclosure of changes in accounting policies, changes in accounting estimates and corrections of errors. The Standard is intended to enhance the relevance and reliability of an entity's financial statements, and the comparability of those financial statements over time and with the financial statements of other entities.

2   Disclosure requirements for accounting policies, except those for changes in accounting policies, are set out in IAS 1 *Presentation of Financial Statements*.

Scope

3   **This Standard shall be applied in selecting and applying accounting policies, and accounting for changes in accounting policies, changes in accounting estimates and corrections of prior period errors.**

4   The tax effects of corrections of prior period errors and of retrospective adjustments made to apply changes in accounting policies are accounted for and disclosed in accordance with IAS 12 *Income Taxes*.

Definitions

5   **The following terms are used in this Standard with the meanings specified:**

Accounting policies **are the specific principles, bases, conventions, rules and practices applied by an entity in preparing and presenting financial statements.**

A *change in accounting estimate* **is an adjustment of the carrying amount of an asset or a liability, or the amount of the periodic consumption of an asset, that results from the assessment of the present status of, and expected future benefits and obligations associated with, assets and liabilities. Changes in accounting estimates result from new information or new developments and, accordingly, are not corrections of errors.**

International Financial Reporting Standards (IFRSs) **are Standards and Interpretations issued by the International Accounting Standards Board (IASB). They comprise:**

(a)   **International Financial Reporting Standards;**

(b)   **International Accounting Standards;**

(c)   **IFRIC Interpretations; and**

(d)   **SIC Interpretations.**[1]

---

1   Definition of IFRSs amended after the name changes introduced by the revised Constitution of the IFRS Foundation in 2010.

Material Omissions or misstatements of items are material if they could, individually or collectively, influence the economic decisions that users make on the basis of the financial statements. Materiality depends on the size and nature of the omission or misstatement judged in the surrounding circumstances. The size or nature of the item, or a combination of both, could be the determining factor.

Prior period errors are omissions from, and misstatements in, the entity's financial statements for one or more prior periods arising from a failure to use, or misuse of, reliable information that:

(a)   was available when financial statements for those periods were authorised for issue; and

(b)   could reasonably be expected to have been obtained and taken into account in the preparation and presentation of those financial statements.

Such errors include the effects of mathematical mistakes, mistakes in applying accounting policies, oversights or misinterpretations of facts, and fraud.

Retrospective application is applying a new accounting policy to transactions, other events and conditions as if that policy had always been applied.

Retrospective restatement is correcting the recognition, measurement and disclosure of amounts of elements of financial statements as if a prior period error had never occurred.

Impracticable Applying a requirement is impracticable when the entity cannot apply it after making every reasonable effort to do so. For a particular prior period, it is impracticable to apply a change in an accounting policy retrospectively or to make a retrospective restatement to correct an error if:

(a)   the effects of the retrospective application or retrospective restatement are not determinable;

(b)   the retrospective application or retrospective restatement requires assumptions about what management's intent would have been in that period; or

(c)   the retrospective application or retrospective restatement requires significant estimates of amounts and it is impossible to distinguish objectively information about those estimates that:

    (i)   provides evidence of circumstances that existed on the date(s) as at which those amounts are to be recognised, measured or disclosed; and

    (ii)   would have been available when the financial statements for that prior period were authorised for issue

from other information.

Prospective application of a change in accounting policy and of recognising the effect of a change in an accounting estimate, respectively, are:

(a)   applying the new accounting policy to transactions, other events and conditions occurring after the date as at which the policy is changed; and

(b)   recognising the effect of the change in the accounting estimate in the current and future periods affected by the change.

6   Assessing whether an omission or misstatement could influence economic decisions of users, and so be material, requires consideration of the characteristics of those users. The *Framework for the Preparation and Presentation of Financial Statements* states in paragraph 25[2] that 'users are assumed to have a reasonable knowledge of business and economic activities and accounting and a willingness to study the information with reasonable diligence.' Therefore, the assessment needs to take into account how users with such attributes could reasonably be expected to be influenced in making economic decisions.

Accounting policies

Selection and application of accounting policies

7   **When an IFRS specifically applies to a transaction, other event or condition, the accounting policy or policies applied to that item shall be determined by applying the IFRS.**

8   IFRSs set out accounting policies that the IASB has concluded result in financial statements containing relevant and reliable information about the transactions, other events and conditions to which they apply. Those policies need not be applied when the effect of applying them is immaterial. However, it is inappropriate to make, or leave uncorrected, immaterial departures from IFRSs to achieve a particular presentation of an entity's financial position, financial performance or cash flows.

9   IFRSs are accompanied by guidance to assist entities in applying their requirements. All such guidance states whether it is an integral part of IFRSs. Guidance that is an integral part of the IFRSs is mandatory. Guidance that is not an integral part of the IFRSs does not contain requirements for financial statements.

10 **In the absence of an IFRS that specifically applies to a transaction, other event or condition, management shall use its judgement in developing and applying an accounting policy that results in information that is:**

   (a)   **relevant to the economic decision-making needs of users; and**

   (b)   **reliable, in that the financial statements:**

      (i)   **represent faithfully the financial position, financial performance and cash flows of the entity;**

      (ii)   **reflect the economic substance of transactions, other events and conditions, and not merely the legal form;**

      (iii) **are neutral, ie free from bias;**

      (iv)   **are prudent; and**

      (v)   **are complete in all material respects.**

---

2   IASC's *Framework for the Preparation and Presentation of Financial Statements* was adopted by the IASB in 2001. In September 2010 the IASB replaced the *Framework* with the *Conceptual Framework for Financial Reporting*. Paragraph 25 was superseded by Chapter 3 of the *Conceptual Framework*.

11   In making the judgement described in paragraph 10, management shall refer to, and consider the applicability of, the following sources in descending order:

    (a)   the requirements in IFRSs dealing with similar and related issues; and

    (b)   the definitions, recognition criteria measurement concepts for assets, liabilities, income and expenses in the *Framework*.[3]

12   In making the judgement described in paragraph 10, management may also consider the most recent pronouncements of other standard-setting bodies that use a similar conceptual framework to develop accounting standards, other accounting literature and accepted industry practices, to the extent that these do not conflict with the sources in paragraph 11.

Consistency of accounting policies

13   An entity shall select and apply its accounting policies consistently for similar transactions, other events and conditions, unless an IFRS specifically requires or permits categorisation of items for which different policies may be appropriate. If an IFRS requires or permits such categorisation, an appropriate accounting policy shall be selected and applied consistently to each category.

Changes in accounting policies

14   An entity shall change an accounting policy only if the change:

    (a)   is required by an IFRS; or

    (b)   results in the financial statements providing reliable and more relevant information about the effects of transactions, other events or conditions on the entity's financial position, financial performance or cash flows.

15   Users of financial statements need to be able to compare the financial statements of an entity over time to identify trends in its financial position, financial performance and cash flows. Therefore, the same accounting policies are applied within each period and from one period to the next unless a change in accounting policy meets one of the criteria in paragraph 14.

16   The following are not changes in accounting policies:

    (a)   the application of an accounting policy for transactions, other events or conditions that differ in substance from those previously occurring; and

    (b)   the application of a new accounting policy for transactions, other events or conditions that did not occur previously or were immaterial.

17   The initial application of a policy to revalue assets in accordance with IAS 16 *Property, Plant and Equipment* or IAS 38 *Intangible Assets* is a change in an accounting policy to be dealt with as a revaluation in accordance with IAS 16 or IAS 38, rather than in accordance with this Standard.

18   Paragraphs 19–31 do not apply to the change in accounting policy described in paragraph 17.

---

3   In September 2010 the IASB replaced the *Framework* with the *Conceptual Framework for Financial Reporting*.

Applying changes in accounting policies

19   Subject to paragraph 23:

(a)   an entity shall account for a change in accounting policy resulting from the initial application of an IFRS in accordance with the specific transitional provisions, if any, in that IFRS; and

(b)   when an entity changes an accounting policy upon initial application of an IFRS that does not include specific transitional provisions applying to that change, or changes an accounting policy voluntarily, it shall apply the change retrospectively.

20   For the purpose of this Standard, early application of an IFRS is not a voluntary change in accounting policy.

21   In the absence of an IFRS that specifically applies to a transaction, other event or condition, management may, in accordance with paragraph 12, apply an accounting policy from the most recent pronouncements of other standard-setting bodies that use a similar conceptual framework to develop accounting standards. If, following an amendment of such a pronouncement, the entity chooses to change an accounting policy, that change is accounted for and disclosed as a voluntary change in accounting policy.

Retrospective application

22   Subject to paragraph 23, when a change in accounting policy is applied retrospectively in accordance with paragraph 19(a) or (b), the entity shall adjust the opening balance of each affected component of equity for the earliest prior period presented and the other comparative amounts disclosed for each prior period presented as if the new accounting policy had always been applied.

Limitations on retrospective application

23   When retrospective application is required by paragraph 19(a) or (b), a change in accounting policy shall be applied retrospectively except to the extent that it is impracticable to determine either the period-specific effects or the cumulative effect of the change.

24   When it is impracticable to determine the period-specific effects of changing an accounting policy on comparative information for one or more prior periods presented, the entity shall apply the new accounting policy to the carrying amounts of assets and liabilities as at the beginning of the earliest period for which retrospective application is practicable, which may be the current period, and shall make a corresponding adjustment to the opening balance of each affected component of equity for that period.

25   When it is impracticable to determine the cumulative effect, at the beginning of the current period, of applying a new accounting policy to all prior periods, the entity shall adjust the comparative information to apply the new accounting policy prospectively from the earliest date practicable.

26   When an entity applies a new accounting policy retrospectively, it applies the new accounting policy to comparative information for prior periods as far back as is practicable. Retrospective application to a prior period is not practicable unless it is practicable to determine the cumulative effect on the amounts in both the opening and closing statements of financial position for that period. The amount of the resulting adjustment relating to periods before those presented in the financial statements is made to the opening balance of each affected component of equity of the earliest prior period presented. Usually the adjustment is made to retained earnings. However, the adjustment may be made to another component of equity (for example, to comply with an IFRS). Any other information about prior periods, such as historical summaries of financial data, is also adjusted as far back as is practicable.

27   When it is impracticable for an entity to apply a new accounting policy retrospectively, because it cannot determine the cumulative effect of applying the policy to all prior periods, the entity, in accordance with paragraph 25, applies the new policy prospectively from the start of the earliest period practicable. It therefore disregards the portion of the cumulative adjustment to assets, liabilities and equity arising before that date. Changing an accounting policy is permitted even if it is impracticable to apply the policy prospectively for any prior period. Paragraphs 50–53 provide guidance on when it is impracticable to apply a new accounting policy to one or more prior periods.

Disclosure

28   **When initial application of an IFRS has an effect on the current period or any prior period, would have such an effect except that it is impracticable to determine the amount of the adjustment, or might have an effect on future periods, an entity shall disclose:**

(a)   **the title of the IFRS;**

(b)   **when applicable, that the change in accounting policy is made in accordance with its transitional provisions;**

(c)   **the nature of the change in accounting policy;**

(d)   **when applicable, a description of the transitional provisions;**

(e)   **when applicable, the transitional provisions that might have an effect on future periods;**

(f)   **for the current period and each prior period presented, to the extent practicable, the amount of the adjustment:**

(i)   **for each financial statement line item affected; and**

(ii)   **if IAS 33 *Earnings per Share* applies to the entity, for basic and diluted earnings per share;**

(g)   **the amount of the adjustment relating to periods before those presented, to the extent practicable; and**

(h)   if retrospective application required by paragraph 19(a) or (b) is impracticable for a particular prior period, or for periods before those presented, the circumstances that led to the existence of that condition and a description of how and from when the change in accounting policy has been applied.

Financial statements of subsequent periods need not repeat these disclosures.

29   When a voluntary change in accounting policy has an effect on the current period or any prior period, would have an effect on that period except that it is impracticable to determine the amount of the adjustment, or might have an effect on future periods, an entity shall disclose:

(a)   the nature of the change in accounting policy;

(b)   the reasons why applying the new accounting policy provides reliable and more relevant information;

(c)   for the current period and each prior period presented, to the extent practicable, the amount of the adjustment:

    (i)   for each financial statement line item affected; and

    (ii)   if IAS 33 applies to the entity, for basic and diluted earnings per share;

(d)   the amount of the adjustment relating to periods before those presented, to the extent practicable; and

(e)   if retrospective application is impracticable for a particular prior period, or for periods before those presented, the circumstances that led to the existence of that condition and a description of how and from when the change in accounting policy has been applied.

Financial statements of subsequent periods need not repeat these disclosures.

30   When an entity has not applied a new IFRS that has been issued but is not yet effective, the entity shall disclose:

(a)   this fact; and

(b)   known or reasonably estimable information relevant to assessing the possible impact that application of the new IFRS will have on the entity's financial statements in the period of initial application.

31   In complying with paragraph 30, an entity considers disclosing:

(a)   the title of the new IFRS;

(b)   the nature of the impending change or changes in accounting policy;

(c)   the date by which application of the IFRS is required;

(d)   the date as at which it plans to apply the IFRS initially; and

(e)   either:

    (i)   a discussion of the impact that initial application of the IFRS is expected to have on the entity's financial statements; or

    (ii)   if that impact is not known or reasonably estimable, a statement to that effect.

Changes in accounting estimates

32   As a result of the uncertainties inherent in business activities, many items in financial statements cannot be measured with precision but can only be estimated. Estimation involves judgements based on the latest available, reliable information. For example, estimates may be required of:

(a)   bad debts;

(b)   inventory obsolescence;

(c)   the fair value of financial assets or financial liabilities;

(d)   the useful lives of, or expected pattern of consumption of the future economic benefits embodied in, depreciable assets; and

(e)   warranty obligations.

33   The use of reasonable estimates is an essential part of the preparation of financial statements and does not undermine their reliability.

34   An estimate may need revision if changes occur in the circumstances on which the estimate was based or as a result of new information or more experience. By its nature, the revision of an estimate does not relate to prior periods and is not the correction of an error.

35   A change in the measurement basis applied is a change in an accounting policy, and is not a change in an accounting estimate. When it is difficult to distinguish a change in an accounting policy from a change in an accounting estimate, the change is treated as a change in an accounting estimate.

36   **The effect of a change in an accounting estimate, other than a change to which paragraph 37 applies, shall be recognised prospectively by including it in profit or loss in:**

(a)   **the period of the change, if the change affects that period only; or**

(b)   **the period of the change and future periods, if the change affects both.**

37   **To the extent that a change in an accounting estimate gives rise to changes in assets and liabilities, or relates to an item of equity, it shall be recognised by adjusting the carrying amount of the related asset, liability or equity item in the period of the change.**

38   Prospective recognition of the effect of a change in an accounting estimate means that the change is applied to transactions, other events and conditions from the date of the change in estimate. A change in an accounting estimate may affect only the current period's profit or loss, or the profit or loss of both the current period and future periods. For example, a change in the estimate of the amount of bad debts affects only the current period's profit or loss and therefore is recognised in the current period. However, a change in the estimated useful life of, or the expected pattern of consumption of the future economic benefits embodied in, a depreciable asset affects depreciation expense for the current period and for each future period during the asset's remaining useful life. In both cases, the effect of the change relating to the current period is recognised as income or expense in the current period. The effect, if any, on future periods is recognised as income or   expense in those future periods.

Disclosure

39 An entity shall disclose the nature and amount of a change in an accounting estimate that has an effect in the current period or is expected to have an effect in future periods, except for the disclosure of the effect on future periods when it is impracticable to estimate that effect.

40 If the amount of the effect in future periods is not disclosed because estimating it is impracticable, an entity shall disclose that fact.

Errors

41 Errors can arise in respect of the recognition, measurement, presentation or disclosure of elements of financial statements. Financial statements do not comply with IFRSs if they contain either material errors or immaterial errors made intentionally to achieve a particular presentation of an entity's financial position, financial performance or cash flows. Potential current period errors discovered in that period are corrected before the financial statements are authorised for issue. However, material errors are sometimes not discovered until a subsequent period, and these prior period errors are corrected in the comparative information presented in the financial statements for that subsequent period (see paragraphs 42–47).

42 Subject to paragraph 43, an entity shall correct material prior period errors retrospectively in the first set of financial statements authorised for issue after their discovery by:

(a) restating the comparative amounts for the prior period(s) presented in which the error occurred; or

(b) if the error occurred before the earliest prior period presented, restating the opening balances of assets, liabilities and equity for the earliest prior period presented.

Limitations on retrospective restatement

43 A prior period error shall be corrected by retrospective restatement except to the extent that it is impracticable to determine either the period-specific effects or the cumulative effect of the error.

44 When it is impracticable to determine the period-specific effects of an error on comparative information for one or more prior periods presented, the entity shall restate the opening balances of assets, liabilities and equity for the earliest period for which retrospective restatement is practicable (which may be the current period).

45 When it is impracticable to determine the cumulative effect, at the beginning of the current period, of an error on all prior periods, the entity shall restate the comparative information to correct the error prospectively from the earliest date practicable.

46   The correction of a prior period error is excluded from profit or loss for the period in which the error is discovered. Any information presented about prior periods, including any historical summaries of financial data, is restated as far back as is practicable.

47   When it is impracticable to determine the amount of an error (eg a mistake in applying an accounting policy) for all prior periods, the entity, in accordance with paragraph 45, restates the comparative information prospectively from the earliest date practicable. It therefore disregards the portion of the cumulative restatement of assets, liabilities and equity arising before that date. Paragraphs 50–53 provide guidance on when it is impracticable to correct an error for one or more prior periods.

48   Corrections of errors are distinguished from changes in accounting estimates. Accounting estimates by their nature are approximations that may need revision as additional information becomes known. For example, the gain or loss recognised on the outcome of a contingency is not the correction of an error.

Disclosure of prior period errors

49   In applying paragraph 42, an entity shall disclose the following:

    (a)   the nature of the prior period error;

    (b)   for each prior period presented, to the extent practicable, the amount of the correction:

        (i)   for each financial statement line item affected; and

        (ii)   if IAS 33 applies to the entity, for basic and diluted earnings per share;

    (c)   the amount of the correction at the beginning of the earliest prior period presented; and

    (d)   if retrospective restatement is impracticable for a particular prior period, the circumstances that led to the existence of that condition and a description of how and from when the error has been corrected.

Financial statements of subsequent periods need not repeat these disclosures.

Impracticability in respect of retrospective application and retrospective restatement

50   In some circumstances, it is impracticable to adjust comparative information for one or more prior periods to achieve comparability with the current period. For example, data may not have been collected in the prior period(s) in a way that allows either retrospective application of a new accounting policy (including, for the purpose of paragraphs 51–53, its prospective application to prior periods) or retrospective restatement to correct a prior period error, and it may be impracticable to recreate the information.

51   It is frequently necessary to make estimates in applying an accounting policy to elements of financial statements recognised or disclosed in respect of transactions, other events or conditions. Estimation is inherently subjective, and estimates may be developed after the reporting period. Developing estimates is potentially more difficult when retrospectively applying an accounting policy or making a retrospective restatement to correct a prior period error, because of the longer period of time that might have passed since the affected transaction, other event or condition occurred. However, the objective of estimates related to prior periods remains the same as for estimates made in the current period, namely, for the estimate to reflect the circumstances that existed when the transaction, other event or condition occurred.

52   Therefore, retrospectively applying a new accounting policy or correcting a prior period error requires distinguishing information that

(a)   provides evidence of circumstances that existed on the date(s) as at which the transaction, other event or condition occurred, and

(b)   would have been available when the financial statements for that prior period were authorised for issue

from other information. For some types of estimates (eg a fair value measurement that uses significant unobservable inputs), it is impracticable to distinguish these types of information. When retrospective application or retrospective restatement would require making a significant estimate for which it is impossible to distinguish these two types of information, it is impracticable to apply the new accounting policy or correct the prior period error retrospectively.

53   Hindsight should not be used when applying a new accounting policy to, or correcting amounts for, a prior period, either in making assumptions about what management's intentions would have been in a prior period or estimating the amounts recognised, measured or disclosed in a prior period. For example, when an entity corrects a prior period error in calculating its liability for employees' accumulated sick leave in accordance with IAS 19 *Employee Benefits*, it disregards information about an unusually severe influenza season during the next period that became available after the financial statements for the prior period were authorised for issue. The fact that significant estimates are frequently required when amending comparative information presented for prior periods does not prevent reliable adjustment or correction of the comparative information.

Effective date

54   An entity shall apply this Standard for annual periods beginning on or after 1 January 2005. Earlier application is encouraged. If an entity applies this Standard for a period beginning before 1 January 2005, it shall disclose that fact.

54A   [Deleted]

54B   IFRS 9 *Financial Instruments*, issued in October 2010, amended paragraph 53 and deleted paragraph 54A. An entity shall apply those amendments when it applies IFRS 9 as issued in October 2010.

54C   IFRS 13 *Fair Value Measurement*, issued in May 2011, amended paragraph 52. An entity shall apply that amendment when it applies IFRS 13.

Withdrawal of other pronouncements

55   This Standard supersedes IAS 8 *Net Profit or Loss for the Period, Fundamental Errors and Changes in Accounting Policies*, revised in 1993.

56   This Standard supersedes the following Interpretations:

(a)   SIC-2 *Consistency—Capitalisation of Borrowing Costs*; and

(b)   SIC-18 *Consistency—Alternative Methods*.

Appendix
Amendments to other pronouncements

The amendments in this appendix shall be applied for annual periods beginning on or after 1 January 2005. If an entity applies this Standard for an earlier period, these amendments shall be applied for that earlier period.

* * * * *

The amendments contained in this appendix when this Standard was revised in 2003 have been incorporated into the relevant pronouncements published in this volume.

International Accounting Standard 10

Events after the Reporting Period

In April 2001 the International Accounting Standards Board (IASB) adopted IAS 10 *Events After the Balance Sheet Date*, which had originally been issued by the International Accounting Standards Committee in May 1999. IAS 10 *Events After the Balance Sheet Date* replaced parts of IAS 10 *Contingencies and Events Occurring After the Balance Sheet Date* (issued in June 1978) that were not replaced by IAS 37 *Provisions and Contingent Assets and Contingent Liabilities* (issued in 1998).

In December 2003 the IASB issued a revised IAS 10 with a modified title—*Events after the Balance Sheet Date*. This revised IAS 10 was part of the IASB's initial agenda of technical projects. As a result of the changes in terminology made by IAS 1 *Presentation of Financial Statements* in 2007, the title of IAS 10 was changed to *Events after the Reporting Period*.

Other IFRSs have made minor consequential amendments to IAS 10. They include IFRS 5 *Non-Current Assets Held for Sale and Discontinued Operations* (issued March 2004) and *Improvements to IFRSs* (issued May 2008).

CONTENTS

FOR THE ACCOMPANYING DOCUMENTS LISTED BELOW, SEE PART B OF THIS EDITION

APPROVAL BY THE BOARD OF IAS 10 ISSUED IN DECEMBER 2003

BASIS FOR CONCLUSIONS

International Accounting Standard 10 *Events after the Reporting Period* (IAS 10) is set out in paragraphs 1–24 and the Appendix. All the paragraphs have equal authority but retain the IASC format of the Standard when it was adopted by the IASB. IAS 10 should be read in the context of its objective and the Basis for Conclusions, the *Preface to International Financial Reporting Standards* and the *Conceptual Framework for Financial Reporting*. IAS 8 *Accounting Policies, Changes in Accounting Estimates and Errors* provides a basis for selecting and applying accounting policies in the absence of explicit guidance.

Introduction

IN1　International Accounting Standard 10 *Events after the Reporting Period* (IAS 10)[1] replaces IAS 10 *Events After the Balance Sheet Date* (revised in 1999) and should be applied for annual periods beginning on or after 1 January 2005. Earlier application is encouraged.

Reasons for revising IAS 10

IN2　The International Accounting Standards Board developed this revised IAS 10 as part of its project on Improvements to International Accounting Standards. The project was undertaken in the light of queries and criticisms raised in relation to the Standards by securities regulators, professional accountants and other interested parties. The objectives of the project were to reduce or eliminate alternatives, redundancies and conflicts within the Standards, to deal with some convergence issues and to make other improvements.

IN3　For IAS 10 the Board's main objective was a limited clarification of the accounting for dividends declared after the reporting period. The Board did not reconsider the fundamental approach to the accounting for events after the reporting period contained in IAS 10.

The main changes

IN4　The main change from the previous version of IAS 10 was a limited clarification of paragraphs 12 and 13 (paragraphs 11 and 12 of the previous version of IAS 10). As revised, those paragraphs state that if an entity declares dividends after the reporting period, the entity shall not recognise those dividends as a liability at the end of the reporting period.

1　In September 2007 the IASB amended the title of IAS 10 from *Events after the Balance Sheet Date* to *Events after the Reporting Period* as a consequence of the revision of IAS 1 *Presentation of Financial Statements* in 2007.

International Accounting Standard 10
Events after the Reporting Period

Objective

1   The objective of this Standard is to prescribe:

    (a)   when an entity should adjust its financial statements for events after the reporting period; and

    (b)   the disclosures that an entity should give about the date when the financial statements were authorised for issue and about events after the reporting period.

    The Standard also requires that an entity should not prepare its financial statements on a going concern basis if events after the reporting period indicate that the going concern assumption is not appropriate.

Scope

2   **This Standard shall be applied in the accounting for, and disclosure of, events after the reporting period.**

Definitions

3   **The following terms are used in this Standard with the meanings specified:**

    ***Events after the reporting period* are those events, favourable and unfavourable, that occur between the end of the reporting period and the date when the financial statements are authorised for issue. Two types of events can be identified:**

    (a)   **those that provide evidence of conditions that existed at the end of the reporting period (*adjusting events after the reporting period*); and**

    (b)   **those that are indicative of conditions that arose after the reporting period (*non-adjusting events after the reporting period*).**

4   The process involved in authorising the financial statements for issue will vary depending upon the management structure, statutory requirements and procedures followed in preparing and finalising the financial statements.

5   In some cases, an entity is required to submit its financial statements to its shareholders for approval after the financial statements have been issued. In such cases, the financial statements are authorised for issue on the date of issue, not the date when shareholders approve the financial statements.

Example

The management of an entity completes draft financial statements for the year to 31 December 20X1 on 28 February 20X2. On 18 March 20X2, the board of directors reviews the financial statements and authorises them for issue. The entity announces its profit and selected other financial information on 19 March 20X2. The financial statements are made available to shareholders and others on 1 April 20X2. The shareholders approve the financial statements at their annual meeting on 15 May 20X2 and the approved financial statements are then filed with a regulatory body on 17 May 20X2.

The financial statements are authorised for issue on 18 March 20X2 (date of board authorisation for issue).

---

6   In some cases, the management of an entity is required to issue its financial statements to a supervisory board (made up solely of non-executives) for approval. In such cases, the financial statements are authorised for issue when the management authorises them for issue to the supervisory board.

Example

On 18 March 20X2, the management of an entity authorises financial statements for issue to its supervisory board. The supervisory board is made up solely of non-executives and may include representatives of employees and other outside interests. The supervisory board approves the financial statements on 26 March 20X2. The financial statements are made available to shareholders and others on 1 April 20X2. The shareholders approve the financial statements at their annual meeting on 15 May 20X2 and the financial statements are then filed with a regulatory body on 17 May 20X2.

The financial statements are authorised for issue on 18 March 20X2 (date of management authorisation for issue to the supervisory board).

---

7   Events after the reporting period include all events up to the date when the financial statements are authorised for issue, even if those events occur after the public announcement of profit or of other selected financial information.

Recognition and measurement

Adjusting events after the reporting period

8   **An entity shall adjust the amounts recognised in its financial statements to reflect adjusting events after the reporting period.**

9   The following are examples of adjusting events after the reporting period that require an entity to adjust the amounts recognised in its financial statements, or to recognise items that were not previously recognised:

(a) the settlement after the reporting period of a court case that confirms that the entity had a present obligation at the end of the reporting period. The entity adjusts any previously recognised provision related to this court case in accordance with IAS 37 *Provisions, Contingent Liabilities and Contingent Assets* or recognises a new provision. The entity does not merely disclose a contingent liability because the settlement provides additional evidence that would be considered in accordance with paragraph 16 of IAS 37.

(b) the receipt of information after the reporting period indicating that an asset was impaired at the end of the reporting period, or that the amount of a previously recognised impairment loss for that asset needs to be adjusted. For example:

   (i) the bankruptcy of a customer that occurs after the reporting period usually confirms that a loss existed at the end of the reporting period on a trade receivable and that the entity needs to adjust the carrying amount of the trade receivable; and

   (ii) the sale of inventories after the reporting period may give evidence about their net realisable value at the end of the reporting period.

(c) the determination after the reporting period of the cost of assets purchased, or the proceeds from assets sold, before the end of the reporting period.

(d) the determination after the reporting period of the amount of profit-sharing or bonus payments, if the entity had a present legal or constructive obligation at the end of the reporting period to make such payments as a result of events before that date (see IAS 19 *Employee Benefits*).

(e) the discovery of fraud or errors that show that the financial statements are incorrect.

Non-adjusting events after the reporting period

10 **An entity shall not adjust the amounts recognised in its financial statements to reflect non-adjusting events after the reporting period.**

11 An example of a non-adjusting event after the reporting period is a decline in fair value of investments between the end of the reporting period and the date when the financial statements are authorised for issue. The decline in fair value does not normally relate to the condition of the investments at the end of the reporting period, but reflects circumstances that have arisen subsequently. Therefore, an entity does not adjust the amounts recognised in its financial statements for the investments. Similarly, the entity does not update the amounts disclosed for the investments as at the end of the reporting period, although it may need to give additional disclosure under paragraph 21.

Dividends

12 **If an entity declares dividends to holders of equity instruments (as defined in IAS 32 *Financial Instruments: Presentation*) after the reporting period, the entity shall not recognise those dividends as a liability at the end of the reporting period.**

13   If dividends are declared after the reporting period but before the financial statements are authorised for issue, the dividends are not recognised as a liability at the end of the reporting period because no obligation exists at that time. Such dividends are disclosed in the notes in accordance with IAS 1 *Presentation of Financial Statements*.

Going concern

14   **An entity shall not prepare its financial statements on a going concern basis if management determines after the reporting period either that it intends to liquidate the entity or to cease trading, or that it has no realistic alternative but to do so.**

15   Deterioration in operating results and financial position after the reporting period may indicate a need to consider whether the going concern assumption is still appropriate. If the going concern assumption is no longer appropriate, the effect is so pervasive that this Standard requires a fundamental change in the basis of accounting, rather than an adjustment to the amounts recognised within the original basis of accounting.

16   IAS 1 specifies required disclosures if:

(a)   the financial statements are not prepared on a going concern basis; or

(b)   management is aware of material uncertainties related to events or conditions that may cast significant doubt upon the entity's ability to continue as a going concern. The events or conditions requiring disclosure may arise after the reporting period.

Disclosure

Date of authorisation for issue

17   **An entity shall disclose the date when the financial statements were authorised for issue and who gave that authorisation. If the entity's owners or others have the power to amend the financial statements after issue, the entity shall disclose that fact.**

18   It is important for users to know when the financial statements were authorised for issue, because the financial statements do not reflect events after this date.

Updating disclosure about conditions at the end of the reporting period

19   **If an entity receives information after the reporting period about conditions that existed at the end of the reporting period, it shall update disclosures that relate to those conditions, in the light of the new information.**

20   In some cases, an entity needs to update the disclosures in its financial statements to reflect information received after the reporting period, even when the information does not affect the amounts that it recognises in its financial statements. One example of the need to update disclosures is when evidence

becomes available after the reporting period about a contingent liability that existed at the end of the reporting period. In addition to considering whether it should recognise or change a provision under IAS 37, an entity updates its disclosures about the contingent liability in the light of that evidence.

Non-adjusting events after the reporting period

21 If non-adjusting events after the reporting period are material, non-disclosure could influence the economic decisions that users make on the basis of the financial statements. Accordingly, an entity shall disclose the following for each material category of non-adjusting event after the reporting period:

(a) the nature of the event; and

(b) an estimate of its financial effect, or a statement that such an estimate cannot be made.

22 The following are examples of non-adjusting events after the reporting period that would generally result in disclosure:

(a) a major business combination after the reporting period (IFRS 3 *Business Combinations* requires specific disclosures in such cases) or disposing of a major subsidiary;

(b) announcing a plan to discontinue an operation;

(c) major purchases of assets, classification of assets as held for sale in accordance with IFRS 5 *Non-current Assets Held for Sale and Discontinued Operations*, other disposals of assets, or expropriation of major assets by government;

(d) the destruction of a major production plant by a fire after the reporting period;

(e) announcing, or commencing the implementation of, a major restructuring (see IAS 37);

(f) major ordinary share transactions and potential ordinary share transactions after the reporting period (IAS 33 *Earnings per Share* requires an entity to disclose a description of such transactions, other than when such transactions involve capitalisation or bonus issues, share splits or reverse share splits all of which are required to be adjusted under IAS 33);

(g) abnormally large changes after the reporting period in asset prices or foreign exchange rates;

(h) changes in tax rates or tax laws enacted or announced after the reporting period that have a significant effect on current and deferred tax assets and liabilities (see IAS 12 *Income Taxes*);

(i) entering into significant commitments or contingent liabilities, for example, by issuing significant guarantees; and

(j) commencing major litigation arising solely out of events that occurred after the reporting period.

Effective date

23   An entity shall apply this Standard for annual periods beginning on or after 1 January 2005. Earlier application is encouraged. If an entity applies this Standard for a period beginning before 1 January 2005, it shall disclose that fact.

23A   IFRS 13, issued in May 2011, amended paragraph 11. An entity shall apply that amendment when it applies IFRS 13.

Withdrawal of IAS 10 (revised 1999)

24   This Standard supersedes IAS 10 *Events After the Balance Sheet Date* (revised in 1999).

Appendix
Amendments to other pronouncements

The amendments in this appendix shall be applied for annual periods beginning on or after 1 January 2005. If an entity applies this Standard for an earlier period, these amendments shall be applied for that earlier period.

* * * * *

The amendments contained in this appendix when this Standard was revised in 2003 have been incorporated into the relevant IFRSs published in this volume.

International Accounting Standard 11

Construction Contracts

In April 2001 the International Accounting Standards Board (IASB) adopted IAS 11 *Construction Contracts*, which had originally been issued by the International Accounting Standards Committee in December 1993. IAS 11 *Construction Contracts* replaced parts of IAS 11 *Accounting for Construction Contracts* (issued in March 1979).

Other IFRSs have made minor consequential amendments to IAS 11. They include IAS 23 *Borrowing Costs* (as revised in March 2007) and IAS 1 *Presentation of Financial Statements* (as revised in September 2007).

CONTENTS

FOR THE ACCOMPANYING DOCUMENTS LISTED BELOW, SEE PART B OF THIS EDITION

ILLUSTRATIVE EXAMPLES

Disclosure of accounting policies
The determination of contract revenue and expenses
Contract disclosures

© IFRS Foundation

International Accounting Standard 11 *Construction Contracts* (IAS 11) is set out in paragraphs 1–46. All the paragraphs have equal authority but retain the IASC format of the Standard when it was adopted by the IASB. IAS 11 should be read in the context of its objective, the *Preface to International Financial Reporting Standards* and the *Conceptual Framework for Financial Reporting*. IAS 8 *Accounting Policies, Changes in Accounting Estimates and Errors* provides a basis for selecting and applying accounting policies in the absence of explicit guidance.

International Accounting Standard 11
Construction Contracts

Objective

The objective of this Standard is to prescribe the accounting treatment of revenue and costs associated with construction contracts. Because of the nature of the activity undertaken in construction contracts, the date at which the contract activity is entered into and the date when the activity is completed usually fall into different accounting periods. Therefore, the primary issue in accounting for construction contracts is the allocation of contract revenue and contract costs to the accounting periods in which construction work is performed. This Standard uses the recognition criteria established in the *Framework for the Preparation and Presentation of Financial Statements*[1] to determine when contract revenue and contract costs should be recognised as revenue and expenses in the statement of comprehensive income. It also provides practical guidance on the application of these criteria.

Scope

1   **This Standard shall be applied in accounting for construction contracts in the financial statements of contractors.**

2   This Standard supersedes IAS 11 *Accounting for Construction Contracts* approved in 1978.

Definitions

3   **The following terms are used in this Standard with the meanings specified:**

A *construction contract* is a contract specifically negotiated for the construction of an asset or a combination of assets that are closely interrelated or interdependent in terms of their design, technology and function or their ultimate purpose or use.

A *fixed price contract* is a construction contract in which the contractor agrees to a fixed contract price, or a fixed rate per unit of output, which in some cases is subject to cost escalation clauses.

A *cost plus contract* is a construction contract in which the contractor is reimbursed for allowable or otherwise defined costs, plus a percentage of these costs or a fixed fee.

4   A construction contract may be negotiated for the construction of a single asset such as a bridge, building, dam, pipeline, road, ship or tunnel. A construction contract may also deal with the construction of a number of assets which are closely interrelated or interdependent in terms of their design, technology and function or their ultimate purpose or use; examples of such contracts include those for the construction of refineries and other complex pieces of plant or equipment.

---

1   IASC's *Framework for the Preparation and Presentation of Financial Statements* was adopted by the IASB in 2001. In September 2010 the IASB replaced the *Framework* with the *Conceptual Framework for Financial Reporting*.

5   For the purposes of this Standard, construction contracts include:

(a)   contracts for the rendering of services which are directly related to the construction of the asset, for example, those for the services of project managers and architects; and

(b)   contracts for the destruction or restoration of assets, and the restoration of the environment following the demolition of assets.

6   Construction contracts are formulated in a number of ways which, for the purposes of this Standard, are classified as fixed price contracts and cost plus contracts. Some construction contracts may contain characteristics of both a fixed price contract and a cost plus contract, for example in the case of a cost plus contract with an agreed maximum price. In such circumstances, a contractor needs to consider all the conditions in paragraphs 23 and 24 in order to determine when to recognise contract revenue and expenses.

Combining and segmenting construction contracts

7   The requirements of this Standard are usually applied separately to each construction contract. However, in certain circumstances, it is necessary to apply the Standard to the separately identifiable components of a single contract or to a group of contracts together in order to reflect the substance of a contract or a group of contracts.

8   When a contract covers a number of assets, the construction of each asset shall be treated as a separate construction contract when:

(a)   separate proposals have been submitted for each asset;

(b)   each asset has been subject to separate negotiation and the contractor and customer have been able to accept or reject that part of the contract relating to each asset; and

(c)   the costs and revenues of each asset can be identified.

9   A group of contracts, whether with a single customer or with several customers, shall be treated as a single construction contract when:

(a)   the group of contracts is negotiated as a single package;

(b)   the contracts are so closely interrelated that they are, in effect, part of a single project with an overall profit margin; and

(c)   the contracts are performed concurrently or in a continuous sequence.

10   A contract may provide for the construction of an additional asset at the option of the customer or may be amended to include the construction of an additional asset. The construction of the additional asset shall be treated as a separate construction contract when:

(a)   the asset differs significantly in design, technology or function from the asset or assets covered by the original contract; or

(b)   the price of the asset is negotiated without regard to the original contract price.

Contract revenue

11   Contract revenue shall comprise:

(a)   the initial amount of revenue agreed in the contract; and

(b)   variations in contract work, claims and incentive payments:

(i)   to the extent that it is probable that they will result in revenue; and

(ii)   they are capable of being reliably measured.

12   Contract revenue is measured at the fair value of the consideration received or receivable. The measurement of contract revenue is affected by a variety of uncertainties that depend on the outcome of future events. The estimates often need to be revised as events occur and uncertainties are resolved. Therefore, the amount of contract revenue may increase or decrease from one period to the next. For example:

(a)   a contractor and a customer may agree variations or claims that increase or decrease contract revenue in a period subsequent to that in which the contract was initially agreed;

(b)   the amount of revenue agreed in a fixed price contract may increase as a result of cost escalation clauses;

(c)   the amount of contract revenue may decrease as a result of penalties arising from delays caused by the contractor in the completion of the contract; or

(d)   when a fixed price contract involves a fixed price per unit of output, contract revenue increases as the number of units is increased.

13   A variation is an instruction by the customer for a change in the scope of the work to be performed under the contract. A variation may lead to an increase or a decrease in contract revenue. Examples of variations are changes in the specifications or design of the asset and changes in the duration of the contract. A variation is included in contract revenue when:

(a)   it is probable that the customer will approve the variation and the amount of revenue arising from the variation; and

(b)   the amount of revenue can be reliably measured.

14   A claim is an amount that the contractor seeks to collect from the customer or another party as reimbursement for costs not included in the contract price. A claim may arise from, for example, customer caused delays, errors in specifications or design, and disputed variations in contract work. The measurement of the amounts of revenue arising from claims is subject to a high level of uncertainty and often depends on the outcome of negotiations. Therefore, claims are included in contract revenue only when:

(a)   negotiations have reached an advanced stage such that it is probable that the customer will accept the claim; and

(b)   the amount that it is probable will be accepted by the customer can be measured reliably.

15   Incentive payments are additional amounts paid to the contractor if specified
      performance standards are met or exceeded. For example, a contract may allow
      for an incentive payment to the contractor for early completion of the contract.
      Incentive payments are included in contract revenue when:

      (a)   the contract is sufficiently advanced that it is probable that the specified
             performance standards will be met or exceeded; and

      (b)   the amount of the incentive payment can be measured reliably.

Contract costs

16   **Contract costs shall comprise:**

      (a)   costs that relate directly to the specific contract;

      **(b)   costs that are attributable to contract activity in general and can be
             allocated to the contract; and**

      **(c)   such other costs as are specifically chargeable to the customer under the
             terms of the contract.**

17   Costs that relate directly to a specific contract include:

      (a)   site labour costs, including site supervision;

      (b)   costs of materials used in construction;

      (c)   depreciation of plant and equipment used on the contract;

      (d)   costs of moving plant, equipment and materials to and from the contract
             site;

      (e)   costs of hiring plant and equipment;

      (f)   costs of design and technical assistance that is directly related to the
             contract;

      (g)   the estimated costs of rectification and guarantee work, including
             expected warranty costs; and

      (h)   claims from third parties.

      These costs may be reduced by any incidental income that is not included in
      contract revenue, for example income from the sale of surplus materials and the
      disposal of plant and equipment at the end of the contract.

18   Costs that may be attributable to contract activity in general and can be allocated
      to specific contracts include:

      (a)   insurance;

      (b)   costs of design and technical assistance that are not directly related to a
             specific contract; and

      (c)   construction overheads.

Such costs are allocated using methods that are systematic and rational and are applied consistently to all costs having similar characteristics. The allocation is based on the normal level of construction activity. Construction overheads include costs such as the preparation and processing of construction personnel payroll. Costs that may be attributable to contract activity in general and can be allocated to specific contracts also include borrowing costs.

19 Costs that are specifically chargeable to the customer under the terms of the contract may include some general administration costs and development costs for which reimbursement is specified in the terms of the contract.

20 Costs that cannot be attributed to contract activity or cannot be allocated to a contract are excluded from the costs of a construction contract. Such costs include:

(a) general administration costs for which reimbursement is not specified in the contract;

(b) selling costs;

(c) research and development costs for which reimbursement is not specified in the contract; and

(d) depreciation of idle plant and equipment that is not used on a particular contract.

21 Contract costs include the costs attributable to a contract for the period from the date of securing the contract to the final completion of the contract. However, costs that relate directly to a contract and are incurred in securing the contract are also included as part of the contract costs if they can be separately identified and measured reliably and it is probable that the contract will be obtained. When costs incurred in securing a contract are recognised as an expense in the period in which they are incurred, they are not included in contract costs when the contract is obtained in a subsequent period.

Recognition of contract revenue and expenses

22 **When the outcome of a construction contract can be estimated reliably, contract revenue and contract costs associated with the construction contract shall be recognised as revenue and expenses respectively by reference to the stage of completion of the contract activity at the end of the reporting period. An expected loss on the construction contract shall be recognised as an expense immediately in accordance with paragraph 36.**

23 **In the case of a fixed price contract, the outcome of a construction contract can be estimated reliably when all the following conditions are satisfied:**

(a) **total contract revenue can be measured reliably;**

(b) **it is probable that the economic benefits associated with the contract will flow to the entity;**

(c) **both the contract costs to complete the contract and the stage of contract completion at the end of the reporting period can be measured reliably; and**

(d)   the contract costs attributable to the contract can be clearly identified and measured reliably so that actual contract costs incurred can be compared with prior estimates.

24   In the case of a cost plus contract, the outcome of a construction contract can be estimated reliably when all the following conditions are satisfied:

(a)   it is probable that the economic benefits associated with the contract will flow to the entity; and

(b)   the contract costs attributable to the contract, whether or not specifically reimbursable, can be clearly identified and measured reliably.

25   The recognition of revenue and expenses by reference to the stage of completion of a contract is often referred to as the percentage of completion method. Under this method, contract revenue is matched with the contract costs incurred in reaching the stage of completion, resulting in the reporting of revenue, expenses and profit which can be attributed to the proportion of work completed. This method provides useful information on the extent of contract activity and performance during a period.

26   Under the percentage of completion method, contract revenue is recognised as revenue in profit or loss in the accounting periods in which the work is performed. Contract costs are usually recognised as an expense in profit or loss in the accounting periods in which the work to which they relate is performed. However, any expected excess of total contract costs over total contract revenue for the contract is recognised as an expense immediately in accordance with paragraph 36.

27   A contractor may have incurred contract costs that relate to future activity on the contract. Such contract costs are recognised as an asset provided it is probable that they will be recovered. Such costs represent an amount due from the customer and are often classified as contract work in progress.

28   The outcome of a construction contract can only be estimated reliably when it is probable that the economic benefits associated with the contract will flow to the entity. However, when an uncertainty arises about the collectibility of an amount already included in contract revenue, and already recognised in profit or loss, the uncollectible amount or the amount in respect of which recovery has ceased to be probable is recognised as an expense rather than as an adjustment of the amount of contract revenue.

29   An entity is generally able to make reliable estimates after it has agreed to a contract which establishes:

(a)   each party's enforceable rights regarding the asset to be constructed;

(b)   the consideration to be exchanged; and

(c)   the manner and terms of settlement.

It is also usually necessary for the entity to have an effective internal financial budgeting and reporting system. The entity reviews and, when necessary, revises the estimates of contract revenue and contract costs as the contract progresses. The need for such revisions does not necessarily indicate that the outcome of the contract cannot be estimated reliably.

30   The stage of completion of a contract may be determined in a variety of ways. The entity uses the method that measures reliably the work performed. Depending on the nature of the contract, the methods may include:

(a)   the proportion that contract costs incurred for work performed to date bear to the estimated total contract costs;

(b)   surveys of work performed; or

(c)   completion of a physical proportion of the contract work.

Progress payments and advances received from customers often do not reflect the work performed.

31   When the stage of completion is determined by reference to the contract costs incurred to date, only those contract costs that reflect work performed are included in costs incurred to date. Examples of contract costs which are excluded are:

(a)   contract costs that relate to future activity on the contract, such as costs of materials that have been delivered to a contract site or set aside for use in a contract but not yet installed, used or applied during contract performance, unless the materials have been made specially for the contract; and

(b)   payments made to subcontractors in advance of work performed under the subcontract.

32   **When the outcome of a construction contract cannot be estimated reliably:**

(a)   **revenue shall be recognised only to the extent of contract costs incurred that it is probable will be recoverable; and**

(b)   **contract costs shall be recognised as an expense in the period in which they are incurred.**

An expected loss on the construction contract shall be recognised as an expense immediately in accordance with paragraph 36.

33   During the early stages of a contract it is often the case that the outcome of the contract cannot be estimated reliably. Nevertheless, it may be probable that the entity will recover the contract costs incurred. Therefore, contract revenue is recognised only to the extent of costs incurred that are expected to be recoverable. As the outcome of the contract cannot be estimated reliably, no profit is recognised. However, even though the outcome of the contract cannot be estimated reliably, it may be probable that total contract costs will exceed total contract revenues. In such cases, any expected excess of total contract costs over total contract revenue for the contract is recognised as an expense immediately in accordance with paragraph 36.

34   Contract costs that are not probable of being recovered are recognised as an expense immediately. Examples of circumstances in which the recoverability of contract costs incurred may not be probable and in which contract costs may need to be recognised as an expense immediately include contracts:

(a)   that are not fully enforceable, ie their validity is seriously in question;

(b)   the completion of which is subject to the outcome of pending litigation or legislation;

(c)   relating to properties that are likely to be condemned or expropriated;

(d)   where the customer is unable to meet its obligations; or

(e)   where the contractor is unable to complete the contract or otherwise meet its obligations under the contract.

35   **When the uncertainties that prevented the outcome of the contract being estimated reliably no longer exist, revenue and expenses associated with the construction contract shall be recognised in accordance with paragraph 22 rather than in accordance with paragraph 32.**

Recognition of expected losses

36   **When it is probable that total contract costs will exceed total contract revenue, the expected loss shall be recognised as an expense immediately.**

37   The amount of such a loss is determined irrespective of:

(a)   whether work has commenced on the contract;

(b)   the stage of completion of contract activity; or

(c)   the amount of profits expected to arise on other contracts which are not treated as a single construction contract in accordance with paragraph 9.

Changes in estimates

38   The percentage of completion method is applied on a cumulative basis in each accounting period to the current estimates of contract revenue and contract costs. Therefore, the effect of a change in the estimate of contract revenue or contract costs, or the effect of a change in the estimate of the outcome of a contract, is accounted for as a change in accounting estimate (see IAS 8 *Accounting Policies, Changes in Accounting Estimates and Errors*). The changed estimates are used in the determination of the amount of revenue and expenses recognised in profit or loss in the period in which the change is made and in subsequent periods.

Disclosure

39   **An entity shall disclose:**

(a)   **the amount of contract revenue recognised as revenue in the period;**

(b)   **the methods used to determine the contract revenue recognised in the period; and**

(c)   **the methods used to determine the stage of completion of contracts in progress.**

40   An entity shall disclose each of the following for contracts in progress at the end of the reporting period:

(a)   the aggregate amount of costs incurred and recognised profits (less recognised losses) to date;

(b)   the amount of advances received; and

(c)   the amount of retentions.

41   Retentions are amounts of progress billings that are not paid until the satisfaction of conditions specified in the contract for the payment of such amounts or until defects have been rectified. Progress billings are amounts billed for work performed on a contract whether or not they have been paid by the customer. Advances are amounts received by the contractor before the related work is performed.

42   An entity shall present:

(a)   the gross amount due from customers for contract work as an asset; and

(b)   the gross amount due to customers for contract work as a liability.

43   The gross amount due from customers for contract work is the net amount of:

(a)   costs incurred plus recognised profits; less

(b)   the sum of recognised losses and progress billings

for all contracts in progress for which costs incurred plus recognised profits (less recognised losses) exceeds progress billings.

44   The gross amount due to customers for contract work is the net amount of:

(a)   costs incurred plus recognised profits; less

(b)   the sum of recognised losses and progress billings

for all contracts in progress for which progress billings exceed costs incurred plus recognised profits (less recognised losses).

45   An entity discloses any contingent liabilities and contingent assets in accordance with IAS 37 *Provisions, Contingent Liabilities and Contingent Assets*. Contingent liabilities and contingent assets may arise from such items as warranty costs, claims, penalties or possible losses.

Effective date

46   This Standard becomes operative for financial statements covering periods beginning on or after 1 January 1995.

International Accounting Standard 12

Income Taxes

In April 2001 the International Accounting Standards Board (IASB) adopted IAS 12 *Income Taxes*, which had originally been issued by the International Accounting Standards Committee in October 1996. IAS 12 *Income Taxes* replaced parts of IAS 12 *Accounting for Income Taxes* (issued in July 1979).

In December 2010, the IASB amended IAS 12 to address an issue that arises when entities apply the measurement principle in IAS 12 to temporary differences relating to investment properties that are measured at fair value. That amendment also incorporated some guidance from a related Interpretation (SIC-25 *Income Taxes—Recovery of Revalued Non-Depreciable Assets*).

Other IFRSs have made minor consequential amendments to IAS 12. They include IAS 1 *Presentation of Financial Statements* (as revised in December 2003 and September 2007), IFRS 3 *Business Combinations* (issued March 2004) and IFRS 9 *Financial Instruments* (issued November 2009 and October 2010).

CONTENTS

FOR THE ACCOMPANYING DOCUMENTS LISTED BELOW, SEE PART B OF THIS EDITION

APPROVAL BY THE BOARD OF *DEFERRED TAX: RECOVERY OF UNDERLYING ASSETS* **(AMENDMENTS TO IAS 12) ISSUED IN DECEMBER 2010**

BASIS FOR CONCLUSIONS

ILLUSTRATIVE EXAMPLES

Examples of temporary differences

Illustrative computations and presentation

International Accounting Standard 12 *Income Taxes* (IAS 12) is set out in paragraphs 1–99. All the paragraphs have equal authority but retain the IASC format of the Standard when it was adopted by the IASB. IAS 12 should be read in the context of its objective and the Basis for Conclusions, the *Preface to International Financial Reporting Standards* and the *Conceptual Framework for Financial Reporting*. IAS 8 *Accounting Policies, Changes in Accounting Estimates and Errors* provides a basis for selecting and applying accounting policies in the absence of explicit guidance.

Introduction

IN1 This Standard ('IAS 12 (revised)') replaces IAS 12 *Accounting for Taxes on Income* ('the original IAS 12'). IAS 12 (revised) is effective for accounting periods beginning on or after 1 January 1998. The major changes from the original IAS 12 are as follows.

IN2 The original IAS 12 required an entity to account for deferred tax using either the deferral method or a liability method which is sometimes known as the income statement liability method. IAS 12 (revised) prohibits the deferral method and requires another liability method which is sometimes known as the balance sheet liability method.

The income statement liability method focuses on timing differences, whereas the balance sheet liability method focuses on temporary differences. Timing differences are differences between taxable profit and accounting profit that originate in one period and reverse in one or more subsequent periods. Temporary differences are differences between the tax base of an asset or liability and its carrying amount in the statement of financial position. The tax base of an asset or liability is the amount attributed to that asset or liability for tax purposes.

All timing differences are temporary differences. Temporary differences also arise in the following circumstances, which do not give rise to timing differences, although the original IAS 12 treated them in the same way as transactions that do give rise to timing differences:

(a) subsidiaries, associates or joint arrangements have not distributed their entire profits to the parent, investor, joint venturer or joint operator;

(b) assets are revalued and no equivalent adjustment is made for tax purposes; and

(c) the identifiable assets acquired and liabilities assumed in a business combination are generally recognised at their fair values in accordance with IFRS 3 *Business Combinations*, but no equivalent adjustment is made for tax purposes.

Furthermore, there are some temporary differences which are not timing differences, for example those temporary differences that arise when:

(a) the non-monetary assets and liabilities of an entity are measured in its functional currency but the taxable profit or tax loss (and, hence, the tax base of its non-monetary assets and liabilities) is determined in a different currency;

(b) non-monetary assets and liabilities are restated under IAS 29 *Financial Reporting in Hyperinflationary Economies*; or

(c) the carrying amount of an asset or liability on initial recognition differs from its initial tax base.

IN3 The original IAS 12 permitted an entity not to recognise deferred tax assets and liabilities where there was reasonable evidence that timing differences would not reverse for some considerable period ahead. IAS 12 (revised) requires an entity to recognise a deferred tax liability or (subject to certain conditions) asset for all temporary differences, with certain exceptions noted below.

IN4 The original IAS 12 required that:

(a) deferred tax assets arising from timing differences should be recognised when there was a reasonable expectation of realisation; and

(b) deferred tax assets arising from tax losses should be recognised as an asset only where there was assurance beyond any reasonable doubt that future taxable income would be sufficient to allow the benefit of the loss to be realised. The original IAS 12 permitted (but did not require) an entity to defer recognition of the benefit of tax losses until the period of realisation.

IAS 12 (revised) requires that deferred tax assets should be recognised when it is probable that taxable profits will be available against which the deferred tax asset can be utilised. Where an entity has a history of tax losses, the entity recognises a deferred tax asset only to the extent that the entity has sufficient taxable temporary differences or there is convincing other evidence that sufficient taxable profit will be available.

IN5 As an exception to the general requirement set out in paragraph IN3 above, IAS 12 (revised) prohibits the recognition of deferred tax liabilities and deferred tax assets arising from certain assets or liabilities whose carrying amount differs on initial recognition from their initial tax base. Because such circumstances do not give rise to timing differences, they did not result in deferred tax assets or liabilities under the original IAS 12.

IN6 The original IAS 12 required that taxes payable on undistributed profits of subsidiaries and associates should be recognised unless it was reasonable to assume that those profits will not be distributed or that a distribution would not give rise to a tax liability. However, IAS 12 (revised) prohibits the recognition of such deferred tax liabilities (and those arising from any related cumulative translation adjustment) to the extent that:

(a) the parent, investor, joint venturer or joint operator is able to control the timing of the reversal of the temporary difference; and

(b) it is probable that the temporary difference will not reverse in the foreseeable future.

Where this prohibition has the result that no deferred tax liabilities have been recognised, IAS 12 (revised) requires an entity to disclose the aggregate amount of the temporary differences concerned.

IN7 The original IAS 12 did not refer explicitly to fair value adjustments made on a business combination. Such adjustments give rise to temporary differences and IAS 12 (revised) requires an entity to recognise the resulting deferred tax liability or (subject to the probability criterion for recognition) deferred tax asset with a corresponding effect on the determination of the amount of goodwill or bargain purchase gain recognised. However, IAS 12 (revised) prohibits the recognition of deferred tax liabilities arising from the initial recognition of goodwill.

IN8   The original IAS 12 permitted, but did not require, an entity to recognise a deferred tax liability in respect of asset revaluations. IAS 12 (revised) requires an entity to recognise a deferred tax liability in respect of asset revaluations.

IN9   The tax consequences of recovering the carrying amount of certain assets or liabilities may depend on the manner of recovery or settlement, for example:

     (a)   in certain countries, capital gains are not taxed at the same rate as other taxable income; and

     (b)   in some countries, the amount that is deducted for tax purposes on sale of an asset is greater than the amount that may be deducted as depreciation.

     The original IAS 12 gave no guidance on the measurement of deferred tax assets and liabilities in such cases. IAS 12 (revised) requires that the measurement of deferred tax liabilities and deferred tax assets should be based on the tax consequences that would follow from the manner in which the entity expects to recover or settle the carrying amount of its assets and liabilities.

IN10   The original IAS 12 did not state explicitly whether deferred tax assets and liabilities may be discounted. IAS 12 (revised) prohibits discounting of deferred tax assets and liabilities.

IN11   The original IAS 12 did not specify whether an entity should classify deferred tax balances as current assets and liabilities or as non-current assets and liabilities. IAS 12 (revised) requires that an entity which makes the current/non-current distinction should not classify deferred tax assets and liabilities as current assets and liabilities.[1]

IN12   The original IAS 12 stated that debit and credit balances representing deferred taxes may be offset. IAS 12 (revised) establishes more restrictive conditions on offsetting, based largely on those for financial assets and liabilities in IAS 32 *Financial Instruments: Disclosure and Presentation*.[2]

IN13   The original IAS 12 required disclosure of an explanation of the relationship between tax expense and accounting profit if not explained by the tax rates effective in the reporting entity's country. IAS 12 (revised) requires this explanation to take either or both of the following forms:

     (a)   a numerical reconciliation between tax expense (income) and the product of accounting profit multiplied by the applicable tax rate(s); or

     (b)   a numerical reconciliation between the average effective tax rate and the applicable tax rate.

     IAS 12 (revised) also requires an explanation of changes in the applicable tax rate(s) compared to the previous accounting period.

---

1   This requirement has been moved to paragraph 56 of IAS 1 *Presentation of Financial Statements* (as revised in 2007).

2   In 2005 the IASB amended IAS 32 as *Financial Instruments: Presentation*.

IN14 New disclosures required by IAS 12 (revised) include:

(a) in respect of each type of temporary difference, unused tax losses and unused tax credits:

(i) the amount of deferred tax assets and liabilities recognised; and

(ii) the amount of the deferred tax income or expense recognised in profit or loss, if this is not apparent from the changes in the amounts recognised in the statement of financial position;

(b) in respect of discontinued operations, the tax expense relating to:

(i) the gain or loss on discontinuance; and

(ii) the profit or loss from the ordinary activities of the discontinued operation; and

(c) the amount of a deferred tax asset and the nature of the evidence supporting its recognition, when:

(i) the utilisation of the deferred tax asset is dependent on future taxable profits in excess of the profits arising from the reversal of existing taxable temporary differences; and

(ii) the entity has suffered a loss in either the current or preceding period in the tax jurisdiction to which the deferred tax asset relates.

International Accounting Standard 12
Income Taxes

Objective

The objective of this Standard is to prescribe the accounting treatment for income taxes. The principal issue in accounting for income taxes is how to account for the current and future tax consequences of:

(a)   the future recovery (settlement) of the carrying amount of assets (liabilities) that are recognised in an entity's statement of financial position; and

(b)   transactions and other events of the current period that are recognised in an entity's financial statements.

It is inherent in the recognition of an asset or liability that the reporting entity expects to recover or settle the carrying amount of that asset or liability. If it is probable that recovery or settlement of that carrying amount will make future tax payments larger (smaller) than they would be if such recovery or settlement were to have no tax consequences, this Standard requires an entity to recognise a deferred tax liability (deferred tax asset), with certain limited exceptions.

This Standard requires an entity to account for the tax consequences of transactions and other events in the same way that it accounts for the transactions and other events themselves. Thus, for transactions and other events recognised in profit or loss, any related tax effects are also recognised in profit or loss. For transactions and other events recognised outside profit or loss (either in other comprehensive income or directly in equity), any related tax effects are also recognised outside profit or loss (either in other comprehensive income or directly in equity, respectively). Similarly, the recognition of deferred tax assets and liabilities in a business combination affects the amount of goodwill arising in that business combination or the amount of the bargain purchase gain recognised.

This Standard also deals with the recognition of deferred tax assets arising from unused tax losses or unused tax credits, the presentation of income taxes in the financial statements and the disclosure of information relating to income taxes.

Scope

1   **This Standard shall be applied in accounting for income taxes.**

2   For the purposes of this Standard, income taxes include all domestic and foreign taxes which are based on taxable profits. Income taxes also include taxes, such as withholding taxes, which are payable by a subsidiary, associate or joint arrangement on distributions to the reporting entity.

3   [Deleted]

4   This Standard does not deal with the methods of accounting for government grants (see IAS 20 *Accounting for Government Grants and Disclosure of Government Assistance*) or investment tax credits. However, this Standard does deal with the accounting for temporary differences that may arise from such grants or investment tax credits.

Definitions

5   **The following terms are used in this Standard with the meanings specified:**

Accounting profit is profit or loss for a period before deducting tax expense.

Taxable profit (tax loss) is the profit (loss) for a period, determined in accordance with the rules established by the taxation authorities, upon which income taxes are payable (recoverable).

Tax expense (tax income) is the aggregate amount included in the determination of profit or loss for the period in respect of current tax and deferred tax.

Current tax is the amount of income taxes payable (recoverable) in respect of the taxable profit (tax loss) for a period.

Deferred tax liabilities are the amounts of income taxes payable in future periods in respect of taxable temporary differences.

Deferred tax assets are the amounts of income taxes recoverable in future periods in respect of:

(a)   deductible temporary differences;

(b)   the carryforward of unused tax losses; and

(c)   the carryforward of unused tax credits.

Temporary differences are differences between the carrying amount of an asset or liability in the statement of financial position and its tax base. Temporary differences may be either:

(a)   *taxable temporary differences*, which are temporary differences that will result in taxable amounts in determining taxable profit (tax loss) of future periods when the carrying amount of the asset or liability is recovered or settled; or

(b)   *deductible temporary differences*, which are temporary differences that will result in amounts that are deductible in determining taxable profit (tax loss) of future periods when the carrying amount of the asset or liability is recovered or settled.

The *tax base* of an asset or liability is the amount attributed to that asset or liability for tax purposes.

6   Tax expense (tax income) comprises current tax expense (current tax income) and deferred tax expense (deferred tax income).

Tax base

7   The tax base of an asset is the amount that will be deductible for tax purposes against any taxable economic benefits that will flow to an entity when it recovers the carrying amount of the asset. If those economic benefits will not be taxable, the tax base of the asset is equal to its carrying amount.

Examples
1   A machine cost 100. For tax purposes, depreciation of 30 has already been deducted in the current and prior periods and the remaining cost will be deductible in future periods, either as depreciation or through a deduction on disposal. Revenue generated by using the machine is taxable, any gain on disposal of the machine will be taxable and any loss on disposal will be deductible for tax purposes. *The tax base of the machine is 70.*
2   Interest receivable has a carrying amount of 100. The related interest revenue will be taxed on a cash basis. *The tax base of the interest receivable is nil.*
3   Trade receivables have a carrying amount of 100. The related revenue has already been included in taxable profit (tax loss). *The tax base of the trade receivables is 100.*
4   Dividends receivable from a subsidiary have a carrying amount of 100. The dividends are not taxable. *In substance, the entire carrying amount of the asset is deductible against the economic benefits. Consequently, the tax base of the dividends receivable is 100.*[a]
5   A loan receivable has a carrying amount of 100. The repayment of the loan will have no tax consequences. *The tax base of the loan is 100.*

(a)   Under this analysis, there is no taxable temporary difference. An alternative analysis is that the accrued dividends receivable have a tax base of nil and that a tax rate of nil is applied to the resulting taxable temporary difference of 100. Under both analyses, there is no deferred tax liability.

8   The tax base of a liability is its carrying amount, less any amount that will be deductible for tax purposes in respect of that liability in future periods. In the case of revenue which is received in advance, the tax base of the resulting liability is its carrying amount, less any amount of the revenue that will not be taxable in future periods.

Examples

1. Current liabilities include accrued expenses with a carrying amount of 100. The related expense will be deducted for tax purposes on a cash basis. *The tax base of the accrued expenses is nil.*

2. Current liabilities include interest revenue received in advance, with a carrying amount of 100. The related interest revenue was taxed on a cash basis. *The tax base of the interest received in advance is nil.*

3. Current liabilities include accrued expenses with a carrying amount of 100. The related expense has already been deducted for tax purposes. *The tax base of the accrued expenses is 100.*

4. Current liabilities include accrued fines and penalties with a carrying amount of 100. Fines and penalties are not deductible for tax purposes. *The tax base of the accrued fines and penalties is 100.*[a]

5. A loan payable has a carrying amount of 100. The repayment of the loan will have no tax consequences. *The tax base of the loan is 100.*

(a) Under this analysis, there is no deductible temporary difference. An alternative analysis is that the accrued fines and penalties payable have a tax base of nil and that a tax rate of nil is applied to the resulting deductible temporary difference of 100. Under both analyses, there is no deferred tax asset.

9 Some items have a tax base but are not recognised as assets and liabilities in the statement of financial position. For example, research costs are recognised as an expense in determining accounting profit in the period in which they are incurred but may not be permitted as a deduction in determining taxable profit (tax loss) until a later period. The difference between the tax base of the research costs, being the amount the taxation authorities will permit as a deduction in future periods, and the carrying amount of nil is a deductible temporary difference that results in a deferred tax asset.

10 Where the tax base of an asset or liability is not immediately apparent, it is helpful to consider the fundamental principle upon which this Standard is based: that an entity shall, with certain limited exceptions, recognise a deferred tax liability (asset) whenever recovery or settlement of the carrying amount of an asset or liability would make future tax payments larger (smaller) than they would be if such recovery or settlement were to have no tax consequences. Example C following paragraph 51A illustrates circumstances when it may be helpful to consider this fundamental principle, for example, when the tax base of an asset or liability depends on the expected manner of recovery or settlement.

11 In consolidated financial statements, temporary differences are determined by comparing the carrying amounts of assets and liabilities in the consolidated financial statements with the appropriate tax base. The tax base is determined by reference to a consolidated tax return in those jurisdictions in which such a return is filed. In other jurisdictions, the tax base is determined by reference to the tax returns of each entity in the group.

Recognition of current tax liabilities and current tax assets

12   Current tax for current and prior periods shall, to the extent unpaid, be recognised as a liability. If the amount already paid in respect of current and prior periods exceeds the amount due for those periods, the excess shall be recognised as an asset.

13   The benefit relating to a tax loss that can be carried back to recover current tax of a previous period shall be recognised as an asset.

14   When a tax loss is used to recover current tax of a previous period, an entity recognises the benefit as an asset in the period in which the tax loss occurs because it is probable that the benefit will flow to the entity and the benefit can be reliably measured.

Recognition of deferred tax liabilities and deferred tax assets

Taxable temporary differences

15   A deferred tax liability shall be recognised for all taxable temporary differences, except to the extent that the deferred tax liability arises from:

(a)   the initial recognition of goodwill; or

(b)   the initial recognition of an asset or liability in a transaction which:

(i)   is not a business combination; and

(ii)   at the time of the transaction, affects neither accounting profit nor taxable profit (tax loss).

However, for taxable temporary differences associated with investments in subsidiaries, branches and associates, and interests in joint arrangements, a deferred tax liability shall be recognised in accordance with paragraph 39.

16   It is inherent in the recognition of an asset that its carrying amount will be recovered in the form of economic benefits that flow to the entity in future periods. When the carrying amount of the asset exceeds its tax base, the amount of taxable economic benefits will exceed the amount that will be allowed as a deduction for tax purposes. This difference is a taxable temporary difference and the obligation to pay the resulting income taxes in future periods is a deferred tax liability. As the entity recovers the carrying amount of the asset, the taxable temporary difference will reverse and the entity will have taxable profit. This makes it probable that economic benefits will flow from the entity in the form of tax payments. Therefore, this Standard requires the recognition of all deferred tax liabilities, except in certain circumstances described in paragraphs 15 and 39.

> **Example**
>
> An asset which cost 150 has a carrying amount of 100. Cumulative depreciation for tax purposes is 90 and the tax rate is 25%.
>
> *The tax base of the asset is 60 (cost of 150 less cumulative tax depreciation of 90). To recover the carrying amount of 100, the entity must earn taxable income of 100, but will only be able to deduct tax depreciation of 60. Consequently, the entity will pay income taxes of 10 (40 at 25%) when it recovers the carrying amount of the asset. The difference between the carrying amount of 100 and the tax base of 60 is a taxable temporary difference of 40. Therefore, the entity recognises a deferred tax liability of 10 (40 at 25%) representing the income taxes that it will pay when it recovers the carrying amount of the asset.*

17   Some temporary differences arise when income or expense is included in accounting profit in one period but is included in taxable profit in a different period. Such temporary differences are often described as timing differences. The following are examples of temporary differences of this kind which are taxable temporary differences and which therefore result in deferred tax liabilities:

(a)   interest revenue is included in accounting profit on a time proportion basis but may, in some jurisdictions, be included in taxable profit when cash is collected. The tax base of any receivable recognised in the statement of financial position with respect to such revenues is nil because the revenues do not affect taxable profit until cash is collected;

(b)   depreciation used in determining taxable profit (tax loss) may differ from that used in determining accounting profit. The temporary difference is the difference between the carrying amount of the asset and its tax base which is the original cost of the asset less all deductions in respect of that asset permitted by the taxation authorities in determining taxable profit of the current and prior periods. A taxable temporary difference arises, and results in a deferred tax liability, when tax depreciation is accelerated (if tax depreciation is less rapid than accounting depreciation, a deductible temporary difference arises, and results in a deferred tax asset); and

(c)   development costs may be capitalised and amortised over future periods in determining accounting profit but deducted in determining taxable profit in the period in which they are incurred. Such development costs have a tax base of nil as they have already been deducted from taxable profit. The temporary difference is the difference between the carrying amount of the development costs and their tax base of nil.

18   Temporary differences also arise when:

(a)   the identifiable assets acquired and liabilities assumed in a business combination are recognised at their fair values in accordance with IFRS 3 *Business Combinations*, but no equivalent adjustment is made for tax purposes (see paragraph 19);

(b)   assets are revalued and no equivalent adjustment is made for tax purposes (see paragraph 20);

(c)   goodwill arises in a business combination (see paragraph 21);

(d) the tax base of an asset or liability on initial recognition differs from its initial carrying amount, for example when an entity benefits from non-taxable government grants related to assets (see paragraphs 22 and 33); or

(e) the carrying amount of investments in subsidiaries, branches and associates or interests in joint arrangements becomes different from the tax base of the investment or interest (see paragraphs 38–45).

Business combinations

19 With limited exceptions, the identifiable assets acquired and liabilities assumed in a business combination are recognised at their fair values at the acquisition date. Temporary differences arise when the tax bases of the identifiable assets acquired and liabilities assumed are not affected by the business combination or are affected differently. For example, when the carrying amount of an asset is increased to fair value but the tax base of the asset remains at cost to the previous owner, a taxable temporary difference arises which results in a deferred tax liability. The resulting deferred tax liability affects goodwill (see paragraph 66).

Assets carried at fair value

20 IFRSs permit or require certain assets to be carried at fair value or to be revalued (see, for example, IAS 16 *Property, Plant and Equipment*, IAS 38 *Intangible Assets*, IAS 40 *Investment Property* and IFRS 9 *Financial Instruments*) . In some jurisdictions, the revaluation or other restatement of an asset to fair value affects taxable profit (tax loss) for the current period. As a result, the tax base of the asset is adjusted and no temporary difference arises. In other jurisdictions, the revaluation or restatement of an asset does not affect taxable profit in the period of the revaluation or restatement and, consequently, the tax base of the asset is not adjusted. Nevertheless, the future recovery of the carrying amount will result in a taxable flow of economic benefits to the entity and the amount that will be deductible for tax purposes will differ from the amount of those economic benefits. The difference between the carrying amount of a revalued asset and its tax base is a temporary difference and gives rise to a deferred tax liability or asset. This is true even if:

(a) the entity does not intend to dispose of the asset. In such cases, the revalued carrying amount of the asset will be recovered through use and this will generate taxable income which exceeds the depreciation that will be allowable for tax purposes in future periods; or

(b) tax on capital gains is deferred if the proceeds of the disposal of the asset are invested in similar assets. In such cases, the tax will ultimately become payable on sale or use of the similar assets.

Goodwill

21 Goodwill arising in a business combination is measured as the excess of (a) over (b) below:

(a) the aggregate of:

(i) the consideration transferred measured in accordance with IFRS 3, which generally requires acquisition-date fair value;

(ii)   the amount of any non-controlling interest in the acquiree recognised in accordance with IFRS 3; and

(iii)   in a business combination achieved in stages, the acquisition-date fair value of the acquirer's previously held equity interest in the acquiree.

(b)   the net of the acquisition-date amounts of the identifiable assets acquired and liabilities assumed measured in accordance with IFRS 3.

Many taxation authorities do not allow reductions in the carrying amount of goodwill as a deductible expense in determining taxable profit. Moreover, in such jurisdictions, the cost of goodwill is often not deductible when a subsidiary disposes of its underlying business. In such jurisdictions, goodwill has a tax base of nil. Any difference between the carrying amount of goodwill and its tax base of nil is a taxable temporary difference. However, this Standard does not permit the recognition of the resulting deferred tax liability because goodwill is measured as a residual and the recognition of the deferred tax liability would increase the carrying amount of goodwill.

21A   Subsequent reductions in a deferred tax liability that is unrecognised because it arises from the initial recognition of goodwill are also regarded as arising from the initial recognition of goodwill and are therefore not recognised under paragraph 15(a). For example, if in a business combination an entity recognises goodwill of CU100 that has a tax base of nil, paragraph 15(a) prohibits the entity from recognising the resulting deferred tax liability. If the entity subsequently recognises an impairment loss of CU20 for that goodwill, the amount of the taxable temporary difference relating to the goodwill is reduced from CU100 to CU80, with a resulting decrease in the value of the unrecognised deferred tax liability. That decrease in the value of the unrecognised deferred tax liability is also regarded as relating to the initial recognition of the goodwill and is therefore prohibited from being recognised under paragraph 15(a).

21B   Deferred tax liabilities for taxable temporary differences relating to goodwill are, however, recognised to the extent they do not arise from the initial recognition of goodwill. For example, if in a business combination an entity recognises goodwill of CU100 that is deductible for tax purposes at a rate of 20 per cent per year starting in the year of acquisition, the tax base of the goodwill is CU100 on initial recognition and CU80 at the end of the year of acquisition. If the carrying amount of goodwill at the end of the year of acquisition remains unchanged at CU100, a taxable temporary difference of CU20 arises at the end of that year. Because that taxable temporary difference does not relate to the initial recognition of the goodwill, the resulting deferred tax liability is recognised.

Initial recognition of an asset or liability

22   A temporary difference may arise on initial recognition of an asset or liability, for example if part or all of the cost of an asset will not be deductible for tax purposes. The method of accounting for such a temporary difference depends on the nature of the transaction that led to the initial recognition of the asset or liability:

(a)   in a business combination, an entity recognises any deferred tax liability or asset and this affects the amount of goodwill or bargain purchase gain it recognises (see paragraph 19);

(b)   if the transaction affects either accounting profit or taxable profit, an entity recognises any deferred tax liability or asset and recognises the resulting deferred tax expense or income in profit or loss (see paragraph 59);

(c)   if the transaction is not a business combination, and affects neither accounting profit nor taxable profit, an entity would, in the absence of the exemption provided by paragraphs 15 and 24, recognise the resulting deferred tax liability or asset and adjust the carrying amount of the asset or liability by the same amount. Such adjustments would make the financial statements less transparent. Therefore, this Standard does not permit an entity to recognise the resulting deferred tax liability or asset, either on initial recognition or subsequently (see example below). Furthermore, an entity does not recognise subsequent changes in the unrecognised deferred tax liability or asset as the asset is depreciated.

Example illustrating paragraph 22(c)

An entity intends to use an asset which cost 1,000 throughout its useful life of five years and then dispose of it for a residual value of nil. The tax rate is 40%. Depreciation of the asset is not deductible for tax purposes. On disposal, any capital gain would not be taxable and any capital loss would not be deductible.

As it recovers the carrying amount of the asset, the entity will earn taxable income of 1,000 and pay tax of 400. The entity does not recognise the resulting deferred tax liability of 400 because it results from the initial recognition of the asset.

In the following year, the carrying amount of the asset is 800. In earning taxable income of 800, the entity will pay tax of 320. The entity does not recognise the deferred tax liability of 320 because it results from the initial recognition of the asset.

---

23   In accordance with IAS 32 *Financial Instruments: Presentation* the issuer of a compound financial instrument (for example, a convertible bond) classifies the instrument's liability component as a liability and the equity component as equity. In some jurisdictions, the tax base of the liability component on initial recognition is equal to the initial carrying amount of the sum of the liability and equity components. The resulting taxable temporary difference arises from the initial recognition of the equity component separately from the liability component. Therefore, the exception set out in paragraph 15(b) does not apply. Consequently, an entity recognises the resulting deferred tax liability. In accordance with paragraph 61A, the deferred tax is charged directly to the carrying amount of the equity component. In accordance with paragraph 58, subsequent changes in the deferred tax liability are recognised in profit or loss as deferred tax expense (income).

Deductible temporary differences

24   **A deferred tax asset shall be recognised for all deductible temporary differences to the extent that it is probable that taxable profit will be available against which the deductible temporary difference can be utilised, unless the deferred tax asset arises from the initial recognition of an asset or liability in a transaction that:**

       (a)   is not a business combination; and

> (b)   at the time of the transaction, affects neither accounting profit nor taxable profit (tax loss).
>
> However, for deductible temporary differences associated with investments in subsidiaries, branches and associates, and interests in joint arrangements, a deferred tax asset shall be recognised in accordance with paragraph 44.

25   It is inherent in the recognition of a liability that the carrying amount will be settled in future periods through an outflow from the entity of resources embodying economic benefits. When resources flow from the entity, part or all of their amounts may be deductible in determining taxable profit of a period later than the period in which the liability is recognised. In such cases, a temporary difference exists between the carrying amount of the liability and its tax base. Accordingly, a deferred tax asset arises in respect of the income taxes that will be recoverable in the future periods when that part of the liability is allowed as a deduction in determining taxable profit. Similarly, if the carrying amount of an asset is less than its tax base, the difference gives rise to a deferred tax asset in respect of the income taxes that will be recoverable in future periods.

Example

An entity recognises a liability of 100 for accrued product warranty costs. For tax purposes, the product warranty costs will not be deductible until the entity pays claims. The tax rate is 25%.

The tax base of the liability is nil (carrying amount of 100, less the amount that will be deductible for tax purposes in respect of that liability in future periods). In settling the liability for its carrying amount, the entity will reduce its future taxable profit by an amount of 100 and, consequently, reduce its future tax payments by 25 (100 at 25%). The difference between the carrying amount of 100 and the tax base of nil is a deductible temporary difference of 100. Therefore, the entity recognises a deferred tax asset of 25 (100 at 25%), provided that it is probable that the entity will earn sufficient taxable profit in future periods to benefit from a reduction in tax payments.

---

26   The following are examples of deductible temporary differences that result in deferred tax assets:

(a)   retirement benefit costs may be deducted in determining accounting profit as service is provided by the employee, but deducted in determining taxable profit either when contributions are paid to a fund by the entity or when retirement benefits are paid by the entity. A temporary difference exists between the carrying amount of the liability and its tax base; the tax base of the liability is usually nil. Such a deductible temporary difference results in a deferred tax asset as economic benefits will flow to the entity in the form of a deduction from taxable profits when contributions or retirement benefits are paid;

(b)   research costs are recognised as an expense in determining accounting profit in the period in which they are incurred but may not be permitted as a deduction in determining taxable profit (tax loss) until a later period. The difference between the tax base of the research costs, being the amount the taxation authorities will permit as a deduction in future periods, and the carrying amount of nil is a deductible temporary difference that results in a deferred tax asset;

(c) with limited exceptions, an entity recognises the identifiable assets acquired and liabilities assumed in a business combination at their fair values at the acquisition date. When a liability assumed is recognised at the acquisition date but the related costs are not deducted in determining taxable profits until a later period, a deductible temporary difference arises which results in a deferred tax asset. A deferred tax asset also arises when the fair value of an identifiable asset acquired is less than its tax base. In both cases, the resulting deferred tax asset affects goodwill (see paragraph 66); and

(d) certain assets may be carried at fair value, or may be revalued, without an equivalent adjustment being made for tax purposes (see paragraph 20). A deductible temporary difference arises if the tax base of the asset exceeds its carrying amount.

27 The reversal of deductible temporary differences results in deductions in determining taxable profits of future periods. However, economic benefits in the form of reductions in tax payments will flow to the entity only if it earns sufficient taxable profits against which the deductions can be offset. Therefore, an entity recognises deferred tax assets only when it is probable that taxable profits will be available against which the deductible temporary differences can be utilised.

28 It is probable that taxable profit will be available against which a deductible temporary difference can be utilised when there are sufficient taxable temporary differences relating to the same taxation authority and the same taxable entity which are expected to reverse:

(a) in the same period as the expected reversal of the deductible temporary difference; or

(b) in periods into which a tax loss arising from the deferred tax asset can be carried back or forward.

In such circumstances, the deferred tax asset is recognised in the period in which the deductible temporary differences arise.

29 When there are insufficient taxable temporary differences relating to the same taxation authority and the same taxable entity, the deferred tax asset is recognised to the extent that:

(a) it is probable that the entity will have sufficient taxable profit relating to the same taxation authority and the same taxable entity in the same period as the reversal of the deductible temporary difference (or in the periods into which a tax loss arising from the deferred tax asset can be carried back or forward). In evaluating whether it will have sufficient taxable profit in future periods, an entity ignores taxable amounts arising from deductible temporary differences that are expected to originate in future periods, because the deferred tax asset arising from these deductible temporary differences will itself require future taxable profit in order to be utilised; or

(b) tax planning opportunities are available to the entity that will create taxable profit in appropriate periods.

30 Tax planning opportunities are actions that the entity would take in order to create or increase taxable income in a particular period before the expiry of a tax loss or tax credit carryforward. For example, in some jurisdictions, taxable profit may be created or increased by:

(a) electing to have interest income taxed on either a received or receivable basis;

(b) deferring the claim for certain deductions from taxable profit;

(c) selling, and perhaps leasing back, assets that have appreciated but for which the tax base has not been adjusted to reflect such appreciation; and

(d) selling an asset that generates non-taxable income (such as, in some jurisdictions, a government bond) in order to purchase another investment that generates taxable income.

Where tax planning opportunities advance taxable profit from a later period to an earlier period, the utilisation of a tax loss or tax credit carryforward still depends on the existence of future taxable profit from sources other than future originating temporary differences.

31 When an entity has a history of recent losses, the entity considers the guidance in paragraphs 35 and 36.

32 [Deleted]

Goodwill

32A If the carrying amount of goodwill arising in a business combination is less than its tax base, the difference gives rise to a deferred tax asset. The deferred tax asset arising from the initial recognition of goodwill shall be recognised as part of the accounting for a business combination to the extent that it is probable that taxable profit will be available against which the deductible temporary difference could be utilised.

Initial recognition of an asset or liability

33 One case when a deferred tax asset arises on initial recognition of an asset is when a non-taxable government grant related to an asset is deducted in arriving at the carrying amount of the asset but, for tax purposes, is not deducted from the asset's depreciable amount (in other words its tax base); the carrying amount of the asset is less than its tax base and this gives rise to a deductible temporary difference. Government grants may also be set up as deferred income in which case the difference between the deferred income and its tax base of nil is a deductible temporary difference. Whichever method of presentation an entity adopts, the entity does not recognise the resulting deferred tax asset, for the reason given in paragraph 22.

Unused tax losses and unused tax credits

34   **A deferred tax asset shall be recognised for the carryforward of unused tax losses and unused tax credits to the extent that it is probable that future taxable profit will be available against which the unused tax losses and unused tax credits can be utilised.**

35   The criteria for recognising deferred tax assets arising from the carryforward of unused tax losses and tax credits are the same as the criteria for recognising deferred tax assets arising from deductible temporary differences. However, the existence of unused tax losses is strong evidence that future taxable profit may not be available. Therefore, when an entity has a history of recent losses, the entity recognises a deferred tax asset arising from unused tax losses or tax credits only to the extent that the entity has sufficient taxable temporary differences or there is convincing other evidence that sufficient taxable profit will be available against which the unused tax losses or unused tax credits can be utilised by the entity. In such circumstances, paragraph 82 requires disclosure of the amount of the deferred tax asset and the nature of the evidence supporting its recognition.

36   An entity considers the following criteria in assessing the probability that taxable profit will be available against which the unused tax losses or unused tax credits can be utilised:

(a)   whether the entity has sufficient taxable temporary differences relating to the same taxation authority and the same taxable entity, which will result in taxable amounts against which the unused tax losses or unused tax credits can be utilised before they expire;

(b)   whether it is probable that the entity will have taxable profits before the unused tax losses or unused tax credits expire;

(c)   whether the unused tax losses result from identifiable causes which are unlikely to recur; and

(d)   whether tax planning opportunities (see paragraph 30) are available to the entity that will create taxable profit in the period in which the unused tax losses or unused tax credits can be utilised.

To the extent that it is not probable that taxable profit will be available against which the unused tax losses or unused tax credits can be utilised, the deferred tax asset is not recognised.

Reassessment of unrecognised deferred tax assets

37   At the end of each reporting period, an entity reassesses unrecognised deferred tax assets. The entity recognises a previously unrecognised deferred tax asset to the extent that it has become probable that future taxable profit will allow the deferred tax asset to be recovered. For example, an improvement in trading conditions may make it more probable that the entity will be able to generate sufficient taxable profit in the future for the deferred tax asset to meet the recognition criteria set out in paragraph 24 or 34. Another example is when an entity reassesses deferred tax assets at the date of a business combination or subsequently (see paragraphs 67 and 68).

Investments in subsidiaries, branches and associates and interests in joint arrangements

38   Temporary differences arise when the carrying amount of investments in subsidiaries, branches and associates or interests in joint arrangements (namely the parent or investor's share of the net assets of the subsidiary, branch, associate or investee, including the carrying amount of goodwill) becomes different from the tax base (which is often cost) of the investment or interest. Such differences may arise in a number of different circumstances, for example:

(a)   the existence of undistributed profits of subsidiaries, branches, associates and joint arrangements;

(b)   changes in foreign exchange rates when a parent and its subsidiary are based in different countries; and

(c)   a reduction in the carrying amount of an investment in an associate to its recoverable amount.

In consolidated financial statements, the temporary difference may be different from the temporary difference associated with that investment in the parent's separate financial statements if the parent carries the investment in its separate financial statements at cost or revalued amount.

39   **An entity shall recognise a deferred tax liability for all taxable temporary differences associated with investments in subsidiaries, branches and associates, and interests in joint arrangements, except to the extent that both of the following conditions are satisfied:**

(a)   **the parent, investor, joint venturer or joint operator is able to control the timing of the reversal of the temporary difference; and**

(b)   **it is probable that the temporary difference will not reverse in the foreseeable future.**

40   As a parent controls the dividend policy of its subsidiary, it is able to control the timing of the reversal of temporary differences associated with that investment (including the temporary differences arising not only from undistributed profits but also from any foreign exchange translation differences). Furthermore, it would often be impracticable to determine the amount of income taxes that would be payable when the temporary difference reverses. Therefore, when the parent has determined that those profits will not be distributed in the foreseeable future the parent does not recognise a deferred tax liability. The same considerations apply to investments in branches.

41   The non-monetary assets and liabilities of an entity are measured in its functional currency (see IAS 21 *The Effects of Changes in Foreign Exchange Rates*). If the entity's taxable profit or tax loss (and, hence, the tax base of its non-monetary assets and liabilities) is determined in a different currency, changes in the exchange rate give rise to temporary differences that result in a recognised deferred tax liability or (subject to paragraph 24) asset. The resulting deferred tax is charged or credited to profit or loss (see paragraph 58).

42   An investor in an associate does not control that entity and is usually not in a position to determine its dividend policy. Therefore, in the absence of an agreement requiring that the profits of the associate will not be distributed in the foreseeable future, an investor recognises a deferred tax liability arising from taxable temporary differences associated with its investment in the associate. In some cases, an investor may not be able to determine the amount of tax that would be payable if it recovers the cost of its investment in an associate, but can determine that it will equal or exceed a minimum amount. In such cases, the deferred tax liability is measured at this amount.

43   The arrangement between the parties to a joint arrangement usually deals with the distribution of the profits and identifies whether decisions on such matters require the consent of all the parties or a group of the parties. When the joint venturer or joint operator can control the timing of the distribution of its share of the profits of the joint arrangement and it is probable that its share of the profits will not be distributed in the foreseeable future, a deferred tax liability is not recognised.

44   An entity shall recognise a deferred tax asset for all deductible temporary differences arising from investments in subsidiaries, branches and associates, and interests in joint arrangements, to the extent that, and only to the extent that, it is probable that:

(a)   the temporary difference will reverse in the foreseeable future; and

(b)   taxable profit will be available against which the temporary difference can be utilised.

45   In deciding whether a deferred tax asset is recognised for deductible temporary differences associated with its investments in subsidiaries, branches and associates, and its interests in joint arrangements, an entity considers the guidance set out in paragraphs 28 to 31.

Measurement

46   Current tax liabilities (assets) for the current and prior periods shall be measured at the amount expected to be paid to (recovered from) the taxation authorities, using the tax rates (and tax laws) that have been enacted or substantively enacted by the end of the reporting period.

47   Deferred tax assets and liabilities shall be measured at the tax rates that are expected to apply to the period when the asset is realised or the liability is settled, based on tax rates (and tax laws) that have been enacted or substantively enacted by the end of the reporting period.

48   Current and deferred tax assets and liabilities are usually measured using the tax rates (and tax laws) that have been enacted. However, in some jurisdictions, announcements of tax rates (and tax laws) by the government have the substantive effect of actual enactment, which may follow the announcement by a period of several months. In these circumstances, tax assets and liabilities are measured using the announced tax rate (and tax laws).

49   When different tax rates apply to different levels of taxable income, deferred tax assets and liabilities are measured using the average rates that are expected to apply to the taxable profit (tax loss) of the periods in which the temporary differences are expected to reverse.

50   [Deleted]

51   **The measurement of deferred tax liabilities and deferred tax assets shall reflect the tax consequences that would follow from the manner in which the entity expects, at the end of the reporting period, to recover or settle the carrying amount of its assets and liabilities.**

51A   In some jurisdictions, the manner in which an entity recovers (settles) the carrying amount of an asset (liability) may affect either or both of:

    (a)   the tax rate applicable when the entity recovers (settles) the carrying amount of the asset (liability); and

    (b)   the tax base of the asset (liability).

In such cases, an entity measures deferred tax liabilities and deferred tax assets using the tax rate and the tax base that are consistent with the expected manner of recovery or settlement.

Example A

An item of property, plant and equipment has a carrying amount of 100 and a tax base of 60. A tax rate of 20% would apply if the item were sold and a tax rate of 30% would apply to other income.

The entity recognises a deferred tax liability of 8 (40 at 20%) if it expects to sell the item without further use and a deferred tax liability of 12 (40 at 30%) if it expects to retain the item and recover its carrying amount through use.

Example B

An item or property, plant and equipment with a cost of 100 and a carrying amount of 80 is revalued to 150. No equivalent adjustment is made for tax purposes. Cumulative depreciation for tax purposes is 30 and the tax rate is 30%. If the item is sold for more than cost, the cumulative tax depreciation of 30 will be included in taxable income but sale proceeds in excess of cost will not be taxable.

The tax base of the item is 70 and there is a taxable temporary difference of 80. If the entity expects to recover the carrying amount by using the item, it must generate taxable income of 150, but will only be able to deduct depreciation of 70. On this basis, there is a deferred tax liability of 24 (80 at 30%). If the entity expects to recover the carrying amount by selling the item immediately for proceeds of 150, the deferred tax liability is computed as follows:

continued...

...continued	Taxable Temporary Difference	Tax Rate	Deferred Tax Liability
Cumulative tax depreciation	30	30%	9
Proceeds in excess of cost	50	nil	–
Total	80		9

(note: in accordance with paragraph 61A, the additional deferred tax that arises on the revaluation is recognised in other comprehensive income)

Example C

The facts are as in example B, except that if the item is sold for more than cost, the cumulative tax depreciation will be included in taxable income (taxed at 30%) and the sale proceeds will be taxed at 40%, after deducting an inflation-adjusted cost of 110.

If the entity expects to recover the carrying amount by using the item, it must generate taxable income of 150, but will only be able to deduct depreciation of 70. On this basis, the tax base is 70, there is a taxable temporary difference of 80 and there is a deferred tax liability of 24 (80 at 30%), as in example B.

If the entity expects to recover the carrying amount by selling the item immediately for proceeds of 150, the entity will be able to deduct the indexed cost of 110. The net proceeds of 40 will be taxed at 40%. In addition, the cumulative tax depreciation of 30 will be included in taxable income and taxed at 30%. On this basis, the tax base is 80 (110 less 30), there is a taxable temporary difference of 70 and there is a deferred tax liability of 25 (40 at 40% plus 30 at 30%). If the tax base is not immediately apparent in this example, it may be helpful to consider the fundamental principle set out in paragraph 10.

(note: in accordance with paragraph 61A, the additional deferred tax that arises on the revaluation is recognised in other comprehensive income)

51B If a deferred tax liability or deferred tax asset arises from a non-depreciable asset measured using the revaluation model in IAS 16, the measurement of the deferred tax liability or deferred tax asset shall reflect the tax consequences of recovering the carrying amount of the non-depreciable asset through sale, regardless of the basis of measuring the carrying amount of that asset. Accordingly, if the tax law specifies a tax rate applicable to the taxable amount derived from the sale of an asset that differs from the tax rate applicable to the taxable amount derived from using an asset, the former rate is applied in measuring the deferred tax liability or asset related to a non-depreciable asset.

51C If a deferred tax liability or asset arises from investment property that is measured using the fair value model in IAS 40, there is a rebuttable presumption that the carrying amount of the investment property will be recovered through sale. Accordingly, unless the presumption is rebutted, the measurement of the deferred tax liability or deferred tax asset shall reflect the tax consequences of recovering the carrying amount of the investment property entirely through sale. This presumption is rebutted if the investment property is depreciable and is held within a business model whose objective is to consume substantially all of the economic benefits embodied in the investment property over time, rather than through sale. If the presumption is rebutted, the requirements of paragraphs 51 and 51A shall be followed.

Example illustrating paragraph 51C

An investment property has a cost of 100 and fair value of 150. It is measured using the fair value model in IAS 40. It comprises land with a cost of 40 and fair value of 60 and a building with a cost of 60 and fair value of 90. The land has an unlimited useful life.

Cumulative depreciation of the building for tax purposes is 30. Unrealised changes in the fair value of the investment property do not affect taxable profit. If the investment property is sold for more than cost, the reversal of the cumulative tax depreciation of 30 will be included in taxable profit and taxed at an ordinary tax rate of 30%. For sales proceeds in excess of cost, tax law specifies tax rates of 25% for assets held for less than two years and 20% for assets held for two years or more.

Because the investment property is measured using the fair value model in IAS 40, there is a rebuttable presumption that the entity will recover the carrying amount of the investment property entirely through sale. If that presumption is not rebutted, the deferred tax reflects the tax consequences of recovering the carrying amount entirely through sale, even if the entity expects to earn rental income from the property before sale.

The tax base of the land if it is sold is 40 and there is a taxable temporary difference of 20 (60 − 40). The tax base of the building if it is sold is 30 (60 − 30) and there is a taxable temporary difference of 60 (90 − 30). As a result, the total taxable temporary difference relating to the investment property is 80 (20 + 60).

In accordance with paragraph 47, the tax rate is the rate expected to apply to the period when the investment property is realised. Thus, the resulting deferred tax liability is computed as follows, if the entity expects to sell the property after holding it for more than two years:

	Taxable Temporary Difference	Tax Rate	Deferred Tax Liability
Cumulative tax depreciation	30	30%	9
Proceeds in excess of cost	50	20%	10
Total	80		19

continued...

> **...continued**
>
> *If the entity expects to sell the property after holding it for less than two years, the above computation would be amended to apply a tax rate of 25%, rather than 20%, to the proceeds in excess of cost.*
>
> *If, instead, the entity holds the building within a business model whose objective is to consume substantially all of the economic benefits embodied in the building over time, rather than through sale, this presumption would be rebutted for the building. However, the land is not depreciable. Therefore the presumption of recovery through sale would not be rebutted for the land. It follows that the deferred tax liability would reflect the tax consequences of recovering the carrying amount of the building through use and the carrying amount of the land through sale.*
>
> *The tax base of the building if it is used is 30 (60 − 30) and there is a taxable temporary difference of 60 (90 − 30), resulting in a deferred tax liability of 18 (60 at 30%).*
>
> *The tax base of the land if it is sold is 40 and there is a taxable temporary difference of 20 (60 − 40), resulting in a deferred tax liability of 4 (20 at 20%).*
>
> *As a result, if the presumption of recovery through sale is rebutted for the building, the deferred tax liability relating to the investment property is 22 (18 + 4)*

51D   The rebuttable presumption in paragraph 51C also applies when a deferred tax liability or a deferred tax asset arises from measuring investment property in a business combination if the entity will use the fair value model when subsequently measuring that investment property.

51E   Paragraphs 51B–51D do not change the requirements to apply the principles in paragraphs 24–33 (deductible temporary differences) and paragraphs 34–36 (unused tax losses and unused tax credits) of this Standard when recognising and measuring deferred tax assets.

52   [moved and renumbered 51A]

52A   In some jurisdictions, income taxes are payable at a higher or lower rate if part or all of the net profit or retained earnings is paid out as a dividend to shareholders of the entity. In some other jurisdictions, income taxes may be refundable or payable if part or all of the net profit or retained earnings is paid out as a dividend to shareholders of the entity. In these circumstances, current and deferred tax assets and liabilities are measured at the tax rate applicable to undistributed profits.

52B   In the circumstances described in paragraph 52A, the income tax consequences of dividends are recognised when a liability to pay the dividend is recognised. The income tax consequences of dividends are more directly linked to past transactions or events than to distributions to owners. Therefore, the income tax consequences of dividends are recognised in profit or loss for the period as required by paragraph 58 except to the extent that the income tax consequences of dividends arise from the circumstances described in paragraph 58(a) and (b).

> **Example illustrating paragraphs 52A and 52B**
>
> The following example deals with the measurement of current and deferred tax assets and liabilities for an entity in a jurisdiction where income taxes are payable at a higher rate on undistributed profits (50%) with an amount being refundable when profits are distributed. The tax rate on distributed profits is 35%. At the end of the reporting period, 31 December 20X1, the entity does not recognise a liability for dividends proposed or declared after the reporting period. As a result, no dividends are recognised in the year 20X1. Taxable income for 20X1 is 100,000. The net taxable temporary difference for the year 20X1 is 40,000.
>
> *The entity recognises a current tax liability and a current income tax expense of 50,000. No asset is recognised for the amount potentially recoverable as a result of future dividends. The entity also recognises a deferred tax liability and deferred tax expense of 20,000 (40,000 at 50%) representing the income taxes that the entity will pay when it recovers or settles the carrying amounts of its assets and liabilities based on the tax rate applicable to undistributed profits.*
>
> Subsequently, on 15 March 20X2 the entity recognises dividends of 10,000 from previous operating profits as a liability.
>
> *On 15 March 20X2, the entity recognises the recovery of income taxes of 1,500 (15% of the dividends recognised as a liability) as a current tax asset and as a reduction of current income tax expense for 20X2.*

53 **Deferred tax assets and liabilities shall not be discounted.**

54 The reliable determination of deferred tax assets and liabilities on a discounted basis requires detailed scheduling of the timing of the reversal of each temporary difference. In many cases such scheduling is impracticable or highly complex. Therefore, it is inappropriate to require discounting of deferred tax assets and liabilities. To permit, but not to require, discounting would result in deferred tax assets and liabilities which would not be comparable between entities. Therefore, this Standard does not require or permit the discounting of deferred tax assets and liabilities.

55 Temporary differences are determined by reference to the carrying amount of an asset or liability. This applies even where that carrying amount is itself determined on a discounted basis, for example in the case of retirement benefit obligations (see IAS 19 *Employee Benefits*).

56 **The carrying amount of a deferred tax asset shall be reviewed at the end of each reporting period. An entity shall reduce the carrying amount of a deferred tax asset to the extent that it is no longer probable that sufficient taxable profit will be available to allow the benefit of part or all of that deferred tax asset to be utilised. Any such reduction shall be reversed to the extent that it becomes probable that sufficient taxable profit will be available.**

Recognition of current and deferred tax

57   Accounting for the current and deferred tax effects of a transaction or other event is consistent with the accounting for the transaction or event itself. Paragraphs 58 to 68C implement this principle.

Items recognised in profit or loss

58   **Current and deferred tax shall be recognised as income or an expense and included in profit or loss for the period, except to the extent that the tax arises from:**

   (a)   **a transaction or event which is recognised, in the same or a different period, outside profit or loss, either in other comprehensive income or directly in equity (see paragraphs 61A to 65); or**

   (b)   **a business combination (see paragraphs 66 to 68).**

59   Most deferred tax liabilities and deferred tax assets arise where income or expense is included in accounting profit in one period, but is included in taxable profit (tax loss) in a different period. The resulting deferred tax is recognised in profit or loss. Examples are when:

   (a)   interest, royalty or dividend revenue is received in arrears and is included in accounting profit on a time apportionment basis in accordance with IAS 18 *Revenue*, but is included in taxable profit (tax loss) on a cash basis; and

   (b)   costs of intangible assets have been capitalised in accordance with IAS 38 and are being amortised in profit or loss, but were deducted for tax purposes when they were incurred.

60   The carrying amount of deferred tax assets and liabilities may change even though there is no change in the amount of the related temporary differences. This can result, for example, from:

   (a)   a change in tax rates or tax laws;

   (b)   a reassessment of the recoverability of deferred tax assets; or

   (c)   a change in the expected manner of recovery of an asset.

   The resulting deferred tax is recognised in profit or loss, except to the extent that it relates to items previously recognised outside profit or loss (see paragraph 63).

Items recognised outside profit or loss

61   [Deleted]

61A   **Current tax and deferred tax shall be recognised outside profit or loss if the tax relates to items that are recognised, in the same or a different period, outside profit or loss. Therefore, current tax and deferred tax that relates to items that are recognised, in the same or a different period:**

   (a)   **in other comprehensive income, shall be recognised in other comprehensive income (see paragraph 62).**

   (b)   **directly in equity, shall be recognised directly in equity (see paragraph 62A).**

62   International Financial Reporting Standards require or permit particular items to be recognised in other comprehensive income. Examples of such items are:

     (a)   a change in carrying amount arising from the revaluation of property, plant and equipment (see IAS 16); and

     (b)   [deleted]

     (c)   exchange differences arising on the translation of the financial statements of a foreign operation (see IAS 21).

     (d)   [deleted]

62A   International Financial Reporting Standards require or permit particular items to be credited or charged directly to equity. Examples of such items are:

     (a)   an adjustment to the opening balance of retained earnings resulting from either a change in accounting policy that is applied retrospectively or the correction of an error (see IAS 8 *Accounting Policies, Changes in Accounting Estimates and Errors*); and

     (b)   amounts arising on initial recognition of the equity component of a compound financial instrument (see paragraph 23).

63   In exceptional circumstances it may be difficult to determine the amount of current and deferred tax that relates to items recognised outside profit or loss (either in other comprehensive income or directly in equity). This may be the case, for example, when:

     (a)   there are graduated rates of income tax and it is impossible to determine the rate at which a specific component of taxable profit (tax loss) has been taxed;

     (b)   a change in the tax rate or other tax rules affects a deferred tax asset or liability relating (in whole or in part) to an item that was previously recognised outside profit or loss; or

     (c)   an entity determines that a deferred tax asset should be recognised, or should no longer be recognised in full, and the deferred tax asset relates (in whole or in part) to an item that was previously recognised outside profit or loss.

     In such cases, the current and deferred tax related to items that are recognised outside profit or loss are based on a reasonable pro rata allocation of the current and deferred tax of the entity in the tax jurisdiction concerned, or other method that achieves a more appropriate allocation in the circumstances.

64   IAS 16 does not specify whether an entity should transfer each year from revaluation surplus to retained earnings an amount equal to the difference between the depreciation or amortisation on a revalued asset and the depreciation or amortisation based on the cost of that asset. If an entity makes such a transfer, the amount transferred is net of any related deferred tax. Similar considerations apply to transfers made on disposal of an item of property, plant or equipment.

65 When an asset is revalued for tax purposes and that revaluation is related to an accounting revaluation of an earlier period, or to one that is expected to be carried out in a future period, the tax effects of both the asset revaluation and the adjustment of the tax base are recognised in other comprehensive income in the periods in which they occur. However, if the revaluation for tax purposes is not related to an accounting revaluation of an earlier period, or to one that is expected to be carried out in a future period, the tax effects of the adjustment of the tax base are recognised in profit or loss.

65A When an entity pays dividends to its shareholders, it may be required to pay a portion of the dividends to taxation authorities on behalf of shareholders. In many jurisdictions, this amount is referred to as a withholding tax. Such an amount paid or payable to taxation authorities is charged to equity as a part of the dividends.

Deferred tax arising from a business combination

66 As explained in paragraphs 19 and 26(c), temporary differences may arise in a business combination. In accordance with IFRS 3, an entity recognises any resulting deferred tax assets (to the extent that they meet the recognition criteria in paragraph 24) or deferred tax liabilities as identifiable assets and liabilities at the acquisition date. Consequently, those deferred tax assets and deferred tax liabilities affect the amount of goodwill or the bargain purchase gain the entity recognises. However, in accordance with paragraph 15(a), an entity does not recognise deferred tax liabilities arising from the initial recognition of goodwill.

67 As a result of a business combination, the probability of realising a pre-acquisition deferred tax asset of the acquirer could change. An acquirer may consider it probable that it will recover its own deferred tax asset that was not recognised before the business combination. For example, the acquirer may be able to utilise the benefit of its unused tax losses against the future taxable profit of the acquiree. Alternatively, as a result of the business combination it might no longer be probable that future taxable profit will allow the deferred tax asset to be recovered. In such cases, the acquirer recognises a change in the deferred tax asset in the period of the business combination, but does not include it as part of the accounting for the business combination. Therefore, the acquirer does not take it into account in measuring the goodwill or bargain purchase gain it recognises in the business combination.

68 The potential benefit of the acquiree's income tax loss carryforwards or other deferred tax assets might not satisfy the criteria for separate recognition when a business combination is initially accounted for but might be realised subsequently. An entity shall recognise acquired deferred tax benefits that it realises after the business combination as follows:

(a) Acquired deferred tax benefits recognised within the measurement period that result from new information about facts and circumstances that existed at the acquisition date shall be applied to reduce the carrying amount of any goodwill related to that acquisition. If the carrying amount of that goodwill is zero, any remaining deferred tax benefits shall be recognised in profit or loss.

(b) All other acquired deferred tax benefits realised shall be recognised in profit or loss (or, if this Standard so requires, outside profit or loss).

Current and deferred tax arising from share-based payment transactions

68A In some tax jurisdictions, an entity receives a tax deduction (ie an amount that is deductible in determining taxable profit) that relates to remuneration paid in shares, share options or other equity instruments of the entity. The amount of that tax deduction may differ from the related cumulative remuneration expense, and may arise in a later accounting period. For example, in some jurisdictions, an entity may recognise an expense for the consumption of employee services received as consideration for share options granted, in accordance with IFRS 2 *Share-based Payment*, and not receive a tax deduction until the share options are exercised, with the measurement of the tax deduction based on the entity's share price at the date of exercise.

68B As with the research costs discussed in paragraphs 9 and 26(b) of this Standard, the difference between the tax base of the employee services received to date (being the amount the taxation authorities will permit as a deduction in future periods), and the carrying amount of nil, is a deductible temporary difference that results in a deferred tax asset. If the amount the taxation authorities will permit as a deduction in future periods is not known at the end of the period, it shall be estimated, based on information available at the end of the period. For example, if the amount that the taxation authorities will permit as a deduction in future periods is dependent upon the entity's share price at a future date, the measurement of the deductible temporary difference should be based on the entity's share price at the end of the period.

68C As noted in paragraph 68A, the amount of the tax deduction (or estimated future tax deduction, measured in accordance with paragraph 68B) may differ from the related cumulative remuneration expense. Paragraph 58 of the Standard requires that current and deferred tax should be recognised as income or an expense and included in profit or loss for the period, except to the extent that the tax arises from (a) a transaction or event that is recognised, in the same or a different period, outside profit or loss, or (b) a business combination. If the amount of the tax deduction (or estimated future tax deduction) exceeds the amount of the related cumulative remuneration expense, this indicates that the tax deduction relates not only to remuneration expense but also to an equity item. In this situation, the excess of the associated current or deferred tax should be recognised directly in equity.

Presentation

Tax assets and tax liabilities

69–70 [Deleted]

Offset

71 **An entity shall offset current tax assets and current tax liabilities if, and only if, the entity:**

(a) **has a legally enforceable right to set off the recognised amounts; and**

(b) intends either to settle on a net basis, or to realise the asset and settle the liability simultaneously.

72 Although current tax assets and liabilities are separately recognised and measured they are offset in the statement of financial position subject to criteria similar to those established for financial instruments in IAS 32. An entity will normally have a legally enforceable right to set off a current tax asset against a current tax liability when they relate to income taxes levied by the same taxation authority and the taxation authority permits the entity to make or receive a single net payment.

73 In consolidated financial statements, a current tax asset of one entity in a group is offset against a current tax liability of another entity in the group if, and only if, the entities concerned have a legally enforceable right to make or receive a single net payment and the entities intend to make or receive such a net payment or to recover the asset and settle the liability simultaneously.

74 **An entity shall offset deferred tax assets and deferred tax liabilities if, and only if:**

   (a) **the entity has a legally enforceable right to set off current tax assets against current tax liabilities; and**

   (b) **the deferred tax assets and the deferred tax liabilities relate to income taxes levied by the same taxation authority on either:**

      (i) **the same taxable entity; or**

      (ii) **different taxable entities which intend either to settle current tax liabilities and assets on a net basis, or to realise the assets and settle the liabilities simultaneously, in each future period in which significant amounts of deferred tax liabilities or assets are expected to be settled or recovered.**

75 To avoid the need for detailed scheduling of the timing of the reversal of each temporary difference, this Standard requires an entity to set off a deferred tax asset against a deferred tax liability of the same taxable entity if, and only if, they relate to income taxes levied by the same taxation authority and the entity has a legally enforceable right to set off current tax assets against current tax liabilities.

76 In rare circumstances, an entity may have a legally enforceable right of set-off, and an intention to settle net, for some periods but not for others. In such rare circumstances, detailed scheduling may be required to establish reliably whether the deferred tax liability of one taxable entity will result in increased tax payments in the same period in which a deferred tax asset of another taxable entity will result in decreased payments by that second taxable entity.

Tax expense

Tax expense (income) related to profit or loss from ordinary activities

77 **The tax expense (income) related to profit or loss from ordinary activities shall be presented as part of profit or loss in the statement(s) of profit or loss and other comprehensive income.**

77A [Deleted]

Exchange differences on deferred foreign tax liabilities or assets

78   IAS 21 requires certain exchange differences to be recognised as income or expense but does not specify where such differences should be presented in the statement of comprehensive income. Accordingly, where exchange differences on deferred foreign tax liabilities or assets are recognised in the statement of comprehensive income, such differences may be classified as deferred tax expense (income) if that presentation is considered to be the most useful to financial statement users.

Disclosure

79   **The major components of tax expense (income) shall be disclosed separately.**

80   Components of tax expense (income) may include:

(a)   current tax expense (income);

(b)   any adjustments recognised in the period for current tax of prior periods;

(c)   the amount of deferred tax expense (income) relating to the origination and reversal of temporary differences;

(d)   the amount of deferred tax expense (income) relating to changes in tax rates or the imposition of new taxes;

(e)   the amount of the benefit arising from a previously unrecognised tax loss, tax credit or temporary difference of a prior period that is used to reduce current tax expense;

(f)   the amount of the benefit from a previously unrecognised tax loss, tax credit or temporary difference of a prior period that is used to reduce deferred tax expense;

(g)   deferred tax expense arising from the write-down, or reversal of a previous write-down, of a deferred tax asset in accordance with paragraph 56; and

(h)   the amount of tax expense (income) relating to those changes in accounting policies and errors that are included in profit or loss in accordance with IAS 8, because they cannot be accounted for retrospectively.

81   **The following shall also be disclosed separately:**

(a)   **the aggregate current and deferred tax relating to items that are charged or credited directly to equity (see paragraph 62A);**

(ae)   **the amount of income tax relating to each component of other comprehensive income (see paragraph 62 and IAS 1 (as revised in 2007));**

(b)   **[deleted];**

(c)   **an explanation of the relationship between tax expense (income) and accounting profit in either or both of the following forms:**

(i)   **a numerical reconciliation between tax expense (income) and the product of accounting profit multiplied by the applicable tax rate(s), disclosing also the basis on which the applicable tax rate(s) is (are) computed; or**

     (ii)   a numerical reconciliation between the average effective tax rate and the applicable tax rate, disclosing also the basis on which the applicable tax rate is computed;

(d)   an explanation of changes in the applicable tax rate(s) compared to the previous accounting period;

(e)   the amount (and expiry date, if any) of deductible temporary differences, unused tax losses, and unused tax credits for which no deferred tax asset is recognised in the statement of financial position;

(f)   the aggregate amount of temporary differences associated with investments in subsidiaries, branches and associates and interests in joint arrangements, for which deferred tax liabilities have not been recognised (see paragraph 39);

(g)   in respect of each type of temporary difference, and in respect of each type of unused tax losses and unused tax credits:

     (i)   the amount of the deferred tax assets and liabilities recognised in the statement of financial position for each period presented;

     (ii)   the amount of the deferred tax income or expense recognised in profit or loss, if this is not apparent from the changes in the amounts recognised in the statement of financial position;

(h)   in respect of discontinued operations, the tax expense relating to:

     (i)   the gain or loss on discontinuance; and

     (ii)   the profit or loss from the ordinary activities of the discontinued operation for the period, together with the corresponding amounts for each prior period presented;

(i)   the amount of income tax consequences of dividends to shareholders of the entity that were proposed or declared before the financial statements were authorised for issue, but are not recognised as a liability in the financial statements;

(j)   if a business combination in which the entity is the acquirer causes a change in the amount recognised for its pre-acquisition deferred tax asset (see paragraph 67), the amount of that change; and

(k)   if the deferred tax benefits acquired in a business combination are not recognised at the acquisition date but are recognised after the acquisition date (see paragraph 68), a description of the event or change in circumstances that caused the deferred tax benefits to be recognised.

82   An entity shall disclose the amount of a deferred tax asset and the nature of the evidence supporting its recognition, when:

(a)   the utilisation of the deferred tax asset is dependent on future taxable profits in excess of the profits arising from the reversal of existing taxable temporary differences; and

(b)   the entity has suffered a loss in either the current or preceding period in the tax jurisdiction to which the deferred tax asset relates.

82A   In the circumstances described in paragraph 52A, an entity shall disclose the nature of the potential income tax consequences that would result from the payment of dividends to its shareholders. In addition, the entity shall disclose the amounts of the potential income tax consequences practically determinable and whether there are any potential income tax consequences not practically determinable.

83   [Deleted]

84   The disclosures required by paragraph 81(c) enable users of financial statements to understand whether the relationship between tax expense (income) and accounting profit is unusual and to understand the significant factors that could affect that relationship in the future. The relationship between tax expense (income) and accounting profit may be affected by such factors as revenue that is exempt from taxation, expenses that are not deductible in determining taxable profit (tax loss), the effect of tax losses and the effect of foreign tax rates.

85   In explaining the relationship between tax expense (income) and accounting profit, an entity uses an applicable tax rate that provides the most meaningful information to the users of its financial statements. Often, the most meaningful rate is the domestic rate of tax in the country in which the entity is domiciled, aggregating the tax rate applied for national taxes with the rates applied for any local taxes which are computed on a substantially similar level of taxable profit (tax loss). However, for an entity operating in several jurisdictions, it may be more meaningful to aggregate separate reconciliations prepared using the domestic rate in each individual jurisdiction. The following example illustrates how the selection of the applicable tax rate affects the presentation of the numerical reconciliation.

Example illustrating paragraph 85

In 19X2, an entity has accounting profit in its own jurisdiction (country A) of 1,500 (19X1: 2,000) and in country B of 1,500 (19X1: 500). The tax rate is 30% in country A and 20% in country B. In country A, expenses of 100 (19X1: 200) are not deductible for tax purposes.

The following is an example of a reconciliation to the domestic tax rate.

	19X1	19X2
Accounting profit	2,500	3,000
Tax at the domestic rate of 30%	750	900
Tax effect of expenses that are not deductible for tax purposes	60	30
Effect of lower tax rates in country B	(50)	(150)
Tax expense	760	780

continued...

> *...continued*
>
> *The following is an example of a reconciliation prepared by aggregating separate reconciliations for each national jurisdiction. Under this method, the effect of differences between the reporting entity's own domestic tax rate and the domestic tax rate in other jurisdictions does not appear as a separate item in the reconciliation. An entity may need to discuss the effect of significant changes in either tax rates, or the mix of profits earned in different jurisdictions, in order to explain changes in the applicable tax rate(s), as required by paragraph 81(d).*
>
> | | | |
> |---|---|---|
> | Accounting profit | 2,500 | 3,000 |
> | Tax at the domestic rates applicable to profits in the country concerned | 700 | 750 |
> | Tax effect of expenses that are not deductible for tax purposes | 60 | 30 |
> | Tax expense | 760 | 780 |

86 The average effective tax rate is the tax expense (income) divided by the accounting profit.

87 It would often be impracticable to compute the amount of unrecognised deferred tax liabilities arising from investments in subsidiaries, branches and associates and interests in joint arrangements (see paragraph 39). Therefore, this Standard requires an entity to disclose the aggregate amount of the underlying temporary differences but does not require disclosure of the deferred tax liabilities. Nevertheless, where practicable, entities are encouraged to disclose the amounts of the unrecognised deferred tax liabilities because financial statement users may find such information useful.

87A Paragraph 82A requires an entity to disclose the nature of the potential income tax consequences that would result from the payment of dividends to its shareholders. An entity discloses the important features of the income tax systems and the factors that will affect the amount of the potential income tax consequences of dividends.

87B It would sometimes not be practicable to compute the total amount of the potential income tax consequences that would result from the payment of dividends to shareholders. This may be the case, for example, where an entity has a large number of foreign subsidiaries. However, even in such circumstances, some portions of the total amount may be easily determinable. For example, in a consolidated group, a parent and some of its subsidiaries may have paid income taxes at a higher rate on undistributed profits and be aware of the amount that would be refunded on the payment of future dividends to shareholders from consolidated retained earnings. In this case, that refundable amount is disclosed. If applicable, the entity also discloses that there are additional potential income tax consequences not practicably determinable. In the parent's separate financial statements, if any, the disclosure of the potential income tax consequences relates to the parent's retained earnings.

87C An entity required to provide the disclosures in paragraph 82A may also be required to provide disclosures related to temporary differences associated with investments in subsidiaries, branches and associates or interests in joint arrangements. In such cases, an entity considers this in determining the information to be disclosed under paragraph 82A. For example, an entity may be required to disclose the aggregate amount of temporary differences associated with investments in subsidiaries for which no deferred tax liabilities have been recognised (see paragraph 81(f)). If it is impracticable to compute the amounts of unrecognised deferred tax liabilities (see paragraph 87) there may be amounts of potential income tax consequences of dividends not practicably determinable related to these subsidiaries.

88 An entity discloses any tax-related contingent liabilities and contingent assets in accordance with IAS 37 *Provisions, Contingent Liabilities and Contingent Assets*. Contingent liabilities and contingent assets may arise, for example, from unresolved disputes with the taxation authorities. Similarly, where changes in tax rates or tax laws are enacted or announced after the reporting period, an entity discloses any significant effect of those changes on its current and deferred tax assets and liabilities (see IAS 10 *Events after the Reporting Period*).

Effective date

89 This Standard becomes operative for financial statements covering periods beginning on or after 1 January 1998, except as specified in paragraph 91. If an entity applies this Standard for financial statements covering periods beginning before 1 January 1998, the entity shall disclose the fact it has applied this Standard instead of IAS 12 *Accounting for Taxes on Income*, approved in 1979.

90 This Standard supersedes IAS 12 *Accounting for Taxes on Income*, approved in 1979.

91 Paragraphs 52A, 52B, 65A, 81(i), 82A, 87A, 87B, 87C and the deletion of paragraphs 3 and 50 become operative for annual financial statements[3] covering periods beginning on or after 1 January 2001. Earlier adoption is encouraged. If earlier adoption affects the financial statements, an entity shall disclose that fact.

92 IAS 1 (as revised in 2007) amended the terminology used throughout IFRSs. In addition it amended paragraphs 23, 52, 58, 60, 62, 63, 65, 68C, 77 and 81, deleted paragraph 61 and added paragraphs 61A, 62A and 77A. An entity shall apply those amendments for annual periods beginning on or after 1 January 2009. If an entity applies IAS 1 (revised 2007) for an earlier period, the amendments shall be applied for that earlier period.

93 Paragraph 68 shall be applied prospectively from the effective date of IFRS 3 (as revised in 2008) to the recognition of deferred tax assets acquired in business combinations.

94 Therefore, entities shall not adjust the accounting for prior business combinations if tax benefits failed to satisfy the criteria for separate recognition as of the acquisition date and are recognised after the acquisition date, unless the benefits are recognised within the measurement period and result from new information about facts and circumstances that existed at the acquisition date. Other tax benefits recognised shall be recognised in profit or loss (or, if this Standard so requires, outside profit or loss).

---

3 Paragraph 91 refers to 'annual financial statements' in line with more explicit language for writing effective dates adopted in 1998. Paragraph 89 refers to 'financial statements'.

95   IFRS 3 (as revised in 2008) amended paragraphs 21 and 67 and added paragraphs 32A and 81(j) and (k). An entity shall apply those amendments for annual periods beginning on or after 1 July 2009. If an entity applies IFRS 3 (revised 2008) for an earlier period, the amendments shall also be applied for that earlier period.

96   [Deleted]

97   IFRS 9, issued in October 2010, amended paragraph 20 and deleted paragraph 96. An entity shall apply those amendments when it applies IFRS 9 as issued in October 2010.

98   Paragraph 52 was renumbered as 51A, paragraph 10 and the examples following paragraph 51A were amended, and paragraphs 51B and 51C and the following example and paragraphs 51D, 51E and 99 were added by *Deferred Tax: Recovery of Underlying Assets*, issued in December 2010. An entity shall apply those amendments for annual periods beginning on or after 1 January 2012. Earlier application is permitted. If an entity applies the amendments for an earlier period, it shall disclose that fact.

98A   IFRS 11 *Joint Arrangements*, issued in May 2011, amended paragraphs 2, 15, 18(e), 24, 38, 39, 43–45, 81(f), 87 and 87C. An entity shall apply those amendments when it applies IFRS 11.

98B   *Presentation of Items of Other Comprehensive Income* (Amendments to IAS 1), issued in June 2011, amended paragraph 77 and deleted paragraph 77A. An entity shall apply those amendments when it applies IAS 1 as amended in June 2011.

Withdrawal of SIC-21

99   The amendments made by *Deferred Tax: Recovery of Underlying Assets*, issued in December 2010, supersede SIC Interpretation 21 *Income Taxes—Recovery of Revalued Non-Depreciable Assets*.

International Accounting Standard 16

Property, Plant and Equipment

In April 2001 the International Accounting Standards Board (IASB) adopted IAS 16 *Property, Plant and Equipment*, which had originally been issued by the International Accounting Standards Committee in December 1993. IAS 16 *Property, Plant and Equipment* replaced IAS 16 *Accounting for Property, Plant and Equipment* (issued in March 1982). IAS 16 that was issued in March 1982 also replaced some parts in IAS 4 *Depreciation Accounting* that was approved in November 1975.

In December 2003 the IASB issued a revised IAS 16 as part of its initial agenda of technical projects. The revised standard also replaced the guidance in three Interpretations (SIC-6 *Costs of Modifying Existing Software*, SIC-14 *Property, Plant and Equipment—Compensation for the Impairment or Loss of Items* and SIC-23 *Property, Plant and Equipment—Major Inspection or Overhaul Costs*).

Other IFRSs have made minor consequential amendments to IAS 16. They include IFRS 3 *Business Combinations* (issued March 2004 and as revised in January 2008), IFRS 5 *Non-Current Assets Held for Sale and Discontinued Operations* (issued March 2004), IAS 1 *Presentation of Financial Statements* (as revised in September 2007), *Improvements to IFRSs* (issued May 2008), IFRS 9 *Financial Instruments* (issued November 2009 and October 2010) and IFRS 13 *Fair Value Measurement* (issued May 2011).

Contents

FOR THE ACCOMPANYING DOCUMENTS LISTED BELOW, SEE PART B OF THIS EDITION

APPROVAL BY THE BOARD OF IAS 16 ISSUED IN DECEMBER 2003

BASIS FOR CONCLUSIONS

International Accounting Standard 16 *Property, Plant and Equipment* (IAS 16) is set out in paragraphs 1–83 and the Appendix. All the paragraphs have equal authority but retain the IASC format of the Standard when it was adopted by the IASB. IAS 16 should be read in the context of its objective and the Basis for Conclusions, the *Preface to International Financial Reporting Standards* and the *Conceptual Framework for Financial Reporting*. IAS 8 *Accounting Policies, Changes in Accounting Estimates and Errors* provides a basis for selecting and applying accounting policies in the absence of explicit guidance.

Introduction

IN1   International Accounting Standard 16 *Property, Plant and Equipment* (IAS 16) replaces IAS 16 *Property, Plant and Equipment* (revised in 1998), and should be applied for annual periods beginning on or after 1 January 2005. Earlier application is encouraged. The Standard also replaces the following Interpretations:

- SIC-6 *Costs of Modifying Existing Software*

- SIC-14 *Property, Plant and Equipment—Compensation for the Impairment or Loss of Items*

- SIC-23 *Property, Plant and Equipment—Major Inspection or Overhaul Costs*.

Reasons for revising IAS 16

IN2   The International Accounting Standards Board developed this revised IAS 16 as part of its project on Improvements to International Accounting Standards. The project was undertaken in the light of queries and criticisms raised in relation to the Standards by securities regulators, professional accountants and other interested parties. The objectives of the project were to reduce or eliminate alternatives, redundancies and conflicts within the Standards, to deal with some convergence issues and to make other improvements.

IN3   For IAS 16 the Board's main objective was a limited revision to provide additional guidance and clarification on selected matters. The Board did not reconsider the fundamental approach to the accounting for property, plant and equipment contained in IAS 16.

The main changes

IN4   The main changes from the previous version of IAS 16 are described below.

Scope

IN5   This Standard clarifies that an entity is required to apply the principles of this Standard to items of property, plant and equipment used to develop or maintain (a) biological assets and (b) mineral rights and mineral reserves such as oil, natural gas and similar non-regenerative resources.

Recognition: subsequent costs

IN6   An entity evaluates under the general recognition principle all property, plant and equipment costs at the time they are incurred. Those costs include costs incurred initially to acquire or construct an item of property, plant and equipment and costs incurred subsequently to add to, replace part of, or service an item. The previous version of IAS 16 contained two recognition principles. An entity applied the second recognition principle to subsequent costs.

Measurement at recognition: asset dismantlement, removal and restoration costs

IN7 The cost of an item of property, plant and equipment includes the costs of its dismantlement, removal or restoration, the obligation for which an entity incurs as a consequence of installing the item. Its cost also includes the costs of its dismantlement, removal or restoration, the obligation for which an entity incurs as a consequence of using the item during a particular period for purposes other than to produce inventories during that period. The previous version of IAS 16 included within its scope only the costs incurred as a consequence of installing the item.

Measurement at recognition: asset exchange transactions

IN8 An entity is required to measure an item of property, plant and equipment acquired in exchange for a non-monetary asset or assets, or a combination of monetary and non-monetary assets, at fair value unless the exchange transaction lacks commercial substance. Under the previous version of IAS 16, an entity measured such an acquired asset at fair value unless the exchanged assets were similar.

Measurement after recognition: revaluation model

IN9 If fair value can be measured reliably, an entity may carry all items of property, plant and equipment of a class at a revalued amount, which is the fair value of the items at the date of the revaluation less any subsequent accumulated depreciation and accumulated impairment losses. Under the previous version of IAS 16, use of revalued amounts did not depend on whether fair values were reliably measurable.

Depreciation: unit of measure

IN10 An entity is required to determine the depreciation charge separately for each significant part of an item of property, plant and equipment. The previous version of IAS 16 did not as clearly set out this requirement.

Depreciation: depreciable amount

IN11 An entity is required to measure the residual value of an item of property, plant and equipment as the amount it estimates it would receive currently for the asset if the asset were already of the age and in the condition expected at the end of its useful life. The previous version of IAS 16 did not specify whether the residual value was to be this amount or the amount, inclusive of the effects of inflation, that an entity expected to receive in the future on the asset's actual retirement date.

Depreciation: depreciation period

IN12 An entity is required to begin depreciating an item of property, plant and equipment when it is available for use and to continue depreciating it until it is derecognised, even if during that period the item is idle. The previous version of

IAS 16 did not specify when depreciation of an item began and specified that an entity should cease depreciating an item that it had retired from active use and was holding for disposal.

Derecognition: derecognition date

IN13   An entity is required to derecognise the carrying amount of an item of property, plant and equipment that it disposes of on the date the criteria for the sale of goods in IAS 18 *Revenue* would be met. The previous version of IAS 16 did not require an entity to use those criteria to determine the date on which it derecognised the carrying amount of a disposed-of item of property, plant and equipment.

IN14   An entity is required to derecognise the carrying amount of a part of an item of property, plant and equipment if that part has been replaced and the entity has included the cost of the replacement in the carrying amount of the item. The previous version of IAS 16 did not extend its derecognition principle to such parts; rather, its recognition principle for subsequent expenditures effectively precluded the cost of a replacement from being included in the carrying amount of the item.

Derecognition: gain classification

IN15   An entity cannot classify as revenue a gain it realises on the disposal of an item of property, plant and equipment. The previous version of IAS 16 did not contain this provision.

International Accounting Standard 16
Property, Plant and Equipment

Objective

1   The objective of this Standard is to prescribe the accounting treatment for property, plant and equipment so that users of the financial statements can discern information about an entity's investment in its property, plant and equipment and the changes in such investment. The principal issues in accounting for property, plant and equipment are the recognition of the assets, the determination of their carrying amounts and the depreciation charges and impairment losses to be recognised in relation to them.

Scope

2   **This Standard shall be applied in accounting for property, plant and equipment except when another Standard requires or permits a different accounting treatment.**

3   This Standard does not apply to:

    (a)   property, plant and equipment classified as held for sale in accordance with IFRS 5 *Non-current Assets Held for Sale and Discontinued Operations*;

    (b)   biological assets related to agricultural activity (see IAS 41 *Agriculture*);

    (c)   the recognition and measurement of exploration and evaluation assets (see IFRS 6 *Exploration for and Evaluation of Mineral Resources*); or

    (d)   mineral rights and mineral reserves such as oil, natural gas and similar non-regenerative resources.

However, this Standard applies to property, plant and equipment used to develop or maintain the assets described in (b)–(d).

4   Other Standards may require recognition of an item of property, plant and equipment based on an approach different from that in this Standard. For example, IAS 17 *Leases* requires an entity to evaluate its recognition of an item of leased property, plant and equipment on the basis of the transfer of risks and rewards. However, in such cases other aspects of the accounting treatment for these assets, including depreciation, are prescribed by this Standard.

5   An entity using the cost model for investment property in accordance with IAS 40 *Investment Property* shall use the cost model in this Standard.

Definitions

6   The following terms are used in this Standard with the meanings specified:

Carrying amount is the amount at which an asset is recognised after deducting any accumulated depreciation and accumulated impairment losses.

Cost is the amount of cash or cash equivalents paid or the fair value of the other consideration given to acquire an asset at the time of its acquisition or construction or, where applicable, the amount attributed to that asset when initially recognised in accordance with the specific requirements of other IFRSs, eg IFRS 2 *Share-based Payment*.

Depreciable amount is the cost of an asset, or other amount substituted for cost, less its residual value.

Depreciation is the systematic allocation of the depreciable amount of an asset over its useful life.

Entity-specific value is the present value of the cash flows an entity expects to arise from the continuing use of an asset and from its disposal at the end of its useful life or expects to incur when settling a liability.

Fair value is the price that would be received to sell an asset or paid to transfer a liability in an orderly transaction between market participants at the measurement date. (See IFRS 13 *Fair Value Measurement*.)

An *impairment loss* is the amount by which the carrying amount of an asset exceeds its recoverable amount.

Property, plant and equipment are tangible items that:

(a)   are held for use in the production or supply of goods or services, for rental to others, or for administrative purposes; and

(b)   are expected to be used during more than one period.

Recoverable amount is the higher of an asset's fair value less costs to sell and its value in use.

The *residual value* of an asset is the estimated amount that an entity would currently obtain from disposal of the asset, after deducting the estimated costs of disposal, if the asset were already of the age and in the condition expected at the end of its useful life.

Useful life is:

(a)   the period over which an asset is expected to be available for use by an entity; or

(b)   the number of production or similar units expected to be obtained from the asset by an entity.

Recognition

7   The cost of an item of property, plant and equipment shall be recognised as an asset if, and only if:

(a)   it is probable that future economic benefits associated with the item will flow to the entity; and

(b)   the cost of the item can be measured reliably.

8   Spare parts and servicing equipment are usually carried as inventory and recognised in profit or loss as consumed. However, major spare parts and stand-by equipment qualify as property, plant and equipment when an entity expects to use them during more than one period. Similarly, if the spare parts and servicing equipment can be used only in connection with an item of property, plant and equipment, they are accounted for as property, plant and equipment.

9   This Standard does not prescribe the unit of measure for recognition, ie what constitutes an item of property, plant and equipment. Thus, judgement is required in applying the recognition criteria to an entity's specific circumstances. It may be appropriate to aggregate individually insignificant items, such as moulds, tools and dies, and to apply the criteria to the aggregate value.

10   An entity evaluates under this recognition principle all its property, plant and equipment costs at the time they are incurred. These costs include costs incurred initially to acquire or construct an item of property, plant and equipment and costs incurred subsequently to add to, replace part of, or service it.

Initial costs

11   Items of property, plant and equipment may be acquired for safety or environmental reasons. The acquisition of such property, plant and equipment, although not directly increasing the future economic benefits of any particular existing item of property, plant and equipment, may be necessary for an entity to obtain the future economic benefits from its other assets. Such items of property, plant and equipment qualify for recognition as assets because they enable an entity to derive future economic benefits from related assets in excess of what could be derived had those items not been acquired. For example, a chemical manufacturer may install new chemical handling processes to comply with environmental requirements for the production and storage of dangerous chemicals; related plant enhancements are recognised as an asset because without them the entity is unable to manufacture and sell chemicals. However, the resulting carrying amount of such an asset and related assets is reviewed for impairment in accordance with IAS 36 *Impairment of Assets*.

Subsequent costs

12   Under the recognition principle in paragraph 7, an entity does not recognise in the carrying amount of an item of property, plant and equipment the costs of the day-to-day servicing of the item. Rather, these costs are recognised in profit or loss as incurred. Costs of day-to-day servicing are primarily the costs of labour and consumables, and may include the cost of small parts. The purpose of these expenditures is often described as for the 'repairs and maintenance' of the item of property, plant and equipment.

13   Parts of some items of property, plant and equipment may require replacement at regular intervals. For example, a furnace may require relining after a specified number of hours of use, or aircraft interiors such as seats and galleys may require replacement several times during the life of the airframe. Items of property, plant and equipment may also be acquired to make a less frequently recurring replacement, such as replacing the interior walls of a building, or to make a nonrecurring replacement. Under the recognition principle in paragraph 7, an

entity recognises in the carrying amount of an item of property, plant and equipment the cost of replacing part of such an item when that cost is incurred if the recognition criteria are met. The carrying amount of those parts that are replaced is derecognised in accordance with the derecognition provisions of this Standard (see paragraphs 67–72).

14   A condition of continuing to operate an item of property, plant and equipment (for example, an aircraft) may be performing regular major inspections for faults regardless of whether parts of the item are replaced. When each major inspection is performed, its cost is recognised in the carrying amount of the item of property, plant and equipment as a replacement if the recognition criteria are satisfied. Any remaining carrying amount of the cost of the previous inspection (as distinct from physical parts) is derecognised. This occurs regardless of whether the cost of the previous inspection was identified in the transaction in which the item was acquired or constructed. If necessary, the estimated cost of a future similar inspection may be used as an indication of what the cost of the existing inspection component was when the item was acquired or constructed.

Measurement at recognition

15   **An item of property, plant and equipment that qualifies for recognition as an asset shall be measured at its cost.**

Elements of cost

16   The cost of an item of property, plant and equipment comprises:

(a)   its purchase price, including import duties and non-refundable purchase taxes, after deducting trade discounts and rebates.

(b)   any costs directly attributable to bringing the asset to the location and condition necessary for it to be capable of operating in the manner intended by management.

(c)   the initial estimate of the costs of dismantling and removing the item and restoring the site on which it is located, the obligation for which an entity incurs either when the item is acquired or as a consequence of having used the item during a particular period for purposes other than to produce inventories during that period.

17   Examples of directly attributable costs are:

(a)   costs of employee benefits (as defined in IAS 19 *Employee Benefits*) arising directly from the construction or acquisition of the item of property, plant and equipment;

(b)   costs of site preparation;

(c)   initial delivery and handling costs;

(d)   installation and assembly costs;

(e) costs of testing whether the asset is functioning properly, after deducting the net proceeds from selling any items produced while bringing the asset to that location and condition (such as samples produced when testing equipment); and

(f) professional fees.

18 An entity applies IAS 2 *Inventories* to the costs of obligations for dismantling, removing and restoring the site on which an item is located that are incurred during a particular period as a consequence of having used the item to produce inventories during that period. The obligations for costs accounted for in accordance with IAS 2 or IAS 16 are recognised and measured in accordance with IAS 37 *Provisions, Contingent Liabilities and Contingent Assets*.

19 Examples of costs that are not costs of an item of property, plant and equipment are:

(a) costs of opening a new facility;

(b) costs of introducing a new product or service (including costs of advertising and promotional activities);

(c) costs of conducting business in a new location or with a new class of customer (including costs of staff training); and

(d) administration and other general overhead costs.

20 Recognition of costs in the carrying amount of an item of property, plant and equipment ceases when the item is in the location and condition necessary for it to be capable of operating in the manner intended by management. Therefore, costs incurred in using or redeploying an item are not included in the carrying amount of that item. For example, the following costs are not included in the carrying amount of an item of property, plant and equipment:

(a) costs incurred while an item capable of operating in the manner intended by management has yet to be brought into use or is operated at less than full capacity;

(b) initial operating losses, such as those incurred while demand for the item's output builds up; and

(c) costs of relocating or reorganising part or all of an entity's operations.

21 Some operations occur in connection with the construction or development of an item of property, plant and equipment, but are not necessary to bring the item to the location and condition necessary for it to be capable of operating in the manner intended by management. These incidental operations may occur before or during the construction or development activities. For example, income may be earned through using a building site as a car park until construction starts. Because incidental operations are not necessary to bring an item to the location and condition necessary for it to be capable of operating in the manner intended by management, the income and related expenses of incidental operations are recognised in profit or loss and included in their respective classifications of income and expense.

22 The cost of a self-constructed asset is determined using the same principles as for an acquired asset. If an entity makes similar assets for sale in the normal course of business, the cost of the asset is usually the same as the cost of constructing an asset for sale (see IAS 2). Therefore, any internal profits are eliminated in arriving at such costs. Similarly, the cost of abnormal amounts of wasted material, labour, or other resources incurred in self-constructing an asset is not included in the cost of the asset. IAS 23 *Borrowing Costs* establishes criteria for the recognition of interest as a component of the carrying amount of a self-constructed item of property, plant and equipment.

Measurement of cost

23 The cost of an item of property, plant and equipment is the cash price equivalent at the recognition date. If payment is deferred beyond normal credit terms, the difference between the cash price equivalent and the total payment is recognised as interest over the period of credit unless such interest is capitalised in accordance with IAS 23.

24 One or more items of property, plant and equipment may be acquired in exchange for a non-monetary asset or assets, or a combination of monetary and non-monetary assets. The following discussion refers simply to an exchange of one non-monetary asset for another, but it also applies to all exchanges described in the preceding sentence. The cost of such an item of property, plant and equipment is measured at fair value unless (a) the exchange transaction lacks commercial substance or (b) the fair value of neither the asset received nor the asset given up is reliably measurable. The acquired item is measured in this way even if an entity cannot immediately derecognise the asset given up. If the acquired item is not measured at fair value, its cost is measured at the carrying amount of the asset given up.

25 An entity determines whether an exchange transaction has commercial substance by considering the extent to which its future cash flows are expected to change as a result of the transaction. An exchange transaction has commercial substance if:

(a) the configuration (risk, timing and amount) of the cash flows of the asset received differs from the configuration of the cash flows of the asset transferred; or

(b) the entity-specific value of the portion of the entity's operations affected by the transaction changes as a result of the exchange; and

(c) the difference in (a) or (b) is significant relative to the fair value of the assets exchanged.

For the purpose of determining whether an exchange transaction has commercial substance, the entity-specific value of the portion of the entity's operations affected by the transaction shall reflect post-tax cash flows. The result of these analyses may be clear without an entity having to perform detailed calculations.

26 The fair value of an asset is reliably measurable if (a) the variability in the range of reasonable fair value measurements is not significant for that asset or (b) the probabilities of the various estimates within the range can be reasonably assessed and used when measuring fair value. If an entity is able to measure reliably the fair value of either the asset received or the asset given up, then the fair value of the asset given up is used to measure the cost of the asset received unless the fair value of the asset received is more clearly evident.

27 The cost of an item of property, plant and equipment held by a lessee under a finance lease is determined in accordance with IAS 17.

28 The carrying amount of an item of property, plant and equipment may be reduced by government grants in accordance with IAS 20 *Accounting for Government Grants and Disclosure of Government Assistance*.

Measurement after recognition

29 **An entity shall choose either the cost model in paragraph 30 or the revaluation model in paragraph 31 as its accounting policy and shall apply that policy to an entire class of property, plant and equipment.**

Cost model

30 **After recognition as an asset, an item of property, plant and equipment shall be carried at its cost less any accumulated depreciation and any accumulated impairment losses.**

Revaluation model

31 **After recognition as an asset, an item of property, plant and equipment whose fair value can be measured reliably shall be carried at a revalued amount, being its fair value at the date of the revaluation less any subsequent accumulated depreciation and subsequent accumulated impairment losses. Revaluations shall be made with sufficient regularity to ensure that the carrying amount does not differ materially from that which would be determined using fair value at the end of the reporting period.**

32–33 [Deleted]

34 The frequency of revaluations depends upon the changes in fair values of the items of property, plant and equipment being revalued. When the fair value of a revalued asset differs materially from its carrying amount, a further revaluation is required. Some items of property, plant and equipment experience significant and volatile changes in fair value, thus necessitating annual revaluation. Such frequent revaluations are unnecessary for items of property, plant and equipment with only insignificant changes in fair value. Instead, it may be necessary to revalue the item only every three or five years.

35 When an item of property, plant and equipment is revalued, any accumulated depreciation at the date of the revaluation is treated in one of the following ways:

(a) restated proportionately with the change in the gross carrying amount of the asset so that the carrying amount of the asset after revaluation equals its revalued amount. This method is often used when an asset is revalued by means of applying an index to determine its depreciated replacement cost (see IFRS 13).

(b) eliminated against the gross carrying amount of the asset and the net amount restated to the revalued amount of the asset. This method is often used for buildings.

The amount of the adjustment arising on the restatement or elimination of accumulated depreciation forms part of the increase or decrease in carrying amount that is accounted for in accordance with paragraphs 39 and 40.

36 **If an item of property, plant and equipment is revalued, the entire class of property, plant and equipment to which that asset belongs shall be revalued.**

37 A class of property, plant and equipment is a grouping of assets of a similar nature and use in an entity's operations. The following are examples of separate classes:

(a) land;

(b) land and buildings;

(c) machinery;

(d) ships;

(e) aircraft;

(f) motor vehicles;

(g) furniture and fixtures; and

(h) office equipment.

38 The items within a class of property, plant and equipment are revalued simultaneously to avoid selective revaluation of assets and the reporting of amounts in the financial statements that are a mixture of costs and values as at different dates. However, a class of assets may be revalued on a rolling basis provided revaluation of the class of assets is completed within a short period and provided the revaluations are kept up to date.

39 **If an asset's carrying amount is increased as a result of a revaluation, the increase shall be recognised in other comprehensive income and accumulated in equity under the heading of revaluation surplus. However, the increase shall be recognised in profit or loss to the extent that it reverses a revaluation decrease of the same asset previously recognised in profit or loss.**

40 **If an asset's carrying amount is decreased as a result of a revaluation, the decrease shall be recognised in profit or loss. However, the decrease shall be recognised in other comprehensive income to the extent of any credit balance existing in the revaluation surplus in respect of that asset. The decrease recognised in other comprehensive income reduces the amount accumulated in equity under the heading of revaluation surplus.**

41 The revaluation surplus included in equity in respect of an item of property, plant and equipment may be transferred directly to retained earnings when the asset is derecognised. This may involve transferring the whole of the surplus when the asset is retired or disposed of. However, some of the surplus may be transferred as the asset is used by an entity. In such a case, the amount of the surplus transferred would be the difference between depreciation based on the revalued carrying amount of the asset and depreciation based on the asset's original cost. Transfers from revaluation surplus to retained earnings are not made through profit or loss.

42 The effects of taxes on income, if any, resulting from the revaluation of property, plant and equipment are recognised and disclosed in accordance with IAS 12 *Income Taxes*.

Depreciation

43 **Each part of an item of property, plant and equipment with a cost that is significant in relation to the total cost of the item shall be depreciated separately.**

44 An entity allocates the amount initially recognised in respect of an item of property, plant and equipment to its significant parts and depreciates separately each such part. For example, it may be appropriate to depreciate separately the airframe and engines of an aircraft, whether owned or subject to a finance lease. Similarly, if an entity acquires property, plant and equipment subject to an operating lease in which it is the lessor, it may be appropriate to depreciate separately amounts reflected in the cost of that item that are attributable to favourable or unfavourable lease terms relative to market terms.

45 A significant part of an item of property, plant and equipment may have a useful life and a depreciation method that are the same as the useful life and the depreciation method of another significant part of that same item. Such parts may be grouped in determining the depreciation charge.

46 To the extent that an entity depreciates separately some parts of an item of property, plant and equipment, it also depreciates separately the remainder of the item. The remainder consists of the parts of the item that are individually not significant. If an entity has varying expectations for these parts, approximation techniques may be necessary to depreciate the remainder in a manner that faithfully represents the consumption pattern and/or useful life of its parts.

47 An entity may choose to depreciate separately the parts of an item that do not have a cost that is significant in relation to the total cost of the item.

48 **The depreciation charge for each period shall be recognised in profit or loss unless it is included in the carrying amount of another asset.**

49 The depreciation charge for a period is usually recognised in profit or loss. However, sometimes, the future economic benefits embodied in an asset are absorbed in producing other assets. In this case, the depreciation charge constitutes part of the cost of the other asset and is included in its carrying amount. For example, the depreciation of manufacturing plant and equipment is included in the costs of conversion of inventories (see IAS 2). Similarly, depreciation of property, plant and equipment used for development activities may be included in the cost of an intangible asset recognised in accordance with IAS 38 *Intangible Assets*.

Depreciable amount and depreciation period

50 **The depreciable amount of an asset shall be allocated on a systematic basis over its useful life.**

51 **The residual value and the useful life of an asset shall be reviewed at least at each financial year-end and, if expectations differ from previous estimates, the change(s) shall be accounted for as a change in an accounting estimate in accordance with IAS 8** *Accounting Policies, Changes in Accounting Estimates and Errors.*

52 Depreciation is recognised even if the fair value of the asset exceeds its carrying amount, as long as the asset's residual value does not exceed its carrying amount. Repair and maintenance of an asset do not negate the need to depreciate it.

53 The depreciable amount of an asset is determined after deducting its residual value. In practice, the residual value of an asset is often insignificant and therefore immaterial in the calculation of the depreciable amount.

54 The residual value of an asset may increase to an amount equal to or greater than the asset's carrying amount. If it does, the asset's depreciation charge is zero unless and until its residual value subsequently decreases to an amount below the asset's carrying amount.

55 Depreciation of an asset begins when it is available for use, ie when it is in the location and condition necessary for it to be capable of operating in the manner intended by management. Depreciation of an asset ceases at the earlier of the date that the asset is classified as held for sale (or included in a disposal group that is classified as held for sale) in accordance with IFRS 5 and the date that the asset is derecognised. Therefore, depreciation does not cease when the asset becomes idle or is retired from active use unless the asset is fully depreciated. However, under usage methods of depreciation the depreciation charge can be zero while there is no production.

56 The future economic benefits embodied in an asset are consumed by an entity principally through its use. However, other factors, such as technical or commercial obsolescence and wear and tear while an asset remains idle, often result in the diminution of the economic benefits that might have been obtained from the asset. Consequently, all the following factors are considered in determining the useful life of an asset:

(a) expected usage of the asset. Usage is assessed by reference to the asset's expected capacity or physical output.

(b) expected physical wear and tear, which depends on operational factors such as the number of shifts for which the asset is to be used and the repair and maintenance programme, and the care and maintenance of the asset while idle.

(c) technical or commercial obsolescence arising from changes or improvements in production, or from a change in the market demand for the product or service output of the asset.

(d) legal or similar limits on the use of the asset, such as the expiry dates of related leases.

57   The useful life of an asset is defined in terms of the asset's expected utility to the entity. The asset management policy of the entity may involve the disposal of assets after a specified time or after consumption of a specified proportion of the future economic benefits embodied in the asset. Therefore, the useful life of an asset may be shorter than its economic life. The estimation of the useful life of the asset is a matter of judgement based on the experience of the entity with similar assets.

58   Land and buildings are separable assets and are accounted for separately, even when they are acquired together. With some exceptions, such as quarries and sites used for landfill, land has an unlimited useful life and therefore is not depreciated. Buildings have a limited useful life and therefore are depreciable assets. An increase in the value of the land on which a building stands does not affect the determination of the depreciable amount of the building.

59   If the cost of land includes the costs of site dismantlement, removal and restoration, that portion of the land asset is depreciated over the period of benefits obtained by incurring those costs. In some cases, the land itself may have a limited useful life, in which case it is depreciated in a manner that reflects the benefits to be derived from it.

Depreciation method

60   **The depreciation method used shall reflect the pattern in which the asset's future economic benefits are expected to be consumed by the entity.**

61   **The depreciation method applied to an asset shall be reviewed at least at each financial year-end and, if there has been a significant change in the expected pattern of consumption of the future economic benefits embodied in the asset, the method shall be changed to reflect the changed pattern. Such a change shall be accounted for as a change in an accounting estimate in accordance with IAS 8.**

62   A variety of depreciation methods can be used to allocate the depreciable amount of an asset on a systematic basis over its useful life. These methods include the straight-line method, the diminishing balance method and the units of production method. Straight-line depreciation results in a constant charge over the useful life if the asset's residual value does not change. The diminishing balance method results in a decreasing charge over the useful life. The units of production method results in a charge based on the expected use or output. The entity selects the method that most closely reflects the expected pattern of consumption of the future economic benefits embodied in the asset. That method is applied consistently from period to period unless there is a change in the expected pattern of consumption of those future economic benefits.

Impairment

63   To determine whether an item of property, plant and equipment is impaired, an entity applies IAS 36 *Impairment of Assets*. That Standard explains how an entity reviews the carrying amount of its assets, how it determines the recoverable amount of an asset, and when it recognises, or reverses the recognition of, an impairment loss.

64   [Deleted]

Compensation for impairment

65 **Compensation from third parties for items of property, plant and equipment that were impaired, lost or given up shall be included in profit or loss when the compensation becomes receivable.**

66 Impairments or losses of items of property, plant and equipment, related claims for or payments of compensation from third parties and any subsequent purchase or construction of replacement assets are separate economic events and are accounted for separately as follows:

(a) impairments of items of property, plant and equipment are recognised in accordance with IAS 36;

(b) derecognition of items of property, plant and equipment retired or disposed of is determined in accordance with this Standard;

(c) compensation from third parties for items of property, plant and equipment that were impaired, lost or given up is included in determining profit or loss when it becomes receivable; and

(d) the cost of items of property, plant and equipment restored, purchased or constructed as replacements is determined in accordance with this Standard.

Derecognition

67 **The carrying amount of an item of property, plant and equipment shall be derecognised:**

(a) **on disposal; or**

(b) **when no future economic benefits are expected from its use or disposal.**

68 **The gain or loss arising from the derecognition of an item of property, plant and equipment shall be included in profit or loss when the item is derecognised (unless IAS 17 requires otherwise on a sale and leaseback). Gains shall not be classified as revenue.**

68A However, an entity that, in the course of its ordinary activities, routinely sells items of property, plant and equipment that it has held for rental to others shall transfer such assets to inventories at their carrying amount when they cease to be rented and become held for sale. The proceeds from the sale of such assets shall be recognised as revenue in accordance with IAS 18 *Revenue*. IFRS 5 does not apply when assets that are held for sale in the ordinary course of business are transferred to inventories.

69 The disposal of an item of property, plant and equipment may occur in a variety of ways (eg by sale, by entering into a finance lease or by donation). In determining the date of disposal of an item, an entity applies the criteria in IAS 18 for recognising revenue from the sale of goods. IAS 17 applies to disposal by a sale and leaseback.

70   If, under the recognition principle in paragraph 7, an entity recognises in the carrying amount of an item of property, plant and equipment the cost of a replacement for part of the item, then it derecognises the carrying amount of the replaced part regardless of whether the replaced part had been depreciated separately. If it is not practicable for an entity to determine the carrying amount of the replaced part, it may use the cost of the replacement as an indication of what the cost of the replaced part was at the time it was acquired or constructed.

71   **The gain or loss arising from the derecognition of an item of property, plant and equipment shall be determined as the difference between the net disposal proceeds, if any, and the carrying amount of the item.**

72   The consideration receivable on disposal of an item of property, plant and equipment is recognised initially at its fair value. If payment for the item is deferred, the consideration received is recognised initially at the cash price equivalent. The difference between the nominal amount of the consideration and the cash price equivalent is recognised as interest revenue in accordance with IAS 18 reflecting the effective yield on the receivable.

Disclosure

73   The financial statements shall disclose, for each class of property, plant and equipment:

(a)   the measurement bases used for determining the gross carrying amount;

(b)   the depreciation methods used;

(c)   the useful lives or the depreciation rates used;

(d)   the gross carrying amount and the accumulated depreciation (aggregated with accumulated impairment losses) at the beginning and end of the period; and

(e)   a reconciliation of the carrying amount at the beginning and end of the period showing:

(i)   additions;

(ii)   assets classified as held for sale or included in a disposal group classified as held for sale in accordance with IFRS 5 and other disposals;

(iii)   acquisitions through business combinations;

(iv)   increases or decreases resulting from revaluations under paragraphs 31, 39 and 40 and from impairment losses recognised or reversed in other comprehensive income in accordance with IAS 36;

(v)   impairment losses recognised in profit or loss in accordance with IAS 36;

(vi)   impairment losses reversed in profit or loss in accordance with IAS 36;

(vii)   depreciation;

(viii) the net exchange differences arising on the translation of the financial statements from the functional currency into a different presentation currency, including the translation of a foreign operation into the presentation currency of the reporting entity; and

(ix) other changes.

74 The financial statements shall also disclose:

(a) the existence and amounts of restrictions on title, and property, plant and equipment pledged as security for liabilities;

(b) the amount of expenditures recognised in the carrying amount of an item of property, plant and equipment in the course of its construction;

(c) the amount of contractual commitments for the acquisition of property, plant and equipment; and

(d) if it is not disclosed separately in the statement of comprehensive income, the amount of compensation from third parties for items of property, plant and equipment that were impaired, lost or given up that is included in profit or loss.

75 Selection of the depreciation method and estimation of the useful life of assets are matters of judgement. Therefore, disclosure of the methods adopted and the estimated useful lives or depreciation rates provides users of financial statements with information that allows them to review the policies selected by management and enables comparisons to be made with other entities. For similar reasons, it is necessary to disclose:

(a) depreciation, whether recognised in profit or loss or as a part of the cost of other assets, during a period; and

(b) accumulated depreciation at the end of the period.

76 In accordance with IAS 8 an entity discloses the nature and effect of a change in an accounting estimate that has an effect in the current period or is expected to have an effect in subsequent periods. For property, plant and equipment, such disclosure may arise from changes in estimates with respect to:

(a) residual values;

(b) the estimated costs of dismantling, removing or restoring items of property, plant and equipment;

(c) useful lives; and

(d) depreciation methods.

77 If items of property, plant and equipment are stated at revalued amounts, the following shall be disclosed in addition to the disclosures required by IFRS 13:

(a) the effective date of the revaluation;

(b) whether an independent valuer was involved;

(c) [deleted]

(d) [deleted]

    (e)   **for each revalued class of property, plant and equipment, the carrying amount that would have been recognised had the assets been carried under the cost model; and**

    (f)   **the revaluation surplus, indicating the change for the period and any restrictions on the distribution of the balance to shareholders.**

78   In accordance with IAS 36 an entity discloses information on impaired property, plant and equipment in addition to the information required by paragraph 73(e)(iv)–(vi).

79   Users of financial statements may also find the following information relevant to their needs:

    (a)   the carrying amount of temporarily idle property, plant and equipment;

    (b)   the gross carrying amount of any fully depreciated property, plant and equipment that is still in use;

    (c)   the carrying amount of property, plant and equipment retired from active use and not classified as held for sale in accordance with IFRS 5; and

    (d)   when the cost model is used, the fair value of property, plant and equipment when this is materially different from the carrying amount.

Therefore, entities are encouraged to disclose these amounts.

Transitional provisions

80   **The requirements of paragraphs 24–26 regarding the initial measurement of an item of property, plant and equipment acquired in an exchange of assets transaction shall be applied prospectively only to future transactions.**

Effective date

81   An entity shall apply this Standard for annual periods beginning on or after 1 January 2005. Earlier application is encouraged. If an entity applies this Standard for a period beginning before 1 January 2005, it shall disclose that fact.

81A   An entity shall apply the amendments in paragraph 3 for annual periods beginning on or after 1 January 2006. If an entity applies IFRS 6 for an earlier period, those amendments shall be applied for that earlier period.

81B   IAS 1 *Presentation of Financial Statements* (as revised in 2007) amended the terminology used throughout IFRSs. In addition it amended paragraphs 39, 40 and 73(e)(iv). An entity shall apply those amendments for annual periods beginning on or after 1 January 2009. If an entity applies IAS 1 (revised 2007) for an earlier period, the amendments shall be applied for that earlier period.

81C   IFRS 3 *Business Combinations* (as revised in 2008) amended paragraph 44. An entity shall apply that amendment for annual periods beginning on or after 1 July 2009. If an entity applies IFRS 3 (revised 2008) for an earlier period, the amendment shall also be applied for that earlier period.

81D   Paragraphs 6 and 69 were amended and paragraph 68A was added by *Improvements to IFRSs* issued in May 2008. An entity shall apply those amendments for annual periods beginning on or after 1 January 2009. Earlier application is permitted. If an entity applies the amendments for an earlier period it shall disclose that fact and at the same time apply the related amendments to IAS 7 *Statement of Cash Flows.*

81E   Paragraph 5 was amended by *Improvements to IFRSs* issued in May 2008. An entity shall apply that amendment prospectively for annual periods beginning on or after 1 January 2009. Earlier application is permitted if an entity also applies the amendments to paragraphs 8, 9, 22, 48, 53, 53A, 53B, 54, 57 and 85B of IAS 40 at the same time. If an entity applies the amendment for an earlier period it shall disclose that fact.

81F   IFRS 13, issued in May 2011, amended the definition of fair value in paragraph 6, amended paragraphs 26, 35 and 77 and deleted paragraphs 32 and 33. An entity shall apply those amendments when it applies IFRS 13.

Withdrawal of other pronouncements

82   This Standard supersedes IAS 16 *Property, Plant and Equipment* (revised in 1998).

83   This Standard supersedes the following Interpretations:

   (a)   SIC-6 *Costs of Modifying Existing Software;*

   (b)   SIC-14 *Property, Plant and Equipment—Compensation for the Impairment or Loss of Items;* and

   (c)   SIC-23 *Property, Plant and Equipment—Major Inspection or Overhaul Costs.*

Appendix
Amendments to other pronouncements

The amendments in this appendix shall be applied for annual periods beginning on or after 1 January 2005. If an entity applies this Standard for an earlier period, these amendments shall be applied for that earlier period.

* * * * *

The amendments contained in this appendix when this Standard was issued in 2003 have been incorporated into the relevant pronouncements published in this volume.

International Accounting Standard 17

Leases

In April 2001 the International Accounting Standards Board (IASB) adopted IAS 17 *Leases*, which had originally been issued by the International Accounting Standards Committee in December 1997. IAS 17 *Leases* replaced IAS 17 *Accounting for Leases* that was issued in September 1982.

In December 2003 the IASB issued a revised IAS 17 as part of its initial agenda of technical projects.

Other IFRSs have made minor consequential amendments to IAS 17. They include the requirements in IAS 1 *Presentation of Financial Statements* (as revised in September 2007), *Improvements to IFRSs* (issued April 2009) and IFRS 9 *Financial Instruments* (issued November 2009 and October 2010).

Contents

> **FOR THE ACCOMPANYING DOCUMENTS LISTED BELOW, SEE PART B OF THIS EDITION**

APPROVAL BY THE BOARD OF IAS 17 ISSUED IN DECEMBER 2003

BASIS FOR CONCLUSIONS

DISSENTING OPINION

IMPLEMENTATION GUIDANCE
Illustrative examples of sale and leaseback transactions that result in operating leases

International Accounting Standard 17 *Leases* (IAS 17) is set out in paragraphs 1–70 and the Appendix. All the paragraphs have equal authority but retain the IASC format of the Standard when it was adopted by the IASB. IAS 17 should be read in the context of its objective and the Basis for Conclusions, the *Preface to International Financial Reporting Standards* and the *Conceptual Framework for Financial Reporting*. IAS 8 *Accounting Policies, Changes in Accounting Estimates and Errors* provides a basis for selecting and applying accounting policies in the absence of explicit guidance.

Introduction

IN1   International Accounting Standard 17 *Leases* (IAS 17) replaces IAS 17 *Leases* (revised in 1997) and should be applied for annual periods beginning on or after 1 January 2005. Earlier application is encouraged.

Reasons for revising IAS 17

IN2   The International Accounting Standards Board developed this revised IAS 17 as part of its project on Improvements to International Accounting Standards. The project was undertaken in the light of queries and criticisms raised in relation to the Standards by securities regulators, professional accountants and other interested parties. The objectives of the project were to reduce or eliminate alternatives, redundancies and conflicts within the Standards, to deal with some convergence issues and to make other improvements.

IN3   For IAS 17 the Board's main objective was a limited revision to clarify the classification of a lease of land and buildings and to eliminate accounting alternatives for initial direct costs in the financial statements of lessors.

IN4   Because the Board's agenda includes a project on leases, the Board did not reconsider the fundamental approach to the accounting for leases contained in IAS 17. For the same reason, the Board decided not to incorporate into IAS 17 relevant SIC Interpretations.

The main changes

Scope

IN5   Although IAS 40 *Investment Property* prescribes the measurement models that can be applied to investment properties held, it requires the finance lease accounting methodology set out in this Standard to be used for investment properties held under leases.

Definitions

Initial direct costs

IN6   Initial direct costs are incremental costs that are directly attributable to negotiating and arranging a lease. The definition of the interest rate implicit in the lease has been amended to clarify that it is the discount rate that results in the present value of the minimum lease payments and any unguaranteed residual value equalling the fair value of the leased asset plus initial direct costs of the lessor.

Inception of the lease/commencement of the lease term

IN7 This Standard distinguishes between the inception of the lease (when leases are classified) and the commencement of the lease term (when recognition takes place).

Unearned finance income/net investment in the lease

IN8 The definitions of these terms have been simplified and articulated more explicitly to complement the changes relating to initial direct costs referred to in paragraphs IN10–IN12 and the change in the definition of the interest rate implicit in the lease referred to in paragraph IN6.

Classification of leases

IN9 When classifying a lease of land and buildings, an entity normally considers the land and buildings elements separately. The minimum lease payments are allocated between the land and buildings elements in proportion to the relative fair values of the leasehold interests in the land and buildings elements of the lease. The land element is normally classified as an operating lease unless title passes to the lessee at the end of the lease term. The buildings element is classified as an operating or finance lease by applying the classification criteria in the Standard.

Initial direct costs

IN10 Lessors include in the initial measurement of finance lease receivables the initial direct costs incurred in negotiating a lease. This treatment does not apply to manufacturer or dealer lessors. Manufacturer or dealer lessors recognise costs of this type as an expense when the selling profit is recognised.

IN11 Initial direct costs incurred by lessors in negotiating an operating lease are added to the carrying amount of the leased asset and recognised over the lease term on the same basis as the lease income.

IN12 The Standard does not permit initial direct costs of lessors to be charged as expenses as incurred.

Transitional provisions

IN13 As discussed in paragraph 68 of the Standard, an entity that has previously applied IAS 17 (revised 1997) is required to apply the amendments made by this Standard retrospectively for all leases, or if IAS 17 (revised 1997) was not applied retrospectively, for all leases entered into since it first applied that Standard.

International Accounting Standard 17
Leases

Objective

1   The objective of this Standard is to prescribe, for lessees and lessors, the appropriate accounting policies and disclosure to apply in relation to leases.

Scope

2   **This Standard shall be applied in accounting for all leases other than:**

(a)   leases to explore for or use minerals, oil, natural gas and similar non-regenerative resources; and

(b)   licensing agreements for such items as motion picture films, video recordings, plays, manuscripts, patents and copyrights.

However, this Standard shall not be applied as the basis of measurement for:

(a)   property held by lessees that is accounted for as investment property (see IAS 40 *Investment Property*);

(b)   investment property provided by lessors under operating leases (see IAS 40);

(c)   biological assets held by lessees under finance leases (see IAS 41 *Agriculture*); or

(d)   biological assets provided by lessors under operating leases (see IAS 41).

3   This Standard applies to agreements that transfer the right to use assets even though substantial services by the lessor may be called for in connection with the operation or maintenance of such assets. This Standard does not apply to agreements that are contracts for services that do not transfer the right to use assets from one contracting party to the other.

Definitions

4   **The following terms are used in this Standard with the meanings specified:**

A *lease* is an agreement whereby the lessor conveys to the lessee in return for a payment or series of payments the right to use an asset for an agreed period of time.

A *finance lease* is a lease that transfers substantially all the risks and rewards incidental to ownership of an asset. Title may or may not eventually be transferred.

An *operating lease* is a lease other than a finance lease.

A *non-cancellable lease* is a lease that is cancellable only:

(a)   upon the occurrence of some remote contingency;

(b)   with the permission of the lessor;

(c)   if the lessee enters into a new lease for the same or an equivalent asset with the same lessor; or

(d)   upon payment by the lessee of such an additional amount that, at inception of the lease, continuation of the lease is reasonably certain.

The *inception of the lease* is the earlier of the date of the lease agreement and the date of commitment by the parties to the principal provisions of the lease. As at this date:

(a)   a lease is classified as either an operating or a finance lease; and

(b)   in the case of a finance lease, the amounts to be recognised at the commencement of the lease term are determined.

The *commencement of the lease term* is the date from which the lessee is entitled to exercise its right to use the leased asset. It is the date of initial recognition of the lease (ie the recognition of the assets, liabilities, income or expenses resulting from the lease, as appropriate).

The *lease term* is the non-cancellable period for which the lessee has contracted to lease the asset together with any further terms for which the lessee has the option to continue to lease the asset, with or without further payment, when at the inception of the lease it is reasonably certain that the lessee will exercise the option.

Minimum lease payments are the payments over the lease term that the lessee is or can be required to make, excluding contingent rent, costs for services and taxes to be paid by and reimbursed to the lessor, together with:

(a)   for a lessee, any amounts guaranteed by the lessee or by a party related to the lessee; or

(b)   for a lessor, any residual value guaranteed to the lessor by:

   (i)   the lessee;

   (ii)   a party related to the lessee; or

   (iii)   a third party unrelated to the lessor that is financially capable of discharging the obligations under the guarantee.

However, if the lessee has an option to purchase the asset at a price that is expected to be sufficiently lower than fair value at the date the option becomes exercisable for it to be reasonably certain, at the inception of the lease, that the option will be exercised, the minimum lease payments comprise the minimum payments payable over the lease term to the expected date of exercise of this purchase option and the payment required to exercise it.

Fair value is the amount for which an asset could be exchanged, or a liability settled, between knowledgeable, willing parties in an arm's length transaction.

Economic life is either:

(a)   the period over which an asset is expected to be economically usable by one or more users; or

(b)   the number of production or similar units expected to be obtained from the asset by one or more users.

Useful life is the estimated remaining period, from the commencement of the lease term, without limitation by the lease term, over which the economic benefits embodied in the asset are expected to be consumed by the entity.

Guaranteed residual value is:

(a)   for a lessee, that part of the residual value that is guaranteed by the lessee or by a party related to the lessee (the amount of the guarantee being the maximum amount that could, in any event, become payable); and

(b)   for a lessor, that part of the residual value that is guaranteed by the lessee or by a third party unrelated to the lessor that is financially capable of discharging the obligations under the guarantee.

Unguaranteed residual value is that portion of the residual value of the leased asset, the realisation of which by the lessor is not assured or is guaranteed solely by a party related to the lessor.

Initial direct costs are incremental costs that are directly attributable to negotiating and arranging a lease, except for such costs incurred by manufacturer or dealer lessors.

Gross investment in the lease is the aggregate of:

(a)   the minimum lease payments receivable by the lessor under a finance lease, and

(b)   any unguaranteed residual value accruing to the lessor.

Net investment in the lease is the gross investment in the lease discounted at the interest rate implicit in the lease.

Unearned finance income is the difference between:

(a)   the gross investment in the lease, and

(b)   the net investment in the lease.

The *interest rate implicit in the lease* is the discount rate that, at the inception of the lease, causes the aggregate present value of (a) the minimum lease payments and (b) the unguaranteed residual value to be equal to the sum of (i) the fair value of the leased asset and (ii) any initial direct costs of the lessor.

The *lessee's incremental borrowing rate of interest* is the rate of interest the lessee would have to pay on a similar lease or, if that is not determinable, the rate that, at the inception of the lease, the lessee would incur to borrow over a similar term, and with a similar security, the funds necessary to purchase the asset.

Contingent rent is that portion of the lease payments that is not fixed in amount but is based on the future amount of a factor that changes other than with the passage of time (eg percentage of future sales, amount of future use, future price indices, future market rates of interest).

5   A lease agreement or commitment may include a provision to adjust the lease payments for changes in the construction or acquisition cost of the leased property or for changes in some other measure of cost or value, such as general price levels, or in the lessor's costs of financing the lease, during the period between the inception of the lease and the commencement of the lease term. If so, the effect of any such changes shall be deemed to have taken place at the inception of the lease for the purposes of this Standard.

6   The definition of a lease includes contracts for the hire of an asset that contain a provision giving the hirer an option to acquire title to the asset upon the fulfilment of agreed conditions. These contracts are sometimes known as hire purchase contracts.

6A   IAS 17 uses the term 'fair value' in a way that differs in some respects from the definition of fair value in IFRS 13 *Fair Value Measurement*. Therefore, when applying IAS 17 an entity measures fair value in accordance with IAS 17, not IFRS 13.

Classification of leases

7   The classification of leases adopted in this Standard is based on the extent to which risks and rewards incidental to ownership of a leased asset lie with the lessor or the lessee. Risks include the possibilities of losses from idle capacity or technological obsolescence and of variations in return because of changing economic conditions. Rewards may be represented by the expectation of profitable operation over the asset's economic life and of gain from appreciation in value or realisation of a residual value.

8   **A lease is classified as a finance lease if it transfers substantially all the risks and rewards incidental to ownership. A lease is classified as an operating lease if it does not transfer substantially all the risks and rewards incidental to ownership.**

9   Because the transaction between a lessor and a lessee is based on a lease agreement between them, it is appropriate to use consistent definitions. The application of these definitions to the differing circumstances of the lessor and lessee may result in the same lease being classified differently by them. For example, this may be the case if the lessor benefits from a residual value guarantee provided by a party unrelated to the lessee.

10   Whether a lease is a finance lease or an operating lease depends on the substance of the transaction rather than the form of the contract.[1] Examples of situations that individually or in combination would normally lead to a lease being classified as a finance lease are:

      (a)   the lease transfers ownership of the asset to the lessee by the end of the lease term;

      (b)   the lessee has the option to purchase the asset at a price that is expected to be sufficiently lower than the fair value at the date the option becomes exercisable for it to be reasonably certain, at the inception of the lease, that the option will be exercised;

---

1   See also SIC-27 *Evaluating the Substance of Transactions Involving the Legal Form of a Lease*.

(c)   the lease term is for the major part of the economic life of the asset even if title is not transferred;

(d)   at the inception of the lease the present value of the minimum lease payments amounts to at least substantially all of the fair value of the leased asset; and

(e)   the leased assets are of such a specialised nature that only the lessee can use them without major modifications.

11   Indicators of situations that individually or in combination could also lead to a lease being classified as a finance lease are:

(a)   if the lessee can cancel the lease, the lessor's losses associated with the cancellation are borne by the lessee;

(b)   gains or losses from the fluctuation in the fair value of the residual accrue to the lessee (for example, in the form of a rent rebate equalling most of the sales proceeds at the end of the lease); and

(c)   the lessee has the ability to continue the lease for a secondary period at a rent that is substantially lower than market rent.

12   The examples and indicators in paragraphs 10 and 11 are not always conclusive. If it is clear from other features that the lease does not transfer substantially all risks and rewards incidental to ownership, the lease is classified as an operating lease. For example, this may be the case if ownership of the asset transfers at the end of the lease for a variable payment equal to its then fair value, or if there are contingent rents, as a result of which the lessee does not have substantially all such risks and rewards.

13   Lease classification is made at the inception of the lease. If at any time the lessee and the lessor agree to change the provisions of the lease, other than by renewing the lease, in a manner that would have resulted in a different classification of the lease under the criteria in paragraphs 7–12 if the changed terms had been in effect at the inception of the lease, the revised agreement is regarded as a new agreement over its term. However, changes in estimates (for example, changes in estimates of the economic life or of the residual value of the leased property), or changes in circumstances (for example, default by the lessee), do not give rise to a new classification of a lease for accounting purposes.

14   [Deleted]

15   [Deleted]

15A   When a lease includes both land and buildings elements, an entity assesses the classification of each element as a finance or an operating lease separately in accordance with paragraphs 7–13. In determining whether the land element is an operating or a finance lease, an important consideration is that land normally has an indefinite economic life.

16   Whenever necessary in order to classify and account for a lease of land and buildings, the minimum lease payments (including any lump-sum upfront payments) are allocated between the land and the buildings elements in proportion to the relative fair values of the leasehold interests in the land element

and buildings element of the lease at the inception of the lease. If the lease payments cannot be allocated reliably between these two elements, the entire lease is classified as a finance lease, unless it is clear that both elements are operating leases, in which case the entire lease is classified as an operating lease.

17   For a lease of land and buildings in which the amount that would initially be recognised for the land element, in accordance with paragraph 20, is immaterial, the land and buildings may be treated as a single unit for the purpose of lease classification and classified as a finance or operating lease in accordance with paragraphs 7–13. In such a case, the economic life of the buildings is regarded as the economic life of the entire leased asset.

18   Separate measurement of the land and buildings elements is not required when the lessee's interest in both land and buildings is classified as an investment property in accordance with IAS 40 and the fair value model is adopted. Detailed calculations are required for this assessment only if the classification of one or both elements is otherwise uncertain.

19   In accordance with IAS 40, it is possible for a lessee to classify a property interest held under an operating lease as an investment property. If it does, the property interest is accounted for as if it were a finance lease and, in addition, the fair value model is used for the asset recognised. The lessee shall continue to account for the lease as a finance lease, even if a subsequent event changes the nature of the lessee's property interest so that it is no longer classified as investment property. This will be the case if, for example, the lessee:

(a)   occupies the property, which is then transferred to owner-occupied property at a deemed cost equal to its fair value at the date of change in use; or

(b)   grants a sublease that transfers substantially all of the risks and rewards incidental to ownership of the interest to an unrelated third party. Such a sublease is accounted for by the lessee as a finance lease to the third party, although it may be accounted for as an operating lease by the third party.

Leases in the financial statements of lessees

Finance leases

Initial recognition

20   At the commencement of the lease term, lessees shall recognise finance leases as assets and liabilities in their statements of financial position at amounts equal to the fair value of the leased property or, if lower, the present value of the minimum lease payments, each determined at the inception of the lease. The discount rate to be used in calculating the present value of the minimum lease payments is the interest rate implicit in the lease, if this is practicable to determine; if not, the lessee's incremental borrowing rate shall be used. Any initial direct costs of the lessee are added to the amount recognised as an asset.

21   Transactions and other events are accounted for and presented in accordance with their substance and financial reality and not merely with legal form. Although the legal form of a lease agreement is that the lessee may acquire no legal title to the leased asset, in the case of finance leases the substance and financial reality are that the lessee acquires the economic benefits of the use of the leased asset for the major part of its economic life in return for entering into an obligation to pay for that right an amount approximating, at the inception of the lease, the fair value of the asset and the related finance charge.

22   If such lease transactions are not reflected in the lessee's statement of financial position, the economic resources and the level of obligations of an entity are understated, thereby distorting financial ratios. Therefore, it is appropriate for a finance lease to be recognised in the lessee's statement of financial position both as an asset and as an obligation to pay future lease payments. At the commencement of the lease term, the asset and the liability for the future lease payments are recognised in the statement of financial position at the same amounts except for any initial direct costs of the lessee that are added to the amount recognised as an asset.

23   It is not appropriate for the liabilities for leased assets to be presented in the financial statements as a deduction from the leased assets. If for the presentation of liabilities in the statement of financial position a distinction is made between current and non-current liabilities, the same distinction is made for lease liabilities.

24   Initial direct costs are often incurred in connection with specific leasing activities, such as negotiating and securing leasing arrangements. The costs identified as directly attributable to activities performed by the lessee for a finance lease are added to the amount recognised as an asset.

Subsequent measurement

25   Minimum lease payments shall be apportioned between the finance charge and the reduction of the outstanding liability. The finance charge shall be allocated to each period during the lease term so as to produce a constant periodic rate of interest on the remaining balance of the liability. Contingent rents shall be charged as expenses in the periods in which they are incurred.

26   In practice, in allocating the finance charge to periods during the lease term, a lessee may use some form of approximation to simplify the calculation.

27   A finance lease gives rise to depreciation expense for depreciable assets as well as finance expense for each accounting period. The depreciation policy for depreciable leased assets shall be consistent with that for depreciable assets that are owned, and the depreciation recognised shall be calculated in accordance with IAS 16 *Property, Plant and Equipment* **and IAS 38** *Intangible Assets*. **If there is no reasonable certainty that the lessee will obtain ownership by the end of the lease term, the asset shall be fully depreciated over the shorter of the lease term and its useful life.**

28   The depreciable amount of a leased asset is allocated to each accounting period during the period of expected use on a systematic basis consistent with the depreciation policy the lessee adopts for depreciable assets that are owned. If there is reasonable certainty that the lessee will obtain ownership by the end of the lease term, the period of expected use is the useful life of the asset; otherwise the asset is depreciated over the shorter of the lease term and its useful life.

29   The sum of the depreciation expense for the asset and the finance expense for the period is rarely the same as the lease payments payable for the period, and it is, therefore, inappropriate simply to recognise the lease payments payable as an expense. Accordingly, the asset and the related liability are unlikely to be equal in amount after the commencement of the lease term.

30   To determine whether a leased asset has become impaired, an entity applies IAS 36 *Impairment of Assets*.

Disclosures

31   Lessees shall, in addition to meeting the requirements of IFRS 7 *Financial Instruments: Disclosures*, make the following disclosures for finance leases:

(a)   for each class of asset, the net carrying amount at the end of the reporting period.

(b)   a reconciliation between the total of future minimum lease payments at the end of the reporting period, and their present value. In addition, an entity shall disclose the total of future minimum lease payments at the end of the reporting period, and their present value, for each of the following periods:

(i)   not later than one year;

(ii)   later than one year and not later than five years;

(iii)   later than five years.

(c)   contingent rents recognised as an expense in the period.

(d)   the total of future minimum sublease payments expected to be received under non-cancellable subleases at the end of the reporting period.

(e)   a general description of the lessee's material leasing arrangements including, but not limited to, the following:

(i)   the basis on which contingent rent payable is determined;

(ii)   the existence and terms of renewal or purchase options and escalation clauses; and

(iii)   restrictions imposed by lease arrangements, such as those concerning dividends, additional debt, and further leasing.

32   In addition, the requirements for disclosure in accordance with IAS 16, IAS 36, IAS 38, IAS 40 and IAS 41 apply to lessees for assets leased under finance leases.

Operating leases

33 **Lease payments under an operating lease shall be recognised as an expense on a straight-line basis over the lease term unless another systematic basis is more representative of the time pattern of the user's benefit.**[2]

34 For operating leases, lease payments (excluding costs for services such as insurance and maintenance) are recognised as an expense on a straight-line basis unless another systematic basis is representative of the time pattern of the user's benefit, even if the payments are not on that basis.

Disclosures

35 Lessees shall, in addition to meeting the requirements of IFRS 7, make the following disclosures for operating leases:

(a) the total of future minimum lease payments under non-cancellable operating leases for each of the following periods:

(i) not later than one year;

(ii) later than one year and not later than five years;

(iii) later than five years.

(b) the total of future minimum sublease payments expected to be received under non-cancellable subleases at the end of the reporting period.

(c) lease and sublease payments recognised as an expense in the period, with separate amounts for minimum lease payments, contingent rents, and sublease payments.

(d) a general description of the lessee's significant leasing arrangements including, but not limited to, the following:

(i) the basis on which contingent rent payable is determined;

(ii) the existence and terms of renewal or purchase options and escalation clauses; and

(iii) restrictions imposed by lease arrangements, such as those concerning dividends, additional debt and further leasing.

Leases in the financial statements of lessors

Finance leases

Initial recognition

36 **Lessors shall recognise assets held under a finance lease in their statements of financial position and present them as a receivable at an amount equal to the net investment in the lease.**

---

2 See also SIC-15 *Operating Leases—Incentives*.

37   Under a finance lease substantially all the risks and rewards incidental to legal ownership are transferred by the lessor, and thus the lease payment receivable is treated by the lessor as repayment of principal and finance income to reimburse and reward the lessor for its investment and services.

38   Initial direct costs are often incurred by lessors and include amounts such as commissions, legal fees and internal costs that are incremental and directly attributable to negotiating and arranging a lease. They exclude general overheads such as those incurred by a sales and marketing team. For finance leases other than those involving manufacturer or dealer lessors, initial direct costs are included in the initial measurement of the finance lease receivable and reduce the amount of income recognised over the lease term. The interest rate implicit in the lease is defined in such a way that the initial direct costs are included automatically in the finance lease receivable; there is no need to add them separately. Costs incurred by manufacturer or dealer lessors in connection with negotiating and arranging a lease are excluded from the definition of initial direct costs. As a result, they are excluded from the net investment in the lease and are recognised as an expense when the selling profit is recognised, which for a finance lease is normally at the commencement of the lease term.

Subsequent measurement

39   **The recognition of finance income shall be based on a pattern reflecting a constant periodic rate of return on the lessor's net investment in the finance lease.**

40   A lessor aims to allocate finance income over the lease term on a systematic and rational basis. This income allocation is based on a pattern reflecting a constant periodic return on the lessor's net investment in the finance lease. Lease payments relating to the period, excluding costs for services, are applied against the gross investment in the lease to reduce both the principal and the unearned finance income.

41   Estimated unguaranteed residual values used in computing the lessor's gross investment in the lease are reviewed regularly. If there has been a reduction in the estimated unguaranteed residual value, the income allocation over the lease term is revised and any reduction in respect of amounts accrued is recognised immediately.

41A   An asset under a finance lease that is classified as held for sale (or included in a disposal group that is classified as held for sale) in accordance with IFRS 5 *Non-current Assets Held for Sale and Discontinued Operations* shall be accounted for in accordance with that IFRS.

42   **Manufacturer or dealer lessors shall recognise selling profit or loss in the period, in accordance with the policy followed by the entity for outright sales. If artificially low rates of interest are quoted, selling profit shall be restricted to that which would apply if a market rate of interest were charged. Costs incurred by manufacturer or dealer lessors in connection with negotiating and arranging a lease shall be recognised as an expense when the selling profit is recognised.**

43   Manufacturers or dealers often offer to customers the choice of either buying or leasing an asset. A finance lease of an asset by a manufacturer or dealer lessor gives rise to two types of income:

(a)   profit or loss equivalent to the profit or loss resulting from an outright sale of the asset being leased, at normal selling prices, reflecting any applicable volume or trade discounts; and

(b)   finance income over the lease term.

44   The sales revenue recognised at the commencement of the lease term by a manufacturer or dealer lessor is the fair value of the asset, or, if lower, the present value of the minimum lease payments accruing to the lessor, computed at a market rate of interest. The cost of sale recognised at the commencement of the lease term is the cost, or carrying amount if different, of the leased property less the present value of the unguaranteed residual value. The difference between the sales revenue and the cost of sale is the selling profit, which is recognised in accordance with the entity's policy for outright sales.

45   Manufacturer or dealer lessors sometimes quote artificially low rates of interest in order to attract customers. The use of such a rate would result in an excessive portion of the total income from the transaction being recognised at the time of sale. If artificially low rates of interest are quoted, selling profit is restricted to that which would apply if a market rate of interest were charged.

46   Costs incurred by a manufacturer or dealer lessor in connection with negotiating and arranging a finance lease are recognised as an expense at the commencement of the lease term because they are mainly related to earning the manufacturer's or dealer's selling profit.

Disclosures

47   **Lessors shall, in addition to meeting the requirements in IFRS 7, disclose the following for finance leases:**

(a)   **a reconciliation between the gross investment in the lease at the end of the reporting period, and the present value of minimum lease payments receivable at the end of the reporting period. In addition, an entity shall disclose the gross investment in the lease and the present value of minimum lease payments receivable at the end of the reporting period, for each of the following periods:**

(i)   **not later than one year;**

(ii)   **later than one year and not later than five years;**

(iii)   **later than five years.**

(b)   **unearned finance income.**

(c)   **the unguaranteed residual values accruing to the benefit of the lessor.**

(d)   **the accumulated allowance for uncollectible minimum lease payments receivable.**

(e)   **contingent rents recognised as income in the period.**

(f)   **a general description of the lessor's material leasing arrangements.**

48   As an indicator of growth it is often useful also to disclose the gross investment less unearned income in new business added during the period, after deducting the relevant amounts for cancelled leases.

Operating leases

49   **Lessors shall present assets subject to operating leases in their statements of financial position according to the nature of the asset.**

50   **Lease income from operating leases shall be recognised in income on a straight-line basis over the lease term, unless another systematic basis is more representative of the time pattern in which use benefit derived from the leased asset is diminished.[3]**

51   Costs, including depreciation, incurred in earning the lease income are recognised as an expense. Lease income (excluding receipts for services provided such as insurance and maintenance) is recognised on a straight-line basis over the lease term even if the receipts are not on such a basis, unless another systematic basis is more representative of the time pattern in which use benefit derived from the leased asset is diminished.

52   **Initial direct costs incurred by lessors in negotiating and arranging an operating lease shall be added to the carrying amount of the leased asset and recognised as an expense over the lease term on the same basis as the lease income.**

53   **The depreciation policy for depreciable leased assets shall be consistent with the lessor's normal depreciation policy for similar assets, and depreciation shall be calculated in accordance with IAS 16 and IAS 38.**

54   To determine whether a leased asset has become impaired, an entity applies IAS 36.

55   A manufacturer or dealer lessor does not recognise any selling profit on entering into an operating lease because it is not the equivalent of a sale.

Disclosures

56   **Lessors shall, in addition to meeting the requirements of IFRS 7, disclose the following for operating leases:**

   (a)   the future minimum lease payments under non-cancellable operating leases in the aggregate and for each of the following periods:

      (i)   not later than one year;

      (ii)   later than one year and not later than five years;

      (iii)   later than five years.

   (b)   total contingent rents recognised as income in the period.

   (c)   a general description of the lessor's leasing arrangements.

57   In addition, the disclosure requirements in IAS 16, IAS 36, IAS 38, IAS 40 and IAS 41 apply to lessors for assets provided under operating leases.

---

3   See also SIC-15 *Operating Leases—Incentives.*

Sale and leaseback transactions

58   A sale and leaseback transaction involves the sale of an asset and the leasing back of the same asset. The lease payment and the sale price are usually interdependent because they are negotiated as a package. The accounting treatment of a sale and leaseback transaction depends upon the type of lease involved.

59   **If a sale and leaseback transaction results in a finance lease, any excess of sales proceeds over the carrying amount shall not be immediately recognised as income by a seller-lessee. Instead, it shall be deferred and amortised over the lease term.**

60   If the leaseback is a finance lease, the transaction is a means whereby the lessor provides finance to the lessee, with the asset as security. For this reason it is not appropriate to regard an excess of sales proceeds over the carrying amount as income. Such excess is deferred and amortised over the lease term.

61   **If a sale and leaseback transaction results in an operating lease, and it is clear that the transaction is established at fair value, any profit or loss shall be recognised immediately. If the sale price is below fair value, any profit or loss shall be recognised immediately except that, if the loss is compensated for by future lease payments at below market price, it shall be deferred and amortised in proportion to the lease payments over the period for which the asset is expected to be used. If the sale price is above fair value, the excess over fair value shall be deferred and amortised over the period for which the asset is expected to be used.**

62   If the leaseback is an operating lease, and the lease payments and the sale price are at fair value, there has in effect been a normal sale transaction and any profit or loss is recognised immediately.

63   **For operating leases, if the fair value at the time of a sale and leaseback transaction is less than the carrying amount of the asset, a loss equal to the amount of the difference between the carrying amount and fair value shall be recognised immediately.**

64   For finance leases, no such adjustment is necessary unless there has been an impairment in value, in which case the carrying amount is reduced to recoverable amount in accordance with IAS 36.

65   Disclosure requirements for lessees and lessors apply equally to sale and leaseback transactions. The required description of material leasing arrangements leads to disclosure of unique or unusual provisions of the agreement or terms of the sale and leaseback transactions.

66   Sale and leaseback transactions may trigger the separate disclosure criteria in IAS 1 *Presentation of Financial Statements.*

Transitional provisions

67   **Subject to paragraph 68, retrospective application of this Standard is encouraged but not required. If the Standard is not applied retrospectively, the balance of any pre-existing finance lease is deemed to have been properly determined by the lessor and shall be accounted for thereafter in accordance with the provisions of this Standard.**

68   An entity that has previously applied IAS 17 (revised 1997) shall apply the amendments made by this Standard retrospectively for all leases or, if IAS 17 (revised 1997) was not applied retrospectively, for all leases entered into since it first applied that Standard.

68A   An entity shall reassess the classification of land elements of unexpired leases at the date it adopts the amendments referred to in paragraph 69A on the basis of information existing at the inception of those leases. It shall recognise a lease newly classified as a finance lease retrospectively in accordance with IAS 8 *Accounting Policies, Changes in Accounting Estimates and Errors*. However, if an entity does not have the information necessary to apply the amendments retrospectively, it shall:

      (a)   apply the amendments to those leases on the basis of the facts and circumstances existing on the date it adopts the amendments; and

      (b)   recognise the asset and liability related to a land lease newly classified as a finance lease at their fair values on that date; any difference between those fair values is recognised in retained earnings.

Effective date

69   An entity shall apply this Standard for annual periods beginning on or after 1 January 2005. Earlier application is encouraged. If an entity applies this Standard for a period beginning before 1 January 2005, it shall disclose that fact.

69A   Paragraphs 14 and 15 were deleted, and paragraphs 15A and 68A were added as part of *Improvements to IFRSs* issued in April 2009. An entity shall apply those amendments for annual periods beginning on or after 1 January 2010. Earlier application is permitted. If an entity applies the amendments for an earlier period it shall disclose that fact.

Withdrawal of IAS 17 (revised 1997)

70   This Standard supersedes IAS 17 *Leases* (revised in 1997).

Appendix
Amendments to other pronouncements

The amendments in this appendix shall be applied for annual periods beginning on or after 1 January 2005. If an entity applies this Standard for an earlier period, these amendments shall be applied for that earlier period.

* * * * *

The amendments contained in this appendix when this Standard was issued in 2003 have been incorporated into the relevant IFRSs published in this volume.

International Accounting Standard 18

Revenue

In April 2001 the International Accounting Standards Board (IASB) adopted IAS 18 *Revenue*, which had originally been issued by the International Accounting Standards Committee in December 1993. IAS 18 *Revenue* replaced IAS 18 *Revenue Recognition* (issued in December 1982).

Other IFRSs have made minor consequential amendments to IAS 18. They include *Cost of an Investment in a Subsidiary, Jointly Controlled Entity or Associate* (Amendments to IFRS 1 and IAS 27) (issued May 2008), *Improvements to IFRSs* (issued April 2009) and IFRS 9 *Financial Instruments* (issued November 2009 and October 2010).

CONTENTS

FOR THE ACCOMPANYING DOCUMENTS LISTED BELOW, SEE PART B OF THIS EDITION

International Accounting Standard 18 *Revenue* (IAS 18) is set out in paragraphs 1–42. All the paragraphs have equal authority but retain the IASC format of the Standard when it was adopted by the IASB. IAS 18 should be read in the context of its objective, the *Preface to International Financial Reporting Standards* and the *Conceptual Framework for Financial Reporting*. IAS 8 *Accounting Policies, Changes in Accounting Estimates and Errors* provides a basis for selecting and applying accounting policies in the absence of explicit guidance.

International Accounting Standard 18
Revenue

Objective

Income is defined in the *Framework for the Preparation and Presentation of Financial Statements*[1] as increases in economic benefits during the accounting period in the form of inflows or enhancements of assets or decreases of liabilities that result in increases in equity, other than those relating to contributions from equity participants. Income encompasses both revenue and gains. Revenue is income that arises in the course of ordinary activities of an entity and is referred to by a variety of different names including sales, fees, interest, dividends and royalties. The objective of this Standard is to prescribe the accounting treatment of revenue arising from certain types of transactions and events.

The primary issue in accounting for revenue is determining when to recognise revenue. Revenue is recognised when it is probable that future economic benefits will flow to the entity and these benefits can be measured reliably. This Standard identifies the circumstances in which these criteria will be met and, therefore, revenue will be recognised. It also provides practical guidance on the application of these criteria.

Scope

1   **This Standard shall be applied in accounting for revenue arising from the following transactions and events:**

    (a)   the sale of goods;

    (b)   the rendering of services; and

    (c)   the use by others of entity assets yielding interest, royalties and dividends.

2   This Standard supersedes IAS 18 *Revenue Recognition* approved in 1982.

3   Goods includes goods produced by the entity for the purpose of sale and goods purchased for resale, such as merchandise purchased by a retailer or land and other property held for resale.

4   The rendering of services typically involves the performance by the entity of a contractually agreed task over an agreed period of time. The services may be rendered within a single period or over more than one period. Some contracts for the rendering of services are directly related to construction contracts, for example, those for the services of project managers and architects. Revenue arising from these contracts is not dealt with in this Standard but is dealt with in accordance with the requirements for construction contracts as specified in IAS 11 *Construction Contracts*.

---

1   IASC's *Framework for the Preparation and Presentation of Financial Statements* was adopted by the IASB in 2001. In September 2010 the IASB replaced the *Framework* with the *Conceptual Framework for Financial Reporting*.

5   The use by others of entity assets gives rise to revenue in the form of:

(a)   interest—charges for the use of cash or cash equivalents or amounts due to the entity;

(b)   royalties—charges for the use of long-term assets of the entity, for example, patents, trademarks, copyrights and computer software; and

(c)   dividends—distributions of profits to holders of equity investments in proportion to their holdings of a particular class of capital.

6   This Standard does not deal with revenue arising from:

(a)   lease agreements (see IAS 17 *Leases*);

(b)   dividends arising from investments which are accounted for under the equity method (see IAS 28 *Investments in Associates and Joint Ventures*);

(c)   insurance contracts within the scope of IFRS 4 *Insurance Contracts*;

(d)   changes in the fair value of financial assets and financial liabilities or their disposal (see IFRS 9 *Financial Instruments*);

(e)   changes in the value of other current assets;

(f)   initial recognition and from changes in the fair value of biological assets related to agricultural activity (see IAS 41 *Agriculture*);

(g)   initial recognition of agricultural produce (see IAS 41); and

(h)   the extraction of mineral ores.

Definitions

7   **The following terms are used in this Standard with the meanings specified:**

Revenue is the gross inflow of economic benefits during the period arising in the course of the ordinary activities of an entity when those inflows result in increases in equity, other than increases relating to contributions from equity participants.

Fair value is the price that would be received to sell an asset or paid to transfer a liability in an orderly transaction between market participants at the measurement date. (See IFRS 13 *Fair Value Measurement*.)

8   Revenue includes only the gross inflows of economic benefits received and receivable by the entity on its own account. Amounts collected on behalf of third parties such as sales taxes, goods and services taxes and value added taxes are not economic benefits which flow to the entity and do not result in increases in equity. Therefore, they are excluded from revenue. Similarly, in an agency relationship, the gross inflows of economic benefits include amounts collected on behalf of the principal and which do not result in increases in equity for the entity. The amounts collected on behalf of the principal are not revenue. Instead, revenue is the amount of commission.

Measurement of revenue

9   **Revenue shall be measured at the fair value of the consideration received or receivable.**[2]

10   The amount of revenue arising on a transaction is usually determined by agreement between the entity and the buyer or user of the asset. It is measured at the fair value of the consideration received or receivable taking into account the amount of any trade discounts and volume rebates allowed by the entity.

11   In most cases, the consideration is in the form of cash or cash equivalents and the amount of revenue is the amount of cash or cash equivalents received or receivable. However, when the inflow of cash or cash equivalents is deferred, the fair value of the consideration may be less than the nominal amount of cash received or receivable. For example, an entity may provide interest-free credit to the buyer or accept a note receivable bearing a below-market interest rate from the buyer as consideration for the sale of goods. When the arrangement effectively constitutes a financing transaction, the fair value of the consideration is determined by discounting all future receipts using an imputed rate of interest. The imputed rate of interest is the more clearly determinable of either:

(a)   the prevailing rate for a similar instrument of an issuer with a similar credit rating; or

(b)   a rate of interest that discounts the nominal amount of the instrument to the current cash sales price of the goods or services.

The difference between the fair value and the nominal amount of the consideration is recognised as interest revenue in accordance with paragraphs 29 and 30 and in accordance with IFRS 9.

12   When goods or services are exchanged or swapped for goods or services which are of a similar nature and value, the exchange is not regarded as a transaction which generates revenue. This is often the case with commodities like oil or milk where suppliers exchange or swap inventories in various locations to fulfil demand on a timely basis in a particular location. When goods are sold or services are rendered in exchange for dissimilar goods or services, the exchange is regarded as a transaction which generates revenue. The revenue is measured at the fair value of the goods or services received, adjusted by the amount of any cash or cash equivalents transferred. When the fair value of the goods or services received cannot be measured reliably, the revenue is measured at the fair value of the goods or services given up, adjusted by the amount of any cash or cash equivalents transferred.

Identification of the transaction

13   The recognition criteria in this Standard are usually applied separately to each transaction. However, in certain circumstances, it is necessary to apply the recognition criteria to the separately identifiable components of a single transaction in order to reflect the substance of the transaction. For example,

---

2   See also SIC-31 *Revenue—Barter Transactions Involving Advertising Services*

when the selling price of a product includes an identifiable amount for subsequent servicing, that amount is deferred and recognised as revenue over the period during which the service is performed. Conversely, the recognition criteria are applied to two or more transactions together when they are linked in such a way that the commercial effect cannot be understood without reference to the series of transactions as a whole. For example, an entity may sell goods and, at the same time, enter into a separate agreement to repurchase the goods at a later date, thus negating the substantive effect of the transaction; in such a case, the two transactions are dealt with together.

Sale of goods

14   Revenue from the sale of goods shall be recognised when all the following conditions have been satisfied:

(a)   the entity has transferred to the buyer the significant risks and rewards of ownership of the goods;

(b)   the entity retains neither continuing managerial involvement to the degree usually associated with ownership nor effective control over the goods sold;

(c)   the amount of revenue can be measured reliably;

(d)   it is probable that the economic benefits associated with the transaction will flow to the entity; and

(e)   the costs incurred or to be incurred in respect of the transaction can be measured reliably.

15   The assessment of when an entity has transferred the significant risks and rewards of ownership to the buyer requires an examination of the circumstances of the transaction. In most cases, the transfer of the risks and rewards of ownership coincides with the transfer of the legal title or the passing of possession to the buyer. This is the case for most retail sales. In other cases, the transfer of risks and rewards of ownership occurs at a different time from the transfer of legal title or the passing of possession.

16   If the entity retains significant risks of ownership, the transaction is not a sale and revenue is not recognised. An entity may retain a significant risk of ownership in a number of ways. Examples of situations in which the entity may retain the significant risks and rewards of ownership are:

(a)   when the entity retains an obligation for unsatisfactory performance not covered by normal warranty provisions;

(b)   when the receipt of the revenue from a particular sale is contingent on the derivation of revenue by the buyer from its sale of the goods;

(c)   when the goods are shipped subject to installation and the installation is a significant part of the contract which has not yet been completed by the entity; and

(d)   when the buyer has the right to rescind the purchase for a reason specified in the sales contract and the entity is uncertain about the probability of return.

17   If an entity retains only an insignificant risk of ownership, the transaction is a sale and revenue is recognised. For example, a seller may retain the legal title to the goods solely to protect the collectibility of the amount due. In such a case, if the entity has transferred the significant risks and rewards of ownership, the transaction is a sale and revenue is recognised. Another example of an entity retaining only an insignificant risk of ownership may be a retail sale when a refund is offered if the customer is not satisfied. Revenue in such cases is recognised at the time of sale provided the seller can reliably estimate future returns and recognises a liability for returns based on previous experience and other relevant factors.

18   Revenue is recognised only when it is probable that the economic benefits associated with the transaction will flow to the entity. In some cases, this may not be probable until the consideration is received or until an uncertainty is removed. For example, it may be uncertain that a foreign governmental authority will grant permission to remit the consideration from a sale in a foreign country. When the permission is granted, the uncertainty is removed and revenue is recognised. However, when an uncertainty arises about the collectibility of an amount already included in revenue, the uncollectible amount or the amount in respect of which recovery has ceased to be probable is recognised as an expense, rather than as an adjustment of the amount of revenue originally recognised.

19   Revenue and expenses that relate to the same transaction or other event are recognised simultaneously; this process is commonly referred to as the matching of revenues and expenses. Expenses, including warranties and other costs to be incurred after the shipment of the goods can normally be measured reliably when the other conditions for the recognition of revenue have been satisfied. However, revenue cannot be recognised when the expenses cannot be measured reliably; in such circumstances, any consideration already received for the sale of the goods is recognised as a liability.

Rendering of services

20   **When the outcome of a transaction involving the rendering of services can be estimated reliably, revenue associated with the transaction shall be recognised by reference to the stage of completion of the transaction at the end of the reporting period. The outcome of a transaction can be estimated reliably when all the following conditions are satisfied:**

(a)   **the amount of revenue can be measured reliably;**

(b)   **it is probable that the economic benefits associated with the transaction will flow to the entity;**

(c)   **the stage of completion of the transaction at the end of the reporting period can be measured reliably; and**

(d)   **the costs incurred for the transaction and the costs to complete the transaction can be measured reliably.[3]**

---

3   See also SIC-27 *Evaluating the Substance of Transactions Involving the Legal Form of a Lease* and SIC-31 *Revenue—Barter Transactions Involving Advertising Services.*

21   The recognition of revenue by reference to the stage of completion of a transaction is often referred to as the percentage of completion method. Under this method, revenue is recognised in the accounting periods in which the services are rendered. The recognition of revenue on this basis provides useful information on the extent of service activity and performance during a period. IAS 11 also requires the recognition of revenue on this basis. The requirements of that Standard are generally applicable to the recognition of revenue and the associated expenses for a transaction involving the rendering of services.

22   Revenue is recognised only when it is probable that the economic benefits associated with the transaction will flow to the entity. However, when an uncertainty arises about the collectibility of an amount already included in revenue, the uncollectible amount, or the amount in respect of which recovery has ceased to be probable, is recognised as an expense, rather than as an adjustment of the amount of revenue originally recognised.

23   An entity is generally able to make reliable estimates after it has agreed to the following with the other parties to the transaction:

      (a)   each party's enforceable rights regarding the service to be provided and received by the parties;

      (b)   the consideration to be exchanged; and

      (c)   the manner and terms of settlement.

      It is also usually necessary for the entity to have an effective internal financial budgeting and reporting system. The entity reviews and, when necessary, revises the estimates of revenue as the service is performed. The need for such revisions does not necessarily indicate that the outcome of the transaction cannot be estimated reliably.

24   The stage of completion of a transaction may be determined by a variety of methods. An entity uses the method that measures reliably the services performed. Depending on the nature of the transaction, the methods may include:

      (a)   surveys of work performed;

      (b)   services performed to date as a percentage of total services to be performed; or

      (c)   the proportion that costs incurred to date bear to the estimated total costs of the transaction. Only costs that reflect services performed to date are included in costs incurred to date. Only costs that reflect services performed or to be performed are included in the estimated total costs of the transaction.

      Progress payments and advances received from customers often do not reflect the services performed.

25   For practical purposes, when services are performed by an indeterminate number of acts over a specified period of time, revenue is recognised on a straight-line basis over the specified period unless there is evidence that some other method better represents the stage of completion. When a specific act is much more significant than any other acts, the recognition of revenue is postponed until the significant act is executed.

26   **When the outcome of the transaction involving the rendering of services cannot be estimated reliably, revenue shall be recognised only to the extent of the expenses recognised that are recoverable.**

27   During the early stages of a transaction, it is often the case that the outcome of the transaction cannot be estimated reliably. Nevertheless, it may be probable that the entity will recover the transaction costs incurred. Therefore, revenue is recognised only to the extent of costs incurred that are expected to be recoverable. As the outcome of the transaction cannot be estimated reliably, no profit is recognised.

28   When the outcome of a transaction cannot be estimated reliably and it is not probable that the costs incurred will be recovered, revenue is not recognised and the costs incurred are recognised as an expense. When the uncertainties that prevented the outcome of the contract being estimated reliably no longer exist, revenue is recognised in accordance with paragraph 20 rather than in accordance with paragraph 26.

Interest, royalties and dividends

29   **Revenue arising from the use by others of entity assets yielding interest, royalties and dividends shall be recognised on the bases set out in paragraph 30 when:**

   (a)   **it is probable that the economic benefits associated with the transaction will flow to the entity; and**

   (b)   **the amount of the revenue can be measured reliably.**

30   **Revenue shall be recognised on the following bases:**

   (a)   **interest shall be recognised using the effective interest method as set out in IAS 39, paragraphs 9 and AG5–AG8;**

   (b)   **royalties shall be recognised on an accrual basis in accordance with the substance of the relevant agreement; and**

   (c)   **dividends shall be recognised when the shareholder's right to receive payment is established.**

31   [Deleted]

32   When unpaid interest has accrued before the acquisition of an interest-bearing investment, the subsequent receipt of interest is allocated between pre-acquisition and post-acquisition periods; only the post-acquisition portion is recognised as revenue.

33 Royalties accrue in accordance with the terms of the relevant agreement and are usually recognised on that basis unless, having regard to the substance of the agreement, it is more appropriate to recognise revenue on some other systematic and rational basis.

34 Revenue is recognised only when it is probable that the economic benefits associated with the transaction will flow to the entity. However, when an uncertainty arises about the collectibility of an amount already included in revenue, the uncollectible amount, or the amount in respect of which recovery has ceased to be probable, is recognised as an expense, rather than as an adjustment of the amount of revenue originally recognised.

Disclosure

35 **An entity shall disclose:**

    (a) **the accounting policies adopted for the recognition of revenue, including the methods adopted to determine the stage of completion of transactions involving the rendering of services;**

    (b) **the amount of each significant category of revenue recognised during the period, including revenue arising from:**

        (i)   **the sale of goods;**

        (ii)   **the rendering of services;**

        (iii) **interest;**

        (iv)   **royalties;**

        (v)   **dividends; and**

    (c) **the amount of revenue arising from exchanges of goods or services included in each significant category of revenue.**

36 An entity discloses any contingent liabilities and contingent assets in accordance with IAS 37 *Provisions, Contingent Liabilities and Contingent Assets*. Contingent liabilities and contingent assets may arise from items such as warranty costs, claims, penalties or possible losses.

Effective date

37 This Standard becomes operative for financial statements covering periods beginning on or after 1 January 1995.

38 *Cost of an Investment in a Subsidiary, Jointly Controlled Entity or Associate* (Amendments to IFRS 1 *First-time Adoption of International Financial Reporting Standards* and IAS 27 *Consolidated and Separate Financial Statements*), issued in May 2008, amended paragraph 32. An entity shall apply that amendment prospectively for annual periods beginning on or after 1 January 2009. Earlier application is permitted. If an entity applies the related amendments in paragraphs 4 and 38A of IAS 27 for an earlier period, it shall apply the amendment in paragraph 32 at the same time.

39 [Deleted]

40   IFRS 9, issued in October 2010, amended paragraphs 6(d) and 11 and deleted paragraph 39. An entity shall apply those amendments when it applies IFRS 9 as issued in October 2010.

41   IFRS 11 *Joint Arrangements*, issued in May 2011, amended paragraph 6(b). An entity shall apply that amendment when it applies IFRS 11.

42   IFRS 13, issued in May 2011, amended the definition of fair value in paragraph 7. An entity shall apply that amendment when it applies IFRS 13.

International Accounting Standard 19

Employee Benefits

In April 2001 the International Accounting Standards Board (IASB) adopted IAS 19 *Employee Benefits*, which had originally been issued by the International Accounting Standards Committee in February 1998. IAS 19 *Employee Benefits* replaced IAS 19 *Accounting for Retirement Benefits in the Financial Statements of Employers* (issued in January 1983). IAS 19 was further amended in 1993 and renamed as IAS 19 *Retirement Benefit Costs*.

The IASB amended the accounting for multi-employer plans and group plans in December 2004. In June 2011 the IASB revised IAS 19; this included eliminating an option that allowed an entity to defer the recognition of changes in net defined benefit liability and amending some of the disclosure requirements for defined benefit plans and multi-employer plans.

Other IFRSs have made minor consequential amendments to IAS 19. They include an amendment to IAS 1 *Presentation of Financial Statements* (as revised in December 2003 and September 2007), IFRS 3 *Business Combinations* (issued March 2004), *Improvements to IFRSs* (issued May 2008), IAS 24 *Related Party Disclosures* (as revised in November 2009) and IFRS 9 *Financial Instruments* (issued November 2009 and October 2010).

CONTENTS

APPENDIX
Amendments to other IFRSs

FOR THE ACCOMPANYING DOCUMENTS LISTED BELOW, SEE PART B OF THIS EDITION

APPROVAL BY THE BOARD OF *ACTUARIAL GAINS AND LOSSES, GROUP PLANS AND DISCLOSURES* (AMENDMENT TO IAS 19) ISSUED IN DECEMBER 2004

APPROVAL BY THE BOARD OF IAS 19 ISSUED IN JUNE 2011

BASIS FOR CONCLUSIONS

APPENDIX
Amendments to the Basis for Conclusions on other IFRSs

DISSENTING OPINIONS

AMENDMENTS TO GUIDANCE ON OTHER IFRSs

TABLE OF CONCORDANCE

International Accounting Standard 19 *Employee Benefits* (IAS 19) is set out in paragraphs 1–174 and the Appendix. All the paragraphs have equal authority but retain the IASC format of the Standard when it was adopted by the IASB. IAS 19 should be read in the context of its objective and the Basis for Conclusions, the *Preface to International Financial Reporting Standards* and the *Conceptual Framework for Financial Reporting*. IAS 8 *Accounting Policies, Changes in Accounting Estimates and Errors* provides a basis for selecting and applying accounting policies in the absence of explicit guidance.

Introduction

IN1 IAS 19 *Employee Benefits* prescribes the accounting and disclosure by employers for employee benefits. The Standard does not deal with reporting by employee benefit plans (see IAS 26 *Accounting and Reporting by Retirement Benefit Plans*).

IN2 The Standard identifies four categories of employee benefits:

(a) short-term employee benefits, such as the following (if expected to be settled wholly before twelve months after the end of the annual reporting period in which the employees render the related services): wages, salaries and social security contributions, paid annual leave and paid sick leave, profit-sharing and bonuses and non-monetary benefits (such as medical care, housing, cars and free or subsidised goods or services) for current employees;

(b) post-employment benefits such as retirement benefits (eg pensions and lump sum payments on retirement), post-employment life insurance and post-employment medical care;

(c) other long-term employee benefits, such as long-service leave or sabbatical leave, jubilee or other long-service benefits, long-term disability benefits; and

(d) termination benefits.

IN3 The Standard requires an entity to recognise short-term employee benefits when an employee has rendered service in exchange for those benefits.

IN4 Post-employment benefit plans are classified as either defined contribution plans or defined benefit plans. The Standard gives specific guidance on the classification of multi-employer plans, state plans and plans with insured benefits.

IN5 Under defined contribution plans, an entity pays fixed contributions into a separate entity (a fund) and will have no legal or constructive obligation to pay further contributions if the fund does not hold sufficient assets to pay all employee benefits relating to employee service in the current and prior periods. The Standard requires an entity to recognise contributions to a defined contribution plan when an employee has rendered service in exchange for those contributions.

IN6 All other post-employment benefit plans are defined benefit plans. Defined benefit plans may be unfunded, or they may be wholly or partly funded. The Standard requires an entity:

(a) to account not only for its legal obligation, but also for any constructive obligation that arises from the entity's practices.

(b) to determine the present value of defined benefit obligations and the fair value of any plan assets with sufficient regularity that the amounts recognised in the financial statements do not differ materially from the amounts that would be determined at the end of the reporting period.

(c) to use the projected unit credit method to measure its obligations and costs.

(d) to attribute benefit to periods of service under the plan's benefit formula, unless an employee's service in later years will lead to a materially higher level of benefit than in earlier years.

(e) to use unbiased and mutually compatible actuarial assumptions about demographic variables (such as employee turnover and mortality) and financial variables (such as future increases in salaries, changes in medical costs and particular changes in state benefits). Financial assumptions should be based on market expectations, at the end of the reporting period, for the period over which the obligations are to be settled.

(f) to determine the discount rate by reference to market yields at the end of the reporting period on high quality corporate bonds (or, in countries where there is no deep market in such bonds, government bonds) of a currency and term consistent with the currency and term of the post-employment benefit obligations.

(g) to deduct the fair value of any plan assets from the carrying amount of the obligation in order to determine the net defined benefit liability (asset). Some reimbursement rights that do not qualify as plan assets are treated in the same way as plan assets, except that they are presented as a separate asset, rather than as a deduction from the obligation.

(h) to limit the carrying amount of a net defined benefit asset so that it does not exceed the economic benefits available in the form of refunds from the plan or reductions in future contributions to the plan.

(i) to recognise all changes in the net defined benefit liability (asset) when they occur, as follows:

(i) service cost and net interest in profit or loss; and

(ii) remeasurements in other comprehensive income.

IN7 Employee benefits other than short-term employee benefits, post-employment benefits and termination benefits are other long-term employee benefits. For other long-term employee benefits, the Standard requires the same recognition and measurement as for post-employment benefits but all changes in the carrying amount of liabilities for other long-term employment benefits are recognised in profit or loss. The Standard does not require specific disclosures about other long-term employee benefits.

IN8 Termination benefits are employee benefits payable as a result of either an entity's decision to terminate an employee's employment before the normal retirement date or an employee's decision to accept an offer of benefits in exchange for the termination of employment. An entity is required to recognise termination benefits at the earlier of when the entity can no longer withdraw an offer of those benefits and when it recognises any related restructuring costs.

International Accounting Standard 19
Employee Benefits

Objective

1   The objective of this Standard is to prescribe the accounting and disclosure for employee benefits. The Standard requires an entity to recognise:

(a)   a liability when an employee has provided service in exchange for employee benefits to be paid in the future; and

(b)   an expense when the entity consumes the economic benefit arising from service provided by an employee in exchange for employee benefits.

Scope

2   **This Standard shall be applied by an employer in accounting for all employee benefits, except those to which IFRS 2 *Share-based Payment* applies.**

3   This Standard does not deal with reporting by employee benefit plans (see IAS 26 *Accounting and Reporting by Retirement Benefit Plans*).

4   The employee benefits to which this Standard applies include those provided:

(a)   under formal plans or other formal agreements between an entity and individual employees, groups of employees or their representatives;

(b)   under legislative requirements, or through industry arrangements, whereby entities are required to contribute to national, state, industry or other multi-employer plans; or

(c)   by those informal practices that give rise to a constructive obligation. Informal practices give rise to a constructive obligation where the entity has no realistic alternative but to pay employee benefits. An example of a constructive obligation is where a change in the entity's informal practices would cause unacceptable damage to its relationship with employees.

5   Employee benefits include:

(a)   short-term employee benefits, such as the following, if expected to be settled wholly before twelve months after the end of the annual reporting period in which the employees render the related services:

(i)   wages, salaries and social security contributions;

(ii)   paid annual leave and paid sick leave;

(iii)   profit-sharing and bonuses; and

(iv)   non-monetary benefits (such as medical care, housing, cars and free or subsidised goods or services) for current employees;

(b)   post-employment benefits, such as the following:

(i)   retirement benefits (eg pensions and lump sum payments on retirement); and

     (ii)   other post-employment benefits, such as post-employment life insurance and post-employment medical care;

  (c)   other long-term employee benefits, such as the following:

     (i)   long-term paid absences such as long-service leave or sabbatical leave;

     (ii)   jubilee or other long-service benefits; and

     (iii)   long-term disability benefits; and

  (d)   termination benefits.

6   Employee benefits include benefits provided either to employees or to their dependants or beneficiaries and may be settled by payments (or the provision of goods or services) made either directly to the employees, to their spouses, children or other dependants or to others, such as insurance companies.

7   An employee may provide services to an entity on a full-time, part-time, permanent, casual or temporary basis. For the purpose of this Standard, employees include directors and other management personnel.

Definitions

8   The following terms are used in this Standard with the meanings specified:

Definitions of employee benefits

Employee benefits are all forms of consideration given by an entity in exchange for service rendered by employees or for the termination of employment.

Short-term employee benefits are employee benefits (other than termination benefits) that are expected to be settled wholly before twelve months after the end of the annual reporting period in which the employees render the related service.

Post-employment benefits are employee benefits (other than termination benefits and short-term employee benefits) that are payable after the completion of employment.

Other long-term employee benefits are all employee benefits other than short-term employee benefits, post-employment benefits and termination benefits.

Termination benefits are employee benefits provided in exchange for the termination of an employee's employment as a result of either:

(a)   an entity's decision to terminate an employee's employment before the normal retirement date; or

(b)   an employee's decision to accept an offer of benefits in exchange for the termination of employment.

Definitions relating to classification of plans

Post-employment benefit plans are formal or informal arrangements under which an entity provides post-employment benefits for one or more employees.

Defined contribution plans are post-employment benefit plans under which an entity pays fixed contributions into a separate entity (a fund) and will have no legal or constructive obligation to pay further contributions if the fund does not hold sufficient assets to pay all employee benefits relating to employee service in the current and prior periods.

Defined benefit plans are post-employment benefit plans other than defined contribution plans.

Multi-employer plans are defined contribution plans (other than state plans) or defined benefit plans (other than state plans) that:

(a)   pool the assets contributed by various entities that are not under common control; and

(b)   use those assets to provide benefits to employees of more than one entity, on the basis that contribution and benefit levels are determined without regard to the identity of the entity that employs the employees.

Definitions relating to the net defined benefit liability (asset)

The *net defined benefit liability (asset)* is the deficit or surplus, adjusted for any effect of limiting a net defined benefit asset to the asset ceiling.

The *deficit or surplus* is:

(a)   the present value of the defined benefit obligation less

(b)   the fair value of plan assets (if any).

The *asset ceiling* is the present value of any economic benefits available in the form of refunds from the plan or reductions in future contributions to the plan.

The *present value of a defined benefit obligation* is the present value, without deducting any plan assets, of expected future payments required to settle the obligation resulting from employee service in the current and prior periods.

Plan assets comprise:

(a)   assets held by a long-term employee benefit fund; and

(b)   qualifying insurance policies.

Assets held by a long-term employee benefit fund are assets (other than non-transferable financial instruments issued by the reporting entity) that:

(a)   are held by an entity (a fund) that is legally separate from the reporting entity and exists solely to pay or fund employee benefits; and

    (b)   are available to be used only to pay or fund employee benefits, are not available to the reporting entity's own creditors (even in bankruptcy), and cannot be returned to the reporting entity, unless either:

        (i)   the remaining assets of the fund are sufficient to meet all the related employee benefit obligations of the plan or the reporting entity; or

        (ii)   the assets are returned to the reporting entity to reimburse it for employee benefits already paid.

A *qualifying insurance policy* is an insurance policy[1] issued by an insurer that is not a related party (as defined in IAS 24 *Related Party Disclosures*) of the reporting entity, if the proceeds of the policy:

    (a)   can be used only to pay or fund employee benefits under a defined benefit plan; and

    (b)   are not available to the reporting entity's own creditors (even in bankruptcy) and cannot be paid to the reporting entity, unless either:

        (i)   the proceeds represent surplus assets that are not needed for the policy to meet all the related employee benefit obligations; or

        (ii)   the proceeds are returned to the reporting entity to reimburse it for employee benefits already paid.

Fair value is the amount for which an asset could be exchanged or a liability settled between knowledgeable, willing parties in an arm's length transaction.

Definitions relating to defined benefit cost

Service cost comprises:

    (a)   *current service cost*, which is the increase in the present value of the defined benefit obligation resulting from employee service in the current period;

    (b)   *past service cost*, which is the change in the present value of the defined benefit obligation for employee service in prior periods, resulting from a plan amendment (the introduction or withdrawal of, or changes to, a defined benefit plan) or a curtailment (a significant reduction by the entity in the number of employees covered by a plan); and

    (c)   any gain or loss on settlement.

Net interest on the net defined benefit liability (asset) is the change during the period in the net defined benefit liability (asset) that arises from the passage of time.

Remeasurements of the net defined benefit liability (asset) comprise:

    (a)   actuarial gains and losses;

    (b)   the return on plan assets, excluding amounts included in net interest on the net defined benefit liability (asset); and

---

1   A qualifying insurance policy is not necessarily an insurance contract, as defined in IFRS 4 *Insurance Contracts*.

(c) any change in the effect of the asset ceiling, excluding amounts included in net interest on the net defined benefit liability (asset).

Actuarial gains and losses are changes in the present value of the defined benefit obligation resulting from:

(a) experience adjustments (the effects of differences between the previous actuarial assumptions and what has actually occurred); and

(b) the effects of changes in actuarial assumptions.

The *return on plan assets* is interest, dividends and other income derived from the plan assets, together with realised and unrealised gains or losses on the plan assets, less:

(a) any costs of managing plan assets; and

(b) any tax payable by the plan itself, other than tax included in the actuarial assumptions used to measure the present value of the defined benefit obligation.

A *settlement* is a transaction that eliminates all further legal or constructive obligations for part or all of the benefits provided under a defined benefit plan, other than a payment of benefits to, or on behalf of, employees that is set out in the terms of the plan and included in the actuarial assumptions.

Short-term employee benefits

9 Short-term employee benefits include items such as the following, if expected to be settled wholly before twelve months after the end of the annual reporting period in which the employees render the related services:

(a) wages, salaries and social security contributions;

(b) paid annual leave and paid sick leave;

(c) profit-sharing and bonuses; and

(d) non-monetary benefits (such as medical care, housing, cars and free or subsidised goods or services) for current employees.

10 An entity need not reclassify a short-term employee benefit if the entity's expectations of the timing of settlement change temporarily. However, if the characteristics of the benefit change (such as a change from a non-accumulating benefit to an accumulating benefit) or if a change in expectations of the timing of settlement is not temporary, then the entity considers whether the benefit still meets the definition of short-term employee benefits.

Recognition and measurement

All short-term employee benefits

11 When an employee has rendered service to an entity during an accounting period, the entity shall recognise the undiscounted amount of short-term employee benefits expected to be paid in exchange for that service:

(a) as a liability (accrued expense), after deducting any amount already paid. If the amount already paid exceeds the undiscounted amount of the benefits, an entity shall recognise that excess as an asset (prepaid expense) to the extent that the prepayment will lead to, for example, a reduction in future payments or a cash refund.

(b)   as an expense, unless another IFRS requires or permits the inclusion of the benefits in the cost of an asset (see, for example, IAS 2 *Inventories* and IAS 16 *Property, Plant and Equipment*).

12   Paragraphs 13, 16 and 19 explain how an entity shall apply paragraph 11 to short-term employee benefits in the form of paid absences and profit-sharing and bonus plans.

Short-term paid absences

13   An entity shall recognise the expected cost of short-term employee benefits in the form of paid absences under paragraph 11 as follows:

(a)   in the case of accumulating paid absences, when the employees render service that increases their entitlement to future paid absences.

(b)   in the case of non-accumulating paid absences, when the absences occur.

14   An entity may pay employees for absence for various reasons including holidays, sickness and short-term disability, maternity or paternity, jury service and military service. Entitlement to paid absences falls into two categories:

(a)   accumulating; and

(b)   non-accumulating.

15   Accumulating paid absences are those that are carried forward and can be used in future periods if the current period's entitlement is not used in full. Accumulating paid absences may be either vesting (in other words, employees are entitled to a cash payment for unused entitlement on leaving the entity) or non-vesting (when employees are not entitled to a cash payment for unused entitlement on leaving). An obligation arises as employees render service that increases their entitlement to future paid absences. The obligation exists, and is recognised, even if the paid absences are non-vesting, although the possibility that employees may leave before they use an accumulated non-vesting entitlement affects the measurement of that obligation.

16   An entity shall measure the expected cost of accumulating paid absences as the additional amount that the entity expects to pay as a result of the unused entitlement that has accumulated at the end of the reporting period.

17   The method specified in the previous paragraph measures the obligation at the amount of the additional payments that are expected to arise solely from the fact that the benefit accumulates. In many cases, an entity may not need to make detailed computations to estimate that there is no material obligation for unused paid absences. For example, a sick leave obligation is likely to be material only if there is a formal or informal understanding that unused paid sick leave may be taken as paid annual leave.

> **Example illustrating paragraphs 16 and 17**
>
> An entity has 100 employees, who are each entitled to five working days of paid sick leave for each year. Unused sick leave may be carried forward for one calendar year. Sick leave is taken first out of the current year's entitlement and then out of any balance brought forward from the previous year (a LIFO basis). At 31 December 20X1 the average unused entitlement is two days per employee. The entity expects, on the basis of experience that is expected to continue, that 92 employees will take no more than five days of paid sick leave in 20X2 and that the remaining eight employees will take an average of six and a half days each.
>
> *The entity expects that it will pay an additional twelve days of sick pay as a result of the unused entitlement that has accumulated at 31 December 20X1 (one and a half days each, for eight employees). Therefore, the entity recognises a liability equal to twelve days of sick pay.*

18 Non-accumulating paid absences do not carry forward: they lapse if the current period's entitlement is not used in full and do not entitle employees to a cash payment for unused entitlement on leaving the entity. This is commonly the case for sick pay (to the extent that unused past entitlement does not increase future entitlement), maternity or paternity leave and paid absences for jury service or military service. An entity recognises no liability or expense until the time of the absence, because employee service does not increase the amount of the benefit.

Profit-sharing and bonus plans

19 **An entity shall recognise the expected cost of profit-sharing and bonus payments under paragraph 11 when, and only when:**

   (a) **the entity has a present legal or constructive obligation to make such payments as a result of past events; and**

   (b) **a reliable estimate of the obligation can be made.**

   A present obligation exists when, and only when, the entity has no realistic alternative but to make the payments.

20 Under some profit-sharing plans, employees receive a share of the profit only if they remain with the entity for a specified period. Such plans create a constructive obligation as employees render service that increases the amount to be paid if they remain in service until the end of the specified period. The measurement of such constructive obligations reflects the possibility that some employees may leave without receiving profit-sharing payments.

> **Example illustrating paragraph 20**
>
> A profit-sharing plan requires an entity to pay a specified proportion of its profit for the year to employees who serve throughout the year. If no employees leave during the year, the total profit-sharing payments for the year will be 3 per cent of profit. The entity estimates that staff turnover will reduce the payments to 2.5 per cent of profit.
>
> *The entity recognises a liability and an expense of 2.5 per cent of profit.*

21   An entity may have no legal obligation to pay a bonus. Nevertheless, in some cases, an entity has a practice of paying bonuses. In such cases, the entity has a constructive obligation because the entity has no realistic alternative but to pay the bonus. The measurement of the constructive obligation reflects the possibility that some employees may leave without receiving a bonus.

22   An entity can make a reliable estimate of its legal or constructive obligation under a profit-sharing or bonus plan when, and only when:

(a)   the formal terms of the plan contain a formula for determining the amount of the benefit;

(b)   the entity determines the amounts to be paid before the financial statements are authorised for issue; or

(c)   past practice gives clear evidence of the amount of the entity's constructive obligation.

23   An obligation under profit-sharing and bonus plans results from employee service and not from a transaction with the entity's owners. Therefore, an entity recognises the cost of profit-sharing and bonus plans not as a distribution of profit but as an expense.

24   If profit-sharing and bonus payments are not expected to be settled wholly before twelve months after the end of the annual reporting period in which the employees render the related service, those payments are other long-term employee benefits (see paragraphs 153–158).

Disclosure

25   Although this Standard does not require specific disclosures about short-term employee benefits, other IFRSs may require disclosures. For example, IAS 24 requires disclosures about employee benefits for key management personnel. IAS 1 *Presentation of Financial Statements* requires disclosure of employee benefits expense.

Post-employment benefits: distinction between defined contribution plans and defined benefit plans

26   Post-employment benefits include items such as the following:

(a)   retirement benefits (eg pensions and lump sum payments on retirement); and

(b)   other post-employment benefits, such as post-employment life insurance and post-employment medical care.

Arrangements whereby an entity provides post-employment benefits are post-employment benefit plans. An entity applies this Standard to all such arrangements whether or not they involve the establishment of a separate entity to receive contributions and to pay benefits.

27   Post-employment benefit plans are classified as either defined contribution plans or defined benefit plans, depending on the economic substance of the plan as derived from its principal terms and conditions.

28   Under defined contribution plans the entity's legal or constructive obligation is limited to the amount that it agrees to contribute to the fund. Thus, the amount of the post-employment benefits received by the employee is determined by the amount of contributions paid by an entity (and perhaps also the employee) to a post-employment benefit plan or to an insurance company, together with investment returns arising from the contributions. In consequence, actuarial risk (that benefits will be less than expected) and investment risk (that assets invested will be insufficient to meet expected benefits) fall, in substance, on the employee.

29   Examples of cases where an entity's obligation is not limited to the amount that it agrees to contribute to the fund are when the entity has a legal or constructive obligation through:

(a)   a plan benefit formula that is not linked solely to the amount of contributions and requires the entity to provide further contributions if assets are insufficient to meet the benefits in the plan benefit formula;

(b)   a guarantee, either indirectly through a plan or directly, of a specified return on contributions; or

(c)   those informal practices that give rise to a constructive obligation. For example, a constructive obligation may arise where an entity has a history of increasing benefits for former employees to keep pace with inflation even where there is no legal obligation to do so.

30   Under defined benefit plans:

(a)   the entity's obligation is to provide the agreed benefits to current and former employees; and

(b)   actuarial risk (that benefits will cost more than expected) and investment risk fall, in substance, on the entity. If actuarial or investment experience are worse than expected, the entity's obligation may be increased.

31   Paragraphs 32–49 explain the distinction between defined contribution plans and defined benefit plans in the context of multi-employer plans, defined benefit plans that share risks between entities under common control, state plans and insured benefits.

Multi-employer plans

32   **An entity shall classify a multi-employer plan as a defined contribution plan or a defined benefit plan under the terms of the plan (including any constructive obligation that goes beyond the formal terms).**

33   **If an entity participates in a multi-employer defined benefit plan, unless paragraph 34 applies, it shall:**

(a)   **account for its proportionate share of the defined benefit obligation, plan assets and cost associated with the plan in the same way as for any other defined benefit plan; and**

(b)   **disclose the information required by paragraphs 135–148 (excluding paragraph 148(d)).**

34   When sufficient information is not available to use defined benefit accounting for a multi-employer defined benefit plan, an entity shall:

(a)   account for the plan in accordance with paragraphs 51 and 52 as if it were a defined contribution plan; and

(b)   disclose the information required by paragraph 148.

35   One example of a multi-employer defined benefit plan is one where:

(a)   the plan is financed on a pay-as-you-go basis: contributions are set at a level that is expected to be sufficient to pay the benefits falling due in the same period; and future benefits earned during the current period will be paid out of future contributions; and

(b)   employees' benefits are determined by the length of their service and the participating entities have no realistic means of withdrawing from the plan without paying a contribution for the benefits earned by employees up to the date of withdrawal. Such a plan creates actuarial risk for the entity: if the ultimate cost of benefits already earned at the end of the reporting period is more than expected, the entity will have either to increase its contributions or to persuade employees to accept a reduction in benefits. Therefore, such a plan is a defined benefit plan.

36   Where sufficient information is available about a multi-employer defined benefit plan, an entity accounts for its proportionate share of the defined benefit obligation, plan assets and post-employment cost associated with the plan in the same way as for any other defined benefit plan. However, an entity may not be able to identify its share of the underlying financial position and performance of the plan with sufficient reliability for accounting purposes. This may occur if:

(a)   the plan exposes the participating entities to actuarial risks associated with the current and former employees of other entities, with the result that there is no consistent and reliable basis for allocating the obligation, plan assets and cost to individual entities participating in the plan; or

(b)   the entity does not have access to sufficient information about the plan to satisfy the requirements of this Standard.

In those cases, an entity accounts for the plan as if it were a defined contribution plan and discloses the information required by paragraph 148.

37   There may be a contractual agreement between the multi-employer plan and its participants that determines how the surplus in the plan will be distributed to the participants (or the deficit funded). A participant in a multi-employer plan with such an agreement that accounts for the plan as a defined contribution plan in accordance with paragraph 34 shall recognise the asset or liability that arises from the contractual agreement and the resulting income or expense in profit or loss.

> **Example illustrating paragraph 37**
>
> An entity participates in a multi-employer defined benefit plan that does not prepare plan valuations on an IAS 19 basis. It therefore accounts for the plan as if it were a defined contribution plan. A non-IAS 19 funding valuation shows a deficit of CU100 million[a] in the plan. The plan has agreed under contract a schedule of contributions with the participating employers in the plan that will eliminate the deficit over the next five years. The entity's total contributions under the contract are CU8 million.
>
> *The entity recognises a liability for the contributions adjusted for the time value of money and an equal expense in profit or loss.*

(a)   In this Standard monetary amounts are denominated in 'currency units (CU)'.

38   Multi-employer plans are distinct from group administration plans. A group administration plan is merely an aggregation of single employer plans combined to allow participating employers to pool their assets for investment purposes and reduce investment management and administration costs, but the claims of different employers are segregated for the sole benefit of their own employees. Group administration plans pose no particular accounting problems because information is readily available to treat them in the same way as any other single employer plan and because such plans do not expose the participating entities to actuarial risks associated with the current and former employees of other entities. The definitions in this Standard require an entity to classify a group administration plan as a defined contribution plan or a defined benefit plan in accordance with the terms of the plan (including any constructive obligation that goes beyond the formal terms).

39   **In determining when to recognise, and how to measure, a liability relating to the wind-up of a multi-employer defined benefit plan, or the entity's withdrawal from a multi-employer defined benefit plan, an entity shall apply IAS 37** *Provisions, Contingent Liabilities and Contingent Assets.*

Defined benefit plans that share risks between entities under common control

40   Defined benefit plans that share risks between entities under common control, for example, a parent and its subsidiaries, are not multi-employer plans.

41   An entity participating in such a plan shall obtain information about the plan as a whole measured in accordance with this Standard on the basis of assumptions that apply to the plan as a whole. If there is a contractual agreement or stated policy for charging to individual group entities the net defined benefit cost for the plan as a whole measured in accordance with this Standard, the entity shall, in its

separate or individual financial statements, recognise the net defined benefit cost so charged. If there is no such agreement or policy, the net defined benefit cost shall be recognised in the separate or individual financial statements of the group entity that is legally the sponsoring employer for the plan. The other group entities shall, in their separate or individual financial statements, recognise a cost equal to their contribution payable for the period.

42   Participation in such a plan is a related party transaction for each individual group entity. An entity shall therefore, in its separate or individual financial statements, disclose the information required by paragraph 149.

State plans

43   **An entity shall account for a state plan in the same way as for a multi-employer plan (see paragraphs 32–39).**

44   State plans are established by legislation to cover all entities (or all entities in a particular category, for example, a specific industry) and are operated by national or local government or by another body (for example, an autonomous agency created specifically for this purpose) that is not subject to control or influence by the reporting entity. Some plans established by an entity provide both compulsory benefits, as a substitute for benefits that would otherwise be covered under a state plan, and additional voluntary benefits. Such plans are not state plans.

45   State plans are characterised as defined benefit or defined contribution, depending on the entity's obligation under the plan. Many state plans are funded on a pay-as-you-go basis: contributions are set at a level that is expected to be sufficient to pay the required benefits falling due in the same period; future benefits earned during the current period will be paid out of future contributions. Nevertheless, in most state plans the entity has no legal or constructive obligation to pay those future benefits: its only obligation is to pay the contributions as they fall due and if the entity ceases to employ members of the state plan, it will have no obligation to pay the benefits earned by its own employees in previous years. For this reason, state plans are normally defined contribution plans. However, when a state plan is a defined benefit plan an entity applies paragraphs 32–39.

Insured benefits

46   **An entity may pay insurance premiums to fund a post-employment benefit plan. The entity shall treat such a plan as a defined contribution plan unless the entity will have (either directly, or indirectly through the plan) a legal or constructive obligation either:**

(a)   **to pay the employee benefits directly when they fall due; or**

(b)   **to pay further amounts if the insurer does not pay all future employee benefits relating to employee service in the current and prior periods.**

If the entity retains such a legal or constructive obligation, the entity shall treat the plan as a defined benefit plan.

47   The benefits insured by an insurance policy need not have a direct or automatic relationship with the entity's obligation for employee benefits. Post-employment benefit plans involving insurance policies are subject to the same distinction between accounting and funding as other funded plans.

48   Where an entity funds a post-employment benefit obligation by contributing to an insurance policy under which the entity (either directly, indirectly through the plan, through the mechanism for setting future premiums or through a related party relationship with the insurer) retains a legal or constructive obligation, the payment of the premiums does not amount to a defined contribution arrangement. It follows that the entity:

(a)   accounts for a qualifying insurance policy as a plan asset (see paragraph 8); and

(b)   recognises other insurance policies as reimbursement rights (if the policies satisfy the criterion in paragraph 116).

49   Where an insurance policy is in the name of a specified plan participant or a group of plan participants and the entity does not have any legal or constructive obligation to cover any loss on the policy, the entity has no obligation to pay benefits to the employees and the insurer has sole responsibility for paying the benefits. The payment of fixed premiums under such contracts is, in substance, the settlement of the employee benefit obligation, rather than an investment to meet the obligation. Consequently, the entity no longer has an asset or a liability. Therefore, an entity treats such payments as contributions to a defined contribution plan.

Post-employment benefits: defined contribution plans

50   Accounting for defined contribution plans is straightforward because the reporting entity's obligation for each period is determined by the amounts to be contributed for that period. Consequently, no actuarial assumptions are required to measure the obligation or the expense and there is no possibility of any actuarial gain or loss. Moreover, the obligations are measured on an undiscounted basis, except where they are not expected to be settled wholly before twelve months after the end of the annual reporting period in which the employees render the related service.

Recognition and measurement

51   **When an employee has rendered service to an entity during a period, the entity shall recognise the contribution payable to a defined contribution plan in exchange for that service:**

(a)   **as a liability (accrued expense), after deducting any contribution already paid. If the contribution already paid exceeds the contribution due for service before the end of the reporting period, an entity shall recognise that excess as an asset (prepaid expense) to the extent that the prepayment will lead to, for example, a reduction in future payments or a cash refund.**

(b)   **as an expense, unless another IFRS requires or permits the inclusion of the contribution in the cost of an asset (see, for example, IAS 2 and IAS 16).**

52 **When contributions to a defined contribution plan are not expected to be settled wholly before twelve months after the end of the annual reporting period in which the employees render the related service, they shall be discounted using the discount rate specified in paragraph 83.**

Disclosure

53 **An entity shall disclose the amount recognised as an expense for defined contribution plans.**

54 Where required by IAS 24 an entity discloses information about contributions to defined contribution plans for key management personnel.

Post-employment benefits: defined benefit plans

55 Accounting for defined benefit plans is complex because actuarial assumptions are required to measure the obligation and the expense and there is a possibility of actuarial gains and losses. Moreover, the obligations are measured on a discounted basis because they may be settled many years after the employees render the related service.

Recognition and measurement

56 Defined benefit plans may be unfunded, or they may be wholly or partly funded by contributions by an entity, and sometimes its employees, into an entity, or fund, that is legally separate from the reporting entity and from which the employee benefits are paid. The payment of funded benefits when they fall due depends not only on the financial position and the investment performance of the fund but also on an entity's ability, and willingness, to make good any shortfall in the fund's assets. Therefore, the entity is, in substance, underwriting the actuarial and investment risks associated with the plan. Consequently, the expense recognised for a defined benefit plan is not necessarily the amount of the contribution due for the period.

57 Accounting by an entity for defined benefit plans involves the following steps:

(a) determining the deficit or surplus. This involves:

(i) using an actuarial technique, the projected unit credit method, to make a reliable estimate of the ultimate cost to the entity of the benefit that employees have earned in return for their service in the current and prior periods (see paragraphs 67–69). This requires an entity to determine how much benefit is attributable to the current and prior periods (see paragraphs 70–74) and to make estimates (actuarial assumptions) about demographic variables (such as employee turnover and mortality) and financial variables (such as future increases in salaries and medical costs) that will affect the cost of the benefit (see paragraphs 75–98).

(ii) discounting that benefit in order to determine the present value of the defined benefit obligation and the current service cost (see paragraphs 67–69 and 83–86).

        (iii)   deducting the fair value of any plan assets (see paragraphs 113–115) from the present value of the defined benefit obligation.

    (b)   determining the amount of the net defined benefit liability (asset) as the amount of the deficit or surplus determined in (a), adjusted for any effect of limiting a net defined benefit asset to the asset ceiling (see paragraph 64).

    (c)   determining amounts to be recognised in profit or loss:

        (i)   current service cost (see paragraphs 70–74).

        (ii)   any past service cost and gain or loss on settlement (see paragraphs 99–112).

        (iii)   net interest on the net defined benefit liability (asset) (see paragraphs 123–126).

    (d)   determining the remeasurements of the net defined benefit liability (asset), to be recognised in other comprehensive income, comprising:

        (i)   actuarial gains and losses (see paragraphs 128 and 129);

        (ii)   return on plan assets, excluding amounts included in net interest on the net defined benefit liability (asset) (see paragraph 130); and

        (iii)   any change in the effect of the asset ceiling (see paragraph 64), excluding amounts included in net interest on the net defined benefit liability (asset).

Where an entity has more than one defined benefit plan, the entity applies these procedures for each material plan separately.

58   **An entity shall determine the net defined benefit liability (asset) with sufficient regularity that the amounts recognised in the financial statements do not differ materially from the amounts that would be determined at the end of the reporting period.**

59   This Standard encourages, but does not require, an entity to involve a qualified actuary in the measurement of all material post-employment benefit obligations. For practical reasons, an entity may request a qualified actuary to carry out a detailed valuation of the obligation before the end of the reporting period. Nevertheless, the results of that valuation are updated for any material transactions and other material changes in circumstances (including changes in market prices and interest rates) up to the end of the reporting period.

60   In some cases, estimates, averages and computational short cuts may provide a reliable approximation of the detailed computations illustrated in this Standard.

Accounting for the constructive obligation

61   An entity shall account not only for its legal obligation under the formal terms of a defined benefit plan, but also for any constructive obligation that arises from the entity's informal practices. Informal practices give rise to a constructive obligation where the entity has no realistic alternative but to pay employee benefits. An example of a constructive obligation is where a change in the entity's informal practices would cause unacceptable damage to its relationship with employees.

62   The formal terms of a defined benefit plan may permit an entity to terminate its obligation under the plan. Nevertheless, it is usually difficult for an entity to terminate its obligation under a plan (without payment) if employees are to be retained. Therefore, in the absence of evidence to the contrary, accounting for post-employment benefits assumes that an entity that is currently promising such benefits will continue to do so over the remaining working lives of employees.

Statement of financial position

63   An entity shall recognise the net defined benefit liability (asset) in the statement of financial position.

64   When an entity has a surplus in a defined benefit plan, it shall measure the net defined benefit asset at the lower of:

    (a)   the surplus in the defined benefit plan; and

    (b)   the asset ceiling, determined using the discount rate specified in paragraph 83.

65   A net defined benefit asset may arise where a defined benefit plan has been overfunded or where actuarial gains have arisen. An entity recognises a net defined benefit asset in such cases because:

    (a)   the entity controls a resource, which is the ability to use the surplus to generate future benefits;

    (b)   that control is a result of past events (contributions paid by the entity and service rendered by the employee); and

    (c)   future economic benefits are available to the entity in the form of a reduction in future contributions or a cash refund, either directly to the entity or indirectly to another plan in deficit. The asset ceiling is the present value of those future benefits.

Recognition and measurement: present value of defined benefit obligations and current service cost

66   The ultimate cost of a defined benefit plan may be influenced by many variables, such as final salaries, employee turnover and mortality, employee contributions and medical cost trends. The ultimate cost of the plan is uncertain and this uncertainty is likely to persist over a long period of time. In order to measure the present value of the post-employment benefit obligations and the related current service cost, it is necessary:

(a)   to apply an actuarial valuation method (see paragraphs 67–69);

(b)   to attribute benefit to periods of service (see paragraphs 70–74); and

(c)   to make actuarial assumptions (see paragraphs 75–98).

Actuarial valuation method

67   **An entity shall use the projected unit credit method to determine the present value of its defined benefit obligations and the related current service cost and, where applicable, past service cost.**

68   The projected unit credit method (sometimes known as the accrued benefit method pro-rated on service or as the benefit/years of service method) sees each period of service as giving rise to an additional unit of benefit entitlement (see paragraphs 70–74) and measures each unit separately to build up the final obligation (see paragraphs 75–98).

Example illustrating paragraph 68

A lump sum benefit is payable on termination of service and equal to 1 per cent of final salary for each year of service. The salary in year 1 is CU10,000 and is assumed to increase at 7 per cent (compound) each year. The discount rate used is 10 per cent per year. The following table shows how the obligation builds up for an employee who is expected to leave at the end of year 5, assuming that there are no changes in actuarial assumptions. For simplicity, this example ignores the additional adjustment needed to reflect the probability that the employee may leave the entity at an earlier or later date.

Year	1	2	3	4	5
	CU	CU	CU	CU	CU
Benefit attributed to:					
– prior years	0	131	262	393	524
– current year (1% of final salary)	131	131	131	131	131
– current and prior years	131	262	393	524	655
Opening obligation	–	89	196	324	476
Interest at 10%	–	9	20	33	48
Current service cost	89	98	108	119	131
Closing obligation	89	196	324	476	655

Note:

1   The opening obligation is the present value of the benefit attributed to prior years.

2   The current service cost is the present value of the benefit attributed to the current year.

3   The closing obligation is the present value of the benefit attributed to current and prior years.

69　An entity discounts the whole of a post-employment benefit obligation, even if part of the obligation is expected to be settled before twelve months after the reporting period.

Attributing benefit to periods of service

70　**In determining the present value of its defined benefit obligations and the related current service cost and, where applicable, past service cost, an entity shall attribute benefit to periods of service under the plan's benefit formula. However, if an employee's service in later years will lead to a materially higher level of benefit than in earlier years, an entity shall attribute benefit on a straight-line basis from:**

(a)　**the date when service by the employee first leads to benefits under the plan (whether or not the benefits are conditional on further service) until**

(b)　**the date when further service by the employee will lead to no material amount of further benefits under the plan, other than from further salary increases.**

71　The projected unit credit method requires an entity to attribute benefit to the current period (in order to determine current service cost) and the current and prior periods (in order to determine the present value of defined benefit obligations). An entity attributes benefit to periods in which the obligation to provide post-employment benefits arises. That obligation arises as employees render services in return for post-employment benefits that an entity expects to pay in future reporting periods. Actuarial techniques allow an entity to measure that obligation with sufficient reliability to justify recognition of a liability.

Examples illustrating paragraph 71

1　A defined benefit plan provides a lump sum benefit of CU100 payable on retirement for each year of service.

　A benefit of CU100 is attributed to each year. The current service cost is the present value of CU100. The present value of the defined benefit obligation is the present value of CU100, multiplied by the number of years of service up to the end of the reporting period.

　If the benefit is payable immediately when the employee leaves the entity, the current service cost and the present value of the defined benefit obligation reflect the date at which the employee is expected to leave. Thus, because of the effect of discounting, they are less than the amounts that would be determined if the employee left at the end of the reporting period.

2　A plan provides a monthly pension of 0.2 per cent of final salary for each year of service. The pension is payable from the age of 65.

　Benefit equal to the present value, at the expected retirement date, of a monthly pension of 0.2 per cent of the estimated final salary payable from the expected retirement date until the expected date of death is attributed to each year of service. The current service cost is the present value of that benefit. The present value of the defined benefit obligation is the present value of monthly pension payments of 0.2 per cent of final salary, multiplied by the number of years of service up to the end of the reporting period. The current service cost and the present value of the defined benefit obligation are discounted because pension payments begin at the age of 65.

---

72   Employee service gives rise to an obligation under a defined benefit plan even if the benefits are conditional on future employment (in other words they are not vested). Employee service before the vesting date gives rise to a constructive obligation because, at the end of each successive reporting period, the amount of future service that an employee will have to render before becoming entitled to the benefit is reduced. In measuring its defined benefit obligation, an entity considers the probability that some employees may not satisfy any vesting requirements. Similarly, although some post-employment benefits, for example, post-employment medical benefits, become payable only if a specified event occurs when an employee is no longer employed, an obligation is created when the employee renders service that will provide entitlement to the benefit if the specified event occurs. The probability that the specified event will occur affects the measurement of the obligation, but does not determine whether the obligation exists.

Examples illustrating paragraph 72

1   A plan pays a benefit of CU100 for each year of service. The benefits vest after ten years of service.

A benefit of CU100 is attributed to each year. In each of the first ten years, the current service cost and the present value of the obligation reflect the probability that the employee may not complete ten years of service.

2   A plan pays a benefit of CU100 for each year of service, excluding service before the age of 25. The benefits vest immediately.

No benefit is attributed to service before the age of 25 because service before that date does not lead to benefits (conditional or unconditional). A benefit of CU100 is attributed to each subsequent year.

---

73   The obligation increases until the date when further service by the employee will lead to no material amount of further benefits. Therefore, all benefit is attributed to periods ending on or before that date. Benefit is attributed to individual accounting periods under the plan's benefit formula. However, if an employee's service in later years will lead to a materially higher level of benefit than in earlier years, an entity attributes benefit on a straight-line basis until the date when further service by the employee will lead to no material amount of further benefits. That is because the employee's service throughout the entire period will ultimately lead to benefit at that higher level.

Examples illustrating paragraph 73

1   A plan pays a lump sum benefit of CU1,000 that vests after ten years of service. The plan provides no further benefit for subsequent service.

A benefit of CU100 (CU1,000 divided by ten) is attributed to each of the first ten years.

The current service cost in each of the first ten years reflects the probability that the employee may not complete ten years of service. No benefit is attributed to subsequent years.

continued...

...continued

Examples illustrating paragraph 73

2   A plan pays a lump sum retirement benefit of CU2,000 to all employees who are still employed at the age of 55 after twenty years of service, or who are still employed at the age of 65, regardless of their length of service.

For employees who join before the age of 35, service first leads to benefits under the plan at the age of 35 (an employee could leave at the age of 30 and return at the age of 33, with no effect on the amount or timing of benefits). Those benefits are conditional on further service. Also, service beyond the age of 55 will lead to no material amount of further benefits. For these employees, the entity attributes benefit of CU100 (CU2,000 divided by twenty) to each year from the age of 35 to the age of 55.

For employees who join between the ages of 35 and 45, service beyond twenty years will lead to no material amount of further benefits. For these employees, the entity attributes benefit of 100 (2,000 divided by twenty) to each of the first twenty years.

For an employee who joins at the age of 55, service beyond ten years will lead to no material amount of further benefits. For this employee, the entity attributes benefit of CU200 (CU2,000 divided by ten) to each of the first ten years.

For all employees, the current service cost and the present value of the obligation reflect the probability that the employee may not complete the necessary period of service.

3   A post-employment medical plan reimburses 40 per cent of an employee's post-employment medical costs if the employee leaves after more than ten and less than twenty years of service and 50 per cent of those costs if the employee leaves after twenty or more years of service.

Under the plan's benefit formula, the entity attributes 4 per cent of the present value of the expected medical costs (40 per cent divided by ten) to each of the first ten years and 1 per cent (10 per cent divided by ten) to each of the second ten years. The current service cost in each year reflects the probability that the employee may not complete the necessary period of service to earn part or all of the benefits. For employees expected to leave within ten years, no benefit is attributed.

4   A post-employment medical plan reimburses 10 per cent of an employee's post-employment medical costs if the employee leaves after more than ten and less than twenty years of service and 50 per cent of those costs if the employee leaves after twenty or more years of service.

Service in later years will lead to a materially higher level of benefit than in earlier years. Therefore, for employees expected to leave after twenty or more years, the entity attributes benefit on a straight-line basis under paragraph 71. Service beyond twenty years will lead to no material amount of further benefits. Therefore, the benefit attributed to each of the first twenty years is 2.5 per cent of the present value of the expected medical costs (50 per cent divided by twenty).

For employees expected to leave between ten and twenty years, the benefit attributed to each of the first ten years is 1 per cent of the present value of the expected medical costs.

For these employees, no benefit is attributed to service between the end of the tenth year and the estimated date of leaving.

For employees expected to leave within ten years, no benefit is attributed.

---

74   Where the amount of a benefit is a constant proportion of final salary for each year of service, future salary increases will affect the amount required to settle the obligation that exists for service before the end of the reporting period, but do not create an additional obligation. Therefore:

(a)   for the purpose of paragraph 70(b), salary increases do not lead to further benefits, even though the amount of the benefits is dependent on final salary; and

(b)   the amount of benefit attributed to each period is a constant proportion of the salary to which the benefit is linked.

Example illustrating paragraph 74

Employees are entitled to a benefit of 3 per cent of final salary for each year of service before the age of 55.

Benefit of 3 per cent of estimated final salary is attributed to each year up to the age of 55. This is the date when further service by the employee will lead to no material amount of further benefits under the plan. No benefit is attributed to service after that age.

Actuarial assumptions

75   **Actuarial assumptions shall be unbiased and mutually compatible.**

76   Actuarial assumptions are an entity's best estimates of the variables that will determine the ultimate cost of providing post-employment benefits. Actuarial assumptions comprise:

(a)   demographic assumptions about the future characteristics of current and former employees (and their dependants) who are eligible for benefits. Demographic assumptions deal with matters such as:

(i)   mortality (see paragraphs 81 and 82);

(ii)   rates of employee turnover, disability and early retirement;

(iii)   the proportion of plan members with dependants who will be eligible for benefits;

(iv)   the proportion of plan members who will select each form of payment option available under the plan terms; and

(v)   claim rates under medical plans.

(b)   financial assumptions, dealing with items such as:

(i)   the discount rate (see paragraphs 83–86);

(ii)   benefit levels, excluding any cost of the benefits to be met by employees, and future salary (see paragraphs 87–95);

(iii)   in the case of medical benefits, future medical costs, including claim handling costs (ie the costs that will be incurred in processing and resolving claims, including legal and adjuster's fees) (see paragraphs 96–98); and

       (iv)   taxes payable by the plan on contributions relating to service before the reporting date or on benefits resulting from that service.

77   Actuarial assumptions are unbiased if they are neither imprudent nor excessively conservative.

78   Actuarial assumptions are mutually compatible if they reflect the economic relationships between factors such as inflation, rates of salary increase and discount rates. For example, all assumptions that depend on a particular inflation level (such as assumptions about interest rates and salary and benefit increases) in any given future period assume the same inflation level in that period.

79   An entity determines the discount rate and other financial assumptions in nominal (stated) terms, unless estimates in real (inflation-adjusted) terms are more reliable, for example, in a hyperinflationary economy (see IAS 29 *Financial Reporting in Hyperinflationary Economies*), or where the benefit is index-linked and there is a deep market in index-linked bonds of the same currency and term.

80   **Financial assumptions shall be based on market expectations, at the end of the reporting period, for the period over which the obligations are to be settled.**

Actuarial assumptions: mortality

81   **An entity shall determine its mortality assumptions by reference to its best estimate of the mortality of plan members both during and after employment.**

82   In order to estimate the ultimate cost of the benefit an entity takes into consideration expected changes in mortality, for example by modifying standard mortality tables with estimates of mortality improvements.

Actuarial assumptions: discount rate

83   **The rate used to discount post-employment benefit obligations (both funded and unfunded) shall be determined by reference to market yields at the end of the reporting period on high quality corporate bonds. In countries where there is no deep market in such bonds, the market yields (at the end of the reporting period) on government bonds shall be used. The currency and term of the corporate bonds or government bonds shall be consistent with the currency and estimated term of the post-employment benefit obligations.**

84   One actuarial assumption that has a material effect is the discount rate. The discount rate reflects the time value of money but not the actuarial or investment risk. Furthermore, the discount rate does not reflect the entity-specific credit risk borne by the entity's creditors, nor does it reflect the risk that future experience may differ from actuarial assumptions.

85   The discount rate reflects the estimated timing of benefit payments. In practice, an entity often achieves this by applying a single weighted average discount rate that reflects the estimated timing and amount of benefit payments and the currency in which the benefits are to be paid.

86   In some cases, there may be no deep market in bonds with a sufficiently long maturity to match the estimated maturity of all the benefit payments. In such cases, an entity uses current market rates of the appropriate term to discount shorter-term payments, and estimates the discount rate for longer maturities by extrapolating current market rates along the yield curve. The total present value of a defined benefit obligation is unlikely to be particularly sensitive to the discount rate applied to the portion of benefits that is payable beyond the final maturity of the available corporate or government bonds.

Actuarial assumptions: salaries, benefits and medical costs

87   An entity shall measure its defined benefit obligations on a basis that reflects:

(a)   the benefits set out in the terms of the plan (or resulting from any constructive obligation that goes beyond those terms) at the end of the reporting period;

(b)   any estimated future salary increases that affect the benefits payable;

(c)   the effect of any limit on the employer's share of the cost of the future benefits;

(d)   contributions from employees or third parties that reduce the ultimate cost to the entity of those benefits; and

(e)   estimated future changes in the level of any state benefits that affect the benefits payable under a defined benefit plan, if, and only if, either:

   (i)   those changes were enacted before the end of the reporting period; or

   (ii)   historical data, or other reliable evidence, indicate that those state benefits will change in some predictable manner, for example, in line with future changes in general price levels or general salary levels.

88   Actuarial assumptions reflect future benefit changes that are set out in the formal terms of a plan (or a constructive obligation that goes beyond those terms) at the end of the reporting period. This is the case if, for example:

(a)   the entity has a history of increasing benefits, for example, to mitigate the effects of inflation, and there is no indication that this practice will change in the future;

(b)   the entity is obliged, by either the formal terms of a plan (or a constructive obligation that goes beyond those terms) or legislation, to use any surplus in the plan for the benefit of plan participants (see paragraph 108(c)); or

(c)   benefits vary in response to a performance target or other criteria. For example, the terms of the plan may state that it will pay reduced benefits or require additional contributions from employees if the plan assets are insufficient. The measurement of the obligation reflects the best estimate of the effect of the performance target or other criteria.

89   Actuarial assumptions do not reflect future benefit changes that are not set out in the formal terms of the plan (or a constructive obligation) at the end of the reporting period. Such changes will result in:

(a)   past service cost, to the extent that they change benefits for service before the change; and

(b)   current service cost for periods after the change, to the extent that they change benefits for service after the change.

90   Estimates of future salary increases take account of inflation, seniority, promotion and other relevant factors, such as supply and demand in the employment market.

91   Some defined benefit plans limit the contributions that an entity is required to pay. The ultimate cost of the benefits takes account of the effect of a limit on contributions. The effect of a limit on contributions is determined over the shorter of:

(a)   the estimated life of the entity; and

(b)   the estimated life of the plan.

92   Some defined benefit plans require employees or third parties to contribute to the cost of the plan. Contributions by employees reduce the cost of the benefits to the entity. An entity considers whether third-party contributions reduce the cost of the benefits to the entity, or are a reimbursement right as described in paragraph 116. Contributions by employees or third parties are either set out in the formal terms of the plan (or arise from a constructive obligation that goes beyond those terms), or are discretionary. Discretionary contributions by employees or third parties reduce service cost upon payment of these contributions to the plan.

93   Contributions from employees or third parties set out in the formal terms of the plan either reduce service cost (if they are linked to service), or reduce remeasurements of the net defined benefit liability (asset) (eg if the contributions are required to reduce a deficit arising from losses on plan assets or actuarial losses). Contributions from employees or third parties in respect of service are attributed to periods of service as a negative benefit in accordance with paragraph 70 (ie the net benefit is attributed in accordance with that paragraph).

94   Changes in employee or third-party contributions in respect of service result in:

(a)   current and past service cost (if changes in employee contributions are not set out in the formal terms of a plan and do not arise from a constructive obligation); or

(b)   actuarial gains and losses (if changes in employee contributions are set out in the formal terms of a plan, or arise from a constructive obligation).

95   Some post-employment benefits are linked to variables such as the level of state retirement benefits or state medical care. The measurement of such benefits reflects the best estimate of such variables, based on historical data and other reliable evidence.

96   **Assumptions about medical costs shall take account of estimated future changes in the cost of medical services, resulting from both inflation and specific changes in medical costs.**

97   Measurement of post-employment medical benefits requires assumptions about the level and frequency of future claims and the cost of meeting those claims. An entity estimates future medical costs on the basis of historical data about the entity's own experience, supplemented where necessary by historical data from other entities, insurance companies, medical providers or other sources. Estimates of future medical costs consider the effect of technological advances, changes in health care utilisation or delivery patterns and changes in the health status of plan participants.

98   The level and frequency of claims is particularly sensitive to the age, health status and sex of employees (and their dependants) and may be sensitive to other factors such as geographical location. Therefore, historical data are adjusted to the extent that the demographic mix of the population differs from that of the population used as a basis for the data. They are also adjusted where there is reliable evidence that historical trends will not continue.

Past service cost and gains and losses on settlement

99   **Before determining past service cost, or a gain or loss on settlement, an entity shall remeasure the net defined benefit liability (asset) using the current fair value of plan assets and current actuarial assumptions (including current market interest rates and other current market prices) reflecting the benefits offered under the plan before the plan amendment, curtailment or settlement.**

100   An entity need not distinguish between past service cost resulting from a plan amendment, past service cost resulting from a curtailment and a gain or loss on settlement if these transactions occur together. In some cases, a plan amendment occurs before a settlement, such as when an entity changes the benefits under the plan and settles the amended benefits later. In those cases an entity recognises past service cost before any gain or loss on settlement.

101   A settlement occurs together with a plan amendment and curtailment if a plan is terminated with the result that the obligation is settled and the plan ceases to exist. However, the termination of a plan is not a settlement if the plan is replaced by a new plan that offers benefits that are, in substance, the same.

Past service cost

102   Past service cost is the change in the present value of the defined benefit obligation resulting from a plan amendment or curtailment.

103   **An entity shall recognise past service cost as an expense at the earlier of the following dates:**

      (a)   **when the plan amendment or curtailment occurs; and**

      (b)   **when the entity recognises related restructuring costs (see IAS 37) or termination benefits (see paragraph 165).**

104   A plan amendment occurs when an entity introduces, or withdraws, a defined benefit plan or changes the benefits payable under an existing defined benefit plan.

105   A curtailment occurs when an entity significantly reduces the number of employees covered by a plan. A curtailment may arise from an isolated event, such as the closing of a plant, discontinuance of an operation or termination or suspension of a plan.

106   Past service cost may be either positive (when benefits are introduced or changed so that the present value of the defined benefit obligation increases) or negative (when benefits are withdrawn or changed so that the present value of the defined benefit obligation decreases).

107   Where an entity reduces benefits payable under an existing defined benefit plan and, at the same time, increases other benefits payable under the plan for the same employees, the entity treats the change as a single net change.

108   Past service cost excludes:

(a)   the effect of differences between actual and previously assumed salary increases on the obligation to pay benefits for service in prior years (there is no past service cost because actuarial assumptions allow for projected salaries);

(b)   underestimates and overestimates of discretionary pension increases when an entity has a constructive obligation to grant such increases (there is no past service cost because actuarial assumptions allow for such increases);

(c)   estimates of benefit improvements that result from actuarial gains or from the return on plan assets that have been recognised in the financial statements if the entity is obliged, by either the formal terms of a plan (or a constructive obligation that goes beyond those terms) or legislation, to use any surplus in the plan for the benefit of plan participants, even if the benefit increase has not yet been formally awarded (there is no past service cost because the resulting increase in the obligation is an actuarial loss, see paragraph 88); and

(d)   the increase in vested benefits (ie benefits that are not conditional on future employment, see paragraph 72) when, in the absence of new or improved benefits, employees complete vesting requirements (there is no past service cost because the entity recognised the estimated cost of benefits as current service cost as the service was rendered).

Gains and losses on settlement

109   The gain or loss on a settlement is the difference between:

(a)   the present value of the defined benefit obligation being settled, as determined on the date of settlement; and

(b)   the settlement price, including any plan assets transferred and any payments made directly by the entity in connection with the settlement.

110   **An entity shall recognise a gain or loss on the settlement of a defined benefit plan when the settlement occurs.**

111 A settlement occurs when an entity enters into a transaction that eliminates all further legal or constructive obligation for part or all of the benefits provided under a defined benefit plan (other than a payment of benefits to, or on behalf of, employees in accordance with the terms of the plan and included in the actuarial assumptions). For example, a one-off transfer of significant employer obligations under the plan to an insurance company through the purchase of an insurance policy is a settlement; a lump sum cash payment, under the terms of the plan, to plan participants in exchange for their rights to receive specified post-employment benefits is not.

112 In some cases, an entity acquires an insurance policy to fund some or all of the employee benefits relating to employee service in the current and prior periods. The acquisition of such a policy is not a settlement if the entity retains a legal or constructive obligation (see paragraph 46) to pay further amounts if the insurer does not pay the employee benefits specified in the insurance policy. Paragraphs 116–119 deal with the recognition and measurement of reimbursement rights under insurance policies that are not plan assets.

Recognition and measurement: plan assets

Fair value of plan assets

113 The fair value of any plan assets is deducted from the present value of the defined benefit obligation in determining the deficit or surplus. When no market price is available, the fair value of plan assets is estimated, for example, by discounting expected future cash flows using a discount rate that reflects both the risk associated with the plan assets and the maturity or expected disposal date of those assets (or, if they have no maturity, the expected period until the settlement of the related obligation).

114 Plan assets exclude unpaid contributions due from the reporting entity to the fund, as well as any non-transferable financial instruments issued by the entity and held by the fund. Plan assets are reduced by any liabilities of the fund that do not relate to employee benefits, for example, trade and other payables and liabilities resulting from derivative financial instruments.

115 Where plan assets include qualifying insurance policies that exactly match the amount and timing of some or all of the benefits payable under the plan, the fair value of those insurance policies is deemed to be the present value of the related obligations (subject to any reduction required if the amounts receivable under the insurance policies are not recoverable in full).

Reimbursements

116 **When, and only when, it is virtually certain that another party will reimburse some or all of the expenditure required to settle a defined benefit obligation, an entity shall:**

(a) **recognise its right to reimbursement as a separate asset. The entity shall measure the asset at fair value.**

(b) **disaggregate and recognise changes in the fair value of its right to reimbursement in the same way as for changes in the fair value of plan** assets (see paragraphs 124 and 125). The components of defined benefit cost recognised in accordance with paragraph 120 may be recognised net of amounts relating to changes in the carrying amount of the right to reimbursement.

117 Sometimes, an entity is able to look to another party, such as an insurer, to pay part or all of the expenditure required to settle a defined benefit obligation. Qualifying insurance policies, as defined in paragraph 8, are plan assets. An entity accounts for qualifying insurance policies in the same way as for all other plan assets and paragraph 116 is not relevant (see paragraphs 46–49 and 115).

118 When an insurance policy held by an entity is not a qualifying insurance policy, that insurance policy is not a plan asset. Paragraph 116 is relevant to such cases: the entity recognises its right to reimbursement under the insurance policy as a separate asset, rather than as a deduction in determining the defined benefit deficit or surplus. Paragraph 140(b) requires the entity to disclose a brief description of the link between the reimbursement right and the related obligation.

119 If the right to reimbursement arises under an insurance policy that exactly matches the amount and timing of some or all of the benefits payable under a defined benefit plan, the fair value of the reimbursement right is deemed to be the present value of the related obligation (subject to any reduction required if the reimbursement is not recoverable in full).

Components of defined benefit cost

120 An entity shall recognise the components of defined benefit cost, except to the extent that another IFRS requires or permits their inclusion in the cost of an asset, as follows:

(a) service cost (see paragraphs 66–112) in profit or loss;

(b) net interest on the net defined benefit liability (asset) (see paragraphs 123–126) in profit or loss; and

(c) remeasurements of the net defined benefit liability (asset) (see paragraphs 127–130) in other comprehensive income.

121 Other IFRSs require the inclusion of some employee benefit costs within the cost of assets, such as inventories and property, plant and equipment (see IAS 2 and IAS 16). Any post-employment benefit costs included in the cost of such assets include the appropriate proportion of the components listed in paragraph 120.

122 Remeasurements of the net defined benefit liability (asset) recognised in other comprehensive income shall not be reclassified to profit or loss in a subsequent period. However, the entity may transfer those amounts recognised in other comprehensive income within equity.

Net interest on the net defined benefit liability (asset)

123 **Net interest on the net defined benefit liability (asset) shall be determined by multiplying the net defined benefit liability (asset) by the discount rate specified in paragraph 83, both as determined at the start of the annual reporting period, taking account of any changes in the net defined benefit liability (asset) during the period as a result of contribution and benefit payments.**

124 Net interest on the net defined benefit liability (asset) can be viewed as comprising interest income on plan assets, interest cost on the defined benefit obligation and interest on the effect of the asset ceiling mentioned in paragraph 64.

125 Interest income on plan assets is a component of the return on plan assets, and is determined by multiplying the fair value of the plan assets by the discount rate specified in paragraph 83, both as determined at the start of the annual reporting period, taking account of any changes in the plan assets held during the period as a result of contributions and benefit payments. The difference between the interest income on plan assets and the return on plan assets is included in the remeasurement of the net defined benefit liability (asset).

126 Interest on the effect of the asset ceiling is part of the total change in the effect of the asset ceiling, and is determined by multiplying the effect of the asset ceiling by the discount rate specified in paragraph 83, both as determined at the start of the annual reporting period. The difference between that amount and the total change in the effect of the asset ceiling is included in the remeasurement of the net defined benefit liability (asset).

Remeasurements of the net defined benefit liability (asset)

127 Remeasurements of the net defined benefit liability (asset) comprise:

    (a)   actuarial gains and losses (see paragraphs 128 and 129);

    (b)   the return on plan assets (see paragraph 130), excluding amounts included in net interest on the net defined benefit liability (asset) (see paragraph 125); and

    (c)   any change in the effect of the asset ceiling, excluding amounts included in net interest on the net defined benefit liability (asset) (see paragraph 126).

128 Actuarial gains and losses result from increases or decreases in the present value of the defined benefit obligation because of changes in actuarial assumptions and experience adjustments. Causes of actuarial gains and losses include, for example:

    (a)   unexpectedly high or low rates of employee turnover, early retirement or mortality or of increases in salaries, benefits (if the formal or constructive terms of a plan provide for inflationary benefit increases) or medical costs;

    (b)   the effect of changes to assumptions concerning benefit payment options;

    (c)   the effect of changes in estimates of future employee turnover, early retirement or mortality or of increases in salaries, benefits (if the formal or constructive terms of a plan provide for inflationary benefit increases) or medical costs; and

    (d)   the effect of changes in the discount rate.

129　Actuarial gains and losses do not include changes in the present value of the defined benefit obligation because of the introduction, amendment, curtailment or settlement of the defined benefit plan, or changes to the benefits payable under the defined benefit plan. Such changes result in past service cost or gains or losses on settlement.

130　In determining the return on plan assets, an entity deducts the costs of managing the plan assets and any tax payable by the plan itself, other than tax included in the actuarial assumptions used to measure the defined benefit obligation (paragraph 76). Other administration costs are not deducted from the return on plan assets.

Presentation

Offset

131　**An entity shall offset an asset relating to one plan against a liability relating to another plan when, and only when, the entity:**

(a)　**has a legally enforceable right to use a surplus in one plan to settle obligations under the other plan; and**

(b)　**intends either to settle the obligations on a net basis, or to realise the surplus in one plan and settle its obligation under the other plan simultaneously.**

132　The offsetting criteria are similar to those established for financial instruments in IAS 32 *Financial Instruments: Presentation*.

Current/non-current distinction

133　Some entities distinguish current assets and liabilities from non-current assets and liabilities. This Standard does not specify whether an entity should distinguish current and non-current portions of assets and liabilities arising from post-employment benefits.

Components of defined benefit cost

134　Paragraph 120 requires an entity to recognise service cost and net interest on the net defined benefit liability (asset) in profit or loss. This Standard does not specify how an entity should present service cost and net interest on the net defined benefit liability (asset). An entity presents those components in accordance with IAS 1.

Disclosure

135　**An entity shall disclose information that:**

(a)　**explains the characteristics of its defined benefit plans and risks associated with them (see paragraph 139);**

(b)　**identifies and explains the amounts in its financial statements arising from its defined benefit plans (see paragraphs 140–144); and**

(c)　**describes how its defined benefit plans may affect the amount, timing and uncertainty of the entity's future cash flows (see paragraphs 145–147).**

136   To meet the objectives in paragraph 135, an entity shall consider all the following:

(a)   the level of detail necessary to satisfy the disclosure requirements;

(b)   how much emphasis to place on each of the various requirements;

(c)   how much aggregation or disaggregation to undertake; and

(d)   whether users of financial statements need additional information to evaluate the quantitative information disclosed.

137   If the disclosures provided in accordance with the requirements in this Standard and other IFRSs are insufficient to meet the objectives in paragraph 135, an entity shall disclose additional information necessary to meet those objectives. For example, an entity may present an analysis of the present value of the defined benefit obligation that distinguishes the nature, characteristics and risks of the obligation. Such a disclosure could distinguish:

(a)   between amounts owing to active members, deferred members, and pensioners.

(b)   between vested benefits and accrued but not vested benefits.

(c)   between conditional benefits, amounts attributable to future salary increases and other benefits.

138   An entity shall assess whether all or some disclosures should be disaggregated to distinguish plans or groups of plans with materially different risks. For example, an entity may disaggregate disclosure about plans showing one or more of the following features:

(a)   different geographical locations.

(b)   different characteristics such as flat salary pension plans, final salary pension plans or post-employment medical plans.

(c)   different regulatory environments.

(d)   different reporting segments.

(e)   different funding arrangements (eg wholly unfunded, wholly or partly funded).

Characteristics of defined benefit plans and risks associated with them

139   An entity shall disclose:

(a)   information about the characteristics of its defined benefit plans, including:

(i)   the nature of the benefits provided by the plan (eg final salary defined benefit plan or contribution-based plan with guarantee).

(ii)   a description of the regulatory framework in which the plan operates, for example the level of any minimum funding requirements, and any effect of the regulatory framework on the plan, such as the asset ceiling (see paragraph 64).

    (iii) a description of any other entity's responsibilities for the governance of the plan, for example responsibilities of trustees or of board members of the plan.

  (b) a description of the risks to which the plan exposes the entity, focused on any unusual, entity-specific or plan-specific risks, and of any significant concentrations of risk. For example, if plan assets are invested primarily in one class of investments, eg property, the plan may expose the entity to a concentration of property market risk.

  (c) a description of any plan amendments, curtailments and settlements.

Explanation of amounts in the financial statements

140   An entity shall provide a reconciliation from the opening balance to the closing balance for each of the following, if applicable:

  (a) the net defined benefit liability (asset), showing separate reconciliations for:

    (i) plan assets.

    (ii) the present value of the defined benefit obligation.

    (iii) the effect of the asset ceiling.

  (b) any reimbursement rights. An entity shall also describe the relationship between any reimbursement right and the related obligation.

141   Each reconciliation listed in paragraph 140 shall show each of the following, if applicable:

  (a) current service cost.

  (b) interest income or expense.

  (c) remeasurements of the net defined benefit liability (asset), showing separately:

    (i) the return on plan assets, excluding amounts included in interest in (b).

    (ii) actuarial gains and losses arising from changes in demographic assumptions (see paragraph 76(a)).

    (iii) actuarial gains and losses arising from changes in financial assumptions (see paragraph 76(b)).

    (iv) changes in the effect of limiting a net defined benefit asset to the asset ceiling, excluding amounts included in interest in (b). An entity shall also disclose how it determined the maximum economic benefit available, ie whether those benefits would be in the form of refunds, reductions in future contributions or a combination of both.

  (d) past service cost and gains and losses arising from settlements. As permitted by paragraph 100, past service cost and gains and losses arising from settlements need not be distinguished if they occur together.

(e)   the effect of changes in foreign exchange rates.

(f)   contributions to the plan, showing separately those by the employer and by plan participants.

(g)   payments from the plan, showing separately the amount paid in respect of any settlements.

(h)   the effects of business combinations and disposals.

142   An entity shall disaggregate the fair value of the plan assets into classes that distinguish the nature and risks of those assets, subdividing each class of plan asset into those that have a quoted market price in an active market (as defined in IFRS 13 *Fair Value Measurement*[2]) and those that do not. For example, and considering the level of disclosure discussed in paragraph 136, an entity could distinguish between:

(a)   cash and cash equivalents;

(b)   equity instruments (segregated by industry type, company size, geography etc);

(c)   debt instruments (segregated by type of issuer, credit quality, geography etc);

(d)   real estate (segregated by geography etc);

(e)   derivatives (segregated by type of underlying risk in the contract, for example, interest rate contracts, foreign exchange contracts, equity contracts, credit contracts, longevity swaps etc);

(f)   investment funds (segregated by type of fund);

(g)   asset-backed securities; and

(h)   structured debt.

143   An entity shall disclose the fair value of the entity's own transferable financial instruments held as plan assets, and the fair value of plan assets that are property occupied by, or other assets used by, the entity.

144   An entity shall disclose the significant actuarial assumptions used to determine the present value of the defined benefit obligation (see paragraph 76). Such disclosure shall be in absolute terms (eg as an absolute percentage, and not just as a margin between different percentages and other variables). When an entity provides disclosures in total for a grouping of plans, it shall provide such disclosures in the form of weighted averages or relatively narrow ranges.

Amount, timing and uncertainty of future cash flows

145   An entity shall disclose:

(a)   a sensitivity analysis for each significant actuarial assumption (as disclosed under paragraph 144) as of the end of the reporting period, showing how

---

2   If an entity has not yet applied IFRS 13, it may refer to paragraph AG71 of IAS 39 *Financial Instruments: Recognition and Measurement*, or paragraph B.5.4.3 of IFRS 9 *Financial Instruments* (October 2010), if applicable.

the defined benefit obligation would have been affected by changes in the relevant actuarial assumption that were reasonably possible at that date.

(b)   the methods and assumptions used in preparing the sensitivity analyses required by (a) and the limitations of those methods.

(c)   changes from the previous period in the methods and assumptions used in preparing the sensitivity analyses, and the reasons for such changes.

146   An entity shall disclose a description of any asset-liability matching strategies used by the plan or the entity, including the use of annuities and other techniques, such as longevity swaps, to manage risk.

147   To provide an indication of the effect of the defined benefit plan on the entity's future cash flows, an entity shall disclose:

(a)   a description of any funding arrangements and funding policy that affect future contributions.

(b)   the expected contributions to the plan for the next annual reporting period.

(c)   information about the maturity profile of the defined benefit obligation. This will include the weighted average duration of the defined benefit obligation and may include other information about the distribution of the timing of benefit payments, such as a maturity analysis of the benefit payments.

Multi-employer plans

148   If an entity participates in a multi-employer defined benefit plan, it shall disclose:

(a)   a description of the funding arrangements, including the method used to determine the entity's rate of contributions and any minimum funding requirements.

(b)   a description of the extent to which the entity can be liable to the plan for other entities' obligations under the terms and conditions of the multi-employer plan.

(c)   a description of any agreed allocation of a deficit or surplus on:

(i)   wind-up of the plan; or

(ii)   the entity's withdrawal from the plan.

(d)   if the entity accounts for that plan as if it were a defined contribution plan in accordance with paragraph 34, it shall disclose the following, in addition to the information required by (a)–(c) and instead of the information required by paragraphs 139–147:

(i)   the fact that the plan is a defined benefit plan.

(ii)   the reason why sufficient information is not available to enable the entity to account for the plan as a defined benefit plan.

(iii) the expected contributions to the plan for the next annual reporting period.

  (iv) information about any deficit or surplus in the plan that may affect the amount of future contributions, including the basis used to determine that deficit or surplus and the implications, if any, for the entity.

  (v) an indication of the level of participation of the entity in the plan compared with other participating entities. Examples of measures that might provide such an indication include the entity's proportion of the total contributions to the plan or the entity's proportion of the total number of active members, retired members, and former members entitled to benefits, if that information is available.

Defined benefit plans that share risks between entities under common control

149 If an entity participates in a defined benefit plan that shares risks between entities under common control, it shall disclose:

  (a) the contractual agreement or stated policy for charging the net defined benefit cost or the fact that there is no such policy.

  (b) the policy for determining the contribution to be paid by the entity.

  (c) if the entity accounts for an allocation of the net defined benefit cost as noted in paragraph 41, all the information about the plan as a whole required by paragraphs 135–147.

  (d) if the entity accounts for the contribution payable for the period as noted in paragraph 41, the information about the plan as a whole required by paragraphs 135–137, 139, 142–144 and 147(a) and (b).

150 The information required by paragraph 149(c) and (d) can be disclosed by cross-reference to disclosures in another group entity's financial statements if:

  (a) that group entity's financial statements separately identify and disclose the information required about the plan; and

  (b) that group entity's financial statements are available to users of the financial statements on the same terms as the financial statements of the entity and at the same time as, or earlier than, the financial statements of the entity.

Disclosure requirements in other IFRSs

151 Where required by IAS 24 an entity discloses information about:

  (a) related party transactions with post-employment benefit plans; and

  (b) post-employment benefits for key management personnel.

152 Where required by IAS 37 an entity discloses information about contingent liabilities arising from post-employment benefit obligations.

Other long-term employee benefits

153 Other long-term employee benefits include items such as the following, if not expected to be settled wholly before twelve months after the end of the annual reporting period in which the employees render the related service:

(a) long-term paid absences such as long-service or sabbatical leave;

(b) jubilee or other long-service benefits;

(c) long-term disability benefits;

(d) profit-sharing and bonuses; and

(e) deferred remuneration.

154 The measurement of other long-term employee benefits is not usually subject to the same degree of uncertainty as the measurement of post-employment benefits. For this reason, this Standard requires a simplified method of accounting for other long-term employee benefits. Unlike the accounting required for post-employment benefits, this method does not recognise remeasurements in other comprehensive income.

Recognition and measurement

155 **In recognising and measuring the surplus or deficit in an other long-term employee benefit plan, an entity shall apply paragraphs 56–98 and 113–115. An entity shall apply paragraphs 116–119 in recognising and measuring any reimbursement right.**

156 **For other long-term employee benefits, an entity shall recognise the net total of the following amounts in profit or loss, except to the extent that another IFRS requires or permits their inclusion in the cost of an asset:**

(a) **service cost (see paragraphs 66–112);**

(b) **net interest on the net defined benefit liability (asset) (see paragraphs 123–126); and**

(c) **remeasurements of the net defined benefit liability (asset) (see paragraphs 127–130).**

157 One form of other long-term employee benefit is long-term disability benefit. If the level of benefit depends on the length of service, an obligation arises when the service is rendered. Measurement of that obligation reflects the probability that payment will be required and the length of time for which payment is expected to be made. If the level of benefit is the same for any disabled employee regardless of years of service, the expected cost of those benefits is recognised when an event occurs that causes a long-term disability.

Disclosure

158 Although this Standard does not require specific disclosures about other long-term employee benefits, other IFRSs may require disclosures. For example, IAS 24 requires disclosures about employee benefits for key management personnel. IAS 1 requires disclosure of employee benefits expense.

Termination benefits

159 This Standard deals with termination benefits separately from other employee benefits because the event that gives rise to an obligation is the termination of employment rather than employee service. Termination benefits result from either an entity's decision to terminate the employment or an employee's decision to accept an entity's offer of benefits in exchange for termination of employment.

160 Termination benefits do not include employee benefits resulting from termination of employment at the request of the employee without an entity's offer, or as a result of mandatory retirement requirements, because those benefits are post-employment benefits. Some entities provide a lower level of benefit for termination of employment at the request of the employee (in substance, a post-employment benefit) than for termination of employment at the request of the entity. The difference between the benefit provided for termination of employment at the request of the employee and a higher benefit provided at the request of the entity is a termination benefit.

161 The form of the employee benefit does not determine whether it is provided in exchange for service or in exchange for termination of the employee's employment. Termination benefits are typically lump sum payments, but sometimes also include:

(a) enhancement of post-employment benefits, either indirectly through an employee benefit plan or directly.

(b) salary until the end of a specified notice period if the employee renders no further service that provides economic benefits to the entity.

162 Indicators that an employee benefit is provided in exchange for services include the following:

(a) the benefit is conditional on future service being provided (including benefits that increase if further service is provided).

(b) the benefit is provided in accordance with the terms of an employee benefit plan.

163 Some termination benefits are provided in accordance with the terms of an existing employee benefit plan. For example, they may be specified by statute, employment contract or union agreement, or may be implied as a result of the employer's past practice of providing similar benefits. As another example, if an entity makes an offer of benefits available for more than a short period, or there is more than a short period between the offer and the expected date of actual termination, the entity considers whether it has established a new employee

benefit plan and hence whether the benefits offered under that plan are termination benefits or post-employment benefits. Employee benefits provided in accordance with the terms of an employee benefit plan are termination benefits if they both result from an entity's decision to terminate an employee's employment and are not conditional on future service being provided.

164 Some employee benefits are provided regardless of the reason for the employee's departure. The payment of such benefits is certain (subject to any vesting or minimum service requirements) but the timing of their payment is uncertain. Although such benefits are described in some jurisdictions as termination indemnities or termination gratuities, they are post-employment benefits rather than termination benefits, and an entity accounts for them as post-employment benefits.

Recognition

165 **An entity shall recognise a liability and expense for termination benefits at the earlier of the following dates:**

(a) **when the entity can no longer withdraw the offer of those benefits; and**

(b) **when the entity recognises costs for a restructuring that is within the scope of IAS 37 and involves the payment of termination benefits.**

166 For termination benefits payable as a result of an employee's decision to accept an offer of benefits in exchange for the termination of employment, the time when an entity can no longer withdraw the offer of termination benefits is the earlier of:

(a) when the employee accepts the offer; and

(b) when a restriction (eg a legal, regulatory or contractual requirement or other restriction) on the entity's ability to withdraw the offer takes effect. This would be when the offer is made, if the restriction existed at the time of the offer.

167 For termination benefits payable as a result of an entity's decision to terminate an employee's employment, the entity can no longer withdraw the offer when the entity has communicated to the affected employees a plan of termination meeting all of the following criteria:

(a) Actions required to complete the plan indicate that it is unlikely that significant changes to the plan will be made.

(b) The plan identifies the number of employees whose employment is to be terminated, their job classifications or functions and their locations (but the plan need not identify each individual employee) and the expected completion date.

(c) The plan establishes the termination benefits that employees will receive in sufficient detail that employees can determine the type and amount of benefits they will receive when their employment is terminated.

168 When an entity recognises termination benefits, the entity may also have to account for a plan amendment or a curtailment of other employee benefits (see paragraph 103).

Measurement

169 **An entity shall measure termination benefits on initial recognition, and shall measure and recognise subsequent changes, in accordance with the nature of the employee benefit, provided that if the termination benefits are an enhancement to post-employment benefits, the entity shall apply the requirements for post-employment benefits. Otherwise:**

    (a) **if the termination benefits are expected to be settled wholly before twelve months after the end of the annual reporting period in which the termination benefit is recognised, the entity shall apply the requirements for short-term employee benefits.**

    (b) **if the termination benefits are not expected to be settled wholly before twelve months after the end of the annual reporting period, the entity shall apply the requirements for other long-term employee benefits.**

170 Because termination benefits are not provided in exchange for service, paragraphs 70–74 relating to the attribution of the benefit to periods of service are not relevant.

Example illustrating paragraphs 159–170

Background

As a result of a recent acquisition, an entity plans to close a factory in ten months and, at that time, terminate the employment of all of the remaining employees at the factory. Because the entity needs the expertise of the employees at the factory to complete some contracts, it announces a plan of termination as follows.

Each employee who stays and renders service until the closure of the factory will receive on the termination date a cash payment of CU30,000. Employees leaving before closure of the factory will receive CU10,000.

There are 120 employees at the factory. At the time of announcing the plan, the entity expects 20 of them to leave before closure. Therefore, the total expected cash outflows under the plan are CU3,200,000 (ie 20 × CU10,000 + 100 × CU30,000). As required by paragraph 160, the entity accounts for benefits provided in exchange for termination of employment as termination benefits and accounts for benefits provided in exchange for services as short-term employee benefits.

continued...

...continued

Example illustrating paragraphs 159–170

Termination benefits

The benefit provided in exchange for termination of employment is CU10,000. This is the amount that an entity would have to pay for terminating the employment regardless of whether the employees stay and render service until closure of the factory or they leave before closure. Even though the employees can leave before closure, the termination of all employees' employment is a result of the entity's decision to close the factory and terminate their employment (ie all employees will leave employment when the factory closes). Therefore the entity recognises a liability of CU1,200,000 (ie 120 × CU10,000) for the termination benefits provided in accordance with the employee benefit plan at the earlier of when the plan of termination is announced and when the entity recognises the restructuring costs associated with the closure of the factory.

Benefits provided in exchange for service

The incremental benefits that employees will receive if they provide services for the full ten-month period are in exchange for services provided over that period. The entity accounts for them as short-term employee benefits because the entity expects to settle them before twelve months after the end of the annual reporting period. In this example, discounting is not required, so an expense of CU200,000 (ie CU2,000,000 ÷ 10) is recognised in each month during the service period of ten months, with a corresponding increase in the carrying amount of the liability.

Disclosure

171 Although this Standard does not require specific disclosures about termination benefits, other IFRSs may require disclosures. For example, IAS 24 requires disclosures about employee benefits for key management personnel. IAS 1 requires disclosure of employee benefits expense.

Transition and effective date

172 An entity shall apply this Standard for annual periods beginning on or after 1 January 2013. Earlier application is permitted. If an entity applies this Standard for an earlier period, it shall disclose that fact.

173 An entity shall apply this Standard retrospectively, in accordance with IAS 8 *Accounting Policies, Changes in Accounting Estimates and Errors*, except that:

(a) an entity need not adjust the carrying amount of assets outside the scope of this Standard for changes in employee benefit costs that were included in the carrying amount before the date of initial application. The date of initial application is the beginning of the earliest prior period presented in the first financial statements in which the entity adopts this Standard.

(b)   in financial statements for periods beginning before 1 January 2014, an entity need not present comparative information for the disclosures required by paragraph 145 about the sensitivity of the defined benefit obligation.

174   IFRS 13, issued in May 2011, amended the definition of fair value in paragraph 8 and amended paragraph 113. An entity shall apply those amendments when it applies IFRS 13.

Appendix
Amendments to other IFRSs

This appendix sets out amendments to other IFRSs that are a consequence of the Board amending IAS 19 in June 2011. An entity shall apply these amendments when it applies IAS 19 as amended. Amended paragraphs are shown with new text underlined and deleted text struck through.

* * * * *

The amendments contained in this appendix when this Standard was amended in 2011 have been incorporated into the relevant IFRSs published in this volume.

International Accounting Standard 20

Accounting for Government Grants and Disclosure of Government Assistance

In April 2001 the International Accounting Standards Board (IASB) adopted IAS 20 *Accounting for Government Grants and Disclosure of Government Assistance*, which had originally been issued by the International Accounting Standards Committee in April 1983.

Other IFRSs have made minor consequential amendments to IAS 20. They include an amendment to IAS 1 *Presentation of Financial Statements* (as revised in September 2007), *Improvements to IFRSs* (issued May 2008) and IFRS 9 *Financial Instruments* (issued October 2010).

CONTENTS

from paragraph

INTERNATIONAL ACCOUNTING STANDARD 20
ACCOUNTING FOR GOVERNMENT GRANTS AND DISCLOSURE OF GOVERNMENT ASSISTANCE

FOR THE ACCOMPANYING DOCUMENTS LISTED BELOW, SEE PART B OF THIS EDITION

BASIS FOR CONCLUSIONS

International Accounting Standard 20 *Accounting for Government Grants and Disclosure of Government Assistance* (IAS 20) is set out in paragraphs 1–46. All the paragraphs have equal authority but retain the IASC format of the Standard when it was adopted by the IASB. IAS 20 should be read in the context of the Basis for Conclusions, the *Preface to International Financial Reporting Standards* and the *Conceptual Framework for Financial Reporting*. IAS 8 *Accounting Policies, Changes in Accounting Estimates and Errors* provides a basis for selecting and applying accounting policies in the absence of explicit guidance.

International Accounting Standard 20
Accounting for Government Grants and Disclosure of Government Assistance[1]

Scope

1   This Standard shall be applied in accounting for, and in the disclosure of, government grants and in the disclosure of other forms of government assistance.

2   This Standard does not deal with:

    (a)   the special problems arising in accounting for government grants in financial statements reflecting the effects of changing prices or in supplementary information of a similar nature.

    (b)   government assistance that is provided for an entity in the form of benefits that are available in determining taxable profit or tax loss, or are determined or limited on the basis of income tax liability. Examples of such benefits are income tax holidays, investment tax credits, accelerated depreciation allowances and reduced income tax rates.

    (c)   government participation in the ownership of the entity.

    (d)   government grants covered by IAS 41 *Agriculture*.

Definitions

3   The following terms are used in this Standard with the meanings specified:

Government refers to government, government agencies and similar bodies whether local, national or international.

Government assistance is action by government designed to provide an economic benefit specific to an entity or range of entities qualifying under certain criteria. Government assistance for the purpose of this Standard does not include benefits provided only indirectly through action affecting general trading conditions, such as the provision of infrastructure in development areas or the imposition of trading constraints on competitors.

Government grants are assistance by government in the form of transfers of resources to an entity in return for past or future compliance with certain conditions relating to the operating activities of the entity. They exclude those forms of government assistance which cannot reasonably have a value placed upon them and transactions with government which cannot be distinguished from the normal trading transactions of the entity.[2]

---

1   As part of *Improvements to IFRSs* issued in May 2008 the Board amended terminology used in this Standard to be consistent with other IFRSs as follows: (a) 'taxable income' was amended to 'taxable profit or tax loss', (b) 'recognised as income/expense' was amended to 'recognised in profit or loss', (c) 'credited directly to shareholders' interests/equity' was amended to 'recognised outside profit or loss', and (d) 'revision to an accounting estimate' was amended to 'change in accounting estimate'.

2   See also SIC-10 *Government Assistance—No Specific Relation to Operating Activities*.

Grants related to assets are government grants whose primary condition is that an entity qualifying for them should purchase, construct or otherwise acquire long-term assets. Subsidiary conditions may also be attached restricting the type or location of the assets or the periods during which they are to be acquired or held.

Grants related to income are government grants other than those related to assets.

Forgivable loans are loans which the lender undertakes to waive repayment of under certain prescribed conditions.

Fair value is the price that would be received to sell an asset or paid to transfer a liability in an orderly transaction between market participants at the measurement date. (See IFRS 13 *Fair Value Measurement*.)

4   Government assistance takes many forms varying both in the nature of the assistance given and in the conditions which are usually attached to it. The purpose of the assistance may be to encourage an entity to embark on a course of action which it would not normally have taken if the assistance was not provided.

5   The receipt of government assistance by an entity may be significant for the preparation of the financial statements for two reasons. Firstly, if resources have been transferred, an appropriate method of accounting for the transfer must be found. Secondly, it is desirable to give an indication of the extent to which the entity has benefited from such assistance during the reporting period. This facilitates comparison of an entity's financial statements with those of prior periods and with those of other entities.

6   Government grants are sometimes called by other names such as subsidies, subventions, or premiums.

Government grants

7   Government grants, including non-monetary grants at fair value, shall not be recognised until there is reasonable assurance that:

(a)   the entity will comply with the conditions attaching to them; and

(b)   the grants will be received.

8   A government grant is not recognised until there is reasonable assurance that the entity will comply with the conditions attaching to it, and that the grant will be received. Receipt of a grant does not of itself provide conclusive evidence that the conditions attaching to the grant have been or will be fulfilled.

9   The manner in which a grant is received does not affect the accounting method to be adopted in regard to the grant. Thus a grant is accounted for in the same manner whether it is received in cash or as a reduction of a liability to the government.

10   A forgivable loan from government is treated as a government grant when there is reasonable assurance that the entity will meet the terms for forgiveness of the loan.

10A The benefit of a government loan at a below-market rate of interest is treated as a government grant. The loan shall be recognised and measured in accordance with IFRS 9 *Financial Instruments*. The benefit of the below-market rate of interest shall be measured as the difference between the initial carrying value of the loan determined in accordance with IFRS 9 and the proceeds received. The benefit is accounted for in accordance with this Standard. The entity shall consider the conditions and obligations that have been, or must be, met when identifying the costs for which the benefit of the loan is intended to compensate.

11 Once a government grant is recognised, any related contingent liability or contingent asset is treated in accordance with IAS 37 *Provisions, Contingent Liabilities and Contingent Assets*.

12 Government grants shall be recognised in profit or loss on a systematic basis over the periods in which the entity recognises as expenses the related costs for which the grants are intended to compensate.

13 There are two broad approaches to the accounting for government grants: the capital approach, under which a grant is recognised outside profit or loss, and the income approach, under which a grant is recognised in profit or loss over one or more periods.

14 Those in support of the capital approach argue as follows:

(a) government grants are a financing device and should be dealt with as such in the statement of financial position rather than be recognised in profit or loss to offset the items of expense that they finance. Because no repayment is expected, such grants should be recognised outside profit or loss.

(b) it is inappropriate to recognise government grants in profit or loss, because they are not earned but represent an incentive provided by government without related costs.

15 Arguments in support of the income approach are as follows:

(a) because government grants are receipts from a source other than shareholders, they should not be recognised directly in equity but should be recognised in profit or loss in appropriate periods.

(b) government grants are rarely gratuitous. The entity earns them through compliance with their conditions and meeting the envisaged obligations. They should therefore be recognised in profit or loss over the periods in which the entity recognises as expenses the related costs for which the grant is intended to compensate.

(c) because income and other taxes are expenses, it is logical to deal also with government grants, which are an extension of fiscal policies, in profit or loss.

16 It is fundamental to the income approach that government grants should be recognised in profit or loss on a systematic basis over the periods in which the entity recognises as expenses the related costs for which the grant is intended to compensate. Recognition of government grants in profit or loss on a receipts basis is not in accordance with the accrual accounting assumption (see IAS 1 *Presentation of Financial Statements*) and would be acceptable only if no basis existed for allocating a grant to periods other than the one in which it was received.

17   In most cases the periods over which an entity recognises the costs or expenses related to a government grant are readily ascertainable. Thus grants in recognition of specific expenses are recognised in profit or loss in the same period as the relevant expenses. Similarly, grants related to depreciable assets are usually recognised in profit or loss over the periods and in the proportions in which depreciation expense on those assets is recognised.

18   Grants related to non-depreciable assets may also require the fulfilment of certain obligations and would then be recognised in profit or loss over the periods that bear the cost of meeting the obligations. As an example, a grant of land may be conditional upon the erection of a building on the site and it may be appropriate to recognise the grant in profit or loss over the life of the building.

19   Grants are sometimes received as part of a package of financial or fiscal aids to which a number of conditions are attached. In such cases, care is needed in identifying the conditions giving rise to costs and expenses which determine the periods over which the grant will be earned. It may be appropriate to allocate part of a grant on one basis and part on another.

20   **A government grant that becomes receivable as compensation for expenses or losses already incurred or for the purpose of giving immediate financial support to the entity with no future related costs shall be recognised in profit or loss of the period in which it becomes receivable.**

21   In some circumstances, a government grant may be awarded for the purpose of giving immediate financial support to an entity rather than as an incentive to undertake specific expenditures. Such grants may be confined to a particular entity and may not be available to a whole class of beneficiaries. These circumstances may warrant recognising a grant in profit or loss of the period in which the entity qualifies to receive it, with disclosure to ensure that its effect is clearly understood.

22   A government grant may become receivable by an entity as compensation for expenses or losses incurred in a previous period. Such a grant is recognised in profit or loss of the period in which it becomes receivable, with disclosure to ensure that its effect is clearly understood.

Non-monetary government grants

23   A government grant may take the form of a transfer of a non-monetary asset, such as land or other resources, for the use of the entity. In these circumstances it is usual to assess the fair value of the non-monetary asset and to account for both grant and asset at that fair value. An alternative course that is sometimes followed is to record both asset and grant at a nominal amount.

Presentation of grants related to assets

24   **Government grants related to assets, including non-monetary grants at fair value, shall be presented in the statement of financial position either by setting up the grant as deferred income or by deducting the grant in arriving at the carrying amount of the asset.**

25 Two methods of presentation in financial statements of grants (or the appropriate portions of grants) related to assets are regarded as acceptable alternatives.

26 One method recognises the grant as deferred income that is recognised in profit or loss on a systematic basis over the useful life of the asset.

27 The other method deducts the grant in calculating the carrying amount of the asset. The grant is recognised in profit or loss over the life of a depreciable asset as a reduced depreciation expense.

28 The purchase of assets and the receipt of related grants can cause major movements in the cash flow of an entity. For this reason and in order to show the gross investment in assets, such movements are often disclosed as separate items in the statement of cash flows regardless of whether or not the grant is deducted from the related asset for presentation purposes in the statement of financial position.

Presentation of grants related to income

29 Grants related to income are presented as part of profit or loss, either separately or under a general heading such as 'Other income'; alternatively, they are deducted in reporting the related expense.

29A [Deleted]

30 Supporters of the first method claim that it is inappropriate to net income and expense items and that separation of the grant from the expense facilitates comparison with other expenses not affected by a grant. For the second method it is argued that the expenses might well not have been incurred by the entity if the grant had not been available and presentation of the expense without offsetting the grant may therefore be misleading.

31 Both methods are regarded as acceptable for the presentation of grants related to income. Disclosure of the grant may be necessary for a proper understanding of the financial statements. Disclosure of the effect of the grants on any item of income or expense which is required to be separately disclosed is usually appropriate.

Repayment of government grants

32 A government grant that becomes repayable shall be accounted for as a change in accounting estimate (see IAS 8 *Accounting Policies, Changes in Accounting Estimates and Errors*). Repayment of a grant related to income shall be applied first against any unamortised deferred credit recognised in respect of the grant. To the extent that the repayment exceeds any such deferred credit, or when no deferred credit exists, the repayment shall be recognised immediately in profit or loss. Repayment of a grant related to an asset shall be recognised by increasing the carrying amount of the asset or reducing the deferred income balance by the amount repayable. The cumulative additional depreciation that would have been recognised in profit or loss to date in the absence of the grant shall be recognised immediately in profit or loss.

33   Circumstances giving rise to repayment of a grant related to an asset may require consideration to be given to the possible impairment of the new carrying amount of the asset.

Government assistance

34   Excluded from the definition of government grants in paragraph 3 are certain forms of government assistance which cannot reasonably have a value placed upon them and transactions with government which cannot be distinguished from the normal trading transactions of the entity.

35   Examples of assistance that cannot reasonably have a value placed upon them are free technical or marketing advice and the provision of guarantees. An example of assistance that cannot be distinguished from the normal trading transactions of the entity is a government procurement policy that is responsible for a portion of the entity's sales. The existence of the benefit might be unquestioned but any attempt to segregate the trading activities from government assistance could well be arbitrary.

36   The significance of the benefit in the above examples may be such that disclosure of the nature, extent and duration of the assistance is necessary in order that the financial statements may not be misleading.

37   [Deleted]

38   In this Standard, government assistance does not include the provision of infrastructure by improvement to the general transport and communication network and the supply of improved facilities such as irrigation or water reticulation which is available on an ongoing indeterminate basis for the benefit of an entire local community.

Disclosure

39   The following matters shall be disclosed:

    (a)   the accounting policy adopted for government grants, including the methods of presentation adopted in the financial statements;

    (b)   the nature and extent of government grants recognised in the financial statements and an indication of other forms of government assistance from which the entity has directly benefited; and

    (c)   unfulfilled conditions and other contingencies attaching to government assistance that has been recognised.

Transitional provisions

40   An entity adopting the Standard for the first time shall:

    (a)   comply with the disclosure requirements, where appropriate; and

    (b)   either:

        (i)   adjust its financial statements for the change in accounting policy in accordance with IAS 8; or

        (ii)   apply the accounting provisions of the Standard only to grants or portions of grants becoming receivable or repayable after the effective date of the Standard.

Effective date

41   This Standard becomes operative for financial statements covering periods beginning on or after 1 January 1984.

42   IAS 1 (as revised in 2007) amended the terminology used throughout IFRSs. In addition it added paragraph 29A. An entity shall apply those amendments for annual periods beginning on or after 1 January 2009. If an entity applies IAS 1 (revised 2007) for an earlier period, the amendments shall be applied for that earlier period.

43   Paragraph 37 was deleted and paragraph 10A added by *Improvements to IFRSs* issued in May 2008. An entity shall apply those amendments prospectively to government loans received in periods beginning on or after 1 January 2009. Earlier application is permitted. If an entity applies the amendments for an earlier period it shall disclose that fact.

44   IFRS 9, issued in October 2010, amended paragraph 10A. An entity shall apply that amendment when it applies IFRS 9 as issued in October 2010.

45   IFRS 13, issued in May 2011, amended the definition of fair value in paragraph 3. An entity shall apply that amendment when it applies IFRS 13.

46   *Presentation of Items of Other Comprehensive Income* (Amendments to IAS 1), issued in June 2011, amended paragraph 29 and deleted paragraph 29A. An entity shall apply those amendments when it applies IAS 1 as amended in June 2011.

International Accounting Standard 21

The Effects of Changes in Foreign Exchange Rates

In April 2001 the International Accounting Standards Board (IASB) adopted IAS 21 *The Effects of Changes in Foreign Exchange Rates*, which had originally been issued by the International Accounting Standards Committee in December 1983. IAS 21 *The Effects of Changes in Foreign Exchange Rates* replaced IAS 21 *Accounting for the Effects of Changes in Foreign Exchange Rates* (issued in July 1983).

In December 2003 the IASB issued a revised IAS 21 as part of its initial agenda of technical projects. The revised IAS 21 also incorporated the guidance contained in three related Interpretations (SIC-11 *Foreign Exchange—Capitalisation of Losses Resulting from Severe Currency Devaluations*, SIC-19 *Reporting Currency—Measurement and Presentation of Financial Statements under IAS 21 and IAS 29* and SIC-30 *Reporting Currency—Translation from Measurement Currency to Presentation Currency*). The IASB also amended SIC-7 *Introduction of the Euro*.

The IASB amended IAS 21 in December 2005 to require that some types of exchange differences arising from a monetary item should be separately recognised as equity.

Other IFRSs have made minor consequential amendments to IAS 21. They include *Cost of an Investment in a Subsidiary, Jointly Controlled Entity or Associate* (Amendments to IFRS 1 and IAS 27) (issued May 2008), IAS 1 *Presentation of Financial Statements* (as revised in September 2007), IFRS 9 *Financial Instruments* (issued November 2009 and October 2010) and *Improvements to IFRSs* (issued May 2010).

Contents

FOR THE ACCOMPANYING DOCUMENTS LISTED BELOW, SEE PART B OF THIS EDITION

APPROVAL BY THE BOARD OF IAS 21 ISSUED IN DECEMBER 2003

APPROVAL BY THE BOARD OF *NET INVESTMENT IN A FOREIGN OPERATION*
(AMENDMENT TO IAS 21) ISSUED IN DECEMBER 2005

BASIS FOR CONCLUSIONS

International Accounting Standard 21 *The Effects of Changes in Foreign Exchange Rates* (IAS 21) is set out in paragraphs 1–62 and the Appendix. All the paragraphs have equal authority but retain the IASC format of the Standard when it was adopted by the IASB. IAS 21 should be read in the context of its objective and the Basis for Conclusions, the *Preface to International Financial Reporting Standards* and the *Conceptual Framework for Financial Reporting*. IAS 8 *Accounting Policies, Changes in Accounting Estimates and Errors* provides a basis for selecting and applying accounting policies in the absence of explicit guidance.

Introduction

IN1 International Accounting Standard 21 *The Effects of Changes in Foreign Exchange Rates* (IAS 21) replaces IAS 21 *The Effects of Changes in Foreign Exchange Rates* (revised in 1993), and should be applied for annual periods beginning on or after 1 January 2005. Earlier application is encouraged. The Standard also replaces the following Interpretations:

- SIC-11 *Foreign Exchange—Capitalisation of Losses Resulting from Severe Currency Devaluations*

- SIC-19 *Reporting Currency—Measurement and Presentation of Financial Statements under IAS 21 and IAS 29*

- SIC-30 *Reporting Currency—Translation from Measurement Currency to Presentation Currency.*

Reasons for revising IAS 21

IN2 The International Accounting Standards Board developed this revised IAS 21 as part of its project on Improvements to International Accounting Standards. The project was undertaken in the light of queries and criticisms raised in relation to the Standards by securities regulators, professional accountants and other interested parties. The objectives of the project were to reduce or eliminate alternatives, redundancies and conflicts within the Standards, to deal with some convergence issues and to make other improvements.

IN3 For IAS 21 the Board's main objective was to provide additional guidance on the translation method and on determining the functional and presentation currencies. The Board did not reconsider the fundamental approach to accounting for the effects of changes in foreign exchange rates contained in IAS 21.

The main changes

IN4 The main changes from the previous version of IAS 21 are described below.

Scope

IN5 The Standard excludes from its scope foreign currency derivatives that are within the scope of IFRS 9 *Financial Instruments*. Similarly, the material on hedge accounting has been moved to IAS 39 *Financial Instruments: Recognition and Measurement*.

Definitions

IN6 The notion of 'reporting currency' has been replaced with two notions:

- functional currency, ie the currency of the primary economic environment in which the entity operates. The term 'functional currency' is used in place of 'measurement currency' (the term used in SIC-19) because it is the more commonly used term, but with essentially the same meaning.

- presentation currency, ie the currency in which financial statements are presented.

Definitions—functional currency

IN7 When a reporting entity prepares financial statements, the Standard requires each individual entity included in the reporting entity—whether it is a stand-alone entity, an entity with foreign operations (such as a parent) or a foreign operation (such as a subsidiary or branch)—to determine its functional currency and measure its results and financial position in that currency. The new material on functional currency incorporates some of the guidance previously included in SIC-19 on how to determine a measurement currency. However, the Standard gives greater emphasis than SIC-19 gave to the currency of the economy that determines the pricing of transactions, as opposed to the currency in which transactions are denominated.

IN8 As a result of these changes and the incorporation of guidance previously in SIC-19:

- an entity (whether a stand-alone entity or a foreign operation) does not have a free choice of functional currency.

- an entity cannot avoid restatement in accordance with IAS 29 *Financial Reporting in Hyperinflationary Economies* by, for example, adopting a stable currency (such as the functional currency of its parent) as its functional currency.

IN9 The Standard revises the requirements in the previous version of IAS 21 for distinguishing between foreign operations that are integral to the operations of the reporting entity (referred to below as 'integral foreign operations') and foreign entities. The requirements are now among the indicators of an entity's functional currency. As a result:

- there is no distinction between integral foreign operations and foreign entities. Rather, an entity that was previously classified as an integral foreign operation will have the same functional currency as the reporting entity.

- only one translation method is used for foreign operations—namely that described in the previous version of IAS 21 as applying to foreign entities (see paragraph IN13).

- the paragraphs dealing with the distinction between an integral foreign operation and a foreign entity and the paragraph specifying the translation method to be used for the former have been deleted.

Reporting foreign currency transactions in the functional currency—recognition of exchange differences

IN10 The Standard removes the limited option in the previous version of IAS 21 to capitalise exchange differences resulting from a severe devaluation or depreciation of a currency against which there is no means of hedging. Under the Standard, such exchange differences are now recognised in profit or loss. Consequently, SIC-11, which outlined restricted circumstances in which such exchange differences may be capitalised, has been superseded since capitalisation of such exchange differences is no longer permitted in any circumstances.

Reporting foreign currency transactions in the functional currency—change in functional currency

IN11 The Standard replaces the previous requirement for accounting for a change in the classification of a foreign operation (which is now redundant) with a requirement that a change in functional currency is accounted for prospectively.

Use of a presentation currency other than the functional currency—translation to the presentation currency

IN12 The Standard permits an entity to present its financial statements in any currency (or currencies). For this purpose, an entity could be a stand-alone entity, a parent preparing consolidated financial statements in accordance with IFRS 10 *Consolidated Financial Statements* or a parent, an investor with joint control of, or significant influence over, an investee preparing separate financial statements in accordance with IAS 27 *Separate Financial Statements*.

IN13 An entity is required to translate its results and financial position from its functional currency into a presentation currency (or currencies) using the method required for translating a foreign operation for inclusion in the reporting entity's financial statements. Under this method, assets and liabilities are translated at the closing rate, and income and expenses are translated at the exchange rates at the dates of the transactions (or at the average rate for the period when this is a reasonable approximation).

IN14 The Standard requires comparative amounts to be translated as follows:

(a) for an entity whose functional currency is not the currency of a hyperinflationary economy:

   (i) assets and liabilities in each statement of financial position presented are translated at the closing rate at the date of that statement of financial position (ie last year's comparatives are translated at last year's closing rate).

   (ii) income and expenses in each statement presenting profit or loss and other comprehensive income are translated at exchange rates at the dates of the transactions (ie last year's comparatives are translated at last year's actual or average rate).

(b)   for an entity whose functional currency is the currency of a hyperinflationary economy, and for which the comparative amounts are translated into the currency of a different hyperinflationary economy, all amounts (eg amounts in a statement of financial position and statement of comprehensive income) are translated at the closing rate of the most recent statement of financial position presented (ie last year's comparatives, as adjusted for subsequent changes in the price level, are translated at this year's closing rate).

(c)   for an entity whose functional currency is the currency of a hyperinflationary economy, and for which the comparative amounts are translated into the currency of a non-hyperinflationary economy, all amounts are those presented in the prior year financial statements (ie not adjusted for subsequent changes in the price level or subsequent changes in exchange rates).

This translation method, like that described in paragraph IN13, applies when translating the financial statements of a foreign operation for inclusion in the financial statements of the reporting entity, and when translating the financial statements of an entity into a different presentation currency.

Use of a presentation currency other than the functional currency—translation of a foreign operation

IN15   The Standard requires goodwill and fair value adjustments to assets and liabilities that arise on the acquisition of a foreign entity to be treated as part of the assets and liabilities of the acquired entity and translated at the closing rate.

Disclosure

IN16   The Standard includes most of the disclosure requirements of SIC-30. These apply when a translation method different from that described in paragraphs IN13 and IN14 is used or other supplementary information (such as an extract from the full financial statements) is displayed in a currency other than the functional currency or the presentation currency.

IN17   In addition, entities must disclose when there has been a change in functional currency, and the reasons for the change.

International Accounting Standard 21
The Effects of Changes in Foreign Exchange Rates

Objective

1   An entity may carry on foreign activities in two ways. It may have transactions in foreign currencies or it may have foreign operations. In addition, an entity may present its financial statements in a foreign currency. The objective of this Standard is to prescribe how to include foreign currency transactions and foreign operations in the financial statements of an entity and how to translate financial statements into a presentation currency.

2   The principal issues are which exchange rate(s) to use and how to report the effects of changes in exchange rates in the financial statements.

Scope

3   **This Standard shall be applied:**[1]

     (a)   **in accounting for transactions and balances in foreign currencies, except for those derivative transactions and balances that are within the scope of IFRS 9** *Financial Instruments***;**

     (b)   **in translating the results and financial position of foreign operations that are included in the financial statements of the entity by consolidation or the equity method; and**

     (c)   **in translating an entity's results and financial position into a presentation currency.**

4   IFRS 9 applies to many foreign currency derivatives and, accordingly, these are excluded from the scope of this Standard. However, those foreign currency derivatives that are not within the scope of IFRS 9 (eg some foreign currency derivatives that are embedded in other contracts) are within the scope of this Standard. In addition, this Standard applies when an entity translates amounts relating to derivatives from its functional currency to its presentation currency.

5   This Standard does not apply to hedge accounting for foreign currency items, including the hedging of a net investment in a foreign operation. IAS 39 applies to hedge accounting.

6   This Standard applies to the presentation of an entity's financial statements in a foreign currency and sets out requirements for the resulting financial statements to be described as complying with International Financial Reporting Standards (IFRSs). For translations of financial information into a foreign currency that do not meet these requirements, this Standard specifies information to be disclosed.

7   This Standard does not apply to the presentation in a statement of cash flows of the cash flows arising from transactions in a foreign currency, or to the translation of cash flows of a foreign operation (see IAS 7 *Statement of Cash Flows*).

---

1   See also SIC-7 *Introduction of the Euro*.

Definitions

8   The following terms are used in this Standard with the meanings specified:

Closing rate is the spot exchange rate at the end of the reporting period.

Exchange difference is the difference resulting from translating a given number of units of one currency into another currency at different exchange rates.

Exchange rate is the ratio of exchange for two currencies.

Fair value is the price that would be received to sell an asset or paid to transfer a liability in an orderly transaction between market participants at the measurement date. (See IFRS 13 *Fair Value Measurement*.)

Foreign currency is a currency other than the functional currency of the entity.

Foreign operation is an entity that is a subsidiary, associate, joint arrangement or branch of a reporting entity, the activities of which are based or conducted in a country or currency other than those of the reporting entity.

Functional currency is the currency of the primary economic environment in which the entity operates.

A *group* is a parent and all its subsidiaries.

Monetary items are units of currency held and assets and liabilities to be received or paid in a fixed or determinable number of units of currency.

Net investment in a foreign operation is the amount of the reporting entity's interest in the net assets of that operation.

Presentation currency is the currency in which the financial statements are presented.

Spot exchange rate is the exchange rate for immediate delivery.

Elaboration on the definitions

Functional currency

9   The primary economic environment in which an entity operates is normally the one in which it primarily generates and expends cash. An entity considers the following factors in determining its functional currency:

    (a)   the currency:

       (i)   that mainly influences sales prices for goods and services (this will often be the currency in which sales prices for its goods and services are denominated and settled); and

       (ii)   of the country whose competitive forces and regulations mainly determine the sales prices of its goods and services.

    (b)   the currency that mainly influences labour, material and other costs of providing goods or services (this will often be the currency in which such costs are denominated and settled).

10   The following factors may also provide evidence of an entity's functional currency:

   (a)   the currency in which funds from financing activities (ie issuing debt and equity instruments) are generated.

   (b)   the currency in which receipts from operating activities are usually retained.

11   The following additional factors are considered in determining the functional currency of a foreign operation, and whether its functional currency is the same as that of the reporting entity (the reporting entity, in this context, being the entity that has the foreign operation as its subsidiary, branch, associate or joint arrangement):

   (a)   whether the activities of the foreign operation are carried out as an extension of the reporting entity, rather than being carried out with a significant degree of autonomy. An example of the former is when the foreign operation only sells goods imported from the reporting entity and remits the proceeds to it. An example of the latter is when the operation accumulates cash and other monetary items, incurs expenses, generates income and arranges borrowings, all substantially in its local currency.

   (b)   whether transactions with the reporting entity are a high or a low proportion of the foreign operation's activities.

   (c)   whether cash flows from the activities of the foreign operation directly affect the cash flows of the reporting entity and are readily available for remittance to it.

   (d)   whether cash flows from the activities of the foreign operation are sufficient to service existing and normally expected debt obligations without funds being made available by the reporting entity.

12   When the above indicators are mixed and the functional currency is not obvious, management uses its judgement to determine the functional currency that most faithfully represents the economic effects of the underlying transactions, events and conditions. As part of this approach, management gives priority to the primary indicators in paragraph 9 before considering the indicators in paragraphs 10 and 11, which are designed to provide additional supporting evidence to determine an entity's functional currency.

13   An entity's functional currency reflects the underlying transactions, events and conditions that are relevant to it. Accordingly, once determined, the functional currency is not changed unless there is a change in those underlying transactions, events and conditions.

14   If the functional currency is the currency of a hyperinflationary economy, the entity's financial statements are restated in accordance with IAS 29 *Financial Reporting in Hyperinflationary Economies*. An entity cannot avoid restatement in accordance with IAS 29 by, for example, adopting as its functional currency a currency other than the functional currency determined in accordance with this Standard (such as the functional currency of its parent).

Net investment in a foreign operation

15 An entity may have a monetary item that is receivable from or payable to a foreign operation. An item for which settlement is neither planned nor likely to occur in the foreseeable future is, in substance, a part of the entity's net investment in that foreign operation, and is accounted for in accordance with paragraphs 32 and 33. Such monetary items may include long-term receivables or loans. They do not include trade receivables or trade payables.

15A The entity that has a monetary item receivable from or payable to a foreign operation described in paragraph 15 may be any subsidiary of the group. For example, an entity has two subsidiaries, A and B. Subsidiary B is a foreign operation. Subsidiary A grants a loan to Subsidiary B. Subsidiary A's loan receivable from Subsidiary B would be part of the entity's net investment in Subsidiary B if settlement of the loan is neither planned nor likely to occur in the foreseeable future. This would also be true if Subsidiary A were itself a foreign operation.

Monetary items

16 The essential feature of a monetary item is a right to receive (or an obligation to deliver) a fixed or determinable number of units of currency. Examples include: pensions and other employee benefits to be paid in cash; provisions that are to be settled in cash; and cash dividends that are recognised as a liability. Similarly, a contract to receive (or deliver) a variable number of the entity's own equity instruments or a variable amount of assets in which the fair value to be received (or delivered) equals a fixed or determinable number of units of currency is a monetary item. Conversely, the essential feature of a non-monetary item is the absence of a right to receive (or an obligation to deliver) a fixed or determinable number of units of currency. Examples include: amounts prepaid for goods and services (eg prepaid rent); goodwill; intangible assets; inventories; property, plant and equipment; and provisions that are to be settled by the delivery of a non-monetary asset.

Summary of the approach required by this Standard

17 In preparing financial statements, each entity—whether a stand-alone entity, an entity with foreign operations (such as a parent) or a foreign operation (such as a subsidiary or branch)—determines its functional currency in accordance with paragraphs 9–14. The entity translates foreign currency items into its functional currency and reports the effects of such translation in accordance with paragraphs 20–37 and 50.

18 Many reporting entities comprise a number of individual entities (eg a group is made up of a parent and one or more subsidiaries). Various types of entities, whether members of a group or otherwise, may have investments in associates or joint arrangements. They may also have branches. It is necessary for the results and financial position of each individual entity included in the reporting entity to be translated into the currency in which the reporting entity presents its financial statements. This Standard permits the presentation currency of a

reporting entity to be any currency (or currencies). The results and financial position of any individual entity within the reporting entity whose functional currency differs from the presentation currency are translated in accordance with paragraphs 38–50.

19   This Standard also permits a stand-alone entity preparing financial statements or an entity preparing separate financial statements in accordance with IAS 27 *Separate Financial Statements* to present its financial statements in any currency (or currencies). If the entity's presentation currency differs from its functional currency, its results and financial position are also translated into the presentation currency in accordance with paragraphs 38–50.

Reporting foreign currency transactions in the functional currency

Initial recognition

20   A foreign currency transaction is a transaction that is denominated or requires settlement in a foreign currency, including transactions arising when an entity:

   (a)   buys or sells goods or services whose price is denominated in a foreign currency;

   (b)   borrows or lends funds when the amounts payable or receivable are denominated in a foreign currency; or

   (c)   otherwise acquires or disposes of assets, or incurs or settles liabilities, denominated in a foreign currency.

21   **A foreign currency transaction shall be recorded, on initial recognition in the functional currency, by applying to the foreign currency amount the spot exchange rate between the functional currency and the foreign currency at the date of the transaction.**

22   The date of a transaction is the date on which the transaction first qualifies for recognition in accordance with IFRSs. For practical reasons, a rate that approximates the actual rate at the date of the transaction is often used, for example, an average rate for a week or a month might be used for all transactions in each foreign currency occurring during that period. However, if exchange rates fluctuate significantly, the use of the average rate for a period is inappropriate.

Reporting at the ends of subsequent reporting periods

23   **At the end of each reporting period:**

   (a)   **foreign currency monetary items shall be translated using the closing rate;**

   (b)   **non-monetary items that are measured in terms of historical cost in a foreign currency shall be translated using the exchange rate at the date of the transaction; and**

   (c)   **non-monetary items that are measured at fair value in a foreign currency shall be translated using the exchange rates at the date when the fair value was measured.**

24   The carrying amount of an item is determined in conjunction with other relevant Standards. For example, property, plant and equipment may be measured in terms of fair value or historical cost in accordance with IAS 16 *Property, Plant and Equipment*. Whether the carrying amount is determined on the basis of historical cost or on the basis of fair value, if the amount is determined in a foreign currency it is then translated into the functional currency in accordance with this Standard.

25   The carrying amount of some items is determined by comparing two or more amounts. For example, the carrying amount of inventories is the lower of cost and net realisable value in accordance with IAS 2 *Inventories*. Similarly, in accordance with IAS 36 *Impairment of Assets*, the carrying amount of an asset for which there is an indication of impairment is the lower of its carrying amount before considering possible impairment losses and its recoverable amount. When such an asset is non-monetary and is measured in a foreign currency, the carrying amount is determined by comparing:

(a)   the cost or carrying amount, as appropriate, translated at the exchange rate at the date when that amount was determined (ie the rate at the date of the transaction for an item measured in terms of historical cost); and

(b)   the net realisable value or recoverable amount, as appropriate, translated at the exchange rate at the date when that value was determined (eg the closing rate at the end of the reporting period).

The effect of this comparison may be that an impairment loss is recognised in the functional currency but would not be recognised in the foreign currency, or vice versa.

26   When several exchange rates are available, the rate used is that at which the future cash flows represented by the transaction or balance could have been settled if those cash flows had occurred at the measurement date. If exchangeability between two currencies is temporarily lacking, the rate used is the first subsequent rate at which exchanges could be made.

Recognition of exchange differences

27   As noted in paragraphs 3(a) and 5, IAS 39 applies to hedge accounting for foreign currency items. The application of hedge accounting requires an entity to account for some exchange differences differently from the treatment of exchange differences required by this Standard. For example, IAS 39 requires that exchange differences on monetary items that qualify as hedging instruments in a cash flow hedge are recognised initially in other comprehensive income to the extent that the hedge is effective.

28   **Exchange differences arising on the settlement of monetary items or on translating monetary items at rates different from those at which they were translated on initial recognition during the period or in previous financial statements shall be recognised in profit or loss in the period in which they arise, except as described in paragraph 32.**

29   When monetary items arise from a foreign currency transaction and there is a change in the exchange rate between the transaction date and the date of settlement, an exchange difference results. When the transaction is settled within the same accounting period as that in which it occurred, all the exchange difference is recognised in that period. However, when the transaction is settled in a subsequent accounting period, the exchange difference recognised in each period up to the date of settlement is determined by the change in exchange rates during each period.

30   **When a gain or loss on a non-monetary item is recognised in other comprehensive income, any exchange component of that gain or loss shall be recognised in other comprehensive income. Conversely, when a gain or loss on a non-monetary item is recognised in profit or loss, any exchange component of that gain or loss shall be recognised in profit or loss.**

31   Other IFRSs require some gains and losses to be recognised in other comprehensive income. For example, IAS 16 requires some gains and losses arising on a revaluation of property, plant and equipment to be recognised in other comprehensive income. When such an asset is measured in a foreign currency, paragraph 23(c) of this Standard requires the revalued amount to be translated using the rate at the date the value is determined, resulting in an exchange difference that is also recognised in other comprehensive income.

32   **Exchange differences arising on a monetary item that forms part of a reporting entity's net investment in a foreign operation (see paragraph 15) shall be recognised in profit or loss in the separate financial statements of the reporting entity or the individual financial statements of the foreign operation, as appropriate. In the financial statements that include the foreign operation and the reporting entity (eg consolidated financial statements when the foreign operation is a subsidiary), such exchange differences shall be recognised initially in other comprehensive income and reclassified from equity to profit or loss on disposal of the net investment in accordance with paragraph 48.**

33   When a monetary item forms part of a reporting entity's net investment in a foreign operation and is denominated in the functional currency of the reporting entity, an exchange difference arises in the foreign operation's individual financial statements in accordance with paragraph 28. If such an item is denominated in the functional currency of the foreign operation, an exchange difference arises in the reporting entity's separate financial statements in accordance with paragraph 28. If such an item is denominated in a currency other than the functional currency of either the reporting entity or the foreign operation, an exchange difference arises in the reporting entity's separate financial statements and in the foreign operation's individual financial statements in accordance with paragraph 28. Such exchange differences are recognised in other comprehensive income in the financial statements that include the foreign operation and the reporting entity (ie financial statements in which the foreign operation is consolidated or accounted for using the equity method).

34   When an entity keeps its books and records in a currency other than its functional currency, at the time the entity prepares its financial statements all amounts are translated into the functional currency in accordance with paragraphs 20–26. This produces the same amounts in the functional currency as would have occurred had the items been recorded initially in the functional currency. For example, monetary items are translated into the functional currency using the closing rate, and non-monetary items that are measured on a historical cost basis are translated using the exchange rate at the date of the transaction that resulted in their recognition.

Change in functional currency

35   **When there is a change in an entity's functional currency, the entity shall apply the translation procedures applicable to the new functional currency prospectively from the date of the change.**

36   As noted in paragraph 13, the functional currency of an entity reflects the underlying transactions, events and conditions that are relevant to the entity. Accordingly, once the functional currency is determined, it can be changed only if there is a change to those underlying transactions, events and conditions. For example, a change in the currency that mainly influences the sales prices of goods and services may lead to a change in an entity's functional currency.

37   The effect of a change in functional currency is accounted for prospectively. In other words, an entity translates all items into the new functional currency using the exchange rate at the date of the change. The resulting translated amounts for non-monetary items are treated as their historical cost. Exchange differences arising from the translation of a foreign operation previously recognised in other comprehensive income in accordance with paragraphs 32 and 39(c) are not reclassified from equity to profit or loss until the disposal of the operation.

Use of a presentation currency other than the functional currency

Translation to the presentation currency

38   An entity may present its financial statements in any currency (or currencies). If the presentation currency differs from the entity's functional currency, it translates its results and financial position into the presentation currency. For example, when a group contains individual entities with different functional currencies, the results and financial position of each entity are expressed in a common currency so that consolidated financial statements may be presented.

39   **The results and financial position of an entity whose functional currency is not the currency of a hyperinflationary economy shall be translated into a different presentation currency using the following procedures:**

     (a)   **assets and liabilities for each statement of financial position presented (ie including comparatives) shall be translated at the closing rate at the date of that statement of financial position;**

(b) income and expenses for each statement presenting profit or loss and other comprehensive income (ie including comparatives) shall be translated at exchange rates at the dates of the transactions; and

(c) all resulting exchange differences shall be recognised in other comprehensive income.

40 For practical reasons, a rate that approximates the exchange rates at the dates of the transactions, for example an average rate for the period, is often used to translate income and expense items. However, if exchange rates fluctuate significantly, the use of the average rate for a period is inappropriate.

41 The exchange differences referred to in paragraph 39(c) result from:

(a) translating income and expenses at the exchange rates at the dates of the transactions and assets and liabilities at the closing rate.

(b) translating the opening net assets at a closing rate that differs from the previous closing rate.

These exchange differences are not recognised in profit or loss because the changes in exchange rates have little or no direct effect on the present and future cash flows from operations. The cumulative amount of the exchange differences is presented in a separate component of equity until disposal of the foreign operation. When the exchange differences relate to a foreign operation that is consolidated but not wholly-owned, accumulated exchange differences arising from translation and attributable to non-controlling interests are allocated to, and recognised as part of, non-controlling interests in the consolidated statement of financial position.

42 The results and financial position of an entity whose functional currency is the currency of a hyperinflationary economy shall be translated into a different presentation currency using the following procedures:

(a) all amounts (ie assets, liabilities, equity items, income and expenses, including comparatives) shall be translated at the closing rate at the date of the most recent statement of financial position, except that

(b) when amounts are translated into the currency of a non-hyperinflationary economy, comparative amounts shall be those that were presented as current year amounts in the relevant prior year financial statements (ie not adjusted for subsequent changes in the price level or subsequent changes in exchange rates).

43 When an entity's functional currency is the currency of a hyperinflationary economy, the entity shall restate its financial statements in accordance with IAS 29 before applying the translation method set out in paragraph 42, except for comparative amounts that are translated into a currency of a non-hyperinflationary economy (see paragraph 42(b)). When the economy ceases to be hyperinflationary and the entity no longer restates its financial statements in accordance with IAS 29, it shall use as the historical costs for translation into the presentation currency the amounts restated to the price level at the date the entity ceased restating its financial statements.

Translation of a foreign operation

44   Paragraphs 45–47, in addition to paragraphs 38–43, apply when the results and financial position of a foreign operation are translated into a presentation currency so that the foreign operation can be included in the financial statements of the reporting entity by consolidation or the equity method.

45   The incorporation of the results and financial position of a foreign operation with those of the reporting entity follows normal consolidation procedures, such as the elimination of intragroup balances and intragroup transactions of a subsidiary (see IFRS 10 *Consolidated Financial Statements*). However, an intragroup monetary asset (or liability), whether short-term or long-term, cannot be eliminated against the corresponding intragroup liability (or asset) without showing the results of currency fluctuations in the consolidated financial statements. This is because the monetary item represents a commitment to convert one currency into another and exposes the reporting entity to a gain or loss through currency fluctuations. Accordingly, in the consolidated financial statements of the reporting entity, such an exchange difference is recognised in profit or loss or, if it arises from the circumstances described in paragraph 32, it is recognised in other comprehensive income and accumulated in a separate component of equity until the disposal of the foreign operation.

46   When the financial statements of a foreign operation are as of a date different from that of the reporting entity, the foreign operation often prepares additional statements as of the same date as the reporting entity's financial statements. When this is not done, IFRS 10 allows the use of a different date provided that the difference is no greater than three months and adjustments are made for the effects of any significant transactions or other events that occur between the different dates. In such a case, the assets and liabilities of the foreign operation are translated at the exchange rate at the end of the reporting period of the foreign operation. Adjustments are made for significant changes in exchange rates up to the end of the reporting period of the reporting entity in accordance with IFRS 10. The same approach is used in applying the equity method to associates and joint ventures in accordance with IAS 28 (as amended in 2011).

47   **Any goodwill arising on the acquisition of a foreign operation and any fair value adjustments to the carrying amounts of assets and liabilities arising on the acquisition of that foreign operation shall be treated as assets and liabilities of the foreign operation. Thus they shall be expressed in the functional currency of the foreign operation and shall be translated at the closing rate in accordance with paragraphs 39 and 42.**

Disposal or partial disposal of a foreign operation

48   **On the disposal of a foreign operation, the cumulative amount of the exchange differences relating to that foreign operation, recognised in other comprehensive income and accumulated in the separate component of equity, shall be reclassified from equity to profit or loss (as a reclassification adjustment) when the gain or loss on disposal is recognised (see IAS 1 *Presentation of Financial Statements* (as revised in 2007)).**

48A   In addition to the disposal of an entity's entire interest in a foreign operation, the following partial disposals are accounted for as disposals:

   (a)   when the partial disposal involves the loss of control of a subsidiary that includes a foreign operation, regardless of whether the entity retains a non-controlling interest in its former subsidiary after the partial disposal; and

   (b)   when the retained interest after the partial disposal of an interest in a joint arrangement or a partial disposal of an interest in an associate that includes a foreign operation is a financial asset that includes a foreign operation.

48B   On disposal of a subsidiary that includes a foreign operation, the cumulative amount of the exchange differences relating to that foreign operation that have been attributed to the non-controlling interests shall be derecognised, but shall not be reclassified to profit or loss.

48C   **On the partial disposal of a subsidiary that includes a foreign operation, the entity shall re-attribute the proportionate share of the cumulative amount of the exchange differences recognised in other comprehensive income to the non-controlling interests in that foreign operation. In any other partial disposal of a foreign operation the entity shall reclassify to profit or loss only the proportionate share of the cumulative amount of the exchange differences recognised in other comprehensive income.**

48D   A partial disposal of an entity's interest in a foreign operation is any reduction in an entity's ownership interest in a foreign operation, except those reductions in paragraph 48A that are accounted for as disposals.

49   An entity may dispose or partially dispose of its interest in a foreign operation through sale, liquidation, repayment of share capital or abandonment of all, or part of, that entity. A write-down of the carrying amount of a foreign operation, either because of its own losses or because of an impairment recognised by the investor, does not constitute a partial disposal. Accordingly, no part of the foreign exchange gain or loss recognised in other comprehensive income is reclassified to profit or loss at the time of a write-down.

Tax effects of all exchange differences

50   Gains and losses on foreign currency transactions and exchange differences arising on translating the results and financial position of an entity (including a foreign operation) into a different currency may have tax effects. IAS 12 *Income Taxes* applies to these tax effects.

Disclosure

51 In paragraphs 53 and 55–57 references to 'functional currency' apply, in the case of a group, to the functional currency of the parent.

52 An entity shall disclose:

(a) the amount of exchange differences recognised in profit or loss except for those arising on financial instruments measured at fair value through profit or loss in accordance with IFRS 9; and

(b) net exchange differences recognised in other comprehensive income and accumulated in a separate component of equity, and a reconciliation of the amount of such exchange differences at the beginning and end of the period.

53 When the presentation currency is different from the functional currency, that fact shall be stated, together with disclosure of the functional currency and the reason for using a different presentation currency.

54 When there is a change in the functional currency of either the reporting entity or a significant foreign operation, that fact and the reason for the change in functional currency shall be disclosed.

55 When an entity presents its financial statements in a currency that is different from its functional currency, it shall describe the financial statements as complying with IFRSs only if they comply with all the requirements of IFRSs including the translation method set out in paragraphs 39 and 42.

56 An entity sometimes presents its financial statements or other financial information in a currency that is not its functional currency without meeting the requirements of paragraph 55. For example, an entity may convert into another currency only selected items from its financial statements. Or, an entity whose functional currency is not the currency of a hyperinflationary economy may convert the financial statements into another currency by translating all items at the most recent closing rate. Such conversions are not in accordance with IFRSs and the disclosures set out in paragraph 57 are required.

57 When an entity displays its financial statements or other financial information in a currency that is different from either its functional currency or its presentation currency and the requirements of paragraph 55 are not met, it shall:

(a) clearly identify the information as supplementary information to distinguish it from the information that complies with IFRSs;

(b) disclose the currency in which the supplementary information is displayed; and

(c) disclose the entity's functional currency and the method of translation used to determine the supplementary information.

Effective date and transition

58 An entity shall apply this Standard for annual periods beginning on or after 1 January 2005. Earlier application is encouraged. If an entity applies this Standard for a period beginning before 1 January 2005, it shall disclose that fact.

58A *Net Investment in a Foreign Operation* (Amendment to IAS 21), issued in December 2005, added paragraph 15A and amended paragraph 33. An entity shall apply those amendments for annual periods beginning on or after 1 January 2006. Earlier application is encouraged.

59 An entity shall apply paragraph 47 prospectively to all acquisitions occurring after the beginning of the financial reporting period in which this Standard is first applied. Retrospective application of paragraph 47 to earlier acquisitions is permitted. For an acquisition of a foreign operation treated prospectively but which occurred before the date on which this Standard is first applied, the entity shall not restate prior years and accordingly may, when appropriate, treat goodwill and fair value adjustments arising on that acquisition as assets and liabilities of the entity rather than as assets and liabilities of the foreign operation. Therefore, those goodwill and fair value adjustments either are already expressed in the entity's functional currency or are non-monetary foreign currency items, which are reported using the exchange rate at the date of the acquisition.

60 All other changes resulting from the application of this Standard shall be accounted for in accordance with the requirements of IAS 8 *Accounting Policies, Changes in Accounting Estimates and Errors*.

60A IAS 1 (as revised in 2007) amended the terminology used throughout IFRSs. In addition it amended paragraphs 27, 30–33, 37, 39, 41, 45, 48 and 52. An entity shall apply those amendments for annual periods beginning on or after 1 January 2009. If an entity applies IAS 1 (revised 2007) for an earlier period, the amendments shall be applied for that earlier period.

60B IAS 27 (as amended in 2008) added paragraphs 48A–48D and amended paragraph 49. An entity shall apply those amendments prospectively for annual periods beginning on or after 1 July 2009. If an entity applies IAS 27 (amended 2008) for an earlier period, the amendments shall be applied for that earlier period.

60C [Deleted]

60D Paragraph 60B was amended by *Improvements to IFRSs* issued in May 2010. An entity shall apply that amendment for annual periods beginning on or after 1 July 2010. Earlier application is permitted.

60E IFRS 9, issued in October 2010, amended paragraphs 3(a), 4 and 52(a) and deleted paragraph 60C. An entity shall apply those amendments when it applies IFRS 9 as issued in October 2010.

60F IFRS 10 and IFRS 11 *Joint Arrangements*, issued in May 2011, amended paragraphs 3(b), 8, 11, 18, 19, 33, 44–46 and 48A. An entity shall apply those amendments when it applies IFRS 10 and IFRS 11.

60G IFRS 13, issued in May 2011, amended the definition of fair value in paragraph 8 and amended paragraph 23. An entity shall apply those amendments when it applies IFRS 13.

60H *Presentation of Items of Other Comprehensive Income* (Amendments to IAS 1), issued in June 2011, amended paragraph 39. An entity shall apply that amendment when it applies IAS 1 as amended in June 2011.

Withdrawal of other pronouncements

61 This Standard supersedes IAS 21 *The Effects of Changes in Foreign Exchange Rates* (revised in 1993).

62 This Standard supersedes the following Interpretations:

(a) SIC-11 *Foreign Exchange—Capitalisation of Losses Resulting from Severe Currency Devaluations*;

(b) SIC-19 *Reporting Currency—Measurement and Presentation of Financial Statements under IAS 21 and IAS 29*; and

(c) SIC-30 *Reporting Currency—Translation from Measurement Currency to Presentation Currency*.

Appendix
Amendments to other pronouncements

The amendments in this appendix shall be applied for annual periods beginning on or after 1 January 2005. If an entity applies this Standard for an earlier period, these amendments shall be applied for that earlier period.

* * * * *

The amendments contained in this appendix when this Standard was issued in 2003 have been incorporated into the relevant pronouncements published in this volume.

International Accounting Standard 23

Borrowing Costs

In April 2001 the International Accounting Standards Board (IASB) adopted IAS 23 *Borrowing Costs*, which had originally been issued by the International Accounting Standards Committee in December 1993. IAS 23 *Borrowing Costs* replaced IAS 23 *Capitalisation of Borrowing Costs* (issued in March 1984).

In March 2007 the IASB issued a revised IAS 23 that eliminated the option of immediate recognition of borrowing costs as an expense.

The IASB made minor consequential amendments to IAS 23 through *Improvements to IFRSs* (issued May 2008).

CONTENTS

> FOR THE ACCOMPANYING DOCUMENTS LISTED BELOW, SEE PART B OF THIS EDITION

International Accounting Standard 23 *Borrowing Costs* (IAS 23) is set out in paragraphs 1–30 and the Appendix. All of the paragraphs have equal authority but retain the IASC format of the Standard when it was adopted by the IASB. IAS 23 should be read in the context of its core principle and the Basis for Conclusions, the *Preface to International Financial Reporting Standards* and the *Conceptual Framework for Financial Reporting*. IAS 8 *Accounting Policies, Changes in Accounting Estimates and Errors* provides a basis for selecting and applying accounting policies in the absence of explicit guidance.

This revised Standard was issued in March 2007. It supersedes IAS 23, revised in 1993. The text of the revised Standard, marked to show changes from the previous version, is available from the IASB's Subscriber Website at www.ifrs.org for a limited period.

International Accounting Standard 23
Borrowing Costs

Core principle

1   Borrowing costs that are directly attributable to the acquisition, construction or production of a qualifying asset form part of the cost of that asset. Other borrowing costs are recognised as an expense.

Scope

2   **An entity shall apply this Standard in accounting for borrowing costs.**

3   The Standard does not deal with the actual or imputed cost of equity, including preferred capital not classified as a liability.

4   An entity is not required to apply the Standard to borrowing costs directly attributable to the acquisition, construction or production of:

(a)   a qualifying asset measured at fair value, for example a biological asset; or

(b)   inventories that are manufactured, or otherwise produced, in large quantities on a repetitive basis.

Definitions

5   **This Standard uses the following terms with the meanings specified:**

Borrowing costs **are interest and other costs that an entity incurs in connection with the borrowing of funds.**

A *qualifying asset* **is an asset that necessarily takes a substantial period of time to get ready for its intended use or sale.**

6   Borrowing costs may include:

(a)   interest expense calculated using the effective interest method as described in IAS 39 *Financial Instruments: Recognition and Measurement*;

(b)   [deleted]

(c)   [deleted]

(d)   finance charges in respect of finance leases recognised in accordance with IAS 17 *Leases*; and

(e)   exchange differences arising from foreign currency borrowings to the extent that they are regarded as an adjustment to interest costs.

7   Depending on the circumstances, any of the following may be qualifying assets:

(a)   inventories

(b)   manufacturing plants

    (c)   power generation facilities

    (d)   intangible assets

    (e)   investment properties.

Financial assets, and inventories that are manufactured, or otherwise produced, over a short period of time, are not qualifying assets. Assets that are ready for their intended use or sale when acquired are not qualifying assets.

Recognition

8   **An entity shall capitalise borrowing costs that are directly attributable to the acquisition, construction or production of a qualifying asset as part of the cost of that asset. An entity shall recognise other borrowing costs as an expense in the period in which it incurs them.**

9   Borrowing costs that are directly attributable to the acquisition, construction or production of a qualifying asset are included in the cost of that asset. Such borrowing costs are capitalised as part of the cost of the asset when it is probable that they will result in future economic benefits to the entity and the costs can be measured reliably. When an entity applies IAS 29 *Financial Reporting in Hyperinflationary Economies*, it recognises as an expense the part of borrowing costs that compensates for inflation during the same period in accordance with paragraph 21 of that Standard.

Borrowing costs eligible for capitalisation

10   The borrowing costs that are directly attributable to the acquisition, construction or production of a qualifying asset are those borrowing costs that would have been avoided if the expenditure on the qualifying asset had not been made. When an entity borrows funds specifically for the purpose of obtaining a particular qualifying asset, the borrowing costs that directly relate to that qualifying asset can be readily identified.

11   It may be difficult to identify a direct relationship between particular borrowings and a qualifying asset and to determine the borrowings that could otherwise have been avoided. Such a difficulty occurs, for example, when the financing activity of an entity is co-ordinated centrally. Difficulties also arise when a group uses a range of debt instruments to borrow funds at varying rates of interest, and lends those funds on various bases to other entities in the group. Other complications arise through the use of loans denominated in or linked to foreign currencies, when the group operates in highly inflationary economies, and from fluctuations in exchange rates. As a result, the determination of the amount of borrowing costs that are directly attributable to the acquisition of a qualifying asset is difficult and the exercise of judgement is required.

12   **To the extent that an entity borrows funds specifically for the purpose of obtaining a qualifying asset, the entity shall determine the amount of borrowing costs eligible for capitalisation as the actual borrowing costs incurred on that borrowing during the period less any investment income on the temporary investment of those borrowings.**

13   The financing arrangements for a qualifying asset may result in an entity obtaining borrowed funds and incurring associated borrowing costs before some or all of the funds are used for expenditures on the qualifying asset. In such circumstances, the funds are often temporarily invested pending their expenditure on the qualifying asset. In determining the amount of borrowing costs eligible for capitalisation during a period, any investment income earned on such funds is deducted from the borrowing costs incurred.

14   **To the extent that an entity borrows funds generally and uses them for the purpose of obtaining a qualifying asset, the entity shall determine the amount of borrowing costs eligible for capitalisation by applying a capitalisation rate to the expenditures on that asset. The capitalisation rate shall be the weighted average of the borrowing costs applicable to the borrowings of the entity that are outstanding during the period, other than borrowings made specifically for the purpose of obtaining a qualifying asset. The amount of borrowing costs that an entity capitalises during a period shall not exceed the amount of borrowing costs it incurred during that period.**

15   In some circumstances, it is appropriate to include all borrowings of the parent and its subsidiaries when computing a weighted average of the borrowing costs; in other circumstances, it is appropriate for each subsidiary to use a weighted average of the borrowing costs applicable to its own borrowings.

Excess of the carrying amount of the qualifying asset over recoverable amount

16   When the carrying amount or the expected ultimate cost of the qualifying asset exceeds its recoverable amount or net realisable value, the carrying amount is written down or written off in accordance with the requirements of other Standards. In certain circumstances, the amount of the write-down or write-off is written back in accordance with those other Standards.

Commencement of capitalisation

17   **An entity shall begin capitalising borrowing costs as part of the cost of a qualifying asset on the commencement date. The commencement date for capitalisation is the date when the entity first meets all of the following conditions:**

     (a)   **it incurs expenditures for the asset;**

     (b)   **it incurs borrowing costs; and**

     (c)   **it undertakes activities that are necessary to prepare the asset for its intended use or sale.**

18   Expenditures on a qualifying asset include only those expenditures that have resulted in payments of cash, transfers of other assets or the assumption of interest-bearing liabilities. Expenditures are reduced by any progress payments received and grants received in connection with the asset (see IAS 20 *Accounting for Government Grants and Disclosure of Government Assistance*). The average carrying amount of the asset during a period, including borrowing costs previously capitalised, is normally a reasonable approximation of the expenditures to which the capitalisation rate is applied in that period.

19   The activities necessary to prepare the asset for its intended use or sale encompass more than the physical construction of the asset. They include technical and administrative work prior to the commencement of physical construction, such as the activities associated with obtaining permits prior to the commencement of the physical construction. However, such activities exclude the holding of an asset when no production or development that changes the asset's condition is taking place. For example, borrowing costs incurred while land is under development are capitalised during the period in which activities related to the development are being undertaken. However, borrowing costs incurred while land acquired for building purposes is held without any associated development activity do not qualify for capitalisation.

Suspension of capitalisation

20   **An entity shall suspend capitalisation of borrowing costs during extended periods in which it suspends active development of a qualifying asset.**

21   An entity may incur borrowing costs during an extended period in which it suspends the activities necessary to prepare an asset for its intended use or sale. Such costs are costs of holding partially completed assets and do not qualify for capitalisation. However, an entity does not normally suspend capitalising borrowing costs during a period when it carries out substantial technical and administrative work. An entity also does not suspend capitalising borrowing costs when a temporary delay is a necessary part of the process of getting an asset ready for its intended use or sale. For example, capitalisation continues during the extended period that high water levels delay construction of a bridge, if such high water levels are common during the construction period in the geographical region involved.

Cessation of capitalisation

22   **An entity shall cease capitalising borrowing costs when substantially all the activities necessary to prepare the qualifying asset for its intended use or sale are complete.**

23   An asset is normally ready for its intended use or sale when the physical construction of the asset is complete even though routine administrative work might still continue. If minor modifications, such as the decoration of a property to the purchaser's or user's specification, are all that are outstanding, this indicates that substantially all the activities are complete.

24   **When an entity completes the construction of a qualifying asset in parts and each part is capable of being used while construction continues on other parts, the entity shall cease capitalising borrowing costs when it completes substantially all the activities necessary to prepare that part for its intended use or sale.**

25   A business park comprising several buildings, each of which can be used individually, is an example of a qualifying asset for which each part is capable of being usable while construction continues on other parts. An example of a qualifying asset that needs to be complete before any part can be used is an industrial plant involving several processes which are carried out in sequence at different parts of the plant within the same site, such as a steel mill.

Disclosure

26 An entity shall disclose:

    (a)   the amount of borrowing costs capitalised during the period; and

    (b)   the capitalisation rate used to determine the amount of borrowing costs eligible for capitalisation.

Transitional provisions

27 When application of this Standard constitutes a change in accounting policy, an entity shall apply the Standard to borrowing costs relating to qualifying assets for which the commencement date for capitalisation is on or after the effective date.

28 However, an entity may designate any date before the effective date and apply the Standard to borrowing costs relating to all qualifying assets for which the commencement date for capitalisation is on or after that date.

Effective date

29 An entity shall apply the Standard for annual periods beginning on or after 1 January 2009. Earlier application is permitted. If an entity applies the Standard from a date before 1 January 2009, it shall disclose that fact.

29A Paragraph 6 was amended by *Improvements to IFRSs* issued in May 2008. An entity shall apply that amendment for annual periods beginning on or after 1 January 2009. Earlier application is permitted. If an entity applies the amendment for an earlier period it shall disclose that fact.

Withdrawal of IAS 23 (revised 1993)

30 This Standard supersedes IAS 23 *Borrowing Costs* revised in 1993.

Appendix
Amendments to other pronouncements

The amendments in this appendix shall be applied for annual periods beginning on or after 1 January 2009. If an entity applies this Standard for an earlier period, the amendments in this appendix shall be applied for that earlier period. In the amended paragraphs, new text is underlined and deleted text is struck through.

* * * * *

The amendments contained in this appendix when this IFRS was issued in 2007 have been incorporated into the relevant IFRSs published in this volume.

International Accounting Standard 24

Related Party Disclosures

In April 2001 the International Accounting Standards Board (IASB) adopted IAS 24 *Related Party Disclosures*, which had originally been issued by the International Accounting Standards Committee in July 1984.

In December 2003 the IASB issued a revised IAS 24 as part of its initial agenda of technical projects that included amending disclosures on management compensation and related party disclosures in separate financial statements. The IASB revised IAS 24 again to address the disclosures in government-related entities.

In December 2009 the IASB issued a revised IAS 24 to simplify the definition of 'related party' and to provide an exemption from the disclosure requirements for some government-related entities.

Other IFRSs have made minor consequential amendments to IAS 21. They include IAS 1 *Presentation of Financial Statements* (as revised in September 2007).

CONTENTS

> FOR THE ACCOMPANYING DOCUMENTS LISTED BELOW, SEE PART B OF THIS EDITION

International Accounting Standard 24 *Related Party Disclosures* (IAS 24) is set out in paragraphs 1–29 and the Appendix. All of the paragraphs have equal authority but retain the IASC format of the Standard when it was adopted by the IASB. IAS 24 should be read in the context of its objective and the Basis for Conclusions, the *Preface to International Financial Reporting Standards* and the *Conceptual Framework for Financial Reporting*. IAS 8 *Accounting Policies, Changes in Accounting Estimates and Errors* provides a basis for selecting and applying accounting policies in the absence of explicit guidance. The revised Standard was issued in November 2009. It supersedes IAS 24 (as revised in 2003). The text of the revised Standard, marked to show changes from the previous version, is available from the IASB's Subscriber Website at www.ifrs.org for a limited period.

Introduction

IN1   International Accounting Standard 24 *Related Party Disclosures* (IAS 24) requires a reporting entity to disclose:

    (a)   transactions with its related parties; and

    (b)   relationships between parents and subsidiaries irrespective of whether there have been transactions between those related parties.

IN2   The International Accounting Standards Board revised IAS 24 in 2009 by:

    (a)   simplifying the definition of a related party, clarifying its intended meaning and eliminating inconsistencies from the definition.

    (b)   providing a partial exemption from the disclosure requirements for government-related entities.

IN3   In making those revisions, the Board did not reconsider the fundamental approach to related party disclosures contained in IAS 24 (as revised in 2003).

International Accounting Standard 24
Related Party Disclosures

Objective

1   The objective of this Standard is to ensure that an entity's financial statements contain the disclosures necessary to draw attention to the possibility that its financial position and profit or loss may have been affected by the existence of related parties and by transactions and outstanding balances, including commitments, with such parties.

Scope

2   **This Standard shall be applied in:**

   (a)   **identifying related party relationships and transactions;**

   (b)   **identifying outstanding balances, including commitments, between an entity and its related parties;**

   (c)   **identifying the circumstances in which disclosure of the items in (a) and (b) is required; and**

   (d)   **determining the disclosures to be made about those items.**

3   **This Standard requires disclosure of related party relationships, transactions and outstanding balances, including commitments, in the consolidated and separate financial statements of a parent or investors with joint control of, or significant influence over, an investee presented in accordance with IFRS 10** *Consolidated Financial Statements* **or IAS 27** *Separate Financial Statements*. **This Standard also applies to individual financial statements.**

4   Related party transactions and outstanding balances with other entities in a group are disclosed in an entity's financial statements. Intragroup related party transactions and outstanding balances are eliminated in the preparation of consolidated financial statements of the group.

Purpose of related party disclosures

5   Related party relationships are a normal feature of commerce and business. For example, entities frequently carry on parts of their activities through subsidiaries, joint ventures and associates. In those circumstances, the entity has the ability to affect the financial and operating policies of the investee through the presence of control, joint control or significant influence.

6   A related party relationship could have an effect on the profit or loss and financial position of an entity. Related parties may enter into transactions that unrelated parties would not. For example, an entity that sells goods to its parent at cost might not sell on those terms to another customer. Also, transactions between related parties may not be made at the same amounts as between unrelated parties.

7 The profit or loss and financial position of an entity may be affected by a related party relationship even if related party transactions do not occur. The mere existence of the relationship may be sufficient to affect the transactions of the entity with other parties. For example, a subsidiary may terminate relations with a trading partner on acquisition by the parent of a fellow subsidiary engaged in the same activity as the former trading partner. Alternatively, one party may refrain from acting because of the significant influence of another—for example, a subsidiary may be instructed by its parent not to engage in research and development.

8 For these reasons, knowledge of an entity's transactions, outstanding balances, including commitments, and relationships with related parties may affect assessments of its operations by users of financial statements, including assessments of the risks and opportunities facing the entity.

Definitions

9 The following terms are used in this Standard with the meanings specified:

A *related party* is a person or entity that is related to the entity that is preparing its financial statements (in this Standard referred to as the 'reporting entity').

(a) A person or a close member of that person's family is related to a reporting entity if that person:

  (i) has control or joint control of the reporting entity;

  (ii) has significant influence over the reporting entity; or

  (iii) is a member of the key management personnel of the reporting entity or of a parent of the reporting entity.

(b) An entity is related to a reporting entity if any of the following conditions applies:

  (i) The entity and the reporting entity are members of the same group (which means that each parent, subsidiary and fellow subsidiary is related to the others).

  (ii) One entity is an associate or joint venture of the other entity (or an associate or joint venture of a member of a group of which the other entity is a member).

  (iii) Both entities are joint ventures of the same third party.

  (iv) One entity is a joint venture of a third entity and the other entity is an associate of the third entity.

  (v) The entity is a post-employment benefit plan for the benefit of employees of either the reporting entity or an entity related to the reporting entity. If the reporting entity is itself such a plan, the sponsoring employers are also related to the reporting entity.

  (vi) The entity is controlled or jointly controlled by a person identified in (a).

(vii) A person identified in (a)(i) has significant influence over the entity or is a member of the key management personnel of the entity (or of a parent of the entity).

A *related party transaction* is a transfer of resources, services or obligations between a reporting entity and a related party, regardless of whether a price is charged.

Close members of the family of a person are those family members who may be expected to influence, or be influenced by, that person in their dealings with the entity and include:

(a) that person's children and spouse or domestic partner;

(b) children of that person's spouse or domestic partner; and

(c) dependants of that person or that person's spouse or domestic partner.

Compensation includes all employee benefits (as defined in IAS 19 *Employee Benefits*) including employee benefits to which IFRS 2 *Share-based Payment* applies. Employee benefits are all forms of consideration paid, payable or provided by the entity, or on behalf of the entity, in exchange for services rendered to the entity. It also includes such consideration paid on behalf of a parent of the entity in respect of the entity. Compensation includes:

(a) short-term employee benefits, such as wages, salaries and social security contributions, paid annual leave and paid sick leave, profit-sharing and bonuses (if payable within twelve months of the end of the period) and non-monetary benefits (such as medical care, housing, cars and free or subsidised goods or services) for current employees;

(b) post-employment benefits such as pensions, other retirement benefits, post-employment life insurance and post-employment medical care;

(c) other long-term employee benefits, including long-service leave or sabbatical leave, jubilee or other long-service benefits, long-term disability benefits and, if they are not payable wholly within twelve months after the end of the period, profit-sharing, bonuses and deferred compensation;

(d) termination benefits; and

(e) share-based payment.

Key management personnel are those persons having authority and responsibility for planning, directing and controlling the activities of the entity, directly or indirectly, including any director (whether executive or otherwise) of that entity.

Government refers to government, government agencies and similar bodies whether local, national or international.

A *government-related entity* is an entity that is controlled, jointly controlled or significant influence by a government.

The terms 'control', 'jointly control' and 'significant influence' are defined in IFRS 10, IFRS 11 *Joint Arrangements* and IAS 28 *Investments in Associates and Joint Ventures* and are used in this Standard with the meanings specified in those IFRSs.

10   In considering each possible related party relationship, attention is directed to the substance of the relationship and not merely the legal form.

11   In the context of this Standard, the following are not related parties:

   (a)   two entities simply because they have a director or other member of key management personnel in common or because a member of key management personnel of one entity has significant influence over the other entity.

   (b)   two joint venturers simply because they share joint control of a joint venture.

   (c)

      (i)   providers of finance,

      (ii)   trade unions,

      (iii) public utilities, and

      (iv)   departments and agencies of a government that does not control, jointly control or significant influence the reporting entity,

         simply by virtue of their normal dealings with an entity (even though they may affect the freedom of action of an entity or participate in its decision-making process).

   (d)   a customer, supplier, franchisor, distributor or general agent with whom an entity transacts a significant volume of business, simply by virtue of the resulting economic dependence.

12   In the definition of a related party, an associate includes subsidiaries of the associate and a joint venture includes subsidiaries of the joint venture. Therefore, for example, an associate's subsidiary and the investor that has significant influence over the associate are related to each other.

Disclosures

All entities

13   **Relationships between a parent and its subsidiaries shall be disclosed irrespective of whether there have been transactions between them. An entity shall disclose the name of its parent and, if different, the ultimate controlling party. If neither the entity's parent nor the ultimate controlling party produces consolidated financial statements available for public use, the name of the next most senior parent that does so shall also be disclosed.**

14   To enable users of financial statements to form a view about the effects of related party relationships on an entity, it is appropriate to disclose the related party relationship when control exists, irrespective of whether there have been transactions between the related parties.

15   The requirement to disclose related party relationships between a parent and its subsidiaries is in addition to the disclosure requirements in IAS 27 and IFRS 12 *Disclosure of Interests in Other Entities*.

16   Paragraph 13 refers to the next most senior parent. This is the first parent in the group above the immediate parent that produces consolidated financial statements available for public use.

17   **An entity shall disclose key management personnel compensation in total and for each of the following categories:**

    (a)   **short-term employee benefits;**

    (b)   **post-employment benefits;**

    (c)   **other long-term benefits;**

    (d)   **termination benefits; and**

    (e)   **share-based payment.**

18   **If an entity has had related party transactions during the periods covered by the financial statements, it shall disclose the nature of the related party relationship as well as information about those transactions and outstanding balances, including commitments, necessary for users to understand the potential effect of the relationship on the financial statements. These disclosure requirements are in addition to those in paragraph 17. At a minimum, disclosures shall include:**

    (a)   **the amount of the transactions;**

    (b)   **the amount of outstanding balances, including commitments, and:**

        (i)   **their terms and conditions, including whether they are secured, and the nature of the consideration to be provided in settlement; and**

        (ii)   **details of any guarantees given or received;**

    (c)   **provisions for doubtful debts related to the amount of outstanding balances; and**

    (d)   **the expense recognised during the period in respect of bad or doubtful debts due from related parties.**

19   **The disclosures required by paragraph 18 shall be made separately for each of the following categories:**

    (a)   **the parent;**

    (b)   **entities with joint control of, or significant influence over, the entity;**

    (c)   **subsidiaries;**

    (d)   **associates;**

    (e)   **joint ventures in which the entity is a joint venturer;**

    (f)   **key management personnel of the entity or its parent; and**

    (g)   **other related parties.**

20   The classification of amounts payable to, and receivable from, related parties in the different categories as required in paragraph 19 is an extension of the disclosure requirement in IAS 1 *Presentation of Financial Statements* for information to be presented either in the statement of financial position or in the notes. The categories are extended to provide a more comprehensive analysis of related party balances and apply to related party transactions.

21   The following are examples of transactions that are disclosed if they are with a related party:

(a)   purchases or sales of goods (finished or unfinished);

(b)   purchases or sales of property and other assets;

(c)   rendering or receiving of services;

(d)   leases;

(e)   transfers of research and development;

(f)   transfers under licence agreements;

(g)   transfers under finance arrangements (including loans and equity contributions in cash or in kind);

(h)   provision of guarantees or collateral;

(i)   commitments to do something if a particular event occurs or does not occur in the future, including executory contracts[1] (recognised and unrecognised); and

(j)   settlement of liabilities on behalf of the entity or by the entity on behalf of that related party.

22   Participation by a parent or subsidiary in a defined benefit plan that shares risks between group entities is a transaction between related parties (see paragraph 42 of IAS 19 (as amended in 2011)).

23   Disclosures that related party transactions were made on terms equivalent to those that prevail in arm's length transactions are made only if such terms can be substantiated.

24   **Items of a similar nature may be disclosed in aggregate except when separate disclosure is necessary for an understanding of the effects of related party transactions on the financial statements of the entity.**

Government-related entities

25   **A reporting entity is exempt from the disclosure requirements of paragraph 18 in relation to related party transactions and outstanding balances, including commitments, with:**

(a)   **a government that has control or joint control of, or significant influence over, the reporting entity; and**

---

1   IAS 37 *Provisions, Contingent Liabilities and Contingent Assets* defines executory contracts as contracts under which neither party has performed any of its obligations or both parties have partially performed their obligations to an equal extent.

(b)   another entity that is a related party because the same government has control or joint control of, or significant influence over, both the reporting entity and the other entity.

26   If a reporting entity applies the exemption in paragraph 25, it shall disclose the following about the transactions and related outstanding balances referred to in paragraph 25:

(a)   the name of the government and the nature of its relationship with the reporting entity (ie control, joint control or significant influence);

(b)   the following information in sufficient detail to enable users of the entity's financial statements to understand the effect of related party transactions on its financial statements:

(i)   the nature and amount of each individually significant transaction; and

(ii)   for other transactions that are collectively, but not individually, significant, a qualitative or quantitative indication of their extent. Types of transactions include those listed in paragraph 21.

27   In using its judgement to determine the level of detail to be disclosed in accordance with the requirements in paragraph 26(b), the reporting entity shall consider the closeness of the related party relationship and other factors relevant in establishing the level of significance of the transaction such as whether it is:

(a)   significant in terms of size;

(b)   carried out on non-market terms;

(c)   outside normal day-to-day business operations, such as the purchase and sale of businesses;

(d)   disclosed to regulatory or supervisory authorities;

(e)   reported to senior management;

(f)   subject to shareholder approval.

Effective date and transition

28   An entity shall apply this Standard retrospectively for annual periods beginning on or after 1 January 2011. Earlier application is permitted, either of the whole Standard or of the partial exemption in paragraphs 25–27 for government-related entities. If an entity applies either the whole Standard or that partial exemption for a period beginning before 1 January 2011, it shall disclose that fact.

28A   IFRS 10, IFRS 11 *Joint Arrangements* and IFRS 12, issued in May 2011, amended paragraphs 3, 9, 11(b), 15, 19(b) and (e) and 25. An entity shall apply those amendments when it applies IFRS 10, IFRS 11 and IFRS 12.

Withdrawal of IAS 24 (2003)

29   This Standard supersedes IAS 24 *Related Party Disclosures* (as revised in 2003).

Appendix
Amendment to IFRS 8 *Operating Segments*

This amendment contained in this appendix when this Standard was issued in 2009 has been incorporated into IFRS 8 as published in this volume.

International Accounting Standard 26

Accounting and Reporting by Retirement Benefit Plans

In April 2001 the International Accounting Standards Board (IASB) adopted IAS 26 *Accounting and Reporting by Retirement Benefit Plans*, which had originally been issued by the International Accounting Standards Committee in January 1987.

CONTENTS

International Accounting Standard 26 *Accounting and Reporting by Retirement Benefit Plans* (IAS 26) is set out in paragraphs 1–37. All the paragraphs have equal authority but retain the IASC format of the Standard when it was adopted by the IASB. IAS 26 should be read in the context of the *Preface to International Financial Reporting Standards* and the *Conceptual Framework for Financial Reporting*. IAS 8 *Accounting Policies, Changes in Accounting Estimates and Errors* provides a basis for selecting and applying accounting policies in the absence of explicit guidance.

International Accounting Standard 26
Accounting and Reporting by Retirement Benefit Plans

Scope

1   **This Standard shall be applied in the financial statements of retirement benefit plans where such financial statements are prepared.**

2   Retirement benefit plans are sometimes referred to by various other names, such as 'pension schemes', 'superannuation schemes' or 'retirement benefit schemes'. This Standard regards a retirement benefit plan as a reporting entity separate from the employers of the participants in the plan. All other Standards apply to the financial statements of retirement benefit plans to the extent that they are not superseded by this Standard.

3   This Standard deals with accounting and reporting by the plan to all participants as a group. It does not deal with reports to individual participants about their retirement benefit rights.

4   IAS 19 *Employee Benefits* is concerned with the determination of the cost of retirement benefits in the financial statements of employers having plans. Hence this Standard complements IAS 19.

5   Retirement benefit plans may be defined contribution plans or defined benefit plans. Many require the creation of separate funds, which may or may not have separate legal identity and may or may not have trustees, to which contributions are made and from which retirement benefits are paid. This Standard applies regardless of whether such a fund is created and regardless of whether there are trustees.

6   Retirement benefit plans with assets invested with insurance companies are subject to the same accounting and funding requirements as privately invested arrangements. Accordingly, they are within the scope of this Standard unless the contract with the insurance company is in the name of a specified participant or a group of participants and the retirement benefit obligation is solely the responsibility of the insurance company.

7   This Standard does not deal with other forms of employment benefits such as employment termination indemnities, deferred compensation arrangements, long-service leave benefits, special early retirement or redundancy plans, health and welfare plans or bonus plans. Government social security type arrangements are also excluded from the scope of this Standard.

Definitions

8   **The following terms are used in this Standard with the meanings specified:**

Retirement benefit plans are arrangements whereby an entity provides benefits for employees on or after termination of service (either in the form of an annual income or as a lump sum) when such benefits, or the contributions towards them, can be determined or estimated in advance of retirement from the provisions of a document or from the entity's practices.

Defined contribution plans are retirement benefit plans under which amounts to be paid as retirement benefits are determined by contributions to a fund together with investment earnings thereon.

Defined benefit plans are retirement benefit plans under which amounts to be paid as retirement benefits are determined by reference to a formula usually based on employees' earnings and/or years of service.

Funding is the transfer of assets to an entity (the *fund*) separate from the employer's entity to meet future obligations for the payment of retirement benefits.

For the purposes of this Standard the following terms are also used:

Participants are the members of a retirement benefit plan and others who are entitled to benefits under the plan.

Net assets available for benefits are the assets of a plan less liabilities other than the actuarial present value of promised retirement benefits.

Actuarial present value of promised retirement benefits is the present value of the expected payments by a retirement benefit plan to existing and past employees, attributable to the service already rendered.

Vested benefits are benefits, the rights to which, under the conditions of a retirement benefit plan, are not conditional on continued employment.

9   Some retirement benefit plans have sponsors other than employers; this Standard also applies to the financial statements of such plans.

10   Most retirement benefit plans are based on formal agreements. Some plans are informal but have acquired a degree of obligation as a result of employers' established practices. While some plans permit employers to limit their obligations under the plans, it is usually difficult for an employer to cancel a plan if employees are to be retained. The same basis of accounting and reporting applies to an informal plan as to a formal plan.

11   Many retirement benefit plans provide for the establishment of separate funds into which contributions are made and out of which benefits are paid. Such funds may be administered by parties who act independently in managing fund assets. Those parties are called trustees in some countries. The term trustee is used in this Standard to describe such parties regardless of whether a trust has been formed.

12   Retirement benefit plans are normally described as either defined contribution plans or defined benefit plans, each having their own distinctive characteristics. Occasionally plans exist that contain characteristics of both. Such hybrid plans are considered to be defined benefit plans for the purposes of this Standard.

Defined contribution plans

13   The financial statements of a defined contribution plan shall contain a statement of net assets available for benefits and a description of the funding policy.

14   Under a defined contribution plan, the amount of a participant's future benefits is determined by the contributions paid by the employer, the participant, or both, and the operating efficiency and investment earnings of the fund. An employer's obligation is usually discharged by contributions to the fund. An actuary's advice is not normally required although such advice is sometimes used to estimate future benefits that may be achievable based on present contributions and varying levels of future contributions and investment earnings.

15   The participants are interested in the activities of the plan because they directly affect the level of their future benefits. Participants are interested in knowing whether contributions have been received and proper control has been exercised to protect the rights of beneficiaries. An employer is interested in the efficient and fair operation of the plan.

16   The objective of reporting by a defined contribution plan is periodically to provide information about the plan and the performance of its investments. That objective is usually achieved by providing financial statements including the following:

(a)   a description of significant activities for the period and the effect of any changes relating to the plan, and its membership and terms and conditions;

(b)   statements reporting on the transactions and investment performance for the period and the financial position of the plan at the end of the period; and

(c)   a description of the investment policies.

Defined benefit plans

17   The financial statements of a defined benefit plan shall contain either:

(a)   a statement that shows:

(i)   the net assets available for benefits;

(ii)   the actuarial present value of promised retirement benefits, distinguishing between vested benefits and non-vested benefits; and

(iii)   the resulting excess or deficit; or

(b)   a statement of net assets available for benefits including either:

(i)   a note disclosing the actuarial present value of promised retirement benefits, distinguishing between vested benefits and non-vested benefits; or

(ii)   a reference to this information in an accompanying actuarial report.

If an actuarial valuation has not been prepared at the date of the financial statements, the most recent valuation shall be used as a base and the date of the valuation disclosed.

18   For the purposes of paragraph 17, the actuarial present value of promised retirement benefits shall be based on the benefits promised under the terms of the plan on service rendered to date using either current salary levels or projected salary levels with disclosure of the basis used. The effect of any changes in actuarial assumptions that have had a significant effect on the actuarial present value of promised retirement benefits shall also be disclosed.

19   The financial statements shall explain the relationship between the actuarial present value of promised retirement benefits and the net assets available for benefits, and the policy for the funding of promised benefits.

20   Under a defined benefit plan, the payment of promised retirement benefits depends on the financial position of the plan and the ability of contributors to make future contributions to the plan as well as the investment performance and operating efficiency of the plan.

21   A defined benefit plan needs the periodic advice of an actuary to assess the financial condition of the plan, review the assumptions and recommend future contribution levels.

22   The objective of reporting by a defined benefit plan is periodically to provide information about the financial resources and activities of the plan that is useful in assessing the relationships between the accumulation of resources and plan benefits over time. This objective is usually achieved by providing financial statements including the following:

(a)   a description of significant activities for the period and the effect of any changes relating to the plan, and its membership and terms and conditions;

(b)   statements reporting on the transactions and investment performance for the period and the financial position of the plan at the end of the period;

(c)   actuarial information either as part of the statements or by way of a separate report; and

(d)   a description of the investment policies.

Actuarial present value of promised retirement benefits

23   The present value of the expected payments by a retirement benefit plan may be calculated and reported using current salary levels or projected salary levels up to the time of retirement of participants.

24   The reasons given for adopting a current salary approach include:

(a)   the actuarial present value of promised retirement benefits, being the sum of the amounts presently attributable to each participant in the plan, can be calculated more objectively than with projected salary levels because it involves fewer assumptions;

(b)   increases in benefits attributable to a salary increase become an obligation of the plan at the time of the salary increase; and

(c)   the amount of the actuarial present value of promised retirement benefits using current salary levels is generally more closely related to the amount payable in the event of termination or discontinuance of the plan.

25   Reasons given for adopting a projected salary approach include:

(a)   financial information should be prepared on a going concern basis, irrespective of the assumptions and estimates that must be made;

(b)   under final pay plans, benefits are determined by reference to salaries at or near retirement date; hence salaries, contribution levels and rates of return must be projected; and

(c)   failure to incorporate salary projections, when most funding is based on salary projections, may result in the reporting of an apparent overfunding when the plan is not overfunded, or in reporting adequate funding when the plan is underfunded.

26   The actuarial present value of promised retirement benefits based on current salaries is disclosed in the financial statements of a plan to indicate the obligation for benefits earned to the date of the financial statements. The actuarial present value of promised retirement benefits based on projected salaries is disclosed to indicate the magnitude of the potential obligation on a going concern basis which is generally the basis for funding. In addition to disclosure of the actuarial present value of promised retirement benefits, sufficient explanation may need to be given so as to indicate clearly the context in which the actuarial present value of promised retirement benefits should be read. Such explanation may be in the form of information about the adequacy of the planned future funding and of the funding policy based on salary projections. This may be included in the financial statements or in the actuary's report.

Frequency of actuarial valuations

27   In many countries, actuarial valuations are not obtained more frequently than every three years. If an actuarial valuation has not been prepared at the date of the financial statements, the most recent valuation is used as a base and the date of the valuation disclosed.

Financial statement content

28   For defined benefit plans, information is presented in one of the following formats which reflect different practices in the disclosure and presentation of actuarial information:

(a)   a statement is included in the financial statements that shows the net assets available for benefits, the actuarial present value of promised retirement benefits, and the resulting excess or deficit. The financial statements of the plan also contain statements of changes in net assets available for benefits and changes in the actuarial present value of promised retirement benefits. The financial statements may be accompanied by a separate actuary's report supporting the actuarial present value of promised retirement benefits;

(b)   financial statements that include a statement of net assets available for benefits and a statement of changes in net assets available for benefits. The actuarial present value of promised retirement benefits is disclosed in a note to the statements. The financial statements may also be accompanied by a report from an actuary supporting the actuarial present value of promised retirement benefits; and

(c)   financial statements that include a statement of net assets available for benefits and a statement of changes in net assets available for benefits with the actuarial present value of promised retirement benefits contained in a separate actuarial report.

In each format a trustees' report in the nature of a management or directors' report and an investment report may also accompany the financial statements.

29   Those in favour of the formats described in paragraph 28(a) and (b) believe that the quantification of promised retirement benefits and other information provided under those approaches help users to assess the current status of the plan and the likelihood of the plan's obligations being met. They also believe that financial statements should be complete in themselves and not rely on accompanying statements. However, some believe that the format described in paragraph 28(a) could give the impression that a liability exists, whereas the actuarial present value of promised retirement benefits does not in their opinion have all the characteristics of a liability.

30   Those who favour the format described in paragraph 28(c) believe that the actuarial present value of promised retirement benefits should not be included in a statement of net assets available for benefits as in the format described in paragraph 28(a) or even be disclosed in a note as in paragraph 28(b), because it will be compared directly with plan assets and such a comparison may not be valid. They contend that actuaries do not necessarily compare actuarial present value of promised retirement benefits with market values of investments but may instead assess the present value of cash flows expected from the investments. Therefore, those in favour of this format believe that such a comparison is unlikely to reflect the actuary's overall assessment of the plan and that it may be misunderstood. Also, some believe that, regardless of whether quantified, the information about promised retirement benefits should be contained solely in the separate actuarial report where a proper explanation can be provided.

31   This Standard accepts the views in favour of permitting disclosure of the information concerning promised retirement benefits in a separate actuarial report. It rejects arguments against the quantification of the actuarial present value of promised retirement benefits. Accordingly, the formats described in paragraph 28(a) and (b) are considered acceptable under this Standard, as is the format described in paragraph 28(c) so long as the financial statements contain a reference to, and are accompanied by, an actuarial report that includes the actuarial present value of promised retirement benefits.

All plans

Valuation of plan assets

32   **Retirement benefit plan investments shall be carried at fair value. In the case of marketable securities fair value is market value. Where plan investments are held for which an estimate of fair value is not possible disclosure shall be made of the reason why fair value is not used.**

33　In the case of marketable securities fair value is usually market value because this is considered the most useful measure of the securities at the report date and of the investment performance for the period. Those securities that have a fixed redemption value and that have been acquired to match the obligations of the plan, or specific parts thereof, may be carried at amounts based on their ultimate redemption value assuming a constant rate of return to maturity. Where plan investments are held for which an estimate of fair value is not possible, such as total ownership of an entity, disclosure is made of the reason why fair value is not used. To the extent that investments are carried at amounts other than market value or fair value, fair value is generally also disclosed. Assets used in the operations of the fund are accounted for in accordance with the applicable Standards.

Disclosure

34　**The financial statements of a retirement benefit plan, whether defined benefit or defined contribution, shall also contain the following information:**

　　(a)　a statement of changes in net assets available for benefits;

　　(b)　a summary of significant accounting policies; and

　　(c)　a description of the plan and the effect of any changes in the plan during the period.

35　Financial statements provided by retirement benefit plans include the following, if applicable:

　　(a)　a statement of net assets available for benefits disclosing:

　　　　(i)　assets at the end of the period suitably classified;

　　　　(ii)　the basis of valuation of assets;

　　　　(iii)　details of any single investment exceeding either 5% of the net assets available for benefits or 5% of any class or type of security;

　　　　(iv)　details of any investment in the employer; and

　　　　(v)　liabilities other than the actuarial present value of promised retirement benefits;

　　(b)　a statement of changes in net assets available for benefits showing the following:

　　　　(i)　employer contributions;

　　　　(ii)　employee contributions;

　　　　(iii)　investment income such as interest and dividends;

　　　　(iv)　other income;

　　　　(v)　benefits paid or payable (analysed, for example, as retirement, death and disability benefits, and lump sum payments);

　　　　(vi)　administrative expenses;

　　　　(vii)　other expenses;

       (viii) taxes on income;

       (ix)   profits and losses on disposal of investments and changes in value of investments; and

       (x)   transfers from and to other plans;

(c)   a description of the funding policy;

(d)   for defined benefit plans, the actuarial present value of promised retirement benefits (which may distinguish between vested benefits and non-vested benefits) based on the benefits promised under the terms of the plan, on service rendered to date and using either current salary levels or projected salary levels; this information may be included in an accompanying actuarial report to be read in conjunction with the related financial statements; and

(e)   for defined benefit plans, a description of the significant actuarial assumptions made and the method used to calculate the actuarial present value of promised retirement benefits.

36   The report of a retirement benefit plan contains a description of the plan, either as part of the financial statements or in a separate report. It may contain the following:

(a)   the names of the employers and the employee groups covered;

(b)   the number of participants receiving benefits and the number of other participants, classified as appropriate;

(c)   the type of plan—defined contribution or defined benefit;

(d)   a note as to whether participants contribute to the plan;

(e)   a description of the retirement benefits promised to participants;

(f)   a description of any plan termination terms; and

(g)   changes in items (a) to (f) during the period covered by the report.

It is not uncommon to refer to other documents that are readily available to users and in which the plan is described, and to include only information on subsequent changes.

Effective date

37   This Standard becomes operative for financial statements of retirement benefit plans covering periods beginning on or after 1 January 1988.

International Accounting Standard 27

Separate Financial Statements

In April 2001 the International Accounting Standards Board adopted IAS 27 *Consolidated Financial Statements and Accounting for Investments in Subsidiaries*, which had originally been issued by the International Accounting Standards Committee in April 1989. That standard replaced IAS 3 *Consolidated Financial Statements* (issued in July 1976), except for those parts that dealt with accounting for investment in associates.

In December 2003, the IASB issued a revised IAS 27 with a new title—*Consolidated and Separate Financial Statements*. This revised IAS 27 was part of the IASB's initial agenda of technical projects. The revised IAS 27 also incorporated the guidance from two related Interpretations (SIC-12 *Consolidation—Special Purpose Entities* and SIC-33 *Consolidation and Equity Method—Potential Voting Rights and Allocation of Ownership Interests*).

The IASB amended IAS 27 in January 2008 to address the accounting for non-controlling interests and loss of control of a subsidiary as part of its business combinations project.

In May 2011 the IASB issued a revised IAS 27 with a modified title—*Separate Financial Statements*. IFRS 10 *Consolidated Financial Statements* addresses the principle of control and the requirements relating to the preparation of consolidated financial statements.

Other IFRSs have made minor consequential amendments to IAS 27. They include IFRS 5 *Non-current Assets Held for Sale and Discontinued Operations* (issued March 2004), IAS 1 *Presentation of Financial Statements* (as revised in September 2007), *Improvements to IFRSs* (issued May 2008) and IFRS 9 *Financial Instruments* (issued November 2009 and October 2010).

Contents

Introduction

IN1 IAS 27 *Separate Financial Statements* contains accounting and disclosure requirements for investments in subsidiaries, joint ventures and associates when an entity prepares separate financial statements. The Standard requires an entity preparing separate financial statements to account for those investments at cost or in accordance with IFRS 9 *Financial Instruments*.

IN2 The Standard is effective for annual periods beginning on or after 1 January 2013. Earlier application is permitted.

International Accounting Standard 27
Separate Financial Statements

Objective

1   The objective of this Standard is to prescribe the accounting and disclosure requirements for investments in subsidiaries, joint ventures and associates when an entity prepares separate financial statements.

Scope

2   **This Standard shall be applied in accounting for investments in subsidiaries, joint ventures and associates when an entity elects, or is required by local regulations, to present separate financial statements.**

3   This Standard does not mandate which entities produce separate financial statements. It applies when an entity prepares separate financial statements that comply with International Financial Reporting Standards.

Definitions

4   **The following terms are used in this Standard with the meanings specified:**

Consolidated financial statements **are the financial statements of a group in which the assets, liabilities, equity, income, expenses and cash flows of the parent and its subsidiaries are presented as those of a single economic entity.**

Separate financial statements **are those presented by a parent (ie an investor with control of a subsidiary) or an investor with joint control of, or significant influence over, an investee, in which the investments are accounted for at cost or in accordance with IFRS 9** *Financial Instruments.*

5   The following terms are defined in Appendix A of IFRS 10 *Consolidated Financial Statements*, Appendix A of IFRS 11 *Joint Arrangements* and paragraph 3 of IAS 28 *Investments in Associates and Joint Ventures*:

*   associate

*   control of an investee

*   group

*   joint control

*   joint venture

*   joint venturer

*   parent

*   significant influence

*   subsidiary.

6   Separate financial statements are those presented in addition to consolidated financial statements or in addition to financial statements in which investments in associates or joint ventures are accounted for using the equity method, other than in the circumstances set out in paragraph 8. Separate financial statements need not be appended to, or accompany, those statements.

7   Financial statements in which the equity method is applied are not separate financial statements. Similarly, the financial statements of an entity that does not have a subsidiary, associate or joint venturer's interest in a joint venture are not separate financial statements.

8   An entity that is exempted in accordance with paragraph 4(a) of IFRS 10 from consolidation or paragraph 17 of IAS 28 (as amended in 2011) from applying the equity method may present separate financial statements as its only financial statements.

Preparation of separate financial statements

9   **Separate financial statements shall be prepared in accordance with all applicable IFRSs, except as provided in paragraph 10.**

10   **When an entity prepares separate financial statements, it shall account for investments in subsidiaries, joint ventures and associates either:**

     (a)   at cost, or

     (b)   in accordance with IFRS 9.

    The entity shall apply the same accounting for each category of investments. Investments accounted for at cost shall be accounted for in accordance with IFRS 5 *Non-current Assets Held for Sale and Discontinued Operations* **when they are classified as held for sale (or included in a disposal group that is classified as held for sale). The measurement of investments accounted for in accordance with IFRS 9 is not changed in such circumstances.**

11   If an entity elects, in accordance with paragraph 18 of IAS 28 (as amended in 2011), to measure its investments in associates or joint ventures at fair value through profit or loss in accordance with IFRS 9, it shall also account for those investments in the same way in its separate financial statements.

12   **An entity shall recognise a dividend from a subsidiary, a joint venture or an associate in profit or loss in its separate financial statements when its right to receive the dividend is established.**

13   When a parent reorganises the structure of its group by establishing a new entity as its parent in a manner that satisfies the following criteria:

     (a)   the new parent obtains control of the original parent by issuing equity instruments in exchange for existing equity instruments of the original parent;

     (b)   the assets and liabilities of the new group and the original group are the same immediately before and after the reorganisation; and

(c)   the owners of the original parent before the reorganisation have the same absolute and relative interests in the net assets of the original group and the new group immediately before and after the reorganisation,

and the new parent accounts for its investment in the original parent in accordance with paragraph 10(a) in its separate financial statements, the new parent shall measure cost at the carrying amount of its share of the equity items shown in the separate financial statements of the original parent at the date of the reorganisation.

14   Similarly, an entity that is not a parent might establish a new entity as its parent in a manner that satisfies the criteria in paragraph 13. The requirements in paragraph 13 apply equally to such reorganisations. In such cases, references to 'original parent' and 'original group' are to the 'original entity'.

Disclosure

15   **An entity shall apply all applicable IFRSs when providing disclosures in its separate financial statements, including the requirements in paragraphs 16 and 17.**

16   **When a parent, in accordance with paragraph 4(a) of IFRS 10, elects not to prepare consolidated financial statements and instead prepares separate financial statements, it shall disclose in those separate financial statements:**

    (a)   **the fact that the financial statements are separate financial statements; that the exemption from consolidation has been used; the name and principal place of business (and country of incorporation, if different) of the entity whose consolidated financial statements that comply with International Financial Reporting Standards have been produced for public use; and the address where those consolidated financial statements are obtainable.**

    (b)   **a list of significant investments in subsidiaries, joint ventures and associates, including:**

        (i)   **the name of those investees.**

        (ii)   **the principal place of business (and country of incorporation, if different) of those investees.**

        (iii)   **its proportion of the ownership interest (and its proportion of the voting rights, if different) held in those investees.**

    (c)   **a description of the method used to account for the investments listed under (b).**

17   **When a parent (other than a parent covered by paragraph 16) or an investor with joint control of, or significant influence over, an investee prepares separate financial statements, the parent or investor shall identify the financial statements prepared in accordance with IFRS 10, IFRS 11 or IAS 28 (as amended in 2011) to which they relate. The parent or investor shall also disclose in its separate financial statements:**

(a) the fact that the statements are separate financial statements and the reasons why those statements are prepared if not required by law.

(b) a list of significant investments in subsidiaries, joint ventures and associates, including:

(i) the name of those investees.

(ii) the principal place of business (and country of incorporation, if different) of those investees.

(iii) its proportion of the ownership interest (and its proportion of the voting rights, if different) held in those investees.

(c) a description of the method used to account for the investments listed under (b).

The parent or investor shall also identify the financial statements prepared in accordance with IFRS 10, IFRS 11 or IAS 28 (as amended in 2011) to which they relate.

Effective date and transition

18 An entity shall apply this Standard for annual periods beginning on or after 1 January 2013. Earlier application is permitted. If an entity applies this Standard earlier, it shall disclose that fact and apply IFRS 10, IFRS 11, IFRS 12 *Disclosure of Interests in Other Entities* and IAS 28 (as amended in 2011) at the same time.

References to IFRS 9

19 If an entity applies this Standard but does not yet apply IFRS 9, any reference to IFRS 9 shall be read as a reference to IAS 39 *Financial Instruments: Recognition and Measurement*.

Withdrawal of IAS 27 (2008)

20 This Standard is issued concurrently with IFRS 10. Together, the two IFRSs supersede IAS 27 *Consolidated and Separate Financial Statements* (as amended in 2008).

International Accounting Standard 28

Investments in Associates and Joint Ventures

In April 2001 the International Accounting Standards Board (IASB) adopted IAS 28 *Accounting for Investments in Associates*, which had originally been issued by the International Accounting Standards Committee in April 1989. IAS 28 *Accounting for Investments in Associates* replaced those parts of IAS 3 *Consolidated Financial Statements* (issued in July 1976) that dealt with accounting for investment in associates.

In December 2003, the IASB issued a revised IAS 28 with a new title—*Investments in Associates*. This revised IAS 27 was part of the IASB's initial agenda of technical projects and also incorporated the guidance contained in two related Interpretations (SIC-3 *Elimination of Unrealised Profits and Losses on Transactions with Associates*, SIC-20 *Equity Accounting Method—Recognition of Losses* and SIC-33 *Consolidation and Equity Method—Potential Voting Rights and Allocation of Ownership Interests*).

Other IFRSs have made minor consequential amendments to IAS 28. They include IFRS 3 *Business Combinations* (issued March 2004 and as revised in January 2008), IAS 1 *Presentation of Financial Statements* (as revised in September 2007), IAS 27 *Consolidated and Separate Financial Statements* (as amended in January 2008), *Improvements to IFRSs* (issued May 2008 and May 2010) and IFRS 9 *Financial Instruments* (issued November 2009 and October 2010).

CONTENTS

FOR THE ACCOMPANYING DOCUMENTS LISTED BELOW, SEE PART B OF THIS EDITION

International Accounting Standard 28 *Investments in Associates and Joint Ventures* (IAS 28) is set out in paragraphs 1–47. All the paragraphs have equal authority but retain the IASC format of the Standard when it was adopted by the IASB. IAS 28 should be read in the context of its objective and the Basis for Conclusions, the *Preface to International Financial Reporting Standards* and the *Conceptual Framework for Financial Reporting*. IAS 8 *Accounting Policies, Changes in Accounting Estimates and Errors* provides a basis for selecting and applying accounting policies in the absence of explicit guidance.

Introduction

IN1 International Accounting Standard 28 *Investments in Associates and Joint Ventures* (IAS 28) prescribes the accounting for investments in associates and sets out the requirements for the application of the equity method when accounting for investments in associates and joint ventures.

IN2 The Standard is effective for annual periods beginning on or after 1 January 2013. Earlier application is permitted.

Main features of the Standard

IN3 IAS 28 (as amended in 2011) is to be applied by all entities that are investors with joint control of, or significant influence over, an investee.

IN4 The Standard defines significant influence as the power to participate in the financial and operating policy decisions of the investee but is not control or joint control of those policies.

IN5 IFRS 11 *Joint Arrangements* establishes principles for the financial reporting of parties to joint arrangements. It defines joint control as the contractually agreed sharing of control of an arrangement, which exists only when decisions about the relevant activities require the unanimous consent of the parties sharing control.

IN6 An entity applies IFRS 11 to determine the type of joint arrangement in which it is involved. Once it has determined that it has an interest in a joint venture, the entity recognises an investment and accounts for it using the equity method in accordance with IAS 28 (as amended in 2011), unless the entity is exempted from applying the equity method as specified in the Standard.

Equity method

IN7 The Standard defines the equity method as a method of accounting whereby the investment is initially recognised at cost and adjusted thereafter for the post-acquisition change in the investor's share of net assets of the investee. The profit or loss of the investor includes its share of the profit or loss of the investee and the other comprehensive income of the investor includes its share of other comprehensive income of the investee.

IN8 An entity uses the equity method to account for its investments in associates or joint ventures in its consolidated financial statements. An entity that does not have any subsidiaries also uses the equity method to account for its investments in associates or joint ventures in its financial statements even though those are not described as consolidated financial statements. The only financial statements to which an entity does not apply the equity method are separate financial statements it presents in accordance with IAS 27 *Separate Financial Statements*.

Exemptions from applying the equity method

IN9 The Standard provides exemptions from applying the equity method similar to those provided in IFRS 10 *Consolidated Financial Statements* for parents not to prepare consolidated financial statements.

IN10   The Standard also provides exemptions from applying the equity method when the investment in the associate or joint venture is held by, or is held indirectly through, venture capital organisations, or mutual funds, unit trusts and similar entities including investment-linked insurance funds. Those investments in associates and joint ventures may be measured at fair value through profit or loss in accordance with IFRS 9 *Financial Instruments*.

Disclosure

IN11   The disclosure requirements for entities with joint control of, or significant influence over, an investee are specified in IFRS 12 *Disclosure of Interests in Other Entities*.

International Accounting Standard 28
Investments in Associates and Joint Ventures

Objective

1   The objective of this Standard is to prescribe the accounting for investments in associates and to set out the requirements for the application of the equity method when accounting for investments in associates and joint ventures.

Scope

2   This Standard shall be applied by all entities that are investors with joint control of, or significant influence over, an investee.

Definitions

3   The following terms are used in this Standard with the meanings specified:

An *associate* is an entity over which the investor has significant influence.

Consolidated financial statements are the financial statements of a group in which assets, liabilities, equity, income, expenses and cash flows of the parent and its subsidiaries are presented as those of a single economic entity.

The *equity method* is a method of accounting whereby the investment is initially recognised at cost and adjusted thereafter for the post-acquisition change in the investor's share of the investee's net assets. The investor's profit or loss includes its share of the investee's profit or loss and the investor's other comprehensive income includes its share of the investee's other comprehensive income.

A *joint arrangement* is an arrangement of which two or more parties have joint control.

Joint control is the contractually agreed sharing of control of an arrangement, which exists only when decisions about the relevant activities require the unanimous consent of the parties sharing control.

A *joint venture* is a joint arrangement whereby the parties that have joint control of the arrangement have rights to the net assets of the arrangement.

A *joint venturer* is a party to a joint venture that has joint control of that joint venture.

Significant influence is the power to participate in the financial and operating policy decisions of the investee but is not control or joint control of those policies.

4   The following terms are defined in paragraph 4 of IAS 27 *Separate Financial Statements* and in Appendix A of IFRS 10 *Consolidated Financial Statements* and are used in this Standard with the meanings specified in the IFRSs in which they are defined:

- control of an investee

- group

- parent
- separate financial statements
- subsidiary.

Significant influence

5   If an entity holds, directly or indirectly (eg through subsidiaries), 20 per cent or more of the voting power of the investee, it is presumed that the entity has significant influence, unless it can be clearly demonstrated that this is not the case. Conversely, if the entity holds, directly or indirectly (eg through subsidiaries), less than 20 per cent of the voting power of the investee, it is presumed that the entity does not have significant influence, unless such influence can be clearly demonstrated. A substantial or majority ownership by another investor does not necessarily preclude an entity from having significant influence.

6   The existence of significant influence by an entity is usually evidenced in one or more of the following ways:

(a)   representation on the board of directors or equivalent governing body of the investee;

(b)   participation in policy-making processes, including participation in decisions about dividends or other distributions;

(c)   material transactions between the entity and its investee;

(d)   interchange of managerial personnel; or

(e)   provision of essential technical information.

7   An entity may own share warrants, share call options, debt or equity instruments that are convertible into ordinary shares, or other similar instruments that have the potential, if exercised or converted, to give the entity additional voting power or to reduce another party's voting power over the financial and operating policies of another entity (ie potential voting rights). The existence and effect of potential voting rights that are currently exercisable or convertible, including potential voting rights held by other entities, are considered when assessing whether an entity has significant influence. Potential voting rights are not currently exercisable or convertible when, for example, they cannot be exercised or converted until a future date or until the occurrence of a future event.

8   In assessing whether potential voting rights contribute to significant influence, the entity examines all facts and circumstances (including the terms of exercise of the potential voting rights and any other contractual arrangements whether considered individually or in combination) that affect potential rights, except the intentions of management and the financial ability to exercise or convert those potential rights.

9   An entity loses significant influence over an investee when it loses the power to participate in the financial and operating policy decisions of that investee. The loss of significant influence can occur with or without a change in absolute or relative ownership levels. It could occur, for example, when an associate becomes subject to the control of a government, court, administrator or regulator. It could also occur as a result of a contractual arrangement.

Equity method

10   Under the equity method, on initial recognition the investment in an associate or a joint venture is recognised at cost, and the carrying amount is increased or decreased to recognise the investor's share of the profit or loss of the investee after the date of acquisition. The investor's share of the investee's profit or loss is recognised in the investor's profit or loss. Distributions received from an investee reduce the carrying amount of the investment. Adjustments to the carrying amount may also be necessary for changes in the investor's proportionate interest in the investee arising from changes in the investee's other comprehensive income. Such changes include those arising from the revaluation of property, plant and equipment and from foreign exchange translation differences. The investor's share of those changes is recognised in the investor's other comprehensive income (see IAS 1 *Presentation of Financial Statements*).

11   The recognition of income on the basis of distributions received may not be an adequate measure of the income earned by an investor on an investment in an associate or a joint venture because the distributions received may bear little relation to the performance of the associate or joint venture. Because the investor has joint control of, or significant influence over, the investee, the investor has an interest in the associate's or joint venture's performance and, as a result, the return on its investment. The investor accounts for this interest by extending the scope of its financial statements to include its share of the profit or loss of such an investee. As a result, application of the equity method provides more informative reporting of the investor's net assets and profit or loss.

12   When potential voting rights or other derivatives containing potential voting rights exist, an entity's interest in an associate or a joint venture is determined solely on the basis of existing ownership interests and does not reflect the possible exercise or conversion of potential voting rights and other derivative instruments, unless paragraph 13 applies.

13   In some circumstances, an entity has, in substance, an existing ownership as a result of a transaction that currently gives it access to the returns associated with an ownership interest. In such circumstances, the proportion allocated to the entity is determined by taking into account the eventual exercise of those potential voting rights and other derivative instruments that currently give the entity access to the returns.

14   IFRS 9 *Financial Instruments* does not apply to interests in associates and joint ventures that are accounted for using the equity method. When instruments containing potential voting rights in substance currently give access to the returns associated with an ownership interest in an associate or a joint venture, the instruments are not subject to IFRS 9. In all other cases, instruments containing potential voting rights in an associate or a joint venture are accounted for in accordance with IFRS 9.

15   Unless an investment, or a portion of an investment, in an associate or a joint venture is classified as held for sale in accordance with IFRS 5 *Non-current Assets Held for Sale and Discontinued Operations*, the investment, or any retained interest in the investment not classified as held for sale, shall be classified as a non-current asset.

Application of the equity method

16   An entity with joint control of, or significant influence over, an investee shall account for its investment in an associate or a joint venture using the equity method except when that investment qualifies for exemption in accordance with paragraphs 17–19.

Exemptions from applying the equity method

17   An entity need not apply the equity method to its investment in an associate or a joint venture if the entity is a parent that is exempt from preparing consolidated financial statements by the scope exception in paragraph 4(a) of IFRS 10 or if all the following apply:

(a)   The entity is a wholly-owned subsidiary, or is a partially-owned subsidiary of another entity and its other owners, including those not otherwise entitled to vote, have been informed about, and do not object to, the entity not applying the equity method.

(b)   The entity's debt or equity instruments are not traded in a public market (a domestic or foreign stock exchange or an over-the-counter market, including local and regional markets).

(c)   The entity did not file, nor is it in the process of filing, its financial statements with a securities commission or other regulatory organisation, for the purpose of issuing any class of instruments in a public market.

(d)   The ultimate or any intermediate parent of the entity produces consolidated financial statements available for public use that comply with IFRSs.

18   When an investment in an associate or a joint venture is held by, or is held indirectly through, an entity that is a venture capital organisation, or a mutual fund, unit trust and similar entities including investment-linked insurance funds, the entity may elect to measure investments in those associates and joint ventures at fair value through profit or loss in accordance with IFRS 9.

19   When an entity has an investment in an associate, a portion of which is held indirectly through a venture capital organisation, or a mutual fund, unit trust and similar entities including investment-linked insurance funds, the entity may elect to measure that portion of the investment in the associate at fair value through profit or loss in accordance with IFRS 9 regardless of whether the venture capital organisation, or the mutual fund, unit trust and similar entities including investment-linked insurance funds, has significant influence over that portion of the investment. If the entity makes that election, the entity shall apply the equity method to any remaining portion of its investment in an associate that is not held through a venture capital organisation, or a mutual fund, unit trust and similar entities including investment-linked insurance funds.

Classification as held for sale

20   An entity shall apply IFRS 5 to an investment, or a portion of an investment, in an associate or a joint venture that meets the criteria to be classified as held for sale. Any retained portion of an investment in an associate or a joint venture that has not been classified as held for sale shall be accounted for using the equity method until disposal of the portion that is classified as held for sale takes place. After the disposal takes place, an entity shall account for any retained interest in the associate or joint venture in accordance with IFRS 9 unless the retained interest continues to be an associate or a joint venture, in which case the entity uses the equity method.

21   When an investment, or a portion of an investment, in an associate or a joint venture previously classified as held for sale no longer meets the criteria to be so classified, it shall be accounted for using the equity method retrospectively as from the date of its classification as held for sale. Financial statements for the periods since classification as held for sale shall be amended accordingly.

Discontinuing the use of the equity method

22   An entity shall discontinue the use of the equity method from the date when its investment ceases to be an associate or a joint venture as follows:

(a)   If the investment becomes a subsidiary, the entity shall account for its investment in accordance with IFRS 3 *Business Combinations* and IFRS 10.

(b)   If the retained interest in the former associate or joint venture is a financial asset, the entity shall measure the retained interest at fair value. The fair value of the retained interest shall be regarded as its fair value on initial recognition as a financial asset in accordance with IFRS 9. The entity shall recognise in profit or loss any difference between:

(i)   the fair value of any retained interest and any proceeds from disposing of a part interest in the associate or joint venture; and

(ii)   the carrying amount of the investment at the date the equity method was discontinued.

(c)   When an entity discontinues the use of the equity method, the entity shall account for all amounts previously recognised in other comprehensive income in relation to that investment on the same basis as would have been required if the investee had directly disposed of the related assets or liabilities.

23   Therefore, if a gain or loss previously recognised in other comprehensive income by the investee would be reclassified to profit or loss on the disposal of the related assets or liabilities, the entity reclassifies the gain or loss from equity to profit or loss (as a reclassification adjustment) when the equity method is discontinued. For example, if an associate or a joint venture has cumulative exchange differences relating to a foreign operation and the entity discontinues the use of the equity method, the entity shall reclassify to profit or loss the gain or loss that had previously been recognised in other comprehensive income in relation to the foreign operation.

24   **If an investment in an associate becomes an investment in a joint venture or an investment in a joint venture becomes an investment in an associate, the entity continues to apply the equity method and does not remeasure the retained interest.**

Changes in ownership interest

25   If an entity's ownership interest in an associate or a joint venture is reduced, but the entity continues to apply the equity method, the entity shall reclassify to profit or loss the proportion of the gain or loss that had previously been recognised in other comprehensive income relating to that reduction in ownership interest if that gain or loss would be required to be reclassified to profit or loss on the disposal of the related assets or liabilities.

Equity method procedures

26   Many of the procedures that are appropriate for the application of the equity method are similar to the consolidation procedures described in IFRS 10. Furthermore, the concepts underlying the procedures used in accounting for the acquisition of a subsidiary are also adopted in accounting for the acquisition of an investment in an associate or a joint venture.

27   A group's share in an associate or a joint venture is the aggregate of the holdings in that associate or joint venture by the parent and its subsidiaries. The holdings of the group's other associates or joint ventures are ignored for this purpose. When an associate or a joint venture has subsidiaries, associates or joint ventures, the profit or loss, other comprehensive income and net assets taken into account in applying the equity method are those recognised in the associate's or joint venture's financial statements (including the associate's or joint venture's share of the profit or loss, other comprehensive income and net assets of its associates and joint ventures), after any adjustments necessary to give effect to uniform accounting policies (see paragraphs 35 and 36).

28   Gains and losses resulting from 'upstream' and 'downstream' transactions between an entity (including its consolidated subsidiaries) and its associate or joint venture are recognised in the entity's financial statements only to the extent of unrelated investors' interests in the associate or joint venture. 'Upstream' transactions are, for example, sales of assets from an associate or a joint venture to the investor. 'Downstream' transactions are, for example, sales or contributions of assets from the investor to its associate or its joint venture. The investor's share in the associate's or joint venture's gains or losses resulting from these transactions is eliminated.

29   When downstream transactions provide evidence of a reduction in the net realisable value of the assets to be sold or contributed, or of an impairment loss of those assets, those losses shall be recognised in full by the investor. When upstream transactions provide evidence of a reduction in the net realisable value of the assets to be purchased or of an impairment loss of those assets, the investor shall recognise its share in those losses.

30   The contribution of a non-monetary asset to an associate or a joint venture in exchange for an equity interest in the associate or joint venture shall be accounted for in accordance with paragraph 28, except when the contribution lacks commercial substance, as that term is described in IAS 16 *Property, Plant and Equipment*. If such a contribution lacks commercial substance, the gain or loss is regarded as unrealised and is not recognised unless paragraph 31 also applies. Such unrealised gains and losses shall be eliminated against the investment accounted for using the equity method and shall not be presented as deferred gains or losses in the entity's consolidated statement of financial position or in the entity's statement of financial position in which investments are accounted for using the equity method.

31   If, in addition to receiving an equity interest in an associate or a joint venture, an entity receives monetary or non-monetary assets, the entity recognises in full in profit or loss the portion of the gain or loss on the non-monetary contribution relating to the monetary or non-monetary assets received.

32   An investment is accounted for using the equity method from the date on which it becomes an associate or a joint venture. On acquisition of the investment, any difference between the cost of the investment and the entity's share of the net fair value of the investee's identifiable assets and liabilities is accounted for as follows:

(a)   Goodwill relating to an associate or a joint venture is included in the carrying amount of the investment. Amortisation of that goodwill is not permitted.

(b)   Any excess of the entity's share of the net fair value of the investee's identifiable assets and liabilities over the cost of the investment is included as income in the determination of the entity's share of the associate or joint venture's profit or loss in the period in which the investment is acquired.

Appropriate adjustments to the entity's share of the associate's or joint venture's profit or loss after acquisition are made in order to account, for example, for depreciation of the depreciable assets based on their fair values at the acquisition date. Similarly, appropriate adjustments to the entity's share of the associate's or joint venture's profit or loss after acquisition are made for impairment losses such as for goodwill or property, plant and equipment.

33   **The most recent available financial statements of the associate or joint venture are used by the entity in applying the equity method. When the end of the reporting period of the entity is different from that of the associate or joint venture, the associate or joint venture prepares, for the use of the entity, financial statements as of the same date as the financial statements of the entity unless it is impracticable to do so.**

34   When, in accordance with paragraph 33, the financial statements of an associate or a joint venture used in applying the equity method are prepared as of a date different from that used by the entity, adjustments shall be made for the effects of significant transactions or events that occur between that date and the date of the entity's financial statements. In any case, the difference between the end of the reporting period of the associate or joint venture and that of the entity shall be no more than three months. The length of the reporting periods and any difference between the ends of the reporting periods shall be the same from period to period.

35   The entity's financial statements shall be prepared using uniform accounting policies for like transactions and events in similar circumstances.

36   If an associate or a joint venture uses accounting policies other than those of the entity for like transactions and events in similar circumstances, adjustments shall be made to make the associate's or joint venture's accounting policies conform to those of the entity when the associate's or joint venture's financial statements are used by the entity in applying the equity method.

37   If an associate or a joint venture has outstanding cumulative preference shares that are held by parties other than the entity and are classified as equity, the entity computes its share of profit or loss after adjusting for the dividends on such shares, whether or not the dividends have been declared.

38   If an entity's share of losses of an associate or a joint venture equals or exceeds its interest in the associate or joint venture, the entity discontinues recognising its share of further losses. The interest in an associate or a joint venture is the carrying amount of the investment in the associate or joint venture determined using the equity method together with any long-term interests that, in substance, form part of the entity's net investment in the associate or joint venture. For example, an item for which settlement is neither planned nor likely to occur in the foreseeable future is, in substance, an extension of the entity's investment in that associate or joint venture. Such items may include preference shares and long-term receivables or loans, but do not include trade receivables, trade payables or any long-term receivables for which adequate collateral exists, such as secured loans. Losses recognised using the equity method in excess of the entity's investment in ordinary shares are applied to the other components of the entity's interest in an associate or a joint venture in the reverse order of their seniority (ie priority in liquidation).

39   After the entity's interest is reduced to zero, additional losses are provided for, and a liability is recognised, only to the extent that the entity has incurred legal or constructive obligations or made payments on behalf of the associate or joint venture. If the associate or joint venture subsequently reports profits, the entity resumes recognising its share of those profits only after its share of the profits equals the share of losses not recognised.

Impairment losses

40   After application of the equity method, including recognising the associate's or joint venture's losses in accordance with paragraph 38, the entity applies IAS 39 *Financial Instruments: Recognition and Measurement* to determine whether it is necessary to recognise any additional impairment loss with respect to its net investment in the associate or joint venture.

41   The entity also applies IAS 39 to determine whether any additional impairment loss is recognised with respect to its interest in the associate or joint venture that does not constitute part of the net investment and the amount of that impairment loss.

42   Because goodwill that forms part of the carrying amount of an investment in an associate or a joint venture is not separately recognised, it is not tested for impairment separately by applying the requirements for impairment testing goodwill in IAS 36 Impairment of Assets. Instead, the entire carrying amount of the investment is tested for impairment in accordance with IAS 36 as a single asset, by comparing its recoverable amount (higher of value in use and fair value less costs to sell) with its carrying amount, whenever application of IAS 39 indicates that the investment may be impaired. An impairment loss recognised in those circumstances is not allocated to any asset, including goodwill, that forms part of the carrying amount of the investment in the associate or joint venture. Accordingly, any reversal of that impairment loss is recognised in accordance with IAS 36 to the extent that the recoverable amount of the investment subsequently increases. In determining the value in use of the investment, an entity estimates:

(a)   its share of the present value of the estimated future cash flows expected to be generated by the associate or joint venture, including the cash flows from the operations of the associate or joint venture and the proceeds from the ultimate disposal of the investment; or

(b)   the present value of the estimated future cash flows expected to arise from dividends to be received from the investment and from its ultimate disposal.

Using appropriate assumptions, both methods give the same result.

43   The recoverable amount of an investment in an associate or a joint venture shall be assessed for each associate or joint venture, unless the associate or joint venture does not generate cash inflows from continuing use that are largely independent of those from other assets of the entity.

Separate financial statements

44   An investment in an associate or a joint venture shall be accounted for in the entity's separate financial statements in accordance with paragraph 10 of IAS 27 (as amended in 2011).

Effective date and transition

45   An entity shall apply this Standard for annual periods beginning on or after 1 January 2013. Earlier application is permitted. If an entity applies this Standard earlier, it shall disclose that fact and apply IFRS 10, IFRS 11 *Joint Arrangements*, IFRS 12 *Disclosure of Interests in Other Entities* and IAS 27 (as amended in 2011) at the same time.

References to IFRS 9

46   If an entity applies this Standard but does not yet apply IFRS 9, any reference to IFRS 9 shall be read as a reference to IAS 39.

Withdrawal of IAS 28 (2003)

47   This Standard supersedes IAS 28 *Investments in Associates* (as revised in 2003).

International Accounting Standard 29

Financial Reporting in Hyperinflationary Economies

In April 2001 the International Accounting Standards Board (IASB) adopted IAS 29 *Financial Reporting in Hyperinflationary Economies*, which had originally been issued by the International Accounting Standards Committee in July 1989.

Other IFRSs have made minor consequential amendments to IAS 29. They include IAS 21 *The Effects of Changes in Foreign Exchange Rates* (as revised in December 2003), IAS 1 *Presentation of Financial Statements* (as revised in September 2007) and *Improvements to IFRSs* (issued May 2008).

CONTENTS

FOR THE ACCOMPANYING DOCUMENTS LISTED BELOW, SEE PART B OF THIS EDITION

BASIS FOR CONCLUSIONS

International Accounting Standard 29 *Financial Reporting in Hyperinflationary Economies* (IAS 29) is set out in paragraphs 1–41. All the paragraphs have equal authority but retain the IASC format of the Standard when it was adopted by the IASB. IAS 29 should be read in the context of the Basis for Conclusions, the *Preface to International Financial Reporting Standards* and the *Conceptual Framework for Financial Reporting*. IAS 8 *Accounting Policies, Changes in Accounting Estimates and Errors* provides a basis for selecting and applying accounting policies in the absence of explicit guidance.

International Accounting Standard 29
Financial Reporting in Hyperinflationary Economies[1]

Scope

1   **This Standard shall be applied to the financial statements, including the consolidated financial statements, of any entity whose functional currency is the currency of a hyperinflationary economy.**

2   In a hyperinflationary economy, reporting of operating results and financial position in the local currency without restatement is not useful. Money loses purchasing power at such a rate that comparison of amounts from transactions and other events that have occurred at different times, even within the same accounting period, is misleading.

3   This Standard does not establish an absolute rate at which hyperinflation is deemed to arise. It is a matter of judgement when restatement of financial statements in accordance with this Standard becomes necessary. Hyperinflation is indicated by characteristics of the economic environment of a country which include, but are not limited to, the following:

   (a)   the general population prefers to keep its wealth in non-monetary assets or in a relatively stable foreign currency. Amounts of local currency held are immediately invested to maintain purchasing power;

   (b)   the general population regards monetary amounts not in terms of the local currency but in terms of a relatively stable foreign currency. Prices may be quoted in that currency;

   (c)   sales and purchases on credit take place at prices that compensate for the expected loss of purchasing power during the credit period, even if the period is short;

   (d)   interest rates, wages and prices are linked to a price index; and

   (e)   the cumulative inflation rate over three years is approaching, or exceeds, 100%.

4   It is preferable that all entities that report in the currency of the same hyperinflationary economy apply this Standard from the same date. Nevertheless, this Standard applies to the financial statements of any entity from the beginning of the reporting period in which it identifies the existence of hyperinflation in the country in whose currency it reports.

---

1   As part of *Improvements to IFRSs* issued in May 2008, the Board changed terms used in IAS 29 to be consistent with other IFRSs as follows: (a) 'market value' was amended to 'fair value', and (b) 'results of operations' and 'net income' were amended to 'profit or loss'.

The restatement of financial statements

5   Prices change over time as the result of various specific or general political, economic and social forces. Specific forces such as changes in supply and demand and technological changes may cause individual prices to increase or decrease significantly and independently of each other. In addition, general forces may result in changes in the general level of prices and therefore in the general purchasing power of money.

6   Entities that prepare financial statements on the historical cost basis of accounting do so without regard either to changes in the general level of prices or to increases in specific prices of recognised assets or liabilities. The exceptions to this are those assets and liabilities that the entity is required, or chooses, to measure at fair value. For example, property, plant and equipment may be revalued to fair value and biological assets are generally required to be measured at fair value. Some entities, however, present financial statements that are based on a current cost approach that reflects the effects of changes in the specific prices of assets held.

7   In a hyperinflationary economy, financial statements, whether they are based on a historical cost approach or a current cost approach, are useful only if they are expressed in terms of the measuring unit current at the end of the reporting period. As a result, this Standard applies to the financial statements of entities reporting in the currency of a hyperinflationary economy. Presentation of the information required by this Standard as a supplement to unrestated financial statements is not permitted. Furthermore, separate presentation of the financial statements before restatement is discouraged.

8   **The financial statements of an entity whose functional currency is the currency of a hyperinflationary economy, whether they are based on a historical cost approach or a current cost approach, shall be stated in terms of the measuring unit current at the end of the reporting period. The corresponding figures for the previous period required by IAS 1** *Presentation of Financial Statements* **(as revised in 2007) and any information in respect of earlier periods shall also be stated in terms of the measuring unit current at the end of the reporting period. For the purpose of presenting comparative amounts in a different presentation currency, paragraphs 42(b) and 43 of IAS 21** *The Effects of Changes in Foreign Exchange Rates* **apply.**

9   **The gain or loss on the net monetary position shall be included in profit or loss and separately disclosed.**

10   The restatement of financial statements in accordance with this Standard requires the application of certain procedures as well as judgement. The consistent application of these procedures and judgements from period to period is more important than the precise accuracy of the resulting amounts included in the restated financial statements.

Historical cost financial statements

Statement of financial position

11   Statement of financial position amounts not already expressed in terms of the measuring unit current at the end of the reporting period are restated by applying a general price index.

12   Monetary items are not restated because they are already expressed in terms of the monetary unit current at the end of the reporting period. Monetary items are money held and items to be received or paid in money.

13   Assets and liabilities linked by agreement to changes in prices, such as index linked bonds and loans, are adjusted in accordance with the agreement in order to ascertain the amount outstanding at the end of the reporting period. These items are carried at this adjusted amount in the restated statement of financial position.

14   All other assets and liabilities are non-monetary. Some non-monetary items are carried at amounts current at the end of the reporting period, such as net realisable value and fair value, so they are not restated. All other non-monetary assets and liabilities are restated.

15   Most non-monetary items are carried at cost or cost less depreciation; hence they are expressed at amounts current at their date of acquisition. The restated cost, or cost less depreciation, of each item is determined by applying to its historical cost and accumulated depreciation the change in a general price index from the date of acquisition to the end of the reporting period. For example, property, plant and equipment, inventories of raw materials and merchandise, goodwill, patents, trademarks and similar assets are restated from the dates of their purchase. Inventories of partly-finished and finished goods are restated from the dates on which the costs of purchase and of conversion were incurred.

16   Detailed records of the acquisition dates of items of property, plant and equipment may not be available or capable of estimation. In these rare circumstances, it may be necessary, in the first period of application of this Standard, to use an independent professional assessment of the value of the items as the basis for their restatement.

17   A general price index may not be available for the periods for which the restatement of property, plant and equipment is required by this Standard. In these circumstances, it may be necessary to use an estimate based, for example, on the movements in the exchange rate between the functional currency and a relatively stable foreign currency.

18   Some non-monetary items are carried at amounts current at dates other than that of acquisition or that of the statement of financial position, for example property, plant and equipment that has been revalued at some earlier date. In these cases, the carrying amounts are restated from the date of the revaluation.

19   The restated amount of a non-monetary item is reduced, in accordance with appropriate IFRSs, when it exceeds its recoverable amount. For example, restated amounts of property, plant and equipment, goodwill, patents and trademarks are reduced to recoverable amount and restated amounts of inventories are reduced to net realisable value.

20   An investee that is accounted for under the equity method may report in the currency of a hyperinflationary economy. The statement of financial position and statement of comprehensive income of such an investee are restated in accordance with this Standard in order to calculate the investor's share of its net assets and profit or loss. When the restated financial statements of the investee are expressed in a foreign currency they are translated at closing rates.

21   The impact of inflation is usually recognised in borrowing costs. It is not appropriate both to restate the capital expenditure financed by borrowing and to capitalise that part of the borrowing costs that compensates for the inflation during the same period. This part of the borrowing costs is recognised as an expense in the period in which the costs are incurred.

22   An entity may acquire assets under an arrangement that permits it to defer payment without incurring an explicit interest charge. Where it is impracticable to impute the amount of interest, such assets are restated from the payment date and not the date of purchase.

23   [Deleted]

24   At the beginning of the first period of application of this Standard, the components of owners' equity, except retained earnings and any revaluation surplus, are restated by applying a general price index from the dates the components were contributed or otherwise arose. Any revaluation surplus that arose in previous periods is eliminated. Restated retained earnings are derived from all the other amounts in the restated statement of financial position.

25   At the end of the first period and in subsequent periods, all components of owners' equity are restated by applying a general price index from the beginning of the period or the date of contribution, if later. The movements for the period in owners' equity are disclosed in accordance with IAS 1.

Statement of comprehensive income

26   This Standard requires that all items in the statement of comprehensive income are expressed in terms of the measuring unit current at the end of the reporting period. Therefore all amounts need to be restated by applying the change in the general price index from the dates when the items of income and expenses were initially recorded in the financial statements.

Gain or loss on net monetary position

27   In a period of inflation, an entity holding an excess of monetary assets over monetary liabilities loses purchasing power and an entity with an excess of monetary liabilities over monetary assets gains purchasing power to the extent the assets and liabilities are not linked to a price level. This gain or loss on the net monetary position may be derived as the difference resulting from the restatement of non-monetary assets, owners' equity and items in the statement of

comprehensive income and the adjustment of index linked assets and liabilities. The gain or loss may be estimated by applying the change in a general price index to the weighted average for the period of the difference between monetary assets and monetary liabilities.

28   The gain or loss on the net monetary position is included in profit or loss. The adjustment to those assets and liabilities linked by agreement to changes in prices made in accordance with paragraph 13 is offset against the gain or loss on net monetary position. Other income and expense items, such as interest income and expense, and foreign exchange differences related to invested or borrowed funds, are also associated with the net monetary position. Although such items are separately disclosed, it may be helpful if they are presented together with the gain or loss on net monetary position in the statement of comprehensive income.

Current cost financial statements

Statement of financial position

29   Items stated at current cost are not restated because they are already expressed in terms of the measuring unit current at the end of the reporting period. Other items in the statement of financial position are restated in accordance with paragraphs 11 to 25.

Statement of comprehensive income

30   The current cost statement of comprehensive income, before restatement, generally reports costs current at the time at which the underlying transactions or events occurred. Cost of sales and depreciation are recorded at current costs at the time of consumption; sales and other expenses are recorded at their money amounts when they occurred. Therefore all amounts need to be restated into the measuring unit current at the end of the reporting period by applying a general price index.

Gain or loss on net monetary position

31   The gain or loss on the net monetary position is accounted for in accordance with paragraphs 27 and 28.

Taxes

32   The restatement of financial statements in accordance with this Standard may give rise to differences between the carrying amount of individual assets and liabilities in the statement of financial position and their tax bases. These differences are accounted for in accordance with IAS 12 *Income Taxes*.

Statement of cash flows

33   This Standard requires that all items in the statement of cash flows are expressed in terms of the measuring unit current at the end of the reporting period.

Corresponding figures

34   Corresponding figures for the previous reporting period, whether they were based on a historical cost approach or a current cost approach, are restated by applying a general price index so that the comparative financial statements are presented in terms of the measuring unit current at the end of the reporting period. Information that is disclosed in respect of earlier periods is also expressed in terms of the measuring unit current at the end of the reporting period. For the purpose of presenting comparative amounts in a different presentation currency, paragraphs 42(b) and 43 of IAS 21 apply.

Consolidated financial statements

35   A parent that reports in the currency of a hyperinflationary economy may have subsidiaries that also report in the currencies of hyperinflationary economies. The financial statements of any such subsidiary need to be restated by applying a general price index of the country in whose currency it reports before they are included in the consolidated financial statements issued by its parent. Where such a subsidiary is a foreign subsidiary, its restated financial statements are translated at closing rates. The financial statements of subsidiaries that do not report in the currencies of hyperinflationary economies are dealt with in accordance with IAS 21.

36   If financial statements with different ends of the reporting periods are consolidated, all items, whether non-monetary or monetary, need to be restated into the measuring unit current at the date of the consolidated financial statements.

Selection and use of the general price index

37   The restatement of financial statements in accordance with this Standard requires the use of a general price index that reflects changes in general purchasing power. It is preferable that all entities that report in the currency of the same economy use the same index.

Economies ceasing to be hyperinflationary

38   When an economy ceases to be hyperinflationary and an entity discontinues the preparation and presentation of financial statements prepared in accordance with this Standard, it shall treat the amounts expressed in the measuring unit current at the end of the previous reporting period as the basis for the carrying amounts in its subsequent financial statements.

Disclosures

39   The following disclosures shall be made:

   (a)   the fact that the financial statements and the corresponding figures for previous periods have been restated for the changes in the general purchasing power of the functional currency and, as a result, are stated in terms of the measuring unit current at the end of the reporting period;

(b)   whether the financial statements are based on a historical cost approach or a current cost approach; and

(c)   the identity and level of the price index at the end of the reporting period and the movement in the index during the current and the previous reporting period.

40   The disclosures required by this Standard are needed to make clear the basis of dealing with the effects of inflation in the financial statements. They are also intended to provide other information necessary to understand that basis and the resulting amounts.

Effective date

41   This Standard becomes operative for financial statements covering periods beginning on or after 1 January 1990.

International Accounting Standard 32

Financial Instruments: Presentation

In April 2001 the International Accounting Standards Board (IASB) adopted IAS 32 *Financial Instruments: Disclosure and Presentation*, which had been issued by the International Accounting Standards Committee in 2000. IAS 32 *Financial Instruments: Disclosure and Presentation* had originally been issued in June 1995 and had been subsequently amended in 1998 and 2000.

The IASB issued a revised IAS 32 in December 2003 as part of its initial agenda of technical projects. This revised IAS 32 also incorporated the guidance contained in related Interpretations (SIC-5 *Classification of Financial Instruments-Contingent Settlement Provisions*, SIC-16 *Share Capital-Reacquired Own Equity Instruments (Treasury Shares)* and SIC-17 *Equity—Costs of an Equity Transaction*). It also incorporated guidance previously proposed in draft SIC Interpretation D34 *Financial Instruments—Instruments or Rights Redeemable by the Holder*.

In December 2005 the IASB amended IAS 32 by relocating all disclosures relating to financial instruments to IFRS 7 *Financial Instruments: Disclosures*. Consequently, the title of IAS 32 changed to *Financial Instruments: Presentation*.

In February 2008 IAS 32 was changed to require some puttable financial instruments and obligations arising on liquidation to be classified as equity. In October 2009 the IASB amended IAS 32 to require some rights that are denominated in a foreign currency to be classified as equity. The application guidance in IAS 32 was amended in December 2011 to address some inconsistencies relating to the offsetting financial assets and financial liabilities criteria.

Other IFRSs have made minor consequential amendments to IAS 32. They include IFRS 2 *Share-based Payments* (issued February 2004), IFRS 3 *Business Combinations* (issued March 2004 and revised in January 2008), IAS 1 *Presentation of Financial Statements* (as revised in September 2007), *Improvements to IFRSs* (issued May 2008 and May 2010), IFRS 9 *Financial Instruments* (issued November 2009 and October 2010) and IFRS 13 *Fair Value Measurement* (issued May 2011).

CONTENTS

FOR THE ACCOMPANYING DOCUMENTS LISTED BELOW, SEE PART B OF THIS EDITION

APPROVAL BY THE BOARD OF IAS 32 ISSUED IN DECEMBER 2003

APPROVAL BY THE BOARD OF AMENDMENTS TO IAS 32:

Puttable Financial Instruments and Obligations Arising on Liquidation (Amendments to IAS 32 and IAS 1) issued in February 2008

Classification of Rights Issues (Amendments to IAS 32) issued in October 2009

Offsetting Financial Assets and Financial Liabilities (Amendments to IAS 32) issued in December 2011

BASIS FOR CONCLUSIONS

DISSENTING OPINIONS

ILLUSTRATIVE EXAMPLES

International Accounting Standard 32 *Financial Instruments: Presentation* (IAS 32) is set out in paragraphs 2–100 and the Appendix. All the paragraphs have equal authority but retain the IASC format of the Standard when it was adopted by the IASB. IAS 32 should be read in the context of its objective and the Basis for Conclusions, the *Preface to International Financial Reporting Standards* and the *Conceptual Framework for Financial Reporting*. IAS 8 *Accounting Policies, Changes in Accounting Estimates and Errors* provides a basis for selecting and applying accounting policies in the absence of explicit guidance.

Introduction

Reasons for revising IAS 32 in December 2003

IN1   International Accounting Standard 32 *Financial Instruments: Disclosure and Presentation* (IAS 32)[1] replaces IAS 32 *Financial Instruments: Disclosure and Presentation* (revised in 2000), and should be applied for annual periods beginning on or after 1 January 2005. Earlier application is permitted. The Standard also replaces the following Interpretations and draft Interpretation:

- SIC-5 *Classification of Financial Instruments—Contingent Settlement Provisions*;

- SIC-16 *Share Capital—Reacquired Own Equity Instruments (Treasury Shares)*;

- SIC-17 *Equity—Costs of an Equity Transaction*; and

- draft SIC-D34 *Financial Instruments—Instruments or Rights Redeemable by the Holder*.

IN2   The International Accounting Standards Board developed this revised IAS 32 as part of its project to improve IAS 32 and IAS 39 *Financial Instruments: Recognition and Measurement*. The objective of the project was to reduce complexity by clarifying and adding guidance, eliminating internal inconsistencies and incorporating into the Standards elements of Standing Interpretations Committee (SIC) Interpretations and IAS 39 implementation guidance published by the Implementation Guidance Committee (IGC).

IN3   For IAS 32, the Board's main objective was a limited revision to provide additional guidance on selected matters—such as the measurement of the components of a compound financial instrument on initial recognition, and the classification of derivatives based on an entity's own shares—and to locate all disclosures relating to financial instruments in one Standard.[2] The Board did not reconsider the fundamental approach to the presentation and disclosure of financial instruments contained in IAS 32.

The main changes

IN4   The main changes from the previous version of IAS 32 are described below.

Scope

IN5   The scope of IAS 32 has, where appropriate, been conformed to the scope of IAS 39.

---

1   This Introduction refers to IAS 32 as revised in December 2003. In August 2005 the IASB amended IAS 32 by relocating all disclosures relating to financial instruments to IFRS 7 *Financial Instruments: Disclosures*. In February 2008 the IASB amended IAS 32 by requiring some puttable financial instruments and some financial instruments that impose on the entity an obligation to deliver to another party a pro rata share of the net assets of the entity only on liquidation to be classified as equity.

2   In August 2005 the IASB relocated all disclosures relating to financial instruments to IFRS 7 *Financial Instruments: Disclosures*.

Principle

IN6   In summary, when an issuer determines whether a financial instrument is a financial liability or an equity instrument, the instrument is an equity instrument if, and only if, both conditions (a) and (b) are met.

(a)   The instrument includes no contractual obligation:

(i)   to deliver cash or another financial asset to another entity; or

(ii)   to exchange financial assets or financial liabilities with another entity under conditions that are potentially unfavourable to the issuer.

(b)   If the instrument will or may be settled in the issuer's own equity instruments, it is:

(i)   a non-derivative that includes no contractual obligation for the issuer to deliver a variable number of its own equity instruments; or

(ii)   a derivative that will be settled by the issuer exchanging a fixed amount of cash or another financial asset for a fixed number of its own equity instruments. For this purpose, the issuer's own equity instruments do not include instruments that are themselves contracts for the future receipt or delivery of the issuer's own equity instruments.

IN7   In addition, when an issuer has an obligation to purchase its own shares for cash or another financial asset, there is a liability for the amount that the issuer is obliged to pay.

IN8   The definitions of a financial asset and a financial liability, and the description of an equity instrument, are amended consistently with this principle.

Classification of contracts settled in an entity's own equity instruments

IN9   The classification of derivative and non-derivative contracts indexed to, or settled in, an entity's own equity instruments has been clarified consistently with the principle in paragraph IN6 above. In particular, when an entity uses its own equity instruments 'as currency' in a contract to receive or deliver a variable number of shares whose value equals a fixed amount or an amount based on changes in an underlying variable (eg a commodity price), the contract is not an equity instrument, but is a financial asset or a financial liability.

Puttable instruments

IN10   IAS 32 incorporates the guidance previously proposed in draft SIC Interpretation 34 *Financial Instruments—Instruments or Rights Redeemable by the Holder*. Consequently, a financial instrument that gives the holder the right to put the instrument back to the issuer for cash or another financial asset (a 'puttable instrument') is a financial liability of the issuer. In response to comments received on the Exposure Draft, the Standard provides additional guidance and illustrative examples for entities that, because of this requirement, have no equity or whose share capital is not equity as defined in IAS 32.

Contingent settlement provisions

IN11   IAS 32 incorporates the conclusion previously in SIC-5 *Classification of Financial Instruments—Contingent Settlement Provisions* that a financial instrument is a financial liability when the manner of settlement depends on the occurrence or non-occurrence of uncertain future events or on the outcome of uncertain circumstances that are beyond the control of both the issuer and the holder. Contingent settlement provisions are ignored when they apply only in the event of liquidation of the issuer or are not genuine.

Settlement options

IN12   Under IAS 32, a derivative financial instrument is a financial asset or a financial liability when it gives one of the parties to it a choice of how it is settled unless all of the settlement alternatives would result in it being an equity instrument.

Measurement of the components of a compound financial instrument on initial recognition

IN13   The revisions eliminate the option previously in IAS 32 to measure the liability component of a compound financial instrument on initial recognition either as a residual amount after separating the equity component, or by using a relative-fair-value method. Thus, any asset and liability components are separated first and the residual is the amount of any equity component. These requirements for separating the liability and equity components of a compound financial instrument are conformed to both the definition of an equity instrument as a residual and the measurement requirements in IFRS 9.

Treasury shares

IN14   IAS 32 incorporates the conclusion previously in SIC-16 *Share Capital—Reacquired Own Equity Instruments (Treasury Shares)* that the acquisition or subsequent resale by an entity of its own equity instruments does not result in a gain or loss for the entity. Rather it represents a transfer between those holders of equity instruments who have given up their equity interest and those who continue to hold an equity instrument.

Interest, dividends, losses and gains

IN15   IAS 32 incorporates the guidance previously in SIC-17 *Equity—Costs of an Equity Transaction*. Transaction costs incurred as a necessary part of completing an equity transaction are accounted for as part of that transaction and are deducted from equity.

Disclosure

IN16–
IN19   [Deleted]

IN19A   In August 2005 the Board revised disclosures about financial instruments and relocated them to IFRS 7 *Financial Instruments: Disclosures*.

Withdrawal of other pronouncements

IN20   As a consequence of the revisions to this Standard, the Board withdrew the three Interpretations and one draft Interpretation of the former Standing Interpretations Committee noted in paragraph IN1.

Potential impact of proposals in exposure drafts

IN21   [Deleted]

Reasons for amending IAS 32 in February 2008

IN22   In February 2008 the IASB amended IAS 32 by requiring some financial instruments that meet the definition of a financial liability to be classified as equity. Entities should apply the amendments for annual periods beginning on or after 1 January 2009. Earlier application is permitted.

IN23   The amendment addresses the classification of some:

(a)   puttable financial instruments, and

(b)   instruments, or components of instruments, that impose on the entity an obligation to deliver to another party a pro rata share of the net assets of the entity only on liquidation.

IN24   The objective was a short-term, limited scope amendment to improve the financial reporting of particular types of financial instruments that meet the definition of a financial liability but represent the residual interest in the net assets of the entity.

International Accounting Standard 32
Financial Instruments: Presentation

Objective

1   [Deleted]

2   The objective of this Standard is to establish principles for presenting financial instruments as liabilities or equity and for offsetting financial assets and financial liabilities. It applies to the classification of financial instruments, from the perspective of the issuer, into financial assets, financial liabilities and equity instruments; the classification of related interest, dividends, losses and gains; and the circumstances in which financial assets and financial liabilities should be offset.

3   The principles in this Standard complement the principles for recognising and measuring financial assets and financial liabilities in IFRS 9 *Financial Instruments*, and for disclosing information about them in IFRS 7 *Financial Instruments: Disclosures*.

Scope

4   **This Standard shall be applied by all entities to all types of financial instruments except:**

    (a)   those interests in subsidiaries, associates or joint ventures that are accounted for in accordance with IFRS 10 *Consolidated Financial Statements*, **IAS 27** *Separate Financial Statements* **or IAS 28** *Investments in Associates and Joint Ventures*. **However, in some cases, IAS 27 or IAS 28 permits an entity to account for an interest in a subsidiary, associate or joint venture using IFRS 9; in those cases, entities shall apply the requirements of this Standard. Entities shall also apply this Standard to all derivatives linked to interests in subsidiaries, associates or joint ventures.**

    (b)   employers' rights and obligations under employee benefit plans, to which IAS 19 *Employee Benefits* **applies.**

    (c)   [deleted]

    (d)   insurance contracts as defined in IFRS 4 *Insurance Contracts*. **However, this Standard applies to derivatives that are embedded in insurance contracts if IFRS 9 requires the entity to account for them separately. Moreover, an issuer shall apply this Standard to financial guarantee contracts if the issuer applies IFRS 9 in recognising and measuring the contracts, but shall apply IFRS 4 if the issuer elects, in accordance with paragraph 4(d) of IFRS 4, to apply IFRS 4 in recognising and measuring them.**

    (e)   financial instruments that are within the scope of IFRS 4 because they contain a discretionary participation feature. The issuer of these instruments is exempt from applying to these features paragraphs 15–32 and AG25–AG35 of this Standard regarding the distinction between financial liabilities and equity instruments. However, these instruments

are subject to all other requirements of this Standard. Furthermore, this Standard applies to derivatives that are embedded in these instruments (see IFRS 9).

(f) financial instruments, contracts and obligations under share-based payment transactions to which IFRS 2 *Share-based Payment* applies, except for

    (i) contracts within the scope of paragraphs 8–10 of this Standard, to which this Standard applies,

    (ii) paragraphs 33 and 34 of this Standard, which shall be applied to treasury shares purchased, sold, issued or cancelled in connection with employee share option plans, employee share purchase plans, and all other share-based payment arrangements.

5–7 [Deleted]

8 This Standard shall be applied to those contracts to buy or sell a non-financial item that can be settled net in cash or another financial instrument, or by exchanging financial instruments, as if the contracts were financial instruments, with the exception of contracts that were entered into and continue to be held for the purpose of the receipt or delivery of a non-financial item in accordance with the entity's expected purchase, sale or usage requirements.

9 There are various ways in which a contract to buy or sell a non-financial item can be settled net in cash or another financial instrument or by exchanging financial instruments. These include:

(a) when the terms of the contract permit either party to settle it net in cash or another financial instrument or by exchanging financial instruments;

(b) when the ability to settle net in cash or another financial instrument, or by exchanging financial instruments, is not explicit in the terms of the contract, but the entity has a practice of settling similar contracts net in cash or another financial instrument, or by exchanging financial instruments (whether with the counterparty, by entering into offsetting contracts or by selling the contract before its exercise or lapse);

(c) when, for similar contracts, the entity has a practice of taking delivery of the underlying and selling it within a short period after delivery for the purpose of generating a profit from short-term fluctuations in price or dealer's margin; and

(d) when the non-financial item that is the subject of the contract is readily convertible to cash.

A contract to which (b) or (c) applies is not entered into for the purpose of the receipt or delivery of the non-financial item in accordance with the entity's expected purchase, sale or usage requirements, and, accordingly, is within the scope of this Standard. Other contracts to which paragraph 8 applies are evaluated to determine whether they were entered into and continue to be held for the purpose of the receipt or delivery of the non-financial item in accordance with the entity's expected purchase, sale or usage requirement, and accordingly, whether they are within the scope of this Standard.

10   A written option to buy or sell a non-financial item that can be settled net in cash or another financial instrument, or by exchanging financial instruments, in accordance with paragraph 9(a) or (d) is within the scope of this Standard. Such a contract cannot be entered into for the purpose of the receipt or delivery of the non-financial item in accordance with the entity's expected purchase, sale or usage requirements.

Definitions (see also paragraphs AG3–AG23)

11   The following terms are used in this Standard with the meanings specified:

A *financial instrument* is any contract that gives rise to a financial asset of one entity and a financial liability or equity instrument of another entity.

A *financial asset* is any asset that is:

(a)   cash;

(b)   an equity instrument of another entity;

(c)   a contractual right:

   (i)   to receive cash or another financial asset from another entity; or

   (ii)   to exchange financial assets or financial liabilities with another entity under conditions that are potentially favourable to the entity; or

(d)   a contract that will or may be settled in the entity's own equity instruments and is:

   (i)   a non-derivative for which the entity is or may be obliged to receive a variable number of the entity's own equity instruments; or

   (ii)   a derivative that will or may be settled other than by the exchange of a fixed amount of cash or another financial asset for a fixed number of the entity's own equity instruments. For this purpose the entity's own equity instruments do not include puttable financial instruments classified as equity instruments in accordance with paragraphs 16A and 16B, instruments that impose on the entity an obligation to deliver to another party a pro rata share of the net assets of the entity only on liquidation and are classified as equity instruments in accordance with paragraphs 16C and 16D, or instruments that are contracts for the future receipt or delivery of the entity's own equity instruments.

A *financial liability* is any liability that is:

(a)   a contractual obligation :

   (i)   to deliver cash or another financial asset to another entity; or

   (ii)   to exchange financial assets or financial liabilities with another entity under conditions that are potentially unfavourable to the entity; or

(b)   a contract that will or may be settled in the entity's own equity instruments and is:

   (i)   a non-derivative for which the entity is or may be obliged to deliver a variable number of the entity's own equity instruments; or

   (ii)   a derivative that will or may be settled other than by the exchange of a fixed amount of cash or another financial asset for a fixed number of the entity's own equity instruments. For this purpose, rights, options or warrants to acquire a fixed number of the entity's own equity instruments for a fixed amount of any currency are equity instruments if the entity offers the rights, options or warrants pro rata to all of its existing owners of the same class of its own non-derivative equity instruments. Also, for these purposes the entity's own equity instruments do not include puttable financial instruments that are classified as equity instruments in accordance with paragraphs 16A and 16B, instruments that impose on the entity an obligation to deliver to another party a pro rata share of the net assets of the entity only on liquidation and are classified as equity instruments in accordance with paragraphs 16C and 16D, or instruments that are contracts for the future receipt or delivery of the entity's own equity instruments.

As an exception, an instrument that meets the definition of a financial liability is classified as an equity instrument if it has all the features and meets the conditions in paragraphs 16A and 16B or paragraphs 16C and 16D.

An *equity instrument* is any contract that evidences a residual interest in the assets of an entity after deducting all of its liabilities.

Fair value is the price that would be received to sell an asset or paid to transfer a liability in an orderly transaction between market participants at the measurement date. (See IFRS 13 *Fair Value Measurement*.)

A *puttable instrument* is a financial instrument that gives the holder the right to put the instrument back to the issuer for cash or another financial asset or is automatically put back to the issuer on the occurrence of an uncertain future event or the death or retirement of the instrument holder.

12   The following terms are defined in Appendix A of IFRS 9 or paragraph 9 of IAS 39 *Financial Instruments: Recognition and Measurement* and are used in this Standard with the meaning specified in IAS 39 and IFRS 9.

- amortised cost of a financial asset or financial liability

- derecognition

- derivative

- effective interest method

- financial guarantee contract

- financial liability at fair value through profit or loss

- firm commitment

© IFRS Foundation

- forecast transaction

- hedge effectiveness

- hedged item

- hedging instrument

- held for trading

- regular way purchase or sale

- transaction costs.

13   In this Standard, 'contract' and 'contractual' refer to an agreement between two or more parties that has clear economic consequences that the parties have little, if any, discretion to avoid, usually because the agreement is enforceable by law. Contracts, and thus financial instruments, may take a variety of forms and need not be in writing.

14   In this Standard, 'entity' includes individuals, partnerships, incorporated bodies, trusts and government agencies.

Presentation

Liabilities and equity (see also paragraphs AG13–AG14J and AG25–AG29A)

15   **The issuer of a financial instrument shall classify the instrument, or its component parts, on initial recognition as a financial liability, a financial asset or an equity instrument in accordance with the substance of the contractual arrangement and the definitions of a financial liability, a financial asset and an equity instrument.**

16   When an issuer applies the definitions in paragraph 11 to determine whether a financial instrument is an equity instrument rather than a financial liability, the instrument is an equity instrument if, and only if, both conditions (a) and (b) below are met.

(a)   The instrument includes no contractual obligation:

(i)   to deliver cash or another financial asset to another entity; or

(ii)   to exchange financial assets or financial liabilities with another entity under conditions that are potentially unfavourable to the issuer.

(b)   If the instrument will or may be settled in the issuer's own equity instruments, it is:

(i)   a non-derivative that includes no contractual obligation for the issuer to deliver a variable number of its own equity instruments; or

(ii)   a derivative that will be settled only by the issuer exchanging a fixed amount of cash or another financial asset for a fixed number of its own equity instruments. For this purpose, rights, options or warrants to acquire a fixed number of the entity's own equity instruments for a fixed amount of any currency are equity instruments if the entity offers the rights, options or warrants pro rata to all of its existing owners of the same class of its own non-derivative equity instruments. Also, for these purposes the issuer's own equity instruments do not include instruments that have all the features and meet the conditions described in paragraphs 16A and 16B or paragraphs 16C and 16D, or instruments that are contracts for the future receipt or delivery of the issuer's own equity instruments.

A contractual obligation, including one arising from a derivative financial instrument, that will or may result in the future receipt or delivery of the issuer's own equity instruments, but does not meet conditions (a) and (b) above, is not an equity instrument. As an exception, an instrument that meets the definition of a financial liability is classified as an equity instrument if it has all the features and meets the conditions in paragraphs 16A and 16B or paragraphs 16C and 16D.

Puttable instruments

16A   A puttable financial instrument includes a contractual obligation for the issuer to repurchase or redeem that instrument for cash or another financial asset on exercise of the put. As an exception to the definition of a financial liability, an instrument that includes such an obligation is classified as an equity instrument if it has all the following features:

(a)   It entitles the holder to a pro rata share of the entity's net assets in the event of the entity's liquidation. The entity's net assets are those assets that remain after deducting all other claims on its assets. A pro rata share is determined by:

(i)   dividing the entity's net assets on liquidation into units of equal amount; and

(ii)   multiplying that amount by the number of the units held by the financial instrument holder.

(b)   The instrument is in the class of instruments that is subordinate to all other classes of instruments. To be in such a class the instrument:

(i)   has no priority over other claims to the assets of the entity on liquidation, and

(ii)   does not need to be converted into another instrument before it is in the class of instruments that is subordinate to all other classes of instruments.

(c)   All financial instruments in the class of instruments that is subordinate to all other classes of instruments have identical features. For example, they must all be puttable, and the formula or other method used to calculate the repurchase or redemption price is the same for all instruments in that class.

(d)   Apart from the contractual obligation for the issuer to repurchase or redeem the instrument for cash or another financial asset, the instrument does not include any contractual obligation to deliver cash or another financial asset to another entity, or to exchange financial assets or financial liabilities with another entity under conditions that are potentially unfavourable to the entity, and it is not a contract that will or may be settled in the entity's own equity instruments as set out in subparagraph (b) of the definition of a financial liability.

(e) The total expected cash flows attributable to the instrument over the life of the instrument are based substantially on the profit or loss, the change in the recognised net assets or the change in the fair value of the recognised and unrecognised net assets of the entity over the life of the instrument (excluding any effects of the instrument).

16B For an instrument to be classified as an equity instrument, in addition to the instrument having all the above features, the issuer must have no other financial instrument or contract that has:

(a) total cash flows based substantially on the profit or loss, the change in the recognised net assets or the change in the fair value of the recognised and unrecognised net assets of the entity (excluding any effects of such instrument or contract) and

(b) the effect of substantially restricting or fixing the residual return to the puttable instrument holders.

For the purposes of applying this condition, the entity shall not consider non-financial contracts with a holder of an instrument described in paragraph 16A that have contractual terms and conditions that are similar to the contractual terms and conditions of an equivalent contract that might occur between a non-instrument holder and the issuing entity. If the entity cannot determine that this condition is met, it shall not classify the puttable instrument as an equity instrument.

Instruments, or components of instruments, that impose on the entity an obligation to deliver to another party a pro rata share of the net assets of the entity only on liquidation

16C Some financial instruments include a contractual obligation for the issuing entity to deliver to another entity a pro rata share of its net assets only on liquidation. The obligation arises because liquidation either is certain to occur and outside the control of the entity (for example, a limited life entity) or is uncertain to occur but is at the option of the instrument holder. As an exception to the definition of a financial liability, an instrument that includes such an obligation is classified as an equity instrument if it has all the following features:

(a) It entitles the holder to a pro rata share of the entity's net assets in the event of the entity's liquidation. The entity's net assets are those assets that remain after deducting all other claims on its assets. A pro rata share is determined by:

(i) dividing the net assets of the entity on liquidation into units of equal amount; and

(ii) multiplying that amount by the number of the units held by the financial instrument holder.

(b)   The instrument is in the class of instruments that is subordinate to all other classes of instruments. To be in such a class the instrument:

    (i)   has no priority over other claims to the assets of the entity on liquidation, and

    (ii)   does not need to be converted into another instrument before it is in the class of instruments that is subordinate to all other classes of instruments.

(c)   All financial instruments in the class of instruments that is subordinate to all other classes of instruments must have an identical contractual obligation for the issuing entity to deliver a pro rata share of its net assets on liquidation.

16D   For an instrument to be classified as an equity instrument, in addition to the instrument having all the above features, the issuer must have no other financial instrument or contract that has:

(a)   total cash flows based substantially on the profit or loss, the change in the recognised net assets or the change in the fair value of the recognised and unrecognised net assets of the entity (excluding any effects of such instrument or contract) and

(b)   the effect of substantially restricting or fixing the residual return to the instrument holders.

For the purposes of applying this condition, the entity shall not consider non-financial contracts with a holder of an instrument described in paragraph 16C that have contractual terms and conditions that are similar to the contractual terms and conditions of an equivalent contract that might occur between a non-instrument holder and the issuing entity. If the entity cannot determine that this condition is met, it shall not classify the instrument as an equity instrument.

Reclassification of puttable instruments and instruments that impose on the entity an obligation to deliver to another party a pro rata share of the net assets of the entity only on liquidation

16E   An entity shall classify a financial instrument as an equity instrument in accordance with paragraphs 16A and 16B or paragraphs 16C and 16D from the date when the instrument has all the features and meets the conditions set out in those paragraphs. An entity shall reclassify a financial instrument from the date when the instrument ceases to have all the features or meet all the conditions set out in those paragraphs. For example, if an entity redeems all its issued non-puttable instruments and any puttable instrument that remain outstanding have all the features and meet all the conditions in paragraphs 16A and 16B, the entity shall reclassify the puttable instruments as equity instruments from the date when it redeems the non-puttable instruments.

16F   An entity shall account as follows for the reclassification of an instrument in accordance with paragraph 16E:

(a)   It shall reclassify an equity instrument as a financial liability from the date when the instrument ceases to have all the features or meet the conditions in paragraphs 16A and 16B or paragraphs 16C and 16D. The financial liability shall be measured at the instrument's fair value at the date of reclassification. The entity shall recognise in equity any difference between the carrying value of the equity instrument and the fair value of the financial liability at the date of reclassification.

(b)   It shall reclassify a financial liability as equity from the date when the instrument has all the features and meets the conditions set out in paragraphs 16A and 16B or paragraphs 16C and 16D. An equity instrument shall be measured at the carrying value of the financial liability at the date of reclassification.

No contractual obligation to deliver cash or another financial asset (paragraph 16(a))

17   With the exception of the circumstances described in paragraphs 16A and 16B or paragraphs 16C and 16D, a critical feature in differentiating a financial liability from an equity instrument is the existence of a contractual obligation of one party to the financial instrument (the issuer) either to deliver cash or another financial asset to the other party (the holder) or to exchange financial assets or financial liabilities with the holder under conditions that are potentially unfavourable to the issuer. Although the holder of an equity instrument may be entitled to receive a pro rata share of any dividends or other distributions of equity, the issuer does not have a contractual obligation to make such distributions because it cannot be required to deliver cash or another financial asset to another party.

18   The substance of a financial instrument, rather than its legal form, governs its classification in the entity's statement of financial position. Substance and legal form are commonly consistent, but not always. Some financial instruments take the legal form of equity but are liabilities in substance and others may combine features associated with equity instruments and features associated with financial liabilities. For example:

(a)   a preference share that provides for mandatory redemption by the issuer for a fixed or determinable amount at a fixed or determinable future date, or gives the holder the right to require the issuer to redeem the instrument at or after a particular date for a fixed or determinable amount, is a financial liability.

(b)   a financial instrument that gives the holder the right to put it back to the issuer for cash or another financial asset (a 'puttable instrument') is a financial liability, except for those instruments classified as equity instruments in accordance with paragraphs 16A and 16B or paragraphs 16C and 16D. The financial instrument is a financial liability even when the amount of cash or other financial assets is determined on the basis of an index or other item that has the potential to increase or decrease. The existence of an option for the holder to put the instrument back to the issuer for cash or another financial asset means that the puttable instrument meets the definition of a financial liability, except for those instruments classified as equity instruments in accordance with paragraphs 16A and 16B or paragraphs 16C and 16D. For example, open-ended mutual funds, unit trusts, partnerships and some co-operative entities may provide their unitholders or members with a right to redeem their interests in the issuer at any time for cash, which results in the unitholders' or members' interests being classified as financial liabilities, except for those instruments classified as equity instruments in accordance with paragraphs 16A and 16B or paragraphs 16C and 16D. However, classification as a financial liability does not preclude the use of descriptors such as 'net asset value attributable to unitholders' and 'change in net asset value attributable to unitholders' in the financial statements of an entity that has no contributed equity (such as some mutual funds and unit trusts, see Illustrative Example 7) or the use of additional disclosure to show that total members' interests comprise items such as reserves that meet the definition of equity and puttable instruments that do not (see Illustrative Example 8).

19   If an entity does not have an unconditional right to avoid delivering cash or another financial asset to settle a contractual obligation, the obligation meets the definition of a financial liability, except for those instruments classified as equity instruments in accordance with paragraphs 16A and 16B or paragraphs 16C and 16D. For example:

(a)   a restriction on the ability of an entity to satisfy a contractual obligation, such as lack of access to foreign currency or the need to obtain approval for payment from a regulatory authority, does not negate the entity's contractual obligation or the holder's contractual right under the instrument.

(b)   a contractual obligation that is conditional on a counterparty exercising its right to redeem is a financial liability because the entity does not have the unconditional right to avoid delivering cash or another financial asset.

20   A financial instrument that does not explicitly establish a contractual obligation to deliver cash or another financial asset may establish an obligation indirectly through its terms and conditions. For example:

(a)   a financial instrument may contain a non-financial obligation that must be settled if, and only if, the entity fails to make distributions or to redeem the instrument. If the entity can avoid a transfer of cash or another financial asset only by settling the non-financial obligation, the financial instrument is a financial liability.

(b)   a financial instrument is a financial liability if it provides that on settlement the entity will deliver either:

(i)   cash or another financial asset; or

(ii)   its own shares whose value is determined to exceed substantially the value of the cash or other financial asset.

Although the entity does not have an explicit contractual obligation to deliver cash or another financial asset, the value of the share settlement alternative is such that the entity will settle in cash. In any event, the holder has in substance been guaranteed receipt of an amount that is at least equal to the cash settlement option (see paragraph 21).

Settlement in the entity's own equity instruments (paragraph 16(b))

21   A contract is not an equity instrument solely because it may result in the receipt or delivery of the entity's own equity instruments. An entity may have a contractual right or obligation to receive or deliver a number of its own shares or other equity instruments that varies so that the fair value of the entity's own equity instruments to be received or delivered equals the amount of the contractual right or obligation. Such a contractual right or obligation may be for a fixed amount or an amount that fluctuates in part or in full in response to changes in a variable other than the market price of the entity's own equity instruments (eg an interest rate, a commodity price or a financial instrument price). Two examples are (a) a contract to deliver as many of the entity's own equity instruments as are equal in value to CU100,[3] and (b) a contract to deliver as many of the entity's own equity instruments as are equal in value to the value of 100 ounces of gold. Such a contract is a financial liability of the entity even though the entity must or can settle it by delivering its own equity instruments. It is not an equity instrument because the entity uses a variable number of its own equity instruments as a means to settle the contract. Accordingly, the contract does not evidence a residual interest in the entity's assets after deducting all of its liabilities.

22   Except as stated in paragraph 22A, a contract that will be settled by the entity (receiving or) delivering a fixed number of its own equity instruments in exchange for a fixed amount of cash or another financial asset is an equity instrument. For example, an issued share option that gives the counterparty a right to buy a fixed number of the entity's shares for a fixed price or for a fixed stated principal amount of a bond is an equity instrument. Changes in the fair value of a contract arising from variations in market interest rates that do not affect the amount of cash or other financial assets to be paid or received, or the number of equity instruments to be received or delivered, on settlement of the contract do not preclude the contract from being an equity instrument. Any consideration received (such as the premium received for a written option or warrant on the entity's own shares) is added directly to equity. Any consideration paid (such as the premium paid for a purchased option) is deducted directly from equity. Changes in the fair value of an equity instrument are not recognised in the financial statements.

22A   If the entity's own equity instruments to be received, or delivered, by the entity upon settlement of a contract are puttable financial instruments with all the features and meeting the conditions described in paragraphs 16A and 16B, or instruments that impose on the entity an obligation to deliver to another party a pro rata share of the net assets of the entity only on liquidation with all the features and meeting the conditions described in paragraphs 16C and 16D, the contract is a financial asset or a financial liability. This includes a contract that will be settled by the entity receiving or delivering a fixed number of such instruments in exchange for a fixed amount of cash or another financial asset.

---

3   In this Standard, monetary amounts are denominated in 'currency units (CU)'.

23   With the exception of the circumstances described in paragraphs 16A and 16B or paragraphs 16C and 16D, a contract that contains an obligation for an entity to purchase its own equity instruments for cash or another financial asset gives rise to a financial liability for the present value of the redemption amount (for example, for the present value of the forward repurchase price, option exercise price or other redemption amount). This is the case even if the contract itself is an equity instrument. One example is an entity's obligation under a forward contract to purchase its own equity instruments for cash. The financial liability is recognised initially at the present value of the redemption amount, and is reclassified from equity. Subsequently, the financial liability is measured in accordance with IFRS 9. If the contract expires without delivery, the carrying amount of the financial liability is reclassified to equity. An entity's contractual obligation to purchase its own equity instruments gives rise to a financial liability for the present value of the redemption amount even if the obligation to purchase is conditional on the counterparty exercising a right to redeem (eg a written put option that gives the counterparty the right to sell an entity's own equity instruments to the entity for a fixed price).

24   A contract that will be settled by the entity delivering or receiving a fixed number of its own equity instruments in exchange for a variable amount of cash or another financial asset is a financial asset or financial liability. An example is a contract for the entity to deliver 100 of its own equity instruments in return for an amount of cash calculated to equal the value of 100 ounces of gold.

Contingent settlement provisions

25   A financial instrument may require the entity to deliver cash or another financial asset, or otherwise to settle it in such a way that it would be a financial liability, in the event of the occurrence or non-occurrence of uncertain future events (or on the outcome of uncertain circumstances) that are beyond the control of both the issuer and the holder of the instrument, such as a change in a stock market index, consumer price index, interest rate or taxation requirements, or the issuer's future revenues, net income or debt-to-equity ratio. The issuer of such an instrument does not have the unconditional right to avoid delivering cash or another financial asset (or otherwise to settle it in such a way that it would be a financial liability). Therefore, it is a financial liability of the issuer unless:

(a)   the part of the contingent settlement provision that could require settlement in cash or another financial asset (or otherwise in such a way that it would be a financial liability) is not genuine;

(b)   the issuer can be required to settle the obligation in cash or another financial asset (or otherwise to settle it in such   a way that it would be a financial liability) only in the event of liquidation of the issuer; or

(c)   the instrument has all the features and meets the conditions in paragraphs 16A and 16B.

Settlement options

26   When a derivative financial instrument gives one party a choice over how it is settled (eg the issuer or the holder can choose settlement net in cash or by exchanging shares for cash), it is a financial asset or a financial liability unless all of the settlement alternatives would result in it being an equity instrument.

27   An example of a derivative financial instrument with a settlement option that is a financial liability is a share option that the issuer can decide to settle net in cash or by exchanging its own shares for cash. Similarly, some contracts to buy or sell a non-financial item in exchange for the entity's own equity instruments are within the scope of this Standard because they can be settled either by delivery of the non-financial item or net in cash or another financial instrument (see paragraphs 8–10). Such contracts are financial assets or financial liabilities and not equity instruments.

Compound financial instruments (see also paragraphs AG30–AG35 and Illustrative examples 9–12)

28   **The issuer of a non-derivative financial instrument shall evaluate the terms of the financial instrument to determine whether it contains both a liability and an equity component. Such components shall be classified separately as financial liabilities, financial assets or equity instruments in accordance with paragraph 15.**

29   An entity recognises separately the components of a financial instrument that (a) creates a financial liability of the entity and (b) grants an option to the holder of the instrument to convert it into an equity instrument of the entity. For example, a bond or similar instrument convertible by the holder into a fixed number of ordinary shares of the entity is a compound financial instrument. From the perspective of the entity, such an instrument comprises two components: a financial liability (a contractual arrangement to deliver cash or another financial asset) and an equity instrument (a call option granting the holder the right, for a specified period of time, to convert it into a fixed number of ordinary shares of the entity). The economic effect of issuing such an instrument is substantially the same as issuing simultaneously a debt instrument with an early settlement provision and warrants to purchase ordinary shares, or issuing a debt instrument with detachable share purchase warrants. Accordingly, in all cases, the entity presents the liability and equity components separately in its statement of financial position.

30   Classification of the liability and equity components of a convertible instrument is not revised as a result of a change in the likelihood that a conversion option will be exercised, even when exercise of the option may appear to have become economically advantageous to some holders. Holders may not always act in the way that might be expected because, for example, the tax consequences resulting from conversion may differ among holders. Furthermore, the likelihood of conversion will change from time to time. The entity's contractual obligation to make future payments remains outstanding until it is extinguished through conversion, maturity of the instrument or some other transaction.

31   IFRS 9 deals with the measurement of financial assets and financial liabilities. Equity instruments are instruments that evidence a residual interest in the assets of an entity after deducting all of its liabilities. Therefore, when the initial carrying amount of a compound financial instrument is allocated to its equity and liability components, the equity component is assigned the residual amount after deducting from the fair value of the instrument as a whole the amount separately determined for the liability component. The value of any derivative features (such as a call option) embedded in the compound financial instrument other than the equity component (such as an equity conversion option) is included in the liability component. The sum of the carrying amounts assigned to the liability and equity components on initial recognition is always equal to the fair value that would be ascribed to the instrument as a whole. No gain or loss arises from initially recognising the components of the instrument separately.

32   Under the approach described in paragraph 31, the issuer of a bond convertible into ordinary shares first determines the carrying amount of the liability component by measuring the fair value of a similar liability (including any embedded non-equity derivative features) that does not have an associated equity component. The carrying amount of the equity instrument represented by the option to convert the instrument into ordinary shares is then determined by deducting the fair value of the financial liability from the fair value of the compound financial instrument as a whole.

Treasury shares (see also paragraph AG36)

33   **If an entity reacquires its own equity instruments, those instruments ('treasury shares') shall be deducted from equity. No gain or loss shall be recognised in profit or loss on the purchase, sale, issue or cancellation of an entity's own equity instruments. Such treasury shares may be acquired and held by the entity or by other members of the consolidated group. Consideration paid or received shall be recognised directly in equity.**

34   The amount of treasury shares held is disclosed separately either in the statement of financial position or in the notes, in accordance with IAS 1 *Presentation of Financial Statements*. An entity provides disclosure in accordance with IAS 24 *Related Party Disclosures* if the entity reacquires its own equity instruments from related parties.

Interest, dividends, losses and gains (see also paragraph AG37)

35   **Interest, dividends, losses and gains relating to a financial instrument or a component that is a financial liability shall be recognised as income or expense in profit or loss. Distributions to holders of an equity instrument shall be debited by the entity directly to equity, net of any related income tax benefit. Transaction costs of an equity transaction shall be accounted for as a deduction from equity, net of any related income tax benefit.**

36　The classification of a financial instrument as a financial liability or an equity instrument determines whether interest, dividends, losses and gains relating to that instrument are recognised as income or expense in profit or loss. Thus, dividend payments on shares wholly recognised as liabilities are recognised as expenses in the same way as interest on a bond. Similarly, gains and losses associated with redemptions or refinancings of financial liabilities are recognised in profit or loss, whereas redemptions or refinancings of equity instruments are recognised as changes in equity. Changes in the fair value of an equity instrument are not recognised in the financial statements.

37　An entity typically incurs various costs in issuing or acquiring its own equity instruments. Those costs might include registration and other regulatory fees, amounts paid to legal, accounting and other professional advisers, printing costs and stamp duties. The transaction costs of an equity transaction are accounted for as a deduction from equity (net of any related income tax benefit) to the extent they are incremental costs directly attributable to the equity transaction that otherwise would have been avoided. The costs of an equity transaction that is abandoned are recognised as an expense.

38　Transaction costs that relate to the issue of a compound financial instrument are allocated to the liability and equity components of the instrument in proportion to the allocation of proceeds. Transaction costs that relate jointly to more than one transaction (for example, costs of a concurrent offering of some shares and a stock exchange listing of other shares) are allocated to those transactions using a basis of allocation that is rational and consistent with similar transactions.

39　The amount of transaction costs accounted for as a deduction from equity in the period is disclosed separately under IAS 1. The related amount of income taxes recognised directly in equity is included in the aggregate amount of current and deferred income tax credited or charged to equity that is disclosed under IAS 12 *Income Taxes*.

40　Dividends classified as an expense may be presented in the statement(s) of profit or loss and other comprehensive income either with interest on other liabilities or as a separate item. In addition to the requirements of this Standard, disclosure of interest and dividends is subject to the requirements of IAS 1 and IFRS 7. In some circumstances, because of the differences between interest and dividends with respect to matters such as tax deductibility, it is desirable to disclose them separately in the statement(s) of profit or loss and other comprehensive income. Disclosures of the tax effects are made in accordance with IAS 12.

41　Gains and losses related to changes in the carrying amount of a financial liability are recognised as income or expense in profit or loss even when they relate to an instrument that includes a right to the residual interest in the assets of the entity in exchange for cash or another financial asset (see paragraph 18(b)). Under IAS 1 the entity presents any gain or loss arising from remeasurement of such an instrument separately in the statement of comprehensive income when it is relevant in explaining the entity's performance.

Offsetting a financial asset and a financial liability (see also paragraphs AG38A–AG38F and AG39)

42   A financial asset and a financial liability shall be offset and the net amount presented in the statement of financial position when, and only when, an entity:

(a)   currently has a legally enforceable right to set off the recognised amounts; and

(b)   intends either to settle on a net basis, or to realise the asset and settle the liability simultaneously.

In accounting for a transfer of a financial asset that does not qualify for derecognition, the entity shall not offset the transferred asset and the associated liability (see IFRS 9, paragraph 3.2.22).

43   This Standard requires the presentation of financial assets and financial liabilities on a net basis when doing so reflects an entity's expected future cash flows from settling two or more separate financial instruments. When an entity has the right to receive or pay a single net amount and intends to do so, it has, in effect, only a single financial asset or financial liability. In other circumstances, financial assets and financial liabilities are presented separately from each other consistently with their characteristics as resources or obligations of the entity. An entity shall disclose the information required in paragraphs 13B–13E of IFRS 7 for recognised financial instruments that are within the scope of paragraph 13A of IFRS 7.

44   Offsetting a recognised financial asset and a recognised financial liability and presenting the net amount differs from the derecognition of a financial asset or a financial liability. Although offsetting does not give rise to recognition of a gain or loss, the derecognition of a financial instrument not only results in the removal of the previously recognised item from the statement of financial position but also may result in recognition of a gain or loss.

45   A right of set-off is a debtor's legal right, by contract or otherwise, to settle or otherwise eliminate all or a portion of an amount due to a creditor by applying against that amount an amount due from the creditor. In unusual circumstances, a debtor may have a legal right to apply an amount due from a third party against the amount due to a creditor provided that there is an agreement between the three parties that clearly establishes the debtor's right of set-off. Because the right of set-off is a legal right, the conditions supporting the right may vary from one legal jurisdiction to another and the laws applicable to the relationships between the parties need to be considered.

46   The existence of an enforceable right to set off a financial asset and a financial liability affects the rights and obligations associated with a financial asset and a financial liability and may affect an entity's exposure to credit and liquidity risk. However, the existence of the right, by itself, is not a sufficient basis for offsetting. In the absence of an intention to exercise the right or to settle simultaneously, the amount and timing of an entity's future cash flows are not affected. When an entity intends to exercise the right or to settle simultaneously, presentation of the asset and liability on a net basis reflects more appropriately the amounts and timing of the expected future cash flows, as well as the risks to which those cash

flows are exposed. An intention by one or both parties to settle on a net basis without the legal right to do so is not sufficient to justify offsetting because the rights and obligations associated with the individual financial asset and financial liability remain unaltered.

47   An entity's intentions with respect to settlement of particular assets and liabilities may be influenced by its normal business practices, the requirements of the financial markets and other circumstances that may limit the ability to settle net or to settle simultaneously. When an entity has a right of set-off, but does not intend to settle net or to realise the asset and settle the liability simultaneously, the effect of the right on the entity's credit risk exposure is disclosed in accordance with paragraph 36 of IFRS 7.

48   Simultaneous settlement of two financial instruments may occur through, for example, the operation of a clearing house in an organised financial market or a face-to-face exchange. In these circumstances the cash flows are, in effect, equivalent to a single net amount and there is no exposure to credit or liquidity risk. In other circumstances, an entity may settle two instruments by receiving and paying separate amounts, becoming exposed to credit risk for the full amount of the asset or liquidity risk for the full amount of the liability. Such risk exposures may be significant even though relatively brief. Accordingly, realisation of a financial asset and settlement of a financial liability are treated as simultaneous only when the transactions occur at the same moment.

49   The conditions set out in paragraph 42 are generally not satisfied and offsetting is usually inappropriate when:

(a)   several different financial instruments are used to emulate the features of a single financial instrument (a 'synthetic instrument');

(b)   financial assets and financial liabilities arise from financial instruments having the same primary risk exposure (for example, assets and liabilities within a portfolio of forward contracts or other derivative instruments) but involve different counterparties;

(c)   financial or other assets are pledged as collateral for non-recourse financial liabilities;

(d)   financial assets are set aside in trust by a debtor for the purpose of discharging an obligation without those assets having been accepted by the creditor in settlement of the obligation (for example, a sinking fund arrangement); or

(e)   obligations incurred as a result of events giving rise to losses are expected to be recovered from a third party by virtue of a claim made under an insurance contract.

50   An entity that undertakes a number of financial instrument transactions with a single counterparty may enter into a 'master netting arrangement' with that counterparty. Such an agreement provides for a single net settlement of all financial instruments covered by the agreement in the event of default on, or termination of, any one contract. These arrangements are commonly used by financial institutions to provide protection against loss in the event of bankruptcy or other circumstances that result in a counterparty being unable to

meet its obligations. A master netting arrangement commonly creates a right of set-off that becomes enforceable and affects the realisation or settlement of individual financial assets and financial liabilities only following a specified event of default or in other circumstances not expected to arise in the normal course of business. A master netting arrangement does not provide a basis for offsetting unless both of the criteria in paragraph 42 are satisfied. When financial assets and financial liabilities subject to a master netting arrangement are not offset, the effect of the arrangement on an entity's exposure to credit risk is disclosed in accordance with paragraph 36 of IFRS 7.

Disclosure

51–95   [Deleted]

Effective date and transition

96   An entity shall apply this Standard for annual periods beginning on or after 1 January 2005. Earlier application is permitted. An entity shall not apply this Standard for annual periods beginning before 1 January 2005 unless it also applies IAS 39 (issued December 2003), including the amendments issued in March 2004. If an entity applies this Standard for a period beginning before 1 January 2005, it shall disclose that fact.

96A   *Puttable Financial Instruments and Obligations Arising on Liquidation* (Amendments to IAS 32 and IAS 1), issued in February 2008, required financial instruments that contain all the features and meet the conditions in paragraphs 16A and 16B or paragraphs 16C and 16D to be classified as an equity instrument, amended paragraphs 11, 16, 17–19, 22, 23, 25, AG13, AG14 and AG27, and inserted paragraphs 16A–16F, 22A, 96B, 96C, 97C, AG14A–AG14J and AG29A. An entity shall apply those amendments for annual periods beginning on or after 1 January 2009. Earlier application is permitted. If an entity applies the changes for an earlier period, it shall disclose that fact and apply the related amendments to IAS 1, IAS 39, IFRS 7 and IFRIC 2 at the same time.

96B   *Puttable Financial Instruments and Obligations Arising on Liquidation* introduced a limited scope exception; therefore, an entity shall not apply the exception by analogy.

96C   The classification of instruments under this exception shall be restricted to the accounting for such an instrument under IAS 1, IAS 32, IAS 39, IFRS 7 and IFRS 9. The instrument shall not be considered an equity instrument under other guidance, for example IFRS 2.

97   This Standard shall be applied retrospectively.

97A   IAS 1 (as revised in 2007) amended the terminology used throughout IFRSs. In addition it amended paragraph 40. An entity shall apply those amendments for annual periods beginning on or after 1 January 2009. If an entity applies IAS 1 (revised 2007) for an earlier period, the amendments shall be applied for that earlier period.

97B   IFRS 3 *Business Combinations* (as revised in 2008) deleted paragraph 4(c). An entity shall apply that amendment for annual periods beginning on or after 1 July 2009. If an entity applies IFRS 3 (revised 2008) for an earlier period, the amendment shall also be applied for that earlier period. However, the amendment does not apply to contingent consideration that arose from a business combination for which the acquisition date preceded the application of IFRS 3 (revised 2008). Instead, an entity shall account for such consideration in accordance with paragraphs 65A–65E of IFRS 3 (as amended in 2010).

97C   When applying the amendments described in paragraph 96A, an entity is required to split a compound financial instrument with an obligation to deliver to another party a pro rata share of the net assets of the entity only on liquidation into separate liability and equity components. If the liability component is no longer outstanding, a retrospective application of those amendments to IAS 32 would involve separating two components of equity. The first component would be in retained earnings and represent the cumulative interest accreted on the liability component. The other component would represent the original equity component. Therefore, an entity need not separate these two components if the liability component is no longer outstanding at the date of application of the amendments.

97D   Paragraph 4 was amended by *Improvements to IFRSs* issued in May 2008. An entity shall apply that amendment for annual periods beginning on or after 1 January 2009. Earlier application is permitted. If an entity applies the amendment for an earlier period it shall disclose that fact and apply for that earlier period the amendments to paragraph 3 of IFRS 7, paragraph 1 of IAS 28 and paragraph 1 of IAS 31 issued in May 2008. An entity is permitted to apply the amendment prospectively.

97E   Paragraphs 11 and 16 were amended by *Classification of Rights Issues* issued in October 2009. An entity shall apply that amendment for annual periods beginning on or after 1 February 2010. Earlier application is permitted. If an entity applies the amendment for an earlier period, it shall disclose that fact.

97F   [Deleted]

97G   Paragraph 97B was amended by *Improvements to IFRSs* issued in May 2010. An entity shall apply that amendment for annual periods beginning on or after 1 July 2010. Earlier application is permitted.

97H   IFRS 9, issued in October 2010, amended paragraphs 3, 4, 12, 23, 31, 42, 96C, AG2 and AG30 and deleted paragraph 97F. An entity shall apply those amendments when it applies IFRS 9 as issued in October 2010.

97I   IFRS 10 and IFRS 11 *Joint Arrangements*, issued in May 2011, amended paragraphs 4(a) and AG29. An entity shall apply those amendments when it applies IFRS 10 and IFRS 11.

97J   IFRS 13, issued in May 2011, amended the definition of fair value in paragraph 11 and amended paragraphs 23 and AG31. An entity shall apply those amendments when it applies IFRS 13.

97K   *Presentation of Items of Other Comprehensive Income* (Amendments to IAS 1), issued in June 2011, amended paragraph 40. An entity shall apply that amendment when it applies IAS 1 as amended in June 2011.

97L   *Offsetting Financial Assets and Financial Liabilities* (Amendments to IAS 32), issued in December 2011, deleted paragraph AG38 and added paragraphs AG38A–AG38F. An entity shall apply those amendments for annual periods beginning on or after 1 January 2014. An entity shall apply those amendments retrospectively. Earlier application is permitted. If an entity applies those amendments from an earlier date, it shall disclose that fact and shall also make the disclosures required by *Disclosures—Offsetting Financial Assets and Financial Liabilities* (Amendments to IFRS 7) issued in December 2011.

Withdrawal of other pronouncements

98   This Standard supersedes IAS 32 *Financial Instruments: Disclosure and Presentation* revised in 2000.[4]

99   This Standard supersedes the following Interpretations:

(a)   SIC-5 *Classification of Financial Instruments—Contingent Settlement Provisions*;

(b)   SIC-16 *Share Capital—Reacquired Own Equity Instruments (Treasury Shares)*; and

(c)   SIC-17 *Equity—Costs of an Equity Transaction*.

100   This Standard withdraws draft SIC Interpretation D34 *Financial Instruments—Instruments or Rights Redeemable by the Holder*.

---

4   In August 2005 the IASB relocated all disclosures relating to financial instruments to IFRS 7 *Financial Instruments: Disclosures*.

Appendix
Application Guidance
IAS 32 *Financial Instruments: Presentation*

This appendix is an integral part of the Standard.

AG1   This Application Guidance explains the application of particular aspects of the Standard.

AG2   The Standard does not deal with the recognition or measurement of financial instruments. Requirements about the recognition and measurement of financial assets and financial liabilities are set out in IFRS 9.

Definitions (paragraphs 11–14)

Financial assets and financial liabilities

AG3   Currency (cash) is a financial asset because it represents the medium of exchange and is therefore the basis on which all transactions are measured and recognised in financial statements. A deposit of cash with a bank or similar financial institution is a financial asset because it represents the contractual right of the depositor to obtain cash from the institution or to draw a cheque or similar instrument against the balance in favour of a creditor in payment of a financial liability.

AG4   Common examples of financial assets representing a contractual right to receive cash in the future and corresponding financial liabilities representing a contractual obligation to deliver cash in the future are:

(a)   trade accounts receivable and payable;

(b)   notes receivable and payable;

(c)   loans receivable and payable; and

(d)   bonds receivable and payable.

In each case, one party's contractual right to receive (or obligation to pay) cash is matched by the other party's corresponding obligation to pay (or right to receive).

AG5   Another type of financial instrument is one for which the economic benefit to be received or given up is a financial asset other than cash. For example, a note payable in government bonds gives the holder the contractual right to receive and the issuer the contractual obligation to deliver government bonds, not cash. The bonds are financial assets because they represent obligations of the issuing government to pay cash. The note is, therefore, a financial asset of the note holder and a financial liability of the note issuer.

AG6   'Perpetual' debt instruments (such as 'perpetual' bonds, debentures and capital notes) normally provide the holder with the contractual right to receive payments on account of interest at fixed dates extending into the indefinite future, either with no right to receive a return of principal or a right to a return of principal under terms that make it very unlikely or very far in the future. For example, an entity may issue a financial instrument requiring it to make annual payments in perpetuity equal to a stated interest rate of 8 per cent applied to a stated par or principal amount of CU1,000.[5] Assuming 8 per cent to be the market rate of interest for the instrument when issued, the issuer assumes a contractual obligation to make a stream of future interest payments having a fair value (present value) of CU1,000 on initial recognition. The holder and issuer of the instrument have a financial asset and a financial liability, respectively.

AG7   A contractual right or contractual obligation to receive, deliver or exchange financial instruments is itself a financial instrument. A chain of contractual rights or contractual obligations meets the definition of a financial instrument if it will ultimately lead to the receipt or payment of cash or to the acquisition or issue of an equity instrument.

AG8   The ability to exercise a contractual right or the requirement to satisfy a contractual obligation may be absolute, or it may be contingent on the occurrence of a future event. For example, a financial guarantee is a contractual right of the lender to receive cash from the guarantor, and a corresponding contractual obligation of the guarantor to pay the lender, if the borrower defaults. The contractual right and obligation exist because of a past transaction or event (assumption of the guarantee), even though the lender's ability to exercise its right and the requirement for the guarantor to perform under its obligation are both contingent on a future act of default by the borrower. A contingent right and obligation meet the definition of a financial asset and a financial liability, even though such assets and liabilities are not always recognised in the financial statements. Some of these contingent rights and obligations may be insurance contracts within the scope of IFRS 4.

AG9   Under IAS 17 *Leases* a finance lease is regarded as primarily an entitlement of the lessor to receive, and an obligation of the lessee to pay, a stream of payments that are substantially the same as blended payments of principal and interest under a loan agreement. The lessor accounts for its investment in the amount receivable under the lease contract rather than the leased asset itself. An operating lease, on the other hand, is regarded as primarily an uncompleted contract committing the lessor to provide the use of an asset in future periods in exchange for consideration similar to a fee for a service. The lessor continues to account for the leased asset itself rather than any amount receivable in the future under the contract. Accordingly, a finance lease is regarded as a financial instrument and an operating lease is not regarded as a financial instrument (except as regards individual payments currently due and payable).

AG10 Physical assets (such as inventories, property, plant and equipment), leased assets and intangible assets (such as patents and trademarks) are not financial assets. Control of such physical and intangible assets creates an opportunity to generate an inflow of cash or another financial asset, but it does not give rise to a present right to receive cash or another financial asset.

---

5   In this guidance, monetary amounts are denominated in 'currency units (CU)'.

AG11   Assets (such as prepaid expenses) for which the future economic benefit is the receipt of goods or services, rather than the right to receive cash or another financial asset, are not financial assets. Similarly, items such as deferred revenue and most warranty obligations are not financial liabilities because the outflow of economic benefits associated with them is the delivery of goods and services rather than a contractual obligation to pay cash or another financial asset.

AG12   Liabilities or assets that are not contractual (such as income taxes that are created as a result of statutory requirements imposed by governments) are not financial liabilities or financial assets. Accounting for income taxes is dealt with in IAS 12. Similarly, constructive obligations, as defined in IAS 37 *Provisions, Contingent Liabilities and Contingent Assets*, do not arise from contracts and are not financial liabilities.

Equity instruments

AG13   Examples of equity instruments include non-puttable ordinary shares, some puttable instruments (see paragraphs 16A and 16B), some instruments that impose on the entity an obligation to deliver to another party a pro rata share of the net assets of the entity only on liquidation (see paragraphs 16C and 16D), some types of preference shares (see paragraphs AG25 and AG26), and warrants or written call options that allow the holder to subscribe for or purchase a fixed number of non-puttable ordinary shares in the issuing entity in exchange for a fixed amount of cash or another financial asset. An entity's obligation to issue or purchase a fixed number of its own equity instruments in exchange for a fixed amount of cash or another financial asset is an equity instrument of the entity (except as stated in paragraph 22A). However, if such a contract contains an obligation for the entity to pay cash or another financial asset (other than a contract classified as equity in accordance with paragraphs 16A and 16B or paragraphs 16C and 16D), it also gives rise to a liability for the present value of the redemption amount (see paragraph AG27(a)). An issuer of non-puttable ordinary shares assumes a liability when it formally acts to make a distribution and becomes legally obliged to the shareholders to do so. This may be the case following the declaration of a dividend or when the entity is being wound up and any assets remaining after the satisfaction of liabilities become distributable to shareholders.

AG14   A purchased call option or other similar contract acquired by an entity that gives it the right to reacquire a fixed number of its own equity instruments in exchange for delivering a fixed amount of cash or another financial asset is not a financial asset of the entity (except as stated in paragraph 22A). Instead, any consideration paid for such a contract is deducted from equity.

The class of instruments that is subordinate to all other classes (paragraphs 16A(b) and 16C(b))

AG14A   One of the features of paragraphs 16A and 16C is that the financial instrument is in the class of instruments that is subordinate to all other classes.

AG14B When determining whether an instrument is in the subordinate class, an entity evaluates the instrument's claim on liquidation as if it were to liquidate on the date when it classifies the instrument. An entity shall reassess the classification if there is a change in relevant circumstances. For example, if the entity issues or redeems another financial instrument, this may affect whether the instrument in question is in the class of instruments that is subordinate to all other classes.

AG14C An instrument that has a preferential right on liquidation of the entity is not an instrument with an entitlement to a pro rata share of the net assets of the entity. For example, an instrument has a preferential right on liquidation if it entitles the holder to a fixed dividend on liquidation, in addition to a share of the entity's net assets, when other instruments in the subordinate class with a right to a pro rata share of the net assets of the entity do not have the same right on liquidation.

AG14D If an entity has only one class of financial instruments, that class shall be treated as if it were subordinate to all other classes.

Total expected cash flows attributable to the instrument over the life of the instrument (paragraph 16A(e))

AG14E The total expected cash flows of the instrument over the life of the instrument must be substantially based on the profit or loss, change in the recognised net assets or fair value of the recognised and unrecognised net assets of the entity over the life of the instrument. Profit or loss and the change in the recognised net assets shall be measured in accordance with relevant IFRSs.

Transactions entered into by an instrument holder other than as owner of the entity (paragraphs 16A and 16C)

AG14F The holder of a puttable financial instrument or an instrument that imposes on the entity an obligation to deliver to another party a pro rata share of the net assets of the entity only on liquidation may enter into transactions with the entity in a role other than that of an owner. For example, an instrument holder may also be an employee of the entity. Only the cash flows and the contractual terms and conditions of the instrument that relate to the instrument holder as an owner of the entity shall be considered when assessing whether the instrument should be classified as equity under paragraph 16A or paragraph 16C.

AG14G An example is a limited partnership that has limited and general partners. Some general partners may provide a guarantee to the entity and may be remunerated for providing that guarantee. In such situations, the guarantee and the associated cash flows relate to the instrument holders in their role as guarantors and not in their roles as owners of the entity. Therefore, such a guarantee and the associated cash flows would not result in the general partners being considered subordinate to the limited partners, and would be disregarded when assessing whether the contractual terms of the limited partnership instruments and the general partnership instruments are identical.

AG14H Another example is a profit or loss sharing arrangement that allocates profit or loss to the instrument holders on the basis of services rendered or business generated during the current and previous years. Such arrangements are transactions with instrument holders in their role as non-owners and should not be considered when assessing the features listed in paragraph 16A or paragraph 16C.

However, profit or loss sharing arrangements that allocate profit or loss to instrument holders based on the nominal amount of their instruments relative to others in the class represent transactions with the instrument holders in their roles as owners and should be considered when assessing the features listed in paragraph 16A or paragraph 16C.

AG14I The cash flows and contractual terms and conditions of a transaction between the instrument holder (in the role as a non-owner) and the issuing entity must be similar to an equivalent transaction that might occur between a non-instrument holder and the issuing entity.

No other financial instrument or contract with total cash flows that substantially fixes or restricts the residual return to the instrument holder (paragraphs 16B and 16D)

AG14J A condition for classifying as equity a financial instrument that otherwise meets the criteria in paragraph 16A or paragraph 16C is that the entity has no other financial instrument or contract that has (a) total cash flows based substantially on the profit or loss, the change in the recognised net assets or the change in the fair value of the recognised and unrecognised net assets of the entity and (b) the effect of substantially restricting or fixing the residual return. The following instruments, when entered into on normal commercial terms with unrelated parties, are unlikely to prevent instruments that otherwise meet the criteria in paragraph 16A or paragraph 16C from being classified as equity:

(a) instruments with total cash flows substantially based on specific assets of the entity.

(b) instruments with total cash flows based on a percentage of revenue.

(c) contracts designed to reward individual employees for services rendered to the entity.

(d) contracts requiring the payment of an insignificant percentage of profit for services rendered or goods provided.

Derivative financial instruments

AG15 Financial instruments include primary instruments (such as receivables, payables and equity instruments) and derivative financial instruments (such as financial options, futures and forwards, interest rate swaps and currency swaps). Derivative financial instruments meet the definition of a financial instrument and, accordingly, are within the scope of this Standard.

AG16 Derivative financial instruments create rights and obligations that have the effect of transferring between the parties to the instrument one or more of the financial risks inherent in an underlying primary financial instrument. On inception, derivative financial instruments give one party a contractual right to exchange financial assets or financial liabilities with another party under conditions that are potentially favourable, or a contractual obligation to exchange financial assets or financial liabilities with another party under conditions that are potentially unfavourable. However, they generally[6] do not result in a transfer of the underlying primary financial instrument on inception of the contract, nor does such a transfer necessarily take place on maturity of the contract. Some instruments embody both a right and an obligation to make an exchange. Because the terms of the exchange are determined on inception of the derivative instrument, as prices in financial markets change those terms may become either favourable or unfavourable.

AG17   A put or call option to exchange financial assets or financial liabilities (ie financial instruments other than an entity's own equity instruments) gives the holder a right to obtain potential future economic benefits associated with changes in the fair value of the financial instrument underlying the contract. Conversely, the writer of an option assumes an obligation to forgo potential future economic benefits or bear potential losses of economic benefits associated with changes in the fair value of the underlying financial instrument. The contractual right of the holder and obligation of the writer meet the definition of a financial asset and a financial liability, respectively. The financial instrument underlying an option contract may be any financial asset, including shares in other entities and interest-bearing instruments. An option may require the writer to issue a debt instrument, rather than transfer a financial asset, but the instrument underlying the option would constitute a financial asset of the holder if the option were exercised. The option-holder's right to exchange the financial asset under potentially favourable conditions and the writer's obligation to exchange the financial asset under potentially unfavourable conditions are distinct from the underlying financial asset to be exchanged upon exercise of the option. The nature of the holder's right and of the writer's obligation are not affected by the likelihood that the option will be exercised.

AG18   Another example of a derivative financial instrument is a forward contract to be settled in six months' time in which one party (the purchaser) promises to deliver CU1,000,000 cash in exchange for CU1,000,000 face amount of fixed rate government bonds, and the other party (the seller) promises to deliver CU1,000,000 face amount of fixed rate government bonds in exchange for CU1,000,000 cash. During the six months, both parties have a contractual right and a contractual obligation to exchange financial instruments. If the market price of the government bonds rises above CU1,000,000, the conditions will be favourable to the purchaser and unfavourable to the seller; if the market price falls below CU1,000,000, the effect will be the opposite. The purchaser has a contractual right (a financial asset) similar to the right under a call option held and a contractual obligation (a financial liability) similar to the obligation under a put option written; the seller has a contractual right (a financial asset) similar to the right under a put option held and a contractual obligation (a financial liability) similar to the obligation under a call option written. As with options, these contractual rights and obligations constitute financial assets and financial liabilities separate and distinct from the underlying financial instruments (the bonds and cash to be exchanged). Both parties to a forward contract have an obligation to perform at the agreed time, whereas performance under an option contract occurs only if and when the holder of the option chooses to exercise it.

---

6   This is true of most, but not all derivatives, eg in some cross-currency interest rate swaps principal is exchanged on inception (and re-exchanged on maturity).

AG19   Many other types of derivative instruments embody a right or obligation to make a future exchange, including interest rate and currency swaps, interest rate caps, collars and floors, loan commitments, note issuance facilities and letters of credit. An interest rate swap contract may be viewed as a variation of a forward contract in which the parties agree to make a series of future exchanges of cash amounts, one amount calculated with reference to a floating interest rate and the other with reference to a fixed interest rate. Futures contracts are another variation of forward contracts, differing primarily in that the contracts are standardised and traded on an exchange.

Contracts to buy or sell non-financial items (paragraphs 8–10)

AG20   Contracts to buy or sell non-financial items do not meet the definition of a financial instrument because the contractual right of one party to receive a non-financial asset or service and the corresponding obligation of the other party do not establish a present right or obligation of either party to receive, deliver or exchange a financial asset. For example, contracts that provide for settlement only by the receipt or delivery of a non-financial item (eg an option, futures or forward contract on silver) are not financial instruments. Many commodity contracts are of this type. Some are standardised in form and traded on organised markets in much the same fashion as some derivative financial instruments. For example, a commodity futures contract may be bought and sold readily for cash because it is listed for trading on an exchange and may change hands many times. However, the parties buying and selling the contract are, in effect, trading the underlying commodity. The ability to buy or sell a commodity contract for cash, the ease with which it may be bought or sold and the possibility of negotiating a cash settlement of the obligation to receive or deliver the commodity do not alter the fundamental character of the contract in a way that creates a financial instrument. Nevertheless, some contracts to buy or sell non-financial items that can be settled net or by exchanging financial instruments, or in which the non-financial item is readily convertible to cash, are within the scope of the Standard as if they were financial instruments (see paragraph 8).

AG21   A contract that involves the receipt or delivery of physical assets does not give rise to a financial asset of one party and a financial liability of the other party unless any corresponding payment is deferred past the date on which the physical assets are transferred. Such is the case with the purchase or sale of goods on trade credit.

AG22   Some contracts are commodity-linked, but do not involve settlement through the physical receipt or delivery of a commodity. They specify settlement through cash payments that are determined according to a formula in the contract, rather than through payment of fixed amounts. For example, the principal amount of a bond may be calculated by applying the market price of oil prevailing at the maturity of the bond to a fixed quantity of oil. The principal is indexed by reference to a commodity price, but is settled only in cash. Such a contract constitutes a financial instrument.

AG23 The definition of a financial instrument also encompasses a contract that gives rise to a non-financial asset or non-financial liability in addition to a financial asset or financial liability. Such financial instruments often give one party an option to exchange a financial asset for a non-financial asset. For example, an oil-linked bond may give the holder the right to receive a stream of fixed periodic interest payments and a fixed amount of cash on maturity, with the option to exchange the principal amount for a fixed quantity of oil. The desirability of exercising this option will vary from time to time depending on the fair value of oil relative to the exchange ratio of cash for oil (the exchange price) inherent in the bond. The intentions of the bondholder concerning the exercise of the option do not affect the substance of the component assets. The financial asset of the holder and the financial liability of the issuer make the bond a financial instrument, regardless of the other types of assets and liabilities also created.

AG24 [Deleted]

Presentation

Liabilities and equity (paragraphs 15–27)

No contractual obligation to deliver cash or another financial asset (paragraphs 17–20)

AG25 Preference shares may be issued with various rights. In determining whether a preference share is a financial liability or an equity instrument, an issuer assesses the particular rights attaching to the share to determine whether it exhibits the fundamental characteristic of a financial liability. For example, a preference share that provides for redemption on a specific date or at the option of the holder contains a financial liability because the issuer has an obligation to transfer financial assets to the holder of the share. The potential inability of an issuer to satisfy an obligation to redeem a preference share when contractually required to do so, whether because of a lack of funds, a statutory restriction or insufficient profits or reserves, does not negate the obligation. An option of the issuer to redeem the shares for cash does not satisfy the definition of a financial liability because the issuer does not have a present obligation to transfer financial assets to the shareholders. In this case, redemption of the shares is solely at the discretion of the issuer. An obligation may arise, however, when the issuer of the shares exercises its option, usually by formally notifying the shareholders of an intention to redeem the shares.

AG26 When preference shares are non-redeemable, the appropriate classification is determined by the other rights that attach to them. Classification is based on an assessment of the substance of the contractual arrangements and the definitions of a financial liability and an equity instrument. When distributions to holders of the preference shares, whether cumulative or non-cumulative, are at the discretion of the issuer, the shares are equity instruments. The classification of a preference share as an equity instrument or a financial liability is not affected by, for example:

(a) a history of making distributions;

(b) an intention to make distributions in the future;

(c) a possible negative impact on the price of ordinary shares of the issuer if distributions are not made (because of restrictions on paying dividends on the ordinary shares if dividends are not paid on the preference shares);

(d) the amount of the issuer's reserves;

(e) an issuer's expectation of a profit or loss for a period; or

(f) an ability or inability of the issuer to influence the amount of its profit or loss for the period.

Settlement in the entity's own equity instruments (paragraphs 21–24)

AG27 The following examples illustrate how to classify different types of contracts on an entity's own equity instruments:

(a) A contract that will be settled by the entity receiving or delivering a fixed number of its own shares for no future consideration, or exchanging a fixed number of its own shares for a fixed amount of cash or another financial asset, is an equity instrument (except as stated in paragraph 22A). Accordingly, any consideration received or paid for such a contract is added directly to or deducted directly from equity. One example is an issued share option that gives the counterparty a right to buy a fixed number of the entity's shares for a fixed amount of cash. However, if the contract requires the entity to purchase (redeem) its own shares for cash or another financial asset at a fixed or determinable date or on demand, the entity also recognises a financial liability for the present value of the redemption amount (with the exception of instruments that have all the features and meet the conditions in paragraphs 16A and 16B or paragraphs 16C and 16D). One example is an entity's obligation under a forward contract to repurchase a fixed number of its own shares for a fixed amount of cash.

(b) An entity's obligation to purchase its own shares for cash gives rise to a financial liability for the present value of the redemption amount even if the number of shares that the entity is obliged to repurchase is not fixed or if the obligation is conditional on the counterparty exercising a right to redeem (except as stated in paragraphs 16A and 16B or paragraphs 16C and 16D). One example of a conditional obligation is an issued option that requires the entity to repurchase its own shares for cash if the counterparty exercises the option.

(c) A contract that will be settled in cash or another financial asset is a financial asset or financial liability even if the amount of cash or another financial asset that will be received or delivered is based on changes in the market price of the entity's own equity (except as stated in paragraphs 16A and 16B or paragraphs 16C and 16D). One example is a net cash-settled share option.

(d) A contract that will be settled in a variable number of the entity's own shares whose value equals a fixed amount or an amount based on changes in an underlying variable (eg a commodity price) is a financial asset or a financial liability. An example is a written option to buy gold that, if exercised, is settled net in the entity's own instruments by the entity delivering as many of those instruments as are equal to the value of the option contract. Such a contract is a financial asset or financial liability even if the underlying variable is the entity's own share price rather than gold. Similarly, a contract that will be settled in a fixed number of the entity's own shares, but the rights attaching to those shares will be varied so that the settlement value equals a fixed amount or an amount based on changes in an underlying variable, is a financial asset or a financial liability.

Contingent settlement provisions (paragraph 25)

AG28   Paragraph 25 requires that if a part of a contingent settlement provision that could require settlement in cash or another financial asset (or in another way that would result in the instrument being a financial liability) is not genuine, the settlement provision does not affect the classification of a financial instrument. Thus, a contract that requires settlement in cash or a variable number of the entity's own shares only on the occurrence of an event that is extremely rare, highly abnormal and very unlikely to occur is an equity instrument. Similarly, settlement in a fixed number of an entity's own shares may be contractually precluded in circumstances that are outside the control of the entity, but if these circumstances have no genuine possibility of occurring, classification as an equity instrument is appropriate.

Treatment in consolidated financial statements

AG29   In consolidated financial statements, an entity presents non-controlling interests—ie the interests of other parties in the equity and income of its subsidiaries—in accordance with IAS 1 and IFRS 10. When classifying a financial instrument (or a component of it) in consolidated financial statements, an entity considers all terms and conditions agreed between members of the group and the holders of the instrument in determining whether the group as a whole has an obligation to deliver cash or another financial asset in respect of the instrument or to settle it in a manner that results in liability classification. When a subsidiary in a group issues a financial instrument and a parent or other group entity agrees additional terms directly with the holders of the instrument (eg a guarantee), the group may not have discretion over distributions or redemption. Although the subsidiary may appropriately classify the instrument without regard to these additional terms in its individual financial statements, the effect of other agreements between members of the group and the holders of the instrument is considered in order to ensure that consolidated financial statements reflect the contracts and transactions entered into by the group as a whole. To the extent that there is such an obligation or settlement provision, the instrument (or the component of it that is subject to the obligation) is classified as a financial liability in consolidated financial statements.

AG29A   Some types of instruments that impose a contractual obligation on the entity are classified as equity instruments in accordance with paragraphs 16A and 16B or paragraphs 16C and 16D. Classification in accordance with those paragraphs is an exception to the principles otherwise applied in this Standard to the classification of an instrument. This exception is not extended to the classification of non-controlling interests in the consolidated financial statements. Therefore, instruments classified as equity instruments in accordance with either paragraphs 16A and 16B or paragraphs 16C and 16D in the separate or individual financial statements that are non-controlling interests are classified as liabilities in the consolidated financial statements of the group.

Compound financial instruments (paragraphs 28–32)

AG30 Paragraph 28 applies only to issuers of non-derivative compound financial instruments. Paragraph 28 does not deal with compound financial instruments from the perspective of holders. IFRS 9 deals with the classification and measurement of financial assets that are compound financial instruments from the holder's perspective.

AG31 A common form of compound financial instrument is a debt instrument with an embedded conversion option, such as a bond convertible into ordinary shares of the issuer, and without any other embedded derivative features. Paragraph 28 requires the issuer of such a financial instrument to present the liability component and the equity component separately in the statement of financial position, as follows:

(a) The issuer's obligation to make scheduled payments of interest and principal is a financial liability that exists as long as the instrument is not converted. On initial recognition, the fair value of the liability component is the present value of the contractually determined stream of future cash flows discounted at the rate of interest applied at that time by the market to instruments of comparable credit status and providing substantially the same cash flows, on the same terms, but without the conversion option.

(b) The equity instrument is an embedded option to convert the liability into equity of the issuer. This option has value on initial recognition even when it is out of the money.

AG32 On conversion of a convertible instrument at maturity, the entity derecognises the liability component and recognises it as equity. The original equity component remains as equity (although it may be transferred from one line item within equity to another). There is no gain or loss on conversion at maturity.

AG33 When an entity extinguishes a convertible instrument before maturity through an early redemption or repurchase in which the original conversion privileges are unchanged, the entity allocates the consideration paid and any transaction costs for the repurchase or redemption to the liability and equity components of the instrument at the date of the transaction. The method used in allocating the consideration paid and transaction costs to the separate components is consistent with that used in the original allocation to the separate components of the proceeds received by the entity when the convertible instrument was issued, in accordance with paragraphs 28–32.

AG34 Once the allocation of the consideration is made, any resulting gain or loss is treated in accordance with accounting principles applicable to the related component, as follows:

(a) the amount of gain or loss relating to the liability component is recognised in profit or loss; and

(b) the amount of consideration relating to the equity component is recognised in equity.

AG35 An entity may amend the terms of a convertible instrument to induce early conversion, for example by offering a more favourable conversion ratio or paying other additional consideration in the event of conversion before a specified date. The difference, at the date the terms are amended, between the fair value of the consideration the holder receives on conversion of the instrument under the revised terms and the fair value of the consideration the holder would have received under the original terms is recognised as a loss in profit or loss.

Treasury shares (paragraphs 33 and 34)

AG36 An entity's own equity instruments are not recognised as a financial asset regardless of the reason for which they are reacquired. Paragraph 33 requires an entity that reacquires its own equity instruments to deduct those equity instruments from equity. However, when an entity holds its own equity on behalf of others, eg a financial institution holding its own equity on behalf of a client, there is an agency relationship and as a result those holdings are not included in the entity's statement of financial position.

Interest, dividends, losses and gains (paragraphs 35–41)

AG37 The following example illustrates the application of paragraph 35 to a compound financial instrument. Assume that a non-cumulative preference share is mandatorily redeemable for cash in five years, but that dividends are payable at the discretion of the entity before the redemption date. Such an instrument is a compound financial instrument, with the liability component being the present value of the redemption amount. The unwinding of the discount on this component is recognised in profit or loss and classified as interest expense. Any dividends paid relate to the equity component and, accordingly, are recognised as a distribution of profit or loss. A similar treatment would apply if the redemption was not mandatory but at the option of the holder, or if the share was mandatorily convertible into a variable number of ordinary shares calculated to equal a fixed amount or an amount based on changes in an underlying variable (eg commodity). However, if any unpaid dividends are added to the redemption amount, the entire instrument is a liability. In such a case, any dividends are classified as interest expense.

Offsetting a financial asset and a financial liability (paragraphs 42–50)

AG38 [Deleted]

Criterion that an entity 'currently has a legally enforceable right to set off the recognised amounts' (paragraph 42(a))

AG38A A right of set-off may be currently available or it may be contingent on a future event (for example, the right may be triggered or exercisable only on the occurrence of some future event, such as the default, insolvency or bankruptcy of one of the counterparties). Even if the right of set-off is not contingent on a future event, it may only be legally enforceable in the normal course of business, or in the event of default, or in the event of insolvency or bankruptcy, of one or all of the counterparties.

AG38B To meet the criterion in paragraph 42(a), an entity must currently have a legally enforceable right of set-off. This means that the right of set-off:

(a) must not be contingent on a future event; and

(b) must be legally enforceable in all of the following circumstances:

(i) the normal course of business;

(ii) the event of default; and

(iii) the event of insolvency or bankruptcy

of the entity and all of the counterparties.

AG38C The nature and extent of the right of set-off, including any conditions attached to its exercise and whether it would remain in the event of default or insolvency or bankruptcy, may vary from one legal jurisdiction to another. Consequently, it cannot be assumed that the right of set-off is automatically available outside of the normal course of business. For example, the bankruptcy or insolvency laws of a jurisdiction may prohibit, or restrict, the right of set-off in the event of bankruptcy or insolvency in some circumstances.

AG38D The laws applicable to the relationships between the parties (for example, contractual provisions, the laws governing the contract, or the default, insolvency or bankruptcy laws applicable to the parties) need to be considered to ascertain whether the right of set-off is enforceable in the normal course of business, in an event of default, and in the event of insolvency or bankruptcy, of the entity and all of the counterparties (as specified in paragraph AG38B(b)).

Criterion that an entity 'intends either to settle on a net basis, or to realise the asset and settle the liability simultaneously' (paragraph 42(b))

AG38E To meet the criterion in paragraph 42(b) an entity must intend either to settle on a net basis or to realise the asset and settle the liability simultaneously. Although the entity may have a right to settle net, it may still realise the asset and settle the liability separately.

AG38F If an entity can settle amounts in a manner such that the outcome is, in effect, equivalent to net settlement, the entity will meet the net settlement criterion in paragraph 42(b). This will occur if, and only if, the gross settlement mechanism has features that eliminate or result in insignificant credit and liquidity risk, and that will process receivables and payables in a single settlement process or cycle. For example, a gross settlement system that has all of the following characteristics would meet the net settlement criterion in paragraph 42(b):

(a) financial assets and financial liabilities eligible for set-off are submitted at the same point in time for processing;

(b) once the financial assets and financial liabilities are submitted for processing, the parties are committed to fulfil the settlement obligation;

(c) there is no potential for the cash flows arising from the assets and liabilities to change once they have been submitted for processing (unless the processing fails—see (d) below);

(d)   assets and liabilities that are collateralised with securities will be settled on a securities transfer or similar system (for example, delivery versus payment), so that if the transfer of securities fails, the processing of the related receivable or payable for which the securities are collateral will also fail (and vice versa);

(e)   any transactions that fail, as outlined in (d), will be re-entered for processing until they are settled;

(f)   settlement is carried out through the same settlement institution (for example, a settlement bank, a central bank or a central securities depository); and

(g)   an intraday credit facility is in place that will provide sufficient overdraft amounts to enable the processing of payments at the settlement date for each of the parties, and it is virtually certain that the intraday credit facility will be honoured if called upon.

AG39   The Standard does not provide special treatment for so-called 'synthetic instruments', which are groups of separate financial instruments acquired and held to emulate the characteristics of another instrument. For example, a floating rate long-term debt combined with an interest rate swap that involves receiving floating payments and making fixed payments synthesises a fixed rate long-term debt. Each of the individual financial instruments that together constitute a 'synthetic instrument' represents a contractual right or obligation with its own terms and conditions and each may be transferred or settled separately. Each financial instrument is exposed to risks that may differ from the risks to which other financial instruments are exposed. Accordingly, when one financial instrument in a 'synthetic instrument' is an asset and another is a liability, they are not offset and presented in an entity's statement of financial position on a net basis unless they meet the criteria for offsetting in paragraph 42.

Disclosure

Financial assets and financial liabilities at fair value through profit or loss (paragraph 94(f))

AG40   [Deleted]

International Accounting Standard 33

Earnings per Share

In April 2001 the International Accounting Standards Board (IASB) adopted IAS 33 *Earnings per Share—Financial Instruments and Other Contracts that May Be Settled in Shares*, which had been issued by the International Accounting Standards Committee in February 1997.

In December 2003 the IASB revised IAS 33 and changed the title to *Earnings per Share*. This IAS 33 also incorporated the guidance contained in a related Interpretation (SIC-24 *Earnings Per Share—Financial Instruments and Other Contracts that May be Settled in Shares*).

Other IFRSs have made minor consequential amendments to IAS 33. They include IFRS 2 *Share-based Payments* (issued February 2004), IFRS 3 *Business Combinations* (issued March 2004 and revised in January 2008) and IAS 1 *Presentation of Financial Statements* (as revised in September 2007).

CONTENTS

FOR THE ACCOMPANYING DOCUMENTS LISTED BELOW, SEE PART B OF THIS EDITION

APPROVAL BY THE BOARD OF IAS 33 ISSUED IN DECEMBER 2003

BASIS FOR CONCLUSIONS

ILLUSTRATIVE EXAMPLES

International Accounting Standard 33 *Earnings per Share* (IAS 33) is set out in paragraphs 1–76 and Appendices A and B. All the paragraphs have equal authority but retain the IASC format of the Standard when it was adopted by the IASB. IAS 33 should be read in the context of its objective and the Basis for Conclusions, the *Preface to International Financial Reporting Standards* and the *Conceptual Framework for Financial Reporting*. IAS 8 *Accounting Policies, Changes in Accounting Estimates and Errors* provides a basis for selecting and applying accounting policies in the absence of explicit guidance.

Introduction

IN1 International Accounting Standard 33 *Earnings per Share* (IAS 33) replaces IAS 33 *Earnings Per Share* (issued in 1997), and should be applied for annual periods beginning on or after 1 January 2005. Earlier application is encouraged. The Standard also replaces SIC-24 *Earnings Per Share—Financial Instruments and Other Contracts that May Be Settled in Shares*.

Reasons for revising IAS 33

IN2 The International Accounting Standards Board has developed this revised IAS 33 as part of its project on Improvements to International Accounting Standards. The project was undertaken in the light of queries and criticisms raised in relation to the Standards by securities regulators, professional accountants and other interested parties. The objectives of the project were to reduce or eliminate alternatives, redundancies and conflicts within the Standards, to deal with some convergence issues and to make other improvements.

IN3 For IAS 33 the Board's main objective was a limited revision to provide additional guidance and illustrative examples on selected complex matters, such as the effects of contingently issuable shares; potential ordinary shares of subsidiaries, joint ventures or associates; participating equity instruments; written put options; purchased put and call options; and mandatorily convertible instruments. The Board did not reconsider the fundamental approach to the determination and presentation of earnings per share contained in IAS 33.

International Accounting Standard 33
Earnings per Share

Objective

1   The objective of this Standard is to prescribe principles for the determination and presentation of earnings per share, so as to improve performance comparisons between different entities in the same reporting period and between different reporting periods for the same entity. Even though earnings per share data have limitations because of the different accounting policies that may be used for determining 'earnings', a consistently determined denominator enhances financial reporting. The focus of this Standard is on the denominator of the earnings per share calculation.

Scope

2   This Standard shall apply to

    (a)   the separate or individual financial statements of an entity:

        (i)   whose ordinary shares or potential ordinary shares are traded in a public market (a domestic or foreign stock exchange or an over-the-counter market, including local and regional markets) or

        (ii)   that files, or is in the process of filing, its financial statements with a securities commission or other regulatory organisation for the purpose of issuing ordinary shares in a public market; and

    (b)   the consolidated financial statements of a group with a parent:

        (i)   whose ordinary shares or potential ordinary shares are traded in a public market (a domestic or foreign stock exchange or an over-the-counter market, including local and regional markets) or

        (ii)   that files, or is in the process of filing, its financial statements with a securities commission or other regulatory organisation for the purpose of issuing ordinary shares in a public market.

3   An entity that discloses earnings per share shall calculate and disclose earnings per share in accordance with this Standard.

4   When an entity presents both consolidated financial statements and separate financial statements prepared in accordance with IFRS 10 *Consolidated Financial Statements* and IAS 27 *Separate Financial Statements* respectively, the disclosures required by this Standard need be presented only on the basis of the consolidated information. An entity that chooses to disclose earnings per share based on its separate financial statements shall present such earnings per share information only in its statement of comprehensive income. An entity shall not present such earnings per share information in the consolidated financial statements.

4A   If an entity presents items of profit or loss in a separate statement as described in paragraph 10A of IAS 1 *Presentation of Financial Statements* (as amended in 2011), it presents earnings per share only in that separate statement.

Definitions

5   The following terms are used in this Standard with the meanings specified:

Antidilution is an increase in earnings per share or a reduction in loss per share resulting from the assumption that convertible instruments are converted, that options or warrants are exercised, or that ordinary shares are issued upon the satisfaction of specified conditions.

A *contingent share agreement* is an agreement to issue shares that is dependent on the satisfaction of specified conditions.

Contingently issuable ordinary shares are ordinary shares issuable for little or no cash or other consideration upon the satisfaction of specified conditions in a contingent share agreement.

Dilution is a reduction in earnings per share or an increase in loss per share resulting from the assumption that convertible instruments are converted, that options or warrants are exercised, or that ordinary shares are issued upon the satisfaction of specified conditions.

Options, warrants and their equivalents are financial instruments that give the holder the right to purchase ordinary shares.

An *ordinary share* is an equity instrument that is subordinate to all other classes of equity instruments.

A *potential ordinary share* is a financial instrument or other contract that may entitle its holder to ordinary shares.

Put options on ordinary shares are contracts that give the holder the right to sell ordinary shares at a specified price for a given period.

6   Ordinary shares participate in profit for the period only after other types of shares such as preference shares have participated. An entity may have more than one class of ordinary shares. Ordinary shares of the same class have the same rights to receive dividends.

7   Examples of potential ordinary shares are:

   (a)   financial liabilities or equity instruments, including preference shares, that are convertible into ordinary shares;

   (b)   options and warrants;

   (c)   shares that would be issued upon the satisfaction of conditions resulting from contractual arrangements, such as the purchase of a business or other assets.

8   Terms defined in IAS 32 *Financial Instruments: Presentation* are used in this Standard with the meanings specified in paragraph 11 of IAS 32, unless otherwise noted. IAS 32 defines financial instrument, financial asset, financial liability and equity instrument, and provides guidance on applying those definitions. IFRS 13 *Fair Value Measurement* defines fair value and sets out requirements for applying that definition.

Measurement

Basic earnings per share

9   **An entity shall calculate basic earnings per share amounts for profit or loss attributable to ordinary equity holders of the parent entity and, if presented, profit or loss from continuing operations attributable to those equity holders.**

10   **Basic earnings per share shall be calculated by dividing profit or loss attributable to ordinary equity holders of the parent entity (the numerator) by the weighted average number of ordinary shares outstanding (the denominator) during the period.**

11   The objective of basic earnings per share information is to provide a measure of the interests of each ordinary share of a parent entity in the performance of the entity over the reporting period.

Earnings

12   **For the purpose of calculating basic earnings per share, the amounts attributable to ordinary equity holders of the parent entity in respect of:**

       (a)   **profit or loss from continuing operations attributable to the parent entity; and**

       (b)   **profit or loss attributable to the parent entity**

       shall be the amounts in (a) and (b) adjusted for the after-tax amounts of preference dividends, differences arising on the settlement of preference shares, and other similar effects of preference shares classified as equity.

13   All items of income and expense attributable to ordinary equity holders of the parent entity that are recognised in a period, including tax expense and dividends on preference shares classified as liabilities are included in the determination of profit or loss for the period attributable to ordinary equity holders of the parent entity (see IAS 1).

14   The after-tax amount of preference dividends that is deducted from profit or loss is:

       (a)   the after-tax amount of any preference dividends on non-cumulative preference shares declared in respect of the period; and

       (b)   the after-tax amount of the preference dividends for cumulative preference shares required for the period, whether or not the dividends have been declared. The amount of preference dividends for the period does not include the amount of any preference dividends for cumulative preference shares paid or declared during the current period in respect of previous periods.

15   Preference shares that provide for a low initial dividend to compensate an entity for selling the preference shares at a discount, or an above-market dividend in later periods to compensate investors for purchasing preference shares at a premium, are sometimes referred to as increasing rate preference shares. Any original issue discount or premium on increasing rate preference shares is amortised to retained earnings using the effective interest method and treated as a preference dividend for the purposes of calculating earnings per share.

16   Preference shares may be repurchased under an entity's tender offer to the holders. The excess of the fair value of the consideration paid to the preference shareholders over the carrying amount of the preference shares represents a return to the holders of the preference shares and a charge to retained earnings for the entity. This amount is deducted in calculating profit or loss attributable to ordinary equity holders of the parent entity.

17   Early conversion of convertible preference shares may be induced by an entity through favourable changes to the original conversion terms or the payment of additional consideration. The excess of the fair value of the ordinary shares or other consideration paid over the fair value of the ordinary shares issuable under the original conversion terms is a return to the preference shareholders, and is deducted in calculating profit or loss attributable to ordinary equity holders of the parent entity.

18   Any excess of the carrying amount of preference shares over the fair value of the consideration paid to settle them is added in calculating profit or loss attributable to ordinary equity holders of the parent entity.

Shares

19   For the purpose of calculating basic earnings per share, the number of ordinary shares shall be the weighted average number of ordinary shares outstanding during the period.

20   Using the weighted average number of ordinary shares outstanding during the period reflects the possibility that the amount of shareholders' capital varied during the period as a result of a larger or smaller number of shares being outstanding at any time. The weighted average number of ordinary shares outstanding during the period is the number of ordinary shares outstanding at the beginning of the period, adjusted by the number of ordinary shares bought back or issued during the period multiplied by a time-weighting factor. The time-weighting factor is the number of days that the shares are outstanding as a proportion of the total number of days in the period; a reasonable approximation of the weighted average is adequate in many circumstances.

21   Shares are usually included in the weighted average number of shares from the date consideration is receivable (which is generally the date of their issue), for example:

(a)   ordinary shares issued in exchange for cash are included when cash is receivable;

(b)   ordinary shares issued on the voluntary reinvestment of dividends on ordinary or preference shares are included when dividends are reinvested;

(c) ordinary shares issued as a result of the conversion of a debt instrument to ordinary shares are included from the date that interest ceases to accrue;

(d) ordinary shares issued in place of interest or principal on other financial instruments are included from the date that interest ceases to accrue;

(e) ordinary shares issued in exchange for the settlement of a liability of the entity are included from the settlement date;

(f) ordinary shares issued as consideration for the acquisition of an asset other than cash are included as of the date on which the acquisition is recognised; and

(g) ordinary shares issued for the rendering of services to the entity are included as the services are rendered.

The timing of the inclusion of ordinary shares is determined by the terms and conditions attaching to their issue. Due consideration is given to the substance of any contract associated with the issue.

22 Ordinary shares issued as part of the consideration transferred in a business combination are included in the weighted average number of shares from the acquisition date. This is because the acquirer incorporates into its statement of comprehensive income the acquiree's profits and losses from that date.

23 Ordinary shares that will be issued upon the conversion of a mandatorily convertible instrument are included in the calculation of basic earnings per share from the date the contract is entered into.

24 Contingently issuable shares are treated as outstanding and are included in the calculation of basic earnings per share only from the date when all necessary conditions are satisfied (ie the events have occurred). Shares that are issuable solely after the passage of time are not contingently issuable shares, because the passage of time is a certainty. Outstanding ordinary shares that are contingently returnable (ie subject to recall) are not treated as outstanding and are excluded from the calculation of basic earnings per share until the date the shares are no longer subject to recall.

25 [Deleted]

26 **The weighted average number of ordinary shares outstanding during the period and for all periods presented shall be adjusted for events, other than the conversion of potential ordinary shares, that have changed the number of ordinary shares outstanding without a corresponding change in resources.**

27 Ordinary shares may be issued, or the number of ordinary shares outstanding may be reduced, without a corresponding change in resources. Examples include:

(a) a capitalisation or bonus issue (sometimes referred to as a stock dividend);

(b) a bonus element in any other issue, for example a bonus element in a rights issue to existing shareholders;

(c) a share split; and

(d) a reverse share split (consolidation of shares).

28 In a capitalisation or bonus issue or a share split, ordinary shares are issued to existing shareholders for no additional consideration. Therefore, the number of ordinary shares outstanding is increased without an increase in resources. The number of ordinary shares outstanding before the event is adjusted for the proportionate change in the number of ordinary shares outstanding as if the event had occurred at the beginning of the earliest period presented. For example, on a two-for-one bonus issue, the number of ordinary shares outstanding before the issue is multiplied by three to obtain the new total number of ordinary shares, or by two to obtain the number of additional ordinary shares.

29 A consolidation of ordinary shares generally reduces the number of ordinary shares outstanding without a corresponding reduction in resources. However, when the overall effect is a share repurchase at fair value, the reduction in the number of ordinary shares outstanding is the result of a corresponding reduction in resources. An example is a share consolidation combined with a special dividend. The weighted average number of ordinary shares outstanding for the period in which the combined transaction takes place is adjusted for the reduction in the number of ordinary shares from the date the special dividend is recognised.

Diluted earnings per share

30 **An entity shall calculate diluted earnings per share amounts for profit or loss attributable to ordinary equity holders of the parent entity and, if presented, profit or loss from continuing operations attributable to those equity holders.**

31 **For the purpose of calculating diluted earnings per share, an entity shall adjust profit or loss attributable to ordinary equity holders of the parent entity, and the weighted average number of shares outstanding, for the effects of all dilutive potential ordinary shares.**

32 The objective of diluted earnings per share is consistent with that of basic earnings per share—to provide a measure of the interest of each ordinary share in the performance of an entity—while giving effect to all dilutive potential ordinary shares outstanding during the period. As a result:

(a) profit or loss attributable to ordinary equity holders of the parent entity is increased by the after-tax amount of dividends and interest recognised in the period in respect of the dilutive potential ordinary shares and is adjusted for any other changes in income or expense that would result from the conversion of the dilutive potential ordinary shares; and

(b) the weighted average number of ordinary shares outstanding is increased by the weighted average number of additional ordinary shares that would have been outstanding assuming the conversion of all dilutive potential ordinary shares.

Earnings

33 **For the purpose of calculating diluted earnings per share, an entity shall adjust profit or loss attributable to ordinary equity holders of the parent entity, as calculated in accordance with paragraph 12, by the after-tax effect of:**

(a)   any dividends or other items related to dilutive potential ordinary shares deducted in arriving at profit or loss attributable to ordinary equity holders of the parent entity as calculated in accordance with paragraph 12;

(b)   any interest recognised in the period related to dilutive potential ordinary shares; and

(c)   any other changes in income or expense that would result from the conversion of the dilutive potential ordinary shares.

34   After the potential ordinary shares are converted into ordinary shares, the items identified in paragraph 33(a)–(c) no longer arise. Instead, the new ordinary shares are entitled to participate in profit or loss attributable to ordinary equity holders of the parent entity. Therefore, profit or loss attributable to ordinary equity holders of the parent entity calculated in accordance with paragraph 12 is adjusted for the items identified in paragraph 33(a)–(c) and any related taxes. The expenses associated with potential ordinary shares include transaction costs and discounts accounted for in accordance with the effective interest method (see paragraph 9 of IAS 39 *Financial Instruments: Recognition and Measurement*, as revised in 2003).

35   The conversion of potential ordinary shares may lead to consequential changes in income or expenses. For example, the reduction of interest expense related to potential ordinary shares and the resulting increase in profit or reduction in loss may lead to an increase in the expense related to a non-discretionary employee profit-sharing plan. For the purpose of calculating diluted earnings per share, profit or loss attributable to ordinary equity holders of the parent entity is adjusted for any such consequential changes in income or expense.

Shares

36   **For the purpose of calculating diluted earnings per share, the number of ordinary shares shall be the weighted average number of ordinary shares calculated in accordance with paragraphs 19 and 26, plus the weighted average number of ordinary shares that would be issued on the conversion of all the dilutive potential ordinary shares into ordinary shares. Dilutive potential ordinary shares shall be deemed to have been converted into ordinary shares at the beginning of the period or, if later, the date of the issue of the potential ordinary shares.**

37   Dilutive potential ordinary shares shall be determined independently for each period presented. The number of dilutive potential ordinary shares included in the year-to-date period is not a weighted average of the dilutive potential ordinary shares included in each interim computation.

38   Potential ordinary shares are weighted for the period they are outstanding. Potential ordinary shares that are cancelled or allowed to lapse during the period are included in the calculation of diluted earnings per share only for the portion of the period during which they are outstanding. Potential ordinary shares that are converted into ordinary shares during the period are included in the calculation of diluted earnings per share from the beginning of the period to the date of conversion; from the date of conversion, the resulting ordinary shares are included in both basic and diluted earnings per share.

39   The number of ordinary shares that would be issued on conversion of dilutive potential ordinary shares is determined from the terms of the potential ordinary shares. When more than one basis of conversion exists, the calculation assumes the most advantageous conversion rate or exercise price from the standpoint of the holder of the potential ordinary shares.

40   A subsidiary, joint venture or associate may issue to parties other than the parent or investors with joint control of, or significant influence over, the investee potential ordinary shares that are convertible into either ordinary shares of the subsidiary, joint venture or associate, or ordinary shares of the parent or investors with joint control of, or significant influence (the reporting entity) over, the investee. If these potential ordinary shares of the subsidiary, joint venture or associate have a dilutive effect on the basic earnings per share of the reporting entity, they are included in the calculation of diluted earnings per share.

Dilutive potential ordinary shares

41   **Potential ordinary shares shall be treated as dilutive when, and only when, their conversion to ordinary shares would decrease earnings per share or increase loss per share from continuing operations.**

42   An entity uses profit or loss from continuing operations attributable to the parent entity as the control number to establish whether potential ordinary shares are dilutive or antidilutive. Profit or loss from continuing operations attributable to the parent entity is adjusted in accordance with paragraph 12 and excludes items relating to discontinued operations.

43   Potential ordinary shares are antidilutive when their conversion to ordinary shares would increase earnings per share or decrease loss per share from continuing operations. The calculation of diluted earnings per share does not assume conversion, exercise, or other issue of potential ordinary shares that would have an antidilutive effect on earnings per share.

44   In determining whether potential ordinary shares are dilutive or antidilutive, each issue or series of potential ordinary shares is considered separately rather than in aggregate. The sequence in which potential ordinary shares are considered may affect whether they are dilutive. Therefore, to maximise the dilution of basic earnings per share, each issue or series of potential ordinary shares is considered in sequence from the most dilutive to the least dilutive, ie dilutive potential ordinary shares with the lowest 'earnings per incremental share' are included in the diluted earnings per share calculation before those with a higher earnings per incremental share. Options and warrants are generally included first because they do not affect the numerator of the calculation.

Options, warrants and their equivalents

45   **For the purpose of calculating diluted earnings per share, an entity shall assume the exercise of dilutive options and warrants of the entity. The assumed proceeds from these instruments shall be regarded as having been received from the issue of ordinary shares at the average market price of ordinary shares during the**

period. **The difference between the number of ordinary shares issued and the number of ordinary shares that would have been issued at the average market price of ordinary shares during the period shall be treated as an issue of ordinary shares for no consideration.**

46   Options and warrants are dilutive when they would result in the issue of ordinary shares for less than the average market price of ordinary shares during the period. The amount of the dilution is the average market price of ordinary shares during the period minus the issue price. Therefore, to calculate diluted earnings per share, potential ordinary shares are treated as consisting of both the following:

(a)   a contract to issue a certain number of the ordinary shares at their average market price during the period. Such ordinary shares are assumed to be fairly priced and to be neither dilutive nor antidilutive. They are ignored in the calculation of diluted earnings per share.

(b)   a contract to issue the remaining ordinary shares for no consideration. Such ordinary shares generate no proceeds and have no effect on profit or loss attributable to ordinary shares outstanding. Therefore, such shares are dilutive and are added to the number of ordinary shares outstanding in the calculation of diluted earnings per share.

47   Options and warrants have a dilutive effect only when the average market price of ordinary shares during the period exceeds the exercise price of the options or warrants (ie they are 'in the money'). Previously reported earnings per share are not retroactively adjusted to reflect changes in prices of ordinary shares.

47A   For share options and other share-based payment arrangements to which IFRS 2 *Share-based Payment* applies, the issue price referred to in paragraph 46 and the exercise price referred to in paragraph 47 shall include the fair value (measured in accordance with IFRS 2) of any goods or services to be supplied to the entity in the future under the share option or other share-based payment arrangement.

48   Employee share options with fixed or determinable terms and non-vested ordinary shares are treated as options in the calculation of diluted earnings per share, even though they may be contingent on vesting. They are treated as outstanding on the grant date. Performance-based employee share options are treated as contingently issuable shares because their issue is contingent upon satisfying specified conditions in addition to the passage of time.

Convertible instruments

49   The dilutive effect of convertible instruments shall be reflected in diluted earnings per share in accordance with paragraphs 33 and 36.

50   Convertible preference shares are antidilutive whenever the amount of the dividend on such shares declared in or accumulated for the current period per ordinary share obtainable on conversion exceeds basic earnings per share. Similarly, convertible debt is antidilutive whenever its interest (net of tax and other changes in income or expense) per ordinary share obtainable on conversion exceeds basic earnings per share.

51   The redemption or induced conversion of convertible preference shares may affect only a portion of the previously outstanding convertible preference shares. In such cases, any excess consideration referred to in paragraph 17 is attributed to those shares that are redeemed or converted for the purpose of determining whether the remaining outstanding preference shares are dilutive. The shares redeemed or converted are considered separately from those shares that are not redeemed or converted.

Contingently issuable shares

52   As in the calculation of basic earnings per share, contingently issuable ordinary shares are treated as outstanding and included in the calculation of diluted earnings per share if the conditions are satisfied (ie the events have occurred). Contingently issuable shares are included from the beginning of the period (or from the date of the contingent share agreement, if later). If the conditions are not satisfied, the number of contingently issuable shares included in the diluted earnings per share calculation is based on the number of shares that would be issuable if the end of the period were the end of the contingency period. Restatement is not permitted if the conditions are not met when the contingency period expires.

53   If attainment or maintenance of a specified amount of earnings for a period is the condition for contingent issue and if that amount has been attained at the end of the reporting period but must be maintained beyond the end of the reporting period for an additional period, then the additional ordinary shares are treated as outstanding, if the effect is dilutive, when calculating diluted earnings per share. In that case, the calculation of diluted earnings per share is based on the number of ordinary shares that would be issued if the amount of earnings at the end of the reporting period were the amount of earnings at the end of the contingency period. Because earnings may change in a future period, the calculation of basic earnings per share does not include such contingently issuable ordinary shares until the end of the contingency period because not all necessary conditions have been satisfied.

54   The number of ordinary shares contingently issuable may depend on the future market price of the ordinary shares. In that case, if the effect is dilutive, the calculation of diluted earnings per share is based on the number of ordinary shares that would be issued if the market price at the end of the reporting period were the market price at the end of the contingency period. If the condition is based on an average of market prices over a period of time that extends beyond the end of the reporting period, the average for the period of time that has lapsed is used. Because the market price may change in a future period, the calculation of basic earnings per share does not include such contingently issuable ordinary shares until the end of the contingency period because not all necessary conditions have been satisfied.

55   The number of ordinary shares contingently issuable may depend on future earnings and future prices of the ordinary shares. In such cases, the number of ordinary shares included in the diluted earnings per share calculation is based on both conditions (ie earnings to date and the current market price at the end of the reporting period). Contingently issuable ordinary shares are not included in the diluted earnings per share calculation unless both conditions are met.

56   In other cases, the number of ordinary shares contingently issuable depends on a condition other than earnings or market price (for example, the opening of a specific number of retail stores). In such cases, assuming that the present status of the condition remains unchanged until the end of the contingency period, the contingently issuable ordinary shares are included in the calculation of diluted earnings per share according to the status at the end of the reporting period.

57   Contingently issuable potential ordinary shares (other than those covered by a contingent share agreement, such as contingently issuable convertible instruments) are included in the diluted earnings per share calculation as follows:

   (a)   an entity determines whether the potential ordinary shares may be assumed to be issuable on the basis of the conditions specified for their issue in accordance with the contingent ordinary share provisions in paragraphs 52–56; and

   (b)   if those potential ordinary shares should be reflected in diluted earnings per share, an entity determines their impact on the calculation of diluted earnings per share by following the provisions for options and warrants in paragraphs 45–48, the provisions for convertible instruments in paragraphs 49–51, the provisions for contracts that may be settled in ordinary shares or cash in paragraphs 58–61, or other provisions, as appropriate.

   However, exercise or conversion is not assumed for the purpose of calculating diluted earnings per share unless exercise or conversion of similar outstanding potential ordinary shares that are not contingently issuable is assumed.

Contracts that may be settled in ordinary shares or cash

58   When an entity has issued a contract that may be settled in ordinary shares or cash at the entity's option, the entity shall presume that the contract will be settled in ordinary shares, and the resulting potential ordinary shares shall be included in diluted earnings per share if the effect is dilutive.

59   When such a contract is presented for accounting purposes as an asset or a liability, or has an equity component and a liability component, the entity shall adjust the numerator for any changes in profit or loss that would have resulted during the period if the contract had been classified wholly as an equity instrument. That adjustment is similar to the adjustments required in paragraph 33.

60   For contracts that may be settled in ordinary shares or cash at the holder's option, the more dilutive of cash settlement and share settlement shall be used in calculating diluted earnings per share.

61   An example of a contract that may be settled in ordinary shares or cash is a debt instrument that, on maturity, gives the entity the unrestricted right to settle the principal amount in cash or in its own ordinary shares. Another example is a written put option that gives the holder a choice of settling in ordinary shares or cash.

Purchased options

62   Contracts such as purchased put options and purchased call options (ie options held by the entity on its own ordinary shares) are not included in the calculation of diluted earnings per share because including them would be antidilutive. The put option would be exercised only if the exercise price were higher than the market price and the call option would be exercised only if the exercise price were lower than the market price.

Written put options

63   **Contracts that require the entity to repurchase its own shares, such as written put options and forward purchase contracts, are reflected in the calculation of diluted earnings per share if the effect is dilutive. If these contracts are 'in the money' during the period (ie the exercise or settlement price is above the average market price for that period), the potential dilutive effect on earnings per share shall be calculated as follows:**

      (a)   **it shall be assumed that at the beginning of the period sufficient ordinary shares will be issued (at the average market price during the period) to raise proceeds to satisfy the contract;**

      (b)   **it shall be assumed that the proceeds from the issue are used to satisfy the contract (ie to buy back ordinary shares); and**

      (c)   **the incremental ordinary shares (the difference between the number of ordinary shares assumed issued and the number of ordinary shares received from satisfying the contract) shall be included in the calculation of diluted earnings per share.**

Retrospective adjustments

64   **If the number of ordinary or potential ordinary shares outstanding increases as a result of a capitalisation, bonus issue or share split, or decreases as a result of a reverse share split, the calculation of basic and diluted earnings per share for all periods presented shall be adjusted retrospectively. If these changes occur after the reporting period but before the financial statements are authorised for issue, the per share calculations for those and any prior period financial statements presented shall be based on the new number of shares. The fact that per share calculations reflect such changes in the number of shares shall be disclosed. In addition, basic and diluted earnings per share of all periods presented shall be adjusted for the effects of errors and adjustments resulting from changes in accounting policies accounted for retrospectively.**

65   An entity does not restate diluted earnings per share of any prior period presented for changes in the assumptions used in earnings per share calculations or for the conversion of potential ordinary shares into ordinary shares.

Presentation

66　**An entity shall present in the statement of comprehensive income basic and diluted earnings per share for profit or loss from continuing operations attributable to the ordinary equity holders of the parent entity and for profit or loss attributable to the ordinary equity holders of the parent entity for the period for each class of ordinary shares that has a different right to share in profit for the period. An entity shall present basic and diluted earnings per share with equal prominence for all periods presented.**

67　Earnings per share is presented for every period for which a statement of comprehensive income is presented. If diluted earnings per share is reported for at least one period, it shall be reported for all periods presented, even if it equals basic earnings per share. If basic and diluted earnings per share are equal, dual presentation can be accomplished in one line in the statement of comprehensive income.

67A　If an entity presents items of profit or loss in a separate statement as described in paragraph 10A of IAS 1 (as amended in 2011), it presents basic and diluted earnings per share, as required in paragraphs 66 and 67, in that separate statement.

68　**An entity that reports a discontinued operation shall disclose the basic and diluted amounts per share for the discontinued operation either in the statement of comprehensive income or in the notes.**

68A　If an entity presents items of profit or loss in a separate statement as described in paragraph 10A of IAS 1 (as amended in 2011), it presents basic and diluted earnings per share for the discontinued operation, as required in paragraph 68, in that separate statement or in the notes.

69　**An entity shall present basic and diluted earnings per share, even if the amounts are negative (ie a loss per share).**

Disclosure

70　**An entity shall disclose the following:**

(a)　the amounts used as the numerators in calculating basic and diluted earnings per share, and a reconciliation of those amounts to profit or loss attributable to the parent entity for the period. The reconciliation shall include the individual effect of each class of instruments that affects earnings per share.

(b)　the weighted average number of ordinary shares used as the denominator in calculating basic and diluted earnings per share, and a reconciliation of these denominators to each other. The reconciliation shall include the individual effect of each class of instruments that affects earnings per share.

(c)   instruments (including contingently issuable shares) that could potentially dilute basic earnings per share in the future, but were not included in the calculation of diluted earnings per share because they are antidilutive for the period(s) presented.

(d)   a description of ordinary share transactions or potential ordinary share transactions, other than those accounted for in accordance with paragraph 64, that occur after the reporting period and that would have changed significantly the number of ordinary shares or potential ordinary shares outstanding at the end of the period if those transactions had occurred before the end of the reporting period.

71   Examples of transactions in paragraph 70(d) include:

(a)   an issue of shares for cash;

(b)   an issue of shares when the proceeds are used to repay debt or preference shares outstanding at the end of the reporting period;

(c)   the redemption of ordinary shares outstanding;

(d)   the conversion or exercise of potential ordinary shares outstanding at the end of the reporting period into ordinary shares;

(e)   an issue of options, warrants, or convertible instruments; and

(f)   the achievement of conditions that would result in the issue of contingently issuable shares.

Earnings per share amounts are not adjusted for such transactions occurring after the reporting period because such transactions do not affect the amount of capital used to produce profit or loss for the period.

72   Financial instruments and other contracts generating potential ordinary shares may incorporate terms and conditions that affect the measurement of basic and diluted earnings per share. These terms and conditions may determine whether any potential ordinary shares are dilutive and, if so, the effect on the weighted average number of shares outstanding and any consequent adjustments to profit or loss attributable to ordinary equity holders. The disclosure of the terms and conditions of such financial instruments and other contracts is encouraged, if not otherwise required (see IFRS 7 *Financial Instruments: Disclosures*).

73   **If an entity discloses, in addition to basic and diluted earnings per share, amounts per share using a reported component of the statement of comprehensive income other than one required by this Standard, such amounts shall be calculated using the weighted average number of ordinary shares determined in accordance with this Standard. Basic and diluted amounts per share relating to such a component shall be disclosed with equal prominence and presented in the notes. An entity shall indicate the basis on which the numerator(s) is (are) determined, including whether amounts per share are before tax or after tax. If a component of the statement of comprehensive income is used that is not reported as a line item in the statement of comprehensive income, a reconciliation shall be provided between the component used and a line item that is reported in the statement of comprehensive income.**

73A   Paragraph 73 applies also to an entity that discloses, in addition to basic and diluted earnings per share, amounts per share using a reported item of profit or loss, other than one required by this Standard.

Effective date

74   An entity shall apply this Standard for annual periods beginning on or after 1 January 2005. Earlier application is encouraged. If an entity applies the Standard for a period beginning before 1 January 2005, it shall disclose that fact.

74A   IAS 1 (as revised in 2007) amended the terminology used throughout IFRSs. In addition it added paragraphs 4A, 67A, 68A and 73A. An entity shall apply those amendments for annual periods beginning on or after 1 January 2009. If an entity applies IAS 1 (revised 2007) for an earlier period, the amendments shall be applied for that earlier period.

74B   IFRS 10 and IFRS 11 *Joint Arrangements*, issued in May 2011, amended paragraphs 4, 40 and A11. An entity shall apply those amendments when it applies IFRS 10 and IFRS 11.

74C   IFRS 13, issued in May 2011, amended paragraphs 8, 47A and A2. An entity shall apply those amendments when it applies IFRS 13.

74D   *Presentation of Items of Other Comprehensive Income* (Amendments to IAS 1), issued in June 2011, amended paragraphs 4A, 67A, 68A and 73A. An entity shall apply those amendments when it applies IAS 1 as amended in June 2011.

Withdrawal of other pronouncements

75   This Standard supersedes IAS 33 *Earnings Per Share* (issued in 1997).

76   This Standard supersedes SIC-24 *Earnings Per Share—Financial Instruments and Other Contracts that May Be Settled in Shares*.

Appendix A
Application guidance

This appendix is an integral part of the Standard.

Profit or loss attributable to the parent entity

A1 For the purpose of calculating earnings per share based on the consolidated financial statements, profit or loss attributable to the parent entity refers to profit or loss of the consolidated entity after adjusting for non-controlling interests.

Rights issues

A2 The issue of ordinary shares at the time of exercise or conversion of potential ordinary shares does not usually give rise to a bonus element. This is because the potential ordinary shares are usually issued for fair value, resulting in a proportionate change in the resources available to the entity. In a rights issue, however, the exercise price is often less than the fair value of the shares. Therefore, as noted in paragraph 27(b), such a rights issue includes a bonus element. If a rights issue is offered to all existing shareholders, the number of ordinary shares to be used in calculating basic and diluted earnings per share for all periods before the rights issue is the number of ordinary shares outstanding before the issue, multiplied by the following factor:

$$\frac{\text{Fair value per share immediately before the exercise of rights}}{\text{Theoretical ex-rights fair value per share}}$$

The theoretical ex-rights fair value per share is calculated by adding the aggregate fair value of the shares immediately before the exercise of the rights to the proceeds from the exercise of the rights, and dividing by the number of shares outstanding after the exercise of the rights. Where the rights are to be publicly traded separately from the shares before the exercise date, fair value is measured at the close of the last day on which the shares are traded together with the rights.

Control number

A3 To illustrate the application of the control number notion described in paragraphs 42 and 43, assume that an entity has profit from continuing operations attributable to the parent entity of CU4,800,[1] a loss from discontinued operations attributable to the parent entity of (CU7,200), a loss attributable to the parent entity of (CU2,400), and 2,000 ordinary shares and 400 potential ordinary shares outstanding. The entity's basic earnings per share is CU2.40 for continuing operations, (CU3.60) for discontinued operations and (CU1.20) for the loss. The 400 potential ordinary shares are included in the diluted earnings per share calculation because the resulting CU2.00 earnings per share for continuing operations is dilutive, assuming no profit or loss impact of those 400 potential ordinary shares. Because profit from continuing operations attributable to the parent entity is the control number, the entity also includes those 400 potential

---

1 In this guidance, monetary amounts are denominated in 'currency units (CU)'.

ordinary shares in the calculation of the other earnings per share amounts, even though the resulting earnings per share amounts are antidilutive to their comparable basic earnings per share amounts, ie the loss per share is less [(CU3.00) per share for the loss from discontinued operations and (CU1.00) per share for the loss].

Average market price of ordinary shares

A4   For the purpose of calculating diluted earnings per share, the average market price of ordinary shares assumed to be issued is calculated on the basis of the average market price of the ordinary shares during the period. Theoretically, every market transaction for an entity's ordinary shares could be included in the determination of the average market price. As a practical matter, however, a simple average of weekly or monthly prices is usually adequate.

A5   Generally, closing market prices are adequate for calculating the average market price. When prices fluctuate widely, however, an average of the high and low prices usually produces a more representative price. The method used to calculate the average market price is used consistently unless it is no longer representative because of changed conditions. For example, an entity that uses closing market prices to calculate the average market price for several years of relatively stable prices might change to an average of high and low prices if prices start fluctuating greatly and the closing market prices no longer produce a representative average price.

Options, warrants and their equivalents

A6   Options or warrants to purchase convertible instruments are assumed to be exercised to purchase the convertible instrument whenever the average prices of both the convertible instrument and the ordinary shares obtainable upon conversion are above the exercise price of the options or warrants. However, exercise is not assumed unless conversion of similar outstanding convertible instruments, if any, is also assumed.

A7   Options or warrants may permit or require the tendering of debt or other instruments of the entity (or its parent or a subsidiary) in payment of all or a portion of the exercise price. In the calculation of diluted earnings per share, those options or warrants have a dilutive effect if (a) the average market price of the related ordinary shares for the period exceeds the exercise price or (b) the selling price of the instrument to be tendered is below that at which the instrument may be tendered under the option or warrant agreement and the resulting discount establishes an effective exercise price below the market price of the ordinary shares obtainable upon exercise. In the calculation of diluted earnings per share, those options or warrants are assumed to be exercised and the debt or other instruments are assumed to be tendered. If tendering cash is more advantageous to the option or warrant holder and the contract permits tendering cash, tendering of cash is assumed. Interest (net of tax) on any debt assumed to be tendered is added back as an adjustment to the numerator.

A8   Similar treatment is given to preference shares that have similar provisions or to other instruments that have conversion options that permit the investor to pay cash for a more favourable conversion rate.

A9   The underlying terms of certain options or warrants may require the proceeds received from the exercise of those instruments to be applied to redeem debt or other instruments of the entity (or its parent or a subsidiary). In the calculation of diluted earnings per share, those options or warrants are assumed to be exercised and the proceeds applied to purchase the debt at its average market price rather than to purchase ordinary shares. However, the excess proceeds received from the assumed exercise over the amount used for the assumed purchase of debt are considered (ie assumed to be used to buy back ordinary shares) in the diluted earnings per share calculation. Interest (net of tax) on any debt assumed to be purchased is added back as an adjustment to the numerator.

Written put options

A10   To illustrate the application of paragraph 63, assume that an entity has outstanding 120 written put options on its ordinary shares with an exercise price of CU35. The average market price of its ordinary shares for the period is CU28. In calculating diluted earnings per share, the entity assumes that it issued 150 shares at CU28 per share at the beginning of the period to satisfy its put obligation of CU4,200. The difference between the 150 ordinary shares issued and the 120 ordinary shares received from satisfying the put option (30 incremental ordinary shares) is added to the denominator in calculating diluted earnings per share.

Instruments of subsidiaries, joint ventures or associates

A11   Potential ordinary shares of a subsidiary, joint venture or associate convertible into either ordinary shares of the subsidiary, joint venture or associate, or ordinary shares of the parent or investors with joint control of, or significant influence (the reporting entity) over, the investee are included in the calculation of diluted earnings per share as follows:

(a)   instruments issued by a subsidiary, joint venture or associate that enable their holders to obtain ordinary shares of the subsidiary, joint venture or associate are included in calculating the diluted earnings per share data of the subsidiary, joint venture or associate. Those earnings per share are then included in the reporting entity's earnings per share calculations based on the reporting entity's holding of the instruments of the subsidiary, joint venture or associate.

(b)   instruments of a subsidiary, joint venture or associate that are convertible into the reporting entity's ordinary shares are considered among the potential ordinary shares of the reporting entity for the purpose of calculating diluted earnings per share. Likewise, options or warrants issued by a subsidiary, joint venture or associate to purchase ordinary shares of the reporting entity are considered among the potential ordinary shares of the reporting entity in the calculation of consolidated diluted earnings per share.

A12   For the purpose of determining the earnings per share effect of instruments issued by a reporting entity that are convertible into ordinary shares of a subsidiary, joint venture or associate, the instruments are assumed to be converted and the numerator (profit or loss attributable to ordinary equity holders of the parent entity) adjusted as necessary in accordance with paragraph 33. In addition to those adjustments, the numerator is adjusted for any change in the profit or loss recorded by the reporting entity (such as dividend income or equity method income) that is attributable to the increase in the number of ordinary shares of the subsidiary, joint venture or associate outstanding as a result of the assumed conversion. The denominator of the diluted earnings per share calculation is not affected because the number of ordinary shares of the reporting entity outstanding would not change upon assumed conversion.

Participating equity instruments and two-class ordinary shares

A13   The equity of some entities includes:

(a)   instruments that participate in dividends with ordinary shares according to a predetermined formula (for example, two for one) with, at times, an upper limit on the extent of participation (for example, up to, but not beyond, a specified amount per share).

(b)   a class of ordinary shares with a different dividend rate from that of another class of ordinary shares but without prior or senior rights.

A14   For the purpose of calculating diluted earnings per share, conversion is assumed for those instruments described in paragraph A13 that are convertible into ordinary shares if the effect is dilutive. For those instruments that are not convertible into a class of ordinary shares, profit or loss for the period is allocated to the different classes of shares and participating equity instruments in accordance with their dividend rights or other rights to participate in undistributed earnings. To calculate basic and diluted earnings per share:

(a)   profit or loss attributable to ordinary equity holders of the parent entity is adjusted (a profit reduced and a loss increased) by the amount of dividends declared in the period for each class of shares and by the contractual amount of dividends (or interest on participating bonds) that must be paid for the period (for example, unpaid cumulative dividends).

(b)   the remaining profit or loss is allocated to ordinary shares and participating equity instruments to the extent that each instrument shares in earnings as if all of the profit or loss for the period had been distributed. The total profit or loss allocated to each class of equity instrument is determined by adding together the amount allocated for dividends and the amount allocated for a participation feature.

(c)   the total amount of profit or loss allocated to each class of equity instrument is divided by the number of outstanding instruments to which the earnings are allocated to determine the earnings per share for the instrument.

For the calculation of diluted earnings per share, all potential ordinary shares assumed to have been issued are included in outstanding ordinary shares.

Partly paid shares

A15 Where ordinary shares are issued but not fully paid, they are treated in the calculation of basic earnings per share as a fraction of an ordinary share to the extent that they were entitled to participate in dividends during the period relative to a fully paid ordinary share.

A16 To the extent that partly paid shares are not entitled to participate in dividends during the period they are treated as the equivalent of warrants or options in the calculation of diluted earnings per share. The unpaid balance is assumed to represent proceeds used to purchase ordinary shares. The number of shares included in diluted earnings per share is the difference between the number of shares subscribed and the number of shares assumed to be purchased.

Appendix B
Amendments to other pronouncements

The amendments in this appendix shall be applied for annual periods beginning on or after 1 January 2005. If an entity applies this Standard for an earlier period, these amendments shall be applied for that earlier period.

* * * * *

The amendments contained in this appendix when this Standard was revised in 2003 have been incorporated into the relevant pronouncements published in this volume.

International Accounting Standard 34

Interim Financial Reporting

In April 2001 the International Accounting Standards Board (IASB) adopted IAS 34 *Interim Financial Reporting*, which had originally been issued by the International Accounting Standards Committee in 2000. IAS 34 that was issued in 2000 replaced the original version that was published in February 1998.

Other IFRSs have made minor consequential amendments to IAS 34. They include IAS 8 *Accounting Policies, Changes in Estimates and Errors* (issued December 2003), IAS 1 *Presentation of Financial Statements* (as revised in December 2003 and September 2007), IAS 21 *The Effects of Changes in Foreign Exchange Rates* (as revised in December 2003), IFRS 8 *Operating Segments* (issued November 2006) and *Improvements to IFRSs* (issued May 2008).

Contents

FOR THE ACCOMPANYING DOCUMENTS LISTED BELOW, SEE PART B OF THIS EDITION

BASIS FOR CONCLUSIONS

ILLUSTRATIVE EXAMPLES

A   Illustration of periods required to be presented

B   Examples of applying the recognition and measurement principles

C   Examples of the use of estimates

International Accounting Standard 34 *Interim Financial Reporting* (IAS 34) is set out in paragraphs 1–51. All the paragraphs have equal authority but retain the IASC format of the Standard when it was adopted by the IASB. IAS 34 should be read in the context of its objective and the Basis for Conclusions, the *Preface to International Financial Reporting Standards* and the *Conceptual Framework for Financial Reporting*. IAS 8 *Accounting Policies, Changes in Accounting Estimates and Errors* provides a basis for selecting and applying accounting policies in the absence of explicit guidance.

Introduction

IN1   This Standard (IAS 34) addresses interim financial reporting, a matter not covered in a prior Standard. IAS 34 is effective for accounting periods beginning on or after 1 January 1999.

IN2   An interim financial report is a financial report that contains either a complete or condensed set of financial statements for a period shorter than an entity's full financial year.

IN3   This Standard does not mandate which entities should publish interim financial reports, how frequently, or how soon after the end of an interim period. In IASC's judgement, those matters should be decided by national governments, securities regulators, stock exchanges, and accountancy bodies. This Standard applies if a company is required or elects to publish an interim financial report in accordance with Standards.

IN4   This Standard:

(a)   defines the minimum content of an interim financial report, including disclosures; and

(b)   identifies the accounting recognition and measurement principles that should be applied in an interim financial report.

IN5   The minimum content of an interim financial report is a condensed statement of financial position, a condensed statement or statements of profit or loss and other comprehensive income, a condensed statement of cash flows, a condensed statement of changes in equity, and selected explanatory notes. If an entity presents the items of profit or loss in a separate statement as described in paragraph 10A of IAS 1 *Presentation of Financial Statements* (as amended in 2011), it presents interim condensed information from that statement.

IN6   On the presumption that anyone who reads an entity's interim report will also have access to its most recent annual report, virtually none of the notes to the annual financial statements are repeated or updated in the interim report. Instead, the interim notes include primarily an explanation of the events and changes that are significant to an understanding of the changes in financial position and performance of the entity since the end of the last annual reporting period.

IN7   An entity should apply the same accounting policies in its interim financial report as are applied in its annual financial statements, except for accounting policy changes made after the date of the most recent annual financial statements that are to be reflected in the next annual financial statements. The frequency of an entity's reporting—annual, half-yearly, or quarterly—should not affect the measurement of its annual results. To achieve that objective, measurements for interim reporting purposes are made on a year-to-date basis.

IN8   Part B of the illustrative examples accompanying the Standard provides guidance for applying the basic recognition and measurement principles at interim dates to various types of asset, liability, income, and expense. Income tax expense for an interim period is based on an estimated average annual effective income tax rate, consistent with the annual assessment of taxes.

IN9   In deciding how to recognise, classify, or disclose an item for interim financial reporting purposes, materiality is to be assessed in relation to the interim period financial data, not forecast annual data.

International Accounting Standard 34
Interim Financial Reporting

Objective

The objective of this Standard is to prescribe the minimum content of an interim financial report and to prescribe the principles for recognition and measurement in complete or condensed financial statements for an interim period. Timely and reliable interim financial reporting improves the ability of investors, creditors, and others to understand an entity's capacity to generate earnings and cash flows and its financial condition and liquidity.

Scope

1   This Standard does not mandate which entities should be required to publish interim financial reports, how frequently, or how soon after the end of an interim period. However, governments, securities regulators, stock exchanges, and accountancy bodies often require entities whose debt or equity securities are publicly traded to publish interim financial reports. This Standard applies if an entity is required or elects to publish an interim financial report in accordance with International Financial Reporting Standards (IFRSs). The International Accounting Standards Committee[1] encourages publicly traded entities to provide interim financial reports that conform to the recognition, measurement, and disclosure principles set out in this Standard. Specifically, publicly traded entities are encouraged:

(a)   to provide interim financial reports at least as of the end of the first half of their financial year; and

(b)   to make their interim financial reports available not later than 60 days after the end of the interim period.

2   Each financial report, annual or interim, is evaluated on its own for conformity to IFRSs. The fact that an entity may not have provided interim financial reports during a particular financial year or may have provided interim financial reports that do not comply with this Standard does not prevent the entity's annual financial statements from conforming to IFRSs if they otherwise do so.

3   If an entity's interim financial report is described as complying with IFRSs, it must comply with all of the requirements of this Standard. Paragraph 19 requires certain disclosures in that regard.

---

1   The International Accounting Standards Committee was succeeded by the International Accounting Standards Board, which began operations in 2001.

Definitions

4   The following terms are used in this Standard with the meanings specified:

Interim period is a financial reporting period shorter than a full financial year.

Interim financial report means a financial report containing either a complete set of financial statements (as described in IAS 1 *Presentation of Financial Statements* (as revised in 2007)) or a set of condensed financial statements (as described in this Standard) for an interim period.

Content of an interim financial report

5   IAS 1 (as revised in 2007) defines a complete set of financial statements as including the following components:

(a)   a statement of financial position as at the end of the period;

(b)   a statement of comprehensive income for the period;

(c)   a statement of changes in equity for the period;

(d)   a statement of cash flows for the period;

(e)   notes, comprising a summary of significant accounting policies and other explanatory information; and

(f)   a statement of financial position as at the beginning of the earliest comparative period when an entity applies an accounting policy retrospectively or makes a retrospective restatement of items in its financial statements, or when it reclassifies items in its financial statements.

6   In the interest of timeliness and cost considerations and to avoid repetition of information previously reported, an entity may be required to or may elect to provide less information at interim dates as compared with its annual financial statements.   This Standard defines the minimum content of an interim financial report as including condensed financial statements and selected explanatory notes. The interim financial report is intended to provide an update on the latest complete set of annual financial statements. Accordingly, it focuses on new activities, events, and circumstances and does not duplicate information previously reported.

7   Nothing in this Standard is intended to prohibit or discourage an entity from publishing a complete set of financial statements (as described in IAS 1) in its interim financial report, rather than condensed financial statements and selected explanatory notes. Nor does this Standard prohibit or discourage an entity from including in condensed interim financial statements more than the minimum line items or selected explanatory notes as set out in this Standard. The recognition and measurement guidance in this Standard applies also to complete financial statements for an interim period, and such statements would include all of the disclosures required by this Standard (particularly the selected note disclosures in paragraph 16) as well as those required by other IFRSs.

Minimum components of an interim financial report

8   An interim financial report shall include, at a minimum, the following components:

(a)   a condensed statement of financial position;

(b)   a condensed statement or condensed statements of profit or loss and other comprehensive income;

(c)   a condensed statement of changes in equity;

(d)   a condensed statement of cash flows; and

(e)   selected explanatory notes.

8A   If an entity presents items of profit or loss in a separate statement as described in paragraph 10A of IAS 1 (as amended in 2011), it presents interim condensed information from that statement.

Form and content of interim financial statements

9   If an entity publishes a complete set of financial statements in its interim financial report, the form and content of those statements shall conform to the requirements of IAS 1 for a complete set of financial statements.

10   If an entity publishes a set of condensed financial statements in its interim financial report, those condensed statements shall include, at a minimum, each of the headings and subtotals that were included in its most recent annual financial statements   and the selected explanatory notes as required by this Standard. Additional line items or notes shall be included if their omission would make the condensed interim financial statements misleading.

11   In the statement that presents the components of profit or loss for an interim period, an entity shall present basic and diluted earnings per share for that period when the entity is within the scope of IAS 33 *Earnings per Share*.[2]

11A If an entity presents items of profit or loss in a separate statement as described in paragraph 10A of IAS 1 (as amended in 2011), it presents basic and diluted earnings per share in that statement.

12   IAS 1 (as revised in 2007) provides guidance on the structure of financial statements. The Implementation Guidance for IAS 1 illustrates ways in which the statement of financial position, statement of comprehensive income and statement of changes in equity may be presented.

13   [Deleted]

14   An interim financial report is prepared on a consolidated basis if the entity's most recent annual financial statements were consolidated statements. The parent's separate financial statements are not consistent or comparable with the consolidated statements in the most recent annual financial report. If an entity's

---

2   This paragraph was amended by Improvements to IFRSs issued in May 2008 to clarify the scope of IAS 34.

annual financial report included the parent's separate financial statements in addition to consolidated financial statements, this Standard neither requires nor prohibits the inclusion of the parent's separate statements in the entity's interim financial report.

Significant events and transactions

15   An entity shall include in its interim financial report an explanation of events and transactions that are significant to an understanding of the changes in financial position and performance of the entity since the end of the last annual reporting period. Information disclosed in relation to those events and transactions shall update the relevant information presented in the most recent annual financial report.

15A   A user of an entity's interim financial report will have access to the most recent annual financial report of that entity. Therefore, it is unnecessary for the notes to an interim financial report to provide relatively insignificant updates to the information that was reported in the notes in the most recent annual financial report.

15B   The following is a list of events and transactions for which disclosures would be required if they are significant: the list is not exhaustive.

(a)   the write-down of inventories to net realisable value and the reversal of such a write-down;

(b)   recognition of a loss from the impairment of financial assets, property, plant and equipment, intangible assets, or other assets, and the reversal of such an impairment loss;

(c)   the reversal of any provisions for the costs of restructuring;

(d)   acquisitions and disposals of items of property, plant and equipment;

(e)   commitments for the purchase of property, plant and equipment;

(f)   litigation settlements;

(g)   corrections of prior period errors;

(h)   changes in the business or economic circumstances that affect the fair value of the entity's financial assets and financial liabilities, whether those assets or liabilities are recognised at fair value or amortised cost;

(i)   any loan default or breach of a loan agreement that has not been remedied on or before the end of the reporting period;

(j)   related party transactions;

(k)   transfers between levels of the fair value hierarchy used in measuring the fair value of financial instruments;

(l)   changes in the classification of financial assets as a result of a change in the purpose or use of those assets; and

(m)   changes in contingent liabilities or contingent assets.

15C   Individual IFRSs provide guidance regarding disclosure requirements for many of the items listed in paragraph 15B. When an event or transaction is significant to an understanding of the changes in an entity's financial position or performance since the last annual reporting period, its interim financial report should provide an explanation of and an update to the relevant information included in the financial statements of the last annual reporting period.

16–18 [Deleted]

Other disclosures

16A   **In addition to disclosing significant events and transactions in accordance with paragraphs 15–15C, an entity shall include the following information, in the notes to its interim financial statements, if not disclosed elsewhere in the interim financial report. The information shall normally be reported on a financial year-to-date basis.**

(a)   a statement that the same accounting policies and methods of computation are followed in the interim financial statements as compared with the most recent annual financial statements or, if those policies or methods have been changed, a description of the nature and effect of the change.

(b)   explanatory comments about the seasonality or cyclicality of interim operations.

(c)   the nature and amount of items affecting assets, liabilities, equity, net income or cash flows that are unusual because of their nature, size or incidence.

(d)   the nature and amount of changes in estimates of amounts reported in prior interim periods of the current financial year or changes in estimates of amounts reported in prior financial years.

(e)   issues, repurchases and repayments of debt and equity securities.

(f)   dividends paid (aggregate or per share) separately for ordinary shares and other shares.

(g)   the following segment information (disclosure of segment information is required in an entity's interim financial report only if IFRS 8 *Operating Segments* requires that entity to disclose segment information in its annual financial statements):

(i)   revenues from external customers, if included in the measure of segment profit or loss reviewed by the chief operating decision maker or otherwise regularly provided to the chief operating decision maker.

(ii)   intersegment revenues, if included in the measure of segment profit or loss reviewed by the chief operating decision maker or otherwise regularly provided to the chief operating decision maker.

(iii) a measure of segment profit or loss.

(iv)   total assets for which there has been a material change from the amount disclosed in the last annual financial statements.

(v)   a description of differences from the last annual financial statements in the basis of segmentation or in the basis of measurement of segment profit or loss.

(vi)   a reconciliation of the total of the reportable segments' measures of profit or loss to the entity's profit or loss before tax expense (tax income) and discontinued operations. However, if an entity allocates to reportable segments items such as tax expense (tax income), the entity may reconcile the total of the segments' measures of profit or loss to profit or loss after those items. Material reconciling items shall be separately identified and described in that reconciliation.

(h)   events after the interim period that have not been reflected in the financial statements for the interim period.

(i)   the effect of changes in the composition of the entity during the interim period, including business combinations, obtaining or losing control of subsidiaries and long-term investments, restructurings, and discontinued operations. In the case of business combinations, the entity shall disclose the information required by IFRS 3 *Business Combinations*.

(j)   for financial instruments, the disclosures about fair value required by paragraphs 91–93(h), 94–96, 98 and 99 of IFRS 13 *Fair Value Measurement* and paragraphs 25, 26 and 28–30 of IFRS 7 *Financial Instruments: Disclosures*.

Disclosure of compliance with IFRSs

19   If an entity's interim financial report is in compliance with this Standard, that fact shall be disclosed. An interim financial report shall not be described as complying with IFRSs unless it complies with all the requirements of IFRSs.

Periods for which interim financial statements are required to be presented

20   Interim reports shall include interim financial statements (condensed or complete) for periods as follows:

(a)   statement of financial position as of the end of the current interim period and a comparative statement of financial position as of the end of the immediately preceding financial year.

(b)   statements of profit or loss and other comprehensive income for the current interim period and cumulatively for the current financial year to date, with comparative statements of profit or loss and other comprehensive income for the comparable interim periods (current and year-to-date) of the immediately preceding financial year. As permitted by IAS 1 (as amended in 2011), an interim report may present for each period a statement or statements of profit or loss and other comprehensive income.

(c)   statement of changes in equity cumulatively for the current financial year to date, with a comparative statement for the comparable year-to-date period of the immediately preceding financial year.

(d) statement of cash flows cumulatively for the current financial year to date, with a comparative statement for the comparable year-to-date period of the immediately preceding financial year.

21 For an entity whose business is highly seasonal, financial information for the twelve months up to the end of the interim period and comparative information for the prior twelve-month period may be useful. Accordingly, entities whose business is highly seasonal are encouraged to consider reporting such information in addition to the information called for in the preceding paragraph.

22 Part A of the illustrative examples accompanying this Standard illustrates the periods required to be presented by an entity that reports half-yearly and an entity that reports quarterly.

Materiality

23 **In deciding how to recognise, measure, classify, or disclose an item for interim financial reporting purposes, materiality shall be assessed in relation to the interim period financial data. In making assessments of materiality, it shall be recognised that interim measurements may rely on estimates to a greater extent than measurements of annual financial data.**

24 IAS 1 and IAS 8 *Accounting Policies, Changes in Accounting Estimates and Errors* define an item as material if its omission or misstatement could influence the economic decisions of users of the financial statements. IAS 1 requires separate disclosure of material items, including (for example) discontinued operations, and IAS 8 requires disclosure of changes in accounting estimates, errors, and changes in accounting policies. The two Standards do not contain quantified guidance as to materiality.

25 While judgement is always required in assessing materiality, this Standard bases the recognition and disclosure decision on data for the interim period by itself for reasons of understandability of the interim figures. Thus, for example, unusual items, changes in accounting policies or estimates, and errors are recognised and disclosed on the basis of materiality in relation to interim period data to avoid misleading inferences that might result from non-disclosure. The overriding goal is to ensure that an interim financial report includes all information that is relevant to understanding an entity's financial position and performance during the interim period.

Disclosure in annual financial statements

26 **If an estimate of an amount reported in an interim period is changed significantly during the final interim period of the financial year but a separate financial report is not published for that final interim period, the nature and amount of that change in estimate shall be disclosed in a note to the annual financial statements for that financial year.**

27 IAS 8 requires disclosure of the nature and (if practicable) the amount of a change in estimate that either has a material effect in the current period or is expected to have a material effect in subsequent periods. Paragraph 16A(d) of this Standard requires similar *disclosure* in an interim financial report. Examples

include changes in estimate in the final interim period relating to inventory write-downs, restructurings, or impairment losses that were reported in an earlier interim period of the financial year. The disclosure required by the preceding paragraph is consistent with the IAS 8 requirement and is intended to be narrow in scope—relating only to the change in estimate. An entity is not required to include additional interim period financial information in its annual financial statements.

Recognition and measurement

Same accounting policies as annual

28 **An entity shall apply the same accounting policies in its interim financial statements as are applied in its annual financial statements, except for accounting policy changes made after the date of the most recent annual financial statements that are to be reflected in the next annual financial statements. However, the frequency of an entity's reporting (annual, half-yearly, or quarterly) shall not affect the measurement of its annual results. To achieve that objective, measurements for interim reporting purposes shall be made on a year-to-date basis.**

29 Requiring that an entity apply the same accounting policies in its interim financial statements as in its annual statements may seem to suggest that interim period measurements are made as if each interim period stands alone as an independent reporting period. However, by providing that the frequency of an entity's reporting shall not affect the measurement of its annual results, paragraph 28 acknowledges that an interim period is a part of a larger financial year. Year-to-date measurements may involve changes in estimates of amounts reported in prior interim periods of the current financial year. But the principles for recognising assets, liabilities, income, and expenses for interim periods are the same as in annual financial statements.

30 To illustrate:

(a) the principles for recognising and measuring losses from inventory write-downs, restructurings, or impairments in an interim period are the same as those that an entity would follow if it prepared only annual financial statements. However, if such items are recognised and measured in one interim period and the estimate changes in a subsequent interim period of that financial year, the original estimate is changed in the subsequent interim period either by accrual of an additional amount of loss or by reversal of the previously recognised amount;

(b) a cost that does not meet the definition of an asset at the end of an interim period is not deferred in the statement of financial position either to await future information as to whether it has met the definition of an asset or to smooth earnings over interim periods within a financial year; and

(c) income tax expense is recognised in each interim period based on the best estimate of the weighted average annual income tax rate expected for the full financial year. Amounts accrued for income tax expense in one interim period may have to be adjusted in a subsequent interim period of that financial year if the estimate of the annual income tax rate changes.

31   Under the *Framework for the Preparation and Presentation of Financial Statements* (the *Framework*),[3] recognition is the 'process of incorporating in the balance sheet or income statement an item that meets the definition of an element and satisfies the criteria for recognition'. The definitions of assets, liabilities, income, and expenses are fundamental to recognition, at the end of both annual and interim financial reporting periods.

32   For assets, the same tests of future economic benefits apply at interim dates and at the end of an entity's financial year. Costs that, by their nature, would not qualify as assets at financial year-end would not qualify at interim dates either. Similarly, a liability at the end of an interim reporting period must represent an existing obligation at that date, just as it must at the end of an annual reporting period.

33   An essential characteristic of income (revenue) and expenses is that the related inflows and outflows of assets and liabilities have already taken place. If those inflows or outflows have taken place, the related revenue and expense are recognised; otherwise they are not recognised. The *Framework* says that 'expenses are recognised in the income statement when a decrease in future economic benefits related to a decrease in an asset or an increase of a liability has arisen that can be measured reliably... [The] *Framework* does not allow the recognition of items in the balance sheet which do not meet the definition of assets or liabilities.'

34   In measuring the assets, liabilities, income, expenses, and cash flows reported in its financial statements, an entity that reports only annually is able to take into account information that becomes available throughout the financial year. Its measurements are, in effect, on a year-to-date basis.

35   An entity that reports half-yearly uses information available by mid-year or shortly thereafter in making the measurements in its financial statements for the first six-month period and information available by year-end or shortly thereafter for the twelve-month period. The twelve-month measurements will reflect possible changes in estimates of amounts reported for the first six-month period. The amounts reported in the interim financial report for the first six-month period are not retrospectively adjusted. Paragraphs 16A(d) and 26 require, however, that the nature and amount of any significant changes in estimates be disclosed.

36   An entity that reports more frequently than half-yearly measures income and expenses on a year-to-date basis for each interim period using information available when each set of financial statements is being prepared. Amounts of income and expenses reported in the current interim period will reflect any changes in estimates of amounts reported in prior interim periods of the financial year. The amounts reported in prior interim periods are not retrospectively adjusted. Paragraphs 16A(d) and 26 require, however, that the nature and amount of any significant changes in estimates be disclosed.

---

3   IASC's *Framework for the Preparation and Presentation of Financial Statements* was adopted by the IASB in 2001. In September 2010 the IASB replaced the *Framework* with the *Conceptual Framework for Financial Reporting*.

Revenues received seasonally, cyclically, or occasionally

37   Revenues that are received seasonally, cyclically, or occasionally within a financial
      year shall not be anticipated or deferred as of an interim date if anticipation or
      deferral would not be appropriate at the end of the entity's financial year.

38   Examples include dividend revenue, royalties, and government grants.
      Additionally, some entities consistently earn more revenues in certain interim
      periods of a financial year than in other interim periods, for example, seasonal
      revenues of retailers. Such revenues are recognised when they occur.

Costs incurred unevenly during the financial year

39   Costs that are incurred unevenly during an entity's financial year shall be
      anticipated or deferred for interim reporting purposes if, and only if, it is also
      appropriate to anticipate or defer that type of cost at the end of the financial year.

Applying the recognition and measurement principles

40   Part B of the illustrative examples accompanying this Standard provides examples
      of applying the general recognition and measurement principles set out in
      paragraphs 28–39.

Use of estimates

41   The measurement procedures to be followed in an interim financial report
      shall be designed to ensure that the resulting information is reliable and that all
      material financial information that is relevant to an understanding of the
      financial position or performance of the entity is appropriately disclosed. While
      measurements in both annual and interim financial reports are often based on
      reasonable estimates, the preparation of interim financial reports generally will
      require a greater use of estimation methods than annual financial reports.

42   Part C of the illustrative examples accompanying this Standard provides examples
      of the use of estimates in interim periods.

Restatement of previously reported interim periods

43   A change in accounting policy, other than one for which the transition is specified
      by a new IFRS, shall be reflected by:

      (a)   restating the financial statements of prior interim periods of the current
             financial year and the comparable interim periods of any prior financial
             years that will be restated in the annual financial statements in accordance
             with IAS 8; or

      (b)   when it is impracticable to determine the cumulative effect at the beginning
             of the financial year of applying a new accounting policy to all prior periods,
             adjusting the financial statements of prior interim periods of the current
             financial year, and comparable interim periods of prior financial years to
             apply the new accounting policy prospectively from the earliest date
             practicable.

44   One objective of the preceding principle is to ensure that a single accounting policy is applied to a particular class of transactions throughout an entire financial year. Under IAS 8, a change in accounting policy is reflected by retrospective application, with restatement of prior period financial data as far back as is practicable. However, if the cumulative amount of the adjustment relating to prior financial years is impracticable to determine, then under IAS 8 the new policy is applied prospectively from the earliest date practicable. The effect of the principle in paragraph 43 is to require that within the current financial year any change in accounting policy is applied either retrospectively or, if that is not practicable, prospectively, from no later than the beginning of the financial year.

45   To allow accounting changes to be reflected as of an interim date within the financial year would allow two differing accounting policies to be applied to a particular class of transactions within a single financial year. The result would be interim allocation difficulties, obscured operating results, and complicated analysis and understandability of interim period information.

Effective date

46   This Standard becomes operative for financial statements covering periods beginning on or after 1 January 1999. Earlier application is encouraged.

47   IAS 1 (as revised in 2007) amended the terminology used throughout IFRSs. In addition it amended paragraphs 4, 5, 8, 11, 12 and 20, deleted paragraph 13 and added paragraphs 8A and 11A. An entity shall apply those amendments for annual periods beginning on or after 1 January 2009. If an entity applies IAS 1 (revised 2007) for an earlier period, the amendments shall be applied for that earlier period.

48   IFRS 3 (as revised in 2008) amended paragraph 16(i). An entity shall apply that amendment for annual periods beginning on or after 1 July 2009. If an entity applies IFRS 3 (revised 2008) for an earlier period, the amendment shall also be applied for that earlier period.

49   Paragraphs 15, 27, 35 and 36 were amended, paragraphs 15A–15C and 16A were added and paragraphs 16–18 were deleted by *Improvements to IFRSs* in May 2010. An entity shall apply those amendments for annual periods beginning on or after 1 January 2011. Earlier application is permitted. If an entity applies the amendments for an earlier period it shall disclose that fact.

50   IFRS 13, issued in May 2011, added paragraph 16A(j). An entity shall apply that amendment when it applies IFRS 13.

51   *Presentation of Items of Other Comprehensive Income* (Amendments to IAS 1), issued in June 2011, amended paragraphs 8, 8A, 11A and 20. An entity shall apply those amendments when it applies IAS 1 as amended in June 2011.

International Accounting Standard 36

Impairment of Assets

In April 2001 the International Accounting Standards Board (IASB) adopted IAS 36 *Impairment of Assets*, which had originally been issued by the International Accounting Standards Committee in June 1998. That standard consolidated all the requirements on how to assess for recoverability of an asset. These requirements were contained in IAS 16 *Property, Plant and Equipment*, IAS 22 *Business Combinations*, IAS 28 *Accounting for Associates* and IAS 31 *Financial Reporting of Interests in Joint Ventures*.

The IASB revised IAS 36 in March 2004 as part of the first phase of its business combinations project. In January 2008 the IASB amended IAS 36 again as part of the second phase of its business combinations project.

Other IFRSs have made minor consequential amendments to IAS 36. They include IAS 16 *Property, Plant and Equipment* (as revised in December 2003), IAS 39 *Financial Instruments: Recognition and Measurement* (as revised in December 2003), IAS 1 *Presentation of Financial Statements* (as revised in September 2007), *Improvements to IFRSs* (issued May 2008 and April 2009) and IFRS 9 *Financial Instruments* (issued November 2009 and October 2010).

CONTENTS

APPENDICES

A   Using present value techniques to measure value in use

B   Amendment to IAS 16

C   Impairment testing cash-generating units with goodwill and non-controlling interests

FOR THE ACCOMPANYING DOCUMENTS LISTED BELOW, SEE PART B OF THIS EDITION

APPROVAL BY THE BOARD OF IAS 36 ISSUED IN MARCH 2004

BASIS FOR CONCLUSIONS

DISSENTING OPINIONS

ILLUSTRATIVE EXAMPLES

International Accounting Standard 36 *Impairment of Assets* (IAS 36) is set out in paragraphs 1–141 and Appendices A–C. All the paragraphs have equal authority but retain the IASC format of the Standard when it was adopted by the IASB. IAS 36 should be read in the context of its objective and the Basis for Conclusions, the *Preface to International Financial Reporting Standards* and the *Conceptual Framework for Financial Reporting*. IAS 8 *Accounting Policies, Changes in Accounting Estimates and Errors* provides a basis for selecting and applying accounting policies in the absence of explicit guidance.

Introduction

IN1 International Accounting Standard 36 *Impairment of Assets* (IAS 36) replaces IAS 36 *Impairment of Assets* (issued in 1998), and should be applied:

(a) on acquisition to goodwill and intangible assets acquired in business combinations for which the agreement date is on or after 31 March 2004.

(b) to all other assets, for annual periods beginning on or after 31 March 2004.

Earlier application is encouraged.

Reasons for revising IAS 36

IN2 The International Accounting Standards Board developed this revised IAS 36 as part of its project on business combinations. The project's objective was to improve the quality of, and seek international convergence on, the accounting for business combinations and the subsequent accounting for goodwill and intangible assets acquired in business combinations.

IN3 The project had two phases. The first phase resulted in the Board issuing simultaneously in 2004 IFRS 3 *Business Combinations* and revised versions of IAS 36 and IAS 38 *Intangible Assets*. The Board's deliberations during the first phase of the project focused primarily on the following issues:

(a) the method of accounting for business combinations;

(b) the initial measurement of the identifiable assets acquired and liabilities and contingent liabilities assumed in a business combination;

(c) the recognition of provisions for terminating or reducing the activities of an acquiree;

(d) the treatment of any excess of the acquirer's interest in the fair values of identifiable net assets acquired in a business combination over the cost of the combination; and

(e) the accounting for goodwill and intangible assets acquired in a business combination.

IN4 The second phase of the project resulted in the Board issuing simultaneously in 2008 a revised IFRS 3 and amendments to IAS 27 *Consolidated and Separate Financial Statements*.[1] The Board's intention while revising IAS 36 was to reflect only those changes related to its decisions in the Business Combinations project, and *not* to reconsider all of the requirements in IAS 36. The changes that have been made in the Standard are primarily concerned with the impairment test for goodwill.

---

1 The consolidation requirements in IAS 27 were superseded by IFRS 10 *Consolidated Financial Statements*, issued in May 2011.

Summary of main changes

Frequency of impairment testing

IN5   The previous version of IAS 36 required the recoverable amount of an asset to be measured whenever there is an indication that the asset may be impaired. This requirement is included in the Standard. However, the Standard also requires:

     (a)   the recoverable amount of an intangible asset with an indefinite useful life to be measured annually, irrespective of whether there is any indication that it may be impaired. The most recent detailed calculation of recoverable amount made in a preceding period may be used in the impairment test for that asset in the current period, provided specified criteria are met.

     (b)   the recoverable amount of an intangible asset not yet available for use to be measured annually, irrespective of whether there is any indication that it may be impaired.

     (c)   goodwill acquired in a business combination to be tested for impairment annually.

Measuring value in use

IN6   The Standard clarifies that the following elements should be reflected in the calculation of an asset's value in use:

     (a)   an estimate of the future cash flows the entity expects to derive from the asset;

     (b)   expectations about possible variations in the amount or timing of those future cash flows;

     (c)   the time value of money, represented by the current market risk-free rate of interest;

     (d)   the price for bearing the uncertainty inherent in the asset; and

     (e)   other factors, such as illiquidity, that market participants would reflect in pricing the future cash flows the entity expects to derive from the asset.

The Standard also clarifies that the second, fourth and fifth of these elements can be reflected either as adjustments to the future cash flows or adjustments to the discount rate.

IN7   The Standard carries forward from the previous version of IAS 36 the requirement for the cash flow projections used to measure value in use to be based on reasonable and supportable assumptions that represent management's best estimate of the economic conditions that will exist over the remaining useful life of the asset. However, the Standard clarifies that management:

     (a)   should assess the reasonableness of the assumptions on which its current cash flow projections are based by examining the causes of differences between past cash flow projections and actual cash flows.

(b)   should ensure that the assumptions on which its current cash flow projections are based are consistent with past actual outcomes, provided the effects of subsequent events or circumstances that did not exist when those actual cash flows were generated make this appropriate.

IN8   The previous version of IAS 36 required the cash flow projections used to measure value in use to be based on the most recent financial budgets/forecasts approved by management. The Standard carries forward this requirement, but clarifies that the cash flow projections exclude any estimated cash inflows or outflows expected to arise from:

(a)   future restructurings to which the entity is not yet committed; or

(b)   improving or enhancing the asset's performance.

IN9   Additional guidance on using present value techniques in measuring an asset's value in use is included in Appendix A of the Standard. In addition, the guidance in the previous version of IAS 36 on estimating the discount rate when an asset-specific rate is not directly available from the market has been relocated to Appendix A.

Identifying the cash-generating unit to which an asset belongs

IN10   The Standard carries forward from the previous version of IAS 36 the requirement that if an active market exists for the output produced by an asset or a group of assets, that asset or group of assets should be identified as a cash-generating unit, even if some or all of the output is used internally. However, the previous version of IAS 36 required that, in such circumstances, management's best estimate of future market prices for the output should be used in estimating the future cash flows used to determine the unit's value in use. It also required that when an entity was estimating future cash flows to determine the value in use of cash-generating units using the output, management's best estimate of future market prices for the output should be used. The Standard requires that if the cash inflows generated by *any* asset or cash-generating unit are affected by internal transfer pricing, an entity should use management's best estimate of future price(s) that could be achieved in arm's length transactions in estimating:

(a)   the future cash inflows used to determine the asset's or cash-generating unit's value in use; and

(b)   the future cash outflows used to determine the value in use of other assets or cash-generating units affected by the internal transfer pricing.

Allocating goodwill to cash-generating units

IN11   The previous version of IAS 36 required goodwill acquired in a business combination to be tested for impairment as part of impairment testing the cash-generating unit(s) to which it related. It employed a 'bottom-up/top-down' approach under which the goodwill was, in effect, tested for impairment by allocating its carrying amount to each cash-generating unit or smallest group of cash-generating units to which a portion of that carrying amount could be allocated on a reasonable and consistent basis. The Standard similarly requires goodwill acquired in a business combination to be tested for impairment as part of impairment testing the cash-generating unit(s) to which it relates. However, the Standard clarifies that:

(a)   the goodwill should, from the acquisition date, be allocated to each of the acquirer's cash-generating units, or groups of cash-generating units, that are expected to benefit from the synergies of the business combination, irrespective of whether other assets or liabilities of the acquiree are assigned to those units or groups of units.

(b)   each unit or group of units to which the goodwill is allocated should:

(i)   represent the lowest level within the entity at which the goodwill is monitored for internal management purposes; and

(ii)   not be larger than an operating segment determined in accordance with IFRS 8 *Operating Segments*.

IN12   The Standard also clarifies the following:

(a)   if the initial allocation of goodwill acquired in a business combination cannot be completed before the end of the annual period in which the business combination occurs, that initial allocation should be completed before the end of the first annual period beginning after the acquisition date.

(b)   when an entity disposes of an operation within a cash-generating unit (group of units) to which goodwill has been allocated, the goodwill associated with that operation should be:

(i)   included in the carrying amount of the operation when determining the gain or loss on disposal; and

(ii)   measured on the basis of the relative values of the operation disposed of and the portion of the cash-generating unit (group of units) retained, unless the entity can demonstrate that some other method better reflects the goodwill associated with the operation disposed of.

(c)   when an entity reorganises its reporting structure in a manner that changes the composition of cash-generating units (groups of units) to which goodwill has been allocated, the goodwill should be reallocated to the units (groups of units) affected. This reallocation should be performed using a relative value approach similar to that used when an entity disposes of an operation within a cash-generating unit (group of units), unless the entity can demonstrate that some other method better reflects the goodwill associated with the reorganised units (groups of units).

Timing of impairment tests for goodwill

IN13   The Standard permits:

(a)   the annual impairment test for a cash-generating unit (group of units) to which goodwill has been allocated to be performed at any time during an annual reporting period, provided the test is performed at the same time every year.

(b) different cash-generating units (groups of units) to be tested for impairment at different times.

However, if some of the goodwill allocated to a cash-generating unit (group of units) was acquired in a business combination during the current annual period, the Standard requires that unit (group of units) to be tested for impairment before the end of the current period.

IN14 The Standard permits the most recent detailed calculation made in a preceding period of the recoverable amount of a cash-generating unit (group of units) to which goodwill has been allocated to be used in the impairment test for that unit (group of units) in the current period, provided specified criteria are met.

Reversals of impairment losses for goodwill

IN15 The previous version of IAS 36 required an impairment loss recognised for goodwill in a previous period to be reversed when the impairment loss was caused by a specific external event of an exceptional nature that is not expected to recur and subsequent external events have occurred that reverse the effect of that event. The Standard prohibits the recognition of reversals of impairment losses for goodwill.

Disclosure

IN16 The Standard requires that if any portion of the goodwill acquired in a business combination during the period has not been allocated to a cash-generating unit at the end of the reporting period, an entity should disclose the amount of the unallocated goodwill together with the reasons why that amount remains unallocated.

IN17 The Standard requires disclosure of information for each cash-generating unit (group of units) for which the carrying amount of goodwill or intangible assets with indefinite useful lives allocated to that unit (group of units) is significant in comparison with the entity's total carrying amount of goodwill or intangible assets with indefinite lives. That information is concerned primarily with the key assumptions used to measure the recoverable amounts of such units (groups of units).

IN18 The Standard also requires specified information to be disclosed if some or all of the carrying amount of goodwill or intangible assets with indefinite lives is allocated across multiple cash-generating units (groups of units), and the amount so allocated to each unit (group of units) is not significant in comparison with the total carrying amount of goodwill or intangible assets with indefinite lives. Further disclosures are required if, in such circumstances, the recoverable amounts of any of those units (groups of units) are based on the same key assumption(s) and the aggregate carrying amount of goodwill or intangible assets with indefinite lives allocated to them is significant in comparison with the entity's total carrying amount of goodwill or intangible assets with indefinite lives.

International Accounting Standard 36
Impairment of Assets

Objective

1   The objective of this Standard is to prescribe the procedures that an entity applies to ensure that its assets are carried at no more than their recoverable amount. An asset is carried at more than its recoverable amount if its carrying amount exceeds the amount to be recovered through use or sale of the asset. If this is the case, the asset is described as impaired and the Standard requires the entity to recognise an impairment loss. The Standard also specifies when an entity should reverse an impairment loss and prescribes disclosures.

Scope

2   **This Standard shall be applied in accounting for the impairment of all assets, other than:**

   (a)   **inventories (see IAS 2 *Inventories*);**

   (b)   **assets arising from construction contracts (see IAS 11 *Construction Contracts*);**

   (c)   **deferred tax assets (see IAS 12 *Income Taxes*);**

   (d)   **assets arising from employee benefits (see IAS 19 *Employee Benefits*);**

   (e)   **financial assets that are within the scope of IFRS 9 *Financial Instruments*;**

   (f)   **investment property that is measured at fair value (see IAS 40 *Investment Property*);**

   (g)   **biological assets related to agricultural activity that are measured at fair value less costs of disposal (see IAS 41 *Agriculture*);**

   (h)   **deferred acquisition costs, and intangible assets, arising from an insurer's contractual rights under insurance contracts within the scope of IFRS 4 *Insurance Contracts*; and**

   (i)   **non-current assets (or disposal groups) classified as held for sale in accordance with IFRS 5 *Non-current Assets Held for Sale and Discontinued Operations*.**

3   This Standard does not apply to inventories, assets arising from construction contracts, deferred tax assets, assets arising from employee benefits, or assets classified as held for sale (or included in a disposal group that is classified as held for sale) because existing IFRSs applicable to these assets contain requirements for recognising and measuring these assets.

4   This Standard applies to financial assets classified as:

   (a)   subsidiaries, as defined in IFRS 10 *Consolidated Financial Statements*;

   (b)   associates, as defined in IAS 28 *Investments in Associates and Joint Ventures*; and

   (c)   joint ventures, as defined in IFRS 11 *Joint Arrangements*.

   For impairment of other financial assets, refer to IAS 39.

5 This Standard does not apply to financial assets within the scope of IFRS 9, investment property measured at fair value within the scope of IAS 40, or biological assets related to agricultural activity measured at fair value less costs of disposal within the scope of IAS 41. However, this Standard applies to assets that are carried at revalued amount (ie fair value at the date of the revaluation less any subsequent accumulated depreciation and subsequent accumulated impairment losses) in accordance with other IFRSs, such as the revaluation model in IAS 16 *Property, Plant and Equipment* and IAS 38 *Intangible Assets*. The only difference between an asset's fair value and its fair value less costs of disposal is the direct incremental costs attributable to the disposal of the asset.

(a) If the disposal costs are negligible, the recoverable amount of the revalued asset is necessarily close to, or greater than, its revalued amount. In this case, after the revaluation requirements have been applied, it is unlikely that the revalued asset is impaired and recoverable amount need not be estimated.

(b) [deleted]

(c) If the disposal costs are not negligible, the fair value less costs of disposal of the revalued asset is necessarily less than its fair value. Therefore, the revalued asset will be impaired if its value in use is less than its revalued amount. In this case, after the revaluation requirements have been applied, an entity applies this Standard to determine whether the asset may be impaired.

Definitions

6 **The following terms are used in this Standard with the meanings specified:**

Carrying amount **is the amount at which an asset is recognised after deducting any accumulated depreciation (amortisation) and accumulated impairment losses thereon.**

A *cash-generating unit* **is the smallest identifiable group of assets that generates cash inflows that are largely independent of the cash inflows from other assets or groups of assets.**

Corporate assets **are assets other than goodwill that contribute to the future cash flows of both the cash-generating unit under review and other cash-generating units.**

Costs of disposal **are incremental costs directly attributable to the disposal of an asset or cash-generating unit, excluding finance costs and income tax expense.**

Depreciable amount **is the cost of an asset, or other amount substituted for cost in the financial statements, less its residual value.**

Depreciation (Amortisation) **is the systematic allocation of the depreciable amount of an asset over its useful life.[2]**

---

2 In the case of an intangible asset, the term 'amortisation' is generally used instead of 'depreciation'. The two terms have the same meaning.

Fair value is the price that would be received to sell an asset or paid to transfer a liability in an orderly transaction between market participants at the measurement date. (See IFRS 13 *Fair Value Measurement*.)

An *impairment loss* is the amount by which the carrying amount of an asset or a cash-generating unit exceeds its recoverable amount.

The *recoverable amount* of an asset or a cash-generating unit is the higher of its fair value less costs of disposal and its value in use.

Useful life is either:

(a)   the period of time over which an asset is expected to be used by the entity; or

(b)   the number of production or similar units expected to be obtained from the asset by the entity.

Value in use is the present value of the future cash flows expected to be derived from an asset or cash-generating unit.

Identifying an asset that may be impaired

7   Paragraphs 8–17 specify when recoverable amount shall be determined. These requirements use the term 'an asset' but apply equally to an individual asset or a cash-generating unit. The remainder of this Standard is structured as follows:

(a)   paragraphs 18–57 set out the requirements for measuring recoverable amount. These requirements also use the term 'an asset' but apply equally to an individual asset and a cash-generating unit.

(b)   paragraphs 58–108 set out the requirements for recognising and measuring impairment losses. Recognition and measurement of impairment losses for individual assets other than goodwill are dealt with in paragraphs 58–64. Paragraphs 65–108 deal with the recognition and measurement of impairment losses for cash-generating units and goodwill.

(c)   paragraphs 109–116 set out the requirements for reversing an impairment loss recognised in prior periods for an asset or a cash-generating unit. Again, these requirements use the term 'an asset' but apply equally to an individual asset or a cash-generating unit. Additional requirements for an individual asset are set out in paragraphs 117–121, for a cash-generating unit in paragraphs 122 and 123, and for goodwill in paragraphs 124 and 125.

(d)   paragraphs 126–133 specify the information to be disclosed about impairment losses and reversals of impairment losses for assets and cash-generating units. Paragraphs 134–137 specify additional disclosure requirements for cash-generating units to which goodwill or intangible assets with indefinite useful lives have been allocated for impairment testing purposes.

8   An asset is impaired when its carrying amount exceeds its recoverable amount. Paragraphs 12–14 describe some indications that an impairment loss may have occurred. If any of those indications is present, an entity is required to make a formal estimate of recoverable amount. Except as described in paragraph 10, this Standard does not require an entity to make a formal estimate of recoverable amount if no indication of an impairment loss is present.

9   **An entity shall assess at the end of each reporting period whether there is any indication that an asset may be impaired. If any such indication exists, the entity shall estimate the recoverable amount of the asset.**

10   **Irrespective of whether there is any indication of impairment, an entity shall also:**

   (a)   **test an intangible asset with an indefinite useful life or an intangible asset not yet available for use for impairment annually by comparing its carrying amount with its recoverable amount. This impairment test may be performed at any time during an annual period, provided it is performed at the same time every year. Different intangible assets may be tested for impairment at different times. However, if such an intangible asset was initially recognised during the current annual period, that intangible asset shall be tested for impairment before the end of the current annual period.**

   (b)   **test goodwill acquired in a business combination for impairment annually in accordance with paragraphs 80–99.**

11   The ability of an intangible asset to generate sufficient future economic benefits to recover its carrying amount is usually subject to greater uncertainty before the asset is available for use than after it is available for use. Therefore, this Standard requires an entity to test for impairment, at least annually, the carrying amount of an intangible asset that is not yet available for use.

12   **In assessing whether there is any indication that an asset may be impaired, an entity shall consider, as a minimum, the following indications:**

   External sources of information

   (a)   **there are observable indications that the asset's value has declined during the period significantly more than would be expected as a result of the passage of time or normal use.**

   (b)   **significant changes with an adverse effect on the entity have taken place during the period, or will take place in the near future, in the technological, market, economic or legal environment in which the entity operates or in the market to which an asset is dedicated.**

   (c)   **market interest rates or other market rates of return on investments have increased during the period, and those increases are likely to affect the discount rate used in calculating an asset's value in use and decrease the asset's recoverable amount materially.**

   (d)   **the carrying amount of the net assets of the entity is more than its market capitalisation.**

   Internal sources of information

   (e)   **evidence is available of obsolescence or physical damage of an asset.**

(f)   significant changes with an adverse effect on the entity have taken place during the period, or are expected to take place in the near future, in the extent to which, or manner in which, an asset is used or is expected to be used. These changes include the asset becoming idle, plans to discontinue or restructure the operation to which an asset belongs, plans to dispose of an asset before the previously expected date, and reassessing the useful life of an asset as finite rather than indefinite.[3]

(g)   evidence is available from internal reporting that indicates that the economic performance of an asset is, or will be, worse than expected.

Dividend from a subsidiary, joint venture or associate

(h)   for an investment in a subsidiary, joint venture or associate, the investor recognises a dividend from the investment and evidence is available that:

    (i)   the carrying amount of the investment in the separate financial statements exceeds the carrying amounts in the consolidated financial statements of the investee's net assets, including associated goodwill; or

    (ii)   the dividend exceeds the total comprehensive income of the subsidiary, joint venture or associate in the period the dividend is declared.

13   The list in paragraph 12 is not exhaustive. An entity may identify other indications that an asset may be impaired and these would also require the entity to determine the asset's recoverable amount or, in the case of goodwill, perform an impairment test in accordance with paragraphs 80–99.

14   Evidence from internal reporting that indicates that an asset may be impaired includes the existence of:

(a)   cash flows for acquiring the asset, or subsequent cash needs for operating or maintaining it, that are significantly higher than those originally budgeted;

(b)   actual net cash flows or operating profit or loss flowing from the asset that are significantly worse than those budgeted;

(c)   a significant decline in budgeted net cash flows or operating profit, or a significant increase in budgeted loss, flowing from the asset; or

(d)   operating losses or net cash outflows for the asset, when current period amounts are aggregated with budgeted amounts for the future.

15   As indicated in paragraph 10, this Standard requires an intangible asset with an indefinite useful life or not yet available for use and goodwill to be tested for impairment, at least annually. Apart from when the requirements in paragraph 10 apply, the concept of materiality applies in identifying whether the recoverable amount of an asset needs to be estimated. For example, if previous calculations show that an asset's recoverable amount is significantly greater than its carrying

---

3   Once an asset meets the criteria to be classified as held for sale (or is included in a disposal group that is classified as held for sale), it is excluded from the scope of this Standard and is accounted for in accordance with IFRS 5 *Non-current Assets Held for Sale and Discontinued Operations*.

amount, the entity need not re-estimate the asset's recoverable amount if no events have occurred that would eliminate that difference. Similarly, previous analysis may show that an asset's recoverable amount is not sensitive to one (or more) of the indications listed in paragraph 12.

16   As an illustration of paragraph 15, if market interest rates or other market rates of return on investments have increased during the period, an entity is not required to make a formal estimate of an asset's recoverable amount in the following cases:

(a)   if the discount rate used in calculating the asset's value in use is unlikely to be affected by the increase in these market rates. For example, increases in short-term interest rates may not have a material effect on the discount rate used for an asset that has a long remaining useful life.

(b)   if the discount rate used in calculating the asset's value in use is likely to be affected by the increase in these market rates but previous sensitivity analysis of recoverable amount shows that:

(i)   it is unlikely that there will be a material decrease in recoverable amount because future cash flows are also likely to increase (eg in some cases, an entity may be able to demonstrate that it adjusts its revenues to compensate for any increase in market rates); or

(ii)   the decrease in recoverable amount is unlikely to result in a material impairment loss.

17   If there is an indication that an asset may be impaired, this may indicate that the remaining useful life, the depreciation (amortisation) method or the residual value for the asset needs to be reviewed and adjusted in accordance with the Standard applicable to the asset, even if no impairment loss is recognised for the asset.

Measuring recoverable amount

18   This Standard defines recoverable amount as the higher of an asset's or cash-generating unit's fair value less costs of disposal and its value in use. Paragraphs 19–57 set out the requirements for measuring recoverable amount. These requirements use the term 'an asset' but apply equally to an individual asset or a cash-generating unit.

19   It is not always necessary to determine both an asset's fair value less costs of disposal and its value in use. If either of these amounts exceeds the asset's carrying amount, the asset is not impaired and it is not necessary to estimate the other amount.

20   It may be possible to measure fair value less costs of disposal, even if there is not a quoted price in an active market for an identical asset. However, sometimes it will not be possible to measure fair value less costs of disposal because there is no basis for making a reliable estimate of the price at which an orderly transaction to sell the asset would take place between market participants at the measurement date under current market conditions. In this case, the entity may use the asset's value in use as its recoverable amount.

21 If there is no reason to believe that an asset's value in use materially exceeds its fair value less costs of disposal, the asset's fair value less costs of disposal may be used as its recoverable amount. This will often be the case for an asset that is held for disposal. This is because the value in use of an asset held for disposal will consist mainly of the net disposal proceeds, as the future cash flows from continuing use of the asset until its disposal are likely to be negligible.

22 Recoverable amount is determined for an individual asset, unless the asset does not generate cash inflows that are largely independent of those from other assets or groups of assets. If this is the case, recoverable amount is determined for the cash-generating unit to which the asset belongs (see paragraphs 65–103), unless either:

(a) the asset's fair value less costs of disposal is higher than its carrying amount; or

(b) the asset's value in use can be estimated to be close to its fair value less costs of disposal and fair value less costs of disposal can be measured.

23 In some cases, estimates, averages and computational short cuts may provide reasonable approximations of the detailed computations illustrated in this Standard for determining fair value less costs of disposal or value in use.

Measuring the recoverable amount of an intangible asset with an indefinite useful life

24 Paragraph 10 requires an intangible asset with an indefinite useful life to be tested for impairment annually by comparing its carrying amount with its recoverable amount, irrespective of whether there is any indication that it may be impaired. However, the most recent detailed calculation of such an asset's recoverable amount made in a preceding period may be used in the impairment test for that asset in the current period, provided all of the following criteria are met:

(a) if the intangible asset does not generate cash inflows from continuing use that are largely independent of those from other assets or groups of assets and is therefore tested for impairment as part of the cash-generating unit to which it belongs, the assets and liabilities making up that unit have not changed significantly since the most recent recoverable amount calculation;

(b) the most recent recoverable amount calculation resulted in an amount that exceeded the asset's carrying amount by a substantial margin; and

(c) based on an analysis of events that have occurred and circumstances that have changed since the most recent recoverable amount calculation, the likelihood that a current recoverable amount determination would be less than the asset's carrying amount is remote.

Fair value less costs of disposal

25–27   [Deleted]

28   Costs of disposal, other than those that have been recognised as liabilities, are deducted in measuring fair value less costs of disposal. Examples of such costs are legal costs, stamp duty and similar transaction taxes, costs of removing the asset, and direct incremental costs to bring an asset into condition for its sale. However, termination benefits (as defined in IAS 19) and costs associated with reducing or reorganising a business following the disposal of an asset are not direct incremental costs to dispose of the asset.

29   Sometimes, the disposal of an asset would require the buyer to assume a liability and only a single fair value less costs of disposal is available for both the asset and the liability. Paragraph 78 explains how to deal with such cases.

Value in use

30   The following elements shall be reflected in the calculation of an asset's value in use:

(a)   an estimate of the future cash flows the entity expects to derive from the asset;

(b)   expectations about possible variations in the amount or timing of those future cash flows;

(c)   the time value of money, represented by the current market risk-free rate of interest;

(d)   the price for bearing the uncertainty inherent in the asset; and

(e)   other factors, such as illiquidity, that market participants would reflect in pricing the future cash flows the entity expects to derive from the asset.

31   Estimating the value in use of an asset involves the following steps:

(a)   estimating the future cash inflows and outflows to be derived from continuing use of the asset and from its ultimate disposal; and

(b)   applying the appropriate discount rate to those future cash flows.

32   The elements identified in paragraph 30(b), (d) and (e) can be reflected either as adjustments to the future cash flows or as adjustments to the discount rate. Whichever approach an entity adopts to reflect expectations about possible variations in the amount or timing of future cash flows, the result shall be to reflect the expected present value of the future cash flows, ie the weighted average of all possible outcomes. Appendix A provides additional guidance on the use of present value techniques in measuring an asset's value in use.

Basis for estimates of future cash flows

33   In measuring value in use an entity shall:

(a)   base cash flow projections on reasonable and supportable assumptions that represent management's best estimate of the range of economic conditions that will exist over the remaining useful life of the asset. Greater weight shall be given to external evidence.

(b) base cash flow projections on the most recent financial budgets/forecasts approved by management, but shall exclude any estimated future cash inflows or outflows expected to arise from future restructurings or from improving or enhancing the asset's performance. Projections based on these budgets/forecasts shall cover a maximum period of five years, unless a longer period can be justified.

(c) estimate cash flow projections beyond the period covered by the most recent budgets/forecasts by extrapolating the projections based on the budgets/forecasts using a steady or declining growth rate for subsequent years, unless an increasing rate can be justified. This growth rate shall not exceed the long-term average growth rate for the products, industries, or country or countries in which the entity operates, or for the market in which the asset is used, unless a higher rate can be justified.

34 Management assesses the reasonableness of the assumptions on which its current cash flow projections are based by examining the causes of differences between past cash flow projections and actual cash flows. Management shall ensure that the assumptions on which its current cash flow projections are based are consistent with past actual outcomes, provided the effects of subsequent events or circumstances that did not exist when those actual cash flows were generated make this appropriate.

35 Detailed, explicit and reliable financial budgets/forecasts of future cash flows for periods longer than five years are generally not available. For this reason, management's estimates of future cash flows are based on the most recent budgets/forecasts for a maximum of five years. Management may use cash flow projections based on financial budgets/forecasts over a period longer than five years if it is confident that these projections are reliable and it can demonstrate its ability, based on past experience, to forecast cash flows accurately over that longer period.

36 Cash flow projections until the end of an asset's useful life are estimated by extrapolating the cash flow projections based on the financial budgets/forecasts using a growth rate for subsequent years. This rate is steady or declining, unless an increase in the rate matches objective information about patterns over a product or industry lifecycle. If appropriate, the growth rate is zero or negative.

37 When conditions are favourable, competitors are likely to enter the market and restrict growth. Therefore, entities will have difficulty in exceeding the average historical growth rate over the long term (say, twenty years) for the products, industries, or country or countries in which the entity operates, or for the market in which the asset is used.

38 In using information from financial budgets/forecasts, an entity considers whether the information reflects reasonable and supportable assumptions and represents management's best estimate of the set of economic conditions that will exist over the remaining useful life of the asset.

Composition of estimates of future cash flows

39   Estimates of future cash flows shall include:

(a)   projections of cash inflows from the continuing use of the asset;

(b)   projections of cash outflows that are necessarily incurred to generate the cash inflows from continuing use of the asset (including cash outflows to prepare the asset for use) and can be directly attributed, or allocated on a reasonable and consistent basis, to the asset; and

(c)   net cash flows, if any, to be received (or paid) for the disposal of the asset at the end of its useful life.

40   Estimates of future cash flows and the discount rate reflect consistent assumptions about price increases attributable to general inflation. Therefore, if the discount rate includes the effect of price increases attributable to general inflation, future cash flows are estimated in nominal terms. If the discount rate excludes the effect of price increases attributable to general inflation, future cash flows are estimated in real terms (but include future specific price increases or decreases).

41   Projections of cash outflows include those for the day-to-day servicing of the asset as well as future overheads that can be attributed directly, or allocated on a reasonable and consistent basis, to the use of the asset.

42   When the carrying amount of an asset does not yet include all the cash outflows to be incurred before it is ready for use or sale, the estimate of future cash outflows includes an estimate of any further cash outflow that is expected to be incurred before the asset is ready for use or sale. For example, this is the case for a building under construction or for a development project that is not yet completed.

43   To avoid double-counting, estimates of future cash flows do not include:

(a)   cash inflows from assets that generate cash inflows that are largely independent of the cash inflows from the asset under review (for example, financial assets such as receivables); and

(b)   cash outflows that relate to obligations that have been recognised as liabilities (for example, payables, pensions or provisions).

44   **Future cash flows shall be estimated for the asset in its current condition. Estimates of future cash flows shall not include estimated future cash inflows or outflows that are expected to arise from:**

(a)   **a future restructuring to which an entity is not yet committed; or**

(b)   **improving or enhancing the asset's performance.**

45   Because future cash flows are estimated for the asset in its current condition, value in use does not reflect:

(a)   future cash outflows or related cost savings (for example reductions in staff costs) or benefits that are expected to arise from a future restructuring to which an entity is not yet committed; or

(b) future cash outflows that will improve or enhance the asset's performance or the related cash inflows that are expected to arise from such outflows.

46 A restructuring is a programme that is planned and controlled by management and materially changes either the scope of the business undertaken by an entity or the manner in which the business is conducted. IAS 37 *Provisions, Contingent Liabilities and Contingent Assets* contains guidance clarifying when an entity is committed to a restructuring.

47 When an entity becomes committed to a restructuring, some assets are likely to be affected by this restructuring. Once the entity is committed to the restructuring:

(a) its estimates of future cash inflows and cash outflows for the purpose of determining value in use reflect the cost savings and other benefits from the restructuring (based on the most recent financial budgets/forecasts approved by management); and

(b) its estimates of future cash outflows for the restructuring are included in a restructuring provision in accordance with IAS 37.

Illustrative Example 5 illustrates the effect of a future restructuring on a value in use calculation.

48 Until an entity incurs cash outflows that improve or enhance the asset's performance, estimates of future cash flows do not include the estimated future cash inflows that are expected to arise from the increase in economic benefits associated with the cash outflow (see Illustrative Example 6).

49 Estimates of future cash flows include future cash outflows necessary to maintain the level of economic benefits expected to arise from the asset in its current condition. When a cash-generating unit consists of assets with different estimated useful lives, all of which are essential to the ongoing operation of the unit, the replacement of assets with shorter lives is considered to be part of the day-to-day servicing of the unit when estimating the future cash flows associated with the unit. Similarly, when a single asset consists of components with different estimated useful lives, the replacement of components with shorter lives is considered to be part of the day-to-day servicing of the asset when estimating the future cash flows generated by the asset.

50 **Estimates of future cash flows shall not include:**

(a) **cash inflows or outflows from financing activities; or**

(b) **income tax receipts or payments.**

51 Estimated future cash flows reflect assumptions that are consistent with the way the discount rate is determined. Otherwise, the effect of some assumptions will be counted twice or ignored. Because the time value of money is considered by discounting the estimated future cash flows, these cash flows exclude cash inflows or outflows from financing activities. Similarly, because the discount rate is determined on a pre-tax basis, future cash flows are also estimated on a pre-tax basis.

52   The estimate of net cash flows to be received (or paid) for the disposal of an asset at the end of its useful life shall be the amount that an entity expects to obtain from the disposal of the asset in an arm's length transaction between knowledgeable, willing parties, after deducting the estimated costs of disposal.

53   The estimate of net cash flows to be received (or paid) for the disposal of an asset at the end of its useful life is determined in a similar way to an asset's fair value less costs of disposal, except that, in estimating those net cash flows:

(a)   an entity uses prices prevailing at the date of the estimate for similar assets that have reached the end of their useful life and have operated under conditions similar to those in which the asset will be used.

(b)   the entity adjusts those prices for the effect of both future price increases due to general inflation and specific future price increases or decreases. However, if estimates of future cash flows from the asset's continuing use and the discount rate exclude the effect of general inflation, the entity also excludes this effect from the estimate of net cash flows on disposal.

53A   Fair value differs from value in use. Fair value reflects the assumptions market participants would use when pricing the asset. In contrast, value in use reflects the effects of factors that may be specific to the entity and not applicable to entities in general. For example, fair value does not reflect any of the following factors to the extent that they would not be generally available to market participants:

(a)   additional value derived from the grouping of assets (such as the creation of a portfolio of investment properties in different locations);

(b)   synergies between the asset being measured and other assets;

(c)   legal rights or legal restrictions that are specific only to the current owner of the asset; and

(d)   tax benefits or tax burdens that are specific to the current owner of the asset.

Foreign currency future cash flows

54   Future cash flows are estimated in the currency in which they will be generated and then discounted using a discount rate appropriate for that currency. An entity translates the present value using the spot exchange rate at the date of the value in use calculation.

Discount rate

55   The discount rate (rates) shall be a pre-tax rate (rates) that reflect(s) current market assessments of:

(a)   the time value of money; and

(b)   the risks specific to the asset for which the future cash flow estimates have not been adjusted.

56   A rate that reflects current market assessments of the time value of money and the risks specific to the asset is the return that investors would require if they were to choose an investment that would generate cash flows of amounts, timing and risk profile equivalent to those that the entity expects to derive from the asset. This rate is estimated from the rate implicit in current market transactions for similar assets or from the weighted average cost of capital of a listed entity that has a single asset (or a portfolio of assets) similar in terms of service potential and risks to the asset under review. However, the discount rate(s) used to measure an asset's value in use shall not reflect risks for which the future cash flow estimates have been adjusted. Otherwise, the effect of some assumptions will be double-counted.

57   When an asset-specific rate is not directly available from the market, an entity uses surrogates to estimate the discount rate. Appendix A provides additional guidance on estimating the discount rate in such circumstances.

Recognising and measuring an impairment loss

58   Paragraphs 59–64 set out the requirements for recognising and measuring impairment losses for an individual asset other than goodwill. Recognising and measuring impairment losses for cash-generating units and goodwill are dealt with in paragraphs 65–108.

59   **If, and only if, the recoverable amount of an asset is less than its carrying amount, the carrying amount of the asset shall be reduced to its recoverable amount. That reduction is an impairment loss.**

60   **An impairment loss shall be recognised immediately in profit or loss, unless the asset is carried at revalued amount in accordance with another Standard (for example, in accordance with the revaluation model in IAS 16). Any impairment loss of a revalued asset shall be treated as a revaluation decrease in accordance with that other Standard.**

61   An impairment loss on a non-revalued asset is recognised in profit or loss. However, an impairment loss on a revalued asset is recognised in other comprehensive income to the extent that the impairment loss does not exceed the amount in the revaluation surplus for that same asset. Such an impairment loss on a revalued asset reduces the revaluation surplus for that asset.

62   **When the amount estimated for an impairment loss is greater than the carrying amount of the asset to which it relates, an entity shall recognise a liability if, and only if, that is required by another Standard.**

63   **After the recognition of an impairment loss, the depreciation (amortisation) charge for the asset shall be adjusted in future periods to allocate the asset's revised carrying amount, less its residual value (if any), on a systematic basis over its remaining useful life.**

64   If an impairment loss is recognised, any related deferred tax assets or liabilities are determined in accordance with IAS 12 by comparing the revised carrying amount of the asset with its tax base (see Illustrative Example 3).

Cash-generating units and goodwill

65 Paragraphs 66–108 and Appendix C set out the requirements for identifying the cash-generating unit to which an asset belongs and determining the carrying amount of, and recognising impairment losses for, cash-generating units and goodwill.

Identifying the cash-generating unit to which an asset belongs

66 **If there is any indication that an asset may be impaired, recoverable amount shall be estimated for the individual asset. If it is not possible to estimate the recoverable amount of the individual asset, an entity shall determine the recoverable amount of the cash-generating unit to which the asset belongs (the asset's cash-generating unit).**

67 The recoverable amount of an individual asset cannot be determined if:

(a) the asset's value in use cannot be estimated to be close to its fair value less costs of disposal (for example, when the future cash flows from continuing use of the asset cannot be estimated to be negligible); and

(b) the asset does not generate cash inflows that are largely independent of those from other assets.

In such cases, value in use and, therefore, recoverable amount, can be determined only for the asset's cash-generating unit.

Example
A mining entity owns a private railway to support its mining activities. The private railway could be sold only for scrap value and it does not generate cash inflows that are largely independent of the cash inflows from the other assets of the mine.
It is not possible to estimate the recoverable amount of the private railway because its value in use cannot be determined and is probably different from scrap value. Therefore, the entity estimates the recoverable amount of the cash-generating unit to which the private railway belongs, ie the mine as a whole.

68 As defined in paragraph 6, an asset's cash-generating unit is the smallest group of assets that includes the asset and generates cash inflows that are largely independent of the cash inflows from other assets or groups of assets. Identification of an asset's cash-generating unit involves judgement. If recoverable amount cannot be determined for an individual asset, an entity identifies the lowest aggregation of assets that generate largely independent cash inflows.

> **Example**
>
> A bus company provides services under contract with a municipality that requires minimum service on each of five separate routes. Assets devoted to each route and the cash flows from each route can be identified separately. One of the routes operates at a significant loss.
>
> *Because the entity does not have the option to curtail any one bus route, the lowest level of identifiable cash inflows that are largely independent of the cash inflows from other assets or groups of assets is the cash inflows generated by the five routes together. The cash-generating unit for each route is the bus company as a whole.*

69 Cash inflows are inflows of cash and cash equivalents received from parties external to the entity. In identifying whether cash inflows from an asset (or group of assets) are largely independent of the cash inflows from other assets (or groups of assets), an entity considers various factors including how management monitors the entity's operations (such as by product lines, businesses, individual locations, districts or regional areas) or how management makes decisions about continuing or disposing of the entity's assets and operations. Illustrative Example 1 gives examples of identification of a cash-generating unit.

70 **If an active market exists for the output produced by an asset or group of assets, that asset or group of assets shall be identified as a cash-generating unit, even if some or all of the output is used internally. If the cash inflows generated by any asset or cash-generating unit are affected by internal transfer pricing, an entity shall use management's best estimate of future price(s) that could be achieved in arm's length transactions in estimating:**

(a) **the future cash inflows used to determine the asset's or cash-generating unit's value in use; and**

(b) **the future cash outflows used to determine the value in use of any other assets or cash-generating units that are affected by the internal transfer pricing.**

71 Even if part or all of the output produced by an asset or a group of assets is used by other units of the entity (for example, products at an intermediate stage of a production process), this asset or group of assets forms a separate cash-generating unit if the entity could sell the output on an active market. This is because the asset or group of assets could generate cash inflows that would be largely independent of the cash inflows from other assets or groups of assets. In using information based on financial budgets/forecasts that relates to such a cash-generating unit, or to any other asset or cash-generating unit affected by internal transfer pricing, an entity adjusts this information if internal transfer prices do not reflect management's best estimate of future prices that could be achieved in arm's length transactions.

72 **Cash-generating units shall be identified consistently from period to period for the same asset or types of assets, unless a change is justified.**

73   If an entity determines that an asset belongs to a cash-generating unit different from that in previous periods, or that the types of assets aggregated for the asset's cash-generating unit have changed, paragraph 130 requires disclosures about the cash-generating unit, if an impairment loss is recognised or reversed for the cash-generating unit.

Recoverable amount and carrying amount of a cash-generating unit

74   The recoverable amount of a cash-generating unit is the higher of the cash-generating unit's fair value less costs of disposal and its value in use. For the purpose of determining the recoverable amount of a cash-generating unit, any reference in paragraphs 19–57 to 'an asset' is read as a reference to 'a cash-generating unit'.

75   **The carrying amount of a cash-generating unit shall be determined on a basis consistent with the way the recoverable amount of the cash-generating unit is determined.**

76   The carrying amount of a cash-generating unit:

(a)   includes the carrying amount of only those assets that can be attributed directly, or allocated on a reasonable and consistent basis, to the cash-generating unit and will generate the future cash inflows used in determining the cash-generating unit's value in use; and

(b)   does not include the carrying amount of any recognised liability, unless the recoverable amount of the cash-generating unit cannot be determined without consideration of this liability.

This is because fair value less costs of disposal and value in use of a cash-generating unit are determined excluding cash flows that relate to assets that are not part of the cash-generating unit and liabilities that have been recognised (see paragraphs 28 and 43).

77   When assets are grouped for recoverability assessments, it is important to include in the cash-generating unit all assets that generate or are used to generate the relevant stream of cash inflows. Otherwise, the cash-generating unit may appear to be fully recoverable when in fact an impairment loss has occurred. In some cases, although some assets contribute to the estimated future cash flows of a cash-generating unit, they cannot be allocated to the cash-generating unit on a reasonable and consistent basis. This might be the case for goodwill or corporate assets such as head office assets. Paragraphs 80–103 explain how to deal with these assets in testing a cash-generating unit for impairment.

78   It may be necessary to consider some recognised liabilities to determine the recoverable amount of a cash-generating unit. This may occur if the disposal of a cash-generating unit would require the buyer to assume the liability. In this case, the fair value less costs of disposal (or the estimated cash flow from ultimate disposal) of the cash-generating unit is the price to sell the assets of the cash-generating unit and the liability together, less the costs of disposal. To perform a meaningful comparison between the carrying amount of the

cash-generating unit and its recoverable amount, the carrying amount of the liability is deducted in determining both the cash-generating unit's value in use and its carrying amount.

Example
A company operates a mine in a country where legislation requires that the owner must restore the site on completion of its mining operations. The cost of restoration includes the replacement of the overburden, which must be removed before mining operations commence. A provision for the costs to replace the overburden was recognised as soon as the overburden was removed. The amount provided was recognised as part of the cost of the mine and is being depreciated over the mine's useful life. The carrying amount of the provision for restoration costs is CU500,[a] which is equal to the present value of the restoration costs.
The entity is testing the mine for impairment. The cash-generating unit for the mine is the mine as a whole. The entity has received various offers to buy the mine at a price of around CU800. This price reflects the fact that the buyer will assume the obligation to restore the overburden. Disposal costs for the mine are negligible. The value in use of the mine is approximately CU1,200, excluding restoration costs. The carrying amount of the mine is CU1,000.
The cash-generating unit's fair value less costs of disposal is CU800. This amount considers restoration costs that have already been provided for. As a consequence, the value in use for the cash-generating unit is determined after consideration of the restoration costs and is estimated to be CU700 (CU1,200 less CU500). The carrying amount of the cash-generating unit is CU500, which is the carrying amount of the mine (CU1,000) less the carrying amount of the provision for restoration costs (CU500). Therefore, the recoverable amount of the cash-generating unit exceeds its carrying amount.

(a) In this Standard, monetary amounts are denominated in 'currency units (CU)'.

79   For practical reasons, the recoverable amount of a cash-generating unit is sometimes determined after consideration of assets that are not part of the cash-generating unit (for example, receivables or other financial assets) or liabilities that have been recognised (for example, payables, pensions and other provisions). In such cases, the carrying amount of the cash-generating unit is increased by the carrying amount of those assets and decreased by the carrying amount of those liabilities.

Goodwill

Allocating goodwill to cash-generating units

80   **For the purpose of impairment testing, goodwill acquired in a business combination shall, from the acquisition date, be allocated to each of the acquirer's cash-generating units, or groups of cash-generating units, that is expected to benefit from the synergies of the combination, irrespective of whether other assets or liabilities of the acquiree are assigned to those units or groups of units. Each unit or group of units to which the goodwill is so allocated shall:**

(a) represent the lowest level within the entity at which the goodwill is monitored for internal management purposes; and

(b) not be larger than an operating segment as defined by paragraph 5 of IFRS 8 *Operating Segments* before aggregation.

81 Goodwill recognised in a business combination is an asset representing the future economic benefits arising from other assets acquired in a business combination that are not individually identified and separately recognised. Goodwill does not generate cash flows independently of other assets or groups of assets, and often contributes to the cash flows of multiple cash-generating units. Goodwill sometimes cannot be allocated on a non-arbitrary basis to individual cash-generating units, but only to groups of cash-generating units. As a result, the lowest level within the entity at which the goodwill is monitored for internal management purposes sometimes comprises a number of cash-generating units to which the goodwill relates, but to which it cannot be allocated. References in paragraphs 83–99 and Appendix C to a cash-generating unit to which goodwill is allocated should be read as references also to a group of cash-generating units to which goodwill is allocated.

82 Applying the requirements in paragraph 80 results in goodwill being tested for impairment at a level that reflects the way an entity manages its operations and with which the goodwill would naturally be associated. Therefore, the development of additional reporting systems is typically not necessary.

83 A cash-generating unit to which goodwill is allocated for the purpose of impairment testing may not coincide with the level at which goodwill is allocated in accordance with IAS 21 *The Effects of Changes in Foreign Exchange Rates* for the purpose of measuring foreign currency gains and losses. For example, if an entity is required by IAS 21 to allocate goodwill to relatively low levels for the purpose of measuring foreign currency gains and losses, it is not required to test the goodwill for impairment at that same level unless it also monitors the goodwill at that level for internal management purposes.

84 **If the initial allocation of goodwill acquired in a business combination cannot be completed before the end of the annual period in which the business combination is effected, that initial allocation shall be completed before the end of the first annual period beginning after the acquisition date.**

85 In accordance with IFRS 3 *Business Combinations*, if the initial accounting for a business combination can be determined only provisionally by the end of the period in which the combination is effected, the acquirer:

(a) accounts for the combination using those provisional values; and

(b) recognises any adjustments to those provisional values as a result of completing the initial accounting within the measurement period, which will not exceed twelve months from the acquisition date.

In such circumstances, it might also not be possible to complete the initial allocation of the goodwill recognised in the combination before the end of the annual period in which the combination is effected. When this is the case, the entity discloses the information required by paragraph 133.

86   If goodwill has been allocated to a cash-generating unit and the entity disposes of an operation within that unit, the goodwill associated with the operation disposed of shall be:

(a)   included in the carrying amount of the operation when determining the gain or loss on disposal; and

(b)   measured on the basis of the relative values of the operation disposed of and the portion of the cash-generating unit retained, unless the entity can demonstrate that some other method better reflects the goodwill associated with the operation disposed of.

> **Example**
>
> An entity sells for CU100 an operation that was part of a cash-generating unit to which goodwill has been allocated. The goodwill allocated to the unit cannot be identified or associated with an asset group at a level lower than that unit, except arbitrarily. The recoverable amount of the portion of the cash-generating unit retained is CU300.
>
> *Because the goodwill allocated to the cash-generating unit cannot be non-arbitrarily identified or associated with an asset group at a level lower than that unit, the goodwill associated with the operation disposed of is measured on the basis of the relative values of the operation disposed of and the portion of the unit retained. Therefore, 25 per cent of the goodwill allocated to the cash-generating unit is included in the carrying amount of the operation that is sold.*

87   If an entity reorganises its reporting structure in a way that changes the composition of one or more cash-generating units to which goodwill has been allocated, the goodwill shall be reallocated to the units affected. This reallocation shall be performed using a relative value approach similar to that used when an entity disposes of an operation within a cash-generating unit, unless the entity can demonstrate that some other method better reflects the goodwill associated with the reorganised units.

> **Example**
>
> Goodwill had previously been allocated to cash-generating unit A. The goodwill allocated to A cannot be identified or associated with an asset group at a level lower than A, except arbitrarily. A is to be divided and integrated into three other cash-generating units, B, C and D.
>
> *Because the goodwill allocated to A cannot be non-arbitrarily identified or associated with an asset group at a level lower than A, it is reallocated to units B, C and D on the basis of the relative values of the three portions of A before those portions are integrated with B, C and D.*

Testing cash-generating units with goodwill for impairment

88   When, as described in paragraph 81, goodwill relates to a cash-generating unit but has not been allocated to that unit, the unit shall be tested for impairment, whenever there is an indication that the unit may be impaired, by comparing the unit's carrying amount, excluding any goodwill, with its recoverable amount. Any impairment loss shall be recognised in accordance with paragraph 104.

89   If a cash-generating unit described in paragraph 88 includes in its carrying amount an intangible asset that has an indefinite useful life or is not yet available for use and that asset can be tested for impairment only as part of the cash-generating unit, paragraph 10 requires the unit also to be tested for impairment annually.

90   **A cash-generating unit to which goodwill has been allocated shall be tested for impairment annually, and whenever there is an indication that the unit may be impaired, by comparing the carrying amount of the unit, including the goodwill, with the recoverable amount of the unit. If the recoverable amount of the unit exceeds the carrying amount of the unit, the unit and the goodwill allocated to that unit shall be regarded as not impaired. If the carrying amount of the unit exceeds the recoverable amount of the unit, the entity shall recognise the impairment loss in accordance with paragraph 104.**

91-95   [Deleted]

Timing of impairment tests

96   **The annual impairment test for a cash-generating unit to which goodwill has been allocated may be performed at any time during an annual period, provided the test is performed at the same time every year. Different cash-generating units may be tested for impairment at different times. However, if some or all of the goodwill allocated to a cash-generating unit was acquired in a business combination during the current annual period, that unit shall be tested for impairment before the end of the current annual period.**

97   **If the assets constituting the cash-generating unit to which goodwill has been allocated are tested for impairment at the same time as the unit containing the goodwill, they shall be tested for impairment before the unit containing the goodwill. Similarly, if the cash-generating units constituting a group of cash-generating units to which goodwill has been allocated are tested for impairment at the same time as the group of units containing the goodwill, the individual units shall be tested for impairment before the group of units containing the goodwill.**

98   At the time of impairment testing a cash-generating unit to which goodwill has been allocated, there may be an indication of an impairment of an asset within the unit containing the goodwill. In such circumstances, the entity tests the asset for impairment first, and recognises any impairment loss for that asset before testing for impairment the cash-generating unit containing the goodwill. Similarly, there may be an indication of an impairment of a cash-generating unit within a group of units containing the goodwill. In such circumstances, the entity tests the cash-generating unit for impairment first, and recognises any impairment loss for that unit, before testing for impairment the group of units to which the goodwill is allocated.

99   **The most recent detailed calculation made in a preceding period of the recoverable amount of a cash-generating unit to which goodwill has been allocated may be used in the impairment test of that unit in the current period provided all of the following criteria are met:**

(a) the assets and liabilities making up the unit have not changed significantly since the most recent recoverable amount calculation;

(b) the most recent recoverable amount calculation resulted in an amount that exceeded the carrying amount of the unit by a substantial margin; and

(c) based on an analysis of events that have occurred and circumstances that have changed since the most recent recoverable amount calculation, the likelihood that a current recoverable amount determination would be less than the current carrying amount of the unit is remote.

Corporate assets

100   Corporate assets include group or divisional assets such as the building of a headquarters or a division of the entity, EDP equipment or a research centre. The structure of an entity determines whether an asset meets this Standard's definition of corporate assets for a particular cash-generating unit. The distinctive characteristics of corporate assets are that they do not generate cash inflows independently of other assets or groups of assets and their carrying amount cannot be fully attributed to the cash-generating unit under review.

101   Because corporate assets do not generate separate cash inflows, the recoverable amount of an individual corporate asset cannot be determined unless management has decided to dispose of the asset. As a consequence, if there is an indication that a corporate asset may be impaired, recoverable amount is determined for the cash-generating unit or group of cash-generating units to which the corporate asset belongs, and is compared with the carrying amount of this cash-generating unit or group of cash-generating units. Any impairment loss is recognised in accordance with paragraph 104.

102   **In testing a cash-generating unit for impairment, an entity shall identify all the corporate assets that relate to the cash-generating unit under review. If a portion of the carrying amount of a corporate asset:**

(a) can be allocated on a reasonable and consistent basis to that unit, the entity shall compare the carrying amount of the unit, including the portion of the carrying amount of the corporate asset allocated to the unit, with its recoverable amount. Any impairment loss shall be recognised in accordance with paragraph 104.

(b) cannot be allocated on a reasonable and consistent basis to that unit, the entity shall:

(i) compare the carrying amount of the unit, excluding the corporate asset, with its recoverable amount and recognise any impairment loss in accordance with paragraph 104;

(ii) identify the smallest group of cash-generating units that includes the cash-generating unit under review and to which a portion of the carrying amount of the corporate asset can be allocated on a reasonable and consistent basis; and

(iii) compare the carrying amount of that group of cash-generating units, including the portion of the carrying amount of the corporate asset allocated to that group of units, with the recoverable amount of the group of units. Any impairment loss shall be recognised in accordance with paragraph 104.

103 Illustrative Example 8 illustrates the application of these requirements to corporate assets.

Impairment loss for a cash-generating unit

104 An impairment loss shall be recognised for a cash-generating unit (the smallest group of cash-generating units to which goodwill or a corporate asset has been allocated) if, and only if, the recoverable amount of the unit (group of units) is less than the carrying amount of the unit (group of units). The impairment loss shall be allocated to reduce the carrying amount of the assets of the unit (group of units) in the following order:

(a) first, to reduce the carrying amount of any goodwill allocated to the cash-generating unit (group of units); and

(b) then, to the other assets of the unit (group of units) pro rata on the basis of the carrying amount of each asset in the unit (group of units).

These reductions in carrying amounts shall be treated as impairment losses on individual assets and recognised in accordance with paragraph 60.

105 In allocating an impairment loss in accordance with paragraph 104, an entity shall not reduce the carrying amount of an asset below the highest of:

(a) its fair value less costs of disposal (if measurable);

(b) its value in use (if determinable); and

(c) zero.

The amount of the impairment loss that would otherwise have been allocated to the asset shall be allocated pro rata to the other assets of the unit (group of units).

106 If it is not practicable to estimate the recoverable amount of each individual asset of a cash-generating unit, this Standard requires an arbitrary allocation of an impairment loss between the assets of that unit, other than goodwill, because all assets of a cash-generating unit work together.

107 If the recoverable amount of an individual asset cannot be determined (see paragraph 67):

(a) an impairment loss is recognised for the asset if its carrying amount is greater than the higher of its fair value less costs of disposal and the results of the allocation procedures described in paragraphs 104 and 105; and

(b) no impairment loss is recognised for the asset if the related cash-generating unit is not impaired. This applies even if the asset's fair value less costs of disposal is less than its carrying amount.

> **Example**
>
> A machine has suffered physical damage but is still working, although not as well as before it was damaged. The machine's fair value less costs of disposal is less than its carrying amount. The machine does not generate independent cash inflows. The smallest identifiable group of assets that includes the machine and generates cash inflows that are largely independent of the cash inflows from other assets is the production line to which the machine belongs. The recoverable amount of the production line shows that the production line taken as a whole is not impaired.
>
> Assumption 1: budgets/forecasts approved by management reflect no commitment of management to replace the machine.
>
> *The recoverable amount of the machine alone cannot be estimated because the machine's value in use:*
>
> *(a)   may differ from its fair value less costs of disposal; and*
>
> *(b)   can be determined only for the cash-generating unit to which the machine belongs (the production line).*
>
> *The production line is not impaired. Therefore, no impairment loss is recognised for the machine. Nevertheless, the entity may need to reassess the depreciation period or the depreciation method for the machine. Perhaps a shorter depreciation period or a faster depreciation method is required to reflect the expected remaining useful life of the machine or the pattern in which economic benefits are expected to be consumed by the entity.*
>
> Assumption 2: budgets/forecasts approved by management reflect a commitment of management to replace the machine and sell it in the near future. Cash flows from continuing use of the machine until its disposal are estimated to be negligible.
>
> *The machine's value in use can be estimated to be close to its fair value less costs of disposal. Therefore, the recoverable amount of the machine can be determined and no consideration is given to the cash-generating unit to which the machine belongs (ie the production line). Because the machine's fair value less costs of disposal is less than its carrying amount, an impairment loss is recognised for the machine.*

108   After the requirements in paragraphs 104 and 105 have been applied, a liability shall be recognised for any remaining amount of an impairment loss for a cash-generating unit if, and only if, that is required by another IFRS.

Reversing an impairment loss

109   Paragraphs 110–116 set out the requirements for reversing an impairment loss recognised for an asset or a cash-generating unit in prior periods. These requirements use the term 'an asset' but apply equally to an individual asset or a cash-generating unit. Additional requirements for an individual asset are set out in paragraphs 117–121, for a cash-generating unit in paragraphs 122 and 123 and for goodwill in paragraphs 124 and 125.

110   An entity shall assess at the end of each reporting period whether there is any indication that an impairment loss recognised in prior periods for an asset other than goodwill may no longer exist or may have decreased. If any such indication exists, the entity shall estimate the recoverable amount of that asset.

111   In assessing whether there is any indication that an impairment loss recognised in prior periods for an asset other than goodwill may no longer exist or may have decreased, an entity shall consider, as a minimum, the following indications:

External sources of information

(a)   there are observable indications that the asset's value has increased significantly during the period.

(b)   significant changes with a favourable effect on the entity have taken place during the period, or will take place in the near future, in the technological, market, economic or legal environment in which the entity operates or in the market to which the asset is dedicated.

(c)   market interest rates or other market rates of return on investments have decreased during the period, and those decreases are likely to affect the discount rate used in calculating the asset's value in use and increase the asset's recoverable amount materially.

Internal sources of information

(d)   significant changes with a favourable effect on the entity have taken place during the period, or are expected to take place in the near future, in the extent to which, or manner in which, the asset is used or is expected to be used. These changes include costs incurred during the period to improve or enhance the asset's performance or restructure the operation to which the asset belongs.

(e)   evidence is available from internal reporting that indicates that the economic performance of the asset is, or will be, better than expected.

112   Indications of a potential decrease in an impairment loss in paragraph 111 mainly mirror the indications of a potential impairment loss in paragraph 12.

113   If there is an indication that an impairment loss recognised for an asset other than goodwill may no longer exist or may have decreased, this may indicate that the remaining useful life, the depreciation (amortisation) method or the residual value may need to be reviewed and adjusted in accordance with the IFRS applicable to the asset, even if no impairment loss is reversed for the asset.

114   An impairment loss recognised in prior periods for an asset other than goodwill shall be reversed if, and only if, there has been a change in the estimates used to determine the asset's recoverable amount since the last impairment loss was recognised. If this is the case, the carrying amount of the asset shall, except as described in paragraph 117, be increased to its recoverable amount. That increase is a reversal of an impairment loss.

115   A reversal of an impairment loss reflects an increase in the estimated service potential of an asset, either from use or from sale, since the date when an entity last recognised an impairment loss for that asset. Paragraph 130 requires an entity to identify the change in estimates that causes the increase in estimated service potential. Examples of changes in estimates include:

    (a)   a change in the basis for recoverable amount (ie whether recoverable amount is based on fair value less costs of disposal or value in use);

    (b)   if recoverable amount was based on value in use, a change in the amount or timing of estimated future cash flows or in the discount rate; or

    (c)   if recoverable amount was based on fair value less costs of disposal, a change in estimate of the components of fair value less costs of disposal.

116   An asset's value in use may become greater than the asset's carrying amount simply because the present value of future cash inflows increases as they become closer. However, the service potential of the asset has not increased. Therefore, an impairment loss is not reversed just because of the passage of time (sometimes called the 'unwinding' of the discount), even if the recoverable amount of the asset becomes higher than its carrying amount.

Reversing an impairment loss for an individual asset

117   **The increased carrying amount of an asset other than goodwill attributable to a reversal of an impairment loss shall not exceed the carrying amount that would have been determined (net of amortisation or depreciation) had no impairment loss been recognised for the asset in prior years.**

118   Any increase in the carrying amount of an asset other than goodwill above the carrying amount that would have been determined (net of amortisation or depreciation) had no impairment loss been recognised for the asset in prior years is a revaluation. In accounting for such a revaluation, an entity applies the IFRS applicable to the asset.

119   **A reversal of an impairment loss for an asset other than goodwill shall be recognised immediately in profit or loss, unless the asset is carried at revalued amount in accordance with another IFRS (for example, the revaluation model in IAS 16). Any reversal of an impairment loss of a revalued asset shall be treated as a revaluation increase in accordance with that other IFRS.**

120   A reversal of an impairment loss on a revalued asset is recognised in other comprehensive income and increases the revaluation surplus for that asset. However, to the extent that an impairment loss on the same revalued asset was previously recognised in profit or loss, a reversal of that impairment loss is also recognised in profit or loss.

121   **After a reversal of an impairment loss is recognised, the depreciation (amortisation) charge for the asset shall be adjusted in future periods to allocate the asset's revised carrying amount, less its residual value (if any), on a systematic basis over its remaining useful life.**

Reversing an impairment loss for a cash-generating unit

122   A reversal of an impairment loss for a cash-generating unit shall be allocated to the assets of the unit, except for goodwill, pro rata with the carrying amounts of those assets. These increases in carrying amounts shall be treated as reversals of impairment losses for individual assets and recognised in accordance with paragraph 119.

123   In allocating a reversal of an impairment loss for a cash-generating unit in accordance with paragraph 122, the carrying amount of an asset shall not be increased above the lower of:

   (a)   its recoverable amount (if determinable); and

   (b)   the carrying amount that would have been determined (net of amortisation or depreciation) had no impairment loss been recognised for the asset in prior periods.

The amount of the reversal of the impairment loss that would otherwise have been allocated to the asset shall be allocated pro rata to the other assets of the unit, except for goodwill.

Reversing an impairment loss for goodwill

124   An impairment loss recognised for goodwill shall not be reversed in a subsequent period.

125   IAS 38 *Intangible Assets* prohibits the recognition of internally generated goodwill. Any increase in the recoverable amount of goodwill in the periods following the recognition of an impairment loss for that goodwill is likely to be an increase in internally generated goodwill, rather than a reversal of the impairment loss recognised for the acquired goodwill.

Disclosure

126   An entity shall disclose the following for each class of assets:

   (a)   the amount of impairment losses recognised in profit or loss during the period and the line item(s) of the statement of comprehensive income in which those impairment losses are included.

   (b)   the amount of reversals of impairment losses recognised in profit or loss during the period and the line item(s) of the statement of comprehensive income in which those impairment losses are reversed.

   (c)   the amount of impairment losses on revalued assets recognised in other comprehensive income during the period.

   (d)   the amount of reversals of impairment losses on revalued assets recognised in other comprehensive income during the period.

127   A class of assets is a grouping of assets of similar nature and use in an entity's operations.

128   The information required in paragraph 126 may be presented with other information disclosed for the class of assets. For example, this information may be included in a reconciliation of the carrying amount of property, plant and equipment, at the beginning and end of the period, as required by IAS 16.

129   An entity that reports segment information in accordance with IFRS 8 shall disclose the following for each reportable segment:

    (a)   the amount of impairment losses recognised in profit or loss and in other comprehensive income during the period.

    (b)   the amount of reversals of impairment losses recognised in profit or loss and in other comprehensive income during the period.

130   An entity shall disclose the following for each material impairment loss recognised or reversed during the period for an individual asset, including goodwill, or a cash-generating unit:

    (a)   the events and circumstances that led to the recognition or reversal of the impairment loss.

    (b)   the amount of the impairment loss recognised or reversed.

    (c)   for an individual asset:

        (i)   the nature of the asset; and

        (ii)   if the entity reports segment information in accordance with IFRS 8, the reportable segment to which the asset belongs.

    (d)   for a cash-generating unit:

        (i)   a description of the cash-generating unit (such as whether it is a product line, a plant, a business operation, a geographical area, or a reportable segment as defined in IFRS 8);

        (ii)   the amount of the impairment loss recognised or reversed by class of assets and, if the entity reports segment information in accordance with IFRS 8, by reportable segment; and

        (iii)   if the aggregation of assets for identifying the cash-generating unit has changed since the previous estimate of the cash-generating unit's recoverable amount (if any), a description of the current and former way of aggregating assets and the reasons for changing the way the cash-generating unit is identified.

    (e)   whether the recoverable amount of the asset (cash-generating unit) is its fair value less costs of disposal or its value in use.

    (f)   if recoverable amount is fair value less costs of disposal, the basis used to measure fair value less costs of disposal (such as whether fair value was measured by reference to a quoted price in an active market for an identical asset). An entity is not required to provide the disclosures required by IFRS 13.

    (g)   if recoverable amount is value in use, the discount rate(s) used in the current estimate and previous estimate (if any) of value in use.

131 An entity shall disclose the following information for the aggregate impairment losses and the aggregate reversals of impairment losses recognised during the period for which no information is disclosed in accordance with paragraph 130:

(a) the main classes of assets affected by impairment losses and the main classes of assets affected by reversals of impairment losses.

(b) the main events and circumstances that led to the recognition of these impairment losses and reversals of impairment losses.

132 An entity is encouraged to disclose assumptions used to determine the recoverable amount of assets (cash-generating units) during the period. However, paragraph 134 requires an entity to disclose information about the estimates used to measure the recoverable amount of a cash-generating unit when goodwill or an intangible asset with an indefinite useful life is included in the carrying amount of that unit.

133 If, in accordance with paragraph 84, any portion of the goodwill acquired in a business combination during the period has not been allocated to a cash-generating unit (group of units) at the end of the reporting period, the amount of the unallocated goodwill shall be disclosed together with the reasons why that amount remains unallocated.

Estimates used to measure recoverable amounts of cash-generating units containing goodwill or intangible assets with indefinite useful lives

134 An entity shall disclose the information required by (a)–(f) for each cash-generating unit (group of units) for which the carrying amount of goodwill or intangible assets with indefinite useful lives allocated to that unit (group of units) is significant in comparison with the entity's total carrying amount of goodwill or intangible assets with indefinite useful lives:

(a) the carrying amount of goodwill allocated to the unit (group of units).

(b) the carrying amount of intangible assets with indefinite useful lives allocated to the unit (group of units).

(c) the recoverable amount of the unit (or group of units) and the basis on which the unit's (group of units') recoverable amount has been determined (ie value in use or fair value less costs of disposal).

(d) if the unit's (group of units') recoverable amount is based on value in use:

(i) each key assumption on which management has based its cash flow projections for the period covered by the most recent budgets/forecasts. Key assumptions are those to which the unit's (group of units') recoverable amount is most sensitive.

(ii) a description of management's approach to determining the value(s) assigned to each key assumption, whether those value(s) reflect past experience or, if appropriate, are consistent with external sources of information, and, if not, how and why they differ from past experience or external sources of information.

(iii) the period over which management has projected cash flows based on financial budgets/forecasts approved by management and, when a period greater than five years is used for a cash-generating unit (group of units), an explanation of why that longer period is justified.

(iv) the growth rate used to extrapolate cash flow projections beyond the period covered by the most recent budgets/forecasts, and the justification for using any growth rate that exceeds the long-term average growth rate for the products, industries, or country or countries in which the entity operates, or for the market to which the unit (group of units) is dedicated.

(v) the discount rate(s) applied to the cash flow projections.

(e) if the unit's (group of units') recoverable amount is based on fair value less costs of disposal, the valuation technique(s) used to measure fair value less costs of disposal. An entity is not required to provide the disclosures required by IFRS 13. If fair value less costs of disposal is not measured using a quoted price for an identical unit (group of units), an entity shall disclose the following information:

(i) each key assumption on which management has based its determination of fair value less costs of disposal. Key assumptions are those to which the unit's (group of units') recoverable amount is most sensitive.

(ii) a description of management's approach to determining the value (or values) assigned to each key assumption, whether those values reflect past experience or, if appropriate, are consistent with external sources of information, and, if not, how and why they differ from past experience or external sources of information.

(iiA) the level of the fair value hierarchy (see IFRS 13) within which the fair value measurement is categorised in its entirety (without giving regard to the observability of 'costs of disposal').

(iiB) if there has been a change in valuation technique, the change and the reason(s) for making it.

If fair value less costs of disposal is measured using discounted cash flow projections, an entity shall disclose the following information:

(iii) the period over which management has projected cash flows.

(iv) the growth rate used to extrapolate cash flow projections.

(v) the discount rate(s) applied to the cash flow projections.

(f) if a reasonably possible change in a key assumption on which management has based its determination of the unit's (group of units') recoverable amount would cause the unit's (group of units') carrying amount to exceed its recoverable amount:

(i) the amount by which the unit's (group of units') recoverable amount exceeds its carrying amount.

(ii) the value assigned to the key assumption.

    (iii)   the amount by which the value assigned to the key assumption must change, after incorporating any consequential effects of that change on the other variables used to measure recoverable amount, in order for the unit's (group of units') recoverable amount to be equal to its carrying amount.

135   If some or all of the carrying amount of goodwill or intangible assets with indefinite useful lives is allocated across multiple cash-generating units (groups of units), and the amount so allocated to each unit (group of units) is not significant in comparison with the entity's total carrying amount of goodwill or intangible assets with indefinite useful lives, that fact shall be disclosed, together with the aggregate carrying amount of goodwill or intangible assets with indefinite useful lives allocated to those units (groups of units). In addition, if the recoverable amounts of any of those units (groups of units) are based on the same key assumption(s) and the aggregate carrying amount of goodwill or intangible assets with indefinite useful lives allocated to them is significant in comparison with the entity's total carrying amount of goodwill or intangible assets with indefinite useful lives, an entity shall disclose that fact, together with:

(a)   the aggregate carrying amount of goodwill allocated to those units (groups of units).

(b)   the aggregate carrying amount of intangible assets with indefinite useful lives allocated to those units (groups of units).

(c)   a description of the key assumption(s).

(d)   a description of management's approach to determining the value(s) assigned to the key assumption(s), whether those value(s) reflect past experience or, if appropriate, are consistent with external sources of information, and, if not, how and why they differ from past experience or external sources of information.

(e)   if a reasonably possible change in the key assumption(s) would cause the aggregate of the units' (groups of units') carrying amounts to exceed the aggregate of their recoverable amounts:

    (i)   the amount by which the aggregate of the units' (groups of units') recoverable amounts exceeds the aggregate of their carrying amounts.

    (ii)   the value(s) assigned to the key assumption(s).

    (iii)   the amount by which the value(s) assigned to the key assumption(s) must change, after incorporating any consequential effects of the change on the other variables used to measure recoverable amount, in order for the aggregate of the units' (groups of units') recoverable amounts to be equal to the aggregate of their carrying amounts.

136   The most recent detailed calculation made in a preceding period of the recoverable amount of a cash-generating unit (group of units) may, in accordance with paragraph 24 or 99, be carried forward and used in the impairment test for that unit (group of units) in the current period provided specified criteria are met. When this is the case, the information for that unit (group of units) that is incorporated into the disclosures required by paragraphs 134 and 135 relate to the carried forward calculation of recoverable amount.

137   Illustrative Example 9 illustrates the disclosures required by paragraphs 134 and 135.

Transitional provisions and effective date

138   [Deleted]

139   An entity shall apply this Standard:

   (a)   to goodwill and intangible assets acquired in business combinations for which the agreement date is on or after 31 March 2004; and

   (b)   to all other assets prospectively from the beginning of the first annual period beginning on or after 31 March 2004.

140   Entities to which paragraph 139 applies are encouraged to apply the requirements of this Standard before the effective dates specified in paragraph 139. However, if an entity applies this Standard before those effective dates, it also shall apply IFRS 3 and IAS 38 (as revised in 2004) at the same time.

140A   IAS 1 *Presentation of Financial Statements* (as revised in 2007) amended the terminology used throughout IFRSs. In addition it amended paragraphs 61, 120, 126 and 129. An entity shall apply those amendments for annual periods beginning on or after 1 January 2009. If an entity applies IAS 1 (revised 2007) for an earlier period, the amendments shall be applied for that earlier period.

140B   IFRS 3 (as revised in 2008) amended paragraphs 65, 81, 85 and 139, deleted paragraphs 91–95 and 138 and added Appendix C. An entity shall apply those amendments for annual periods beginning on or after 1 July 2009. If an entity applies IFRS 3 (revised 2008) for an earlier period, the amendments shall also be applied for that earlier period.

140C   Paragraph 134(e) was amended by *Improvements to IFRSs* issued in May 2008. An entity shall apply that amendment for annual periods beginning on or after 1 January 2009. Earlier application is permitted. If an entity applies the amendment for an earlier period it shall disclose that fact.

140D   *Cost of an Investment in a Subsidiary, Jointly Controlled Entity or Associate* (Amendments to IFRS 1 *First-time Adoption of International Financial Reporting Standards* and IAS 27), issued in May 2008, added paragraph 12(h). An entity shall apply that amendment prospectively for annual periods beginning on or after 1 January 2009. Earlier application is permitted. If an entity applies the related amendments in paragraphs 4 and 38A of IAS 27 for an earlier period, it shall apply the amendment in paragraph 12(h) at the same time.

140E   *Improvements to IFRSs* issued in April 2009 amended paragraph 80(b). An entity shall apply that amendment prospectively for annual periods beginning on or after 1 January 2010. Earlier application is permitted. If an entity applies the amendment for an earlier period it shall disclose that fact.

140F   [Deleted]

140G   IFRS 9, issued in October 2010, amended paragraphs 2(e) and 5 and deleted paragraph 140F. An entity shall apply those amendments when it applies IFRS 9 as issued in October 2010.

140H   IFRS 10 and IFRS 11, issued in May 2011, amended paragraph 4, the heading above paragraph 12(h) and paragraph 12(h). An entity shall apply those amendments when it applies IFRS 10 and IFRS 11.

140I   IFRS 13, issued in May 2011, amended paragraphs 5, 6, 12, 20, 28, 78, 105, 111, 130 and 134, deleted paragraphs 25–27 and added paragraph 53A. An entity shall apply those amendments when it applies IFRS 13.

Withdrawal of IAS 36 (issued 1998)

141   This Standard supersedes IAS 36 *Impairment of Assets* (issued in 1998).

Appendix A
Using present value techniques to measure value in use

This appendix is an integral part of the Standard. It provides guidance on the use of present value techniques in measuring value in use. Although the guidance uses the term 'asset', it equally applies to a group of assets forming a cash-generating unit.

The components of a present value measurement

A1 The following elements together capture the economic differences between assets:

    (a) an estimate of the future cash flow, or in more complex cases, series of future cash flows the entity expects to derive from the asset;

    (b) expectations about possible variations in the amount or timing of those cash flows;

    (c) the time value of money, represented by the current market risk-free rate of interest;

    (d) the price for bearing the uncertainty inherent in the asset; and

    (e) other, sometimes unidentifiable, factors (such as illiquidity) that market participants would reflect in pricing the future cash flows the entity expects to derive from the asset.

A2 This appendix contrasts two approaches to computing present value, either of which may be used to estimate the value in use of an asset, depending on the circumstances. Under the 'traditional' approach, adjustments for factors (b)–(e) described in paragraph A1 are embedded in the discount rate. Under the 'expected cash flow' approach, factors (b), (d) and (e) cause adjustments in arriving at risk-adjusted expected cash flows. Whichever approach an entity adopts to reflect expectations about possible variations in the amount or timing of future cash flows, the result should be to reflect the expected present value of the future cash flows, ie the weighted average of all possible outcomes.

General principles

A3 The techniques used to estimate future cash flows and interest rates will vary from one situation to another depending on the circumstances surrounding the asset in question. However, the following general principles govern any application of present value techniques in measuring assets:

    (a) interest rates used to discount cash flows should reflect assumptions that are consistent with those inherent in the estimated cash flows. Otherwise, the effect of some assumptions will be double-counted or ignored. For example, a discount rate of 12 per cent might be applied to contractual cash flows of a loan receivable. That rate reflects expectations about future defaults from loans with particular characteristics. That same 12 per cent rate should not be used to discount expected cash flows because those cash flows already reflect assumptions about future defaults.

(b)   estimated cash flows and discount rates should be free from both bias and factors unrelated to the asset in question. For example, deliberately understating estimated net cash flows to enhance the apparent future profitability of an asset introduces a bias into the measurement.

(c)   estimated cash flows or discount rates should reflect the range of possible outcomes rather than a single most likely, minimum or maximum possible amount.

Traditional and expected cash flow approaches to present value

Traditional approach

A4   Accounting applications of present value have traditionally used a single set of estimated cash flows and a single discount rate, often described as 'the rate commensurate with the risk'. In effect, the traditional approach assumes that a single discount rate convention can incorporate all the expectations about the future cash flows and the appropriate risk premium. Therefore, the traditional approach places most of the emphasis on selection of the discount rate.

A5   In some circumstances, such as those in which comparable assets can be observed in the marketplace, a traditional approach is relatively easy to apply. For assets with contractual cash flows, it is consistent with the manner in which marketplace participants describe assets, as in 'a 12 per cent bond'.

A6   However, the traditional approach may not appropriately address some complex measurement problems, such as the measurement of non-financial assets for which no market for the item or a comparable item exists. A proper search for 'the rate commensurate with the risk' requires analysis of at least two items—an asset that exists in the marketplace and has an observed interest rate and the asset being measured. The appropriate discount rate for the cash flows being measured must be inferred from the observable rate of interest in that other asset. To draw that inference, the characteristics of the other asset's cash flows must be similar to those of the asset being measured. Therefore, the measurer must do the following:

(a)   identify the set of cash flows that will be discounted;

(b)   identify another asset in the marketplace that appears to have similar cash flow characteristics;

(c)   compare the cash flow sets from the two items to ensure that they are similar (for example, are both sets contractual cash flows, or is one contractual and the other an estimated cash flow?);

(d)   evaluate whether there is an element in one item that is not present in the other (for example, is one less liquid than the other?); and

(e)   evaluate whether both sets of cash flows are likely to behave (ie vary) in a similar fashion in changing economic conditions.

Expected cash flow approach

A7 The expected cash flow approach is, in some situations, a more effective measurement tool than the traditional approach. In developing a measurement, the expected cash flow approach uses all expectations about possible cash flows instead of the single most likely cash flow. For example, a cash flow might be CU100, CU200 or CU300 with probabilities of 10 per cent, 60 per cent and 30 per cent, respectively. The expected cash flow is CU220. The expected cash flow approach thus differs from the traditional approach by focusing on direct analysis of the cash flows in question and on more explicit statements of the assumptions used in the measurement.

A8 The expected cash flow approach also allows use of present value techniques when the timing of cash flows is uncertain. For example, a cash flow of CU1,000 may be received in one year, two years or three years with probabilities of 10 per cent, 60 per cent and 30 per cent, respectively. The example below shows the computation of expected present value in that situation.

Present value of CU1,000 in 1 year at 5%	CU952.38	
Probability	10.00%	CU95.24
Present value of CU1,000 in 2 years at 5.25%	CU902.73	
Probability	60.00%	CU541.64
Present value of CU1,000 in 3 years at 5.50%	CU851.61	
Probability	30.00%	CU255.48
Expected present value		CU892.36

A9 The expected present value of CU892.36 differs from the traditional notion of a best estimate of CU902.73 (the 60 per cent probability). A traditional present value computation applied to this example requires a decision about which of the possible timings of cash flows to use and, accordingly, would not reflect the probabilities of other timings. This is because the discount rate in a traditional present value computation cannot reflect uncertainties in timing.

A10 The use of probabilities is an essential element of the expected cash flow approach. Some question whether assigning probabilities to highly subjective estimates suggests greater precision than, in fact, exists. However, the proper application of the traditional approach (as described in paragraph A6) requires the same estimates and subjectivity without providing the computational transparency of the expected cash flow approach.

A11 Many estimates developed in current practice already incorporate the elements of expected cash flows informally. In addition, accountants often face the need to measure an asset using limited information about the probabilities of possible cash flows. For example, an accountant might be confronted with the following situations:

(a) the estimated amount falls somewhere between CU50 and CU250, but no amount in the range is more likely than any other amount. Based on that limited information, the estimated expected cash flow is CU150 [(50 + 250)/2].

(b)   the estimated amount falls somewhere between CU50 and CU250, and the most likely amount is CU100. However, the probabilities attached to each amount are unknown. Based on that limited information, the estimated expected cash flow is CU133.33 [(50 + 100 + 250)/3].

(c)   the estimated amount will be CU50 (10 per cent probability), CU250 (30 per cent probability), or CU100 (60 per cent probability). Based on that limited information, the estimated expected cash flow is CU140 [(50 × 0.10) + (250 × 0.30) + (100 × 0.60)].

In each case, the estimated expected cash flow is likely to provide a better estimate of value in use than the minimum, most likely or maximum amount taken alone.

A12   The application of an expected cash flow approach is subject to a cost-benefit constraint. In some cases, an entity may have access to extensive data and may be able to develop many cash flow scenarios. In other cases, an entity may not be able to develop more than general statements about the variability of cash flows without incurring substantial cost. The entity needs to balance the cost of obtaining additional information against the additional reliability that information will bring to the measurement.

A13   Some maintain that expected cash flow techniques are inappropriate for measuring a single item or an item with a limited number of possible outcomes. They offer an example of an asset with two possible outcomes: a 90 per cent probability that the cash flow will be CU10 and a 10 per cent probability that the cash flow will be CU1,000. They observe that the expected cash flow in that example is CU109 and criticise that result as not representing either of the amounts that may ultimately be paid.

A14   Assertions like the one just outlined reflect underlying disagreement with the measurement objective. If the objective is accumulation of costs to be incurred, expected cash flows may not produce a representationally faithful estimate of the expected cost. However, this Standard is concerned with measuring the recoverable amount of an asset. The recoverable amount of the asset in this example is not likely to be CU10, even though that is the most likely cash flow. This is because a measurement of CU10 does not incorporate the uncertainty of the cash flow in the measurement of the asset. Instead, the uncertain cash flow is presented as if it were a certain cash flow. No rational entity would sell an asset with these characteristics for CU10.

Discount rate

A15   Whichever approach an entity adopts for measuring the value in use of an asset, interest rates used to discount cash flows should not reflect risks for which the estimated cash flows have been adjusted. Otherwise, the effect of some assumptions will be double-counted.

A16   When an asset-specific rate is not directly available from the market, an entity uses surrogates to estimate the discount rate. The purpose is to estimate, as far as possible, a market assessment of:

(a)   the time value of money for the periods until the end of the asset's useful life; and

(b)   factors (b), (d) and (e) described in paragraph A1, to the extent those factors have not caused adjustments in arriving at estimated cash flows.

A17   As a starting point in making such an estimate, the entity might take into account the following rates:

(a)   the entity's weighted average cost of capital determined using techniques such as the Capital Asset Pricing Model;

(b)   the entity's incremental borrowing rate; and

(c)   other market borrowing rates.

A18   However, these rates must be adjusted:

(a)   to reflect the way that the market would assess the specific risks associated with the asset's estimated cash flows; and

(b)   to exclude risks that are not relevant to the asset's estimated cash flows or for which the estimated cash flows have been adjusted.

Consideration should be given to risks such as country risk, currency risk and price risk.

A19   The discount rate is independent of the entity's capital structure and the way the entity financed the purchase of the asset, because the future cash flows expected to arise from an asset do not depend on the way in which the entity financed the purchase of the asset.

A20   Paragraph 55 requires the discount rate used to be a pre-tax rate. Therefore, when the basis used to estimate the discount rate is post-tax, that basis is adjusted to reflect a pre-tax rate.

A21   An entity normally uses a single discount rate for the estimate of an asset's value in use. However, an entity uses separate discount rates for different future periods where value in use is sensitive to a difference in risks for different periods or to the term structure of interest rates.

Appendix B
Amendment to IAS 16

The amendment in this appendix shall be applied when an entity applies IAS 16 Property, Plant and Equipment *(as revised in 2003). It is superseded when IAS 36* Impairment of Assets *(as revised in 2004) becomes effective. This appendix replaces the consequential amendments made by IAS 16 (as revised in 2003) to IAS 36* Impairment of Asset *(issued in 1998). IAS 36 (as revised in 2004) incorporates the requirements of the paragraphs in this appendix. Consequently, the amendments from IAS 16 (as revised in 2003) are not necessary once an entity is subject to IAS 36 (as revised in 2004). Accordingly, this appendix is applicable only to entities that elect to apply IAS 16 (as revised in 2003) before its effective date.*

* * * * *

The text of this appendix has been omitted from this volume.

Appendix C
Impairment testing cash-generating units with goodwill and non-controlling interests

This appendix is an integral part of the Standard.

C1   In accordance with IFRS 3 (as revised in 2008), the acquirer measures and recognises goodwill as of the acquisition date as the excess of (a) over (b) below:

      (a)   the aggregate of:

          (i)   the consideration transferred measured in accordance with IFRS 3, which generally requires acquisition-date fair value;

          (ii)   the amount of any non-controlling interest in the acquiree measured in accordance with IFRS 3; and

          (iii)   in a business combination achieved in stages, the acquisition-date fair value of the acquirer's previously held equity interest in the acquiree.

      (b)   the net of the acquisition-date amounts of the identifiable assets acquired and liabilities assumed measured in accordance with IFRS 3.

Allocation of goodwill

C2   Paragraph 80 of this Standard requires goodwill acquired in a business combination to be allocated to each of the acquirer's cash-generating units, or groups of cash-generating units, expected to benefit from the synergies of the combination, irrespective of whether other assets or liabilities of the acquiree are assigned to those units, or groups of units. It is possible that some of the synergies resulting from a business combination will be allocated to a cash-generating unit in which the non-controlling interest does not have an interest.

Testing for impairment

C3   Testing for impairment involves comparing the recoverable amount of a cash-generating unit with the carrying amount of the cash-generating unit.

C4   If an entity measures non-controlling interests as its proportionate interest in the net identifiable assets of a subsidiary at the acquisition date, rather than at fair value, goodwill attributable to non-controlling interests is included in the recoverable amount of the related cash-generating unit but is not recognised in the parent's consolidated financial statements. As a consequence, an entity shall gross up the carrying amount of goodwill allocated to the unit to include the goodwill attributable to the non-controlling interest. This adjusted carrying amount is then compared with the recoverable amount of the unit to determine whether the cash-generating unit is impaired.

Allocating an impairment loss

C5 Paragraph 104 requires any identified impairment loss to be allocated first to reduce the carrying amount of goodwill allocated to the unit and then to the other assets of the unit pro rata on the basis of the carrying amount of each asset in the unit.

C6 If a subsidiary, or part of a subsidiary, with a non-controlling interest is itself a cash-generating unit, the impairment loss is allocated between the parent and the non-controlling interest on the same basis as that on which profit or loss is allocated.

C7 If a subsidiary, or part of a subsidiary, with a non-controlling interest is part of a larger cash-generating unit, goodwill impairment losses are allocated to the parts of the cash-generating unit that have a non-controlling interest and the parts that do not. The impairment losses should be allocated to the parts of the cash-generating unit on the basis of:

(a) to the extent that the impairment relates to goodwill in the cash-generating unit, the relative carrying values of the goodwill of the parts before the impairment; and

(b) to the extent that the impairment relates to identifiable assets in the cash-generating unit, the relative carrying values of the net identifiable assets of the parts before the impairment. Any such impairment is allocated to the assets of the parts of each unit pro rata on the basis of the carrying amount of each asset in the part.

In those parts that have a non-controlling interest, the impairment loss is allocated between the parent and the non-controlling interest on the same basis as that on which profit or loss is allocated.

C8 If an impairment loss attributable to a non-controlling interest relates to goodwill that is not recognised in the parent's consolidated financial statements (see paragraph C4), that impairment is not recognised as a goodwill impairment loss. In such cases, only the impairment loss relating to the goodwill that is allocated to the parent is recognised as a goodwill impairment loss.

C9 Illustrative Example 7 illustrates the impairment testing of a non-wholly-owned cash-generating unit with goodwill.

International Accounting Standard 37

Provisions, Contingent Liabilities and Contingent Assets

In April 2001 the International Accounting Standards Board (IASB) adopted IAS 37 *Provisions, Contingent Liabilities and Contingent Assets*, which had originally been issued by the International Accounting Standards Committee in September 1998. That standard replaced parts of IAS 10 *Contingencies and Events Occurring after the Balance Sheet Date* that was issued in 1978 and that dealt with contingencies.

Other IFRSs have made minor consequential amendments to IAS 37. They include IAS 16 *Property, Plant and Equipment* (as revised in December 2003), IAS 39 *Financial Instruments: Recognition and Measurement* (as revised in December 2003), IFRS 3 *Business Combinations* (issued March 2004 and revised in January 2008), IAS 1 *Presentation of Financial Statements* (as revised in September 2007) and IFRS 9 *Financial Instruments* (issued in October 2010).

Contents

FOR THE ACCOMPANYING DOCUMENTS LISTED BELOW, SEE PART B OF THIS EDITION

IMPLEMENTATION GUIDANCE

A Tables – Provisions, contingent liabilities, contingent assets and reimbursements

B Decision tree

C Examples: recognition

D Examples: disclosures

International Accounting Standard 37 *Provisions, Contingent Liabilities and Contingent Assets* (IAS 37) is set out in paragraphs 1–97. All the paragraphs have equal authority but retain the IASC format of the Standard when it was adopted by the IASB. IAS 37 should be read in the context of its objective, the *Preface to International Financial Reporting Standards* and the *Conceptual Framework for Financial Reporting*. IAS 8 *Accounting Policies, Changes in Accounting Estimates and Errors* provides a basis for selecting and applying accounting policies in the absence of explicit guidance.

Introduction

IN1 IAS 37 prescribes the accounting and disclosure for all provisions, contingent liabilities and contingent assets, except:

    (a) those resulting from financial instruments that are carried at fair value;

    (b) those resulting from executory contracts, except where the contract is onerous. Executory contracts are contracts under which neither party has performed any of its obligations or both parties have partially performed their obligations to an equal extent;

    (c) those arising in insurance entities from contracts with policyholders; or

    (d) those covered by another Standard.

Provisions

IN2 The Standard defines provisions as liabilities of uncertain timing or amount. A provision should be recognised when, and only when:

    (a) an entity has a present obligation (legal or constructive) as a result of a past event;

    (b) it is probable (ie more likely than not) that an outflow of resources embodying economic benefits will be required to settle the obligation; and

    (c) a reliable estimate can be made of the amount of the obligation. The Standard notes that it is only in extremely rare cases that a reliable estimate will not be possible.

IN3 The Standard defines a constructive obligation as an obligation that derives from an entity's actions where:

    (a) by an established pattern of past practice, published policies or a sufficiently specific current statement, the entity has indicated to other parties that it will accept certain responsibilities; and

    (b) as a result, the entity has created a valid expectation on the part of those other parties that it will discharge those responsibilities.

IN4 In rare cases, for example in a lawsuit, it may not be clear whether an entity has a present obligation. In these cases, a past event is deemed to give rise to a present obligation if, taking account of all available evidence, it is more likely than not that a present obligation exists at the end of the reporting period. An entity recognises a provision for that present obligation if the other recognition criteria described above are met. If it is more likely than not that no present obligation exists, the entity discloses a contingent liability, unless the possibility of an outflow of resources embodying economic benefits is remote.

IN5   The amount recognised as a provision should be the best estimate of the expenditure required to settle the present obligation at the end of the reporting period, in other words, the amount that an entity would rationally pay to settle the obligation at the end of the reporting period or to transfer it to a third party at that time.

IN6   The Standard requires that an entity should, in measuring a provision:

(a)   take risks and uncertainties into account. However, uncertainty does not justify the creation of excessive provisions or a deliberate overstatement of liabilities;

(b)   discount the provisions, where the effect of the time value of money is material, using a pre-tax discount rate (or rates) that reflect(s) current market assessments of the time value of money and those risks specific to the liability that have not been reflected in the best estimate of the expenditure. Where discounting is used, the increase in the provision due to the passage of time is recognised as an interest expense;

(c)   take future events, such as changes in the law and technological changes, into account where there is sufficient objective evidence that they will occur; and

(d)   not take gains from the expected disposal of assets into account, even if the expected disposal is closely linked to the event giving rise to the provision.

IN7   An entity may expect reimbursement of some or all of the expenditure required to settle a provision (for example, through insurance contracts, indemnity clauses or suppliers' warranties). An entity should:

(a)   recognise a reimbursement when, and only when, it is virtually certain that reimbursement will be received if the entity settles the obligation. The amount recognised for the reimbursement should not exceed the amount of the provision; and

(b)   recognise the reimbursement as a separate asset. In the statement of comprehensive income, the expense relating to a provision may be presented net of the amount recognised for a reimbursement.

IN8   Provisions should be reviewed at the end of each reporting period and adjusted to reflect the current best estimate. If it is no longer probable that an outflow of resources embodying economic benefits will be required to settle the obligation, the provision should be reversed.

IN9   A provision should be used only for expenditures for which the provision was originally recognised.

Provisions – specific applications

IN10 The Standard explains how the general recognition and measurement requirements for provisions should be applied in three specific cases: future operating losses; onerous contracts ; and restructurings.

IN11 Provisions should not be recognised for future operating losses. An expectation of future operating losses is an indication that certain assets of the operation may be impaired. In this case, an entity tests these assets for impairment under IAS 36 *Impairment of Assets*.

IN12 If an entity has a contract that is onerous, the present obligation under the contract should be recognised and measured as a provision. An onerous contract is one in which the unavoidable costs of meeting the obligations under the contract exceed the economic benefits expected to be received under it.

IN13 The Standard defines a restructuring as a programme that is planned and controlled by management, and materially changes either:

(a) the scope of a business undertaken by an entity; or

(b) the manner in which that business is conducted.

IN14 A provision for restructuring costs is recognised only when the general recognition criteria for provisions are met. In this context, a constructive obligation to restructure arises only when an entity:

(a) has a detailed formal plan for the restructuring identifying at least:

(i) the business or part of a business concerned;

(ii) the principal locations affected;

(iii) the location, function, and approximate number of employees who will be compensated for terminating their services;

(iv) the expenditures that will be undertaken; and

(v) when the plan will be implemented; and

(b) has raised a valid expectation in those affected that it will carry out the restructuring by starting to implement that plan or announcing its main features to those affected by it.

IN15 A management or board decision to restructure does not give rise to a constructive obligation at the end of the reporting period unless the entity has, before the end of the reporting period:

(a) started to implement the restructuring plan; or

(b) communicated the restructuring plan to those affected by it in a sufficiently specific manner to raise a valid expectation in them that the entity will carry out the restructuring.

IN16 Where a restructuring involves the sale of an operation, no obligation arises for the sale until the entity is committed to the sale, ie there is a binding sale agreement.

IN17 A restructuring provision should include only the direct expenditures arising from the restructuring, which are those that are both:

    (a) necessarily entailed by the restructuring; and

    (b) not associated with the ongoing activities of the entity. Thus, a restructuring provision does not include such costs as: retraining or relocating continuing staff; marketing; or investment in new systems and distribution networks.

Contingent liabilities

IN18 The Standard defines a contingent liability as:

    (a) a possible obligation that arises from past events and whose existence will be confirmed only by the occurrence or non-occurrence of one or more uncertain future events not wholly within the control of the entity; or

    (b) a present obligation that arises from past events but is not recognised because:

        (i) it is not probable that an outflow of resources embodying economic benefits will be required to settle the obligation; or

        (ii) the amount of the obligation cannot be measured with sufficient reliability.

IN19 An entity should not recognise a contingent liability. An entity should disclose a contingent liability, unless the possibility of an outflow of resources embodying economic benefits is remote.

Contingent assets

IN20 The Standard defines a contingent asset as a possible asset that arises from past events and whose existence will be confirmed only by the occurrence or non-occurrence of one or more uncertain future events not wholly within the control of the entity. An example is a claim that an entity is pursuing through legal processes, where the outcome is uncertain.

IN21 An entity should not recognise a contingent asset. A contingent asset should be disclosed where an inflow of economic benefits is probable.

IN22 When the realisation of income is virtually certain, then the related asset is not a contingent asset and its recognition is appropriate.

Effective date

IN23 The Standard becomes operative for annual financial statements covering periods beginning on or after 1 July 1999. Earlier application is encouraged.

International Accounting Standard 37
Provisions, Contingent Liabilities and Contingent Assets

Objective

The objective of this Standard is to ensure that appropriate recognition criteria and measurement bases are applied to provisions, contingent liabilities and contingent assets and that sufficient information is disclosed in the notes to enable users to understand their nature, timing and amount.

Scope

1 **This Standard shall be applied by all entities in accounting for provisions, contingent liabilities and contingent assets, except:**

   (a) **those resulting from executory contracts, except where the contract is onerous; and**

   (b) [deleted]

   (c) **those covered by another Standard.**

2 This Standard does not apply to financial instruments (including guarantees) that are within the scope of IFRS 9 *Financial Instruments*.

3 Executory contracts are contracts under which neither party has performed any of its obligations or both parties have partially performed their obligations to an equal extent. This Standard does not apply to executory   contracts unless they are onerous.

4 [Deleted]

5 When another Standard deals with a specific type of provision, contingent liability or contingent asset, an entity applies that Standard instead of this Standard. For example, some types of provisions are addressed in Standards on:

   (a) construction contracts (see IAS 11 *Construction Contracts*);

   (b) income taxes (see IAS 12 *Income Taxes*);

   (c) leases (see IAS 17 *Leases*). However, as IAS 17 contains no specific requirements to deal with operating leases that have become onerous, this Standard applies to such cases;

   (d) employee benefits (see IAS 19 *Employee Benefits*); and

   (e) insurance contracts (see IFRS 4 *Insurance Contracts*). However, this Standard applies to provisions, contingent liabilities and contingent assets of an insurer, other than those arising from its contractual obligations and rights under insurance contracts within the scope of IFRS 4.

6   Some amounts treated as provisions may relate to the recognition of revenue, for example where an entity gives guarantees in exchange for a fee. This Standard does not address the recognition of revenue. IAS 18 *Revenue* identifies the circumstances in which revenue is recognised and provides practical guidance on the application of the recognition criteria. This Standard does not change the requirements of IAS 18.

7   This Standard defines provisions as liabilities of uncertain timing or amount. In some countries the term 'provision' is also used in the context of items such as depreciation, impairment of assets and doubtful debts: these are adjustments to the carrying amounts of assets and are not addressed in this Standard.

8   Other Standards specify whether expenditures are treated as assets or as expenses. These issues are not addressed in this Standard. Accordingly, this Standard neither prohibits nor requires capitalisation of the costs recognised when a provision is made.

9   This Standard applies to provisions for restructurings (including discontinued operations). When a restructuring meets the definition of a discontinued operation, additional disclosures may be required by IFRS 5 *Non-current Assets Held for Sale and Discontinued Operations*.

Definitions

10   The following terms are used in this Standard with the meanings specified:

A *provision* is a liability of uncertain timing or amount.

A *liability* is a present obligation of the entity arising from past events, the settlement of which is expected to result in an outflow from the entity of resources embodying economic benefits.

An *obligating event* is an event that creates a legal or constructive obligation that results in an entity having no realistic alternative to settling that obligation.

A *legal obligation* is an obligation that derives from:

(a)   a contract (through its explicit or implicit terms);

(b)   legislation; or

(c)   other operation of law.

A *constructive obligation* is an obligation that derives from an entity's actions where:

(a)   by an established pattern of past practice, published policies or a sufficiently specific current statement, the entity has indicated to other parties that it will accept certain responsibilities; and

(b)   as a result, the entity has created a valid expectation on the part of those other parties that it will discharge those responsibilities.

A *contingent liability* is:

(a)   a possible obligation that arises from past events and whose existence will be confirmed only by the occurrence or non-occurrence of one or more uncertain future events not wholly within the control of the entity; or

(b)   a present obligation that arises from past events but is not recognised because:

    (i)   it is not probable that an outflow of resources embodying economic benefits will be required to settle the obligation; or

    (ii)   the amount of the obligation cannot be measured with sufficient reliability.

A *contingent asset* is a possible asset that arises from past events and whose existence will be confirmed only by the occurrence or non-occurrence of one or more uncertain future events not wholly within the control of the entity.

An *onerous contract* is a contract in which the unavoidable costs of meeting the obligations under the contract exceed the economic benefits expected to be received under it.

A *restructuring* is a programme that is planned and controlled by management, and materially changes either:

(a)   the scope of a business undertaken by an entity; or

(b)   the manner in which that business is conducted.

Provisions and other liabilities

11   Provisions can be distinguished from other liabilities such as trade payables and accruals because there is uncertainty about the timing or amount of the future expenditure required in settlement. By contrast:

(a)   trade payables are liabilities to pay for goods or services that have been received or supplied and have been invoiced or formally agreed with the supplier; and

(b)   accruals are liabilities to pay for goods or services that have been received or supplied but have not been paid, invoiced or formally agreed with the supplier, including amounts due to employees (for example, amounts relating to accrued vacation pay). Although it is sometimes necessary to estimate the amount or timing of accruals, the uncertainty is generally much less than for provisions.

Accruals are often reported as part of trade and other payables, whereas provisions are reported separately.

Relationship between provisions and contingent liabilities

12   In a general sense, all provisions are contingent because they are uncertain in timing or amount. However, within this Standard the term 'contingent' is used for liabilities and assets that are not recognised because their existence will be confirmed only by the occurrence or non-occurrence of one or more uncertain future events not wholly within the control of the entity. In addition, the term 'contingent liability' is used for liabilities that do not meet the recognition criteria.

13   This Standard distinguishes between:

   (a)   provisions – which are recognised as liabilities (assuming that a reliable estimate can be made) because they are present obligations and it is probable that an outflow of resources embodying economic benefits will be required to settle the obligations; and

   (b)   contingent liabilities – which are not recognised as liabilities because they are either:

      (i)   possible obligations, as it has yet to be confirmed whether the entity has a present obligation that could lead to an outflow of resources embodying economic benefits; or

      (ii)   present obligations that do not meet the recognition criteria in this Standard (because either it is not probable that an outflow of resources embodying economic benefits will be required to settle the obligation, or a sufficiently reliable estimate of the amount of the obligation cannot be made).

Recognition

Provisions

14   A provision shall be recognised when:

   (a)   an entity has a present obligation (legal or constructive) as a result of a past event;

   (b)   it is probable that an outflow of resources embodying economic benefits will be required to settle the obligation; and

   (c)   a reliable estimate can be made of the amount of the obligation.

If these conditions are not met, no provision shall be recognised.

Present obligation

15   In rare cases it is not clear whether there is a present obligation. In these cases, a past event is deemed to give rise to a present obligation if, taking account of all available evidence, it is more likely than not that a present obligation exists at the end of the reporting period.

16   In almost all cases it will be clear whether a past event has given rise to a present obligation. In rare cases, for example in a lawsuit, it may be disputed either whether certain events have occurred or whether those events result in a present obligation. In such a case, an entity determines whether a present obligation exists at the end of the reporting period by taking account of all available evidence, including, for example, the opinion of experts. The evidence considered includes any additional evidence provided by events after the reporting period. On the basis of such evidence:

(a)   where it is more likely than not that a present obligation exists at the end of the reporting period, the entity recognises a provision (if the recognition criteria are met); and

(b)   where it is more likely that no present obligation exists at the end of the reporting period, the entity discloses a contingent liability, unless the possibility of an outflow of resources embodying economic benefits is remote (see paragraph 86).

Past event

17   A past event that leads to a present obligation is called an obligating event. For an event to be an obligating event, it is necessary that the entity has no realistic alternative to settling the obligation created by the event. This is the case only:

(a)   where the settlement of the obligation can be enforced by law; or

(b)   in the case of a constructive obligation, where the event (which may be an action of the entity) creates valid expectations in other parties that the entity will discharge the obligation.

18   Financial statements deal with the financial position of an entity at the end of its reporting period and not its possible position in the future. Therefore, no provision is recognised for costs that need to be incurred to operate in the future. The only liabilities recognised in an entity's statement of financial position are those that exist at the end of the reporting period.

19   It is only those obligations arising from past events existing independently of an entity's future actions (ie the future conduct of its business) that are recognised as provisions. Examples of such obligations are penalties or clean-up costs for unlawful environmental damage, both of which would lead to an outflow of resources embodying economic benefits in settlement regardless of the future actions of the entity. Similarly, an entity recognises a provision for the decommissioning costs of an oil installation or a nuclear power station to the extent that the entity is obliged to rectify damage already caused. In contrast, because of commercial pressures or legal requirements, an entity may intend or need to carry out expenditure to operate in a particular way in the future (for example, by fitting smoke filters in a certain type of factory). Because the entity can avoid the future expenditure by its future actions, for example by changing its method of operation, it has no present obligation for that future expenditure and no provision is recognised.

20   An obligation always involves another party to whom the obligation is owed. It is not necessary, however, to know the identity of the party to whom the obligation is owed—indeed the obligation may be to the public at large. Because an obligation always involves a commitment to another party, it follows that a management or board decision does not give rise to a constructive obligation at the end of the reporting period unless the decision has been communicated before the end of the reporting period to those affected by it in a sufficiently specific manner to raise a valid expectation in them that the entity will discharge its responsibilities.

21   An event that does not give rise to an obligation immediately may do so at a later date, because of changes in the law or because an act (for example, a sufficiently specific public statement) by the entity gives rise to a constructive obligation. For example, when environmental damage is caused there may be no obligation to remedy the consequences. However, the causing of the damage will become an obligating event when a new law requires the existing damage to be rectified or when the entity publicly accepts responsibility for rectification in a way that creates a constructive obligation.

22   Where details of a proposed new law have yet to be finalised, an obligation arises only when the legislation is virtually certain to be enacted as drafted. For the purpose of this Standard, such an obligation is treated as a legal obligation. Differences in circumstances surrounding enactment make it impossible to specify a single event that would make the enactment of a law virtually certain. In many cases it will be impossible to be virtually certain of the enactment of a law until it is enacted.

Probable outflow of resources embodying economic benefits

23   For a liability to qualify for recognition there must be not only a present obligation   but also the probability of an outflow of resources embodying economic benefits to settle that obligation. For the purpose of this Standard,[1] an outflow of resources or other event is regarded as probable if the event is more likely than not to occur, ie the probability that the event will occur is greater than the probability that it will not. Where it is not probable that a present obligation exists, an entity discloses a contingent liability, unless the possibility of an outflow of resources embodying economic benefits is remote (see paragraph 86).

24   Where there are a number of similar obligations (eg product warranties or similar contracts) the probability that an outflow will be required in settlement is determined by considering the class of obligations as a whole. Although the likelihood of outflow for any one item may be small, it may well be probable that some outflow of resources will be needed to settle the class of obligations as a whole. If that is the case, a provision is recognised (if the other recognition criteria are met).

---

[1]   The interpretation of 'probable' in this Standard as 'more likely than not' does not necessarily apply in other Standards.

© IFRS Foundation

Reliable estimate of the obligation

25   The use of estimates is an essential part of the preparation of financial statements and does not undermine their reliability. This is especially true in the case of provisions, which by their nature are more uncertain than most other items in the statement of financial position. Except in extremely rare cases, an entity will be able to determine a range of possible outcomes and can therefore make an estimate of the obligation that is sufficiently reliable to use in recognising a provision.

26   In the extremely rare case where no reliable estimate can be made, a liability exists that cannot be recognised. That liability is disclosed as a contingent liability (see paragraph 86).

Contingent liabilities

27   **An entity shall not recognise a contingent liability.**

28   A contingent liability is disclosed, as required by paragraph 86, unless the possibility of an outflow of resources embodying economic benefits is remote.

29   Where an entity is jointly and severally liable for an obligation, the part of the obligation that is expected to be met by other parties is treated as a contingent liability. The entity recognises a provision for the part of the obligation for which an outflow of resources embodying economic benefits is probable, except in the extremely rare circumstances where no reliable estimate can be made.

30   Contingent liabilities may develop in a way not initially expected. Therefore, they are assessed continually to determine whether an outflow of resources embodying economic benefits has become probable. If it becomes probable that an outflow of future economic benefits will be required for an item previously dealt with as a contingent liability, a provision is recognised in the financial statements of the period in which the change in probability occurs (except in the extremely rare circumstances where no reliable estimate can be made).

Contingent assets

31   **An entity shall not recognise a contingent asset.**

32   Contingent assets usually arise from unplanned or other unexpected events that give rise to the possibility of an inflow of economic benefits to the entity. An example is a claim that an entity is pursuing through legal processes, where the outcome is uncertain.

33   Contingent assets are not recognised in financial statements since this may result in the recognition of income that may never be realised. However, when the realisation of income is virtually certain, then the related asset is not a contingent asset and its recognition is appropriate.

34   A contingent asset is disclosed, as required by paragraph 89, where an inflow of economic benefits is probable.

35   Contingent assets are assessed continually to ensure that developments are appropriately reflected in the financial statements. If it has become virtually certain that an inflow of economic benefits will arise, the asset and the related income are recognised in the financial statements of the period in which the change occurs. If an inflow of economic benefits has become probable, an entity discloses the contingent asset (see paragraph 89).

Measurement

Best estimate

36   **The amount recognised as a provision shall be the best estimate of the expenditure required to settle the present obligation at the end of the reporting period.**

37   The best estimate of the expenditure required to settle the present obligation is the amount that an entity would rationally pay to settle the obligation at the end of the reporting period or to transfer it to a third party at that time. It will often be impossible or prohibitively expensive to settle or transfer an obligation at the end of the reporting period. However, the estimate of the amount that an entity would rationally pay to settle or transfer the obligation gives the best estimate of the expenditure required to settle the present obligation at the end of the reporting period.

38   The estimates of outcome and financial effect are determined by the judgement of the management of the entity, supplemented by experience of similar transactions and, in some cases, reports from independent experts. The evidence considered includes any additional evidence provided by events after the reporting period.

39   Uncertainties surrounding the amount to be recognised as a provision are dealt with by various means according to the circumstances. Where the provision being measured involves a large population of items, the obligation is estimated by weighting all possible outcomes by their associated probabilities. The name for this statistical method of estimation is 'expected value'. The provision will therefore be different depending on whether the probability of a loss of a given amount is, for example, 60 per cent or 90 per cent. Where there is a continuous range of possible outcomes, and each point in that range is as likely as any other, the mid-point of the range is used.

Example

An entity sells goods with a warranty under which customers are covered for the cost of repairs of any manufacturing defects that become apparent within the first six months after purchase. If minor defects were detected in all products sold, repair costs of 1 million would result. If major defects were detected in all products sold, repair costs of 4 million would result. The entity's past experience and future expectations indicate that, for the coming year, 75 per cent of the goods sold will have no defects, 20 per cent of the goods sold will have minor defects and 5 per cent of the goods sold will have major defects. In accordance with paragraph 24, an entity assesses the probability of an outflow for the warranty obligations as a whole.

The expected value of the cost of repairs is:

(75% of nil) + (20% of 1m) + (5% of 4m) = 400,000

---

40   Where a single obligation is being measured, the individual most likely outcome may be the best estimate of the liability. However, even in such a case, the entity considers other possible outcomes. Where other possible outcomes are either mostly higher or mostly lower than the most likely outcome, the best estimate will be a higher or lower amount. For example, if an entity has to rectify a serious fault in a major plant that it has constructed for a customer, the individual most likely outcome may be for the repair to succeed at the first attempt at a cost of 1,000, but a provision for a larger amount is made if there is a significant chance that further attempts will be necessary.

41   The provision is measured before tax, as the tax consequences of the provision, and changes in it, are dealt with under IAS 12.

Risks and uncertainties

42   **The risks and uncertainties that inevitably surround many events and circumstances shall be taken into account in reaching the best estimate of a provision.**

43   Risk describes variability of outcome. A risk adjustment may increase the amount at which a liability is measured. Caution is needed in making judgements under conditions of uncertainty, so that income or assets are not overstated and expenses or liabilities are not understated. However, uncertainty does not justify the creation of excessive provisions or a deliberate overstatement of liabilities. For example, if the projected costs of a particularly adverse outcome are estimated on a prudent basis, that outcome is not then deliberately treated as more probable than is realistically the case. Care is needed to avoid duplicating adjustments for risk and uncertainty with consequent overstatement of a provision.

44   Disclosure of the uncertainties surrounding the amount of the expenditure is made under paragraph 85(b).

Present value

45   **Where the effect of the time value of money is material, the amount of a provision shall be the present value of the expenditures expected to be required to settle the obligation.**

46   Because of the time value of money, provisions relating to cash outflows that arise soon after the reporting period are more onerous than those where cash outflows of the same amount arise later. Provisions are therefore discounted, where the effect is material.

47   **The discount rate (or rates) shall be a pre-tax rate (or rates) that reflect(s) current market assessments of the time value of money and the risks specific to the liability. The discount rate(s) shall not reflect risks for which future cash flow estimates have been adjusted.**

Future events

48   **Future events that may affect the amount required to settle an obligation shall be reflected in the amount of a provision where there is sufficient objective evidence that they will occur.**

49   Expected future events may be particularly important in measuring provisions. For example, an entity may believe that the cost of cleaning up a site at the end of its life will be reduced by future changes in technology. The amount recognised reflects a reasonable expectation of technically qualified, objective observers, taking account of all available evidence as to the technology that will be available at the time of the clean-up. Thus it is appropriate to include, for example, expected cost reductions associated with increased experience in applying existing technology or the expected cost of applying existing technology to a larger or more complex clean-up operation than has previously been carried out. However, an entity does not anticipate the development of a completely new technology for cleaning up unless it is supported by sufficient objective evidence.

50   The effect of possible new legislation is taken into consideration in measuring an existing obligation when sufficient objective evidence exists that the legislation is virtually certain to be enacted. The variety of circumstances that arise in practice makes it impossible to specify a single event that will provide sufficient, objective evidence in every case. Evidence is required both of what legislation will demand and of whether it is virtually certain to be enacted and implemented in due course. In many cases sufficient objective evidence will not exist until the new legislation is enacted.

Expected disposal of assets

51   **Gains from the expected disposal of assets shall not be taken into account in measuring a provision.**

52   Gains on the expected disposal of assets are not taken into account in measuring a provision, even if the expected disposal is closely linked to the event giving rise to the provision. Instead, an entity recognises gains on expected disposals of assets at the time specified by the Standard dealing with the assets concerned.

Reimbursements

53   Where some or all of the expenditure required to settle a provision is expected to be reimbursed by another party, the reimbursement shall be recognised when, and only when, it is virtually certain that reimbursement will be received if the entity settles the obligation. The reimbursement shall be treated as a separate asset. The amount recognised for the reimbursement shall not exceed the amount of the provision.

54   In the statement of comprehensive income, the expense relating to a provision may be presented net of the amount recognised for a reimbursement.

55   Sometimes, an entity is able to look to another party to pay part or all of the expenditure required to settle a provision (for example, through insurance contracts, indemnity clauses or suppliers' warranties). The other party may either reimburse amounts paid by the entity or pay the amounts directly.

56   In most cases the entity will remain liable for the whole of the amount in question so that the entity would have to settle the full amount if the third party failed to pay for any reason. In this situation, a provision is recognised for the full amount of the liability, and a separate asset for the expected reimbursement is recognised when it is virtually certain that reimbursement will be received if the entity settles the liability.

57   In some cases, the entity will not be liable for the costs in question if the third party fails to pay. In such a case the entity has no liability for those costs and they are not included in the provision.

58   As noted in paragraph 29, an obligation for which an entity is jointly and severally liable is a contingent liability to the extent that it is expected that the obligation will be settled by the other parties.

Changes in provisions

59   Provisions shall be reviewed at the end of each reporting period and adjusted to reflect the current best estimate. If it is no longer probable that an outflow of resources embodying economic benefits will be required to settle the obligation, the provision shall be reversed.

60   Where discounting is used, the carrying amount of a provision increases in each period to reflect the passage of time. This increase is recognised as borrowing cost.

Use of provisions

61   A provision shall be used only for expenditures for which the provision was originally recognised.

62   Only expenditures that relate to the original provision are set against it. Setting expenditures against a provision that was originally recognised for another purpose would conceal the impact of two different events.

Application of the recognition and measurement rules

Future operating losses

63   **Provisions shall not be recognised for future operating losses.**

64   Future operating losses do not meet the definition of a liability in paragraph 10 and the general recognition criteria set out for provisions in paragraph 14.

65   An expectation of future operating losses is an indication that certain assets of the operation may be impaired. An entity tests these assets for impairment under IAS 36 *Impairment of Assets*.

Onerous contracts

66   **If an entity has a contract that is onerous, the present obligation under the contract shall be recognised and measured as a provision.**

67   Many contracts (for example, some routine purchase orders) can be cancelled without paying compensation to the other party, and therefore there is no obligation. Other contracts establish both rights and obligations for each of the contracting parties. Where events make such a contract onerous, the contract falls within the scope of this Standard and a liability exists which is recognised. Executory contracts that are not onerous fall outside the scope of this Standard.

68   This Standard defines an onerous contract as a contract in which the unavoidable costs of meeting the obligations under the contract exceed the economic benefits expected to be received under it. The unavoidable costs under a contract reflect the least net cost of exiting from the contract, which is the lower of the cost of fulfilling it and any compensation or penalties arising from failure to fulfil it.

69   Before a separate provision for an onerous contract is established, an entity recognises any impairment loss that has occurred on assets dedicated to that contract (see IAS 36).

Restructuring

70   The following are examples of events that may fall under the definition of restructuring:

     (a)   sale or termination of a line of business;

     (b)   the closure of business locations in a country or region or the relocation of business activities from one country or region to another;

     (c)   changes in management structure, for example, eliminating a layer of management; and

     (d)   fundamental reorganisations that have a material effect on the nature and focus of the entity's operations.

71   A provision for restructuring costs is recognised only when the general recognition criteria for provisions set out in paragraph 14 are met. Paragraphs 72–83 set out how the general recognition criteria apply to restructurings.

72   **A constructive obligation to restructure arises only when an entity:**

     (a)   **has a detailed formal plan for the restructuring identifying at least:**

         (i)   **the business or part of a business concerned;**

         (ii)   **the principal locations affected;**

         (iii)   **the location, function, and approximate number of employees who will be compensated for terminating their services;**

         (iv)   **the expenditures that will be undertaken; and**

         (v)   **when the plan will be implemented; and**

     (b)   **has raised a valid expectation in those affected that it will carry out the restructuring by starting to implement that plan or announcing its main features to those affected by it.**

73   Evidence that an entity has started to implement a restructuring plan would be provided, for example, by dismantling plant or selling assets or by the public announcement of the main features of the plan. A public announcement of a detailed plan to restructure constitutes a constructive obligation to restructure only if it is made in such a way and in sufficient detail (ie setting out the main features of the plan) that it gives rise to valid expectations in other parties such as customers, suppliers and employees (or their representatives) that the entity will carry out the restructuring.

74   For a plan to be sufficient to give rise to a constructive obligation when communicated to those affected by it, its implementation needs to be planned to begin as soon as possible and to be completed in a timeframe that makes significant changes to the plan unlikely. If it is expected that there will be a long delay before the restructuring begins or that the restructuring will take an unreasonably long time, it is unlikely that the plan will raise a valid expectation on the part of others that the entity is at present committed to restructuring, because the timeframe allows opportunities for the entity to change its plans.

75   A management or board decision to restructure taken before the end of the reporting period does not give rise to a constructive obligation at the end of the reporting period unless the entity has, before the end of the reporting period:

     (a)   started to implement the restructuring plan; or

     (b)   announced the main features of the restructuring plan to those affected by it in a sufficiently specific manner to raise a valid expectation in them that the entity will carry out the restructuring.

If an entity starts to implement a restructuring plan, or announces its main features to those affected, only after the reporting period, disclosure is required under IAS 10 *Events after the Reporting Period*, if the restructuring is material and non-disclosure could influence the economic decisions that users make on the basis of the financial statements.

76   Although a constructive obligation is not created solely by a management decision, an obligation may result from other earlier events together with such a decision. For example, negotiations with employee representatives for termination payments, or with purchasers for the sale of an operation, may have been concluded subject only to board approval. Once that approval has been obtained and communicated to the other parties, the entity has a constructive obligation to restructure, if the conditions of paragraph 72 are met.

77   In some countries, the ultimate authority is vested in a board whose membership includes representatives of interests other than those of management (eg employees) or notification to such representatives may be necessary before the board decision is taken. Because a decision by such a board involves communication to these representatives, it may result in a constructive obligation to restructure.

78   No obligation arises for the sale of an operation until the entity is committed to the sale, ie there is a binding sale agreement.

79   Even when an entity has taken a decision to sell an operation and announced that decision publicly, it cannot be committed to the sale until a purchaser has been identified and there is a binding sale agreement. Until there is a binding sale agreement, the entity will be able to change its mind and indeed will have to take another course of action if a purchaser cannot be found on acceptable terms. When the sale of an operation is envisaged as part of a restructuring, the assets of the operation are reviewed for impairment, under IAS 36. When a sale is only part of a restructuring, a constructive obligation can arise for the other parts of the restructuring before a binding sale agreement exists.

80   A restructuring provision shall include only the direct expenditures arising from the restructuring, which are those that are both:

    (a)   necessarily entailed by the restructuring; and

    (b)   not associated with the ongoing activities of the entity.

81   A restructuring provision does not include such costs as:

    (a)   retraining or relocating continuing staff;

    (b)   marketing; or

    (c)   investment in new systems and distribution networks.

These expenditures relate to the future conduct of the business and are not liabilities for restructuring at the end of the reporting period. Such expenditures are recognised on the same basis as if they arose independently of a restructuring.

82   Identifiable future operating losses up to the date of a restructuring are not included in a provision, unless they relate to an onerous contract as defined in paragraph 10.

83   As required by paragraph 51, gains on the expected disposal of assets are not taken into account in measuring a restructuring provision, even if the sale of assets is envisaged as part of the restructuring.

Disclosure

84   For each class of provision, an entity shall disclose:

(a)   the carrying amount at the beginning and end of the period;

(b)   additional provisions made in the period, including increases to existing provisions;

(c)   amounts used (ie incurred and charged against the provision) during the period;

(d)   unused amounts reversed during the period; and

(e)   the increase during the period in the discounted amount arising from the passage of time and the effect of any change in the discount rate.

Comparative information is not required.

85   An entity shall disclose the following for each class of provision:

(a)   a brief description of the nature of the obligation and the expected timing of any resulting outflows of economic benefits;

(b)   an indication of the uncertainties about the amount or timing of those outflows. Where necessary to provide adequate information, an entity shall disclose the major assumptions made concerning future events, as addressed in paragraph 48; and

(c)   the amount of any expected reimbursement, stating the amount of any asset that has been recognised for that expected reimbursement.

86   Unless the possibility of any outflow in settlement is remote, an entity shall disclose for each class of contingent liability at the end of the reporting period a brief description of the nature of the contingent liability and, where practicable:

(a)   an estimate of its financial effect, measured under paragraphs 36–52;

(b)   an indication of the uncertainties relating to the amount or timing of any outflow; and

(c)   the possibility of any reimbursement.

87   In determining which provisions or contingent liabilities may be aggregated to form a class, it is necessary to consider whether the nature of the items is sufficiently similar for a single statement about them to fulfil the requirements of paragraphs 85(a) and (b) and 86(a) and (b). Thus, it may be appropriate to treat as a single class of provision amounts relating to warranties of different products, but it would not be appropriate to treat as a single class amounts relating to normal warranties and amounts that are subject to legal proceedings.

88   Where a provision and a contingent liability arise from the same set of circumstances, an entity makes the disclosures required by paragraphs 84–86 in a way that shows the link between the provision and the contingent liability.

89   Where an inflow of economic benefits is probable, an entity shall disclose a brief description of the nature of the contingent assets at the end of the reporting period, and, where practicable, an estimate of their financial effect, measured using the principles set out for provisions in paragraphs 36–52.

90   It is important that disclosures for contingent assets avoid giving misleading indications of the likelihood of income arising.

91   Where any of the information required by paragraphs 86 and 89 is not disclosed because it is not practicable to do so, that fact shall be stated.

92   In extremely rare cases, disclosure of some or all of the information required by paragraphs 84–89 can be expected to prejudice seriously the position of the entity in a dispute with other parties on the subject matter of the provision, contingent liability or contingent asset. In such cases, an entity need not disclose the information, but shall disclose the general nature of the dispute, together with the fact that, and reason why, the information has not been disclosed.

Transitional provisions

93   The effect of adopting this Standard on its effective date (or earlier) shall be reported as an adjustment to the opening balance of retained earnings for the period in which the Standard is first adopted. Entities are encouraged, but not required, to adjust the opening balance of retained earnings for the earliest period presented and to restate comparative information. If comparative information is not restated, this fact shall be disclosed.

94   [Deleted]

Effective date

95   This Standard becomes operative for annual financial statements covering periods beginning on or after 1 July 1999. Earlier application is encouraged. If an entity applies this Standard for periods beginning before 1 July 1999, it shall disclose that fact.

96   [Deleted]

97   IFRS 9, issued in October 2010, amended paragraph 2. An entity shall apply that amendment when it applies IFRS 9 as issued in October 2010.

International Accounting Standard 38

Intangible Assets

In April 2001 the International Accounting Standards Board (IASB) adopted IAS 38 *Intangible Assets*, which had originally been issued by the International Accounting Standards Committee in September 1998. That standard had replaced IAS 9 *Research and Development Costs*, which had been issued in 1993, which itself replaced an earlier version called *Accounting for Research and Development Activities* that had been issued in July 1978.

The IASB revised IAS 38 in March 2004 as part of the first phase of its business combinations project. In January 2008 the IASB amended IAS 36 again as part of the second phase of its business combinations project

Other IFRSs have made minor consequential amendments to IAS 38. They include IAS 16 *Property, Plant and Equipment* (issued December 2003), IAS 1 *Presentation of Financial Statements* (as revised in September 2007) and *Improvements to IFRSs* (issued May 2008 and April 2009).

CONTENTS

International Accounting Standard 38 *Intangible Assets* (IAS 38) is set out in paragraphs 1–133. All the paragraphs have equal authority but retain the IASC format of the Standard when it was adopted by the IASB. IAS 38 should be read in the context of its objective and the Basis for Conclusions, the *Preface to International Financial Reporting Standards* and the *Conceptual Framework for Financial Reporting*. IAS 8 *Accounting Policies, Changes in Accounting Estimates and Errors* provides a basis for selecting and applying accounting policies in the absence of explicit guidance.

Introduction

IN1 International Accounting Standard 38 *Intangible Assets* (IAS 38) replaces IAS 38 *Intangible Assets* (issued in 1998), and should be applied:

(a) on acquisition to the accounting for intangible assets acquired in business combinations for which the agreement date is on or after 31 March 2004.

(b) to all other intangible assets, for annual periods beginning on or after 31 March 2004.

Earlier application is encouraged.

Reasons for revising IAS 38

IN2 The International Accounting Standards Board developed this revised IAS 38 as part of its project on business combinations. The project's objective is to improve the quality of, and seek international convergence on, the accounting for business combinations and the subsequent accounting for goodwill and intangible assets acquired in business combinations.

IN3 The project has two phases. The first phase resulted in the Board issuing simultaneously IFRS 3 *Business Combinations* and revised versions of IAS 38 and IAS 36 *Impairment of Assets*. The Board's deliberations during the first phase of the project focused primarily on:

(a) the method of accounting for business combinations;

(b) the initial measurement of the identifiable assets acquired and liabilities and contingent liabilities assumed in a business combination;

(c) the recognition of provisions for terminating or reducing the activities of an acquiree;

(d) the treatment of any excess of the acquirer's interest in the fair values of identifiable net assets acquired in a business combination over the cost of the combination; and

(e) the accounting for goodwill and intangible assets acquired in a business combination.

IN4 Therefore, the Board's intention while revising IAS 38 was to reflect only those changes related to its decisions in the Business Combinations project, and *not* to reconsider all of the requirements in IAS 38. The changes that have been made in the Standard are primarily concerned with clarifying the notion of 'identifiability' as it relates to intangible assets, the useful life and amortisation of intangible assets, and the accounting for in-process research and development projects acquired in business combinations.

Summary of main changes

Definition of an intangible asset

IN5   The previous version of IAS 38 defined an intangible asset as an identifiable non-monetary asset without physical substance held for use in the production or supply of goods or services, for rental to others, or for administrative purposes. The requirement for the asset to be held for use in the production or supply of goods or services, for rental to others, or for administrative purposes has been removed from the definition of an intangible asset.

IN6   The previous version of IAS 38 did not define 'identifiability', but stated that an intangible asset could be distinguished clearly from goodwill if the asset was separable, but that separability was not a necessary condition for identifiability. The Standard states that an asset meets the identifiability criterion in the definition of an intangible asset when it:

    (a)   is separable, ie capable of being separated or divided from the entity and sold, transferred, licensed, rented or exchanged, either individually or together with a related contract, asset or liability; or

    (b)   arises from contractual or other legal rights, regardless of whether those rights are transferable or separable from the entity or from other rights and obligations.

Criteria for initial recognition

IN7   The previous version of IAS 38 required an intangible asset to be recognised if, and only if, it was probable that the expected future economic benefits attributable to the asset would flow to the entity, and its cost could be measured reliably. These recognition criteria have been included in the Standard. However, additional guidance has been included to clarify that:

    (a)   the probability recognition criterion is always considered to be satisfied for intangible assets that are acquired separately or in a business combination.

    (b)   the fair value of an intangible asset acquired in a business combination can be measured with sufficient reliability to be recognised separately from goodwill.

Subsequent expenditure

IN8   Under the previous version of IAS 38, the treatment of subsequent expenditure on an in-process research and development project acquired in a business combination and recognised as an asset separately from goodwill was unclear. The Standard requires such expenditure to be:

    (a)   recognised as an expense when incurred if it is research expenditure;

    (b)   recognised as an expense when incurred if it is development expenditure that does not satisfy the criteria in IAS 38 for recognising such expenditure as an intangible asset; and

(c)   recognised as an intangible asset if it is development expenditure that satisfies the criteria in IAS 38 for recognising such expenditure as an intangible asset.

Useful life

IN9   The previous version of IAS 38 was based on the assumption that the useful life of an intangible asset is always finite, and included a rebuttable presumption that the useful life cannot exceed twenty years from the date the asset is available for use. That rebuttable presumption has been removed. The Standard requires an intangible asset to be regarded as having an indefinite useful life when, based on an analysis of all of the relevant factors, there is no foreseeable limit to the period over which the asset is expected to generate net cash inflows for the entity.

IN10 The previous version of IAS 38 required that if control over the future economic benefits from an intangible asset was achieved through legal rights granted for a finite period, the useful life of the intangible asset could not exceed the period of those rights, unless the rights were renewable and renewal was virtually certain. The Standard requires that:

(a)   the useful life of an intangible asset arising from contractual or other legal rights should not exceed the period of those rights, but may be shorter depending on the period over which the asset is expected to be used by the entity; and

(b)   if the rights are conveyed for a limited term that can be renewed, the useful life should include the renewal period(s) only if there is evidence to support renewal by the entity without significant cost.

Intangible assets with indefinite useful lives

IN11 The Standard requires that:

(a)   an intangible asset with an indefinite useful life should not be amortised.

(b)   the useful life of such an asset should be reviewed each reporting period to determine whether events and circumstances continue to support an indefinite useful life assessment for that asset. If they do not, the change in the useful life assessment from indefinite to finite should be accounted for as a change in an accounting estimate.

Impairment testing intangible assets with finite useful lives

IN12 The previous version of IAS 38 required the recoverable amount of an intangible asset that was amortised over a period exceeding twenty years from the date it was available for use to be estimated at least at each financial year-end, even if there was no indication that the asset was impaired. This requirement has been removed. Therefore, an entity needs to determine the recoverable amount of an intangible asset with a finite useful life that is amortised over a period exceeding twenty years from the date it is available for use only when, in accordance with IAS 36, there is an indication that the asset may be impaired.

Disclosure

IN13 If an intangible asset is assessed as having an indefinite useful life, the Standard
requires an entity to disclose the carrying amount of that asset and the reasons
supporting the indefinite useful life assessment.

International Accounting Standard 38
Intangible Assets

Objective

1   The objective of this Standard is to prescribe the accounting treatment for intangible assets that are not dealt with specifically in another Standard. This Standard requires an entity to recognise an intangible asset if, and only if, specified criteria are met. The Standard also specifies how to measure the carrying amount of intangible assets and requires specified disclosures about intangible assets.

Scope

2   This Standard shall be applied in accounting for intangible assets, except:

    (a)   intangible assets that are within the scope of another Standard;

    (b)   financial assets, as defined in IAS 32 *Financial Instruments: Presentation*;

    (c)   the recognition and measurement of exploration and evaluation assets (see IFRS 6 *Exploration for and Evaluation of Mineral Resources*); and

    (d)   expenditure on the development and extraction of minerals, oil, natural gas and similar non-regenerative resources.

3   If another Standard prescribes the accounting for a specific type of intangible asset, an entity applies that Standard instead of this Standard. For example, this Standard does not apply to:

    (a)   intangible assets held by an entity for sale in the ordinary course of business (see IAS 2 *Inventories* and IAS 11 *Construction Contracts*).

    (b)   deferred tax assets (see IAS 12 *Income Taxes*).

    (c)   leases that are within the scope of IAS 17 *Leases*.

    (d)   assets arising from employee benefits (see IAS 19 *Employee Benefits*).

    (e)   financial assets as defined in IAS 32. The recognition and measurement of some financial assets are covered by IFRS 10 *Consolidated Financial Statements*, IAS 27 *Separate Financial Statements* and IAS 28 *Investments in Associates and Joint Ventures*.

    (f)   goodwill acquired in a business combination (see IFRS 3 *Business Combinations*).

    (g)   deferred acquisition costs, and intangible assets, arising from an insurer's contractual rights under insurance contracts within the scope of IFRS 4 *Insurance Contracts*. IFRS 4 sets out specific disclosure requirements for those deferred acquisition costs but not for those intangible assets. Therefore, the disclosure requirements in this Standard apply to those intangible assets.

    (h)   non-current intangible assets classified as held for sale (or included in a disposal group that is classified as held for sale) in accordance with IFRS 5 *Non-current Assets Held for Sale and Discontinued Operations*.

4   Some intangible assets may be contained in or on a physical substance such as a compact disc (in the case of computer software), legal documentation (in the case of a licence or patent) or film. In determining whether an asset that incorporates both intangible and tangible elements should be treated under IAS 16 *Property, Plant and Equipment* or as an intangible asset under this Standard, an entity uses judgement to assess which element is more significant. For example, computer software for a computer-controlled machine tool that cannot operate without that specific software is an integral part of the related hardware and it is treated as property, plant and equipment. The same applies to the operating system of a computer. When the software is not an integral part of the related hardware, computer software is treated as an intangible asset.

5   This Standard applies to, among other things, expenditure on advertising, training, start-up, research and development activities. Research and development activities are directed to the development of knowledge. Therefore, although these activities may result in an asset with physical substance (eg a prototype), the physical element of the asset is secondary to its intangible component, ie the knowledge embodied in it.

6   In the case of a finance lease, the underlying asset may be either tangible or intangible. After initial recognition, a lessee accounts for an intangible asset held under a finance lease in accordance with this Standard. Rights under licensing agreements for items such as motion picture films, video recordings, plays, manuscripts, patents and copyrights are excluded from the scope of IAS 17 and are within the scope of this Standard.

7   Exclusions from the scope of a Standard may occur if activities or transactions are so specialised that they give rise to accounting issues that may need to be dealt with in a different way. Such issues arise in the accounting for expenditure on the exploration for, or development and extraction of, oil, gas and mineral deposits in extractive industries and in the case of insurance contracts. Therefore, this Standard does not apply to expenditure on such activities and contracts. However, this Standard applies to other intangible assets used (such as computer software), and other expenditure incurred (such as start-up costs), in extractive industries or by insurers.

Definitions

8   The following terms are used in this Standard with the meanings specified:

Amortisation is the systematic allocation of the depreciable amount of an intangible asset over its useful life.

An *asset* is a resource:

(a)   controlled by an entity as a result of past events; and

(b)   from which future economic benefits are expected to flow to the entity.

Carrying amount is the amount at which an asset is recognised in the statement of financial position after deducting any accumulated amortisation and accumulated impairment losses thereon.

Cost is the amount of cash or cash equivalents paid or the fair value of other consideration given to acquire an asset at the time of its acquisition or construction, or, when applicable, the amount attributed to that asset when initially recognised in accordance with the specific requirements of other IFRSs, eg IFRS 2 *Share-based Payment.*

Depreciable amount is the cost of an asset, or other amount substituted for cost, less its residual value.

Development is the application of research findings or other knowledge to a plan or design for the production of new or substantially improved materials, devices, products, processes, systems or services before the start of commercial production or use.

Entity-specific value is the present value of the cash flows an entity expects to arise from the continuing use of an asset and from its disposal at the end of its useful life or expects to incur when settling a liability.

Fair value is the price that would be received to sell an asset or paid to transfer a liability in an orderly transaction between market participants at the measurement date. (See IFRS 13 *Fair Value Measurement.*)

An *impairment loss* is the amount by which the carrying amount of an asset exceeds its recoverable amount.

An *intangible asset* is an identifiable non-monetary asset without physical substance.

Monetary assets are money held and assets to be received in fixed or determinable amounts of money.

Research is original and planned investigation undertaken with the prospect of gaining new scientific or technical knowledge and understanding.

The *residual value* of an intangible asset is the estimated amount that an entity would currently obtain from disposal of the asset, after deducting the estimated costs of disposal, if the asset were already of the age and in the condition expected at the end of its useful life.

Useful life is:

(a)   the period over which an asset is expected to be available for use by an entity; or

(b)   the number of production or similar units expected to be obtained from the asset by an entity.

Intangible assets

9   Entities frequently expend resources, or incur liabilities, on the acquisition, development, maintenance or enhancement of intangible resources such as scientific or technical knowledge, design and implementation of new processes or systems, licences, intellectual property, market knowledge and trademarks (including brand names and publishing titles). Common examples of items

encompassed by these broad headings are computer software, patents, copyrights, motion picture films, customer lists, mortgage servicing rights, fishing licences, import quotas, franchises, customer or supplier relationships, customer loyalty, market share and marketing rights.

10 Not all the items described in paragraph 9 meet the definition of an intangible asset, ie identifiability, control over a resource and existence of future economic benefits. If an item within the scope of this Standard does not meet the definition of an intangible asset, expenditure to acquire it or generate it internally is recognised as an expense when it is incurred. However, if the item is acquired in a business combination, it forms part of the goodwill recognised at the acquisition date (see paragraph 68).

Identifiability

11 The definition of an intangible asset requires an intangible asset to be identifiable to distinguish it from goodwill. Goodwill recognised in a business combination is an asset representing the future economic benefits arising from other assets acquired in a business combination that are not individually identified and separately recognised. The future economic benefits may result from synergy between the identifiable assets acquired or from assets that, individually, do not qualify for recognition in the financial statements.

12 **An asset is identifiable if it either:**

    (a)   is separable, ie is capable of being separated or divided from the entity and sold, transferred, licensed, rented or exchanged, either individually or together with a related contract, identifiable asset or liability, regardless of whether the entity intends to do so; or

    (b)   arises from contractual or other legal rights, regardless of whether those rights are transferable or separable from the entity or from other rights and obligations.

Control

13 An entity controls an asset if the entity has the power to obtain the future economic benefits flowing from the underlying resource and to restrict the access of others to those benefits. The capacity of an entity to control the future economic benefits from an intangible asset would normally stem from legal rights that are enforceable in a court of law. In the absence of legal rights, it is more difficult to demonstrate control. However, legal enforceability of a right is not a necessary condition for control because an entity may be able to control the future economic benefits in some other way.

14 Market and technical knowledge may give rise to future economic benefits. An entity controls those benefits if, for example, the knowledge is protected by legal rights such as copyrights, a restraint of trade agreement (where permitted) or by a legal duty on employees to maintain confidentiality.

15 An entity may have a team of skilled staff and may be able to identify incremental staff skills leading to future economic benefits from training. The entity may also expect that the staff will continue to make their skills available to the entity. However, an entity usually has insufficient control over the expected future

economic benefits arising from a team of skilled staff and from training for these items to meet the definition of an intangible asset. For a similar reason, specific management or technical talent is unlikely to meet the definition of an intangible asset, unless it is protected by legal rights to use it and to obtain the future economic benefits expected from it, and it also meets the other parts of the definition.

16   An entity may have a portfolio of customers or a market share and expect that, because of its efforts in building customer relationships and loyalty, the customers will continue to trade with the entity. However, in the absence of legal rights to protect, or other ways to control, the relationships with customers or the loyalty of the customers to the entity, the entity usually has insufficient control over the expected economic benefits from customer relationships and loyalty for such items (eg portfolio of customers, market shares, customer relationships and customer loyalty) to meet the definition of intangible assets. In the absence of legal rights to protect customer relationships, exchange transactions for the same or similar non-contractual customer relationships (other than as part of a business combination) provide evidence that the entity is nonetheless able to control the expected future economic benefits flowing from the customer relationships. Because such exchange transactions also provide evidence that the customer relationships are separable, those customer relationships meet the definition of an intangible asset.

Future economic benefits

17   The future economic benefits flowing from an intangible asset may include revenue from the sale of products or services, cost savings, or other benefits resulting from the use of the asset by the entity. For example, the use of intellectual property in a production process may reduce future production costs rather than increase future revenues.

Recognition and measurement

18   The recognition of an item as an intangible asset requires an entity to demonstrate that the item meets:

(a)   the definition of an intangible asset (see paragraphs 8–17); and

(b)   the recognition criteria (see paragraphs 21–23).

This requirement applies to costs incurred initially to acquire or internally generate an intangible asset and those incurred subsequently to add to, replace part of, or service it.

19   Paragraphs 25–32 deal with the application of the recognition criteria to separately acquired intangible assets, and paragraphs 33–43 deal with their application to intangible assets acquired in a business combination. Paragraph 44 deals with the initial measurement of intangible assets acquired by way of a government grant, paragraphs 45–47 with exchanges of intangible assets, and paragraphs 48–50 with the treatment of internally generated goodwill. Paragraphs 51–67 deal with the initial recognition and measurement of internally generated intangible assets.

20 The nature of intangible assets is such that, in many cases, there are no additions to such an asset or replacements of part of it. Accordingly, most subsequent expenditures are likely to maintain the expected future economic benefits embodied in an existing intangible asset rather than meet the definition of an intangible asset and the recognition criteria in this Standard. In addition, it is often difficult to attribute subsequent expenditure directly to a particular intangible asset rather than to the business as a whole. Therefore, only rarely will subsequent expenditure—expenditure incurred after the initial recognition of an acquired intangible asset or after completion of an internally generated intangible asset—be recognised in the carrying amount of an asset. Consistently with paragraph 63, subsequent expenditure on brands, mastheads, publishing titles, customer lists and items similar in substance (whether externally acquired or internally generated) is always recognised in profit or loss as incurred. This is because such expenditure cannot be distinguished from expenditure to develop the business as a whole.

21 **An intangible asset shall be recognised if, and only if:**

    (a) **it is probable that the expected future economic benefits that are attributable to the asset will flow to the entity; and**

    (b) **the cost of the asset can be measured reliably.**

22 **An entity shall assess the probability of expected future economic benefits using reasonable and supportable assumptions that represent management's best estimate of the set of economic conditions that will exist over the useful life of the asset.**

23 An entity uses judgement to assess the degree of certainty attached to the flow of future economic benefits that are attributable to the use of the asset on the basis of the evidence available at the time of initial recognition, giving greater weight to external evidence.

24 **An intangible asset shall be measured initially at cost.**

Separate acquisition

25 Normally, the price an entity pays to acquire separately an intangible asset will reflect expectations about the probability that the expected future economic benefits embodied in the asset will flow to the entity. In other words, the entity expects there to be an inflow of economic benefits, even if there is uncertainty about the timing or the amount of the inflow. Therefore, the probability recognition criterion in paragraph 21(a) is always considered to be satisfied for separately acquired intangible assets.

26 In addition, the cost of a separately acquired intangible asset can usually be measured reliably. This is particularly so when the purchase consideration is in the form of cash or other monetary assets.

27 The cost of a separately acquired intangible asset comprises:

    (a) its purchase price, including import duties and non-refundable purchase taxes, after deducting trade discounts and rebates; and

    (b) any directly attributable cost of preparing the asset for its intended use.

28   Examples of directly attributable costs are:

    (a)   costs of employee benefits (as defined in IAS 19) arising directly from bringing the asset to its working condition;

    (b)   professional fees arising directly from bringing the asset to its working condition; and

    (c)   costs of testing whether the asset is functioning properly.

29   Examples of expenditures that are not part of the cost of an intangible asset are:

    (a)   costs of introducing a new product or service (including costs of advertising and promotional activities);

    (b)   costs of conducting business in a new location or with a new class of customer (including costs of staff training); and

    (c)   administration and other general overhead costs.

30   Recognition of costs in the carrying amount of an intangible asset ceases when the asset is in the condition necessary for it to be capable of operating in the manner intended by management. Therefore, costs incurred in using or redeploying an intangible asset are not included in the carrying amount of that asset. For example, the following costs are not included in the carrying amount of an intangible asset:

    (a)   costs incurred while an asset capable of operating in the manner intended by management has yet to be brought into use; and

    (b)   initial operating losses, such as those incurred while demand for the asset's output builds up.

31   Some operations occur in connection with the development of an intangible asset, but are not necessary to bring the asset to the condition necessary for it to be capable of operating in the manner intended by management. These incidental operations may occur before or during the development activities. Because incidental operations are not necessary to bring an asset to the condition necessary for it to be capable of operating in the manner intended by management, the income and related expenses of incidental operations are recognised immediately in profit or loss, and included in their respective classifications of income and expense.

32   If payment for an intangible asset is deferred beyond normal credit terms, its cost is the cash price equivalent. The difference between this amount and the total payments is recognised as interest expense over the period of credit unless it is capitalised in accordance with IAS 23 *Borrowing Costs*.

Acquisition as part of a business combination

33   In accordance with IFRS 3 *Business Combinations*, if an intangible asset is acquired in a business combination, the cost of that intangible asset is its fair value at the acquisition date. The fair value of an intangible asset will reflect market participants' expectations at the acquisition date about the probability that the expected future economic benefits embodied in the asset will flow to the entity. In other words, the entity expects there to be an inflow of economic benefits, even

if there is uncertainty about the timing or the amount of the inflow. Therefore, the probability recognition criterion in paragraph 21(a) is always considered to be satisfied for intangible assets acquired in business combinations. If an asset acquired in a business combination is separable or arises from contractual or other legal rights, sufficient information exists to measure reliably the fair value of the asset. Thus, the reliable measurement criterion in paragraph 21(b) is always considered to be satisfied for intangible assets acquired in business combinations.

34   In accordance with this Standard and IFRS 3 (as revised in 2008), an acquirer recognises at the acquisition date, separately from goodwill, an intangible asset of the acquiree, irrespective of whether the asset had been recognised by the acquiree before the business combination. This means that the acquirer recognises as an asset separately from goodwill an in-process research and development project of the acquiree if the project meets the definition of an intangible asset. An acquiree's in-process research and development project meets the definition of an intangible asset when it:

(a)   meets the definition of an asset; and

(b)   is identifiable, ie is separable or arises from contractual or other legal rights.

Intangible asset acquired in a business combination

35   If an intangible asset acquired in a business combination is separable or arises from contractual or other legal rights, sufficient information exists to measure reliably the fair value of the asset. When, for the estimates used to measure an intangible asset's fair value, there is a range of possible outcomes with different probabilities, that uncertainty enters into the measurement of the asset's fair value.

36   An intangible asset acquired in a business combination might be separable, but only together with a related contract, identifiable asset or liability. In such cases, the acquirer recognises the intangible asset separately from goodwill, but together with the related item.

37   The acquirer may recognise a group of complementary intangible assets as a single asset provided the individual assets have similar useful lives. For example, the terms 'brand' and 'brand name' are often used as synonyms for trademarks and other marks. However, the former are general marketing terms that are typically used to refer to a group of complementary assets such as a trademark (or service mark) and its related trade name, formulas, recipes and technological expertise.

38–41   [Deleted]

Subsequent expenditure on an acquired in-process research and development project

42   Research or development expenditure that:

(a)   relates to an in-process research or development project acquired separately or in a business combination and recognised as an intangible asset; and

(b)   is incurred after the acquisition of that project

shall be accounted for in accordance with paragraphs 54–62.

43　Applying the requirements in paragraphs 54–62 means that subsequent expenditure on an in-process research or development project acquired separately or in a business combination and recognised as an intangible asset is:

(a)　recognised as an expense when incurred if it is research expenditure;

(b)　recognised as an expense when incurred if it is development expenditure that does not satisfy the criteria for recognition as an intangible asset in paragraph 57; and

(c)　added to the carrying amount of the acquired in-process research or development project if it is development expenditure that satisfies the recognition criteria in paragraph 57.

Acquisition by way of a government grant

44　In some cases, an intangible asset may be acquired free of charge, or for nominal consideration, by way of a government grant. This may happen when a government transfers or allocates to an entity intangible assets such as airport landing rights, licences to operate radio or television stations, import licences or quotas or rights to access other restricted resources. In accordance with IAS 20 *Accounting for Government Grants and Disclosure of Government Assistance*, an entity may choose to recognise both the intangible asset and the grant initially at fair value. If an entity chooses not to recognise the asset initially at fair value, the entity recognises the asset initially at a nominal amount (the other treatment permitted by IAS 20) plus any expenditure that is directly attributable to preparing the asset for its intended use.

Exchanges of assets

45　One or more intangible assets may be acquired in exchange for a non-monetary asset or assets, or a combination of monetary and non-monetary assets. The following discussion refers simply to an exchange of one non-monetary asset for another, but it also applies to all exchanges described in the preceding sentence. The cost of such an intangible asset is measured at fair value unless (a) the exchange transaction lacks commercial substance or (b) the fair value of neither the asset received nor the asset given up is reliably measurable. The acquired asset is measured in this way even if an entity cannot immediately derecognise the asset given up. If the acquired asset is not measured at fair value, its cost is measured at the carrying amount of the asset given up.

46　An entity determines whether an exchange transaction has commercial substance by considering the extent to which its future cash flows are expected to change as a result of the transaction. An exchange transaction has commercial substance if:

(a)　the configuration (ie risk, timing and amount) of the cash flows of the asset received differs from the configuration of the cash flows of the asset transferred; or

(b)　the entity-specific value of the portion of the entity's operations affected by the transaction changes as a result of the exchange; and

(c)   the difference in (a) or (b) is significant relative to the fair value of the assets exchanged.

For the purpose of determining whether an exchange transaction has commercial substance, the entity-specific value of the portion of the entity's operations affected by the transaction shall reflect post-tax cash flows. The result of these analyses may be clear without an entity having to perform detailed calculations.

47   Paragraph 21(b) specifies that a condition for the recognition of an intangible asset is that the cost of the asset can be measured reliably. The fair value of an intangible asset is reliably measurable if (a) the variability in the range of reasonable fair value measurements is not significant for that asset or (b) the probabilities of the various estimates within the range can be reasonably assessed and used when measuring fair value. If an entity is able to measure reliably the fair value of either the asset received or the asset given up, then the fair value of the asset given up is used to measure cost unless the fair value of the asset received is more clearly evident.

Internally generated goodwill

48   **Internally generated goodwill shall not be recognised as an asset.**

49   In some cases, expenditure is incurred to generate future economic benefits, but it does not result in the creation of an intangible asset that meets the recognition criteria in this Standard. Such expenditure is often described as contributing to internally generated goodwill. Internally generated goodwill is not recognised as an asset because it is not an identifiable resource (ie it is not separable nor does it arise from contractual or other legal rights) controlled by the entity that can be measured reliably at cost.

50   Differences between the fair value of an entity and the carrying amount of its identifiable net assets at any time may capture a range of factors that affect the fair value of the entity. However, such differences do not represent the cost of intangible assets controlled by the entity.

Internally generated intangible assets

51   It is sometimes difficult to assess whether an internally generated intangible asset qualifies for recognition because of problems in:

(a)   identifying whether and when there is an identifiable asset that will generate expected future economic benefits; and

(b)   determining the cost of the asset reliably. In some cases, the cost of generating an intangible asset internally cannot be distinguished from the cost of maintaining or enhancing the entity's internally generated goodwill or of running day-to-day operations.

Therefore, in addition to complying with the general requirements for the recognition and initial measurement of an intangible asset, an entity applies the requirements and guidance in paragraphs 52–67 to all internally generated intangible assets.

52   To assess whether an internally generated intangible asset meets the criteria for recognition, an entity classifies the generation of the asset into:

(a)   a research phase; and

(b)   a development phase.

Although the terms 'research' and 'development' are defined, the terms 'research phase' and 'development phase' have a broader meaning for the purpose of this Standard.

53   If an entity cannot distinguish the research phase from the development phase of an internal project to create an intangible asset, the entity treats the expenditure on that project as if it were incurred in the research phase only.

Research phase

54   **No intangible asset arising from research (or from the research phase of an internal project) shall be recognised. Expenditure on research (or on the research phase of an internal project) shall be recognised as an expense when it is incurred.**

55   In the research phase of an internal project, an entity cannot demonstrate that an intangible asset exists that will generate probable future economic benefits. Therefore, this expenditure is recognised as an expense when it is incurred.

56   Examples of research activities are:

(a)   activities aimed at obtaining new knowledge;

(b)   the search for, evaluation and final selection of, applications of research findings or other knowledge;

(c)   the search for alternatives for materials, devices, products, processes, systems or services; and

(d)   the formulation, design, evaluation and final selection of possible alternatives for new or improved materials, devices, products, processes, systems or services.

Development phase

57   **An intangible asset arising from development (or from the development phase of an internal project) shall be recognised if, and only if, an entity can demonstrate all of the following:**

(a)   **the technical feasibility of completing the intangible asset so that it will be available for use or sale.**

(b)   **its intention to complete the intangible asset and use or sell it.**

(c)   **its ability to use or sell the intangible asset.**

(d)   **how the intangible asset will generate probable future economic benefits. Among other things, the entity can demonstrate the existence of a market for the output of the intangible asset or the intangible asset itself or, if it is to be used internally, the usefulness of the intangible asset.**

(e)   the availability of adequate technical, financial and other resources to complete the development and to use or sell the intangible asset.

(f)   its ability to measure reliably the expenditure attributable to the intangible asset during its development.

58   In the development phase of an internal project, an entity can, in some instances, identify an intangible asset and demonstrate that the asset will generate probable future economic benefits. This is because the development phase of a project is further advanced than the research phase.

59   Examples of development activities are:

(a)   the design, construction and testing of pre-production or pre-use prototypes and models;

(b)   the design of tools, jigs, moulds and dies involving new technology;

(c)   the design, construction and operation of a pilot plant that is not of a scale economically feasible for commercial production; and

(d)   the design, construction and testing of a chosen alternative for new or improved materials, devices, products, processes, systems or services.

60   To demonstrate how an intangible asset will generate probable future economic benefits, an entity assesses the future economic benefits to be received from the asset using the principles in IAS 36 *Impairment of Assets*. If the asset will generate economic benefits only in combination with other assets, the entity applies the concept of cash-generating units in IAS 36.

61   Availability of resources to complete, use and obtain the benefits from an intangible asset can be demonstrated by, for example, a business plan showing the technical, financial and other resources needed and the entity's ability to secure those resources. In some cases, an entity demonstrates the availability of external finance by obtaining a lender's indication of its willingness to fund the plan.

62   An entity's costing systems can often measure reliably the cost of generating an intangible asset internally, such as salary and other expenditure incurred in securing copyrights or licences or developing computer software.

63   **Internally generated brands, mastheads, publishing titles, customer lists and items similar in substance shall not be recognised as intangible assets.**

64   Expenditure on internally generated brands, mastheads, publishing titles, customer lists and items similar in substance cannot be distinguished from the cost of developing the business as a whole. Therefore, such items are not recognised as intangible assets.

Cost of an internally generated intangible asset

65   The cost of an internally generated intangible asset for the purpose of paragraph 24 is the sum of expenditure incurred from the date when the intangible asset first meets the recognition criteria in paragraphs 21, 22 and 57. Paragraph 71 prohibits reinstatement of expenditure previously recognised as an expense.

66   The cost of an internally generated intangible asset comprises all directly attributable costs necessary to create, produce, and prepare the asset to be capable of operating in the manner intended by management. Examples of directly attributable costs are:

(a)   costs of materials and services used or consumed in generating the intangible asset;

(b)   costs of employee benefits (as defined in IAS 19) arising from the generation of the intangible asset;

(c)   fees to register a legal right; and

(d)   amortisation of patents and licences that are used to generate the intangible asset.

IAS 23 specifies criteria for the recognition of interest as an element of the cost of an internally generated intangible asset.

67   The following are not components of the cost of an internally generated intangible asset:

(a)   selling, administrative and other general overhead expenditure unless this expenditure can be directly attributed to preparing the asset for use;

(b)   identified inefficiencies and initial operating losses incurred before the asset achieves planned performance; and

(c)   expenditure on training staff to operate the asset.

Example illustrating paragraph 65

An entity is developing a new production process. During 20X5, expenditure incurred was CU1,000ᵃ, of which CU900 was incurred before 1 December 20X5 and CU100 was incurred between 1 December 20X5 and 31 December 20X5. The entity is able to demonstrate that, at 1 December 20X5, the production process met the criteria for recognition as an intangible asset. The recoverable amount of the know-how embodied in the process (including future cash outflows to complete the process before it is available for use) is estimated to be CU500.

At the end of 20X5, the production process is recognised as an intangible asset at a cost of CU100 (expenditure incurred since the date when the recognition criteria were met, ie 1 December 20X5). The CU900 expenditure incurred before 1 December 20X5 is recognised as an expense because the recognition criteria were not met until 1 December 20X5. This expenditure does not form part of the cost of the production process recognised in the statement of financial position.

During 20X6, expenditure incurred is CU2,000. At the end of 20X6, the recoverable amount of the know-how embodied in the process (including future cash outflows to complete the process before it is available for use) is estimated to be CU1,900.

At the end of 20X6, the cost of the production process is CU2,100 (CU100 expenditure recognised at the end of 20X5 plus CU2,000 expenditure recognised in 20X6). The entity recognises an impairment loss of CU200 to adjust the carrying amount of the process before impairment loss (CU2,100) to its recoverable amount (CU1,900). This impairment loss will be reversed in a subsequent period if the requirements for the reversal of an impairment loss in IAS 36 are met.

(a) In this Standard, monetary amounts are denominated in 'currency units (CU)'.

Recognition of an expense

68   Expenditure on an intangible item shall be recognised as an expense when it is incurred unless:

    (a)   it forms part of the cost of an intangible asset that meets the recognition criteria (see paragraphs 18–67); or

    (b)   the item is acquired in a business combination and cannot be recognised as an intangible asset. If this is the case, it forms part of the amount recognised as goodwill at the acquisition date (see IFRS 3).

69   In some cases, expenditure is incurred to provide future economic benefits to an entity, but no intangible asset or other asset is acquired or created that can be recognised. In the case of the supply of goods, the entity recognises such expenditure as an expense when it has a right to access those goods. In the case of the supply of services, the entity recognises the expenditure as an expense when it receives the services. For example, expenditure on research is recognised as an expense when it is incurred (see paragraph 54), except when it is acquired as part of a business combination. Other examples of expenditure that is recognised as an expense when it is incurred include:

    (a)   expenditure on start-up activities (ie start-up costs), unless this expenditure is included in the cost of an item of property, plant and equipment in accordance with IAS 16. Start-up costs may consist of establishment costs such as legal and secretarial costs incurred in establishing a legal entity, expenditure to open a new facility or business (ie pre-opening costs) or expenditures for starting new operations or launching new products or processes (ie pre-operating costs).

    (b)   expenditure on training activities.

    (c)   expenditure on advertising and promotional activities (including mail order catalogues).

    (d)   expenditure on relocating or reorganising part or all of an entity.

69A   An entity has a right to access goods when it owns them. Similarly, it has a right to access goods when they have been constructed by a supplier in accordance with the terms of a supply contract and the entity could demand delivery of them in return for payment. Services are received when they are performed by a supplier in accordance with a contract to deliver them to the entity and not when the entity uses them to deliver another service, for example, to deliver an advertisement to customers.

70   Paragraph 68 does not preclude an entity from recognising a prepayment as an asset when payment for goods has been made in advance of the entity obtaining a right to access those goods. Similarly, paragraph 68 does not preclude an entity from recognising a prepayment as an asset when payment for services has been made in advance of the entity receiving those services.

Past expenses not to be recognised as an asset

71   **Expenditure on an intangible item that was initially recognised as an expense shall not be recognised as part of the cost of an intangible asset at a later date.**

Measurement after recognition

72   **An entity shall choose either the cost model in paragraph 74 or the revaluation model in paragraph 75 as its accounting policy. If an intangible asset is accounted for using the revaluation model, all the other assets in its class shall also be accounted for using the same model, unless there is no active market for those assets.**

73   A class of intangible assets is a grouping of assets of a similar nature and use in an entity's operations. The items within a class of intangible assets are revalued simultaneously to avoid selective revaluation of assets and the reporting of amounts in the financial statements representing a mixture of costs and values as at different dates.

Cost model

74   **After initial recognition, an intangible asset shall be carried at its cost less any accumulated amortisation and any accumulated impairment losses.**

Revaluation model

75   After initial recognition, an intangible asset shall be carried at a revalued amount, being its fair value at the date of the revaluation less any subsequent accumulated amortisation and any subsequent accumulated impairment losses. For the purpose of revaluations under this Standard, fair value shall be measured by reference to an active market. Revaluations shall be made with such regularity that at the end of the reporting period the carrying amount of the asset does not differ materially from its fair value.

76   The revaluation model does not allow:

(a)   the revaluation of intangible assets that have not previously been recognised as assets; or

(b)   the initial recognition of intangible assets at amounts other than cost.

77   The revaluation model is applied after an asset has been initially recognised at cost. However, if only part of the cost of an intangible asset is recognised as an asset because the asset did not meet the criteria for recognition until part of the way through the process (see paragraph 65), the revaluation model may be applied to the whole of that asset. Also, the revaluation model may be applied to an intangible asset that was received by way of a government grant and recognised at a nominal amount (see paragraph 44).

78   It is uncommon for an active market to exist for an intangible asset, although this may happen. For example, in some jurisdictions, an active market may exist for freely transferable taxi licences, fishing licences or production quotas. However, an active market cannot exist for brands, newspaper mastheads, music and film publishing rights, patents or trademarks, because each such asset is unique. Also, although intangible assets are bought and sold, contracts are negotiated between individual buyers and sellers, and transactions are relatively infrequent. For these reasons, the price paid for one asset may not provide sufficient evidence of the fair value of another. Moreover, prices are often not available to the public.

79   The frequency of revaluations depends on the volatility of the fair values of the intangible assets being revalued. If the fair value of a revalued asset differs materially from its carrying amount, a further revaluation is necessary. Some intangible assets may experience significant and volatile movements in fair value, thus necessitating annual revaluation. Such frequent revaluations are unnecessary for intangible assets with only insignificant movements in fair value.

80   If an intangible asset is revalued, any accumulated amortisation at the date of the revaluation is either:

(a)   restated proportionately with the change in the gross carrying amount of the asset so that the carrying amount of the asset after revaluation equals its revalued amount; or

(b)   eliminated against the gross carrying amount of the asset and the net amount restated to the revalued amount of the asset.

81   If an intangible asset in a class of revalued intangible assets cannot be revalued because there is no active market for this asset, the asset shall be carried at its cost less any accumulated amortisation and impairment losses.

82   If the fair value of a revalued intangible asset can no longer be measured by reference to an active market, the carrying amount of the asset shall be its revalued amount at the date of the last revaluation by reference to the active market less any subsequent accumulated amortisation and any subsequent accumulated impairment losses.

83   The fact that an active market no longer exists for a revalued intangible asset may indicate that the asset may be impaired and that it needs to be tested in accordance with IAS 36.

84   If the fair value of the asset can be measured by reference to an active market at a subsequent measurement date, the revaluation model is applied from that date.

85   If an intangible asset's carrying amount is increased as a result of a revaluation, the increase shall be recognised in other comprehensive income and accumulated in equity under the heading of revaluation surplus. However, the increase shall be recognised in profit or loss to the extent that it reverses a revaluation decrease of the same asset previously recognised in profit or loss.

86   If an intangible asset's carrying amount is decreased as a result of a revaluation, the decrease shall be recognised in profit or loss. However, the decrease shall be recognised in other comprehensive income to the extent of any credit balance in the revaluation surplus in respect of that asset. The decrease recognised in other comprehensive income reduces the amount accumulated in equity under the heading of revaluation surplus.

87   The cumulative revaluation surplus included in equity may be transferred directly to retained earnings when the surplus is realised. The whole surplus may be realised on the retirement or disposal of the asset. However, some of the surplus may be realised as the asset is used by the entity; in such a case, the amount of the surplus realised is the difference between amortisation based on the revalued carrying amount of the asset and amortisation that would have been recognised based on the asset's historical cost. The transfer from revaluation surplus to retained earnings is not made through profit or loss.

Useful life

88   An entity shall assess whether the useful life of an intangible asset is finite or indefinite and, if finite, the length of, or number of production or similar units constituting, that useful life. An intangible asset shall be regarded by the entity as having an indefinite useful life when, based on an analysis of all of the relevant factors, there is no foreseeable limit to the period over which the asset is expected to generate net cash inflows for the entity.

89   The accounting for an intangible asset is based on its useful life. An intangible asset with a finite useful life is amortised (see paragraphs 97–106), and an intangible asset with an indefinite useful life is not (see paragraphs 107–110). The Illustrative Examples accompanying this Standard illustrate the determination of useful life for different intangible assets, and the subsequent accounting for those assets based on the useful life determinations.

90   Many factors are considered in determining the useful life of an intangible asset, including:

(a)   the expected usage of the asset by the entity and whether the asset could be managed efficiently by another management team;

(b)   typical product life cycles for the asset and public information on estimates of useful lives of similar assets that are used in a similar way;

(c)   technical, technological, commercial or other types of obsolescence;

(d)   the stability of the industry in which the asset operates and changes in the market demand for the products or services output from the asset;

(e)   expected actions by competitors or potential competitors;

(f)   the level of maintenance expenditure required to obtain the expected future economic benefits from the asset and the entity's ability and intention to reach such a level;

(g)   the period of control over the asset and legal or similar limits on the use of the asset, such as the expiry dates of related leases; and

(h)   whether the useful life of the asset is dependent on the useful life of other assets of the entity.

91   The term 'indefinite' does not mean 'infinite'. The useful life of an intangible asset reflects only that level of future maintenance expenditure required to maintain the asset at its standard of performance assessed at the time of estimating the asset's useful life, and the entity's ability and intention to reach such a level. A conclusion that the useful life of an intangible asset is indefinite should not depend on planned future expenditure in excess of that required to maintain the asset at that standard of performance.

92   Given the history of rapid changes in technology, computer software and many other intangible assets are susceptible to technological obsolescence. Therefore, it is likely that their useful life is short.

93   The useful life of an intangible asset may be very long or even indefinite. Uncertainty justifies estimating the useful life of an intangible asset on a prudent basis, but it does not justify choosing a life that is unrealistically short.

94   **The useful life of an intangible asset that arises from contractual or other legal rights shall not exceed the period of the contractual or other legal rights, but may be shorter depending on the period over which the entity expects to use the asset. If the contractual or other legal rights are conveyed for a limited term that can be renewed, the useful life of the intangible asset shall include the renewal period(s) only if there is evidence to support renewal by the entity without significant cost. The useful life of a reacquired right recognised as an intangible asset in a business combination is the remaining contractual period of the contract in which the right was granted and shall not include renewal periods.**

95   There may be both economic and legal factors influencing the useful life of an intangible asset. Economic factors determine the period over which future economic benefits will be received by the entity. Legal factors may restrict the period over which the entity controls access to these benefits. The useful life is the shorter of the periods determined by these factors.

96   Existence of the following factors, among others, indicates that an entity would be able to renew the contractual or other legal rights without significant cost:

(a)   there is evidence, possibly based on experience, that the contractual or other legal rights will be renewed. If renewal is contingent upon the consent of a third party, this includes evidence that the third party will give its consent;

(b)   there is evidence that any conditions necessary to obtain renewal will be satisfied; and

(c)   the cost to the entity of renewal is not significant when compared with the future economic benefits expected to flow to the entity from renewal.

If the cost of renewal is significant when compared with the future economic benefits expected to flow to the entity from renewal, the 'renewal' cost represents, in substance, the cost to acquire a new intangible asset at the renewal date.

Intangible assets with finite useful lives

Amortisation period and amortisation method

97   **The depreciable amount of an intangible asset with a finite useful life shall be allocated on a systematic basis over its useful life. Amortisation shall begin when the asset is available for use, ie when it is in the location and condition necessary for it to be capable of operating in the manner intended by management. Amortisation shall cease at the earlier of the date that the asset is classified as held for sale (or included in a disposal group that is classified as held for sale) in accordance with IFRS 5 and the date that the asset is derecognised. The amortisation method used shall reflect the pattern in which the asset's future economic benefits are expected to be consumed by the entity. If that pattern cannot be determined reliably, the straight-line method shall be used. The amortisation charge for each period shall be recognised in profit or loss unless this or another Standard permits or requires it to be included in the carrying amount of another asset.**

98   A variety of amortisation methods can be used to allocate the depreciable amount of an asset on a systematic basis over its useful life. These methods include the straight-line method, the diminishing balance method and the unit of production method. The method used is selected on the basis of the expected pattern of consumption of the expected future economic benefits embodied in the asset and is applied consistently from period to period, unless there is a change in the expected pattern of consumption of those future economic benefits.

99   Amortisation is usually recognised in profit or loss. However, sometimes the future economic benefits embodied in an asset are absorbed in producing other assets. In this case, the amortisation charge constitutes part of the cost of the other asset and is included in its carrying amount. For example, the amortisation of intangible assets used in a production process is included in the carrying amount of inventories (see IAS 2 *Inventories*).

Residual value

100   The residual value of an intangible asset with a finite useful life shall be assumed to be zero unless:

    (a)   there is a commitment by a third party to purchase the asset at the end of its useful life; or

    (b)   there is an active market (as defined in IFRS 13) for the asset and:

        (i)   residual value can be determined by reference to that market; and

        (ii)   it is probable that such a market will exist at the end of the asset's useful life.

101   The depreciable amount of an asset with a finite useful life is determined after deducting its residual value. A residual value other than zero implies that an entity expects to dispose of the intangible asset before the end of its economic life.

102   An estimate of an asset's residual value is based on the amount recoverable from disposal using prices prevailing at the date of the estimate for the sale of a similar asset that has reached the end of its useful life and has operated under conditions similar to those in which the asset will be used. The residual value is reviewed at least at each financial year-end. A change in the asset's residual value is accounted for as a change in an accounting estimate in accordance with IAS 8 *Accounting Policies, Changes in Accounting Estimates and Errors.*

103   The residual value of an intangible asset may increase to an amount equal to or greater than the asset's carrying amount. If it does, the asset's amortisation charge is zero unless and until its residual value subsequently decreases to an amount below the asset's carrying amount.

Review of amortisation period and amortisation method

104   The amortisation period and the amortisation method for an intangible asset with a finite useful life shall be reviewed at least at each financial year-end. If the expected useful life of the asset is different from previous estimates, the amortisation period shall be changed accordingly. If there has been a change in the expected pattern of consumption of the future economic benefits embodied in the asset, the amortisation method shall be changed to reflect the changed pattern. Such changes shall be accounted for as changes in accounting estimates in accordance with IAS 8.

105   During the life of an intangible asset, it may become apparent that the estimate of its useful life is inappropriate. For example, the recognition of an impairment loss may indicate that the amortisation period needs to be changed.

106   Over time, the pattern of future economic benefits expected to flow to an entity from an intangible asset may change. For example, it may become apparent that a diminishing balance method of amortisation is appropriate rather than a straight-line method. Another example is if use of the rights represented by a licence is deferred pending action on other components of the business plan. In this case, economic benefits that flow from the asset may not be received until later periods.

Intangible assets with indefinite useful lives

107 **An intangible asset with an indefinite useful life shall not be amortised.**

108 In accordance with IAS 36, an entity is required to test an intangible asset with an indefinite useful life for impairment by comparing its recoverable amount with its carrying amount

(a) annually, and

(b) whenever there is an indication that the intangible asset may be impaired.

Review of useful life assessment

109 **The useful life of an intangible asset that is not being amortised shall be reviewed each period to determine whether events and circumstances continue to support an indefinite useful life assessment for that asset. If they do not, the change in the useful life assessment from indefinite to finite shall be accounted for as a change in an accounting estimate in accordance with IAS 8.**

110 In accordance with IAS 36, reassessing the useful life of an intangible asset as finite rather than indefinite is an indicator that the asset may be impaired. As a result, the entity tests the asset for impairment by comparing its recoverable amount, determined in accordance with IAS 36, with its carrying amount, and recognising any excess of the carrying amount over the recoverable amount as an impairment loss.

Recoverability of the carrying amount—impairment losses

111 To determine whether an intangible asset is impaired, an entity applies IAS 36. That Standard explains when and how an entity reviews the carrying amount of its assets, how it determines the recoverable amount of an asset and when it recognises or reverses an impairment loss.

Retirements and disposals

112 **An intangible asset shall be derecognised:**

(a) **on disposal; or**

(b) **when no future economic benefits are expected from its use or disposal.**

113 **The gain or loss arising from the derecognition of an intangible asset shall be determined as the difference between the net disposal proceeds, if any, and the carrying amount of the asset. It shall be recognised in profit or loss when the asset is derecognised (unless IAS 17 requires otherwise on a sale and leaseback.) Gains shall not be classified as revenue.**

114 The disposal of an intangible asset may occur in a variety of ways (eg by sale, by entering into a finance lease, or by donation). In determining the date of disposal of such an asset, an entity applies the criteria in IAS 18 *Revenue* for recognising revenue from the sale of goods. IAS 17 applies to disposal by a sale and leaseback.

115   If in accordance with the recognition principle in paragraph 21 an entity recognises in the carrying amount of an asset the cost of a replacement for part of an intangible asset, then it derecognises the carrying amount of the replaced part. If it is not practicable for an entity to determine the carrying amount of the replaced part, it may use the cost of the replacement as an indication of what the cost of the replaced part was at the time it was acquired or internally generated.

115A   In the case of a reacquired right in a business combination, if the right is subsequently reissued (sold) to a third party, the related carrying amount, if any, shall be used in determining the gain or loss on reissue.

116   The consideration receivable on disposal of an intangible asset is recognised initially at its fair value. If payment for the intangible asset is deferred, the consideration received is recognised initially at the cash price equivalent. The difference between the nominal amount of the consideration and the cash price equivalent is recognised as interest revenue in accordance with IAS 18 reflecting the effective yield on the receivable.

117   Amortisation of an intangible asset with a finite useful life does not cease when the intangible asset is no longer used, unless the asset has been fully depreciated or is classified as held for sale (or included in a disposal group that is classified as held for sale) in accordance with IFRS 5.

Disclosure

General

118   An entity shall disclose the following for each class of intangible assets, distinguishing between internally generated intangible assets and other intangible assets:

(a)   whether the useful lives are indefinite or finite and, if finite, the useful lives or the amortisation rates used;

(b)   the amortisation methods used for intangible assets with finite useful lives;

(c)   the gross carrying amount and any accumulated amortisation (aggregated with accumulated impairment losses) at the beginning and end of the period;

(d)   the line item(s) of the statement of comprehensive income in which any amortisation of intangible assets is included;

(e)   a reconciliation of the carrying amount at the beginning and end of the period showing:

(i)   additions, indicating separately those from internal development, those acquired separately, and those acquired through business combinations;

(ii)   assets classified as held for sale or included in a disposal group classified as held for sale in accordance with IFRS 5 and other disposals;

    (iii)   **increases or decreases during the period resulting from revaluations under paragraphs 75, 85 and 86 and from impairment losses recognised or reversed in other comprehensive income in accordance with IAS 36 (if any);**

    (iv)   **impairment losses recognised in profit or loss during the period in accordance with IAS 36 (if any);**

    (v)   **impairment losses reversed in profit or loss during the period in accordance with IAS 36 (if any);**

    (vi)   **any amortisation recognised during the period;**

    (vii)   **net exchange differences arising on the translation of the financial statements into the presentation currency, and on the translation of a foreign operation into the presentation currency of the entity; and**

    (viii)   **other changes in the carrying amount during the period.**

119   A class of intangible assets is a grouping of assets of a similar nature and use in an entity's operations. Examples of separate classes may include:

    (a)   brand names;

    (b)   mastheads and publishing titles;

    (c)   computer software;

    (d)   licences and franchises;

    (e)   copyrights, patents and other industrial property rights, service and operating rights;

    (f)   recipes, formulae, models, designs and prototypes; and

    (g)   intangible assets under development.

The classes mentioned above are disaggregated (aggregated) into smaller (larger) classes if this results in more relevant information for the users of the financial statements.

120   An entity discloses information on impaired intangible assets in accordance with IAS 36 in addition to the information required by paragraph 118(e)(iii)–(v).

121   IAS 8 requires an entity to disclose the nature and amount of a change in an accounting estimate that has a material effect in the current period or is expected to have a material effect in subsequent periods. Such disclosure may arise from changes in:

    (a)   the assessment of an intangible asset's useful life;

    (b)   the amortisation method; or

    (c)   residual values.

122   **An entity shall also disclose:**

    (a)   **for an intangible asset assessed as having an indefinite useful life, the carrying amount of that asset and the reasons supporting the assessment of an indefinite useful life. In giving these reasons, the entity shall describe the factor(s) that played a significant role in determining that the asset has an indefinite useful life.**

(b) a description, the carrying amount and remaining amortisation period of any individual intangible asset that is material to the entity's financial statements.

(c) for intangible assets acquired by way of a government grant and initially recognised at fair value (see paragraph 44):

(i) the fair value initially recognised for these assets;

(ii) their carrying amount; and

(iii) whether they are measured after recognition under the cost model or the revaluation model.

(d) the existence and carrying amounts of intangible assets whose title is restricted and the carrying amounts of intangible assets pledged as security for liabilities.

(e) the amount of contractual commitments for the acquisition of intangible assets.

123 When an entity describes the factor(s) that played a significant role in determining that the useful life of an intangible asset is indefinite, the entity considers the list of factors in paragraph 90.

Intangible assets measured after recognition using the revaluation model

124 If intangible assets are accounted for at revalued amounts, an entity shall disclose the following:

(a) by class of intangible assets:

(i) the effective date of the revaluation;

(ii) the carrying amount of revalued intangible assets; and

(iii) the carrying amount that would have been recognised had the revalued class of intangible assets been measured after recognition using the cost model in paragraph 74; and

(b) the amount of the revaluation surplus that relates to intangible assets at the beginning and end of the period, indicating the changes during the period and any restrictions on the distribution of the balance to shareholders.

(c) [deleted]

125 It may be necessary to aggregate the classes of revalued assets into larger classes for disclosure purposes. However, classes are not aggregated if this would result in the combination of a class of intangible assets that includes amounts measured under both the cost and revaluation models.

Research and development expenditure

126 An entity shall disclose the aggregate amount of research and development expenditure recognised as an expense during the period.

127　　Research and development expenditure comprises all expenditure that is directly attributable to research or development activities (see paragraphs 66 and 67 for guidance on the type of expenditure to be included for the purpose of the disclosure requirement in paragraph 126).

Other information

128　　An entity is encouraged, but not required, to disclose the following information:

(a)　a description of any fully amortised intangible asset that is still in use; and

(b)　a brief description of significant intangible assets controlled by the entity but not recognised as assets because they did not meet the recognition criteria in this Standard or because they were acquired or generated before the version of IAS 38 *Intangible Assets* issued in 1998 was effective.

Transitional provisions and effective date

129　　[Deleted]

130　　An entity shall apply this Standard:

(a)　to the accounting for intangible assets acquired in business combinations for which the agreement date is on or after 31 March 2004; and

(b)　to the accounting for all other intangible assets prospectively from the beginning of the first annual period beginning on or after 31 March 2004. Thus, the entity shall not adjust the carrying amount of intangible assets recognised at that date. However, the entity shall, at that date, apply this Standard to reassess the useful lives of such intangible assets. If, as a result of that reassessment, the entity changes its assessment of the useful life of an asset, that change shall be accounted for as a change in an accounting estimate in accordance with IAS 8.

130A　An entity shall apply the amendments in paragraph 2 for annual periods beginning on or after 1 January 2006. If an entity applies IFRS 6 for an earlier period, those amendments shall be applied for that earlier period.

130B　IAS 1 *Presentation of Financial Statements* (as revised in 2007) amended the terminology used throughout IFRSs. In addition it amended paragraphs 85, 86 and 118(e)(iii). An entity shall apply those amendments for annual periods beginning on or after 1 January 2009. If an entity applies IAS 1 (revised 2007) for an earlier period, the amendments shall be applied for that earlier period.

130C　IFRS 3 (as revised in 2008) amended paragraphs 12, 33–35, 68, 69, 94 and 130, deleted paragraphs 38 and 129 and added paragraph 115A. *Improvements to IFRSs* issued in April 2009 amended paragraphs 36 and 37. An entity shall apply those amendments prospectively for annual periods beginning on or after 1 July 2009. Therefore, amounts recognised for intangible assets and goodwill in prior business combinations shall not be adjusted. If an entity applies IFRS 3 (revised 2008) for an earlier period, it shall apply the amendments for that earlier period and disclose that fact.

130D   Paragraphs 69, 70 and 98 were amended and paragraph 69A was added by
        Improvements to IFRSs issued in May 2008. An entity shall apply those amendments
        for annual periods beginning on or after 1 January 2009. Earlier application is
        permitted. If an entity applies the amendments for an earlier period it shall
        disclose that fact.

130E   [Deleted]

130F   IFRS 10 and IFRS 11 *Joint Arrangements*, issued in May 2011, amended paragraph 3(e).
        An entity shall apply that amendment when it applies IFRS 10 and IFRS 11.

130G   IFRS 13, issued in May 2011, amended paragraphs 8, 33, 47, 50, 75, 78, 82, 84, 100
        and 124 and deleted paragraphs 39–41 and 130E. An entity shall apply those
        amendments when it applies IFRS 13.

Exchanges of similar assets

131   The requirement in paragraphs 129 and 130(b) to apply this Standard
        prospectively means that if an exchange of assets was measured before the
        effective date of this Standard on the basis of the carrying amount of the asset
        given up, the entity does not restate the carrying amount of the asset acquired to
        reflect its fair value at the acquisition date.

Early application

132   Entities to which paragraph 130 applies are encouraged to apply the
        requirements of this Standard before the effective dates specified in paragraph 130.
        However, if an entity applies this Standard before those effective dates, it also
        shall apply IFRS 3 and IAS 36 (as revised in 2004) at the same time.

Withdrawal of IAS 38 (issued 1998)

133   This Standard supersedes IAS 38 *Intangible Assets* (issued in 1998).

International Accounting Standard 39

Financial Instruments: Recognition and Measurement

In April 2001 the International Accounting Standards Board (IASB) adopted IAS 38 *Intangible Assets*, which had originally been issued by the International Accounting Standards Committee (IASC) in March 1999. That standard had replaced the original IAS 39 *Recognition and Measurement*, which had been issued in December 1998. That original IAS 39 had replaced some parts of IAS 25 *Accounting for Investments*, which had been issued in March 1986.

In December 2003 the IASB issued a revised IAS 39 as part of its initial agenda of technical projects. The revised IAS 27 also incorporated an Implementation Guidance section, which replaced a series of Questions & Answers that had been developed by the IAS 39 Implementation Guidance Committee (IGC).

Following that, the IASB made further amendments to IAS 39:

(a)   in March 2004, to enable fair value hedge accounting to be used for a portfolio hedge of interest rate risk;

(b)   in June 2005, relating to when the fair value option could be applied;

(c)   in July 2008, to provide application guidance to illustrate how the principles underlying hedge accounting should be applied;

(d)   in October 2008, to allow some types of financial assets to be reclassified; and

(e)   in March 2009, to address how some embedded derivatives should be measured if they were previously reclassified.

In August 2005 the IASB issued IFRS 7 *Financial Instruments: Disclosures*. Consequently, the disclosure requirements that were in IAS 39 were moved to IFRS 7.

The IASB intends ultimately to replace IAS 39 in its entirety. However, in response to requests from interested parties that the accounting for financial instruments should be improved quickly, the IASB divided the project into phases. As the IASB completes each phase, it will create chapters in IFRS 9 that replace the relevant requirements in IAS 39.

In November 2009, the IASB issued the chapters of IFRS 9 *Financial Instruments* relating to the classification and measurement of financial assets. In October 2010 the IASB added to IFRS 9 the requirements related to the classification and measurement of financial liabilities. When those chapters were issued, the IASB withdrew those relevant requirements from IAS 39.

In October 2010 the IASB also moved the requirements related to the derecognition of financial assets and financial liabilities and embedded derivatives from IAS 39 to IFRS 9.

Other IFRSs have made minor consequential amendments to IAS 39. They include IFRS 7 *Financial Instruments: Disclosures* (issued August 2005), IAS 1 *Presentation of Financial Statements* (as revised in September 2007), *Improvements to IFRSs* (issued May 2008 and April 2009) and IFRS 13 *Fair Value Measurement* (issued May 2011).

CONTENTS

from paragraph

FOR THE ACCOMPANYING DOCUMENTS LISTED BELOW, SEE PART B OF THIS EDITION

APPROVAL BY THE BOARD OF IAS 39 ISSUED IN DECEMBER 2003

APPROVAL BY THE BOARD OF AMENDMENTS TO IAS 39:

Fair Value Hedge Accounting for a Portfolio Hedge of Interest Rate Risk
issued in March 2004

Transition and Initial Recognition of Financial Assets and Financial Liabilities
issued in December 2004

Cash Flow Hedge Accounting of Forecast Intragroup Transactions
issued in April 2005

The Fair Value Option issued in June 2005

Financial Guarantee Contracts (Amendments to IAS 39 and IFRS 4) issued in August 2005

Eligible Hedged Items issued in July 2008

Embedded Derivatives (Amendments to IFRIC 9 and IAS 39) issued in March 2009[1]

BASIS FOR CONCLUSIONS

DISSENTING OPINIONS

ILLUSTRATIVE EXAMPLE

IMPLEMENTATION GUIDANCE

---

1   IFRIC 9 was superseded by IFRS 9 *Financial Instruments*, issued in October 2010.

International Accounting Standard 39 *Financial Instruments: Recognition and Measurement* (IAS 39) is set out in paragraphs 2–110 and Appendices A and B. All the paragraphs have equal authority but retain the IASC format of the Standard when it was adopted by the IASB. IAS 39 should be read in the context of its objective and the Basis for Conclusions, the *Preface to International Financial Reporting Standards* and the *Conceptual Framework for Financial Reporting*. IAS 8 *Accounting Policies, Changes in Accounting Estimates and Errors* provides a basis for selecting and applying accounting policies in the absence of explicit guidance.

Introduction

The International Accounting Standards Board has decided to replace IAS 39 *Financial Instruments: Recognition and Measurement* over a period of time. The first instalment, dealing with classification and measurement of financial assets, was issued as IFRS 9 *Financial Instruments* in November 2009. The requirements for classification and measurement of financial liabilities and derecognition of financial assets and liabilities were added to IFRS 9 in October 2010. As a consequence, parts of IAS 39 are being superseded and will become obsolete for annual periods beginning on or after 1 January 2013. Proposals to replace the requirements on impairment have been published and proposals on hedge accounting are expected to be published in 2010. The remaining requirements of IAS 39 continue in effect until superseded by future instalments of IFRS 9. The Board expects to replace IAS 39 in its entirety.

International Accounting Standard 39
Financial Instruments: Recognition and Measurement

1   [Deleted]

Scope

2   This Standard shall be applied by all entities to all types of financial instruments
       except:

    (a)   those interests in subsidiaries, associates and joint ventures that are
accounted for in accordance with IFRS 10 *Consolidated Financial Statements*,
IAS 27 *Separate Financial Statements* or IAS 28 *Investments in Associates and
Joint Ventures*. However, entities shall apply this Standard to an interest in a
subsidiary, associate or joint venture that according to IAS 27 or IAS 28 is
accounted for under this Standard. Entities shall also apply this Standard
to derivatives on an interest in a subsidiary, associate or joint venture
unless the derivative meets the definition of an equity instrument of the
entity in IAS 32 *Financial Instruments: Presentation*.

    (b)   rights and obligations under leases to which IAS 17 *Leases* applies.
However:

        (i)   lease receivables recognised by a lessor are subject to the
derecognition and impairment provisions of this Standard;

        (ii)   finance lease payables recognised by a lessee are subject to the
derecognition provisions of this Standard; and

        (iii)   derivatives that are embedded in leases are subject to the embedded
derivatives provisions of this Standard.

    (c)   employers' rights and obligations under employee benefit plans, to which
IAS 19 *Employee Benefits* applies.

    (d)   financial instruments issued by the entity that meet the definition of an
equity instrument in IAS 32 (including options and warrants) or that are
required to be classified as an equity instrument in accordance with
paragraphs 16A and 16B or paragraphs 16C and 16D of IAS 32. However, the
holder of such equity instruments shall apply this Standard to those
instruments, unless they meet the exception in (a) above.

    (e)   rights and obligations arising under (i) an insurance contract as defined in
IFRS 4 *Insurance Contracts*, other than an issuer's rights and obligations
arising under an insurance contract that meets the definition of a financial
guarantee contract in Appendix A of IFRS 9 *Financial Instruments*, or (ii) a
contract that is within the scope of IFRS 4 because it contains
a discretionary participation feature. However, this Standard applies to a
derivative that is embedded in a contract within the scope of IFRS 4 if the
derivative is not itself a contract within the scope of IFRS 4. Moreover, if an
issuer of financial guarantee contracts has previously asserted explicitly
that it regards such contracts as insurance contracts and has used

accounting applicable to insurance contracts, the issuer may elect to apply either this Standard or IFRS 4 to such financial guarantee contracts (see paragraphs AG4 and AG4A). The issuer may make that election contract by contract, but the election for each contract is irrevocable.

(f)   [deleted]

(g)   any forward contract between an acquirer and a selling shareholder to buy or sell an acquiree that will result in a business combination at a future acquisition date. The term of the forward contract should not exceed a reasonable period normally necessary to obtain any required approvals and to complete the transaction.

(h)   loan commitments other than those loan commitments described in paragraph 4. An issuer of loan commitments shall apply IAS 37 *Provisions, Contingent Liabilities and Contingent Assets* to loan commitments that are not within the scope of this Standard. However, all loan commitments are subject to the derecognition provisions of this Standard.

(i)   financial instruments, contracts and obligations under share-based payment transactions to which IFRS 2 *Share-based Payment* applies, except for contracts within the scope of paragraphs 5–7 of this Standard, to which this Standard applies.

(j)   rights to payments to reimburse the entity for expenditure it is required to make to settle a liability that it recognises as a provision in accordance with IAS 37, or for which, in an earlier period, it recognised a provision in accordance with IAS 37.

3   [Deleted]

4   The following loan commitments are within the scope of this Standard:

(a)   loan commitments that the entity designates as financial liabilities at fair value through profit or loss (see paragraph 4.2.2 of IFRS 9). An entity that has a past practice of selling the assets resulting from its loan commitments shortly after origination shall apply this Standard to all its loan commitments in the same class.

(b)   loan commitments that can be settled net in cash or by delivering or issuing another financial instrument. These loan commitments are derivatives. A loan commitment is not regarded as settled net merely because the loan is paid out in instalments (for example, a mortgage construction loan that is paid out in instalments in line with the progress of construction).

(c)   commitments to provide a loan at a below-market interest rate (see paragraph 4.2.1 of IFRS 9).

5   This Standard shall be applied to those contracts to buy or sell a non-financial item that can be settled net in cash or another financial instrument, or by exchanging financial instruments, as if the contracts were financial instruments, with the exception of contracts that were entered into and continue to be held for the purpose of the receipt or delivery of a non-financial item in accordance with the entity's expected purchase, sale or usage requirements.

6   There are various ways in which a contract to buy or sell a non-financial item can be settled net in cash or another financial instrument or by exchanging financial instruments. These include:

(a)   when the terms of the contract permit either party to settle it net in cash or another financial instrument or by exchanging financial instruments;

(b)   when the ability to settle net in cash or another financial instrument, or by exchanging financial instruments, is not explicit in the terms of the contract, but the entity has a practice of settling similar contracts net in cash or another financial instrument or by exchanging financial instruments (whether with the counterparty, by entering into offsetting contracts or by selling the contract before its exercise or lapse);

(c)   when, for similar contracts, the entity has a practice of taking delivery of the underlying and selling it within a short period after delivery for the purpose of generating a profit from short-term fluctuations in price or dealer's margin; and

(d)   when the non-financial item that is the subject of the contract is readily convertible to cash.

A contract to which (b) or (c) applies is not entered into for the purpose of the receipt or delivery of the non-financial item in accordance with the entity's expected purchase, sale or usage requirements and, accordingly, is within the scope of this Standard. Other contracts to which paragraph 5 applies are evaluated to determine whether they were entered into and continue to be held for the purpose of the receipt or delivery of the non-financial item in accordance with the entity's expected purchase, sale or usage requirements and, accordingly, whether they are within the scope of this Standard.

7   A written option to buy or sell a non-financial item that can be settled net in cash or another financial instrument, or by exchanging financial instruments, in accordance with paragraph 6(a) or (d) is within the scope of this Standard. Such a contract cannot be entered into for the purpose of the receipt or delivery of the non-financial item in accordance with the entity's expected purchase, sale or usage requirements.

Definitions

8   The terms defined in IFRS 9 and IAS 32 are used in this Standard with the meanings specified in Appendix A of IFRS 9 and paragraph 11 of IAS 32. IFRS 9 and IAS 32 define the following terms:

- derecognition

- derivative

- equity instrument

- fair value

- financial asset

- financial guarantee contract
- financial instrument
- financial liability

and provide guidance on applying those definitions.

9 The following terms are used in this Standard with the meanings specified:

Definitions relating to recognition and measurement

The *amortised cost of a financial asset or financial liability* is the amount at which the financial asset or financial liability is measured at initial recognition minus principal repayments, plus or minus the cumulative amortisation using the effective interest method of any difference between that initial amount and the maturity amount, and minus any reduction (directly or through the use of an allowance account) for impairment or uncollectibility.

The *effective interest method* is a method of calculating the amortised cost of a financial asset or a financial liability (or group of financial assets or financial liabilities) and of allocating the interest income or interest expense over the relevant period.

The *effective interest rate* is the rate that exactly discounts estimated future cash payments or receipts through the expected life of the financial instrument or, when appropriate, a shorter period to the net carrying amount of the financial asset or financial liability. When calculating the effective interest rate, an entity shall estimate cash flows considering all contractual terms of the financial instrument (for example, prepayment, call and similar options) but shall not consider future credit losses. The calculation includes all fees and points paid or received between parties to the contract that are an integral part of the effective interest rate (see IAS 18 *Revenue*), transaction costs, and all other premiums or discounts. There is a presumption that the cash flows and the expected life of a group of similar financial instruments can be estimated reliably. However, in those rare cases when it is not possible to estimate reliably the cash flows or the expected life of a financial instrument (or group of financial instruments), the entity shall use the contractual cash flows over the full contractual term of the financial instrument (or group of financial instruments).

Transaction costs are incremental costs that are directly attributable to the acquisition, issue or disposal of a financial asset or financial liability (see Appendix A paragraph AG13). An incremental cost is one that would not have been incurred if the entity had not acquired, issued or disposed of the financial instrument.

Definitions relating to hedge accounting

A *firm commitment* is a binding agreement for the exchange of a specified quantity of resources at a specified price on a specified future date or dates.

A *forecast transaction* is an uncommitted but anticipated future transaction.

A *hedging instrument* is a designated derivative or (for a hedge of the risk of changes in foreign currency exchange rates only) a designated non-derivative financial asset or non-derivative financial liability whose fair value or cash flows are expected to offset changes in the fair value or cash flows of a designated hedged item (paragraphs 72–77 and Appendix A paragraphs AG94–AG97 elaborate on the definition of a hedging instrument).

A *hedged item* is an asset, liability, firm commitment, highly probable forecast transaction or net investment in a foreign operation that (a) exposes the entity to risk of changes in fair value or future cash flows and (b) is designated as being hedged (paragraphs 78–84 and Appendix A paragraphs AG98–AG101 elaborate on the definition of hedged items).

Hedge effectiveness is the degree to which changes in the fair value or cash flows of the hedged item that are attributable to a hedged risk are offset by changes in the fair value or cash flows of the hedging instrument (see Appendix A paragraphs AG105–AG113).

10–57   [Deleted]

Impairment and uncollectibility of financial assets measured at amortised cost

58   An entity shall assess at the end of each reporting period whether there is any objective evidence that a financial asset or group of financial assets measured at amortised cost is impaired. If any such evidence exists, the entity shall apply paragraph 63 to determine the amount of any impairment loss.

59   A financial asset or a group of financial assets is impaired and impairment losses are incurred if, and only if, there is objective evidence of impairment as a result of one or more events that occurred after the initial recognition of the asset (a 'loss event') and that loss event (or events) has an impact on the estimated future cash flows of the financial asset or group of financial assets that can be reliably estimated. It may not be possible to identify a single, discrete event that caused the impairment. Rather the combined effect of several events may have caused the impairment. Losses expected as a result of future events, no matter how likely, are not recognised. Objective evidence that a financial asset or group of assets is impaired includes observable data that comes to the attention of the holder of the asset about the following loss events:

(a)   significant financial difficulty of the issuer or obligor;

(b)   a breach of contract, such as a default or delinquency in interest or principal payments;

(c)   the lender, for economic or legal reasons relating to the borrower's financial difficulty, granting to the borrower a concession that the lender would not otherwise consider;

(d)   it becoming probable that the borrower will enter bankruptcy or other financial reorganisation;

(e)   the disappearance of an active market for that financial asset because of financial difficulties; or

(f)   observable data indicating that there is a measurable decrease in the estimated future cash flows from a group of financial assets since the initial recognition of those assets, although the decrease cannot yet be identified with the individual financial assets in the group, including:

(i)   adverse changes in the payment status of borrowers in the group (eg an increased number of delayed payments or an increased number of credit card borrowers who have reached their credit limit and are paying the minimum monthly amount); or

(ii) national or local economic conditions that correlate with defaults on the assets in the group (eg an increase in the unemployment rate in the geographical area of the borrowers, a decrease in property prices for mortgages in the relevant area, a decrease in oil prices for loan assets to oil producers, or adverse changes in industry conditions that affect the borrowers in the group).

60 The disappearance of an active market because an entity's financial instruments are no longer publicly traded is not evidence of impairment. A downgrade of an entity's credit rating is not, of itself, evidence of impairment, although it may be evidence of impairment when considered with other available information. A decline in the fair value of a financial asset below its cost or amortised cost is not necessarily evidence of impairment (for example, a decline in the fair value of an investment in a debt instrument that results from an increase in the risk-free interest rate).

61 [Deleted]

62 In some cases the observable data required to estimate the amount of an impairment loss on a financial asset may be limited or no longer fully relevant to current circumstances. For example, this may be the case when a borrower is in financial difficulties and there are few available historical data relating to similar borrowers. In such cases, an entity uses its experienced judgement to estimate the amount of any impairment loss. Similarly an entity uses its experienced judgement to adjust observable data for a group of financial assets to reflect current circumstances (see paragraph AG89). The use of reasonable estimates is an essential part of the preparation of financial statements and does not undermine their reliability.

63 **If there is objective evidence that an impairment loss on financial assets measured at amortised cost has been incurred, the amount of the loss is measured as the difference between the asset's carrying amount and the present value of estimated future cash flows (excluding future credit losses that have not been incurred) discounted at the financial asset's original effective interest rate (ie the effective interest rate computed at initial recognition). The carrying amount of the asset shall be reduced either directly or through use of an allowance account. The amount of the loss shall be recognised in profit or loss.**

64 An entity first assesses whether objective evidence of impairment exists individually for financial assets that are individually significant, and individually or collectively for financial assets that are not individually significant (see paragraph 59). If an entity determines that no objective evidence of impairment exists for an individually assessed financial asset, whether significant or not, it includes the asset in a group of financial assets with similar credit risk characteristics and collectively assesses them for impairment. Assets that are individually assessed for impairment and for which an impairment loss is or continues to be recognised are not included in a collective assessment of impairment.

65   **If, in a subsequent period, the amount of the impairment loss decreases and the decrease can be related objectively to an event occurring after the impairment was recognised (such as an improvement in the debtor's credit rating), the previously recognised impairment loss shall be reversed either directly or by adjusting an allowance account. The reversal shall not result in a carrying amount of the financial asset that exceeds what the amortised cost would have been had the impairment not been recognised at the date the impairment is reversed. The amount of the reversal shall be recognised in profit or loss.**

66–70   [Deleted]

Hedging

71   **If there is a designated hedging relationship between a hedging instrument and a hedged item as described in paragraphs 85–88 and Appendix A paragraphs AG102–AG104, accounting for the gain or loss on the hedging instrument and the hedged item shall follow paragraphs 89–102.**

Hedging instruments

Qualifying instruments

72   This Standard does not restrict the circumstances in which a derivative may be designated as a hedging instrument provided the conditions in paragraph 88 are met, except for some written options (see Appendix A paragraph AG94). However, a non-derivative financial asset or non-derivative financial liability may be designated as a hedging instrument only for a hedge of a foreign currency risk.

73   For hedge accounting purposes, only instruments that involve a party external to the reporting entity (ie external to the group or individual entity that is being reported on) can be designated as hedging instruments. Although individual entities within a consolidated group or divisions within an entity may enter into hedging transactions with other entities within the group or divisions within the entity, any such intragroup transactions are eliminated on consolidation. Therefore, such hedging transactions do not qualify for hedge accounting in the consolidated financial statements of the group. However, they may qualify for hedge accounting in the individual or separate financial statements of individual entities within the group provided that they are external to the individual entity that is being reported on.

Designation of hedging instruments

74   There is normally a single fair value measure for a hedging instrument in its entirety, and the factors that cause changes in fair value are co-dependent. Thus, a hedging relationship is designated by an entity for a hedging instrument in its entirety. The only exceptions permitted are:

(a)   separating the intrinsic value and time value of an option contract and designating as the hedging instrument only the change in intrinsic value of an option and excluding change in its time value; and

(b)   separating the interest element and the spot price of a forward contract.

These exceptions are permitted because the intrinsic value of the option and the premium on the forward can generally be measured separately. A dynamic hedging strategy that assesses both the intrinsic value and time value of an option contract can qualify for hedge accounting.

75   A proportion of the entire hedging instrument, such as 50 per cent of the notional amount, may be designated as the hedging instrument in a hedging relationship. However, a hedging relationship may not be designated for only a portion of the time period during which a hedging instrument remains outstanding.

76   A single hedging instrument may be designated as a hedge of more than one type of risk provided that (a) the risks hedged can be identified clearly; (b) the effectiveness of the hedge can be demonstrated; and (c) it is possible to ensure that there is specific designation of the hedging instrument and different risk positions.

77   Two or more derivatives, or proportions of them (or, in the case of a hedge of currency risk, two or more non-derivatives or proportions of them, or a combination of derivatives and non-derivatives or proportions of them), may be viewed in combination and jointly designated as the hedging instrument, including when the risk(s) arising from some derivatives offset(s) those arising from others. However, an interest rate collar or other derivative instrument that combines a written option and a purchased option does not qualify as a hedging instrument if it is, in effect, a net written option (for which a net premium is received). Similarly, two or more instruments (or proportions of them) may be designated as the hedging instrument only if none of them is a written option or a net written option.

Hedged items

Qualifying items

78   A hedged item can be a recognised asset or liability, an unrecognised firm commitment, a highly probable forecast transaction or a net investment in a foreign operation. The hedged item can be (a) a single asset, liability, firm commitment, highly probable forecast transaction or net investment in a foreign operation, (b) a group of assets, liabilities, firm commitments, highly probable forecast transactions or net investments in foreign operations with similar risk characteristics or (c) in a portfolio hedge of interest rate risk only, a portion of the portfolio of financial assets or financial liabilities that share the risk being hedged.

79   [Deleted]

80   For hedge accounting purposes, only assets, liabilities, firm commitments or highly probable forecast transactions that involve a party external to the entity can be designated as hedged items. It follows that hedge accounting can be applied to transactions between entities in the same group only in the individual or separate financial statements of those entities and not in the consolidated financial statements of the group. As an exception, the foreign currency risk of an intragroup monetary item (eg a payable/receivable between two subsidiaries) may qualify as a hedged item in the consolidated financial statements if it results in an exposure to foreign exchange rate gains or losses that are not fully

eliminated on consolidation in accordance with IAS 21 *The Effects of Changes in Foreign Exchange Rates*. In accordance with IAS 21, foreign exchange rate gains and losses on intragroup monetary items are not fully eliminated on consolidation when the intragroup monetary item is transacted between two group entities that have different functional currencies. In addition, the foreign currency risk of a highly probable forecast intragroup transaction may qualify as a hedged item in consolidated financial statements provided that the transaction is denominated in a currency other than the functional currency of the entity entering into that transaction and the foreign currency risk will affect consolidated profit or loss.

Designation of financial items as hedged items

81   If the hedged item is a financial asset or financial liability, it may be a hedged item with respect to the risks associated with only a portion of its cash flows or fair value (such as one or more selected contractual cash flows or portions of them or a percentage of the fair value) provided that effectiveness can be measured. For example, an identifiable and separately measurable portion of the interest rate exposure of an interest-bearing asset or interest-bearing liability may be designated as the hedged risk (such as a risk-free interest rate or benchmark interest rate component of the total interest rate exposure of a hedged financial instrument).

81A   In a fair value hedge of the interest rate exposure of a portfolio of financial assets or financial liabilities (and only in such a hedge), the portion hedged may be designated in terms of an amount of a currency (eg an amount of dollars, euro, pounds or rand) rather than as individual assets (or liabilities). Although the portfolio may, for risk management purposes, include assets and liabilities, the amount designated is an amount of assets or an amount of liabilities. Designation of a net amount including assets and liabilities is not permitted. The entity may hedge a portion of the interest rate risk associated with this designated amount. For example, in the case of a hedge of a portfolio containing prepayable assets, the entity may hedge the change in fair value that is attributable to a change in the hedged interest rate on the basis of expected, rather than contractual, repricing dates. When the portion hedged is based on expected repricing dates, the effect that changes in the hedged interest rate have on those expected repricing dates shall be included when determining the change in the fair value of the hedged item. Consequently, if a portfolio that contains prepayable items is hedged with a non-prepayable derivative, ineffectiveness arises if the dates on which items in the hedged portfolio are expected to prepay are revised, or actual prepayment dates differ from those expected.

Designation of non-financial items as hedged items

82   **If the hedged item is a non-financial asset or non-financial liability, it shall be designated as a hedged item (a) for foreign currency risks, or (b) in its entirety for all risks, because of the difficulty of isolating and measuring the appropriate portion of the cash flows or fair value changes attributable to specific risks other than foreign currency risks.**

Designation of groups of items as hedged items

83   Similar assets or similar liabilities shall be aggregated and hedged as a group only if the individual assets or individual liabilities in the group share the risk exposure that is designated as being hedged. Furthermore, the change in fair value attributable to the hedged risk for each individual item in the group shall be expected to be approximately proportional to the overall change in fair value attributable to the hedged risk of the group of items.

84   Because an entity assesses hedge effectiveness by comparing the change in the fair value or cash flow of a hedging instrument (or group of similar hedging instruments) and a hedged item (or group of similar hedged items), comparing a hedging instrument with an overall net position (eg the net of all fixed rate assets and fixed rate liabilities with similar maturities), rather than with a specific hedged item, does not qualify for hedge accounting.

Hedge accounting

85   Hedge accounting recognises the offsetting effects on profit or loss of changes in the fair values of the hedging instrument and the hedged item.

86   **Hedging relationships are of three types:**

    (a) *fair value hedge*: **a hedge of the exposure to changes in fair value of a recognised asset or liability or an unrecognised firm commitment, or an identified portion of such an asset, liability or firm commitment, that is attributable to a particular risk and could affect profit or loss.**

    (b) *cash flow hedge*: **a hedge of the exposure to variability in cash flows that (i) is attributable to a particular risk associated with a recognised asset or liability (such as all or some future interest payments on variable rate debt) or a highly probable forecast transaction and (ii) could affect profit or loss.**

    (c) *hedge of a net investment in a foreign operation* **as defined in IAS 21.**

87   A hedge of the foreign currency risk of a firm commitment may be accounted for as a fair value hedge or as a cash flow hedge.

88   **A hedging relationship qualifies for hedge accounting under paragraphs 89–102 if, and only if, all of the following conditions are met.**

    (a) **At the inception of the hedge there is formal designation and documentation of the hedging relationship and the entity's risk management objective and strategy for undertaking the hedge. That documentation shall include identification of the hedging instrument, the hedged item or transaction, the nature of the risk being hedged and how the entity will assess the hedging instrument's effectiveness in offsetting the exposure to changes in the hedged item's fair value or cash flows attributable to the hedged risk.**

    (b) **The hedge is expected to be highly effective (see Appendix A paragraphs AG105–AG113) in achieving offsetting changes in fair value or cash flows attributable to the hedged risk, consistently with the originally documented risk management strategy for that particular hedging relationship.**

(c) For cash flow hedges, a forecast transaction that is the subject of the hedge must be highly probable and must present an exposure to variations in cash flows that could ultimately affect profit or loss.

(d) The effectiveness of the hedge can be reliably measured, ie the fair value or cash flows of the hedged item that are attributable to the hedged risk and the fair value of the hedging instrument can be reliably measured.

(e) The hedge is assessed on an ongoing basis and determined actually to have been highly effective throughout the financial reporting periods for which the hedge was designated.

Fair value hedges

89 If a fair value hedge meets the conditions in paragraph 88 during the period, it shall be accounted for as follows:

(a) the gain or loss from remeasuring the hedging instrument at fair value (for a derivative hedging instrument) or the foreign currency component of its carrying amount measured in accordance with IAS 21 (for a non-derivative hedging instrument) shall be recognised in profit or loss; and

(b) the gain or loss on the hedged item attributable to the hedged risk shall adjust the carrying amount of the hedged item and be recognised in profit or loss. This applies if the hedged item is otherwise measured at cost.

89A For a fair value hedge of the interest rate exposure of a portion of a portfolio of financial assets or financial liabilities (and only in such a hedge), the requirement in paragraph 89(b) may be met by presenting the gain or loss attributable to the hedged item either:

(a) in a single separate line item within assets, for those repricing time periods for which the hedged item is an asset; or

(b) in a single separate line item within liabilities, for those repricing time periods for which the hedged item is a liability.

The separate line items referred to in (a) and (b) above shall be presented next to financial assets or financial liabilities. Amounts included in these line items shall be removed from the statement of financial position when the assets or liabilities to which they relate are derecognised.

90 If only particular risks attributable to a hedged item are hedged, recognised changes in the fair value of the hedged item unrelated to the hedged risk are recognised as set out in paragraph 5.7.1 of IFRS 9.

91 An entity shall discontinue prospectively the hedge accounting specified in paragraph 89 if:

(a) the hedging instrument expires or is sold, terminated or exercised (for this purpose, the replacement or rollover of a hedging instrument into another hedging instrument is not an expiration or termination if such replacement or rollover is part of the entity's documented hedging strategy);

(b) the hedge no longer meets the criteria for hedge accounting in paragraph 88; or

(c)   the entity revokes the designation.

92   Any adjustment arising from paragraph 89(b) to the carrying amount of a hedged financial instrument for which the effective interest method is used (or, in the case of a portfolio hedge of interest rate risk, to the separate line item in the statement of financial position described in paragraph 89A) shall be amortised to profit or loss. Amortisation may begin as soon as an adjustment exists and shall begin no later than when the hedged item ceases to be adjusted for changes in its fair value attributable to the risk being hedged. The adjustment is based on a recalculated effective interest rate at the date amortisation begins. However, if, in the case of a fair value hedge of the interest rate exposure of a portfolio of financial assets or financial liabilities (and only in such a hedge), amortising using a recalculated effective interest rate is not practicable, the adjustment shall be amortised using a straight-line method. The adjustment shall be amortised fully by maturity of the financial instrument or, in the case of a portfolio hedge of interest rate risk, by expiry of the relevant repricing time period.

93   When an unrecognised firm commitment is designated as a hedged item, the subsequent cumulative change in the fair value of the firm commitment attributable to the hedged risk is recognised as an asset or liability with a corresponding gain or loss recognised in profit or loss (see paragraph 89(b)). The changes in the fair value of the hedging instrument are also recognised in profit or loss.

94   When an entity enters into a firm commitment to acquire an asset or assume a liability that is a hedged item in a fair value hedge, the initial carrying amount of the asset or liability that results from the entity meeting the firm commitment is adjusted to include the cumulative change in the fair value of the firm commitment attributable to the hedged risk that was recognised in the statement of financial position.

Cash flow hedges

95   If a cash flow hedge meets the conditions in paragraph 88 during the period, it shall be accounted for as follows:

(a)   the portion of the gain or loss on the hedging instrument that is determined to be an effective hedge (see paragraph 88) shall be recognised in other comprehensive income; and

(b)   the ineffective portion of the gain or loss on the hedging instrument shall be recognised in profit or loss.

96   More specifically, a cash flow hedge is accounted for as follows:

(a)   the separate component of equity associated with the hedged item is adjusted to the lesser of the following (in absolute amounts):

(i)   the cumulative gain or loss on the hedging instrument from inception of the hedge; and

(ii)   the cumulative change in fair value (present value) of the expected future cash flows on the hedged item from inception of the hedge;

(b) any remaining gain or loss on the hedging instrument or designated component of it (that is not an effective hedge) is recognised in profit or loss; and

(c) if an entity's documented risk management strategy for a particular hedging relationship excludes from the assessment of hedge effectiveness a specific component of the gain or loss or related cash flows on the hedging instrument (see paragraphs 74, 75 and 88(a)), that excluded component of gain or loss is recognised in accordance with paragraph 5.7.1 of IFRS 9.

97   If a hedge of a forecast transaction subsequently results in the recognition of a financial asset or a financial liability, the associated gains or losses that were recognised in other comprehensive income in accordance with paragraph 95 shall be reclassified from equity to profit or loss as a reclassification adjustment (see IAS 1 (as revised in 2007)) in the same period or periods during which the hedged forecast cash flows affect profit or loss (such as in the periods that interest income or interest expense is recognised). However, if an entity expects that all or a portion of a loss recognised in other comprehensive income will not be recovered in one or more future periods, it shall reclassify into profit or loss as a reclassification adjustment the amount that is not expected to be recovered.

98   If a hedge of a forecast transaction subsequently results in the recognition of a non-financial asset or a non-financial liability, or a forecast transaction for a non-financial asset or non-financial liability becomes a firm commitment for which fair value hedge accounting is applied, then the entity shall adopt (a) or (b) below:

(a) It reclassifies the associated gains and losses that were recognised in other comprehensive income in accordance with paragraph 95 to profit or loss as a reclassification adjustment (see IAS 1 (revised 2007)) in the same period or periods during which the asset acquired or liability assumed affects profit or loss (such as in the periods that depreciation expense or cost of sales is recognised). However, if an entity expects that all or a portion of a loss recognised in other comprehensive income will not be recovered in one or more future periods, it shall reclassify from equity to profit or loss as a reclassification adjustment the amount that is not expected to be recovered.

(b) It removes the associated gains and losses that were recognised in other comprehensive income in accordance with paragraph 95, and includes them in the initial cost or other carrying amount of the asset or liability.

99   An entity shall adopt either (a) or (b) in paragraph 98 as its accounting policy and shall apply it consistently to all hedges to which paragraph 98 relates.

100   For cash flow hedges other than those covered by paragraphs 97 and 98, amounts that had been recognised in other comprehensive income shall be reclassified from equity to profit or loss as a reclassification adjustment (see IAS 1 (revised 2007)) in the same period or periods during which the hedged forecast cash flows affect profit or loss (for example, when a forecast sale occurs).

101   In any of the following circumstances an entity shall discontinue prospectively the hedge accounting specified in paragraphs 95–100:

(a) The hedging instrument expires or is sold, terminated or exercised (for this purpose, the replacement or rollover of a hedging instrument into another hedging instrument is not an expiration or termination if such replacement or rollover is part of the entity's documented hedging strategy). In this case, the cumulative gain or loss on the hedging instrument that has been recognised in other comprehensive income from the period when the hedge was effective (see paragraph 95(a)) shall remain separately in equity until the forecast transaction occurs. When the transaction occurs, paragraph 97, 98 or 100 applies.

(b) The hedge no longer meets the criteria for hedge accounting in paragraph 88. In this case, the cumulative gain or loss on the hedging instrument that has been recognised in other comprehensive income from the period when the hedge was effective (see paragraph 95(a)) shall remain separately in equity until the forecast transaction occurs. When the transaction occurs, paragraph 97, 98 or 100 applies.

(c) The forecast transaction is no longer expected to occur, in which case any related cumulative gain or loss on the hedging instrument that has been recognised in other comprehensive income from the period when the hedge was effective (see paragraph 95(a)) shall be reclassified from equity to profit or loss as a reclassification adjustment. A forecast transaction that is no longer highly probable (see paragraph 88(c)) may still be expected to occur.

(d) The entity revokes the designation. For hedges of a forecast transaction, the cumulative gain or loss on the hedging instrument that has been recognised in other comprehensive income from the period when the hedge was effective (see paragraph 95(a)) shall remain separately in equity until the forecast transaction occurs or is no longer expected to occur. When the transaction occurs, paragraph 97, 98 or 100 applies. If the transaction is no longer expected to occur, the cumulative gain or loss that had been recognised in other comprehensive income shall be reclassified from equity to profit or loss as a reclassification adjustment.

Hedges of a net investment

102 Hedges of a net investment in a foreign operation, including a hedge of a monetary item that is accounted for as part of the net investment (see IAS 21), shall be accounted for similarly to cash flow hedges:

(a) the portion of the gain or loss on the hedging instrument that is determined to be an effective hedge (see paragraph 88) shall be recognised in other comprehensive income; and

(b) the ineffective portion shall be recognised in profit or loss.

The gain or loss on the hedging instrument relating to the effective portion of the hedge that has been recognised in other comprehensive income shall be reclassified from equity to profit or loss as a reclassification adjustment (see IAS 1 (revised 2007)) in accordance with paragraphs 48–49 of IAS 21 on the disposal or partial disposal of the foreign operation.

Effective date and transition

103 An entity shall apply this Standard (including the amendments issued in March 2004) for annual periods beginning on or after 1 January 2005. Earlier application is permitted. An entity shall not apply this Standard (including the amendments issued in March 2004) for annual periods beginning before 1 January 2005 unless it also applies IAS 32 (issued December 2003). If an entity applies this Standard for a period beginning before 1 January 2005, it shall disclose that fact.

103A An entity shall apply the amendment in paragraph 2(j) for annual periods beginning on or after 1 January 2006. If an entity applies IFRIC 5 *Rights to Interests arising from Decommissioning, Restoration and Environmental Rehabilitation Funds* for an earlier period, this amendment shall be applied for that earlier period.

103B *Financial Guarantee Contracts* (Amendments to IAS 39 and IFRS 4), issued in August 2005, amended paragraphs 2(e) and (h), 4 and AG4, added paragraph AG4A, added a new definition of financial guarantee contracts and deleted paragraph 3. An entity shall apply those amendments for annual periods beginning on or after 1 January 2006. Earlier application is encouraged. If an entity applies these changes for an earlier period, it shall disclose that fact and apply the related amendments to IAS 32² and IFRS 4 at the same time.

103C IAS 1 (as revised in 2007) amended the terminology used throughout IFRSs. In addition it amended paragraphs 95(a), 97, 98, 100, 102, 108 and AG99B. An entity shall apply those amendments for annual periods beginning on or after 1 January 2009. If an entity applies IAS 1 (revised 2007) for an earlier period, the amendments shall be applied for that earlier period.

103D IFRS 3 (as revised in 2008) deleted paragraph 2(f). An entity shall apply that amendment for annual periods beginning on or after 1 July 2009. If an entity applies IFRS 3 (revised 2008) for an earlier period, the amendment shall also be applied for that earlier period. However, the amendment does not apply to contingent consideration that arose from a business combination for which the acquisition date preceded the application of IFRS 3 (revised 2008). Instead, an entity shall account for such consideration in accordance with paragraphs 65A–65E of IFRS 3 (as amended in 2010).

103E IAS 27 (as amended in 2008) amended paragraph 102. An entity shall apply that amendment for annual periods beginning on or after 1 July 2009. If an entity applies IAS 27 (amended 2008) for an earlier period, the amendment shall be applied for that earlier period.

103F An entity shall apply the amendment in paragraph 2 for annual periods beginning on or after 1 January 2009. If an entity applies *Puttable Financial Instruments and Obligations Arising on Liquidation* (Amendments to IAS 32 and IAS 1), issued in February 2008, for an earlier period, the amendment in paragraph 2 shall be applied for that earlier period.

---

2 When an entity applies IFRS 7, the reference to IAS 32 is replaced by a reference to IFRS 7.

103G   An entity shall apply paragraphs AG99BA, AG99E, AG99F, AG110A and AG110B retrospectively for annual periods beginning on or after 1 July 2009, in accordance with IAS 8 *Accounting Policies, Changes in Accounting Estimates and Errors.* Earlier application is permitted. If an entity applies *Eligible Hedged Items* (Amendment to IAS 39) for periods beginning before 1 July 2009, it shall disclose that fact.

103H–103J   [Deleted]

103K   *Improvements to IFRSs* issued in April 2009 amended paragraphs 2(g), 97 and 100. An entity shall apply the amendments to those paragraphs prospectively to all unexpired contracts for annual periods beginning on or after 1 January 2010. Earlier application is permitted. If an entity applies the amendment for an earlier period it shall disclose that fact.

103L   [Deleted]

103M   [Deleted]

103N   Paragraph 103D was amended by *Improvements to IFRSs* issued in May 2010. An entity shall apply that amendment for annual periods beginning on or after 1 July 2010. Earlier application is permitted.

103O   IFRS 9, issued in October 2010, amended paragraphs 2, 4, 8, 9, 58, 63, 88(d), 89(b), 90, 96(c), 103B, 103C, 103K, 104, 108C, AG3–AG4, AG8, AG84, AG95, AG114(a) and AG118(b) and deleted paragraphs 1, 10–57, 61, 66–70, 79, 103H–103J, 103L, 103M, 105–107A, AG4B–AG4K, AG9–AG12A, AG14, AG15, AG27–AG83 and AG96. An entity shall apply those amendments when it applies IFRS 9 as issued in October 2010.

103P   IFRS 10 and IFRS 11 *Joint Arrangements,* issued in May 2011, amended paragraphs 2(a), 15, AG3, AG36–AG38 and AG4I(a). An entity shall apply those amendments when it applies IFRS 10 and IFRS 11.

103Q   IFRS 13, issued in May 2011, amended paragraphs 9, 13, 28, 47, 88, AG46, AG52, AG64, AG76, AG76A, AG80, AG81 and AG96, added paragraph 43A and deleted paragraphs 48–49, AG69–AG75, AG77–AG79 and AG82. An entity shall apply those amendments when it applies IFRS 13.

104   This Standard shall be applied retrospectively except as specified in paragraph 108. The opening balance of retained earnings for the earliest prior period presented and all other comparative amounts shall be adjusted as if this Standard had always been in use unless restating the information would be impracticable. If restatement is impracticable, the entity shall disclose that fact and indicate the extent to which the information was restated.

105–107A   [Deleted]

108   An entity shall not adjust the carrying amount of non-financial assets and non-financial liabilities to exclude gains and losses related to cash flow hedges that were included in the carrying amount before the beginning of the financial year in which this Standard is first applied. At the beginning of the financial period in which this Standard is first applied, any amount recognised

outside profit or loss (in other comprehensive income or directly in equity) for a hedge of a firm commitment that under this Standard is accounted for as a fair value hedge shall be reclassified as an asset or liability, except for a hedge of foreign currency risk that continues to be treated as a cash flow hedge.

108A   An entity shall apply the last sentence of paragraph 80, and paragraphs AG99A and AG99B, for annual periods beginning on or after 1 January 2006. Earlier application is encouraged. If an entity has designated as the hedged item an external forecast transaction that

(a)   is denominated in the functional currency of the entity entering into the transaction,

(b)   gives rise to an exposure that will have an effect on consolidated profit or loss (ie is denominated in a currency other than the group's presentation currency), and

(c)   would have qualified for hedge accounting had it not been denominated in the functional currency of the entity entering into it,

it may apply hedge accounting in the consolidated financial statements in the period(s) before the date of application of the last sentence of paragraph 80, and paragraphs AG99A and AG99B.

108B   An entity need not apply paragraph AG99B to comparative information relating to periods before the date of application of the last sentence of paragraph 80 and paragraph AG99A.

108C   Paragraphs 73 and AG8 were amended by *Improvements to IFRSs*, issued in May 2008. Paragraph 80 was amended by *Improvements to IFRSs* issued in April 2009. An entity shall apply those amendments for annual periods beginning on or after 1 January 2009. Earlier application of all the amendments is permitted. If an entity applies the amendments for an earlier period it shall disclose that fact.

Withdrawal of other pronouncements

109   This Standard supersedes IAS 39 *Financial Instruments: Recognition and Measurement* revised in October 2000.

110   This Standard and the accompanying Implementation Guidance supersede the Implementation Guidance issued by the IAS 39 Implementation Guidance Committee, established by the former IASC.

Appendix A
Application guidance

This appendix is an integral part of the Standard.

Scope (paragraphs 2–7)

AG1   Some contracts require a payment based on climatic, geological or other physical variables. (Those based on climatic variables are sometimes referred to as 'weather derivatives'.) If those contracts are not within the scope of IFRS 4, they are within the scope of this Standard.

AG2   This Standard does not change the requirements relating to employee benefit plans that comply with IAS 26 *Accounting and Reporting by Retirement Benefit Plans* and royalty agreements based on the volume of sales or service revenues that are accounted for under IAS 18.

AG3   Sometimes, an entity makes what it views as a 'strategic investment' in equity instruments issued by another entity, with the intention of establishing or maintaining a long-term operating relationship with the entity in which the investment is made. The investor or joint venturer entity uses IAS 28 to determine whether the equity method of accounting is appropriate for such an investment. If the equity method is not appropriate, the entity applies this Standard and IFRS 9 to that strategic investment.

AG3A   This Standard and IFRS 9 apply to the financial assets and financial liabilities of insurers, other than rights and obligations that paragraph 2(e) excludes because they arise under contracts within the scope of IFRS 4.

AG4   Financial guarantee contracts may have various legal forms, such as a guarantee, some types of letter of credit, a credit default contract or an insurance contract. Their accounting treatment does not depend on their legal form. The following are examples of the appropriate treatment (see paragraph 2(e)):

(a)   Although a financial guarantee contract meets the definition of an insurance contract in IFRS 4 if the risk transferred is significant, the issuer applies this Standard and IFRS 9. Nevertheless, if the issuer has previously asserted explicitly that it regards such contracts as insurance contracts and has used accounting applicable to insurance contracts, the issuer may elect to apply either this Standard and IFRS 9 or IFRS 4 to such financial guarantee contracts. If this Standard and IFRS 9 apply, paragraph 5.1.1 of IFRS 9 requires the issuer to recognise a financial guarantee contract initially at fair value. If the financial guarantee contract was issued to an unrelated party in a stand-alone arm's length transaction, its fair value at inception is likely to equal the premium received, unless there is evidence to the contrary. Subsequently, unless the financial guarantee contract was designated at inception as at fair value through profit or loss or unless paragraphs 3.2.15–3.2.23 and B3.2.12–B3.2.17 of IFRS 9 apply (when a transfer of a financial asset does not qualify for derecognition or the continuing involvement approach applies), the issuer measures it at the higher of:

(i)   the amount determined in accordance with IAS 37; and

(ii)   the amount initially recognised less, when appropriate, cumulative amortisation recognised in accordance with IAS 18 (see paragraph 4.2.1(c) of IFRS 9).

(b)   Some credit-related guarantees do not, as a precondition for payment, require that the holder is exposed to, and has incurred a loss on, the failure of the debtor to make payments on the guaranteed asset when due. An example of such a guarantee is one that requires payments in response to changes in a specified credit rating or credit index. Such guarantees are not financial guarantee contracts as defined in IFRS 9 and are not insurance contracts as defined in IFRS 4. Such guarantees are derivatives and the issuer applies this Standard and IFRS 9 to them.

(c)   If a financial guarantee contract was issued in connection with the sale of goods, the issuer applies IAS 18 in determining when it recognises the revenue from the guarantee and from the sale of goods.

AG4A   Assertions that an issuer regards contracts as insurance contracts are typically found throughout the issuer's communications with customers and regulators, contracts, business documentation and financial statements. Furthermore, insurance contracts are often subject to accounting requirements that are distinct from the requirements for other types of transaction, such as contracts issued by banks or commercial companies. In such cases, an issuer's financial statements typically include a statement that the issuer has used those accounting requirements.

Definitions (paragraphs 8 and 9)

AG4B–   [Deleted]
AG4K

Effective interest rate

AG5   In some cases, financial assets are acquired at a deep discount that reflects incurred credit losses. Entities include such incurred credit losses in the estimated cash flows when computing the effective interest rate.

AG6   When applying the effective interest method, an entity generally amortises any fees, points paid or received, transaction costs and other premiums or discounts included in the calculation of the effective interest rate over the expected life of the instrument. However, a shorter period is used if this is the period to which the fees, points paid or received, transaction costs, premiums or discounts relate. This will be the case when the variable to which the fees, points paid or received, transaction costs, premiums or discounts relate is repriced to market rates before the expected maturity of the instrument. In such a case, the appropriate amortisation period is the period to the next such repricing date. For example, if a premium or discount on a floating rate instrument reflects interest that has accrued on the instrument since interest was last paid, or changes in market rates since the floating interest rate was reset to market rates, it will be amortised to the next date when the floating interest is reset to market rates. This is because the premium or discount relates to the period to the next interest reset date because, at that date, the variable to which the premium or discount relates (ie interest rates) is reset to market rates. If, however, the premium or discount results from a change in the credit spread over the floating rate specified in the instrument, or other variables that are not reset to market rates, it is amortised over the expected life of the instrument.

AG7   For floating rate financial assets and floating rate financial liabilities, periodic re-estimation of cash flows to reflect movements in market rates of interest alters the effective interest rate. If a floating rate financial asset or floating rate financial liability is recognised initially at an amount equal to the principal receivable or payable on maturity, re-estimating the future interest payments normally has no significant effect on the carrying amount of the asset or liability.

AG8   If an entity revises its estimates of payments or receipts, the entity shall adjust the carrying amount of the financial asset or financial liability (or group of financial instruments) to reflect actual and revised estimated cash flows. The entity recalculates the carrying amount by computing the present value of estimated future cash flows at the financial instrument's original effective interest rate or, when applicable, the revised effective interest rate calculated in accordance with paragraph 92. The adjustment is recognised in profit or loss as income or expense.

AG9–   [Deleted]
AG12A

Transaction costs

AG13   Transaction costs include fees and commissions paid to agents (including employees acting as selling agents), advisers, brokers and dealers, levies by regulatory agencies and securities exchanges, and transfer taxes and duties. Transaction costs do not include debt premiums or discounts, financing costs or internal administrative or holding costs.

AG14–   [Deleted]
AG83

Impairment and uncollectibility of financial assets measured at amortised cost (paragraphs 58–65)

AG84   Impairment of a financial asset measured at amortised cost is measured using the financial instrument's original effective interest rate because discounting at the current market rate of interest would, in effect, impose fair value measurement on financial assets that are otherwise measured at amortised cost. If the terms of a financial asset measured at amortised cost are renegotiated or otherwise modified because of financial difficulties of the borrower or issuer, impairment is measured using the original effective interest rate before the modification of terms. Cash flows relating to short-term receivables are not discounted if the effect of discounting is immaterial. If a financial asset measured at amortised cost has a variable interest rate, the discount rate for measuring any impairment loss under paragraph 63 is the current effective interest rate(s) determined under the contract. As a practical expedient, a creditor may measure impairment of a financial asset measured at amortised cost on the basis of an instrument's fair value using an observable market price. The calculation of the present value of the estimated future cash flows of a collateralised financial asset reflects the cash flows that may result from foreclosure less costs for obtaining and selling the collateral, whether or not foreclosure is probable.

AG85   The process for estimating impairment considers all credit exposures, not only those of low credit quality. For example, if an entity uses an internal credit grading system it considers all credit grades, not only those reflecting a severe credit deterioration.

AG86   The process for estimating the amount of an impairment loss may result either in a single amount or in a range of possible amounts. In the latter case, the entity recognises an impairment loss equal to the best estimate within the range[3] taking into account all relevant information available before the financial statements are issued about conditions existing at the end of the reporting period.

AG87   For the purpose of a collective evaluation of impairment, financial assets are grouped on the basis of similar credit risk characteristics that are indicative of the debtors' ability to pay all amounts due according to the contractual terms (for example, on the basis of a credit risk evaluation or grading process that considers asset type, industry, geographical location, collateral type, past-due status and other relevant factors). The characteristics chosen are relevant to the estimation of future cash flows for groups of such assets by being indicative of the debtors' ability to pay all amounts due according to the contractual terms of the assets being evaluated. However, loss probabilities and other loss statistics differ at a group level between (a) assets that have been individually evaluated for impairment and found not to be impaired and (b) assets that have not been individually evaluated for impairment, with the result that a different amount of impairment may be required. If an entity does not have a group of assets with similar risk characteristics, it does not make the additional assessment.

AG88   Impairment losses recognised on a group basis represent an interim step pending the identification of impairment losses on individual assets in the group of financial assets that are collectively assessed for impairment. As soon as information is available that specifically identifies losses on individually impaired assets in a group, those assets are removed from the group.

AG89   Future cash flows in a group of financial assets that are collectively evaluated for impairment are estimated on the basis of historical loss experience for assets with credit risk characteristics similar to those in the group. Entities that have no entity-specific loss experience or insufficient experience, use peer group experience for comparable groups of financial assets. Historical loss experience is adjusted on the basis of current observable data to reflect the effects of current conditions that did not affect the period on which the historical loss experience is based and to remove the effects of conditions in the historical period that do not exist currently. Estimates of changes in future cash flows reflect and are directionally consistent with changes in related observable data from period to period (such as changes in unemployment rates, property prices, commodity

---

3   IAS 37, paragraph 39 contains guidance on how to determine the best estimate in a range of possible outcomes.

prices, payment status or other factors that are indicative of incurred losses in the group and their magnitude). The methodology and assumptions used for estimating future cash flows are reviewed regularly to reduce any differences between loss estimates and actual loss experience.

AG90   As an example of applying paragraph AG89, an entity may determine, on the basis of historical experience, that one of the main causes of default on credit card loans is the death of the borrower. The entity may observe that the death rate is unchanged from one year to the next. Nevertheless, some of the borrowers in the entity's group of credit card loans may have died in that year, indicating that an impairment loss has occurred on those loans, even if, at the year-end, the entity is not yet aware which specific borrowers have died. It would be appropriate for an impairment loss to be recognised for these 'incurred but not reported' losses. However, it would not be appropriate to recognise an impairment loss for deaths that are expected to occur in a future period, because the necessary loss event (the death of the borrower) has not yet occurred.

AG91   When using historical loss rates in estimating future cash flows, it is important that information about historical loss rates is applied to groups that are defined in a manner consistent with the groups for which the historical loss rates were observed. Therefore, the method used should enable each group to be associated with information about past loss experience in groups of assets with similar credit risk characteristics and relevant observable data that reflect current conditions.

AG92   Formula-based approaches or statistical methods may be used to determine impairment losses in a group of financial assets (eg for smaller balance loans) as long as they are consistent with the requirements in paragraphs 63–65 and AG87–AG91. Any model used would incorporate the effect of the time value of money, consider the cash flows for all of the remaining life of an asset (not only the next year), consider the age of the loans within the portfolio and not give rise to an impairment loss on initial recognition of a financial asset.

Interest income after impairment recognition

AG93   Once a financial asset or a group of similar financial assets has been written down as a result of an impairment loss, interest income is thereafter recognised using the rate of interest used to discount the future cash flows for the purpose of measuring the impairment loss.

Hedging (paragraphs 71–102)

Hedging instruments (paragraphs 72–77)

Qualifying instruments (paragraphs 72 and 73)

AG94   The potential loss on an option that an entity writes could be significantly greater than the potential gain in value of a related hedged item. In other words, a written option is not effective in reducing the profit or loss exposure of a hedged item. Therefore, a written option does not qualify as a hedging instrument unless it is designated as an offset to a purchased option, including one that is embedded in another financial instrument (for example, a written call option used to hedge a callable liability). In contrast, a purchased option has potential gains equal to or greater than losses and therefore has the potential to reduce profit or loss exposure from changes in fair values or cash flows. Accordingly, it can qualify as a hedging instrument.

AG95   A financial asset measured at amortised cost may be designated as a hedging instrument in a hedge of foreign currency risk.

AG96   [Deleted]

AG97   An entity's own equity instruments are not financial assets or financial liabilities of the entity and therefore cannot be designated as hedging instruments.

Hedged items (paragraphs 78–84)

Qualifying items (paragraphs 78–80)

AG98   A firm commitment to acquire a business in a business combination cannot be a hedged item, except for foreign exchange risk, because the other risks being hedged cannot be specifically identified and measured. These other risks are general business risks.

AG99   An equity method investment cannot be a hedged item in a fair value hedge because the equity method recognises in profit or loss the investor's share of the associate's profit or loss, rather than changes in the investment's fair value. For a similar reason, an investment in a consolidated subsidiary cannot be a hedged item in a fair value hedge because consolidation recognises in profit or loss the subsidiary's profit or loss, rather than changes in the investment's fair value. A hedge of a net investment in a foreign operation is different because it is a hedge of the foreign currency exposure, not a fair value hedge of the change in the value of the investment.

AG99A   Paragraph 80 states that in consolidated financial statements the foreign currency risk of a highly probable forecast intragroup transaction may qualify as a hedged item in a cash flow hedge, provided the transaction is denominated in a currency other than the functional currency of the entity entering into that transaction and the foreign currency risk will affect consolidated profit or loss. For this purpose an entity can be a parent, subsidiary, associate, joint venture or branch. If the foreign currency risk of a forecast intragroup transaction does not affect consolidated profit or loss, the intragroup transaction cannot qualify as a hedged item. This is usually the case for royalty payments, interest payments or management charges between members of the same group unless there is a related external transaction. However, when the foreign currency risk of a forecast intragroup transaction will affect consolidated profit or loss, the intragroup transaction can qualify as a hedged item. An example is forecast sales or purchases of inventories between members of the same group if there is an onward sale of the inventory to a party external to the group. Similarly, a forecast intragroup sale of plant and equipment from the group entity that manufactured it to a group entity that will use the plant and equipment in its operations may affect consolidated profit or loss. This could occur, for example, because the plant and equipment will be depreciated by the purchasing entity and the amount initially recognised for the plant and equipment may change if the forecast intragroup transaction is denominated in a currency other than the functional currency of the purchasing entity.

AG99B   If a hedge of a forecast intragroup transaction qualifies for hedge accounting, any gain or loss that is recognised in other comprehensive income in accordance with paragraph 95(a) shall be reclassified from equity to profit or loss as a reclassification adjustment in the same period or periods during which the foreign currency risk of the hedged transaction affects consolidated profit or loss.

AG99BA An entity can designate all changes in the cash flows or fair value of a hedged item in a hedging relationship. An entity can also designate only changes in the cash flows or fair value of a hedged item above or below a specified price or other variable (a one-sided risk). The intrinsic value of a purchased option hedging instrument (assuming that it has the same principal terms as the designated risk), but not its time value, reflects a one-sided risk in a hedged item. For example, an entity can designate the variability of future cash flow outcomes resulting from a price increase of a forecast commodity purchase. In such a situation, only cash flow losses that result from an increase in the price above the specified level are designated. The hedged risk does not include the time value of a purchased option because the time value is not a component of the forecast transaction that affects profit or loss (paragraph 86(b)).

Designation of financial items as hedged items (paragraphs 81 and 81A)

AG99C   If a portion of the cash flows of a financial asset or financial liability is designated as the hedged item, that designated portion must be less than the total cash flows of the asset or liability. For example, in the case of a liability whose effective interest rate is below LIBOR, an entity cannot designate (a) a portion of the liability equal to the principal amount plus interest at LIBOR and (b) a negative residual portion. However, the entity may designate all of the cash flows of the entire financial asset or financial liability as the hedged item and hedge them for only one particular risk (eg only for changes that are attributable to changes in LIBOR). For example, in the case of a financial liability whose effective interest rate is 100 basis points below LIBOR, an entity can designate as the hedged item the entire liability (ie principal plus interest at LIBOR minus 100 basis points) and hedge the change in the fair value or cash flows of that entire liability that is attributable to changes in LIBOR. The entity may also choose a hedge ratio of other than one to one in order to improve the effectiveness of the hedge as described in paragraph AG100.

AG99D   In addition, if a fixed rate financial instrument is hedged some time after its origination and interest rates have changed in the meantime, the entity can designate a portion equal to a benchmark rate that is higher than the contractual rate paid on the item. The entity can do so provided that the benchmark rate is less than the effective interest rate calculated on the assumption that the entity had purchased the instrument on the day it first designates the hedged item. For example, assume an entity originates a fixed rate financial asset of CU100 that has an effective interest rate of 6 per cent at a time when LIBOR is 4 per cent. It begins to hedge that asset some time later when LIBOR has increased to 8 per cent and the fair value of the asset has decreased to CU90. The entity calculates that if it had purchased the asset on the date it first designates it as the hedged item for its then fair value of CU90, the effective yield would have been 9.5 per cent. Because LIBOR is less than this effective yield, the entity can designate a LIBOR portion of 8 per cent that consists partly of the contractual interest cash flows and partly of the difference between the current fair value (ie CU90) and the amount repayable on maturity (ie CU100).

AG99E   Paragraph 81 permits an entity to designate something other than the entire fair value change or cash flow variability of a financial instrument. For example:

(a)   all of the cash flows of a financial instrument may be designated for cash flow or fair value changes attributable to some (but not all) risks; or

(b)   some (but not all) of the cash flows of a financial instrument may be designated for cash flow or fair value changes attributable to all or only some risks (ie a 'portion' of the cash flows of the financial instrument may be designated for changes attributable to all or only some risks).

AG99F   To be eligible for hedge accounting, the designated risks and portions must be separately identifiable components of the financial instrument, and changes in the cash flows or fair value of the entire financial instrument arising from changes in the designated risks and portions must be reliably measurable. For example:

(a)   for a fixed rate financial instrument hedged for changes in fair value attributable to changes in a risk-free or benchmark interest rate, the risk-free or benchmark rate is normally regarded as both a separately identifiable component of the financial instrument and reliably measurable.

(b)   inflation is not separately identifiable and reliably measurable and cannot be designated as a risk or a portion of a financial instrument unless the requirements in (c) are met.

(c)   a contractually specified inflation portion of the cash flows of a recognised inflation-linked bond (assuming there is no requirement to account for an embedded derivative separately) is separately identifiable and reliably measurable as long as other cash flows of the instrument are not affected by the inflation portion.

Designation of non-financial items as hedged items (paragraph 82)

AG100   Changes in the price of an ingredient or component of a non-financial asset or non-financial liability generally do not have a predictable, separately measurable effect on the price of the item that is comparable to the effect of, say, a change in market interest rates on the price of a bond. Thus, a non-financial asset or non-financial liability is a hedged item only in its entirety or for foreign exchange risk. If there is a difference between the terms of the hedging instrument and the hedged item (such as for a hedge of the forecast purchase of Brazilian coffee using a forward contract to purchase Colombian coffee on otherwise similar terms), the hedging relationship nonetheless can qualify as a hedge relationship provided all the conditions in paragraph 88 are met, including that the hedge is expected to be highly effective. For this purpose, the amount of the hedging instrument may be greater or less than that of the hedged item if this improves the effectiveness of the hedging relationship. For example, a regression analysis could be performed to establish a statistical relationship between the hedged item (eg a transaction in Brazilian coffee) and the hedging instrument (eg a transaction in Colombian coffee). If there is a valid statistical relationship between the two variables (ie between the unit prices of Brazilian coffee and Colombian coffee), the slope of the regression line can be used to establish the hedge ratio that will maximise expected effectiveness. For example, if the slope of the regression line is 1.02, a hedge ratio based on 0.98 quantities of hedged items to 1.00 quantities of the hedging instrument maximises expected effectiveness. However, the hedging relationship may result in ineffectiveness that is recognised in profit or loss during the term of the hedging relationship.

Designation of groups of items as hedged items (paragraphs 83 and 84)

AG101 A hedge of an overall net position (eg the net of all fixed rate assets and fixed rate liabilities with similar maturities), rather than of a specific hedged item, does not qualify for hedge accounting. However, almost the same effect on profit or loss of hedge accounting for this type of hedging relationship can be achieved by designating as the hedged item part of the underlying items. For example, if a bank has CU100 of assets and CU90 of liabilities with risks and terms of a similar nature and hedges the net CU10 exposure, it can designate as the hedged item CU10 of those assets. This designation can be used if such assets and liabilities are fixed rate instruments, in which case it is a fair value hedge, or if they are variable rate instruments, in which case it is a cash flow hedge. Similarly, if an entity has a firm commitment to make a purchase in a foreign currency of CU100 and a firm commitment to make a sale in the foreign currency of CU90, it can hedge the net amount of CU10 by acquiring a derivative and designating it as a hedging instrument associated with CU10 of the firm purchase commitment of CU100.

Hedge accounting (paragraphs 85–102)

AG102 An example of a fair value hedge is a hedge of exposure to changes in the fair value of a fixed rate debt instrument as a result of changes in interest rates. Such a hedge could be entered into by the issuer or by the holder.

AG103 An example of a cash flow hedge is the use of a swap to change floating rate debt to fixed rate debt (ie a hedge of a future transaction where the future cash flows being hedged are the future interest payments).

AG104 A hedge of a firm commitment (eg a hedge of the change in fuel price relating to an unrecognised contractual commitment by an electric utility to purchase fuel at a fixed price) is a hedge of an exposure to a change in fair value. Accordingly, such a hedge is a fair value hedge. However, under paragraph 87 a hedge of the foreign currency risk of a firm commitment could alternatively be accounted for as a cash flow hedge.

Assessing hedge effectiveness

AG105   A hedge is regarded as highly effective only if both of the following conditions are met:

(a)   At the inception of the hedge and in subsequent periods, the hedge is expected to be highly effective in achieving offsetting changes in fair value or cash flows attributable to the hedged risk during the period for which the hedge is designated. Such an expectation can be demonstrated in various ways, including a comparison of past changes in the fair value or cash flows of the hedged item that are attributable to the hedged risk with past changes in the fair value or cash flows of the hedging instrument, or by demonstrating a high statistical correlation between the fair value or cash flows of the hedged item and those of the hedging instrument. The entity may choose a hedge ratio of other than one to one in order to improve the effectiveness of the hedge as described in paragraph AG100.

(b)   The actual results of the hedge are within a range of 80–125 per cent. For example, if actual results are such that the loss on the hedging instrument is CU120 and the gain on the cash instrument is CU100, offset can be measured by 120/100, which is 120 per cent, or by 100/120, which is 83 per cent. In this example, assuming the hedge meets the condition in (a), the entity would conclude that the hedge has been highly effective.

AG106   Effectiveness is assessed, at a minimum, at the time an entity prepares its annual or interim financial statements.

AG107   This Standard does not specify a single method for assessing hedge effectiveness. The method an entity adopts for assessing hedge effectiveness depends on its risk management strategy. For example, if the entity's risk management strategy is to adjust the amount of the hedging instrument periodically to reflect changes in the hedged position, the entity needs to demonstrate that the hedge is expected to be highly effective only for the period until the amount of the hedging instrument is next adjusted. In some cases, an entity adopts different methods for different types of hedges. An entity's documentation of its hedging strategy includes its procedures for assessing effectiveness. Those procedures state whether the assessment includes all of the gain or loss on a hedging instrument or whether the instrument's time value is excluded.

AG107A   If an entity hedges less than 100 per cent of the exposure on an item, such as 85 per cent, it shall designate the hedged item as being 85 per cent of the exposure and shall measure ineffectiveness based on the change in that designated 85 per cent exposure. However, when hedging the designated 85 per cent exposure, the entity may use a hedge ratio of other than one to one if that improves the expected effectiveness of the hedge, as explained in paragraph AG100.

AG108   If the principal terms of the hedging instrument and of the hedged asset, liability, firm commitment or highly probable forecast transaction are the same, the changes in fair value and cash flows attributable to the risk being hedged may be likely to offset each other fully, both when the hedge is entered into and afterwards. For example, an interest rate swap is likely to be an effective hedge if the notional and principal amounts, term, repricing dates, dates of interest and principal receipts and payments, and basis for measuring interest rates are the same for the hedging instrument and the hedged item. In addition, a hedge of a highly probable forecast purchase of a commodity with a forward contract is likely to be highly effective if:

(a)   the forward contract is for the purchase of the same quantity of the same commodity at the same time and location as the hedged forecast purchase;

(b)   the fair value of the forward contract at inception is zero; and

(c)   either the change in the discount or premium on the forward contract is excluded from the assessment of effectiveness and recognised in profit or loss or the change in expected cash flows on the highly probable forecast transaction is based on the forward price for the commodity.

AG109   Sometimes the hedging instrument offsets only part of the hedged risk. For example, a hedge would not be fully effective if the hedging instrument and hedged item are denominated in different currencies that do not move in tandem. Also, a hedge of interest rate risk using a derivative would not be fully effective if part of the change in the fair value of the derivative is attributable to the counterparty's credit risk.

AG110   To qualify for hedge accounting, the hedge must relate to a specific identified and designated risk, and not merely to the entity's general business risks, and must ultimately affect the entity's profit or loss. A hedge of the risk of obsolescence of a physical asset or the risk of expropriation of property by a government is not eligible for hedge accounting; effectiveness cannot be measured because those risks are not measurable reliably.

AG110A Paragraph 74(a) permits an entity to separate the intrinsic value and time value of an option contract and designate as the hedging instrument only the change in the intrinsic value of the option contract. Such a designation may result in a hedging relationship that is perfectly effective in achieving offsetting changes in cash flows attributable to a hedged one-sided risk of a forecast transaction, if the principal terms of the forecast transaction and hedging instrument are the same.

AG110B If an entity designates a purchased option in its entirety as the hedging instrument of a one-sided risk arising from a forecast transaction, the hedging relationship will not be perfectly effective. This is because the premium paid for the option includes time value and, as stated in paragraph AG99BA, a designated one-sided risk does not include the time value of an option. Therefore, in this situation, there will be no offset between the cash flows relating to the time value of the option premium paid and the designated hedged risk.

AG111   In the case of interest rate risk, hedge effectiveness may be assessed by preparing a maturity schedule for financial assets and financial liabilities that shows the net interest rate exposure for each time period, provided that the net exposure is associated with a specific asset or liability (or a specific group of assets or liabilities or a specific portion of them) giving rise to the net exposure, and hedge effectiveness is assessed against that asset or liability.

AG112 In assessing the effectiveness of a hedge, an entity generally considers the time value of money. The fixed interest rate on a hedged item need not exactly match the fixed interest rate on a swap designated as a fair value hedge. Nor does the variable interest rate on an interest-bearing asset or liability need to be the same as the variable interest rate on a swap designated as a cash flow hedge. A swap's fair value derives from its net settlements. The fixed and variable rates on a swap can be changed without affecting the net settlement if both are changed by the same amount.

AG113 If an entity does not meet hedge effectiveness criteria, the entity discontinues hedge accounting from the last date on which compliance with hedge effectiveness was demonstrated. However, if the entity identifies the event or change in circumstances that caused the hedging relationship to fail the effectiveness criteria, and demonstrates that the hedge was effective before the event or change in circumstances occurred, the entity discontinues hedge accounting from the date of the event or change in circumstances.

Fair value hedge accounting for a portfolio hedge of interest rate risk

AG114 For a fair value hedge of interest rate risk associated with a portfolio of financial assets or financial liabilities, an entity would meet the requirements of this Standard if it complies with the procedures set out in (a)–(i) and paragraphs AG115–AG132 below.

(a) As part of its risk management process the entity identifies a portfolio of items whose interest rate risk it wishes to hedge. The portfolio may comprise only assets, only liabilities or both assets and liabilities. The entity may identify two or more portfolios, in which case it applies the guidance below to each portfolio separately.

(b) The entity analyses the portfolio into repricing time periods based on expected, rather than contractual, repricing dates. The analysis into repricing time periods may be performed in various ways including scheduling cash flows into the periods in which they are expected to occur, or scheduling notional principal amounts into all periods until repricing is expected to occur.

(c) On the basis of this analysis, the entity decides the amount it wishes to hedge. The entity designates as the hedged item an amount of assets or liabilities (but not a net amount) from the identified portfolio equal to the amount it wishes to designate as being hedged. This amount also determines the percentage measure that is used for testing effectiveness in accordance with paragraph AG126(b).

(d) The entity designates the interest rate risk it is hedging. This risk could be a portion of the interest rate risk in each of the items in the hedged position, such as a benchmark interest rate (eg LIBOR).

(e) The entity designates one or more hedging instruments for each repricing time period.

(f) Using the designations made in (c)–(e) above, the entity assesses at inception and in subsequent periods, whether the hedge is expected to be highly effective during the period for which the hedge is designated.

(g)   Periodically, the entity measures the change in the fair value of the hedged item (as designated in (c)) that is attributable to the hedged risk (as designated in (d)), on the basis of the expected repricing dates determined in (b). Provided that the hedge is determined actually to have been highly effective when assessed using the entity's documented method of assessing effectiveness, the entity recognises the change in fair value of the hedged item as a gain or loss in profit or loss and in one of two line items in the statement of financial position as described in paragraph 89A. The change in fair value need not be allocated to individual assets or liabilities.

(h)   The entity measures the change in fair value of the hedging instrument(s) (as designated in (e)) and recognises it as a gain or loss in profit or loss. The fair value of the hedging instrument(s) is recognised as an asset or liability in the statement of financial position.

(i)   Any ineffectiveness[4] will be recognised in profit or loss as the difference between the change in fair value referred to in (g) and that referred to in (h).

AG115   This approach is described in more detail below. The approach shall be applied only to a fair value hedge of the interest rate risk associated with a portfolio of financial assets or financial liabilities.

AG116   The portfolio identified in paragraph AG114(a) could contain assets and liabilities. Alternatively, it could be a portfolio containing only assets, or only liabilities. The portfolio is used to determine the amount of the assets or liabilities the entity wishes to hedge. However, the portfolio is not itself designated as the hedged item.

AG117   In applying paragraph AG114(b), the entity determines the expected repricing date of an item as the earlier of the dates when that item is expected to mature or to reprice to market rates. The expected repricing dates are estimated at the inception of the hedge and throughout the term of the hedge, based on historical experience and other available information, including information and expectations regarding prepayment rates, interest rates and the interaction between them. Entities that have no entity-specific experience or insufficient experience use peer group experience for comparable financial instruments. These estimates are reviewed periodically and updated in the light of experience. In the case of a fixed rate item that is prepayable, the expected repricing date is the date on which the item is expected to prepay unless it reprices to market rates on an earlier date. For a group of similar items, the analysis into time periods based on expected repricing dates may take the form of allocating a percentage of the group, rather than individual items, to each time period. An entity may apply other methodologies for such allocation purposes. For example, it may use a prepayment rate multiplier for allocating amortising loans to time periods based on expected repricing dates. However, the methodology for such an allocation shall be in accordance with the entity's risk management procedures and objectives.

---

4   The same materiality considerations apply in this context as apply throughout IFRSs.

AG118　As an example of the designation set out in paragraph AG114(c), if in a particular repricing time period an entity estimates that it has fixed rate assets of CU100 and fixed rate liabilities of CU80 and decides to hedge all of the net position of CU20, it designates as the hedged item assets in the amount of CU20 (a portion of the assets).[5] The designation is expressed as an 'amount of a currency' (eg an amount of dollars, euro, pounds or rand) rather than as individual assets. It follows that all of the assets (or liabilities) from which the hedged amount is drawn—ie all of the CU100 of assets in the above example—must be:

(a)　items whose fair value changes in response to changes in the interest rate being hedged; and

(b)　items that could have qualified for fair value hedge accounting if they had been designated as hedged individually. In particular, because IFRS 9 specifies that the fair value of a financial liability with a demand feature (such as demand deposits and some types of time deposits) is not less than the amount payable on demand, discounted from the first date that the amount could be required to be paid, such an item cannot qualify for fair value hedge accounting for any time period beyond the shortest period in which the holder can demand payment. In the above example, the hedged position is an amount of assets. Hence, such liabilities are not a part of the designated hedged item, but are used by the entity to determine the amount of the asset that is designated as being hedged. If the position the entity wished to hedge was an amount of liabilities, the amount representing the designated hedged item must be drawn from fixed rate liabilities other than liabilities that the entity can be required to repay in an earlier time period, and the percentage measure used for assessing hedge effectiveness in accordance with paragraph AG126(b) would be calculated as a percentage of these other liabilities. For example, assume that an entity estimates that in a particular repricing time period it has fixed rate liabilities of CU100, comprising CU40 of demand deposits and CU60 of liabilities with no demand feature, and CU70 of fixed rate assets. If the entity decides to hedge all of the net position of CU30, it designates as the hedged item liabilities of CU30 or 50 per cent[6] of the liabilities with no demand feature.

AG119　The entity also complies with the other designation and documentation requirements set out in paragraph 88(a). For a portfolio hedge of interest rate risk, this designation and documentation specifies the entity's policy for all of the variables that are used to identify the amount that is hedged and how effectiveness is measured, including the following:

(a)　which assets and liabilities are to be included in the portfolio hedge and the basis to be used for removing them from the portfolio.

(b)　how the entity estimates repricing dates, including what interest rate assumptions underlie estimates of prepayment rates and the basis for changing those estimates. The same method is used for both the initial estimates made at the time an asset or liability is included in the hedged portfolio and for any later revisions to those estimates.

5　The Standard permits an entity to designate any amount of the available qualifying assets or liabilities, ie in this example any amount of assets between CU0 and CU100.

6　$CU30 \div (CU100 - CU40) = 50$ per cent

(c)   the number and duration of repricing time periods.

(d)   how often the entity will test effectiveness and which of the two methods in paragraph AG126 it will use.

(e)   the methodology used by the entity to determine the amount of assets or liabilities that are designated as the hedged item and, accordingly, the percentage measure used when the entity tests effectiveness using the method described in paragraph AG126(b).

(f)   when the entity tests effectiveness using the method described in paragraph AG126(b), whether the entity will test effectiveness for each repricing time period individually, for all time periods in aggregate, or by using some combination of the two.

The policies specified in designating and documenting the hedging relationship shall be in accordance with the entity's risk management procedures and objectives. Changes in policies shall not be made arbitrarily. They shall be justified on the basis of changes in market conditions and other factors and be founded on and consistent with the entity's risk management procedures and objectives.

AG120   The hedging instrument referred to in paragraph AG114(e) may be a single derivative or a portfolio of derivatives all of which contain exposure to the hedged interest rate risk designated in paragraph AG114(d) (eg a portfolio of interest rate swaps all of which contain exposure to LIBOR). Such a portfolio of derivatives may contain offsetting risk positions. However, it may not include written options or net written options, because the Standard[7] does not permit such options to be designated as hedging instruments (except when a written option is designated as an offset to a purchased option). If the hedging instrument hedges the amount designated in paragraph AG114(c) for more than one repricing time period, it is allocated to all of the time periods that it hedges. However, the whole of the hedging instrument must be allocated to those repricing time periods because the Standard[8] does not permit a hedging relationship to be designated for only a portion of the time period during which a hedging instrument remains outstanding.

AG121   When the entity measures the change in the fair value of a prepayable item in accordance with paragraph AG114(g), a change in interest rates affects the fair value of the prepayable item in two ways: it affects the fair value of the contractual cash flows and the fair value of the prepayment option that is contained in a prepayable item. Paragraph 81 of the Standard permits an entity to designate a portion of a financial asset or financial liability, sharing a common risk exposure, as the hedged item, provided effectiveness can be measured. For prepayable items, paragraph 81A permits this to be achieved by designating the hedged item in terms of the change in the fair value that is attributable to changes in the designated interest rate on the basis of *expected*, rather than *contractual*, repricing dates. However, the effect that changes in the hedged interest rate have on those expected repricing dates shall be included when determining the change in the fair value of the hedged item.

---

7   see paragraphs 77 and AG94

8   see paragraph 75

Consequently, if the expected repricing dates are revised (eg to reflect a change in expected prepayments), or if actual repricing dates differ from those expected, ineffectiveness will arise as described in paragraph AG126. Conversely, changes in expected repricing dates that (a) clearly arise from factors other than changes in the hedged interest rate, (b) are uncorrelated with changes in the hedged interest rate and (c) can be reliably separated from changes that are attributable to the hedged interest rate (eg changes in prepayment rates clearly arising from a change in demographic factors or tax regulations rather than changes in interest rate) are excluded when determining the change in the fair value of the hedged item, because they are not attributable to the hedged risk. If there is uncertainty about the factor that gave rise to the change in expected repricing dates or the entity is not able to separate reliably the changes that arise from the hedged interest rate from those that arise from other factors, the change is assumed to arise from changes in the hedged interest rate.

AG122 The Standard does not specify the techniques used to determine the amount referred to in paragraph AG114(g), namely the change in the fair value of the hedged item that is attributable to the hedged risk. If statistical or other estimation techniques are used for such measurement, management must expect the result to approximate closely that which would have been obtained from measurement of all the individual assets or liabilities that constitute the hedged item. It is not appropriate to assume that changes in the fair value of the hedged item equal changes in the value of the hedging instrument.

AG123 Paragraph 89A requires that if the hedged item for a particular repricing time period is an asset, the change in its value is presented in a separate line item within assets. Conversely, if the hedged item for a particular repricing time period is a liability, the change in its value is presented in a separate line item within liabilities. These are the separate line items referred to in paragraph AG114(g). Specific allocation to individual assets (or liabilities) is not required.

AG124 Paragraph AG114(i) notes that ineffectiveness arises to the extent that the change in the fair value of the hedged item that is attributable to the hedged risk differs from the change in the fair value of the hedging derivative. Such a difference may arise for a number of reasons, including:

(a) actual repricing dates being different from those expected, or expected repricing dates being revised;

(b) items in the hedged portfolio becoming impaired or being derecognised;

(c) the payment dates of the hedging instrument and the hedged item being different; and

(d) other causes (eg when a few of the hedged items bear interest at a rate below the benchmark rate for which they are designated as being hedged, and the resulting ineffectiveness is not so great that the portfolio as a whole fails to qualify for hedge accounting).

Such ineffectiveness[9] shall be identified and recognised in profit or loss.

---

9   The same materiality considerations apply in this context as apply throughout IFRSs.

AG125 Generally, the effectiveness of the hedge will be improved:

   (a)   if the entity schedules items with different prepayment characteristics in a way that takes account of the differences in prepayment behaviour.

   (b)   when the number of items in the portfolio is larger. When only a few items are contained in the portfolio, relatively high ineffectiveness is likely if one of the items prepays earlier or later than expected. Conversely, when the portfolio contains many items, the prepayment behaviour can be predicted more accurately.

   (c)   when the repricing time periods used are narrower (eg 1-month as opposed to 3-month repricing time periods). Narrower repricing time periods reduce the effect of any mismatch between the repricing and payment dates (within the repricing time period) of the hedged item and those of the hedging instrument.

   (d)   the greater the frequency with which the amount of the hedging instrument is adjusted to reflect changes in the hedged item (eg because of changes in prepayment expectations).

AG126 An entity tests effectiveness periodically. If estimates of repricing dates change between one date on which an entity assesses effectiveness and the next, it shall calculate the amount of effectiveness either:

   (a)   as the difference between the change in the fair value of the hedging instrument (see paragraph AG114(h)) and the change in the value of the entire hedged item that is attributable to changes in the hedged interest rate (including the effect that changes in the hedged interest rate have on the fair value of any embedded prepayment option); or

   (b)   using the following approximation. The entity:

      (i)   calculates the percentage of the assets (or liabilities) in each repricing time period that was hedged, on the basis of the estimated repricing dates at the last date it tested effectiveness.

      (ii)   applies this percentage to its revised estimate of the amount in that repricing time period to calculate the amount of the hedged item based on its revised estimate.

      (iii)   calculates the change in the fair value of its revised estimate of the hedged item that is attributable to the hedged risk and presents it as set out in paragraph AG114(g).

      (iv)   recognises ineffectiveness equal to the difference between the amount determined in (iii) and the change in the fair value of the hedging instrument (see paragraph AG114(h)).

AG127 When measuring effectiveness, the entity distinguishes revisions to the estimated repricing dates of existing assets (or liabilities) from the origination of new assets (or liabilities), with only the former giving rise to ineffectiveness. All revisions to estimated repricing dates (other than those excluded in accordance with paragraph AG121), including any reallocation of existing items between time periods, are included when revising the estimated amount in a time period in accordance with paragraph AG126(b)(ii) and hence when measuring effectiveness.

Once ineffectiveness has been recognised as set out above, the entity establishes a new estimate of the total assets (or liabilities) in each repricing time period, including new assets (or liabilities) that have been originated since it last tested effectiveness, and designates a new amount as the hedged item and a new percentage as the hedged percentage. The procedures set out in paragraph AG126(b) are then repeated at the next date it tests effectiveness.

AG128 Items that were originally scheduled into a repricing time period may be derecognised because of earlier than expected prepayment or write-offs caused by impairment or sale. When this occurs, the amount of change in fair value included in the separate line item referred to in paragraph AG114(g) that relates to the derecognised item shall be removed from the statement of financial position, and included in the gain or loss that arises on derecognition of the item. For this purpose, it is necessary to know the repricing time period(s) into which the derecognised item was scheduled, because this determines the repricing time period(s) from which to remove it and hence the amount to remove from the separate line item referred to in paragraph AG114(g). When an item is derecognised, if it can be determined in which time period it was included, it is removed from that time period. If not, it is removed from the earliest time period if the derecognition resulted from higher than expected prepayments, or allocated to all time periods containing the derecognised item on a systematic and rational basis if the item was sold or became impaired.

AG129 In addition, any amount relating to a particular time period that has not been derecognised when the time period expires is recognised in profit or loss at that time (see paragraph 89A). For example, assume an entity schedules items into three repricing time periods. At the previous redesignation, the change in fair value reported in the single line item in the statement of financial position was an asset of CU25. That amount represents amounts attributable to periods 1, 2 and 3 of CU7, CU8 and CU10, respectively. At the next redesignation, the assets attributable to period 1 have been either realised or rescheduled into other periods. Therefore, CU7 is derecognised from the statement of financial position and recognised in profit or loss. CU8 and CU10 are now attributable to periods 1 and 2, respectively. These remaining periods are then adjusted, as necessary, for changes in fair value as described in paragraph AG114(g).

AG130 As an illustration of the requirements of the previous two paragraphs, assume that an entity scheduled assets by allocating a percentage of the portfolio into each repricing time period. Assume also that it scheduled CU100 into each of the first two time periods. When the first repricing time period expires, CU110 of assets are derecognised because of expected and unexpected repayments. In this case, all of the amount contained in the separate line item referred to in paragraph AG114(g) that relates to the first time period is removed from the statement of financial position, plus 10 per cent of the amount that relates to the second time period.

AG131 If the hedged amount for a repricing time period is reduced without the related assets (or liabilities) being derecognised, the amount included in the separate line item referred to in paragraph AG114(g) that relates to the reduction shall be amortised in accordance with paragraph 92.

AG132 An entity may wish to apply the approach set out in paragraphs AG114–AG131 to a portfolio hedge that had previously been accounted for as a cash flow hedge in accordance with IAS 39. Such an entity would revoke the previous designation of a cash flow hedge in accordance with paragraph 101(d), and apply the requirements set out in that paragraph. It would also redesignate the hedge as a fair value hedge and apply the approach set out in paragraphs AG114–AG131 prospectively to subsequent accounting periods.

Transition (paragraphs 103–108C)

AG133 An entity may have designated a forecast intragroup transaction as a hedged item at the start of an annual period beginning on or after 1 January 2005 (or, for the purpose of restating comparative information, the start of an earlier comparative period) in a hedge that would qualify for hedge accounting in accordance with this Standard (as amended by the last sentence of paragraph 80). Such an entity may use that designation to apply hedge accounting in consolidated financial statements from the start of the annual period beginning on or after 1 January 2005 (or the start of the earlier comparative period). Such an entity shall also apply paragraphs AG99A and AG99B from the start of the annual period beginning on or after 1 January 2005. However, in accordance with paragraph 108B, it need not apply paragraph AG99B to comparative information for earlier periods.

Appendix B
Amendments to other pronouncements

The amendments in this appendix shall be applied for annual periods beginning on or after 1 January 2005. If an entity applies this Standard for an earlier period, these amendments shall be applied for that earlier period.

* * * * *

The amendments contained in this appendix when this Standard was revised in 2003 have been incorporated into the relevant pronouncements.

International Accounting Standard 40

Investment Property

In April 2001 the International Accounting Standards Board (IASB) adopted IAS 40 *Investment Property*, which had originally been issued by the International Accounting Standards Committee (IASC) in April 2000. That standard had replaced some parts of IAS 25 *Accounting for Investments*, which had been issued in March 1986 and had not already been replaced by IAS 39 *Financial Instruments: Recognition and Measurement*.

In December 2003 the IASB issued a revised IAS 40 as part of its initial agenda of technical projects.

Other IFRSs have made minor consequential amendments to IAS 40. They include IAS 1 *Presentation of Financial Statements* (as revised in September 2007), *Improvements to IFRSs* (issued May 2008) and IFRS 13 *Fair Value Measurement* (issued May 2011).

Contents

FOR THE ACCOMPANYING DOCUMENTS LISTED BELOW, SEE PART B OF THIS EDITION

APPROVAL BY THE BOARD OF IAS 40 ISSUED IN DECEMBER 2003

IASB BASIS FOR CONCLUSIONS ON IAS 40 (AS REVISED IN 2003)

IASC BASIS FOR CONCLUSIONS ON IAS 40 (2000)

International Accounting Standard 40 *Investment Property* (IAS 40) is set out in paragraphs 1–86. All the paragraphs have equal authority but retain the IASC format of the Standard when it was adopted by the IASB. IAS 40 should be read in the context of its objective and the IASB's Basis for Conclusions, the *Preface to International Financial Reporting Standards* and the *Conceptual Framework for Financial Reporting*. IAS 8 *Accounting Policies, Changes in Accounting Estimates and Errors* provides a basis for selecting and applying accounting policies in the absence of explicit guidance.

Introduction

IN1　International Accounting Standard 40 *Investment Property* (IAS 40) replaces IAS 40 *Investment Property* (issued in 2000), and should be applied for annual periods beginning on or after 1 January 2005. Earlier application is encouraged.

Reasons for revising IAS 40

IN2　The International Accounting Standards Board developed this revised IAS 40 as part of its project on Improvements to International Accounting Standards. The project was undertaken in the light of queries and criticisms raised in relation to the Standards by securities regulators, professional accountants and other interested parties. The objectives of the project were to reduce or eliminate alternatives, redundancies and conflicts within the Standards, to deal with some convergence issues and to make other improvements.

IN3　For IAS 40 the Board's main objective was a limited revision to permit a property interest held by a lessee under an operating lease to qualify as investment property under specified conditions. Those conditions include requirements that the property must otherwise meet the definition of an investment property, and that the lessee must account for the lease as if it were a finance lease and measure the resulting lease asset using the fair value model. The Board did not reconsider the fundamental approach to the accounting for investment property contained in IAS 40.

The main changes

IN4　The main changes from the previous version of IAS 40 are described below.

IN5　A property interest that is held by a lessee under an operating lease may be classified and accounted for as investment property provided that:

(a)　the rest of the definition of investment property is met;

(b)　the operating lease is accounted for as if it were a finance lease in accordance with IAS 17 *Leases*; and

(c)　the lessee uses the fair value model set out in this Standard for the asset recognised.

IN6　The classification alternative described in paragraph IN5 is available on a property-by-property basis. However, because it is a general requirement of the Standard that all investment property should be consistently accounted for using the fair value or cost model, once this alternative is selected for one such property, all property classified as investment property is to be accounted for consistently on a fair value basis.

IN7　The Standard requires an entity to disclose:

(a)　whether it applies the fair value model or the cost model; and

© IFRS Foundation

(b) if it applies the fair value model, whether, and in what circumstances, property interests held under operating leases are classified and accounted for as investment property.

IN8 When a valuation obtained for investment property is adjusted significantly for the purpose of the financial statements, a reconciliation is required between the valuation obtained and the valuation included in the financial statements.

IN9 The Standard clarifies that if a property interest held under a lease is classified as investment property, the item accounted for at fair value is that interest and not the underlying property.

IN10 Comparative information is required for all disclosures.

IN11 Some significant changes have been incorporated into the Standard as a result of amendments that the Board made to IAS 16 *Property, Plant and Equipment* as part of the Improvements project:

(a) to specify what costs are included in the cost of investment property and when replaced items should be derecognised;

(b) to specify when exchange transactions (ie transactions in which investment property is acquired in exchange for non-monetary assets, in whole or in part) have commercial substance and how such transactions, with or without commercial substance, are accounted for; and

(c) to specify the accounting for compensation from third parties for investment property that was impaired, lost or given up.

Summary of the approach required by the Standard

IN12 The Standard permits entities to choose either:

(a) a fair value model, under which an investment property is measured, after initial measurement, at fair value with changes in fair value recognised in profit or loss; or

(b) a cost model. The cost model is specified in IAS 16 and requires an investment property to be measured after initial measurement at depreciated cost (less any accumulated impairment losses). An entity that chooses the cost model discloses the fair value of its investment property.

IN13 The choice between the cost and fair value models is not available to a lessee accounting for a property interest held under an operating lease that it has elected to classify and account for as investment property. The Standard requires such investment property to be measured using the fair value model.

IN14 The fair value model differs from the revaluation model that is permitted for some non-financial assets. Under the revaluation model, increases in carrying amount above a cost-based measure are recognised as revaluation surplus. However, under the fair value model, all changes in fair value are recognised in profit or loss.

IN15 The Standard requires an entity to apply its chosen model to all of its investment property. However, this does not mean that all eligible operating leases must be classified as investment properties.

IN16   In exceptional cases, when an entity has adopted the fair value model, there may be clear evidence when an entity first acquires an investment property (or when an existing property first becomes investment property following the completion of construction or development, or after a change in use) that its fair value will not be reliably measurable on a continuing basis. In such cases, the Standard requires the entity to measure that investment property using the cost model in IAS 16 until disposal of the investment property. The residual value of the investment property is assumed to be zero.

IN17   A change from one model to the other is made only if the change results in a more relevant presentation. The Standard states that this is highly unlikely to be the case for a change from the fair value model to the cost model.

IN18   IAS 40 depends upon IAS 17 for requirements for the classification of leases, the accounting for finance and operating leases and for some of the disclosures relevant to leased investment properties. When a property interest held under an operating lease is classified and accounted for as an investment property, IAS 40 overrides IAS 17 by requiring that the lease is accounted for as if it were a finance lease. Paragraphs 14–18 of IAS 17 apply to the classification of leases of land and buildings. In particular, paragraph 18 specifies when it is not necessary to measure separately the land and building elements of such a lease.

International Accounting Standard 40
Investment Property

Objective

1. The objective of this Standard is to prescribe the accounting treatment for investment property and related disclosure requirements.

Scope

2. **This Standard shall be applied in the recognition, measurement and disclosure of investment property.**

3. Among other things, this Standard applies to the measurement in a lessee's financial statements of investment property interests held under a lease accounted for as a finance lease and to the measurement in a lessor's financial statements of investment property provided to a lessee under an operating lease. This Standard does not deal with matters covered in IAS 17 *Leases*, including:

    (a) classification of leases as finance leases or operating leases;

    (b) recognition of lease income from investment property (see also IAS 18 *Revenue*);

    (c) measurement in a lessee's financial statements of property interests held under a lease accounted for as an operating lease;

    (d) measurement in a lessor's financial statements of its net investment in a finance lease;

    (e) accounting for sale and leaseback transactions; and

    (f) disclosure about finance leases and operating leases.

4. This Standard does not apply to:

    (a) biological assets related to agricultural activity (see IAS 41 *Agriculture*); and

    (b) mineral rights and mineral reserves such as oil, natural gas and similar non-regenerative resources.

Definitions

5. **The following terms are used in this Standard with the meanings specified:**

    Carrying amount is the amount at which an asset is recognised in the statement of financial position.

    Cost is the amount of cash or cash equivalents paid or the fair value of other consideration given to acquire an asset at the time of its acquisition or construction or, where applicable, the amount attributed to that asset when initially recognised in accordance with the specific requirements of other IFRSs, eg IFRS 2 *Share-based Payment*.

Fair value is the price that would be received to sell an asset or paid to transfer a liability in an orderly transaction between market participants at the measurement date. (See IFRS 13 *Fair Value Measurement*).

Investment property is property (land or a building—or part of a building—or both) held (by the owner or by the lessee under a finance lease) to earn rentals or for capital appreciation or both, rather than for:

(a) use in the production or supply of goods or services or for administrative purposes; or

(b) sale in the ordinary course of business.

Owner-occupied property is property held (by the owner or by the lessee under a finance lease) for use in the production or supply of goods or services or for administrative purposes.

6 A *property interest* that is held by a lessee under an operating lease may be classified and accounted for as investment property if, and only if, the property would otherwise meet the definition of an investment property and the lessee uses the fair value model set out in paragraphs 33–55 for the asset recognised. This classification alternative is available on a property-by-property basis. However, once this classification alternative is selected for one such property interest held under an operating lease, all property classified as investment property shall be accounted for using the fair value model. When this classification alternative is selected, any interest so classified is included in the disclosures required by paragraphs 74–78.

7 Investment property is held to earn rentals or for capital appreciation or both. Therefore, an investment property generates cash flows largely independently of the other assets held by an entity. This distinguishes investment property from owner-occupied property. The production or supply of goods or services (or the use of property for administrative purposes) generates cash flows that are attributable not only to property, but also to other assets used in the production or supply process. IAS 16 *Property, Plant and Equipment* applies to owner-occupied property.

8 The following are examples of investment property:

(a) land held for long-term capital appreciation rather than for short-term sale in the ordinary course of business.

(b) land held for a currently undetermined future use. (If an entity has not determined that it will use the land as owner-occupied property or for short-term sale in the ordinary course of business, the land is regarded as held for capital appreciation.)

(c) a building owned by the entity (or held by the entity under a finance lease) and leased out under one or more operating leases.

(d) a building that is vacant but is held to be leased out under one or more operating leases.

(e) property that is being constructed or developed for future use as investment property.

9   The following are examples of items that are not investment property and are therefore outside the scope of this Standard:

(a)   property intended for sale in the ordinary course of business or in the process of construction or development for such sale (see IAS 2 *Inventories*), for example, property acquired exclusively with a view to subsequent disposal in the near future or for development and resale.

(b)   property being constructed or developed on behalf of third parties (see IAS 11 *Construction Contracts*).

(c)   owner-occupied property (see IAS 16), including (among other things) property held for future use as owner-occupied property, property held for future development and subsequent use as owner-occupied property, property occupied by employees (whether or not the employees pay rent at market rates) and owner-occupied property awaiting disposal.

(d)   [deleted]

(e)   property that is leased to another entity under a finance lease.

10   Some properties comprise a portion that is held to earn rentals or for capital appreciation and another portion that is held for use in the production or supply of goods or services or for administrative purposes. If these portions could be sold separately (or leased out separately under a finance lease), an entity accounts for the portions separately. If the portions could not be sold separately, the property is investment property only if an insignificant portion is held for use in the production or supply of goods or services or for administrative purposes.

11   In some cases, an entity provides ancillary services to the occupants of a property it holds. An entity treats such a property as investment property if the services are insignificant to the arrangement as a whole. An example is when the owner of an office building provides security and maintenance services to the lessees who occupy the building.

12   In other cases, the services provided are significant. For example, if an entity owns and manages a hotel, services provided to guests are significant to the arrangement as a whole. Therefore, an owner-managed hotel is owner-occupied property, rather than investment property.

13   It may be difficult to determine whether ancillary services are so significant that a property does not qualify as investment property. For example, the owner of a hotel sometimes transfers some responsibilities to third parties under a management contract. The terms of such contracts vary widely. At one end of the spectrum, the owner's position may, in substance, be that of a passive investor. At the other end of the spectrum, the owner may simply have outsourced day-to-day functions while retaining significant exposure to variation in the cash flows generated by the operations of the hotel.

14   Judgement is needed to determine whether a property qualifies as investment property. An entity develops criteria so that it can exercise that judgement consistently in accordance with the definition of investment property and with the related guidance in paragraphs 7–13. Paragraph 75(c) requires an entity to disclose these criteria when classification is difficult.

15 In some cases, an entity owns property that is leased to, and occupied by, its parent or another subsidiary. The property does not qualify as investment property in the consolidated financial statements, because the property is owner-occupied from the perspective of the group. However, from the perspective of the entity that owns it, the property is investment property if it meets the definition in paragraph 5. Therefore, the lessor treats the property as investment property in its individual financial statements.

Recognition

16 **Investment property shall be recognised as an asset when, and only when:**

(a) **it is probable that the future economic benefits that are associated with the investment property will flow to the entity; and**

(b) **the cost of the investment property can be measured reliably.**

17 An entity evaluates under this recognition principle all its investment property costs at the time they are incurred. These costs include costs incurred initially to acquire an investment property and costs incurred subsequently to add to, replace part of, or service a property.

18 Under the recognition principle in paragraph 16, an entity does not recognise in the carrying amount of an investment property the costs of the day-to-day servicing of such a property. Rather, these costs are recognised in profit or loss as incurred. Costs of day-to-day servicing are primarily the cost of labour and consumables, and may include the cost of minor parts. The purpose of these expenditures is often described as for the 'repairs and maintenance' of the property.

19 Parts of investment properties may have been acquired through replacement. For example, the interior walls may be replacements of original walls. Under the recognition principle, an entity recognises in the carrying amount of an investment property the cost of replacing part of an existing investment property at the time that cost is incurred if the recognition criteria are met. The carrying amount of those parts that are replaced is derecognised in accordance with the derecognition provisions of this Standard.

Measurement at recognition

20 **An investment property shall be measured initially at its cost. Transaction costs shall be included in the initial measurement.**

21 The cost of a purchased investment property comprises its purchase price and any directly attributable expenditure. Directly attributable expenditure includes, for example, professional fees for legal services, property transfer taxes and other transaction costs.

22 [Deleted]

23 The cost of an investment property is not increased by:

(a) start-up costs (unless they are necessary to bring the property to the condition necessary for it to be capable of operating in the manner intended by management),

(b) operating losses incurred before the investment property achieves the planned level of occupancy, or

(c) abnormal amounts of wasted material, labour or other resources incurred in constructing or developing the property.

24 If payment for an investment property is deferred, its cost is the cash price equivalent. The difference between this amount and the total payments is recognised as interest expense over the period of credit.

25 The initial cost of a property interest held under a lease and classified as an investment property shall be as prescribed for a finance lease by paragraph 20 of IAS 17, ie the asset shall be recognised at the lower of the fair value of the property and the present value of the minimum lease payments. An equivalent amount shall be recognised as a liability in accordance with that same paragraph.

26 Any premium paid for a lease is treated as part of the minimum lease payments for this purpose, and is therefore included in the cost of the asset, but is excluded from the liability. If a property interest held under a lease is classified as investment property, the item accounted for at fair value is that interest and not the underlying property. Guidance on measuring the fair value of a property interest is set out for the fair value model in paragraphs 33–35, 40, 41, 48, 50 and 52 and in IFRS 13. That guidance is also relevant to the measurement of fair value when that value is used as cost for initial recognition purposes.

27 One or more investment properties may be acquired in exchange for a non-monetary asset or assets, or a combination of monetary and non-monetary assets. The following discussion refers to an exchange of one non-monetary asset for another, but it also applies to all exchanges described in the preceding sentence. The cost of such an investment property is measured at fair value unless (a) the exchange transaction lacks commercial substance or (b) the fair value of neither the asset received nor the asset given up is reliably measurable. The acquired asset is measured in this way even if an entity cannot immediately derecognise the asset given up. If the acquired asset is not measured at fair value, its cost is measured at the carrying amount of the asset given up.

28 An entity determines whether an exchange transaction has commercial substance by considering the extent to which its future cash flows are expected to change as a result of the transaction. An exchange transaction has commercial substance if:

(a) the configuration (risk, timing and amount) of the cash flows of the asset received differs from the configuration of the cash flows of the asset transferred, or

(b) the entity-specific value of the portion of the entity's operations affected by the transaction changes as a result of the exchange, and

(c) the difference in (a) or (b) is significant relative to the fair value of the assets exchanged.

For the purpose of determining whether an exchange transaction has commercial substance, the entity-specific value of the portion of the entity's operations affected by the transaction shall reflect post-tax cash flows. The result of these analyses may be clear without an entity having to perform detailed calculations.

29   The fair value of an asset is reliably measurable if (a) the variability in the range of reasonable fair value measurements is not significant for that asset or (b) the probabilities of the various estimates within the range can be reasonably assessed and used when measuring fair value. If the entity is able to measure reliably the fair value of either the asset received or the asset given up, then the fair value of the asset given up is used to measure cost unless the fair value of the asset received is more clearly evident.

Measurement after recognition

Accounting policy

30   **With the exceptions noted in paragraphs 32A and 34, an entity shall choose as its accounting policy either the fair value model in paragraphs 33–55 or the cost model in paragraph 56 and shall apply that policy to all of its investment property.**

31   IAS 8 *Accounting Policies, Changes in Accounting Estimates and Errors* states that a voluntary change in accounting policy shall be made only if the change results in the financial statements providing reliable and more relevant information about the effects of transactions, other events or conditions on the entity's financial position, financial performance or cash flows. It is highly unlikely that a change from the fair value model to the cost model will result in a more relevant presentation.

32   This Standard requires all entities to measure the fair value of investment property, for the purpose of either measurement (if the entity uses the fair value model) or disclosure (if it uses the cost model). An entity is encouraged, but not required, to measure the fair value of investment property on the basis of a valuation by an independent valuer who holds a recognised and relevant professional qualification and has recent experience in the location and category of the investment property being valued.

32A   **An entity may:**

(a)   **choose either the fair value model or the cost model for all investment property backing liabilities that pay a return linked directly to the fair value of, or returns from, specified assets including that investment property; and**

(b)   **choose either the fair value model or the cost model for all other investment property, regardless of the choice made in (a).**

32B   Some insurers and other entities operate an internal property fund that issues notional units, with some units held by investors in linked contracts and others held by the entity. Paragraph 32A does not permit an entity to measure the property held by the fund partly at cost and partly at fair value.

32C   If an entity chooses different models for the two categories described in paragraph 32A, sales of investment property between pools of assets measured using different models shall be recognised at fair value and the cumulative change in fair value shall be recognised in profit or loss. Accordingly, if an investment property is sold from a pool in which the fair value model is used into a pool in which the cost model is used, the property's fair value at the date of the sale becomes its deemed cost.

Fair value model

33   **After initial recognition, an entity that chooses the fair value model shall measure all of its investment property at fair value, except in the cases described in paragraph 53.**

34   **When a property interest held by a lessee under an operating lease is classified as an investment property under paragraph 6, paragraph 30 is not elective; the fair value model shall be applied.**

35   **A gain or loss arising from a change in the fair value of investment property shall be recognised in profit or loss for the period in which it arises.**

36–39   [Deleted]

40   When measuring the fair value of investment property in accordance with IFRS 13, an entity shall ensure that the fair value reflects, among other things, rental income from current leases and other assumptions that market participants would use when pricing investment property under current market conditions.

41   Paragraph 25 specifies the basis for initial recognition of the cost of an interest in a leased property. Paragraph 33 requires the interest in the leased property to be remeasured, if necessary, to fair value. In a lease negotiated at market rates, the fair value of an interest in a leased property at acquisition, net of all expected lease payments (including those relating to recognised liabilities), should be zero. This fair value does not change regardless of whether, for accounting purposes, a leased asset and liability are recognised at fair value or at the present value of minimum lease payments, in accordance with paragraph 20 of IAS 17. Thus, remeasuring a leased asset from cost in accordance with paragraph 25 to fair value in accordance with paragraph 33 should not give rise to any initial gain or loss, unless fair value is measured at different times. This could occur when an election to apply the fair value model is made after initial recognition.

42–47   [Deleted]

48   In exceptional cases, there is clear evidence when an entity first acquires an investment property (or when an existing property first becomes investment property after a change in use) that the variability in the range of reasonable fair value measurements will be so great, and the probabilities of the various outcomes so difficult to assess, that the usefulness of a single measure of fair value is negated. This may indicate that the fair value of the property will not be reliably measurable on a continuing basis (see paragraph 53).

49   [Deleted]

50 In determining the carrying amount of investment property under the fair value model, an entity does not double-count assets or liabilities that are recognised as separate assets or liabilities. For example:

(a) equipment such as lifts or air-conditioning is often an integral part of a building and is generally included in the fair value of the investment property, rather than recognised separately as property, plant and equipment.

(b) if an office is leased on a furnished basis, the fair value of the office generally includes the fair value of the furniture, because the rental income relates to the furnished office. When furniture is included in the fair value of investment property, an entity does not recognise that furniture as a separate asset.

(c) the fair value of investment property excludes prepaid or accrued operating lease income, because the entity recognises it as a separate liability or asset.

(d) the fair value of investment property held under a lease reflects expected cash flows (including contingent rent that is expected to become payable). Accordingly, if a valuation obtained for a property is net of all payments expected to be made, it will be necessary to add back any recognised lease liability, to arrive at the carrying amount of the investment property using the fair value model.

51 [Deleted]

52 In some cases, an entity expects that the present value of its payments relating to an investment property (other than payments relating to recognised liabilities) will exceed the present value of the related cash receipts. An entity applies IAS 37 *Provisions, Contingent Liabilities and Contingent Assets* to determine whether to recognise a liability and, if so, how to measure it.

Inability to measure fair value reliably

53 **There is a rebuttable presumption that an entity can reliably measure the fair value of an investment property on a continuing basis. However, in exceptional cases, there is clear evidence when an entity first acquires an investment property (or when an existing property first becomes investment property after a change in use) that the fair value of the investment property is not reliably measurable on a continuing basis. This arises when, and only when, the market for comparable properties is inactive (eg there are few recent transactions, price quotations are not current or observed transaction prices indicate that the seller was forced to sell) and alternative reliable measurements of fair value (for example, based on discounted cash flow projections) are not available. If an entity determines that the fair value of an investment property under construction is not reliably measurable but expects the fair value of the property to be reliably measurable when construction is complete, it shall measure that investment property under construction at cost until either its fair value becomes reliably measurable or construction is completed (whichever is earlier). If an entity determines that the fair value of an investment property (other than an investment property under**

construction) is not reliably measurable on a continuing basis, the entity shall measure that investment property using the cost model in IAS 16. The residual value of the investment property shall be assumed to be zero. The entity shall apply IAS 16 until disposal of the investment property.

53A Once an entity becomes able to measure reliably the fair value of an investment property under construction that has previously been measured at cost, it shall measure that property at its fair value. Once construction of that property is complete, it is presumed that fair value can be measured reliably. If this is not the case, in accordance with paragraph 53, the property shall be accounted for using the cost model in accordance with IAS 16.

53B The presumption that the fair value of investment property under construction can be measured reliably can be rebutted only on initial recognition. An entity that has measured an item of investment property under construction at fair value may not conclude that the fair value of the completed investment property cannot be measured reliably.

54 In the exceptional cases when an entity is compelled, for the reason given in paragraph 53, to measure an investment property using the cost model in accordance with IAS 16, it measures at fair value all its other investment property, including investment property under construction. In these cases, although an entity may use the cost model for one investment property, the entity shall continue to account for each of the remaining properties using the fair value model.

55 If an entity has previously measured an investment property at fair value, it shall continue to measure the property at fair value until disposal (or until the property becomes owner-occupied property or the entity begins to develop the property for subsequent sale in the ordinary course of business) even if comparable market transactions become less frequent or market prices become less readily available.

Cost model

56 After initial recognition, an entity that chooses the cost model shall measure all of its investment properties in accordance with IAS 16's requirements for that model, other than those that meet the criteria to be classified as held for sale (or are included in a disposal group that is classified as held for sale) in accordance with IFRS 5 *Non-current Assets Held for Sale and Discontinued Operations*. Investment properties that meet the criteria to be classified as held for sale (or are included in a disposal group that is classified as held for sale) shall be measured in accordance with IFRS 5.

Transfers

57 Transfers to, or from, investment property shall be made when, and only when, there is a change in use, evidenced by:

(a) commencement of owner-occupation, for a transfer from investment property to owner-occupied property;

(b) commencement of development with a view to sale, for a transfer from investment property to inventories;

(c)   **end of owner-occupation, for a transfer from owner-occupied property to investment property; or**

(d)   **commencement of an operating lease to another party, for a transfer from inventories to investment property.**

(e)   [deleted]

58   Paragraph 57(b) requires an entity to transfer a property from investment property to inventories when, and only when, there is a change in use, evidenced by commencement of development with a view to sale. When an entity decides to dispose of an investment property without development, it continues to treat the property as an investment property until it is derecognised (eliminated from the statement of financial position) and does not treat it as inventory. Similarly, if an entity begins to redevelop an existing investment property for continued future use as investment property, the property remains an investment property and is not reclassified as owner-occupied property during the redevelopment.

59   Paragraphs 60–65 apply to recognition and measurement issues that arise when an entity uses the fair value model for investment property. When an entity uses the cost model, transfers between investment property, owner-occupied property and inventories do not change the carrying amount of the property transferred and they do not change the cost of that property for measurement or disclosure purposes.

60   **For a transfer from investment property carried at fair value to owner-occupied property or inventories, the property's deemed cost for subsequent accounting in accordance with IAS 16 or IAS 2 shall be its fair value at the date of change in use.**

61   **If an owner-occupied property becomes an investment property that will be carried at fair value, an entity shall apply IAS 16 up to the date of change in use. The entity shall treat any difference at that date between the carrying amount of the property in accordance with IAS 16 and its fair value in the same way as a revaluation in accordance with IAS 16.**

62   Up to the date when an owner-occupied property becomes an investment property carried at fair value, an entity depreciates the property and recognises any impairment losses that have occurred. The entity treats any difference at that date between the carrying amount of the property in accordance with IAS 16 and its fair value in the same way as a revaluation in accordance with IAS 16. In other words:

(a)   any resulting decrease in the carrying amount of the property is recognised in profit or loss. However, to the extent that an amount is included in revaluation surplus for that property, the decrease is recognised in other comprehensive income and reduces the revaluation surplus within equity.

(b)   any resulting increase in the carrying amount is treated as follows:

    (i)   to the extent that the increase reverses a previous impairment loss for that property, the increase is recognised in profit or loss. The amount recognised in profit or loss does not exceed the amount needed to restore the carrying amount to the carrying amount that would have been determined (net of depreciation) had no impairment loss been recognised.

    (ii)   any remaining part of the increase is recognised in other comprehensive income and increases the revaluation surplus within equity. On subsequent disposal of the investment property, the revaluation surplus included in equity may be transferred to retained earnings. The transfer from revaluation surplus to retained earnings is not made through profit or loss.

63   **For a transfer from inventories to investment property that will be carried at fair value, any difference between the fair value of the property at that date and its previous carrying amount shall be recognised in profit or loss.**

64   The treatment of transfers from inventories to investment property that will be carried at fair value is consistent with the treatment of sales of inventories.

65   **When an entity completes the construction or development of a self-constructed investment property that will be carried at fair value, any difference between the fair value of the property at that date and its previous carrying amount shall be recognised in profit or loss.**

Disposals

66   **An investment property shall be derecognised (eliminated from the statement of financial position) on disposal or when the investment property is permanently withdrawn from use and no future economic benefits are expected from its disposal.**

67   The disposal of an investment property may be achieved by sale or by entering into a finance lease. In determining the date of disposal for investment property, an entity applies the criteria in IAS 18 for recognising revenue from the sale of goods and considers the related guidance in the illustrative examples accompanying IAS 18. IAS 17 applies to a disposal effected by entering into a finance lease and to a sale and leaseback.

68   If, in accordance with the recognition principle in paragraph 16, an entity recognises in the carrying amount of an asset the cost of a replacement for part of an investment property, it derecognises the carrying amount of the replaced part. For investment property accounted for using the cost model, a replaced part may not be a part that was depreciated separately. If it is not practicable for an entity to determine the carrying amount of the replaced part, it may use the cost of the replacement as an indication of what the cost of the replaced part was at the time it was acquired or constructed. Under the fair value model, the fair value of the investment property may already reflect that the part to be replaced has lost its value. In other cases it may be difficult to discern how much fair value should be reduced for the part being replaced. An alternative to reducing fair value for the replaced part, when it is not practical to do so, is to include the cost of the replacement in the carrying amount of the asset and then to reassess the fair value, as would be required for additions not involving replacement.

69   Gains or losses arising from the retirement or disposal of investment property shall be determined as the difference between the net disposal proceeds and the carrying amount of the asset and shall be recognised in profit or loss (unless IAS 17 requires otherwise on a sale and leaseback) in the period of the retirement or disposal.

70   The consideration receivable on disposal of an investment property is recognised initially at fair value. In particular, if payment for an investment property is deferred, the consideration received is recognised initially at the cash price equivalent. The difference between the nominal amount of the consideration and the cash price equivalent is recognised as interest revenue in accordance with IAS 18 using the effective interest method.

71   An entity applies IAS 37 or other Standards, as appropriate, to any liabilities that it retains after disposal of an investment property.

72   Compensation from third parties for investment property that was impaired, lost or given up shall be recognised in profit or loss when the compensation becomes receivable.

73   Impairments or losses of investment property, related claims for or payments of compensation from third parties and any subsequent purchase or construction of replacement assets are separate economic events and are accounted for separately as follows:

      (a)   impairments of investment property are recognised in accordance with IAS 36;

      (b)   retirements or disposals of investment property are recognised in accordance with paragraphs 66–71 of this Standard;

      (c)   compensation from third parties for investment property that was impaired, lost or given up is recognised in profit or loss when it becomes receivable; and

      (d)   the cost of assets restored, purchased or constructed as replacements is determined in accordance with paragraphs 20–29 of this Standard.

Disclosure

Fair value model and cost model

74   The disclosures below apply in addition to those in IAS 17. In accordance with IAS 17, the owner of an investment property provides lessors' disclosures about leases into which it has entered. An entity that holds an investment property under a finance or operating lease provides lessees' disclosures for finance leases and lessors' disclosures for any operating leases into which it has entered.

75   An entity shall disclose:

      (a)   whether it applies the fair value model or the cost model.

      (b)   if it applies the fair value model, whether, and in what circumstances, property interests held under operating leases are classified and accounted for as investment property.

(c) when classification is difficult (see paragraph 14), the criteria it uses to distinguish investment property from owner-occupied property and from property held for sale in the ordinary course of business.

(d) [deleted]

(e) the extent to which the fair value of investment property (as measured or disclosed in the financial statements) is based on a valuation by an independent valuer who holds a recognised and relevant professional qualification and has recent experience in the location and category of the investment property being valued. If there has been no such valuation, that fact shall be disclosed.

(f) the amounts recognised in profit or loss for:

    (i) rental income from investment property;

    (ii) direct operating expenses (including repairs and maintenance) arising from investment property that generated rental income during the period; and

    (iii) direct operating expenses (including repairs and maintenance) arising from investment property that did not generate rental income during the period.

    (iv) the cumulative change in fair value recognised in profit or loss on a sale of investment property from a pool of assets in which the cost model is used into a pool in which the fair value model is used (see paragraph 32C).

(g) the existence and amounts of restrictions on the realisability of investment property or the remittance of income and proceeds of disposal.

(h) contractual obligations to purchase, construct or develop investment property or for repairs, maintenance or enhancements.

Fair value model

76 In addition to the disclosures required by paragraph 75, an entity that applies the fair value model in paragraphs 33–55 shall disclose a reconciliation between the carrying amounts of investment property at the beginning and end of the period, showing the following:

(a) additions, disclosing separately those additions resulting from acquisitions and those resulting from subsequent expenditure recognised in the carrying amount of an asset;

(b) additions resulting from acquisitions through business combinations;

(c) assets classified as held for sale or included in a disposal group classified as held for sale in accordance with IFRS 5 and other disposals;

(d) net gains or losses from fair value adjustments;

(e) the net exchange differences arising on the translation of the financial statements into a different presentation currency, and on translation of a foreign operation into the presentation currency of the reporting entity;

(f)   transfers to and from inventories and owner-occupied property; and

(g)   other changes.

77   When a valuation obtained for investment property is adjusted significantly for the purpose of the financial statements, for example to avoid double-counting of assets or liabilities that are recognised as separate assets and liabilities as described in paragraph 50, the entity shall disclose a reconciliation between the valuation obtained and the adjusted valuation included in the financial statements, showing separately the aggregate amount of any recognised lease obligations that have been added back, and any other significant adjustments.

78   In the exceptional cases referred to in paragraph 53, when an entity measures investment property using the cost model in IAS 16, the reconciliation required by paragraph 76 shall disclose amounts relating to that investment property separately from amounts relating to other investment property. In addition, an entity shall disclose:

(a)   a description of the investment property;

(b)   an explanation of why fair value cannot be measured reliably;

(c)   if possible, the range of estimates within which fair value is highly likely to lie; and

(d)   on disposal of investment property not carried at fair value:

(i)   the fact that the entity has disposed of investment property not carried at fair value;

(ii)   the carrying amount of that investment property at the time of sale; and

(iii)   the amount of gain or loss recognised.

Cost model

79   In addition to the disclosures required by paragraph 75, an entity that applies the cost model in paragraph 56 shall disclose:

(a)   the depreciation methods used;

(b)   the useful lives or the depreciation rates used;

(c)   the gross carrying amount and the accumulated depreciation (aggregated with accumulated impairment losses) at the beginning and end of the period;

(d)   a reconciliation of the carrying amount of investment property at the beginning and end of the period, showing the following:

(i)   additions, disclosing separately those additions resulting from acquisitions and those resulting from subsequent expenditure recognised as an asset;

(ii)   additions resulting from acquisitions through business combinations;

(iii)   assets classified as held for sale or included in a disposal group classified as held for sale in accordance with IFRS 5 and other disposals;

(iv)   depreciation;

(v)   the amount of impairment losses recognised, and the amount of impairment losses reversed, during the period in accordance with IAS 36;

(vi)   the net exchange differences arising on the translation of the financial statements into a different presentation currency, and on translation of a foreign operation into the presentation currency of the reporting entity;

(vii)   transfers to and from inventories and owner-occupied property; and

(viii)   other changes; and

(e)   the fair value of investment property. In the exceptional cases described in paragraph 53, when an entity cannot measure the fair value of the investment property reliably, it shall disclose:

(i)   a description of the investment property;

(ii)   an explanation of why fair value cannot be measured reliably; and

(iii)   if possible, the range of estimates within which fair value is highly likely to lie.

Transitional provisions

Fair value model

80   An entity that has previously applied IAS 40 (2000) and elects for the first time to classify and account for some or all eligible property interests held under operating leases as investment property shall recognise the effect of that election as an adjustment to the opening balance of retained earnings for the period in which the election is first made. In addition:

(a)   if the entity has previously disclosed publicly (in financial statements or otherwise) the fair value of those property interests in earlier periods (measured on a basis that satisfies the definition of fair value in IFRS 13), the entity is encouraged, but not required:

(i)   to adjust the opening balance of retained earnings for the earliest period presented for which such fair value was disclosed publicly; and

(ii)   to restate comparative information for those periods; and

(b)   if the entity has not previously disclosed publicly the information described in (a), it shall not restate comparative information and shall disclose that fact.

81   This Standard requires a treatment different from that required by IAS 8. IAS 8 requires comparative information to be restated unless such restatement is impracticable.

82　　When an entity first applies this Standard, the adjustment to the opening balance of retained earnings includes the reclassification of any amount held in revaluation surplus for investment property.

Cost model

83　　IAS 8 applies to any change in accounting policies that is made when an entity first applies this Standard and chooses to use the cost model. The effect of the change in accounting policies includes the reclassification of any amount held in revaluation surplus for investment property.

84　　**The requirements of paragraphs 27–29 regarding the initial measurement of an investment property acquired in an exchange of assets transaction shall be applied prospectively only to future transactions.**

Effective date

85　　An entity shall apply this Standard for annual periods beginning on or after 1 January 2005. Earlier application is encouraged. If an entity applies this Standard for a period beginning before 1 January 2005, it shall disclose that fact.

85A　　IAS 1 *Presentation of Financial Statements* (as revised in 2007) amended the terminology used throughout IFRSs. In addition it amended paragraph 62. An entity shall apply those amendments for annual periods beginning on or after 1 January 2009. If an entity applies IAS 1 (revised 2007) for an earlier period, the amendments shall be applied for that earlier period.

85B　　Paragraphs 8, 9, 48, 53, 54 and 57 were amended, paragraph 22 was deleted and paragraphs 53A and 53B were added by *Improvements to IFRSs* issued in May 2008. An entity shall apply those amendments prospectively for annual periods beginning on or after 1 January 2009. An entity is permitted to apply the amendments to investment property under construction from any date before 1 January 2009 provided that the fair values of investment properties under construction were measured at those dates. Earlier application is permitted. If an entity applies the amendments for an earlier period it shall disclose that fact and at the same time apply the amendments to paragraphs 5 and 81E of IAS 16 *Property, Plant and Equipment*.

85C　　IFRS 13, issued in May 2011, amended the definition of fair value in paragraph 5, amended paragraphs 26, 29, 32, 40, 48, 53, 53B, 78–80 and 85B and deleted paragraphs 36–39, 42–47, 49, 51 and 75(d). An entity shall apply those amendments when it applies IFRS 13.

Withdrawal of IAS 40 (2000)

86　　This Standard supersedes IAS 40 *Investment Property* (issued in 2000).

International Accounting Standard 41

Agriculture

In April 2001 the International Accounting Standards Board (IASB) adopted IAS 41 *Agriculture*, which had originally been issued by the International Accounting Standards Committee (IASC) in February 2001.

In December 2003 the IASB issued a revised IAS 41 as part of its initial agenda of technical projects.

Other IFRSs have made minor consequential amendments to IAS 41. They include IAS 1 *Presentation of Financial Statements* (as revised in December 2003 and September 2007), IAS 2 *Inventories* (as revised in December 2003), *Improvements to IFRSs* (issued May 2008) and IFRS 13 *Fair Value Measurement* (issued May 2011).

CONTENTS

FOR THE ACCOMPANYING DOCUMENTS LISTED BELOW, SEE PART B OF THIS EDITION

BASIS FOR CONCLUSIONS

BASIS FOR IASC'S CONCLUSIONS

ILLUSTRATIVE EXAMPLES

International Accounting Standard 41 *Agriculture* (IAS 41) is set out in paragraphs 1–61. All the paragraphs have equal authority but retain the IASC format of the Standard when it was adopted by the IASB. IAS 41 should be read in the context of its objective and the Basis for Conclusions, the *Preface to International Financial Reporting Standards* and the *Conceptual Framework for Financial Reporting*. IAS 8 *Accounting Policies, Changes in Accounting Estimates and Errors* provides a basis for selecting and applying accounting policies in the absence of explicit guidance.

Introduction

IN1   IAS 41 prescribes the accounting treatment, financial statement presentation, and disclosures related to agricultural activity, a matter not covered in other Standards. Agricultural activity is the management by an entity of the biological transformation of living animals or plants (biological assets) for sale, into agricultural produce, or into additional biological assets.

IN2   IAS 41 prescribes, among other things, the accounting treatment for biological assets during the period of growth, degeneration, production, and procreation, and for the initial measurement of agricultural produce at the point of harvest. It requires measurement at fair value less costs to sell from initial recognition of biological assets up to the point of harvest, other than when fair value cannot be measured reliably on initial recognition. However, IAS 41 does not deal with processing of agricultural produce after harvest; for example, processing grapes into wine and wool into yarn.

IN3   There is a presumption that fair value can be measured reliably for a biological asset. However, that presumption can be rebutted only on initial recognition for a biological asset for which quoted market prices are not available and for which alternative fair value measurements are determined to be clearly unreliable. In such a case, IAS 41 requires an entity to measure that biological asset at its cost less any accumulated depreciation and any accumulated impairment losses. Once the fair value of such a biological asset becomes reliably measurable, an entity should measure it at its fair value less costs to sell. In all cases, an entity should measure agricultural produce at the point of harvest at its fair value less costs to sell.

IN4   IAS 41 requires that a change in fair value less costs to sell of a biological asset be included in profit or loss for the period in which it arises. In agricultural activity, a change in physical attributes of a living animal or plant directly enhances or diminishes economic benefits to the entity. Under a transaction-based, historical cost accounting model, a plantation forestry entity might report no income until first harvest and sale, perhaps 30 years after planting. On the other hand, an accounting model that recognises and measures biological growth using current fair values reports changes in fair value throughout the period between planting and harvest.

IN5   IAS 41 does not establish any new principles for land related to agricultural activity. Instead, an entity follows IAS 16 *Property, Plant and Equipment* or IAS 40 *Investment Property*, depending on which standard is appropriate in the circumstances. IAS 16 requires land to be measured either at its cost less any accumulated impairment losses, or at a revalued amount. IAS 40 requires land that is investment property to be measured at its fair value, or cost less any accumulated impairment losses. Biological assets that are physically attached to land (for example, trees in a plantation forest) are measured at their fair value less costs to sell separately from the land.

IN6   IAS 41 requires an unconditional government grant related to a biological asset measured at its fair value less costs to sell to be recognised in profit or loss when, and only when, the government grant becomes receivable. If a government grant is conditional, including when a government grant requires an entity not to engage in specified agricultural activity, an entity should recognise the government grant in profit or loss when, and only when, the conditions attaching to the government grant are met. If a government grant relates to a biological asset measured at its cost less any accumulated depreciation and any accumulated impairment losses, the entity applies IAS 20 *Accounting for Government Grants and Disclosure of Government Assistance*.

IN7 IAS 41 is effective for annual financial statements covering periods beginning on or after 1 January 2003. Earlier application is encouraged.

IN8 IAS 41 does not establish any specific transitional provisions. The adoption of IAS 41 is accounted for in accordance with IAS 8 *Accounting Policies, Changes in Accounting Estimates and Errors*.

IN9 The illustrative examples accompanying IAS 41 provide examples of the application of the Standard. The Basis for Conclusions summarises the Board's reasons for adopting the requirements set out in IAS 41.

International Accounting Standard 41
Agriculture

Objective

The objective of this Standard is to prescribe the accounting treatment and disclosures related to agricultural activity.

Scope

1   **This Standard shall be applied to account for the following when they relate to agricultural activity:**

 (a)   **biological assets;**

 (b)   **agricultural produce at the point of harvest; and**

 (c)   **government grants covered by paragraphs 34 and 35.**

2   This Standard does not apply to:

 (a)   land related to agricultural activity (see IAS 16 *Property, Plant and Equipment* and IAS 40 *Investment Property*); and

 (b)   intangible assets related to agricultural activity (see IAS 38 *Intangible Assets*).

3   This Standard is applied to agricultural produce, which is the harvested product of the entity's biological assets, only at the point of harvest. Thereafter, IAS 2 *Inventories* or another applicable Standard is applied. Accordingly, this Standard does not deal with the processing of agricultural produce after harvest; for example, the processing of grapes into wine by a vintner who has grown the grapes. While such processing may be a logical and natural extension of agricultural activity, and the events taking place may bear some similarity to biological transformation, such processing is not included within the definition of agricultural activity in this Standard.

4   The table below provides examples of biological assets, agricultural produce, and products that are the result of processing after harvest:

Biological assets	Agricultural produce	Products that are the result of processing after harvest
Sheep	Wool	Yarn, carpet
Trees in a plantation forest	Felled trees	Logs, lumber
Plants	Cotton	Thread, clothing
	Harvested cane	Sugar
Dairy cattle	Milk	Cheese
Pigs	Carcass	Sausages, cured hams
Bushes	Leaf	Tea, cured tobacco
Vines	Grapes	Wine
Fruit trees	Picked fruit	Processed fruit

Definitions

Agriculture-related definitions

5   The following terms are used in this Standard with the meanings specified:

Agricultural activity is the management by an entity of the biological transformation and harvest of biological assets for sale or for conversion into agricultural produce or into additional biological assets.

Agricultural produce is the harvested product of the entity's biological assets.

A *biological asset* is a living animal or plant.

Biological transformation comprises the processes of growth, degeneration, production, and procreation that cause qualitative or quantitative changes in a biological asset.

Costs to sell are the incremental costs directly attributable to the disposal of an asset, excluding finance costs and income taxes.

A *group of biological assets* is an aggregation of similar living animals or plants.

Harvest is the detachment of produce from a biological asset or the cessation of a biological asset's life processes.

6   Agricultural activity covers a diverse range of activities; for example, raising livestock, forestry, annual or perennial cropping, cultivating orchards and plantations, floriculture and aquaculture (including fish farming). Certain common features exist within this diversity:

(a)   *Capability to change.* Living animals and plants are capable of biological transformation;

(b)   *Management of change.* Management facilitates biological transformation by enhancing, or at least stabilising, conditions necessary for the process to take place (for example, nutrient levels, moisture, temperature, fertility, and light). Such management distinguishes agricultural activity from other activities. For example, harvesting from unmanaged sources (such as ocean fishing and deforestation) is not agricultural activity; and

(c)   *Measurement of change.* The change in quality (for example, genetic merit, density, ripeness, fat cover, protein content, and fibre strength) or quantity (for example, progeny, weight, cubic metres, fibre length or diameter, and number of buds) brought about by biological transformation or harvest is measured and monitored as a routine management function.

7   Biological transformation results in the following types of outcomes:

(a)   asset changes through (i) growth (an increase in quantity or improvement in quality of an animal or plant), (ii) degeneration (a decrease in the quantity or deterioration in quality of an animal or plant), or (iii) procreation (creation of additional living animals or plants); or

(b)   production of agricultural produce such as latex, tea leaf, wool, and milk.

General definitions

8   The following terms are used in this Standard with the meanings specified:

Carrying amount is the amount at which an asset is recognised in the statement of financial position.

Fair value is the price that would be received to sell an asset or paid to transfer a liability in an orderly transaction between market participants at the measurement date. (See IFRS 13 *Fair Value Measurement*.)

Government grants are as defined in IAS 20 *Accounting for Government Grants and Disclosure of Government Assistance*.

9   [Deleted]

Recognition and measurement

10   An entity shall recognise a biological asset or agricultural produce when, and only when:

(a)   the entity controls the asset as a result of past events;

(b)   it is probable that future economic benefits associated with the asset will flow to the entity; and

(c)   the fair value or cost of the asset can be measured reliably.

11   In agricultural activity, control may be evidenced by, for example, legal ownership of cattle and the branding or otherwise marking of the cattle on acquisition, birth, or weaning. The future benefits are normally assessed by measuring the significant physical attributes.

12   A biological asset shall be measured on initial recognition and at the end of each reporting period at its fair value less costs to sell, except for the case described in paragraph 30 where the fair value cannot be measured reliably.

13   Agricultural produce harvested from an entity's biological assets shall be measured at its fair value less costs to sell at the point of harvest. Such measurement is the cost at that date when applying IAS 2 *Inventories* or another applicable Standard.

14   [Deleted]

15   The fair value measurement of a biological asset or agricultural produce may be facilitated by grouping biological assets or agricultural produce according to significant attributes; for example, by age or quality. An entity selects the attributes corresponding to the attributes used in the market as a basis for pricing.

16   Entities often enter into contracts to sell their biological assets or agricultural produce at a future date. Contract prices are not necessarily relevant in measuring fair value, because fair value reflects the current market conditions in which market participant buyers and sellers would enter into a transaction. As a result, the fair value of a biological asset or agricultural produce is not

adjusted because of the existence of a contract. In some cases, a contract for the sale of a biological asset or agricultural produce may be an onerous contract, as defined in IAS 37 *Provisions, Contingent Liabilities and Contingent Assets*. IAS 37 applies to onerous contracts.

17–21 [Deleted]

22 An entity does not include any cash flows for financing the assets, taxation, or re-establishing biological assets after harvest (for example, the cost of replanting trees in a plantation forest after harvest).

23 [Deleted]

24 Cost may sometimes approximate fair value, particularly when:

(a) little biological transformation has taken place since initial cost incurrence (for example, for fruit tree seedlings planted immediately prior to the end of a reporting period); or

(b) the impact of the biological transformation on price is not expected to be material (for example, for the initial growth in a 30-year pine plantation production cycle).

25 Biological assets are often physically attached to land (for example, trees in a plantation forest). There may be no separate market for biological assets that are attached to the land but an active market may exist for the combined assets, that is, the biological assets, raw land, and land improvements, as a package. An entity may use information regarding the combined assets to measure the fair value of the biological assets. For example, the fair value of raw land and land improvements may be deducted from the fair value of the combined assets to arrive at the fair value of biological assets.

Gains and losses

26 **A gain or loss arising on initial recognition of a biological asset at fair value less costs to sell and from a change in fair value less costs to sell of a biological asset shall be included in profit or loss for the period in which it arises.**

27 A loss may arise on initial recognition of a biological asset, because costs to sell are deducted in determining fair value less costs to sell of a biological asset. A gain may arise on initial recognition of a biological asset, such as when a calf is born.

28 **A gain or loss arising on initial recognition of agricultural produce at fair value less costs to sell shall be included in profit or loss for the period in which it arises.**

29 A gain or loss may arise on initial recognition of agricultural produce as a result of harvesting.

Inability to measure fair value reliably

30 **There is a presumption that fair value can be measured reliably for a biological asset. However, that presumption can be rebutted only on initial recognition for a biological asset for which quoted market prices are not available and for which alternative fair value measurements are determined to be clearly unreliable.**

In such a case, that biological asset shall be measured at its cost less any accumulated depreciation and any accumulated impairment losses. Once the fair value of such a biological asset becomes reliably measurable, an entity shall measure it at its fair value less costs to sell. Once a non-current biological asset meets the criteria to be classified as held for sale (or is included in a disposal group that is classified as held for sale) in accordance with IFRS 5 *Non-current Assets Held for Sale and Discontinued Operations*, it is presumed that fair value can be measured reliably.

31 The presumption in paragraph 30 can be rebutted only on initial recognition. An entity that has previously measured a biological asset at its fair value less costs to sell continues to measure the biological asset at its fair value less costs to sell until disposal.

32 In all cases, an entity measures agricultural produce at the point of harvest at its fair value less costs to sell. This Standard reflects the view that the fair value of agricultural produce at the point of harvest can always be measured reliably.

33 In determining cost, accumulated depreciation and accumulated impairment losses, an entity considers IAS 2, IAS 16 and IAS 36 *Impairment of Assets*.

Government grants

34 **An unconditional government grant related to a biological asset measured at its fair value less costs to sell shall be recognised in profit or loss when, and only when, the government grant becomes receivable.**

35 **If a government grant related to a biological asset measured at its fair value less costs to sell is conditional, including when a government grant requires an entity not to engage in specified agricultural activity, an entity shall recognise the government grant in profit or loss when, and only when, the conditions attaching to the government grant are met.**

36 Terms and conditions of government grants vary. For example, a grant may require an entity to farm in a particular location for five years and require the entity to return all of the grant if it farms for a period shorter than five years. In this case, the grant is not recognised in profit or loss until the five years have passed. However, if the terms of the grant allow part of it to be retained according to the time that has elapsed, the entity recognises that part in profit or loss as time passes.

37 If a government grant relates to a biological asset measured at its cost less any accumulated depreciation and any accumulated impairment losses (see paragraph 30), IAS 20 is applied.

38 This Standard requires a different treatment from IAS 20, if a government grant relates to a biological asset measured at its fair value less costs to sell or a government grant requires an entity not to engage in specified agricultural activity. IAS 20 is applied only to a government grant related to a biological asset measured at its cost less any accumulated depreciation and any accumulated impairment losses.

Disclosure

39 [Deleted]

General

40 An entity shall disclose the aggregate gain or loss arising during the current period on initial recognition of biological assets and agricultural produce and from the change in fair value less costs to sell of biological assets.

41 An entity shall provide a description of each group of biological assets.

42 The disclosure required by paragraph 41 may take the form of a narrative or quantified description.

43 An entity is encouraged to provide a quantified description of each group of biological assets, distinguishing between consumable and bearer biological assets or between mature and immature biological assets, as appropriate. For example, an entity may disclose the carrying amounts of consumable biological assets and bearer biological assets by group. An entity may further divide those carrying amounts between mature and immature assets. These distinctions provide information that may be helpful in assessing the timing of future cash flows. An entity discloses the basis for making any such distinctions.

44 Consumable biological assets are those that are to be harvested as agricultural produce or sold as biological assets. Examples of consumable biological assets are livestock intended for the production of meat, livestock held for sale, fish in farms, crops such as maize and wheat, and trees being grown for lumber. Bearer biological assets are those other than consumable biological assets; for example, livestock from which milk is produced, grape vines, fruit trees, and trees from which firewood is harvested while the tree remains. Bearer biological assets are not agricultural produce but, rather, are self-regenerating.

45 Biological assets may be classified either as mature biological assets or immature biological assets. Mature biological assets are those that have attained harvestable specifications (for consumable biological assets) or are able to sustain regular harvests (for bearer biological assets).

46 If not disclosed elsewhere in information published with the financial statements, an entity shall describe:

   (a)   the nature of its activities involving each group of biological assets; and

   (b)   non-financial measures or estimates of the physical quantities of:

      (i)   each group of the entity's biological assets at the end of the period; and

      (ii)   output of agricultural produce during the period.

47–48 [Deleted]

49   An entity shall disclose:

    (a)   the existence and carrying amounts of biological assets whose title is restricted, and the carrying amounts of biological assets pledged as security for liabilities;

    (b)   the amount of commitments for the development or acquisition of biological assets; and

    (c)   financial risk management strategies related to agricultural activity.

50   An entity shall present a reconciliation of changes in the carrying amount of biological assets between the beginning and the end of the current period. The reconciliation shall include:

    (a)   the gain or loss arising from changes in fair value less costs to sell;

    (b)   increases due to purchases;

    (c)   decreases attributable to sales and biological assets classified as held for sale (or included in a disposal group that is classified as held for sale) in accordance with IFRS 5;

    (d)   decreases due to harvest;

    (e)   increases resulting from business combinations;

    (f)   net exchange differences arising on the translation of financial statements into a different presentation currency, and on the translation of a foreign operation into the presentation currency of the reporting entity; and

    (g)   other changes.

51   The fair value less costs to sell of a biological asset can change due to both physical changes and price changes in the market. Separate disclosure of physical and price changes is useful in appraising current period performance and future prospects, particularly when there is a production cycle of more than one year. In such cases, an entity is encouraged to disclose, by group or otherwise, the amount of change in fair value less costs to sell included in profit or loss due to physical changes and due to price changes. This information is generally less useful when the production cycle is less than one year (for example, when raising chickens or growing cereal crops).

52   Biological transformation results in a number of types of physical change—growth, degeneration, production, and procreation, each of which is observable and measurable. Each of those physical changes has a direct relationship to future economic benefits. A change in fair value of a biological asset due to harvesting is also a physical change.

53   Agricultural activity is often exposed to climatic, disease and other natural risks. If an event occurs that gives rise to a material item of income or expense, the nature and amount of that item are disclosed in accordance with IAS 1 *Presentation of Financial Statements*. Examples of such an event include an outbreak of a virulent disease, a flood, a severe drought or frost, and a plague of insects.

Additional disclosures for biological assets where fair value cannot be measured reliably

54 If an entity measures biological assets at their cost less any accumulated depreciation and any accumulated impairment losses (see paragraph 30) at the end of the period, the entity shall disclose for such biological assets:

(a) a description of the biological assets;

(b) an explanation of why fair value cannot be measured reliably;

(c) if possible, the range of estimates within which fair value is highly likely to lie;

(d) the depreciation method used;

(e) the useful lives or the depreciation rates used; and

(f) the gross carrying amount and the accumulated depreciation (aggregated with accumulated impairment losses) at the beginning and end of the period.

55 If, during the current period, an entity measures biological assets at their cost less any accumulated depreciation and any accumulated impairment losses (see paragraph 30), an entity shall disclose any gain or loss recognised on disposal of such biological assets and the reconciliation required by paragraph 50 shall disclose amounts related to such biological assets separately. In addition, the reconciliation shall include the following amounts included in profit or loss related to those biological assets:

(a) impairment losses;

(b) reversals of impairment losses; and

(c) depreciation.

56 If the fair value of biological assets previously measured at their cost less any accumulated depreciation and any accumulated impairment losses becomes reliably measurable during the current period, an entity shall disclose for those biological assets:

(a) a description of the biological assets;

(b) an explanation of why fair value has become reliably measurable; and

(c) the effect of the change.

Government grants

57 An entity shall disclose the following related to agricultural activity covered by this Standard:

(a) the nature and extent of government grants recognised in the financial statements;

(b) unfulfilled conditions and other contingencies attaching to government grants; and

(c) significant decreases expected in the level of government grants.

Effective date and transition

58   This Standard becomes operative for annual financial statements covering periods beginning on or after 1 January 2003. Earlier application is encouraged. If an entity applies this Standard for periods beginning before 1 January 2003, it shall disclose that fact.

59   This Standard does not establish any specific transitional provisions. The adoption of this Standard is accounted for in accordance with IAS 8 *Accounting Policies, Changes in Accounting Estimates and Errors.*

60   Paragraphs 5, 6, 17, 20 and 21 were amended and paragraph 14 deleted by *Improvements to IFRSs* issued in May 2008. An entity shall apply those amendments prospectively for annual periods beginning on or after 1 January 2009. Earlier application is permitted. If an entity applies the amendments for an earlier period it shall disclose that fact.

61   IFRS 13, issued in May 2011, amended paragraphs 8, 15, 16, 25 and 30 and deleted paragraphs 9, 17–21, 23, 47 and 48. An entity shall apply those amendments when it applies IFRS 13.

IFRIC Interpretation 1

Changes in Existing Decommissioning, Restoration and Similar Liabilities

In May 2004 the International Accounting Standards Board issued IFRIC 1 *Changes in Existing Decommissioning, Restoration and Similar Liabilities*. It was developed by the Interpretations Committee.

Other IFRSs have made minor consequential amendments to IFRIC 1. These include IAS 23 *Borrowing Costs* (as revised in March 2007) and IAS 1 *Presentation of Financial Statements* (as revised in September 2007).

CONTENTS

> FOR THE ACCOMPANYING DOCUMENTS LISTED BELOW, SEE PART B OF THIS EDITION

IFRIC Interpretation 1 *Changes in Existing Decommissioning, Restoration and Similar Liabilities* (IFRIC 1) is set out in paragraphs 1–10 and the Appendix. IFRIC 1 is accompanied by illustrative examples and a Basis for Conclusions. The scope and authority of Interpretations are set out in paragraphs 2 and 7–16 of the *Preface to International Financial Reporting Standards*.

IFRIC Interpretation 1
Changes in Existing Decommissioning, Restoration and Similar Liabilities

References

- IAS 1 *Presentation of Financial Statements* (as revised in 2007)
- IAS 8 *Accounting Policies, Changes in Accounting Estimates and Errors*
- IAS 16 *Property, Plant and Equipment* (as revised in 2003)
- IAS 23 *Borrowing Costs*
- IAS 36 *Impairment of Assets* (as revised in 2004)
- IAS 37 *Provisions, Contingent Liabilities and Contingent Assets*

Background

1   Many entities have obligations to dismantle, remove and restore items of property, plant and equipment. In this Interpretation such obligations are referred to as 'decommissioning, restoration and similar liabilities'. Under IAS 16, the cost of an item of property, plant and equipment includes the initial estimate of the costs of dismantling and removing the item and restoring the site on which it is located, the obligation for which an entity incurs either when the item is acquired or as a consequence of having used the item during a particular period for purposes other than to produce inventories during that period. IAS 37 contains requirements on how to measure decommissioning, restoration and similar liabilities. This Interpretation provides guidance on how to account for the effect of changes in the measurement of existing decommissioning, restoration and similar liabilities.

Scope

2   This Interpretation applies to changes in the measurement of any existing decommissioning, restoration or similar liability that is both:

(a)   recognised as part of the cost of an item of property, plant and equipment in accordance with IAS 16; and

(b)   recognised as a liability in accordance with IAS 37.

For example, a decommissioning, restoration or similar liability may exist for decommissioning a plant, rehabilitating environmental damage in extractive industries, or removing equipment.

Issue

3   This Interpretation addresses how the effect of the following events that change the measurement of an existing decommissioning, restoration or similar liability should be accounted for:

(a)   a change in the estimated outflow of resources embodying economic benefits (eg cash flows) required to settle the obligation;

(b)   a change in the current market-based discount rate as defined in paragraph 47 of IAS 37 (this includes changes in the time value of money and the risks specific to the liability); and

(c)   an increase that reflects the passage of time (also referred to as the unwinding of the discount).

Consensus

4   Changes in the measurement of an existing decommissioning, restoration and similar liability that result from changes in the estimated timing or amount of the outflow of resources embodying economic benefits required to settle the obligation, or a change in the discount rate, shall be accounted for in accordance with paragraphs 5–7 below.

5   If the related asset is measured using the cost model:

(a)   subject to (b), changes in the liability shall be added to, or deducted from, the cost of the related asset in the current period.

(b)   the amount deducted from the cost of the asset shall not exceed its carrying amount. If a decrease in the liability exceeds the carrying amount of the asset, the excess shall be recognised immediately in profit or loss.

(c)   if the adjustment results in an addition to the cost of an asset, the entity shall consider whether this is an indication that the new carrying amount of the asset may not be fully recoverable. If it is such an indication, the entity shall test the asset for impairment by estimating its recoverable amount, and shall account for any impairment loss, in accordance with IAS 36.

6   If the related asset is measured using the revaluation model:

(a)   changes in the liability alter the revaluation surplus or deficit previously recognised on that asset, so that:

(i)   a decrease in the liability shall (subject to (b)) be recognised in other comprehensive income and increase the revaluation surplus within equity, except that it shall be recognised in profit or loss to the extent that it reverses a revaluation deficit on the asset that was previously recognised in profit or loss;

(ii)   an increase in the liability shall be recognised in profit or loss, except that it shall be recognised in other comprehensive income and reduce the revaluation surplus within equity to the extent of any credit balance existing in the revaluation surplus in respect of that asset.

(b)   in the event that a decrease in the liability exceeds the carrying amount that would have been recognised had the asset been carried under the cost model, the excess shall be recognised immediately in profit or loss.

   (c)   a change in the liability is an indication that the asset may have to be revalued in order to ensure that the carrying amount does not differ materially from that which would be determined using fair value at the end of the reporting period. Any such revaluation shall be taken into account in determining the amounts to be recognised in profit or loss or in other comprehensive income under (a). If a revaluation is necessary, all assets of that class shall be revalued.

   (d)   IAS 1 requires disclosure in the statement of comprehensive income of each component of other comprehensive income or expense. In complying with this requirement, the change in the revaluation surplus arising from a change in the liability shall be separately identified and disclosed as such.

7   The adjusted depreciable amount of the asset is depreciated over its useful life. Therefore, once the related asset has reached the end of its useful life, all subsequent changes in the liability shall be recognised in profit or loss as they occur. This applies under both the cost model and the revaluation model.

8   The periodic unwinding of the discount shall be recognised in profit or loss as a finance cost as it occurs. Capitalisation under IAS 23 is not permitted.

Effective date

9   An entity shall apply this Interpretation for annual periods beginning on or after 1 September 2004. Earlier application is encouraged. If an entity applies the Interpretation for a period beginning before 1 September 2004, it shall disclose that fact.

9A   IAS 1 (as revised in 2007) amended the terminology used throughout IFRSs. In addition it amended paragraph 6. An entity shall apply those amendments for annual periods beginning on or after 1 January 2009. If an entity applies IAS 1 (revised 2007) for an earlier period, the amendments shall be applied for that earlier period.

Transition

10   Changes in accounting policies shall be accounted for according to the requirements of IAS 8 *Accounting Policies, Changes in Accounting Estimates and Errors*.[1]

---

1   If an entity applies this Interpretation for a period beginning before 1 January 2005, the entity shall follow the requirements of the previous version of IAS 8, which was entitled *Net Profit or Loss for the Period, Fundamental Errors and Changes in Accounting Policies*, unless the entity is applying the revised version of that Standard for that earlier period.

          © IFRS Foundation

Appendix
Amendments to IFRS 1 *First-time Adoption of International Financial Reporting Standards*

The amendments in this appendix shall be applied for annual periods beginning on or after 1 September 2004. If an entity applies this Interpretation for an earlier period, these amendments shall be applied for that earlier period.

* * * * *

The amendments contained in this appendix when this Interpretation was issued in 2004 have been incorporated into IFRS 1 as issued on and after 27 May 2004. In November 2008 a revised version of IFRS 1 was issued.

IFRIC Interpretation 2

Members' Shares in Co-operative Entities and Similar Instruments

In November 2004 the International Accounting Standards Board issued IFRIC 2 *Members' Shares in Co-operative Entities and Similar Instruments*. It was developed by the Interpretations Committee.

Other IFRSs have made minor consequential amendments to IFRIC 2. These include *Puttable Financial Instruments and Obligations Arising on Liquidation* (Amendments to IAS 32 and IAS 1) (issued February 2008) and IFRS 9 *Financial Instruments* (issued October 2010).

CONTENTS

FOR THE ACCOMPANYING DOCUMENTS LISTED BELOW, SEE PART B OF THIS EDITION

BASIS FOR CONCLUSIONS

IFRIC Interpretation 2 *Members' Shares in Co-operative Entities and Similar Instruments* (IFRIC 2) is set out in paragraphs 1–16 and the Appendix. IFRIC 2 is accompanied by a Basis for Conclusions. The scope and authority of Interpretations are set out in paragraphs 2 and 7–16 of the *Preface to International Financial Reporting Standards*.

IFRIC Interpretation 2
Members' Shares in Co-operative Entities and Similar Instruments

References

- IAS 32 *Financial Instruments: Disclosure and Presentation* (as revised in 2003)[1]
- IFRS 9 *Financial Instruments* (issued October 2010)
- IFRS 13 *Fair Value Measurement*

Background

1   Co-operatives and other similar entities are formed by groups of persons to meet common economic or social needs. National laws typically define a co-operative as a society endeavouring to promote its members' economic advancement by way of a joint business operation (the principle of self-help). Members' interests in a co-operative are often characterised as members' shares, units or the like, and are referred to below as 'members' shares'.

2   IAS 32 establishes principles for the classification of financial instruments as financial liabilities or equity. In particular, those principles apply to the classification of puttable instruments that allow the holder to put those instruments to the issuer for cash or another financial instrument. The application of those principles to members' shares in co-operative entities and similar instruments is difficult. Some of the International Accounting Standards Board's constituents have asked for help in understanding how the principles in IAS 32 apply to members' shares and similar instruments that have certain features, and the circumstances in which those features affect the classification as liabilities or equity.

Scope

3   This Interpretation applies to financial instruments within the scope of IAS 32, including financial instruments issued to members of co-operative entities that evidence the members' ownership interest in the entity. This Interpretation does not apply to financial instruments that will or may be settled in the entity's own equity instruments.

Issue

4   Many financial instruments, including members' shares, have characteristics of equity, including voting rights and rights to participate in dividend distributions.

---

1   In August 2005, IAS 32 was amended as IAS 32 *Financial Instruments: Presentation*. In February 2008 the IASB amended IAS 32 by requiring instruments to be classified as equity if those instruments have all the features and meet the conditions in paragraphs 16A and 16B or paragraphs 16C and 16D of IAS 32.

Some financial instruments give the holder the right to request redemption for cash or another financial asset, but may include or be subject to limits on whether the financial instruments will be redeemed. How should those redemption terms be evaluated in determining whether the financial instruments should be classified as liabilities or equity?

Consensus

5   The contractual right of the holder of a financial instrument (including members' shares in co-operative entities) to request redemption does not, in itself, require that financial instrument to be classified as a financial liability. Rather, the entity must consider all of the terms and conditions of the financial instrument in determining its classification as a financial liability or equity. Those terms and conditions include relevant local laws, regulations and the entity's governing charter in effect at the date of classification, but not expected future amendments to those laws, regulations or charter.

6   Members' shares that would be classified as equity if the members did not have a right to request redemption are equity if either of the conditions described in paragraphs 7 and 8 is present or the members' shares have all the features and meet the conditions in paragraphs 16A and 16B or paragraphs 16C and 16D of IAS 32. Demand deposits, including current accounts, deposit accounts and similar contracts that arise when members act as customers are financial liabilities of the entity.

7   Members' shares are equity if the entity has an unconditional right to refuse redemption of the members' shares.

8   Local law, regulation or the entity's governing charter can impose various types of prohibitions on the redemption of members' shares, eg unconditional prohibitions or prohibitions based on liquidity criteria. If redemption is unconditionally prohibited by local law, regulation or the entity's governing charter, members' shares are equity. However, provisions in local law, regulation or the entity's governing charter that prohibit redemption only if conditions—such as liquidity constraints—are met (or are not met) do not result in members' shares being equity.

9   An unconditional prohibition may be absolute, in that all redemptions are prohibited. An unconditional prohibition may be partial, in that it prohibits redemption of members' shares if redemption would cause the number of members' shares or amount of paid-in capital from members' shares to fall below a specified level. Members' shares in excess of the prohibition against redemption are liabilities, unless the entity has the unconditional right to refuse redemption as described in paragraph 7 or the members' shares have all the features and meet the conditions in paragraphs 16A and 16B or paragraphs 16C and 16D of IAS 32. In some cases, the number of shares or the amount of paid-in capital subject to a redemption prohibition may change from time to time. Such a change in the redemption prohibition leads to a transfer between financial liabilities and equity.

10   At initial recognition, the entity shall measure its financial liability for redemption at fair value. In the case of members' shares with a redemption feature, the entity measures the fair value of the financial liability for redemption at no less than the maximum amount payable under the redemption provisions of its governing charter or applicable law discounted from the first date that the amount could be required to be paid (see example 3).

11   As required by paragraph 35 of IAS 32, distributions to holders of equity instruments are recognised directly in equity, net of any income tax benefits. Interest, dividends and other returns relating to financial instruments classified as financial liabilities are expenses, regardless of whether those amounts paid are legally characterised as dividends, interest or otherwise.

12   The Appendix, which is an integral part of the consensus, provides examples of the application of this consensus.

Disclosure

13   When a change in the redemption prohibition leads to a transfer between financial liabilities and equity, the entity shall disclose separately the amount, timing and reason for the transfer.

Effective date

14   The effective date and transition requirements of this Interpretation are the same as those for IAS 32 (as revised in 2003). An entity shall apply this Interpretation for annual periods beginning on or after 1 January 2005. If an entity applies this Interpretation for a period beginning before 1 January 2005, it shall disclose that fact. This Interpretation shall be applied retrospectively.

14A   An entity shall apply the amendments in paragraphs 6, 9, A1 and A12 for annual periods beginning on or after 1 January 2009. If an entity applies *Puttable Financial Instruments and Obligations Arising on Liquidation* (Amendments to IAS 32 and IAS 1), issued in February 2008, for an earlier period, the amendments in paragraphs 6, 9, A1 and A12 shall be applied for that earlier period.

15   IFRS 9, issued in October 2010, amended paragraphs A8 and A10. An entity shall apply those amendments when it applies IFRS 9 as issued in October 2010.

16   IFRS 13, issued in May 2011, amended paragraph A8. An entity shall apply that amendment when it applies IFRS 13.

Appendix
Examples of application of the consensus

This appendix is an integral part of the Interpretation.

A1   This appendix sets out seven examples of the application of the IFRIC consensus. The examples do not constitute an exhaustive list; other fact patterns are possible. Each example assumes that there are no conditions other than those set out in the facts of the example that would require the financial instrument to be classified as a financial liability and that the financial instrument does not have all the features or does not meet the conditions in paragraphs 16A and 16B or paragraphs 16C and 16D of IAS 32.

Unconditional right to refuse redemption (paragraph 7)

Example 1

Facts

A2   The entity's charter states that redemptions are made at the sole discretion of the entity. The charter does not provide further elaboration or limitation on that discretion. In its history, the entity has never refused to redeem members' shares, although the governing board has the right to do so.

Classification

A3   The entity has the unconditional right to refuse redemption and the members' shares are equity. IAS 32 establishes principles for classification that are based on the terms of the financial instrument and notes that a history of, or intention to make, discretionary payments does not trigger liability classification. Paragraph AG26 of IAS 32 states:

> When preference shares are non-redeemable, the appropriate classification is determined by the other rights that attach to them. Classification is based on an assessment of the substance of the contractual arrangements and the definitions of a financial liability and an equity instrument. When distributions to holders of the preference shares, whether cumulative or non-cumulative, are at the discretion of the issuer, the shares are equity instruments. The classification of a preference share as an equity instrument or a financial liability is not affected by, for example:
>
> (a)   a history of making distributions;
>
> (b)   an intention to make distributions in the future;
>
> (c)   a possible negative impact on the price of ordinary shares of the issuer if distributions are not made (because of restrictions on paying dividends on the ordinary shares if dividends are not paid on the preference shares);
>
> (d)   the amount of the issuer's reserves;
>
> (e)   an issuer's expectation of a profit or loss for a period; or
>
> (f)   an ability or inability of the issuer to influence the amount of its profit or loss for the period.

Example 2

Facts

A4   The entity's charter states that redemptions are made at the sole discretion of the entity. However, the charter further states that approval of a redemption request is automatic unless the entity is unable to make payments without violating local regulations regarding liquidity or reserves.

Classification

A5   The entity does not have the unconditional right to refuse redemption and the members' shares are a financial liability. The restrictions described above are based on the entity's ability to settle its liability. They restrict redemptions only if the liquidity or reserve requirements are not met and then only until such time as they are met. Hence, they do not, under the principles established in IAS 32, result in the classification of the financial instrument as equity. Paragraph AG25 of IAS 32 states:

> Preference shares may be issued with various rights. In determining whether a preference share is a financial liability or an equity instrument, an issuer assesses the particular rights attaching to the share to determine whether it exhibits the fundamental characteristic of a financial liability. For example, a preference share that provides for redemption on a specific date or at the option of the holder contains a financial liability because the issuer has an obligation to transfer financial assets to the holder of the share. *The potential inability of an issuer to satisfy an obligation to redeem a preference share when contractually required to do so, whether because of a lack of funds, a statutory restriction or insufficient profits or reserves, does not negate the obligation.* [Emphasis added]

Prohibitions against redemption (paragraphs 8 and 9)

Example 3

Facts

A6   A co-operative entity has issued shares to its members at different dates and for different amounts in the past as follows:

    (a)   1 January 20X1 100,000 shares at CU10 each (CU1,000,000);

    (b)   1 January 20X2 100,000 shares at CU20 each (a further CU2,000,000, so that the total for shares issued is CU3,000,000).

Shares are redeemable on demand at the amount for which they were issued.

A7   The entity's charter states that cumulative redemptions cannot exceed 20 per cent of the highest number of its members' shares ever outstanding. At 31 December 20X2 the entity has 200,000 of outstanding shares, which is the highest number of members' shares ever outstanding and no shares have been redeemed in the past. On 1 January 20X3 the entity amends its governing charter and increases the permitted level of cumulative redemptions to 25 per cent of the highest number of its members' shares ever outstanding.

Classification

Before the governing charter is amended

A8 Members' shares in excess of the prohibition against redemption are financial liabilities. The co-operative entity measures this financial liability at fair value at initial recognition. Because these shares are redeemable on demand, the co-operative entity measures the fair value of such financial liabilities as required by paragraph 47 of IFRS 13, which states: 'The fair value of a financial liability with a demand feature (eg a demand deposit) is not less than the amount payable on demand ...' Accordingly, the co-operative entity classifies as financial liabilities the maximum amount payable on demand under the redemption provisions.

A9 On 1 January 20X1 the maximum amount payable under the redemption provisions is 20,000 shares at CU10 each and accordingly the entity classifies CU200,000 as financial liability and CU800,000 as equity. However, on 1 January 20X2 because of the new issue of shares at CU20, the maximum amount payable under the redemption provisions increases to 40,000 shares at CU20 each. The issue of additional shares at CU20 creates a new liability that is measured on initial recognition at fair value. The liability after these shares have been issued is 20 per cent of the total shares in issue (200,000), measured at CU20, or CU800,000. This requires recognition of an additional liability of CU600,000. In this example no gain or loss is recognised. Accordingly the entity now classifies CU800,000 as financial liabilities and CU2,200,000 as equity. This example assumes these amounts are not changed between 1 January 20X1 and 31 December 20X2.

After the governing charter is amended

A10 Following the change in its governing charter the co-operative entity can now be required to redeem a maximum of 25 per cent of its outstanding shares or a maximum of 50,000 shares at CU20 each. Accordingly, on 1 January 20X3 the co-operative entity classifies as financial liabilities an amount of CU1,000,000 being the maximum amount payable on demand under the redemption provisions, as determined in accordance with paragraph 5.4.3 of IFRS 9. It therefore transfers on 1 January 20X3 from equity to financial liabilities an amount of CU200,000, leaving CU2,000,000 classified as equity. In this example the entity does not recognise a gain or loss on the transfer.

Example 4

Facts

A11 Local law governing the operations of co-operatives, or the terms of the entity's governing charter, prohibit an entity from redeeming members' shares if, by redeeming them, it would reduce paid-in capital from members' shares below 75 per cent of the highest amount of paid-in capital from members' shares. The highest amount for a particular co-operative is CU1,000,000. At the end of the reporting period the balance of paid-in capital is CU900,000.

Classification

A12 In this case, CU750,000 would be classified as equity and CU150,000 would be classified as financial liabilities. In addition to the paragraphs already cited, paragraph 18(b) of IAS 32 states in part:

> ... a financial instrument that gives the holder the right to put it back to the issuer for cash or another financial asset (a 'puttable instrument') is a financial liability, except for those instruments classified as equity instruments in accordance with paragraphs 16A and 16B or paragraphs 16C and 16D. The financial instrument is a financial liability even when the amount of cash or other financial assets is determined on the basis of an index or other item that has the potential to increase or decrease. The existence of an option for the holder to put the instrument back to the issuer for cash or another financial asset means that the puttable instrument meets the definition of a financial liability, except for those instruments classified as equity instruments in accordance with paragraphs 16A and 16B or paragraphs 16C and 16D.

A13 The redemption prohibition described in this example is different from the restrictions described in paragraphs 19 and AG25 of IAS 32. Those restrictions are limitations on the ability of the entity to pay the amount due on a financial liability, ie they prevent payment of the liability only if specified conditions are met. In contrast, this example describes an unconditional prohibition on redemptions beyond a specified amount, regardless of the entity's ability to redeem members' shares (eg given its cash resources, profits or distributable reserves). In effect, the prohibition against redemption prevents the entity from incurring any financial liability to redeem more than a specified amount of paid-in capital. Therefore, the portion of shares subject to the redemption prohibition is not a financial liability. While each member's shares may be redeemable individually, a portion of the total shares outstanding is not redeemable in any circumstances other than liquidation of the entity.

Example 5

Facts

A14 The facts of this example are as stated in example 4. In addition, at the end of the reporting period, liquidity requirements imposed in the local jurisdiction prevent the entity from redeeming any members' shares unless its holdings of cash and short-term investments are greater than a specified amount. The effect of these liquidity requirements at the end of the reporting period is that the entity cannot pay more than CU50,000 to redeem the members' shares.

Classification

A15 As in example 4, the entity classifies CU750,000 as equity and CU150,000 as a financial liability. This is because the amount classified as a liability is based on the entity's unconditional right to refuse redemption and not on conditional restrictions that prevent redemption only if liquidity or other conditions are not met and then only until such time as they are met. The provisions of paragraphs 19 and AG25 of IAS 32 apply in this case.

Example 6

Facts

A16 The entity's governing charter prohibits it from redeeming members' shares, except to the extent of proceeds received from the issue of additional members' shares to new or existing members during the preceding three years. Proceeds from issuing members' shares must be applied to redeem shares for which members have requested redemption. During the three preceding years, the proceeds from issuing members' shares have been CU12,000 and no member's shares have been redeemed.

Classification

A17 The entity classifies CU12,000 of the members' shares as financial liabilities. Consistently with the conclusions described in example 4, members' shares subject to an unconditional prohibition against redemption are not financial liabilities. Such an unconditional prohibition applies to an amount equal to the proceeds of shares issued before the preceding three years, and accordingly, this amount is classified as equity. However, an amount equal to the proceeds from any shares issued in the preceding three years is not subject to an unconditional prohibition on redemption. Accordingly, proceeds from the issue of members' shares in the preceding three years give rise to financial liabilities until they are no longer available for redemption of members' shares. As a result the entity has a financial liability equal to the proceeds of shares issued during the three preceding years, net of any redemptions during that period.

Example 7

Facts

A18 The entity is a co-operative bank. Local law governing the operations of co-operative banks state that at least 50 per cent of the entity's total 'outstanding liabilities' (a term defined in the regulations to include members' share accounts) has to be in the form of members' paid-in capital. The effect of the regulation is that if all of a co-operative's outstanding liabilities are in the form of members' shares, it is able to redeem them all. On 31 December 20X1 the entity has total outstanding liabilities of CU200,000, of which CU125,000 represent members' share accounts. The terms of the members' share accounts permit the holder to redeem them on demand and there are no limitations on redemption in the entity's charter.

Classification

A19 In this example members' shares are classified as financial liabilities. The redemption prohibition is similar to the restrictions described in paragraphs 19 and AG25 of IAS 32. The restriction is a conditional limitation on the ability of the entity to pay the amount due on a financial liability, ie they prevent payment of the liability only if specified conditions are met. More specifically, the entity could be required to redeem the entire amount of members' shares (CU125,000) if it repaid all of its other liabilities (CU75,000). Consequently, the prohibition against redemption does not prevent the entity from incurring a financial liability to redeem more than a specified number of members' shares or amount of paid-in capital. It allows the entity only to defer redemption until a condition is met, ie the repayment of other liabilities. Members' shares in this example are not subject to an unconditional prohibition against redemption and are therefore classified as financial liabilities.

IFRIC Interpretation 4

Determining whether an Arrangement contains a Lease

In December 2004 the International Accounting Standards Board issued IFRIC 4 *Determining whether an Arrangement contains a Lease*. It was developed by the Interpretations Committee.

Other IFRSs have made minor consequential amendments to IFRIC 4. These include IFRIC 12 *Service Concession Arrangements* (issued November 2006) and IFRS 9 *Financial Instruments* (issued November 2009 and October 2010).

CONTENTS

FOR THE ACCOMPANYING DOCUMENTS LISTED BELOW, SEE PART B OF THIS EDITION

ILLUSTRATIVE EXAMPLES

Example of an arrangement that contains a lease

Example of an arrangement that does not contain a lease

BASIS FOR CONCLUSIONS

IFRIC Interpretation 4 *Determining whether an Arrangement contains a Lease* (IFRIC 4) is set out in paragraphs 1–17 and the Appendix. IFRIC 4 is accompanied by illustrative examples and a Basis for Conclusions. The scope and authority of Interpretations are set out in paragraphs 2 and 7–16 of the *Preface to International Financial Reporting Standards.*

IFRIC Interpretation 4
Determining whether an Arrangement contains a Lease

References

- IFRS 13 *Fair Value Measurement*

- IAS 8 *Accounting Policies, Changes in Accounting Estimates and Errors*

- IAS 16 *Property, Plant and Equipment* (as revised in 2003)

- IAS 17 *Leases* (as revised in 2003)

- IAS 38 *Intangible Assets* (as revised in 2004)

- IFRIC 12 *Service Concession Arrangements*

Background

1   An entity may enter into an arrangement, comprising a transaction or a series of
     related transactions, that does not take the legal form of a lease but conveys a
     right to use an asset (eg an item of property, plant or equipment) in return for a
     payment or series of payments. Examples of arrangements in which one entity
     (the supplier) may convey such a right to use an asset to another entity (the
     purchaser), often together with related services, include:

- outsourcing arrangements (eg the outsourcing of the data processing
  functions of an entity).

- arrangements in the telecommunications industry, in which suppliers of
  network capacity enter into contracts to provide purchasers with rights to
  capacity.

- take-or-pay and similar contracts, in which purchasers must make specified
  payments regardless of whether they take delivery of the contracted
  products or services (eg a take-or-pay contract to acquire substantially all of
  the output of a supplier's power generator).

2   This Interpretation provides guidance for determining whether such arrangements
     are, or contain, leases that should be accounted for in accordance with IAS 17. It
     does not provide guidance for determining how such a lease should be classified
     under that Standard.

3   In some arrangements, the underlying asset that is the subject of the lease is a
     portion of a larger asset. This Interpretation does not address how to determine
     when a portion of a larger asset is itself the underlying asset for the purposes of
     applying IAS 17. Nevertheless, arrangements in which the underlying asset would
     represent a unit of account in either IAS 16 or IAS 38 are within the scope of this
     Interpretation.

Scope

4   This Interpretation does not apply to arrangements that:

    (a)   are, or contain, leases excluded from the scope of IAS 17; or

    (b)   are public-to-private service concession arrangements within the scope of IFRIC 12.

Issues

5   The issues addressed in this Interpretation are:

    (a)   how to determine whether an arrangement is, or contains, a lease as defined in IAS 17;

    (b)   when the assessment or a reassessment of whether an arrangement is, or contains, a lease should be made; and

    (c)   if an arrangement is, or contains, a lease, how the payments for the lease should be separated from payments for any other elements in the arrangement.

Consensus

Determining whether an arrangement is, or contains, a lease

6   Determining whether an arrangement is, or contains, a lease shall be based on the substance of the arrangement and requires an assessment of whether:

    (a)   fulfilment of the arrangement is dependent on the use of a specific asset or assets (the asset); and

    (b)   the arrangement conveys a right to use the asset.

Fulfilment of the arrangement is dependent on the use of a specific asset

7   Although a specific asset may be explicitly identified in an arrangement, it is not the subject of a lease if fulfilment of the arrangement is not dependent on the use of the specified asset. For example, if the supplier is obliged to deliver a specified quantity of goods or services and has the right and ability to provide those goods or services using other assets not specified in the arrangement, then fulfilment of the arrangement is not dependent on the specified asset and the arrangement does not contain a lease. A warranty obligation that permits or requires the substitution of the same or similar assets when the specified asset is not operating properly does not preclude lease treatment. In addition, a contractual provision (contingent or otherwise) permitting or requiring the supplier to substitute other assets for any reason on or after a specified date does not preclude lease treatment before the date of substitution.

8   An asset has been implicitly specified if, for example, the supplier owns or leases only one asset with which to fulfil the obligation and it is not economically feasible or practicable for the supplier to perform its obligation through the use of alternative assets.

Arrangement conveys a right to use the asset

9   An arrangement conveys the right to use the asset if the arrangement conveys to the purchaser (lessee) the right to control the use of the underlying asset. The right to control the use of the underlying asset is conveyed if any one of the following conditions is met:

(a) The purchaser has the ability or right to operate the asset or direct others to operate the asset in a manner it determines while obtaining or controlling more than an insignificant amount of the output or other utility of the asset.

(b) The purchaser has the ability or right to control physical access to the underlying asset while obtaining or controlling more than an insignificant amount of the output or other utility of the asset.

(c) Facts and circumstances indicate that it is remote that one or more parties other than the purchaser will take more than an insignificant amount of the output or other utility that will be produced or generated by the asset during the term of the arrangement, and the price that the purchaser will pay for the output is neither contractually fixed per unit of output nor equal to the current market price per unit of output as of the time of delivery of the output.

Assessing or reassessing whether an arrangement is, or contains, a lease

10   The assessment of whether an arrangement contains a lease shall be made at the inception of the arrangement, being the earlier of the date of the arrangement and the date of commitment by the parties to the principal terms of the arrangement, on the basis of all of the facts and circumstances. A reassessment of whether the arrangement contains a lease after the inception of the arrangement shall be made only if any one of the following conditions is met:

(a) There is a change in the contractual terms, unless the change only renews or extends the arrangement.

(b) A renewal option is exercised or an extension is agreed to by the parties to the arrangement, unless the term of the renewal or extension had initially been included in the lease term in accordance with paragraph 4 of IAS 17. A renewal or extension of the arrangement that does not include modification of any of the terms in the original arrangement before the end of the term of the original arrangement shall be evaluated under paragraphs 6–9 only with respect to the renewal or extension period.

(c) There is a change in the determination of whether fulfilment is dependent on a specified asset.

(d) There is a substantial change to the asset, for example a substantial physical change to property, plant or equipment.

© IFRS Foundation

11 A reassessment of an arrangement shall be based on the facts and circumstances as of the date of reassessment, including the remaining term of the arrangement. Changes in estimate (for example, the estimated amount of output to be delivered to the purchaser or other potential purchasers) would not trigger a reassessment. If an arrangement is reassessed and is determined to contain a lease (or not to contain a lease), lease accounting shall be applied (or cease to apply) from:

(a)   in the case of (a), (c) or (d) in paragraph 10, when the change in circumstances giving rise to the reassessment occurs;

(b)   in the case of (b) in paragraph 10, the inception of the renewal or extension period.

Separating payments for the lease from other payments

12 If an arrangement contains a lease, the parties to the arrangement shall apply the requirements of IAS 17 to the lease element of the arrangement, unless exempted from those requirements in accordance with paragraph 2 of IAS 17. Accordingly, if an arrangement contains a lease, that lease shall be classified as a finance lease or an operating lease in accordance with paragraphs 7–19 of IAS 17. Other elements of the arrangement not within the scope of IAS 17 shall be accounted for in accordance with other Standards.

13 For the purpose of applying the requirements of IAS 17, payments and other consideration required by the arrangement shall be separated at the inception of the arrangement or upon a reassessment of the arrangement into those for the lease and those for other elements on the basis of their relative fair values. The minimum lease payments as defined in paragraph 4 of IAS 17 include only payments for the lease (ie the right to use the asset) and exclude payments for other elements in the arrangement (eg for services and the cost of inputs).

14 In some cases, separating the payments for the lease from payments for other elements in the arrangement will require the purchaser to use an estimation technique. For example, a purchaser may estimate the lease payments by reference to a lease agreement for a comparable asset that contains no other elements, or by estimating the payments for the other elements in the arrangement by reference to comparable agreements and then deducting these payments from the total payments under the arrangement.

15 If a purchaser concludes that it is impracticable to separate the payments reliably, it shall:

(a)   in the case of a finance lease, recognise an asset and a liability at an amount equal to the fair value[1] of the underlying asset that was identified in paragraphs 7 and 8 as the subject of the lease. Subsequently the liability shall be reduced as payments are made and an imputed finance charge on the liability recognised using the purchaser's incremental borrowing rate of interest.[2]

---

1   IAS 17 uses the term 'fair value' in a way that differs in some respects from the definition of fair value in IFRS 13. Therefore, when applying IAS 17 an entity measures fair value in accordance with IAS 17, not IFRS 13.

2   ie the lessee's incremental borrowing rate of interest as defined in paragraph 4 of IAS 17.

(b) in the case of an operating lease, treat all payments under the arrangement as lease payments for the purposes of complying with the disclosure requirements of IAS 17, but

    (i) disclose those payments separately from minimum lease payments of other arrangements that do not include payments for non-lease elements, and

    (ii) state that the disclosed payments also include payments for non-lease elements in the arrangement.

Effective date

16   An entity shall apply this Interpretation for annual periods beginning on or after 1 January 2006. Earlier application is encouraged. If an entity applies this Interpretation for a period beginning before 1 January 2006, it shall disclose that fact.

16A   An entity shall apply the amendment in paragraph 4(b) for annual periods beginning on or after 1 January 2008. If an entity applies IFRIC 12 for an earlier period, the amendment shall be applied for that earlier period.

Transition

17   IAS 8 specifies how an entity applies a change in accounting policy resulting from the initial application of an Interpretation. An entity is not required to comply with those requirements when first applying this Interpretation. If an entity uses this exemption, it shall apply paragraphs 6–9 of the Interpretation to arrangements existing at the start of the earliest period for which comparative information under IFRSs is presented on the basis of facts and circumstances existing at the start of that period.

Appendix
Amendments to IFRS 1 *First-time Adoption of International Financial Reporting Standards*

The amendments in this appendix shall be applied for annual periods beginning on or after 1 September 2004. If an entity applies this Interpretation for an earlier period, these amendments shall be applied for that earlier period.

* * * * *

The amendments contained in this appendix when this Interpretation was issued in 2004 were incorporated into IFRS 1 as issued on and after 2 December 2004. In November 2008 a revised version of IFRS 1 was issued.

IFRIC Interpretation 5

Rights to Interests arising from Decommissioning, Restoration and Environmental Rehabilitation Funds

In December 2004 the International Accounting Standards Board issued IFRIC 5 *Rights to Interests arising from Decommissioning, Restoration and Environmental Rehabilitation Funds*. It was developed by the Interpretations Committee.

Other IFRSs have made minor consequential amendments to IFRIC 5. These include IAS 1 *Presentation of Financial Statements* (as revised in September 2007) and IFRS 9 *Financial Instruments* (issued November 2009 and October 2010).

CONTENTS

from paragraph

FOR THE ACCOMPANYING DOCUMENT LISTED BELOW, SEE PART B OF THIS EDITION

BASIS FOR CONSLUSIONS

IFRIC Interpretation 5 *Rights to Interests arising from Decommissioning, Restoration and Environmental Rehabilitation Funds* (IFRIC 5) is set out in paragraphs 1–15 and the Appendix. IFRIC 5 is accompanied by a Basis for Conclusions. The scope and authority of Interpretations are set out in paragraphs 2 and 7–16 of the *Preface to International Financial Reporting Standards*.

IFRIC Interpretation 5
Rights to Interests arising from Decommissioning, Restoration and Environmental Rehabilitation Funds

References

- IAS 8 *Accounting Policies, Changes in Accounting Estimates and Errors*
- IAS 28 *Investments in Associates and Joint Ventures*
- IAS 37 *Provisions, Contingent Liabilities and Contingent Assets*
- IFRS 9 *Financial Instruments* (issued in October 2010)
- IFRS 10 *Consolidated Financial Statements*
- IFRS 11 *Joint Arrangements*
- SIC-12 *Consolidation—Special Purpose Entities* (as revised in 2004)

Background

1   The purpose of decommissioning, restoration and environmental rehabilitation funds, hereafter referred to as 'decommissioning funds' or 'funds', is to segregate assets to fund some or all of the costs of decommissioning plant (such as a nuclear plant) or certain equipment (such as cars), or in undertaking environmental rehabilitation (such as rectifying pollution of water or restoring mined land), together referred to as 'decommissioning'.

2   Contributions to these funds may be voluntary or required by regulation or law. The funds may have one of the following structures:

   (a)   funds that are established by a single contributor to fund its own decommissioning obligations, whether for a particular site, or for a number of geographically dispersed sites.

   (b)   funds that are established with multiple contributors to fund their individual or joint decommissioning obligations, when contributors are entitled to reimbursement for decommissioning expenses to the extent of their contributions plus any actual earnings on those contributions less their share of the costs of administering the fund. Contributors may have an obligation to make additional contributions, for example, in the event of the bankruptcy of another contributor.

   (c)   funds that are established with multiple contributors to fund their individual or joint decommissioning obligations when the required level of contributions is based on the current activity of a contributor and the benefit obtained by that contributor is based on its past activity. In such cases there is a potential mismatch in the amount of contributions made by a contributor (based on current activity) and the value realisable from the fund (based on past activity).

3   Such funds generally have the following features:

(a)   the fund is separately administered by independent trustees.

(b)   entities (contributors) make contributions to the fund, which are invested in a range of assets that may include both debt and equity investments, and are available to help pay the contributors' decommissioning costs. The trustees determine how contributions are invested, within the constraints set by the fund's governing documents and any applicable legislation or other regulations.

(c)   the contributors retain the obligation to pay decommissioning costs. However, contributors are able to obtain reimbursement of decommissioning costs from the fund up to the lower of the decommissioning costs incurred and the contributor's share of assets of the fund.

(d)   the contributors may have restricted access or no access to any surplus of assets of the fund over those used to meet eligible decommissioning costs.

Scope

4   This Interpretation applies to accounting in the financial statements of a contributor for interests arising from decommissioning funds that have both of the following features:

(a)   the assets are administered separately (either by being held in a separate legal entity or as segregated assets within another entity); and

(b)   a contributor's right to access the assets is restricted.

5   A residual interest in a fund that extends beyond a right to reimbursement, such as a contractual right to distributions once all the decommissioning has been completed or on winding up the fund, may be an equity instrument within the scope of IFRS 9 and is not within the scope of this Interpretation.

Issues

6   The issues addressed in this Interpretation are:

(a)   how should a contributor account for its interest in a fund?

(b)   when a contributor has an obligation to make additional contributions, for example, in the event of the bankruptcy of another contributor, how should that obligation be accounted for?

Consensus

Accounting for an interest in a fund

7   The contributor shall recognise its obligation to pay decommissioning costs as a liability and recognise its interest in the fund separately unless the contributor is not liable to pay decommissioning costs even if the fund fails to pay.

8   The contributor shall determine whether it has control or joint control of, or significant influence over, the fund by reference to IFRS 10, IFRS 11 and IAS 28. If it does, the contributor shall account for its interest in the fund in accordance with those Standards.

9   If a contributor does not have control or joint control of, or significant influence over, the fund, the contributor shall recognise the right to receive reimbursement from the fund as a reimbursement in accordance with IAS 37. This reimbursement shall be measured at the lower of:

   (a)   the amount of the decommissioning obligation recognised; and

   (b)   the contributor's share of the fair value of the net assets of the fund attributable to contributors.

   Changes in the carrying value of the right to receive reimbursement other than contributions to and payments from the fund shall be recognised in profit or loss in the period in which these changes occur.

Accounting for obligations to make additional contributions

10   When a contributor has an obligation to make potential additional contributions, for example, in the event of the bankruptcy of another contributor or if the value of the investment assets held by the fund decreases to an extent that they are insufficient to fulfil the fund's reimbursement obligations, this obligation is a contingent liability that is within the scope of IAS 37. The contributor shall recognise a liability only if it is probable that additional contributions will be made.

Disclosure

11   A contributor shall disclose the nature of its interest in a fund and any restrictions on access to the assets in the fund.

12   When a contributor has an obligation to make potential additional contributions that is not recognised as a liability (see paragraph 10), it shall make the disclosures required by paragraph 86 of IAS 37.

13   When a contributor accounts for its interest in the fund in accordance with paragraph 9, it shall make the disclosures required by paragraph 85(c) of IAS 37.

Effective date

14   An entity shall apply this Interpretation for annual periods beginning on or after 1 January 2006. Earlier application is encouraged. If an entity applies this Interpretation to a period beginning before 1 January 2006, it shall disclose that fact.

14A IFRS 9 issued in October 2010, amended paragraph 5. An entity shall apply that amendment when it applies IFRS 9 as issued in October 2010.

14B IFRS 10 and IFRS 11, issued in May 2011, amended paragraphs 8 and 9. An entity shall apply those amendments when it applies IFRS 10 and IFRS 11.

Transition

15 Changes in accounting policies shall be accounted for in accordance with the requirements of IAS 8.

Appendix
Amendment to IAS 39 *Financial Instruments: Recognition and Measurement*

The amendment in this appendix shall be applied for annual periods beginning on or after 1 January 2006. If an entity applies this Interpretation for an earlier period, the amendment shall be applied for that earlier period.

* * * * *

The amendment contained in this appendix when this Interpretation was issued in 2004 was incorporated into IAS 39 as issued on and after 16 December 2004.

IFRIC Interpretation 6

Liabilities arising from Participating in a Specific Market—Waste Electrical and Electronic Equipment

In September 2005 the International Accounting Standards Board issued IFRIC 6 *Liabilities arising from Participating in a Specific Market—Waste Electrical and Electronic Equipment*. It was developed by the Interpretations Committee.

CONTENTS

IFRIC Interpretation 6 *Liabilities arising from Participating in a Specific Market—Waste Electrical and Electronic Equipment* (IFRIC 6) is set out in paragraphs 1–11. IFRIC 6 is accompanied by a Basis for Conclusions. The scope and authority of Interpretations are set out in paragraphs 2 and 7–16 of the *Preface to International Financial Reporting Standards*.

IFRIC Interpretation 6
Liabilities arising from Participating in a Specific Market—Waste Electrical and Electronic Equipment

References

- IAS 8 *Accounting Policies, Changes in Accounting Estimates and Errors*
- IAS 37 *Provisions, Contingent Liabilities and Contingent Assets*

Background

1 Paragraph 17 of IAS 37 specifies that an obligating event is a past event that leads to a present obligation that an entity has no realistic alternative to settling.

2 Paragraph 19 of IAS 37 states that provisions are recognised only for 'obligations arising from past events existing independently of an entity's future actions'.

3 The European Union's Directive on Waste Electrical and Electronic Equipment (WE&EE), which regulates the collection, treatment, recovery and environmentally sound disposal of waste equipment, has given rise to questions about when the liability for the decommissioning of WE&EE should be recognised. The Directive distinguishes between 'new' and 'historical' waste and between waste from private households and waste from sources other than private households. New waste relates to products sold after 13 August 2005. All household equipment sold before that date is deemed to give rise to historical waste for the purposes of the Directive.

4 The Directive states that the cost of waste management for historical household equipment should be borne by producers of that type of equipment that are in the market during a period to be specified in the applicable legislation of each Member State (the measurement period). The Directive states that each Member State shall establish a mechanism to have producers contribute to costs proportionately 'e.g. in proportion to their respective share of the market by type of equipment.'

5 Several terms used in the Interpretation such as 'market share' and 'measurement period' may be defined very differently in the applicable legislation of individual Member States. For example, the length of the measurement period might be a year or only one month. Similarly, the measurement of market share and the formulae for computing the obligation may differ in the various national legislations. However, all of these examples affect only the measurement of the liability, which is not within the scope of the Interpretation.

Scope

6 This Interpretation provides guidance on the recognition, in the financial statements of producers, of liabilities for waste management under the EU Directive on WE&EE in respect of sales of historical household equipment.

7   The Interpretation addresses neither new waste nor historical waste from sources other than private households. The liability for such waste management is adequately covered in IAS 37. However, if, in national legislation, new waste from private households is treated in a similar manner to historical waste from private households, the principles of the Interpretation apply by reference to the hierarchy in paragraphs 10–12 of IAS 8. The IAS 8 hierarchy is also relevant for other regulations that impose obligations in a way that is similar to the cost attribution model specified in the EU Directive.

Issue

8   The IFRIC was asked to determine in the context of the decommissioning of WE&EE what constitutes the obligating event in accordance with paragraph 14(a) of IAS 37 for the recognition of a provision for waste management costs:

- the manufacture or sale of the historical household equipment?

- participation in the market during the measurement period?

- the incurrence of costs in the performance of waste management activities?

Consensus

9   Participation in the market during the measurement period is the obligating event in accordance with paragraph 14(a) of IAS 37. As a consequence, a liability for waste management costs for historical household equipment does not arise as the products are manufactured or sold. Because the obligation for historical household equipment is linked to participation in the market during the measurement period, rather than to production or sale of the items to be disposed of, there is no obligation unless and until a market share exists during the measurement period. The timing of the obligating event may also be independent of the particular period in which the activities to perform the waste management are undertaken and the related costs incurred.

Effective date

10   An entity shall apply this Interpretation for annual periods beginning on or after 1 December 2005. Earlier application is encouraged. If an entity applies the Interpretation for a period beginning before 1 December 2005, it shall disclose that fact.

Transition

11   Changes in accounting policies shall be accounted for in accordance with IAS 8.

IFRIC Interpretation 7

Applying the Restatement Approach under IAS 29
Financial Reporting in Hyperinflationary Economies

In November 2005 the International Accounting Standards Board issued IFRIC 7 *Applying the Restatement Approach under IAS 29* Financial Reporting in Hyperinflationary Economies. It was developed by the Interpretations Committee.

IAS 1 *Presentation of Financial Statements* (as revised in September 2007) made minor consequential amendments to IFRIC 7.

CONTENTS

© IFRS Foundation

IFRIC Interpretation 7 *Applying the Restatement Approach under IAS 29* Financial Reporting in Hyperinflationary Economies (IFRIC 7) is set out in paragraphs 1–6. IFRIC 7 is accompanied by an illustrative example and a Basis for Conclusions. The scope and authority of Interpretations are set out in paragraphs 2 and 7–16 of the *Preface to International Financial Reporting Standards*.

IFRIC Interpretation 7
Applying the Restatement Approach under IAS 29
Financial Reporting in Hyperinflationary Economies

References

- IAS 12 *Income Taxes*

- IAS 29 *Financial Reporting in Hyperinflationary Economies*

Background

1   This Interpretation provides guidance on how to apply the requirements of IAS 29 in a reporting period in which an entity identifies[1] the existence of hyperinflation in the economy of its functional currency, when that economy was not hyperinflationary in the prior period, and the entity therefore restates its financial statements in accordance with IAS 29.

Issues

2   The questions addressed in this Interpretation are:

   (a)   how should the requirement '... stated in terms of the measuring unit current at the end of the reporting period' in paragraph 8 of IAS 29 be interpreted when an entity applies the Standard?

   (b)   how should an entity account for opening deferred tax items in its restated financial statements?

Consensus

3   In the reporting period in which an entity identifies the existence of hyperinflation in the economy of its functional currency, not having been hyperinflationary in the prior period, the entity shall apply the requirements of IAS 29 as if the economy had always been hyperinflationary. Therefore, in relation to non-monetary items measured at historical cost, the entity's opening statement of financial position at the beginning of the earliest period presented in the financial statements shall be restated to reflect the effect of inflation from the date the assets were acquired and the liabilities were incurred or assumed until the end of the reporting period. For non-monetary items carried in the opening statement of financial position at amounts current at dates other than those of acquisition or incurrence, that restatement shall reflect instead the effect of inflation from the dates those carrying amounts were determined until the end of the reporting period.

---

1   The identification of hyperinflation is based on the entity's judgement of the criteria in paragraph 3 of IAS 29.

4   At the end of the reporting period, deferred tax items are recognised and measured in accordance with IAS 12. However, the deferred tax figures in the opening statement of financial position for the reporting period shall be determined as follows:

(a)   the entity remeasures the deferred tax items in accordance with IAS 12 after it has restated the nominal carrying amounts of its non-monetary items at the date of the opening statement of financial position of the reporting period by applying the measuring unit at that date.

(b)   the deferred tax items remeasured in accordance with (a) are restated for the change in the measuring unit from the date of the opening statement of financial position of the reporting period to the end of that reporting period.

The entity applies the approach in (a) and (b) in restating the deferred tax items in the opening statement of financial position of any comparative periods presented in the restated financial statements for the reporting period in which the entity applies IAS 29.

5   After an entity has restated its financial statements, all corresponding figures in the financial statements for a subsequent reporting period, including deferred tax items, are restated by applying the change in the measuring unit for that subsequent reporting period only to the restated financial statements for the previous reporting period.

Effective date

6   An entity shall apply this Interpretation for annual periods beginning on or after 1 March 2006. Earlier application is encouraged. If an entity applies this Interpretation to financial statements for a period beginning before 1 March 2006, it shall disclose that fact.

IFRIC Interpretation 10

Interim Financial Reporting and Impairment

In July 2006 the International Accounting Standards Board issued IFRIC 10 *Interim Financial Reporting and Impairment*. It was developed by the Interpretations Committee.

IFRIC 10 has been amended by IAS 1 *Presentation of Financial Statements* (as revised in September 2007) and IFRS 9 *Financial Instruments* (issued November 2009 and October 2010).

CONTENTS

FOR THE ACCOMPANYING DOCUMENT LISTED BELOW, SEE PART B OF THIS EDITION

BASIS FOR CONCLUSIONS

© IFRS Foundation

IFRIC Interpretation 10 *Interim Financial Reporting and Impairment* (IFRIC 10) is set out in paragraphs 1–12. IFRIC 10 is accompanied by a Basis for Conclusions. The scope and authority of Interpretations are set out in paragraphs 2 and 7–16 of the *Preface to International Financial Reporting Standards*.

IFRIC Interpretation 10
Interim Financial Reporting and Impairment

References

- IFRS 9 *Financial Instruments*
- IAS 34 *Interim Financial Reporting*
- IAS 36 *Impairment of Assets*
- IFRS 9 *Financial Instruments* (issued October 2010)

Background

1   An entity is required to assess goodwill for impairment at the end of each reporting period and, if required, to recognise an impairment loss at that date in accordance with IAS 36. However, at the end of a subsequent reporting period, conditions may have so changed that the impairment loss would have been reduced or avoided had the impairment assessment been made only at that date. This Interpretation provides guidance on whether such impairment losses should ever be reversed.

2   The Interpretation addresses the interaction between the requirements of IAS 34 and the recognition of impairment losses on goodwill in IAS 36, and the effect of that interaction on subsequent interim and annual financial statements.

Issue

3   IAS 34 paragraph 28 requires an entity to apply the same accounting policies in its interim financial statements as are applied in its annual financial statements. It also states that 'the frequency of an entity's reporting (annual, half-yearly, or quarterly) shall not affect the measurement of its annual results. To achieve that objective, measurements for interim reporting purposes shall be made on a year-to-date basis.'

4   IAS 36 paragraph 124 states that 'An impairment loss recognised for goodwill shall not be reversed in a subsequent period.'

5–6   [Deleted]

7   The Interpretation addresses the following issue:

        Should an entity reverse impairment losses recognised in an interim period on goodwill if a loss would not have been recognised, or a smaller loss would have been recognised, had an impairment assessment been made only at the end of a subsequent reporting period?

Consensus

8   An entity shall not reverse an impairment loss recognised in a previous interim period in respect of goodwill.

9   An entity shall not extend this consensus by analogy to other areas of potential conflict between IAS 34 and other standards.

Effective date and transition

10   An entity shall apply the Interpretation for annual periods beginning on or after 1 November 2006. Earlier application is encouraged. If an entity applies the Interpretation for a period beginning before 1 November 2006, it shall disclose that fact. An entity shall apply the Interpretation to goodwill prospectively from the date at which it first applied IAS 36; it shall apply the Interpretation to investments in equity instruments or in financial assets carried at cost prospectively from the date at which it first applied the measurement criteria of IAS 39.

11   [Deleted]

12   IFRS 9, issued in October 2010, amended paragraphs 1, 2, 7 and 8 and deleted paragraphs 5, 6 and 11. An entity shall apply those amendments when it applies IFRS 9 as issued in October 2010.

IFRIC Interpretation 12

Service Concession Arrangements

In November 2006 the International Accounting Standards Board issued IFRIC 12 *Service Concession Arrangements*. It was developed by the Interpretations Committee.

Other IFRSs have made minor consequential amendments to IFRIC 12. These include IAS 1 *Presentation of Financial Statements* (as revised in September 2007) and IFRS 9 *Financial Instruments* (issued November 2009 and October 2010).

CONTENTS

FOR THE ACCOMPANYING DOCUMENTS LISTED BELOW, SEE PART B OF THIS EDITION

INFORMATION NOTES

1 Accounting framework for public-to-private service arrangements

2 References to IFRSs that apply to typical types of public-to-private arrangements

ILLUSTRATIVE EXAMPLES

BASIS FOR CONCLUSIONS

IFRIC Interpretation 12 *Service Concession Arrangements* (IFRIC 12) is set out in paragraphs 1–30 and Appendices A and B. IFRIC 12 is accompanied by information notes, illustrative examples and a Basis for Conclusions. The scope and authority of Interpretations are set out in paragraphs 2 and 7–16 of the *Preface to International Financial Reporting Standards*.

IFRIC Interpretation 12
Service Concession Arrangements

References

- *Framework for the Preparation and Presentation of Financial Statements*[1]

- IFRS 1 *First-time Adoption of International Financial Reporting Standards*

- IFRS 7 *Financial Instruments: Disclosures*

- IFRS 9 *Financial Instruments* (issued October 2010)

- IAS 8 *Accounting Policies, Changes in Accounting Estimates and Errors*

- IAS 11 *Construction Contracts*

- IAS 16 *Property, Plant and Equipment*

- IAS 17 *Leases*

- IAS 18 *Revenue*

- IAS 20 *Accounting for Government Grants and Disclosure of Government Assistance*

- IAS 23 *Borrowing Costs*

- IAS 32 *Financial Instruments: Presentation*

- IAS 36 *Impairment of Assets*

- IAS 37 *Provisions, Contingent Liabilities and Contingent Assets*

- IAS 38 *Intangible Assets*

- IFRIC 4 *Determining whether an Arrangement contains a Lease*

- SIC-29 *Service Concession Arrangements: Disclosures*[2]

Background

1   In many countries, infrastructure for public services—such as roads, bridges, tunnels, prisons, hospitals, airports, water distribution facilities, energy supply and telecommunication networks—has traditionally been constructed, operated and maintained by the public sector and financed through public budget appropriation.

2   In some countries, governments have introduced contractual service arrangements to attract private sector participation in the development, financing, operation and maintenance of such infrastructure. The infrastructure may already exist, or may be constructed during the period of the service arrangement. An arrangement within the scope of this Interpretation typically involves a private sector entity (an operator) constructing the infrastructure used

---

1   In September 2010 the IASB replaced the *Framework* with the *Conceptual Framework for Financial Reporting*.

2   The title of SIC-29, formerly *Disclosure—Service Concession Arrangements*, was amended by IFRIC 12.

to provide the public service or upgrading it (for example, by increasing its capacity) and operating and maintaining that infrastructure for a specified period of time. The operator is paid for its services over the period of the arrangement. The arrangement is governed by a contract that sets out performance standards, mechanisms for adjusting prices, and arrangements for arbitrating disputes. Such an arrangement is often described as a 'build-operate-transfer', a 'rehabilitate-operate-transfer' or a 'public-to-private' service concession arrangement.

3   A feature of these service arrangements is the public service nature of the obligation undertaken by the operator. Public policy is for the services related to the infrastructure to be provided to the public, irrespective of the identity of the party that operates the services. The service arrangement contractually obliges the operator to provide the services to the public on behalf of the public sector entity. Other common features are:

(a)   the party that grants the service arrangement (the grantor) is a public sector entity, including a governmental body, or a private sector entity to which the responsibility for the service has been devolved.

(b)   the operator is responsible for at least some of the management of the infrastructure and related services and does not merely act as an agent on behalf of the grantor.

(c)   the contract sets the initial prices to be levied by the operator and regulates price revisions over the period of the service arrangement.

(d)   the operator is obliged to hand over the infrastructure to the grantor in a specified condition at the end of the period of the arrangement, for little or no incremental consideration, irrespective of which party initially financed it.

Scope

4   This Interpretation gives guidance on the accounting by operators for public-to-private service concession arrangements.

5   This Interpretation applies to public-to-private service concession arrangements if:

(a)   the grantor controls or regulates what services the operator must provide with the infrastructure, to whom it must provide them, and at what price; and

(b)   the grantor controls—through ownership, beneficial entitlement or otherwise—any significant residual interest in the infrastructure at the end of the term of the arrangement.

6   Infrastructure used in a public-to-private service concession arrangement for its entire useful life (whole of life assets) is within the scope of this Interpretation if the conditions in paragraph 5(a) are met. Paragraphs AG1–AG8 provide guidance on determining whether, and to what extent, public-to-private service concession arrangements are within the scope of this Interpretation.

7   This Interpretation applies to both:

(a)   infrastructure that the operator constructs or acquires from a third party for the purpose of the service arrangement; and

(b)   existing infrastructure to which the grantor gives the operator access for the purpose of the service arrangement.

8   This Interpretation does not specify the accounting for infrastructure that was held and recognised as property, plant and equipment by the operator before entering the service arrangement. The derecognition requirements of IFRSs (set out in IAS 16) apply to such infrastructure.

9   This Interpretation does not specify the accounting by grantors.

Issues

10   This Interpretation sets out general principles on recognising and measuring the obligations and related rights in service concession arrangements. Requirements for disclosing information about service concession arrangements are in SIC-29. The issues addressed in this Interpretation are:

(a)   treatment of the operator's rights over the infrastructure;

(b)   recognition and measurement of arrangement consideration;

(c)   construction or upgrade services;

(d)   operation services;

(e)   borrowing costs;

(f)   subsequent accounting treatment of a financial asset and an intangible asset; and

(g)   items provided to the operator by the grantor.

Consensus

Treatment of the operator's rights over the infrastructure

11   Infrastructure within the scope of this Interpretation shall not be recognised as property, plant and equipment of the operator because the contractual service arrangement does not convey the right to control the use of the public service infrastructure to the operator. The operator has access to operate the infrastructure to provide the public service on behalf of the grantor in accordance with the terms specified in the contract.

Recognition and measurement of arrangement consideration

12   Under the terms of contractual arrangements within the scope of this Interpretation, the operator acts as a service provider. The operator constructs or upgrades infrastructure (construction or upgrade services) used to provide a public service and operates and maintains that infrastructure (operation services) for a specified period of time.

13   The operator shall recognise and measure revenue in accordance with IASs 11 and 18 for the services it performs. If the operator performs more than one service (ie construction or upgrade services and operation services) under a single contract or arrangement, consideration received or receivable shall be allocated by reference to the relative fair values of the services delivered, when the amounts are separately identifiable. The nature of the consideration determines its subsequent accounting treatment. The subsequent accounting for consideration received as a financial asset and as an intangible asset is detailed in paragraphs 23–26 below.

Construction or upgrade services

14   The operator shall account for revenue and costs relating to construction or upgrade services in accordance with IAS 11.

Consideration given by the grantor to the operator

15   If the operator provides construction or upgrade services the consideration received or receivable by the operator shall be recognised at its fair value. The consideration may be rights to:

(a)   a financial asset, or

(b)   an intangible asset.

16   The operator shall recognise a financial asset to the extent that it has an unconditional contractual right to receive cash or another financial asset from or at the direction of the grantor for the construction services; the grantor has little, if any, discretion to avoid payment, usually because the agreement is enforceable by law. The operator has an unconditional right to receive cash if the grantor contractually guarantees to pay the operator (a) specified or determinable amounts or (b) the shortfall, if any, between amounts received from users of the public service and specified or determinable amounts, even if payment is contingent on the operator ensuring that the infrastructure meets specified quality or efficiency requirements.

17   The operator shall recognise an intangible asset to the extent that it receives a right (a licence) to charge users of the public service. A right to charge users of the public service is not an unconditional right to receive cash because the amounts are contingent on the extent that the public uses the service.

18   If the operator is paid for the construction services partly by a financial asset and partly by an intangible asset it is necessary to account separately for each component of the operator's consideration. The consideration received or receivable for both components shall be recognised initially at the fair value of the consideration received or receivable.

19   The nature of the consideration given by the grantor to the operator shall be determined by reference to the contract terms and, when it exists, relevant contract law.

Operation services

20   The operator shall account for revenue and costs relating to operation services in accordance with IAS 18.

Contractual obligations to restore the infrastructure to a specified level of serviceability

21　The operator may have contractual obligations it must fulfil as a condition of its licence (a) to maintain the infrastructure to a specified level of serviceability or (b) to restore the infrastructure to a specified condition before it is handed over to the grantor at the end of the service arrangement. These contractual obligations to maintain or restore infrastructure, except for any upgrade element (see paragraph 14), shall be recognised and measured in accordance with IAS 37, ie at the best estimate of the expenditure that would be required to settle the present obligation at the end of the reporting period.

Borrowing costs incurred by the operator

22　In accordance with IAS 23, borrowing costs attributable to the arrangement shall be recognised as an expense in the period in which they are incurred unless the operator has a contractual right to receive an intangible asset (a right to charge users of the public service). In this case borrowing costs attributable to the arrangement shall be capitalised during the construction phase of the arrangement in accordance with that Standard.

Financial asset

23　IAS 32 and IFRSs 7 and 9 apply to the financial asset recognised under paragraphs 16 and 18.

24　The amount due from or at the direction of the grantor is accounted for in accordance with IFRS 9 as:

(a)　at amortised cost; or

(b)　measured at fair value through profit or loss.

25　If the amount due from the grantor is accounted for at amortised cost, IFRS 9 requires interest calculated using the effective interest method to be recognised in profit or loss.

Intangible asset

26　IAS 38 applies to the intangible asset recognised in accordance with paragraphs 17 and 18. Paragraphs 45–47 of IAS 38 provide guidance on measuring intangible assets acquired in exchange for a non-monetary asset or assets or a combination of monetary and non-monetary assets.

Items provided to the operator by the grantor

27　In accordance with paragraph 11, infrastructure items to which the operator is given access by the grantor for the purposes of the service arrangement are not recognised as property, plant and equipment of the operator. The grantor may also provide other items to the operator that the operator can keep or deal with as it wishes. If such assets form part of the consideration payable by the grantor for the services, they are not government grants as defined in IAS 20. They are recognised as assets of the operator, measured at fair value on initial recognition. The operator shall recognise a liability in respect of unfulfilled obligations it has assumed in exchange for the assets.

Effective date

28 An entity shall apply this Interpretation for annual periods beginning on or after 1 January 2008. Earlier application is permitted. If an entity applies this Interpretation for a period beginning before 1 January 2008, it shall disclose that fact.

28A [Deleted]

28B IFRS 9, issued in October 2010, amended paragraphs 23–25 and deleted paragraph 28A. An entity shall apply those amendments when it applies IFRS 9 as issued in October 2010.

Transition

29 Subject to paragraph 30, changes in accounting policies are accounted for in accordance with IAS 8, ie retrospectively.

30 If, for any particular service arrangement, it is impracticable for an operator to apply this Interpretation retrospectively at the start of the earliest period presented, it shall:

(a) recognise financial assets and intangible assets that existed at the start of the earliest period presented;

(b) use the previous carrying amounts of those financial and intangible assets (however previously classified) as their carrying amounts as at that date; and

(c) test financial and intangible assets recognised at that date for impairment, unless this is not practicable, in which case the amounts shall be tested for impairment as at the start of the current period.

Appendix A
Application guidance

This appendix is an integral part of the Interpretation.

Scope (paragraph 5)

AG1 Paragraph 5 of this Interpretation specifies that infrastructure is within the scope of the Interpretation when the following conditions apply:

(a) the grantor controls or regulates what services the operator must provide with the infrastructure, to whom it must provide them, and at what price; and

(b) the grantor controls—through ownership, beneficial entitlement or otherwise—any significant residual interest in the infrastructure at the end of the term of the arrangement.

AG2 The control or regulation referred to in condition (a) could be by contract or otherwise (such as through a regulator), and includes circumstances in which the grantor buys all of the output as well as those in which some or all of the output is bought by other users. In applying this condition, the grantor and any related parties shall be considered together. If the grantor is a public sector entity, the public sector as a whole, together with any regulators acting in the public interest, shall be regarded as related to the grantor for the purposes of this Interpretation.

AG3 For the purpose of condition (a), the grantor does not need to have complete control of the price: it is sufficient for the price to be regulated by the grantor, contract or regulator, for example by a capping mechanism. However, the condition shall be applied to the substance of the agreement. Non-substantive features, such as a cap that will apply only in remote circumstances, shall be ignored. Conversely, if for example, a contract purports to give the operator freedom to set prices, but any excess profit is returned to the grantor, the operator's return is capped and the price element of the control test is met.

AG4 For the purpose of condition (b), the grantor's control over any significant residual interest should both restrict the operator's practical ability to sell or pledge the infrastructure and give the grantor a continuing right of use throughout the period of the arrangement. The residual interest in the infrastructure is the estimated current value of the infrastructure as if it were already of the age and in the condition expected at the end of the period of the arrangement.

AG5 Control should be distinguished from management. If the grantor retains both the degree of control described in paragraph 5(a) and any significant residual interest in the infrastructure, the operator is only managing the infrastructure on the grantor's behalf—even though, in many cases, it may have wide managerial discretion.

AG6 Conditions (a) and (b) together identify when the infrastructure, including any replacements required (see paragraph 21), is controlled by the grantor for the whole of its economic life. For example, if the operator has to replace part of an item of infrastructure during the period of the arrangement (eg the top layer of a road or

© IFRS Foundation

the roof of a building), the item of infrastructure shall be considered as a whole. Thus condition (b) is met for the whole of the infrastructure, including the part that is replaced, if the grantor controls any significant residual interest in the final replacement of that part.

AG7   Sometimes the use of infrastructure is partly regulated in the manner described in paragraph 5(a) and partly unregulated. However, these arrangements take a variety of forms:

(a)   any infrastructure that is physically separable and capable of being operated independently and meets the definition of a cash-generating unit as defined in IAS 36 shall be analysed separately if it is used wholly for unregulated purposes. For example, this might apply to a private wing of a hospital, where the remainder of the hospital is used by the grantor to treat public patients.

(b)   when purely ancillary activities (such as a hospital shop) are unregulated, the control tests shall be applied as if those services did not exist, because in cases in which the grantor controls the services in the manner described in paragraph 5, the existence of ancillary activities does not detract from the grantor's control of the infrastructure.

AG8   The operator may have a right to use the separable infrastructure described in paragraph AG7(a), or the facilities used to provide ancillary unregulated services described in paragraph AG7(b). In either case, there may in substance be a lease from the grantor to the operator; if so, it shall be accounted for in accordance with IAS 17.

Appendix B
Amendments to IFRS 1 and to other Interpretations

The amendments in this appendix shall be applied for annual periods beginning on or after 1 January 2008. If an entity applies this Interpretation for an earlier period, these amendments shall be applied for that earlier period.

* * * * *

The amendments contained in this appendix when this Interpretation was issued in 2006 have been incorporated into the text of IFRS 1, IFRIC 4 and SIC-29 as issued on or after 30 November 2006. In November 2008 a revised version of IFRS 1 was issued.

IFRIC Interpretation 13

Customer Loyalty Programmes

In June 2007 the International Accounting Standards Board issued IFRIC 13 *Customer Loyalty Programmes*. It was developed by the Interpretations Committee.

Improvements to IFRSs (issued May 2010) made minor consequential amendments to IFRIC 13.

CONTENTS

FOR THE ACCOMPANYING DOCUMENTS LISTED BELOW, SEE PART B OF THIS EDITION

IFRIC Interpretation 13 *Customer Loyalty Programmes* (IFRIC 13) is set out in paragraphs 1–11 and the Appendix. IFRIC 13 is accompanied by illustrative examples and a Basis for Conclusions. The scope and authority of Interpretations are set out in paragraphs 2 and 7–16 of the *Preface to International Financial Reporting Standards*.

IFRIC Interpretation 13
Customer Loyalty Programmes

References

- IAS 8 *Accounting Policies, Changes in Accounting Estimates and Errors*

- IAS 18 *Revenue*

- IAS 37 *Provisions, Contingent Liabilities and Contingent Assets*

- IFRS 13 *Fair Value Measurement*

Background

1   Customer loyalty programmes are used by entities to provide customers with incentives to buy their goods or services. If a customer buys goods or services, the entity grants the customer award credits (often described as 'points'). The customer can redeem the award credits for awards such as free or discounted goods or services.

2   The programmes operate in a variety of ways. Customers may be required to accumulate a specified minimum number or value of award credits before they are able to redeem them. Award credits may be linked to individual purchases or groups of purchases, or to continued custom over a specified period. The entity may operate the customer loyalty programme itself or participate in a programme operated by a third party. The awards offered may include goods or services supplied by the entity itself and/or rights to claim goods or services from a third party.

Scope

3   This Interpretation applies to customer loyalty award credits that:

(a)   an entity grants to its customers as part of a sales transaction, ie a sale of goods, rendering of services or use by a customer of entity assets; and

(b)   subject to meeting any further qualifying conditions, the customers can redeem in the future for free or discounted goods or services.

The Interpretation addresses accounting by the entity that grants award credits to its customers.

Issues

4   The issues addressed in this Interpretation are:

    (a)   whether the entity's obligation to provide free or discounted goods or services ('awards') in the future should be recognised and measured by:

        (i)   allocating some of the consideration received or receivable from the sales transaction to the award credits and deferring the recognition of revenue (applying paragraph 13 of IAS 18); or

        (ii)   providing for the estimated future costs of supplying the awards (applying paragraph 19 of IAS 18); and

    (b)   if consideration is allocated to the award credits:

        (i)   how much should be allocated to them;

        (ii)   when revenue should be recognised; and

        (iii)   if a third party supplies the awards, how revenue should be measured.

Consensus

5   An entity shall apply paragraph 13 of IAS 18 and account for award credits as a separately identifiable component of the sales transaction(s) in which they are granted (the 'initial sale'). The fair value of the consideration received or receivable in respect of the initial sale shall be allocated between the award credits and the other components of the sale.

6   The consideration allocated to the award credits shall be measured by reference to their fair value.

7   If the entity supplies the awards itself, it shall recognise the consideration allocated to award credits as revenue when award credits are redeemed and it fulfils its obligations to supply awards. The amount of revenue recognised shall be based on the number of award credits that have been redeemed in exchange for awards, relative to the total number expected to be redeemed.

8   If a third party supplies the awards, the entity shall assess whether it is collecting the consideration allocated to the award credits on its own account (ie as the principal in the transaction) or on behalf of the third party (ie as an agent for the third party).

    (a)   If the entity is collecting the consideration on behalf of the third party, it shall:

        (i)   measure its revenue as the net amount retained on its own account, ie the difference between the consideration allocated to the award credits and the amount payable to the third party for supplying the awards; and

        (ii)   recognise this net amount as revenue when the third party becomes obliged to supply the awards and entitled to receive consideration for doing so. These events may occur as soon as the award credits are granted. Alternatively, if the customer can choose to claim awards from either the entity or a third party, these events may occur only when the customer chooses to claim awards from the third party.

(b) If the entity is collecting the consideration on its own account, it shall measure its revenue as the gross consideration allocated to the award credits and recognise the revenue when it fulfils its obligations in respect of the awards.

9 If at any time the unavoidable costs of meeting the obligations to supply the awards are expected to exceed the consideration received and receivable for them (ie the consideration allocated to the award credits at the time of the initial sale that has not yet been recognised as revenue plus any further consideration receivable when the customer redeems the award credits), the entity has onerous contracts. A liability shall be recognised for the excess in accordance with IAS 37. The need to recognise such a liability could arise if the expected costs of supplying awards increase, for example if the entity revises its expectations about the number of award credits that will be redeemed.

Effective date and transition

10 An entity shall apply this Interpretation for annual periods beginning on or after 1 July 2008. Earlier application is permitted. If an entity applies the Interpretation for a period beginning before 1 July 2008, it shall disclose that fact.

10A Paragraph AG2 was amended by *Improvements to IFRSs* issued in May 2010. An entity shall apply that amendment for annual periods beginning on or after 1 January 2011. Earlier application is permitted. If an entity applies the amendment for an earlier period it shall disclose that fact.

10B IFRS 13, issued in May 2011, amended paragraphs 6 and AG1–AG3. An entity shall apply those amendments when it applies IFRS 13.

11 Changes in accounting policy shall be accounted for in accordance with IAS 8.

Appendix
Application guidance

This appendix is an integral part of the Interpretation.

Measuring the fair value of award credits

AG1 Paragraph 6 of the consensus requires the consideration allocated to award credits to be measured by reference to their fair value. If there is not a quoted market price for an identical award credit, fair value must be measured using another valuation technique.

AG2 An entity may measure the fair value of award credits by reference to the fair value of the awards for which they could be redeemed. The fair value of the award credits takes into account, as appropriate:

(a) the amount of the discounts or incentives that would otherwise be offered to customers who have not earned award credits from an initial sale;

(b) the proportion of award credits that are not expected to be redeemed by customers; and

(c) non-performance risk.

If customers can choose from a range of different awards, the fair value of the award credits reflects the fair values of the range of available awards, weighted in proportion to the frequency with which each award is expected to be selected.

AG3 In some circumstances, other valuation techniques may be used. For example, if a third party will supply the awards and the entity pays the third party for each award credit it grants, it could measure the fair value of the award credits by reference to the amount it pays the third party, adding a reasonable profit margin. Judgement is required to select and apply the valuation technique that satisfies the requirements of paragraph 6 of the consensus and is most appropriate in the circumstances.

IFRIC Interpretation 14

IAS 19—The Limit on a Defined Benefit Asset, Minimum Funding Requirements and their Interaction

In July 2007 the International Accounting Standards Board issued IFRIC 14 *IAS 19—The Limit on a Defined Benefit Asset, Minimum Funding Requirements and their Interaction*. It was developed by the Interpretations Committee. In November 2009, IFRIC 14 was amended to address prepayments of future minimum funding requirement contributions.

IAS 1 *Presentation of Financial Statements* (as revised in September 2007) made minor consequential amendments to IFRIC 14.

CONTENTS

FOR THE ACCOMPANYING DOCUMENTS LISTED BELOW, SEE PART B OF THIS EDITION

APPROVAL BY THE BOARD OF *PREPAYMENTS OF A MINIMUM FUNDING REQUIREMENT* ISSUED IN NOVEMBER 2009

ILLUSTRATIVE EXAMPLES

BASIS FOR CONCLUSIONS

IFRIC Interpretation 14 *IAS 19—The Limit on a Defined Benefit Asset, Minimum Funding Requirements and their Interaction* (IFRIC 14) is set out in paragraphs 1–29. IFRIC 14 is accompanied by illustrative examples and a Basis for Conclusions. The scope and authority of Interpretations are set out in paragraphs 2 and 7–16 of the *Preface to International Financial Reporting Standards*.

IFRIC Interpretation 14
IAS 19—The Limit on a Defined Benefit Asset, Minimum Funding Requirements and their Interaction

References

- IAS 1 *Presentation of Financial Statements*
- IAS 8 *Accounting Policies, Changes in Accounting Estimates and Errors*
- IAS 19 *Employee Benefits* (as amended in 2011)
- IAS 37 *Provisions, Contingent Liabilities and Contingent Assets*

Background

1   Paragraph 64 of IAS 19 limits the measurement of a net defined benefit asset to the lower of the surplus in the defined benefit plan and the asset ceiling. Paragraph 8 of IAS 19 defines the asset ceiling as 'the present value of any economic benefits available in the form of refunds from the plan or reductions in future contributions to the plan'. Questions have arisen about when refunds or reductions in future contributions should be regarded as available, particularly when a minimum funding requirement exists.

2   Minimum funding requirements exist in many countries to improve the security of the post-employment benefit promise made to members of an employee benefit plan. Such requirements normally stipulate a minimum amount or level of contributions that must be made to a plan over a given period. Therefore, a minimum funding requirement may limit the ability of the entity to reduce future contributions.

3   Further, the limit on the measurement of a defined benefit asset may cause a minimum funding requirement to be onerous. Normally, a requirement to make contributions to a plan would not affect the measurement of the defined benefit asset or liability. This is because the contributions, once paid, will become plan assets and so the additional net liability is nil. However, a minimum funding requirement may give rise to a liability if the required contributions will not be available to the entity once they have been paid.

3A   In November 2009 the International Accounting Standards Board amended IFRIC 14 to remove an unintended consequence arising from the treatment of prepayments of future contributions in some circumstances when there is a minimum funding requirement.

Scope

4   This Interpretation applies to all post-employment defined benefits and other long-term employee defined benefits.

5   For the purpose of this Interpretation, minimum funding requirements are any requirements to fund a post-employment or other long-term defined benefit plan.

Issues

6   The issues addressed in this Interpretation are:

   (a)   when refunds or reductions in future contributions should be regarded as available in accordance with the definition of the asset ceiling in paragraph 8 of IAS 19.

   (b)   how a minimum funding requirement might affect the availability of reductions in future contributions.

   (c)   when a minimum funding requirement might give rise to a liability.

Consensus

Availability of a refund or reduction in future contributions

7   An entity shall determine the availability of a refund or a reduction in future contributions in accordance with the terms and conditions of the plan and any statutory requirements in the jurisdiction of the plan.

8   An economic benefit, in the form of a refund or a reduction in future contributions, is available if the entity can realise it at some point during the life of the plan or when the plan liabilities are settled. In particular, such an economic benefit may be available even if it is not realisable immediately at the end of the reporting period.

9   The economic benefit available does not depend on how the entity intends to use the surplus. An entity shall determine the maximum economic benefit that is available from refunds, reductions in future contributions or a combination of both. An entity shall not recognise economic benefits from a combination of refunds and reductions in future contributions based on assumptions that are mutually exclusive.

10   In accordance with IAS 1, the entity shall disclose information about the key sources of estimation uncertainty at the end of the reporting period that have a significant risk of causing a material adjustment to the carrying amount of the net asset or liability recognised in the statement of financial position. This might include disclosure of any restrictions on the current realisability of the surplus or disclosure of the basis used to determine the amount of the economic benefit available.

The economic benefit available as a refund

The right to a refund

11   A refund is available to an entity only if the entity has an unconditional right to a refund:

   (a)   during the life of the plan, without assuming that the plan liabilities must be settled in order to obtain the refund (eg in some jurisdictions, the entity may have a right to a refund during the life of the plan, irrespective of whether the plan liabilities are settled); or

(b)   assuming the gradual settlement of the plan liabilities over time until all members have left the plan; or

(c)   assuming the full settlement of the plan liabilities in a single event (ie as a plan wind-up).

An unconditional right to a refund can exist whatever the funding level of a plan at the end of the reporting period.

12   If the entity's right to a refund of a surplus depends on the occurrence or non-occurrence of one or more uncertain future events not wholly within its control, the entity does not have an unconditional right and shall not recognise an asset.

Measurement of the economic benefit

13   An entity shall measure the economic benefit available as a refund as the amount of the surplus at the end of the reporting period (being the fair value of the plan assets less the present value of the defined benefit obligation) that the entity has a right to receive as a refund, less any associated costs. For instance, if a refund would be subject to a tax other than income tax, an entity shall measure the amount of the refund net of the tax.

14   In measuring the amount of a refund available when the plan is wound up (paragraph 11(c)), an entity shall include the costs to the plan of settling the plan liabilities and making the refund. For example, an entity shall deduct professional fees if these are paid by the plan rather than the entity, and the costs of any insurance premiums that may be required to secure the liability on wind-up.

15   If the amount of a refund is determined as the full amount or a proportion of the surplus, rather than a fixed amount, an entity shall make no adjustment for the time value of money, even if the refund is realisable only at a future date.

The economic benefit available as a contribution reduction

16   If there is no minimum funding requirement for contributions relating to future service, the economic benefit available as a reduction in future contributions is the future service cost to the entity for each period over the shorter of the expected life of the plan and the expected life of the entity. The future service cost to the entity excludes amounts that will be borne by employees.

17   An entity shall determine the future service costs using assumptions consistent with those used to determine the defined benefit obligation and with the situation that exists at the end of the reporting period as determined by IAS 19. Therefore, an entity shall assume no change to the benefits to be provided by a plan in the future until the plan is amended and shall assume a stable workforce in the future unless the entity makes a reduction in the number of employees covered by the plan. In the latter case, the assumption about the future workforce shall include the reduction.

The effect of a minimum funding requirement on the economic benefit available as a reduction in future contributions

18   An entity shall analyse any minimum funding requirement at a given date into contributions that are required to cover (a) any existing shortfall for past service on the minimum funding basis and (b) future service.

19   Contributions to cover any existing shortfall on the minimum funding basis in respect of services already received do not affect future contributions for future service. They may give rise to a liability in accordance with paragraphs 23–26.

20   If there is a minimum funding requirement for contributions relating to future service, the economic benefit available as a reduction in future contributions is the sum of:

(a)   any amount that reduces future minimum funding requirement contributions for future service because the entity made a prepayment (ie paid the amount before being required to do so); and

(b)   the estimated future service cost in each period in accordance with paragraphs 16 and 17, less the estimated minimum funding requirement contributions that would be required for future service in those periods if there were no prepayment as described in (a).

21   An entity shall estimate the future minimum funding requirement contributions for future service taking into account the effect of any existing surplus determined using the minimum funding basis but excluding the prepayment described in paragraph 20(a). An entity shall use assumptions consistent with the minimum funding basis and, for any factors not specified by that basis, assumptions consistent with those used to determine the defined benefit obligation and with the situation that exists at the end of the reporting period as determined by IAS 19. The estimate shall include any changes expected as a result of the entity paying the minimum contributions when they are due. However, the estimate shall not include the effect of expected changes in the terms and conditions of the minimum funding basis that are not substantively enacted or contractually agreed at the end of the reporting period.

22   When an entity determines the amount described in paragraph 20(b), if the future minimum funding requirement contributions for future service exceed the future IAS 19 service cost in any given period, that excess reduces the amount of the economic benefit available as a reduction in future contributions. However, the amount described in paragraph 20(b) can never be less than zero.

When a minimum funding requirement may give rise to a liability

23   If an entity has an obligation under a minimum funding requirement to pay contributions to cover an existing shortfall on the minimum funding basis in respect of services already received, the entity shall determine whether the contributions payable will be available as a refund or reduction in future contributions after they are paid into the plan.

24   To the extent that the contributions payable will not be available after they are paid into the plan, the entity shall recognise a liability when the obligation arises. The liability shall reduce the net defined benefit asset or increase the net defined benefit liability so that no gain or loss is expected to result from applying paragraph 64 of IAS 19 when the contributions are paid.

25–26   [Deleted]

Effective date

27   An entity shall apply this Interpretation for annual periods beginning on or after 1 January 2008. Earlier application is permitted.

27A   IAS 1 (as revised in 2007) amended the terminology used throughout IFRSs. In addition it amended paragraph 26. An entity shall apply those amendments for annual periods beginning on or after 1 January 2009. If an entity applies IAS 1 (revised 2007) for an earlier period, the amendments shall be applied for that earlier period.

27B   *Prepayments of a Minimum Funding Requirement* added paragraph 3A and amended paragraphs 16–18 and 20–22. An entity shall apply those amendments for annual periods beginning on or after 1 January 2011. Earlier application is permitted. If an entity applies the amendments for an earlier period, it shall disclose that fact.

27C   IAS 19 (as amended in 2011) amended paragraphs 1, 6, 17 and 24 and deleted paragraphs 25 and 26. An entity shall apply those amendments when it applies IAS 19 (as amended in 2011).

Transition

28   An entity shall apply this Interpretation from the beginning of the first period presented in the first financial statements to which the Interpretation applies. An entity shall recognise any initial adjustment arising from the application of this Interpretation in retained earnings at the beginning of that period.

29   An entity shall apply the amendments in paragraphs 3A, 16–18 and 20–22 from the beginning of the earliest comparative period presented in the first financial statements in which the entity applies this Interpretation. If the entity had previously applied this Interpretation before it applies the amendments, it shall recognise the adjustment resulting from the application of the amendments in retained earnings at the beginning of the earliest comparative period presented.

IFRIC Interpretation 15

Agreements for the Construction of Real Estate

In July 2008 the International Accounting Standards Board issued IFRIC 15 *Agreement for the Construction of Real Estate*. It was developed by the Interpretations Committee.

CONTENTS

IFRIC Interpretation 15 *Agreements for the Construction of Real Estate* (IFRIC 15) is set out in paragraphs 1–25. IFRIC 15 is accompanied by an information note, illustrative examples and a Basis for Conclusions. The scope and authority of Interpretations are set out in paragraphs 2 and 7–16 of the *Preface to International Financial Reporting Standards*.

IFRIC Interpretation 15
Agreements for the Construction of Real Estate

References

- IAS 1 *Presentation of Financial Statements* (as revised in 2007)
- IAS 8 *Accounting Policies, Changes in Accounting Estimates and Errors*
- IAS 11 *Construction Contracts*
- IAS 18 *Revenue*
- IAS 37 *Provisions, Contingent Liabilities and Contingent Assets*
- IFRIC 12 *Service Concession Arrangements*
- IFRIC 13 *Customer Loyalty Programmes*

Background

1   In the real estate industry, entities that undertake the construction of real estate, directly or through subcontractors, may enter into agreements with one or more buyers before construction is complete. Such agreements take diverse forms.

2   For example, entities that undertake the construction of residential real estate may start to market individual units (apartments or houses) 'off plan', ie while construction is still in progress, or even before it has begun. Each buyer enters into an agreement with the entity to acquire a specified unit when it is ready for occupation. Typically, the buyer pays a deposit to the entity that is refundable only if the entity fails to deliver the completed unit in accordance with the contracted terms. The balance of the purchase price is generally paid to the entity only on contractual completion, when the buyer obtains possession of the unit.

3   Entities that undertake the construction of commercial or industrial real estate may enter into an agreement with a single buyer. The buyer may be required to make progress payments between the time of the initial agreement and contractual completion. Construction may take place on land the buyer owns or leases before construction begins.

Scope

4   This Interpretation applies to the accounting for revenue and associated expenses by entities that undertake the construction of real estate directly or through subcontractors.

5   Agreements in the scope of this Interpretation are agreements for the construction of real estate. In addition to the construction of real estate, such agreements may include the delivery of other goods or services.

Issues

6   The Interpretation addresses two issues:

     (a)   Is the agreement within the scope of IAS 11 or IAS 18?

     (b)   When should revenue from the construction of real estate be recognised?

Consensus

7   The following discussion assumes that the entity has previously analysed the agreement for the construction of real estate and any related agreements and concluded that it will retain neither continuing managerial involvement to the degree usually associated with ownership nor effective control over the constructed real estate to an extent that would preclude recognition of some or all of the consideration as revenue. If recognition of some of the consideration as revenue is precluded, the following discussion applies only to the part of the agreement for which revenue will be recognised.

8   Within a single agreement, an entity may contract to deliver goods or services in addition to the construction of real estate (eg a sale of land or provision of property management services). In accordance with paragraph 13 of IAS 18, such an agreement may need to be split into separately identifiable components including one for the construction of real estate. The fair value of the total consideration received or receivable for the agreement shall be allocated to each component. If separate components are identified, the entity applies paragraphs 10–12 of this Interpretation to the component for the construction of real estate in order to determine whether that component is within the scope of IAS 11 or IAS 18. The segmenting criteria of IAS 11 then apply to any component of the agreement that is determined to be a construction contract.

9   The following discussion refers to an agreement for the construction of real estate but it also applies to a component for the construction of real estate identified within an agreement that includes other components.

Determining whether the agreement is within the scope of IAS 11 or IAS 18

10   Determining whether an agreement for the construction of real estate is within the scope of IAS 11 or IAS 18 depends on the terms of the agreement and all the surrounding facts and circumstances. Such a determination requires judgement with respect to each agreement.

11   IAS 11 applies when the agreement meets the definition of a construction contract set out in paragraph 3 of IAS 11: 'a contract specifically negotiated for the construction of an asset or a combination of assets ...' An agreement for the construction of real estate meets the definition of a construction contract when the buyer is able to specify the major structural elements of the design of the real estate before construction begins and/or specify major structural changes once construction is in progress (whether or not it exercises that ability). When

IAS 11 applies, the construction contract also includes any contracts or components for the rendering of services that are directly related to the construction of the real estate in accordance with paragraph 5(a) of IAS 11 and paragraph 4 of IAS 18.

12   In contrast, an agreement for the construction of real estate in which buyers have only limited ability to influence the design of the real estate, eg to select a design from a range of options specified by the entity, or to specify only minor variations to the basic design, is an agreement for the sale of goods within the scope of IAS 18.

Accounting for revenue from the construction of real estate

The agreement is a construction contract

13   When the agreement is within the scope of IAS 11 and its outcome can be estimated reliably, the entity shall recognise revenue by reference to the stage of completion of the contract activity in accordance with IAS 11.

14   The agreement may not meet the definition of a construction contract and therefore be within the scope of IAS 18. In this case, the entity shall determine whether the agreement is for the rendering of services or for the sale of goods.

The agreement is an agreement for the rendering of services

15   If the entity is not required to acquire and supply construction materials, the agreement may be only an agreement for the rendering of services in accordance with IAS 18. In this case, if the criteria in paragraph 20 of IAS 18 are met, IAS 18 requires revenue to be recognised by reference to the stage of completion of the transaction using the percentage of completion method. The requirements of IAS 11 are generally applicable to the recognition of revenue and the associated expenses for such a transaction (IAS 18 paragraph 21).

The agreement is an agreement for the sale of goods

16   If the entity is required to provide services together with construction materials in order to perform its contractual obligation to deliver the real estate to the buyer, the agreement is an agreement for the sale of goods and the criteria for recognition of revenue set out in paragraph 14 of IAS 18 apply.

17   The entity may transfer to the buyer control and the significant risks and rewards of ownership of the work in progress in its current state as construction progresses. In this case, if all the criteria in paragraph 14 of IAS 18 are met continuously as construction progresses, the entity shall recognise revenue by reference to the stage of completion using the percentage of completion method. The requirements of IAS 11 are generally applicable to the recognition of revenue and the associated expenses for such a transaction.

18   The entity may transfer to the buyer control and the significant risks and rewards of ownership of the real estate in its entirety at a single time (eg at completion, upon or after delivery). In this case, the entity shall recognise revenue only when all the criteria in paragraph 14 of IAS 18 are satisfied.

19 When the entity is required to perform further work on real estate already delivered to the buyer, it shall recognise a liability and an expense in accordance with paragraph 19 of IAS 18. The liability shall be measured in accordance with IAS 37. When the entity is required to deliver further goods or services that are separately identifiable from the real estate already delivered to the buyer, it would have identified the remaining goods or services as a separate component of the sale, in accordance with paragraph 8 of this Interpretation.

Disclosures

20 When an entity recognises revenue using the percentage of completion method for agreements that meet all the criteria in paragraph 14 of IAS 18 continuously as construction progresses (see paragraph 17 of the Interpretation), it shall disclose:

(a) how it determines which agreements meet all the criteria in paragraph 14 of IAS 18 continuously as construction progresses;

(b) the amount of revenue arising from such agreements in the period; and

(c) the methods used to determine the stage of completion of agreements in progress.

21 For the agreements described in paragraph 20 that are in progress at the reporting date, the entity shall also disclose:

(a) the aggregate amount of costs incurred and recognised profits (less recognised losses) to date; and

(b) the amount of advances received.

Amendments to the illustrative examples accompanying IAS 18

22–23 [Amendments incorporated in the illustrative examples accompanying IAS 18]

Effective date and transition

24 An entity shall apply this Interpretation for annual periods beginning on or after 1 January 2009. Earlier application is permitted. If an entity applies the Interpretation for a period beginning before 1 January 2009, it shall disclose that fact.

25 Changes in accounting policy shall be accounted for retrospectively in accordance with IAS 8.

IFRIC Interpretation 16

Hedges of a Net Investment in a Foreign Operation

In July 2008 the International Accounting Standards Board issued IFRIC 16 *Hedges of a Net Investment in a Foreign Operation*. It was developed by the Interpretations Committee.

Improvements to IFRSs (issued April 2009) made minor consequential amendments to IFRIC 16.

CONTENTS

FOR THE ACCOMPANYING DOCUMENTS LISTED BELOW, SEE PART B OF THIS EDITION

ILLUSTRATIVE EXAMPLE

BASIS FOR CONCLUSIONS

IFRIC Interpretation 16 *Hedges of a Net Investment in a Foreign Operation* (IFRIC 16) is set out in paragraphs 1–19 and the Appendix. IFRIC 16 is accompanied by an illustrative example and a Basis for Conclusions. The scope and authority of Interpretations are set out in paragraphs 2 and 7–16 of the *Preface to International Financial Reporting Standards*.

IFRIC Interpretation 16
Hedges of a Net Investment in a Foreign Operation

References

- IAS 8 *Accounting Policies, Changes in Accounting Estimates and Errors*
- IAS 21 *The Effects of Changes in Foreign Exchange Rates*
- IAS 39 *Financial Instruments: Recognition and Measurement*

Background

1   Many reporting entities have investments in foreign operations (as defined in IAS 21 paragraph 8). Such foreign operations may be subsidiaries, associates, joint ventures or branches. IAS 21 requires an entity to determine the functional currency of each of its foreign operations as the currency of the primary economic environment of that operation. When translating the results and financial position of a foreign operation into a presentation currency, the entity is required to recognise foreign exchange differences in other comprehensive income until it disposes of the foreign operation.

2   Hedge accounting of the foreign currency risk arising from a net investment in a foreign operation will apply only when the net assets of that foreign operation are included in the financial statements.[1] The item being hedged with respect to the foreign currency risk arising from the net investment in a foreign operation may be an amount of net assets equal to or less than the carrying amount of the net assets of the foreign operation.

3   IAS 39 requires the designation of an eligible hedged item and eligible hedging instruments in a hedge accounting relationship. If there is a designated hedging relationship, in the case of a net investment hedge, the gain or loss on the hedging instrument that is determined to be an effective hedge of the net investment is recognised in other comprehensive income and is included with the foreign exchange differences arising on translation of the results and financial position of the foreign operation.

4   An entity with many foreign operations may be exposed to a number of foreign currency risks. This Interpretation provides guidance on identifying the foreign currency risks that qualify as a hedged risk in the hedge of a net investment in a foreign operation.

5   IAS 39 allows an entity to designate either a derivative or a non-derivative financial instrument (or a combination of derivative and non-derivative financial instruments) as hedging instruments for foreign currency risk. This Interpretation provides guidance on where, within a group, hedging instruments that are hedges of a net investment in a foreign operation can be held to qualify for hedge accounting.

---

1   This will be the case for consolidated financial statements, financial statements in which investments such as associates or joint ventures are accounted for using the equity method and financial statements that include a branch or a joint operation as defined in IFRS 11 *Joint Arrangements*.

6   IAS 21 and IAS 39 require cumulative amounts recognised in other comprehensive income relating to both the foreign exchange differences arising on translation of the results and financial position of the foreign operation and the gain or loss on the hedging instrument that is determined to be an effective hedge of the net investment to be reclassified from equity to profit or loss as a reclassification adjustment when the parent disposes of the foreign operation. This Interpretation provides guidance on how an entity should determine the amounts to be reclassified from equity to profit or loss for both the hedging instrument and the hedged item.

Scope

7   This Interpretation applies to an entity that hedges the foreign currency risk arising from its net investments in foreign operations and wishes to qualify for hedge accounting in accordance with IAS 39. For convenience this Interpretation refers to such an entity as a parent entity and to the financial statements in which the net assets of foreign operations are included as consolidated financial statements. All references to a parent entity apply equally to an entity that has a net investment in a foreign operation that is a joint venture, an associate or a branch.

8   This Interpretation applies only to hedges of net investments in foreign operations; it should not be applied by analogy to other types of hedge accounting.

Issues

9   Investments in foreign operations may be held directly by a parent entity or indirectly by its subsidiary or subsidiaries. The issues addressed in this Interpretation are:

(a)   *the nature of the hedged risk and the amount of the hedged item for which a hedging relationship may be designated:*

       (i)   whether the parent entity may designate as a hedged risk only the foreign exchange differences arising from a difference between the functional currencies of the parent entity and its foreign operation, or whether it may also designate as the hedged risk the foreign exchange differences arising from the difference between the presentation currency of the parent entity's consolidated financial statements and the functional currency of the foreign operation;

       (ii)   if the parent entity holds the foreign operation indirectly, whether the hedged risk may include only the foreign exchange differences arising from differences in functional currencies between the foreign operation and its immediate parent entity, or whether the hedged risk may also include any foreign exchange differences between the functional currency of the foreign operation and any intermediate or ultimate parent entity (ie whether the fact that the net investment in the foreign operation is held through an intermediate parent affects the economic risk to the ultimate parent).

(b) *where in a group the hedging instrument can be held:*

    (i) whether a qualifying hedge accounting relationship can be established only if the entity hedging its net investment is a party to the hedging instrument or whether any entity in the group, regardless of its functional currency, can hold the hedging instrument;

    (ii) whether the nature of the hedging instrument (derivative or non-derivative) or the method of consolidation affects the assessment of hedge effectiveness.

(c) *what amounts should be reclassified from equity to profit or loss as reclassification adjustments on disposal of the foreign operation:*

    (i) when a foreign operation that was hedged is disposed of, what amounts from the parent entity's foreign currency translation reserve in respect of the hedging instrument and in respect of that foreign operation should be reclassified from equity to profit or loss in the parent entity's consolidated financial statements;

    (ii) whether the method of consolidation affects the determination of the amounts to be reclassified from equity to profit or loss.

Consensus

Nature of the hedged risk and amount of the hedged item for which a hedging relationship may be designated

10   Hedge accounting may be applied only to the foreign exchange differences arising between the functional currency of the foreign operation and the parent entity's functional currency.

11   In a hedge of the foreign currency risks arising from a net investment in a foreign operation, the hedged item can be an amount of net assets equal to or less than the carrying amount of the net assets of the foreign operation in the consolidated financial statements of the parent entity. The carrying amount of the net assets of a foreign operation that may be designated as the hedged item in the consolidated financial statements of a parent depends on whether any lower level parent of the foreign operation has applied hedge accounting for all or part of the net assets of that foreign operation and that accounting has been maintained in the parent's consolidated financial statements.

12   The hedged risk may be designated as the foreign currency exposure arising between the functional currency of the foreign operation and the functional currency of any parent entity (the immediate, intermediate or ultimate parent entity) of that foreign operation. The fact that the net investment is held through an intermediate parent does not affect the nature of the economic risk arising from the foreign currency exposure to the ultimate parent entity.

13   An exposure to foreign currency risk arising from a net investment in a foreign operation may qualify for hedge accounting only once in the consolidated financial statements. Therefore, if the same net assets of a foreign operation are hedged by more than one parent entity within the group (for example, both a direct and an indirect parent entity) for the same risk, only one hedging relationship will qualify for hedge accounting in the consolidated financial statements of the ultimate parent. A hedging relationship designated by one parent entity in its consolidated financial statements need not be maintained by another higher level parent entity. However, if it is not maintained by the higher level parent entity, the hedge accounting applied by the lower level parent must be reversed before the higher level parent's hedge accounting is recognised.

Where the hedging instrument can be held

14   A derivative or a non-derivative instrument (or a combination of derivative and non-derivative instruments) may be designated as a hedging instrument in a hedge of a net investment in a foreign operation. The hedging instrument(s) may be held by any entity or entities within the group, as long as the designation, documentation and effectiveness requirements of IAS 39 paragraph 88 that relate to a net investment hedge are satisfied. In particular, the hedging strategy of the group should be clearly documented because of the possibility of different designations at different levels of the group.

15   For the purpose of assessing effectiveness, the change in value of the hedging instrument in respect of foreign exchange risk is computed by reference to the functional currency of the parent entity against whose functional currency the hedged risk is measured, in accordance with the hedge accounting documentation. Depending on where the hedging instrument is held, in the absence of hedge accounting the total change in value might be recognised in profit or loss, in other comprehensive income, or both. However, the assessment of effectiveness is not affected by whether the change in value of the hedging instrument is recognised in profit or loss or in other comprehensive income. As part of the application of hedge accounting, the total effective portion of the change is included in other comprehensive income. The assessment of effectiveness is not affected by whether the hedging instrument is a derivative or a non-derivative instrument or by the method of consolidation.

Disposal of a hedged foreign operation

16   When a foreign operation that was hedged is disposed of, the amount reclassified to profit or loss as a reclassification adjustment from the foreign currency translation reserve in the consolidated financial statements of the parent in respect of the hedging instrument is the amount that IAS 39 paragraph 102 requires to be identified. That amount is the cumulative gain or loss on the hedging instrument that was determined to be an effective hedge.

17   The amount reclassified to profit or loss from the foreign currency translation reserve in the consolidated financial statements of a parent in respect of the net investment in that foreign operation in accordance with IAS 21 paragraph 48 is the amount included in that parent's foreign currency translation reserve in respect of that foreign operation. In the ultimate parent's consolidated financial

statements, the aggregate net amount recognised in the foreign currency translation reserve in respect of all foreign operations is not affected by the consolidation method. However, whether the ultimate parent uses the direct or the step-by-step method of consolidation[2] may affect the amount included in its foreign currency translation reserve in respect of an individual foreign operation. The use of the step-by-step method of consolidation may result in the reclassification to profit or loss of an amount different from that used to determine hedge effectiveness. This difference may be eliminated by determining the amount relating to that foreign operation that would have arisen if the direct method of consolidation had been used. Making this adjustment is not required by IAS 21. However, it is an accounting policy choice that should be followed consistently for all net investments.

Effective date

18   An entity shall apply this Interpretation for annual periods beginning on or after 1 October 2008. An entity shall apply the amendment to paragraph 14 made by *Improvements to IFRSs* issued in April 2009 for annual periods beginning on or after 1 July 2009. Earlier application of both is permitted. If an entity applies this Interpretation for a period beginning before 1 October 2008, or the amendment to paragraph 14 before 1 July 2009, it shall disclose that fact.

Transition

19   IAS 8 specifies how an entity applies a change in accounting policy resulting from the initial application of an Interpretation. An entity is not required to comply with those requirements when first applying the Interpretation. If an entity had designated a hedging instrument as a hedge of a net investment but the hedge does not meet the conditions for hedge accounting in this Interpretation, the entity shall apply IAS 39 to discontinue that hedge accounting prospectively.

---

2   The direct method is the method of consolidation in which the financial statements of the foreign operation are translated directly into the functional currency of the ultimate parent. The step-by-step method is the method of consolidation in which the financial statements of the foreign operation are first translated into the functional currency of any intermediate parent(s) and then translated into the functional currency of the ultimate parent (or the presentation currency if different).

Appendix
Application guidance

This appendix is an integral part of the Interpretation.

AG1　This appendix illustrates the application of the Interpretation using the corporate structure illustrated below. In all cases the hedging relationships described would be tested for effectiveness in accordance with IAS 39, although this testing is not discussed in this appendix. Parent, being the ultimate parent entity, presents its consolidated financial statements in its functional currency of euro (EUR). Each of the subsidiaries is wholly owned. Parent's £500 million net investment in Subsidiary B (functional currency pounds sterling (GBP)) includes the £159 million equivalent of Subsidiary B's US$300 million net investment in Subsidiary C (functional currency US dollars (USD)). In other words, Subsidiary B's net assets other than its investment in Subsidiary C are £341 million.

Nature of hedged risk for which a hedging relationship may be designated (paragraphs 10–13)

AG2　Parent can hedge its net investment in each of Subsidiaries A, B and C for the foreign exchange risk between their respective functional currencies (Japanese yen (JPY), pounds sterling and US dollars) and euro. In addition, Parent can hedge the USD/GBP foreign exchange risk between the functional currencies of Subsidiary B and Subsidiary C. In its consolidated financial statements, Subsidiary B can hedge its net investment in Subsidiary C for the foreign exchange risk between their functional currencies of US dollars and pounds sterling. In the following examples the designated risk is the spot foreign exchange risk because the hedging instruments are not derivatives. If the hedging instruments were forward contracts, Parent could designate the forward foreign exchange risk.

Amount of hedged item for which a hedging relationship may be designated (paragraphs 10–13)

AG3   Parent wishes to hedge the foreign exchange risk from its net investment in Subsidiary C. Assume that Subsidiary A has an external borrowing of US$300 million. The net assets of Subsidiary A at the start of the reporting period are ¥400,000 million including the proceeds of the external borrowing of US$300 million.

AG4   The hedged item can be an amount of net assets equal to or less than the carrying amount of Parent's net investment in Subsidiary C (US$300 million) in its consolidated financial statements. In its consolidated financial statements Parent can designate the US$300 million external borrowing in Subsidiary A as a hedge of the EUR/USD spot foreign exchange risk associated with its net investment in the US$300 million net assets of Subsidiary C. In this case, both the EUR/USD foreign exchange difference on the US$300 million external borrowing in Subsidiary A and the EUR/USD foreign exchange difference on the US$300 million net investment in Subsidiary C are included in the foreign currency translation reserve in Parent's consolidated financial statements after the application of hedge accounting.

AG5   In the absence of hedge accounting, the total USD/EUR foreign exchange difference on the US$300 million external borrowing in Subsidiary A would be recognised in Parent's consolidated financial statements as follows:

- USD/JPY spot foreign exchange rate change, translated to euro, in profit or loss, and

- JPY/EUR spot foreign exchange rate change in other comprehensive income.

Instead of the designation in paragraph AG4, in its consolidated financial statements Parent can designate the US$300 million external borrowing in Subsidiary A as a hedge of the GBP/USD spot foreign exchange risk between Subsidiary C and Subsidiary B. In this case, the total USD/EUR foreign exchange difference on the US$300 million external borrowing in Subsidiary A would instead be recognised in Parent's consolidated financial statements as follows:

- the GBP/USD spot foreign exchange rate change in the foreign currency translation reserve relating to Subsidiary C,

- GBP/JPY spot foreign exchange rate change, translated to euro, in profit or loss, and

- JPY/EUR spot foreign exchange rate change in other comprehensive income.

AG6   Parent cannot designate the US$300 million external borrowing in Subsidiary A as a hedge of both the EUR/USD spot foreign exchange risk and the GBP/USD spot foreign exchange risk in its consolidated financial statements. A single hedging instrument can hedge the same designated risk only once. Subsidiary B cannot apply hedge accounting in its consolidated financial statements because the hedging instrument is held outside the group comprising Subsidiary B and Subsidiary C.

Where in a group can the hedging instrument be held (paragraphs 14 and 15)?

AG7   As noted in paragraph AG5, the total change in value in respect of foreign exchange risk of the US$300 million external borrowing in Subsidiary A would be recorded in both profit or loss (USD/JPY spot risk) and other comprehensive income (EUR/JPY spot risk) in Parent's consolidated financial statements in the absence of hedge accounting. Both amounts are included for the purpose of assessing the effectiveness of the hedge designated in paragraph AG4 because the change in value of both the hedging instrument and the hedged item are computed by reference to the euro functional currency of Parent against the US dollar functional currency of Subsidiary C, in accordance with the hedge documentation. The method of consolidation (ie direct method or step-by-step method) does not affect the assessment of the effectiveness of the hedge.

Amounts reclassified to profit or loss on disposal of a foreign operation (paragraphs 16 and 17)

AG8   When Subsidiary C is disposed of, the amounts reclassified to profit or loss in Parent's consolidated financial statements from its foreign currency translation reserve (FCTR) are:

(a)   in respect of the US$300 million external borrowing of Subsidiary A, the amount that IAS 39 requires to be identified, ie the total change in value in respect of foreign exchange risk that was recognised in other comprehensive income as the effective portion of the hedge; and

(b)   in respect of the US$300 million net investment in Subsidiary C, the amount determined by the entity's consolidation method. If Parent uses the direct method, its FCTR in respect of Subsidiary C will be determined directly by the EUR/USD foreign exchange rate. If Parent uses the step-by-step method, its FCTR in respect of Subsidiary C will be determined by the FCTR recognised by Subsidiary B reflecting the GBP/USD foreign exchange rate, translated to Parent's functional currency using the EUR/GBP foreign exchange rate. Parent's use of the step-by-step method of consolidation in prior periods does not require it to or preclude it from determining the amount of FCTR to be reclassified when it disposes of Subsidiary C to be the amount that it would have recognised if it had always used the direct method, depending on its accounting policy.

Hedging more than one foreign operation (paragraphs 11, 13 and 15)

AG9   The following examples illustrate that in the consolidated financial statements of Parent, the risk that can be hedged is always the risk between its functional currency (euro) and the functional currencies of Subsidiaries B and C. No matter how the hedges are designated, the maximum amounts that can be effective hedges to be included in the foreign currency translation reserve in Parent's consolidated financial statements when both foreign operations are hedged are US$300 million for EUR/USD risk and £341 million for EUR/GBP risk. Other changes in value due to changes in foreign exchange rates are included in Parent's consolidated profit or loss. Of course, it would be possible for Parent to designate US$300 million only for changes in the USD/GBP spot foreign exchange rate or £500 million only for changes in the GBP/EUR spot foreign exchange rate.

Parent holds both USD and GBP hedging instruments

AG10   Parent may wish to hedge the foreign exchange risk in relation to its net investment in Subsidiary B as well as that in relation to Subsidiary C. Assume that Parent holds suitable hedging instruments denominated in US dollars and pounds sterling that it could designate as hedges of its net investments in Subsidiary B and Subsidiary C. The designations Parent can make in its consolidated financial statements include, but are not limited to, the following:

(a)   US$300 million hedging instrument designated as a hedge of the US$300 million of net investment in Subsidiary C with the risk being the spot foreign exchange exposure (EUR/USD) between Parent and Subsidiary C and up to £341 million hedging instrument designated as a hedge of £341 million of the net investment in Subsidiary B with the risk being the spot foreign exchange exposure (EUR/GBP) between Parent and Subsidiary B.

(b)   US$300 million hedging instrument designated as a hedge of the US$300 million of net investment in Subsidiary C with the risk being the spot foreign exchange exposure (GBP/USD) between Subsidiary B and Subsidiary C and up to £500 million hedging instrument designated as a hedge of £500 million of the net investment in Subsidiary B with the risk being the spot foreign exchange exposure (EUR/GBP) between Parent and Subsidiary B.

AG11   The EUR/USD risk from Parent's net investment in Subsidiary C is a different risk from the EUR/GBP risk from Parent's net investment in Subsidiary B. However, in the case described in paragraph AG10(a), by its designation of the USD hedging instrument it holds, Parent has already fully hedged the EUR/USD risk from its net investment in Subsidiary C. If Parent also designated a GBP instrument it holds as a hedge of its £500 million net investment in Subsidiary B, £159 million of that net investment, representing the GBP equivalent of its USD net investment in Subsidiary C, would be hedged twice for GBP/EUR risk in Parent's consolidated financial statements.

AG12   In the case described in paragraph AG10(b), if Parent designates the hedged risk as the spot foreign exchange exposure (GBP/USD) between Subsidiary B and Subsidiary C, only the GBP/USD part of the change in the value of its US$300 million hedging instrument is included in Parent's foreign currency translation reserve relating to Subsidiary C. The remainder of the change (equivalent to the GBP/EUR change on £159 million) is included in Parent's consolidated profit or loss, as in paragraph AG5. Because the designation of the USD/GBP risk between Subsidiaries B and C does not include the GBP/EUR risk, Parent is also able to designate up to £500 million of its net investment in Subsidiary B with the risk being the spot foreign exchange exposure (GBP/EUR) between Parent and Subsidiary B.

Subsidiary B holds the USD hedging instrument

AG13 Assume that Subsidiary B holds US$300 million of external debt the proceeds of which were transferred to Parent by an inter-company loan denominated in pounds sterling. Because both its assets and liabilities increased by £159 million, Subsidiary B's net assets are unchanged. Subsidiary B could designate the external debt as a hedge of the GBP/USD risk of its net investment in Subsidiary C in its consolidated financial statements. Parent could maintain Subsidiary B's designation of that hedging instrument as a hedge of its US$300 million net investment in Subsidiary C for the GBP/USD risk (see paragraph 13) and Parent could designate the GBP hedging instrument it holds as a hedge of its entire £500 million net investment in Subsidiary B. The first hedge, designated by Subsidiary B, would be assessed by reference to Subsidiary B's functional currency (pounds sterling) and the second hedge, designated by Parent, would be assessed by reference to Parent's functional currency (euro). In this case, only the GBP/USD risk from Parent's net investment in Subsidiary C has been hedged in Parent's consolidated financial statements by the USD hedging instrument, not the entire EUR/USD risk. Therefore, the entire EUR/GBP risk from Parent's £500 million net investment in Subsidiary B may be hedged in the consolidated financial statements of Parent.

AG14 However, the accounting for Parent's £159 million loan payable to Subsidiary B must also be considered. If Parent's loan payable is not considered part of its net investment in Subsidiary B because it does not satisfy the conditions in IAS 21 paragraph 15, the GBP/EUR foreign exchange difference arising on translating it would be included in Parent's consolidated profit or loss. If the £159 million loan payable to Subsidiary B is considered part of Parent's net investment, that net investment would be only £341 million and the amount Parent could designate as the hedged item for GBP/EUR risk would be reduced from £500 million to £341 million accordingly.

AG15 If Parent reversed the hedging relationship designated by Subsidiary B, Parent could designate the US$300 million external borrowing held by Subsidiary B as a hedge of its US$300 million net investment in Subsidiary C for the EUR/USD risk and designate the GBP hedging instrument it holds itself as a hedge of only up to £341 million of the net investment in Subsidiary B. In this case the effectiveness of both hedges would be computed by reference to Parent's functional currency (euro). Consequently, both the USD/GBP change in value of the external borrowing held by Subsidiary B and the GBP/EUR change in value of Parent's loan payable to Subsidiary B (equivalent to USD/EUR in total) would be included in the foreign currency translation reserve in Parent's consolidated financial statements. Because Parent has already fully hedged the EUR/USD risk from its net investment in Subsidiary C, it can hedge only up to £341 million for the EUR/GBP risk of its net investment in Subsidiary B.

IFRIC Interpretation 17

Distributions of Non-cash Assets to Owners

In November 2008 the International Accounting Standards Board issued IFRIC 17 *Distributions of Non-cash Assets to Owners*. It was developed by the Interpretations Committee.

The Basis for Conclusions on IFRIC 17 was amended to reflect IFRS 9 *Financial Instruments* (issued November 2009 and October 2010).

Contents

IFRIC Interpretation 17 *Distributions of Non-cash Assets to Owners* (IFRIC 17) is set out in paragraphs 1–20 and the Appendix. IFRIC 17 is accompanied by illustrative examples and a Basis for Conclusions. The scope and authority of Interpretations are set out in paragraphs 2 and 7–16 of the *Preface to International Financial Reporting Standards*.

IFRIC Interpretation 17
Distributions of Non-cash Assets to Owners

References

- IFRS 3 *Business Combinations* (as revised in 2008)
- IFRS 5 *Non-current Assets Held for Sale and Discontinued Operations*
- IFRS 7 *Financial Instruments: Disclosures*
- IFRS 10 *Consolidated Financial Statements*
- IFRS 13 *Fair Value Measurement*
- IAS 1 *Presentation of Financial Statements* (as revised in 2007)
- IAS 10 *Events after the Reporting Period*
- IAS 27 *Consolidated and Separate Financial Statements* (as amended in May 2008)

Background

1   Sometimes an entity distributes assets other than cash (non-cash assets) as dividends to its owners[1] acting in their capacity as owners. In those situations, an entity may also give its owners a choice of receiving either non-cash assets or a cash alternative. The IFRIC received requests for guidance on how an entity should account for such distributions.

2   International Financial Reporting Standards (IFRSs) do not provide guidance on how an entity should measure distributions to its owners (commonly referred to as dividends). IAS 1 requires an entity to present details of dividends recognised as distributions to owners either in the statement of changes in equity or in the notes to the financial statements.

Scope

3   This Interpretation applies to the following types of non-reciprocal distributions of assets by an entity to its owners acting in their capacity as owners:

   (a)   distributions of non-cash assets (eg items of property, plant and equipment, businesses as defined in IFRS 3, ownership interests in another entity or disposal groups as defined in IFRS 5); and

   (b)   distributions that give owners a choice of receiving either non-cash assets or a cash alternative.

4   This Interpretation applies only to distributions in which all owners of the same class of equity instruments are treated equally.

---

1   Paragraph 7 of IAS 1 defines owners as holders of instruments classified as equity.

© IFRS Foundation

5 This Interpretation does not apply to a distribution of a non-cash asset that is ultimately controlled by the same party or parties before and after the distribution. This exclusion applies to the separate, individual and consolidated financial statements of an entity that makes the distribution.

6 In accordance with paragraph 5, this Interpretation does not apply when the non-cash asset is ultimately controlled by the same parties both before and after the distribution. Paragraph B2 of IFRS 3 states that 'A group of individuals shall be regarded as controlling an entity when, as a result of contractual arrangements, they collectively have the power to govern its financial and operating policies so as to obtain benefits from its activities.' Therefore, for a distribution to be outside the scope of this Interpretation on the basis that the same parties control the asset both before and after the distribution, a group of individual shareholders receiving the distribution must have, as a result of contractual arrangements, such ultimate collective power over the entity making the distribution.

7 In accordance with paragraph 5, this Interpretation does not apply when an entity distributes some of its ownership interests in a subsidiary but retains control of the subsidiary. The entity making a distribution that results in the entity recognising a non-controlling interest in its subsidiary accounts for the distribution in accordance with IFRS 10.

8 This Interpretation addresses only the accounting by an entity that makes a non-cash asset distribution. It does not address the accounting by shareholders who receive such a distribution.

Issues

9 When an entity declares a distribution and has an obligation to distribute the assets concerned to its owners, it must recognise a liability for the dividend payable. Consequently, this Interpretation addresses the following issues:

   (a) When should the entity recognise the dividend payable?

   (b) How should an entity measure the dividend payable?

   (c) When an entity settles the dividend payable, how should it account for any difference between the carrying amount of the assets distributed and the carrying amount of the dividend payable?

Consensus

When to recognise a dividend payable

10 The liability to pay a dividend shall be recognised when the dividend is appropriately authorised and is no longer at the discretion of the entity, which is the date:

   (a) when declaration of the dividend, eg by management or the board of directors, is approved by the relevant authority, eg the shareholders, if the jurisdiction requires such approval, or

(b)   when the dividend is declared, eg by management or the board of directors, if the jurisdiction does not require further approval.

Measurement of a dividend payable

11   An entity shall measure a liability to distribute non-cash assets as a dividend to its owners at the fair value of the assets to be distributed.

12   If an entity gives its owners a choice of receiving either a non-cash asset or a cash alternative, the entity shall estimate the dividend payable by considering both the fair value of each alternative and the associated probability of owners selecting each alternative.

13   At the end of each reporting period and at the date of settlement, the entity shall review and adjust the carrying amount of the dividend payable, with any changes in the carrying amount of the dividend payable recognised in equity as adjustments to the amount of the distribution.

Accounting for any difference between the carrying amount of the assets distributed and the carrying amount of the dividend payable when an entity settles the dividend payable

14   When an entity settles the dividend payable, it shall recognise the difference, if any, between the carrying amount of the assets distributed and the carrying amount of the dividend payable in profit or loss.

Presentation and disclosures

15   An entity shall present the difference described in paragraph 14 as a separate line item in profit or loss.

16   An entity shall disclose the following information, if applicable:

(a)   the carrying amount of the dividend payable at the beginning and end of the period; and

(b)   the increase or decrease in the carrying amount recognised in the period in accordance with paragraph 13 as result of a change in the fair value of the assets to be distributed.

17   If, after the end of a reporting period but before the financial statements are authorised for issue, an entity declares a dividend to distribute a non-cash asset, it shall disclose:

(a)   the nature of the asset to be distributed;

(b)   the carrying amount of the asset to be distributed as of the end of the reporting period; and

(c)   the fair value of the asset to be distributed as of the end of the reporting period, if it is different from its carrying amount, and the information about the method(s) used to measure that fair value required by paragraphs 93(b), (d), (g) and (i) and 99 of IFRS 13.

Effective date

18   An entity shall apply this Interpretation prospectively for annual periods beginning on or after 1 July 2009. Retrospective application is not permitted. Earlier application is permitted. If an entity applies this Interpretation for a period beginning before 1 July 2009, it shall disclose that fact and also apply IFRS 3 (as revised in 2008), IAS 27 (as amended in May 2008) and IFRS 5 (as amended by this Interpretation).

19   IFRS 10, issued in May 2011, amended paragraph 7. An entity shall apply that amendment when it applies IFRS 10.

20   IFRS 13, issued in May 2011, amended paragraph 17. An entity shall apply that amendment when it applies IFRS 13.

Appendix
Amendments to IFRS 5 *Non-current Assets Held for Sale and Discontinued Operations* and IAS 10 *Events after the Reporting Period*

The amendments contained in this appendix when this Interpretation was issued in 2008 have been incorporated into IFRS 5 and IAS 10 as published in this volume.

IFRIC Interpretation 18

Transfers of Assets from Customers

In January 2009 the International Accounting Standards Board issued IFRIC 18 *Transfers of Assets from Customers*. It was developed by the Interpretations Committee.

Contents

FOR THE ACCOMPANYING DOCUMENTS LISTED BELOW, SEE PART B OF THIS EDITION

ILLUSTRATIVE EXAMPLES

BASIS FOR CONCLUSIONS

IFRIC Interpretation 18 *Transfers of Assets from Customers* (IFRIC 18) is set out in paragraphs 1–22 and the Appendix. IFRIC 18 is accompanied by illustrative examples and a Basis for Conclusions. The scope and authority of Interpretations are set out in paragraphs 2 and 7–16 of the *Preface to International Financial Reporting Standards*.

IFRIC Interpretation 18
Transfers of Assets from Customers

References

- *Framework for the Preparation and Presentation of Financial Statements*[1]
- IFRS 1 *First-time Adoption of International Financial Reporting Standards* (as revised in 2008)
- IAS 8 *Accounting Policies, Changes in Accounting Estimates and Errors*
- IAS 16 *Property, Plant and Equipment*
- IAS 18 *Revenue*
- IAS 20 *Accounting for Government Grants and Disclosure of Government Assistance*
- IFRIC 12 *Service Concession Arrangements*

Background

1   In the utilities industry, an entity may receive from its customers items of property, plant and equipment that must be used to connect those customers to a network and provide them with ongoing access to a supply of commodities such as electricity, gas or water. Alternatively, an entity may receive cash from customers for the acquisition or construction of such items of property, plant and equipment. Typically, customers are required to pay additional amounts for the purchase of goods or services based on usage.

2   Transfers of assets from customers may also occur in industries other than utilities. For example, an entity outsourcing its information technology functions may transfer its existing items of property, plant and equipment to the outsourcing provider.

3   In some cases, the transferor of the asset may not be the entity that will eventually have ongoing access to the supply of goods or services and will be the recipient of those goods or services. However, for convenience this Interpretation refers to the entity transferring the asset as the customer.

Scope

4   This Interpretation applies to the accounting for transfers of items of property, plant and equipment by entities that receive such transfers from their customers.

5   Agreements within the scope of this Interpretation are agreements in which an entity receives from a customer an item of property, plant and equipment that the entity must then use either to connect the customer to a network or to provide the customer with ongoing access to a supply of goods or services, or to do both.

---

1   In September 2010 the IASB replaced the *Framework* with the *Conceptual Framework for Financial Reporting*.

6　　This Interpretation also applies to agreements in which an entity receives cash from a customer when that amount of cash must be used only to construct or acquire an item of property, plant and equipment and the entity must then use the item of property, plant and equipment either to connect the customer to a network or to provide the customer with ongoing access to a supply of goods or services, or to do both.

7　　This Interpretation does not apply to agreements in which the transfer is either a government grant as defined in IAS 20 or infrastructure used in a service concession arrangement that is within the scope of IFRIC 12.

Issues

8　　The Interpretation addresses the following issues:

    (a)　　Is the definition of an asset met?

    (b)　　If the definition of an asset is met, how should the transferred item of property, plant and equipment be measured on initial recognition?

    (c)　　If the item of property, plant and equipment is measured at fair value on initial recognition, how should the resulting credit be accounted for?

    (d)　　How should the entity account for a transfer of cash from its customer?

Consensus

Is the definition of an asset met?

9　　When an entity receives from a customer a transfer of an item of property, plant and equipment, it shall assess whether the transferred item meets the definition of an asset set out in the *Framework*. Paragraph 49(a) of the *Framework*[2] states that 'an asset is a resource controlled by the entity as a result of past events and from which future economic benefits are expected to flow to the entity.' In most circumstances, the entity obtains the right of ownership of the transferred item of property, plant and equipment. However, in determining whether an asset exists, the right of ownership is not essential. Therefore, if the customer continues to control the transferred item, the asset definition would not be met despite a transfer of ownership.

10　　An entity that controls an asset can generally deal with that asset as it pleases. For example, the entity can exchange that asset for other assets, employ it to produce goods or services, charge a price for others to use it, use it to settle liabilities, hold it, or distribute it to owners. The entity that receives from a customer a transfer of an item of property, plant and equipment shall consider all relevant facts and circumstances when assessing control of the transferred item. For example, although the entity must use the transferred item of property, plant and equipment to provide one or more services to the customer, it may have the ability to decide how the transferred item of property, plant and

---

2　　now paragraph 4.4(a) of the *Conceptual Framework*

equipment is operated and maintained and when it is replaced. In this case, the entity would normally conclude that it controls the transferred item of property, plant and equipment.

How should the transferred item of property, plant and equipment be measured on initial recognition?

11   If the entity concludes that the definition of an asset is met, it shall recognise the transferred asset as an item of property, plant and equipment in accordance with paragraph 7 of IAS 16 and measure its cost on initial recognition at its fair value in accordance with paragraph 24 of that Standard.

How should the credit be accounted for?

12   The following discussion assumes that the entity receiving an item of property, plant and equipment has concluded that the transferred item should be recognised and measured in accordance with paragraphs 9–11.

13   Paragraph 12 of IAS 18 states that 'When goods are sold or services are rendered in exchange for dissimilar goods or services, the exchange is regarded as a transaction which generates revenue.' According to the terms of the agreements within the scope of this Interpretation, a transfer of an item of property, plant and equipment would be an exchange for dissimilar goods or services. Consequently, the entity shall recognise revenue in accordance with IAS 18.

Identifying the separately identifiable services

14   An entity may agree to deliver one or more services in exchange for the transferred item of property, plant and equipment, such as connecting the customer to a network, providing the customer with ongoing access to a supply of goods or services, or both. In accordance with paragraph 13 of IAS 18, the entity shall identify the separately identifiable services included in the agreement.

15   Features that indicate that connecting the customer to a network is a separately identifiable service include:

   (a)   a service connection is delivered to the customer and represents stand-alone value for that customer;

   (b)   the fair value of the service connection can be measured reliably.

16   A feature that indicates that providing the customer with ongoing access to a supply of goods or services is a separately identifiable service is that, in the future, the customer making the transfer receives the ongoing access, the goods or services, or both at a price lower than would be charged without the transfer of the item of property, plant and equipment.

17   Conversely, a feature that indicates that the obligation to provide the customer with ongoing access to a supply of goods or services arises from the terms of the entity's operating licence or other regulation rather than from the agreement relating to the transfer of an item of property, plant and equipment is that customers that make a transfer pay the same price as those that do not for the ongoing access, or for the goods or services, or for both.

Revenue recognition

18 If only one service is identified, the entity shall recognise revenue when the service is performed in accordance with paragraph 20 of IAS 18.

19 If more than one separately identifiable service is identified, paragraph 13 of IAS 18 requires the fair value of the total consideration received or receivable for the agreement to be allocated to each service and the recognition criteria of IAS 18 are then applied to each service.

20 If an ongoing service is identified as part of the agreement, the period over which revenue shall be recognised for that service is generally determined by the terms of the agreement with the customer. If the agreement does not specify a period, the revenue shall be recognised over a period no longer than the useful life of the transferred asset used to provide the ongoing service.

How should the entity account for a transfer of cash from its customer?

21 When an entity receives a transfer of cash from a customer, it shall assess whether the agreement is within the scope of this Interpretation in accordance with paragraph 6. If it is, the entity shall assess whether the constructed or acquired item of property, plant and equipment meets the definition of an asset in accordance with paragraphs 9 and 10. If the definition of an asset is met, the entity shall recognise the item of property, plant and equipment at its cost in accordance with IAS 16 and shall recognise revenue in accordance with paragraphs 13–20 at the amount of cash received from the customer.

Effective date and transition

22 An entity shall apply this Interpretation prospectively to transfers of assets from customers received on or after 1 July 2009. Earlier application is permitted provided the valuations and other information needed to apply the Interpretation to past transfers were obtained at the time those transfers occurred. An entity shall disclose the date from which the Interpretation was applied.

Appendix
Amendment to IFRS 1 *First-time Adoption of International Financial Reporting Standards* (as revised in 2008)

The amendment contained in this appendix when this Interpretation was issued in 2009 has been incorporated into the text of IFRS 1 as issued on or after 29 January 2009.

IFRIC Interpretation 19

Extinguishing Financial Liabilities with Equity Instruments

In November 2009 the International Accounting Standards Board issued IFRIC 19 *Extinguishing Financial Liabilities with Equity Instruments*. It was developed by the Interpretations Committee.

IFRS 9 *Financial Instruments* (issued October 2010) made minor consequential amendments to IFRIC 19.

Contents

FOR THE ACCOMPANYING DOCUMENT LISTED BELOW, SEE PART B OF THIS EDITION

BASIS FOR CONCLUSIONS

IFRIC Interpretation 19 *Extinguishing Financial Liabilities with Equity Instruments* (IFRIC 19) is set out in paragraphs 1–15 and the Appendix. IFRIC 19 is accompanied by a Basis for Conclusions. The scope and authority of Interpretations are set out in paragraphs 2 and 7–16 of the *Preface to International Financial Reporting Standards*.

IFRIC Interpretation 19
Extinguishing Financial Liabilities with Equity Instruments

References

- *Framework for the Preparation and Presentation of Financial Statements*[1]
- IFRS 2 *Share-based Payment*
- IFRS 3 *Business Combinations*
- IFRS 9 *Financial Instruments* (issued October 2010)
- IFRS 13 *Fair Value Measurement*
- IAS 1 *Presentation of Financial Statements*
- IAS 8 *Accounting Policies, Changes in Accounting Estimates and Errors*
- IAS 32 *Financial Instruments: Presentation*

Background

1   A debtor and creditor might renegotiate the terms of a financial liability with the result that the debtor extinguishes the liability fully or partially by issuing equity instruments to the creditor. These transactions are sometimes referred to as 'debt for equity swaps'. The IFRIC has received requests for guidance on the accounting for such transactions.

Scope

2   This Interpretation addresses the accounting by an entity when the terms of a financial liability are renegotiated and result in the entity issuing equity instruments to a creditor of the entity to extinguish all or part of the financial liability. It does not address the accounting by the creditor.

3   An entity shall not apply this Interpretation to transactions in situations where:

(a)   the creditor is also a direct or indirect shareholder and is acting in its capacity as a direct or indirect existing shareholder.

(b)   the creditor and the entity are controlled by the same party or parties before and after the transaction and the substance of the transaction includes an equity distribution by, or contribution to, the entity.

(c)   extinguishing the financial liability by issuing equity shares is in accordance with the original terms of the financial liability.

---

1   In September 2010 the IASB replaced the *Framework* with the *Conceptual Framework for Financial Reporting*.

Issues

4   This Interpretation addresses the following issues:

(a)   Are an entity's equity instruments issued to extinguish all or part of a financial liability 'consideration paid' in accordance with paragraph 3.3.3 of IFRS 9?

(b)   How should an entity initially measure the equity instruments issued to extinguish such a financial liability?

(c)   How should an entity account for any difference between the carrying amount of the financial liability extinguished and the initial measurement amount of the equity instruments issued?

Consensus

5   The issue of an entity's equity instruments to a creditor to extinguish all or part of a financial liability is consideration paid in accordance with paragraph 3.3.3 of IFRS 9. An entity shall remove a financial liability (or part of a financial liability) from its statement of financial position when, and only when, it is extinguished in accordance with paragraph 3.3.1 of IFRS 9.

6   When equity instruments issued to a creditor to extinguish all or part of a financial liability are recognised initially, an entity shall measure them at the fair value of the equity instruments issued, unless that fair value cannot be reliably measured.

7   If the fair value of the equity instruments issued cannot be reliably measured then the equity instruments shall be measured to reflect the fair value of the financial liability extinguished. In measuring the fair value of a financial liability extinguished that includes a demand feature (eg a demand deposit), paragraph 47 of IFRS 13 is not applied.

8   If only part of the financial liability is extinguished, the entity shall assess whether some of the consideration paid relates to a modification of the terms of the liability that remains outstanding. If part of the consideration paid does relate to a modification of the terms of the remaining part of the liability, the entity shall allocate the consideration paid between the part of the liability extinguished and the part of the liability that remains outstanding. The entity shall consider all relevant facts and circumstances relating to the transaction in making this allocation.

9   The difference between the carrying amount of the financial liability (or part of a financial liability) extinguished, and the consideration paid, shall be recognised in profit or loss, in accordance with paragraph 3.3.3 of IFRS 9. The equity instruments issued shall be recognised initially and measured at the date the financial liability (or part of that liability) is extinguished.

10   When only part of the financial liability is extinguished, consideration shall be allocated in accordance with paragraph 8. The consideration allocated to the remaining liability shall form part of the assessment of whether the terms of that remaining liability have been substantially modified. If the remaining liability has been substantially modified, the entity shall account for the modification as the extinguishment of the original liability and the recognition of a new liability as required by paragraph 3.3.2 of IFRS 9.

11   An entity shall disclose a gain or loss recognised in accordance with paragraphs 9 and 10 as a separate line item in profit or loss or in the notes.

Effective date and transition

12   An entity shall apply this Interpretation for annual periods beginning on or after 1 July 2010. Earlier application is permitted. If an entity applies this Interpretation for a period beginning before 1 July 2010, it shall disclose that fact.

13   An entity shall apply a change in accounting policy in accordance with IAS 8 from the beginning of the earliest comparative period presented.

14   IFRS 9, issued in October 2010, amended paragraphs 4(a), 5, 7, 9 and 10. An entity shall apply those amendments when it applies IFRS 9 as issued in October 2010.

15   IFRS 13, issued in May 2011, amended paragraph 7. An entity shall apply that amendment when it applies IFRS 13.

Appendix
Amendment to IFRS 1 *First-time Adoption of International Financial Reporting Standards*

The amendment in this appendix shall be applied for annual periods beginning on or after 1 July 2010. If an entity applies this Interpretation for an earlier period, the amendment shall be applied for that earlier period.

* * * * *

The amendment contained in this appendix when this Interpretation was issued in 2009 has been incorporated into the text of IFRS 1 as issued on or after 26 November 2009.

IFRIC Interpretation 20

Stripping Costs in the Production Phase of a Surface Mine

In October 2011 the International Accounting Standards Board issued IFRIC 20 *Stripping Costs in the Production Phase of a Surface Mine*. It was developed by the Interpretations Committee.

CONTENTS

FOR THE ACCOMPANYING DOCUMENTS LISTED BELOW, SEE PART B OF THIS EDITION

BASIS FOR CONCLUSIONS

IFRIC Interpretation 20 *Stripping Costs in the Production Phase of a Surface Mine* (IFRIC 20) is set out in paragraphs 1–16 and appendices A–B. IFRIC 20 is accompanied by a Basis for Conclusions. The scope and authority of Interpretations are set out in paragraphs 2 and 7–16 of the *Preface to International Financial Reporting Standards*.

IFRIC Interpretation 20
Stripping Costs in the Production Phase of a Surface Mine

References

- *Conceptual Framework for Financial Reporting*
- IAS 1 *Presentation of Financial Statements*
- IAS 2 *Inventories*
- IAS 16 *Property, Plant and Equipment*
- IAS 38 *Intangible Assets*

Background

1   In surface mining operations, entities may find it necessary to remove mine waste materials ('overburden') to gain access to mineral ore deposits. This waste removal activity is known as 'stripping'.

2   During the development phase of the mine (before production begins), stripping costs are usually capitalised as part of the depreciable cost of building, developing and constructing the mine. Those capitalised costs are depreciated or amortised on a systematic basis, usually by using the units of production method, once production begins.

3   A mining entity may continue to remove overburden and to incur stripping costs during the production phase of the mine.

4   The material removed when stripping in the production phase will not necessarily be 100 per cent waste; often it will be a combination of ore and waste. The ratio of ore to waste can range from uneconomic low grade to profitable high grade. Removal of material with a low ratio of ore to waste may produce some usable material, which can be used to produce inventory. This removal might also provide access to deeper levels of material that have a higher ratio of ore to waste. There can therefore be two benefits accruing to the entity from the stripping activity: usable ore that can be used to produce inventory and improved access to further quantities of material that will be mined in future periods.

5   This Interpretation considers when and how to account separately for these two benefits arising from the stripping activity, as well as how to measure these benefits both initially and subsequently.

Scope

6   This Interpretation applies to waste removal costs that are incurred in surface mining activity during the production phase of the mine ('production stripping costs').

Issues

7 This Interpretation addresses the following issues:

    (a) recognition of production stripping costs as an asset;

    (b) initial measurement of the stripping activity asset; and

    (c) subsequent measurement of the stripping activity asset.

Consensus

Recognition of production stripping costs as an asset

8 To the extent that the benefit from the stripping activity is realised in the form of inventory produced, the entity shall account for the costs of that stripping activity in accordance with the principles of IAS 2 *Inventories*. To the extent the benefit is improved access to ore, the entity shall recognise these costs as a non-current asset, if the criteria in paragraph 9 below are met. This Interpretation refers to the non-current asset as the 'stripping activity asset'.

9 An entity shall recognise a stripping activity asset if, and only if, all of the following are met:

    (a) it is probable that the future economic benefit (improved access to the ore body) associated with the stripping activity will flow to the entity;

    (b) the entity can identify the component of the ore body for which access has been improved; and

    (c) the costs relating to the stripping activity associated with that component can be measured reliably.

10 The stripping activity asset shall be accounted for as an addition to, or as an enhancement of, an existing asset. In other words, the stripping activity asset will be accounted for as *part* of an existing asset.

11 The stripping activity asset's classification as a tangible or intangible asset is the same as the existing asset. In other words, the nature of this existing asset will determine whether the entity shall classify the stripping activity asset as tangible or intangible.

Initial measurement of the stripping activity asset

12 The entity shall initially measure the stripping activity asset at cost, this being the accumulation of costs directly incurred to perform the stripping activity that improves access to the identified component of ore, plus an allocation of directly attributable overhead costs. Some incidental operations may take place at the same time as the production stripping activity, but which are not necessary for the production stripping activity to continue as planned. The costs associated with these incidental operations shall not be included in the cost of the stripping activity asset.

13   When the costs of the stripping activity asset and the inventory produced are not separately identifiable, the entity shall allocate the production stripping costs between the inventory produced and the stripping activity asset by using an allocation basis that is based on a relevant production measure. This production measure shall be calculated for the identified component of the ore body, and shall be used as a benchmark to identify the extent to which the additional activity of creating a future benefit has taken place. Examples of such measures include:

(a)   cost of inventory produced compared with expected cost;

(b)   volume of waste extracted compared with expected volume, for a given volume of ore production; and

(c)   mineral content of the ore extracted compared with expected mineral content to be extracted, for a given quantity of ore produced.

Subsequent measurement of the stripping activity asset

14   After initial recognition, the stripping activity asset shall be carried at either its cost or its revalued amount less depreciation or amortisation and less impairment losses, in the same way as the existing asset of which it is a part.

15   The stripping activity asset shall be depreciated or amortised on a systematic basis, over the expected useful life of the identified component of the ore body that becomes more accessible as a result of the stripping activity. The units of production method shall be applied unless another method is more appropriate.

16   The expected useful life of the identified component of the ore body that is used to depreciate or amortise the stripping activity asset will differ from the expected useful life that is used to depreciate or amortise the mine itself and the related life-of-mine assets. The exception to this are those limited circumstances when the stripping activity provides improved access to the whole of the remaining ore body. For example, this might occur towards the end of a mine's useful life when the identified component represents the final part of the ore body to be extracted.

Appendix A

Effective date and transition

This appendix is an integral part of the Interpretation and has the same authority as the other parts of the Interpretation.

A1 An entity shall apply this Interpretation for annual periods beginning on or after 1 January 2013. Earlier application is permitted. If an entity applies this Interpretation for an earlier period, it shall disclose that fact.

A2 An entity shall apply this Interpretation to production stripping costs incurred on or after the beginning of the earliest period presented.

A3 As at the beginning of the earliest period presented, any previously recognised asset balance that resulted from stripping activity undertaken during the production phase ('predecessor stripping asset') shall be reclassified as a part of an existing asset to which the stripping activity related, to the extent that there remains an identifiable component of the ore body with which the predecessor stripping asset can be associated. Such balances shall be depreciated or amortised over the remaining expected useful life of the identified component of the ore body to which each predecessor stripping asset balance relates.

A4 If there is no identifiable component of the ore body to which that predecessor stripping asset relates, it shall be recognised in opening retained earnings at the beginning of the earliest period presented.

Appendix B
Amendments to IFRS 1 *First-time Adoption of International Financial Reporting Standards*

The amendments in this appendix shall be applied for annual periods beginning on or after 1 January 2013. If an entity applies this Interpretation for an earlier period these amendments shall be applied for that earlier period.

* * * * *

The amendments contained in this appendix with this Interpretation was issued in 2011 have been incorporated into IFRS 1 as issued on and after 27 May 2004. In November 2008 a revised version of IFRS 1 was issued.

SIC Interpretation 7

Introduction of the Euro

In April 2001 the International Accounting Standards Board adopted SIC-7 *Introduction of the Euro*, which had originally been issued by the Standing Interpretations Committee of the International Accounting Standards Committee in May 1998.

Other IFRSs have made minor consequential amendments to SIC-7. These include IAS 21 *The Effects of Changes in Foreign Exchange Rates* (as revised in December 2003) and IAS 1 *Presentation of Financial Statements* (as revised in September 2007).

SIC Interpretation 7 *Introduction of the Euro* (SIC-7) is set out in paragraphs 3 and 4. SIC-7 is accompanied by a Basis for Conclusions. The scope and authority of Interpretations are set out in paragraphs 2 and 7–16 of the *Preface to International Financial Reporting Standards*.

FOR THE BASIS FOR CONCLUSIONS ON SIC-7 SEE PART B OF THIS EDITION

SIC Interpretation 7
Introduction of the Euro

References

- IAS 1 *Presentation of Financial Statements* (as revised in 2007)
- IAS 8 *Accounting Policies, Changes in Accounting Estimates and Errors*
- IAS 10 *Events after the Reporting Period*
- IAS 21 *The Effects of Changes in Foreign Exchange Rates* (as revised in 2003)
- IAS 27 *Consolidated and Separate Financial Statements* (as amended in 2008)

Issue

1   From 1 January 1999, the effective start of Economic and Monetary Union (EMU), the euro will become a currency in its own right and the conversion rates between the euro and the participating national currencies will be irrevocably fixed, ie the risk of subsequent exchange differences related to these currencies is eliminated from this date on.

2   The issue is the application of IAS 21 to the changeover from the national currencies of participating Member States of the European Union to the euro ('the changeover').

Consensus

3   The requirements of IAS 21 regarding the translation of foreign currency transactions and financial statements of foreign operations should be strictly applied to the changeover. The same rationale applies to the fixing of exchange rates when countries join EMU at later stages.

4   This means that, in particular:

(a)   foreign currency monetary assets and liabilities resulting from transactions shall continue to be translated into the functional currency at the closing rate. Any resultant exchange differences shall be recognised as income or expense immediately, except that an entity shall continue to apply its existing accounting policy for exchange gains and losses related to hedges of the currency risk of a forecast transaction;

(b)   cumulative exchange differences relating to the translation of financial statements of foreign operations, recognised in other comprehensive income, shall be accumulated in equity and shall be reclassified from equity to profit or loss only on the disposal or partial disposal of the net investment in the foreign operation; and

(c)   exchange differences resulting from the translation of liabilities denominated in participating currencies shall not be included in the carrying amount of related assets.

Date of consensus

October 1997

Effective date

This Interpretation becomes effective on 1 June 1998. Changes in accounting policies shall be accounted for according to the requirements of IAS 8.

IAS 1 (as revised in 2007) amended the terminology used throughout IFRSs. In addition it amended paragraph 4. An entity shall apply those amendments for annual periods beginning on or after 1 January 2009. If an entity applies IAS 1 (revised 2007) for an earlier period, the amendments shall be applied for that earlier period.

IAS 27 (as amended in 2008) amended paragraph 4(b). An entity shall apply that amendment for annual periods beginning on or after 1 July 2009. If an entity applies IAS 27 (amended 2008) for an earlier period, the amendment shall be applied for that earlier period.

SIC Interpretation 10

Government Assistance—No Specific Relation to Operating Activities

In April 2001 the International Accounting Standards Board adopted SIC-10 *Government Assistance—No Specific Relation to Operating Activities*, which had originally been issued by the Standing Interpretations Committee of the International Accounting Standards Committee in July 1998.

IAS 1 *Presentation of Financial Statements* (as revised in September 2007) made minor consequential amendments to SIC-10.

SIC Interpretation 10 *Government Assistance—No Specific Relation to Operating Activities* (SIC-10) is set out in paragraph 3. SIC-10 is accompanied by a Basis for Conclusions. The scope and authority of Interpretations are set out in paragraphs 2 and 7–16 of the *Preface to International Financial Reporting Standards*.

FOR THE BASIS FOR CONCLUSIONS ON SIC-10 SEE PART B OF THIS EDITION

SIC Interpretation 10
Government Assistance—No Specific Relation to Operating Activities

References

- IAS 8 *Accounting Policies, Changes in Accounting Estimates and Errors*
- IAS 20 *Accounting for Government Grants and Disclosure of Government Assistance*

Issue

1　In some countries government assistance to entities may be aimed at encouragement or long-term support of business activities either in certain regions or industry sectors. Conditions to receive such assistance may not be specifically related to the operating activities of the entity. Examples of such assistance are transfers of resources by governments to entities which:

    (a)　operate in a particular industry;

    (b)　continue operating in recently privatised industries; or

    (c)　start or continue to run their business in underdeveloped areas.

2　The issue is whether such government assistance is a 'government grant' within the scope of IAS 20 and, therefore, should be accounted for in accordance with this Standard.

Consensus

3　Government assistance to entities meets the definition of government grants in IAS 20, even if there are no conditions specifically relating to the operating activities of the entity other than the requirement to operate in certain regions or industry sectors. Such grants shall therefore not be credited directly to shareholders' interests.

Date of consensus

January 1998

Effective date

This Interpretation becomes effective on 1 August 1998. Changes in accounting policies shall be accounted for in accordance with IAS 8.

SIC Interpretation 15

Operating Leases—Incentives

In April 2001 the International Accounting Standards Board adopted SIC-15 *Operating Leases—Incentives*, which had originally been issued by the Standing Interpretations Committee of the International Accounting Standards Committee in December 1998.

Other IFRSs have made minor consequential amendments to SIC-15. These include IAS 17 *Leases* (as revised in December 2003) and IAS 1 *Presentation of Financial Statements* (as revised in September 2007).

SIC Interpretation 15 *Operating Leases—Incentives* (SIC-15) is set out in paragraphs 3–6. SIC-15 is accompanied by a Basis for Conclusions and illustrative examples. The scope and authority of Interpretations are set out in paragraphs 2 and 7–16 of the *Preface to International Financial Reporting Standards*.

FOR THE FOLLOWING MATERIAL ACCOMPANYING SIC-15:
- **BASIS FOR CONCLUSIONS**
- **ILLUSTRATIVE EXAMPLE**

SEE PART B OF THIS EDITION

SIC Interpretation 15
Operating Leases—Incentives

References

- IAS 1 *Presentation of Financial Statements* (as revised in 2007)
- IAS 8 *Accounting Policies, Changes in Accounting Estimates and Errors*
- IAS 17 *Leases* (as revised in 2003)

Issue

1   In negotiating a new or renewed operating lease, the lessor may provide incentives for the lessee to enter into the agreement. Examples of such incentives are an up-front cash payment to the lessee or the reimbursement or assumption by the lessor of costs of the lessee (such as relocation costs, leasehold improvements and costs associated with a pre-existing lease commitment of the lessee). Alternatively, initial periods of the lease term may be agreed to be rent-free or at a reduced rent.

2   The issue is how incentives in an operating lease should be recognised in the financial statements of both the lessee and the lessor.

Consensus

3   All incentives for the agreement of a new or renewed operating lease shall be recognised as an integral part of the net consideration agreed for the use of the leased asset, irrespective of the incentive's nature or form or the timing of payments.

4   The lessor shall recognise the aggregate cost of incentives as a reduction of rental income over the lease term, on a straight-line basis unless another systematic basis is representative of the time pattern over which the benefit of the leased asset is diminished.

5   The lessee shall recognise the aggregate benefit of incentives as a reduction of rental expense over the lease term, on a straight-line basis unless another systematic basis is representative of the time pattern of the lessee's benefit from the use of the leased asset.

6   Costs incurred by the lessee, including costs in connection with a pre-existing lease (for example costs for termination, relocation or leasehold improvements), shall be accounted for by the lessee in accordance with the Standards applicable to those costs, including costs which are effectively reimbursed through an incentive arrangement.

Date of consensus

June 1998

Effective date

This Interpretation becomes effective for lease terms beginning on or after 1 January 1999.

SIC Interpretation 25

Income Taxes—Changes in the Tax Status of an Entity or its Shareholders

In April 2001 the International Accounting Standards Board adopted SIC-25 *Income Taxes— Changes in the Tax Status of an Entity or its Shareholders*, which had originally been issued by the Standing Interpretations Committee of the International Accounting Standards Committee in July 2000.

Other IFRSs have made minor consequential amendments to SIC-25. These include IAS 8 *Accounting Policies, Changes in Accounting Estimates and Errors* (issued December 2003), IFRS 3 *Business Combinations* (issued March 2004) and IAS 1 *Presentation of Financial Statements* (as revised in September 2007).

SIC Interpretation 25 *Income Taxes—Changes in the Tax Status of an Entity or its Shareholders* (SIC-25) is set out in paragraph 4. SIC-25 is accompanied by a Basis for Conclusions. The scope and authority of Interpretations are set out in paragraphs 2 and 7–16 of the *Preface to International Financial Reporting Standards.*

FOR THE BASIS FOR CONCLUSIONS ON SIC-25 SEE PART B OF THIS EDITION

SIC Interpretation 25
Income Taxes—Changes in the Tax Status of an Entity or its Shareholders

References

- IAS 1 *Presentation of Financial Statements* (as revised in 2007)
- IAS 8 *Accounting Policies, Changes in Accounting Estimates and Errors*
- IAS 12 *Income Taxes*

Issue

1   A change in the tax status of an entity or of its shareholders may have consequences for an entity by increasing or decreasing its tax liabilities or assets. This may, for example, occur upon the public listing of an entity's equity instruments or upon the restructuring of an entity's equity. It may also occur upon a controlling shareholder's move to a foreign country. As a result of such an event, an entity may be taxed differently; it may for example gain or lose tax incentives or become subject to a different rate of tax in the future.

2   A change in the tax status of an entity or its shareholders may have an immediate effect on the entity's current tax liabilities or assets. The change may also increase or decrease the deferred tax liabilities and assets recognised by the entity, depending on the effect the change in tax status has on the tax consequences that will arise from recovering or settling the carrying amount of the entity's assets and liabilities.

3   The issue is how an entity should account for the tax consequences of a change in its tax status or that of its shareholders.

Consensus

4   A change in the tax status of an entity or its shareholders does not give rise to increases or decreases in amounts recognised outside profit or loss. The current and deferred tax consequences of a change in tax status shall be included in profit or loss for the period, unless those consequences relate to transactions and events that result, in the same or a different period, in a direct credit or charge to the recognised amount of equity or in amounts recognised in other comprehensive income. Those tax consequences that relate to changes in the recognised amount of equity, in the same or a different period (not included in profit or loss), shall be charged or credited directly to equity. Those tax consequences that relate to amounts recognised in other comprehensive income shall be recognised in other comprehensive income.

Date of consensus

August 1999

Effective date

This consensus becomes effective on 15 July 2000. Changes in accounting policies shall be accounted for in accordance with IAS 8.

IAS 1 (as revised in 2007) amended the terminology used throughout IFRSs. In addition it amended paragraph 4. An entity shall apply those amendments for annual periods beginning on or after 1 January 2009. If an entity applies IAS 1 (revised 2007) for an earlier period, the amendments shall be applied for that earlier period.

SIC Interpretation 27

Evaluating the Substance of Transactions Involving the Legal Form of a Lease

In April 2001 the International Accounting Standards Board adopted SIC-27 *Evaluating the Substance of Transactions Involving the Legal Form of a Lease*, which had originally been issued by the Standing Interpretations Committee of the International Accounting Standards Committee in December 2001.

Other IFRSs have made minor consequential amendments to SIC-27. These include IAS 8 *Accounting Policies, Changes in Accounting Estimates and Errors* (issued December 2003), IAS 1 *Presentation of Financial Statements* (as revised in September 2007) and IFRS 9 *Financial Instruments* (issued October 2010).

SIC Interpretation 27 *Evaluating the Substance of Transactions Involving the Legal Form of a Lease* (SIC-27) is set out in paragraphs 3–11. SIC-27 is accompanied by a Basis for Conclusions and implementation guidance. The scope and authority of Interpretations are set out in paragraphs 2 and 7–16 of the *Preface to International Financial Reporting Standards*.

FOR THE FOLLOWING MATERIAL ACCOMPANYING SIC-27:
- **BASIS FOR CONCLUSIONS**
- **IMPLEMENTATION GUIDANCE**
  - A Linked transactions
  - B The substance of an agreement

SEE PART B OF THIS EDITION

SIC Interpretation 27
Evaluating the Substance of Transactions Involving the Legal Form of a Lease

References

- IAS 8 *Accounting Policies, Changes in Accounting Estimates and Errors*
- IAS 11 *Construction Contracts*
- IAS 17 *Leases* (as revised in 2003)
- IAS 18 *Revenue*
- IAS 37 *Provisions, Contingent Liabilities and Contingent Assets*
- IFRS 4 *Insurance Contracts*
- IFRS 9 *Financial Instruments* (issued October 2010)[1]

Issue

1   An Entity may enter into a transaction or a series of structured transactions (an arrangement) with an unrelated party or parties (an Investor) that involves the legal form of a lease. For example, an Entity may lease assets to an Investor and lease the same assets back, or alternatively, legally sell assets and lease the same assets back. The form of each arrangement and its terms and conditions can vary significantly. In the lease and leaseback example, it may be that the arrangement is designed to achieve a tax advantage for the Investor that is shared with the Entity in the form of a fee, and not to convey the right to use an asset.

2   When an arrangement with an Investor involves the legal form of a lease, the issues are:

   (a)   how to determine whether a series of transactions is linked and should be accounted for as one transaction;

   (b)   whether the arrangement meets the definition of a lease under IAS 17; and, if not,

      (i)   whether a separate investment account and lease payment obligations that might exist represent assets and liabilities of the Entity (eg consider the example described in paragraph A2(a) of the guidance accompanying the Interpretation);

      (ii)   how the Entity should account for other obligations resulting from the arrangement; and

      (iii)   how the Entity should account for a fee it might receive from an Investor.

---

1   effective date 1 January 2013 (earlier application permitted)

Consensus

3   A series of transactions that involve the legal form of a lease is linked and shall be accounted for as one transaction when the overall economic effect cannot be understood without reference to the series of transactions as a whole. This is the case, for example, when the series of transactions are closely interrelated, negotiated as a single transaction, and takes place concurrently or in a continuous sequence. (Part A of the accompanying guidance provides illustrations of application of this Interpretation.)

4   The accounting shall reflect the substance of the arrangement. All aspects and implications of an arrangement shall be evaluated to determine its substance, with weight given to those aspects and implications that have an economic effect.

5   IAS 17 applies when the substance of an arrangement includes the conveyance of the right to use an asset for an agreed period of time. Indicators that individually demonstrate that an arrangement may not, in substance, involve a lease under IAS 17 include (Part B of the accompanying guidance provides illustrations of application of this Interpretation):

   (a)   an Entity retains all the risks and rewards incident to ownership of an underlying asset and enjoys substantially the same rights to its use as before the arrangement;

   (b)   the primary reason for the arrangement is to achieve a particular tax result, and not to convey the right to use an asset; and

   (c)   an option is included on terms that make its exercise almost certain (eg a put option that is exercisable at a price sufficiently higher than the expected fair value when it becomes exercisable).

6   The definitions and guidance in paragraphs 49–64 of the *Framework*[2] shall be applied in determining whether, in substance, a separate investment account and lease payment obligations represent assets and liabilities of the Entity. Indicators that collectively demonstrate that, in substance, a separate investment account and lease payment obligations do not meet the definitions of an asset and a liability and shall not be recognised by the Entity include:

   (a)   the Entity is not able to control the investment account in pursuit of its own objectives and is not obligated to pay the lease payments. This occurs when, for example, a prepaid amount is placed in a separate investment account to protect the Investor and may only be used to pay the Investor, the Investor agrees that the lease payment obligations are to be paid from funds in the investment account, and the Entity has no ability to withhold payments to the Investor from the investment account;

   (b)   the Entity has only a remote risk of reimbursing the entire amount of any fee received from an Investor and possibly paying some additional amount, or, when a fee has not been received, only a remote risk of paying an

---

2   The reference to the *Framework* is to IASC's *Framework for the Preparation and Presentation of Financial Statements*, adopted by the IASB in 2001. In September 2010 the IASB replaced the *Framework* with the *Conceptual Framework for Financial Reporting*. Paragraphs 49–64 are now paragraphs 4.4–4.19 of the *Conceptual Framework*.

amount under other obligations (eg a guarantee). Only a remote risk of payment exists when, for example, the terms of the arrangement require that a prepaid amount is invested in risk-free assets that are expected to generate sufficient cash flows to satisfy the lease payment obligations; and

(c) other than the initial cash flows at inception of the arrangement, the only cash flows expected under the arrangement are the lease payments that are satisfied solely from funds withdrawn from the separate investment account established with the initial cash flows.

7 Other obligations of an arrangement, including any guarantees provided and obligations incurred upon early termination, shall be accounted for under IAS 37, IFRS 4 or IFRS 9, depending on the terms.

8 The criteria in paragraph 20 of IAS 18 shall be applied to the facts and circumstances of each arrangement in determining when to recognise a fee as income that an Entity might receive. Factors such as whether there is continuing involvement in the form of significant future performance obligations necessary to earn the fee, whether there are retained risks, the terms of any guarantee arrangements, and the risk of repayment of the fee, shall be considered. Indicators that individually demonstrate that recognition of the entire fee as income when received, if received at the beginning of the arrangement, is inappropriate include:

(a) obligations either to perform or to refrain from certain significant activities are conditions of earning the fee received, and therefore execution of a legally binding arrangement is not the most significant act required by the arrangement;

(b) limitations are put on the use of the underlying asset that have the practical effect of restricting and significantly changing the Entity's ability to use (eg deplete, sell or pledge as collateral) the asset;

(c) the possibility of reimbursing any amount of the fee and possibly paying some additional amount is not remote. This occurs when, for example,

(i) the underlying asset is not a specialised asset that is required by the Entity to conduct its business, and therefore there is a possibility that the Entity may pay an amount to terminate the arrangement early; or

(ii) the Entity is required by the terms of the arrangement, or has some or total discretion, to invest a prepaid amount in assets carrying more than an insignificant amount of risk (eg currency, interest rate or credit risk). In this circumstance, the risk of the investment's value being insufficient to satisfy the lease payment obligations is not remote, and therefore there is a possibility that the Entity may be required to pay some amount.

9 The fee shall be presented in the statement of comprehensive income based on its economic substance and nature.

Disclosure

10   All aspects of an arrangement that does not, in substance, involve a lease under IAS 17 shall be considered in determining the appropriate disclosures that are necessary to understand the arrangement and the accounting treatment adopted. An Entity shall disclose the following in each period that an arrangement exists:

   (a)   a description of the arrangement including:

      (i)   the underlying asset and any restrictions on its use;

      (ii)   the life and other significant terms of the arrangement;

      (iii)   the transactions that are linked together, including any options; and

   (b)   the accounting treatment applied to any fee received, the amount recognised as income in the period, and the line item of the statement of comprehensive income in which it is included.

11   The disclosures required in accordance with paragraph 10 of this Interpretation shall be provided individually for each arrangement or in aggregate for each class of arrangement. A class is a grouping of arrangements with underlying assets of a similar nature (eg power plants).

Date of consensus

February 2000

Effective date

This Interpretation becomes effective on 31 December 2001. Changes in accounting policies shall be accounted for in accordance with IAS 8.

IFRS 9, issued in October 2010, amended paragraph 7. An entity shall apply that amendment when it applies IFRS 9 as issued in October 2010.

SIC Interpretation 29

Service Concession Arrangements: Disclosures

In April 2001 the International Accounting Standards Board (IASB) adopted SIC-29 *Disclosure—Service Concession Arrangements*, which had originally been issued by the Standing Interpretations Committee of the International Accounting Standards Committee in December 2001.

In November 2006, when the IASB issued IFRIC 12 *Service Concession Arrangements*, SIC-29's title was changed to *Service Concession Arrangements: Disclosures*.

Other IFRSs have made minor consequential amendments to SIC-29. These include IAS 1 *Presentation of Financial Statements* (as revised in December 2003 and September 2007) and IFRIC 12 *Service Concession Arrangements* (issued November 2006).

SIC Interpretation 29 *Service Concession Arrangements: Disclosures* (SIC-29) is set out in paragraphs 6–7. SIC-29 is accompanied by a Basis for Conclusions. The scope and authority of Interpretations are set out in paragraphs 2 and 7–16 of the *Preface to International Financial Reporting Standards*.

FOR THE BASIS FOR CONCLUSIONS ON SIC-29 SEE PART B OF THIS EDITION

SIC Interpretation 29
Service Concession Arrangements: Disclosures

References

- IAS 1 *Presentation of Financial Statements* (as revised in 2007)

- IAS 16 *Property, Plant and Equipment* (as revised in 2003)

- IAS 17 *Leases* (as revised in 2003)

- IAS 37 *Provisions, Contingent Liabilities and Contingent Assets*

- IAS 38 *Intangible Assets* (as revised in 2004)

- IFRIC 12 *Service Concession Arrangements*

Issue

1   An entity (the operator) may enter into an arrangement with another entity (the grantor) to provide services that give the public access to major economic and social facilities. The grantor may be a public or private sector entity, including a governmental body. Examples of service concession arrangements involve water treatment and supply facilities, motorways, car parks, tunnels, bridges, airports and telecommunication networks. Examples of arrangements that are not service concession arrangements include an entity outsourcing the operation of its internal services (eg employee cafeteria, building maintenance, and accounting or information technology functions).

2   A service concession arrangement generally involves the grantor conveying for the period of the concession to the operator:

   (a)   the right to provide services that give the public access to major economic and social facilities, and

   (b)   in some cases, the right to use specified tangible assets, intangible assets, or financial assets,

   in exchange for the operator:

   (c)   committing to provide the services according to certain terms and conditions during the concession period, and

   (d)   when applicable, committing to return at the end of the concession period the rights received at the beginning of the concession period and/or acquired during the concession period.

3   The common characteristic of all service concession arrangements is that the operator both receives a right and incurs an obligation to provide public services.

4   The issue is what information should be disclosed in the notes in the financial statements of an operator and a grantor.

5   Certain aspects and disclosures relating to some service concession arrangements
       are already addressed by existing International Financial Reporting Standards (eg
       IAS 16 applies to acquisitions of items of property, plant and equipment, IAS 17
       applies to leases of assets, and IAS 38 applies to acquisitions of intangible assets).
       However, a service concession arrangement may involve executory contracts that
       are not addressed in International Financial Reporting Standards, unless the
       contracts are onerous, in which case IAS 37 applies. Therefore, this Interpretation
       addresses additional disclosures of service concession arrangements.

Consensus

6   All aspects of a service concession arrangement shall be considered in
       determining the appropriate disclosures in the notes. An operator and a grantor
       shall disclose the following in each period:

    (a)   a description of the arrangement;

    (b)   significant terms of the arrangement that may affect the amount, timing
        and certainty of future cash flows (eg the period of the concession,
        re-pricing dates and the basis upon which re-pricing or re-negotiation is
        determined);

    (c)   the nature and extent (eg quantity, time period or amount as appropriate)
        of:

        (i)   rights to use specified assets;

        (ii)   obligations to provide or rights to expect provision of services;

        (iii)   obligations to acquire or build items of property, plant and
            equipment;

        (iv)   obligations to deliver or rights to receive specified assets at the end of
            the concession period;

        (v)   renewal and termination options; and

        (vi)   other rights and obligations (eg major overhauls);

    (d)   changes in the arrangement occurring during the period; and

    (e)   how the service arrangement has been classified.

6A   An operator shall disclose the amount of revenue and profits or losses recognised
       in the period on exchanging construction services for a financial asset or an
       intangible asset.

7   The disclosures required in accordance with paragraph 6 of this Interpretation
       shall be provided individually for each service concession arrangement or in
       aggregate for each class of service concession arrangements. A class is a grouping
       of service concession arrangements involving services of a similar nature (eg toll
       collections, telecommunications and water treatment services).

Date of consensus

May 2001

Effective date

This Interpretation becomes effective on 31 December 2001.

An entity shall apply the amendment in paragraphs 6(e) and 6A for annual periods beginning on or after 1 January 2008. If an entity applies IFRIC 12 for an earlier period, the amendment shall be applied for that earlier period.

SIC Interpretation 31

Revenue—Barter Transactions Involving Advertising Services

In April 2001 the International Accounting Standards Board adopted SIC-31 *Revenue—Barter Transactions Involving Advertising Services*, which had originally been issued by the Standing Interpretations Committee of the International Accounting Standards Committee in December 2001.

IAS 8 *Accounting Policies, Changes in Accounting Estimates and Errors* (issued December 2003), made some consequential amendments to SIC-31.

SIC Interpretation 31 *Revenue—Barter Transactions Involving Advertising Services* (SIC-31) is set out in paragraph 5. SIC-31 is accompanied by a Basis for Conclusions. The scope and authority of Interpretations are set out in paragraphs 2 and 7–16 of the *Preface to International Financial Reporting Standards*.

FOR THE BASIS FOR CONCLUSIONS ON SIC-31 SEE PART B OF THIS EDITION

SIC Interpretation 31
Revenue—Barter Transactions Involving Advertising Services

References

- IAS 8 *Accounting Policies, Changes in Accounting Estimates and Errors*
- IAS 18 *Revenue*

Issue

1 An entity (Seller) may enter into a barter transaction to provide advertising services in exchange for receiving advertising services from its customer (Customer). Advertisements may be displayed on the Internet or poster sites, broadcast on the television or radio, published in magazines or journals, or presented in another medium.

2 In some cases, no cash or other consideration is exchanged between the entities. In some other cases, equal or approximately equal amounts of cash or other consideration are also exchanged.

3 A Seller that provides advertising services in the course of its ordinary activities recognises revenue under IAS 18 from a barter transaction involving advertising when, amongst other criteria, the services exchanged are dissimilar (IAS 18.12) and the amount of revenue can be measured reliably (IAS 18.20(a)). This Interpretation only applies to an exchange of dissimilar advertising services. An exchange of similar advertising services is not a transaction that generates revenue under IAS 18.

4 The issue is under what circumstances can a Seller reliably measure revenue at the fair value of advertising services received or provided in a barter transaction.

Consensus

5 Revenue from a barter transaction involving advertising cannot be measured reliably at the fair value of advertising services received. However, a Seller can reliably measure revenue at the fair value of the advertising services it provides in a barter transaction, by reference only to non-barter transactions that:

(a) involve advertising similar to the advertising in the barter transaction;

(b) occur frequently;

(c) represent a predominant number of transactions and amount when compared to all transactions to provide advertising that is similar to the advertising in the barter transaction;

(d) involve cash and/or another form of consideration (eg marketable securities, non-monetary assets, and other services) that has a reliably measurable fair value; and

(e) do not involve the same counterparty as in the barter transaction.

Date of consensus

May 2001

Effective date

This Interpretation becomes effective on 31 December 2001. Changes in accounting policies shall be accounted for in accordance with IAS 8.

SIC Interpretation 32

Intangible Assets—Web Site Costs

In April 2001 the International Accounting Standards Board adopted SIC-32 *Intangible Assets—Web Site Costs*, which had originally been issued by the Standing Interpretations Committee of the International Accounting Standards Committee in March 2002.

Other IFRSs have made minor consequential amendments to SIC-32. These include IAS 16 *Property, Plant and Equipment* (as revised in December 2003), IFRS 3 *Business Combinations* (issued March 2004) and IAS 1 *Presentation of Financial Statements* (as revised in September 2007).

SIC Interpretation 32 *Intangible Assets—Web Site Costs* (SIC-32) is set out in paragraphs 7–10. SIC-32 is accompanied by a Basis for Conclusions and an example illustrating the application of the Interpretation. The scope and authority of Interpretations are set out in paragraphs 2 and 7–16 of the *Preface to International Financial Reporting Standards*.

FOR THE FOLLOWING MATERIAL ACCOMPANYING SIC-32:
- **BASIS FOR CONCLUSIONS**
- **ILLUSTRATIVE EXAMPLE**

SEE PART B OF THIS EDITION

SIC Interpretation 32
Intangible Assets—Web Site Costs

References

* IAS 1 *Presentation of Financial Statements* (as revised in 2007)
* IAS 2 *Inventories* (as revised in 2003)
* IAS 11 *Construction Contracts*
* IAS 16 *Property, Plant and Equipment* (as revised in 2003)
* IAS 17 *Leases* (as revised in 2003)
* IAS 36 *Impairment of Assets* (as revised in 2004)
* IAS 38 *Intangible Assets* (as revised in 2004)
* IFRS 3 *Business Combinations*

Issue

1   An entity may incur internal expenditure on the development and operation of its own web site for internal or external access. A web site designed for external access may be used for various purposes such as to promote and advertise an entity's own products and services, provide electronic services, and sell products and services. A web site designed for internal access may be used to store company policies and customer details, and search relevant information.

2   The stages of a web site's development can be described as follows:

(a)   Planning – includes undertaking feasibility studies, defining objectives and specifications, evaluating alternatives and selecting preferences.

(b)   Application and Infrastructure Development – includes obtaining a domain name, purchasing and developing hardware and operating software, installing developed applications and stress testing.

(c)   Graphical Design Development – includes designing the appearance of web pages.

(d)   Content Development – includes creating, purchasing, preparing and uploading information, either textual or graphical in nature, on the web site before the completion of the web site's development. This information may either be stored in separate databases that are integrated into (or accessed from) the web site or coded directly into the web pages.

3   Once development of a web site has been completed, the Operating stage begins. During this stage, an entity maintains and enhances the applications, infrastructure, graphical design and content of the web site.

4   When accounting for internal expenditure on the development and operation of an entity's own web site for internal or external access, the issues are:

     (a)   whether the web site is an internally generated intangible asset that is subject to the requirements of IAS 38; and

     (b)   the appropriate accounting treatment of such expenditure.

5   This Interpretation does not apply to expenditure on purchasing, developing, and operating hardware (eg web servers, staging servers, production servers and Internet connections) of a web site. Such expenditure is accounted for under IAS 16. Additionally, when an entity incurs expenditure on an Internet service provider hosting the entity's web site, the expenditure is recognised as an expense under IAS 1.88 and the *Framework*[1] when the services are received.

6   IAS 38 does not apply to intangible assets held by an entity for sale in the ordinary course of business (see IAS 2 and IAS 11) or leases that fall within the scope of IAS 17. Accordingly, this Interpretation does not apply to expenditure on the development or operation of a web site (or web site software) for sale to another entity. When a web site is leased under an operating lease, the lessor applies this Interpretation. When a web site is leased under a finance lease, the lessee applies this Interpretation after initial recognition of the leased asset.

Consensus

7   An entity's own web site that arises from development and is for internal or external access is an internally generated intangible asset that is subject to the requirements of IAS 38.

8   A web site arising from development shall be recognised as an intangible asset if, and only if, in addition to complying with the general requirements described in IAS 38.21 for recognition and initial measurement, an entity can satisfy the requirements in IAS 38.57. In particular, an entity may be able to satisfy the requirement to demonstrate how its web site will generate probable future economic benefits in accordance with IAS 38.57(d) when, for example, the web site is capable of generating revenues, including direct revenues from enabling orders to be placed. An entity is not able to demonstrate how a web site developed solely or primarily for promoting and advertising its own products and services will generate probable future economic benefits, and consequently all expenditure on developing such a web site shall be recognised as an expense when incurred.

9   Any internal expenditure on the development and operation of an entity's own web site shall be accounted for in accordance with IAS 38. The nature of each activity for which expenditure is incurred (eg training employees and maintaining the web site) and the web site's stage of development or post-development shall be evaluated to determine the appropriate accounting treatment (additional guidance is provided in the illustrative example accompanying this Interpretation). For example:

---

1   The reference to the *Framework* is to IASC's *Framework for the Preparation and Presentation of Financial Statements*, adopted by the IASB in 2001. In September 2010 the IASB replaced the *Framework* with the *Conceptual Framework for Financial Reporting*.

(a) the Planning stage is similar in nature to the research phase in IAS 38.54–.56. Expenditure incurred in this stage shall be recognised as an expense when it is incurred.

(b) the Application and Infrastructure Development stage, the Graphical Design stage and the Content Development stage, to the extent that content is developed for purposes other than to advertise and promote an entity's own products and services, are similar in nature to the development phase in IAS 38.57–.64. Expenditure incurred in these stages shall be included in the cost of a web site recognised as an intangible asset in accordance with paragraph 8 of this Interpretation when the expenditure can be directly attributed and is necessary to creating, producing or preparing the web site for it to be capable of operating in the manner intended by management. For example, expenditure on purchasing or creating content (other than content that advertises and promotes an entity's own products and services) specifically for a web site, or expenditure to enable use of the content (eg a fee for acquiring a licence to reproduce) on the web site, shall be included in the cost of development when this condition is met. However, in accordance with IAS 38.71, expenditure on an intangible item that was initially recognised as an expense in previous financial statements shall not be recognised as part of the cost of an intangible asset at a later date (eg if the costs of a copyright have been fully amortised, and the content is subsequently provided on a web site).

(c) expenditure incurred in the Content Development stage, to the extent that content is developed to advertise and promote an entity's own products and services (eg digital photographs of products), shall be recognised as an expense when incurred in accordance with IAS 38.69(c). For example, when accounting for expenditure on professional services for taking digital photographs of an entity's own products and for enhancing their display, expenditure shall be recognised as an expense as the professional services are received during the process, not when the digital photographs are displayed on the web site.

(d) the Operating stage begins once development of a web site is complete. Expenditure incurred in this stage shall be recognised as an expense when it is incurred unless it meets the recognition criteria in IAS 38.18.

10 A web site that is recognised as an intangible asset under paragraph 8 of this Interpretation shall be measured after initial recognition by applying the requirements of IAS 38.72–.87. The best estimate of a web site's useful life should be short.

Date of consensus

May 2001

Effective date

This Interpretation becomes effective on 25 March 2002. The effects of adopting this Interpretation shall be accounted for using the transition requirements in the version of IAS 38 that was issued in 1998. Therefore, when a web site does not meet the criteria for recognition as an intangible asset, but was previously recognised as an asset, the item shall be derecognised at the date when this Interpretation becomes effective. When a web site exists and the expenditure to develop it meets the criteria for recognition as an intangible asset, but was not previously recognised as an asset, the intangible asset shall not be recognised at the date when this Interpretation becomes effective. When a web site exists and the expenditure to develop it meets the criteria for recognition as an intangible asset, was previously recognised as an asset and initially measured at cost, the amount initially recognised is deemed to have been properly determined.

IAS 1 (as revised in 2007) amended the terminology used throughout IFRSs. In addition it amended paragraph 5. An entity shall apply those amendments for annual periods beginning on or after 1 January 2009. If an entity applies IAS 1 (revised 2007) for an earlier period, the amendments shall be applied for that earlier period.

Glossary of Terms

This glossary is extracted from the International Financial Reporting Standards (IFRSs) including International Accounting Standards (IASs) issued by the IASB as at 31 December 2011. References are by Standard and paragraph number.

The glossary also includes extracts from the *Conceptual Framework for Financial Reporting*. References to the *Conceptual Framework* are preceded by CF.

References set out below in (brackets) indicate minor variations in wording.

accounting policies	The specific principles, bases, conventions, rules and practices applied by an entity in preparing and presenting financial statements.	IAS 8.5
accounting profit	Profit or loss for a period before deducting tax expense.	IAS 12.5
acquiree	The business or businesses that the acquirer obtains control of in a business combination.	IFRS 3.A
acquirer	The entity that obtains control of the acquiree.	IFRS 3.A
acquisition date	The date on which the acquirer obtains control of the acquiree.	IFRS 3.A
active market	A market in which transactions for the asset or liability take place with sufficient frequency and volume to provide pricing information on an ongoing basis.	IFRS 13.A
actuarial gains and losses	The changes in the present value of the defined benefit obligation resulting from: (a) Experience adjustments (the effects of differences between the previous actuarial assumptions and what has actually occurred); and (b) the effects of changes in actuarial assumptions.	IAS 19.8
actuarial present value of promised retirement benefits	The present value of the expected payments by a retirement benefit plan to existing and past employees, attributable to the service already rendered.	IAS 26.8
agricultural activity	The management by an entity of the biological transformation and harvest of biological assets for sale or for conversion into agricultural produce or into additional biological assets.	IAS 41.5

agricultural produce	The harvested product of the entity's biological assets.	IAS 41.5
amortisation (depreciation)[1]	The systematic allocation of the depreciable amount of an asset over its useful life.	IAS 36.6, IAS 38.8
amortised cost of a financial asset or financial liability	The amount at which the financial asset or financial liability is measured at initial recognition minus principal repayments, plus or minus the cumulative amortisation using the effective interest method of any difference between that initial amount and the maturity amount, and minus any reduction (directly or through the use of an allowance account) for impairment or uncollectibility.	IAS 39.9
antidilution	An increase in earnings per share or a reduction in loss per share resulting from the assumption that convertible instruments are converted, that options or warrants are exercised, or that ordinary shares are issued upon the satisfaction of specified conditions.	IAS 33.5
asset	A resource:	IAS 38.8, (CF.4.4(a))
	(a) controlled by an entity as a result of past events; and	
	(b) from which future economic benefits are expected to flow to the entity.	
assets held by a long-term employee benefit fund	Assets (other than non-transferable financial instruments issued by the reporting entity) that:	IAS 19.8
	(a) are held by an entity (a fund) that is legally separate from the reporting entity and exists solely to pay or fund employee benefits; and	
	(b) are available to be used only to pay or fund employee benefits, are not available to the reporting entity's own creditors (even in bankruptcy), and cannot be returned to the reporting entity, unless either:	
	(i) the remaining assets of the fund are sufficient to meet all the related employee benefit obligations of the plan or the reporting entity; or	
	(ii) the assets are returned to the reporting entity to reimburse it for employee benefits already paid.	

---

1 In the case of an intangible asset, the term 'amortisation' is generally used instead of 'depreciation'. The two terms have the same meaning.

associate	An entity, over which the investor has significant influence.	IAS 28.3
biological asset	A living animal or plant.	IAS 41.5
biological transformation	The processes of growth, degeneration, production, and procreation that cause qualitative or quantitative changes in a biological asset.	IAS 41.5
borrowing costs	Interest and other costs that an entity incurs in connection with the borrowing of funds.	IAS 23.5
business	An integrated set of activities and assets that is capable of being conducted and managed for the purpose of providing a return in the form of dividends, lower costs or other economic benefits directly to investors or other owners, members or participants.	IFRS 3.A
business combination	A transaction or other event in which an acquirer obtains control of one or more businesses. Transactions sometimes referred to as 'true mergers' or 'mergers of equals' are also business combinations as that term is used in IFRS 3.	IFRS 3.A
carrying amount	The amount at which an asset is recognised after deducting any accumulated depreciation (amortisation) and accumulated impairment losses thereon.	IAS 16.6, IAS 36.6, IAS 38.8
carrying amount	The amount at which an asset is recognised in the statement of financial position.	IAS 40.5, IAS 41.8
cash	Cash on hand and demand deposits.	IAS 7.6
cash equivalents	Short-term, highly liquid investments that are readily convertible to known amounts of cash and which are subject to an insignificant risk of changes in value.	IAS 7.6
cash flows	Inflows and outflows of cash and cash equivalents.	IAS 7.6
cash-generating unit	The smallest identifiable group of assets that generates cash inflows that are largely independent of the cash inflows from other assets or groups of assets.	IAS 36.6, IFRS 5.A
cash-settled share-based payment transaction	A share-based payment transaction in which the entity acquires goods or services by incurring a liability to transfer cash or other assets to the supplier of those goods or services for amounts that are based on the price (or value) of equity instruments (including shares or share options) of the entity or another group entity.	IFRS 2.A

cedant	The policyholder under a reinsurance contract.	IFRS 4.A
change in accounting estimate	An adjustment of the carrying amount of an asset or a liability, or the amount of the periodic consumption of an asset, that results from the assessment of the present status of, and expected future benefits and obligations associated with, assets and liabilities. Changes in accounting estimates result from new information or new developments and, accordingly, are not corrections of errors.	IAS 8.5
close members of the family of a person	Those family members who may be expected to influence, or be influenced by, that person in their dealings with the entity and include: (a) that person's children and spouse or domestic partner; (b) children of that person's spouse or domestic partner; (c) dependants of that person or that person's spouse or domestic partner.	IAS 24.9
closing rate	The spot exchange rate at the end of the reporting period.	IAS 21.8
commencement of the lease term	The date from which the lessee is entitled to exercise its right to use the leased asset. It is the date of initial recognition of the lease (ie the recognition of the assets, liabilities, income or expenses resulting from the lease, as appropriate).	IAS 17.4

compensation	Includes all employee benefits (as defined in IAS 19) including employee benefits to which IFRS 2 applies. Employee benefits are all forms of consideration paid, payable or provided by the entity, or on behalf of the entity, in exchange for services rendered to the entity. It also includes such consideration paid on behalf of a parent of the entity in respect of the entity. Compensation includes:	IAS 24.9

    (a)   short-term employee benefits, such as wages, salaries and social security contributions, paid annual leave and paid sick leave, profit sharing and bonuses (if payable within twelve months of the end of the period) and non-monetary benefits (such as medical care, housing, cars and free or subsidised goods or services) for current employees;

    (b)   post-employment benefits such as pensions, other retirement benefits, post-employment life insurance and post-employment medical care;

    (c)   other long-term employee benefits, including long service leave or sabbatical leave, jubilee or other long service benefits, long-term disability benefits and, if they are not payable wholly within twelve months after the end of the period, profit sharing, bonuses and deferred compensation;

    (d)   termination benefits; and

    (e)   share-based payment.

component of an entity	Operations and cash flows that can be clearly distinguished, operationally and for financial reporting purposes, from the rest of the entity.	IFRS 5.A
consolidated financial statements	The financial statements of a group in which assets, liabilities, equity, income, expenses and cash flow of the parent and its subsidiaries are presented as those of a single economic entity.	IAS 27.4, IAS 28.3, IFRS 10.A
construction contract	A contract specifically negotiated for the construction of an asset or a combination of assets that are closely interrelated or interdependent in terms of their design, technology and function or their ultimate purpose or use.	IAS 11.3

constructive obligation	An obligation that derives from an entity's actions where:	IAS 37.10

(a) by an established pattern of past practice, published policies or a sufficiently specific current statement, the entity has indicated to other parties that it will accept certain responsibilities; and

(b) as a result, the entity has created a valid expectation on the part of those other parties that it will discharge those responsibilities.

contingent asset	A possible asset that arises from past events and whose existence will be confirmed only by the occurrence or non-occurrence of one or more uncertain future events not wholly within the control of the entity.	IAS 37.10
contingent consideration	Usually, an obligation of the acquirer to transfer additional assets or equity interests to the former owners of an acquiree as part of the exchange for control of the acquiree if specified future events occur or conditions are met. However, contingent consideration also may give the acquirer the right to the return of previously transferred consideration if specified conditions are met.	IFRS 3.A
contingent liability	(a) A possible obligation that arises from past events and whose existence will be confirmed only by the occurrence or non-occurrence of one or more uncertain future events not wholly within the control of the entity; or	IAS 37.10

(b) a present obligation that arises from past events but is not recognised because:

(i) it is not probable that an outflow of resources embodying economic benefits will be required to settle the obligation; or

(ii) the amount of the obligation cannot be measured with sufficient reliability.

contingent rent	That portion of the lease payments that is not fixed in amount but is based on the future amount of a factor that changes other than with the passage of time (eg percentage of future sales, amount of future use, future price indices, future market rates of interest).	IAS 17.4

contingent share agreement	An agreement to issue shares that is dependent on the satisfaction of specified conditions.	IAS 33.5
contingently issuable ordinary shares	Ordinary shares issuable for little or no cash or other consideration upon the satisfaction of specified conditions in a contingent share agreement.	IAS 33.5
control of an investee	An investor controls an investee when the investor is exposed, or has rights, to variable returns from its involvement with the investee and has the ability to affect those returns through its power over the investee.	IFRS 10.A
corporate assets	Assets other than goodwill that contribute to the future cash flows of both the cash generating unit under review and other cash generating units.	IAS 36.6
cost	The amount of cash or cash equivalents paid or the fair value of the other consideration given to acquire an asset at the time of its acquisition or construction, or, when applicable, the amount attributed to that asset when initially recognised in accordance with the specific requirements of other IFRSs, eg IFRS 2.	IAS 16.6, IAS 38.8, IAS 40.5
cost approach	A valuation technique that reflects the amount that would be required currently to replace the service capacity of an asset (often referred to as current replacement cost).	IFRS 13.A
cost plus contract	A construction contract in which the contractor is reimbursed for allowable or otherwise defined costs, plus a percentage of these costs or a fixed fee.	IAS 11.3
costs of disposal	Incremental costs directly attributable to the disposal of an asset, excluding finance costs and income tax expense.	IAS 36.6
costs to sell	The incremental costs directly attributable to the disposal of an asset (or disposal group), excluding finance costs and income tax expense.	IFRS 5.A (IAS 41.5)
credit risk	The risk that one party to a financial instrument will cause a financial loss for the other party by failing to discharge an obligation.	IFRS 7.A
currency risk	The risk that the fair value or future cash flows of a financial instrument will fluctuate because of changes in foreign exchange rates.	IFRS 7.A

current asset	An entity shall classify an asset as current when:	IAS 1.66, (IFRS 5.A)

(a) it expects to realise the asset or intends to sell or consume it in its normal operating cycle;

(b) it holds the asset primarily for the purpose of trading;

(c) it expects to realise the asset within twelve months after the reporting period; or

(d) the asset is cash or a cash equivalent (as defined in IAS 7) unless the asset is restricted from being exchanged or used to settle a liability for at least twelve months after the reporting period.

An entity shall classify all other assets as non-current.

current service cost	The increase in the present value of the defined benefit obligation resulting from employee service in the current period.	IAS 19.8
current tax	The amount of income taxes payable (recoverable) in respect of the taxable profit (tax loss) for a period.	IAS 12.5
date of transition to IFRSs	The beginning of the earliest period for which an entity presents full comparative information under IFRSs in its first IFRS financial statements.	IFRS 1.A
decision maker	An entity with decision-making rights that is either a principal or an agent for other parties.	IFRS 10.A
deductible temporary differences	Temporary differences between the carrying amount of an asset or liability in the balance sheet and its tax base that will result in amounts that are deductible in determining taxable profit (tax loss) of future periods when the carrying amount of the asset or liability is recovered or settled.	IAS 12.5
deemed cost	An amount used as a surrogate for cost or depreciated cost at a given date. Subsequent depreciation or amortisation assumes that the entity had initially recognised the asset or liability at the given date and that its cost was equal to the deemed cost.	IFRS 1.A

deferred tax assets	The amounts of income taxes recoverable in future periods in respect of: (a) deductible temporary differences; (b) the carryforward of unused tax losses; and (c) the carryforward of unused tax credits.	IAS 12.5
deferred tax liabilities	The amounts of income taxes payable in future periods in respect of taxable temporary differences.	IAS 12.5
deficit or surplus (of defined benefit liability (asset))	The deficit or surplus is: (a) the present value of the defined benefit obligation less (b) the fair value of the plan assets (if any).	IAS 19.8
defined benefit plans	Post-employment benefit plans other than defined contribution plans.	IAS 19.8
defined benefit plans	Retirement benefit plans under which amounts to be paid as retirement benefits are determined by reference to a formula usually based on employees' earnings and/or years of service.	IAS 26.8
defined contribution plans	Post-employment benefit plans under which an entity pays fixed contributions into a separate entity (a fund) and will have no legal or constructive obligation to pay further contributions if the fund does not hold sufficient assets to pay all employee benefits relating to employee service in the current and prior periods.	IAS 19.8
defined contribution plans	Retirement benefit plans under which amounts to be paid as retirement benefits are determined by contributions to a fund together with investment earnings thereon.	IAS 26.8
deposit component	A contractual component that is not accounted for as a derivative under IFRS 9 and would be within the scope of IFRS 9 if it were a separate instrument.	IFRS 4.A
depreciable amount	The cost of an asset, or other amount substituted for cost (in the financial statements), less its residual value.	IAS 16.6, (IAS 36.6, IAS 38.8)
depreciation (amortisation)[2]	The systematic allocation of the depreciable amount of an asset over its useful life.	IAS 16.6, IAS 36.6

2 In the case of an intangible asset, the term 'amortisation' is generally used instead of 'depreciation'. The two terms have the same meaning.

derecognition (of a financial instrument)	The removal of a previously recognised financial asset or financial liability from an entity's statement of financial position.	IFRS 9.A
derivative	A financial instrument or other contract within the scope of IFRS 9 (see paragraph 2.1) with all three of the following characteristics:	IFRS 9.A

(a) Its value changes in response to the change in a specified interest rate, financial instrument price, commodity price, foreign exchange rate, index of prices or rates, credit rating or credit index, or other variable, provided in the case of a non-financial variable that the variable is not specific to a party to the contract (sometimes called the 'underlying').

(b) It requires no initial net investment or an initial net investment that is smaller than would be required for other types of contracts that would be expected to have a similar response to changes in market factors.

(c) It is settled at a future date.

development	The application of research findings or other knowledge to a plan or design for the production of new or substantially improved materials, devices, products, processes, systems or services before the start of commercial production or use.	IAS 38.8
dilution	A reduction in earnings per share or an increase in loss per share resulting from the assumption that convertible instruments are converted, that options or warrants are exercised, or that ordinary shares are issued upon the satisfaction of specified conditions.	IAS 33.5
direct insurance contract	An insurance contract that is not a reinsurance contract.	IFRS 4.A
discontinued operation	A component of an entity that either has been disposed of or is classified as held for sale and:	IFRS 5.A

(a) represents a separate major line of business or geographical area of operations,

(b) is part of a single co-ordinated plan to dispose of a separate major line of business or geographical area of operations or

(c) is a subsidiary acquired exclusively with a view to resale.

discretionary participation feature	A contractual right to receive, as a supplement to guaranteed benefits, additional benefits:	IFRS 4.A

(a) that are likely to be a significant portion of the total contractual benefits;

(b) whose amount or timing is contractually at the discretion of the issuer; and

(c) that are contractually based on:

   (i) the performance of a specified pool of contracts or a specified type of contract;

   (ii) realised and/or unrealised investment returns on a specified pool of assets held by the issuer; or

   (iii) the profit or loss of the company, fund or other entity that issues the contract.

disposal group	A group of assets to be disposed of, by sale or otherwise, together as a group in a single transaction, and liabilities directly associated with those assets that will be transferred in the transaction. The group includes goodwill acquired in a business combination if the group is a cash generating unit to which goodwill has been allocated in accordance with the requirements of paragraphs 80–87 of IAS 36 or if it is an operation within such a cash generating unit.	IFRS 5.A

economic life	Either:	IAS 17.4

(a) the period over which an asset is expected to be economically usable by one or more users; or

(b) the number of production or similar units expected to be obtained from the asset by one or more users.

effective interest method	A method of calculating the amortised cost of a financial asset or a financial liability (or group of financial assets or financial liabilities) and of allocating the interest income or interest expense over the relevant period.	IAS 39.9

effective interest rate	The rate that exactly discounts estimated future cash payments or receipts through the expected life of the financial instrument or, when appropriate, a shorter period to the net carrying amount of the financial asset or financial liability. When calculating the effective interest rate, an entity shall estimate cash flows considering all contractual terms of the financial instrument (for example, prepayment, call and similar options) but shall not consider future credit losses. The calculation includes all fees and points paid or received between parties to the contract that are an integral part of the effective interest rate (see IAS 18), transaction costs, and all other premiums or discounts. There is a presumption that the cash flows and the expected life of a group of similar financial instruments can be estimated reliably. However, in those rare cases when it is not possible to estimate reliably the cash flows or the expected life of a financial instrument (or group of financial instruments), the entity shall use the contractual cash flows over the full contractual term of the financial instrument (or group of financial instruments).	IAS 39.9
employee benefits	All forms of consideration given by an entity in exchange for service rendered by employees or for the termination of employment.	IAS 19.8
employees and others providing similar services	Individuals who render personal services to the entity and either (a) the individuals are regarded as employees for legal or tax purposes, (b) the individuals work for the entity under its direction in the same way as individuals who are regarded as employees for legal or tax purposes, or (c) the services rendered are similar to those rendered by employees. For example, the term encompasses all management personnel, ie those persons having authority and responsibility for planning, directing and controlling the activities of the entity, including non-executive directors.	IFRS 2.A
entity-specific value	The present value of the cash flows an entity expects to arise from the continuing use of an asset and from its disposal at the end of its useful life or expects to incur when settling a liability.	IAS 16.6, IAS 38.8
entry price	The price paid to acquire an asset or received to assume a liability in an exchange transaction.	IFRS 13.A
equity instrument	A contract that evidences a residual interest in the assets of an entity after deducting all of its liabilities.	IAS 32.11, IFRS 2.A

equity instrument granted	The right (conditional or unconditional) to an equity instrument of the entity conferred by the entity on another party, under a share-based payment arrangement.	IFRS 2.A
equity interests	In IFRS 3, is used broadly to mean ownership interests of investor-owned entities and owner, member or participant interests of mutual entities.	IFRS 3.A
equity method	A method of accounting whereby the investment is initially recognised at cost and adjusted thereafter for the post-acquisition change in the investor's share of the investee's net assets. The investor's profit or loss includes its share of the investee's profit or loss and the investor's other comprehensive income includes its share of the investee's other comprehensive income.	IAS 28.3
equity-settled share-based payment transaction	A share-based payment transaction in which the entity	IFRS 2.A
	(a) receives goods or services as consideration for its own equity instruments (including shares or share options), or	
	(b) receives goods or services but has no obligation to settle the transaction with the supplier.	
events after the reporting period	Those events, favourable and unfavourable, that occur between the end of the reporting period and the date when the financial statements are authorised for issue. Two types of events can be identified:	IAS 10.3
	(a) those that provide evidence of conditions that existed at the end of the reporting period (adjusting events after the reporting period); and	
	(b) those that are indicative of conditions that arose after the reporting period (non-adjusting events after the reporting period).	
exchange difference	The difference resulting from translating a given number of units of one currency into another currency at different exchange rates.	IAS 21.8
exchange rate	The ratio of exchange for two currencies.	IAS 21.8
exit price	The price that would be received to sell an asset or paid to transfer a liability.	IFRS 13.A

expected cash flows	The probability-weighed average (ie mean of the distribution) of possible future cash flows.	IFRS 13.A
expenses	Decreases in economic benefits during the accounting period in the form of outflows or depletions of assets or incurrences of liabilities that result in decreases in equity, other than those relating to distributions to equity participants.	CF.4.25(b)
experience adjustments	The effects of differences between previous actuarial assumptions and what has actually occurred.	IAS 19.8
exploration and evaluation assets	Exploration and evaluation expenditures recognised as assets in accordance with the entity's accounting policy.	IFRS 6.A
exploration and evaluation expenditures	Expenditures incurred by an entity in connection with the exploration for and evaluation of mineral resources before the technical feasibility and commercial viability of extracting a mineral resource are demonstrable.	IFRS 6.A
exploration for and evaluation of mineral resources	The search for mineral resources, including minerals, oil, natural gas and similar non-regenerative resources after the entity has obtained legal rights to explore in a specific area, as well as the determination of the technical feasibility and commercial viability of extracting the mineral resource.	IFRS 6.A
fair value	The price that would be received to sell an asset or paid to transfer a liability in an orderly transaction between market participants at the measurement date.	IAS 2.6, (IAS 16.6), IAS 17.8, IAS 18.7, (IAS 19.7), (IAS 20.3), IAS 21.8, IAS 32.11, (IAS 36.6), (IAS 38.8), (IAS 40.5), IAS 41.8, IFRS 1.A, IFRS 3.A, IFRS 4.A, IFRS 5.A, IFRS 9.A, IFRS 13.A

fair value	The amount for which an asset could be exchanged, a liability settled, or an equity instrument granted could be exchanged, between knowledgeable, willing parties in an arm's length transaction.	IFRS 2.A
fair value less costs to sell	The amount obtainable from the sale of an asset or cash-generating unit in an arm's length transaction between knowledgeable, willing parties, less the costs of disposal.	IAS 36.6
finance lease	A lease that transfers substantially all the risks and rewards incidental to ownership of an asset. Title may or may not eventually be transferred.	IAS 17.4

financial asset   Any asset that is: IAS 32.11

(a)   cash;

(b)   an equity instrument of another entity;

(c)   a contractual right:

(i)   to receive cash or another financial asset from another entity; or

(ii)   to exchange financial assets or financial liabilities with another entity under conditions that are potentially favourable to the entity; or

(d)   a contract that will or may be settled in the entity's own equity instruments and is:

(i)   a non-derivative for which the entity is or may be obliged to receive a variable number of the entity's own equity instruments; or

(ii)   a derivative that will or may be settled other than by the exchange of a fixed amount of cash or another financial asset for a fixed number of the entity's own equity instruments. For this purpose the entity's own equity instruments do not include puttable financial instruments classified as equity instruments in accordance with paragraphs 16A and 16B of IAS 32, instruments that impose on the entity an obligation to deliver to another party a pro rata share of the net assets of the entity only on liquidation and are classified as equity instruments in accordance with paragraphs 16C and 16D of IAS 32, or instruments that are contracts for the future receipt or delivery of the entity's own equity instruments.

financial asset or financial liability held for trading	A financial asset or financial liability that:	IFRS 9.A

(a) is acquired or incurred principally for the purpose of selling or repurchasing it in the near term;

(b) on initial recognition is part of a portfolio of identified financial instruments that are managed together and for which there is evidence of a recent actual pattern of short-term profit-taking; or

(c) is a derivative (except for a derivative that is a financial guarantee contract or a designated and effective hedging instrument).

financial guarantee contract	A contract that requires the issuer to make specified payments to reimburse the holder for a loss it incurs because a specified debtor fails to make payment when due in accordance with the original or modified terms of a debt instrument.	IFRS 4.A, IFRS 9.A
financial instrument	Any contract that gives rise to a financial asset of one entity and a financial liability or equity instrument of another entity.	IAS 32.11

financial liability   Any liability that is: IAS 32.11

    (a)   a contractual obligation:

        (i)   to deliver cash or another financial asset to another entity; or

        (ii)   to exchange financial assets or financial liabilities with another entity under conditions that are potentially unfavourable to the entity; or

    (b)   a contract that will or may be settled in the entity's own equity instruments and is:

        (i)   a non-derivative for which the entity is or may be obliged to deliver a variable number of the entity's own equity instruments; or

        (ii)   a derivative that will or may be settled other than by the exchange of a fixed amount of cash or another financial asset for a fixed number of the entity's own equity instruments. For this purpose, rights, options or warrants to acquire a fixed number of the entity's own equity instruments for a fixed amount of any currency are equity instruments if the entity offers the rights, options or warrants pro rata to all of its existing owners of the same class of its own non-derivative equity instruments. Also, for these purposes the entity's own equity instruments do not include puttable financial instruments that are classified as equity instruments in accordance with paragraphs 16A and 16B of IAS 32, instruments that impose on the entity an obligation to deliver to another party a pro rata share of the net assets of the entity only on liquidation and are classified as equity instruments in accordance with paragraphs 16C and 16D of IAS 32, or instruments that are contracts for the future receipt or delivery of the entity's own equity instruments.

As an exception, an instrument that meets the definition of a financial liability is classified as an equity instrument if it has all the features and meets the conditions in paragraphs 16A and 16B or paragraphs 16C and 16D of IAS 32.

financial liability at fair value through profit or loss	A financial liability that meets either of the following conditions.	IFRS 9.A

(a) It meets the definition of held for trading.

(b) Upon initial recognition it is designated by the entity as at fair value through profit or loss. An entity may use this designation only when permitted by IFRS 9 paragraph 4.3.5 (embedded derivatives) or when doing so results in more relevant information, because either

    (i) it eliminates or significantly reduces a measurement or recognition inconsistency (sometimes referred to as 'an accounting mismatch') that would otherwise arise from measuring assets or liabilities or recognising the gains and losses on them on different bases; or

    (ii) a group of financial liabilities or financial assets and financial liabilities is managed and its performance is evaluated on a fair value basis, in accordance with a documented risk management or investment strategy, and information about the group is provided internally on that basis to the entity's key management personnel (as defined in IAS 24).

financial risk	The risk of a possible future change in one or more of a specified interest rate, financial instrument price, commodity price, foreign exchange rate, index of prices or rates, credit rating or credit index or other variable, provided in the case of a non-financial variable that the variable is not specific to a party to the contract.	IFRS 4.A
financing activities	Activities that result in changes in the size and composition of the contributed equity and borrowings of the entity.	IAS 7.6
firm commitment	A binding agreement for the exchange of a specified quantity of resources at a specified price on a specified future date or dates.	IAS 39.9

firm purchase commitment	An agreement with an unrelated party, binding on both parties and usually legally enforceable, that (a) specifies all significant terms, including the price and timing of the transactions, and (b) includes a disincentive for non-performance that is sufficiently large to make performance highly probable.	IFRS 5.A
first IFRS financial statements	The first annual financial statements in which an entity adopts International Financial Reporting Standards (IFRSs), by an explicit and unreserved statement of compliance with IFRSs.	IFRS 1.A
first IFRS reporting period	The latest reporting period covered by an entity's first IFRS financial statements.	IFRS 1.A
first-time adopter	An entity that presents its first IFRS financial statements.	IFRS 1.A
fixed price contract	A construction contract in which the contractor agrees to a fixed contract price, or a fixed rate per unit of output, which in some cases is subject to cost escalation clauses.	IAS 11.3
forecast transaction	An uncommitted but anticipated future transaction.	IAS 39.9
foreign currency	A currency other than the functional currency of the entity.	IAS 21.8
foreign currency transaction	A transaction that is denominated in or requires settlement in a foreign currency.	IAS 21.20
foreign operation	An entity that is a subsidiary, associate, joint venture or branch of the reporting entity, the activities of which are based or conducted in a country or currency other than those of the reporting entity.	IAS 21.8
forgivable loans	Loans which the lender undertakes to waive repayment of under certain prescribed conditions.	IAS 20.3
functional currency	The currency of the primary economic environment in which the entity operates.	IAS 21.8
funding (of retirement benefits)	The transfer of assets to an entity (the fund) separate from the employer's entity to meet future obligations for the payment of retirement benefits.	IAS 26.8
general purpose financial statements	Financial statements that are intended to meet the needs of users who are not in a position to require an entity to prepare reports tailored to their particular information needs.	IAS 1.7

goodwill	An asset representing the future economic benefits arising from other assets acquired in a **business combination** that are not individually identified and separately recognised.	IFRS 3.A
government	Government, government agencies and similar bodies whether local, national or international.	IAS 20.3, IAS 24.9
government assistance	Action by government designed to provide an economic benefit specific to an entity or range of entities qualifying under certain criteria.	IAS 20.3
government grants	Assistance by government in the form of transfers of resources to an entity in return for past or future compliance with certain conditions relating to the operating activities of the entity. They exclude those forms of government assistance which cannot reasonably have a value placed upon them and transactions with government which cannot be distinguished from the normal trading transactions of the entity.	IAS 20.3
government-related entity	An entity that is controlled, jointly controlled or significantly influenced by a government.	IAS 24.9
grant date	The date at which the entity and another party (including an employee) agree to a share-based payment arrangement, being when the entity and the counterparty have a shared understanding of the terms and conditions of the arrangement. At grant date the entity confers on the counterparty the right to cash, other assets, or equity instruments of the entity, provided the specified vesting conditions, if any, are met. If that agreement is subject to an approval process (for example, by shareholders), grant date is the date when that approval is obtained.	IFRS 2.A
grants related to assets	Government grants whose primary condition is that an entity qualifying for them should purchase, construct or otherwise acquire long-term assets. Subsidiary conditions may also be attached restricting the type or location of the assets or the periods during which they are to be acquired or held.	IAS 20.3
grants related to income	Government grants other than those related to assets.	IAS 20.3

gross investment in the lease	The aggregate of: (a) the minimum lease payments receivable by the lessor under a finance lease, and (b) any unguaranteed residual value accruing to the lessor.	IAS 17.4
group	A parent and all its subsidiaries.	IAS 21.8
group	A parent and its subsidiaries.	IFRS 10.A
group of biological assets	An aggregation of similar living animals or plants.	IAS 41.5
guaranteed benefits	Payments or other benefits to which a particular policyholder or investor has an unconditional right that is not subject to the contractual discretion of the issuer.	IFRS 4.A
guaranteed element	An obligation to pay guaranteed benefits, included in a contract that contains a discretionary participation feature.	IFRS 4.A
guaranteed residual value	(a) For a lessee, that part of the residual value that is guaranteed by the lessee or by a party related to the lessee (the amount of the guarantee being the maximum amount that could, in any event, become payable); and (b) for a lessor, that part of the residual value that is guaranteed by the lessee or by a third party unrelated to the lessor that is financially capable of discharging the obligations under the guarantee.	IAS 17.4
harvest	The detachment of produce from a biological asset or the cessation of a biological asset's life processes.	IAS 41.5
hedge effectiveness	The degree to which changes in the fair value or cash flows of the hedged item that are attributable to a hedged risk are offset by changes in the fair value or cash flows of the hedging instrument (see IAS 39 paragraphs AG105–AG113).	IAS 39.9
hedged item	An asset, liability, firm commitment, highly probable forecast transaction or net investment in a foreign operation that (a) exposes the entity to risk of changes in fair value or future cash flows and (b) is designated as being hedged (IAS 39 paragraphs 78–84 and AG98–AG101 elaborate on the definition of hedged items).	IAS 39.9

hedging instrument	A designated derivative or (for a hedge of the risk of changes in foreign currency exchange rates only) a designated non-derivative financial asset or non-derivative financial liability whose fair value or cash flows are expected to offset changes in the fair value or cash flows of a designated hedged item (IAS 39 paragraphs 72–77 and AG94–AG97 elaborate on the definition of a hedging instrument).	IAS 39.9
held for trading	See 'financial asset or financial liability held for trading.'	IFRS 9.A
highest and best use	The use of a non-financial asset by market participants that would maximise the value of the asset or the group of assets and liabilities (eg a business) within which the asset would be used.	IFRS 13.A
highly probable	Significantly more likely than probable.	IFRS 5.A
hire purchase contract	The definition of a lease includes contracts for the hire of an asset that contain a provision giving the hirer an option to acquire title to the asset upon the fulfilment of agreed conditions. These contracts are sometimes known as hire purchase contracts.	IAS 17.6

| **hyperinflation** | Loss of purchasing power of money at such a rate that comparison of amounts from transactions and other events that have occurred at different times, even within the same accounting period, is misleading. | IAS 29.2–3 |

Hyperinflation is indicated by characteristics of the economic environment of a country which include, but are not limited to, the following:

(a)   the general population prefers to keep its wealth in non-monetary assets or in a relatively stable foreign currency. Amounts of local currency held are immediately invested to maintain purchasing power.

(b)   the general population regards monetary amounts not in terms of the local currency but in terms of a relatively stable foreign currency. Prices may be quoted in that currency.

(c)   sales and purchases on credit take place at prices that compensate for the expected loss of purchasing power during the credit period, even if the period is short.

(d)   interest rates, wages and prices are linked to a price index.

(e)   the cumulative inflation rate over three years is approaching, or exceeds, 100%.

| **identifiable** | An asset is identifiable if it either: | IFRS 3.A |

(a)   is separable, ie capable of being separated or divided from the entity and sold, transferred, licensed, rented or exchanged, either individually or together with a related contract, identifiable asset or liability, regardless of whether the entity intends to do so; or

(b)   arises from contractual or other legal rights, regardless of whether those rights are transferable or separable from the entity or from other rights and obligations.

| **impairment loss** | The amount by which the carrying amount of an asset exceeds its recoverable amount. | IAS 16.6, (IAS 36.6), IAS 38.8 |

impracticable	Applying a requirement is impracticable when the entity cannot apply it after making every reasonable effort to do so.	IAS 1.7, (IAS 8.5)
inception of a lease	The earlier of the date of the lease agreement and the date of commitment by the parties to the principal provisions of the lease.	IAS 17.4
income approach	Valuation techniques that convert future amounts (eg cash flows or income and expenses) to a single current (eg discounted) amount. The fair value measurement is determined on the basis of the value indicated by current market expectations about those future amounts.	IFRS 13.A
income from a structured entity	For the purpose of IFRS 12, income from a structured entity includes, but is not limited to, recurring and non-recurring fees, interest, dividends, gains or losses on the remeasurement or derecognition of interests in structured entities and gains or losses from the transfer of assets and liabilities to the structured entity.	IFRS 12.A
incremental borrowing rate of interest (lessee's)	The rate of interest the lessee would have to pay on a similar lease or, if that is not determinable, the rate that, at the inception of the lease, the lessee would incur to borrow over a similar term, and with a similar security, the funds necessary to purchase the asset.	IAS 17.4
initial direct costs	Incremental costs that are directly attributable to negotiating and arranging a lease, except for such costs incurred by manufacturer or dealer lessors.	IAS 17.4
inputs	The assumptions that market participants would use when pricing the asset or liability, including assumptions about risk, such as the following:	IFRS 13.A

inputs (continued):

(a) the risk inherent in a particular valuation technique used to measure fair value (such as pricing model); and

(b) the risk inherent in the inputs to the valuation technique.

Inputs may be observable or unobservable.

insurance asset	An insurer's net contractual rights under an insurance contract.	IFRS 4.A

insurance contract	A contract under which one party (the insurer) accepts significant insurance risk from another party (the policyholder) by agreeing to compensate the policyholder if a specified uncertain future event (the insured event) adversely affects the policyholder. (See IFRS 4 Appendix B for guidance on this definition.)	IFRS 4.A
insurance liability	An insurer's net contractual obligations under an insurance contract.	IFRS 4.A
insurance risk	Risk, other than financial risk, transferred from the holder of a contract to the issuer.	IFRS 4.A
insured event	An uncertain future event that is covered by an insurance contract and creates insurance risk.	IFRS 4.A
insurer	The party that has an obligation under an insurance contract to compensate a policyholder if an insured event occurs.	IFRS 4.A
intangible asset	An identifiable non-monetary asset without physical substance.	IAS 38.8, IFRS 3.A
interest in another entity	For the purpose of IFRS 12, an interest in another entity refers to contractual and non-contractual involvement that exposes an entity to variability of returns from the performance of the other entity. An interest in another entity can be evidenced by, but is not limited to, the holding of equity or debt instruments as well as other forms of involvement such as the provision of funding, liquidity support, credit enhancement and guarantees. It includes the means by which an entity has control or joint control of, or significant influence over, another entity. An entity does not necessarily have an interest in another entity solely because of a typical customer supplier relationship.	IFRS 12.A
	Paragraphs B7–B9 of IFRS 12 provide further information about interests in other entities.	
	Paragraphs B55–B57 of IFRS 10 explain variability of returns.	
interest rate implicit in the lease	The discount rate that, at the inception of the lease, causes the aggregate present value of (a) the minimum lease payments and (b) the unguaranteed residual value to be equal to the sum of (i) the fair value of the leased asset and (ii) any initial direct costs of the lessor.	IAS 17.4

interest rate risk	The risk that the fair value or future cash flows of a financial instrument will fluctuate because of changes in market interest rates.	IFRS 7.A
interim financial report	A financial report containing either a complete set of financial statements (as described in IAS 1) or a set of condensed financial statements (as described in IAS 34) for an interim period.	IAS 34.4
interim period	A financial reporting period shorter than a full financial year.	IAS 34.4
International Financial Reporting Standards (IFRSs)	Standards and Interpretations issued by the International Accounting Standards Board. They comprise:	IAS 1.7, IAS 8.5, IFRS 1.A

(a)   International Financial Reporting Standards;

(b)   International Accounting Standards;

(c)   IFRIC Interpretations; and

(d)   SIC Interpretations.

intrinsic value	The difference between the fair value of the shares to which the counterparty has the (conditional or unconditional) right to subscribe or which it has the right to receive, and the price (if any) the counterparty is (or will be) required to pay for those shares. For example, a share option with an exercise price of CU15,[3] on a share with a fair value of CU20, has an intrinsic value of CU5.	IFRS 2.A

---

3 Monetary items are denominated in 'currency units (CU)'.

inventories	Assets:	IAS 2.6, IAS 2.8
	(a) held for sale in the ordinary course of business;	
	(b) in the process of production for such sale; or	
	(c) in the form of materials or supplies to be consumed in the production process or in the rendering of services.	
	Inventories encompass goods purchased and held for resale including, for example, merchandise purchased by a retailer and held for resale, or land and other property held for resale. Inventories also encompass finished goods produced, or work in progress being produced, by the entity and include materials and supplies awaiting use in the production process. In the case of a service provider, inventories include the costs of the service, as described in IAS 2 paragraph 19, for which the entity has not yet recognised the related revenue (see IAS 18).	
investing activities	The acquisition and disposal of long-term assets and other investments not included in cash equivalents.	IAS 7.6
investment property	Property (land or a building—or part of a building—or both) held (by the owner or by the lessee under a finance lease) to earn rentals or for capital appreciation or both, rather than for:	IAS 40.5
	(a) use in the production or supply of goods or services or for administrative purposes; or	
	(b) sale in the ordinary course of business.	
joint arrangement	An arrangement of which two or more parties have joint control.	IAS 28.3, IFRS 11.A
joint control	The contractually agreed sharing of control over an economic activity.	IAS 24.9
joint control	The contractually agreed sharing of control of an arrangement, which exists only when decisions about the relevant activities require the unanimous consent of the parties sharing control.	IAS 28.3, IFRS 11.A
joint operation	A joint arrangement whereby the parties that have joint control of the arrangement have rights to the assets, and obligations for the liabilities, relating to the arrangement.	IFRS 11.A

joint operator	A party to a joint operation that has joint control of that joint operation.	IFRS 11.A
joint venture	A joint arrangement whereby the parties that have joint control of the arrangement have rights to the net assets off the arrangement.	IAS 28.3, IFRS 11.A
joint venturer	A party to a joint venture that has joint control of the joint venture.	IAS 28.3, IFRS 11.A
key management personnel	Those persons having authority and responsibility for planning, directing and controlling the activities of the entity, directly or indirectly, including any director (whether executive or otherwise) of that entity.	IAS 24.9
lease	An agreement whereby the lessor conveys to the lessee in return for a payment or series of payments the right to use an asset for an agreed period of time.	IAS 17.4
lease term	The non-cancellable period for which the lessee has contracted to lease the asset together with any further terms for which the lessee has the option to continue to lease the asset, with or without further payment, when at the inception of the lease it is reasonably certain that the lessee will exercise the option.	IAS 17.4
legal obligation	An obligation that derives from: (a) a contract (through its explicit or implicit terms); (b) legislation; or (c) other operation of law.	IAS 37.10
lessee's incremental borrowing rate of interest	The rate of interest the lessee would have to pay on a similar lease or, if that is not determinable, the rate that, at the inception of the lease, the lessee would incur to borrow over a similar term, and with a similar security, the funds necessary to purchase the asset.	IAS 17.4
Level 1 inputs	Quoted prices (unadjusted) in active markets for identical assets or liabilities that the entity can access at the measurement date.	IFRS 13.A
Level 2 inputs	Inputs other than quoted prices included within Level 1 that are observable for the asset or liability, either directly or indirectly.	IFRS 13.A
Level 3 inputs	Unobservable inputs for the asset or liability.	IFRS 13.A

liability	A present obligation of the entity arising from past events, the settlement of which is expected to result in an outflow from the entity of resources embodying economic benefits.	IAS 37.10, CF.4.4(b)
liability adequacy test	An assessment of whether the carrying amount of an insurance liability needs to be increased (or the carrying amount of related deferred acquisition costs or related intangible assets decreased), based on a review of future cash flows.	IFRS 4.A
liquidity risk	The risk that an entity will encounter difficulty in meeting obligations associated with financial liabilities that are settled by delivering cash or another financial asset.	IFRS 7.A
loans payable	Financial liabilities other than short-term trade payables on normal credit terms.	IFRS 7.A
losses	Decreases in economic benefits and as such no different in nature from other expenses.	CF.4.35
market approach	A valuation technique that uses prices and other relevant information generated by market transactions involving identical or comparable (ie similar) assets, liabilities or a group of assets and liabilities, such as a business.	IFRS 13.A
market condition	A condition upon which the exercise price, vesting or exercisability of an equity instrument depends that is related to the market price of the entity's equity instruments, such as attaining a specified share price or a specified amount of intrinsic value of a share option, or achieving a specified target that is based on the market price of the entity's equity instruments relative to an index of market prices of equity instruments of other entities.	IFRS 2.A
market-corroborated inputs	Inputs that are derived principally from or corroborated by observable market data by correlation or other means.	IFRS 13.A
market risk	The risk that the fair value or future cash flows of a financial instrument will fluctuate because of changes in market prices. Market risk comprises three types of risk: currency risk, interest rate risk and other price risk.	IFRS 7.A

material	Omissions or misstatements of items are material if they could, individually or collectively, influence the economic decisions that users make on the basis of the financial statements. Materiality depends on the size and nature of the omission or misstatement judged in the surrounding circumstances. The size or nature of the item, or a combination of both, could be the determining factor.	IAS 1.7, IAS 8.5
measurement	The process of determining the monetary amounts at which the elements of the financial statements are to be recognised and carried in the balance sheet [statement of financial position] and income statement [statement of comprehensive income].	CF.4.54
measurement date	The date at which the fair value of the equity instruments granted is measured for the purposes of IFRS 2. For transactions with employees and others providing similar services, the measurement date is grant date. For transactions with parties other than employees (and those providing similar services), the measurement date is the date the entity obtains the goods or the counterparty renders service.	IFRS 2.A
minimum lease payments	The payments over the lease term that the lessee is or can be required to make, excluding contingent rent, costs for services and taxes to be paid by and reimbursed to the lessor, together with:	IAS 17.4

(a) for a lessee, any amounts guaranteed by the lessee or by a party related to the lessee; or

(b) for a lessor, any residual value guaranteed to the lessor by:

    (i) the lessee;

    (ii) a party related to the lessee; or

    (iii) a third party unrelated to the lessor that is financially capable of discharging the obligations under the guarantee.

minority interest	See 'non-controlling interest'.	
monetary assets	Money held and assets to be received in fixed or determinable amounts of money.	IAS 38.8
monetary items	Units of currency held and assets and liabilities to be received or paid in a fixed or determinable number of units of currency.	IAS 21.8
monetary items	Money held and items to be received or paid in money.	IAS 29.12

multi-employer (benefit) plans	Defined contribution plans (other than state plans) or defined benefit plans (other than state plans) that:	IAS 19.8
	(a) pool the assets contributed by various entities that are not under common control; and	
	(b) use those assets to provide benefits to employees of more than one entity, on the basis that contribution and benefit levels are determined without regard to the identity of the entity that employs the employees concerned.	
mutual entity	An entity, other than an investor-owned entity, that provides dividends, lower costs or other economic benefits directly to its owners, members or participants. For example, a mutual insurance company, a credit union and a co-operative entity are all mutual entities.	IFRS 3.A
net assets available for benefits	The assets of a plan less liabilities other than the actuarial present value of promised retirement benefits.	IAS 26.8
net defined benefit liability (asset)	The deficit or surplus, adjusted for any effects of limiting a net defined benefit assets to the asset ceiling.	IAS 19.8
net interest on the net defined benefit liability (asset)	The change during the period in the net defined benefit liability (asset) that arises from the passage of time.	IAS 19.8
net investment in a foreign operation	The amount of the reporting entity's interest in the net assets of that operation.	IAS 21.8
net investment in the lease	The gross investment in the lease discounted at the interest rate implicit in the lease.	IAS 17.4
net realisable value	The estimated selling price in the ordinary course of business less the estimated costs of completion and the estimated costs necessary to make the sale.	IAS 2.6–7
	Net realisable value refers to the net amount that an entity expects to realise from the sale of inventory in the ordinary course of business. Fair value reflects the amount for which the same inventory could be exchanged between knowledgeable and willing buyers and sellers in the marketplace. The former is an entity specific value; the latter is not. Net realisable value for inventories may not equal fair value less costs to sell.	

non-adjusting events after the reporting period	See 'events after the reporting period'.	
non-cancellable lease	A lease that is cancellable only:	IAS 17.4
	(a) upon the occurrence of some remote contingency;	
	(b) with the permission of the lessor;	
	(c) if the lessee enters into a new lease for the same or an equivalent asset with the same lessor; or	
	(d) upon payment by the lessee of such an additional amount that, at inception of the lease, continuation of the lease is reasonably certain.	
non-controlling interest	Equity in a subsidiary not attributable, directly or indirectly, to a parent.	IFRS 3.A, IFRS 10.A
non-current asset	An asset that does not meet the definition of a current asset.	IFRS 5.A
notes	Notes contain information in addition to that presented in the statement of financial position, statement of comprehensive income, separate income statement (if presented), statement of changes in equity and statement of cash flows. Notes provide narrative descriptions or disaggregations of items presented in those statements and information about items that do not qualify for recognition in those statements.	IAS 1.7
obligating event	An event that creates a legal or constructive obligation that results in an entity having no realistic alternative to settling that obligation.	IAS 37.10
offsetting	See 'set off, legal right of'.	
onerous contract	A contract in which the unavoidable costs of meeting the obligations under the contract exceed the economic benefits expected to be received under it.	IAS 37.10
opening IFRS statement of financial position	An entity's statement of financial position at the date of transition to IFRSs.	IFRS 1.A
operating activities	The principal revenue producing activities of an entity and other activities that are not investing or financing activities.	IAS 7.6

operating lease	A lease other than a finance lease.	IAS 17.4
operating segment	An operating segment is a component of an entity:	IFRS 8

    (a)   that engages in business activities from which it may earn revenues and incur expenses (including revenues and expenses relating to transactions with other components of the same entity),

    (b)   whose operating results are regularly reviewed by the entity's chief operating decision maker to make decisions about resources to be allocated to the segment and assess its performance, and

    (c)   for which discrete financial information is available.

options, warrants and their equivalents	Financial instruments that give the holder the right to purchase ordinary shares.	IAS 33.5
ordinary equity holders	Holders of ordinary shares.	IAS 33.5–9
ordinary share	An equity instrument that is subordinate to all other classes of equity instruments.	IAS 33.5
originated loans and shares	See 'loans and receivables'.	
other comprehensive income	Items of income and expense (including reclassification adjustments) that are not recognised in profit or loss as required or permitted by other IFRSs.	IAS 1.7
other long-term employee benefits	All employee benefits other than short-term employee benefits, post-employment benefits and termination benefits.	IAS 19.8
other price risk	The risk that the fair value or future cash flows of a financial instrument will fluctuate because of changes in market prices (other than those arising from interest rate risk or currency risk), whether those changes are caused by factors specific to the individual financial instrument or its issuer, or factors affecting all similar financial instruments traded in the market.	IFRS 7.A
owner-occupied property	Property held (by the owner or by the lessee under a finance lease) for use in the production or supply of goods or services or for administrative purposes.	IAS 40.5

owners	Holders of instruments classified as equity.	IAS 1.7
owners	In IFRS 3 owners is used broadly to include holders of equity interests of investor-owned entities and owners or members of, or participants in, mutual entities.	IFRS 3.A
parent	An entity that controls one or more entities.	IFRS 10.A
participants	The members of a retirement benefit plan and others who are entitled to benefits under the plan.	IAS 26.8
party to a joint arrangement	An entity that participates in a joint arrangement, regardless of whether that entity has joint control of the arrangement.	IFRS 11.A
past due	A financial asset is past due when a counterparty has failed to make a payment when contractually due.	IFRS 7.A
past service cost	The change in the present value of the defined benefit obligation for employee service in prior periods, resulting from a plan amendment (the introduction or withdrawal of, or change to, a defined benefit plan) or a curtailment (a significant reduction by the entity in the number of employees covered by a plan).	IAS 19.8
plan assets (of an employee benefit plan)	(a) Assets held by a long-term employee benefit fund; and (b) qualifying insurance policies.	IAS 19.8
policyholder	A party that has a right to compensation under an insurance contract if an insured event occurs.	IFRS 4.A
post-employment benefits	Employee benefits (other than termination benefits and short-term employee benefits) that are payable after the completion of employment.	IAS 19.8
post-employment benefit plans	Formal or informal arrangements under which an entity provides post-employment benefits for one or more employees.	IAS 19.8
potential ordinary share	A financial instrument or other contract that may entitle its holder to ordinary shares.	IAS 33.5
power	Existing rights that give the current ability to direct the relevant activities.	IFRS 10.A
presentation currency	The currency in which the financial statements are presented.	IAS 21.8

present value of a defined benefit obligation	The present value, without deducting any plan assets, of expected future payments required to settle the obligation resulting from employee service in the current and prior periods.	IAS 19.8
previous GAAP	The basis of accounting that a first-time adopter used immediately before adopting IFRSs.	IFRS 1.A
prior period errors	Omissions from, and misstatements in, the entity's financial statements for one or more prior periods arising from a failure to use, or misuse of, reliable information that:	IAS 8.5

(a) was available when financial statements for those periods were authorised for issue; and

(b) could reasonably be expected to have been obtained and taken into account in the preparation and presentation of those financial statements.

Such errors include the effects of mathematical mistakes, mistakes in applying accounting policies, oversights or misinterpretations of facts, and fraud.

probable	More likely than not.	IFRS 5.A, (IAS 37.23)
profit or loss	The total of income less expenses, excluding the components of other comprehensive income.	IAS 1.7
property, plant and equipment	Tangible items that:	IAS 16.6

(a) are held for use in the production or supply of goods or services, for rental to others, or for administrative purposes; and

(b) are expected to be used during more than one period.

prospective application	Prospective application of a change in accounting policy and of recognising the effect of a change in an accounting estimate, respectively, are:	IAS 8.5

(a) applying the new accounting policy to transactions, other events and conditions occurring after the date as at which the policy is changed; and

(b) recognising the effect of the change in the accounting estimate in the current and future periods affected by the change.

protective rights	Rights designed to protect the interest of the party holding those rights without giving that party power over the entity to which those rights relate.	IFRS 10.A
provision	A liability of uncertain timing or amount.	IAS 37.10
put options (on ordinary shares)	Contracts that give the holder the right to sell ordinary shares at a specified price for a given period.	IAS 33.5
puttable instrument	A financial instrument that gives the holder the right to put the instrument back to the issuer for cash or another financial asset or is automatically put back to the issuer on the occurrence of an uncertain future event or the death or retirement of the instrument holder.	IAS 32.11
qualifying asset	An asset that necessarily takes a substantial period of time to get ready for its intended use or sale.	IAS 23.5
qualifying insurance policy	An insurance policy issued by an insurer that is not a related party (as defined in IAS 24) of the reporting entity, if the proceeds of the policy:	IAS 19.8

    (a)   can be used only to pay or fund employee benefits under a defined benefit plan;

    (b)   are not available to the reporting entity's own creditors (even in bankruptcy) and cannot be paid to the reporting entity, unless either:

        (i)   the proceeds represent surplus assets that are not needed for the policy to meet all the related employee benefit obligations; or

        (ii)   the proceeds are returned to the reporting entity to reimburse it for employee benefits already paid.

realisable value	The amount of cash or cash equivalents that could currently be obtained by selling an asset in an orderly disposal.	CF.4.55(c)
reclassification adjustments	Amounts reclassified to profit or loss in the current period that were recognised in other comprehensive income in the current or previous periods.	IAS 1.7
reclassification date	The first day of the first reporting period following the change in business model that results in an entity reclassifying financial assets.	IFRS 9.A

recoverable amount	The higher of an asset's (or cash generating unit's) fair value less costs to sell and its value in use.	IAS 16.6, IAS 36.6, IFRS 5.A
regular way purchase or sale	A purchase or sale of a financial asset under a contract whose terms require delivery of the asset within the time frame established generally by regulation or convention in the marketplace concerned.	IFRS 9.A
reinsurance assets	A cedant's net contractual rights under a reinsurance contract.	IFRS 4.A
reinsurance contract	An insurance contract issued by one insurer (the reinsurer) to compensate another insurer (the cedant) for losses on one or more contracts issued by the cedant.	IFRS 4.A
reinsurer	The party that has an obligation under a reinsurance contract to compensate a cedant if an insured event occurs.	IFRS 4.A

related party	A person or entity that is related to the entity that is preparing its financial statements (in IAS 24 referred to as the 'reporting entity').	IAS 24.9

(a) A person or a close member of that person's family is related to a reporting entity if that person:

    (i) has control or joint control over the reporting entity;

    (ii) has significant influence over the reporting entity; or

    (iii) is a member of the key management personnel of the reporting entity or of a parent of the reporting entity.

(b) An entity is related to a reporting entity if any of the following conditions applies:

    (i) The entity and the reporting entity are members of the same group (which means that each parent, subsidiary and fellow subsidiary is related to the others).

    (ii) One entity is an associate or joint venture of the other entity (or an associate or joint venture of a member of a group of which the other entity is a member).

    (iii) Both entities are joint ventures of the same third party.

    (iv) One entity is a joint venture of a third entity and the other entity is an associate of the third entity.

    (v) The entity is a post-employment benefit plan for the benefit of employees of either the reporting entity or an entity related to the reporting entity. If the reporting entity is itself such a plan, the sponsoring employers are also related to the reporting entity.

    (vi) The entity is controlled or jointly controlled by a person identified in (a).

    (vii) A person identified in (a)(i) has significant influence over the entity or is a member of the key management personnel of the entity (or of a parent of the entity).

related party transaction	A transfer of resources, services or obligations between a reporting entity and a related party, regardless of whether a price is charged.	IAS 24.9
relevant activities	For the purpose of IFRS 10, relevant activities are activities of the investee that significantly affect the investee's returns.	IFRS 10.A
reload feature	A feature that provides for an automatic grant of additional share options whenever the option holder exercises previously granted options using the entity's shares, rather than cash, to satisfy the exercise price.	IFRS 2.A
reload option	A new share option granted when a share is used to satisfy the exercise price of a previous share option.	IFRS 2.A
remeasurement of the net defined benefit liability (asset)	Comprises: (a) actuarial gains and losses; (b) the return on plan assets, excluding amounts included in net interest on the net defined benefit liability (asset); and (c) any change in the effect of the asset ceiling, excluding amounts included in net interest on the net defined benefit liability (asset).	IAS 19.8
removal rights	Rights to deprive the decisions maker of its decision-making authority.	IFRS 10.A
reportable segment	An operating segment for which IFRS 8 requires information to be disclosed.	IFRS 8.11
research	Original and planned investigation undertaken with the prospect of gaining new scientific or technical knowledge and understanding.	IAS 38.8
residual value (of an asset)	The estimated amount that an entity would currently obtain from disposal of an asset, after deducting the estimated costs of disposal, if the asset were already of the age and in the condition expected at the end of its useful life.	IAS 16.6, (IAS 38.8)
restructuring	A programme that is planned and controlled by management, and materially changes either: (a) the scope of a business undertaken by an entity; or (b) the manner in which that business is conducted.	IAS 37.10

retirement benefit plans	Arrangements whereby an entity provides benefits for its employees on or after termination of service (either in the form of an annual income or as a lump sum) when such benefits, or the employer's contributions towards them, can be determined or estimated in advance of retirement from the provisions of a document or from the entity's practices. (See also 'post-employment benefit plans'.)	IAS 26.8
retrospective application	Applying a new accounting policy to transactions, other events and conditions as if that policy had always been applied.	IAS 8.5
retrospective restatement	Correcting the recognition, measurement and disclosure of amounts of elements of financial statements as if a prior period error had never occurred.	IAS 8.5
return on plan assets (of an employee benefit plan)	Interest, dividends and other revenue derived from the plan assets, together with realised and unrealised gains or losses on the plan assets, less: (a) any cost of managing plan assets; and (b) any tax payable by the plan itself, other than tax included in the actuarial assumptions used to measure the present value of the defined benefit obligation.	IAS 19.8
revenue	The gross inflow of economic benefits during the period arising in the course of the ordinary activities of an entity when those inflows result in increases in equity, other than increases relating to contributions from equity participants.	IAS 18.7
separate financial statements	Those presented by a parent (ie an investor with control of a subsidiary) or an investor with joint control of, or significant influence over, an investee, in which the investments are accounted for at cost or in accordance with IFRS 9.	IAS 27.4
separate vehicle	A separately identifiable financial structure, including separate legal entities or entities recognised by statue, regardless of whether those entities have a legal personality.	IFRS 11.A
service cost	Comprises: (a) current service cost; (b) past service cost; and (c) any gain or loss on settlement.	IAS 19.8

settlement (of employee benefit obligations)	A transaction that eliminates all further legal or constructive obligation for part or all of the benefits provided under a defined benefit plan, other than a payment of benefits to, or on behalf of, employees that is set out in the terms of the plan and included in the actuarial assumptions.	IAS 19.8
settlement date	The date that a financial asset is delivered to or by an entity.	IFRS 9.B3.1.6
share-based payment arrangement	An agreement between the entity or another group[4] entity or any shareholder of the group entity and another party (including an employee) that entitles the other party to receive	IFRS 2.A
	(a) cash or other assets of the entity for amounts that are based on the price (or value) of equity instruments (including shares or share options) of the entity or another group entity, or	
	(b) equity instruments (including shares or share options) of the entity or another group entity,	
	provided the specified vesting conditions, if any, are met.	
share-based payment transaction	A transaction in which the entity	IFRS 2.A
	(a) receives goods or services from the supplier of those goods or services (including an employee) in a share-based payment arrangement, or	
	(b) incurs an obligation to settle the transaction with the supplier in a share-based payment arrangement when another group entity receives those goods or services.	
share option	A contract that gives the holder the right, but not the obligation, to subscribe to the entity's shares at a fixed or determinable price for a specific period of time.	IFRS 2.A
short seller	An entity that sells financial assets that it has borrowed and does not yet own.	IFRS 9.BA.7(b)
short-term employee benefits	Employee benefits (other than termination benefits) that are expected to be settled wholly before twelve months after the end of the annual reporting period in which the employees render the related service.	IAS 19.8

---

4 A 'group' is defined in paragraph 4 of IAS 27 *Consolidated and Separate Financial Statements* as 'a parent and all its subsidiaries' from the perspective of the reporting entity's ultimate parent.

significant influence	The power to participate in the financial and operating policy decisions of an the investee but is not control or joint control of those policies.	IAS 28.3
spot exchange rate	The exchange rate for immediate delivery.	IAS 21.8
structured entity	An entity that has been designed so that voting or similar rights are not the dominant factor in deciding who controls the entity, such as when any voting rights relate to administrative tasks only and the relevant activities are directed by means of contractual arrangements.	IFRS 12.A
	Paragraphs B22–B24 of IFRS 12 provide further information about structured entities.	
subsidiary	An entity that is controlled by another entity.	IFRS 10.A
tax base of an asset or liability	The amount attributed to that asset or liability for tax purposes.	IAS 12.5
tax expense (tax income)	The aggregate amount included in the determination of profit or loss for the period in respect of current tax and deferred tax. Tax expense (tax income) comprises current tax expense (current tax income) and deferred tax expense (deferred tax income).	IAS 12.5, IAS 12.6
taxable profit (tax loss)	The profit (loss) for a period, determined in accordance with the rules established by the taxation authorities, upon which income taxes are payable (recoverable).	IAS 12.5
taxable temporary differences	Temporary differences that will result in taxable amounts in determining taxable profit (tax loss) of future periods when the carrying amount of the asset or liability is recovered or settled.	IAS 12.5
temporary differences	Differences between the carrying amount of an asset or liability in the statement of financial position and its tax base. Temporary differences may be either:	IAS 12.5
	(a) taxable temporary differences; or	
	(b) deductible temporary differences.	

termination benefits	Employee benefits provided in exchange for the termination of an employee's employment as a result of either:	IAS 19.8
	(a) an entity's decision to terminate an employee's employment before the normal retirement date; or	
	(b) an employee's decision to accept an offer of benefits in exchange for the termination of employment.	
total comprehensive income	The change in equity during a period resulting from transactions and other events, other than those changes resulting from transactions with owners in their capacity as owners.	IAS 1.7
trade date	The date that an entity commits itself to purchase or sell an asset.	IFRS 9.B3.15
transaction costs (financial instruments)	Incremental costs that are directly attributable to the acquisition, issue or disposal of a financial asset or financial liability (see IAS 39 paragraph AG13). An incremental cost is one that would not have been incurred if the entity had not acquired, issued or disposed of the financial instrument.	IAS 39.9
unbundle	Account for the components of a contract as if they were separate contracts.	IFRS 4.A
unearned finance income	The difference between:	IAS 17.4
	(a) the gross investment in the lease, and	
	(b) the net investment in the lease.	
unguaranteed residual value	That portion of the residual value of the leased asset, the realisation of which by the lessor is not assured or is guaranteed solely by a party related to the lessor.	IAS 17.4
useful life	The estimated remaining period, from the commencement of the lease term, without limitation by the lease term, over which the economic benefits embodied in the asset are expected to be consumed by the entity.	IAS 17.4

useful life	Either:	IAS 16.6, IAS 36.6, IAS 38.8
	(a) the period over which an asset is expected to be available for use by an entity; or	
	(b) the number of production or similar units expected to be obtained from the asset by the entity.	
value in use	The present value of estimated future cash flows expected to arise from the continuing use of an asset and from its disposal at the end of its useful life.	IFRS 5.A
value in use	The present value of the future cash flows expected to be derived from an asset or cash generating unit.	IAS 36.6
vest	To become an entitlement. Under a share-based payment arrangement, a counterparty's right to receive cash, other assets or equity instruments of the entity vests when the counterparty's entitlement is no longer conditional on the satisfaction of any vesting conditions.	IFRS 2.A
vested benefits	Benefits, the rights to which, under the conditions of a retirement benefit plan, are not conditional on continued employment.	IAS 26.8
vesting conditions	The conditions that determine whether the entity receives the services that entitle the counterparty to receive cash, other assets or equity instruments of the entity, under a share-based payment arrangement. Vesting conditions are either service conditions or performance conditions. Service conditions require the counterparty to complete a specified period of service. Performance conditions require the counterparty to complete a specified period of service and specified performance targets to be met (such as a specified increase in the entity's profit over a specified period of time). A performance condition might include a market condition.	IFRS 2.A
vesting period	The period during which all the specified vesting conditions of a share-based payment arrangement are to be satisfied.	IFRS 2.A
warrant	A financial instrument that gives the holder the right to purchase ordinary shares.	IAS 33.5

Index

The index to this volume is a comprehensive index. It references not only all International Financial Reporting Standards—IFRSs, IASs and Interpretations—but also all related documentation including Bases for Conclusions, implementation guidance and illustrative examples. In addition, it includes references to the IFRS Foundation Constitution, the IASB *Conceptual Framework for Financial Reporting*, the *Preface to IFRSs*, an IFRS Practice Statement and the Due Process Handbooks for the IASB and the IFRS Interpretations Committee.

References to IFRSs, IASs, Interpretations and supporting documentation are by document number and paragraph number. The index uses prefix notations to identify the document to which paragraphs and subparagraphs belong. These prefix notations are as follows:

Section	Prefix	Examples	Reference
International Financial Reporting Standards (IFRSs) 1–9	IF	**IF1**.1—47A **IF3**.3A(c)	IFRS 1, paragraphs 1 to 47A IFRS 3, paragraph 3A subparagraph (c)
International Accounting Standards (IASs) 1–41	no prefix	**12**.26(a) **37**.10	IAS 12, paragraph 26 subparagraph (a) IAS 37, paragraph 10
Basis for Conclusions on IFRSs	BC or BCZ	**IF2**.BC19–22 **IF9**.BCZ5.31(d)	Basis for Conclusions on IFRS 2, paragraphs BC19 to BC22 Basis for Conclusions on IFRS 9, paragraph BCZ5.31 subparagraph (d)
Basis for Conclusions on IASs	B, BC or BCZ	**24**.BC8–14 **36**.BCZ108–112	Basis for Conclusions on IAS 24, paragraphs BC8 to BC14 Basis for Conclusions on IAS 36, paragraphs BCZ108 to BCZ112
Implementation guidance on IFRSs and IASs	IG	**39**.IG Q&A E.4.2 **IF4**.IG6–10	Implementation guidance on IAS 39 Q&A E.4.2, Implementation guidance on IFRS 4, paragraphs IG6 to IG10
Illustrative examples on IFRSs and IASs	IE	**33**.IE1	IAS 33, Illustrative example 1
Application guidance	AG	**32**.AG25–26 **39**.Appendix A AG84–93	Application guidance on IAS 32, paragraphs AG25 to AG26 IAS 39.Appendix A: Application guidance on IAS 39, paragraphs AG84 to AG93
Appendices to IFRSs and IASs	Appendix	**IF1** Appendices A–C **36**.Appendix A4	IFRS 1, Appendices A to C IAS 36,.Appendix A, paragraph A4

Other prefixes are: IFRS Foundation Constitution–**CN**; Preface to International Financial Reporting Standards–**IFRS Preface**; Due Process Handbook for the IASB–**DPH**; IFRIC Interpretation–**IFRIC**; SIC Interpretation–**SIC**; Due Process Handbook for the IFRS Interpretations Committee–**IDPH**; IASB *Conceptual Framework*–**F**; IFRS Practice Statement–**PS**

© IFRS Foundation

© IFRS Foundation

© IFRS Foundation

© IFRS Foundation

NOTES

NOTES

NOTES

NOTES

NOTES

NOTES

NOTES

NOTES

NOTES

NOTES

NOTES

NOTES